PRENTICE HALL
LITERATURE

BRONZE

Annotated Teacher's Edition
Teaching Portfolio
Novel Study Guides

SILVER

Annotated Teacher's Edition
Teaching Portfolio
Novel Study Guides

GOLD

Annotated Teacher's Edition
Teaching Portfolio
Novel Study Guides

PLATINUM

Annotated Teacher's Edition
Teaching Portfolio
Novel Study Guides

THE AMERICAN EXPERIENCE

Annotated Teacher's Edition
Teaching Portfolio
Novel Study Guides

THE ENGLISH TRADITION

Annotated Teacher's Edition
Teaching Portfolio
Novel Study Guides

PRENTICE HALL
LITERATURE
SILVER

 PRENTICE HALL, Englewood Cliffs, New Jersey 07632

ISBN 0-13-698523-8

10 9 8

Art credits begin on page 870.

COVER AND TITLE PAGE: **YOUNG LINCOLN**, 1868, Eastman Johnson, University of Michigan, Museum of Art

PRENTICE HALL
A Division of Simon & Schuster
Englewood Cliffs, New Jersey 07632

ACKNOWLEDGMENTS

Grateful acknowledgment is made to the following for permission to reprint copyrighted material:

American Way
"Dial Versus Digital" by Isaac Asimov. Reprinted by permission of *American Way*, inflight magazine of American Airlines, copyright 1985 by American Airlines.

Atheneum Publishers, Inc.
Patricia Hubbell, "Concrete Mixers" from *8 A.M. Shadows*. Copyright © 1965 Patricia Hubbell. Reprinted with the permission of Atheneum Publishers, Inc.

Robert Bly
"Driving to Town Late To Mail a Letter" from *Silence In the Snowy Fields*, Wesleyan University Press, 1962. Copyright © 1962 by Robert Bly, reprinted with his permission.

Dorothy Boles and Triangle Communications, Inc.
"The House Guest" by Paul Darcy Boles, copyright 1975 by Triangle Communications, Inc. All rights reserved. Originally appeared in *Seventeen* Magazine.

Borden Publishing Company
From "Hokusai: The Old Man Mad About Drawing" reproduced from *The Drawings of Hokusai* by Stephen Longstreet published by Borden Publishing Co., Alhambra, California.

Brandt & Brandt Literary Agents, Inc.
"Johnny Appleseed" from *A Book of Americans*, copyright 1933 by Rosemary and Stephen Vincent Benét; copyright renewed 1961 by Rosemary Carr Benét. "The Land and the Water" from *The Wind Shifting West* by Shirley Ann Grau, copyright © 1973 by Shirley Ann Grau. Reprinted by permission of Brandt & Brandt Literary Agents, Inc.

The Caxton Printers, Ltd.
"The Six Rows of Pompons" from *Yokohama, California* by Toshio Mori. The Caxton Printers, Ltd., Caldwell, Idaho.

Coward-McCann, Inc.
"Desert Noon" by Elizabeth Coatsworth, reprinted by permission of Coward-McCann, Inc., from *Compass Rose* by Elizabeth Coatsworth, copyright 1929 by Coward-McCann, Inc.; copyright renewed © 1957 by Elizabeth Coatsworth.

Curtis Brown Ltd., London
"Journey to the Interior" from *A Short History of the Fur Trade* by Adrien Stoutenburg. Copyright © 1968 by Adrien Stoutenburg. Reprinted by permission of Curtis Brown, Ltd.

Curtis Brown Ltd., London
"The Ugly Duckling" by A. A. Milne. Copyright 1941 by A. A. Milne. Reprinted by permission of Curtis Brown Ltd., London.

Dodd, Mead & Company, Inc.
"Grass Fire" from *The Edge of Time* by Loula Grace Erdman. Copyright 1950 by Loula Grace Erdman. Copyright renewed 1978 by the Amarillo National Bank. Reprinted by permission of Dodd, Mead & Company, Inc.

Doubleday & Company, Inc.
"Rain, Rain, Go Away" by Isaac Asimov copyright © 1959 by King-Size Publishing, Inc. from *Buy Jupiter and Other Stories*. "A Retrieved Reformation" from *Roads of Destiny* by O. Henry. "My Wild Irish Mother" by Jean Kerr. Copyright © 1960 by McCall Corp. From *How I Got to be Perfect*.

(continued on page 868)

CONTENTS

DRAMA

NONFICTION

POETRY

AMERICAN MYTHS, LEGENDS, AND FOLKTALES

THE NOVEL

HANDBOOK OF CRITICAL THINKING AND READING TERMS   840
Selection Illustrating Term

PRENTICE HALL
LITERATURE
SILVER

CHILDREN AND PIGEONS IN THE PARK, CENTRAL PARK, 1907
Millard Sheets
Photograph Courtesy of Kennedy Galleries, New York

SHORT STORIES

A short story is one of the most popular forms of literature. Even though it is fiction, a product of the author's imagination, you may become interested in reading it because it deals with people, places, actions, and events that seem familiar. At other times it may stir your imagination because it deals with the fantastic—or unusual. Whatever your reason for enjoying a particular short story, you will find that because it is short, you can usually read it in one sitting.

A short story is made up of elements: plot, character, setting, point of view, and theme. The plot is the sequence of events in the story. The characters are the people, and sometimes the animals, that play a role in the story. The setting is where and when the events take place. Often the plot, characters, and setting work together to reveal a theme, or insight into life.

Adventure stories, mysteries, science-fiction, animal tales—these are just a few of the varied types of short stories that authors write. In this unit you will encounter many of these types, and you will learn strategies to help you understand and appreciate short stories more thoroughly.

The Short Story

Good readers become actively involved. They read not only with their eyes but, more important, with a questioning mind. This means that they interact with the story, considering the events, the characters, where the story takes place, and the story's meaning.

Question

As you read, ask questions and then read to find the answers to these questions. What questions does the title bring to mind? Ask how a situation came about. Question why a character acts a certain way or makes a particular remark. Wonder about how the setting affects the characters and the events. Then read to find the answers to your questions.

Predict

Make predictions about what will happen. Base these predictions on clues in the story, on your own experience, and on your knowledge of how a story works. For example, when reading an action-filled adventure story, you may predict "I'm sure he will get off that runaway train before it goes over the cliff." Of course, some predictions will turn out to be true, while others, as in life, will not.

Clarify

Take time to clarify points. Stop to find the answers to your own questions. Check your predictions to see if they turned out to be true. Then discard predictions that turned out to be inaccurate and make new predictions based on your latest information.

Summarize

Occasionally, stop to summarize. At appropriate points in the story, review the main events. Identify what seems to be important, and consider the significance of this information.

Pull It Together

Think about the story after you are done reading. Pull together all the details and consider the effect of the story as a whole. What does the story mean to you? How do you feel about it?

Using these strategies will help you become a more effective reader. You will be better able to recall details, interpret meaning, and apply this meaning to your life.

On the following pages is a model of how an active reader might read a story.

The Story-Teller

Saki

Question: Who is the storyteller? Will this story be about this character?

It was a hot afternoon, and the railway carriage was correspondingly sultry, and the next stop was at Temple-combe, nearly an hour ahead. The occupants of the carriage were a small girl, and a smaller girl, and a small boy. An aunt belonging to the children occupied one corner seat, and the further corner seat on the opposite side was occupied by a bachelor who was a stranger to their party, but the small girls and the small boy emphatically occupied the compartment. Both the aunt and the children were conversational in a limited, persistent way, reminding one of the attentions of a housefly that refused to be discouraged. Most of the aunt's remarks seemed to begin with ''Don't,'' and nearly all of the children's remarks began with ''Why?'' The bachelor said nothing out loud.

Question: Why does the author compare the group to a housefly? What does this comparison indicate about the group?

''Don't, Cyril, don't,'' exclaimed the aunt, as the small boy began smacking the cushions of the seat, producing a cloud of dust at each blow.

''Come and look out of the window,'' she added.

The child moved reluctantly to the window. ''Why are those sheep being driven out of that field?'' he asked.

''I expect they are being driven to another field where there is more grass,'' said the aunt weakly.

''But there is lots of grass in that field,'' protested the boy; ''there's nothing else but grass there. Aunt, there's lots of grass in that field.''

''Perhaps the grass in the other field is better,'' suggested the aunt fatuously.[1]

''Why is it better?'' came the swift, inevitable question.

''Oh, look at those cows!'' exclaimed the aunt. Nearly every field along the line had contained cows or bullocks, but she spoke as though she were drawing attention to a rarity.

---

1. fatuously (fach′ oo wəs′ lē) *adv.*: In a foolish way.

"Why is the grass in the other field better?" persisted Cyril.

The frown on the bachelor's face was deepening to a scowl. He was a hard, unsympathetic man, the aunt decided in her mind. She was utterly unable to come to any satisfactory decision about the grass in the other field.

The smaller girl created a diversion by beginning to recite "On the Road to Mandalay."[2] She only knew the first line, but she put her limited knowledge to the fullest possible use. She repeated the line over and over again in a dreamy but resolute and very audible voice; it seemed to the bachelor as though someone had had a bet with her that she could not repeat the line aloud two thousand times without stopping. Whoever it was who had made the wager was likely to lose his bet.

"Come over here and listen to a story," said the aunt, when the bachelor had looked twice at her and once at the communication cord.[3]

---

2. "On the Road to Mandalay": Poem by Rudyard Kipling. Its first line is "By the old Moulmain Pagoda, lookin' eastward to the sea . . . ."
3. communication cord: Signal switch pulled to call the conductor.

Prediction: The bachelor will not put up with this behavior for long.

Clarification: This group is really annoying. So this is what the author was suggesting by comparing them to a fly.

Question: Is the aunt the storyteller that the title refers to?

The children moved listlessly toward the aunt's end of the carriage. Evidently her reputation as a story-teller did not rank high in their estimation.

In a low, confidential voice, interrupted at frequent intervals by loud, petulant[4] questions from her listeners, she began an unenterprising and deplorably uninteresting story about a little girl who was good, and made friends with everyone on account of her goodness, and was finally saved from a mad bull by a number of rescuers who admired her moral character.

Prediction: The aunt's story will not prove a success.

"Wouldn't they have saved her if she hadn't been good?" demanded the bigger of the small girls. It was exactly the question that the bachelor had wanted to ask.

"Well, yes," admitted the aunt lamely, "but I don't think they would have run quite so fast to her help if they had not liked her so much."

"It's the stupidest story I've ever heard," said the bigger of the small girls, with immense conviction.

"I didn't listen after the first bit, it was so stupid," said Cyril.

The smaller girl made no actual comment on the story, but she had long ago recommenced a murmured repetition of her favorite line.

Clarification: The aunt's story is a failure. It does not keep the children interested or quiet.

"You don't seem to be a success as a story-teller," said the bachelor suddenly from his corner.

The aunt bristled in instant defense at this unexpected attack.

"It's a very difficult thing to tell stories that children can both understand and appreciate," she said stiffly.

"I don't agree with you," said the bachelor.

Prediction: The bachelor will tell a story the children will like.

"Perhaps *you* would like to tell them a story," was the aunt's retort.

"Tell us a story," demanded the bigger of the small girls.

"Once upon a time," began the bachelor, "there was a little girl called Bertha, who was extraordinarily good."

Clarification: So there are two storytellers—the aunt and the bachelor.

The children's momentarily aroused interest began at once to flicker; all stories seemed dreadfully alike, no matter who told them.

"She did all that she was told, she was always truthful, she kept her clothes clean, ate milk puddings as though they

---

4. petulant (pech′ ōō lənt) *adj.*: Impatient.

were jam tarts, learned her lessons perfectly, and was polite in her manners."

"Was she pretty?" asked the bigger of the small girls.

"Not as pretty as any of you," said the bachelor, "but she was horribly good."

There was a wave of reaction in favor of the story; the word horrible in connection with goodness was a novelty that commended itself. It seemed to introduce a ring of truth that was absent from the aunt's tales of infant life.

"She was so good," continued the bachelor, "that she won several medals for goodness, which she always wore, pinned on to her dress. There was a medal for obedience, another medal for punctuality, and a third for good behavior. They were large metal medals and they clinked against one another as she walked. No other child in town where she lived had as many as three medals, so everybody knew that she must be an extra good child."

"Horribly good," quoted Cyril.

"Everybody talked about her goodness, and the Prince of the country got to hear about it, and he said that as she was so very good she might be allowed once a week to walk in his park, which was just outside the town. It was a beautiful park, and no children were ever allowed in it, so it was a great honor for Bertha to be allowed to go there."

"Were there any sheep in the park?" demanded Cyril.

"No," said the bachelor, "there were no sheep."

"Why weren't there any sheep?" came the inevitable question arising out of that answer.

The aunt permitted herself a smile, which might almost have been described as a grin.

Clarification: The bachelor is a good storyteller. The children *do* like his story.

"There were no sheep in the park," said the bachelor, "because the Prince's mother had once had a dream that her son would either be killed by a sheep or else by a clock falling on him. For that reason the Prince never kept a sheep in his park or a clock in his palace."

The aunt suppressed a gasp of admiration.

"Was the Prince killed by a sheep or by a clock?" asked Cyril.

"He is still alive, so we can't tell whether the dream will come true," said the bachelor unconcernedly; "anyway, there were no sheep in the park, but there were lots of little pigs running all over the place."

"What color were they?"

"Black with white faces, white with black spots, black all over, gray with white patches, and some were white all over."

The story-teller paused to let a full idea of the park's treasures sink into the children's imaginations; then he resumed:

"Bertha was rather sorry to find that there were no flowers in the park. She had promised her aunts, with tears in her eyes, that she would not pick any of the kind Prince's flowers, and she had meant to keep her promise, so of course it made her feel silly to find that there were no flowers to pick."

"Why weren't there any flowers?"

"Because the pigs had eaten them all," said the bachelor promptly. "The gardeners had told the Prince that you

couldn't have pigs and flowers, so he decided to have pigs and no flowers.''

There was a murmur of approval at the excellence of the Prince's decision; so many people would have decided the other way.

"There were lots of other delightful things in the park. There were ponds with gold and blue and green fish in them, and trees with beautiful parrots that said clever things at a moment's notice, and hummingbirds that hummed all the popular tunes of the day. Bertha walked up and down and enjoyed herself immensely, and thought to herself: 'If I were not so extraordinarily good, I should not have been allowed to come into this beautiful park and enjoy all that there is to be seen in it,' and her three medals clinked against one another as she walked and helped to remind her how very good she really was. Just then an enormous wolf came prowling into the park to see if it could catch a fat little pig for its supper.''

"What color was it?'' asked the children, amid an immediate quickening of interest.

"Mud color all over, with a black tongue and pale gray eyes that gleamed with unspeakable ferocity. The first thing that it saw in the park was Bertha; her pinafore[5] was so spotlessly white and clean that it could be seen from a great distance. Bertha saw the wolf and saw that it was stealing toward her, and she began to wish that she had never been allowed to come into the park. She ran as hard as she could, and the wolf came after her with huge leaps and bounds. She managed to reach a shrubbery of myrtle bushes, and she hid herself in one of the thickest of the bushes. The wolf came sniffing among the branches, its black tongue lolling out of its mouth and its pale gray eyes glaring with rage. Bertha was terribly frightened, and thought to herself: 'If I had not been so extraordinarily good, I should have been safe in the town at this moment.' However, the scent of the myrtle was so strong that the wolf could not sniff out where Bertha was hiding, and the bushes were so thick that he might have hunted about in them for a long time without catching sight of her, so he thought he might as well go off and catch a little pig instead. Bertha was trembling very much at having the wolf

Prediction: This story is quite different from the aunt's. Perhaps the good little girl will not be saved this time.

Question: Will Bertha escape?

---

5. pinafore (pin′ ə fôr′) *n.*: A sleeveless, apronlike garment worn by little girls over a dress.

prowling and sniffing so near her, and as she trembled the medal for obedience clinked against the medals for good conduct and punctuality. The wolf was just moving away when he heard the sound of the medals clinking and stopped to listen; they clinked again in a bush quite near him. He dashed into the bush, his pale gray eyes gleaming with ferocity and triumph, and dragged Bertha out and devoured her to the last morsel. All that was left of her were her shoes, bits of clothing, and the three medals for goodness."

Clarification: So Bertha does meet with a bad end after all.

"Were any of the little pigs killed?"

"No, they all escaped."

"The story began badly," said the smaller of the small girls, "but it had a beautiful ending."

"It is the most beautiful story that I ever heard," said the bigger of the small girls, with immense decision.

"It is the *only* beautiful story I have ever heard," said Cyril.

Question: Why do the children like this story so much?

A dissentient[6] opinion came from the aunt.

"A most improper story to tell to young children! You have undermined the effect of years of careful teaching."

"At any rate," said the bachelor, collecting his belongings preparatory to leaving the carriage, "I kept them quiet for ten minutes, which was more than you were able to do."

"Unhappy woman!" he observed to himself as he walked down the platform of Templecombe station; "for the next six months or so those children will assail her in public with demands for an improper story!"

Putting It Together: The bachelor's story is much better than the aunt's. Perhaps children prefer stories that stir their imagination to ones that teach a lesson.

---

6. dissentient (di sen′ shənt) *adj.*: Differing from the majority.

Saki (1870–1916) is the pen name of H. H. Munro, one of England's finest short-story writers. Born in Burma, after his mother's death he was sent to England, where he was brought up by his grandmother and two strict aunts. In 1893 he moved back to Burma, where he received a posting in the military police. However, ill health forced him to leave this posting and return to England. Here he began his career as a writer. Did you notice how Saki poked fun at aunts in "The Story-Teller"?

THINKING ABOUT THE SELECTION
Recalling

1. Describe the children's behavior at the beginning of the trip.
2. Why does the aunt decide to tell the children a story? Why are the children unexcited by this prospect?
3. How does the aunt react to the bachelor's story? What was he able to accomplish with his story that the aunt had not been able to do?

Interpreting

4. Why are the children never satisfied by the aunt's answers to their questions? How are the bachelor's answers different?
5. What makes the aunt's story "deplorably uninteresting"?
6. How does the word *horribly* inject "a ring of truth" into the bachelor's story? What other details of the bachelor's story do the children particularly like?

Applying

7. Why do people tell stories to children that teach moral lessons? Are these stories effective? Explain your answer.

ANALYZING LITERATURE
Understanding the Title

The author of a story usually chooses the title very carefully. It may call attention to a character or suggest something about the plot. It may even hint at the theme, or central idea, that the story expresses. The title of this story calls attention to the storytellers in it.

1. Describe the first storyteller. Include in your description as many key features of this character's personality as you can.

2. Describe the second storyteller. Indicate as many key features as you can.
3. There is also a third storyteller—one who does not appear as a character. Who is this storyteller?
4. What does the third storyteller's tale suggest about the art of telling stories?

CRITICAL THINKING AND READING
Comparing and Contrasting Stories

When you compare two things you show how they are alike. When you contrast, you show how they are different. Think about the story the aunt tells and the story the bachelor tells.

1. Compare and contrast the girl in each story.
2. Compare and contrast what happens in each story.
3. Compare and contrast the use of descriptive detail.
4. Compare and contrast the moral, or lesson.
5. Why do the children enjoy the bachelor's story so much more than the aunt's?
6. Which story did you enjoy more? Explain your answer.

THINKING AND WRITING
Creating a Story

Imagine you, like the bachelor in this story, have to entertain a group of unruly children. Create a story that would stir their imagination and keep them involved. First decide on your main character. Will this character be horribly good, or impossibly perfect, or wonderfully bratty? Next decide what happens to this character. Write the first draft of this story. Revise it, making sure it holds enough details to keep your audience interested. Prepare a final draft and share it with your classmates.

Plot

JAMES FOLLY GENERAL STORE AND POST OFFICE
Winfield Scott Clime
Three Lions

Rain, Rain, Go Away

Isaac Asimov (1920–   ), born in the Soviet Union, came to the United States when he was three. Asimov once remarked, "I imagine there must be such a thing as a born writer; at least, I can't remember when I wasn't on fire to write." Asimov has the ability to combine science with fiction to create astounding science-fiction and fantasy stories. He has won a Locus Award, a National Science Fiction Writers Award, a Nebula Award, and a Hugo Award. In "Rain, Rain, Go Away," Asimov gives a new twist to an old song.

Plot

Plot is the series of related actions or events in a short story. This sequence of events centers on a **conflict,** which is a struggle between opposing forces, or on a problem that must be solved. The plot includes exposition, in which the situation is revealed. The events build toward a **climax,** the point of highest interest. They continue toward a **resolution,** in which the story comes to a close.

Look For

As you read "Rain, Rain, Go Away," look for clues that indicate what makes the Sakkaros special. How does one action or event lead to another as the plot develops? How does each event make you curious about what will happen next? What is the climax?

Writing

Why do you think children sing the song "Rain, Rain, Go Away"? Freewrite about rain and its effect on you. Are you usually pleased when it rains? Does your feeling about rain depend on what you want to do when it rains? Do you always feel the same about rain?

Vocabulary

Knowing the following words will help you as you read "Rain, Rain, Go Away."

forestall (fôr stôl') v.: Prevent (p. 13)

meticulous (mə tik'yoo ləs) adj.: Extremely careful about details (p. 15)

affectation (af'ek tā'shən) n.: Artificial behavior intended to impress others (p. 15)

semblance (sem'bləns) n.: Outward appearance (p. 16)

centrifugal (sen trif'yə gəl) adj.: Tending to move away from the center (p. 16)

celestial (səl es'chəl) adj.: Of the sky (p. 18)

Rain, Rain, Go Away

Isaac Asimov

"There she is again," said Lillian Wright as she adjusted the venetian blinds carefully. "There she is, George."

"There who is?" asked her husband, trying to get satisfactory contrast on the TV so that he might settle down to the ball game.

"Mrs. Sakkaro," she said, and then, to forestall her husband's inevitable "Who's that?" added hastily, "The new neighbors, for goodness sake."

"Oh."

"Sunbathing. Always sunbathing. I wonder where her boy is. He's usually out on a nice day like this, standing in that tremendous yard of theirs and throwing the ball against the house. Did you ever see him, George?"

"I've heard him. It's a version of the Chinese water torture.[1] Bang on the wall, biff on the ground, smack in the hand. Bang, biff, smack, bang, biff—"

"He's a *nice* boy, quiet and well-behaved. I wish Tommie would make friends with him. He's the right age, too, just about ten, I should say."

"I didn't know Tommie was backward about making friends."

"Well, it's hard with the Sakkaros. They keep so to themselves. I don't even know what Mr. Sakkaro does."

"Why should you? It's not really anyone's business what he does."

"It's odd that I never see him go to work."

"No one ever sees me go to work."

"You stay home and write. What does *he* do?"

"I dare say Mrs. Sakkaro knows what Mr. Sakkaro does and is all upset because she doesn't know what *I* do."

"Oh, George." Lillian retreated from the window and glanced with distaste at the television. (Schoendienst was at bat.) "I think we should make an effort; the neighborhood should."

"What kind of an effort?" George was comfortable on the couch now.

"To get to know them."

"Well, didn't you, when she first moved in? You said you called."

"I said hello but, well, she'd just moved in and the house was still upset, so that's all it could be, just hello. It's been two months now and it's still nothing more than hello, sometimes.—She's so odd."

"Is she?"

"She's always looking at the sky; I've seen her do it a hundred times and she's never been out when it's the least bit cloudy. Once, when the boy was out playing, she called to him to come in, shouting that it was going to rain. I happened to hear her

---

1. Chinese water torture: A form of torture in which the slow, steady drip of water on the victim's head can drive him or her mad.

"He talked to their boy, in between ball chucks, I guess, and he told Tommie they came from Arizona and then the boy was called in. At least, Tommie says it might have been Arizona, or maybe Alabama or some place like that. You know Tommie and his nontotal recall. But if they're that nervous about the weather, I guess it's Arizona and they don't know what to make of a good rainy climate like ours."

"But why didn't you ever tell me?"

"Because Tommie only told me this morning and because I thought he must have told you already and, to tell the absolute truth, because I thought you could just manage to drag out a normal existence even if you never found out. Wow——"

The ball went sailing into the right field stands and that was that for the pitcher.

Lillian went back to the venetian blinds and said, "I'll simply just have to make her acquaintance. She looks *very* nice.—Oh, look at that, George."

George was looking at nothing but the TV.

Lillian said, "I know she's staring at that cloud. And now she'll be going in. Honestly."

George was out two days later on a reference search in the library and came home with a load of books. Lillian greeted him jubilantly.

She said, "Now, you're not doing anything tomorrow."

"That sounds like a statement, not a question."

"It *is* a statement. We're going out with the Sakkaros to Murphy's Park."

"With——"

"With the next-door neighbors, George. *How* can you never remember the name?"

"I'm gifted. How did it happen?"

and I thought, Oh no, wouldn't you know and me with a wash on the line, so I hurried out and, you know, it was broad sunlight. Oh, there were some clouds, but nothing, really."

"Did it rain, eventually?"

"Of course not. I just had to run out in the yard for nothing."

George was lost amid a couple of base hits and a most embarrassing bobble that meant a run. When the excitement was over and the pitcher was trying to regain his composure, George called out after Lillian, who was vanishing into the kitchen, "Well, since they're from Arizona, I dare say they don't know rainclouds from any other kind."

Lillian came back into the living room. "From where?"

"From Arizona, according to Tommie."

"How did Tommie know?"

"I just went up to their house this morning and rang the bell."

"That easy?"

"It wasn't easy. It was hard. I stood there, jittering, with my finger on the doorbell, till I thought that ringing the bell would be easier than having the door open and being caught standing there like a fool."

"And she didn't kick you out?"

"No. She was sweet as she could be. Invited me in, knew who I was, said she was so glad I had come to visit. *You* know."

"And you suggested we go to Murphy's Park."

"Yes. I thought if I suggested something that would let the children have fun, it would be easier for her to go along with it. She wouldn't want to spoil a chance for her boy."

"A mother's psychology."

"But you should see her home."

"Ah. You had a reason for all this. It comes out. You wanted the Cook's tour.[2] But, please, spare me the color-scheme details. I'm not interested in the bedspreads, and the size of the closets is a topic with which I can dispense."

It was the secret of their happy marriage that Lillian paid no attention to George. She went into the color-scheme details, was most meticulous about the bedspreads, and gave him an inch-by-inch description of closet-size.

"And *clean?* I have never seen any place so spotless."

"If you get to know her, then, she'll be setting you impossible standards and you'll have to drop her in self-defense."

---

2. **Cook's tour:** A brief, well-organized tour named after a British travel agent.

"Her kitchen," said Lillian, ignoring him, "was so spanking clean you just couldn't believe she ever used it. I asked for a drink of water and she held the glass underneath the tap and poured slowly so that not one drop fell in the sink itself. It wasn't affectation. She did it so casually that I just knew she always did it that way. And when she gave me the glass she held it with a clean napkin. Just hospital-sanitary."

"She must be a lot of trouble to herself. Did she agree to come with us right off?"

"Well—not right off. She called to her husband about what the weather forecast was, and he said that the newspapers all said it would be fair tomorrow but that he was waiting for the latest report on the radio."

"*All* the newspapers said so, eh?"

"Of course, they all just print the official weather forecast, so they would all agree. But I think they do subscribe to all the newspapers. At least I've watched the bundle the newsboy leaves—"

"There isn't much you miss, is there?"

"Anyway," said Lillian severely, "she called up the weather bureau and had them tell her the latest and she called it out to her husband and they said they'd go, except they said they'd phone us if there were any unexpected changes in the weather."

"All right. Then we'll go."

The Sakkaros were young and pleasant, dark and handsome. In fact, as they came down the long walk from their home to where the Wright automobile was parked, George leaned toward his wife and breathed into her ear, "So *he's* the reason."

"I wish he were," said Lillian. "Is that a handbag he's carrying?"

"Pocket-radio. To listen to weather forecasts, I bet."

The Sakkaro boy came running after them, waving something which turned out to be an aneroid barometer,[3] and all three got into the back seat. Conversation was turned on and lasted, with neat give-and-take on impersonal subjects, to Murphy's Park.

The Sakkaro boy was so polite and reasonable that even Tommie Wright, wedged between his parents in the front seat, was subdued by example into a semblance of civilization. Lillian couldn't recall when she had spent so serenely pleasant a drive.

She was not the least disturbed by the fact that, barely to be heard under the flow of the conversation, Mr. Sakkaro's small radio was on, and she never actually saw him put it occasionally to his ear.

It was a beautiful day at Murphy's Park; hot and dry without being too hot; and with a cheerfully bright sun in a blue, blue sky. Even Mr. Sakkaro, though he inspected every quarter of the heavens with a careful eye and then stared piercingly at the barometer, seemed to have no fault to find.

Lillian ushered the two boys to the amusement section and bought enough tickets to allow one ride for each on every variety of centrifugal thrill that the park offered.

"Please," she had said to a protesting Mrs. Sakkaro, "let this be my treat. I'll let you have your turn next time."

When she returned, George was alone. "Where—" she began.

"Just down there at the refreshment stand. I told them I'd wait here for you and we would join them." He sounded gloomy.

"Anything wrong?"

"No, not really, except that I think he must be independently wealthy."

"What?"

"I don't know what he does for a living. I hinted—"

"Now who's curious?"

"I was doing it for you. He said he's just a student of human nature."

---

3. aneroid (an′ ər oid) **barometer:** An instrument that registers air pressure changes on a dial and is used to predict weather changes. A "falling barometer" indicates an increase in air pressure and the likelihood of rain.

He looked so surprised, it was obvious he didn't. Then he laughed and asked if he had an Arizona accent."

Lillian said thoughtfully, "He has some kind of accent, you know. There are lots of Spanish-ancestry people in the Southwest so he could still be from Arizona. Sakkaro could be a Spanish name."

"Sounds Japanese to me.—Come on, they're waving. Oh, look what they've bought."

The Sakkaros were each holding three sticks of cotton candy, huge swirls of pink foam consisting of threads of sugar dried out of frothy syrup that had been whipped about in a warm vessel. It melted sweetly in the mouth and left one feeling sticky.

The Sakkaros held one out to each Wright, and out of politeness the Wrights accepted.

They went down the midway, tried their hand at darts, at the kind of poker game where balls were rolled into holes, at knocking wooden cylinders off pedestals. They took pictures of themselves and recorded their voices and tested the strength of their handgrips.

Eventually they collected the youngsters, who had been reduced to a satisfactorily breathless state of roiled-up[4] insides, and the Sakkaros ushered theirs off instantly to the refreshment stand. Tommie hinted the extent of his pleasure at the possible purchase of a hot-dog and George tossed him a quarter. He ran off, too.

"Frankly," said George, "I prefer to stay here. If I see them biting away at another cotton candy stick I'll turn green and sicken on the spot. If they haven't had a dozen apiece, I'll eat a dozen myself."

"I know, and they're buying a handful for the child now."

"How philosophical. That would explain all those newspapers."

"Yes, but with a handsome, wealthy man next door, it looks as though I'll have impossible standards set for me, too."

"Don't be silly."

"And he doesn't come from Arizona."

"He doesn't?"

"I said I heard he was from Arizona.

_____

4. roiled-up *adj.*: Stirred up, agitated, unsettled.

"I offered to stand Sakkaro a hamburger and he just looked grim and shook his head. Not that a hamburger's much, but after enough cotton candy, it ought to be a feast."

"I know. I offered her an orange drink and the way she jumped when she said no, you'd think I'd thrown it in her face.—Still, I suppose they've never been to a place like this before and they'll need time to adjust to the novelty. They'll fill up on cotton candy and then never eat it again for ten years."

"Well, maybe." They strolled toward the Sakkaros. "You know, Lil, it's clouding up."

Mr. Sakkaro had the radio to his ear and was looking anxiously toward the west.

"Uh-oh," said George, "he's seen it. One gets you fifty, he'll want to go home."

All three Sakkaros were upon him, polite but insistent. They were sorry, they had had a wonderful time, a marvelous time, the Wrights would have to be their guests as soon as it could be managed, but now, really, they had to go home. It looked stormy. Mrs. Sakkaro wailed that all the forecasts had been for fair weather.

George tried to console them. "It's hard to predict a local thunderstorm, but even if it were to come, and it mightn't, it wouldn't last more than half an hour on the outside."

At which comment, the Sakkaro youngster seemed on the verge of tears, and Mrs. Sakkaro's hand, holding a handkerchief, trembled visibly.

"Let's go home," said George in resignation.

The drive back seemed to stretch interminably. There was no conversation to speak of. Mr. Sakkaro's radio was quite loud now as he switched from station to station, catching a weather report every time. They were mentioning "local thundershowers" now.

The Sakkaro youngster piped up that the barometer was falling, and Mrs. Sakkaro, chin in the palm of her hand, stared dolefully at the sky and asked if George could not drive faster, please.

"It does look rather threatening, doesn't it?" said Lillian in a polite attempt to share their guests' attitude. But then George heard her mutter, "Honestly!" under her breath.

A wind had sprung up, driving the dust of the weeks-dry road before it, when they entered the street on which they lived, and the leaves rustled ominously. Lightning flickered.

George said, "You'll be indoors in two minutes, friends. We'll make it."

He pulled up at the gate that opened onto the Sakkaro's spacious front yard and got out of the car to open the back door. He thought he felt a drop. They were *just* in time.

The Sakkaros tumbled out, faces drawn with tension, muttering thanks, and started off toward their long front walk at a dead run.

"Honestly," began Lillian, "you would think they were—"

The heavens opened and the rain came down in giant drops as though some celestial dam had suddenly burst. The top of their car was pounded with a hundred drum sticks, and halfway to their front door the Sakkaros stopped and looked despairingly upward.

Their faces blurred as the rain hit; blurred and shrank and ran together. All three shriveled, collapsing within their clothes, which sank down into three sticky-wet heaps.

And while the Wrights sat there, transfixed with horror, Lillian found herself unable to stop the completion of her remark: "—made of sugar and afraid they would melt."

THINKING ABOUT THE SELECTION

Recalling

1. Name two events involving the Sakkaros that make the Wrights curious about them, even before the outing to Murphy's Park.
2. Why does Mrs. Wright suggest Murphy's Park for an outing with the Sakkaros?
3. How do the Sakkaros show their nervousness about the weather on their trip?
4. Why do the Sakkaros insist on going home?

Interpreting

5. Why does Mrs. Sakkaro fill the glass of water for Mrs. Wright so carefully?
6. What is unusual about what the Sakkaros eat at the park? Why do they refuse other food?
7. What does Mr. Sakkaro probably mean when he says he is a student of human nature?
8. Where do you think the Sakkaros are from? Find evidence to support your answer.
9. How is Mrs. Wright's statement at the end of the story truer than even she expects?

Applying

10. Mrs. Wright's last sentence describes people who are behaving almost too carefully. A similar common saying is, "He looks as if he is walking on eggs." What other expressions describe especially careful behavior?

ANALYZING LITERATURE

Understanding Plot

Plot is a sequence of events or related actions. Usually, a **conflict** or a problem, such as Mrs. Wright's desire to know about the Sakkaros, is presented. Next, the action builds up to the high point, or **climax,** of the story. Finally, the action moves to a **resolution,** or final outcome.

1. Name two events that move the plot toward the climax of the story.
2. What is the climax of the story?
3. How is the conflict resolved?

CRITICAL THINKING AND READING

Understanding the Sequence of Events

Authors carefully plan the **sequence,** or order, of events in stories. Often they arrange events in **chronological order,** which shows how one event follows another in time. For example, Lillian first invites the Sakkaros to Murphy's Park; then the families go there.

On a piece of paper, write the numbers of the following events in chronological order:

1. The Wrights discuss their new neighbors.
2. The adults play games on the midway.
3. The Wrights and the Sakkaros go to the park.
4. The Sakkaros move to the neighborhood.
5. The Sakkaros race for their front door.

UNDERSTANDING LANGUAGE

Using Negative Prefixes

A **prefix** is a letter or group of letters added at the beginning of words to form a new word or to change the meaning of the original word. A **negative prefix** reverses the meaning of the original word. For example, *un-* added to *happy* creates the negative word *unhappy.*

Add one of the following negative prefixes to each word below: *mis-, non-, dis-, in-, il-, im-.*

1. agreeable
2. possible
3. active
4. logical
5. spell
6. sense

THINKING AND WRITING

Writing a Short Story

Sometimes a story starts by an author wondering "What if?" Use your imagination to complete the statement: What if the people next door really were _____. Then imagine an outing with your neighbors. Write the first draft of a short story telling about the consequences of their true identity. Include dialogue between the characters. When you revise, be sure to start a new paragraph when you change speakers.

GUIDE FOR READING

Christmas Day in the Morning

Pearl S. Buck (1892–1973) grew up in China where her parents were missionaries. After teaching in China and the United States, she became a full-time writer of nonfiction and fiction. Her most famous novel, *The Good Earth,* earned her a Pulitzer Prize, and in 1938 she won the Nobel Prize for Literature. Buck was active throughout her life in child welfare work. Her caring about people is clearly seen in "Christmas Day in the Morning," where Buck shows that the greatest gift we have to give one another is love.

Flashback

A **flashback** is a scene inserted into a story showing events that occurred in the past. Usually the events in a story are arranged **chronologically;** that is, the order in which the events occurred in time is the order in which they appear in the story. Sometimes, however, an author might want to show something that happened at an earlier time than the events of the story. To do so, the author uses a flashback. In "Christmas Day in the Morning," the author uses a flashback to show why Robert, now an aging grandfather, has had special feelings about Christmas since he was fifteen.

Look For

As you read "Christmas Day in the Morning," look for the flashback. Why do you think the author includes this flashback in the story? How does it help explain Robert's actions?

Writing

Think of a movie or television program you have seen recently that contained a flashback. Explain why you think the flashback was included. Would the story have been as effective if the author had told it in strict time order?

Vocabulary

Knowing the following words will help you as you read "Christmas Day in the Morning."
placidly (plas'id lē) *adv.:* Calmly; quietly (p. 22)

acquiescent (ak'we es'ənt) *adj.:* Agreeing without protest (p. 22)

Christmas Day in the Morning

Pearl S. Buck

He woke suddenly and completely. It was four o'clock, the hour at which his father had always called him to get up and help with the milking. Strange how the habits of his youth clung to him still! Fifty years ago, and his father had been dead for thirty years, and yet he waked at four o'clock in the morning. He had trained himself to turn over and go to sleep, but this morning, because it was Christmas, he did not try to sleep.

Yet what was the magic of Christmas now? His childhood and youth were long past, and his own children had grown up and gone. Some of them lived only a few miles away but they had their own families, and though they would come in as usual toward the end of the day, they had explained with infinite gentleness that they wanted their children to build Christmas memories about *their* houses, not his. He was left alone with his wife.

Yesterday she had said, "It isn't worthwhile, perhaps—"

And he had said, "Oh, yes, Alice, even if there are only the two of us, let's have a Christmas of our own."

Then she had said, "Let's not trim the tree until tomorrow, Robert—just so it's ready when the children come. I'm tired."

He had agreed, and the tree was still out in the back entry.

Why did he feel so awake tonight? For it was still night, a clear and starry night. No moon, of course, but the stars were extraordinary! Now that he thought of it, the stars seemed always large and clear before the dawn of Christmas Day. There was one star now that was certainly larger and brighter than any of the others. He could even imagine it moving, as it had seemed to him to move one night long ago.

He slipped back in time, as he did so easily nowadays. He was fifteen years old and still on his father's farm. He loved his father. He had not known it until one day a few days before Christmas, when he had overheard what his father was saying to his mother.

"Mary, I hate to call Rob in the mornings. He's growing so fast and he needs his sleep. If you could see how he sleeps when I go in to wake him up! I wish I could manage alone."

"Well, you can't, Adam." His mother's voice was brisk. "Besides, he isn't a child anymore. It's time he took his turn."

"Yes," his father said slowly. "But I sure do hate to wake him."

When he heard these words, something in him woke: his father loved him! He had never thought of it before, taking for granted the tie of their blood. Neither his father nor his mother talked about loving their children—they had no time for such things. There was always so much to do on a farm.

Now that he knew his father loved him, there would be no more loitering in the mornings and having to be called again. He got up after that, stumbling blind with sleep, and pulled on his clothes, his eyes tight shut, but he got up.

And then on the night before Christmas, that year when he was fifteen, he lay for a few minutes thinking about the next day. They were poor, and most of the excitement was in the turkey they had raised themselves and in the mince pies his mother made. His sisters sewed presents and his mother and father always bought something he needed, not only a warm jacket, maybe, but something more, such as a book. And he saved and bought them each something, too.

He wished, that Christmas he was fifteen, he had a better present for his father. As usual he had gone to the ten-cent store and bought a tie. It had seemed nice enough until he lay thinking the night before Christmas, and then he wished that he had heard his father and mother talking in time for him to save for something better.

He lay on his side, his head supported by his elbow, and looked out of his attic window. The stars were bright, much brighter than he ever remembered seeing them, and one star in particular was so bright that he wondered if it were really the Star of Bethlehem.

"Dad," he had once asked when he was a little boy, "what is a stable?"

"It's just a barn," his father had replied, "like ours."

Then Jesus had been born in a barn, and to a barn the shepherds and the Wise Men had come, bringing their Christmas gifts!

The thought struck him like a silver dagger. Why should he not give his father a special gift too, out there in the barn? He could get up early, earlier than four o'clock, and he could creep into the barn and get all the milking done. He'd do it alone, milk and clean up, and then when his father went in to start the milking, he'd see it all done. And he would know who had done it.

He laughed to himself as he gazed at the stars. It was what he would do, and he mustn't sleep too sound.

He must have waked twenty times, scratching a match each time to look at his old watch—midnight, and half past one, and then two o'clock.

At a quarter to three he got up and put on his clothes. He crept downstairs, careful of the creaky boards, and let himself out. The big star hung lower over the barn roof, a reddish gold. The cows looked at him, sleepy and surprised. It was early for them too.

"So, boss," he whispered. They accepted him placidly and he fetched some hay for each cow and then got the milking pail and the big milk cans.

He had never milked all alone before, but it seemed almost easy. He kept thinking about his father's surprise. His father would come in and call him, saying that he would get things started while Rob was getting dressed. He'd go to the barn, open the door, and then he'd go to get the two big empty milk cans. But they wouldn't be waiting or empty; they'd be standing in the milkhouse, filled.

"What the—" he could hear his father exclaiming.

He smiled and milked steadily, two strong streams rushing into the pail, frothing and fragrant. The cows were still surprised but acquiescent. For once they were behaving well, as though they knew it was Christmas.

The task went more easily than he had ever known it to before. Milking for once was not a chore. It was something else, a gift to

his father who loved him. He finished, the two milk cans were full, and he covered them and closed the milkhouse door carefully, making sure of the latch. He put the stool in its place by the door and hung up the clean milk pail. Then he went out of the barn and barred the door behind him.

Back in his room he had only a minute to pull off his clothes in the darkness and jump into bed, for he heard his father up. He put the covers over his head to silence his quick breathing. The door opened.

"Rob!" his father called. "We have to get up, son, even if it is Christmas."

"Aw-right," he said sleepily.

"I'll go on out," his father said. "I'll get things started."

The door closed and he lay still, laughing to himself. In just a few minutes his father would know. His dancing heart was ready to jump from his body.

The minutes were endless—ten, fifteen, he did not know how many—and he heard his father's footsteps again. The door opened and he lay still.

"Rob!"

"Yes, Dad—"

"You son of a—" His father was laughing, a queer sobbing sort of a laugh. "Thought you'd fool me, did you?" His father was standing beside his bed, feeling for him, pulling away the cover.

"It's for Christmas, Dad!"

He found his father and clutched him in a great hug. He felt his father's arms go around him. It was dark and they could not see each other's faces.

"Son, I thank you. Nobody ever did a nicer thing—"

"Oh, Dad, I want you to know—I do want to be good!" The words broke from him of their own will. He did not know what to say. His heart was bursting with love.

"Well, I reckon I can go back to bed and sleep," his father said after a moment. "No, hark—the little ones are waked up. Come to think of it, son, I've never seen you children when you first saw the Christmas tree. I was always in the barn. Come on!"

He got up and pulled on his clothes again and they went down to the Christmas tree, and soon the sun was creeping up to where the star had been. Oh, what a Christmas, and how his heart had nearly burst again with shyness and pride as his father told his mother and made the younger children listen about how he, Rob, had got up all by himself.

"The best Christmas gift I ever had, and I'll remember it, son, every year on Christmas morning, so long as I live."

They had both remembered it, and now that his father was dead he remembered it alone: that blessed Christmas dawn when, alone with the cows in the barn, he had made his first gift of true love.

Outside the window now the great star slowly sank. He got up out of bed and put on his slippers and bathrobe and went softly upstairs to the attic and found the box of Christmas-tree decorations. He took them downstairs into the living room. Then he brought in the tree. It was a little one—they had not had a big tree since the children went away—but he set it in the holder and put it in the middle of the long table under the window. Then carefully he began to trim it.

It was done very soon, the time passing as quickly as it had that morning long ago in the barn. He went to his library and fetched the little box that contained his special gift to his wife, a star of diamonds, not large but dainty in design. He had written the card for it the day before. He tied the gift on the tree and then stood back. It was pretty, very pretty, and she would be surprised.

But he was not satisfied. He wanted to tell her—to tell her how much he loved her. It had been a long time since he had really told her, although he loved her in a very special way, much more than he ever had when they were young.

He had been fortunate that she had loved him—and how fortunate that he had been able to love! Ah, that was the true joy of life, the ability to love! For he was quite sure that some people were genuinely unable to love anyone. But love was alive in him, it still was.

It occurred to him suddenly that it was alive because long ago it had been born in him when he knew his father loved him. That was it: love alone could waken love.

And he could give the gift again and again. This morning, this blessed Christmas morning, he would give it to his beloved wife. He could write it down in a letter for her to read and keep forever. He went to his desk and began his love letter to his wife: *My dearest love . . .*

When it was finished he sealed it and tied it on the tree where she would see it the first thing when she came into the room. She would read it, surprised and then moved, and realize how very much he loved her.

He put out the light and went tiptoeing up the stairs. The star in the sky was gone, and the first rays of the sun were gleaming in the sky. Such a happy, happy Christmas!

THINKING ABOUT THE SELECTION

Recalling

1. How does Robert spend Christmas now?
2. Why did young Rob's father wake him every morning at 4:00 A.M.?
3. How did Rob learn that he loved his father?
4. What gift did young Rob plan to give his father? Why does he alter his plan?
5. How did Rob's father show his gratitude for Rob's gift?

Interpreting

6. Why is the gift young Rob gives his father special? How does giving it make Rob feel?
7. Explain the significance of the two gifts the adult Robert gives his wife.
8. When Robert first awakens at the beginning of the story, he wonders where the magic of Christmas is now. How do his feelings change by the end of the story? What has brought about the change?

Applying

9. Do you agree with Robert that people who can love are fortunate? Explain your answer.
10. This story tells of one gift of love. What other gifts of love are there?

ANALYZING LITERATURE

Understanding a Flashback

A **flashback** presents events of the past in the midst of a story in the present. Pearl Buck uses a flashback to relate a Christmas in Robert's youth to a Christmas today. As a reader, you need to be able to tell when a flashback begins and when it ends.

1. When does the flashback begin in "Christmas Day in the Morning"?
2. How does the reader know when it is over?
3. What is the effect of the flashback?
4. How does the flashback prove Robert's statement: "Love alone could waken love"?

CRITICAL THINKING AND READING

Understanding Time Order

When an author uses flashbacks, events in the plot are not all in time or chronological order. To understand the story, you must mentally put the events in chronological order as you read.

Tell whether each event happens in the past as part of the flashback or in the present.

1. Robert overhears his father talking about him.
2. Robert writes a love letter to his wife.
3. Rob gets up at quarter to three to milk cows.

UNDERSTANDING LANGUAGE

Using Context Clues

One way to find the meaning of unfamiliar words is to use the context. The **context** of a word is the words and phrases that surround it. Often, the context gives clues to the meaning. Notice the context clue for *auburn:* "Her auburn hair gleamed like copper." The word *copper* indicates that auburn hair is the color of copper.

Use the context to determine the meanings of the following italicized words.

1. ". . . there would be no more *loitering* in the mornings and having to be called again."
2. "The cows were still surprised but *acquiescent.* For once they were behaving well, as though they knew it was Christmas."

THINKING AND WRITING

Writing an Extended Definition

An **extended definition** includes examples of what you are defining and points out important aspects that cannot be explained in a brief definition. Brainstorm about what the word *love* means to you. Make a list of examples of kinds of love with which you are familiar. Then, write an extended definition of the word *love.* Use specific examples from your list to illustrate your definition. Check carefully to see that you have covered as many types of love as you can.

GUIDE FOR READING

The Adventure of the Speckled Band

Arthur Conan Doyle (1859–1950) was born in Edinburgh, Scotland. He began to study medicine and took up writing mystery stories in his early twenties. According to one of his professors, Doyle was often more accurate in guessing the occupation of patients than in diagnosing their illnesses. By 1886 Doyle had published his first Sherlock Holmes mystery, "A Study in Scarlet." In "The Adventure of the Speckled Band," you will see that Holmes, like Doyle himself, displays extraordinary powers of observation.

Conflict

A **conflict** is a struggle between opposing forces or characters. Often a conflict occurs between two characters or between a character and the forces of nature. Conflict adds interest to a story, since it makes us wonder who will win.

Look For

In "The Adventure of the Speckled Band" Sherlock Holmes stands in the way of Dr. Roylott's achieving his goal. Look for the way the conflict is developed. Are the characters evenly matched? Why does one character finally win over the other?

Writing

When Holmes's client offers to pay him, Holmes responds, "As to my reward, my profession is its own reward." Do you think you would enjoy being a detective as much as Holmes does? Freewrite, exploring your thoughts about being a detective.

Vocabulary

Knowing the following words will help you as you read "The Adventure of the Speckled Band."

defray (di frā′) v.: Pay the money for the cost of (p. 29)
manifold (man′ə fōld′) adj.: Many and varied (p. 29)
dissolute (dis′ə lo͞ot′) adj.: Unrestrained (p. 30)
morose (mə rōs′) adj.: Ill-tempered; gloomy; sullen (p. 30)
convulsed (kən vuls′d′) v.: Suffered a violent, involuntary spasm (p. 32)

imperturbably (im′pər tʉr′bə blē) adv.: Unexcitedly; calmly (p. 35)
reverie (rev′ər ē) n.: Daydreaming (p. 40)
tangible (tan′jə b′l) adj.: Having form and substance; that can be touched or felt by touch (p. 40)

The Adventure of the Speckled Band

Sir Arthur Conan Doyle

On glancing over my notes of the seventy odd cases in which I have during the last eight years studied the methods of my friend Sherlock Holmes, I find many tragic, some comic, a large number merely strange, but none commonplace; for, working as he did rather for the love of his art than for the acquirement of wealth, he refused to associate himself with any investigation which did not tend towards the unusual, and even the fantastic. Of all these varied cases, however, I cannot recall any which presented more singular features than that which was associated with the well-known Surrey family of the Roylotts of Stoke Moran. The events in question occurred in the early days of my association with Holmes when we were sharing rooms as bachelors in Baker Street. It is possible that I might have placed them upon record before but a promise of secrecy was made at the time, from which I have only been freed during the last month by the untimely death of the lady to whom the pledge was given. It is perhaps as well that the facts should now come to light, for I have reasons to know that there are widespread rumors as to the death of Dr. Grimesby Roylott which tend to make the matter even more terrible than the truth.

It was early in April in the year 1883 that I woke one morning to find Sherlock Holmes standing, fully dressed, by the side of my bed. He was a late riser, as a rule, and as the clock on the mantelpiece showed me that it was only a quarter past seven, I blinked up at him in some surprise, and perhaps just a little resentment, for I was myself regular in my habits.

"Very sorry to wake you up, Watson," said he, "but it's the common lot this morning. Mrs. Hudson has been awakened, she retorted upon me, and I on you."

"What is it, then—a fire?"

"No; a client. It seems that a young lady has arrived in a considerable state of excitement who insists upon seeing me. She is waiting now in the sitting room. Now, when young ladies wander about the metropolis at this hour of the morning, and get sleepy people up out of their beds, I presume that it is something very pressing which they have to communicate. Should it prove to be an interesting case, you would, I am sure, wish to follow it from the outset. I thought, at any rate, that I should call you and give you the chance."

"My dear fellow, I would not miss it for anything."

I had no keener pleasure than in following Holmes in his professional investigations, and in admiring the rapid deductions, as swift as intuitions, and yet always founded on a logical basis, with which he unraveled the problems which were submitted to him. I rapidly threw on my clothes and was ready in a few minutes to accompany my friend down to the sitting room. A lady dressed in black and heavily veiled, who had been sitting in the window, rose as we entered.

"Good morning, madam," said Holmes cheerily. "My name is Sherlock Holmes. This is my intimate friend and associate, Dr. Watson, before whom you can speak as freely as before myself. Ha! I am glad to see that Mrs. Hudson has had the good sense to light the fire. Pray draw up to it, and I shall order you a cup of hot coffee, for I observe that you are shivering."

"It is not cold which makes me shiver," said the woman in a low voice, changing her seat as requested.

"What, then?"

"It is fear, Mr. Holmes. It is terror." She raised her veil as she spoke, and we could see that she was indeed in a pitiable state of agitation, her face all drawn and gray, with restless, frightened eyes, like those of some hunted animal. Her features and figure were those of a woman of thirty, but her hair was shot with premature gray, and her expression was weary and haggard. Sherlock Holmes ran her over with one of his quick, all-comprehensive glances.

"You must not fear," said he soothingly, bending forward and patting her forearm. "We shall soon set matters right, I have no doubt. You have come in by train this morning, I see."

"You know me, then?"

"No, but I observe the second half of a return ticket in the palm of your left glove. You must have started early, and yet you had a good drive in a dogcart[1] along heavy roads, before you reached the station."

---

1. dogcart: Small horse-drawn carriage with seats arranged back-to-back.

The lady gave a violent start and stared in bewilderment at my companion.

"There is no mystery, my dear madam," said he, smiling. "The left arm of your jacket is spattered with mud in no less than seven places. The marks are perfectly fresh. There is no vehicle save a dogcart which throws up mud in that way, and then only when you sit on the left-hand side of the driver."

"Whatever your reasons may be, you are perfectly correct," said she. "I started from home before six, reached Leatherhead at twenty past, and came in by the first train to Waterloo. Sir, I can stand this strain no longer; I shall go mad if it continues. I have no one to turn to—none, save only one, who cares for me, and he, poor fellow, can be of little aid. I have heard of you, Mr. Holmes, I

have heard of you from Mrs. Farintosh, whom you helped in the hour of her sore need. It was from her that I had your address. Oh, sir, do you not think that you could help me, too, and at least throw a little light through the dense darkness which surrounds me? At present it is out of my power to reward you for your service, but in a month or six weeks I shall be married, with the control of my own income, and then at least you shall not find me ungrateful."

Holmes turned to his desk and, unlocking it, drew out a small case book, which he consulted.

"Farintosh," said he. "Ah yes, I recall the case; it was concerned with an opal tiara. I think it was before your time, Watson. I can only say, madam, that I shall be happy to devote the same care to your case as I did to that of your friend. As to reward, my profession is its own reward; but you are at liberty to defray whatever expenses I may be put to, at the time which suits you best. And now I beg that you will lay before us everything that may help us in forming an opinion upon the matter."

"Alas!" replied our visitor, "the very horror of my situation lies in the fact that my fears are so vague, and my suspicions depend so entirely upon small points, which might seem trivial to another, that even he to whom of all others I have a right to look for help and advice looks upon all that I tell him about it as fancy. He does not say so, but I can read it from his soothing answers and averted eyes. But I have heard, Mr. Holmes, that you can see deeply into the manifold wickedness of the human heart. You may advise me how to walk amid the dangers which encompass me."

"I am all attention, madam."

"My name is Helen Stoner, and I am living with my stepfather, who is the last survivor of one of the oldest Saxon families in England; the Roylotts of Stoke Moran, on the western border of Surrey."

Holmes nodded his head. "The name is familiar to me," said he.

"The family was at one time among the richest in England, and the estates extended over the borders into Berkshire in the north, and Hampshire in the west. In the last century, however, four successive heirs were of a dissolute and wasteful disposition, and the family ruin was eventually completed by a gambler in the days of the Regency. Nothing was left save a few acres of ground, and the two-hundred-year-old house, which is itself crushed under a heavy mortgage. The last squire dragged out his existence there, living the horrible life of an aristocratic pauper; but his only son, my stepfather, seeing that he must adapt himself to the new conditions, obtained an advance from a relative, which enabled him to take a medical degree and went out to Calcutta, where, by his professional skill and his force of character, he established a large practice. In a fit of anger, however, caused by some robberies which had been perpetrated in the house, he beat his native butler to death and narrowly escaped a capital sentence. As it was, he suffered a long term of imprisonment and afterwards returned to England a morose and disappointed man.

"When Dr. Roylott was in India he married my mother, Mrs. Stoner, the young widow of Major-General Stoner, of the Bengal Artillery. My sister Julia and I were twins, and we were only two years old at the time of my mother's remarriage. She had a considerable sum of money—not less than £1000 a year[2]—and this she bequeathed to Dr. Roylott entirely while we resided with him, with a provision that a certain annual

sum should be allowed to each of us in the event of our marriage. Shortly after our return to England my mother died—she was killed eight years ago in a railway accident near Crewe. Dr. Roylott then abandoned his attempts to establish himself in practice in London and took us to live with him in the old ancestral house at Stoke Moran. The money which my mother had left was enough for all our wants, and there seemed to be no obstacle to our happiness.

"But a terrible change came over our stepfather about this time. Instead of making friends and exchanging visits with our neighbors, who had at first been overjoyed to see a Roylott of Stoke Moran back in the old family seat, he shut himself up in his house and seldom came out save to indulge in ferocious quarrels with whoever might cross his path. Violence of temper approaching to mania has been hereditary in the men of the family, and in my stepfather's case it had, I believe, been intensified by his long residence in the tropics. A series of disgraceful brawls took place, two of which ended in the police court, until at last he became the terror of the village, and the folks would fly at his approach, for he is a man of immense strength, and absolutely uncontrollable in his anger.

"Last week he hurled the local blacksmith over a parapet into a stream, and it was only by paying over all the money which I could gather together that I was able to avert another public exposure. He had no friends at all save the wandering gypsies, and he would give these vagabonds leave to encamp upon the few acres of bramble-covered land which represent the family estate, and would accept in return the hospitality of their tents, wandering away with them sometimes for weeks on end. He has a passion also for Indian animals, which are sent over to him by a correspondent, and he

---

2. £1000: One thousand pounds. £ is the symbol for pound or pounds, the British unit of money.

has at this moment a cheetah and a baboon, which wander freely over his grounds and are feared by the villagers almost as much as is their master.

"You can imagine from what I say that my poor sister Julia and I had no great pleasure in our lives. No servant would stay with us, and for a long time we did all the work of the house. She was but thirty at the time of her death, and yet her hair had already begun to whiten, even as mine has."

"Your sister is dead, then?"

"She died just two years ago, and it is of her death that I wish to speak to you. You can understand that, living the life which I have described, we were little likely to see anyone of our own age and position. We had, however, an aunt, my mother's maiden sister, Miss Honoria Westphail, who lives near Harrow, and we were occasionally allowed to pay short visits at this lady's house. Julia went there at Christmas two years ago, and met there a major in the Marines, to whom she became engaged. My stepfather learned of the engagement when my sister returned and offered no objection to the marriage; but within a fortnight of the day which had been fixed for the wedding, the terrible event occurred which has deprived me of my only companion."

Sherlock Holmes had been leaning back in his chair with his eyes closed and his head sunk in a cushion, but he half opened his lids now and glanced across at his visitor.

"Pray be precise as to details," said he.

"It is easy for me to be so, for every event of that dreadful time is seared into my memory. The manor house is, as I have already said, very old, and only one wing is now inhabited. The bedrooms in this wing are on the ground floor, the sitting rooms being in the central block of the buildings. Of these bedrooms the first is Dr. Roylott's, the sec-

ond my sister's, and the third my own. There is no communication between them, but they all open out into the same corridor. Do I make myself plain?"

"Perfectly so."

"The windows of the three rooms open out upon the lawn. That fatal night Dr. Roylott had gone to his room early, though we knew that he had not retired to rest, for my sister was troubled by the smell of the strong Indian cigars which it was his custom to smoke. She left her room, therefore, and came into mine, where she sat for some time, chatting about her approaching wedding. At eleven o'clock she rose to leave me, but she paused at the door and looked back.

" 'Tell me, Helen,' said she, 'have you ever heard anyone whistle in the dead of the night?'

" 'Never,' said I.

" 'I suppose that you could not possibly whistle, yourself, in your sleep?'

" 'Certainly not. But why?'

" 'Because during the last few nights I have always, about three in the morning, heard a low, clear whistle. I am a light sleeper, and it has awakened me. I cannot tell where it came from—perhaps from the next room, perhaps from the lawn. I thought that I would just ask you whether you had heard it.'

" 'No, I have not. It must be the gypsies in the plantation.'

" 'Very likely. And yet if it were on the lawn, I wonder that you did not hear it also.'

" 'Ah, but I sleep more heavily than you.'

" 'Well, it is of no great consequence, at any rate.' She smiled back at me, closed my door, and a few moments later I heard her key turn in the lock."

"Indeed," said Holmes. "Was it your custom always to lock yourselves in at night?"

"Always."

"And why?"

"I think that I mentioned to you that the doctor kept a cheetah and a baboon. We had no feeling of security unless our doors were locked."

"Quite so. Pray proceed with your statement."

"I could not sleep that night. A vague feeling of impending misfortune impressed me. My sister and I, you will recollect, were twins, and you know how subtle are the links which bind two souls which are so closely allied. It was a wild night. The wind was howling outside, and the rain was beating and splashing against the windows. Suddenly, amid all the hubbub of the gale, there burst forth the wild scream of a terrified woman. I knew that it was my sister's voice. I sprang from my bed, wrapped a shawl round me, and rushed into the corridor. As I opened my door I seemed to hear a low whistle, such as my sister described, and a few moments later a clanging sound, as if a mass of metal had fallen. As I ran down the passage, my sister's door was unlocked, and revolved slowly upon its hinges. I stared at it horror-stricken, not knowing what was about to issue from it. By the light of the corridor lamp I saw my sister appear at the opening, her face blanched with terror, her hands groping for help, her whole figure swaying to and fro like that of a drunkard. I ran to her and threw my arms round her, but at that moment her knees seemed to give way and she fell to the ground. She writhed as one who is in terrible pain, and her limbs were dreadfully convulsed. At first I thought that she had not recognized me, but as I bent over her she suddenly shrieked out in a voice which I shall never forget, 'Oh, Helen! It was the band! The speckled band!' There was something else which she would fain have said, and she stabbed with her finger into the air in the direction of the doctor's room, but a fresh convulsion seized her and choked her words. I rushed out, calling loudly for my stepfather, and I met him hastening from his room in his dressing gown. When he reached my sister's side she was unconscious, and though he poured brandy down her throat and sent for medical aid from the village, all efforts were in vain, for she slowly sank and died without having recovered her consciousness. Such was the dreadful end of my beloved sister."

"One moment," said Holmes; "are you sure about this whistle and metallic sound? Could you swear to it?"

"That was what the county coroner asked me at the inquiry. It is my strong impression that I heard it, and yet, among the crash of the gale and the creaking of an old house, I may possibly have been deceived."

"Was your sister dressed?"

"No, she was in her nightdress. In her right hand was found the charred stump of a match, and in her left a matchbox."

"Showing that she had struck a light and looked about her when the alarm took place. That is important. And what conclusions did the coroner come to?"

"He investigated the case with great care, for Dr. Roylott's conduct had long been notorious in the county, but he was unable to find any satisfactory cause of death. My evidence showed that the door had been fastened upon the inner side, and the windows were blocked by old-fashioned shutters with broad iron bars, which were secured every night. The walls were carefully sounded, and were shown to be quite solid all round, and the flooring was also thoroughly examined, with the same result. The chimney is wide, but is barred up by four large staples. It is certain, therefore, that my sister was quite alone when she met her end. Besides, there were no marks of any violence upon her."

"How about poison?"

"The doctors examined her for it, but without success."

"What do you think that this unfortunate lady died of, then?"

"It is my belief that she died of pure fear and nervous shock, though what it was that frightened her I cannot imagine."

"Were there gypsies in the plantation at the time?"

"Yes, there are nearly always some there."

"Ah, and what did you gather from this allusion to a band—a speckled band?"

"Sometimes I have thought that it was merely the wild talk of delirium, sometimes that it may have referred to some band of people, perhaps to these very gypsies in the plantation. I do not know whether the spotted handkerchiefs which so many of them wear over their heads might have suggested the strange adjective which she used."

Holmes shook his head like a man who is far from being satisfied.

"These are very deep waters," said he; "pray go on with your narrative."

"Two years have passed since then, and my life has been until lately lonelier than ever. A month ago, however, a dear friend, whom I have known for many years, has done me the honor to ask my hand in marriage. His name is Armitage—Percy Armitage—the second son of Mr. Armitage, of Crane Water, near Reading. My stepfather has offered no opposition to the match, and we are to be married in the course of the spring. Two days ago some repairs were started in the west wing of the building, and my bedroom wall has been pierced, so that I have had to move into the chamber in which my sister died, and to sleep in the very bed in which she slept. Imagine, then, my thrill of terror when last night, as I lay awake, thinking over her terrible fate, I suddenly heard in the silence of the night the low whistle which had been the herald of her own death. I sprang up and lit the lamp, but nothing was to be seen in the room. I was too shaken to go to bed again, however, so I dressed, and as soon as it was daylight I slipped down, got a dogcart at the Crown Inn, which is opposite, and drove to Leatherhead, from whence I have come on this morning with the one object of seeing you and asking your advice."

"You have done wisely," said my friend. "But have you told me all?"

"Yes, all."

"Miss Roylott, you have not. You are screening your stepfather."

"Why, what do you mean?"

For answer Holmes pushed back the frill of black lace which fringed the hand that lay upon our visitor's knee. Five little livid spots, the marks of four fingers and a thumb, were printed upon the white wrist.

"You have been cruelly used," said Holmes.

The lady colored deeply and covered over her injured wrist. "He is a hard man," she said, "and perhaps he hardly knows his own strength."

There was a long silence, during which Holmes leaned his chin upon his hands and stared into the crackling fire.

"This is a very deep business," he said at last. "There are a thousand details which I should desire to know before I decide upon our course of action. Yet we have not a moment to lose. If we were to come to Stoke Moran today, would it be possible for us to look over these rooms without the knowledge of your stepfather?"

"As it happens, he spoke of coming into town today upon some most important business. It is probable that he will be away all day, and that there would be nothing to disturb you. We have a housekeeper now, but I could easily get her out of the way."

"Excellent. You are not averse to this trip, Watson?"

"By no means."

"Then we shall both come. What are you going to do yourself?"

"I have one or two things which I would wish to do now that I am in town. But I shall return by the twelve o'clock train, so as to be there in time for your coming."

"And you may expect us early in the afternoon. I have myself some small business matters to attend to. Will you not wait and breakfast?"

"No, I must go. My heart is lightened already since I have confided my trouble to you. I shall look forward to seeing you again this afternoon." She dropped her thick black veil over her face and glided from the room.

"And what do you think of it all, Watson?" asked Sherlock Holmes, leaning back in his chair.

"It seems to me to be a most dark and sinister business."

"Dark enough and sinister enough."

"Yet if the lady is correct in saying that the flooring and walls are sound, and that the door, window, and chimney are impassable, then her sister must have been undoubtedly alone when she met her mysterious end."

"What becomes, then, of these nocturnal whistles, and what of the very peculiar words of the dying woman?"

"I cannot think."

"When you combine the ideas of whistles at night, the presence of a band of gypsies who are on intimate terms with this old doctor, the fact that we have every reason to believe that the doctor has an interest in preventing his stepdaughter's marriage,

the dying allusion to a band, and, finally, the fact that Miss Helen Stoner heard a metallic clang, which might have been caused by one of those metal bars that secured the shutters, falling back into its place, I think that there is good ground to think that the mystery may be cleared along those lines."

"But what, then, did the gypsies do?"

"I cannot imagine."

"I see many objections to any such theory."

"And so do I. It is precisely for that reason that we are going to Stoke Moran this day. I want to see whether the objections are fatal, or if they may be explained away. But what in the name of the devil!"

The ejaculation had been drawn from my companion by the fact that our door had been suddenly dashed open, and that a huge man had framed himself in the aperture. His costume was a peculiar mixture of the professional and of the agricultural, having a black top hat, a long frock coat, and a pair of high gaiters,[3] with a hunting crop swinging in his hand. So tall was he that his hat actually brushed the crossbar of the doorway, and his breadth seemed to span it across from side to side. A large face, seared with a thousand wrinkles, burned yellow with the sun, and marked with every evil passion, was turned from one to the other of us, while his deep-set, bile-shot eyes, and his high, thin, fleshless nose, gave him somewhat the resemblance to a fierce old bird of prey.

"Which of you is Holmes?" asked this apparition.

"My name, sir; but you have the advantage of me," said my companion quietly.

---

3. gaiters (gāt′ ərz) *n.*: A high overshoe with a cloth upper.

"I am Dr. Grimesby Roylott, of Stoke Moran."

"Indeed, Doctor," said Holmes blandly. "Pray take a seat."

"I will do nothing of the kind. My step-daughter has been here. I have traced her. What has she been saying to you?"

"It is a little cold for the time of the year," said Holmes.

"What has she been saying to you?" screamed the old man furiously.

"But I have heard that the crocuses promise well," continued my companion imperturbably.

"Ha! You put me off, do you?" said our new visitor, taking a step forward and shaking his hunting crop. "I know you, you scoundrel! I have heard of you before. You are Holmes, the meddler."

My friend smiled.

"Holmes, the busybody!"

His smile broadened.

"Holmes, the Scotland Yard Jack-in-office!"

Holmes chuckled heartily. "Your conversation is most entertaining," said he. "When you go out close the door, for there is a decided draft."

"I will go when I have said my say. Don't you dare to meddle with my affairs. I know that Miss Stoner has been here. I traced her! I am a dangerous man to fall foul of! See here." He stepped swiftly forward, seized the poker, and bent it into a curve with his huge brown hands.

"See that you keep yourself out of my grip," he snarled, and hurling the twisted poker into the fireplace he strode out of the room.

"He seems a very amiable person," said Holmes, laughing. "I am not quite so bulky, but if he had remained I might have shown him that my grip was not much more feeble than his own." As he spoke he picked up the steel poker and, with a sudden effort, straightened it out again.

"Fancy his having the insolence to confound me with[4] the official detective force! This incident gives zest to our investigation, however, and I only trust that our little friend will not suffer from her imprudence in allowing this brute to trace her. And now, Watson, we shall order breakfast, and afterwards I shall walk down to Doctors' Commons, where I hope to get some data which may help us in this matter."

It was nearly one o'clock when Sherlock Holmes returned from his excursion. He held in his hand a sheet of blue paper, scrawled over with notes and figures.

"I have seen the will of the deceased wife," said he. "To determine its exact meaning I have been obliged to work out the present prices of the investments with which it is concerned. The total income, which at the time of the wife's death was little short of £1100, is now, through the fall in agricultural prices, not more than £750. Each daughter can claim an income of £250, in case of marriage. It is evident, therefore, that if both girls had married, this beauty would have had a mere pittance,[5] while even one of them would cripple him to a very serious extent. My morning's work has not been wasted, since it has proved that he has the very strongest motives for standing in the way of anything of the sort. And now, Watson, this is too serious for dawdling, especially as the old man is aware that we are interesting ourselves in his affairs; so if you are ready, we shall call a cab and drive to Waterloo. I should be very much obliged if you would slip your revolver into your pocket. An Eley's No. 2 is an excellent argument with gentlemen who can twist steel pokers

into knots. That and a toothbrush are, I think, all that we need."

At Waterloo we were fortunate in catching a train for Leatherhead, where we hired a trap at the station inn and drove for four or five miles through the lovely Surrey lanes. It was a perfect day, with a bright sun and a few fleecy clouds in the heavens. The trees and wayside hedges were just throwing out their first green shoots, and the air was full of the pleasant smell of the moist earth. To me at least there was a strange contrast between the sweet promise of the spring and this sinister quest upon which we were engaged. My companion sat in the front of the trap, his arms folded, his hat pulled down over his eyes, and his chin sunk upon his breast, buried in the deepest thought. Suddenly, however, he started, tapped me on the shoulder, and pointed over the meadows.

"Look there!" said he.

A heavily timbered park stretched up in a gentle slope, thickening into a grove at the highest point. From amid the branches there jutted out the gray gables and high rooftop of a very old mansion.

"Stoke Moran?" said he.

"Yes, sir, that be the house of Dr. Grimesby Roylott," remarked the driver.

"There is some building going on there," said Holmes; "that is where we are going."

"There's the village," said the driver, pointing to a cluster of roofs some distance to the left; "but if you want to get to the house, you'll find it shorter to get over this stile, and so by the footpath over the fields. There it is, where the lady is walking."

"And the lady, I fancy, is Miss Stoner," observed Holmes, shading his eyes. "Yes, I think we had better do as you suggest."

We got off, paid our fare, and the trap rattled back on its way to Leatherhead.

"I thought it as well," said Holmes as we

---

4. confound . . . with: Mistake me for.
5. pittance (pit′ 'ns) *n*.: A small or barely sufficient allowance of money.

climbed the stile, "that this fellow should think we had come here as architects, or on some definite business. It may stop his gossip. Good afternoon, Miss Stoner. You see that we have been as good as our word."

Our client of the morning had hurried forward to meet us with a face which spoke her joy. "I have been waiting so eagerly for you," she cried, shaking hands with us warmly. "All has turned out splendidly. Dr. Roylott has gone to town, and it is unlikely that he will be back before evening."

"We have had the pleasure of making the doctor's acquaintance," said Holmes, and in a few words he sketched out what had occurred. Miss Stoner turned white to the lips as she listened.

"Good heavens!" she cried, "he has followed me, then."

"So it appears."

"He is so cunning that I never know when I am safe from him. What will he say when he returns?"

"He must guard himself, for he may find that there is someone more cunning than himself upon his track. You must lock yourself up from him tonight. If he is violent, we shall take you away to your aunt's at Harrow. Now, we must make the best use of our time, so kindly take us at once to the rooms which we are to examine."

The building was of gray, lichen-blotched[6] stone, with a high central portion and two curving wings, like the claws of a crab, thrown out on each side. In one of these wings the windows were broken and blocked with wooden boards, while the roof was partly caved in, a picture of ruin. The central portion was in little better repair, but the right-hand block was comparatively modern, and the blinds in the windows,

with the blue smoke curling up from the chimneys, showed that this was where the family resided. Some scaffolding had been erected against the end wall, and the stonework had been broken into, but there were no signs of any workmen at the moment of our visit. Holmes walked slowly up and down the ill-trimmed lawn and examined with deep attention the outsides of the windows.

"This, I take it, belongs to the room in which you used to sleep, the center one to your sister's, and the one next to the main building to Dr. Roylott's chamber?"

"Exactly so. But I am now sleeping in the middle one."

"Pending the alterations, as I understand. By the way, there does not seem to be any very pressing need for repairs at that end wall."

"There were none. I believe that it was an excuse to move me from my room."

"Ah! that is suggestive. Now, on the other side of this narrow wing runs the corridor from which these three rooms open. There are windows in it, of course?"

"Yes, but very small ones. Too narrow for anyone to pass through."

"As you both locked your doors at night, your rooms were unapproachable from that side. Now, would you have the kindness to go into your room and bar your shutters?"

Miss Stoner did so, and Holmes, after a careful examination through the open window, endeavored in every way to force the shutter open, but without success. There was no slit through which a knife could be passed to raise the bar. Then with his lens he tested the hinges, but they were of solid iron, built firmly into the massive masonry. "Hum!" said he, scratching his chin in some perplexity, "My theory certainly presents some difficulties. No one could pass through these shutters if they were bolted. Well, we

---

6. lichen-blotched (lī′ kən blächt) *adj.*: Covered with patches of fungus.

shall see if the inside throws any light upon the matter.''

A small side door led into the white-washed corridor from which the three bed-rooms opened. Holmes refused to examine the third chamber, so we passed at once to the second, that in which Miss Stoner was now sleeping, and in which her sister had met with her fate. It was a homely little room, with a low ceiling and a gaping fire-place, after the fashion of old country hous-es. A brown chest of drawers stood in one corner, a narrow white-counterpaned bed in another, and a dressing table on the left-hand side of the window. These articles, with two small wickerwork chairs, made up all the furniture in the room save for a square of Wilton carpet in the center. The boards round and the paneling of the walls were of brown, worm-eaten oak, so old and discolored that it may have dated from the original building of the house. Holmes drew one of the chairs into a corner and sat silent, while his eyes traveled round and round and up and down, taking in every detail of the apartment.

"Where does that bell communicate with?" he asked at last, pointing to a thick bell-rope which hung down beside the bed, the tassel actually lying upon the pillow.

"It goes to the housekeeper's room."

"It looks newer than the other things?"

"Yes, it was only put there a couple of years ago."

"Your sister asked for it, I suppose?"

"No, I never heard of her using it. We used always to get what we wanted for our-selves."

"Indeed, it seemed unnecessary to put so nice a bell-pull there. You will excuse me for a few minutes while I satisfy myself as to this floor." He threw himself down upon his face with his lens in his hand and crawled swiftly backward and forward, examining

minutely the cracks between the boards. Then he did the same with the woodwork with which the chamber was paneled. Fi-nally he walked over to the bed and spent some time in staring at it and in running his eye up and down the wall. Finally he took the bell-rope in his hand and gave it a brisk tug.

"Why, it's a dummy," said he.

"Won't it ring?"

"No, it is not even attached to a wire. This is very interesting. You can see now

"Done about the same time as the bell-rope?" remarked Holmes.

"Yes, there were several little changes carried out about that time."

"They seem to have been of a most interesting character—dummy bell-ropes, and ventilators which do not ventilate. With your permission, Miss Stoner, we shall now carry our researches into the inner apartment."

Dr. Grimesby Roylott's chamber was larger than that of his stepdaughter, but was as plainly furnished. A camp bed, a small wooden shelf full of books, mostly of a technical character, an armchair beside the bed, a plain wooden chair against the wall, a round table, and a large iron safe were the principal things which met the eye. Holmes walked slowly round and examined each and all of them with the keenest interest.

"What's in here?" he asked, tapping the safe.

"My stepfather's business papers."

"Oh! you have seen inside, then?"

"Only once, some years ago. I remember that it was full of papers."

"There isn't a cat in it, for example?"

"No. What a strange idea!"

"Well, look at this!" He took up a small saucer of milk which stood on the top of it.

"No; we don't keep a cat. But there is a cheetah and a baboon."

"Ah, yes, of course! Well, a cheetah is just a big cat, and yet a saucer of milk does not go very far in satisfying its wants, I daresay. There is one point which I should wish to determine." He squatted down in front of the wooden chair and examined the seat of it with the greatest attention.

"Thank you. That is quite settled," said he, rising and putting his lens in his pocket. "Hello! Here is something interesting!"

The object which had caught his eye was a small dog lash hung on one corner of the

that it is fastened to a hook just above where the little opening for the ventilator is."

"How very absurd! I never noticed that before!"

"Very strange!" muttered Holmes, pulling at the rope. "There are one or two very singular points about this room. For example, what a fool a builder must be to open a ventilator into another room, when, with the same trouble, he might have communicated with the outside air!"

"That is also quite modern," said the lady.

bed. The lash, however, was curled upon itself and tied so as to make a loop of whipcord.

"What do you make of that, Watson?"

"It's a common enough lash. But I don't know why it should be tied."

"That is not quite so common, is it? Ah, me! it's a wicked world, and when a clever man turns his brains to crime it is the worst of all. I think that I have seen enough now, Miss Stoner, and with your permission we shall walk out upon the lawn."

I had never seen my friend's face so grim or his brow so dark as it was when we turned from the scene of this investigation. We had walked several times up and down the lawn, neither Miss Stoner nor myself liking to break in upon his thoughts before he roused himself from his reverie.

"It is very essential, Miss Stoner," said he, "that you should absolutely follow my advice in every respect."

"I shall most certainly do so."

"The matter is too serious for any hesitation. Your life may depend upon your compliance."[7]

"I assure you that I am in your hands."

"In the first place, both my friend and I must spend the night in your room."

Both Miss Stoner and I gazed at him in astonishment.

"Yes, it must be so. Let me explain. I believe that that is the village inn over there?"

"Yes, that is the Crown."

"Very good. Your windows would be visible from there?"

"Certainly."

"You must confine yourself to your room, on pretense of a headache, when your stepfather comes back. Then when you hear him retire for the night, you must open the shutters of your window, undo the hasp,[8] put your lamp there as a signal to us, and then withdraw quietly with everything which you are likely to want into the room which you used to occupy. I have no doubt that, in spite of the repairs, you could manage there for one night."

"Oh, yes, easily."

"The rest you will leave in our hands."

"But what will you do?"

"We shall spend the night in your room, and we shall investigate the cause of this noise which has disturbed you."

"I believe, Mr. Holmes, that you have already made up your mind," said Miss Stoner, laying her hand upon my companion's sleeve.

"Perhaps I have."

"Then, for pity's sake, tell me what was the cause of my sister's death."

"I should prefer to have clearer proofs before I speak."

"You can at least tell me whether my own thought is correct, and if she died from some sudden fright."

"No, I do not think so. I think that there was probably some more tangible cause. And now, Miss Stoner, we must leave you, for if Dr. Roylott returned and saw us our journey would be in vain. Goodbye, and be brave, for if you will do what I have told you, you may rest assured that we shall soon drive away the dangers that threaten you."

Sherlock Holmes and I had no difficulty in engaging a bedroom and sitting room at the Crown Inn. They were on the upper floor, and from our window we could command a view of the avenue gate, and of the inhabited wing of Stoke Moran Manor House. At dusk we saw Dr. Grimesby Roylott drive past, his huge form looming up beside

---

7. compliance (kəm pli′ əns) *n.*: Agreeing to a request.

8. hasp *n.*: Hinged metal fastening of a window.

the little figure of the lad who drove him. The boy had some slight difficulty in undoing the heavy iron gates, and we heard the hoarse roar of the doctor's voice and saw the fury with which he shook his clinched fists at him. The trap drove on, and a few minutes later we saw a sudden light spring up among the trees as the lamp was lit in one of the sitting rooms.

"Do you know, Watson," said Holmes as we sat together in the gathering darkness, "I have really some scruples as to taking you tonight. There is a distinct element of danger."

"Can I be of assistance?"

"Your presence might be invaluable."

"Then I shall certainly come."

"It is very kind of you."

"You speak of danger. You have evidently seen more in these rooms than was visible to me."

"No, but I fancy that I may have deduced a little more. I imagine that you saw all that I did."

"I saw nothing remarkable save the bellrope, and what purpose that could answer I confess is more than I can imagine."

"You saw the ventilator, too?"

"Yes, but I do not think that it is such a very unusual thing to have a small opening between two rooms. It was so small that a rat could hardly pass through."

"I knew that we should find a ventilator before ever we came to Stoke Moran."

"My dear Holmes!"

"Oh, yes, I did. You remember in her statement she said that her sister could smell Dr. Roylott's cigar. Now, of course that suggested at once that there must be a communication between the two rooms. It could only be a small one, or it would have been remarked upon at the coroner's inquiry. I deduced a ventilator."

"But what harm can there be in that?"

"Well, there is at least a curious coincidence of dates. A ventilator is made, a cord is hung, and a lady who sleeps in the bed dies. Does not that strike you?"

"I cannot as yet see any connection."

"Did you observe anything very peculiar about that bed?"

"No."

"It was clamped to the floor. Did you ever see a bed fastened like that before?"

"I cannot say that I have."

"The lady could not move her bed. It must always be in the same relative position to the ventilator and to the rope—or so we may call it, since it was clearly never meant for a bell-pull."

"Holmes," I cried, "I seem to see dimly what you are hinting at. We are only just in time to prevent some subtle and horrible crime."

"Subtle enough and horrible enough. When a doctor does go wrong he is the first of criminals. He has nerve and he has knowledge. Palmer and Pritchard were among the heads of their profession. This man strikes even deeper, but I think, Watson, that we shall be able to strike deeper still. But we shall have horrors enough before the night is over; for goodness' sake let us have a quiet pipe and turn our minds for a few hours to something more cheerful."

About nine o'clock the light among the trees was extinguished, and all was dark in the direction of the Manor House. Two hours passed slowly away, and then, suddenly, just at the stroke of eleven, a single bright light shone out right in front of us.

"That is our signal," said Holmes, springing to his feet; "it comes from the middle window."

As we passed out he exchanged a few words with the landlord, explaining that we were going on a late visit to an acquaintance, and that it was possible that we might spend the night there. A moment later we were out on the dark road, a chill wind blowing in our faces, and one yellow light twinkling in front of us through the gloom to guide us on our somber errand.

There was little difficulty in entering the grounds; for unrepaired breaches gaped in the old park wall. Making our way among the trees, we reached the lawn, crossed it, and were about to enter through the window when out from a clump of laurel bushes there darted what seemed to be a hideous and distorted child, who threw itself upon the grass with writhing limbs and then ran swiftly across the lawn into the darkness.

"My God!" I whispered; "did you see it?"

Holmes was for the moment as startled as I. His hand closed like a vise upon my wrist in his agitation. Then he broke into a low laugh and put his lips to my ear.

"It is a nice household," he murmured. "That is the baboon."

I had forgotten the strange pets which the doctor affected. There was a cheetah, too; perhaps we might find it upon our shoulders at any moment. I confess that I felt easier in my mind when, after following Holmes's example and slipping off my shoes, I found myself inside the bedroom. My companion noiselessly closed the shutters, moved the lamp onto the table, and cast his eyes round the room. All was as we had seen it in the daytime. Then creeping up to me and making a trumpet of his hand, he whispered into my ear again so gently that it was all that I could do to distinguish the words:

"The least sound would be fatal to our plans."

I nodded to show that I had heard.

"We must sit without light. He would see it through the ventilator."

I nodded again.

"Do not go asleep; your very life may depend upon it. Have your pistol ready in case we should need it. I will sit on the side of the bed, and you in that chair."

I took out my revolver and laid it on the corner of the table.

Holmes had brought up a long thin cane, and this he placed upon the bed beside him. By it he laid the box of matches and the stump of a candle. Then he turned down the lamp, and we were left in darkness.

How shall I ever forget that dreadful vigil? I could not hear a sound, not even the drawing of a breath, and yet I knew that my companion sat open-eyed, within a few feet of me, in the same state of nervous tension in which I was myself. The shutters cut off the least ray of light, and we waited in absolute darkness. From outside came the occasional cry of a night bird, and once at our very window a long-drawn catlike whine, which told us that the cheetah was indeed at liberty. Far away we could hear the deep tones of the parish clock, which boomed out every quarter of an hour. How long they seemed, those quarters! Twelve struck, and one and two and three, and still we sat waiting silently for whatever might befall.

Suddenly there was the momentary gleam of a light up in the direction of the ventilator, which vanished immediately, but was succeeded by a strong smell of burning oil and heated metal. Someone in the next room had lit a dark lantern.[9] I heard a gentle sound of movement, and then all was silent once more, though the smell grew stronger. For half an hour I sat with straining ears.

---

9. dark lantern: A lantern with a shutter that can hide the light.

Then suddenly another sound became audible—a very gentle, soothing sound, like that of a small jet of steam escaping continually from a kettle. The instant that we heard it, Holmes sprang from the bed, struck a match, and lashed furiously with his cane at the bell-pull.

"You see it, Watson?" he yelled. "You see it?"

But I saw nothing. At the moment when Holmes struck the light I heard a low, clear whistle, but the sudden glare flashing into my weary eyes made it impossible for me to tell what it was at which my friend lashed so savagely. I could, however, see that his face was deadly pale and filled with horror and loathing.

He had ceased to strike and was gazing up at the ventilator when suddenly there broke from the silence of the night the most horrible cry to which I have ever listened. It swelled up louder and louder, a hoarse yell of pain and fear and anger all mingled in the one dreadful shriek. They say that away down in the village, and even in the distant parsonage, that cry raised the sleepers from their beds. It struck cold to our hearts, and I stood gazing at Holmes, and he at me, until the last echoes of it had died away into the silence from which it rose.

"What can it mean?" I gasped.

"It means that it is all over," Holmes answered. "And perhaps, after all, it is for the best. Take your pistol, and we will enter Dr. Roylott's room."

With a grave face he lit the lamp and led the way down the corridor. Twice he struck at the chamber door without any reply from within. Then he turned the handle and entered, I at his heels, with the cocked pistol in my hand.

It was a singular sight which met our eyes. On the table stood a dark lantern with the shutter half open, throwing a brilliant beam of light upon the iron safe, the door of which was ajar. Beside this table, on the wooden chair, sat Dr. Grimesby Roylott, clad in a long gray dressing gown, his bare ankles protruding beneath, and his feet thrust into red heelless Turkish slippers. Across his lap lay the short stock with the long lash which we had noticed during the day. His chin was cocked upward and his eyes were fixed in a dreadful, rigid stare at the corner of the ceiling. Round his brow he had a peculiar yellow band, with brownish speckles, which seemed to be bound tightly round his head. As we entered he made neither sound nor motion.

"The band! the speckled band!" whispered Holmes.

I took a step forward. In an instant his strange headgear began to move, and there reared itself from among his hair the squat diamond-shaped head and puffed neck of a loathsome serpent.

"It is a swamp adder!" cried Holmes; "the deadliest snake in India. He has died within ten seconds of being bitten. Violence does, in truth, recoil upon the violent, and the schemer falls into the pit which he digs for another. Let us thrust this creature back into its den, and we can then remove Miss Stoner to some place of shelter and let the county police know what has happened."

As he spoke he drew the dog whip swiftly from the dead man's lap, and throwing the noose round the reptile's neck he drew it from its horrid perch and, carrying it at arm's length, threw it into the iron safe, which he closed upon it.

Such are the true facts of the death of Dr. Grimesby Roylott, of Stoke Moran. It is not necessary that I should prolong a narrative which has already run to too great a length by telling how we broke the sad news to the terrified girl, how we conveyed her by the morning train to the care of her good aunt at Harrow, of how the slow process of official inquiry came to the conclusion that the doctor met his fate while indiscreetly playing with a dangerous pet. The little which I had yet to learn of the case was told me by Sherlock Holmes as we traveled back next day.

"I had," said he, "come to an entirely erroneous conclusion which shows, my dear Watson, how dangerous it always is to reason from insufficient data. The presence of the gypsies, and the use of the word *band*, which was used by the poor girl, no doubt to explain the appearance which she had caught a hurried glimpse of by the light of her match, were sufficient to put me upon an entirely wrong scent. I can only claim the merit that I instantly reconsidered my position when, however, it became clear to me that whatever danger threatened an occupant of the room could not come either from the window or the door. My attention was speedily drawn, as I have already remarked to you, to this ventilator, and to the bell-rope which hung down to the bed. The discovery that this was a dummy, and that the bed was clamped to the floor, instantly gave rise to the suspicion that the rope was there as a bridge for something passing through the hole and coming to the bed. The idea of a snake instantly occurred to me, and when I coupled it with my knowledge that the doctor was furnished with a supply of creatures from India, I felt that I was probably on the right track. The idea of using a form of poison which could not possibly be discovered by any chemical test was just such a one as would occur to a clever and ruthless man who had had an Eastern training. The rapidity with which such a poison would take effect would also, from his point of view, be an advantage. It would be a sharp-eyed coroner, indeed, who could distinguish the two little dark punctures which would show where the poison fangs had done their work. Then I thought of the whistle. Of course he must recall the snake before the morning light revealed it to the victim. He had trained it, probably by the use of the milk which we saw, to return to him when summoned. He would put it through this ventilator at the hour that he thought best, with the certainty that it would crawl down the rope and land on the bed. It might or might not bite the occupant, perhaps she might escape every night for a week, but sooner or later she must fall a victim.

"I had come to these conclusions before ever I had entered his room. An inspection of his chair showed me that he had been in the habit of standing on it, which of course would be necessary in order that he should reach the ventilator. The sight of the safe, the saucer of milk, and the loop of whipcord were enough to finally dispel any doubts which may have remained. The metallic clang heard by Miss Stoner was obviously caused by her stepfather hastily closing the door of his safe upon its terrible occupant. Having once made up my mind, you know the steps which I took in order to put the matter to the proof. I heard the creature hiss as I have no doubt that you did also, and I instantly lit the light and attacked it."

"With the result of driving it through the ventilator."

"And also with the result of causing it to turn upon its master at the other side. Some of the blows of my cane came home and roused its snakish temper, so that it flew upon the first person it saw. In this way I am no doubt indirectly responsible for Dr. Grimesby Roylott's death, and I cannot say that it is likely to weigh very heavily upon my conscience."

THINKING ABOUT THE SELECTION

Recalling

1. Why has Helen Stoner come to see Holmes?
2. What does Holmes learn about Helen by observing her?
3. What does Dr. Roylott do shortly after his wife's death? What are the terms of her will?
4. What two sounds did Helen hear after she was awakened by her sister's scream? What are her sister's last words?
5. Why does Dr. Roylott pay a visit to Holmes? How does Holmes react to Roylott's visit?
6. How do Holmes and Watson spend the night at Stoke Moran?
7. What is the speckled band?

Interpreting

8. What had Holmes thought was the significance of Julia's last words? How is this an example of reasoning from insufficient data?
9. Name three ways that Helen's situation now is similar to Julia's just before Julia's death.
10. Explain the significance of the dummy bell rope, the ventilator leading to Dr. Roylott's room, and the bed anchored to the floor in Julia's room.
11. Explain the significance of each of the four clues Holmes finds in Roylott's room.
12. What is Roylott's motive for the crimes?
13. How does Roylott's plan backfire?

Applying

14. Sherlock Holmes uses his powers of observation well. Name three ways to improve your own powers of observation.

ANALYZING LITERATURE

Examining Conflict

Conflict is a struggle between opposing forces or characters. One type of conflict involves a struggle of one character with another. Often the characters are fairly evenly matched.

1. How does Roylott prove his physical strength? How does Holmes prove to be his match?
2. In what way does Holmes's nerve, or courage, help him win the conflict?
3. How does his superior intellect help him win?
4. What does Holmes say that indicates he recognizes nerve and intellect in Dr. Roylott?

CRITICAL THINKING AND READING

Understanding Logical Reasoning

A detective reasons in a logical way to solve a crime. Holmes uses a process of elimination. First he gathers all the information he can about Julia's death. Then he tests each piece of information to see if it leads to the truth. If not, Holmes eliminates it from his thinking. For example, when Holmes realizes that gypsies could not have gotten into Julia's room, he stops thinking they might be responsible for her death. In this way, he can focus his skills on fewer and fewer facts or clues, fitting them together in a sequence of events that will lead to the solution.

1. What early clues suggest that Dr. Roylott has something to hide from the authorities?
2. How did you know Dr. Roylott would make an attempt on Helen's life that very night?

THINKING AND WRITING

Understanding Your Thinking

Holmes uses deductive reasoning to solve problems. For example, after observing Helen, he concludes that she drove in a dogcart along heavy roads before reaching the train station. He bases his conclusion on evidence: Her jacket is splattered with fresh mud and the only vehicle that throws up mud that way is a dogcart.

Write the first draft of a composition explaining how you have solved a problem through deductive reasoning, such as solving a television mystery. Revise to make sure your reasoning is clear. Prepare a final draft.

GUIDE FOR READING

Accounts Settled

Paul Annixter (1894–   ) was born in Minnesota. Annixter often writes about the wilderness and its creatures. Perhaps this is because he has had personal experience with the woods. As a young man, Annixter spent a year and a half alone on a timber claim in northern Minnesota where he cut wood to make money and hunted game for his food. Annixter used his knowledge of the wilderness to write "Accounts Settled," the story you are about to read.

Suspense and Foreshadowing

Suspense is the quality of a story that makes the reader curious and excited about what will happen next. One way an author can build suspense is by using foreshadowing. **Foreshadowing** means giving the reader clues that hint at later events in the plot without actually revealing them.

Paul Annixter uses foreshadowing to increase the suspense in "Accounts Settled." In the very first paragraph, he refers to a "sinister feeling" and "a sense of something watching, waiting." These details foreshadow later events by hinting at the possibility that the hero is not alone.

Look For

As you read "Accounts Settled," watch for language that creates suspense and for hints that foreshadow what will happen to Gordon as he spends a lonely night in the silent, forbidding woods.

Writing

In "Accounts Settled" sixteen-year-old Gordon Bent faces his fears and shows courage. Freewrite for five minutes about what the word *courage* means to you. Include examples of courage with which you are familiar.

Vocabulary

Knowing the following words will help you as you read "Accounts Settled."

sinister (sin'is tər) *adj.*: Threatening harm, evil, or misfortune (p. 47)

initiation (i nish'ē ā'shən) *n.*: The events or process during which a person becomes admitted as a member of a club or special group (p. 48)

Accounts Settled

Paul Annixter

There it was again, that sinister feeling in the pine shadows and a sense of something watching, waiting among the dense trees up ahead. This spruce valley was a dark, forbidding place even in summer; now the winter silence under the blue-black trees was more than silence—it was like a spell. Queer, they had had to choose this place to lay their trapline, just a week before his father had come down with flu-pneumonia, leaving Gordon to cover the long line during the worst weeks of winter. He wouldn't have minded tending the old line along the lake shore, but this haunted place—

Gordon Bent was sixteen, turning seventeen, already six feet tall and scantling thin.[1] The first fuzz of beard showed like a faint gray lichen[2] along his lean cheek. Timber-bred, he knew the woods and creatures as well as his father, and never before had he feared any of them. But something about this valley had filled him with dread from the first.

It would have been all right but for the nights. The valley was a mile from home, and it took him two days to cover the trapline properly. So twice a week he had to make snow camp in the deep woods near the valley's head, sleeping out in the bark-

covered, half-faced lean-to he and his father had set up for the storing of trapping gear.

Almost too much to bear, it had been at first—the deathly diamond stillness of the night, the tremendous onslaught of the cold, the emptiness and the loneliness. And then he began to see and feel all the things he had longed to know: the deep woods showing him their dark and secret face, their winter side, which few men ever had

---

1. scantling thin: As thin as a small timber or beam in a structure.
2. lichen (lī′ kən) n.: Small plants of fungus and alga growing on rocks, wood, or soil.

the need or hardihood to learn. Only because he had been raised to like the lonely places had he grown accustomed to it. Then, in the past week or so, had come this other thing—the growing sense that he was not alone, that inimical eyes were watching him from some unguessed vantage. The feeling was so strong that he would stop often to look behind him and sometimes go back over his trail, but he saw nothing; the silence of the winter woods remained enigmatic and complete.

Once he spoke to his father about it.

"Might be some young lynx, playin' hide an' seek with you," the elder Bent had smiled. "A lynx is a tomfool for followin' humans."

Gordon had let it go at that, but he knew by the occasional fuzz of nerves along his back that the secret shadowing still went on, and that it was more than an inquisitive surveillance.[3] There was threat and danger in it. He had thought at first it might be a wolverine, that bane[4] of all trappers, whose cunning is beyond belief; but a wolverine would have played hob with[5] his traps, and this prowler did not molest his line. His catch of fur continued to mount, and he was inordinately proud, for ill luck had long dogged the backwoods family, culminating in his father's illness coming just as the high tide of the trapping season began. Each outjourney now netted him from six to a dozen prime pelts.[6] His father, lying in his cord bunk, would carefully examine every pelt that spilled from Gordon's filled sack with expert appraisal, while Gordon would stand by, the faint

sweat of pride on his frost-darkened face. The elder Bent would hold up the skins, blowing expertly into the piled nap where it was deepest, estimating their value, each one a rare mint of the secret woods.

"How many now, Son?" he would ask, and Gordon, who kept careful record, would study his list. "Sixty-seven now, Pa. Thirty-five of them prime number ones, I figure."

"We're getting out of the woods for fair," his father would smile. "'Spite of my lying here hog-tied and halted. Old Hard Luck went and hunted him another range after layin' me low, I guess. Couldn't cope with you nohow."

"I aim to have more skins curing here than a body'll know what to do with, come February," Gordon would say largely, holding hard against the tide of feeling roused by all this praise. He was bowed these days beneath the care of the line and all the chores about the place, trying to act like the man of the house, fighting against the undermining gnawing of exhaustion and the subtler gnawing of self-importance. At all times he was aware of his father's silent appraisal.[7] Not for anything would he have shown by word or look the fear he felt in the lonely valley. For these were the crucial days that marked his initiation into the cult of finished woodsmen.

And the valley had kept giving up its daily tithe of treasure, the skins had kept coming in. Three great bundles of them now hung in the storehouse suspended from chains against the inroads of rodents, and the cabin walls were pegged with them from floor to rafter. More than pelts, they were furry flags and banners of victory, proclaiming that the Bents were winning out at last in their long handicap fight against

---

3. inquisitive (in kwiz′ə tiv) **surveillance** (sər vā′ləns): Curious inspection.
4. bane (bān) *n.*: Ruin.
5. played hob with: Interfered with.
6. pelts (peltz) *n.*: The skin, including the fur, of a fur-bearing animal.

---

7. appraisal (ə prā′ z'l) *n.*: Evaluation; judgment.

poverty, proclaiming, too, that Gordon was no longer a stripling, but a man.

Now it was late afternoon and Gordon was making another lonely round of the line. Tonight he was to sleep in the woods again. As the short winter day drew to a close, he felt the clutch of the empty solitude like a hand squeezing the valves of his heart. He came to his night camp in a dense stand of hemlocks. As usual, he stood for a time in silence, gazing down the blue-black aisles between the trees, listening to the ancient dirge[8] of the breeze in the treetops. Always he felt the deep woods here as nowhere else in the valley, and always that sense of surveillance was stronger here.

All around his camp the dark conifers stood quiet, listening, as if they were tranced and hearing something too. They talked softly among themselves in winter tones. The tall firs with their heads together whispered and creaked; the hoary matted hemlocks muttered low. Sometimes they sighed.

Abruptly Gordon became aware of another sound, not of the trees. His nerves tautened, and automatically he loosed the safety catch of his rifle. Then high above him he saw the source of the sound. A porcupine had just emerged from a hole high up in the big hemlock. Gordon's rifle went up and he was about to shoot the animal in nervous reaction to the start it had given him, when he recalled something his father had told him. "Never kill a porcupine," the elder Bent had counseled him, and later Gordon had found that it was a sort of unwritten law among woodsmen to let the quill-pig go unmolested. The porcupine was an utterly harmless animal, abroad at all seasons, and many a time, according to

record, hunters' lives had been saved in a pinch when they killed a porcupine for food.

Gordon let his rifle drop into the crook of his arm and watched the porky slowly descending the tree trunk, accompanied by the rasping of claws on bark and a total disregard for who or what might see him. Every now and then it emitted small grunts and chatterings of petulance or satisfaction. Once it turned its gray-black, gnomelike face to eye Gordon with an expression at once mild and ludicrously irate. Its quills rose and rattled and the whole animal seemed to pale with anger and irritation, as the gray-white underfur came into view. Then it continued its downward progress, calm with a containment that few but the

8. **dirge** (dʉrj) *n.:* Slow, sad song of mourning.

great achieve. About him, if one were sensitive enough to catch it, was the sense that he was as mystically attuned to nature as the silent, grand march of the forest trees.

Gordon passed on up the valley, for he had three more traps to cover before he turned in. Darkness had fallen when he returned, and it was then that he found out why the porky had been hanging around. His grub cache[9] had been robbed. He made a hurried checkup. Nearly all of his precious supply of bacon was gone. With infinite pains, Quills had gnawed a hole clear through the split-log cache with big yellow chisels, in search of food. In an uprush of anger, Gordon rated himself for a fool, for not having shot the porcupine. If he crossed the animal's trail again, he vowed, he would kill it on sight.

Because of the robbery, he rolled into his blankets with scarcely any supper. He did not sleep for a long time, but lay looking up through the hemlock branches to the cold sky pollened with stars. Finally he drowsed off. How long afterward it was that he awakened he never knew, nor what it was that seemed to cry a sharp warning through the mists of the unconscious. It must have been something akin to those guardian instincts that animals know, and without which all wild things would soon become extinct. The same thing that had warned him brought him back to full consciousness smoothly and subtly so that not the slightest jerk or start accompanied it. Almost before his eyelids parted, he was aware of the nature of the danger that threatened.

A segment of waning moon shone through the branches overhead and into the open-ended lean-to. In the faint light, Gordon half doubted the testimony of his eyes, though at the same time something

within him did not. Something about the outline of the hemlock branch directly above him drew and fixed his attention. And all at once he knew that a great cougar was crouching up there; that it had been the grim fixity of the beast's regard that had jerked him out of sleep.

The limb was nine feet above him, and Gordon knew in a flash how the cougar had reached it—by climbing a tree some hundreds of feet away and picking his way among the overlapping branches. The big cat was stretched out along the branch, its powerful foreclaws unsheathed and gripping the bark in tense but silent savagery. Its yellow-notch eyes glowed lambently in the flat, down-thrust head. By the savage hunger of those eyes and by every contour of the crouching form, Gordon knew that

_____

9. grub cache (kash): Hidden supply of food.

had he made a single abrupt movement on awakening, the cat would have sprung.

Gordon knew the nature of the cougar to be about eighty percent ferocity, which is just another name for cowardice, and that under ordinary circumstances a man had nothing to fear from him. But there were certain times, under certain conditions, when there was no enemy in the wilderness more dangerous. Let age slow his speed and spoil his timing and hunger have its way with him, and the lion of America leans toward man-killing, just as the lion of Africa. In the eyes of this one, Gordon sensed fear and murder struggling for mastery. Here, he knew, was the unseen shadower that had been playing havoc with his nerves.

Instinct dictated his actions in the grim moments that followed. He kept his eyes almost closed, that the beast might not catch their gleam; and his whole body remained still, in a semblance of sleep. He knew that if he so much as stirred a hand the cat would spring. But if he remained utterly still there was a slim chance that the animal might go away.

Then began an ordeal which taxed every atom of Gordon's physical and mental control. His body was numb and full of aches from sleeping in one position. Already his muscles cried out to be eased and stretched. Yet he dared not move an inch.

Moments passed, horrible heart-thudding moments, during which neither man nor animal stirred. The cougar remained frozen in his attitude of vigilance, head sunk on paws, every muscle set except for the slow, unconscious twitching of his rounded tail tip. His eyes held the boy unwinkingly as he waited in the fiendish way of cats for the moment when the man must stir, or make an attempt to escape, the moment when his ingrained fear of man would be swallowed up by the rising tide of his blood-lust.

Gordon began to feel that he was going mad. Sweat stood out on his body now, prickling sensations ran along his cramped limbs, and he could hear the pumping of blood in his temples like the beating of a great drum. He knew he could not hold out much longer, that soon his tormented nerves and muscles must assert an involuntary rebellion of their own, even though his will stood out against it.

He had located the exact position of his rifle, propped against the side of the lean-to, but he knew that a single move to reach it would precipitate[10] a lightning spring. An almost overwhelming impulse to risk all on a desperate grab for the gun obsessed him; but his cooler faculties told him he would never live to fire a shot. The cougar would be on him in a flash, his great claws like steel hooks, ripping, tearing. Yet the torture was too great for calm judgment now. He must move, in another minute, another second—.

And then, even as he was on the verge of desperate action, came interruption.

A sound smote upon his overstretched nerves—slight, yet magnified a hundred times in the breathless stillness of the forest night. It was exactly timed to upset the dramatic situation at the moment of crisis, for it electrified the cougar on his high perch.

Gordon saw a tremor pass over the lithe form of the killer. For a taut instant he held his breath. The slightest thing now, he knew, might draw a swift attack. Then he gasped in silent relief, for he had located the sound. So had the cougar. The flat head lifted in attention; then the eyes glared downward on the other side of the branch.

---

10. precipitate (pri sip′ə tāt′) *v*.: Cause to happen.

Quills, the porcupine, had recalled his stolen meal of bacon in Gordon's cache, and was returning in search of more. He had approached from behind the lean-to and was investigating the hole he had gnawed, giving vent to short grunts and faint rodent-like chatterings of anticipation. Fearless and one-pointed in his quest, he was oblivious to both man and cougar.

Above him, Gordon saw the cougar quiver slightly, its tail lashing softly. For a moment or two, he knew, the cat would not leap; for its shallow brain could focus upon but one thing at a time, and the porcupine now held the stage.

Stealthily Gordon lifted the blankets and reached for his rifle, his eyes never leaving the crouched form above. His hand closed on the weapon and with a single follow-through movement he dropped to his back again and fired.

Almost in the same instant the cougar launched himself frenziedly downward. Gordon fired again from his prone position, and in mid-air the lithe outstretched body buckled and crumpled, the leap falling just short of the boy, who had flung himself aside. Again the rifle blazed death at the writhing body in the snow, and that shot took vengeance for the ordeal Gordon had undergone, and the weeks of fear that had gone before.

As the breathless silence of the night and the forest fell once more over the camp, Gordon found himself trembling all over with a cold that had nothing to do with the frost. A sort of whimper escaped him, the first sound he had made, and two hot tears sprang from his eyes and bounced off his cheeks. They were the final tears of boyhood, and he was glad he was alone with them. Never would he cry again, and never

again, he felt, would he be afraid of any beast that prowled.

His eye was drawn now to the squat form of the porcupine, every quill erect and faintly limned[11] in the patch of milky moonlight. At the report of the rifle, Quills had quickly doubled up in self-defense, thrusting his nose between his forefeet. As Gordon watched, the panoply[12] of spines began slowly to lower and the little meddler took a crafty look around. The unseemly ruckus that had startled him was apparently over. Disregarding the watching boy, he returned to his rummaging, and Gordon, grinning, made no move to stop him.

Sleep was gone for him for the night. Dawn was not far off. He built a fire near the opening of the lean-to and got out his skinning knife. Only then did he sense how very near the end he had been. In the light of the flames, he saw the yellowed and broken fangs in the cougar's open jaws, the ragged, moulting look of the fur and other signs of age. It had been a long time since the killer had been able to bring down his usual prey among the deer herds. Months of desperate hunger had led up to the big cat's act of daring madness.

Gordon thought with a shiver of the inevitable outcome had he shot the porcupine that afternoon as he had been tempted to do. The porcupine had repaid his little act of tolerance a hundredfold.

What a tale he'd have to tell when people gathered round hearth or campfire. No longer would he be a stripling, sitting back in the shadows, listening to the sights and feats of other hunters. He'd have a marvel to relate that matched the oldest of them now, and a pelt to prove it, as a trophy.

---

11. limned (limd) *adj.*: Outlined.
12. panoply (pan′ə plē) *n.*: Magnificent covering or array.

THINKING ABOUT THE SELECTION

Recalling

1. Why is Gordon alone in the woods?
2. Why does Gordon spare the porcupine?
3. Why does Gordon wake up suddenly? Of what is he aware before he opens his eyes?
4. Explain how instinct helps Gordon avoid the cougar's attack?
5. How does the porcupine help Gordon escape?

Interpreting

6. Explain how this incident marks Gordon's passage from boyhood to manhood.
7. Explain the meaning of the story's title.

Applying

8. Do you agree with Gordon's claim that ferocity is another name for cowardice? Explain.
9. Some of Gordon's qualities would serve him well in places other than the woods. Name three of these traits and tell how they would be useful no matter where Gordon was.

ANALYZING LITERATURE

Investigating Suspense

Suspense is the quality of a story that keeps you wondering what will happen next. One way an author increases suspense is by the use of **foreshadowing,** or hinting at what is to come.

1. When did you first think Gordon was in danger?
2. Find two clues that hint at the cougar's presence.
3. How does Gordon having to lie perfectly still to avoid the attack increase the suspense?

CRITICAL THINKING AND READING

Making Predictions

As you read, you make predictions about what will happen next. **Predictions** are intelli- gent guesses based on evidence you already have. For example, you may predict Gordon will run into trouble when you read about the "sinister feeling" he has in the "dark, forbidding place."

1. What clue helped you predict the porcupine would play an important role in this story?
2. What would have happened to Gordon if he had killed the porcupine? Explain your answer.

UNDERSTANDING LANGUAGE

Interpreting Metaphors

A **metaphor** is an implied comparison be- tween unlike things. For example, look at the following sentence: "With infinite pains, Quills had gnawed a hole clear through the split-log cache with big yellow chisels, in search of food." The author compares the porcupine's teeth to chisels, which are used for splitting wood, to describe how effectively a porcupine can chew.

Find the metaphor in the following sentence and explain what it means: "More than pelts, they were furry flags and banners of victory, pro- claiming that the Bents were winning out at last in their long handicap fight against poverty, pro- claiming, too, that Gordon was no longer a stripling, but a man."

THINKING AND WRITING

Writing About Suspense

The writer Max Lerner has said: "The turning point in the process of growing up is when you discover the core strength within you. . . ." Think about the meaning of Lerner's words. Discuss them with your classmates. How do these words relate to Gordon? How do they relate to you? Write the first draft of a composition about an incident that marks your passage from child- hood. (If you prefer, create a fictional character and a fictional incident.) Revise your composi- tion, making sure you have retold the incident in a logical order. Finally, proofread your paper.

GUIDE FOR READING

A Retrieved Reformation

O. Henry (1862–1910) was born William Sidney Porter in North Carolina. In his youth he worked as a reporter, a bank teller, and a draftsman. He lived in Austin, Texas, in the country of Honduras, in Pittsburgh, and in New York City. He even spent three years in an Ohio penitentiary. It was there that he wrote his first short stories. It was also there that he learned about a bank robber and a safecracker who became models for Jimmy Valentine, the hero of "A Retrieved Reformation."

The Surprise Ending

Sometimes writers surprise you at the ending of a story. A **surprise ending** is an unexpected twist at the end of a story that you did not predict. Even though an ending is a surprise, it must be believable. Writers make surprise endings believable by giving you a few hints about the ending without giving it away. O. Henry is known for startling his readers with surprise endings.

Look For

As you read "A Retrieved Reformation," look for the clues that point to the surprise ending.

Writing

Look up the words *retrieve* and *reformation* in a dictionary and write their definitions. Then write a short paragraph predicting what this story is about by considering its title "A Retrieved Reformation."

Vocabulary

Knowing the following words will help you as you read "A Retrieved Reformation."

assiduously (ə sij'yoo wəs lē) *adv.*: Carefully and busily (p. 55)

eminent (em'ə nənt) *adj.*: Well-known; of high achievement (p. 56)

retribution (ret'rə byoo'shən) *n.*: A punishment deserved for a wrong done (p. 56)

specious (spē'shəs) *adj.*: Seeming to be true without really being so (p. 57)

guile (gīl) *n.*: Craftiness (p. 57)

alterative (ôl'tə rāt'iv) *adj.*: Causing a change (p. 57)

unobtrusively (un əb troo'siv lē) *adv.*: Without calling attention to oneself (p. 58)

A Retrieved Reformation

O. Henry

A guard came to the prison shoe-shop, where Jimmy Valentine was assiduously stitching uppers, and escorted him to the front office. There the warden handed Jimmy his pardon, which had been signed that morning by the governor. Jimmy took it in a tired kind of way. He had served nearly ten months of a four-year sentence. He had expected to stay only about three months, at the longest. When a man with as many friends on the outside as Jimmy Valentine had is received in the "stir" it is hardly worthwhile to cut his hair.

"Now, Valentine," said the warden, "you'll go out in the morning. Brace up, and make a man of yourself. You're not a bad fellow at heart. Stop cracking safes, and live straight."

"Me?" said Jimmy, in surprise. "Why, I never cracked a safe in my life."

"Oh, no," laughed the warden. "Of course not. Let's see, now. How was it you happened to get sent up on that Springfield job? Was it because you wouldn't prove an alibi for fear of compromising somebody in extremely high-toned society? Or was it simply a case of a mean old jury that had it in for you? It's always one or the other with you innocent victims."

"Me?" said Jimmy, still blankly virtuous. "Why, warden, I never was in Springfield in my life!"

"Take him back, Cronin," smiled the warden, "and fix him up with outgoing clothes. Unlock him at seven in the morning, and let him come to the bullpen.[1] Better think over my advice, Valentine."

At a quarter past seven on the next morning Jimmy stood in the warden's outer office. He had on a suit of the villainously fitting, ready-made clothes and a pair of the stiff, squeaky shoes that the state furnishes to its discharged compulsory guests.

The clerk handed him a railroad ticket and the five-dollar bill with which the law expected him to rehabilitate himself into good citizenship and prosperity. The warden gave him a cigar, and shook hands. Valentine, 9762, was chronicled on the books "Pardoned by Governor," and Mr. James Valentine walked out into the sunshine.

Disregarding the song of the birds, the waving green trees, and the smell of the flowers, Jimmy headed straight for a restaurant. There he tasted the first sweet joys of liberty in the shape of a chicken dinner. From there he proceeded leisurely to the depot and boarded his train. Three hours set him down in a little town near the state line. He went to the café of one Mike Dolan and shook hands with Mike, who was alone behind the bar.

"Sorry we couldn't make it sooner, Jimmy, me boy," said Mike. "But we had

---

1. bullpen *n*.: A barred room in a jail, where prisoners are kept temporarily.

that protest from Springfield to buck against, and the governor nearly balked. Feeling all right?''

"Fine," said Jimmy. "Got my key?"

He got his key and went upstairs, unlocking the door of a room at the rear. Everything was just as he had left it. There on the floor was still Ben Price's collar-button that had been torn from that eminent detective's shirt-band when they had overpowered Jimmy to arrest him.

Pulling out from the wall a folding-bed, Jimmy slid back a panel in the wall and dragged out a dust-covered suitcase. He opened this and gazed fondly at the finest set of burglar's tools in the East. It was a complete set, made of specially tempered steel, the latest designs in drills, punches, braces and bits, jimmies, clamps, and augers,[2] with two or three novelties invented by Jimmy himself, in which he took pride. Over nine hundred dollars they had cost him to have made at—, a place where they make such things for the profession.

In half an hour Jimmy went downstairs and through the café. He was now dressed in tasteful and well-fitting clothes, and carried his dusted and cleaned suitcase in his hand.

"Got anything on?" asked Mike Dolan, genially.

"Me?" said Jimmy, in a puzzled tone. "I don't understand. I'm representing the New York Amalgamated Short Snap Biscuit Cracker and Frazzled Wheat Company."

This statement delighted Mike to such an extent that Jimmy had to take a seltzer-and-milk on the spot. He never touched "hard" drinks.

A week after the release of Valentine, 9762, there was a neat job of safe-burglary done in Richmond, Indiana, with no clue to the author. A scant eight hundred dollars was all that was secured. Two weeks after that a patented, improved, burglar-proof safe in Logansport was opened like a cheese to the tune of fifteen hundred dollars, currency; securities and silver untouched. That began to interest the rogue-catchers.[3] Then an old-fashioned bank-safe in Jefferson City became active and threw out of its crater an eruption of bank-notes amounting to five thousand dollars. The losses were now high enough to bring the matter up into Ben Price's class of work. By comparing notes, a remarkable similarity in the methods of the burglaries was noticed. Ben Price investigated the scenes of the robberies, and was heard to remark:

"That's Dandy Jim Valentine's autograph. He's resumed business. Look at that combination knob—jerked out as easy as pulling up a radish in wet weather. He's got the only clamps that can do it. And look how clean those tumblers were punched out! Jimmy never has to drill but one hole. Yes, I guess I want Mr. Valentine. He'll do his bit next time without any short-time or clemency foolishness.''

Ben Price knew Jimmy's habits. He had learned them while working up the Springfield case. Long jumps, quick getaways, no confederates,[4] and a taste for good society —these ways had helped Mr. Valentine to become noted as a successful dodger of retribution. It was given out that Ben Price had taken up the trail of the elusive cracksman, and other people with burglar-proof safes felt more at ease.

One afternoon, Jimmy Valentine and his suitcase climbed out of the mail hack[5] in

---

2. **drills . . . augers** (ô′ gərz): Tools used in metalwork.

3. **rogue-catchers** n.: The police.
4. **confederates** (kən fed′ər its) n.: Accomplices; partners in crime.
5. **mail hack:** A horse and carriage used to deliver mail to surrounding towns.

Elmore, a little town five miles off the railroad down in the blackjack country of Arkansas. Jimmy, looking like an athletic young senior just home from college, went down the board sidewalk toward the hotel.

A young lady crossed the street, passed him at the corner and entered a door over which was the sign "The Elmore Bank." Jimmy Valentine looked into her eyes, forgot what he was, and became another man. She lowered her eyes and colored slightly. Young men of Jimmy's style and looks were scarce in Elmore.

Jimmy collared a boy that was loafing on the steps of the bank as if he were one of the stockholders, and began to ask him questions about the town, feeding him dimes at intervals. By and by the young lady came out, looking royally unconscious of the young man with the suitcase, and went her way.

"Isn't that young lady Miss Polly Simpson?" asked Jimmy, with specious guile.

"Naw," said the boy. "She's Annabel Adams. Her pa owns this bank. What'd you come to Elmore for? Is that a gold watch chain? I'm going to get a bulldog. Got any more dimes?"

Jimmy went to the Planters' Hotel, registered as Ralph D. Spencer, and engaged a room. He leaned on the desk and declared his platform[6] to the clerk. He said he had come to Elmore to look for a location to go into business. How was the shoe business, now, in the town? He had thought of the shoe business. Was there an opening?

The clerk was impressed by the clothes and manner of Jimmy. He, himself, was something of a pattern of fashion to the thinly gilded[7] youth of Elmore, but he now perceived his shortcomings. While trying to figure out Jimmy's manner of tying his four-in-hand,[8] he cordially gave information.

Yes, there ought to be a good opening in the shoe line. There wasn't an exclusive shoe store in the place. The dry-goods and general stores handled them. Business in all lines was fairly good. Hoped Mr. Spencer would decide to locate in Elmore. He would find it a pleasant town to live in, and the people very sociable.

Mr. Spencer thought he would stop over in the town a few days and look over the situation. No, the clerk needn't call the boy. He would carry up his suitcase, himself; it was rather heavy.

Mr. Ralph Spencer, the phoenix[9] that arose from Jimmy Valentine's ashes—ashes left by the flame of a sudden and alterative attack of love—remained in Elmore, and prospered. He opened a shoe store and secured a good run of trade.

Socially he was also a success, and made many friends. And he accomplished the wish of his heart. He met Miss Annabel Adams, and became more and more captivated by her charms.

At the end of a year the situation of Mr. Ralph Spencer was this: he had won the respect of the community, his shoe store was flourishing, and he and Annabel were engaged to be married in two weeks. Mr. Adams, the typical, plodding, country banker, approved of Spencer. Annabel's pride in him almost equalled her affection. He was as much at home in the family of Mr. Adams and that of Annabel's married sister as if he were already a member.

---

6. platform *n*.: Here, statement of intention.
7. thinly gilded *adj*.: Coated with a thin layer of gold; here, appearing well-dressed.

8. four-in-hand *n*.: A necktie.
9. phoenix (fē′niks), *n*.: In Egyptian mythology, a beautiful bird that lived for about 600 years and then burst into flames; a new bird arose from its ashes.

One day Jimmy sat down in his room and wrote this letter, which he mailed to the safe address of one of his old friends in St. Louis:

Dear Old Pal:

I want you to be at Sullivan's place, in Little Rock, next Wednesday night, at nine o'clock. I want you to wind up some little matters for me. And, also, I want to make you a present of my kit of tools. I know you'll be glad to get them—you couldn't duplicate the lot for a thousand dollars. Say, Billy, I've quit the old business—a year ago. I've got a nice store. I'm making an honest living, and I'm going to marry the finest girl on earth two weeks from now. It's the only life, Billy—the straight one. I wouldn't touch a dollar of another man's money now for a million. After I get married I'm going to sell out and go West, where there won't be so much danger of having old scores brought up against me. I tell you, Billy, she's an angel. She believes in me; and I wouldn't do another crooked thing for the whole world. Be sure to be at Sully's, for I must see you. I'll bring along the tools with me.

Your old friend,

Jimmy.

On the Monday night after Jimmy wrote this letter, Ben Price jogged unobtrusively into Elmore in a livery buggy.[10] He lounged about town in his quiet way until he found out what he wanted to know. From the drugstore across the street from Spencer's shoe store he got a good look at Ralph D. Spencer.

"Going to marry the banker's daughter are you, Jimmy?" said Ben to himself, softly. "Well, I don't know!"

The next morning Jimmy took breakfast at the Adamses. He was going to Little Rock that day to order his wedding suit and buy something nice for Annabel. That would be the first time he had left town since he came to Elmore. It had been more than a year now since those last professional "jobs," and he thought he could safely venture out.

After breakfast quite a family party went downtown together—Mr. Adams, Annabel, Jimmy, and Annabel's married sister with her two little girls, aged five and nine. They came by the hotel where Jimmy still boarded, and he ran up to his room and brought along his suitcase. Then they went on to the bank. There stood Jimmy's horse and buggy and Dolph Gibson, who was going to drive him over to the railroad station.

All went inside the high, carved oak railings into the banking-room—Jimmy included, for Mr. Adam's future son-in-law was welcome anywhere. The clerks were pleased to be greeted by the good-looking, agreeable young man who was going to marry Miss Annabel. Jimmy set his suitcase down. Annabel, whose heart was bubbling with happiness and lively youth, put on Jimmy's hat, and picked up the suitcase. "Wouldn't I make a nice drummer?[11] said Annabel. "My! Ralph, how heavy it is! Feels like it was full of gold bricks."

"Lot of nickel-plated shoehorns in there," said Jimmy, coolly, "that I'm going to return. Thought I'd save express charges by taking them up. I'm getting awfully economical."

---

10. livery buggy: A horse and carriage for hire.

11. drummer *n.*: A traveling salesman.

The Elmore Bank had just put in a new safe and vault. Mr. Adams was very proud of it, and insisted on an inspection by everyone. The vault was a small one, but it had a new, patented door. It fastened with three solid steel bolts thrown simultaneously with a single handle, and had a time lock. Mr. Adams beamingly explained its workings to Mr. Spencer, who showed a courteous but not too intelligent interest. The two children, May and Agatha, were delighted by the shining metal and funny clock and knobs.

While they were thus engaged Ben Price sauntered in and leaned on his elbow, looking casually inside between the railings. He

told the teller that he didn't want anything; he was just waiting for a man he knew.

Suddenly there was a scream or two from the women, and a commotion. Unperceived by the elders, May, the nine-year-old girl, in a spirit of play, had shut Agatha in the vault. She had then shot the bolts and turned the knob of the combination as she had seen Mr. Adams do.

The old banker sprang to the handle and tugged at it for a moment. "The door can't be opened," he groaned. "The clock hasn't been wound nor the combination set."

Agatha's mother screamed again, hysterically.

"Hush!" said Mr. Adams, raising his trembling hand. "All be quiet for a moment. Agatha!" he called as loudly as he could. "Listen to me." During the following silence they could just hear the faint sound of the child wildly shrieking in the dark vault in a panic of terror.

"My precious darling!" wailed the mother. "She will die of fright! Open the door! Oh, break it open! Can't you men do something?"

"There isn't a man nearer than Little Rock who can open that door," said Mr. Adams, in a shaky voice. "My God! Spencer, what shall we do? That child—she can't stand it long in there. There isn't enough air, and, besides, she'll go into convulsions from fright."

Agatha's mother, frantic now, beat the door of the vault with her hands. Somebody wildly suggested dynamite. Annabel turned to Jimmy, her large eyes full of anguish, but not yet despairing. To a woman nothing seems quite impossible to the powers of the man she worships.

"Can't you do something, Ralph—*try*, won't you?"

He looked at her with a queer, soft smile on his lips and in his keen eyes.

"Annabel," he said, "give me that rose you are wearing, will you?"

Hardly believing that she heard him aright, she unpinned the bud from the bosom of her dress, and placed it in his hand. Jimmy stuffed it into his vest pocket, threw off his coat and pulled up his shirt sleeves. With that act Ralph D. Spencer passed away and Jimmy Valentine took his place.

"Get away from the door, all of you," he commanded, shortly.

He set his suitcase on the table, and opened it out flat. From that time on he seemed to be unconscious of the presence of anyone else. He laid out the shining, queer implements swiftly and orderly, whistling softly to himself as he always did when at work. In a deep silence and immovable, the others watched him as if under a spell.

In a minute Jimmy's pet drill was biting smoothly into the steel door. In ten minutes —breaking his own burglarious record—he threw back the bolts and opened the door.

Agatha, almost collapsed, but safe, was gathered into her mother's arms.

Jimmy Valentine put on his coat, and walked outside the railings toward the front door. As he went he thought he heard a far-away voice that he once knew call "Ralph!" But he never hesitated.

At the door a big man stood somewhat in his way.

"Hello, Ben!" said Jimmy, still with his strange smile. "Got around at last, have you? Well, let's go. I don't know that it makes much difference, now."

And then Ben Price acted rather strangely.

"Guess you're mistaken, Mr. Spencer," he said. "Don't believe I recognize you. Your buggy's waiting for you, ain't it?"

And Ben Price turned and strolled down the street.

THINKING ABOUT THE SELECTION

Recalling

1. Why is Valentine in prison? Why is he pardoned?
2. Out of prison, how does Valentine support himself?
3. Why does Ben start looking for Jimmy again?
4. At what point in the story does Valentine become another man? What causes this change?
5. Why does Valentine use his old talents once again?

Interpreting

6. Find three details in the story that support the idea that Valentine really has changed.
7. Why does Ben pretend not to know Jimmy?
8. Explain the meaning of the story's title.

Applying

9. People speak of turning points in their lives, when they seem to change greatly. Can people really change? Support your answer.

ANALYZING LITERATURE

Understanding the Surprise Ending

A **surprise ending** depends on an unexpected resolution of the main conflict. To make the surprise ending believable, authors include hints in the story that point toward the ending.

1. How did you think this story would end? Which clues led you to expect this ending?
2. How did the story really end? What clues did the author plant leading to this ending?

CRITICAL THINKING AND READING

Recognizing Allusions

An **allusion** is a reference in a work of literature to a person, place, or thing in another work, such as literature, art, music, history, painting, mythology. For example, O. Henry writes, "Mr. Ralph Spencer, the phoenix that arose from Jimmy Valentine's ashes—ashes left by the flame of a sudden and alterative attack of love—remained in Elmore, and prospered." The phoenix is a mythical bird that lived in the Arabian wilderness. Every 500 or 600 years it would burn itself up and rise from its ashes anew.

1. In what way is Valentine like a phoenix?
2. How does this allusion help you predict that Valentine is now truly Ralph Spencer?

UNDERSTANDING LANGUAGE

Finding Meanings to Fit the Context

One unabridged dictionary lists thirty-four meanings for the word *serve*. In the following sentence you can tell the appropriate meaning of *served* from its context: "He had *served* nearly ten months of a four-year sentence." Here *serve* means "spent."

Use the context to choose the correct definitions for the following italicized words.

1. "After breakfast quite a family *party* went downtown together. . . ."
   a. social gathering   c. defendant in a suit
   b. group of people
2. "Or was it simply a *case* of a mean old jury that had it in for you?"
   a. problem   b. instance   c. legal claim

THINKING AND WRITING

Writing About A Surprise Ending

Stephen Leacock, a writer and critic, once wrote about O. Henry: "No one better than he can hold the reader in suspense. Nay, more than that, the reader scarcely knows that he is 'suspended,' until at the very close of the story, O. Henry, so to speak, turns on the lights, and the whole tale is revealed as an entirety." Discuss Leacock's statement with your classmates. Then write a paper using examples from the story to agree or disagree with this opinion. Revise your paper to make sure you have organized your support in a logical order. Proofread for correct sentence structure, spelling, and punctuation.

GUIDE FOR READING

The Rule of Names

Ursula K. Le Guin (1929–   ) was born in California and earned her undergraduate and graduate degrees from eastern universities. Her first published writings appeared when she was thirty-two years old. Since then she has received a Science Fiction Writers Award for best short story, a Nebula Award, and a Hugo Award. Le Guin writes mainly science fiction and fantasy. "The Rule of Names," while a complete story on its own, sets the scene for three of Le Guin's later novels.

Fantasy

Fantasy is a type of fiction that is based on the impossible. The plot of a fantasy may take place in an imaginary place, such as a make-believe country, and have imaginary characters, often with supernatural powers, such as wizards. While fantasy is similar to science fiction, it does not need to be based on scientific reality. Instead, it may use magic or other unnatural powers in the plot.

Look For

As you read "The Rule of Names," look for the events that could not possibly happen in real life. Which characters have supernatural powers? How does the author make these characters appear real?

Writing

Why do we like to imagine creatures like dragons and wizards that cannot possibly exist? Freewrite about your answer.

Vocabulary

Knowing the following words will help you as you read "The Rule of Names."

walleyed (wôl'īd') *adj.*: Having eyes that turn outward (p. 64)

damask (dam'əsk) *n.*: A fine fabric of silk or linen with a woven design; tablecloth and napkins made of damask (p. 64)

incantation (in'kan tā'shən) *n.*: Magic words used to cast a spell (p. 65)

taciturn (tas'ə tʉrn') *adj.*: Not likely to talk (p. 67)

stolid (stäl'id) *adj.*: Showing little or no emotion (p. 67)

crockery (kräk'ər ē) *n.*: Earthenware dishes, pots, and so on (p. 69)

cataract (kat'ə rakt') *n.*: Large waterfall (p. 70)

taunted (tônt'əd) *v.*: Jeered at; mocked (p. 70)

The Rule of Names

Ursula K. Le Guin

Mr. Underhill came out from under his hill, smiling and breathing hard. Each breath shot out of his nostrils as a double puff of steam, snow-white in the morning sunshine. Mr. Underhill looked up at the bright December sky and smiled wider than ever, showing snow-white teeth. Then he went down to the village.

"Morning, Mr. Underhill," said the villagers as he passed them in the narrow street between houses with conical, overhanging roofs like the fat red caps of toadstools. "Morning, morning!" he replied to each. (It was of course bad luck to wish anyone a *good* morning; a simple statement of the time of day was quite enough, in a place so permeated with Influences as Sat-

tins Island, where a careless adjective might change the weather for a week.) All of them spoke to him, some with affection, some with affectionate disdain. He was all the little island had in the way of a wizard, and so deserved respect—but how could you respect a little fat man of fifty who waddled along with his toes turned in, breathing steam and smiling? He was no great shakes

as a workman either. His fireworks were fairly elaborate but his elixirs[1] were weak. Warts he charmed off frequently reappeared after three days; tomatoes he enchanted grew no bigger than cantaloupes; and those rare times when a strange ship stopped at Sattins Harbor, Mr. Underhill always stayed under his hill—for fear, he explained, of the evil eye. He was, in other words, a wizard the way walleyed Gan was a carpenter: by default. The villagers made do with badly-hung doors and inefficient spells, for this generation, and relieved their annoyance by treating Mr. Underhill quite familiarly, as a mere fellow-villager. They even asked him to dinner. Once he asked some of them to dinner, and served a splendid repast, with silver, crystal, damask, roast goose, sparkling Andrades '639, and plum pudding with hard sauce; but he was so nervous all through the meal that it took the joy out of it, and besides, everybody was hungry again half an hour afterward. He did not like anyone to visit his cave, not even the anteroom, beyond which in fact nobody had ever got. When he saw people approaching the hill he always came trotting out to meet them. "Let's sit out here under the pine trees!" he would say, smiling and waving towards the fir grove, or if it was raining, "Let's go have a drink at the inn, eh?" though everybody knew he drank nothing stronger than well-water.

Some of the village children, teased by that locked cave, poked and pried and made raids while Mr. Underhill was away; but the small door that led into the inner chamber was spell-shut, and it seemed for once to be an effective spell. Once a couple of boys, thinking the wizard was over on the West Shore curing Mrs. Ruuna's sick donkey,

brought a crowbar and a hatchet up there, but at the first whack of the hatchet on the door there came a roar of wrath from inside, and a cloud of purple steam. Mr. Underhill had got home early. The boys fled. He did not come out, and the boys came to no harm, though they said you couldn't believe what a huge hooting howling hissing horrible bellow that little fat man could make unless you'd heard it.

His business in town this day was three dozen fresh eggs and a pound of liver; also a stop at Seacaptain Fogeno's cottage to renew the seeing-charm on the old man's eyes (quite useless when applied to a case of detached retina,[2] but Mr. Underhill kept trying), and finally a chat with old Goody[3] Guld, the concertina-maker's[4] widow. Mr. Underhill's friends were mostly old people. He was timid with the strong young men of the village, and the girls were shy of him. "He makes me nervous, he smiles so much," they all said, pouting, twisting silky ringlets round a finger. "Nervous" was a newfangled word, and their mothers all replied grimly, "Nervous my foot, silliness is the word for it. Mr. Underhill is a very respectable wizard!"

After leaving Goody Guld, Mr. Underhill passed by the school, which was being held this day out on the common. Since no one on Sattins Island was literate, there were no books to learn to read from and no desks to carve initials on and no blackboards to erase, and in fact no schoolhouse. On rainy days the children met in the loft of the Communal Barn, and got hay in their pants; on sunny days the schoolteacher, Palani,

---

1. elixirs (i lik' sərz) *n.*: Magic potions.

2. detached retina: A serious visual disorder due to damaged nerve tissue at the back of the eyeball.
3. Goody *n.*: Short form of *goodwife*, a term formerly used for married women of low social standing.
4. concertina (kän' sər tē'nə) **maker's** *adj.*: Belonging to the person who makes a musical instrument like a small accordion.

took them anywhere she felt like. Today, surrounded by thirty interested children under twelve and forty uninterested sheep under five, she was teaching an important item on the curriculum: the Rules of Names. Mr. Underhill, smiling shyly, paused to listen and watch. Palani, a plump, pretty girl of twenty, made a charming picture there in the wintry sunlight, sheep and children around her, a leafless oak above her, and behind her the dunes and sea and clear, pale sky. She spoke earnestly, her face flushed pink by wind and words. "Now you know the Rules of Names already, children. There are two, and they're the same on every island in the world. What's one of them?"

"It ain't polite to ask anybody what his name is," shouted a fat, quick boy, interrupted by a little girl shrieking, "You can't never tell your own name to nobody my ma says!"

"Yes, Suba. Yes, Popi dear, don't screech. That's right. You never ask anybody his name. You never tell your own. Now think about that a minute and then tell me why we call our wizard Mr. Underhill." She smiled across the curly heads and the woolly backs at Mr. Underhill, who beamed, and nervously clutched his sack of eggs.

"'Cause he lives under a hill!" said half the children.

"But is it his truename?"

"No!" said the fat boy, echoed by little Popi shrieking, "No!"

"How do you know it's not?"

"'Cause he came here all alone and so there wasn't anybody knew his truename so they couldn't tell us, and *he* couldn't—"

"Very good, Suba. Popi, don't shout. That's right. Even a wizard can't tell his truename. When you children are through school and go through the Passage, you'll leave your childnames behind and keep only your truenames, which you must never ask for and never give away. Why is that the rule?"

The children were silent. The sheep bleated gently. Mr. Underhill answered the question: "Because the name is the thing," he said in his shy, soft, husky voice, "and the truename is the true thing. To speak the name is to control the thing. Am I right, Schoolmistress?"

She smiled and curtseyed, evidently a little embarrassed by his participation. And he trotted off towards his hill, clutching his eggs to his bosom. Somehow the minute spent watching Palani and the children had made him very hungry. He locked his inner door behind him with a hasty incantation, but there must have been a leak or two in the spell, for soon the bare anteroom of the cave was rich with the smell of frying eggs and sizzling liver.

The wind that day was light and fresh out of the west, and on it at noon a little boat came skimming the bright waves into Sattins Harbor. Even as it rounded the point a sharp-eyed boy spotted it, and knowing, like every child on the island, every sail and spar of the forty boats of the fishing fleet, he ran down the street calling out, "A foreign boat, a foreign boat!" Very seldom was the lonely isle visited by a boat from some equally lonely isle of the East Reach, or an adventurous trader from the Archipelago.[5] By the time the boat was at the pier half the village was there to greet it, and fishermen were following it homewards, and cowherds and clam-diggers and herb-hunters were puffing up and down all the rocky hills, heading towards the harbor.

But Mr. Underhill's door stayed shut.

There was only one man aboard the

---

5. archipelago (ar′kə pel′ ə gō′) *n.*: A chain of many islands.

boat. Old Seacaptain Fogeno, when they told him that, drew down a bristle of white brows over his unseeing eyes. "There's only one kind of man," he said, "that sails the Outer Reach alone. A wizard, or a warlock, or a Mage . . ."

So the villagers were breathless hoping to see for once in their lives a Mage, one of the mighty White Magicians of the rich, towered, crowded inner islands of the Archipelago. They were disappointed, for the voyager was quite young, a handsome black-bearded fellow who hailed them cheerfully from his boat, and leaped ashore like any sailor glad to have made port. He introduced himself at once as a sea-peddlar. But when they told Seacaptain Fogeno that he carried an oaken walking-stick around with him, the old man nodded. "Two wizards in one town," he said. "Bad!" And his mouth snapped shut like an old carp's.

As the stranger could not give them his name, they gave him one right away: Blackbeard. And they gave him plenty of attention. He had a small mixed cargo of cloth and sandals and piswi feathers for trimming cloaks and cheap incense and levity stones and fine herbs and great glass beads from Venway—the usual peddlar's lot. Everyone on Sattins Island came to look, to chat with the voyager, and perhaps to buy something —"Just to remember him by!" cackled Goody Guld, who like all the women and girls of the village was smitten with Blackbeard's bold good looks. All the boys hung round him too, to hear him tell of his voyages to far, strange islands of the Reach or describe the great rich islands of the Archipelago, the Inner Lanes, the roadsteads white with ships, and the golden roofs of Havnor. The men willingly listened to his tales; but some of them wondered why a trader should sail alone, and kept their eyes thoughtfully upon his oaken staff.

But all this time Mr. Underhill stayed under his hill.

"This is the first island I've ever seen that had no wizard," said Blackbeard one evening to Goody Guld, who had invited him and her nephew and Palani in for a cup of rushwash tea. "What do you do when you get a toothache, or the cow goes dry?"

"Why, we've got Mr. Underhill!" said the old woman.

"For what that's worth," muttered her nephew Birt, and then blushed purple and spilled his tea. Birt was a fisherman, a large, brave, wordless young man. He loved the schoolmistress, but the nearest he had come to telling her of his love was to give baskets of fresh mackerel to her father's cook.

"Oh, you do have a wizard?" Blackbeard asked. "Is he invisible?"

"No, he's just very shy," said Palani. "You've only been here a week, you know, and we see so few strangers here. . . ." She also blushed a little, but did not spill her tea.

Blackbeard smiled at her. "He's a good Sattinsman, then, eh?"

"No," said Goody Guld, "no more than you are. Another cup, nevvy?[6] Keep it in the cup this time. No, my dear, he came in a little bit of a boat, four years ago was it? Just a day after the end of the shad run, I recall, for they was taking up the nets over in East Creek, and Pondi Cowherd broke his leg that very morning—five years ago it must be. No, four. No, five it is, 'twas the year the garlic didn't sprout. So he sails in on a bit of a sloop loaded full up with great chests and boxes and says to Seacaptain Fogeno, who wasn't blind then, though old enough goodness knows to be blind twice over, 'I hear tell,' he says, 'you've got no wizard nor warlock at all, might you be

---

6. nevvy n.: *Nephew* in dialect form.

wanting one?' 'Indeed, if the magic's white!' says the Captain, and before you could say cuttlefish Mr. Underhill had settled down in the cave under the hill and was charming the mange off Goody Beltow's cat. Though the fur grew in grey, and 'twas an orange cat. Queer-looking thing it was after that. It died last winter in the cold spell. Goody Beltow took on so at that cat's death, poor thing, worse than when her man was drowned on the Long Banks, the year of the long herring-runs, when nevvy Birt here was but a babe in petticoats." Here Birt spilled his tea again, and Blackbeard grinned, but Goody Guld proceeded undismayed, and talked on till nightfall.

Next day Blackbeard was down at the pier, seeing after the sprung board in his boat which he seemed to take a long time fixing, and as usual drawing the taciturn Sattinsmen into talk. "Now which of these is your wizard's craft?" he asked. "Or has he got one of those the Mages fold up into a walnut shell when they're not using it?"

"Nay," said a stolid fisherman. "She's oop in his cave, under hill."

"He carried the boat he came in up to his cave?"

"Aye. Clear oop. I helped. Heavier as lead she was. Full oop with great boxes, and they full oop with books o' spells, he says. Heavier as lead she was." And the stolid fisherman turned his back, sighing stolidly. Goody Guld's nephew, mending a net nearby, looked up from his work and asked with equal stolidity, "Would ye like to meet Mr. Underhill, maybe?"

Blackbeard returned Birt's look. Clever black eyes met candid blue ones for a long moment; then Blackbeard smiled and said, "Yes. Will you take me up to the hill, Birt?"

"Aye, when I'm done with this," said the fisherman. And when the net was mended, he and the Archipelagan set off up the village street towards the high green hill above it. But as they crossed the common Blackbeard said, "Hold on a while, friend Birt. I have a tale to tell you, before we meet your wizard."

"Tell away," says Birt, sitting down in the shade of a live-oak.

"It's a story that started a hundred years ago, and isn't finished yet—though it soon will be, very soon. . . . In the very heart of the Archipelago, where the islands crowd thick as flies on honey, there's a little isle called Pendor. The sealords of Pendor were mighty men, in the old days of war before the League. Loot and ransom and tribute came pouring into Pendor, and they gathered a great treasure there, long ago. Then from somewhere away out in the West Reach, where dragons breed on the lava isles, came one day a very mighty dragon. Not one of those overgrown lizards most of you Outer Reach folk call dragons, but a big, black, winged, wise, cunning monster, full of strength and subtlety, and like all dragons loving gold and precious stones above all things. He killed the Sealord and his soldiers, and the people of Pendor fled in their ships by night. They all fled away and left the dragon coiled up in Pendor Towers. And there he stayed for a hundred years, dragging his scaly belly over the emeralds and sapphires and coins of gold, coming forth only once in a year or two when he must eat. He'd raid nearby islands for his food. You know what dragons eat?"

Birt nodded and said in a whisper, "Maidens."

"Right," said Blackbeard. "Well, that couldn't be endured forever, nor the thought of nim sitting on all that treasure. So after the League grew strong, and the Archipelago wasn't so busy with wars and piracy, it was decided to attack Pendor, drive out the dragon, and get the gold and jewels for the treasury of the League. They're forever wanting money, the League is. So a huge fleet gathered from fifty islands, and seven Mages stood in the prows of the seven strongest ships, and they sailed towards Pendor. . . . They got there. They landed. Nothing stirred. The houses all stood empty, the dishes on the tables full of a hundred years' dust. The bones of the old Sealord and his men lay about in the castle courts and on the stairs. And the Tower rooms reeked of dragon. But there was no dragon. And no treasure, not a diamond the size of a poppyseed, not a single silver bead . . . Knowing that he couldn't stand up to seven Mages, the dragon had skipped out. They tracked him, and found he'd flown to a deserted island up north called Udrath; they followed his trail there, and what did they find? Bones again. His bones—the dragon's. But no treasure. A wizard, some unknown wizard from somewhere, must have met him single-handed, and defeated him—and then made off with the treasure, right under the League's nose!''

The fisherman listened, attentive and expressionless.

"Now that must have been a powerful wizard and a clever one, first to kill a dragon, and second to get off without leaving a trace. The lords and Mages of the Archipelago couldn't track him at all, neither where he'd come from nor where he'd made off to. They were about to give up. That was last spring; I'd been off on a three-year voyage up in the North Reach, and got back about that time. And they asked me to help them find the unknown wizard. That was clever of them. Because I'm not only a wizard myself, as I think some of the oafs here have guessed, but I am also a descendant of the Lords of Pendor. That treasure is mine. It's mine, and knows that it's mine. Those fools of the League couldn't find it, because

it's not theirs. It belongs to the House of Pendor, and the great emerald, the star of the hoard, Inalkil the Greenstone, knows its master. Behold!'' Blackbeard raised his oaken staff and cried aloud, "Inalkil!'' The tip of the staff began to glow green, a fiery green radiance, a dazzling haze the color of April grass, and at the same moment the staff tipped in the wizard's hand, leaning, slanting till it pointed straight at the side of the hill above them.

"It wasn't so bright a glow, far away in Havnor,'' Blackbeard murmured, "but the staff pointed true. Inalkil answered when I called. The jewel knows its master. And I know the thief, and I shall conquer him. He's a mighty wizard, who could overcome a dragon. But I am mightier. Do you want to know why, oaf? Because I know his name!''

As Blackbeard's tone got more arrogant, Birt had looked duller and duller, blanker and blanker; but at this he gave a twitch, shut his mouth, and stared at the Archipelagan. "How did you . . . learn it?'' he asked very slowly.

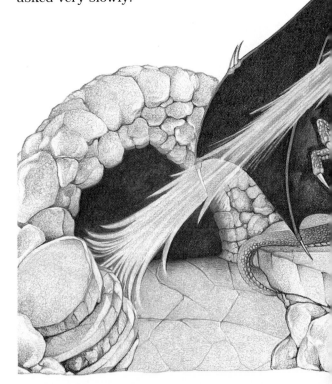

Blackbeard grinned, and did not answer.

"Black magic?"

"How else?"

Birt looked pale, and said nothing.

"I am the Sealord of Pendor, oaf, and I will have the gold my fathers won, and the jewels my mothers wore, and the Greenstone! For they are mine. —Now, you can tell your village boobies the whole story

after I have defeated this wizard and gone. Wait here. Or you can come and watch, if you're not afraid. You'll never get the chance again to see a great wizard in all his power." Blackbeard turned, and without a backward glance strode off up the hill towards the entrance to the cave.

Very slowly, Birt followed. A good distance from the cave he stopped, sat down under a hawthorn tree, and watched. The Archipelagan had stopped; a stiff, dark figure alone on the green swell of the hill before the gaping cave-mouth, he stood perfectly still. All at once he swung his staff up over his head, and the emerald radiance shone about him as he shouted, "Thief, thief of the Hoard of Pendor, come forth!"

There was a crash, as of dropped crockery, from inside the cave, and a lot of dust came spewing out. Scared, Birt ducked. When he looked again he saw Blackbeard still standing motionless, and at the mouth of the cave, dusty and dishevelled, stood Mr. Underhill. He looked small and pitiful, with his toes turned in as usual, and his little bowlegs in black tights, and no staff—he never had had one, Birt suddenly thought. Mr. Underhill spoke. "Who are you?" he said in his husky little voice.

"I am the Sealord of Pendor, thief, come to claim my treasure!"

At that, Mr. Underhill slowly turned pink, as he always did when people were rude to him. But he then turned something else. He turned yellow. His hair bristled out, he gave a coughing roar—and was a yellow lion leaping down the hill at Blackbeard, white fangs gleaming.

But Blackbeard no longer stood there. A gigantic tiger, color of night and lightning, bounded to meet the lion. . . .

The lion was gone. Below the cave all of a sudden stood a high grove of trees, black in the winter sunshine. The tiger, checking himself in mid-leap just before he entered the shadow of the trees, caught fire in the air, became a tongue of flame lashing out at the dry black branches. . . .

But where the trees had stood a sudden cataract leaped from the hillside, an arch of silvery crashing water, thundering down upon the fire. But the fire was gone. . . .

For just a moment before the fisherman's staring eyes two hills rose—the green one he knew, and a new one, a bare, brown hillock ready to drink up the rushing waterfall. That passed so quickly it made Birt blink, and after blinking he blinked again, and moaned, for what he saw now was a great deal worse. Where the cataract had been there hovered a dragon. Black wings darkened all the hill, steel claws reached groping, and from the dark, scaly, gaping lips fire and steam shot out.

Beneath the monstrous creature stood Blackbeard, laughing.

"Take any shape you please, little Mr. Underhill!" he taunted. "I can match you. But the game grows tiresome. I want to look upon my treasure, upon Inalkil. Now, big dragon, little wizard, take your true shape. I command you by the power of your true name—Yevaud!"

Birt could not move at all, not even to blink. He cowered, staring whether he would or not. He saw the black dragon hang there in the air above Blackbeard. He saw the fire lick like many tongues from the scaly mouth, the steam jet from the red nostrils. He saw Blackbeard's face grow white, white as chalk, and the beard-fringed lips trembling.

"Your name is Yevaud!"

"Yes," said a great, husky, hissing voice. "My truename is Yevaud, and my true shape is this shape."

"But the dragon was killed—they found dragon-bones on Udrath Island—"

"That was another dragon," said the dragon, and then stooped like a hawk, talons outstretched. And Birt shut his eyes.

When he opened them the sky was clear, the hillside empty, except for a reddish-blackish trampled spot, and a few talon-marks in the grass.

Birt the fisherman got to his feet and ran. He ran across the common, scattering sheep to right and left, and straight down the village street to Palani's father's house. Palani was out in the garden weeding the nasturtiums. "Come with me!" Birt gasped. She stared. He grabbed her wrist and dragged her with him. She screeched a little, but did not resist. He ran with her straight to the pier, pushed her into his fishing-sloop the *Queenie*, untied the painter,[7] took up the oars and set off rowing like a demon. The last that Sattins Island saw of him and Palani was the *Queenie*'s sail vanishing in the direction of the nearest island westward.

The villagers thought they would never stop talking about it, how Goody Guld's nephew Birt had lost his mind and sailed off with the schoolmistress on the very same day that the peddlar Blackbeard disappeared without a trace, leaving all his feathers and beads behind. But they did stop talking about it, three days later. They had other things to talk about, when Mr. Underhill finally came out of his cave.

Mr. Underhill had decided that since his truename was no longer a secret, he might as well drop his disguise. Walking was a lot harder than flying, and besides, it was a long, long time since he had had a real meal.

---

7. painter *n.:* Here, a rope tied to a boat.

THINKING ABOUT THE SELECTION
Recalling

1. What is Mr. Underhill's role in the village?
2. Give two examples that indicate how well Mr. Underhill performs his job.
3. What are the two Rules of Names?
4. Why does Blackbeard come to Sattins Island? How is he guided there?
5. What shapes does Mr. Underhill take during the battle? What is his true shape?
6. What happens to Blackbeard at the end of the story?

Interpreting

7. Why does Blackbeard feel that knowing Mr. Underhill's true name would enable him to defeat Underhill?
8. What "other things" do the villagers have to talk about at the end of the story?
9. What clues does the author provide throughout the story to Mr. Underhill's true identity?

Applying

10. Explain why names used for people or things do or do not affect the way you feel about them.

ANALYZING LITERATURE
Investigating Fantasy

The elements of **fantasy** include imaginary places, strange characters, and the use of magic and supernatural powers in plots.

1. What powers do the villagers know Mr. Underhill to have?
2. What are his true powers?
3. What powers does Blackbeard have?
4. Why does he lose the battle to Mr. Underhill?

CRITICAL THINKING AND READING
Separating Realistic and Fantastic Details

Although the details in a work of fiction may all be products of the author's imagination, some might possibly happen in life. These are realistic details. Others are simply fantastic; those could not possibly happen in real life. Label the following details from "The Rule of Names" as either realistic or fantastic.

1. "A careless adjective might change the weather for a week."
2. "He loved the schoolmistress, but the nearest he had come to telling her of his love was to give baskets of fresh mackerel to her father's cook."
3. "A stiff dark figure alone on the green swell of the hill before the gaping cave-mouth, he stood perfectly still."
4. "Where the cataract had been there hovered a dragon."

UNDERSTANDING LANGUAGE
Identifying Synonyms

Synonyms are words that mean almost the same thing. *Happy* and *joyful* are synonyms, for example.

Identify the synonym for each italicized word in these sentences:

1. The wizard asked some of the villagers to *dinner* where he served a splendid repast of roast goose.
2. The staff was *leaning,* slanting so that it pointed at the side of the hill.

THINKING AND WRITING
Writing a Fantasy

Think of an event that could not possibly happen in real life. Use it as the plot of a short fantasy. Write your fantasy, including characters and details that will make your story interesting as well as fantastic. When you have written your first draft, revise it to make sure that your ideas are presented clearly and that what you have written is fantasy. Finally, share your fantasy with your classmates.

GUIDE FOR READING

Charles

Shirley Jackson (1919–1965) was born in San Francisco and was graduated from Syracuse University. Jackson was married and had four children. As a writer, she produced mainly two types of stories—spine-tingling tales of supernatural events and hilarious stories about family life. She once said that she wrote because "It's the only chance I get to sit down" and because it gave her an excuse not to clean her closets. The main character in "Charles" is patterned after Jackson's own son Laurie.

Point of View

In writing a short story, the author chooses the character through whose eyes he or she wants you to see the story. **Point of view** is the way an author chooses to see and tell a story. One point of view an author may use is first-person narrative. In a **first-person narrative,** a character tells the story, referring to himself or herself as "I," and presenting only what he or she knows about events.

"Charles" is a first-person narrative, told by Laurie's mother. You learn at the same time as she does about the events in Laurie's kindergarten class.

Look For

As you read "Charles," look for all the details the mother learns about Charles. Think about why the author may have decided to tell her story using first-person narrative point of view.

Writing

"Charles" tells the story of an unforgettable boy. Think about people you know who are unforgettable. What is it that makes them unforgettable? Write about some of the things that make a person unforgettable to you.

Vocabulary

Knowing the following words can help you as you read "Charles."

renounced (ri nouns'′d) v.: Gave up (p. 73)

swaggering (swag'ər iŋ) v.: Strutting; walking with a bold step (p. 73)

insolently (in′sə lənt lē) adv.: Boldly disrespectful in speech or behavior (p. 73)

simultaneously (sī′məl tā′nē əs lē) adv.: At the same time (p. 74)

elaborately (i lab'ər it lē) adv.: Painstakingly (p. 74)

incredulously (in krej′oo ləs lē) adv.: With doubt or disbelief (p. 75)

haggard (hag'ərd) adj.: Having a tired look (p. 75)

Charles

Shirley Jackson

The day my son Laurie started kindergarten he renounced corduroy overalls with bibs and began wearing blue jeans with a belt; I watched him go off the first morning with the older girl next door, seeing clearly that an era of my life was ended, my sweet-voiced nursery-school tot replaced by a long-trousered, swaggering character who forgot to stop at the corner and wave good-bye to me.

He came home the same way, the front door slamming open, his cap on the floor, and the voice suddenly become raucous[1] shouting, "Isn't anybody *here*?"

At lunch he spoke insolently to his father, spilled his baby sister's milk, and remarked that his teacher said we were not to take the name of the Lord in vain.

"How *was* school today?" I asked, elaborately casual.

"All right," he said.

"Did you learn anything?" his father asked.

Laurie regarded his father coldly. "I didn't learn nothing," he said.

"Anything," I said. "Didn't learn anything."

"The teacher spanked a boy, though," Laurie said, addressing his bread and butter. "For being fresh," he added, with his mouth full.

"What did he do?" I asked. "Who was it?"

Laurie thought. "It was Charles," he said. "He was fresh. The teacher spanked him and made him stand in a corner. He was awfully fresh."

"What did he do?" I asked again, but Laurie slid off his chair, took a cookie, and left, while his father was still saying, "See here, young man."

The next day Laurie remarked at lunch, as soon as he sat down, "Well, Charles was bad again today." He grinned enormously and said, "Today Charles hit the teacher."

"Good heavens," I said, mindful of the Lord's name, "I suppose he got spanked again?"

"He sure did," Laurie said. "Look up," he said to his father.

"What?" his father said, looking up.

"Look down," Laurie said. "Look at my thumb. Gee, you're dumb." He began to laugh insanely.

"Why did Charles hit the teacher?" I asked quickly.

"Because she tried to make him color with red crayons," Laurie said. "Charles wanted to color with green crayons so he hit the teacher and she spanked him and said nobody play with Charles but everybody did."

The third day—it was Wednesday of the first week—Charles bounced a see-saw on to the head of a little girl and made her bleed, and the teacher made him stay inside all during recess. Thursday Charles had to stand in a corner during story-time because he kept pounding his feet on the

---

1. raucous (rô′ kəs) *adj.*: Boisterous; disorderly.

floor. Friday Charles was deprived of black-board privileges because he threw chalk.

On Saturday I remarked to my husband, "Do you think kindergarten is too unsettling for Laurie? All this toughness, and bad grammar, and this Charles boy sounds like such a bad influence."

"It'll be all right," my husband said reassuringly. "Bound to be people like Charles in the world. Might as well meet them now as later."

On Monday Laurie came home late, full of news. "Charles," he shouted as he came up the hill; I was waiting anxiously on the front steps. "Charles," Laurie yelled all the way up the hill, "Charles was bad again."

"Come right in," I said, as soon as he came close enough. "Lunch is waiting."

"You know what Charles did?" he demanded, following me through the door. "Charles yelled so in school they sent a boy in from first grade to tell the teacher she had to make Charles keep quiet, and so Charles had to stay after school. And so all the children stayed to watch him."

"What did he do?" I asked.

"He just sat there," Laurie said, climbing into his chair at the table. "Hi, Pop, y'old dust mop."

"Charles had to stay after school today," I told my husband. "Everyone stayed with him."

"What does this Charles look like?" my husband asked Laurie. "What's his other name?"

"He's bigger than me," Laurie said. "And he doesn't have any rubbers and he doesn't ever wear a jacket."

Monday night was the first Parent-Teachers meeting, and only the fact that the baby had a cold kept me from going; I wanted passionately to meet Charles's mother. On Tuesday Laurie remarked suddenly, "Our teacher had a friend come to see her in school today."

"Charles's mother?" my husband and I asked simultaneously.

"Naaah," Laurie said scornfully. "It was a man who came and made us do exercises, we had to touch our toes. Look." He climbed down from his chair and squatted down and touched his toes. "Like this," he said. He got solemnly back into his chair and said, picking up his fork, "Charles didn't even *do* exercises."

"That's fine," I said heartily. "Didn't Charles want to do exercises?"

"Naaah," Laurie said. "Charles was so fresh to the teacher's friend he wasn't *let* do exercises."

"Fresh again?" I said.

"He kicked the teacher's friend," Laurie said. "The teacher's friend told Charles to touch his toes like I just did and Charles kicked him."

"What are they going to do about Charles, do you suppose?" Laurie's father asked him.

Laurie shrugged elaborately. "Throw him out of school, I guess," he said.

Wednesday and Thursday were routine; Charles yelled during story hour and hit a boy in the stomach and made him cry. On Friday Charles stayed after school again and so did all the other children.

With the third week of kindergarten Charles was an institution in our family; the baby was being a Charles when she cried all afternoon; Laurie did a Charles when he filled his wagon full of mud and pulled it through the kitchen; even my husband, when he caught his elbow in the telephone cord and pulled the telephone and a bowl of flowers off the table, said, after the first minute, "Looks like Charles."

During the third and fourth weeks it looked like a reformation in Charles; Laurie reported grimly at lunch on Thursday of the third week, "Charles was so good today the teacher gave him an apple."

"What?" I said, and my husband added warily, "You mean Charles?"

"Charles," Laurie said. "He gave the crayons around and he picked up the books afterward and the teacher said he was her helper."

"What happened?" I asked incredulously.

"He was her helper, that's all," Laurie said, and shrugged.

"Can this be true, about Charles?" I asked my husband that night. "Can something like this happen?"

"Wait and see," my husband said cynically.[2] "When you've got a Charles to deal with, this may mean he's only plotting." He seemed to be wrong. For over a week Charles was the teacher's helper; each day he handed things out and he picked things up; no one had to stay after school.

"The PTA meeting's next week again," I told my husband one evening. "I'm going to find Charles's mother there."

"Ask her what happened to Charles," my husband said. "I'd like to know."

"I'd like to know myself," I said.

On Friday of that week things were back to normal. "You know what Charles did today?" Laurie demanded at the lunch table, in a voice slightly awed. "He told a little girl to say a word and she said it and the teacher washed her mouth out with soap and Charles laughed."

"What word?" his father asked unwisely, and Laurie said, "I'll have to whisper it to you, it's so bad." He got down off his chair and went around to his father. His father bent his head down and Laurie whispered joyfully. His father's eyes widened.

"Did Charles tell the little girl to say that?" he asked respectfully.

"She said it twice," Laurie said. "Charles told her to say it twice."

"What happened to Charles?" my husband asked.

"Nothing," Laurie said. "He was passing out the crayons."

Monday morning Charles abandoned the little girl and said the evil word himself three or four times, getting his mouth washed out with soap each time. He also threw chalk.

My husband came to the door with me that evening as I set out for the PTA meeting. "Invite her over for a cup of tea after the meeting," he said. "I want to get a look at her."

"If only she's there," I said prayerfully.

"She'll be there," my husband said. "I don't see how they could hold a PTA meeting without Charles's mother."

At the meeting I sat restlessly, scanning each comfortable matronly face, trying to determine which one hid the secret of Charles. None of them looked to me haggard enough. No one stood up in the meeting and apologized for the way her son had been acting. No one mentioned Charles.

After the meeting I identified and sought out Laurie's kindergarten teacher. She had a plate with a cup of tea and a piece of chocolate cake; I had a plate with a cup of tea and a piece of marshmallow cake. We maneuvered[3] up to one another cautiously, and smiled.

"I've been so anxious to meet you," I said. "I'm Laurie's mother."

"We're all so interested in Laurie," she said.

"Well, he certainly likes kindergarten," I said. "He talks about it all the time."

"We had a little trouble adjusting, the

---

2. cynically (sin′ i k'l ē) *adv*.: With disbelief as to the sincerity of people's intentions or actions.

3. maneuvered (mə n$\overline{oo}$′ vərd) *v*.: Moved in a planned way.

first week or so," she said primly, "but now he's a fine little helper. With occasional lapses, of course."

"Laurie usually adjusts very quickly," I said. "I suppose this time it's Charles's influence."

"Charles?"

"Yes," I said, laughing, "you must have your hands full in that kindergarten, with Charles."

"Charles?" she said. "We don't have any Charles in the kindergarten."

THINKING ABOUT THE SELECTION

Recalling

1. Give three examples of Charles's poor behavior in school.
2. Give three examples of Laurie's poor behavior at home.
3. How does Charles's teacher deal with him?
4. What does Laurie's mother learn when she goes to the PTA meeting?

Interpreting

5. Why did Laurie act the way he did in school?
6. What clues to Laurie's behavior in school can you find in his behavior at home?
7. Why do you think Laurie invented Charles?

Applying

8. Imagine you were Laurie's parent. What would you do about Laurie's behavior?

ANALYZING LITERATURE

Investigating Point of View

"Charles" is a **first-person narrative.** A character, Laurie's mother, tells the story. As the narrator, she uses language such as "my son" and "I said." The plot reveals information only as Laurie's mother learns it. The story's ending is as much of a surprise to her as it is to you.

1. Before the PTA meeting, how does Laurie's mother learn about incidents in school?

2. Why is a first-person point of view effective for developing the plot of "Charles"?

CRITICAL THINKING AND READING

Making Inferences About the Plot

An **inference** is a conclusion based on evidence. Sometimes an author does not state directly everything that is happening. The reader must make inferences based on clues given. For example, the author does not tell you directly that Laurie's behavior at home changes after he starts kindergarten, but you infer it.

Find and list four clues from which you can make the inference that Charles is Laurie.

THINKING AND WRITING

Writing from Another Point of View

Make a list of several questions you might want to ask the parents of Laurie if you were his kindergarten teacher. Use the questions to write a new scene at the PTA meeting between Laurie's mother and his teacher. Instead of writing the episode from the point of view of Laurie's mother, write your episode from the point of view of Laurie's teacher. The pronouns "I" and "me" will refer to the teacher in your scene. Remember that she knows only about what has happened at school.

Revise your story to make sure you have maintained a consistent point of view. Finally, proofread your story and share it with your classmates.

Character

WOMAN WITH PARASOL
Claude Monet
Scala/Art Resource

GUIDE FOR READING

The House Guest

Paul Darcy Boles (1916–1984) was born in Ashley-Hudson, Indiana, and was the author of novels, short stories, plays, and criticism. Some of his short stories were first published in magazines. Among these stories was "The House Guest," which first appeared in *Seventeen* in 1975. During that year, the problems of unrest and conflict in Northern Ireland were frequently reported in the news. The house guest in this story is a young girl from Northern Ireland.

Character Traits

Character traits are the qualities that make up a character's personality. For example, a character may be honest, generous, stubborn, or scheming. You can discover these character traits through a character's actions and words and through the writer's description of the character. Some characters may show only one major character trait, while others, like real people, show a number of different traits.

Look For

As you read "The House Guest," pay attention to the characters of Bridgie and Mitch. Look for the ways in which their character traits are revealed. What are they like? Do you think you would enjoy knowing them?

Writing

"The House Guest" tells of a young Irish girl who comes to live with an American family for a few weeks and touches their lives. Think of someone you have met who stands out in your mind. List that person's character traits in order of importance—from what is most outstanding about the person to what is least memorable. Then describe the person's full character.

Vocabulary

Knowing the meaning of the following words will help you as you read "The House Guest."

intern (in'tərn) *n.:* A doctor serving a training period in a hospital after completing medical school (p. 79)

mammoth (mam'əth) *adj.:* Huge (p. 81)

crooning (kroon'iŋ) *adj.:* Singing or humming in a low, gentle way (p. 84)

mutual (myoo'choo wəl) *adj.:* Having the same relationship toward each other (p. 84)

The House Guest

Paul Darcy Boles

I'm writing this at the downstairs desk where I do homework or just fool around. It's the same desk Bridgie used to come up to and stand behind sometimes. After a second or so I would feel her standing there. Then I would turn around, making it slow because she's a kid you don't want to scare. She has big dark blue eyes, red hair about the color of the sun before it's really up. She doesn't have much of a chin; her cheekbones are high and like smooth little rocks under the clear skin. She's no beauty. I mean, she's just what she is.

When I turned around and she was there as I'd thought, I would say, "Can I help you, Bridgie?" She would shake her head; she'd just wanted to see if *I* was all right. And when she'd made sure I was, she would just turn around and walk off. My mother and father told me she did the same thing with them: stood and looked at them for a couple of seconds, then walked off . . . satisfied they were still themselves and handy.

She was only with us for six short weeks. It was one of these red-tape deals through the United States government: you signed up to keep a kid from Northern Ireland in your home as a guest. The idea was to show the kids what America was like, as if anybody could do that even in six years. Anyhow, I was all for it; my brother is an intern and he's working in Rome for a year, and I never had a sister.

The night Bridgie first came, after my parents brought her from the city to our town, she didn't talk much at all. I don't mean she ducked her head or looked awkward or fiddled with her feet or hid behind the furniture. It was just that she clammed up.

She had a small green bag with some extra clothes in it and an old doll that had been whacked around quite a bit. That was the whole works, except for the clothes she wore. Next day my mother took her to a couple of shops in town and bought her some new stuff. She still wasn't talking a lot, only pleases and thank-yous, and when my mother took the new clothes out of the boxes to hang them up, Bridgie touched them, very politely, as if they belonged to somebody else and she shouldn't make any fuss. She was nine years old.

At first it kept on being kind of eggshelly around her. You see, we weren't supposed to ask her anything heavy about how things were in the place she'd come from. She'd been born in Belfast, grew up there. She had four brothers and two sisters. She was next to the oldest. Her mother had died a year and a half before and her father took care of the family the best he could.

We got all that from the bunch of statis-

tics that came before we even saw her. The people running this show wanted the kids to "fit easily into the American environment" without being pestered. I guess that was a noble idea, but it left an awful lot you couldn't say or ask.

You can hear a good deal of traffic from our dining room, not anything thunderous, but backfires and people pretending they're A. J. Foyt[1] when they zoom down the street. And a couple of times at dinner when this happened, you could see Bridgie stiffen up. She'd get quiet as a rabbit, and it wasn't even that so much as it was the way she

---

1. A. J. Foyt: A race-car driver.

looked out of the corners of her eyes. As if she were searching for a neat, dark place to hide in.

It didn't wreck her appetite, though. I don't mean she was a born pig, I just mean she always ate fast and never left anything on the plate. Oh, sure, my mother is a decent cook, but this was a different thing. I noticed she never asked for second helpings, either, but she'd take them when they were handed to her, even if she looked kind of amazed about getting them.

It was not until the third day she was with us that she really started to open up a little. We were all sitting around yakking after the evening's parade of news on TV. There had been a clip of a building, or what was left of it, that had been bombed in Dublin. The commentator had said, in that level voice they use for good news, terrible news and in between, that the trouble was moving out of Belfast, that it wasn't "contained" anymore. Bridgie had been sitting straight as six o'clock, hands in her lap, and suddenly she said, "My da was in Dublin the once."

There was a good-sized stop in the talk; then my mother asked, "Did he go on a holiday?"

She gave her head a small shake. She wore her hair in two braids wound tight around her head like pale silk ropes. "Nah, ma'am. He went there in a van to help his mate he worked with down at the docks. His mate was movin' to Dublin. When my da come back he brought us a dog."

"What kind?" I asked. "What'd he look like?"

Her eyes went a pretty fair distance away, "Ah, I was a kid then. I hardly remember ut." She looked around blinking, her eyes that same way, as if she were looking into the fireplace where the fire was jumping around in some pine logs and trying to see backward. Then she said, "But soft he was, with fine ears that stuck up when he was happy." She turned back from the fire and her shoulders went up in little wings, shrugging. "He come up missin' inside the week though. My ma never took to him, him makin' messes and all. But he couldn't o' helped it, so young."

That night after Bridgie had been tucked in bed by my mother in the room next to my parents', I asked my mother whether we could adopt Bridgie or something. My mother said that wasn't possible, she'd already asked about it. Bridgie's family needed her too much, for one thing. There were a lot of those big, iron reasons. After my mother explained them we just sat there thinking about her. I kept wishing it was the kind of world where I happened to be President, or anyhow head of the State Department or something, and could cut through some rules.

The next day was Saturday. My mother took Bridgie into the city for lunch and a flick and some sight-seeing. The flick was something made for kids, very ha-ha, and my mother said that all through it Bridgie sat without moving and not laughing either, with the buttered-popcorn-and-soft-drink bunch hollering around them.

She liked the Carl Akeley elephants and the stuffed-looking Eskimo families in the Field Museum, but the thing she liked best was a bunch of puppies in a pet-shop window. She had to be just about dragged away. "But we can't get her a dog; it would be too cruel when she had to give it up," my mother said. "She couldn't take it back to Ireland . . ."

After that my mother took her to one of the mammoth toy stores. She walked her through the doll section, but Bridgie wasn't hot about dolls. "I've got the one already," she said. "Ut's good enough."

Finally they got to the crafts part of the store, and there Bridgie finally found something she was really warm for. It was a big leatherworking set with a lot of colored chunks of leather in red, blue, green and yellow, and the knives and tooling instruments and all the rest. It was about the most advanced leatherworking set I'd ever seen, and I asked Bridgie if she'd like me to help her get started with it.

"Nah," she said, "I'm quick at the readin' and I can soak in the directions. Don't put yourself out for me, Mitch."

I wanted to put myself out for her all right, though, so a few nights after that I talked her into going ice skating with me down at the town lake. She didn't exactly skate when we got there, but I pushed her around on the skates I rented for her. After a while it started to snow, and going home I carried Bridgie on my back and she carried my skates. I pranced like a horse in the snow and once I heard her laugh.

But on the porch back home when I was brushing snow off her shoulders she said, "I shouldn't 'a gone. I've missed out a whole night o' my leatherin'."

"That's supposed to be fun too," I said. "Like skating. How're you coming with it?"

"I'm learnin'," she said. "It went slow at the first. Them directions was set down by a blitherin' lump. But now I'm swarmin' around it." Then she said, fast, "Please, Mitch, I'd like a place to work outside the fine room where I do my sleepin'."

I'd happened to look in that room and see her working, chewing her tongue and frowning and fierce. She'd been so into it she hadn't even seen me. Now she said, "It's not the need o' elbow room, there's plenty o' that. It's I'm afraid o' carvin' up the pretty floor. There's the workshop out in your garage, the one next to where ya keep the ottomobiles. It's even got the heater, if ya could spare the oil for that."

I swept out the workroom and got the heater jets open and working the next morning before I went to school. It was a place I'd spent a whole lot of my own time in as a young child, working like a fiend on model airplanes and boats. When I got home that afternoon I found she'd spent most of the day out there; I walked out of the back door and went to the workroom window, but she wasn't inside. Then she came around the corner of the garage from the lane in back of it. Her hair was mussed and she looked as though she'd been doing a hundred-yard dash. "Ah, I had to take me a walk,"

she said. "Ut gets scrooged up, laborin' so over the bench the many hours."

I started into the workroom to turn off the lights, but she ran ahead of me. "Here, I'll do ut." She flipped them off. I could see she didn't want me to see what she was making. She shut the door. On the way back to the house she said, looking at the ground, "Ya won't peach[2] on me? Ya won't tell? Sometimes I just like swingin' around the neighborhood. I won't get lost and shame ya."

We were almost at the back porch steps. She said, "It's fine, walkin' where ya please. Not havin' to stay in the District."

"District?" I said.

"Ah, that's the boundaries. You don't go past 'em unless you're a fool bent on destruction. The District is where you and your people stay inside of."

I'd never even started to think how it would be living inside a few blocks and not stepping over a line. I did then.

She was out in the workroom the next day after breakfast; my mother told me she came in for lunch and then swept right out again. She did the same thing after dinner till I went out and called her in because it was her bedtime. My mother said she was a little worried about all this hangup with leathercraft, but my father said, "Maybe privacy is the rarest thing we can give her," and my mother gave in to that. I didn't tell them about the walks around the neighborhood; Bridgie could take care of Bridgie, all right.

A couple of days before it was time for her to go back—something we weren't mentioning, any of us—my mother and father sailed off in the evening to visit some town friends. Then about nine-thirty my mother called to tell me they were going to stay

---

2. peach v.: To inform against someone.

longer than they'd planned, and to be sure to get Bridgie in from the workroom by around ten. After that, though, the phone rang again; it was some mad, dashing girl I'd been interested in for what seemed a hundred years. It wasn't till we'd finally said good night that I sat up and noticed it was ten-thirty.

I bolted[3] out in the night, down the back porch steps and yelled for Bridgie. There wasn't any answer; the whole night seemed quiet as a piece of white steel. I crunched through the snow that had fallen the day before and looked in at the workroom window. The bench light was off.

A second later, I saw her footprints, leading back to the lane.

Halfway down the lane, though, the footprints started to get mixed up with tire tracks and were harder to make out. But that was all right because by then I could see Bridgie herself. She was easy to spot, down at the end of the lane where the boulevard started and not far from the streetlight, kneeling down beside a ribby old black and tan dog. The dog looked as though it might have had Airedale in it, along with four or five other breeds; on its hind legs it would have been about as tall as Bridgie was.

She didn't turn around, maybe didn't hear me, when I came up closer. She was fitting a new collar around the dog's neck. It was acting pretty patient; she talked to it in a kind of low crooning-scolding way. "Hold your head up," she was saying. "You'll be proud and solid as the Rock of Cashel now, and don't be tryin' to scrape ut off or lose ut. Ut's your ticket to some fine homes. They'll feed ya up. They'll think ya been a pet, they'll b'lieve you're valuable . . ."

About that time, she saw me. She gave the green leather collar another pat, just the same, before she stood up. It was tooled with a lot of careful flowers, and I recognized one of the brass buckles from the giant leatherworking set.

"Well, you've caught me out," she said. "That was the last of the leather, so ut's just as well. I fitted out an even dozen creatures. It was hard findin' 'em all, some I had to folla for blocks. But none had the collars before, and now they have. It makes their chances o' havin' a home much grander. You're not angered?"

I didn't say anything. I just stuck a hand down to her and she took it. We went back along the lane. She said, "The collar's a kind o' door key. Ya'd be faster to take in a dog with a collar, wouldn't ya, now?" I still didn't say anything and she looked up at me. "There's no hard feelin's, for the immense cost o' the leatherin' outfit?"

I said, "It's okay, Bridgie."

Then I lifted her up (for nine she doesn't weigh a lot) and carried her home.

Before she went up to bed she said, "You're glad o' me? You'll ask me back some day when ut's allowed by our mutual governments?"

"Sure," I said. I kissed her on the forehead. She grinned quickly and broadly, and said, "Yah! Mush!" then backed away and skipped off and upstairs.

I'm writing this at the desk Bridgie used to come up to and stand behind while she looked at me to make sure I was still here. I'm still here. Tonight on the news there were some cut-ins from Belfast: bombings and shootings. A while ago I heard a dog outside in the dark howling a little, then going away. I don't know if it had a collar on or not. I turned around when I heard it, but Bridgie wasn't there, of course. She's back home in her District, but maybe that's not exactly true either . . . because I think Bridgie's District is the world.

---

3. bolted v.: Dashed out suddenly.

THINKING ABOUT THE SELECTION

Recalling

1. Why is Bridgie staying with Mitch's family?
2. Which gift does she like the most?
3. Why does Bridgie go for walks alone?

Interpreting

4. Why do you think Bridgie stiffens when she hears cars backfire?
5. Bridgie eats fast and never leaves anything. What does this indicate about her life in Belfast? Find another detail that supports this idea.
6. Find three details that indicate she remembers well the dog she had at home but is covering up her feelings.
7. What does Bridgie mean when she says, "The collar's a kind o' door key." Draw a comparison between Bridgie and dogs she collars.
8. Explain Mitch's statement that "Bridgie's District is the world."

Applying

9. Mitch says, "I'd never even started to think how it would be living inside a few blocks and not stepping over a line. I did then." Discuss what such a life must be like.

ANALYZING LITERATURE

Understanding Character Traits

Character traits are the qualities of a character's personality. They are revealed through a character's actions and words. For example, in "The House Guest," Mitch says about Bridgie, "I noticed she never asked for second helpings, either, but she'd take them when they were handed to her, even if she looked kind of amazed about getting them." This passage shows that Mitch is being perceptive, or observant.

What traits about the character indicated are shown by the following lines from the story?
1. Bridgie: "The night Bridgie first came . . . she didn't talk much at all . . . It was just that she clammed up."

2. Mitch: "I wanted to put myself out for her all right, though, so a few nights after that I talked her into going ice skating with me. . . . "

CRITICAL THINKING AND READING

Comparing and Contrasting Characters

A **comparison** shows the similarities between two or more characters. A **contrast** shows the differences between them.
1. Mitch can walk where he pleases, have second helpings, and live in a peaceful area. How is Bridgie's home life different from Mitch's?
2. Bridgie shows kindness to dogs. How does Mitch similarly show kindness to Bridgie?

UNDERSTANDING LANGUAGE

Showing Contrast

Certain words and phrases such as *although, but, different, however, whereas, on the other hand, unlike, while,* and *yet* indicate contrast.

Combine the pairs of sentences into one sentence by using a word or phrase that shows a contrast. Use a comma or semicolon, if needed.
1. In Ireland, Bridgie's family is confined to their district. In the U.S., Mitch's family is free to travel wherever they wish.
2. Mother worries Bridgie is spending too much time at her leatherworking. Father feels privacy may be the best thing they can give Bridgie.

THINKING AND WRITING

Writing as a Character

Imagine that you are Bridgie back in Northern Ireland. Write a letter to Mitch telling him about how your stay with his family affected you. Give specific examples of the experiences that meant the most to you.

GUIDE FOR READING

Gentleman of Río en Medio

Juan A. A. Sedillo (1902–1982) was born in New Mexico and lived in the Southwest. He was a lawyer and public servant, as well as a writer. "Gentleman of Río en Medio" is based on an actual legal case that arose over a conflict about the ownership of some property. In this story, Sedillo makes use of his legal background and his understanding of people.

Major and Minor Characters

A story usually has both major and minor characters. A **major character** is the most important person in the story. You learn the most about this character when you read the story. A **minor character** is a person of less importance in the story, but who is necessary for the story to develop. You learn only a little about each minor character in the story.

Look For

As you read "Gentleman of Río en Medio," look for what you learn about Don Anselmo. Why is he so important to the story? Who are the less important characters?

Writing

Don Anselmo is called "the *gentleman* of Río en Medio." What makes someone a gentleman? Freewrite, exploring your thoughts on this matter.

Vocabulary

Knowing the following words will help you as you read "Gentleman of Río en Medio."

negotiation (ni gō′shē ā′shən) *n.*: Bargaining or discussing to reach an agreement (p. 87)

gnarled (närld) *adj.*: Knotty and twisted (p. 87)

innumerable (i nōō′mər ə b′l) *adj.*: Too many to be counted (p. 87)

broached (brōcht) *v.*: To start a discussion about a topic (p. 88)

Gentleman of Río en Medio

Juan A. A. Sedillo

It took months of negotiation to come to an understanding with the old man. He was in no hurry. What he had the most of was time. He lived up in Río en Medio,[1] where his people had been for hundreds of years. He tilled the same land they had tilled. His house was small and wretched, but quaint. The little creek ran through his land. His orchard was gnarled and beautiful.

The day of the sale he came into the office. His coat was old, green and faded. I thought of Senator Catron,[2] who had been such a power with these people up there in the mountains. Perhaps it was one of his old Prince Alberts.[3] He also wore gloves. They were old and torn and his finger tips showed through them. He carried a cane, but it was only the skeleton of a worn-out umbrella. Behind him walked one of his innumerable kin—a dark young man with eyes like a gazelle.

The old man bowed to all of us in the room. Then he removed his hat and gloves, slowly and carefully. Chaplin[4] once did that in a picture, in a bank—he was the janitor. Then he handed his things to the boy, who stood obediently behind the old man's chair.

THE SACRISTAN OF TRAMPAS (detail)
Paul Burlin
Museum of New Mexico

There was a great deal of conversation, about rain and about his family. He was very proud of his large family. Finally we got down to business. Yes, he would sell, as he had agreed, for twelve hundred dollars, in cash. We would buy, and the money was ready. "Don[5] Anselmo," I said to him in Spanish, "We have made a discovery. You remember that we sent that surveyor, that

---

1. Río en Medio (rē′ ō en mā′ dē ō)
2. Senator Catron (ka′trən): Thomas Benton Catron, senator from New Mexico, 1912–1917.
3. Prince Alberts: Long, double-breasted coats.
4. Chaplin: Charlie Chaplin (1889–1977), actor and producer of silent films in the United States.

---

5. don: A Spanish title of respect, similar to *Sir* in English.

engineer, up there to survey your land so as to make the deed. Well, he finds that you own more than eight acres. He tells us that your land extends across the river and that you own almost twice as much as you thought." He didn't know that. "And now, Don Anselmo," I added, "These Americans are *buena gente*,[6] they are good people, and they are willing to pay you for the additional land as well, at the same rate per acre, so that instead of twelve hundred dollars you will get almost twice as much, and the money is here for you."

The old man hung his head for a moment in thought. Then he stood up and stared at me. "Friend," he said, "I do not like to have you speak to me in that manner." I kept still and let him have his say. "I know these Americans are good people, and that is why I have agreed to sell to them. But I do not care to be insulted. I have agreed to sell my house and land for twelve hundred dollars and that is the price."

I argued with him but it was useless. Finally he signed the deed and took the money but refused to take more than the amount agreed upon. Then he shook hands all around, put on his ragged gloves, took his stick and walked out with the boy behind him.

A month later my friends had moved into Río en Medio. They had replastered the old adobe house, pruned the trees, patched the fence, and moved in for the summer. One day they came back to the office to complain. The children of the village were overrunning their property. They came every day and played under the trees, built little play fences around them, and took blossoms. When they were spoken to they only laughed and talked back good-naturedly in Spanish.

I sent a messenger up to the mountains for Don Anselmo. It took a week to arrange another meeting. When he arrived he repeated his previous preliminary performance. He wore the same faded cutaway,[7] carried the same stick and was accompanied by the boy again. He shook hands all around, sat down with the boy behind his chair, and talked about the weather. Finally I broached the subject. "Don Anselmo, about the ranch you sold to these people. They are good people and want to be your friends and neighbors always. When you sold to them you signed a document, a deed, and in that deed you agreed to several things. One thing was that they were to have the complete possession of the property. Now, Don Anselmo, it seems that every day the children of the village overrun the orchard and spend most of their time there. We would like to know if you, as the most respected man in the village, could not stop them from doing so in order that these people may enjoy their new home more in peace."

Don Anselmo stood up. "We have all learned to love these Americans," he said, "Because they are good people and good neighbors. I sold them my property because I knew they were good people, but I did not sell them the trees in the orchard."

This was bad. "Don Anselmo," I pleaded, "When one signs a deed and sells real property one sells also everything that grows on the land, and those trees, every one of them, are on the land and inside the boundaries of what you sold."

"Yes, I admit that," he said. "You know," he added, "I am the oldest man in the village. Almost everyone there is my relative and all the children of Río en Medio

---

6. *buena gente* (bwā′ nä hen′ tä)

7. cutaway (kut′ ə wā′) *n*.: A coat worn by men for formal daytime occasions.

are my *sobrinos* and *nietos*,[8] my descendants. Every time a child has been born in Río en Medio since I took possession of that house from my mother I have planted a tree for that child. The trees in that orchard are not mine, *Señor*, they belong to the children of the village. Every person in Río en Medio born since the railroad came to Santa Fé owns a tree in that orchard. I did not sell the trees because I could not. They are not mine.''

There was nothing we could do. Legally we owned the trees but the old man had been so generous, refusing what amounted to a fortune for him. It took most of the following winter to buy the trees, individually, from the descendants of Don Anselmo in the valley of Río en Medio.

---

8. sobrinos (sō brē′ nōs) and **nietos** (nyā′ tōs): Spanish for ''nieces and nephews'' and ''grandchildren.''

THINKING ABOUT THE SELECTION
Recalling

1. Why does it take months to reach the first agreement with Don Anselmo?
2. Why do the Americans offer additional money for the property? How does Don Anselmo react to the offer?
3. What complaint do the Americans have after they have bought the property? What is Don Anselmo's response to their complaint?
4. How do the Americans solve their problem?
5. Describe how Don Anselmo acts when he comes into the office to finalize the sale. What does his behavior suggest about him?

Interpreting

6. What does Don Anselmo's refusal of more money for the land suggest about him? Find one other detail that supports this impression.
7. What does the Americans' solution to the problem suggest about them? Find one other detail that supports this impression.
8. What makes Don Anselmo the ''Gentleman of Río en Medio''?

Applying

9. Put yourself in the Americans' place. Explain how you would have solved their problem.

ANALYZING LITERATURE
Identifying Major and Minor Characters

In a work of literature, the **major** character is the person the story is about—the one about whom you learn the most and who plays the largest role in the tale. The **minor** characters play less essential roles.
1. What role does Don Anselmo play in this story?
2. What do you learn about him as the story progresses?
3. What role do the Americans play in the story?
4. What role does the narrator play?

THINKING AND WRITING
Comparing and Contrasting Cultures

Imagine that you have just received a letter from a pen pal in Mexico. Your pen pal has described his or her birthday celebration and has asked you how you celebrate your birthday. Write a letter to your pen pal explaining how you celebrate birthdays. Include not only what you do but your attitude about birthdays. After you have drafted your letter, revise it to make sure that your explanation is clear. Proofread your letter and prepare a final draft.

GUIDE FOR READING

Raymond's Run

Toni Cade Bambara (1939–   ) was born in New York City and educated in the United States and Europe. She has studied mime and dance and has taught students of all ages, from preschoolers to college students. A critic has said that Bambara writes of "black women at the edge of a new awareness, who create their own choices about the kinds of women they will be." In "Raymond's Run," Squeaky reaches that point and makes a clear choice about the kind of person she intends to be.

Round and Flat Characters

Characters are sometimes described as being round or flat. **Round** characters are like real people. They are complex, revealing several sides to their personality and growing and changing as the story progresses. **Flat** characters are one-dimensional, often revealing a single personal quality and staying the same throughout the story.

Look For

As you read "Raymond's Run," look for the descriptive details that make Squeaky come alive for you. Does she seem like a real person, someone you might know? What sides do you see to her personality? How does she change as the story progresses?

Writing

Think of a television show or movie that you like. List all the characters. Which ones seem round or fully developed? Select one of the round characters and freewrite, exploring all the aspects of his or her personality.

Vocabulary

Knowing the meaning of the following words will help you as you read "Raymond's Run."

prodigy (präd′ə jē) *n.*: A child of extraordinary genius (p. 93)
glockenspiels (gläk′ən spēlz′) *n.*: Musical instruments, like xylophones, that are carried upright and often used in marching bands (p. 94)

periscope (per′ə skōp′) *n.*: An instrument containing mirrors and lenses to see objects not in a direct line from the viewer; often used in submarines to see objects above the water (p. 95)

Raymond's Run

Toni Cade Bambara

I don't have much work to do around the house like some girls. My mother does that. And I don't have to earn my pocket money by hustling; George runs errands for the big boys and sells Christmas cards. And anything else that's got to get done, my father does. All I have to do in life is mind my brother Raymond, which is enough.

Sometimes I slip and say my little brother Raymond. But as any fool can see he's much bigger and he's older too. But a lot of people call him my little brother cause he needs looking after cause he's not quite right. And a lot of smart mouths got lots to say about that too, especially when George was minding him. But now, if anybody has anything to say to Raymond, anything to say about his big head, they have to come by me. And I don't play the dozens[1] or believe in standing around with somebody in my face doing a lot of talking. I much rather just knock you down and take my chances even if I am a little girl with skinny arms and a squeaky voice, which is how I got the name Squeaky. And if things get too rough, I run. And as anybody can tell you, I'm the fastest thing on two feet.

There is no track meet that I don't win the first place medal. I use to win the twenty-yard dash when I was a little kid in kindergarten. Nowadays it's the fifty-yard dash. And tomorrow I'm subject to run the quarter-meter relay all by myself and come in first, second, and third. The big kids call me Mercury[2] cause I'm the swiftest thing in the neighborhood. Everybody knows that —except two people who know better, my father and me.

---

1. the dozens: A game in which the players insult one another; the first to show anger loses.

2. Mercury *n.*: In Roman mythology, the messenger of the gods, known for great speed.

He can beat me to Amsterdam Avenue with me having a two fire-hydrant headstart and him running with his hands in his pockets and whistling. But that's private information. Cause can you imagine some thirty-five-year-old man stuffing himself into PAL[3] shorts to race little kids? So as far as everyone's concerned, I'm the fastest and that goes for Gretchen, too, who has put out the tale that she is going to win the first place medal this year. Ridiculous. In the second place, she's got short legs. In the third place, she's got freckles. In the first place, no one can beat me and that's all there is to it.

I'm standing on the corner admiring the weather and about to take a stroll down Broadway so I can practice my breathing exercises, and I've got Raymond walking on the inside close to the buildings cause he's subject to fits of fantasy and starts thinking he's a circus performer and that the curb is a tight-rope strung high in the air. And sometimes after a rain, he likes to step down off his tightrope right into the gutter and slosh around getting his shoes and cuffs wet. Or sometimes if you don't watch him, he'll dash across traffic to the island in the middle of Broadway and give the pigeons a fit. Then I have to go behind him apologizing to all the old people sitting around trying to get some sun and getting all upset with the pigeons fluttering around them, scattering their newspapers and upsetting the wax-paper lunches in their laps. So I keep Raymond on the inside of me, and he plays like he's driving a stagecoach, which is O.K. by me so long as he doesn't run me over or interrupt my breathing exercises, which I have to do on account of I'm serious about my running and don't care who knows it.

Now some people like to act like things come easy to them, won't let on that they practice. Not me. I'll high prance down 34th Street like a rodeo pony to keep my knees strong even if it does get my mother uptight so that she walks ahead like she's not with me, don't know me, is all by herself on a shopping trip, and I am somebody else's crazy child.

Now you take Cynthia Procter for instance. She's just the opposite. If there's a test tomorrow, she'll say something like, "Oh I guess I'll play handball this afternoon and watch television tonight," just to let you know she ain't thinking about the test. Or like last week when she won the spelling bee for the millionth time, "A good thing you got 'receive,' Squeaky, cause I would have got it wrong. I completely forgot about the spelling bee." And she'll clutch the lace on her blouse like it was a narrow escape. Oh, brother.

But of course when I pass her house on my early morning trots around the block, she is practicing the scales on the piano over and over and over and over. Then in music class, she always lets herself get bumped around so she falls accidently on purpose onto the piano stool and is so surprised to find herself sitting there, and so decides just for fun to try out the ole keys and

3. PAL *adj.*: Police Athletic League.

what do you know—Chopin's[4] waltzes just spring out of her fingertips and she's the most surprised thing in the world. A regular prodigy. I could kill people like that.

I stay up all night studying the words for the spelling bee. And you can see me anytime of day practicing running. I never walk if I can trot and shame on Raymond if he can't keep up. But of course he does, cause if he hangs back someone's liable to walk up to him and get smart, or take his allowance from him, or ask him where he got that great big pumpkin head. People are so stupid sometimes.

So I'm strolling down Broadway breathing out and breathing in on counts of seven, which is my lucky number, and here comes Gretchen and her sidekicks—Mary Louise who used to be a friend of mine when she first moved to Harlem from Baltimore and got beat up by everybody till I took up for her on account of her mother and my mother used to sing in the same choir when they were young girls, but people ain't grateful, so now she hangs out with the new girl Gretchen and talks about me like a dog; and Rosie who is as fat as I am skinny and has a big mouth where Raymond is concerned and is too stupid to know that there is not a big deal of difference between herself and Raymond and that she can't afford to throw stones. So they are steady coming up Broadway and I see right away that it's going to be one of those Dodge City[5] scenes cause the street ain't that big and they're close to the buildings just as we are. First I think I'll step into the candy store and look over the new comics and let them pass. But that's chicken and I've got a reputation to consider. So

then I think I'll just walk straight on through them or over them if necessary. But as they get to me, they slow down. I'm ready to fight, cause like I said I don't feature a whole lot of chit-chat, I much prefer to just knock you down right from the jump and save everybody a lotta precious time.

"You signing up for the May Day races?" smiles Mary Louise, only it's not a smile at all.

A dumb question like that doesn't deserve an answer. Besides, there's just me and Gretchen standing there really, so no use wasting my breath talking to shadows.

"I don't think you're going to win this time," says Rosie, trying to signify with her hands on her hips all salty, completely forgetting that I have whupped her many times for less salt than that.

"I always win cause I'm the best," I say straight at Gretchen who is, as far as I'm concerned, the only one talking in this ventriloquist-dummy routine.

Gretchen smiles but it's not a smile and I'm thinking that girls never really smile at each other because they don't know how and don't want to know how and there's probably no one to teach us how cause grown-up girls don't know either. Then they all look at Raymond who has just brought his mule team to a standstill. And they're about to see what trouble they can get into through him.

"What grade you in now, Raymond?"

"You got anything to say to my brother, you say it to me, Mary Louise Williams of Raggedy Town, Baltimore."

"What are you, his mother?" sasses Rosie.

"That's right, Fatso. And the next word out of anybody and I'll be *their* mother too." So they just stand there and Gretchen shifts from one leg to the other and so do they. Then Gretchen puts her hands on her hips

4. **Chopin** (shō′ pǎn): Frédéric François Chopin (1810–1849), Polish composer and pianist.
5. **Dodge City:** The location of the television program "Gunsmoke," which often presented a gunfight between the sheriff and an outlaw.

and is about to say something with her freckle-face self but doesn't. Then she walks around me looking me up and down but keeps walking up Broadway, and her sidekicks follow her. So me and Raymond smile at each other and he says, "Gidyap" to his team and I continue with my breathing exercises, strolling down Broadway toward the ice man on 145th with not a care in the world cause I am Miss Quicksilver herself.

I take my time getting to the park on May Day because the track meet is the last thing on the program. The biggest thing on the program is the May Pole dancing, which I can do without, thank you, even if my mother thinks it's a shame I don't take part and act like a girl for a change. You'd think my mother'd be grateful not to have to make me a white organdy dress with a big satin sash and buy me new white baby-doll shoes that can't be taken out of the box till the big day. You'd think she'd be glad her daughter ain't out there prancing around a May Pole getting the new clothes all dirty and sweaty and trying to act like a fairy or a flower or whatever you're supposed to be when you should be trying to be yourself, whatever that is, which is, as far as I am concerned, a poor black girl who really can't afford to buy shoes and a new dress you only wear once a lifetime cause it won't fit next year.

I was once a strawberry in a Hansel and Gretel pageant when I was in nursery school and didn't have no better sense than to dance on tiptoe with my arms in a circle over my head doing umbrella steps and being a perfect fool just so my mother and father could come dressed up and clap. You'd think they'd know better than to encourage that kind of nonsense. I am not a strawberry. I do not dance on my toes. I run. That is what I am all about. So I always come late to the May Day program, just in time to get my number pinned on and lay in the grass till they announce the fifty-yard dash.

I put Raymond in the little swings, which is a tight squeeze this year and will be impossible next year. Then I look around for Mr. Pearson, who pins the numbers on. I'm really looking for Gretchen if you want to know the truth, but she's not around. The park is jam-packed. Parents in hats and corsages and breast-pocket handkerchiefs peeking up. Kids in white dresses and light-blue suits. The parkees unfolding chairs and chasing the rowdy kids from Lenox as if they had no right to be there. The big guys with their caps on backwards, leaning against the fence swirling the basketballs on the tips of their fingers, waiting for all these crazy people to clear out the park so they can play. Most of the kids in my class are carrying bass drums and glockenspiels and flutes. You'd think they'd put in a few bongos or something for real like that.

Then here comes Mr. Pearson with his clipboard and his cards and pencils and whistles and safety pins and fifty million other things he's always dropping all over the place with his clumsy self. He sticks out in a crowd cause he's on stilts. We used to call him Jack and the Beanstalk to get him mad. But I'm the only one that can outrun him and get away, and I'm too grown for that silliness now.

"Well, Squeaky," he says checking my name off the list and handing me number seven and two pins. And I'm thinking he's got no right to call me Squeaky, if I can't call him Beanstalk.

"Hazel Elizabeth Deborah Parker," I correct him and tell him to write it down on his board.

"Well, Hazel Elizabeth Deborah Parker, going to give someone else a break this year?" I squint at him real hard to see if he is

seriously thinking I should lose the race on purpose just to give someone else a break.

"Only six girls running this time," he continues, shaking his head sadly like it's my fault all of New York didn't turn out in sneakers. "That new girl should give you a run for your money." He looks around the park for Gretchen like a periscope in a submarine movie. "Wouldn't it be a nice gesture if you were . . . to ahhh . . . ."

I give him such a look he couldn't finish putting that idea into words. Grownups got a lot of nerve sometimes. I pin number seven to myself and stomp away—I'm so burnt. And I go straight for the track and stretch out on the grass while the band winds up with "Oh the Monkey Wrapped His Tail Around the Flag Pole," which my teacher calls by some other name. The man on the loudspeaker is calling everyone over to the track and I'm on my back looking at the sky trying to pretend I'm in the country, but I can't, because even grass in the city feels hard as sidewalk and there's just no pretending you are anywhere but in a "concrete jungle" as my grandfather says.

The twenty-yard dash takes all of the two minutes cause most of the little kids don't know no better than to run off the track or run the wrong way or run smack into the fence and fall down and cry. One little kid, though, has got the good sense to run straight for the white ribbon up ahead, so he wins. Then the second-graders line up for the thirty-yard dash and I don't even bother to turn my head to watch cause Raphael Perez always wins. He wins before he even begins by psyching the runners, telling them they're going to trip on their shoelaces and fall on their faces or lose their shorts or something, which he doesn't really have to do since he is very fast, almost as fast as I am. After that is the forty-yard dash, which I use to run when I was in first grade. Raymond is hollering from the swings cause he knows I'm about to do my thing cause the man on the loudspeaker has just announced the fifty-yard dash, although he might just as well be giving a recipe for angel food cake cause you can hardly make out what he's saying for the static. I get up and slip off my sweat pants and then I see Gretchen standing at the starting line kicking her legs out like a pro. Then as I get into place I see that ole Raymond is in line on the other side of the fence, bending down with his fingers on the ground just like he knew what he was doing. I was going to yell at him but then I didn't. It burns up your energy to holler.

Every time, just before I take off in a race, I always feel like I'm in a dream, the kind of dream you have when you're sick with fever and feel all hot and weightless. I dream I'm flying over a sandy beach in the early morning sun, kissing the leaves of the trees as I fly by. And there's always the smell of apples, just like in the country when I was little and use to think I was a choo-choo train, running through the fields of corn and chugging up the hill to the orchard. And all the time I'm dreaming this, I get lighter and lighter until I'm flying over the beach again, getting blown through the sky like a feather that weighs nothing at all. But once I spread my fingers in the dirt and crouch over for the Get on Your Mark, the dream goes and I am solid again and am telling myself, Squeaky you must win, you must win, you are the fastest thing in the world, you can even beat your father up Amsterdam if you really try. And then I feel my weight coming back just behind my knees then down to my feet then into the earth and the pistol shot explodes in my blood and I am off and weightless again, flying past the other runners, my arms pumping up and down and the whole world is quiet except for the crunch as I zoom over the gravel in the track. I glance to my left and there is no one. To the right a blurred Gretchen, who's got her chin jutting out as if it would win the race all by itself. And on the other side of the fence is Raymond with his arms down to his side and the palms tucked up behind him, running in his very own style and the first time I ever saw that and I almost stop to watch my brother Raymond on his first run. But the white ribbon is bouncing toward me and I tear past it racing into the distance till my feet with a mind of their own start digging up footfuls of dirt and brake me short. Then all the kids standing on the side pile on me, banging me on the back and slapping my head with their May Day programs, for I have won again and everybody on 151st Street can walk tall for another year.

"In first place . . ." the man on the loud-speaker is clear as a bell now. But then he pauses and the loudspeaker starts to whine. Then static. And I lean down to catch my breath and here comes Gretchen walking back for she's overshot the finish line too, huffing and puffing with her hands on her hips taking it slow, breathing in steady time like a real pro and I sort of like her a little for the first time. "In first place . . ." and then three or four voices get all mixed up on the loudspeaker and I dig my sneaker into the grass and stare at Gretchen who's staring back, we both wondering just who did win. I can hear old Beanstalk arguing with the man on the loudspeaker and then a few others running their mouths about what the stop watches say.

Then I hear Raymond yanking at the fence to call me and I wave to shush him, but he keeps rattling the fence like a gorilla in a cage like in them gorilla movies, but then like a dancer or something he starts climbing up nice and easy but very fast. And it occurs to me, watching how smoothly he climbs hand over hand and remembering how he looked running with his arms down to his side and with the wind pulling his mouth back and his teeth showing and all, it occurred to me that Raymond would make a very fine runner. Doesn't he always keep up with me on my trots? And he surely knows how to breathe in counts of seven cause he's always doing it at the dinner table, which drives my brother George up the wall. And I'm smiling to beat the band cause if I've lost this race, or if me and Gretchen tied, or even if I've won, I can always retire as a runner and begin a whole new career as a coach with Raymond as my champion. After all, with a little more study I can beat Cynthia and her phony self at the spelling bee. And if I bugged my mother, I could get piano lessons and become a star. And I have a big rep as the baddest thing around. And I've got a roomful of ribbons and medals and awards. But what has Raymond got to call his own?

So I stand there with my new plan, laughing out loud by this time as Raymond

jumps down from the fence and runs over with his teeth showing and his arms down to the side, which no one before him has quite mastered as a running style. And by the time he comes over I'm jumping up and down so glad to see him—my brother Raymond, a great runner in the family tradition. But of course everyone thinks I'm jumping up and down because the men on the loudspeaker have finally gotten themselves together and compared notes and are announcing "In first place—Miss Hazel Elizabeth Deborah Parker." (Dig that.) "In second place—Miss Gretchen P. Lewis." And I look over at Gretchen wondering what the P stands for. And I smile. Cause she's good, no doubt about it. Maybe she'd like to help me coach Raymond; she obviously is serious about running, as any fool can see. And she nods to congratulate me and then she smiles. And I smile. We stand there with this big smile of respect between us. It's about as real a smile as girls can do for each other, considering we don't practice real smiling every day you know, cause maybe we too busy being flowers or fairies or strawberries instead of something honest and worthy of respect . . . you know . . . like being people.

THINKING ABOUT THE SELECTION

Recalling

1. How did Squeaky gain her name? Why is she also called Mercury? Why does she refer to herself as "Miss Quicksilver"?
2. What would Squeaky's mother like her to do in the May Day program? Why doesn't Squeaky do this?
3. What does Mr. Pearson want her to do during the race? How does she react even before he can finish putting this idea into words?
4. How does Squeaky feel before each race? How does she "psych herself up" or encourage herself to win?
5. What does Squeaky realize about herself at the end of the race? What does she realize about Raymond?

Interpreting

6. Squeaky's main responsibility is taking care of Raymond. How does she feel about this responsibility? Find evidence to support your answer.
7. How does Squeaky act toward people who talk smart to her? What does this behavior suggest about her?
8. When Squeaky runs into Gretchen, Mary Louise, and Rosie, she thinks, "Besides, there's just me and Gretchen standing there really. . . ." What does this thought indicate about her feelings toward the other girls? Why does she feel this way about them?
9. Early in the story, how did Squeaky feel about girls smiling at each other? Why do she and Gretchen smile at each other at the end of the race? What does this change suggest that Squeaky has learned?
10. Why is this story called "Raymond's Run" instead of "Squeaky's Run"?

Applying

11. What makes you respect other people?
12. Squeaky suggests that it is difficult for girls in

our society to be "something honest and worthy of respect." Explain why you agree or disagree with her opinion.

ANALYZING LITERATURE
Recognizing Round and Flat Characters

Writers often people their stories with both round and flat characters. The **round** characters grow and change as the story progresses. The **flat** characters generally reveal only one side of their personality and may serve to highlight the positive qualities of the round characters.

1. Describe how Squeaky grows and changes as the story progresses.
2. In what way does Cynthia Procter serve as a foil to Squeaky? That is, how does she serve to point up Squeaky's positive characteristics?
3. In what way do Mary Louise and Rosie serve as a foil to Squeaky? In what way do they also serve as a foil to Gretchen?

CRITICAL THINKING AND READING
Identifying Reasons

A **reason** is the information that explains or justifies a condition, an action, or a decision. A reason may be a fact, an opinion, a situation, or an occurrence. In "Raymond's Run," for example, the reason for Squeaky's nickname is that she has a squeaky voice.

Give the reasons for the following situations in "Raymond's Run."

1. Squeaky changes her view of Gretchen.
2. At the end, Squeaky feels that winning the race does not matter.

UNDERSTANDING LANGUAGE
Understanding Idioms

An **idiom** is an expression that has a meaning all its own. This meaning is different from the literal meaning of the words. For example, *to catch one's eye* is an idiom that means "to get one's attention." To take this meaning literally can mean making a serious mistake.

The meaning of idioms is generally understood. Sometimes you can understand that words are being used as idioms from the context, or surrounding words and ideas. Often an idiom can give the flavor of a character, or a clearer idea of what the character is like.

What is the meaning of each *italicized* idiom?

1. "Rosie is too stupid to know that there is not a big deal of difference between herself and Raymond and that she can't afford *to throw stones.*"
2. "Grown-ups got a lot of nerve sometimes. I pin number seven to myself and stomp away, I'm so *burnt.*"

THINKING AND WRITING
Writing an Extension of the Story

Imagine Squeaky in a different situation—for example, during Raymond's first race after she has coached him. Write about the race from Squeaky's point of view, speaking as "I." First make an outline of what you will write. Think about what advice Squeaky will give Raymond: how she will feel and think before, during, and after the race; and how the race will end. Then write this part of the story. Revise your story, making sure you have told it consistently from Squeaky's point of view. Proofread your story and share it with your classmates.

GUIDE FOR READING

The Day the Sun Came Out

Dorothy M. Johnson (1905–1984) lived most of her life in Montana where she was born. Many of her stories have western or Indian themes. In fact, Johnson was an honorary member of the Blackfoot tribe; her Indian name is Kills-Both-Places. Two of Johnson's books were adapted in the popular movies "The Man Who Shot Liberty Valance" and "A Man Called Horse." "The Day the Sun Came Out" is one of her many stories about courage and strength in ordinary people.

Direct and Indirect Characterization

Characterization is the way a writer presents a character in a story. A writer may use direct or indirect characterization. In **direct characterization,** the writer tells you what a character is like. For example, the writer might state that Joe is a stubborn man.

In **indirect characterization,** the writer reveals a character through what he or she looks like, says, and does, and lets you draw conclusions about what the character is like. For example, the writer might describe an incident in which Joe acts stubbornly.

Look For

As you read "The Day the Sun Came Out," look for the methods the author uses to create the characters. What do you learn in particular about Mary? How do you learn this? See if you agree that she is heroic.

Writing

Think about someone you consider a hero. Freewrite about the reasons why you consider this person a hero.

Vocabulary

Knowing the meaning of the following words will help you as you read "The Day the Sun Came Out."

teamsters (tēm′ stərz) *n*.: People who drive teams of horses to haul a load (p. 101)
homesteaders (hōm′ sted′ ərz) *n*.: Settlers who received land from the United States government in exchange for living on it and farming it for a period of time (p. 101)
savoring (sā′ vər iŋ) *v*.: Enjoying; appreciating (p. 104)

The Day the Sun Came Out

Dorothy M. Johnson

We left the home place behind, mile by slow mile, heading for the mountains, across the prairie where the wind blew forever.

At first there were four of us with the one-horse wagon and its skimpy load. Pa and I walked, because I was a big boy of eleven. My two little sisters romped and trotted until they got tired and had to be boosted up into the wagon bed.

That was no covered Conestoga, like Pa's folks came West in, but just an old farm wagon, drawn by one weary horse, creaking and rumbling westward to the mountains, toward the little woods town where Pa thought he had an old uncle who owned a little two-bit sawmill.

Two weeks we had been moving when we picked up Mary, who had run away from somewhere that she wouldn't tell. Pa didn't want her along, but she stood up to him with no fear in her voice.

"I'd rather go with a family and look after kids," she said, "but I ain't going back. If you won't take me, I'll travel with any wagon that will."

Pa scowled at her, and her wide blue eyes stared back.

"How old are you?" he demanded.

"Eighteen," she said. "There's team-sters come this way sometimes. I'd rather go with you folks. But I won't go back."

"We're prid'near out of grub," my father told her. "We're clean out of money. I got all I can handle without taking anybody else." He turned away as if he hated the sight of her. "You'll have to walk," he said.

So she went along with us and looked after the little girls, but Pa wouldn't talk to her.

On the prairie, the wind blew. But in the mountains, there was rain. When we stopped at little timber claims along the way, the homesteaders said it had rained all summer. Crops among the blackened stumps were rotted and spoiled. There was no cheer anywhere, and little hospitality. The people we talked to were past worrying. They were scared and desperate.

So was Pa. He traveled twice as far each day as the wagon, ranging through the woods with his rifle, but he never saw game. He had been depending on venison, but we never got any except as a grudging gift from the homesteaders.

He brought in a porcupine once, and that was fat meat and good. Mary roasted it in chunks over the fire, half crying with the smoke. Pa and I rigged up the tarp sheet for a shelter to keep the rain from putting the fire clean out.

The porcupine was long gone, except for some of the tried-out[1] fat that Mary had saved, when we came to an old, empty cabin. Pa said we'd have to stop. The horse was wore out, couldn't pull anymore up those grades on the deep-rutted roads in the mountains.

At the cabin, at least there was shelter. We had a few potatoes left and some corn-meal. There was a creek that probably had fish in it, if a person could catch them. Pa tried it for half a day before he gave up. To this day I don't care for fishing. I remember my father's sunken eyes in his gaunt, grim face.

He took Mary and me outside the cabin to talk. Rain dripped on us from branches overhead.

"I think I know where we are," he said. "I calculate to get to old John's and back in about four days. There'll be grub in the town, and they'll let me have some whether old John's still there or not."

He looked at me. "You do like she tells you," he warned. It was the first time he had admitted Mary was on earth since we picked her up two weeks before.

"You're my pardner," he said to me, "but it might be she's got more brains. You mind what she says."

He burst out with bitterness, "There ain't anything good left in the world, or people to care if you live or die. But I'll get grub in the town and come back with it."

He took a deep breath and added, "If you get too all-fired hungry, butcher the horse. It'll be better than starvin'."

---

1. **tried-out fat:** Fat or lard that has been boiled or melted.

He kissed the little girls good-by and plodded off through the woods with one blanket and the rifle.

The cabin was moldy and had no floor. We kept a fire going under a hole in the roof, so it was full of blinding smoke, but we had to keep the fire so as to dry out the wood.

The third night, we lost the horse. A bear scared him. We heard the racket, and Mary and I ran out, but we couldn't see anything in the pitch-dark.

In gray daylight I went looking for him, and I must have walked fifteen miles. It seemed like I had to have that horse at the cabin when Pa came or he'd whip me. I got plumb lost two or three times and thought maybe I was going to die there alone and nobody would ever know it, but I found the way back to the clearing.

That was the fourth day, and Pa didn't come. That was the day we ate up the last of the grub.

The fifth day, Mary went looking for the horse. My sisters whimpered, huddled in a quilt by the fire, because they were scared and hungry.

I never did get dried out, always having to bring in more damp wood and going out to yell to see if Mary would hear me and not get lost. But I couldn't cry like the little girls did, because I was a big boy, eleven years old.

It was near dark when there was an answer to my yelling, and Mary came into the clearing.

Mary didn't have the horse—we never saw hide nor hair of that old horse again —but she was carrying something big and white that looked like a pumpkin with no color to it.

She didn't say anything, just looked around and saw Pa wasn't there yet, at the end of the fifth day.

"What's that thing?" my sister Elizabeth demanded.

"Mushroom," Mary answered. "I bet it hefts ten pounds."

"What are you going to do with it now?" I sneered. "Play football here?"

"Eat it—maybe," she said, putting it in a corner. Her wet hair hung over her shoulders. She huddled by the fire.

My sister Sarah began to whimper again. "I'm hungry!" she kept saying.

"Mushrooms ain't good eating," I said. "They can kill you."

"Maybe," Mary answered. "Maybe they can. I don't set up to know all about everything, like some people."

"What's that mark on your shoulder?" I asked her. "You tore your dress on the brush."

"What do you think it is?" she said, her head bowed in the smoke.

"Looks like scars," I guessed.

"'Tis scars. They whipped me, them I used to live with. Now mind your own business. I want to think."

Elizabeth whimpered, "Why don't Pa come back?"

"He's coming," Mary promised. "Can't come in the dark. Your pa'll take care of you soon's he can."

She got up and rummaged around in the grub box.

"Nothing there but empty dishes," I growled. "If there was anything, we'd know it."

Mary stood up. She was holding the can with the porcupine grease.

"I'm going to have something to eat," she said coolly. "You kids can't have any yet. And I don't want any squalling,[2] mind."

---

2. squalling (skwôl'lin) *n.*: Crying or screaming.

It was a cruel thing, what she did then. She sliced that big, solid mushroom and heated grease in a pan.

The smell of it brought the little girls out of their quilt, but she told them to go back in so fierce a voice that they obeyed. They cried to break your heart.

I didn't cry. I watched, hating her.

I endured the smell of the mushroom frying as long as I could. Then I said, "Give me some."

"Tomorrow," Mary answered. "Tomorrow, maybe. But not tonight." She turned to me with a sharp command: "Don't bother me! Just leave me be."

She knelt there by the fire and finished frying the slice of mushroom.

If I'd had Pa's rifle, I'd have been willing to kill her right then and there.

She didn't eat right away. She looked at the brown, fried slice for a while and said, "By tomorrow morning, I guess you can tell whether you want any."

The little girls stared at her as she ate. Sarah was chewing an old leather glove.

When Mary crawled into the quilts with them, they moved away as far as they could get.

I was so scared that my stomach heaved, empty as it was.

Mary didn't stay in the quilts long. She took a drink out of the water bucket and sat down by the fire and looked through the smoke at me.

She said in a low voice, "I don't know how it will be if it's poison. Just do the best you can with the girls. Because your pa will come back, you know. . . . You better go to bed. I'm going to sit up."

And so would you sit up. If it might be your last night on earth and the pain of death might seize you at any moment, you

A LOG CABIN IN A CLEARING ON THE AMERICAN FRONTIER, 1826
The Granger Collection

would sit up by the smoky fire, wide-awake, remembering whatever you had to remember, savoring life.

We sat in silence after the girls had gone to sleep. Once I asked, "How long does it take?"

"I never heard," she answered. "Don't think about it."

I slept after a while, with my chin on my chest. Maybe Peter dozed that way at Gethsemane as the Lord knelt praying.

Mary's moving around brought me wide-awake. The black of night was fading.

"I guess it's all right." Mary said. "I'd be able to tell by now, wouldn't I?"

I answered gruffly, "I don't know."

Mary stood in the doorway for a while, looking out at the dripping world as if she found it beautiful. Then she fried slices of the mushroom while the little girls danced with anxiety.

We feasted, we three, my sisters and I, until Mary ruled, "That'll hold you," and would not cook any more. She didn't touch any of the mushroom herself.

That was a strange day in the moldy cabin. Mary laughed and was gay; she told stories, and we played "Who's Got the Thimble?" with a pine cone.

In the afternoon we heard a shout, and my sisters screamed and I ran ahead of them across the clearing.

The rain had stopped. My father came plunging out of the woods leading a pack horse—and well I remember the treasures of food in that pack.

He glanced at us anxiously as he tore at the ropes that bound the pack.

"Where's the other one?" he demanded.

Mary came out of the cabin then, walking sedately. As she came toward us, the sun began to shine.

My stepmother was a wonderful woman.

THINKING ABOUT THE SELECTION
Recalling

1. Describe how the family travels.
2. Why doesn't Pa want Mary to join them?
3. Why does Pa leave his family and Mary alone?
4. Why does Mary go looking for the horse?
5. How do the children feel about Mary as she eats the mushroom?

Interpreting

6. Find two details indicating that Pa has come to respect Mary by the time he leaves.
7. Why won't Mary let the children eat the mushroom until the next day?
8. The Bible says Peter dozed while Jesus waited for the soldiers to take him. Why does the boy in this story compare himself to Peter?
9. Explain the significance of the last line: "My stepmother was a wonderful woman."
10. Why does this story have the title it does?

Applying

11. Would you have told the children why they couldn't have the mushroom? Explain.
12. Explain why you think Mary is heroic or not.

ANALYZING LITERATURE
Understanding Characterization

In **direct characterization,** writers state directly what a character is like. For example, Johnson has the boy say, "I was so scared that my stomach heaved, empty as it was." When the writer uses **indirect characterization,** she shows the character's personality through the character's words and actions. For example, Mary says, "If you won't take me, I'll travel with any wagon who will." This suggests Mary is determined. Tell whether the writer is using direct or indirect characterization in the following:

1. "Pa didn't want her along, but she stood up to him with no fear in her voice."
2. "I don't know how it will be if it's poison. Just do the best you can with the girls."

CRITICAL THINKING AND READING
Making Inferences About Characters

Inferences are conclusions draw from evidence. When writers use indirect characterization, you must make inferences about the character's feelings and personality.

1. When Mary crawls into the quilts after eating the mushroom, the two girls move as far away from her as they can. What are they feeling?
2. When Mary looks at the dripping world the morning after she ate the mushroom, she finds it beautiful. What was she feeling the night before? What is she feeling now?
3. When Pa returns he looks anxiously for Mary. How do you think he is feeling about Mary?

UNDERSTANDING LANGUAGE
Appreciating Dialect

Dialect is a way of speaking found in a particular region or group. It usually differs from the standard language in grammar, vocabulary, or pronunciation. Writers use dialect to place characters in a certain time and to give them local color.

Pa says, "If you get too all-fired hungry, butcher the horse." Such dialect was used by Americans in the 1800's.

Rewrite these sentences in standard English:

1. '"We're prid'near out of food. We're clean out of money.'"
2. "And I don't want any squalling, mind."

THINKING AND WRITING
Comparing and Contrasting Characters

Mary displays great courage. Select a courageous character from another story. First list the ways in which Mary and this character are alike. Then list the ways in which they are different. Write the first draft of a composition comparing and contrasting the two characters. Revise, making sure your details are in a logical order. Finally, proofread your paper.

What Stumped the Blue-jays

Mark Twain (1835–1910) was born Samuel Clemens near Hannibal, Missouri. He wrote books that have become American classics, such as *The Adventures of Tom Sawyer* and *The Adventures of Huckleberry Finn.* Many of Twain's short stories, including the famous "The Notorious Jumping Frog of Calaveras County," are examples of his humorous, sometimes outrageous, style. "What Stumped the Blue-jays" combines Twain's humor with one of his favorite settings—the West.

Humorous Characters

In this short humorous tale, called a *yarn,* Twain creates humor by exaggerating the characters, or overstating what they look like, say, and do. In addition, the serious way in which the narrator, Jim Baker, relates these outrageous events also adds to the story's humor, since the tale is so hard to believe that no one would take it seriously.

Look For

As you read "What Stumped the Blue-jays," look for the ways in which characters' appearance, words, and actions are exaggerated to create humor. Does this yarn make you laugh? Why or why not?

Writing

Many yarns use animal characters and exaggerate the characters of these animals. For example, they may tell about a cat that is overly curious or a monkey that is too good at mimicking human behavior. Choose an animal about which you could write a yarn. Freewrite about the animal's character. Select traits that you have observed about that animal and exaggerate them.

Vocabulary

Knowing the following words will help you as you read "What Stumped the Blue-jays."

lockjaw (läk′ jô′) *n.:* A disease that causes jaw and neck muscles to become rigid, or locked (p. 107)

countenance (koun′ tə nəns) *n.:* A facial expression (p. 108)

singular (sin′ gyə lər) *adj.:* Exceptional; peculiar (p. 109)

guffawed (gə fôd′) *v.:* Laughed in a loud, coarse way (p. 110)

What Stumped the Blue-jays

Mark Twain

Animals talk to each other, of course. There can be no question about that; but I suppose there are very few people who can understand them. I never knew but one man who could. I knew he could, however, because he told me so himself. He was a middle-aged, simple-hearted miner who had lived in a lonely corner of California, among the woods and mountains, a good many years, and had studied the ways of his only neighbors, the beasts and the birds, until he believed he could accurately translate any remark which they made. This was Jim Baker. According to Jim Baker, some animals have only a limited education, and use only very simple words, and scarcely ever a comparison or a flowery figure; whereas, certain other animals have a large vocabulary, a fine command of language and a ready and fluent delivery; consequently these latter talk a great deal; they like it; they are conscious of their talent, and enjoy "showing off." Baker said, that after long and careful observation, he had come to the conclusion that the blue-jays were the best talkers he had found among birds and beasts. Said he:—

"There's more *to* a blue-jay than any other creature. He has got more moods, and more different kinds of feelings than any other creature; and mind you, whatever a blue-jay feels, he can put into language. And no mere commonplace language, either, but rattling, out-and-out book-talk—and bris-

tling with metaphor, too—just bristling! And as for command of language—why *you* never see a blue-jay get stuck for a word. No man ever did. They just boil out of him! And another thing: I've noticed a good deal, and there's no bird, or cow, or anything that uses as good grammar as a blue-jay. You may say a cat uses good grammar. Well, a cat does—but you let a cat get excited once; you let a cat get to pulling fur with another cat on a shed, nights, and you'll hear grammar that will give you the lock-jaw. Ignorant people think it's the *noise* which fighting cats make that is so aggravating, but it ain't so; it's the sickening grammar they use. Now I've never heard a jay use bad grammar but very seldom; and when they do, they are as ashamed as a human; they shut right down and leave.

"When I first begun to understand jay language correctly, there was a little incident happened here. Seven years ago, the last man in this region but me, moved away. There stands his house,—been empty ever since; a log house, with a plank roof—just one big room, and no more; no ceiling—nothing between the rafters and the floor. Well, one Sunday morning I was sitting out here in front of my cabin, with my cat, taking the sun, and looking at the blue hills, and listening to the leaves rustling so lonely in the trees, and thinking of the home away yonder in the States, and I hadn't heard from in thirteen years, when a blue-jay lit on that house, with an acorn in his mouth, and says, 'Hello, I reckon I've struck[1] something.' When he spoke, the acorn dropped out of his mouth and rolled down the roof, of course, but he didn't care; his mind was all on the thing he had struck. It was a knothole[2] in the roof. He cocked his head to one side, shut one eye and put the other one to the hole, like a 'possum looking down a jug; then he glanced up with his bright eyes, gave a wink or two with his wings—which signifies gratification, you understand,—and says, 'It looks like a hole, it's located like a hole,—blamed if I don't believe it *is* a hole!'

"Then he cocked his head down and took another look; he glances up perfectly joyful, this time; winks his wings and his tail both, and says, 'O, no, this ain't no fat thing, I reckon! If I ain't in luck!—why it's a perfectly elegant hole!' So he flew down and got that acorn, and fetched it up and dropped it in, and was just tilting his head back, with the heavenliest smile on his face, when all of a sudden he was paralyzed into a listening attitude and that smile faded gradually out of his countenance like breath off'n a razor, and the queerest look of surprise took its place. Then he says, 'Why, I didn't hear it fall!' He cocked his eye at the hole again, and took a long look; raised up and shook his head; stepped around to the other side of the hole and took another look from that side; shook his head again. He studied a while, then he just went into the *de*tails—walked round and round the hole and spied into it from every point of the compass. No use. Now he took a thinking attitude on the comb of the roof and scratched the back of his head with his right foot a minute, and finally says, 'Well, it's too many for *me*, that's certain; must be a mighty long hole; however, I ain't got no time to fool around here, I got to 'tend to business; I reckon it's all right—chance it, anyway.'

"So he flew off and fetched another acorn and dropped it in, and tried to flirt his eye to the hole quick enough to see what become of it, but he was too late. He held his eye there as much as a minute; then he raised up and sighed, and says, 'Consound it, I don't seem to understand this thing, no way; however, I'll tackle her again.' He fetched another acorn, and done his level best to see what become of it, but he couldn't. He says, 'Well, *I* never struck no such a hole as this, before; I'm of the opinion it's a totally new kind of a hole.' Then he begun to get mad. He held in for a spell, walking up and down the comb of the roof and shaking his head and muttering to himself; but his feelings got the upper hand of him, presently, and he broke loose and cussed himself black in the face. I never see a bird take on so about a little thing.

---

1. struck *v.*: Found.
2. knothole (nät' hōl) *n.*: A hole in a board where a knot has fallen out.

When he got through he walks to the hole and looks in again for half a minute; then he says, 'Well, you're a long hole, and a deep hole, and a mighty singular hole altogether—but I've started in to fill you, if it takes a hundred years!'

"And with that, away he went. You never see a bird work so since you was born. He laid into his work, and the way he hove[3]

---

3. hove (hōv) *v*.: Heaved; threw.

acorns into that hole for about two hours and a half was one of the most exciting and astonishing spectacles I ever struck. He never stopped to take a look any more—he just hove 'em in and went for more. Well at last he could hardly flop his wings, he was so tuckered out. He comes a drooping down, once more, sweating like an ice-pitcher, drops his acorn in and says, '*Now* I guess I've got the bulge on you by this time!' So he bent down for a look. If you'll believe me, when his head come up again he was just pale with rage. He says, 'I've shoveled acorns enough in there to keep the family thirty years, and if I can see a sign of one of 'em I wish I may land in a museum with a belly full of sawdust in two minutes!'

"He just had strength enough to crawl up on to the comb and lean his back agin the chimbly, and then he collected his impressions and begun to free his mind.

"Another jay was going by, and stops to inquire what was up. The sufferer told him the whole circumstance, and says, 'Now yonder's the hole, and if you don't believe me, go and look for yourself.' So this fellow went and looked, and comes back and says, 'How many did you say you put in there?' 'Not any less than two tons,' says the sufferer. The other jay went and looked again. He couldn't seem to make it out, so he raised a yell, and three more jays come. They all examined the hole, they all made the sufferer tell it over again, then they all discussed it, and got off as many leather-headed opinions about it as an average crowd of humans could have done.

"They called in more jays; then more and more, till pretty soon this whole region 'peared to have a blue flush[4] about it. There must have been five thousand of them; and such another jawing and disputing and ripping and cussing, you never heard. Every jay in the whole lot put his eye to the hole and delivered a more chuckle-headed opinion about the mystery than the jay that went there before him. They examined the house all over, too. The door was standing half open, and at last one old jay happened to go and light on it and look in. Of course that knocked the mystery galley-west[5] in a second. There lay the acorns, scattered all over the floor. He flopped his wings and raised a whoop. 'Come here!' he says, 'Come here, everybody; hang'd if this fool hasn't been trying to fill up a house with acorns!' They all came a-swooping down like a blue cloud, and as each fellow lit on the door and took a glance, the whole absurdity of the contract that that first jay had tackled hit him home and he fell over backwards suffocating with laughter, and the next jay took his place and done the same.

"Well, sir, they roosted around here on the house-top and the trees for an hour, and guffawed over that thing like human beings. It ain't any use to tell me a blue-jay hasn't got a sense of humor, because I know better. And memory, too. They brought jays here from all over the United States to look down that hole, every summer for three years. Other birds, too. And they could all see the point, except an owl that come from Nova Scotia to visit the Yosemite[6] and he took this thing in on his way back. He said he couldn't see anything funny in it. But then he was a good deal disappointed about Yosemite, too."

---

5. knocked . . . galley-west: Cleared up the mystery.
6. Yosemite (yō sem′ ə tē): A great ravine, including Yosemite Falls, in Yosemite National Park, east central California.

---

4. flush *n.*: A blush or glow.

THINKING ABOUT THE SELECTION

Recalling

1. What special talent does Jim Baker have? Why is this talent unusual?
2. According to Baker, in what ways are blue-jays special?
3. What does the blue-jay find on the roof?
4. What enrages the blue-jay about the hole?
5. Explain what stumped the blue-jay.

Interpreting

6. Compare and contrast Jim Baker's use of language with what he appreciates about the blue-jay's use of language.
7. Describe the blue-jay's personality.
8. Jim Baker tells this tale in a deadpan, or serious, manner. What is the effect of Jim Baker's manner of telling the story?

Applying

9. Yarns were told on the American frontier to get rid of loneliness, to entertain others, and to enliven a hardworking existence. What do Americans do today that has the same effect?

ANALYZING LITERATURE

Understanding Humorous Characters

In this yarn Twain creates humor by exaggerating, or overstating, characters—what they look like, say, and do. For example, the exasperated blue-jay says that he put "Not any less than two tons" of acorns into the hole. This unbelievable statement, spoken in a serious way, helps create a humorous picture of the angry blue-jay.

1. Explain the trait exaggerated in this passage:
    "Then he begun to get mad. He held in for a spell, walking up and down the comb of the roof and shaking his head and muttering to himself; but his feelings got the upper hand of him, presently, and he broke loose and cussed himself black in the face. I never see a bird take on so about a little thing."

2. What is the effect of this exaggeration?
3. Find two other passages exaggerating what the blue-jay looks like, says, or does. Explain why each passage is effective.

CRITICAL THINKING AND READING

Identifying the Writer's Purpose

The writer's purpose is his or her reason for writing. There are many purposes for writing; for example, to inform, to entertain, or to persuade the reader.

Twain's purpose in spinning this yarn is to entertain. Did he succeed? Explain your answer.

UNDERSTANDING LANGUAGE

Appreciating Synonyms

A **synonym** is a word that has almost the same meaning as another word. For example, *furious* is a synonym for *angry*. Although they are similar in meaning, these two words also have a difference: *furious* is stronger in meaning than *angry*. Selecting the stronger synonym can be useful for exaggeration.

Select the strongest of the following synonyms in each numbered item.

1. laugh   chuckle   guffaw
2. disturbed   exasperated   bothered
3. hollered   called   shouted

THINKING AND WRITING

Writing a Yarn

Refer to your freewriting assignment for your description of an animal character with exaggerated traits. Then think of a humorous, outrageous situation involving the animal. Write a yarn about it. Make your tone serious, even though the situation is unbelievable. Have a yarn day in your class. Pretend you are Jim Baker and tell your yarn to your classmates.

The Day I Got Lost

Isaac Bashevis Singer (1904–   ) was born in Poland, where he received a traditional Jewish education. In 1935 he settled in New York City, where he became a U.S. citizen. Singer writes in Yiddish, a language of some East European Jews and their descendants. In 1978 he was awarded the Nobel Prize for literature. Many of his stories involve people with exaggerated traits. In "The Day I Got Lost," the professor typifies a shlemiel, a Yiddish word for a bungler or unlucky person.

Narrator

A **narrator** is the person who tells a story. In this story, the narrator speaks in the first person as "I." He tells the story as he experiences it, presenting only his own thoughts, feelings, observations, and interpretations of events.

In "The Day I Got Lost" the way the narrator tells the story adds to its humor. Professor Shlemiel tells his story matter-of-factly; he does not realize how utterly ridiculous it is.

Look For

As you read "The Day I Got Lost," look for the differences between the way Professor Shlemiel sees the situation he is in and the way you see it. How does this difference make his story even funnier?

Writing

Freewrite for five minutes about a day in the life of any forgetful person. Think about all the funny things that could happen and exaggerate them. Make your tone light, not serious.

Vocabulary

Knowing the following words will help you as you read "The Day I Got Lost."

eternal (i tur′ n'l) *adj.*: Everlasting (p. 114)

destined (des′ tind) *v.*: Determined by fate (p. 114)

forsaken (fər sā′ kən) *adj.*: Abandoned; desolate (p. 115)

pandemonium (pan′ də mō′ nē əm) *n.*: A scene of wild disorder (p. 115)

The Day I Got Lost

Isaac Bashevis Singer

It is easy to recognize me. See a man in the street wearing a too long coat, too large shoes, a crumpled hat with a wide brim, spectacles with one lens missing, and carrying an umbrella though the sun is shining, and that man will be me, Professor Shlemiel.[1] There are other unmistakable clues to my identity. My pockets are always bulging with newspapers, magazines, and just papers. I carry an overstuffed briefcase, and I'm forever making mistakes. I've been living in New York City for over forty years, yet whenever I want to go uptown, I find myself walking downtown, and when I want to go east, I go west. I'm always late and I never recognize anybody.

I'm always misplacing things. A hundred times a day I ask myself, Where is my pen? Where is my money? Where is my handkerchief? Where is my address book? I am what is known as an absentminded professor.

For many years I have been teaching philosophy in the same university, and I still have difficulty in locating my classrooms. Elevators play strange tricks on me. I want to go to the top floor and I land in the basement. Hardly a day passes when an elevator door doesn't close on me. Elevator doors are my worst enemies.

In addition to my constant blundering and losing things, I'm forgetful. I enter a coffee shop, hang up my coat, and leave without it. By the time I remember to go back for it, I've forgotten where I've been. I lose hats, books, umbrellas, rubbers, and above all manuscripts. Sometimes I even forget my own address. One evening I took a taxi because I was in a hurry to get home. The taxi driver said, "Where to?" And I could not remember where I lived.

"Home!" I said.

"Where is home?" he asked in astonishment.

"I don't remember," I replied.

"What is your name?"

"Professor Shlemiel."

"Professor," the driver said, "I'll get you

1. Shlemiel (shlə mēl′): Version of the slang word schlemiel, an ineffectual, bungling person.

to a telephone booth. Look in the telephone book and you'll find your address.''

He drove me to the nearest drugstore with a telephone booth in it, but he refused to wait. I was about to enter the store when I realized I had left my briefcase behind. I ran after the taxi, shouting, ''My briefcase, my briefcase!'' But the taxi was already out of earshot.

In the drugstore, I found a telephone book, but when I looked under S, I saw to my horror that though there were a number of Shlemiels listed, I was not among them. At that moment I recalled that several months before, Mrs. Shlemiel had decided that we should have an unlisted telephone number. The reason was that my students thought nothing of calling me in the middle of the night and waking me up. It also happened quite frequently that someone wanted to call another Shlemiel and got me by mistake. That was all very well—but how was I going to get home?

I usually had some letters addressed to me in my breast pocket. But just that day I had decided to clean out my pockets. It was my birthday and my wife had invited friends in for the evening. She had baked a huge cake and decorated it with birthday candles. I could see my friends sitting in our living room, waiting to wish me a happy birthday. And here I stood in some drugstore, for the life of me not able to remember where I lived.

Then I recalled the telephone number of a friend of mine, Dr. Motherhead, and I decided to call him for help. I dialed and a young girl's voice answered.

''Is Dr. Motherhead at home?''

''No,'' she replied.

''Is his wife at home?''

''They're both out,'' the girl said.

''Perhaps you can tell me where they can be reached?'' I said.

''I'm only the babysitter, but I think they went to a party at Professor Shlemiel's.

Would you like to leave a message?'' she said. ''Who shall I say called, please?''

''Professor Shlemiel,'' I said.

''They left for your house about an hour ago,'' the girl said.

''Can you tell me where they went?'' I asked.

''I've just told you,'' she said. ''They went to your house.''

''But where do I live?''

''You must be kidding!'' the girl said, and hung up.

I tried to call a number of friends (those whose telephone numbers I happened to think of), but wherever I called, I got the same reply: ''They've gone to a party at Professor Shlemiel's.''

As I stood in the street wondering what to do, it began to rain. ''Where's my umbrella?'' I said to myself. And I knew the answer at once. I'd left it—somewhere. I got under a nearby canopy. It was now raining cats and dogs. It lightninged and thundered. All day it had been sunny and warm, but now that I was lost and my umbrella was lost, it had to storm. And it looked as if it would go on for the rest of the night.

To distract myself, I began to ponder the ancient philosophical problem. A mother chicken lays an egg, I thought to myself, and when it hatches, there is a chicken. That's how it has always been. Every chicken comes from an egg and every egg comes from a chicken. But was there a chicken first? Or an egg first? No philosopher has ever been able to solve this eternal question. Just the same, there must be an answer. Perhaps I, Shlemiel, am destined to stumble on it.

It continued to pour buckets. My feet were getting wet and I was chilled. I began to sneeze and I wanted to wipe my nose, but my handkerchief, too, was gone.

At that moment I saw a big black dog. He was standing in the rain getting soaked and looking at me with sad eyes. I knew immediately what the trouble was. The dog was lost. He, too, had forgotten his address. I felt a great love for that innocent animal. I called to him and he came running to me. I talked to him as if he were human. "Fellow, we're in the same boat," I said. "I'm a man shlemiel and you're a dog shlemiel. Perhaps it's also your birthday, and there's a party for you, too. And here you stand shivering and forsaken in the rain, while your loving master is searching for you everywhere. You're probably just as hungry as I am."

I patted the dog on his wet head and he wagged his tail. "Whatever happens to me will happen to you," I said. "I'll keep you with me until we both find our homes. If we don't find your master, you'll stay with me. Give me your paw," I said. The dog lifted his right paw. There was no question that he understood.

A taxi drove by and splattered us both. Suddenly it stopped and I heard someone shouting, "Shlemiel! Shlemiel!" I looked up and saw the taxi door open, and the head of a friend of mine appeared. "Shlemiel," he called. "What are you doing here? Who are you waiting for?"

"Where are you going?" I asked.

"To your house, of course. I'm sorry I'm late, but I was detained. Anyhow, better late than never. But why aren't you at home? And whose dog is that?"

"Only God could have sent you!" I exclaimed. "What a night! I've forgotten my address, I've left my briefcase in a taxi, I've lost my umbrella, and I don't know where my rubbers are."

"Shlemiel," my friend said, "if there was ever an absentminded professor, you're it!"

When I rang the bell of my apartment, my wife opened the door. "Shlemiel!" she shrieked. "Everybody is waiting for you. Where have you been? Where is your brief-case? Your umbrella? Your rubbers? And who is this dog?"

Our friends surrounded me. "Where have you been?" they cried. "We were so worried. We thought surely something had happened to you!"

"Who is this dog?" my wife kept repeating.

"I don't know," I said finally. "I found him in the street. Let's just call him Bow Wow for the time being."

"Bow Wow, indeed!" my wife scolded. "You know our cat hates dogs. And what about the parakeets? He'll scare them to death."

"He's a quiet dog," I said. "He'll make friends with the cat. I'm sure he loves parakeets. I could not leave him shivering in the rain. He's a good soul."

The moment I said this the dog let out a bloodcurdling howl. The cat ran into the room. When she saw the dog, she arched her back and spat at him, ready to scratch out his eyes. The parakeets in their cage began flapping their wings and screeching. Everybody started talking at once. There was pandemonium.

Would you like to know how it all ended?

Bow Wow still lives with us. He and the cat are great friends. The parakeets have learned to ride on his back as if he were a horse. As for my wife, she loves Bow Wow even more than I do. Whenever I take the dog out, she says, "Now, don't forget your address, both of you."

I never did find my briefcase, or my umbrella, or my rubbers. Like many philosophers before me, I've given up trying to solve the riddle of which came first, the chicken or the egg. Instead, I've started writing a book called *The Memoirs of Shlemiel*. If I don't forget the manuscript in a taxi, or a restaurant, or on a bench in the park, you may read them someday. In the meantime, here is a sample chapter.

THINKING ABOUT THE SELECTION

Recalling

1. What is Shlemiel's most outstanding trait?
2. In what two ways does Professor Shlemiel try to find out his own address?
3. Why can't he get in touch with anybody?
4. How does Professor Shlemiel get home?
5. Why does he bring the dog home with him?

Interpreting

6. In what ways are Shlemiel and the dog alike?
7. In what ways is the professor a true shlemiel, or bungler?
8. Explain what is ridiculous about the outcome of Professor Shlemiel's day.

Applying

9. Describe a character from books, movies, or television whose traits are exaggerated to be funny. An example is the classic comic strip character Popeye the Sailor Man, whose strength is exaggerated to create humor.

ANALYZING LITERATURE

Understanding Narrator

The **narrator,** or person who tells the story, is Professor Shlemiel, who speaks in the first person as "I." You experience the story through his eyes, knowing only his thoughts and feelings; you do not learn the views of anyone else, such as his wife or his friend in the taxi. However, as an active reader, you read between the lines, and see humor where Schlemiel does not.

The serious way in which Professor Shlemiel tells his ridiculous story adds to its humor.

1. What does Shlemiel tell you about himself?
2. How do you think Professor Schlemiel's wife views him? How do you think his friends view him? Find evidence to support your answer.
3. How do you think this story would have been different if Mrs. Schlemiel had told it?

CRITICAL THINKING AND READING

Understanding Caricature

Caricature is the distortion or exaggeration of the peculiarities in a character's personality. Often a writer will use caricature to create a humorous effect. The exaggerated traits can be amusing or ridiculous in themselves, or they can cause preposterous situations.

1. A schlemiel is a bungler. How is Schlemiel a perfect example of this type of person?
2. In what way is he a perfect example of an absent-minded professor?
3. The author reveals only one side of the Professor's personality and blows this side out of proportion. Would this story have been as amusing if the author had presented the Professor as a well-rounded individual? Explain.

SPEAKING AND LISTENING

Reporting on Caricature in Advertising

Advertisements, and television commercials often show people selling products who are caricatures of some sort: the harried housewife, the helpful salesperson. Caricatures appeal to people because they are easily understood.

Collect several advertisements that show people selling a product. Give an oral report describing the caricature of people portrayed.

THINKING AND WRITING

Writing a Story

Write a story telling of another day in the life of Shlemiel. First freewrite for three minutes about what an absent-minded professor might do. Imagine as many ridiculous incidents as you can. Using this freewriting, write in the first person. Make your tone serious as you describe the humorous events. Revise, making sure you have used exaggeration. Proofread your story and share it with your classmates.

Setting

LAVENDER AND OLD LACE
Charles Burchfield
From the collection of the New Britain Museum of American Art

GUIDE FOR READING

The Land and the Water

Shirley Ann Grau (1929–   ) has lived in New Orleans most of her life. She attended Tulane University and raised four children while writing novels, short stories, and journal articles. *Black Prince and Other Stories* is a collection of stories Grau has written especially for teen-agers. "The Land and the Water," like many of her other short stories, is set in Louisiana. This story is an example of the importance of nature and its forces in stories Grau creates.

Setting

The **setting** of a story is the time and place of the action. In a short story the setting is usually presented through detailed descriptions. In some stories the setting plays a very important role. It affects what happens to the characters and what they learn about life.

Look For

"The Land and the Water" takes place by the ocean. As you read, look for ways the ocean affects the plot and the characters. What role does weather play in the story? What feeling does it create?

Writing

Think of times you have seen an ocean or pictures of an ocean. How does weather or the season affect the ocean? List words and phrases that describe the ocean in all its different moods.

Vocabulary

Knowing the following words will help you as you read "The Land and the Water."

stifled (stī′ f'ld) *adj.*: Muffled; suppressed (p. 119)
luminous (lo͞o′ mə nəs) *adj.*: Glowing in the dark (p. 122)
scuttling (skut′ 'liŋ) *v.*: Running or moving quickly (p. 122)
lee (lē) *n.*: Sheltered place; the side away from the wind (p. 122)
spume (spyo͞om) *n.*: Foam; froth (p. 122)

swamped (swämp'd) *v.*: Sank by filling with water (p. 123)
tousled-looking (tou′ z'ld lo͞o′kiŋ) *adj.*: Rumpled or mussed (p. 123)
impenetrable (im pen′ i trə b'l) *adj.*: Not able to be passed through (p. 126)

The Land and the Water

Shirley Ann Grau

From the open Atlantic beyond Timbalier Head a few scattered foghorns grunted, muffled and faint. That bank[1] had been hanging offshore for days. We'd been watching the big draggers[2] chug up to it, get dimmer and dimmer, and finally disappear in its grayness, leaving only the stifled sounds of their horns behind. It had been there so long we got used to it, and came to think of it as always being there, like another piece of land, maybe.

The particular day I'm thinking about started out clear and hot with a tiny breeze —a perfect day for a Snipe or a Sailfish.[3] There were a few of them moving on the big bay, not many. And they stayed close to shore, for the barometer was drifting slowly down in its tube and the wind was shifting slowly backward around the compass.[4]

Larger sailboats never came into the bay—it was too shallow for them—and these small ones, motorless, moving with the smallest stir of air, could sail for home, if the fog came in, by following the shore—or if there was really no wind at all, they could be paddled in and beached. Then their crews could walk to the nearest phone and call to be picked up. You had to do it that way, because the fog always came in so quick. As it did that morning.

My sister and I were working by our dock, scraping and painting the little dinghy.[5] Because the spring tides washed over this stretch, there were no trees, no bushes even, just snail grass and beach lettuce and pink flowering sea lavender, things that liked salt. All morning it had been bright and blue and shining. Then all at once it turned gray and wet, like an unfalling rain, moveless and still. We went right on sanding and from being sweaty hot we turned sweaty cold, the fog chilling and dripping off our faces.

"It isn't worth the money," my sister said. She is ten and that is her favorite sentence. This time it wasn't even true. She was the one who'd talked my father into giving us the job.

I wouldn't give her the satisfaction of an answer, though I didn't like the wet any more than she did. It was sure to make my hair roll up in tight little curls all over my

---

1. bank *n.*: Mass of fog.
2. draggers *n.*: Fishing boats that use large nets to catch fish.
3. Snipe . . . Sailfish: names of sailboats.
4. barometer . . . compass: The decrease in barometric pressure and change in wind direction indicate that a storm is approaching.

5. dinghy (din′ gē) *n.*: Small rowboat.

PERKINS COVE
Jane Betts
Collection of Wendy Betts

head and I would have to wash it again and sleep on the hard metal curlers to get it back in shape.

Finally my sister said, "Let's go get something to drink."

When we turned around to go back up to the house, we found that it had disappeared. It was only a couple of hundred yards away, right behind us and up a little grade, a long slope of beach plum and poison ivy, salt burned and scrubby. You couldn't see a thing now, except gray. The land and the water all looked the same; the fog was that thick.

There wasn't anything to drink. Just a lot of empty bottles waiting in cases on the back porch. "Well," my sister said, "let's go tell her."

She meant my mother of course, and we didn't have to look for her very hard. The house wasn't big, and being a summer house, it had very thin walls: we could hear her playing cards with my father in the living room.

They were sitting by the front window. On a clear day there was really something to see out there: the sweep of the bay and the pattern of the inlets and, beyond it all, the dark blue of the Atlantic. Today there was nothing, not even a bird, if you didn't count the occasional yelp of a seagull off high overhead somewhere.

"There's nothing to drink," my sister said. "Not a single thing."

"Tomorrow's grocery day," my mother said. "Go make a lemonade."

"Look," my father said, "why not go back to work on the dinghy? You'll get your money faster."

So we went, only stopping first to get our oilskin hats. And pretty soon, fog was dripping from the brims like a kind of very gentle rain.

But we didn't go back to work on the dinghy. For a while we sat on the edge of the dock and looked at the minnow-flecked water, and then we got out the crab nets and went over to the tumbled heap of rocks to see if we could catch anything. We spent a couple of hours out there, skinning our knees against the rough barnacled[6] surfaces. Once a seagull swooped down so low he practically touched the tops of our hats. Almost but not quite. I don't think we even saw a crab, though we dragged our nets around in the water just for the fun of it. Finally we dug a dozen or so clams, ate them, and tried to skip the shells along the water. That was how the afternoon passed, with one thing or the other, and us not hurrying, not having anything we'd rather be doing.

We didn't have a watch with us, but it must have been late afternoon when they all came down from the house. We heard them before we saw them, heard the brush of their feet on the grass path.

It was my mother and my father and Robert, my biggest brother, the one who is eighteen. My father had the round black compass and a coil of new line. Robert had a couple of gas lanterns and a big battery one. My mother had the life jackets and a little wicker basket and a thermos bottle. They all went out along the narrow rickety dock and began to load the gear into my father's *Sea Skiff*. It wasn't a big boat and my father had to take a couple of minutes to pack it, stowing the basket way up forward under the cowling[7] and wedging the thermos bottle on top of that. Robert, who'd left his lanterns on the ground to help him, came back to fetch them.

"I thought you were at the McKays," I said. "How'd you get over here?"

"Dad called me." He lifted one eyebrow. "Remember about something called the telephone?" And he picked up his gear and walked away.

"Well," my sister said.

They cast off, the big outboard sputtered gently, throttled way down. They would have to move very slowly in the fog. As they swung away, Robert at the tiller, we saw my father set out his compass and take a bearing off it.

My mother watched them out of sight, which didn't take more than a half minute. Then she stood watching the fog for a while and, I guess, following the sound of the steady put-put. It seemed to me, listening to it move off and blend with the sounds of the bay—the sounds of a lot of water, of tiny waves and fish feeding—that I could pick out two or three other motors.

Finally my mother got tired of standing on the end of the dock and she turned around and walked up to us. I expected her to pass right by and go on up to the house. But she didn't. We could hear her stop and stand looking at us. My sister and I just scraped a little harder, pretending we hadn't noticed.

"I guess you're wondering what that was all about?" she said finally.

"I don't care," my sister said. She was lying. She was just as curious as I was.

---

6. barnacled (bär′ nə k'ld) *adj.*: Covered with small shellfish that attach themselves to rocks, ships, wood, and whales.

7. cowling *n.*: A removable metal covering for an engine.

My mother didn't seem to have heard her. "It's Linda Holloway and Stan Mitchell and Butch Rodgers."

We knew them. They were sailing people, a little older than I, a little younger than my brother Robert. They lived in three houses lined up one by the other on the north shore of Marshall's Inlet. They were all right kids, nothing special either way, sort of a gang, living as close as they did. This year they had turned up with a new sailboat, a twelve-foot fiberglass job that somebody had designed and built for Stan Mitchell as a birthday present.

"What about them?" my sister asked, forgetting that she wasn't interested.

"They haven't come home."

"Oh," I said.

"They were sailing," my mother said. "The Brewers think they saw them off their place just before the fog. They were sort of far out."

"You mean Dad's gone to look for them?"

She nodded.

"Is that all?" my sister said. "Just somebody going to have to sit in their boat and wait until the fog lifts."

My mother looked at us. Her curly red hair was dripping with the damp of the fog and her face was smeared with dust. "The Lord save me from children," she said quietly. "The glass is twenty-nine eighty and it's still going down fast."

We went back up to the house with her, to help fix supper—a quiet nervous kind of supper. The thick luminous fish-colored fog turned into deep solid night fog. Just after supper, while we were drying the dishes, the wind sprang up. It shook the whole line of windows in the kitchen and knocked over every single pot of geraniums on the back porch.

"Well," my mother said, "it's square into the east now."

A low barometer and a wind that had gone backwards into the east—there wasn't one of us didn't know what that meant. And it wasn't more than half an hour before there was a grumble of approaching thunder and the fog began to swirl around the windows, streaming like torn cotton as the wind increased.

"Dad'll come back now, huh?" my sister asked.

"Yes," my mother said. "All the boats'll have to come back now."

We settled down to television, half watching it and half listening to the storm outside. In a little while, an hour or so, my mother said, "Turn off that thing."

"What?"

"Turn it off, quick." She hurried on the porch, saying over her shoulder: "I hear something."

The boards of the wide platform were wet and slippery under our feet, and the eaves of the house poured water in steady small streams that the wind grabbed and tore away. Between the crashes of thunder, we heard it too. There was a boat coming into our cove. By the sound of it, it would be my father and Robert.

"Is that the motor?" my mother asked.

"Sure," I said. It had a little tick and it was higher pitched than any of the others. You couldn't miss it.

Without another word to us she went scuttling across the porch and down the stairs toward the cove. We followed and stood close by, off the path and a little to one side. It was tide marsh there, and salt mud oozed over the tops of our sneakers. The cove itself was sheltered—it was in the lee of Cedar Tree Neck—but even so it was pretty choppy. Whitecaps were beginning to run high and broken, wind against tide, and the spume from them stung as it hit your face and your eyes. You could hear the real stuff blowing overhead, with the

CLOUDS AND WATER, 1930
Arthur Dove
Metropolitan Museum of Art, The Alfred Stieglitz Collection,
1949 © 1979 by the Metropolitan Museum of Art

peculiar sound wind has when it gets past half a gale.

My father's boat was sidling up to the dock now, pitching and rolling in the broken water. Its motor sputtered into reverse and then the hull rubbed gently against the pilings. They had had a bad time. In the quick lightning flashes you could see every scupper[8] pouring water. You could see the slow weary way they made the lines fast.

"There wasn't anything else to do," my father was saying as they came up the path, beating their arms for warmth, "with it blowing straight out the east, we had to come in."

Robert stopped a moment to pull off his

oilskins. Under them his shirt was as drenched as if he hadn't had any protection at all.

"We came the long way around," my father said, "hugging the lee as much as we could."

"We almost swamped," Robert said.

Then we were at the house and they went off to dry their clothes, and that was that. They told us later that everybody had come in, except only for the big Coast Guard launch. And with only one boat it was no wonder they didn't find them.

The next morning was bright and clear and a lot cooler. The big stretch of bay was still shaken and tousled-looking, spotted with whitecaps. Soon as it was light, my father went to the front porch and looked

---

8. scupper *n.*: An opening in a ship's side that allows water to run off the deck.

and looked with his glasses. He checked the anemometer[9] dial, and shook his head. "It's still too rough for us." In a bit the Coast Guard boats—two of them—appeared, and a helicopter began its chopping noisy circling.

It was marketing day too, so my mother, my sister, and I went off, as we always did. We stopped at the laundromat and the hardware, and then my mother had to get some pine trees for the slope behind the house. It was maybe four o'clock before we got home.

---

9. **anemometer** (an′ ə mäm′ ə tər) **dial:** The dial on an instrument that determines wind speed and sometimes direction.

The wind had dropped, the bay was almost quiet again. Robert and my father were gone, and so was the boat. "I thought they'd go out again," my mother said. She got a cup of coffee and the three of us sat watching the fleet of boats work their way back and forth across the bay, searching.

Just before dark—just when the sky was beginning to take its twilight color—my father and Robert appeared. They were burned lobster red with great white circles around their eyes where their glasses had been.

"Did you find anything?" my sister asked.

My father looked at my mother.

SOFTLY
Vivian Caldwell
Private Collection

"You might as well tell them," she said. "They'll know anyway."

"Well," my father said, "they found the boat."

"That's what they were expecting to find, wasn't it?" my mother asked quietly.

He nodded. "It's kind of hard to say what happened. But it looks like they got blown on East Shoal with the tide going down and the chop tearing the keel out."[10]

"Oh," my mother said.

"Oh," my sister said.

"They found the boat around noon."

My mother said: "Have they found them?"

"Not that I heard."

"You think," my mother said, "they could have got to shore way out on Gull Point or some place like that?"

"No place is more than a four-hour walk," my father said. "They'd have turned up by now."

And it was later still, after dark, ten o'clock or so, that Mr. Robinson, who lived next door, stopped by the porch on his way home. "Found one," he said wearily. "The Mitchell boy."

"Oh," my mother said, "oh, oh."

"Where?" my father asked.

"Just off the shoal,[11] they said, curled up in the eel grass."

"My God," my mother said softly.

Mr. Robinson moved off without so much as a good-by. And after a while my sister and I went to bed.

But not to sleep. We played cards for an hour or so, until we couldn't stand that any more. Then we did a couple of crossword puzzles together. Finally we just sat in our beds, in the chilly night, and listened. There were the usual sounds from outside the open windows, sounds of the land and the water. Deer moving about in the brush on their way to eat the wild watercress and wild lettuce that grew around the spring. The deep pumping sounds of an owl's wings in the air. Little splashes from the bay—the fishes and the muskrats and the otters.

"I didn't know there'd be so many things moving at night," my sister said.

"You just weren't ever awake."

"What do you reckon it's like," she said, "being on the bottom in the eel grass?"

"Shut up," I told her.

"Well," she said, "I just asked. Because I was wondering."

"Don't."

Her talking had started a funny shaking quivering feeling from my navel right straight back to my backbone. The tips of my fingers hurt too, the way they always did.

"I thought the dogs would howl," she said.

"They can't smell anything from the water," I told her. "Now quit."

She fell asleep then and maybe I did too, because the night seemed awful short. Or maybe the summer dawns really come that quick. Not dawn, no. The quiet deep dark that means dawn is just about to come. The birds started whistling and the gulls started shrieking. I got up and looked out at the dripping beach plum bushes and the twisted, salt-burned jack pines, then I slipped out the window. I'd done it before. You lifted the screen, and lowered yourself down. It wasn't anything of a drop—all you had to watch was the patch of poison ivy. I circled around the house and took the old deer trail down to the bay. It was chilly, and I began to wish I had brought my robe or a coat. With just cotton pajamas my teeth would begin chattering very soon.

I don't know what I expected to see. And

10. the chop tearing the keel out: The choppy waves tearing out the beam supporting the boat frame.

11. shoal (shōl) *n.*: Sand bar.

I didn't see anything at all. Just some morning fog in the hollows and around the spring. And the dock, with my father's boat bobbing in the run of the tide.

The day was getting close now. The sky overhead turned a sort of luminous dark blue. As it did, the water darkened to a lead-colored gray. It looked heavy and oily and impenetrable. I tried to imagine what would be under it. I always thought I knew. There would be horsehoe crabs and hermit crabs and blue crabs, and scallops squirting their way along, and there'd be all the different kinds of fish, and the eels. I kept telling myself that that was all.

But this time I couldn't seem to keep my thoughts straight. I kept wondering what it must be like to be dead and cold and down in the sand and mud with the eel grass brushing you and the crabs bumping you and the fish—I had felt their little sucking mouths sometimes when I swam.

The water was thick and heavy and the color of a mirror in a dark room. Minnows broke the surface right under the wharf. I jumped. I couldn't help it.

And I got to thinking that something might come out of the water. It didn't have a name or a shape. But it was there.

I stood where I was for a while, trying to fight down the idea. When I found I couldn't do that, I decided to walk slowly back to the house. At least I thought I was going to walk, but the way the boards of the wharf shook under my feet I know that I must have been running. On the path up to the house my bare feet hit some of the sharp cut-off stubs of the rosa rugosa bushes, but I didn't stop. I went crashing into the kitchen because that was the closest door.

The room was thick with the odor of frying bacon, the softness of steam: my mother had gotten up early. She turned around when I came in, not seeming surprised—as if it was the most usual thing in the world for me to be wandering around before daylight in my pajamas.

"Go take those things off, honey," she said. "You're drenched."

"Yes ma'am," I told her.

I stripped off the clothes and saw that they really were soaking. I knew it was just the dew and the fog. But I couldn't help thinking it was something else. Something that had reached for me, and missed. Something that was wet, that had come from the water, something that had splashed me as it went past.

THINKING ABOUT THE SELECTION

Recalling

1. What are the two girls doing at the beginning of the story?
2. Why do the girls' father and brother go out in the boat?
3. Why do they return when they do?
4. What happens to the three lost people?

Interpreting

5. How does the girl react to the boy's death? Why does she slip out of her house just before dawn?
6. What comparison is the author suggesting when the girl's clothing gets wet at the end of the story? What is the "something else" the girl feels has reached for her and missed?

7. What does the girl learn about life?
8. What do you think the land represents to the girl? What do you think the water represents? Why is this story called "The Land and the Water"?

Applying

9. The author Joseph Conrad has written, ". . . for all the celebration it has been the object of . . . , the sea has never been friendly to man." Explain the meaning of these words. How do they relate to this story?

ANALYZING LITERATURE
Understanding Setting

Setting is the time and place of a story. Sometimes the setting is so important it affects what the characters do and what they feel. In "The Land and the Water," for example, the ocean almost becomes a character in the story.

1. At what time of year does "The Land and the Water" take place? How do you know this?
2. Describe the weather during the course of this story.
3. In what way does the setting affect what the characters do and what they feel?
4. In what way can the setting be thought of as almost a character in this story?

CRITICAL THINKING AND READING
Making Inferences About Setting

An **inference** is a judgment or conclusion based on evidence. Not all information about the setting of a story is stated directly by the author. You must also make inferences about the setting from the clues given by the author just as you do about the other elements of a story.

1. What evidence helped you make the inference that this is not the family's first summer here?

2. What clues indicate that the land and sea are unaffected by what has happened?

UNDERSTANDING LANGUAGE
Choosing Meaning To Fit the Context

When you look up an unfamiliar word in a dictionary, you may find more than one definition. Then you must decide which definition fits the context in which the word appears. Try substituting each definition for the word in the sentence and see which one makes the most sense.

For example, in the sentence "The Grand Canyon is a *singular* tourist attraction," *singular* can mean "one of a kind," "odd; peculiar" or "extraordinary." By replacing the word with each definition, you can see that in this sentence *singular* means "one of a kind."

From a dictionary choose the best definition for each of the following italicized words.
1. "That *bank* had been hanging offshore for days."
2. The motor "had a little tick and it was higher *pitched* than any of the others."
3. "And I didn't see anything at all. Just some morning fog in the hollows and around the *spring*."

THINKING AND WRITING
Describing a Setting

Choose one of the pieces of art used to illustrate "The Land and the Water." List descriptive details about it. Include details about the way the picture makes you feel—or your mood. Use your list to write a description of the art. Use vivid, specific words so that a friend who has not seen the picture will be able to envision it. When you finish read over your paper to be sure your friend will be able to visualize the illustration you described.

GUIDE FOR READING

Grass Fire

Loula Grace Erdman (1884–1976) was born in Missouri and later moved to Texas. There she became a school teacher and a professor and novelist-in-residence at West Texas State University. Erdman's novels have been translated into many languages, including German, Italian, Arabic, and Indonesian. She once wrote, "I tend to write about people I could ask in for a cup of coffee or a spot of tea." Her characters, ordinary people who can show extraordinary courage, may help to explain the popularity of her works.

Descriptive Details

A writer can make a story come alive by using vivid descriptive details to describe a character's appearance, the setting, or the actions of characters in a story. In "Grass Fire" the author uses descriptive details to tell of the struggle to stop a grass fire on the prairie. She describes in detail each implement used to fight the fire so that you can see them clearly in your mind.

Look For

As you read "Grass Fire," look for the descriptive details that make you feel you are caught in the fire yourself. What impression do you get of the fire? How do the descriptive details make you feel?

Writing

Fire! The word immediately brings us to attention. Freewrite about the effect of the word *fire*.

Vocabulary

Knowing the following words will help you as you read "Grass Fire."

nesters (nest' ərz) *n.*: Homesteaders on the prairies in the mid-1800's (p. 129)

dugout (dug″ out') *n.*: A shelter built into a hillside (p. 130)

carcass (kär' kəs) *n.*: The dead body of an animal (p. 131)

acrid (ak' rid) *adj.*: Sharp, bitter; stinging to the taste or smell (p. 132)

distended (dis tend' id) *adj.*: Stretched out; swollen (p. 133)

horde (hôrd) *n.*: A large moving crowd or throng (p. 133)

divested (də vest' id) *adj.*: stripped; (p. 133)

cower (kou' ər) *v.*: To crouch or huddle from fear (p. 134)

Grass Fire

from *The Edge of Time*

Loula Grace Erdman

They said, "It's a big one—look at the smoke—"

As a single unit the men moved to their horses, the party forgotten. Where there had been only a light a few moments ago, now there were little red tongues of flame, licking scallops[1] against the sky. Like imps dancing they formed a solid line against the horizon.

"It's headed north," someone said. "And with the wind the way it is—"

North. Away from the river. And, Bethany thought—knew Wade was thinking, too —toward their place. North. For Wade and her, that was the direction in which fear lay.

They set about fighting the fire, ranchers, cowboys and nesters alike, moving together in an undivided attack, held by a common purpose. In their approach there was no talk of me and mine. They saw the fire against the horizon and they moved toward it, determined to use every cunning as if they were fighting an enemy half-human, half-demon. For the fire, indeed, had about it a human-like cunning, a diabolical cruelty.

"You stay here," Wade said to Bethany. "Later you can help bring us something to eat, and some water."

He didn't say, "You couldn't get home now if you wanted to. Not without riding miles out of your way, you couldn't—"

They stayed at the Newsome place, waiting. The men fought, and they used whatever weapons they could lay their hands upon.

They took the plow and put it to a new use. They plowed strips of prairie sod, not for seeding, but to prevent the growth of the seeds of fire. Fireguards, they called these plowed strips. But the red monster hurdled them as if they were not there. Sometimes the wind picked up cow chips, tossing them lightly across the barrier, starting a new fire in fresh fuel. Even the cow chips, which had served them well, seemed to turn against them—friends until now, they had joined the enemy.

The men made backfires[2] between the main blaze and the territory they wished to protect, placing them with cunning, watching them with a care a doctor shows a patient to whom he has given a problematical medicine in a last desperate effort to save him. There was no water here, the

---

1. **licking scallops:** Making a pattern of curves against the sky.

2. **backfire** *n*.: A fire started to stop or check advancing prairie fire or forest fire.

HERD OF BUFFALO FLEEING FROM PRAIRIE FIRE
M. Straus
Amon Carter Museum

natural enemy of fire, so they must make a semblance of that enemy.

It was Lizzie Dillon who took command of the women. She, who had weathered everything, felt no great fear of a grass fire.

"They'll stop it," she said calmly. "They always do. Sometimes it takes longer'n others, but they do it—"

She could be calm, Bethany thought rebelliously. About her place there were no row crops drying, no curtains at dugout windows. No maiden blush rose was taking root beside her door. For Lizzie Dillon, there was nothing to lose. If her burrow was destroyed, she and her mate and her young would move to another.

It was as simple as that.

"Come morning," Lizzie went on. "I reckon we'd best take them a bite to eat—we can load it in my wagon—"

"I'll go with you," Bethany said. "I'll ride Star—"

Morning came, eerie and unreal. The sun rose red in the east, in the west was that other grim redness.

"It ain't quite so big," Lizzie said. "They're a-whippin it; I knowed they would. We'll take the stuff to eat now, and the water."

They packed the food left from the party into pans and boxes. Among them, they got a small barrel on the wagon, filled it with water. Mrs. Newsome's face showed gray and old in the light of dawn. Bethany knew that she herself should be tired, but she was beyond fatigue, beyond feeling of any kind.

Mrs. Dillon awakened the children and got them into the wagon.

"Shouldn't some of us go with you?" Milly asked uncertainly.

"You best stay here and take care of the baby," Lizzie Dillon said kindly. "And you ought to lay down and rest, Mrs. Newsome. You're plum wore out from the party. Git up, Bess. Git up, Kate—"

Lizzie Dillon drove on. The woman did not look back; she drove with sureness and confidence. Bethany followed her, never questioning her decisions. The children sat quiet in the wagon as if they too were sure of her rightness. Afterwards Bethany remembered that not once during all that trip did the children make any trouble, grow restless, ask for some of the food or water which was in the wagon with them. They had been trained in a sort of quiet acceptance of what came. They had been schooled to follow without question the ways of their elders in times of emergency.

They came upon the firefighters by midmorning. The men had just killed an old bull and split him wide open, so that his carcass formed a large flat surface. They had tied ropes to his legs, and two men rode to a side, with the other ends of the ropes tied to their saddle horns.

Four cowboys whom Bethany remembered only vaguely were making ready to drag this strange piece of fire-fighting equipment across the grass, where it was burning farther up the line.

"Wouldn't you like some water?" Bethany asked. "And—and something to eat?"

She felt a little embarrassed to be offering them the dainty remnants of the New-

some party supper. Working men needed real food, not party stuff.

They swung down off their horses, which stood with eyes turned questioningly toward their masters, as if they would know the reason for this strange burden they carried. Live cows they knew—plunging and kicking. They could brace their weights with them, even almost anticipate their movements. But this dead thing—

"Yes, ma'am," they said. "We could use some water and some grub, all right."

Bethany looked at the dead bull, tied fast between the horses.

"Seems sort of a shame," she said. "Killing cattle, I mean—"

"Well, Ma'am," one of them said softly, "maybe so. But I reckon this one would be right proud to know he helped stop a fire."

They would drag this carcass across the burning grass, putting out the flames with it. Maybe it was like that everywhere, Bethany was thinking. A few have to suffer so that things will be easier for others.

"How are they a-comin'?" Lizzie asked. "They are a-stoppin' it, ain't they?"

"I can't say, Ma'am," he told her. "Sometimes we think so, and then the wind changes and blows it back into new places —like as not where none of us are working."

He bent over to beat out a small spark with his slicker. The gesture was automatic. The spark had landed on the trail, was out almost before it struck. But all the same, you put out a fire, however small, when and where you saw it. The monster they were fighting now had probably been a spark no larger than this one at one time.

"Seems like the wind blows from all directions at once when we get to fighting a fire," he said. He got back on his horse. "Guess we'd better be getting along. Thanks for the grub and water.''

"We'll drive on up the trail,'' Lizzie told him. "No fire up thataway, is there?''

"Haven't heard of one.''

"Tell the others where we're headed, and that we got stuff to eat.''

"That's right kind of you, Ma'am,'' he said. "Most of them are back a ways where the fire is worst, but I'll tell them. Maybe they can sort of spell each other off and come for some.''

"Tell them I'm workin' on toward home,'' she said. "I'll git them kids out of the wagon and then bring back some fresh grub and water.''

"That's fine,'' the boy said. "Looks like we may be at this for quite a spell yet. So long—''

He rode off.

"If you see my husband,'' Bethany called after him, "will you tell him I've gone home?''

Home! It seemed like weeks, like years, since she had seen the little dugout. She felt she could not wait to be back there again. And if she went, as she knew now she must, Wade should have word so that he would not go back to Newsomes' looking for her, once the fire was over.

"I'm Mrs. Cameron,'' she added.

"Yes, Ma'am, I know,'' the boy called back to her. "I danced with you last night.''

Last night! That was an eon ago. She rode off, trying to remember what had happened in that long-gone time.

The trail over which they passed, Lizzie driving the rickety wagon and Bethany riding Star, ran through the grass already blackened by fire. It looked like soft, dark cloth, thick and heavy. When the horses' feet touched it, a black dust arose. The smell was acrid, choking, like the smell of fire itself. Off to their right they could see flames against the sky; the fire,

then, was on two sides of them—to the right and behind them. Where it would go next, or whether it would spread at all, was a matter that rested not only with the zeal of the fighters, but on that archvillain, the wind. At any time a new fire could break out, seemingly without cause, sometimes in places widely separated. What was it Tobe Dillon had said one time? "Sometimes I think fire jest breaks out by itself, here—''

Ahead of them now an expanse of unburned grass fanned out. Seeing it, Lizzie said, "Looks like we ain't a-goin' to have a chance to git rid of this grub.''

She had turned to speak to Bethany, and what she saw when she looked around brought a strange expression to her face. She stopped the wagon, stood up. She put her forefinger in her mouth, then held it up to the air. Her face was quiet and intent as she waited for her judgment to tell her what she wanted to know. Finally she turned to Bethany.

"Miz Cameron,'' she said, "the wind is a-changin'. We'd best git down the trail as fast as we can. It don't look so good—back of us—''

Bethany looked around. The thing she saw made panic well up in her.

On three sides of them was fire—behind, to the left, and to the right. More than that—the wind was behind them, pushing the fire forward as a child would roll a hoop. Only the way ahead was clear. And, even as they faced front again, it seemed that the bright edge of fire was spreading closer to the trail.

"I think you'd best tie your horse to the endgate and git in the wagon with the kids,'' Lizzie said quietly.

There was something about her voice that made Bethany obey instantly, without question. She tied Star's reins to the back of the wagon; she got in the wagon and sat down with the Dillon children. They received her with unblinking regard, as they would have received any other fresh discomfort. One of the older girls reached over to pick up the baby. She held it close to her, dropped her face against its head.

Lizzie slapped the lines over the horses' backs. They started off at a smart trot, tossing their heads in nervous excitement. Star, following behind, also seemed uneasy. Bethany hoped she had tied him securely. It would be too bad if he broke loose in his nervousness and fright. Turning to check the knot, she saw what was probably the strangest sight she had ever beheld.

The wild things were coming—running swiftly, with terror-distended nostrils. Side by side they ran, the coyote, the antelope, the lobo,[3] the deer. Cattle came too, and the birds, and the jack rabbits, their great ears erect. Hunted and hunter were as one, joined in a great exodus[4] of fear and horror, fleeing the thing that was more fearful than fear itself. Desire to kill was lost in desire to live. The strange horde passed the wagon as if they knew that man, their enemy, was fleeing as they fled.

And now the fright of the horses almost matched that of their wild brothers. Only Lizzie's expert handling of the lines kept them steady at all. The wagon rattled perilously. *What if it falls to pieces entirely,* Bethany thought. *We'll be left in the path of the fire!* Why hadn't she stayed on Star? She heard Lizzie's voice calling to her. The woman did not turn, but kept her eyes on the fear-maddened horses.

"Now listen, Miz Cameron, and you kids —you do what I tell you to—"

Lizzie had long since lost the last of her

hairpins. Her black hair was hanging loose, whipping back from her face like some strange banner which they must all follow. And, as if she knew they felt this, she gave her directions, quick and tense, like a general who sees one chance to win a battle, and that only if his men obey him without question.

The boys were to peel off their shirts, she said, and Bethany was to take them and wetten them with what was left of the water they had fetched for the men. One of the shirts Bethany must put on her head, protecting her face with it as much as possible. The other she was to hand Lizzie, who would do the same. The kids were to get under the quilt.

"—and Eli, you shuck out of them britches of yores—"

Eli, already divested of his shirt, hung back.

"Eli—" His mother's voice was terrible. Eli, hearing it, forgot false modesty. He pulled off his pants, and then plunged under the quilt.

"Now you git them britches real wet, too," she told Bethany, "and when a spark blows in on the wagon, you beat it out with them. See—?"

"Yes," Bethany said, dipping Eli's pants into the keg of water.

"And if the wind lands a burning chip in the wagon, you jest shovel it out with one of them plates Miz Newsome put the grub on."

"Yes," Bethany said again, locating a plate from the box of food. Part of the cake was still on it, that fancy party cake which looked all the more foolish now in the face of the red terror that menaced them.

Bethany looked around. The red wall was closing in. By now it was a sound and a smell and a red light. She realized what had happened—a new fire had broken out so swiftly and unexpectedly that there were no

3. lobo (lō′ bō) *n.*: Gray wolf.
4. exodus (ek′ sə dəs) *n.*: Departure.

fighters near it. If they came out of this, it would be because Lizzie Dillon brought them out.

"And now," Lizzie said, knowing that her commands were understood and heeded, "now—we'll jest make a run fur it."

She stood up in the wagon and struck the horses. "Git up," she said, although it did not seem possible that they were capable of any greater speed.

The road was a narrowing wedge whose outlines were sketched in fire. The fire did not seem so much to come toward them as they seemed themselves to drive into the face of it. Even through the wet shirt, Bethany could feel the heat. The smoke stung her nostrils; water streamed from her eyes. A flying disc of fire shot into the wagon—a burning cow chip which hit the quilt under which the children were cowering. Bethany scooped it up on Mrs. Newsome's plate, threw it over the side of the wagon. She beat out the smoking place on the quilt with Eli's wet pants.

By now, the team was frantic. They sped across the prairie, down the trail. Lizzie Dillon still stood up in the wagon, leaning forward slightly, as if she would push them along with her own stout heart. The air was full of chips, flaming like meteors. The wagon swayed from side to side. Once Star stumbled. Maybe he had stepped in a prairie dog hole, broken his leg. If he had, Bethany knew what she must do—at once, and with no holding back. She must untie him, leave him there to perish in the fire.

He righted himself, came on after the wagon, as if he knew that in that action lay safety, lay life itself.

"Good old Star," she whispered, feeling her cheeks wet, knowing it was not moisture from the Dillon boy's shirt.

Could they make it?

Lizzie had said they would. She was matching her instinct, her wisdom, against the cunning of the fire. More than that —she was matching the courage of a mother who was taking her children to safety. They had a chance.

The path was very narrow now. The path was not there at all. There was only a line—a thin line—a line through which no human being could pass, and live.

Bethany shut her eyes. Her lips moved stiffly; she knew she was praying, but did not know what words she said. The texture of them was there, though, the need, the appeal.

To perish by fire! To die in a blaze, there in the wagon with Lizzie and the children, with little Eli and the girl who held the baby against her breast. A wave of love for the doomed children passed over her; she wished that she, too, might reach under the quilt and hold one of them close to comfort it in this last hour.

To die by fire. Never to see Wade again. Never.

She felt the slowing pace of the horses. All was over. Lizzie, too, had given up. Lizzie knew it was no use. Bethany reached out blindly for one of the children.

"Well, Miz Cameron," she heard Lizzie say shakily, "we're through—"

Bethany opened her eyes. The prairie stretched out ahead of them, free of fire. Behind them, a red wall had closed in.

"Looks like it's already burned off here," Lizzie said, surveying the burnt grass ahead of them. "Must have happened last night."

They were on burnt grass. They were safe.

"You kids can come out now if you are a mind to," Lizzie said. "Eli, we'll turn our backs whilst you put on yore britches. And don't you fret about 'em being wet—"

THINKING ABOUT THE SELECTION
Recalling

1. Why does the fact that the fire is heading north frighten Bethany?
2. Find three methods the men use to fight the fire.
3. Describe how the wild animals behave during the fire.
4. Why did Bethany, Lizzie, and the children have to race to escape the fire?
5. How do Lizzie and Bethany know that they have escaped the grass fire?

Interpreting

6. What kind of person is Lizzie Dillon? Why is she able to command the women?
7. At one point Bethany thinks, "A few have to suffer so that things will be easier for others." What does this statement indicate about prairie life?
8. How can you tell from the story that grass fires are common occurrences on the prairie? What makes them so dangerous on the prairie?

Applying

9. "Grass Fire" portrays one of the terrible dangers of prairie life in the 1800's. What other dangers did the settlers face? What might have been some benefits of life on the prairie?

ANALYZING LITERATURE
Understanding Descriptive Details

Descriptive details create a picture of an event, character, or place. Erdman uses descriptive details, for example, to help you to picture Lizzie: "Lizzie Dillon still stood up in the wagon, leaning forward slightly, as if she would push them along with her own stout heart."

1. Find three details that show how frightened the prairie animals are by the approaching fire.
2. Give three examples of details describing the last frantic race to escape the fire.

CRITICAL THINKING AND READING
Analyzing the Effect of Setting on Plot

"Grass Fire" could take place only on a prairie. The setting, therefore, causes the plot to develop as it does.

1. Why do grass fires spread so rapidly on a prairie?
2. Why is it difficult to extinguish a grass fire on the prairie?

UNDERSTANDING LANGUAGE
Understanding Similes

A **simile** is a figure of speech that compares two unlike things. A simile uses the words *like* or *as* in the comparison. Read the following simile: "More than that—the wind was behind them, pushing the fire forward as a child would roll a hoop." Here the word *as* is used to compare the way the wind pushes the fire to the way a child rolls a hoop.

1. Identify the simile in this sentence: "The air was full of chips, flaming like meteors." What is the effect of this simile?
2. Write a simile comparing each of the following people or things with something else: Lizzie; the wagon on which Lizzie, Bethany, and the children rode; the men who fought the fire.

THINKING AND WRITING
Using Descriptive Details

Look at the picture that illustrates "Grass Fire." List details about the picture that you could use to help a friend who had not seen it envision the scene. Write a description for your friend using the details you have listed. If possible, include a simile. Revise your writing to be sure your description is clear and vivid. Proofread your writing and share it with your classmates.

GUIDE FOR READING

Crime on Mars

Arthur C. Clarke (1917–   ) grew up in England. Now he lives in Sri Lanka, a small island country off the coast of India. Because he lives in a remote area, Clarke keeps up with world events by subscribing to twenty scientific journals, by listening to the news on his shortwave radio, and by using a modem with his computer. Author of countless science-fiction novels and short stories, Clarke also wrote the screenplay of *2001: A Space Odyssey.* "Crime on Mars" is not only a science-fiction story but also a mystery story.

Time as an Element of Setting

Setting includes the time as well as the location of a story. In some stories the time period is important, and it is therefore reflected in the characters' dress, customs, actions, and beliefs. The time of a story can be any time in the past, present, or future. Science-fiction stories, like "Crime on Mars," are usually set in the future.

Look For

This story has also been published under another title, "The Trouble with Time." As you read, look for reasons why this title is also appropriate.

Writing

Time sometimes causes trouble right here on earth. Having time zones that differ from one section of the country to another and changing from daylight savings time to another time can cause confusion. Freewrite about how traveling from one time zone to another or turning the clocks forward or backward can cause trouble.

Vocabulary

Knowing the following words can help you as you read "Crime on Mars."

enigma (ə nig′ mə) *n.:* An unexplainable matter or event (p. 138)

sects (sekts) *n.:* Small groups of people with the same leaders and beliefs (p. 138)

crustaceans (krus tā′ shəns) *n.:* Shellfish, such as lobsters, crabs, or shrimp (p. 138)

aboriginal (ab′ə rij′ə n′l) *adj.:* First; native (p. 138)

reconnoitering (rē′ kə noit′ ər iŋ) *v.:* Making an exploratory examination to get information about a place (p. 139)

artifacts (är′ tə fakts′) *n.:* Any objects made by human work, left behind by a civilization (p. 139)

discreet surveillance (dis krēt′ sər vā′ ləns): careful, unobserved watch kept over a person, especially one who is a suspect or a prisoner (p. 142)

Crime on Mars

Arthur C. Clarke

"We don't have much crime on Mars," said Detective Inspector Rawlings, a little sadly. "In fact, that's the chief reason I'm going back to the Yard.[1] If I stayed here much longer, I'd get completely out of practice."

We were sitting in the main observation lounge of the Phobos Spaceport, looking out across the jagged, sun-drenched crags of the tiny moon. The ferry rocket that had brought us up from Mars had left ten minutes ago, and was now beginning the long fall back to the ocher-tinted[2] globe hanging there against the stars. In half an hour we would be boarding the liner for Earth—a world upon which most of the passengers had never set foot, but which they still called "home."

"At the same time," continued the Inspector, "now and then there's a case that makes life interesting. You're an art dealer, Mr. Maccar; I'm sure you heard about that spot of bother at Meridian City a couple of months ago."

"I don't think so," replied the plump, olive-skinned little man I'd taken for just another returning tourist. Presumably the Inspector had already checked through the passenger list; I wondered how much he knew about me, and tried to reassure myself that my conscience was—well—reasonably clear. After all, everybody took *something* out through Martian Customs—

"It's been rather well hushed up," said the Inspector, "but you can't keep these things quiet for long. Anyway, a jewel thief from Earth tried to steal Meridian Museum's greatest treasure—the Siren Goddess."

"But that's absurd!" I objected. "It's priceless, of course—but it's only a lump of sandstone. You couldn't sell it to anyone—you might just as well steal the Mona Lisa."[3]

The Inspector grinned, rather mirthlessly. *"That's* happened once," he said. "Maybe the motive was the same. There are collectors who would give a fortune for such an object, even if they could only look at it themselves. Don't you agree, Mr. Maccar?"

"That's perfectly true. In my business, you meet all sorts of crazy people."

"Well, this chappie—name's Danny Weaver—had been well paid by one of them. And if it hadn't been for a piece of fantastically bad luck, he might have brought it off."

The Spaceport P.A. system apologized for a further slight delay owing to final fuel checks, and asked a number of passengers to report to Information. While we were waiting for the announcement to finish, I

---

1. Yard: Scotland Yard, headquarters of the London police force.
2. ocher (ō′ kər)-**tinted** *adj.*: Yellow-colored.

3. Mona Lisa: Priceless portrait by Leonardo da Vinci (1452-1519), an Italian painter.

recalled what little I knew about the Siren
Goddess. Though I'd never seen the original,
like most other departing tourists I had a
replica[4] in my baggage. It bore the certificate
of the Mars Bureau of Antiquities, guaran-
teeing that "this full-scale reproduction is
an exact copy of the so-called Siren Goddess, discovered in the Mare Sirenium by
the Third Expedition, A.D. 2012 (A.M. 23)."

It's quite a tiny thing to have caused so
much controversy. Only eight or nine inches
high—you wouldn't look at it twice if you
saw it in a museum on Earth. The head of a
young woman, with slightly oriental features, elongated earlobes, hair curled in

tight ringlets close to the scalp, lips half
parted in an expression of pleasure or
surprise—that's all. But it's an enigma so
baffling that it's inspired a hundred religious sects, and driven quite a few archaeologists[5] round the bend. For a perfectly
human head has no right whatsoever to be
found on Mars, whose only intelligent inhabitants were crustaceans—"educated
lobsters," as the newspapers are fond of
calling them. The aboriginal Martians never
came near to achieving space flight, and in
any event their civilization died before men
existed on Earth. No wonder the Goddess is

---

4. replica (rep′ li kə) *n*.: A copy of a work of art.

5. archaeologists (är′ kē äl′ ə jistz) *n*.: Scientists who
study the life and culture of ancient peoples.

the solar system's number-one mystery; I don't suppose we'll find the answer in my lifetime—if we ever do.

"Danny's plan was beautifully simple," continued the Inspector. "You know how absolutely dead a Martian city gets on Sunday, when everything closes down and the colonists stay home to watch the TV from Earth. Danny was counting on this, when he checked into the hotel in Meridian West, late Friday afternoon. He'd have Saturday for reconnoitering the Museum, an undisturbed Sunday for the job itself, and on Monday morning he'd be just another tourist leaving town. . . .

"Early Saturday he strolled through the little park and crossed over into Meridian East, where the Museum stands. In case you don't know, the city gets its name because it's exactly on longitude one hundred and eighty degrees; there's a big stone slab in the park with the prime meridian engraved on it, so that visitors can get themselves photographed standing in two hemispheres at once. Amazing what simple things amuse some people.

"Danny spent the day going over the Museum, exactly like any other tourist determined to get his money's worth. But at closing time he didn't leave; he'd holed up in one of the galleries not open to the public, where the Museum had been arranging a Late Canal Period reconstruction but had run out of money before the job could be finished. He stayed there until about midnight, just in case there were any enthusiastic researchers still in the building. Then he emerged and got to work."

"Just a minute," I interrupted. "What about the night watchman?"

The Inspector laughed.

"My dear chap! They don't have such luxuries on Mars. There weren't even any alarms, for who would bother to steal lumps of stone? True, the Goddess was sealed up neatly in a strong glass-and-metal cabinet, just in case some souvenir hunter took a fancy to her. But even if she were stolen, there was nowhere the thief could hide, and of course all outgoing traffic would be searched as soon as the statue was missed."

That was true enough. I'd been thinking in terms of Earth, forgetting that every city on Mars is a closed little world of its own beneath the force-field that protects it from the freezing near-vacuum. Beyond those electronic shields is the utterly hostile emptiness of the Martian Outback, where a man will die in seconds without protection. That makes law enforcement very easy; no wonder there's so little crime on Mars. . . .

"Danny had a beautiful set of tools, as specialized as a watchmaker's. The main item was a microsaw no bigger than a soldering iron; it had a wafer-thin blade, driven at a million cycles a second by an ultrasonic power pack. It would go through glass or metal like butter—and left a cut only about as thick as a hair. Which was very important for Danny, since he had to leave no traces of his handiwork.

"I suppose you've guessed how he intended to operate. He was going to cut through the base of the cabinet, and substitute one of those souvenir replicas for the real Goddess. It might be a couple of years before some inquisitive expert discovered the awful truth; long before then the original would have traveled back to Earth, perfectly disguised as a copy of itself, with a genuine certificate of authenticity. Pretty neat, eh?

"It must have been a weird business, working in that darkened gallery with all those million-year-old carvings and unexplainable artifacts around him. A museum on Earth is bad enough at night, but at least it's—well—*human*. And Gallery Three, which houses the Goddess, is particularly unsettling. It's full of bas-reliefs[6] showing quite incredible animals fighting each other; they look rather like giant beetles, and most paleontologists[7] flatly deny that they could ever have existed. But imaginary or not, they belonged to this world, and they didn't disturb Danny as much as the Goddess, staring at him across the ages and defying him to explain her presence here. She gave him the creeps. How do I know? He told me.

"Danny set to work on that cabinet as carefully as any diamond cutter preparing to cleave a gem. It took most of the night to slice out the trap door, and it was nearly dawn when he relaxed and put down the saw. There was still a lot of work to do, but the hardest part was over. Putting the replica into the case, checking its appearance against the photos he'd thoughtfully brought with him, and covering up his traces might take most of Sunday but that didn't worry him in the least. He had another twenty-four hours, and would positively welcome Monday's first visitors so that he could mingle with them and make his inconspicuous exit.

"It was a perfectly horrible shock to his nervous system, therefore, when the main

---

6. bas-reliefs (bä′ rə lēfs′) *n.*: Sculpture in which figures are carved on a flat surface, such as a wall, so that they stand out from the background.
7. paleontologists (pā′ lē än täl′ ə jists) *n.*: Scientists who investigate prehistoric forms of life by studying plant and animal fossils.

doors were noisily unbarred at eight-thirty and the museum staff—all six of them—started to open up for the day. Danny bolted for the emergency exit, leaving everything behind—tools, Goddesses, the lot. He had another big surprise when he found himself in the street; it should have been completely deserted at this time of day, with everyone at home reading the Sunday papers. But here were the citizens of Meridian East, as large as life, heading for plant or office on what was obviously a normal working day.

"By the time poor Danny got back to his hotel, we were waiting for him. We couldn't claim much credit for deducing that only a visitor from Earth—and a very recent one at that—could have overlooked Meridian City's chief claim to fame. And I presume you know what *that* is."

"Frankly, I don't," I answered. "You can't see much of Mars in six weeks, and I never went east of the Syrtis Major."

"Well, it's absurdly simple, but we shouldn't be too hard on Danny; even the locals occasionally fall into the same trap. It's something that doesn't bother us on Earth, where we've been able to dump the problem in the Pacific Ocean. But Mars, of course, is all dry land; and that means that *somebody* has to live with the International Date Line. . . .[8]

"Danny, you see, had worked from Meridian West. It was Sunday over there all right—and it was still Sunday when we picked him up back at the hotel. But over in Meridian East, half a mile away, it was only Saturday. That little trip across the park had made all the difference; I told you it was rotten luck."

There was a long moment of silent sympathy; then I asked, "What did he get?"

"Three years," said Inspector Rawlings.

"That doesn't seem very much."

"Mars years; that makes it almost six of ours. And a whacking fine which, by an odd coincidence, came to just the refund value of his return ticket to Earth. He isn't in jail, of course; Mars can't afford that kind of nonproductive luxury. Danny has to work for a living, under discreet surveillance. I told you that the Meridian Museum couldn't afford a night watchman. Well, it has one now. Guess who."

"All passengers prepare to board in ten minutes! Please collect your hand baggage!" ordered the loud-speakers.

As we started to move toward the air lock,[9] I couldn't help asking one more question.

"What about the people who put Danny up to it? There must have been a lot of money behind him. Did you get them?"

"Not yet; they'd covered their tracks pretty thoroughly, and I believe Danny was telling the truth when he said he couldn't give us any leads. Still, it's not my case; as I told you, I'm going back to my old job at the Yard. But a policeman always keeps his eyes open—like an art dealer, eh, Mr. Maccar? Why, you look a bit green about the gills. Have one of my space-sickness tablets."

"No, thank you," answered Mr. Maccar, "I'm quite all right."

His tone was distinctly unfriendly; the social temperature seemed to have dropped below zero in the last few minutes. I looked at Mr. Maccar, and I looked at the Inspector. And suddenly I realized that we were going to have a very interesting trip.

---

8. International Date Line: Imaginary line drawn north and south that marks the beginning of different time zones. When it is Sunday on one side of the line, it is Saturday on the other.

9. air lock: An airtight compartment between two places that have different air pressures.

THINKING ABOUT THE SELECTION
Recalling

1. About what crime does the Inspector tell the narrator and Mr. Maccar?
2. Why does the narrator consider such a crime absurd? What is the Inspector's explanation for the motive?
3. Describe the Goddess. Why is it an enigma?
4. How did Danny plan to steal the Goddess?
5. What goes wrong with Danny's plan? Why are the police able to find him so easily?

Interpreting

6. Which detail at the beginning of the story indicates that the Inspector has checked through the passenger list?
7. For what two reasons does the Inspector tell this story?
8. What does the narrator mean when he says, "And suddenly I realized that we were going to have a very interesting trip"?

Applying

9. Compare and contrast the life of the settlers on Mars as shown in this story with the life of settlers of the American frontier.

ANALYZING LITERATURE
Understanding Time as Part of Setting

The setting of a short story includes both its location and the time in which it takes place. Both are very important in "Crime on Mars."
1. Why is there so little crime on Mars?
2. Why is the city named Meridian City?
3. How does time foil Danny's plot?

CRITICAL THINKING AND READING
Identifying Scientific Details

"Crime on Mars" is a science-fiction story set in a spaceport. The spaceport is on one of the moons of the planet Mars. In a science-fiction story, many of the details are based on scientific information. Upon this scientific base, however, the author's imagination creates imaginary characters and situations. Some details in science fiction have a scientific base and some are imaginary.

Label each of the following details as based on science or purely imaginary.
1. "The ferry rocket that had brought us up from Mars had left ten minutes ago, and was now beginning the long fall back to the ocher-tinted globe hanging there against the stars."
2. "For a perfectly human head has no right whatsoever to be found on Mars, whose only intelligent inhabitants were crustaceans —'educated lobsters,' as the newspapers are fond of calling them."
3. "Beyond those electronic shields is the utterly hostile emptiness of the Martian Outback, where a man will die in seconds without protection."

UNDERSTANDING LANGUAGE
Recognizing New Words

Languages grow to accommodate changes in the world. New words are added to the English language as the need for them arises. The areas of science and technology, in particular, have produced words that would not have appeared in any dictionary twenty-five years ago.

Look up the following words in a recent dictionary. Write the meaning of each.
1. camcorder   2. modem   3. condominium

THINKING AND WRITING
Continuing a Science-Fiction Story

Imagine that you are the person telling the story "Crime on Mars." Continue the story by writing a newspaper account of what happened between the Inspector and Mr. Maccar during their trip from Mars and after they landed on earth. Make sure your account contains enough details to be clear and interesting. Proofread your account and share it with your classmates.

GUIDE FOR READING

The Tell-Tale Heart

Edgar Allan Poe (1809–1849) was born in Boston. He wrote many short stories, poems, and essays before he died at the age of 40. During his life Poe endured personal tragedies including the death of his mother, a difficult stay in a foster home, a college career shortened by debts and misconduct, the death of his wife at a young age, and years of poverty. These tragedies influenced Poe's writing so that his short stories were filled with horror. "The Tell-Tale Heart" is one of the best examples of Poe's tales of terror.

Atmosphere and Mood

The **atmosphere** or **mood** of a story is the overall emotional feeling that the details the author uses create. Sometimes you may be able to describe the atmosphere in a single word—sad, frightening, or mysterious, for example. Authors create atmosphere by their descriptions of settings, characters, and events. They choose their words carefully so that you will be affected by their writing in the way they want you to be.

Look For

As you read "The Tell-Tale Heart," look for the descriptive details that help create the atmosphere of the story. How do these details make you feel? What emotions do they stir up in you?

Writing

Make notes about words or descriptions you might include in a story to create an atmosphere or mood of horror. You will probably want to include descriptions of the weather, the time, and the place where your story takes place.

Vocabulary

Knowing the following words will help you as you read "The Tell-Tale Heart."

acute (ə kyo͞ot′) *adj.*: Sensitive (p. 145)

dissimulation (di sim′ yə lā′ shən) *n.*: The hiding of one's feelings or purposes (p. 145)

profound (prə found′) *adj.*: Seeing beyond what is obvious (p. 145)

sagacity (sə gas′ ə tē) *n.*: High intelligence and sound judgment (p. 146)

crevice (krev′ is) *n.*: A narrow opening (p. 147)

suavity (swä′ və tē) *n.*: Graceful politeness (p. 148)

gesticulations (jes tik′ yə lā′ shəns) *n.*: Energetic hand or arm gestures (p. 148)

derision (di rizh′ ən) *n.*: Contempt; ridicule (p. 148)

The Tell-Tale Heart

Edgar Allan Poe

True!—nervous—very, very dreadfully nervous I had been and am; but why *will* you say that I am mad? The disease had sharpened my senses—not destroyed—not dulled them. Above all was the sense of hearing acute. I heard all things in the heaven and in the earth. I heard many things in hell. How, then, am I mad? Hearken![1] and observe how healthily—how calmly I can tell you the whole story.

It is impossible to say how first the idea entered my brain; but once conceived, it haunted me day and night. Object there was none. Passion there was none. I loved the old man. He had never wronged me. He had never given me insult. For his gold I had no desire. I think it was his eye! yes, it was this! One of his eyes resembled that of a vulture—a pale blue eye, with a film over it. Whenever it fell upon me, my blood ran cold; and so by degrees—very gradually—I made up my mind to take the life of the old man, and thus rid myself of the eye forever.

Now this is the point. You fancy me mad. Madmen know nothing. But you should have seen *me*. You should have seen how wisely I proceeded—with what caution—with what foresight—with what dissimulation I went to work! I was never kinder to the old man than during the whole week before I killed him. And every night, about midnight, I turned the latch of his door and opened it—oh, so gently! And then, when I had made an opening sufficient for my head, I put in a dark lantern, all closed, closed, so that no light shone out, and then I thrust in my head. Oh, you would have laughed to see how cunningly I thrust it in! I moved it slowly—very, very slowly, so that I might not disturb the old man's sleep. It took me an hour to place my whole head within the opening so far that I could see him as he lay upon his bed. Ha!—would a madman have been so wise as this? And then, when my head was well in the room, I undid the lantern cautiously—oh, so cautiously—cautiously (for the hinges creaked)—I undid it just so much that a single thin ray fell upon the vulture eye. And this I did for seven long nights—every night just at midnight—but I found the eye always closed; and so it was impossible to do the work; for it was not the old man who vexed me, but his evil eye. And every morning, when the day broke, I went boldly into the chamber, and spoke courageously to him, calling him by name in a hearty tone, and inquiring how he had passed the night. So you see he would have been a very profound old man, indeed, to suspect that every night, just at twelve, I looked in upon him while he slept.

Upon the eighth night I was more than usually cautious in opening the door. A watch's minute hand moves more quickly

---

1. Hearken (här′ kən) *v.*: Listen.

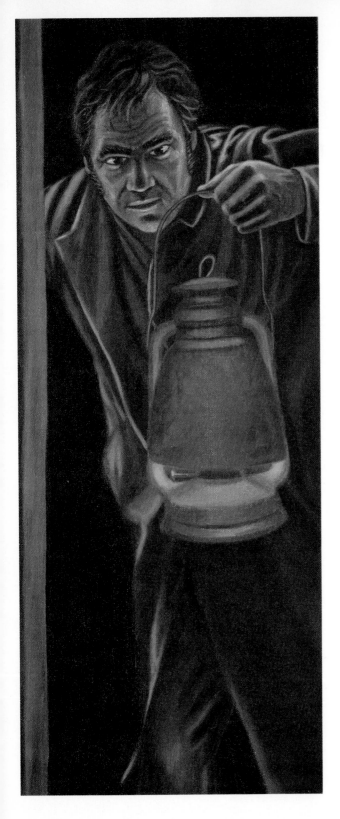

than did mine. Never, before that night, had I *felt* the extent of my own powers—of my sagacity. I could scarcely contain my feelings of triumph. To think that there I was, opening the door, little by little, and he not even to dream of my secret deeds or thoughts. I fairly chuckled at the idea; and perhaps he heard me; for he moved on the bed suddenly, as if startled. Now you may think that I drew back—but no. His room was as black as pitch with the thick darkness (for the shutters were close fastened, through fear of robbers), and so I knew that he could not see the opening of the door, and I kept pushing it on steadily, steadily.

I had my head in, and was about to open the lantern, when my thumb slipped upon the tin fastening, and the old man sprang up in the bed, crying out—"Who's there?"

I kept quite still and said nothing. For a whole hour I did not move a muscle, and in the meantime I did not hear him lie down. He was still sitting up in the bed, listening;—just as I have done, night after night, hearkening to the deathwatches[2] in the wall.

Presently I heard a slight groan, and I knew it was the groan of mortal terror. It was not a groan of pain or of grief—oh, no!—it was the low stifled sound that arises from the bottom of the soul when overcharged with awe. I knew the sound well. Many a night, just at midnight, when all the world slept, it has welled up from my own bosom, deepening, with its dreadful echo, the terrors that distracted me. I say I knew it well. I knew what the old man felt, and pitied him, although I chuckled at heart. I knew that he had been lying

---

2. deathwatches (deth′ woch′ əz) *n*.: Wood-boring beetles that make a tapping noise in the wood they invade. They are thought to predict death.

awake ever since the first slight noise, when he had turned in the bed. His fears had been ever since growing upon him. He had been trying to fancy them causeless, but could not. He had been saying to himself—"It is nothing but the wind in the chimney—it is only a mouse crossing the floor," or "it is merely a cricket which has made a single chirp." Yes, he has been trying to comfort himself with these suppositions: but he had found all in vain. *All in vain;* because Death, in approaching him, had stalked with his black shadow before him, and enveloped the victim. And it was the mournful influence of the unperceived shadow that caused him to feel—although he neither saw nor heard—to *feel* the presence of my head within the room.

When I had waited a long time, very patiently, without hearing him lie down, I resolved to open a little—a very, very little crevice in the lantern. So I opened it—you cannot imagine how stealthily, stealthily —until, at length, a single dim ray, like the thread of the spider, shot from out the crevice and fell upon the vulture eye.

It was open—wide, wide open—and I grew furious as I gazed upon it. I saw it with perfect distinctness—all a dull blue, with a hideous veil over it that chilled the very marrow in my bones; but I could see nothing else of the old man's face or person for I had directed the ray as if by instinct, precisely upon the spot.

And now—have I not told you that what you mistake for madness is but over-acuteness of the senses?—now, I say, there came to my ears a low, dull, quick sound, such as a watch makes when enveloped in cotton. I knew *that* sound well, too. It was the beating of the old man's heart. It increased my fury, as the beating of a drum stimulates the soldier into courage.

But even yet I refrained and kept still. I scarcely breathed. I held the lantern motionless. I tried how steadily I could maintain the ray upon the eye. Meantime the hellish tattoo of the heart increased. It grew quicker and quicker, and louder and louder every instant. The old man's terror *must* have been extreme! It grew louder, I say, louder every moment!—do you mark me well? I have told you that I am nervous: so I am. And now at the dead hour of the night, amid the dreadful silence of that old house, so strange a noise as this excited me to uncontrollable terror. Yet, for some minutes longer I refrained and stood still. But the beating grew louder, louder! I thought the heart must burst. And now a new anxiety seized me—the sound would be heard by a neighbor! The old man's hour had come! With a loud yell, I threw open the lantern and leaped into the room. He shrieked once —once only. In an instant I dragged him to the floor, and pulled the heavy bed over him. I then smiled gaily, to find the deed so far done. But, for many minutes, the heart beat on with a muffled sound. This, however, did not vex me; it would not be heard through the wall. At length it ceased. The old man was dead. I removed the bed and examined the corpse. Yes, he was stone, stone dead. I placed my hand upon the heart and held it there many minutes. There was no pulsation. He was stone dead. His eye would trouble me no more.

If still you think me mad, you will think so no longer when I describe the wise precautions I took for the concealment of the body. The night waned, and I worked hastily, but in silence. First of all I dismembered the corpse. I cut off the head and the arms and the legs.

I then took up three planks from the flooring of the chamber, and deposited all between the scantlings.[3] I then replaced the boards so cleverly, so cunningly, that no human eye—not even *his*—could have detected anything wrong. There was nothing to wash out—no stain of any kind—no blood-spot whatever. I had been too wary for that. A tub had caught all—ha! ha!

When I had made an end of these labors, it was four o'clock—still dark as midnight. As the bell sounded the hour, there came a knocking at the street door. I went down to open it with a light heart—for what had I *now* to fear? There entered three men, who introduced themselves, with perfect suavity, as officers of the police. A shriek had been heard by a neighbor during the night; suspicion of foul play had been aroused; information had been lodged at the police office, and they (the officers) had been deputed to search the premises.

I smiled—for *what* had I to fear? I bade the gentlemen welcome. The shriek, I said, was my own in a dream. The old man, I mentioned, was absent in the country. I took my visitors all over the house. I bade them search—search *well.* I led them, at length, to *his* chamber. I showed them his treasures, secure, undisturbed. In the enthusiasm of my confidence, I brought chairs into the room, and desired them *here* to rest from their fatigues, while I myself, in the wild audacity of my perfect triumph, placed my own seat upon the very spot beneath which reposed the corpse of the victim.

The officers were satisfied. My *manner* had convinced them. I was singularly at ease. They sat, and while I answered cheerily, they chatted of familiar things. But, ere long, I felt myself getting pale and wished them gone. My head ached, and I fancied a ringing in my ears: but still they sat and still chatted. The ringing became more distinct:—it continued and became more distinct: I talked more freely to get rid of the feeling: but it continued and gained definitiveness—until, at length, I found that the noise was *not* within my ears.

No doubt I now grew *very* pale—but I talked more fluently, and with a heightened voice. Yet the sound increased—and what could I do? It was *a low, dull, quick sound—much such a sound as a watch makes when enveloped in cotton.* I gasped for breath—and yet the officers heard it not. I talked more quickly—more vehemently; but the noise steadily increased. I arose and argued about trifles, in a high key and with violent gesticulations; but the noise steadily increased. Why *would* they not be gone? I paced the floor to and fro with heavy strides, as if excited to fury by the observations of the men—but the noise steadily increased. Oh! what *could* I do? I foamed—I raved—I swore! I swung the chair upon which I had been sitting, and grated it upon the boards, but the noise arose over all, and continually increased. It grew louder—louder—*louder!* And still the men chatted pleasantly, and smiled. Was it possible they heard not?—no, no! They heard!—they suspected!—they *knew!*—they were making a mockery of my horror!—this I thought, and this I think. But anything was better than this agony! Anything was more tolerable than this derision! I could bear those hypocritical smiles no longer! I felt that I must scream or die!—and now again! hark! louder! louder! louder! *louder!*—

"Villains!" I shrieked, "dissemble[4] no more! I admit the deed!—tear up the planks!—here, here!—it is the beating of his hideous heart!"

---

3. scantling (skant' lin) *n.*: A small beam or timber.

4. dissemble (di sem' b'l) *v.*: To conceal under a false appearance; to conceal the truth of one's true feelings or motives.

THINKING ABOUT THE SELECTION

Recalling

1. Why does the narrator decide to kill the old man?
2. How long does it take him to accomplish his plan?
3. Why do the police arrive, even though the narrator planned the murder so carefully?

Interpreting

4. How does the narrator reveal his cunning throughout the course of the crime? How does he reveal his powers of concentration?
5. When the police arrive, why does the narrator place his chair over the spot where the old man lies buried?
6. Do you think the police suspect the truth from the beginning? Explain your answer.
7. Do you think anyone but the narrator hears the beating of the old man's heart? Explain your answer. Why does he hear it so loudly?
8. What finally drives the narrator to confess?
9. At the beginning of the story, the narrator says that he is not mad. Explain why you agree or disagree with him.
10. To whom may he be recounting his tale?

Applying

11. Why do people like to read tales of terror?

ANALYZING LITERATURE

Describing Atmosphere or Mood

Atmosphere or **mood** is the overall feeling created in a story. Poe builds the atmosphere by the use of words, details, and pictures that allow you to feel what the characters feel. In the scene where the old man awakes, for instance, Poe includes these details and pictures: ". . . he moved on the bed suddenly, as if startled," "His room was as black as pitch," and "I kept pushing it in, steadily, steadily." These details help you to feel the atmosphere of terror.

1. Look at the paragraph that begins "Presently I heard a slight groan" (page 146). List three details that help you to feel what the old man feels at this time.
2. Look at the paragraph that begins "I then took up three planks from the flooring" (page 147). List three details that create the mood of the narrator at this time.
3. Look at the paragraph that begins "No doubt I now grew *very* pale" (page 148). List three details that create the narrator's mood at this point.

CRITICAL THINKING AND READING

Choosing Words to Create Atmosphere

To create a particular atmosphere, you must choose words carefully. For example, notice the word *vulture* in the following sentence by Poe: "One of his eyes resembled that of a *vulture*." To create a different atmosphere an author might say: "His eyes resembled those of a *puppy*."

For each of the following words, a comparison is given that creates a mood. Create a different mood by writing another sentence comparing the item to something different.

1. *moon:* The golden globe of the moon lit up the road as though it were a street light.
2. *store:* The tiny store displays so many jewels that it resembles a huge jewelry box.
3. *cat:* The eyes of the cat gleamed like stars.

THINKING AND WRITING

Writing to Create Atmosphere

Imagine that Edgar Allan Poe were writing a story using the descriptions you wrote before you read this story. Write one scene as he might have written it. When you have finished, check your scene to make sure that you have used words and phrases that create a mood of horror.

The Drummer Boy of Shiloh

Ray Bradbury (1920–   ) was born in Waukegan, Illinois, and began his working life as a newsboy. Bradbury writes chiefly science-fiction and fantasy stories, such as his famous book *The Martian Chronicles*. The feelings and people that Bradbury writes about, however, could exist in any time or place. He writes stories of people—real, honest people—such as the Civil War drummer boy and the general in the "The Drummer Boy of Shiloh." This story is not science fiction, however; it is an example of historical fiction.

Historical Setting

Stories may be set in a real place in a past time. If these stories are accurate in the way the places, times, and historical events are described, the stories are said to have a **historical setting.** Though the setting and some characters and events may be realistic, most of the characters and events are fictional. "The Drummer Boy of Shiloh," for example, has as its setting the battlefield at Shiloh, Tennessee, on the night before a famous Civil War battle. Although drummer boys and generals really were there, the ones you will meet in the story are creations of the author's imagination.

Look For

As you read "The Drummer Boy of Shiloh," look for details about when and where the story takes place. Does the historical setting change the way you view the story?

Writing

How do you think young soldiers feel the night before a major battle? Freewrite about how they might feel and what they might think about.

Vocabulary

Knowing the following words will help you as you read "The Drummer Boy of Shiloh."

askew (ə skyo͞o′) *adv.*: Crookedly (p. 151)

benediction (ben′ ə dik′ shən) *n.*: A blessing (p. 151)

riveted (riv′ it əd) *adj.*: Fastened or made firm (p. 153)

compounded (käm pound′ əd) *adj.*: Mixed or combined (p. 153)

remote (ri mōt′) *adj.*: Distant (p. 153)

resolute (rez′ ə lo͞ot′) *adj.*: Showing a firm purpose; determined (p. 154)

tremor (trem′ ər) *n.*: Shaking or vibration (p. 155)

muted (myo͞ot′ əd) *adj.*: Muffled; subdued (p. 155)

The Drummer Boy of Shiloh

Ray Bradbury

In the April night, more than once, blossoms fell from the orchard trees and lit with rustling taps on the drumskin. At midnight a peach stone left miraculously on a branch through winter, flicked by a bird, fell swift and unseen, struck once, like panic, which jerked the boy upright. In silence he listened to his own heart ruffle away, away—at last gone from his ears and back in his chest again.

After that, he turned the drum on its side, where its great lunar face peered at him whenever he opened his eyes.

His face, alert or at rest, was solemn. It was indeed a solemn time and a solemn night for a boy just turned fourteen in the peach field near the Owl Creek not far from the church at Shiloh.[1]

"... thirty-one, thirty-two, thirty-three . . . "

Unable to see, he stopped counting.

Beyond the thirty-three familiar shadows, forty thousand men, exhausted by nervous expectation, unable to sleep for romantic dreams of battles yet unfought, lay crazily askew in their uniforms. A mile yet farther on, another army was strewn helter-skelter, turning slow, basting themselves[2] with the thought of what they would do when the time came: a leap, a yell, a blind plunge their strategy, raw youth their protection and benediction.

Now and again the boy heard a vast wind come up, that gently stirred the air. But he knew what it was—the army here, the army there, whispering to itself in the dark. Some men talking to others, others murmuring to themselves, and all so quiet it was like a natural element arisen from South or North with the motion of the earth toward dawn.

What the men whispered the boy could only guess, and he guessed that it was: "Me, I'm the one, I'm the one of all the rest who won't die. I'll live through it. I'll go home. The band will play. And I'll be there to hear it."

Yes, thought the boy, that's all very well for them, they can give as good as they get!

For with the careless bones of the young men harvested by night and bindled[3] around campfires were the similarly strewn steel bones of their rifles, with bayonets fixed like eternal lightning lost in the orchard grass.

---

1. Shiloh (shī′ lō): The site of a Civil War battle in 1862; now a national military park in southwest Tennessee.

2. basting themselves: Here, letting their thoughts pour over them as they turn in their sleep.
3. bindled (bin′ d′ld) *adj.*: Bedded.

DRUMMER BOY
Julian Scott
N. S. Mayer

Me, thought the boy, I got only a drum, two sticks to beat it, and no shield.

There wasn't a man-boy on this ground tonight who did not have a shield he cast, riveted or carved himself on his way to his first attack, compounded of remote but nonetheless firm and fiery family devotion, flag-blown patriotism and cocksure immortality strengthened by the touchstone of very real gunpowder, ramrod, Minié ball[4] and flint. But without these last, the boy felt his family move yet farther off away in the dark, as if one of those great prairie-burning trains had chanted them away never to return—leaving him with this drum which was worse than a toy in the game to be played tomorrow or some day much too soon.

The boy turned on his side. A moth brushed his face, but it was a peach blossom. A peach blossom flicked him, but it was a moth. Nothing stayed put. Nothing had a name. Nothing was as it once was.

If he lay very still, when the dawn came up and the soldiers put on their bravery with their caps, perhaps they might go away, the war with them, and not notice him lying small here, no more than a toy himself.

"Well, now," said a voice.

The boy shut up his eyes, to hide inside himself, but it was too late. Someone, walking by in the night, stood over him.

"Well," said the voice quietly, "here's a soldier crying *before* the fight. Good. Get it over. Won't be time once it all starts."

And the voice was about to move on when the boy, startled, touched the drum at his elbow. The man above, hearing this, stopped. The boy could feel his eyes, sense him slowly bending near. A hand must have come down out of the night, for there was a

4. **Minié** (min′ ē), ball: A cone-shaped rifle bullet that expands when fired.

little *rat-tat* as the fingernails brushed and the man's breath fanned his face.

"Why, it's the drummer boy, isn't it?"

The boy nodded, not knowing if his nod was seen. "Sir, is that *you?*" he said.

"I assume it is." The man's knees cracked as he bent still closer.

He smelled as all fathers should smell, of salt sweat, ginger tobacco, horse and boot leather, and the earth he walked upon. He had many eyes. No, not eyes—brass buttons that watched the boy.

He could only be, and was, the general.

"What's your name, boy?" he asked.

"Joby," whispered the boy, starting to sit up.

"All right, Joby, don't stir." A hand pressed his chest gently, and the boy relaxed. "How long you been with us, Joby?"

"Three weeks, sir."

"Run off from home or joined legitimately, boy?"

Silence.

"Fool question," said the general. "Do you shave yet, boy? Even more of a fool. There's your cheek, fell right off the tree overhead. And the others here not much older. Raw, raw, the lot of you. You ready for tomorrow or the next day, Joby?"

"I think so, sir."

"You want to cry some more, go on ahead. I did the same last night."

"*You,* sir?"

"It's the truth. Thinking of everything ahead. Both sides figuring the other side will just give up, and soon, and the war done in weeks, and us all home. Well, that's not how it's going to be. And maybe that's why I cried."

"Yes, sir," said Joby.

The general must have taken out a cigar now, for the dark was suddenly filled with the smell of tobacco unlit as yet, but chewed as the man thought what next to say.

"It's going to be a crazy time," said the general. "Counting both sides, there's a hundred thousand men, give or take a few thousand out there tonight, not one as can spit a sparrow off a tree, or knows a horse clod from a Minié ball. Stand up, bare the breast, ask to be a target, thank them and sit down, that's us, that's them. We should turn tail and train four months, they should do the same. But here we are, taken with spring fever and thinking it blood lust, taking our sulfur with cannons instead of with molasses, as it should be, going to be a hero, going to live forever. And I can see all of them over there nodding agreement, save the other way around. It's wrong, boy, it's wrong as a head put on hindside front and a man marching backward through life. More innocents will get shot out of pure enthusiasm than ever got shot before. Owl Creek was full of boys splashing around in the noonday sun just a few hours ago. I fear it will be full of boys again, just floating, at sundown tomorrow, not caring where the tide takes them."

The general stopped and made a little pile of winter leaves and twigs in the darkness, as if he might at any moment strike fire to them to see his way through the coming days when the sun might not show its face because of what was happening here and just beyond.

The boy watched the hand stirring the leaves and opened his lips to say something, but did not say it. The general heard the boy's breath and spoke himself.

"Why am I telling you this? That's what you wanted to ask, eh? Well, when you got a bunch of wild horses on a loose rein somewhere, somehow you got to bring order, rein them in. These lads, fresh out of the milkshed, don't know what I know, and I can't tell them: men actually die, in war. So each is his own army. I got to make *one* army of them. And for that, boy, I need you."

"Me!" The boy's lips barely twitched.

"Now, boy," said the general quietly, "you are the heart of the army. Think of that. You're the heart of the army. Listen, now."

And, lying there, Joby listened. And the general spoke on.

If he, Joby, beat slow tomorrow, the heart would beat slow in the men. They would lag by the wayside. They would drowse in the fields on their muskets. They would sleep forever, after that, in those same fields—their hearts slowed by a drummer boy and stopped by enemy lead.

But if he beat a sure, steady, ever faster rhythm, then, then their knees would come up in a long line down over that hill, one knee after the other, like a wave on the ocean shore! Had he seen the ocean ever? Seen the waves rolling in like a well-ordered cavalry charge to the sand? Well, that was it, that's what he wanted, that's what was needed! Joby was his right hand and his left. He gave the orders, but Joby set the pace!

So bring the right knee up and the right foot out and the left knee up and the left foot out. One following the other in good time, in brisk time. Move the blood up the body and make the head proud and the spine stiff and the jaw resolute. Focus the eye and set the teeth, flare the nostrils and tighten the hands, put steel armor all over the men, for blood moving fast in them does indeed make men feel as if they'd put on steel. He must keep at it, at it! Long and steady, steady and long! Then, even though shot or torn, those wounds got in hot blood—in blood he'd helped stir—would feel less pain. If their blood was cold, it would be more than slaughter, it would be murderous nightmare and pain best not told and no one to guess.

The general spoke and stopped, letting his breath slack off. Then, after a moment,

THE BATTLE OF SHILOH, TENNESSEE (6–7 APRIL 1862), 1886
Kurz and Allison
The Granger Collection

he said, "So there you are, that's it. Will you do that, boy? Do you know now you're general of the army when the general's left behind?"

The boy nodded mutely.

"You'll run them through for me then, boy?"

"Yes, sir."

"Good. And, maybe, many nights from tonight, many years from now, when you're as old or far much older than me, when they ask you what you did in this awful time, you will tell them—one part humble and one part proud—'I was the drummer boy at the battle of Owl Creek,' or the Tennessee River, or maybe they'll just name it after the church there. 'I was the drummer boy at Shiloh.' Good grief, that has a beat and sound to it fitting for Mr. Longfellow. 'I was the drummer boy at Shiloh.' Who will ever hear those words and not know you, boy, or

what you thought this night, or what you'll think tomorrow or the next day when we must get up on our legs and *move!*"

The general stood up. "Well, then. Bless you, boy. Good night."

"Good night, sir." And tobacco, brass, boot polish, salt sweat and leather, the man moved away through the grass.

Joby lay for a moment, staring but unable to see where the man had gone. He swallowed. He wiped his eyes. He cleared his throat. He settled himself. Then, at last, very slowly and firmly, he turned the drum so that it faced up toward the sky.

He lay next to it, his arm around it, feeling the tremor, the touch, the muted thunder as, all the rest of the April night in the year 1862, near the Tennessee River, not far from the Owl Creek, very close to the church named Shiloh, the peach blossoms fell on the drum.

The Drummer Boy of Shiloh   155

THINKING ABOUT THE SELECTION

Recalling

1. How old is the drummer boy?
2. What is the boy thinking about as he lies in the orchard?
3. Why has the general cried the night before?
4. Why does the general say he needs Joby?

Interpreting

5. Why do you think Joby joined the army?
6. Why do you think the general stops to talk to the boy?
7. In what way is Joby "the heart of the army"?
8. What does the general mean when he says, "Do you know now you're general of the army when the general's left behind?"
9. How do you think the boy felt after his talk with the general?

Applying

10. Mark Twain once said, "Courage is resistance to fear, mastery of fear—not absence of fear." How does this quotation apply to "The Drummer Boy of Shiloh"?

ANALYZING LITERATURE

Recognizing Historical Details

To create a historical setting, an author includes details that help you recognize and visualize the setting of the story accurately. When Bradbury says "in the peach field near the Owl Creek not far from the church at Shiloh," he introduces a setting where a historical event occurred. As the story continues, he includes other details that are historically accurate.

1. List at least five details in the story that place the setting geographically.
2. List at least five details in the story that place the setting in time.

CRITICAL THINKING AND READING

Identifying Appropriate Historical Details

Authors must be careful to include only details that describe a place and time accurately if they want their historical settings to be true.

Name the item in each of the following groups that does not belong in the same historical setting with the others.

1. battlefield at Shiloh; drummer boy; Jeep; general
2. Cape Canaveral; rocket; television crew; General Custer
3. George Washington; Benjamin Franklin; Douglas MacArthur; Patrick Henry

SPEAKING AND LISTENING

Preparing a Program of Civil War Songs

Look in the card catalog of the public or school library to find song books or records with Civil War songs. List the call numbers and other important information for each book and record. Then, locate the song books and records. Working with some of your classmates, arrange and present a program of Civil War music for your class.

THINKING AND WRITING

Writing About a Historical Setting

Suppose you were preparing a time capsule for someone to open one hundred years from now. List and write about the items you would include in it to give people of the future a clear picture of the place and time you live in today. Explain why you would include each item. Make sure your spelling, grammar, and punctuation are correct.

Theme

ROOMS BY THE SEA
Edward Hopper
Yale University Art Gallery

GUIDE FOR READING

The Ninny

Anton Pavlovich Chekhov (1860–1904), a twentieth-century master storyteller and playwright, was born in southern Russia. He studied medicine in Moscow, supporting his family by writing comic stories. After Chekhov published his first book in 1886, he concentrated on writing. He also wrote plays, among them the classics *The Three Sisters* and *The Cherry Orchard*. That Chekhov sought to "paint life in its true aspects, and to show how far this life falls short of the ideal life" can be seen in "The Ninny."

Theme

Theme is the central idea of a story, or the general idea about life that is revealed through a story. Sometimes the theme of a story is stated directly. Sometimes you must draw a conclusion about it—by considering all of the story's elements. In "The Ninny" the theme is stated directly in the conclusion that the employer draws about certain people.

Look For

As you read "The Ninny," look for what it reveals about life. How does Chekhov show that this life "falls short of the ideal life"?

Writing

What makes people stand up for themselves? Freewrite, exploring your thoughts on this question.

Vocabulary

Knowing the meaning of the following words will help you as you read "The Ninny."

perspiration (pur′ spə rā′ shən) *n*.: Sweat (p. 159)

nitwit (nit′ wit′) *n*.: Stupid or silly person (p. 160)

ninny (nin′ ē) *n*.: Fool (p. 160)

The Ninny

Anton Chekhov

Translated by Robert Payne

Just a few days ago I invited Yulia Vassilyevna, the governess of my children, to come to my study. I wanted to settle my account with her.

"Sit down, Yulia Vassilyevna," I said to her. "Let's get our accounts settled. I'm sure you need some money, but you keep standing on ceremony and never ask for it. Let me see. We agreed to give you thirty rubles[1] a month, didn't we?"

"Forty."

"No, thirty. I made a note of it. I always pay the governess thirty. Now, let me see. You have been with us for two months?"

"Two months and five days."

"Two months exactly. I made a note of it. So you have sixty rubles coming to you. Subtract nine Sundays. You know you don't tutor Kolya on Sundays, you just go out for a walk. And then the three holidays . . ."

Yulia Vassilyevna blushed and picked at the trimmings of her dress, but said not a word.

"Three holidays. So we take off twelve rubles. Kolya was sick for four days—those days you didn't look after him. You looked after Vanya, only Vanya. Then there were the three days you had toothache, when my wife gave you permission to stay away from the children after dinner. Twelve and seven makes nineteen. Subtract. . . . That leaves . . . hm . . . forty-one rubles. Correct?"

Yulia Vassilyevna's left eye reddened and filled with tears. Her chin trembled. She began to cough nervously, blew her nose, and said nothing.

"Then around New Year's Day you broke a cup and saucer. Subtract two rubles. The cup cost more than that—it was an heirloom, but we won't bother about that. We're the ones who pay. Another matter. Due to your carelessness Kolya climbed a tree and tore his coat. Subtract ten. Also, due to your carelessness the chambermaid ran off with Vanya's boots. You ought to have kept your eyes open. You get a good salary. So we dock off five more. . . . On the tenth of January you took ten rubles from me."

"I didn't," Yulia Vassilyevna whispered.

"But I made a note of it."

"Well, yes—perhaps . . ."

"From forty-one we take twenty-seven. That leaves fourteen."

Her eyes filled with tears, and her thin, pretty little nose was shining with perspiration. Poor little child!

"I only took money once," she said in a trembling voice. "I took three rubles from your wife . . . never anything more."

---

1. rubles (roo′ b'lz) *n.:* Units of money used in Russia, now the Soviet Union.

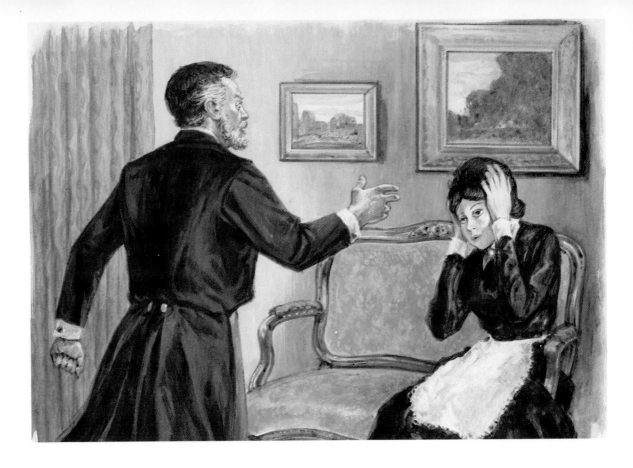

"Did you now? You see, I never made a note of it. Take three from fourteen. That leaves eleven. Here's your money, my dear. Three, three, three . . . one and one. Take it, my dear."

I gave her the eleven rubles. With trembling fingers she took them and slipped them into her pocket.

"*Merci*,"[2] she whispered.

I jumped up, and began pacing up and down the room. I was in a furious temper.

"Why did you say '*merci*'?" I asked.

"For the money."

"Don't you realize I've been cheating you? I steal your money, and all you can say is '*merci*'!"

"In my other places they gave me nothing."

"They gave you nothing! Well, no wonder! I was playing a trick on you—a dirty trick. . . . I'll give you your eighty rubles, they are all here in an envelope made out for you. Is it possible for anyone to be such a nitwit? Why didn't you protest? Why did you keep your mouth shut? Is it possible that there is anyone in this world who is so spineless? Why are you such a ninny?"

She gave me a bitter little smile. On her face I read the words: "Yes, it is possible."

I apologized for having played this cruel trick on her, and to her great surprise gave her the eighty rubles. And then she said "*merci*" again several times, always timidly, and went out. I gazed after her, thinking how very easy it is in this world to be strong.

---

2. *Merci* (mer sē'): French for "Thank you."

THINKING ABOUT THE SELECTION

Recalling

1. According to the governess, how much should she be paid per month?
2. Name three reasons why the employer subtracts money from the governess's salary.
3. How does the governess behave as the employer goes over their accounts?
4. What amount is left after the accounting?
5. How much money does the employer actually pay the governess?

Interpreting

6. Why does the governess not protest her employer's actions?
7. Why does the employer trick the governess?

Applying

8. How would you help a friend like the governess stand up for himself or herself if, for example, this person were not rewarded as had been promised for doing extra work?

ANALYZING LITERATURE

Understanding Theme

Theme is the general idea or insight about life that is revealed through a story. Theme may be directly stated, or it may be revealed through dialogue and events. In "The Ninny," the theme is stated directly by a character.

1. What is the theme of this story?
2. State the theme in your own words.
3. Do you agree with this theme? Give reasons for your answers.

CRITICAL THINKING AND READING

Making Inferences Based on Dialogue

An **inference** is a conclusion that can be drawn from information you are given. In a story you can make inferences about a character based on what he or she says—or does not say.

For example, if a character chatters endlessly, you might infer that this character is nervous or self-centered. If another character observes people quietly and says little; you might infer that this character is serious and thoughtful.

1. In this story, the governess whispers or speaks hesitantly "in a trembling voice"—or says nothing at all. On the basis of this, what do you infer about her character?
2. What can you infer about the employer from his "furious" speech at the end of the story?
3. What do you infer about him from his trick?

UNDERSTANDING LANGUAGE

Finding the Meaning from the Context

One way to figure out the meaning of a word is by looking at its **context**—the words and sentences that surround it. Suppose you did not know the meaning of *nervously*. In the story, the governess's eye reddens, she begins to cry, her chin trembles, and she coughs *nervously*. Clearly she is upset and anxious. You might conclude, from the context, that *nervously* means "uneasily," "restlessly," or "fearfully."

Choose the best definition for the following italicized words, based on context.

1. Mr. Breen stormed and shouted, his face red, his hair flying, his manner *berserk*.
   a. surprised   b. hurt   c. frenzied
2. Cheryl, smiling and nodding pleasantly, *acquiesced to* any plan, rather than refuse.
   a. rejected   b. agreed to   c. opposed

THINKING AND WRITING

Writing an Extension of the Story

How do you think the governess will act the next time she is paid by the employer? Freewrite for three minutes about this scene as you imagine it. Then turn your freewriting into a draft of this scene. Include description and dialogue. When you revise your draft, be sure that the characters' actions are shown clearly. Proofread your story and share it with your classmates.

GUIDE FOR READING

The Six Rows of Pompons

Toshio Mori (1910–1980) wrote short stories and novels about the Japanese-Americans of northern California. Mori was born in Oakland, California; his parents were Japanese immigrants. Mori's collection of stories, *Yokohama, California,* was published in 1949. The stories—including "The Six Rows of Pompons"—take place in the years before World War II. This story shows the qualities that the author William Saroyan has identified in Mori's writing: "understanding sympathy, generosity and kindliness."

Key Statements

Theme is the central idea of a story, or the general idea about life that is revealed through a story. Sometimes the theme is implied, or suggested. A **key statement** in the story is a sentence that may point to the implied theme or help you see what the theme is. A key statement may be made directly by a character.

Look For

As you read "The Six Rows of Pompons," look for key statements by the characters that suggest the theme of the story.

Writing

In "The Six Rows of Pompons" a young boy learns responsibility. Imagine someone has been given a serious responsibility for the first time. Freewrite about how this person would feel.

Vocabulary

Knowing the following words will help you as you read "The Six Rows of Pompons."

rampage (ram′ pāj) *n.*: An outbreak of violent behavior (p. 163)

enthusiasm (in thōo zē az′m) *n.*: Intense or eager interest (p. 165)

lagged (lagd) *v.*: Fell behind (p. 165)

anxious (a ŋk′ sнəs) *adj.*: Eagerly wishing (p. 165)

The Six Rows of Pompons

Toshio Mori

When little Nephew Tatsuo[1] came to live with us he liked to do everything the adults were doing on the nursery, and although his little mind did not know it, everything he did was the opposite of adult conduct, unknowingly destructive and disturbing. So Uncle Hiroshi[2] after witnessing several weeks of rampage said, "This has got to stop, this sawing the side of a barn and nailing the doors to see if it would open. But we must not whip him. We must not crush his curiosity by any means."

And when Nephew Tatsuo, who was seven and in high second grade, got used to the place and began coming out into the fields and pestering us with difficult questions as "What are the plants here for? What is water? Why are the bugs made for? What are the birds and why do the birds sing?" and so on, I said to Uncle Hiroshi, "We must do something about this. We cannot answer questions all the time and we cannot be correct all the time and so we will do harm. But something must be done about this beyond a doubt."

"Let us take him in our hands," Uncle Hiroshi said.

So Uncle Hiroshi took little Nephew Tatsuo aside, and brought him out in the fields and showed him the many rows of pompons[3] growing. "Do you know what these are?" Uncle Hiroshi said. "These things here?"

"Yes. Very valuable," Nephew Tatsuo said. "Plants."

"Do you know when these plants grow up and flower, we eat?" Uncle Hiroshi said.

Nephew Tatsuo nodded. "Yes," he said, "I knew that."

"All right. Uncle Hiroshi will give you six rows of pompons," Uncle Hiroshi said. "You own these six rows. You take care of them. Make them grow and flower like your uncle's."

"Gee!" Nephew Tatsuo said.

"Do you want to do it?" Uncle Hiroshi said.

"Sure!" he said.

"Then jump right in and start working," Uncle Hiroshi said. "But first, let me tell you something. You cannot quit once you start. You must not let it die, you must make it grow and flower like your uncles'."

"All right," little Nephew Tatsuo said, "I will."

"Every day you must tend to your plants. Even after the school opens, rain or shine," Uncle Hiroshi said.

"All right," Nephew Tatsuo said. "You'll see!"

---

1. Tatsuo (tät soo′ ō).
2. Hiroshi (hēr ō′ shē).

3. pompons (päm′ pänz′) *n.*: Flowers that have small, rounded heads, such as chrysanthemums.

So the old folks once more began to work peacefully, undisturbed, and Nephew Tatsuo began to work on his plot. However, every now and then Nephew Tatsuo would run to Uncle Hiroshi with much excitement.

"Uncle Hiroshi, come!" he said. "There's bugs on my plants! Big bugs, green bugs with black dots and some brown bugs. What shall I do?"

"They're bad bugs," Uncle Hiroshi said. "Spray them."

"I have no spray," Nephew Tatsuo said excitedly.

"All right. I will spray them for you today," Uncle Hiroshi said. "Tomorrow I will get you a small hand spray. Then you must spray your own plants."

Several tall grasses shot above the pompons and Uncle Hiroshi noticed this. Also, he saw the beds beginning to fill with young weeds.

"Those grasses attract the bugs," he said. "Take them away. Keep the place clean."

It took Nephew Tatsuo days to pick the weeds out of the six beds. And since the weeds were not picked cleanly, several weeks later it looked as if it was not touched at all. Uncle Hiroshi came around sometimes to feel the moisture in the soil. "Tatsuo," he said, "your plants need water. Give it plenty, it is summer. Soon it will be too late."

Nephew Tatsuo began watering his plants with the three-quarter hose.

"Don't hold the hose long in one place and short in another," Uncle Hiroshi said. "Keep it even and wash the leaves often."

In October Uncle Hiroshi's plants stood tall and straight and the buds began to appear. Nephew Tatsuo kept at it through summer and autumn, although at times he looked wearied and indifferent. And each time Nephew Tatsuo's enthusiasm lagged Uncle Hiroshi took him over to the six rows of pompons and appeared greatly surprised.

"Gosh," he said, "your plants are coming up! It is growing rapidly; pretty soon the flowers will come."

"Do you think so?" Nephew Tatsuo said.

"Sure, can't you see it coming?" Uncle Hiroshi said. "You will have lots of flowers. When you have enough to make a bunch I will sell it for you at the flower market."

"Really?" Nephew Tatsuo said. "In the flower market?"

Uncle Hiroshi laughed. "Sure," he said. "That's where the plant business goes on, isn't it?"

One day Nephew Tatsuo wanted an awful lot to have us play catch with him with a tennis ball. It was at the time when the nursery was the busiest and even Sundays were all work.

"Nephew Tatsuo, don't you realize we are all men with responsibilities?" Uncle Hiroshi said. "Uncle Hiroshi has lots of work to do today. Now is the busiest time. You also have lots of work to do in your beds. And this should be your busiest time. Do you know whether your pompons are dry or wet?"

"No, Uncle Hiroshi," he said. "I don't quite remember."

"Then attend to it. Attend to it," Uncle Hiroshi said.

Nephew Tatsuo ran to the six rows of pompons to see if it was dry or wet. He came running back. "Uncle Hiroshi, it is still wet," he said.

"All right," Uncle Hiroshi said, "but did you see those holes in the ground with the piled-up mounds of earth?"

"Yes. They're gopher holes," Nephew Tatsuo said.

"Right," Uncle Hiroshi said. "Did you catch the gopher?"

"No," said Nephew Tatsuo.

"Then attend to it, attend to it right away," Uncle Hiroshi said.

One day in late October Uncle Hiroshi's pompons began to bloom. He began to cut and bunch and take them early in the morning to the flower market in Oakland.[4] And by this time Nephew Tatsuo was anxious to see his pompons bloom. He was anxious to see how it feels to cut the flowers of his plants. And by this time Nephew Tatsuo's six beds of pompons looked like a patch of tall weeds left uncut through the summer. Very few pompon buds stood out above the tangle.

Few plants survived out of the six rows. In some parts of the beds where the pompons had plenty of water and freedom, the stems grew strong and tall and the buds were big and round. Then there were parts where the plants looked shriveled and the leaves were wilted and brown. The majority of the plants were dead before the cool weather arrived. Some died by dryness, some by gophers or moles, and some were dwarfed by the great big grasses which covered the pompons altogether.

When Uncle Hiroshi's pompons began to flower everywhere the older folks became worried.

"We must do something with Tatsuo's six beds. It is worthless and his bugs are coming over to our beds," Tatsuo's father said. "Let's cut it down and burn them today."

"No," said Uncle Hiroshi. "That will be a very bad thing to do. It will kill Nephew Tatsuo. Let the plants stay."

So the six beds of Nephew Tatsuo remained intact, the grasses, the gophers, the bugs, the buds and the plants and all. Soon

---

4. Oakland (ōk′ lənd): A port city in western California, on San Francisco Bay.

after, the buds began to flower and Nephew Tatsuo began to run around calling Uncle Hiroshi. He said the flowers are coming. Big ones, good ones. He wanted to know when can he cut them.

"Today," Uncle Hiroshi said. "Cut it today and I will sell it for you at the market tomorrow."

Next day at the flower market Uncle Hiroshi sold the bunch of Nephew Tatsuo's pompons for twenty-five cents. When he came home Nephew Tatsuo ran to the car.

"Did you sell it, Uncle Hiroshi?" Nephew Tatsuo said.

"Sure. Why would it not sell?" Uncle Hiroshi said. "They are healthy, carefully cultured pompons."

Nephew Tatsuo ran around excitedly. First, he went to his father. "Papa!" he said, "someone bought my pompons!" Then he ran over to my side and said, "The bunch was sold! Uncle Hiroshi sold my pompons!"

At noontime, after the lunch was over, Uncle Hiroshi handed over the quarter to Nephew Tatsuo.

"What shall I do with this money?" asked Nephew Tatsuo, addressing all of us, with shining eyes.

"Put it in your toy bank," said Tatsuo's father.

"No," said Uncle Hiroshi. "Let him do what he wants. Let him spend and have a taste of his money."

"Do you want to spend your quarter, Nephew Tatsuo?" I said.

"Yes," he said.

"Then do anything you wish with it," Uncle Hiroshi said. "Buy anything you want. Go and have a good time. It is your money."

On the following Sunday we did not see Nephew Tatsuo all day. When he came back late in the afternoon Uncle Hiroshi said, "Nephew Tatsuo, what did you do today?"

"I went to a show, then I bought an ice cream cone and then on my way home I watched the baseball game at the school, and then I bought a popcorn from the candy man. I have five cents left," Nephew Tatsuo said.

"Good," Uncle Hiroshi said. "That shows a good spirit."

Uncle Hiroshi, Tatsuo's father, and I sat in the shade. It was still hot in the late afternoon that day. We sat and watched Nephew Tatsuo riding around and around the yard on his red tricycle, making a furious dust.

"Next year he will forget what he is doing this year and will become a wild animal and go on a rampage again," the father of Tatsuo said.

"Next year is not yet here," said Uncle Hiroshi.

"Do you think he will be interested to raise pompons again?" the father said.

"He enjoys praise," replied Uncle Hiroshi, "and he takes pride in good work well done. We will see."

"He is beyond a doubt the worst gardener in the country," I said. "Probably he is the worst in the world."

"Probably," said Uncle Hiroshi.

"Tomorrow he will forget how he enjoyed spending his year's income," the father of Tatsuo said.

"Let him forget," Uncle Hiroshi said. "One year is nothing. We will keep this six rows of pompon business up till he comes to his senses."

We sat that night the whole family of us, Uncle Hiroshi, Nephew Tatsuo's father, I, Nephew Tatsuo, and the rest, at the table and ate, and talked about the year and the prospect of the flower business, about Uncle Hiroshi's pompon crop, and about Nephew Tatsuo's work and, also, his unfinished work in this world.

THINKING ABOUT THE SELECTION

Recalling

1. What instructions does Uncle Hiroshi give Tatsuo about growing pompons?
2. What problems does Tatsuo have with his pompons?
3. Why does Tatsuo's father suggest cutting Tatsuo's flowers down and burning them?
4. What does Hiroshi encourage Tatsuo to do with the money he got for his flowers?

Interpreting

5. Why do the older folks dislike Tatsuo's questions? How is Hiroshi different from them?
6. Why does Hiroshi give Tatsuo the pompons?
7. Why does Hiroshi ask Tatsuo, "Don't you realize we are all men with responsibilities"?
8. Compare and contrast Tatsuo at the beginning and the end of the story. Will he remember the lesson next spring? Explain.

Applying

9. How can someone be taught responsibility?

ANALYZING LITERATURE

Understanding Key Statements

Key statements are those that help you understand the theme of a story, especially a story whose theme is implied, or suggested. In "The Six Rows of Pompons," for example, Uncle Hiroshi says, "You cannot quit once you start." This key statement says that staying with a project to the end is part of being responsible. It points to the implied theme that responsibility can be taught lovingly through experience rather than through punishment.

Explain how the following key statements lead you to understand the implied theme.

1. "That will be a very bad thing to do. It will kill Nephew Tatsuo."
2. "One year is nothing. We will keep this six rows of pompons business up till he comes to his senses."

CRITICAL THINKING AND READING

Comparing and Contrasting Attitudes

When you look at similarities, you **compare.** When you look at differences, you **contrast.** Comparing and contrasting characters' attitudes can help you understand the implied theme. Tatsuo's father and Uncle Hiroshi both want to teach Tatsuo responsibility, but their attitudes differ on how to teach it.

Contrast their attitudes on the following, and explain what this suggests about theme.

1. Bugs from Tatsuo's bed start going over to the other beds.
2. Tatsuo earns money for his flowers.

UNDERSTANDING LANGUAGE

Understanding Meaning from Context

Many words have more than one meaning. You can tell from the **context,** or surrounding words and ideas, which meaning is correct.

Using the context in the sentences, choose the correct meaning of the italicized words.

1. "Some died by dryness, some by gophers or *moles* . . ."
   a. a dark-colored spot on the human skin
   b. a small, insect-eating mammal
2. "Let him spend and have a *taste* of his money."
   a. sense stimulated by the taste buds
   b. a slight experience of something

THINKING AND WRITING

Writing an Essay About Theme

Imagine that you are Tatsuo recalling this experience when you are thirteen. First freewrite for three minutes about your pompon-growing experience. Then use these ideas to draft a letter to Uncle Hiroshi describing what the experience taught you about responsibility. Proofread your letter and prepare a final draft.

GUIDE FOR READING

Thank You, M'am

Langston Hughes (1902–1967) was born in Joplin, Missouri. He attended Columbia University for a year and held a number of odd jobs before the publication of his first collection of poetry in 1926. Hughes published many volumes of poetry and fiction, as well as essays, histories, and dramas. He was awarded numerous prizes and grants and is often called the "Poet Laureate of Harlem," which is a section of New York City in northern Manhattan. "Thank You, M'am" is one of Hughes's many stories about city life for blacks.

Key to Theme: Character

The way that a character in a story changes and grows often can be a key to theme. Sometimes a character may grow through being helped by others. In "Thank You, M'am," Mrs. Jones helps Roger by treating him with respect and understanding. By thinking about what Mrs. Jones says to Roger, you can understand the implied theme of the story.

Look For

As you read "Thank You, M'am," look for the reasons the characters may have for behaving as they do. How does understanding the reasons behind their actions help you infer the theme?

Writing

In "Thank You, M'am," Mrs. Luella Bates Washington Jones changes a young boy's life. Freewrite about what makes a person memorable.

Vocabulary

Knowing the following words will help you as you read "Thank You, M'am."

willow-wild (wil' ō wild') *adj.*: Slender and pliant, like a reed blowing in the wind (p. 169)
kitchenette-furnished (kich ə net' fur' nisht) *n.*: Having a small, compact kitchen (p. 171)
presentable (pri zen' tə b'l) *adj.*: Suitable to be seen by others (p. 172)

Thank You, M'am

Langston Hughes

She was a large woman with a large purse that had everything in it but hammer and nails. It had a long strap and she carried it slung across her shoulder. It was about eleven o'clock at night, and she was walking alone, when a boy ran up behind her and tried to snatch her purse. The strap broke with the single tug the boy gave it from behind. But the boy's weight, and the weight of the purse combined caused him to lose his balance so, instead of taking off full blast as he had hoped, the boy fell on his back on the sidewalk, and his legs flew up. The large woman simply turned around and kicked him right square in his blue-jeaned sitter. Then she reached down, picked the boy up by his shirt front, and shook him until his teeth rattled.

After that the woman said, "Pick up my pocketbook, boy, and give it here."

She still held him. But she bent down enough to permit him to stoop and pick up her purse. Then she said, "Now ain't you ashamed of yourself?"

Firmly gripped by his shirt front, the boy said, "Yes'm."

The woman said, "What did you want to do it for?"

The boy said, "I didn't aim to."

She said, "You a lie!"

By that time two or three people passed, stopped, turned to look, and some stood watching.

"If I turn you loose, will you run?" asked the woman.

"Yes'm," said the boy.

"Then I won't turn you loose," said the woman. She did not release him.

"I'm very sorry, lady, I'm sorry," whispered the boy.

"Um-hum! And your face is dirty. I got a great mind to wash your face for you. Ain't you got nobody home to tell you to wash your face?"

"No'm," said the boy.

"Then it will get washed this evening," said the large woman starting up the street, dragging the frightened boy behind her.

He looked as if he were fourteen or fifteen, frail and willow-wild, in tennis shoes and blue jeans.

The woman said, "You ought to be my son. I would teach you right from wrong. Least I can do right now is to wash your face. Are you hungry?"

"No'm," said the being-dragged boy. "I just want you to turn me loose."

"Was I bothering *you* when I turned that corner?" asked the woman.

"No'm."

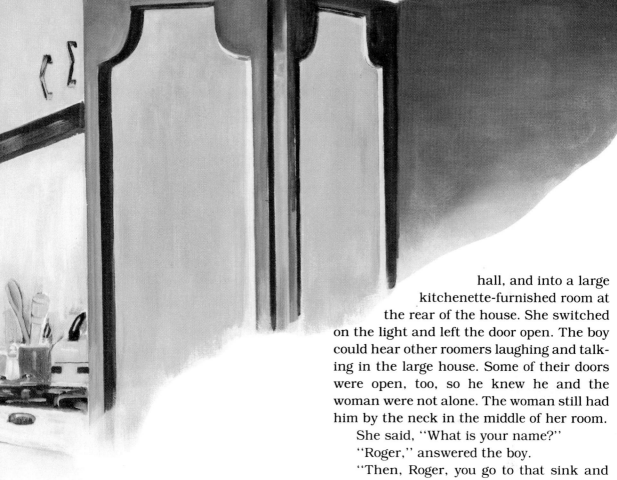

"But you put yourself in contact with *me,*" said the woman. "If you think that that contact is not going to last awhile, you got another thought coming. When I get through with you, sir, you are going to remember Mrs. Luella Bates Washington Jones."

Sweat popped out on the boy's face and he began to struggle. Mrs. Jones stopped, jerked him around in front of her, put a half nelson[1] about his neck, and continued to drag him up the street. When she got to her door, she dragged the boy inside, down a

hall, and into a large kitchenette-furnished room at the rear of the house. She switched on the light and left the door open. The boy could hear other roomers laughing and talking in the large house. Some of their doors were open, too, so he knew he and the woman were not alone. The woman still had him by the neck in the middle of her room.

She said, "What is your name?"

"Roger," answered the boy.

"Then, Roger, you go to that sink and wash your face," said the woman, whereupon she turned him loose—at last. Roger looked at the door—looked at the woman —looked at the door—*and went to the sink.*

"Let the water run until it gets warm," she said. "Here's a clean towel."

"You gonna take me to jail?" asked the boy, bending over the sink.

"Not with that face, I would not take you nowhere," said the woman. "Here I am trying to get home to cook me a bite to eat and you snatch my pocketbook! Maybe you ain't been to your supper either, late as it be. Have you?"

"There's nobody home at my house," said the boy.

---

1. half nelson: A wrestling hold using one arm.

"Then we'll eat," said the woman. "I believe you're hungry—or been hungry—to try to snatch my pocketbook."

"I wanted a pair of blue suede shoes," said the boy.

"Well, you didn't have to snatch *my* pocketbook to get some suede shoes," said Mrs. Luella Bates Washington Jones. "You could of asked me."

"M'am?"

The water dripping from his face, the boy looked at her. There was a long pause. A very long pause. After he had dried his face and not knowing what else to do dried it again, the boy turned around, wondering what next. The door was open. He could make a dash for it down the hall. He could run, run, run, run, *run!*

The woman was sitting on the day bed. After awhile she said, "I were young once and I wanted things I could not get."

There was another long pause. The boy's mouth opened. Then he frowned, but not knowing he frowned.

The woman said, "Um-hum! You thought I was going to say *but*, didn't you? You thought I was going to say, *but I didn't snatch people's pocketbooks.* Well, I wasn't going to say that." Pause. Silence. "I have done things, too, which I would not tell you, son—neither tell God, if He didn't already know. So you set down while I fix us something to eat. You might run that comb through your hair so you will look presentable."

In another corner of the room behind a screen was a gas plate and an icebox. Mrs. Jones got up and went behind the screen. The woman did not watch the boy to see if he was going to run now, nor did she watch her purse which she left behind her on the day bed. But the boy took care to sit on the far side of the room where he thought she could easily see him out of the corner of her eye, if she wanted to. He did not trust the woman *not* to trust him. And he did not want to be mistrusted now.

"Do you need somebody to go to the store," asked the boy, "maybe to get some milk or something?"

"Don't believe I do," said the woman, "unless you just want sweet milk yourself. I was going to make cocoa out of this canned milk I got here."

"That will be fine," said the boy.

She heated some lima beans and ham she had in the icebox, made the cocoa, and set the table. The woman did not ask the boy anything about where he lived, or his folks, or anything else that would embarrass him. Instead, as they ate, she told him about her job in a hotel beauty shop that stayed open late, what the work was like, and how all kinds of women came in and out, blondes, redheads, and brunettes. Then she cut him a half of her ten-cent cake.

"Eat some more, son," she said.

When they were finished eating she got up and said, "Now, here, take this ten dollars and buy yourself some blue suede shoes. And next time, do not make the mistake of latching onto *my* pocketbook *nor nobody else's*—because shoes come by devilish like that will burn your feet. I got to get my rest now. But I wish you would behave yourself, son, from here on in."

She led him down the hall to the front door and opened it. "Goodnight! Behave yourself, boy!" she said, looking out into the street.

The boy wanted to say something else other than, "Thank you, m'am," to Mrs. Luella Bates Washington Jones, but he couldn't do so as he turned at the barren stoop and looked back at the large woman in the door. He barely managed to say, "Thank you," before she shut the door. And he never saw her again.

THINKING ABOUT THE SELECTION

Recalling

1. What does Mrs. Jones do when Roger tries to steal her purse?
2. What does she say she would teach Roger if he were her son?
3. What reason does Roger give for trying to steal her purse? How does Mrs. Jones respond to this reason?
4. Why does Mrs. Jones give Roger ten dollars?

Interpreting

5. Why doesn't Roger run away from Mrs. Jones's apartment at the first opportunity?
6. What does the following tell about Roger: "He did not trust the woman *not* to trust him. And he did not want to be mistrusted now."
7. Early in the story, Mrs. Jones says, "When I get through with you, sir, you are going to remember Mrs. Luella Bates Washington Jones." How do her words turn out to be true?
8. At the end of the story, why does Roger want to say more than just "Thank you, m'am"?

Applying

9. Can you change people's behavior through kindness and understanding? Explain.

ANALYZING LITERATURE

Using Character to Understand Theme

The way that a character changes is often a clue to the theme of a story. In this story, Mrs. Jones's treatment of Roger brings about a change in him that points to the theme.

1. How does Mrs. Jones show that she respects Roger? In what ways does she treat him with understanding and kindness?
2. Explain how you think Mrs. Jones's treatment makes Roger feel about himself.
3. How does Roger change?
4. What do you think is the theme of this story?

CRITICAL THINKING AND READING

Identifying Generalizations

A **generalization** is a conclusion you draw from similarities among a large number of cases. A **hasty generalization** is a conclusion that is based on too few cases. For example, if the pizza is good the first time you eat at a new pizza parlor, you might conclude that the pizza there is *always* good. This would be a hasty generalization, because the number of cases is too small.

1. What generalization had Roger made about older women walking alone at night?
2. What did Roger learn about applying this generalization to this particular case?

SPEAKING AND LISTENING

Presenting Readers' Theater

In Readers' Theater, two or more speakers give a dramatic reading of a literature selection. The words and the way they are spoken are more important than the gestures used.

With classmates, prepare and present a Readers' Theater version of "Thank You, M'am." Decide how the characters will speak or present themselves. Then write a script and practice reading, putting emphasis on oral interpretation of the characters and their actions. Finally, present your Readers' Theater to your classmates.

THINKING AND WRITING

Writing About a Character

Imagine that you are Roger twenty years after the story. You decide to write a letter to Mrs. Jones describing why the event in the story was so important to you. In your letter, include a statement about how the event helped shape your future decisions and actions. Revise your letter, making sure that your reasoning is clear. Proofread your letter and prepare a final draft.

GUIDE FOR READING

The Gift-Giving

Joan Aiken (1924–   ), born in the English village of Rye, Sussex, is known for her tales of fantasy and suspense. As a child, she often made up stories to amuse herself and her brother on long walks. But she reached a much larger audience at age seventeen, when her fantasy story "But Today Is Tuesday" was read on a children's radio program. Joan Aiken believes stories should never pretend that life is not tough, but virtue should triumph in the end.

Significant Actions

A **significant action** is one that stands out from the other actions and events in a story as being particularly important. A significant action may not be extraordinary in itself, but it can point to the story's theme, or central idea. Recognizing significant actions can lead you to the theme of the story.

Look For

As you read "The Gift-Giving," look for actions that seem important. What do they suggest about the story's theme?

Writing

Think about what you would choose as a gift for a friend. Freewrite for five minutes about this meaningful gift.

Vocabulary

Knowing the following words will help you as you read "The Gift-Giving."

hummock (hum′ ək) n.: A mound or small hill (p. 176)
ingots (iŋ′ gətz) n.: Metal cast into bars for storage or transportation (p. 177)
crevasse (kri vas′) n.: A deep, narrow opening from a split or a crack, as in a cliff (p. 178)
gentians (jen′ chənz) n.: Herbs with blue flowers (p. 178)

expound (ik spound′) v.: To explain in careful detail (p. 178)
wizened (wiz′ ənd) adj.: Shrunken, and wrinkled with age (p. 179)
keystone (kē′ stōn) n.: A wedge-shaped piece at the top of an arch that locks into place other pieces (p. 180)
muslin (muz′ lin) n.: Plain-woven, cotton fabric (p. 182)

The Gift-Giving

Joan Aiken

The weeks leading up to Christmas were always full of excitement, and tremendous anxiety too, as the family waited in suspense for the Uncles, who had set off in the spring of the year, to return from their summer's traveling and trading: Uncle Emer, Uncle Acraud, Uncle Gonfil, and Uncle Mark. They always started off together, down the steep mountainside, but then, at the bottom, they took different routes along the deep narrow valley, Uncle Mark and Uncle Acraud riding eastward, toward the great plains, while Uncle Emer and Uncle Gonfil turned west, toward the towns and rivers and the western sea.

Then, before they were clear of the mountains, they would separate once more, Uncle Acraud turning south, Uncle Emer taking his course northward, so that, the children occasionally thought, their family was scattered over the whole world, netted out like a spider's web.

Spring and summer would go by in the usual occupations, digging and sowing the steep hillside garden beds, fishing, hunting for hares, picking wild strawberries, making hay. Then, toward St. Drimma's Day,[1] when the winds began to blow and the snow crept down, lower and lower, from the high peaks, Grandmother would begin to grow restless.

Silent and calm all summer long she sat in her rocking chair on the wide wooden porch, wrapped in a patchwork comforter, with her blind eyes turned eastward toward the lands where Mark, her dearest and first-born, had gone. But when the winds of Michaelmas[2] began to blow, and the wolves grew bolder, and the children dragged in sacks of logs day after day, and the cattle were brought down to the stable under the house, then Grandmother grew agitated indeed.

When Sammle, the eldest granddaughter, brought her hot milk, she would grip the girl's slender brown wrist and demand: "Tell me, child, how many days now to St. Froida's Day?" (which was the first of December).

"Eighteen, Grandmother," Sammle would answer, stooping to kiss the wrinkled cheek.

"So many, still? So many till we may hope to see them?"

"Don't worry, Granny, the Uncles are *certain* to return safely. Perhaps they will be early this year. Perhaps we may see them before the feast of St. Melin" (which was December the fourteenth).

And then, sure enough, sometime during the middle weeks of December, their

---

tall pine
over a high
cliff, would catch
the flash of a baggage-
mule's brass browmedal,
or the sun glancing on the barrel
of a carbine, and would come joyfully
dashing back to report. "Granny! Granny!
The Uncles are almost here!"

Then the whole household, the whole
village, would be filled with as much turmoil
as that of a kingdom of ants when the spade
breaks open their hummock. Wives would
build the fires higher, and fetch out the best
linen, wine, dried meat, pickled eggs; set
dough to rising, mix cakes of honey and

great carts would
come jingling and trampling along
the winding valleys. Young Mark (son of
Uncle Emer), from his watchpoint up a

oats, bring up stone jars of preserved strawberries from the cellars; and the children, with the servants and half the village, would go racing down the perilous zigzag track to meet the cavalcade at the bottom.

The track was far too steep for the heavy carts, which would be dismissed and the carters paid off to go about their business. Then with laughter and shouting, amid a million questions from the children, the loads would be divided and carried up the mountainside on muleback, or on human shoulders. Sometimes the Uncles came home at night, through falling snow, by the smoky light of torches; but the children and the household always knew of their arrival beforehand, and were always there to meet them.

"Did you bring Granny's Chinese shawl, Uncle Mark? Uncle Emer, have you the enameled box for her snuff that Aunt Grippa begged you to get? Uncle Acraud, did you find the glass candlesticks? Uncle Gonfil, did you bring the books?"

"Yes, yes, keep calm, don't deafen us! Poor tired travelers that we are, leave us in peace to climb this devilish hill! Everything is there, set your minds at rest—the shawl, the box, the books—besides a few other odds and ends, pins and needles and fruit and a bottle or two of wine, and

a few trifles for the village. Now, just give us a few minutes to get our breath, will you, kindly—" as the children danced round them, helping each other with the smaller bundles, never ceasing to pour out questions: "Did you see the Grand Cham? The Akond of Swat? The Fon of Bikom? The Seljuk of Rum? Did you go to Cathay? To Muskovy? To Dalai?[3] Did you travel by ship, by camel, by llama, by elephant?"

And, at the top of the hill, Grandmother would be waiting for them, out on her roofed porch, no matter how wild the weather or how late the time, seated in majesty with her furs and patchwork quilt around her, while the Aunts ran to and fro with hot stones to place under her feet. And the Uncles always embraced her first, very fondly and respectfully, before turning to hug their wives and sisters-in-law.

Then the goods they had brought would be distributed through the village—the scissors, tools, medicines, plants, bales of cloth, ingots of metal, cordials, firearms, and musical instruments; after that there would be a great feast.

Not until Christmas morning did Grandmother and the children receive the special gifts that had been brought for them by the Uncles; and this giving always took the same ceremonial form.

Uncle Mark stood behind Grandmother's chair, playing on a small pipe that he had acquired somewhere during his travels; it was made from hard black polished wood, with silver stops, and it had a mouthpiece made of amber. Uncle Mark invariably[4] played the same tune on it at these times, very softly. It was a tune that he had heard for the first time, he said, when he was

---

3. Grand Cham . . . Dalai: Throughout this story, Aiken interweaves imaginary and real place names.
4. invariably (in ver′ ē ə blē) *adv.*: Without change.

much younger, once when he had narrowly escaped falling into a crevasse on the hillside, and a voice had spoken to him, as it seemed, out of the mountain itself, bidding him watch where he set his feet and have a care, for the family depended on him. It was a gentle, thoughtful tune, which reminded Sandri, the middle granddaughter, of springtime sounds, warm wind, water from melted snow dripping off the gabled roofs, birds trying out their mating calls.

While Uncle Mark played on his pipe, Uncle Emer would hand each gift to Grandmother. And she—here was the strange thing—she, who was stone-blind all the year long, could not see her own hand in front of her face, she would take the object in her fingers and instantly identify it. "A mother-of-pearl comb, with silver studs, for Tassy . . . it comes from Babylon. A silk shawl, blue and rose, from Hind, for Argilla. A wooden game, with ivory pegs, for young Emer, from Damascus. A gold brooch, from Hangku, for Grippa. A book of rhymes, from Paris, for Sammle, bound in a scarlet leather cover."

By stroking each gift with her old, blotched, clawlike fingers, frail as quills, Grandmother, who lived all the year round in darkness, could discover not only what the thing was and where it came from, but also the color of it, and that in the most precise and particular manner, correct to a shade. "It is a jacket of stitched and pleated cotton, printed over with leaves and flowers; it comes from the island of Haranati, in the eastern ocean; the colors are leaf-brown and gold and a dark, dark blue, darker than mountain gentians—" for Grandmother had not always been blind; when she was a young girl she had been able to see as well as anybody else.

"And this is for you, Mother, from your son Mark," Uncle Emer would say, handing her a tissue-wrapped bundle, and she would exclaim, "Ah, how beautiful! A coat of tribute silk, of the very palest green, so that the color shows only in the folds, like shadows on snow; the buttons and the button-toggles are of worked silk, lavender-gray, like pearl, and the stiff collar is embroidered with white roses."

"Put it on, Mother!" her sons and daughters-in-law would urge her, and the children, dancing 'round her chair, clutching their own treasures, would chorus, "Yes, put it on, put it on! Ah, you look like a queen, Granny, in that beautiful coat! The highest queen in the world! The queen of the mountain!"

Those months after Christmas were Grandmother's happiest time. Secure, thankful, with her sons safe at home, she would sit in the warm fireside corner of the big wooden family room. The wind might shriek, the snow gather higher and higher out of doors, but that did not concern her, for her family, and all the village, were well supplied with flour, oil, firewood, meat, herbs, and roots. The children had their books and toys, they learned lessons with the old priest, or made looms and spinning wheels, carved stools and chairs and chests with the tools their uncles had brought them. The Uncles rested and told tales of their travels; Uncle Mark played his pipe for hours together, Uncle Acraud drew pictures in charcoal of the places he had seen, and Granny, laying her hand on the paper covered with lines, would expound while Uncle Mark played: "A huge range of mountains, like wrinkled brown lines across the horizon; a wide plain of sand, silvery blond in color, with patches of pale, pale blue; I think it is not water but air the color of water. Here are strange lines across the sand where men once plowed it, long, long ago; and a great patch of crystal green, with what seems like a road crossing it. Now here is a smaller region of plum-pink, bordered by an area of rusty red. I think these are the colors of the earth in these territories; it is very high up, dry from height, and the soil glittering with little particles of metal."

"You have described it better than I could myself!" Uncle Acraud would exclaim, while the children, breathless with wonder and curiosity, sat cross-legged 'round her chair. And she would answer, "Yes, but I cannot see it at all, Acraud, unless your eyes have seen it first, and I cannot see it without Mark's music to help me."

"How does Grandmother *do* it?" the children would demand of their mothers, and Argilla, or Grippa, or Tassy would answer, "Nobody knows. It is Grandmother's gift. She alone can do it."

The people of the village might come in, whenever they chose, and on many evenings thirty or forty would be there, silently listening, and when Grandmother retired to bed, which she did early for the seeing made her weary, the audience would turn to one another with deep sighs, and murmur, "The world is indeed a wide place."

But with the first signs of spring the Uncles would become restless again, and begin looking over their equipment, discussing maps and routes, mending saddlebags and boots, gazing up at the high peaks for signs that the snow was in retreat.

Then Granny would grow very silent. She never asked them to stay longer, she never disputed their going, but her face seemed to shrivel, she grew smaller, wizened and huddled inside her quilted patchwork.

And on St. Petrag's Day, when the Uncles set off, when the farewells were said and they clattered off down the mountain through the melting snow and the trees with pink luminous buds, Grandmother would fall into a silence that lasted, sometimes, for as much as five or six weeks; all day she would sit with her face turned to the east, wordless, motionless, and would drink her milk and go to her bed-place at night still silent and dejected; it took the warm sun and sweet wild hyacinths of May to raise her spirits.

Then, by degrees, she would grow animated, and begin to say, "Only six months, now, till they come back."

But young Mark observed to his cousin Sammle, "It takes longer, every year, for Grandmother to grow accustomed."

And Sammle said, shivering though it was warm May weather, "Perhaps one year, when they come back, she will not be here. She is becoming so tiny and thin; you can see right through her hands, as if they were leaves." And Sammle held up her own thin brown young hand against the sunlight to see the blood glow under the translucent skin.

"I don't know how they would bear it," said Mark thoughtfully, "if when they came back we had to tell them that she had died."

But that was not what happened.

One December the Uncles arrived much later than usual. They did not climb the mountain until St. Misham's Day, and when they reached the house it was in silence. There was none of the usual joyful commotion.

Grandmother knew instantly that there was something wrong. "Where is my son Mark?" she demanded. "Why do I not hear him among you?" And Uncle Acraud had to tell her: "Mother, he is dead. Your son Mark will not come home, ever again."

"How do you *know*? How can you be *sure*? You were not there when he died?"

"I waited and waited at our meeting place, and a messenger came to tell me. His caravan had been attacked by wild tribesmen, riding north from the Lark Mountains. Mark was killed, and all his people. Only this one man escaped and came to bring me the story."

"But how can you be *sure?* How do you know he told the *truth?*"

"He brought Mark's ring."

Emer put it into her hand. As she turned it about in her thin fingers, a long moan went through her.

"Yes, he is dead. My son Mark is dead."

"The man gave me this little box," Acraud said, "which Mark was bringing for you."

Emer put it into her hand, opening the box for her. Inside lay an ivory fan. On it, when it was spread out, you could see a bird, with eyes made of sapphires, flying across a valley, but Grandmother held it listlessly, as if her hands were numb.

"What is it?" she said. "I do not know what it is. Help me to bed, Argilla. I do not know what it is. I do not wish to know. My son Mark is dead."

Her grief infected the whole village. It was as if the keystone of an arch had been knocked out; there was nothing to hold the people together.

That year spring came early, and the three remaining Uncles, melancholy and restless, were glad to leave on their travels. Grandmother hardly noticed their going.

Sammle said to Mark: "You are clever with your hands. Could you not make a pipe—like the one my father had?"

"*I?*" he said. "Make a pipe? Like Uncle Mark's pipe? Why? What would be the point of doing so?"

"Perhaps you might learn to play on it. As he did."

"*I?* Play on a pipe?"

"I think you could," she said. "I have heard you whistle tunes of your own."

"But where would I find the right kind of wood?"

"There is a chest, in which Uncle Gonfil once brought books and music from Leiden. I think it is the same kind of wood. I think you could make a pipe from it."

"But how can I remember the shape?"

"I will make a drawing," Sammle said, and she drew with a stick of charcoal on the whitewashed wall of the cowshed. As soon as Mark looked at her drawing he began to contradict.

"No! I remember now. It was not like that. The stops came here—and the mouthpiece was like this."

Now the other children flocked 'round to help and advise.

"The stops were farther apart," said Creusie. "And there were more of them and they were bigger."

"The pipe was longer than that," said

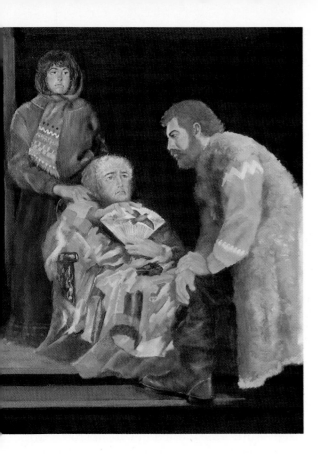

The second pipe was much better than the first. By September, Mark was able to play a few notes on it; by October he was playing simple tunes made up out of his head.

"But," he said, "if I am to play so that Grandmother can see with her fingers—if I am to do *that*—I must remember your father's special tune. Can *you* remember it, Sammle?"

She thought and thought. "Sometimes," she said, "it seems as if it is just beyond the edge of my hearing—as if somebody were playing it, far, far away, in the woods. Oh, if only I could stretch my hearing a little farther!"

"Oh, Sammle! Try!"

For days and days she sat silent or wandered in the woods, frowning, knotting her forehead, willing her ears to hear the tune again; and the women of the household said, "That girl is not doing her fair share of the task."

They scolded her and set her to spin, weave, milk the goats, throw grain to the hens. But all the while she continued silent, listening, listening, to a sound she could not hear. At night, in her dreams, she sometimes thought she could hear the tune, and she would wake with tears on her cheeks, wordlessly calling her father to come back and play his music to her, so that she could remember it.

In September the autumn winds blew cold and fierce; by October snow was piled around the walls and up to the windowsills. On St. Felin's Day the three Uncles returned, but sadly and silently, without the former festivities; although, as usual, they brought many bales and boxes of gifts and merchandise. The children went down, as usual, to help carry the bundles up the mountain. The joy had gone out of this tradition, though, and they toiled silently up the track with their loads.

Sandri. "I have held it. It was as long as my arm."

"How will you ever make the stops?" said young Emer.

"You can have my silver bracelets that Father gave me," said Sammle.

"I'll ask Finn the smith to help me," said Mark.

Once Mark had got the notion of making a pipe into his head, he was eager to begin. But it took him several weeks of difficult carving; the black wood of the chest proved hard as iron. And when the pipe was made, and the stops fitted, it would not play; try as he would, not a note could he fetch out of it.

Mark was dogged, though, once he had set himself to a task; he took another piece of the black chest and began again. Only Sammle stayed to help him now; the other children had lost hope, or interest, and gone back to their summer occupations.

It was a wild, windy evening; the sun set in fire, the wind moaned among the fir trees, and gusts of sleet every now and then dashed in their faces.

"Take care, children!" called Uncle Emer as they skirted along the side of a deep gully, and his words were caught by an echo and flung back and forth between the rocky walls: "Take care—care—care—care— care . . ."

"Oh!" cried Sammle, stopping precipitately and clutching the bag that she was carrying. "I have it! I can remember it! *Now* I know how it went!"

And, as they stumbled on up the snowy hillside, she hummed the melody to her cousin Mark, who was just ahead of her.

"Yes, that is it, yes!" he said. "Or, no, wait a minute, that is not *quite* right—but it is close, it is very nearly the way it went. Only the notes were a little faster, and there were more of them—they went up, not down—before the ending tied them in a knot—"

"No, no, they went down at the end, I am almost sure—"

Arguing, interrupting each other, disputing, agreeing, they dropped their bundles in the family room and ran away to the cowhouse where Mark kept his pipe hidden.

For three days they discussed and argued and tried a hundred different versions; they were so occupied that they hardly took the trouble to eat. But at last, by Christmas morning, they had reached agreement.

"I *think* it is right," said Sammle. "And if it is not, I do not believe there is anything more that we can do about it."

"Perhaps it will not work in any case," said Mark sadly. He was tired out with arguing and practicing.

Sammle was equally tired, but she said, "Oh, it *must* work. Oh, let it work! Please let it work! For otherwise I don't think I can bear the sadness. Go now, Mark, quietly and quickly, go and stand behind Granny's chair."

The family had gathered, according to Christmas habit, around Grandmother's rocking chair, but the faces of the Uncles were glum and reluctant, their wives dejected and hopeless. Only the children showed eagerness, as the cloth-wrapped bundles were brought and laid at Grandmother's feet.

She herself looked wholly dispirited and cast down. When Uncle Emer handed her a slender, soft package, she received it apathetically,[5] almost with dislike, as if she would prefer not to be bothered by this tiresome gift ceremony.

Then Mark, who had slipped through the crowd without being noticed, began to play on his pipe just behind Grandmother's chair.

The Uncles looked angry and scandalized; Aunt Tassy cried out in horror: "Oh, Mark, wicked boy, how *dare* you?" but Grandmother lifted her head, more alertly than she had done for months past, and began to listen.

Mark played on. His mouth was quivering so badly that it was hard to grip the amber mouthpiece, but he played with all the breath that was in him. Meanwhile, Sammle, kneeling by her grandmother, held, with her own warm young hands, the old, brittle ones against the fabric of the gift. And, as she did so, she began to feel what Grandmother felt.

Grandmother said softly and distinctly: "It is a muslin shawl, embroidered in gold thread, from Lebanon. It is colored a soft brick red, with pale roses of sunset pink, and thorns of silver-green. It is for Sammle . . ."

---

5. apathetically (ap′ ə thet′ ik lē), *adv.*: Indifferently.

THINKING ABOUT THE SELECTION

Recalling

1. Describe the gift-giving ceremony that enables Grandmother to see.
2. When does Grandmother lose this ability?
3. What do Sammle and Mark do that enables Grandmother to see again?

Interpreting

4. Grandmother is the central figure that holds the family together. Why is it important for her to resume this role?
5. At the end of the story, "Sammle, kneeling by her grandmother, held, with her own warm young hands, the old brittle ones against the fabric of the gift. And, as she did so, she began to feel what Grandmother felt." What does this suggest about Sammle?
6. Describe what each of the following characters sees in "The Gift-Giving": Grandmother, the Uncles, Sammle.
7. What are two possible meanings of the title "The Gift-Giving"?

Applying

8. Some families pass down traditions that enrich the family, such as a special ceremony or an annual family reunion. What are some other traditions that are passed down in families?

ANALYZING LITERATURE

Understanding Significant Actions

A **significant action** is any action or event in a story that gives you a clue to the theme. A significant action stands out from the others as more important.

1. What ceremony seems significant in "The Gift-Giving"?
2. What are the parts of this ceremony?

3. How often does the ceremony occur?
4. What do you think is the theme of "The Gift-Giving"?

CRITICAL THINKING AND READING

Summarizing

A **summary** is a brief report covering the main points of a story. When you summarize, you must distinguish between the major and minor details. For example, that the Uncles returned home once a year near Christmas is a major detail; that they carried their bundles on mules or on their backs is a minor detail. All of the major details should be in a summary.

1. Which of the following details would you include in a summary of "The Gift-Giving"?
   a. The uncles bring gifts for the family.
   b. During the gift-giving ceremony, Grandmother, who is blind, magically can see.
   c. Uncle Mark first hears the pipe tune when he escapes falling into a crevasse.
   d. Uncle Mark dies.
   e. Uncle Acraud brings Uncle Mark's ring to prove that he had died.
   f. Grandmother loses her ability to see.
   g. Sammle and Mark make a new pipe and song for Grandmother, enabling her to see again.
2. Using the details you selected, write a summary of "The Gift-Giving."

THINKING AND WRITING

Writing About Theme

Select another story that you have read. State the themes of "The Gift-Giving" and the story you chose. List the similarities and differences between them. Then use these ideas to write an essay comparing and contrasting the themes of the two stories. Revise your essay. Proofread it, checking carefully for correct spelling and punctuation.

GUIDE FOR READING

The Man Without a Country

Edward Everett Hale (1822–1909), the grandnephew of American Revolutionary War hero Nathan Hale, began writing stories when he was a boy. He later published his own small newspaper. After graduating from Harvard University, Hale became a Unitarian minister and a journalist, but continued writing short stories, essays, and novels. His well-known story "The Man Without a Country" seemed so realistic that many people who read it in *The Atlantic Monthly* in 1863 believed it was true.

Symbols

A **symbol** is an object, an action, or an idea that stands for something other than itself. For example, a lion is an animal that lives in Africa and Asia, but it is also a symbol of courage and strength. In a story, a writer may use symbols that are familiar to most readers or symbols that occur only in that story. Recognizing and understanding symbols can help you understand a story's theme, or central idea.

Look For

As you read "The Man Without a Country," look for objects, actions, or ideas that stand for something other than themselves. How do they point to the theme?

Writing

In "The Man Without a Country" Philip Nolan claims he never wants to hear of home again. There have been many sayings about the idea of home, such as "Home is where the heart is." Freewrite for three minutes about what *home* means to you. Write down any thoughts, feelings, words, or images that you associate with *home*.

Vocabulary

Knowing the following words will help you as you read "The Man Without a Country."

obscure (äb skyoor') *adj.*: Hidden; not obvious (p. 185)
availed (ə vāld') *v.*: Made use of (p. 185)
stilted (stil' təd) *adj.*: Unnatural; very formal (p. 185)
swagger (swag' ər) *n.*: Arro-gance or boastfulness (p. 187)
intercourse (int' ər kôrs) *n.*: Communication between people (p. 188)
blunders (blun' dərz) *n.*: Foolish or stupid mistakes (p. 191)

The Man Without a Country

Edward Everett Hale

I suppose that very few casual readers of the *New York Herald* of August 13, 1863, observed, in an obscure corner, among the "Deaths," the announcement:

NOLAN. Died, on board U.S. Corvette *Levant*, Lat. 2° 11′ S., Long. 131° W., on the 11th of May, PHILIP NOLAN.

Hundreds of readers would have paused at the announcement had it read thus: "Died, May 11, THE MAN WITHOUT A COUNTRY." For it was as "The Man Without a Country" that poor Philip Nolan had generally been known by the officers who had him in charge during some fifty years, as, indeed, by all the men who sailed under them.

There can now be no possible harm in telling this poor creature's story. Reason enough there has been till now for very strict secrecy, the secrecy of honor itself, among the gentlemen of the Navy who have had Nolan in charge. And certainly it speaks well for the profession and the personal honor of its members that to the press this man's story has been wholly unknown —and, I think, to the country at large also. This I do know, that no naval officer has mentioned Nolan in his report of a cruise.

But there is no need for secrecy any longer. Now the poor creature is dead, it seems to me worthwhile to tell a little of his story, by way of showing young Americans of today what it is to be "A Man Without a Country."

Philip Nolan was as fine a young officer as there was in the "Legion of the West," as the Western division of our army was then called. When Aaron Burr[1] made his first dashing expedition down to New Orleans in 1805, he met this gay, dashing, bright young fellow. Burr marked[2] him, talked to him, walked with him, took him a day or two's voyage in his flatboat,[3] and, in short, fascinated him. For the next year, barrack life was very tame to poor Nolan. He occasionally availed himself of the permission the great man had given him to write to him. Long, stilted letters the poor boy wrote and rewrote and copied. But never a line did he have in reply. The other boys in the garrison[4] sneered at him, because he lost the fun which they found in shooting or rowing while he was working away on these grand letters to his grand friend. But before long the young fellow had his revenge. For this

---

1. Aaron Burr: American political leader (1756–1836). Burr was U.S. Vice-President from 1801 to 1805. He was believed to have plotted to build an empire in the Southwest.
2. marked *v.*: Here, paid attention to.
3. flatboat *n.*: Boat with a flat bottom.
4. garrison (gar′ ə s'n) *n.*: Military post or station.

OFFICER OF THE WATCH ON THE HORSEBLOCK
Heck's Iconographic Encyclopedia, 1851
The New York Public Library

time His Excellency, the Honorable Aaron Burr, appeared again under a very different aspect. There were rumors that he had an army behind him and an empire before him. At that time the youngsters all envied him. Burr had not been talking twenty minutes with the commander before he asked him to send for Lieutenant Nolan. Then, after a little talk, he asked Nolan if he could show him something of the great river and the plans for the new post. He asked Nolan to take him out in his skiff to show him a canebrake[5] or a cottonwood tree, as he said —really to win him over; and by the time the sail was over, Nolan was enlisted body and soul. From that time, though he did not yet know it, he lived as a man without a country.

What Burr meant to do I know no more than you. It is none of our business just now. Only, when the grand catastrophe came —Burr's great treason trial at Richmond —some of the lesser fry at Fort Adams[6] got up a string of court-martials on the officers there. One and another of the colonels and majors were tried, and, to fill out the list, little Nolan, against whom there was evidence enough that he was sick of the service, had been willing to be false to it, and would have obeyed any order to march anywhere had the order been signed "By command of His Exc. A. Burr." The courts dragged on. The big flies[7] escaped—rightly, for all I know. Nolan was proved guilty enough, yet you and I would never have heard of him but that, when the president

---

5. canebrake (kān′ brāk′) *n.*: A dense area of cane plants.

6. Fort Adams: The fort at which Nolan was stationed.
7. big flies: Burr and the other important men who may have been involved in his scheme.

of the court asked him at the close whether he wished to say anything to show that he had always been faithful to the United States, he cried out, in a fit of frenzy:

"Damn the United States! I wish I may never hear of the United States again!"

I suppose he did not know how the words shocked old Colonel Morgan, who was holding the court. Half the officers who sat in it had served through the Revolution, and their lives had been risked for the very idea which he cursed in his madness. He, on his part, had grown up in the West of those days. He had been educated on a plantation where the finest company was a Spanish officer or a French merchant from Orleans. His education had been perfected in commercial expeditions to Vera Cruz, and I think he told me his father once hired an Englishman to be a private tutor for a winter on the plantation. He had spent half his youth with an older brother, hunting horses in Texas; and to him "United States" was scarcely a reality. I do not excuse Nolan; I only explain to the reader why he cursed his country and wished he might never hear her name again.

From that moment, September 23, 1807, till the day he died, May 11, 1863, he never heard her name again. For that half-century and more he was a man without a country.

Old Morgan, as I said, was terribly shocked. If Nolan had compared George Washington to Benedict Arnold, or had cried, "God save King George," Morgan would not have felt worse. He called the court into his private room, and returned in fifteen minutes, with a face like a sheet, to say: "Prisoner, hear the sentence of the Court! The Court decides, subject to the approval of the President, that you never hear the name of the United States again."

Nolan laughed. But nobody else laughed. Old Morgan was too solemn, and the whole room was hushed dead as night for a minute. Even Nolan lost his swagger in a moment. Then Morgan added: "Mr. Marshal, take the prisoner to Orleans in an armed boat, and deliver him to the naval commander there."

The marshal gave his orders and the prisoner was taken out of court.

"Mr. Marshal," continued old Morgan, "see that no one mentions the United States to the prisoner. Mr. Marshal, make my repects to Lieutenant Mitchell at Orleans, and request him to order that no one shall mention the United States to the prisoner while he is on board ship. You will receive your written orders from the officer on duty here this evening. The court is adjourned."

Before the *Nautilus*[8] got round from New Orleans to the Northern Atlantic coast with the prisoner on board, the sentence had been approved, and he was a man without a country.

The plan then adopted was substantially the same which was necessarily followed ever after. The Secretary of the Navy was requested to put Nolan on board a government vessel bound on a long cruise, and to direct that he should be only so far confined there as to make it certain that he never saw or heard of the country. We had few long cruises then, and I do not know certainly what his first cruise was. But the commander to whom he was entrusted regulated the etiquette and the precautions of the affair, and according to his scheme they were carried out till Nolan died.

When I was second officer of the *Intrepid,* some thirty years after, I saw the original paper of instructions. I have been sorry ever since that I did not copy the whole of it. It ran, however, much in this way:

---

8. Nautilus: The naval ship to which Nolan was assigned.

Washington (with a date, which must have been late in 1807).

Sir:

You will receive from Lieutenant Neale the person of Philip Nolan, late a lieutenant in the United States Army.

This person on his trial by court-martial expressed, with an oath, the wish that he might "never hear of the United States again."

The court sentenced him to have his wish fulfilled.

For the present, the execution of the order is entrusted by the President to this department.

You will take the prisoner on board your ship, and keep him there with such precautions as shall prevent his escape.

You will provide him with such quarters, rations, and clothing as would be proper for an officer of his late rank, if he were a passenger on your vessel on the business of his government.

The gentlemen on board will make any arrangements agreeable to themselves regarding his society. He is to be exposed to no indignity of any kind, nor is he ever unnecessarily to be reminded that he is a prisoner.

But under no circumstances is he ever to hear of his country or to see any information regarding it; and you will especially caution all the officers under your command to take care that this rule, in which his punishment is involved, shall not be broken.

It is the intention of the government that he shall never again see the country which he has disowned. Before the end of your cruise you will receive orders which will give effect to this intention.

Respectfully yours,

W. SOUTHARD,
for the Secretary of the Navy.

The rule adopted on board the ships on which I have met "the man without a country" was, I think, transmitted from the beginning. No mess[9] liked to have him permanently, because his presence cut off all talk of home or of the prospect of return, of politics or letters, of peace or of war—cut off more than half the talk men liked to have at sea. But it was always thought too hard that he should never meet the rest of us, except to touch hats, and we finally sank into one system. He was not permitted to talk with the men, unless an officer was by. With officers he had unrestrained intercourse, as far as they and he chose. But he grew shy, though he had favorites: I was one. Then the captain always asked him to dinner on Monday. Every mess in succession took up the invitation in its turn. According to the size of the ship, you had him at your mess more or less often at dinner. His breakfast he ate in his own stateroom. Whatever else he ate or drank, he ate or drank alone. Sometimes, when the marines or sailors had any special jollification,[10] they were permitted to invite "Plain Buttons," as they called him. Then Nolan was sent with some officer, and the men were forbidden to speak of home while he was there. I believe the theory was that the sight of his punishment did them good. They called him "Plain But-

---

9. mess *n.*: Here, a group of people who routinely have their meals together.
10. jollification (jäl′ ə fi kā′ shən) *n.*: Merry-making.

tons," because, while he always chose to wear a regulation army uniform, he was not permitted to wear the army button, for the reason that it bore either the initials or the insignia of the country he had disowned.

I remember, soon after I joined the Navy, I was on shore with some of the older officers from our ship and some of the gentlemen fell to talking about Nolan. Someone told of the system which was adopted from the first about his books and other reading. As he was almost never permitted to go on shore, even though the vessel lay in port for months, his time at the best hung heavy. Everybody was permitted to lend him books, if they were not published in America and made no allusion to it. These were common enough in the old days. He had almost all the foreign papers that came into the ship, sooner or later; only somebody must go over them first, and cut out any advertisement or stray paragraph that referred to America. This was a little cruel sometimes, when the back of what was cut out might be innocent. Right in the midst of one of Napoleon's battles poor Nolan would find a great hole, because on the back of the page of that paper there had been an advertisement of a packet[11] for New York, or a scrap from the President's message. This was the first time I ever heard of this plan. I remember it, because poor Phillips, who was of the party, told a story of something which happened at the Cape of Good Hope on Nolan's first voyage. They had touched at the Cape, paid their respects to the English Admiral and the fleet, and then Phillips had borrowed a lot of English books from an officer. Among them was *The*

Lay of the Last Minstrel,[12] which they had all of them heard of, but which most of them had never seen. I think it could not have been published long. Well, nobody thought there could be any risk of anything national in that. So Nolan was permitted to join the circle one afternoon when a lot of them sat on deck reading aloud. In his turn, Nolan took the book and read to the others; and he read very well. Nobody in the circle knew a line of the poem, only it was all magic and chivalry, and was ten thousand years ago. Poor Nolan read steadily through the fifth canto,[13] stopped a minute and drank something, and then began, without a thought of what was coming:

> Breathes there the man, with soul so
>   dead
> Who never to himself hath said,—

It seems impossible to us that anybody ever heard this for the first time; but all these fellows did then, and poor Nolan himself went on, still unconsciously or mechanically:

> This is my own, my native land!

Then they all saw that something was to pay; but he expected to get through, I suppose, turned a little pale, but plunged on:

> Whose heart hath ne'er within him
>   burned,
> As home his footsteps he hath
>   turned
> From wandering on a foreign
>   strand?—
> If such there breathe, go, mark him
>   well,—

---

11. packet *n*.: A boat that carries passengers, freight, and mail along a regular route.
12. *The Lay of the Last Minstrel*: Narrative poem by Sir Walter Scott, Scottish poet and novelist (1771–1832).

13. canto (kan' tō) *n*.: A main division of certain long poems.

By this time the men were all beside themselves, wishing there was any way to make him turn over two pages; but he had not quite presence of mind for that; he gagged a little, colored crimson, and staggered on:

For him no minstrel raptures swell;
High though his titles, proud his
  name,
Boundless his wealth as wish can
  claim,
Despite these titles, power, and
  pelf,[14]
The wretch, concentered all in
  self,—

and here the poor fellow choked, could not go on, but started up, swung the book into the sea, vanished into his stateroom, "And by Jove," said Phillips, "we did not see him for two months again. And I had to make up some beggarly story to that English surgeon why I did not return his Walter Scott to him."

That story shows about the time when Nolan's braggadocio[15] must have broken down. At first, they said, he took a very high tone, considered his imprisonment a mere farce, affected to enjoy the voyage, and all that; but Phillips said that after he came out of his stateroom he never was the same man again. He never read aloud again, unless it was the Bible or Shakespeare, or something else he was sure of. But it was not that merely. He never entered in with the other young men exactly as a companion again. He was always shy afterwards, when I knew him—very seldom spoke unless he was spoken to, except to a

very few friends. Generally he had the nervous, tired look of a heart-wounded man.

When Captain Shaw was coming home, rather to the surprise of everybody they made one of the Windward Islands, and lay off and on for nearly a week. The boys said the officers were sick of salt-junk,[16] and meant to have turtle-soup before they came home. But after several days the *Warren* came to the same rendezvous;[17] they exchanged signals; she told them she was outward bound, perhaps to the Mediterranean, and took poor Nolan and his traps[18] on the boat to try his second cruise. He looked very blank when he was told to get ready to join her. He had known enough of the signs of the sky to know that till that moment he was going "home." But this was a distinct evidence of something he had not thought of, perhaps—that there was no going home for him, even to a prison. And this was the first of some twenty such transfers, which brought him sooner or later into half our best vessels, but which kept him all his life at least some hundred miles from the country he had hoped he might never hear of again.

It may have been on that second cruise —it was once when he was up the Mediterranean—that Mrs. Graff, the celebrated Southern beauty of those days, danced with him. The ship had been lying a long time in the Bay of Naples, and the officers were very intimate in the English fleet, and there had been great festivities, and our men thought they must give a great ball on board the ship. They wanted to use Nolan's stateroom for something, and they hated to do it without asking him to the ball; so the captain said they might ask

---

14. pelf *n*.: Ill-gotten wealth.
15. braggadocio (brag′ ə dō′ shē ō) *n*.: Here, pretense of bravery; Nolan acts as if he does not mind his imprisonment.

16. salt-junk *n*.: Hard salted meat.
17. rendezvous (rän′ dā vōō) *n*.: Meeting place.
18. traps *n*.: Here, bags or luggage.

him, if they would be responsible that he did not talk with the wrong people, "who would give him intelligence."[19] So the dance went on. For ladies they had the family of the American consul, one or two travelers who had adventured so far, and a nice bevy of English girls and matrons.

Well, different officers relieved each other in standing and talking with Nolan in a friendly way, so as to be sure that nobody else spoke to him. The dancing went on with spirit, and after a while even the fellows who took this honorary guard of Nolan ceased to fear any trouble.

As the dancing went on, Nolan and our fellows all got at ease—so much so, that it seemed quite natural for him to bow to that splendid Mrs. Graff, and say, "I hope you have not forgotten me, Miss Rutledge. Shall I have the honor of dancing?"

He did it so quickly, that Fellows, who was with him, could not hinder him. She laughed and said, "I am not Miss Rutledge any longer, Mr. Nolan; but I will dance all the same." She nodded to Fellows, as if to say he must leave Mr. Nolan to her, and led him off to the place where the dance was forming.

Nolan thought he had got his chance. He had known her at Philadelphia, and at other places had met her. He began with her travels, and Europe, and then he said boldly—a little pale, she said, as she told me the story years after—"And what do you hear from home, Mrs. Graff?"

And that splendid creature looked through him. How she must have looked through him!

"Home! Mr. Nolan! I thought you were the man who never wanted to hear of home again!"—and she walked directly up the deck to her husband, and left poor Nolan alone. He did not dance again.

A happier story than either of these I have told is of the war.[20] That came along soon after. I have heard this affair told in three or four ways—and, indeed, it may have happened more than once. In one of the great frigate[21] duels with the English, in which the navy was really baptized, it happened that a round-shot[22] from the enemy entered one of our ports[23] square, and took right down the officer of the gun himself, and almost every man of the gun's crew. Now you may say what you choose about courage, but that is not a nice thing to see. But, as the men who were not killed picked themselves up, and as they and the surgeon's people were carrying off the bodies, there appeared Nolan in his shirt sleeves, with the rammer in his hand, and, just as if he had been the officer, told them off with authority—who should go to the cockpit with the wounded men, who should stay with him—perfectly cheery, and with that way which makes men feel sure all is right and is going to be right. And he finished loading the gun with his own hands, aimed it, and bade the men fire. And there he stayed, captain of that gun, keeping those fellows in spirits, till the enemy struck[24] —sitting on the carriage while the gun was cooling, though he was exposed all the time —showing them easier ways to handle heavy shot—making the raw hands laugh at their own blunders—and when the gun cooled again, getting it loaded and fired

---

19. intelligence n.: Here, news about his country.

20. the war: The War of 1812 between the United States and Great Britain.
21. frigate (frĭg′ it) n.: A fast-sailing warship equipped with guns.
22. round-shot: A cannonball.
23. ports n.: Here, portholes or openings for cannonballs.
24. struck, (struk) v.: Lowered their flag to admit defeat.

USS CONSTITUTION AND HMS GUERRIERE (Aug. 19, 1812)
Thomas Birch
U.S. Naval Academy Museum

twice as often as any other gun on the ship. The captain walked forward by way of encouraging the men, and Nolan touched his hat and said, "I am showing them how we do this in the artillery, sir."

And this is the part of the story where all the legends agree; the commodore said, "I see you do, and I thank you, sir; and I shall never forget this day, sir, and you never shall, sir."

And after the whole thing was over, and the commodore had the Englishman's sword[25] in the midst of the state and ceremony of the quarter-deck, he said, "Where is Mr. Nolan? Ask Mr. Nolan to come here."

And when Nolan came, he said, "Mr. Nolan, we are all very grateful to you today; you are one of us today; you will be named in the dispatches."

---

25. the Englishman's sword: A defeated commander would turn over his sword to the victor.

And then the old man took off his own sword of ceremony, gave it to Nolan, and made him put it on. The man told me this who saw it. Nolan cried like a baby, and well he might. He had not worn a sword since that infernal day at Fort Adams. But always afterwards on occasions of ceremony, he wore that quaint old French sword of the commodore's.

The captain did mention him in the dispatches. It was always said he asked that Nolan might be pardoned. He wrote a special letter to the Secretary of War, but nothing ever came of it.

All that was nearly fifty years ago. If Nolan was thirty then, he must have been near eighty when he died. He looked sixty when he was forty. But he never seemed to me to change a hair afterwards. As I imagine his life, from what I have seen and heard of it, he must have been in every sea, and yet almost never on land. Till he grew very old, he went aloft a great deal. He always kept up his exercise, and I never heard that he was ill. If any other man was ill, he was the kindest nurse in the world; and he knew more than half the surgeons do. Then if anybody was sick or died, or if the captain wanted him to, on any other occasion, he was always ready to read prayers. I have said that he read beautifully.

My own acquaintance with Philip Nolan began six or eight years after the English war, on my first voyage after I was appointed a midshipman. From the time I joined, I thought Nolan was a sort of lay chaplain—a chaplain with a blue coat. I never asked about him. Everything in the ship was strange to me. I knew it was green to ask questions, and I suppose I thought there was a "Plain Buttons" on every ship. We had him to dine in our mess once a week, and the caution was given that on that day nothing was to be said about home. But if they had told us not to say anything about the planet Mars or the Book of Deuteronomy,[26] I should not have asked why; there were a great many things which seemed to me to have as little reason. I first came to understand anything about "The Man Without a Country" one day when we overhauled a dirty little schooner which had slaves[27] on board. An officer named Vaughan was sent to take charge of her, and after a few minutes, he sent back his boat to ask that someone might be sent to him who could speak Portuguese. None of the officers did; and just as the captain was sending forward to ask if any of the people could, Nolan stepped out and said he should be glad to interpret, if the captain wished, as he understood the language. The captain thanked him, fitted out another boat with him, and in this boat it was my luck to go.

When we got there, it was such a scene as you seldom see, and never want to. Nastiness beyond account, and chaos run loose in the midst of the nastiness. There were not a great many of the Negroes; but by way of making what there were understand that they were free, Vaughan had had their handcuffs and anklecuffs knocked off. The Negroes were, most of them, out of the hold and swarming all round the dirty deck, with a central throng surrounding Vaughan and addressing him in every dialect.

As we came on deck, Vaughan looked down from a hogshead,[28] which he had mounted in desperation, and said, "Is there anybody who can make these people understand something?"

---

26. Book of Deuteronomy (doot′ ər än′ ə mē): The fifth book of the Bible.
27. slaves: In 1808 it became illegal to bring slaves into the United States. In 1842 the U.S. and Great Britain agreed to use ships to patrol the African coast, to prevent slaves being taken.
28. hogshead (hôgz′ hed′) n.: A large barrel or cask.

Nolan said he could speak Portuguese, and one or two fine-looking Kroomen who had worked for the Portuguese on the coast were dragged out.

"Tell them they are free," said Vaughan.

Nolan explained it in such Portuguese as the Kroomen could understand, and they in turn to such of the Negroes as could understand them. Then there was a yell of delight, clenching of fists, and leaping and dancing by way of celebration.

"Tell them," said Vaughan, well pleased, "that I will take them all to Cape Palmas."

This did not answer so well. Cape Palmas was practically as far from the homes of most of them as New Orleans or Rio de Janeiro was; that is, they would be eternally separated from home there. And their interpreters, as we could understand, instantly said, *"Ah, non Palmas,"* and began to protest volubly. Vaughan was rather disappointed at this result of his liberality, and asked Nolan eagerly what they said. The drops stood on poor Nolan's white forehead, as he hushed the men down, and said, "He says, 'Not Palmas.' He says, 'Take us home; take us to our own country; take us to our own house; take us to our own children and our own women.' He says he has an old father and mother who will die if they do not see him. And this one says he left his people all sick, and paddled down to Fernando to beg the white doctor to come and help them, and that these devils caught him in the bay just in sight of home, and that he has never seen anybody from home since then. And this one says," choked out Nolan, "that he has not heard a word from his home in six months."

Vaughan always said he grew gray himself while Nolan struggled through this interpretation. I, who did not understand anything of the passion involved in it, saw that the very elements were melting with fervent heat and that something was to pay somewhere. Even the Negroes themselves stopped howling, as they saw Nolan's agony and Vaughan's almost equal agony of sympathy. As quick as he could get words, Vaughan said, "Tell them yes, yes, yes; tell them they shall go to the Mountains of the Moon, if they will. If I sail the schooner through the Great White Desert, they shall go home!"

And after some fashion Nolan said so. And then they all fell to kissing him again.

But he could not stand it long; and getting Vaughan to say he might go back, he beckoned me down into our boat. As we started back he said to me, "Youngster, let that show you what it is to be without a family, without a home, and without a country. And if you are ever tempted to say a word or to do a thing that shall put a bar between you and your family, your home, and your country, pray God in His mercy to take you that instant home to His own heaven. Think of your home, boy; write and send, and talk about it. Let it be nearer and nearer to your thought the farther you have to travel from it, and rush back to it when you are free, as that poor slave is doing now. And for your country, boy" and the words rattled in his throat, "and for that flag," and he pointed to the ship, "never dream a dream but of serving her as she bids you, though the service carry you through a thousand hells. No matter what happens to you, no matter who flatters you or who abuses you, never look at another flag, never let a night pass but you pray God to bless that flag. Remember, boy, that behind all these men you have to do with, behind officers, and government, and people even, there is the Country herself, your Country, and that you belong to her as you belong to your own mother. Stand by her, boy, as you would stand by your mother!"

I was frightened to death by his calm, hard passion; but I blundered out that I would, by all that was holy, and that I had never thought of doing anything else. He hardly seemed to hear me; but he did, almost in a whisper, say, "Oh, if anybody had said so to me when I was of your age!"

I think it was this half-confidence of his, which I never abused, that afterward made us great friends. He was very kind to me. Often he sat up, or even got up, at night, to walk the deck with me, when it was my watch. He explained to me a great deal of my mathematics, and I owe to him my taste for mathematics. He lent me books and helped me about my reading. He never referred so directly to his story again; but from one and another officer I have learned, in thirty years, what I am telling.

After that cruise I never saw Nolan again. The other men tell me that in those fifteen years he aged very fast, but he was still the same gentle, uncomplaining, silent sufferer that he ever was, bearing as best he could his self-appointed punishment. And now it seems the dear old fellow is dead. He has found a home at last, and a country.

Since writing this, and while considering whether or not I would print it, as a warning to the young Nolans of today of what it is to throw away a country, I have received from Danforth, who is on board the *Levant*, a letter which gives an account of Nolan's last hours. It removes all my doubts about telling this story.

Here is the letter:

Dear Fred,

I try to find heart and life to tell you that it is all over with dear old

WARRANT OFFICERS' MESS
from Heck's Iconographic Encyclopedia, 1851
New York Public Library

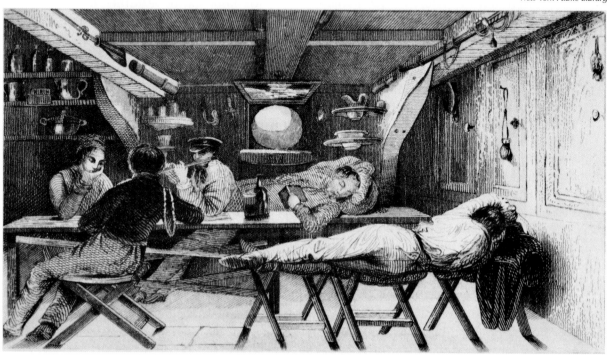

Nolan. I have been with him on this voyage more than I ever was, and I can understand wholly now the way in which you used to speak of the dear old fellow. I could see that he was not strong, but I had no idea the end was so near. The doctor has been watching him very carefully, and yesterday morning came to me and told me that Nolan was not so well, and had not left his stateroom —a thing I never remember before. He had let the doctor come and see him as he lay there—the first time the doctor had been in the stateroom —and he said he should like to see me. Do you remember the mysteries we boys used to invent about his room in the old *Intrepid* days? Well, I went in, and there, to be sure, the poor fellow lay in his berth, smiling pleasantly as he gave me his hand, but looking very frail. I could not help a glance round, which showed me what a little shrine he had made of the box he was lying in. The Stars and Stripes were draped up above and around a picture of Washington and he had painted a majestic eagle, with lightning blazing from his beak and his foot just clasping the whole globe, which his wings overshadowed. The dear old boy saw my glance, and said, with a sad smile, "Here, you see I have a country!" And then he pointed to the foot of his bed, where I had not seen before a great map of the United States, as he had drawn it from memory, and which he had there to look upon as he lay. Quaint, queer old names were on it, in large letters: "Indiana Territory," "Mississippi Territory," and "Louisiana Territory," as I suppose our fathers learned such things: but the old fellow had patched in Texas, too: he had carried his western boundary all the way to the Pacific, but on that shore he had defined nothing.

"O Captain," he said, "I know I am dying. I cannot get home. Surely you will tell me something now? —Stop! stop! Do not speak till I say what I am sure you know, that there is not in this ship, that there is not in America a more loyal man than I. There cannot be a man who loves the old flag as I do, or prays for it as I do, or hopes for it as I do. There are thirty-four stars in it now, Danforth, though I do not know what their names are. There has never been one taken away. I know by that that there has never been any successful Burr. O Danforth, Danforth," he sighed out, "how like a wretched night's dream a boy's idea of personal fame or of separate sovereignty seems, when one looks back on it after such a life as mine! But tell me—tell me something—tell me everything, Danforth, before I die!"

I swear to you that I felt like a monster that I had not told him everything before. "Mr. Nolan," said I, "I will tell you everything you ask about. Only, where shall I begin?"

Oh, the blessed smile that crept over his white face! He pressed my hand and said, "Bless you! Tell me their names," and he pointed to the stars on the flag. "The last I know is Ohio. My father lived in Kentucky. But I have guessed Michigan and Indiana and Mississippi—that was where Fort Adams was—they make twenty. But where are your other fourteen? You have not cut up any of the old ones, I hope?''

Well, that was not a bad text, and I told him the names in as good order as I could, and he bade me take down his beautiful map and draw them in as I best could with my pencil. He was wild with delight about Texas, told me how his cousin died there; he had marked a gold cross near where he supposed his grave was; and he had guessed at Texas. Then he was delighted as he saw California and Oregon;—that, he said, he had suspected partly, because he had never been permitted to land on that shore, though the ships were there so much. Then he asked whether Burr ever tried again—and he ground his teeth with the only passion he showed. But in a moment that was over. He asked about the old war —told me the story of his serving the gun the day we took the *Java*. Then he settled down more quietly, and very happily, to hear me tell in an hour the history of fifty years.

How I wished it had been somebody who knew something! But I did as well as I could. I told him of the English war. I told him about Fulton[29] and the steamboat beginning. I told him about old Scott,[30] and Jackson:[31] told him all I could think of about the Mississippi, and New Orleans, and Texas, and his own old Kentucky.

I tell you, it was a hard thing to condense the history of half a century into that talk with a sick man. And I do not now know what I told him—of emigration, and the means of it—of steamboats, and railroads, and telegraphs—of inventions, and books, and literature—of the colleges, and West Point, and the Naval School—but with the queerest interruptions that ever you heard. You see it was Robinson Crusoe asking all the accumulated questions of fifty-six years!

I remember he asked, all of a sudden, who was President now; and when I told him, he asked if Old Abe was General Benjamin Lincoln's son. He said he met old General Lincoln, when he was quite a boy himself, at some Indian treaty. I said no, that Old Abe was a Kentuckian like himself, but I could not tell him of what family; he had worked up from the ranks. ''Good for him!'' cried Nolan; ''I am glad of that.'' Then I got talking about my visit to Washington. I told him about the Smithsonian, and the Capitol. I told him everything I could think of that would show the grandeur of his country and its prosperity.

And he drank it in and enjoyed it as I cannot tell you. He grew more and more silent, yet I never thought he was tired or faint. I gave him a glass of water, but he just wet his lips, and told me not to go away. Then he asked me to bring the Presbyterian Book of Public Prayer which lay there, and said, with a smile, that it would open at the right place —and so it did. There was his double red mark down the page; and I knelt

---

29. Fulton: Robert Fulton (1765–1815), who invented the steamboat.
30. Scott: General Winfield Scott (1786–1866), who served in the War of 1812 and the Mexican War.
31. Jackson: Andrew Jackson (1767–1845), seventh President of the United States (1829–1837) and a general in the War of 1812.

down and read, and he repeated with me:

For ourselves and our country, O gracious God, we thank Thee, that, notwithstanding our manifold transgressions of Thy holy laws, Thou hast continued to us Thy marvelous kindness . . .

and so to the end of that thanksgiving. Then he turned to the end of the same book, and I read the words more familiar to me:

Most heartily we beseech Thee with Thy favor to behold and bless Thy servant, the President of the United States, and all others in authority.

"Danforth," said he, "I have repeated those prayers night and morning—it is now fifty-five years." And then he said he would go to sleep. He bent me down over him and kissed me; and he said, "Look in my Bible, Captain, when I am gone." And I went away.

But I had no thought it was the end. I thought he was tired and would sleep. I knew he was happy, and I wanted him to be alone.

But in an hour, when the doctor went in gently, he found Nolan had breathed his life away with a smile.

We looked in his Bible, and there was a slip of paper at the place where he had marked the text:

They desire a country, even a heavenly: where God is not ashamed to be called their God: for He hath prepared for them a city.[32]

On this slip of paper he had written:

Bury me in the sea; it has been my home, and I love it. But will not someone set up a stone for my memory at Fort Adams or at Orleans, that my disgrace may not be more than I ought to bear? Say on it:

In Memory of
PHILIP NOLAN,
Lieutenant in the Army of the United States.
He loved his country as no other man has loved her; but no man deserved less at her hands.

---

32. They desire . . . a city: A passage from Hebrews 11:16.

THINKING ABOUT THE SELECTION
Recalling

1. Who is the narrator of this story? What is the narrator's purpose in telling the story?
2. Why is Nolan brought to trial?
3. What rash words does Nolan utter when the judge asks him if he wishes to say anything? What effect do these words have on the judge?
4. What is Nolan's sentence? Explain the plan to carry out the sentence.
5. What precautions have to be taken with Nolan before giving him books? What precautions have to be taken before giving him periodicals?
6. How does Nolan create a country for himself in his stateroom?
7. What is Nolan's last wish?

Interpreting

8. How is it that Aaron Burr is able to win over the young Nolan so easily?
9. Why does the poem *The Lay of the Last Minstrel* have such an effect on Nolan? Why does Nolan cry when he receives the sword of the commodore?
10. After interpreting for the slaves to be sent home, why does Nolan advise the narrator to love and serve his country?
11. How has Nolan changed during the course of the story?

Applying

12. What epitaph would you write for Nolan?
13. Do you think Nolan's punishment fit his crime? Explain your answer.

ANALYZING LITERATURE
Recognizing Symbols

A **symbol** can be a word, an object, or an action in a story that represents, or stands for, something else. For example, a snake is a reptile, but it can also symbolize evil.

The writer usually emphasizes or repeats a symbol, or places it in a particular place in the story. The symbol's meaning depends on the context of the story. A story may have more than one symbol.

1. What do Nolan's plain buttons symbolize?
2. What symbol of honor does the commodore of Philip Nolan's ship give him for bravery in the battle with a British frigate?
3. What do the Stars and Stripes draped in Philip Nolan's stateroom symbolize?
4. What do these symbols suggest about the importance of one's country?

CRITICAL THINKING AND READING
Paraphrasing

Paraphrasing is restating in your own words something you read or hear; you do not repeat the words *exactly*.

Paraphrasing may help you understand better what you read or hear. To paraphrase the theme, or central idea, of a story, read and consider what the story is about. Then state its main points in your own words.

1. Paraphrase the story's theme: "And for your country . . . never dream a dream but of serving her as she bids you, though the service carry you through a thousand hells."
2. Paraphrase Nolan's epitaph: "He loved his country as no other man has loved her; but no man deserved less at her hands."

THINKING AND WRITING
Writing About Theme

Suppose Fred read the obituary in *The New York Herald* and wanted to set the record straight about Philip Nolan's true feelings about his country. List examples from the story of how Nolan felt about the U.S. Then, as Fred, write a letter to the editor describing Nolan's feelings and giving the examples. Revise your letter, making sure you have stated your points clearly. Revise your essay and prepare a final draft.

GUIDE FOR READING

Flowers for Algernon

Daniel Keyes (1927–   ), raised in Brooklyn, New York, is an English professor. He has worked at many jobs, including that of photographer, merchant seaman, and editor. His many works of fiction include the novels *The Touch* (1968) and *The Fifth Sally* (1980). Keyes's best-known story, "Flowers for Algernon," won the Hugo Award of the Science Fiction Writers of America in 1959. It was later adapted for the movie *Charly* and the Broadway musical *Charlie and Algernon*.

Point of View and Theme

Theme is the central insight into life communicated by the events in the story. Sometimes we see the events unfold from one character's point of view. It is as though we stand in this character's shoes and see with this character's eyes. In a story that unfolds this way, we come to understand the theme gradually, as we see what this character sees and sometimes even more than what he or she sees.

Look For

As you read "Flowers for Algernon," look for the way in which the theme emerges from the story. How does Charlie's view of the world change as the story progresses? What do you see in the characters and events Charlie encounters that he does not?

Writing

Charlie takes part in an experiment to make him smart. What makes a person smart? Freewrite about the meaning of the word *intelligence*.

Vocabulary

Knowing the following words will help you as you read "Flowers for Algernon."

tangible (tan′ jə bəl) *adj*.: Observable; understandable (p. 213)

specter (spek′ tər) *n*.: A disturbing thought (p. 213)

refute (ri fyo͞ot′) *v*.: Disprove (p. 214)

vacuous (vak′ yo͞o wəs) *adj*.: Empty; shallow (p. 215)

obscure (äb skyo͞or′) *v*.: Hide (p. 217)

convolutions (kän′ və lo͞o′ shəns) *n*.: Uneven ridges on the brain's surface (p. 218)

fissures (fish′ ərs) *n*.: Narrow openings (p. 218)

introspective (in′ trə spek′ tiv) *adj*.: Looking into one's own thoughts and feelings (p. 218)

Flowers for Algernon

Daniel Keyes

progris riport 1—martch 5 1965

Dr. Strauss says I shud rite down what I think and evrey thing that happins to me from now on. I dont know why but he says its importint so they will see if they will use me. I hope they use me. Miss Kinnian says maybe they can make me smart. I want to be smart. My name is Charlie Gordon. I am 37 years old and 2 weeks ago was my brithday. I have nuthing more to rite now so I will close for today.

progris riport 2—martch 6

I had a test today. I think I faled it. and I think that maybe now they wont use me. What happind is a nice young man was in the room and he had some white cards with ink spillled all over them. He sed Charlie what do you see on this card. I was very skared even tho I had my rabits foot in my pockit because when I was a kid I always faled tests in school and I spillled ink to.

I told him I saw a inkblot. He said yes and it made me feel good. I thot that was all but when I got up to go he stopped me. He said now sit down Charlie we are not thru yet. Then I dont remember so good but he wantid me to say what was in the ink. I dint see nuthing in the ink but he said there was picturs there other pepul saw some picturs. I coudnt see any picturs. I reely tryed to see. I held the card close up and then far away. Then I said if I had my glases I coud see better I usally only ware my glases in the movies or TV but I said they are in the closit in the hall. I got them. Then I said let me see that card agen I bet Ill find it now.

I tryed hard but I still coudnt find the picturs I only saw the ink. I told him maybe I need new glases. He rote somthing down on a paper and I got skared of faling the test. I told him it was a very nice inkblot with littel points all around the eges. He looked very sad so that wasnt it. I said please let me try agen. Ill get it in a few minits becaus Im not so fast somtimes. Im a slow reeder too in Miss Kinnians class for slow adults but I'm trying very hard.

He gave me a chance with another card that had 2 kinds of ink spilled on it red and blue.

He was very nice and talked slow like Miss Kinnian does and he explaned it to me that it was a *raw shok.*[1] He said pepul see things in the ink. I said show me where. He said think. I told him I think a inkblot but that wasnt rite eather. He said what does it remind you—pretend somthing. I closd my eyes for a long time to pretend. I told him I pretned a fowntan pen with ink leeking all over a table cloth. Then he got up and went out.

I dont think I passd the *raw shok* test.

---

[1] **raw shok:** A misspelling of Rorschach (rôr′ sнäk) test, a psychological test involving inkblots that the subject describes.

Edited for this edition.

Dr Strauss and Dr Nemur say it dont matter about the inkblots. I told them I dint spill the ink on the cards and I coudnt see anything in the ink. They said that maybe they will still use me. I said Miss Kinnian never gave me tests like that one only spelling and reading. They said Miss Kinnian told that I was her bestist pupil in the adult nite scool becaus I tryed the hardist and I reely wantid to lern. They said how come you went to the adult nite scool all by yourself Charlie. How did you find it. I said I askd pepul and sumbody told me where I shud go to lern to read and spell good. They said why did you want to. I told them becaus all my life I wantid to be smart and not dumb. But its very hard to be smart. They said you know it will probly be tempirery. I said yes. Miss Kinnian told me. I dont care if it herts.

Later I had more crazy tests today. The nice lady who gave it me told me the name and I asked her how do you spellit so I can rite it in my progris riport. THEMATIC APPERCEPTION TEST.[2] I dont know the frist 2 words but I know what *test* means. You got to pass it or you get bad marks. This test lookd easy becaus I coud see the picturs. Only this time she dint want me to tell her the picturs. That mixd me up. I said the man yesterday said I shoud tell him what I saw in the ink she said that dont make no difrence. She said make up storys about the pepul in the picturs.

I told her how can you tell storys about pepul you never met. I said why shud I make up lies. I never tell lies any more becaus I always get caut.

She told me this test and the other one the raw-shok was for getting personalty. I laffed so hard. I said how can you get that thing from inkblots and fotos. She got sore and put her picturs away. I dont care. It was sily. I gess I faled that test too.

Later some men in white coats took me to a difernt part of the hospitil and gave me a game to play. It was like a race with a white mouse. They called the mouse Algernon. Algernon was in a box with a lot of twists and turns like all kinds of walls and they gave me a pencil and a paper with lines and lots of boxes. On one side it said START and on the other end it said FINISH. They said it was *amazed*[3] and that Algernon and me had the same *amazed* to do. I dint see how we could have the same *amazed* if Algernon had a box and I had a paper but I dint say nothing. Anyway there wasnt time because the race started.

One of the men had a watch he was trying to hide so I woudnt see it so I tryed not to look and that made me nervus.

Anyway that test made me feel worser than all the others because they did it over 10 times with difernt *amazeds* and Algernon won every time. I dint know that mice were so smart. Maybe thats because Algernon is a white mouse. Maybe white mice are smarter than other mice.

progris riport 4—Mar 8

Their going to use me! Im so exited I can hardly write. Dr Nemur and Dr Strauss had a argament about it first. Dr Nemur was in the office when Dr Strauss brot me in. Dr Nemur was worryed about using me but Dr Strauss told him Miss Kinnian rekem-

---

2. THEMATIC (*thē* mat′ ik) **APPERCEPTION** (ap′ ər sep′ sʰən) **TEST:** A personality test in which the subject makes up stories about a series of pictures.

3. amazed: A maze, or confusing series of paths. Often, the intelligence of animals is assessed by how fast they go through a maze.

mended me the best from all the pepul who she was teaching. I like Miss Kinnian becaus shes a very smart teacher. And she said Charlie your going to have a second chance. If you volenteer for this experament you mite get smart. They dont know if it will be perminint but theirs a chance. Thats why I said ok even when I was scared because she said it was an operashun. She said dont be scared Charlie you done so much with so little I think you deserv it most of all.

So I got scaird when Dr Nemur and Dr Strauss argud about it. Dr Strauss said I had something that was very good. He said I had a good *motor-vation*.[4] I never even knew I had that. I felt proud when he said that not every body with an *eye-q*[5] of 68 had that thing. I dont know what it is or where I got it but he said Algernon had it too. Algernons *motor-vation* is the cheese they put in his box. But it cant be that because I didnt eat any cheese this week.

---

4. motor-vation: Motivation, or desire to work hard and achieve a goal.
5. eye-q: I.Q., intelligence quotient, a way of measuring human intelligence.

Then he told Dr Nemur something I dint understand so while they were talking I wrote down some of the words.

He said Dr Nemur I know Charlie is not what you had in mind as the first of your new brede of intelek** (coudnt get the word) superman. But most people of his low ment** are host** and uncoop** they are usualy dull apath** and hard to reach. He has a good natcher hes intristed and eager to please.

Dr Nemur said remember he will be the first human beeng ever to have his intelijence trippled by surgicle meens.

Dr Strauss said exakly. Look at how well hes lerned to read and write for his low mentel age its as grate an acheve** as you and I lerning einstines therey of **vity without help. That shows the intenss motorvation. Its comparat** a tremen** achev** I say we use Charlie.

I dint get all the words and they were talking to fast but it sounded like Dr Strauss was on my side and like the other one wasnt.

Then Dr Nemur nodded he said all right maybe your right. We will use Charlie. When he said that I got so exited I jumped up and shook his hand for being so good to me. I told him thank you doc you wont be sorry for giving me a second chance. And I mean it like I told him. After the operashun Im gonna try to be smart. Im gonna try awful hard.

progris ript 5—Mar 10

Im skared. Lots of people who work here and the nurses and the people who gave me the tests came to bring me candy and wish me luck. I hope I have luck. I got my rabits foot and my lucky penny and my horse shoe. Only a black cat crossed me when I was comming to the hospitil. Dr Strauss says dont be supersitis Charlie this is sience. Anyway Im keeping my rabits foot with me.

I asked Dr Strauss if Ill beat Algernon in the race after the operashun and he said maybe. If the operashun works Ill show that mouse I can be as smart as he is. Maybe smarter. Then Ill be abel to read better and spell the words good and know lots of things and be like other people. I want to be smart like other people. If it works perminint they will make everybody smart all over the wurld.

They dint give me anything to eat this morning. I dont know what that eating has to do with getting smart. Im very hungry and Dr Nemur took away my box of candy. That Dr Nemur is a grouch. Dr Strauss says I can have it back after the operashun. You cant eat befor a operashun . . .

Progress Report 6—Mar 15

The operashun dint hurt. He did it while I was sleeping. They took off the bandijis from my eyes and my head today so I can make a PROGRESS REPORT. Dr Nemur who looked at some of my other ones says I spell PROGRESS wrong and he told me how to spell it and REPORT too. I got to try and remember that.

I have a very bad memary for spelling. Dr Strauss says its ok to tell about all the things that happin to me but he says I shoud tell more about what I feel and what I think. When I told him I dont know how to think he said try. All the time when the bandijis were on my eyes I tryed to think. Nothing happened. I dont know what to think about. Maybe if I ask him he will tell me how I can think now that Im suppose to get smart. What do smart people think about. Fancy things I suppose. I wish I knew some fancy things alredy.

Progress Report 7—mar 19

Nothing is happining. I had lots of tests and different kinds of races with Algernon. I hate that mouse. He always beats me. Dr Strauss said I got to play those games. And he said some time I got to take those tests over again. Thse inkblots are stupid. And those pictures are stupid too. I like to draw a picture of a man and a woman but I wont make up lies about people.

I got a headache from trying to think so much. I thot Dr Strauss was my frend but he dont help me. He dont tell me what to think or when Ill get smart. Miss Kinnian dint come to see me. I think writing these progress reports are stupid too.

Progress Report 8—Mar 23

Im going back to work at the factery. They said it was better I shud go back to work but I cant tell anyone what the operashun was for and I have to come to the hospitil for an hour evry night after work. They are gonna pay me mony every month for lerning to be smart.

Im glad Im going back to work because I miss my job and all my frends and all the fun we have there.

Dr Strauss says I shud keep writing things down but I dont have to do it every day just when I think of something or something speshul happins. He says dont get discoridged because it takes time and it happins slow. He says it took a long time with Algernon before he got 3 times smarter then he was before. Thats why Algernon beats me all the time because he had that operashun too. That makes me feel better. I coud probly do that *amazed* faster than a reglar mouse. Maybe some day Ill beat Algernon. Boy that would be something. So far Algernon looks like he mite be smart perminent.

Mar 25 (I dont have to write PROGRESS REPORT on top any more just when I hand it in once a week for Dr Nemur to read. I just have to put the date on. That saves time)

We had a lot of fun at the factery today. Joe Carp said hey look where Charlie had his operashun what did they do Charlie put some brains in. I was going to tell him but I remembered Dr Strauss said no. Then Frank Reilly said what did you do Charlie forget your key and open your door the hard way. That made me laff. Their really my friends and they like me.

Sometimes somebody will say hey look at Joe or Frank or George he really pulled a Charlie Gordon. I dont know why they say that but they always laff. This morning Amos Borg who is the 4 man at Donnegans used my name when he shouted at Ernie the office boy. Ernie lost a packige. He said Ernie what are you trying to be a Charlie Gordon. I dont understand why he said that. I never lost any packiges.

Mar 28 Dr Straus came to my room tonight to see why I dint come in like I was suppose to. I told him I dont like to race with Algernon any more. He said I dont have to for a while but I shud come in. He had a present for me only it wasnt a present but just for lend. I thot it was a little television but it wasnt. He said I got to turn it on when I go to sleep. I said your kidding why shud I turn it on when Im going to sleep. Who ever herd of a thing like that. But he said if I want to get smart I got to do what he says. I told him I dint think I was going to get smart and he put his hand on my sholder and said Charlie you dont know it yet but your getting smarter all the time. You wont notice for a while. I think he was just being nice to make me feel good because I dont look any smarter.

Oh yes I almost forgot. I asked him when I can go back to the class at Miss Kinnians school. He said I wont go their. He said that soon Miss Kinnian will come to the hospitil to start and teach me speshul. I was mad at her for not comming to see me when I got the operashun but I like her so maybe we will be frends again.

Mar 29 That crazy TV kept me up all night. How can I sleep with something yelling crazy things all night in my ears. And the nutty pictures. Wow. I dont know what it says when Im up so how am I going to know when Im sleeping.

Dr Strauss says its ok. He says my brains are lerning when I sleep and that will help me when Miss Kinnian starts my lessons in the hospitl only I found out it isnt a hospitil its a labatory. I think its all crazy. If you can get smart when your sleeping why do people go to school. That thing I dont think will work. I use to watch the late show and the late late show on TV all the time and it never made me smart. Maybe you have to sleep while you watch it.

PROGRESS REPORT 9—April 3

Dr Strauss showed me how to keep the TV turned low so now I can sleep. I don't hear a thing. And I still dont understand what it says. A few times I play it over in the morning to find out what I lerned when I was sleeping and I dont think so. Miss Kinnian says Maybe its another langwidge or something. But most times it sounds american. It talks so fast faster then even Miss Gold who was my teacher in 6 grade and I remember she talked so fast I coudnt understand her.

I told Dr Strauss what good is it to get smart in my sleep. I want to be smart when Im awake. He says its the same thing and I have two minds. Theres the *subconscious* and the *conscious* (thats how you spell it). And one dont tell the other one what its doing. They dont even talk to each other.

Thats why I dream. And boy have I been having crazy dreams. Wow. Ever since that night TV. The late late late late late show.

I forgot to ask him if it was only me or if everybody had those two minds.

(I just looked up the word in the dictionary Dr Strauss gave me. The word is *subconscious. adj. Of the nature of mental operations yet not present in consciousness; as, subconscious conflict of desires.*) There's more but I still dont know what it means. This isnt a very good dictionary for dumb people like me.

Anyway the headache is from the party. My frends from the factery Joe Carp and Frank Reilly invited me to go with them to Muggsys Saloon for some drinks. I dont like to drink but they said we will have lots of fun. I had a good time.

Joe Carp said I shoud show the girls how I mop out the toilet in the factory and he got me a mop. I showed them and everyone laffed when I told that Mr Donnegan said I was the best janiter he ever had because I like my job and do it good and never come late or miss a day except for my operashun.

I said Miss Kinnian always said Charlie be proud of your job because you do it good.

Everybody laffed and we had a good time and they gave me lots of drinks and Joe said Charlie is a card when hes potted. I dont know what that means but everybody likes me and we have fun. I cant wait to be smart like my best frends Joe Carp and Frank Reilly.

I dont remember how the party was over but I think I went out to buy a newspaper and coffe for Joe and Frank and when I came back there was no one their. I looked for them all over till late. Then I dont remember so good but I think I got sleepy or sick. A nice cop brot me back home. Thats what my landlady Mrs Flynn says.

But I got a headache and a big lump on my head and black and blue all over. I think maybe I fell. Anyway I got a bad headache and Im sick and hurt all over. I dont think Ill drink anymore.

April 6 I beat Algernon! I dint even know I beat him until Burt the tester told me. Then the second time I lost because I got so exited I fell off the chair before I finished. But after that I beat him 8 more times. I must be getting smart to beat a smart mouse like Algernon. But I dont *feel* smarter.

I wanted to race Algernon some more but Burt said thats enough for one day. They let me hold him for a minit. Hes not so bad. Hes soft like a ball of cotton. He blinks and when he opens his eyes their black and pink on the eges.

I said can I feed him because I felt bad to beat him and I wanted to be nice and make frends. Burt said no Algernon is a very specshul mouse with an operashun like mine, and he was the first of all the animals to stay smart so long. He told me Algernon is so smart that every day he has to solve a test to get his food. Its a thing like a lock on a door that changes every time Algernon goes in to eat so he has to lern something new to get his food. That made me sad because if he coudnt lern he woud be hungry.

I dont think its right to make you pass a test to eat. How woud Dr Nemur like it to have to pass a test every time he wants to eat. I think Ill be frends with Algernon.

April 9 Tonight after work Miss Kinnian was at the laboratory. She looked like she was glad to see me but scared. I told her dont worry Miss Kinnian Im not smart yet and she laffed. She said I have confidence in you Charlie the way you struggled so hard to read and right better than all the others. At werst you will have it for a littel wile and your doing something for sience.

We are reading a very hard book. I never read such a hard book before. Its called *Robinson Crusoe*[6] about a man who gets merooned on a dessert Iland. Hes smart and figers out all kinds of things so he can have a house and food and hes a good swimmer. Only I feel sorry because hes all alone and has no frends. But I think their must be somebody else on the iland because theres a picture with his funny umbrella looking at footprints. I hope he gets a frend and not be lonly.

April 10 Miss Kinnian teaches me to spell better. She says look at a word and close your eyes and say it over and over until you remember. I have lots of truble with *through* that you say *threw* and *enough* and *tough* that you dont say *enew* and *tew*. You got to say *enuff* and *tuff*. Thats how I use to write it before I started to get smart. Im confused but Miss Kinnian says theres no reason in spelling.

Apr 14 Finished Robinson Crusoe. I want to find out more about what happens to him but Miss Kinnian says thats all there is. *Why*

Apr 15 Miss Kinnian says Im lerning fast. She read some of the Progress Reports and she looked at me kind of funny. She says Im a fine person and Ill show them all. I asked her why. She said never mind but I shoudnt feel bad if I find out that everybody isnt nice like I think. She said for a person who god gave so little to you done more then

---

6. Robinson Crusoe (kro͞o′ sō): Novel written in 1719 by Daniel Defoe, a British author.

a lot of people with brains they never even used. I said all my frends are smart people but there good. They like me and they never did anything that wasnt nice. Then she got something in her eye and she had to run out to the ladys room.

Apr 16 Today, I lerned, the *comma*, this is a comma (,) a period, with a tail, Miss Kinnian, says its importent, because, it makes writing, better, she said, sombeody, coud lose, a lot of money, if a comma, isnt, in the, right place, I dont have, any money, and I dont see, how a comma, keeps you, from losing it,

But she says, everybody, uses commas, so Ill use, them too,

Apr 17 I used the comma wrong. Its punctuation. Miss Kinnian told me to look up long words in the dictionary to lern to spell them. I said whats the difference if you can read it anyway. She said its part of your education so now on Ill look up all the words Im not sure how to spell. It takes a long time to write that way but I think Im remembering. I only have to look up once and after that I get it right. Anyway thats how come I got the word *punctuation* right. (Its that way in the dictionary). Miss Kinnian says a period is punctuation too, and there are lots of other marks to lern. I told her I thot all the periods had to have tails but she said no.

You got to mix them up, she showed? me" how. to mix! them(up,. and now; I can! mix up all kinds" of punctuation, in! my writing? There, are lots! of rules? to lern; but Im gettin'g them in my head.

One thing I? like about, Dear Miss Kinnian: (thats the way it goes in a business letter if I ever go into business) is she, always gives me' a reason" when—I ask. She's a gen'ius! I wish! I cou'd be smart" like, her;

(Punctuation, is; fun!)

April 18 What a dope I am! I didn't even understand what she was talking about. I read the grammar book last night and it explanes the whole thing. Then I saw it was the same way as Miss Kinnian was trying to tell me, but I didn't get it. I got up in the middle of the night, and the whole thing straightened out in my mind.

Miss Kinnian said that the TV working in my sleep helped out. She said I reached a plateau. Thats like the flat top of a hill.

After I figgered out how punctuation worked, I read over all my old Progress Reports from the beginning. Boy, did I have crazy spelling and punctuation! I told Miss Kinnian I ought to go over the pages and fix all the mistakes but she said, "No, Charlie, Dr. Nemur wants them just as they are. That's why he let you keep them after they were photostated, to see your own progress. You're coming along fast, Charlie."

That made me feel good. After the lesson I went down and played with Algernon. We don't race any more.

April 20 I feel sick inside. Not sick like for a doctor, but inside my chest it feels empty like getting punched and a heartburn at the same time.

I wasn't going to write about it, but I guess I got to, because its important. Today was the first time I ever stayed home from work.

Last night Joe Carp and Frank Reilly invited me to a party. There were lots of girls and some men from the factory. I remembered how sick I got last time I drank too much, so I told Joe I didn't want anything to drink. He gave me a plain coke instead. It tasted funny, but I thought it was just a bad taste in my mouth.

We had a lot of fun for a while. Joe said I should dance with Ellen and she would teach me the steps. I fell a few times and I couldn't understand why because no one else was dancing besides Ellen and me. And all the time I was tripping because somebody's foot was always sticking out.

Then when I got up I saw the look on Joe's face and it gave me a funny feeling in my stomack. "He's a scream," one of the girls said. Everybody was laughing.

Frank said, "I ain't laughed so much since we sent him off for the newspaper that night at Muggsy's and ditched him."

"Look at him. His face is red."

"He's blushing. Charlie is blushing."

"Hey, Ellen, what'd you do to Charlie? I never saw him act like that before."

I didn't know what to do or where to turn. Everyone was looking at me and laughing and I felt naked. I wanted to hide myself. I ran out into the street and I threw up. Then I walked home. It's a funny thing I never knew that Joe and Frank and the others liked to have me around all the time to make fun of me.

Now I know what it means when they say "to pull a Charlie Gordon."

I'm ashamed.

April 21   Still didn't go into the factory. I told Mrs. Flynn my landlady to call and tell Mr. Donnegan I was sick. Mrs. Flynn looks at me very funny lately like she's scared of me.

I think it's a good thing about finding out how everybody laughs at me. I thought about it a lot. It's because I'm so dumb and I don't even know when I'm doing something dumb. People think it's funny when a dumb person can't do things the same way they can.

Anyway, now I know I'm getting smarter every day. I know punctuation and I can spell good. I like to look up all the hard words in the dictionary and I remember them. I'm reading a lot now, and Miss Kinnian says I read very fast. Sometimes I even understand what I'm reading about, and it stays in my mind. There are times when I can close my eyes and think of a page and it all comes back like a picture.

Besides history, geography and arithmetic, Miss Kinnian said I should start to learn a few foreign languages. Dr. Strauss gave me some more tapes to play while I sleep. I still don't understand how that conscious and unconscious mind works, but Dr. Strauss says not to worry yet. He asked me to promise that when I start learning college subjects next week I wouldn't read any books on psychology—that is, until he gives me permission.

I feel a lot better today, but I guess I'm still a little angry that all the time people were laughing and making fun of me because I wasn't so smart. When I become intelligent like Dr. Strauss says, with three times my I.Q. of 68, then maybe I'll be like everyone else and people will like me and be friendly.

I'm not sure what an *I.Q.* is. Dr. Nemur said it was something that measured how intelligent you were—like a scale in the drugstore weighs pounds. But Dr. Strauss had a big arguement with him and said an I.Q. didn't weigh intelligence at all. He said an I.Q. showed how much intelligence you could get, like the numbers on the outside of a measuring cup. You still had to fill the cup up with stuff.

Then when I asked Burt, who gives me my intelligence tests and works with Algernon, he said that both of them were wrong (only I had to promise not to tell them he said so). Burt says that the I.Q. measures a lot of different things including some of the things you learned already, and it really isn't any good at all.

So I still don't know what I.Q. is except that mine is going to be over 200 soon. I didn't want to say anything, but I don't see how if they don't know *what* it is, or *where* it is—I don't see how they know *how much* of it you've got.

Dr. Nemur says I have to take a *Rorshach Test* tomorrow. I wonder what *that* is.

April 22   I found out what a *Rorshach* is. It's the test I took before the operation—the one with the inkblots on the pieces of cardboard. The man who gave me the test was the same one.

I was scared to death of those inkblots. I knew he was going to ask me to find the pictures and I knew I wouldn't be able to. I was thinking to myself, if only there was some way of knowing what kind of pictures were hidden there. Maybe there weren't any pictures at all. Maybe it was just a trick to see if I was dumb enough too look for something that wasn't there. Just thinking about that made me sore at him.

"All right, Charlie," he said, "you've seen these cards before, remember?"

"Of course I remember."

The way I said it, he knew I was angry,

and he looked surprised. "Yes, of course. Now I want you to look at this one. What might this be? What do you see on this card? People see all sorts of things in these inkblots. Tell me what it might be for you—what it makes you think of."

I was shocked. That wasn't what I had expected him to say at all. "You mean there are no pictures hidden in those inkblots?"

He frowned and took off his glasses. "What?"

"Pictures. Hidden in the inkblots. Last time you told me that everyone could see them and you wanted me to find them too."

He explained to me that the last time he had used almost the exact same words he was using now. I didn't believe it, and I still have the suspicion that he misled me at the time just for the fun of it. Unless—I don't know any more—could I have been *that* feeble-minded?

We went through the cards slowly. One of them looked like a pair of bats tugging at some thing. Another one looked like two men fencing with swords. I imagined all sorts of things. I guess I got carried away. But I didn't trust him any more, and I kept turning them around and even looking on the back to see if there was anything there I was supposed to catch. While he was making his notes, I peeked out of the corner of my eye to read it. But it was all in code that looked like this:

WF + A DdF-Ad orig. WF-A
SF + obj

The test still doesn't make sense to me. It seems to me that anyone could make up lies about things that they didn't really see. How could he know I wasn't making a fool of him by mentioning things that I didn't really imagine? Maybe I'll understand it when Dr. Strauss lets me read up on psychology.

April 25   I figured out a new way to line up the machines in the factory, and Mr. Donnegan says it will save him ten thousand dollars a year in labor and increased production. He gave me a $25 bonus.

I wanted to take Joe Carp and Frank Reilly out to lunch to celebrate, but Joe said he had to buy some things for his wife, and Frank said he was meeting his cousin for lunch. I guess it'll take a little time for them to get used to the changes in me. Everybody seems to be frightened of me. When I went over to Amos Borg and tapped him on the shoulder, he jumped up in the air.

People don't talk to me much any more or kid around the way they used to. It makes the job kind of lonely.

April 27   I got up the nerve today to ask Miss Kinnian to have dinner with me tomorrow night to celebrate my bonus.

At first she wasn't sure it was right, but I asked Dr. Strauss and he said it was okay. Dr. Strauss and Dr. Nemur don't seem to be getting along so well. They're arguing all the time. This evening when I came in to ask Dr. Strauss about having dinner with Miss Kinnian, I heard them shouting. Dr. Nemur was saying that it was *his* experiment and *his* research, and Dr. Strauss was shouting back that he contributed just as much, because he found me through Miss Kinnian and he performed the operation. Dr. Strauss said that someday thousands of neurosurgeons[7] might be using his technique all over the world.

Dr. Nemur wanted to publish the results of the experiment at the end of this month. Dr. Strauss wanted to wait a while longer to be sure. Dr. Strauss said that Dr. Nemur

---

7. neurosurgeons (noor′ ō sʉr′ jənz) *n.*: Doctors who operate on the nervous system, including the brain and spine.

was more interested in the Chair[8] of Psychology at Princeton than he was in the experiment. Dr. Nemur said that Dr. Strauss was nothing but an opportunist who was trying to ride to glory on *his* coattails.

When I left afterwards, I found myself trembling. I don't know why for sure, but it was as if I'd seen both men clearly for the first time. I remember hearing Burt say that Dr. Nemur had a shrew of a wife who was pushing him all the time to get things published so that he could become famous. Burt said that the dream of her life was to have a big shot husband.

Was Dr. Strauss really trying to ride on his coattails?

April 28 I don't understand why I never noticed how beautiful Miss Kinnian really is. She has brown eyes and feathery brown hair that comes to the top of her neck. She's only thirty-four! I think from the beginning I had the feeling that she was an unreachable genius—and very, very old. Now, every time I see her she grows younger and more lovely.

We had dinner and a long talk. When she said that I was coming along so fast that soon I'd be leaving her behind, I laughed.

"It's true, Charlie. You're already a better reader than I am. You can read a whole page at a glance while I can take in only a few lines at a time. And you remember every single thing you read. I'm lucky if I can recall the main thoughts and the general meaning."

"I don't feel intelligent. There are so many things I don't understand."

She took out a cigarette and I lit it for her.

"You've got to be a *little* patient. You're accomplishing in days and weeks what it takes normal people to do in half a lifetime.

That's what makes it so amazing. You're like a giant sponge now, soaking things in. Facts, figures, general knowledge. And soon you'll begin to connect them, too. You'll see how the different branches of learning are related. There are many levels, Charlie, like steps on a giant ladder that take you up higher and higher to see more and more of the world around you.

"I can see only a little bit of that, Charlie, and I won't go much higher than I am now, but you'll keep climbing up and up, and see more and more, and each step will open new worlds that you never even knew existed." She frowned. "I hope . . . I just hope to God—"

"What?"

"Never mind, Charles. I just hope I wasn't wrong to advise you to go into this in the first place."

I laughed. "How could that be? It worked, didn't it? Even Algernon is still smart."

We sat there silently for a while and I knew what she was thinking about as she watched me toying with the chain of my rabbit's foot and my keys. I didn't want to think of that possibility any more than elderly people want to think of death. I *knew* that this was only the beginning. I knew what she meant about levels because I'd seen some of them already. The thought of leaving her behind made me sad.

I'm in love with Miss Kinnian.

PROGRESS REPORT 12

April 30 I've quit my job with Donnegan's Plastic Box Company. Mr. Donnegan insisted that it would be better for all concerned if I left. What did I do to make them hate me so?

The first I knew of it was when Mr. Donnegan showed me the petition. Eight hundred and forty names, everyone con-

---

8. chair: Professorship.

nected with the factory, except Fanny Girden. Scanning the list quickly, I saw at once that hers was the only missing name. All the rest demanded that I be fired.

Joe Carp and Frank Reilly wouldn't talk to me about it. No one else would either, except Fanny. She was one of the few people I'd known who set her mind to something and believed it no matter what the rest of the world proved, said or did—and Fanny did not believe that I should have been fired. She had been against the petition on principle and despite the pressure and threats she'd held out.

"Which don't mean to say," she remarked, "that I don't think there's something mighty strange about you, Charlie. Them changes. I don't know. You used to be a good, dependable, ordinary man—not too bright maybe, but honest. Who knows what you done to yourself to get so smart all of a sudden. Like everybody around here's been saying, Charlie, it's not right."

"But how can you say that, Fanny? What's wrong with a man becoming intelligent and wanting to acquire knowledge and understanding of the world around him?"

She stared down at her work, and I turned to leave. Without looking at me, she said: "It was evil when Eve listened to the snake and ate from the tree of knowledge. It was evil when she saw that she was naked. If not for that none of us would ever have to grow old and sick, and die."

Once again now I have the feeling of shame burning inside me. This intelligence has driven a wedge between me and all the people I once knew and loved. Before, they laughed at me and despised me for my ignorance and dullness; now, they hate me for my knowledge and understanding. What do they want of me?

They've driven me out of the factory. Now I'm more alone than ever before . . .

May 15   Dr. Strauss is very angry at me for not having written any progress reports in two weeks. He's justified because the lab is now paying me a regular salary. I told him I was too busy thinking and reading. When I pointed out that writing was such a slow process that it made me impatient with my poor handwriting, he suggested that I learn to type. It's much easier to write now because I can type nearly seventy-five words a minute. Dr. Strauss continually reminds me of the need to speak and write simply so that people will be able to understand me.

I'll try to review all the things that happened to me during the last two weeks. Algernon and I were presented to the American Psychological Association sitting in convention with the World Psychological Association last Tuesday. We created quite a sensation. Dr. Nemur and Dr. Strauss were proud of us.

I suspect that Dr. Nemur, who is sixty —ten years older than Dr. Strauss—finds it necessary to see tangible results of his work. Undoubtedly the result of pressure by Mrs. Nemur.

Contrary to my earlier impressions of him, I realize that Dr. Nemur is not at all a genius. He has a very good mind, but it struggles under the specter of self-doubt. He wants people to take him for a genius. Therefore, it is important for him to feel that his work is accepted by the world. I believe that Dr. Nemur was afraid of further delay because he worried that someone else might make a discovery along these lines and take the credit from him.

Dr. Strauss on the other hand might be called a genius, although I feel that his areas of knowledge are too limited. He was educated in the tradition of narrow specialization; the broader aspects of background were neglected far more than necessary—even for a neurosurgeon.

I was shocked to learn that the only ancient languages he could read were Latin, Greek and Hebrew, and that he knows almost nothing of mathematics beyond the elementary levels of the calculus of variations. When he admitted this to me, I found myself almost annoyed. It was as if he'd hidden this part of himself in order to deceive me, pretending—as do many people I've discovered—to be what he is not. No one I've ever known is what he appears to be on the surface.

Dr. Nemur appears to be uncomfortable around me. Sometimes when I try to talk to him, he just looks at me strangely and turns away. I was angry at first when Dr. Strauss told me I was giving Dr. Nemur an inferiority complex. I thought he was mocking me and I'm oversensitive at being made fun of.

How was I to know that a highly respected psychoexperimentalist like Nemur was unacquainted with Hindustani[9] and Chinese? It's absurd when you consider the work that is being done in India and China today in the very field of his study.

I asked Dr. Strauss how Nemur could refute Rahajamati's attack on his method and results if Nemur couldn't even read them in the first place. That strange look on Dr. Strauss' face can mean only one of two things. Either he doesn't want to tell Nemur what they're saying in India, or else—and this worries me—Dr. Strauss doesn't know either. I must be careful to speak and write clearly and simply so that people won't laugh.

May 18 I am very disturbed. I saw Miss Kinnian last night for the first time in over a week. I tried to avoid all discussions of intellectual concepts and to keep the conversation on a simple, everyday level, but she just stared at me blankly and asked me what I meant about the mathematical variance equivalent in Dorbermann's *Fifth Concerto.*

When I tried to explain she stopped me and laughed. I guess I got angry, but I suspect I'm approaching her on the wrong level. No matter what I try to discuss with her, I am unable to communicate. I must review Vrostadt's equations on *Levels of Semantic Progression.* I find that I don't communicate with people much any more. Thank God for books and music and things I can think about. I am alone in my apartment at Mrs. Flynn's boarding house most of the time and seldom speak to anyone.

May 20 I would not have noticed the new dishwasher, a boy of about sixteen, at the corner diner where I take my evening meals if not for the incident of the broken dishes.

They crashed to the floor, shattering and sending bits of white china under the tables. The boy stood there, dazed and frightened, holding the empty tray in his hand. The whistles and catcalls from the customers (the cries of "hey, there go the profits!" . . . "*Mazeltov!*" . . . and "well, *he* didn't work here very long . . ." which invariably seems to follow the breaking of glass or dishware in a public restaurant) all seemed to confuse him.

When the owner came to see what the excitement was about, the boy cowered as if he expected to be struck and threw up his arms as if to ward off the blow.

"All right! All right, you dope," shouted the owner, "don't just stand there! Get the broom and sweep that mess up. A broom . . . a broom, you idiot! It's in the kitchen. Sweep up all the pieces."

The boy saw that he was not going to be

---

9. Hindustani (hin' dōo stan' ē) *n.*: A language of northern India.

punished. His frightened expression disappeared and he smiled and hummed as he came back with the broom to sweep the floor. A few of the rowdier customers kept up the remarks, amusing themselves at his expense.

"Here, sonny, over here there's a nice piece behind you . . ."

"C'mon, do it again . . ."

"He's not so dumb. It's easier to break 'em than to wash 'em . . ."

As his vacant eyes moved across the crowd of amused onlookers, he slowly mirrored their smiles and finally broke into an uncertain grin at the joke which he obviously did not understand.

I felt sick inside as I looked at his dull, vacuous smile, the wide, bright eyes of a child, uncertain but eager to please. They were laughing at him because he was mentally retarded.

And I had been laughing at him too.

Suddenly, I was furious at myself and all those who were smirking at him. I jumped up and shouted, "Shut up! Leave him alone! It's not his fault he can't understand! He can't help what he is! But . . . he's still a human being!"

The room grew silent. I cursed myself for losing control and creating a scene. I tried not to look at the boy as I paid my check and walked out without touching my food. I felt ashamed for both of us.

How strange it is that people of honest feelings and sensibility, who would not take advantage of a man born without arms or legs or eyes—how such people think nothing of abusing a man born with low intelligence. It infuriated me to think that not too long ago I, like this boy, had foolishly played the clown.

And I had almost forgotten.

I'd hidden the picture of the old Charlie Gordon from myself because now that I was intelligent it was something that had to be pushed out of my mind. But today in looking at that boy, for the first time I saw what I had been. *I was just like him!*

Only a short time ago, I learned that people laughed at me. Now I can see that unknowingly I joined with them in laughing at myself. That hurts most of all.

I have often reread my progress reports and seen the illiteracy, the childish naïveté,[10] the mind of low intelligence peering from a dark room, through the keyhole, at the dazzling light outside. I see that even in my dullness I knew that I was inferior, and that other people had something I lacked— something denied me. In my mental blindness, I thought that it was somehow connected with the ability to read and write, and I was sure that if I could get those skills I would automatically have intelligence too.

Even a feeble-minded man wants to be like other men.

A child may not know how to feed itself, or what to eat, yet it knows of hunger.

This then is what I was like. I never knew. Even with my gift of intellectual awareness, I never really knew.

This day was good for me. Seeing the past more clearly, I have decided to use my knowledge and skills to work in the field of increasing human intelligence levels. Who is better equipped for this work? Who else has lived in both worlds? These are my people. Let me use my gift to do something for them.

Tomorrow, I will discuss with Dr. Strauss the manner in which I can work in this area. I may be able to help him work out the problems of widespread use of the technique which was used on me. I have several good ideas of my own.

---

10. naiveté (nä ēv′ tā) *n.*: Simplicity.

There is so much that might be done with this technique. If I could be made into a genius, what about thousands of others like myself? What fantastic levels might be achieved by using this technique on normal people? On *geniuses*?

There are so many doors to open. I am impatient to begin.

PROGRESS REPORT 13

May 23 It happened today. Algernon bit me. I visited the lab to see him as I do occasionally, and when I took him out of his cage, he snapped at my hand. I put him back and watched him for a while. He was unusually disturbed and vicious.

May 24 Burt, who is in charge of the experimental animals, tells me that Algernon is changing. He is less cooperative; he refuses to run the maze any more; general motivation has decreased. And he hasn't been eating. Everyone is upset about what this may mean.

May 25 They've been feeding Algernon, who now refuses to work the shifting-lock problem. Everyone identifies me with Algernon. In a way we're both the first of our kind. They're all pretending that Algernon's behavior is not necessarily significant for me. But it's hard to hide the fact that some of the other animals who were used in this experiment are showing strange behavior.

Dr. Strauss and Dr. Nemur have asked me not to come to the lab any more. I know what they're thinking but I can't accept it. I am going ahead with my plans to carry their research forward. With all due respect to both of these fine scientists, I am well aware of their limitations. If there is an answer, I'll have to find it out for myself. Suddenly, time has become very important to me.

May 29 I have been given a lab of my own and permission to go ahead with the research. I'm on to something. Working day and night. I've had a cot moved into the lab. Most of my writing time is spent on the notes which I keep in a separate folder, but from time to time I feel it necessary to put down my moods and my thoughts out of sheer habit.

I find the *calculus of intelligence* to be a fascinating study. Here is the place for the application of all the knowledge I have acquired. In a sense it's the problem I've been concerned with all my life.

May 31 Dr. Strauss thinks I'm working too hard. Dr. Nemur says I'm trying to cram a lifetime of research and thought into a few weeks. I know I should rest, but I'm driven on by something inside that won't let me stop. I've got to find the reason for the sharp regression in Algernon. I've got to know *if* and *when* it will happen to me.

June 4

Letter to Dr. Strauss *(copy)*

Dear Dr. Strauss:

Under separate cover I am sending you a copy of my report entitled, "The Algernon-Gordon Effect: A Study of Structure and Function of Increased Intelligence," which I would like to have you read and have published.

As you see, my experiments are completed. I have included in my report all of my formulae, as well as mathematical analysis in the appendix. Of course, these should be verified.

Because of its importance to both you and Dr. Nemur (and need I say to

myself, too?) I have checked and re-checked my results a dozen times in the hope of finding an error. I am sorry to say the results must stand. Yet for the sake of science, I am grateful for the little bit that I here add to the knowledge of the function of the human mind and of the laws governing the artificial increase of human intelligence.

I recall your once saying to me that an experimental *failure* or the *disproving* of a theory was as important to the advancement of learning as a success would be. I know now that this is true. I am sorry, however, that my own contribution to the field must rest upon the ashes of the work of two men I regard so highly.

Yours truly,

Charles Gordon

encl.: rept.

June 5 I must not become emotional. The facts and the results of my experiments are clear, and the more sensational aspects of my own rapid climb cannot obscure the fact that the tripling of intelligence by the surgical technique developed by Drs. Strauss and Nemur must be viewed as having little or no practical applicability (at the present time) to the increase of human intelligence.

As I review the records and data on Algernon, I see that although he is still in his physical infancy, he has regressed mentally. Motor activity[11] is impaired; there is a general reduction of glandular activity; there is an accelerated loss of coordination.

There are also strong indications of progressive amnesia.

As will be seen by my report, these and other physical and mental deterioration syndromes can be predicted with statistically significant results by the application of my formula.

The surgical stimulus to which we were both subjected has resulted in an intensification and acceleration of all mental processes. The unforeseen development, which I have taken the liberty of calling the "Algernon-Gordon Effect," is the logical extension of the entire intelligence speedup. The hypothesis here proven may be described simply in the following terms: Artificially increased intelligence deteriorates at a rate of time directly proportional to the quantity of the increase.

I feel that this, in itself, is an important discovery.

As long as I am able to write, I will continue to record my thoughts in these progress reports. It is one of my few pleasures. However, by all indications, my own mental deterioration will be very rapid.

I have already begun to notice signs of emotional instability and forgetfulness, the first symptoms of the burnout.

June 10 Deterioration progressing. I have become absent-minded. Algernon died two days ago. Dissection shows my predic-

tions were right. His brain had decreased in weight and there was a general smoothing out of cerebral convolutions as well as a deepening and broadening of brain fissures.

I guess the same thing is or will soon be happening to me. Now that it's definite, I don't want it to happen.

I put Algernon's body in a cheese box and buried him in the back yard. I cried.

June 15 Dr. Strauss came to see me again. I wouldn't open the door and I told him to go away. I want to be left to myself. I have become touchy and irritable. I feel the darkness closing in. I keep telling myself how important this introspective journal will be.

It's a strange sensation to pick up a book that you've read and enjoyed just a few months ago and discover that you don't remember it. I remembered how great I thought John Milton[12] was, but when I picked up *Paradise Lost* I couldn't understand it at all. I got so angry I threw the book across the room.

I've got to try to hold on to some of it. Some of the things I've learned. Oh, God, please don't take it all away.

June 19 Sometimes, at night, I go out for a walk. Last night I couldn't remember where I lived. A policeman took me home. I have the strange feeling that this has all happened to me before—a long time ago. I keep telling myself I'm the only person in the world who can describe what's happening to me.

June 21 Why can't I remember? I've got to fight. I lie in bed for days and I don't know who or where I am. Then it all comes

---

11. motor activity: Movement, physical coordination.

12. John Milton: British poet (1608–1674).
13. fugues (fyo͞ogz) **of amnesia** (am nē′ zhə): Periods of loss of memory.

back to me in a flash. Fugues of amnesia.[13] Symptoms of senility—second childhood. I can watch them coming on. It's so cruelly logical. I learned so much and so fast. Now my mind is deteriorating rapidly. I won't let it happen. I'll fight it. I can't help thinking of the boy in the restaurant, the blank expression, the silly smile, the people laughing at him. No—please—not that again . . .

June 22 I'm forgetting things that I learned recently. It seems to be following the classic pattern—the last things learned are the first things forgotten. Or is that the pattern? I'd better look it up again . . .

I reread my paper on the "Algernon-Gordon Effect" and I get the strange feeling that it was written by someone else. There are parts I don't even understand.

Motor activity impaired. I keep tripping over things, and it becomes increasingly difficult to type.

June 23 I've given up using the typewriter completely. My coordination is bad. I feel that I'm moving slower and slower. Had a terrible shock today. I picked up a copy of an article I used in my research, Krueger's "Uber psychische Ganzheit," to see if it would help me understand what I had done. First I thought there was something wrong with my eyes. Then I realized I could no longer read German. I tested myself in other languages. All gone.

June 30 A week since I dared to write again. It's slipping away like sand through my fingers. Most of the books I have are too hard for me now. I get angry with them because I know that I read and understood them just a few weeks ago.

I keep telling myself I must keep writing these reports so that somebody will know what is happening to me. But it gets harder to form the words and remember spellings. I have to look up even simple words in the dictionary now and it makes me impatient with myself.

Dr. Strauss comes around almost every day, but I told him I wouldn't see or speak to anybody. He feels guilty. They all do. But I don't blame anyone. I knew what might happen. But how it hurts.

July 7 I don't know where the week went. Todays Sunday I know because I can see through my window, people going to church. I think I stayed in bed all week but I remember Mrs. Flynn bringing food to me a few times. I keep saying over and over Ive got to do something but then I forget or maybe its just easier not to do what I say Im going to do.

I think of my mother and father a lot these days. I found a picture of them with me taken at a beach. My father has a big ball under his arm and my mother is holding me by the hand. I dont remember them the way they are in the picture. All I remember is my father arguing with mom about money.

He never shaved much and he used to scratch my face when he hugged me. He said he was going to take me to see cows on a farm once but he never did. He never kept his promises . . .

July 10 My landlady Mrs Flynn is very worried about me. She said she doesnt like loafers. If Im sick its one thing, but if Im a loafer thats another thing and she wont have it. I told her I think Im sick.

I try to read a little bit every day, mostly stories, but sometimes I have to read the same thing over and over again because I dont know what it means. And its hard to write. I know I should look up all the words in the dictionary but its so hard and Im so tired all the time.

Then I got the idea that I would only use the easy words instead of the long hard ones. That saves time. I put flowers on Algernons grave about once a week. Mrs. Flynn thinks Im crazy to put flowers on a mouses grave but I told her that Algernon was special.

July 14 Its sunday again. I dont have anything to do to keep me busy now because my television set is broke and I dont have any money to get it fixed. (I think I lost this months check from the lab. I dont remember)

I get awful headaches and asperin doesnt help me much. Mrs. Flynn knows Im really sick and she feels very sorry for me. Shes a wonderful woman whenever someone is sick.

July 22 Mrs. Flynn called a strange doctor to see me. She was afraid I was going to die. I told the doctor I wasnt too sick and that I only forget sometimes. He asked me did I have any friends or relatives and I said no I dont have any. I told him I had a friend called Algernon once but he was a mouse and we used to run races together. He looked at me kind of funny like he thought I was crazy.

He smiled when I told him I used to be a genius. He talked to me like I was a baby and he winked at Mrs Flynn. I got mad and chased him out because he was making fun of me the way they all used to.

July 24 I have no more money and Mrs Flynn says I got to go to work somewhere and pay the rent because I havent paid for over two months. I dont know any work but the job I used to have at Donnegans Plastic Box Company. I dont want to go back there because they all knew me when I was smart and maybe they'll laugh at me. But I dont know what else to do to get money.

July 25 I was looking at some of my old progress reports and its very funny but I cant read what I wrote. I can make out some of the words but they dont make sense.

Miss Kinnian came to the door but I said go away I dont want to see you. She cried and I cried too but I wouldnt let her in because I didnt want her to laugh at me. I told her I didn't like her any more. I told her I didn't want to be smart any more. Thats not true. I still love her and I still want to be smart but I had to say that so shed go away. She gave Mrs. Flynn money to pay the rent. I dont want that. I got to get a job.

Please . . . please let me not forget how to read and write . . .

July 27 Mr. Donnegan was very nice when I came back and asked him for my old job of janitor. First he was very suspicious but I told him what happened to me then he looked very sad and put his hand on my shoulder and said Charlie Gordon you got guts.

Everybody looked at me when I came downstairs and started working in the toilet sweeping it out like I used to. I told myself Charlie if they make fun of you dont get sore because you remember their not so smart as you once thot they were. And besides they were once your friends and if they laughed at you that doesnt mean anything because they liked you too.

One of the new men who came to work there after I went away made a nasty crack he said hey Charlie I hear your a very smart fella a real quiz kid. Say something intelligent. I felt bad but Joe Carp came over and grabbed him by the shirt and said leave him alone or Ill break your neck. I didnt expect

Joe to take my part so I guess hes really my friend.

Later Frank Reilly came over and said Charlie if anybody bothers you or trys to take advantage you call me or Joe and we will set em straight. I said thanks Frank and I got choked up so I had to turn around and go into the supply room so he wouldnt see me cry. Its good to have friends.

July 28 I did a dumb thing today I forgot I wasnt in Miss Kinnians class at the adult center any more like I use to be. I went in and sat down in my old seat in the back of the room and she looked at me funny and she said Charles. I dint remember she ever called me that before only Charlie so I said hello Miss Kinnian Im ready for my lesin today only I lost my reader that we was using. She startid to cry and run out of the room and everybody looked at me and I saw they wasnt the same pepul who use to be in my class.

Then all of a suddin I rememberd some things about the operashun and me getting smart and I said holy smoke I reely pulled a Charlie Gordon that time. I went away before she come back to the room.

Thats why Im going away from New York for good. I dont want to do nothing like that agen. I dont want Miss Kinnian to feel sorry for me. Evry body feels sorry at the factery and I dont want that eather so Im going someplace where nobody knows that Charlie Gordon was once a genus and now he cant even reed a book or rite good.

Im taking a cuple of books along and even if I cant reed them Ill practise hard and maybe I wont forget every thing I lerned. If I try reel hard maybe Ill be a littel bit smarter then I was before the operashun. I got my rabits foot and my luky penny and maybe they will help me.

If you ever reed this Miss Kinnian dont be sorry for me Im glad I got a second chanse to be smart becaus I lerned a lot of things that I never even new were in this world and Im grateful that I saw it all for a littel bit. I dont know why Im dumb agen or what I did wrong maybe its becaus I dint try hard enuff. But if I try and practis very hard maybe Ill get a littl smarter and know what all the words are. I remember a littel bit how nice I had a feeling with the blue book that has the torn cover when I red it. Thats why Im gonna keep trying to get smart so I can have that feeling agen. Its a good feeling to know things and be smart. I wish I had it rite now if I did I woud sit down and reed all the time. Anyway I bet Im the first dumb person in the world who ever found out somthing importent for sience. I remember I did somthing but I dont remember what. So I gess its like I did it for all the dumb pepul like me.

Goodbye Miss Kinnian and Dr Strauss and evreybody. And P.S. please tell Dr Nemur not to be such a grouch when pepul laff at him and he woud have more frends. Its easy to make frends if you let pepul laff at you. Im going to have lots of frends where I go.

P.P.S. Please if you get a chanse put some flowrs on Algernons grave in the bak yard . . .

THINKING ABOUT THE SELECTION

Recalling

1. Why is Charlie keeping a journal?
2. Why does Miss Kinnian believe Charlie should take part in this experiment? Why does she also fear for him?
3. Why does Charlie believe he failed the Rorschach test? What does he come to learn about the Rorschach test?
4. Why does Dr. Strauss think that Charlie is a fit subject for the experiment? Why does Dr. Nemur disagree?
5. How do Charlie's coworkers treat him after he becomes smart? Why does he leave his job?
6. In his June 22 report, what feeling about his scientific paper does Charlie reveal?
7. Why does Charlie decide to leave New York?

Interpreting

8. Explain how Charlie's development parallels Algernon's.
9. How do the spelling and punctuation in Charlie's reports contribute to your view of his progress? How do the books he reads contribute?
10. How is Charlie at the end of the story different from Charlie at the beginning?
11. Do you think "Flowers for Algernon" is a good title for this story? Explain your answer.

Applying

12. As Charlie grows smarter, he asks questions. Explain why the ability to ask questions is an important part of intelligence.

ANALYZING LITERATURE

Understanding Point of View and Theme

When a story is told by a character in it, you see events through this character's eyes. What this character learns helps reveal the theme.

1. What kind of person is Charlie?
2. At the beginning of the story, Charlie views Miss Kinnian, Dr. Strauss, and Dr. Nemur as almost perfect human beings. How does he view them as he grows smarter? How does he view them at the end of the story?
3. Find three examples in the story of how Charlie's views of friendship change.
4. What is the theme of this story?

CRITICAL THINKING AND READING

Comparing and Contrasting Views

When you examine the similarities between two subjects, you **compare** them. When you examine the differences, you **contrast** them.

In "Flowers for Algernon," Charlie's perceptions change as he moves from unintelligence to genius and back again. The views of the people around him also change.

1. Contrast Charlie's reaction to the first party (page 206) with the second (page 209).
2. Compare Charlie's general attitude at the end when he visits the classroom by mistake (page 221) with his attitude at the beginning.
3. Contrast Miss Kinnian's attitude toward Charlie before his operation with that on April 28 (page 212).

THINKING AND WRITING

Writing About Theme

Assume that at the time of the June 10 progress report, Charlie learns another retarded person has the opportunity to undergo the same operation. Freewrite for three minutes as Charlie about his feelings about the operation. Then write a letter in which Charlie gives the person advice on whether to have the operation. Revise your letter, making sure you have presented your case clearly. Proofread, checking for spelling, grammar, and punctuation.

PUTTING IT TOGETHER

The Short Story

A short story is a brief work of fiction made up of elements known as plot, characters, setting, and theme. All these elements should combine to create a single effect. You will gain the most enjoyment by reading actively. Like a detective, an active reader looks for clues to elements of a story and discovers how they work together.

Plot

The plot is the sequence of events. While reading a story, make sure you follow the sequence of events. Do you know the order in which events occur? Do you understand how they are related to each other? Can you identify the conflict, or central problem? How does the author create suspense and keep you interested in the events? Can you identify the climax and resolution of the conflict? Do you understand how the actions affect the characters?

Characters

The characters are the people, and sometimes the animals, who take part in the story's events. Who is the main character? Who are the minor characters? What are the character traits and motivations of the different characters? Does the author use both direct and indirect characterization? Which of the characters seem most lifelike? How are the characters influenced by the setting?

Setting

The setting is the place and time of the events. As you read, visualize the setting. Where does the story take place? How much detail does the author give you about the setting? Do events occur in the present, the past, or the future? Do events occur over a long or short period of time? What kind of atmosphere or mood does the author create? How does this mood affect the whole story?

Theme

The theme is a general idea about life that a story communicates. Ask yourself whether the story you are reading has a theme. Not all stories do. Does the main character change in a significant way that reveals the theme? Does the main character learn something about life? Is the theme stated directly or implied?

The comments in the margin of the story that follows review for you the elements of the short story. They also show questions an active reader might ask about these elements while reading.

The Medicine Bag

Virginia Driving Hawk Sneve

Theme: The title may provide an important clue to the theme. What is a medicine bag?

My kid sister Cheryl and I always bragged about our Sioux[1] grandpa, Joe Iron Shell. Our friends, who had always lived in the city and only knew about Indians from movies and TV, were impressed by our stories. Maybe we exaggerated and made Grandpa and the reservation sound glamorous, but when we'd return home to Iowa after our yearly summer visit to Grandpa, we always had some exciting tale to tell.

We always had some authentic Sioux article to show our listeners. One year Cheryl had new moccasins[2] that Grandpa had made. On another visit he gave me a small, round, flat, rawhide drum that was decorated with a painting of a warrior riding a horse. He taught me a real Sioux chant to sing while I beat the drum with a leather-covered stick that had a feather on the end. Man, that really made an impression.

Character: The main character seems to be a teen-age boy who enjoys impressing his friends with his Sioux heritage. What does his desire to impress his friends indicate about him?

We never showed our friends Grandpa's picture. Not that we were ashamed of him, but because we knew that the glamorous tales we told didn't go with the real thing. Our friends would have laughed at the picture because Grandpa wasn't tall and stately like TV Indians. His hair wasn't in braids but hung in stringy, gray strands on his neck, and he was old. He was our great-grandfather, and he didn't live in a tepee,[3] but all by himself in a part log, part tar-paper shack on the Rosebud Reservation[4] in South Dakota. So when Grandpa came to visit us, I was so ashamed and embarrassed I could've died.

Plot: The boy is experiencing an internal conflict. He loves his grandfather but is also embarrassed by him. How will he work out his problem?

There are a lot of yippy poodles and other fancy little dogs in our neighborhood, but they usually barked singly

---

1. Sioux (soo) *n.*: Native-American tribes of the northern plains of the United States and nearby southern Canada.
2. moccasins (mäk′ ə s′nz) *n.*: Heeless slippers of soft flexible leather, originally worn by native Americans.
3. tepee (tē′ pē) *n.*: A cone-shaped tent of animal skins, used by the Plains Indians.
4. Rosebud Reservation: A small Indian reservation in south-central South Dakota.

at the mailman from the safety of their own yards. Now it sounded as if a whole pack of mutts were barking together in one place.

I got up and walked to the curb to see what the commotion was. About a block away I saw a crowd of little kids yelling, with the dogs yipping and growling around someone who was walking down the middle of the street.

I watched the group as it slowly came closer and saw that in the center of the strange procession was a man wearing a tall black hat. He'd pause now and then to peer at something in his hand and then at the houses on either side of the street. I felt cold and hot at the same time as I recognized the man. "Oh, no!" I whispered. "It's Grandpa!"

I stood on the curb, unable to move even though I wanted to run and hide. Then I got mad when I saw how the yippy dogs were growling and nipping at the old man's baggy pant legs and how wearily he poked them away with his cane. "Stupid mutts," I said as I ran to rescue Grandpa.

When I kicked and hollered at the dogs to get away, they put their tails between their legs and scattered. The kids ran to the curb where they watched me and the old man.

"Grandpa," I said and felt pretty dumb when my voice cracked. I reached for his beat-up old tin suitcase, which was tied shut with a rope. But he set it down right in the street and shook my hand.

"*Hau, Takoza,* Grandchild," he greeted me formally in Sioux.

All I could do was stand there with the whole neighborhood watching and shake the hand of the leather-brown old man. I saw how his gray hair straggled from under his big black hat, which had a drooping feather in its crown. His rumpled black suit hung like a sack over his stooped frame. As he shook my hand, his coat fell open to expose a bright red satin shirt with a beaded bolo tie[5] under the collar. His get-up wasn't out of place on the reservation, but it sure was here, and I wanted to sink right through the pavement.

"Hi," I muttered with my head down. I tried to pull my hand away when I felt his bony hand trembling, and looked up to see fatigue in his face. I felt like crying. I couldn't think of

---

Plot: Notice how this internal conflict is shown by his feeling hot and cold at the same time. Will he go to his grandfather's assistance?

Setting: The confusion in this scene reflects the confusion in the boy's mind. Which sensory details are especially vivid?

---

5. bolo (bō' lō) **tie,** *n.*: A man's string tie, held together with a decorated sliding device.

anything to say so I picked up Grandpa's suitcase, took his arm, and guided him up the driveway to our house.

Mom was standing on the steps. I don't know how long she'd been watching, but her hand was over her mouth and she looked as if she couldn't believe what she saw. Then she ran to us.

"Grandpa," she gasped. "How in the world did you get here?"

She checked her move to embrace Grandpa and I remembered that such a display of affection is unseemly to the Sioux and would embarrass him.

"*Hau,* Marie," he said as he shook Mom's hand. She smiled and took his other arm.

As we supported him up the steps, the door banged open and Cheryl came bursting out of the house. She was all smiles and was so obviously glad to see Grandpa that I was ashamed of how I felt.

Character: Cheryl's reaction to Grandpa is very different from the boy's. How does this contrast make the boy feel?

"Grandpa!" she yelled happily. "You came to see us!"

Grandpa smiled, and Mom and I let go of him as he stretched out his arms to my ten-year-old sister, who was still young enough to be hugged.

"*Wicincala,* little girl," he greeted her and then collapsed.

He had fainted. Mom and I carried him into her sewing room, where we had a spare bed.

After we had Grandpa on the bed, Mom stood there helplessly patting his shoulder.

"Shouldn't we call the doctor, Mom?" I suggested, since she didn't seem to know what to do.

"Yes," she agreed with a sigh. "You make Grandpa comfortable, Martin."

I reluctantly moved to the bed. I knew Grandpa wouldn't want to have Mom undress him, but I didn't want to, either. He was so skinny and frail that his coat slipped off easily. When I loosened his tie and opened his shirt collar, I felt a small leather pouch that hung from a thong[6] around his neck. I left it alone and moved to remove his boots. The scuffed old cowboy boots were tight, and he moaned as I put pressure on his legs to jerk them off.

Plot: Grandpa appears to be ill. Will his illness play a role in the plot?

I put the boots on the floor and saw why they fit so tight.

---

6. thong, *n.*: A narrow strip of leather.

Each one was stuffed with money. I looked at the bills that lined the boots and started to ask about them, but Grandpa's eyes were closed again.

Mom came back with a basin of water. "The doctor thinks Grandpa is suffering from heat exhaustion," she explained as she bathed Grandpa's face. Mom gave a big sigh, *"Oh, hinh, Martin. How do you suppose he got here?"*

We found out after the doctor's visit. Grandpa was angrily sitting up in bed while Mom tried to feed him some soup.

"Tonight you let Marie feed you, Grandpa," spoke my dad, who had gotten home from work just as the doctor was leaving. "You're not really sick," he said as he gently pushed Grandpa back against the pillows. "The doctor said you just got too tired and hot after your long trip."

Grandpa relaxed, and between sips of soup, he told us of his journey. Soon after our visit to him, Grandpa decided that he would like to see where his only living descendants lived and what our home was like. Besides, he admitted sheepishly, he was lonesome after we left.

Theme: The characters in this story come from two different cultures. Will the importance of heritage be an aspect of theme?

I knew that everybody felt as guilty as I did—especially Mom. Mom was all Grandpa had left. So even after she married my dad, who's a white man and teaches in the college in our city, and after Cheryl and I were born, Mom made sure that every summer we spent a week with Grandpa.

I never thought that Grandpa would be lonely after our visits, and none of us noticed how old and weak he had become. But Grandpa knew, and so he came to us. He had ridden on buses for two and a half days. When he arrived in the city, tired and stiff from sitting for so long, he set out, walking, to find us.

He had stopped to rest on the steps of some building downtown, and a policeman found him. The cop, according to Grandpa, was a good man who took him to the bus stop and waited until the bus came and told the driver to let Grandpa out at Bell View Drive. After Grandpa got off the bus, he started walking again. But he couldn't see the house numbers on the other side when he walked on the sidewalk, so he walked in the middle of the street. That's when all the little kids and dogs followed him.

Character: Here the boy feels proud of his grandfather. What qualities does he admire?

I knew everybody felt as bad as I did. Yet I was so proud of this eighty-six-year-old man, who had never been away from the reservation, having the courage to travel so far alone.

"You found the money in my boots?" he asked Mom.

"Martin did," she answered, and roused herself to scold. "Grandpa, you shouldn't have carried so much money. What if someone had stolen it from you?"

Grandpa laughed. "I would've known if anyone tried to take the boots off my feet. The money is what I've saved for a long time—a hundred dollars—for my funeral. But you take it now to buy groceries so that I won't be a burden to you while I am here."

"That won't be necessary, Grandpa," Dad said. "We are honored to have you with us, and you will never be a burden. I am only sorry that we never thought to bring you home with us this summer and spare you the discomfort of a long trip."

Grandpa was pleased. "Thank you," he answered. "But do not feel bad that you didn't bring me with you, for I would not have come then. It was not time." He said this in such a way that no one could argue with him. To Grandpa and the Sioux, he once told me, a thing would be done when it was the right time to do it, and that's the way it was.

Theme: The last sentence here seems significant. What does it mean?

"Also," Grandpa went on, looking at me, "I have come because it is soon time for Martin to have the medicine bag."

We all knew what that meant. Grandpa thought he was going to die, and he had to follow the tradition of his family to pass the medicine bag, along with its history, to the oldest male child.

Theme: Here is the medicine bag mentioned in the title. What does the medicine bag mean to Grandpa? What will it mean to Martin?

"Even though the boy," he said still looking at me, "bears a white man's name, the medicine bag will be his."

I didn't know what to say. I had the same hot and cold feeling that I had when I first saw Grandpa in the street. The medicine bag was the dirty leather pouch I had found around his neck. "I could never wear such a thing," I almost said aloud. I thought of having my friends see it in gym class or at the swimming pool and could imagine the smart things they would say. But I just swallowed hard and took a step toward the bed. I knew I would have to take it.

But Grandpa was tired. "Not now, Martin," he said, waving his hand in dismissal. "It is not time. Now I will sleep."

So that's how Grandpa came to be with us for two months. My friends kept asking to come see the old man, but I put them off. I told myself that I didn't want them laughing at Grandpa. But even as I made excuses, I knew it wasn't Grandpa that I was afraid they'd laugh at.

Nothing bothered Cheryl about bringing her friends to see Grandpa. Every day after school started, there'd be a crew of giggling little girls or round-eyed little boys crowded around the old man on the patio, where he'd gotten in the habit of sitting every afternoon.

Grandpa would smile in his gentle way and patiently answer their questions, or he'd tell them stories of brave warriors, ghosts, animals; and the kids listened in awed silence. Those little guys thought Grandpa was great.

Finally, one day after school, my friends came home with me because nothing I said stopped them. "We're going to see the great Indian of Bell View Drive," said Hank, who was supposed to be my best friend. "My brother has seen him three times so he oughta be well enough to see us."

When we got to my house, Grandpa was sitting on the patio. He had on his red shirt, but today he also wore a fringed leather vest that was decorated with beads. Instead of his usual cowboy boots, he had solidly beaded moccasins on his feet that stuck out of his black trousers. Of course, he had his old black hat on—he was seldom without it. But it had been brushed, and the feather in the beaded headband was proudly erect, its tip a brighter white. His hair lay in silver strands over the red shirt collar.

I stared just as my friends did, and I heard one of them murmur, "Wow!"

Grandpa looked up, and, when his eyes met mine, they twinkled as if he were laughing inside. He nodded to me, and my face got all hot. I could tell that he had known all along I was afraid he'd embarrass me in front of my friends.

"*Hau, hoksilas,* boys," he greeted and held out his hand.

My buddies passed in a single file and shook his hand as I introduced them. They were so polite I almost laughed. "How, there, Grandpa," and even a "How-do-you-do, sir."

"You look fine, Grandpa," I said as the guys sat on the lawn chairs or on the patio floor.

"*Hanh,* yes," he agreed. "When I woke up this morning, it seemed the right time to dress in the good clothes. I knew that my grandson would be bringing his friends."

"You guys want some lemonade or something?" I offered. No one answered. They were listening to Grandpa as he started telling how he'd killed the deer from which his vest was made.

Grandpa did most of the talking while my friends were there. I was so proud of him and amazed at how respectfully quiet my buddies were. Mom had to chase them home at supper time. As they left, they shook Grandpa's hand again and said to me,

"Martin, he's really great!"

"Yeah, man! Don't blame you for keeping him to yourself."

"Can we come back?"

But after they left, Mom said, "No more visitors for a while, Martin. Grandpa won't admit it, but his strength hasn't returned. He likes having company, but it tires him."

That evening Grandpa called me to his room before he went to sleep. "Tomorrow," he said, "when you come home, it will be time to give you the medicine bag."

I felt a hard squeeze from where my heart is supposed to be and was scared, but I answered, "OK, Grandpa."

All night I had weird dreams about thunder and lightning on a high hill. From a distance I heard the slow beat of a drum. When I woke up in the morning, I felt as if I hadn't slept at all. At school it seemed as if the day would never end and, when it finally did, I ran home.

Plot: The writer vividly portrays the turmoil going on in Martin's mind. Will Martin learn anything from Grandpa the next day that helps him?

Grandpa was in his room, sitting on the bed. The shades were down, and the place was dim and cool. I sat on the floor in front of Grandpa, but he didn't even look at me. After what seemed a long time he spoke.

"I sent your mother and sister away. What you will hear today is only for a man's ears. What you will receive is only for a man's hands." He fell silent, and I felt shivers down my back.

"My father in his early manhood," Grandpa began, "made a vision quest[7] to find a spirit guide for his life. You cannot understand how it was in that time, when the great Teton Sioux were first made to stay on the reservation. There was a strong need for guidance from *Wakantanka*,[8] the Great Spirit. But too many of the young men were filled with despair and hatred. They thought it was hopeless to search for a vision when the glorious life was gone and only the hated confines of a reservation lay ahead. But my father held to the old ways.

"He carefully prepared for his quest with a purifying sweat bath, and then he went alone to a high butte top[9] to fast and pray. After three days he received his sacred dream—in which he found, after long searching, the white man's iron. He did not understand his vision of finding something belonging to the white people, for in that time they were the enemy. When he came down from the butte to cleanse himself at the stream below, he found the remains of a campfire and the broken shell of an iron kettle. This was a sign that reinforced his dream. He took a piece of the iron for his medicine bag, which he had made of elk skin years before, to prepare for his quest.

"He returned to his village, where he told his dream to the wise old men of the tribe. They gave him the name *Iron Shell*, but neither did they understand the meaning of the dream. The first Iron Shell kept the piece of iron with him at all times and believed it gave him protection from the evils of those unhappy days.

Theme: This anecdote helps clarify the theme. What does the iron shell represent? How did his vision help him reconcile, or make peace between, the Indian world and the white world?

---

7. vision quest: A search for a revelation that would aid understanding.
8. Wakantanka (wä′ kən tank′ ə) *n.*: The Sioux religion's most important spirit—the creator of the world.
9. butte (byoot) **top,** *n.*: The top of a steep hill standing alone in a plain.

"Then a terrible thing happened to Iron Shell. He and several other young men were taken from their homes by the soldiers and sent far away to a white man's boarding school. He was angry and lonesome for his parents and the young girl he had wed before he was taken away. At first Iron Shell resisted the teacher's attempts to change him, and he did not try to learn. One day it was his turn to work in the school's blacksmith shop. As he walked into the place, he knew that his medicine had brought him there to learn and work with the white man's iron.

"Iron Shell became a blacksmith and worked at the trade when he returned to the reservation. All of his life he treasured the medicine bag. When he was old, and I was a man, he gave it to me, for no one made the vision quest any more."

Grandpa quit talking, and I stared in disbelief as he covered his face with his hands. His shoulders were shaking with quiet sobs, and I looked away until he began to speak again.

"I kept the bag until my son, your mother's father, was a man and had to leave us to fight in the war across the ocean. I gave him the bag, for I believed it would protect him in battle, but he did not take it with him. He was afraid that he would lose it. He died in a faraway place."

Again Grandpa was still, and I felt his grief around me.

"My son," he went on after clearing his throat, "had only a daughter, and it is not proper for her to know of these things."

He unbuttoned his shirt, pulled out the leather pouch, and lifted it over his head. He held it in his hand, turning it over and over as if memorizing how it looked.

"In the bag," he said as he opened it and removed two objects, "is the broken shell of the iron kettle, a pebble from the butte, and a piece of the sacred sage."[10] He held the pouch upside down and dust drifted down.

"After the bag is yours you must put a piece of prairie sage within and never open it again until you pass it on to your son." He replaced the pebble and the piece of iron, and tied the bag.

I stood up, somehow knowing I should. Grandpa slowly rose from the bed and stood upright in front of me holding the bag before my face. I closed my eyes and waited for him to slip it over my head. But he spoke.

"No, you need not wear it." He placed the soft leather bag in my right hand and closed my other hand over it. "It would not be right to wear it in this time and place where no one will understand. Put it safely away until you are again on the reservation. Wear it then, when you replace the sacred sage."

Grandpa turned and sat again on the bed. Wearily he leaned his head against the pillow. "Go," he said. "I will sleep now."

"Thank you, Grandpa," I said softly and left with the bag in my hands.

That night Mom and Dad took Grandpa to the hospital. Two weeks later I stood alone on the lonely prairie of the reservation and put the sacred sage in my medicine bag.

---

10. **sage** (sāj) *n.*: Plant belonging to the mint family.

Virginia Driving Hawk Sneve (1933–   ) grew up on the Sioux Reservation in South Dakota. This writer and teacher has won many awards for her fiction, including the Council on Interracial Books Award and the Western Writers of America award. In books such as *Jimmy Yellow Hawk*, *High Elk's Treasure*, and *When the Thunder Spoke*, she draws on her intimate knowledge of Sioux life. Her Sioux heritage also plays an important role in "The Medicine Bag."

Theme: The medicine bag serves as a symbol? What does it symbolize?

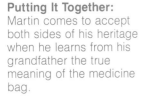

Putting It Together: Martin comes to accept both sides of his heritage when he learns from his grandfather the true meaning of the medicine bag.

THINKING ABOUT THE SELECTION

Recalling

1. Why is Martin embarrassed when Grandpa comes to visit? How is Cheryl's reaction to Grandpa's visit different from Martin's?
2. What three reasons does Grandpa give for his visit?
3. What is the purpose of a vision quest? How did Grandfather's father receive the name Iron Shell?
4. What does Martin do at the end of the story?

Interpreting

5. Compare and contrast the real Grandpa with the Grandpa Martin at first brags to his friends about.
6. How is the Sioux heritage Martin at first brags about different from the Sioux heritage he learns about from Grandpa?
7. What happens to Grandpa at the end of the story?
8. Explain how Martin comes to stand alone on the lonely prairie?

Applying

9. Why is it important for people to maintain their cultural heritage?

ANALYZING LITERATURE

Reviewing the Short Story

The elements of plot, character, setting, and theme all work together to create a total effect. Think of all of these elements and apply them to "The Medicine Bag."

1. Give a brief summary of the story, focusing on the conflict and the resolution.
2. Compare and contrast Martin and his grandfather.
3. Explain how time and place are important in this story.
4. How would you express the theme?

CRITICAL THINKING AND READING

Evaluating a Story

To evaluate a story means to judge how successfully it works. Using your knowledge of literary elements and how they work in short stories, you can comment on what you think works best in any story.

Prepare an answer to one of the following questions. Present your answer in a brief oral report to your classmates.

1. Do you think the characters in "The Medicine Bag" were well drawn?
2. Do you think the conflict was presented successfully?
3. What does the story say about the importance of a cultural heritage?

UNDERSTANDING LANGUAGE

Appreciating Another Language

A writer will sometimes use words from another language to help draw the characters more vividly. For example, in "The Medicine Bag" the author peppers Grandpa's speech with Sioux words.

1. What words does Grandpa use to greet Martin?
2. What word does he use to greet Cheryl?
3. What word does he use for the Great Spirit?

THINKING AND WRITING

Continuing a Story

Imagine you are Martin thirty years in the future. You now have a son of your own and want to pass on the medicine bag. Write a continuation of this story telling what you would say to your son. Revise your story, making sure you have clearly expressed the importance of the medicine bag to you. Finally, proofread your story and share it with your classmates.

Understanding Relationships

One way to increase your understanding of what you read it is to understand the relationships that exist in the plot, setting, and characters. **Time order, cause and effect,** and **comparison and contrast** are the most important relationships you will need to know.

Time Order

Time order refers to the sequence of events. In most stories events are arranged chronologically, that is, in the order in which they occurred. Writers often use signal words to help you see the sequence of events. Be aware of the following time-order signal words:

first	then	before	later	during	when	previously
at last	next	after	earlier	finally	now	preceding

Activity

Read the following paragraph and jot down the time-order signal words. Then list the events in chronological order.

> At first Charlie thought they wouldn't use him, for he was sure he had failed the inkblot test. And what is more, Algernon kept beating him in the mazes. Consequently, when Miss Kinnian told him he had been chosen for the operation, he had been ecstatic because he wanted to be smart. Now that his intelligence had tripled, he was amazed by how different things were from the way he once saw them. First he found out that his old spelling and punctuation were all wrong. Next he realized that Joe and Frank had been making fun of him. Then he saw what Dr. Nemur and Dr. Strauss were really like. Finally he perceived that Miss Kinnian was beautiful.

Cause and Effect

Cause-and-effect relationships help you understand why something occurs and how it is connected to other events. A **cause** is a reason for something happening. An **effect** is the result of some action or cause. Watch for the following signal words.

as	so	therefore	accordingly	consequently	so that
for	thus	as a result	in order that	because	since

Read these sentences:

At first Charlie thought they wouldn't use him, for he was sure he had failed the inkblot test.

Charlie thought they wouldn't use him because Algernon kept beating him in the mazes.

Because he was now smart, he perceived that Miss Kinnian was beautiful.

Note that the first two sentences have the same effect but two different causes. Often there are several reasons for something happening. In the first two sentences, the cause falls at the end of the sentence. In the third, it falls at the beginning.

Activity

Look again at the activity paragraph on page 236. Find at least five cause-and-effect relationships in the paragraph and write them in complete sentences, using one of the signal words.

Comparison and Contrast

Comparing involves finding ways that things are similar, while **contrasting** involves noting ways that they are different. Words such as *both, similar,* and *just as much* indicate a comparison relationship. The following words are used to show contrasting relationships:

but although in contrast   in spite of on the contrary   whereas yet however nevertheless instead   on the other hand while

Activity

Write a well-developed paragraph comparing and contrasting Charlie as he appeared at the beginning of the story and at the end. Brainstorm to determine how the two Charlies are alike and how they are different. Jot down words that would describe the first Charlie and ones that would characterize the last Charlie. Write your paragraph, including signal words to indicate the relationships. Use the information in this paragraph to write a second paragraph in which you determine whether Charlie was better off before the operation or after. Give reasons to support your decision.

YOU THE WRITER

Assignment

1. Select a character other than the narrator in one of the short stories and retell part of the story from his or her point of view. Use first-person narration.

Prewriting. Select one episode, or event, from the story. List the main action in that part of the story. Include the thoughts of the character you chose. Do not list other characters' thoughts.

Writing. Write the first draft of your episode. Remember to use first-person point of view.

Revising. Ask another student to read your episode. Can the person tell from which character's point of view you wrote? If not, you need to rewrite that section of your story. Reveal only what one character knows.

Assignment

2. The setting can contribute to the mood of a short story. Choose a particular mood you want to convey—tension? hostility? joy? peacefulness? Then describe a story setting that reflects that mood. Use specific details of time and place. Do not describe a character. Write only a physical description of time and place.

Prewriting. Record your mood in the middle of the page. Jot down details of a setting that creates this mood. Cluster these details.

Writing. Write the first draft of your description of a setting. Make sure the details you include help create the mood.

Revising. Review your first draft. Check to see that your description is unified; that is, that all the details help create a single impression, or mood.

Assignment

3. Mysteries are popular because they challenge the reader to solve the crime before the detective does. Try writing a short mystery. Think about how your "perfect crime" might be committed and what clues a detective would need in order to solve it.

Prewriting. Brainstorm to form a list of "perfect crimes." Choose one and list some clues a detective would need.

Writing. Write the first draft of your story. Be sure you clearly explain the problem that is to be solved.

Revising. Revise your story to make sure you have included enough background to the crime and all the necessary clues. Make sure that the solution is logical.

YOU THE CRITIC

Assignment

1. Choose a short story in which the main character faces a challenge. Write an essay describing the challenge, how the character deals with it, and the outcome.

Prewriting. Prepare an outline, with an emphasis on challenge. Use the outline to organize your thoughts.

Writing. Begin your essay with an extended definition of the word *challenge*. End this introductory paragraph with your premise. Use your outline to explain the challenge, fill in details of the character's actions, and flesh out how the challenge was met and its outcome.

Revising. Read over your essay. Check to see that you have presented your points clearly and arranged them in logical order.

Assignment

2. A symbol is an object, an action, or an idea that stands for something other than itself. Choose one of the short stories and write an essay exploring how symbolism is used.

Prewriting. Freewrite about the story you chose. Let your mind roam freely, jotting down thoughts about anything that might be a symbol.

Writing. Write the first draft of an essay. Be sure your essay deals with the symbols in a logical order. Try organizing your ideas according to an order-of-importance pattern.

Revising. Revise your first draft. Check to see that you have stated clearly what the symbols are and what they represent.

Assignment

3. Some of the short stories you read focus on a young person's viewpoint. Choose two young people from either two different stories or the same one. Compare these two characters, explaining how they are alike and what they learn about life.

Prewriting. Make two lists, one for each character. List the qualities and characteristics each person has.

Writing. Begin your essay by telling how the two characters are alike. Include at least three details from your lists. Use key words such as *similar, both,* and *comparison* to tell how the two characters relate. Then tell what they learn about life. Again, include details from your lists. Conclude with a sentence that summarizes the comparison of the two characters.

Revising. Revise your writing. Check to see that you used several key words to signal the comparisons.

FIRST ROW ORCHESTRA, 1951
Edward Hopper
Hirshhorn Museum and Sculpture Garden, Smithsonian Institution

DRAMA

What do you think of when you hear the word *drama?* Do you think of the theater with actors, a stage, costumes, sets, and a live audience? Do you think of the movies with action presented on a large screen? Do you think of the pleasure of sitting home and watching a drama unfold on television? Or do you think of hearing a play over the radio? The live theater, the movies, television, and radio—all are means by which drama comes to us.

A play is written to be performed. Therefore, when you read a play, you must visualize how it would appear and sound to an audience. By using your imagination, you can build a theater in your mind. Because a play is written to be performed, it uses certain conventions you do not encounter in short stories. It contains stage directions that tell the actors how to speak and how to move upon the stage. Most of the story is presented through dialogue, the words the characters speak. In addition it is divided into short units of action called "scenes" and larger ones called "acts."

In this unit you will encounter three short plays: a twist on a fairy tale, a romance, and a play with a social comment. In addition you will read one full-length play based on the diary of a young girl.

Drama

The word *drama* brings to mind the world of the theater. It is an exciting world—a curtain rising on a stage with sets, lights, and actors in costume. But drama includes more than the theater. Because drama is a story told in dialogue by performers before an audience, the definition includes television plays, radio plays, and even movies. In all these kinds of drama, actors make a world come alive before an audience.

Plays are meant to be performed, but it is possible just to read a play. When you read a play, you can make it come alive by staging it in your imagination. The play that you are reading is a script. It contains not only the words that the actors speak but also the stage directions the playwright provides to indicate how to put on the play. Stage directions tell what the stage should look like, what the characters wear, how they speak their lines, and where they move.

Stage directions use a particular vocabulary. *Right, left, up, down,* and *center* refer to areas of the stage as the actors see it. To help you visualize what is meant when a stage direction tells an actor to move down left, for example, picture the stage like this:

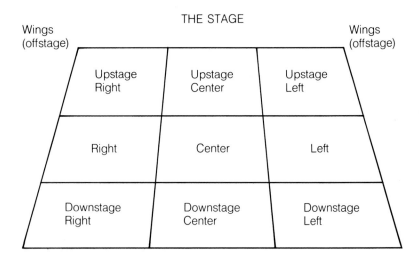

THE STAGE

Wings (offstage)

Wings (offstage)

Upstage Right	Upstage Center	Upstage Left
Right	Center	Left
Downstage Right	Downstage Center	Downstage Left

Curtain

When you are reading drama, right and left are the opposite of what you know. Remember that these are directions for actors, not viewers. Whether as reader, viewer, or actor, though, you too can enjoy the world of drama.

Becoming an active reader of drama will increase your understanding and enjoyment of plays. Reading actively includes seeing the play in your mind while you continually question the meaning of what the characters are saying and doing.

Use the following strategies to help you read drama actively. These strategies will help you to enjoy and appreciate the plays in this unit.

Visualize
Use the directions and information supplied by the playwright to picture the stage and the characters in action. Create the scene in your mind. Hear the characters' voices. See their gestures. Doing so will give meaning to their words.

Question
Question the meaning of each character's words and actions. What motives and traits do the words and actions reveal? What situation does each character face?

Predict
Once you recognize the conflict and understand the characters' motives, predict what you think will happen. How will the conflict be resolved? What will become of each character?

Clarify
If a character's words or actions are not clear to you, stop and try to make sense of them. You may need to look for clues in earlier words or actions. As you read, look also for answers to your questions, and check your predictions.

Summarize
Pause occasionally to review what has happened. What do you know about the story being told through the characters' actions and words?

Pull It Together
Pull together all the elements of the play. What does the play mean? Is there a message, or is the play purely entertainment? What does the play say to you about life?

GUIDE FOR READING

The Ugly Duckling

Alan Alexander Milne (1882–1956) was a British writer best remembered for his children's books featuring Winnie the Pooh and Christopher Robin, which he wrote for his son. Most of Milne's writing, however, was done for an adult audience. From 1906 to 1914, he was an assistant editor and contributor to the British humor magazine *Punch*. In addition to writing many mystery stories, Milne wrote nearly thirty plays. In *The Ugly Duckling* Milne presents a love story with a humorous twist.

The One-Act Play

A one-act play is similar in some ways to a short story. Like a short story, it presents only a few characters and its plot develops quickly. It usually takes place on a single set. Often it has a single theme, or general idea about life, which is presented through dialogue.

Look For

As you read *The Ugly Duckling,* look for the ways in which it is similar to a short story. What is the plot? Who are the main characters? Where does it take place? What does it reveal about life? Also look for the ways in which the characters and situations are not quite what you expected.

Writing

You have probably heard the expression "Beauty is in the eye of the beholder," which means that each person sees beauty somewhat differently. Freewrite for five minutes about what beauty means to you.

Vocabulary

Knowing the following words will help you as you read *The Ugly Duckling.*

profound (prə found′) *adj.*: Deep (p. 246)

posterity (päs ter′ ə tē) *n.*: Future generations (p. 246)

predecessor (pred′ ə ses′ ər) *n.*: One who comes before another in time (p. 246)

homage (häm′ ij) *n.*: Public expression of honor (p. 247)

nonchalantly (nän′ shə länt′ lē) *adv.*: In a casual way (p. 248)

cryptic (krip′ tik) *adj.*: Having hidden meaning (p. 248)

ruse (rōōz) *n.*: A trick or plan for fooling someone (p. 251)

The Ugly Duckling

A. A. Milne

CHARACTERS

The King	**The Chancellor**[1]	**Prince Simon**
The Queen	**Dulcibella**	**Carlo**
The Princess Camilla		

[*The* SCENE *is the Throne Room of the Palace; a room of many doors, or, if preferred, curtain-openings: simply furnished with three thrones for Their Majesties and Her Royal Highness the* PRINCESS CAMILLA—*in other words, with three handsome chairs. At each side is a long seat: reserved, as it might be, for His Majesty's Council (if any), but useful, as to-day, for other purposes. The* KING *is asleep on his throne with a handkerchief over his face. He is a king of any country from any story-book, in whatever costume you please. But he should be wearing his crown.*]

A VOICE. [*Announcing*] His Excellency the Chancellor! [*The* CHANCELLOR, *an elderly man in hornrimmed spectacles, enters, bowing. The* KING *wakes up with a start and removes the handkerchief from his face.*]

KING. [*With simple dignity*] I was thinking.

CHANCELLOR. [*Bowing*] Never, Your Majesty, was greater need for thought than now.

KING. That's what I was thinking. [*He struggles into a more dignified position.*] Well, what is it? More trouble?

CHANCELLOR. What we might call the old trouble, Your Majesty.

---

1. chancellor (chan′ sə lər) *n.*: An official secretary.

KING. It's what I was saying last night to the Queen. "Uneasy lies the head that wears a crown," was how I put it.[2]

CHANCELLOR. A profound and original thought, which may well go down to posterity.

KING. You mean it may go down well with posterity. I hope so. Remind me to tell you some time of another little thing I said to Her Majesty: something about a fierce light beating on a throne.[3] Posterity would like that, too. Well, what is it?

CHANCELLOR. It is in the matter of Her Royal Highness' wedding.

KING. Oh . . . yes.

CHANCELLOR. As Your Majesty is aware, the young Prince Simon arrives today to seek Her Royal Highness' hand in marriage. He has been traveling in distant lands and, as I understand, has not—er—has not—

KING. You mean he hasn't heard anything.

CHANCELLOR. It is a little difficult to put this tactfully, Your Majesty.

KING. Do your best, and I will tell you afterwards how you got on.

CHANCELLOR. Let me put it this way. The Prince Simon will naturally assume that Her Royal Highness has the customary—so customary as to be, in my own poor opinion, slightly monotonous—has what one might call the inevitable[4]—so inevitable as to be, in my opinion again, almost mechanical—will assume, that she has the, as I think

---

2. This quotation is actually from the play *King Henry IV* by William Shakespeare.
3. This reference was actually made by Alfred, Lord Tennyson, in the "Dedication" to his epic poem *Idylls of the King*.
4. inevitable (in ev′ ə tə b'l) *adj.*: Unavoidable.

---

of it, faultily faultless, icily regular, splendidly—

KING. What you are trying to say in the fewest words possible is that my daughter is not beautiful.

CHANCELLOR. Her beauty is certainly elusive,[5] Your Majesty.

KING. It is. It has eluded you, it has eluded me, it has eluded everybody who has seen her. It even eluded the Court Painter. His last words were, "Well, I did my best." His successor[6] is now painting the view across the water-meadows from the West Turret. He says that his doctor has advised him to keep to landscape.

CHANCELLOR. It is unfortunate, Your Majesty, but there it is. One just cannot understand how it can have occurred.

KING. You don't think she takes after *me*, at all? You don't detect a likeness?

CHANCELLOR. Most certainly not, Your Majesty.

KING. Good. . . . Your predecessor did.

CHANCELLOR. I have often wondered what happened to my predecessor.

KING. Well, now you know. [*There is a short silence.*]

CHANCELLOR. Looking at the bright side, although Her Royal Highness is not, strictly speaking, beautiful—

KING. Not, truthfully speaking, beautiful—

CHANCELLOR. Yet she has great beauty of character.

KING. My dear Chancellor, we are not consid-

---

5. elusive (i loo′ siv) *adj.*: Hard to grasp mentally.
6. successor (sək ses′ ər) *n.*: A person that follows or comes after another.

ering Her Royal Highness' character, but her chances of getting married. You observe that there is a distinction.

CHANCELLOR. Yes, Your Majesty.

KING. Look at it from the suitor's[7] point of view. If a girl is beautiful, it is easy to assume that she has, tucked away inside her, an equally beautiful character. But it is impossible to assume that an unattractive girl, however elevated in character, has, tucked away inside her, an equally beautiful face. That is, so to speak, not where you want it—tucked away.

CHANCELLOR. Quite so, Your Majesty.

KING. This doesn't, of course, alter the fact that the Princess Camilla is quite the nicest person in the Kingdom.

CHANCELLOR. [*Enthusiastically*] She is indeed, Your Majesty. [*Hurriedly*] With the exception,[8] I need hardly say, of Your Majesty—and Her Majesty.

KING. Your exceptions are tolerated[9] for their loyalty and condemned[10] for their extreme fatuity.[11]

CHANCELLOR. Thank you, Your Majesty.

KING. As an adjective for your King, the word "nice" is ill-chosen. As an adjective for Her Majesty, it is—ill-chosen. [*At which moment* HER MAJESTY *comes in. The* KING *rises. The* CHANCELLOR *puts himself at right angles.*]

QUEEN. [*Briskly*] Ah. Talking about Camilla? [*She sits down.*]

---

7. suitor (soot′ ər) *n.*: A man courting or wooing a woman.
8. exception (ik sep′ shən) *n.*: Exclusion.
9. tolerated (täl′ ə rāt′ 'd) *v.*: Allowed; permitted.
10. condemned (kən dem″d) *v.*: Disapproved of.
11. fatuity (fə too′ ə tē) *n.*: Stupidity.

KING. [*Returning to his throne*] As always, my dear, you are right.

QUEEN. [*To* CHANCELLOR] This fellow, Simon —What's he like?

CHANCELLOR. Nobody has seen him, Your Majesty.

QUEEN. How old is he?

CHANCELLOR. Five-and-twenty, I understand.

QUEEN. In twenty-five years he must have been seen by somebody.

KING. [*To the* CHANCELLOR] Just a fleeting glimpse.

CHANCELLOR. I meant, Your Majesty, that no detailed report of him has reached this country, save that he has the usual personal advantages and qualities expected of a Prince, and has been traveling in distant and dangerous lands.

QUEEN. Ah! Nothing gone wrong with his eyes? Sunstroke or anything?

CHANCELLOR. Not that I am aware of, Your Majesty. At the same time, as I was venturing[12] to say to His Majesty, Her Royal Highness' character and disposition are so outstandingly—

QUEEN. Stuff and nonsense. You remember what happened when we had the Tournament of Love last year.

CHANCELLOR. I was not myself present, Your Majesty. I had not then the honor of—I was abroad, and never heard the full story.

QUEEN. No; it was the other fool. They all rode up to Camilla to pay their homage—it was the first time they had seen her. The heralds blew their trumpets, and announced that

---

12. venturing (ven′ chər iŋ) *v.*: Expressing at the risk of criticism, objection, or denial.

she would marry whichever Prince was left master of the field when all but one had been unhorsed. The trumpets were blown again, they charged enthusiastically into the fight, and—[*The* KING *looks nonchalantly at the ceiling and whistles a few bars.*]—don't do that.

KING. I'm sorry, my dear.

QUEEN. [*To* CHANCELLOR] And what happened? They all simultaneously fell off their horses and assumed a posture of defeat.

KING. One of them was not quite so quick as the others. I was very quick. I proclaimed him the victor.

QUEEN. At the Feast of Betrothal held that night—

KING. We were all very quick.

QUEEN. The Chancellor announced that by the laws of the country the successful suitor had to pass a further test. He had to give the correct answer to a riddle.

CHANCELLOR. Such undoubtedly is the fact, Your Majesty.

KING. There are times for announcing facts, and times for looking at things in a broad-minded way. Please remember that, Chancellor.

CHANCELLOR. Yes, Your Majesty.

QUEEN. I invented the riddle myself. Quite an easy one. What is it which has four legs and barks like a dog? The answer is, "A dog."

KING. [*To* CHANCELLOR] You see that?

CHANCELLOR. Yes, Your Majesty.

KING. It isn't difficult.

QUEEN. He, however, seemed to find it so. He said an eagle. Then he said a serpent; a very high mountain with slippery sides; two pea-cocks; a moonlight night; the day after tomorrow—

KING. Nobody could accuse him of not trying.

QUEEN. I did.

KING. I *should* have said that nobody could fail to recognize in his attitude an appearance of doggedness.[13]

QUEEN. Finally he said "Death." I nudged the King—

KING. Accepting the word "nudge" for the moment, I rubbed my ankle with one hand, clapped him on the shoulder with the other, and congratulated him on the correct answer. He disappeared under the table, and, personally, I never saw him again.

QUEEN. His body was found in the moat next morning.

CHANCELLOR. But what was he doing in the moat, Your Majesty?

KING. Bobbing about. Try not to ask needless questions.

CHANCELLOR. It all seems so strange.

QUEEN. What does?

CHANCELLOR. That Her Royal Highness, alone of all the Princesses one has ever heard of, should lack that invariable[14] attribute of Royalty, supreme beauty.

QUEEN. [*To the* KING] That was your Great-Aunt Malkin. She came to the christening. You know what she said.

KING. It was cryptic. Great-Aunt Malkin's besetting weakness. She came to *my* christening—she was one hundred and one then, and that was fifty-one years ago. [*To*

---

13. doggedness (dôg′ id nis) *n.*: Stubbornness.
14. invariable (in ver′ ē ə b'l) *adj.*: Not changing; constant.

the CHANCELLOR] How old would that make her?

CHANCELLOR. One hundred and fifty-two, Your Majesty.

KING. [*After thought*] About that, yes. She promised me that when I grew up I should have all the happiness which my wife deserved. It struck me at the time—well, when I say "at the time," I was only a week old—but it did strike me as soon as anything could strike me—I mean of that nature—well, work it out for yourself, Chancellor. It opens up a most interesting field of speculation. Though naturally I have not liked to go into it at all deeply with Her Majesty.

QUEEN. I never heard anything less cryptic. She was wishing you extreme happiness.

KING. I don't think she was *wishing* me anything. However.

CHANCELLOR. [*To the* QUEEN] But what, Your Majesty, did she wish Her Royal Highness?

QUEEN. Her other godmother—on my side —had promised her the dazzling beauty for which all the women in my family are famous—[*She pauses, and the* KING *snaps his fingers surreptitiously in the direction of the* CHANCELLOR.]

CHANCELLOR. [*Hurriedly*] Indeed, yes, Your Majesty. [*The* KING *relaxes.*]

QUEEN. And Great-Aunt Malkin said—[*To the* KING]—what were the words?

KING.   I give you with this kiss
          A wedding-day surprise.
          Where ignorance is bliss
          'Tis folly to be wise.

I thought the last two lines rather neat. But what it *meant*—

QUEEN. We can all see what it meant. She was given beauty—and where is it? Great-Aunt Malkin took it away from her. The wedding-day surprise is that there will never be a wedding day.

KING. Young men being what they are, my dear, it would be much more surprising if there *were* a wedding day. So how— [*The* PRINCESS *comes in. She is young, happy, healthy, but not beautiful. Or let us say that by some trick of make-up or arrangement of hair she seems plain to us: unlike the* PRINCESS *of the story books.*]

PRINCESS. [*To the* KING] Hallo, darling! [*Seeing the others*] Oh, I say! Affairs of state? Sorry.

KING. [*Holding out his hand*] Don't go, Camilla. [*She takes his hand.*]

CHANCELLOR. Shall I withdraw, Your Majesty?

QUEEN. You are aware, Camilla, that Prince Simon arrives today?

PRINCESS. He has arrived. They're just letting down the drawbridge.

KING. [*Jumping up*] Arrived! I must—

PRINCESS. Darling, you know what the drawbridge is like. It takes at *least* half an hour to let it down.

KING. [*Sitting down*] It wants oil. [*To the* CHANCELLOR] Have *you* been grudging it oil?

PRINCESS. It wants a new drawbridge, darling.

CHANCELLOR. Have I Your Majesty's permission—

KING. Yes, yes. [*The* CHANCELLOR *bows and goes out.*]

QUEEN. You've told him, of course? It's the only chance.

KING. Er—no. I was just going to, when—

QUEEN. Then I'd better. [*She goes to the door.*] You can explain to the girl; I'll have her sent to you. You've told Camilla?

KING. Er—no. I was just going to, when—

QUEEN. Then you'd better tell her now.

KING. My dear, are you sure—

QUEEN. It's the only chance left. [*Dramatically to heaven*] My daughter! [*She goes out. There is a little silence when she is gone.*]

KING. Camilla, I want to talk seriously to you about marriage.

PRINCESS. Yes, father.

KING. It is time that you learnt some of the facts of life.

PRINCESS. Yes, father.

KING. Now the great fact about marriage is that once you're married you live happy ever after. All our history books affirm this.

PRINCESS. And your own experience too, darling.

KING. [*With dignity*] Let us confine ourselves to history for the moment.

PRINCESS. Yes, father.

KING. Of course, there *may* be an exception here and there, which, as it were, proves the rule; just as—oh, well, never mind.

PRINCESS. [*Smiling*] Go on, darling. You were going to say that an exception here and there proves the rule that all princesses are beautiful.

KING. Well—leave that for the moment. The point is that it doesn't matter *how* you marry, or *who* you marry, as long as you *get* married. Because you'll be happy ever after in any case. Do you follow me so far?

PRINCESS. Yes, father.

KING. Well, your mother and I have a little plan—

PRINCESS. Was that it, going out of the door just now?

KING. Er—yes. It concerns your waiting-maid.

PRINCESS. Darling, I have several.

KING. Only one that leaps to the eye, so to speak. The one with the—well, with every-thing.

PRINCESS. Dulcibella?

KING. That's the one. It is our little plan that at the first meeting she should pass herself off as the Princess—a harmless ruse, of which you will find frequent record in the history books—and allure[15] Prince Simon to his—that is to say, bring him up to the—In other words, the wedding will take place immediately afterwards, and as quiet-ly as possible—well, naturally in view of the fact that your Aunt Malkin is one hundred and fifty-two; and since you will be wearing the family bridal veil—which is no doubt how the custom arose—the surprise after the ceremony will be his. Are you following me at all? Your attention seems to be wandering.

PRINCESS. I was wondering why you needed to tell me.

KING. Just a precautionary measure, in case you happened to meet the Prince or his attendant before the ceremony; in which

---

15. allure (ə loor′) *v*.: Tempt; attract.

case, of course, you would pass yourself off as the maid—

PRINCESS. A harmless ruse, of which, also, you will find frequent record in the history books.

KING. Exactly. But the occasion need not arise.

A VOICE. [*Announcing*] The woman Dulcibella!

KING. Ah! [*To the* PRINCESS] Now, Camilla, if you will just retire to your own apartments, I will come to you there when we are ready for the actual ceremony. [*He leads her out as he is talking; and as he returns calls out.*] Come in, my dear! [DULCIBELLA *comes in. She is beautiful, but dumb.*] Now don't be frightened, there is nothing to be frightened about. Has Her Majesty told you what you have to do?

DULCIBELLA. Y-yes, Your Majesty.

KING. Well now, let's see how well you can do it. You are sitting here, we will say. [*He leads her to a seat.*] Now imagine that I am Prince Simon. [*He curls his moustache and puts his stomach in. She giggles.*] You are the beautiful Princess Camilla whom he has never seen. [*She giggles again.*] This is a serious moment in your life, and you will find that a giggle will not be helpful. [*He goes to the door.*] I am announced: "His Royal Highness Prince Simon!" That's me being announced. Remember what I said about giggling. You should have a far-away look upon the face. [*She does her best.*] Farther away than that. [*She tries again.*] No, that's too far. You are sitting there, thinking beautiful thoughts—in maiden meditation,[16] fancy-free,[17] as I remember

saying to Her Majesty once . . . speaking of somebody else . . . fancy-free, but with the mouth definitely shut—that's better. I advance and fall upon one knee. [*He does so.*] You extend your hand graciously —*graciously;* you're not trying to push him in the face—that's better, and I raise it to my lips—so—and I kiss it—[*He kisses it warmly.*]—no, perhaps not so ardently[18] as that, more like this [*He kisses it again.*], and I say, "Your Royal Highness, this is the most—er—Your Royal Highness, I shall ever be—no—Your Royal Highness, it is the proudest—" Well, the point is that *he* will say it, and it will be something complimentary, and then he will take your hand in both of his, and press it to his heart. [*He does so.*] And then—what do *you* say?

DULCIBELLA. Coo!

KING. No, *not* Coo.

DULCIBELLA. Never had anyone do *that* to me before.

KING. That also strikes the wrong note. What you want to say is, "Oh, Prince Simon!" . . . Say it.

DULCIBELLA. [*Loudly*] Oh, Prince Simon!

KING. No, no. You don't need to shout until he has said "What?" two or three times. Always consider the possibility that he *isn't* deaf. Softly, and giving the words a dying fall, letting them play around his head like a flight of doves.

DULCIBELLA. [*Still a little overloud*] O-o-o-o-h, Prinsimon!

KING. Keep the idea in your mind of a flight of *doves* rather than a flight of panic-stricken elephants, and you will be all right. Now I'm going to get up and you must, as it

---

16. meditation (med′ ə tā′ shən) *n.*: Deep thought.
17. fancy-free: Carefree.

18. ardently (är′ d'nt lē) *adv.*: Passionately; with intense feeling.

were, *waft*[19] me into a seat by your side. [*She starts wafting.*] *Not* rescuing a drowning man, that's another idea altogether, useful at times, but at the moment inappropriate. Wafting. Prince Simon will put the necessary muscles into play—all you require to do is to indicate by a gracious movement of the hand the seat you require him to take. Now! [*He gets up, a little stiffly, and sits next to her.*] That was better. Well, here we are. Now, I think you give me a look: something, let us say, half-way between a worshipful attitude and wild abandonment,[20] with an undertone of regal dignity, touched, as it were, with good comradeship. Now try that. [*She gives him a vacant look of bewilderment.*] Frankly, that didn't quite get it. There was just a little something missing. An absence, as it were, of all the qualities I asked for, and in their place an odd resemblance to an unsatisfied fish. Let us try to get at it another way. Dulcibella, have you a young man of your own?

DULCIBELLA. [*Eagerly, seizing his hand*] Oo, yes, he's ever so smart, he's an archer,[21] well not as you might say a real archer, he works in the armory,[22] but old Bottlenose, *you* know who I mean, the Captain of the Guard, says the very next man they ever has to shoot, my Eg shall take his place, knowing Father and how it is with Eg and me, and me being maid to Her Royal Highness and can't marry me till he's a real soldier, but ever so loving, and funny like, the things he says, I said to him once, "Eg," I said—

KING. [*Getting up*] I rather fancy, Dulcibella,

that if you think of Eg all the time, *say* as little as possible, and, when thinking of Eg, see that the mouth is not more than partially open, you will do very well. I will show you where you are to sit and wait for His Royal Highness. [*He leads her out. On the way he is saying*] Now remember—*waft*—*waft*—not *hoick*.[23] [PRINCE SIMON *wanders in from the back unannounced. He is a very ordinary-looking young man in rather dusty clothes. He gives a deep sigh of relief as he sinks into the* KING's *throne. . . .* CAMILLA, *a new and strangely beautiful* CAMILLA, *comes in.*]

PRINCESS. [*Surprised*] Well!

PRINCE. Oh, hallo!

PRINCESS. Ought you?

PRINCE. [*Getting up*] Do sit down, won't you?

PRINCESS. Who are you, and how did you get here?

PRINCE. Well, that's rather a long story. Couldn't we sit down? You could sit here if you liked, but it isn't very comfortable.

PRINCESS. That is the King's Throne.

PRINCE. Oh, is that what it is?

PRINCESS. Thrones are not meant to be comfortable.

PRINCE. Well, I don't know if they're meant to be, but they certainly aren't.

PRINCESS. Why were you sitting on the King's Throne, and who are you?

PRINCE. My name is Carlo.

PRINCESS. Mine is Dulcibella.

PRINCE. Good. And now couldn't we sit down?

---

19. waft (waft) *v*.: Signal to; wave.
20. abandonment (ə ban' dən mənt) *n*.: Unrestrained freedom of actions or emotions; surrender to one's impulses.
21. archer (är' chər) *n*.: A person who shoots with bow and arrow.
22. armory (är' mər ē) *n*.: A storehouse for weapons; arsenal.

23. hoick (hoik) *interj*.: A hunter's call to the hounds.

PRINCESS. [*Sitting down on the long seat to the left of the throne, and, as it were, wafting him to a place next to her*] You may sit here, if you like. Why are you so tired? [*He sits down.*]

PRINCE. I've been taking very strenuous exercise.

PRINCESS. Is that part of the long story?

PRINCE. It is.

PRINCESS. [*Settling herself*] I love stories.

PRINCE. This isn't a story really. You see, I'm attendant on Prince Simon who is visiting here.

PRINCESS. Oh? I'm attendant on Her Royal Highness.

PRINCE. Then you know what he's here for.

PRINCESS. Yes.

PRINCE. She's very beautiful, I hear.

PRINCESS. Did you hear that? Where have you been lately?

PRINCE. Traveling in distant lands—with Prince Simon.

PRINCESS. Ah! All the same, I don't understand. Is Prince Simon in the Palace now? The drawbridge *can't* be down yet!

PRINCE. I don't suppose it is. *And* what a noise it makes coming down!

PRINCESS. Isn't it terrible?

PRINCE. I couldn't stand it any more. I just had to get away. That's why I'm here.

PRINCESS. But how?

PRINCE. Well, there's only one way, isn't there? That beech tree, and then a swing and a grab for the battlements, and don't ask me to remember it all—[*He shudders.*]

PRINCESS. You mean you came across the moat by that beech tree?

PRINCE. Yes. I got so tired of hanging about.

PRINCESS. But it's terribly dangerous!

PRINCE. That's why I'm so exhausted. Nervous shock. [*He lies back and breathes loudly.*]

PRINCESS. Of course, it's different for *me*.

PRINCE. [*Sitting up*] Say that again. I must have got it wrong.

PRINCESS. It's different for me, because I'm used to it. Besides, I'm so much lighter.

PRINCE. You don't mean that *you*—

PRINCESS. Oh yes, often.

PRINCE. And I thought I was a brave man! At least, I didn't until five minutes ago, and now I don't again.

PRINCESS. Oh, but you are! And I think it's wonderful to do it straight off the first time.

PRINCE. Well, *you* did.

PRINCESS. Oh no, not the first time. When I was a child.

PRINCE. You mean that you crashed?

PRINCESS. Well, you only fall into the moat.

PRINCE. Only! Can you *swim*?

PRINCESS. Of course.

PRINCE. So you swam to the castle walls, and yelled for help, and they fished you out and walloped you. And next day you tried again. Well, if *that* isn't pluck[24]—

PRINCESS. Of course I didn't. I swam back, and did it at once; I mean I tried again at once. It wasn't until the third time that I

_____

24. pluck (pluk) *n.*: Courage.

actually did it. You see, I was afraid I might lose my nerve.

PRINCE. Afraid she might lose her nerve!

PRINCESS. There's a way of getting over from this side, too; a tree grows out from the wall and you jump into another tree—I don't think it's quite so easy.

PRINCE. Not quite so easy. Good. You must show me.

PRINCESS. Oh, I will.

PRINCE. Perhaps it might be as well if you taught me how to swim first. I've often heard about swimming but never—

PRINCESS. You can't swim?

PRINCE. No. Don't look so surprised. There are a lot of other things which I can't do. I'll tell you about them as soon as you have a couple of years to spare.

PRINCESS. You can't swim and yet you crossed by the beech-tree! And you're *ever* so much heavier than I am! Now who's brave?

PRINCE. [*Getting up*] You keep talking about how light you are. I must see if there's anything to it. Stand up! [*She stands obediently and he picks her up.*] You're right, Dulcibella. I could hold you here forever. [*Looking at her*] You're very lovely. Do you know how lovely you are?

PRINCESS. Yes. [*She laughs suddenly and happily.*]

PRINCE. Why do you laugh?

PRINCESS. Aren't you tired of holding me?

PRINCE. Frankly, yes. I exaggerated when I said I could hold you forever. When you've been hanging by the arms for ten minutes over a very deep moat, wondering if it's too late to learn how to swim—[*He puts her down.*]—what I meant was that I should *like* to hold you forever. Why did you laugh?

PRINCESS. Oh, well, it was a little private joke of mine.

PRINCE. If it comes to that, I've got a private joke too. Let's exchange them.

PRINCESS. Mine's very private. One other woman in the whole world knows, and that's all.

PRINCE. Mine's just as private. One other man knows, and that's all.

PRINCESS. What fun. I love secrets. . . . Well, here's mine. When I was born, one of my godmothers promised that I should be very beautiful.

PRINCE. How right she was.

PRINCESS. But the other one said this:

> I give you with this kiss
> A wedding-day surprise.
> Where ignorance is bliss
> 'Tis folly to be wise.

And nobody knew what it meant. And I grew up very plain. And then, when I was about ten, I met my godmother in the forest one day. It was my tenth birthday. Nobody knows this—except you.

PRINCE. Except us.

PRINCESS. Except us. And she told me what her gift meant. It meant that I *was* beautiful —but everybody else was to go on being ignorant, and thinking me plain, until my wedding-day. Because, she said, she didn't want me to grow up spoiled and willful and vain, as I should have done if everybody had always been saying how beautiful I was; and the best thing in the world, she said, was to be quite sure of yourself, but not to expect admiration from other people. So ever since then my mirror has told me

I'm beautiful, and everybody else thinks me ugly, and I get a lot of fun out of it.

PRINCE. Well, seeing that Dulcibella is the result, I can only say that your godmother was very, very wise.

PRINCESS. And now tell me *your* secret.

PRINCE. It isn't such a pretty one. You see, Prince Simon was going to woo Princess Camilla, and he'd heard that she was beautiful and haughty and imperious—all *you* would have been if your godmother hadn't been so wise. And being a very ordinary-looking fellow himself, he was afraid she wouldn't think much of him, so he suggested to one of his attendants, a man called Carlo, of extremely attractive appearance, that *he* should pretend to be the Prince, and win the Princess's hand; and then at the last moment they would change places—

PRINCESS. How would they do that?

PRINCE. The Prince was going to have been married in full armor—with his visor[25] down.

PRINCESS. [*Laughing happily*] Oh, what fun!

PRINCE. Neat, isn't it?

PRINCESS. [*Laughing*] Oh, very . . . very . . . very.

PRINCE. Neat, but not so terribly *funny.* Why do you keep laughing?

PRINCESS. Well, that's another secret.

PRINCE. If it comes to that, *I've* got another one up my sleeve. Shall we exchange again?

PRINCESS. All right. You go first this time.

PRINCE. Very well. . . . I am not Carlo.

---

25. visor (vī′ zər) *n.*: In ancient armor, a movable part of the helmet that could be lowered to cover the upper part of the face, with slits for seeing.

[*Standing up and speaking dramatically*] I am Simon!—ow! [*He sits down and rubs his leg violently.*]

PRINCESS. [*Alarmed*] What is it?

PRINCE. Cramp. [*In a mild voice, still rubbing*] I was saying that I was Prince Simon.

PRINCESS. Shall I rub it for you? [*She rubs.*]

PRINCE. [*Still hopefully*] I am Simon.

PRINCESS. Is that better?

PRINCE. [*Despairingly*] I am Simon.

PRINCESS. I know.

PRINCE. How did you know?

PRINCESS. Well, you told me.

PRINCE. But oughtn't you to swoon[26] or something?

PRINCESS. Why? History records many similar ruses.

PRINCE. [*Amazed*] Is that so? I've never read history. I thought I was being profoundly original.

PRINCESS. Oh, no! Now I'll tell you *my* secret. For reasons very much like your own the Princess Camilla, who is held to be extremely plain, feared to meet Prince Simon. Is the drawbridge down yet?

PRINCE. Do your people give a faint, surprised cheer every time it gets down?

PRINCESS. Naturally.

PRINCE. Then it came down about three minutes ago.

PRINCESS. Ah! Then at this very moment your man Carlo is declaring his passionate love for my maid, Dulcibella. That, I think, is funny. [*So does the* PRINCE. *He laughs heartily.*] Dulcibella, by the way, is in love with a man she calls Eg, so I hope Carlo isn't getting carried away.

PRINCE. Carlo is married to a girl he calls "the little woman," so Eg has nothing to fear.

PRINCESS. By the way, I don't know if you heard, but I said, or as good as said, that I am the Princess Camilla.

PRINCE. I wasn't surprised. History, of which I read a great deal, records many similar ruses.

PRINCESS. [*Laughing*] Simon!

PRINCE. [*Laughing*] Camilla! [*He stands up.*] May I try holding you again? [*She nods. He takes her in his arms and kisses her.*] Sweetheart!

PRINCESS. You see, when you lifted me up before, you said, "You're very lovely," and my godmother said that the first person to whom I would seem lovely was the man I should marry; so I knew then that you were Simon and I should marry you.

PRINCE. I knew directly I saw you that I should marry you, even if you were Dulcibella. By the way, which of you *am* I marrying?

PRINCESS. When she lifts her veil, it will be Camilla. [*Voices are heard outside.*] Until then it will be Dulcibella.

PRINCE. [*In a whisper*] Then good-bye, Camilla, until you lift your veil.

PRINCESS. Good-bye, Simon, until you raise your visor. [*The* KING *and* QUEEN *come in arm-in-arm, followed by* CARLO *and* DULCIBELLA *also arm-in-arm. The* CHANCELLOR *precedes them, walking backwards, at a loyal angle.*]

PRINCE. [*Supporting the* CHANCELLOR *as an*

---

26. swoon (swo͞on) v.: Faint.

accident seems inevitable] Careful! [*The* CHANCELLOR *turns indignantly round.*]

KING. Who and what is this? More accurately who and what are all these?

CARLO. My attendant, Carlo, Your Majesty. He will, with Your Majesty's permission, prepare me for the ceremony. [*The* PRINCE *bows.*]

KING. Of course, of course!

QUEEN. [*To* DULCIBELLA] Your maid, Dulcibella, is it not, my love? [DULCIBELLA *nods violently.*] I thought so. [*To* CARLO] She will prepare Her Royal Highness. [*The* PRINCESS *curtsies.*]

KING. Ah, yes. Yes. *Most* important.

PRINCESS. [*Curtsying*] I beg pardon, Your Majesty, if I've done wrong, but I found the gentleman wandering—

KING. [*Crossing to her*] Quite right, my dear, quite right. [*He pinches her cheek, and takes advantage of this kingly gesture to say in a loud whisper*] We've pulled it off! [*They sit down; the* KING *and* QUEEN *on their thrones,* DULCIBELLA *on the* PRINCESS'*s throne.* CARLO *stands behind* DULCIBELLA, *the* CANCELLOR *on the right of the* QUEEN, *and the* PRINCE *and* PRINCESS *behind the long seat on the left.*]

CHANCELLOR. [*Consulting documents*] H'r'm! Have I Your Majesty's authority to put the final test to His Royal Highness?

QUEEN. [*Whispering to* KING] Is this safe?

KING. [*Whispering*] Perfectly, my dear. I told him the answer a minute ago. [*Over his shoulder to* CARLO] Don't forget. *Dog.* [*Aloud*] Proceed, Your Excellency. It is my desire that the affairs of my country should ever be conducted in a strictly constitutional manner.

CHANCELLOR. [*Oratorically[27]*] By the constitution of the country, a suitor to Her Royal Highness's hand cannot be deemed successful until he has given the correct answer to a riddle. [*Conversationally*] The last suitor answered incorrectly, and thus failed to win his bride.

KING. By a coincidence he fell into the moat.

CHANCELLOR. [*To* CARLO] I have now to ask Your Royal Highness if you are prepared for the ordeal?

CARLO. [*Cheerfully*] Absolutely.

CHANCELLOR. I may mention, as a matter, possibly, of some slight historical interest to our visitor, that by the constitution of the country the same riddle is not allowed to be asked on two successive occasions.

KING. [*Startled*] What's that?

CHANCELLOR. This one, it is interesting to recall, was propounded[28] exactly a century ago, and we must take it as a fortunate omen[29] that it was well and truly solved.

KING. [*To* QUEEN] I may want my sword directly.

CHANCELLOR. The riddle is this. What is it which has four legs and mews like a cat?

CARLO. [*Promptly*] A dog.

KING. [*Still more promptly*] Bravo, bravo! [*He claps loudly and nudges the* QUEEN, *who claps too.*]

CHANCELLOR. [*Peering at his documents*] According to the records of the occasion to

---

27. oratorically (ôr′ ə tôr′ i k′l ē) *adv.*: In a lofty, high-sounding way.
28. propounded (prə pound′ 'd) *v.*: Proposed; put forward for consideration.
29. omen (ō′ mən) *n.*: A thing or happening supposed to foretell a future event.

which I referred, the correct answer would seem to be—

PRINCESS. [*To* PRINCE] Say something, quick!

CHANCELLOR. —not dog, but—

PRINCE. Your Majesty, have I permission to speak? Naturally His Royal Highness could not think of justifying himself on such an occasion, but I think that with Your Majesty's gracious permission, I could—

KING. Certainly, certainly.

PRINCE. In our country, we have an animal to which we have given the name "dog," or, in the local dialect of the more mountainous districts, "doggie." It sits by the fireside and purrs.

CARLO. That's right. It purrs like anything.

PRINCE. When it needs milk, which is its staple food, it mews.

CARLO. [*Enthusiastically*] Mews like nobody's business.

PRINCE. It also has four legs.

CARLO. One at each corner.

PRINCE. In some countries, I understand, this animal is called a "cat." In one distant country to which His Royal Highness and I penetrated, it was called by the very curious name of "hippopotamus."

CARLO. That's right. [*To the* PRINCE] Do you remember that ginger-colored hippopotamus which used to climb on to my shoulder and lick my ear?

PRINCE. I shall never forget it, sir. [*To the* KING] So you see, Your Majesty—

KING. Thank you. I think that makes it perfectly clear. [*Firmly to the* CHANCELLOR] You are about to agree?

CHANCELLOR. Undoubtedly, Your Majesty. May I be the first to congratulate His Royal Highness on solving the riddle so accurately?

KING. You may be the first to see that all is in order for an immediate wedding.

CHANCELLOR. Thank you, Your Majesty. [*He bows and withdraws. The* KING *rises, as do the* QUEEN *and* DULCIBELLA.]

KING. [*To* CARLO] Doubtless, Prince Simon, you will wish to retire and prepare yourself for the ceremony.

CARLO. Thank you, sir.

PRINCE. Have I Your Majesty's permission to attend His Royal Highness? It is the custom of his country for Princes of the royal blood to be married in full armor, a matter which requires a certain adjustment—

KING. Of course, of course. [CARLO *bows to the* KING *and* QUEEN *and goes out. As the* PRINCE *is about to follow, the* KING *stops him.*] Young man, you have a quality of quickness which I admire. It is my pleasure to reward it in any way which commends itself to you.

PRINCE. Your Majesty is ever gracious. May I ask for my reward *after* the ceremony? [*He catches the eye of the* PRINCESS, *and they give each other a secret smile.*]

KING. Certainly. [*The* PRINCE *bows and goes out. To* DUCIBELLA] Now, young woman, make yourself scarce. You've done your work excellently, and we will see that you and your —what was his name?

DULCIBELLA. Eg, Your Majesty.

KING. —that you and your Eg are not forgotten.

DULCIBELLA. Coo! [*She curtsies and goes out.*]

PRINCESS. [*Calling*] Wait for me, Dulcibella!

KING. [*To* QUEEN] Well, my dear, we may congratulate ourselves. As I remember saying to somebody once, "You have not lost a daughter, you have gained a son." How does he strike you?

QUEEN. Stupid.

KING. They made a very handsome pair, I thought, he and Dulcibella.

QUEEN. Both stupid.

KING. I said nothing about stupidity. What I *said* was that they were both extremely handsome. That is the important thing. [*Struck by a sudden idea*] Or isn't it?

QUEEN. What do *you* think of Prince Simon, Camilla?

PRINCESS. I adore him. We shall be so happy together.

KING. Well, of course you will. I told you so. Happy ever after.

QUEEN. Run along now and get ready.

PRINCESS. Yes, mother. [*She throws a kiss to them and goes out.*]

KING. [*Anxiously*] My dear, have we been wrong about Camilla all this time? It seemed to me that she wasn't looking *quite* so plain as usual just now. Did *you* notice anything?

QUEEN. [*Carelessly*] Just the excitement of the marriage.

KING. [*Relieved*] Ah, yes, that would account for it.

THINKING ABOUT THE SELECTION

Recalling

1. What has the godmother on the Queen's side promised the princess at the christening?
2. What has Great-Aunt Malkin promised?
3. Why is the prince impressed when he first meets the princess?
4. Why is the princess impressed when she first meets the prince?
5. How does the princess know that the young man who says he is Carlo is Prince Simon before he even tells her?

Interpreting

6. The king says Camilla's beauty "has eluded everybody who has seen her." How does this relate to Great-Aunt Malkin's promise?
7. In the fairy tale "The Ugly Duckling" by Hans Christian Andersen, a young swan in a group of ducks feels ugly. Only when it finds swans does it realize that it is beautiful. How is the swan similar to the Princess in the play?
8. The King tells the Princess: "It doesn't matter how you marry or who you marry, as long as you get married. Because you'll be happy ever after in any case." Do you think the playwright expects you to take this statement seriously? Explain your answer.

Applying

9. Would you have liked to receive Great-Aunt Malkin's gift? Explain your answer.

ANALYZING LITERATURE

Understanding the One-Act Play

The **one-act play,** a form of drama with a single act, is in some ways like a short story. Because of its short length, it has only a few vivid characters and a plot that develops quickly. Like *The Ugly Duckling,* it usually has a single theme, presented through dialogue, and a single set.

1. Who are the main characters in this play?
2. Summarize the plot.
3. Describe the setting.
4. What span of time is covered in the play?
5. What is revealed about the idea of beauty?
6. What is the theme of the play?

CRITICAL THINKING AND READING

Recognizing Parody

A **parody** is a humorous mimicking of a serious piece of literature. *The Ugly Duckling* pokes gentle fun at the elements of the traditional fairy tale, although it takes one element seriously.

1. How are the King and Queen in this play different from traditional characters in a fairy tale? How does this difference add to the humor?
2. How are the Prince and Princess in this play different from traditional fairy-tale characters? How does this difference add to the humor?
3. How do the drawbridge and other details of setting in this play differ from those you would expect to find in a traditional fairy tale? How does this difference add to the humor?
4. In fairy tales, the suitor often has to win the hand of the princess. What makes the tournament in this play humorous? What makes the answering of the riddle humorous?
5. Many fairy tales center on a trick. How does the trick in this play contribute to the humor?
6. Does Milne expect you to take the theme of this play seriously? Explain your answer.

THINKING AND WRITING

Writing to Cast the Characters

Pretend that you are a movie producer who is going to produce *The Ugly Duckling.* Choose an actor who is appropriate for a major part. List reasons why this person could play the role well. Then draft a letter asking this actor to play the part and including your reasons. When you revise your letter, make sure your reasons could persuade this actor to accept the role.

GUIDE FOR READING

The Romancers

Edmond Rostand (1868–1918) was born in Marseille, France, and later moved to Paris. Rostand was the youngest writer elected to the famous French Academy (l'Académie Française). His first volume was a book of verses written as a wedding gift for his wife, also a poet. Rostand's best-known play, *Cyrano de Bergerac,* is still frequently performed today. *The Romancers,* written in 1894, was made in 1960 into the musical *The Fantasticks,* which has been playing in New York for more than twenty-seven years.

Staging

A play is written to be performed by actors before an audience. In a live stage performance, **staging** makes the play come alive. Staging includes costumes, props, lighting or sound effects, and the actors' movements and gestures.

"The Romancers" is a comedy—a type of literature that presents life in a humorous way and that usually has a happy ending.

Look For

As you read *The Romancers,* imagine how the play might actually look on the stage. The stage directions will help you visualize how the characters look and move and what the set is like. How does the staging contribute to the humor?

Writing

You have probably heard the saying: The path to true love never runs smoothly. Freewrite about the meaning of this saying. Do you agree with it or disagree?

Vocabulary

Knowing the following words will help you as you read *The Romancers.*

jocund (jäk' ənd) *adj.:* Cheerful; merry (p. 263)

gout (gout) *n.:* Inflammation of the joints (p. 269)

bravado (brə vä' dō) *n.:* Bold, bragging behavior; in this case, one who demonstrates such behavior (p. 270)

ad-lib (ad' lib') *v.:* Say or do things not in a script (p. 270)

discreet (dis krēt') *adj.:* Careful about what one says or does (p. 270)

elders (el' dərz) *n.:* Shrubs or small trees with clusters of small white flowers and red or black berries (p. 273)

The Romancers

Edmond Rostand

CHARACTERS

Sylvette
Percinet
Straforel
Bergamin . . . . Percinet's father
Pasquinot . . . . Sylvette's father

A Wall (Not a speaking part)

Swordsmen, musicians, and torch-bearers

[*The action takes place anywhere, provided the costumes are pretty.*]

[Scene:*The stage is divided by an old wall, covered with vines and flowers. At the right, a corner of* BERGAMIN'S *private park is seen; at the left, a corner of* PASQUINOT'S*. On each side of the wall, and against it, is a rustic bench.*

As the curtain rises, PERCINET *is seated on the top of the wall. On his knee is a book, out of which he is reading to* SYLVETTE, *who stands attentively listening on the bench which is on the other side of the wall.*]

SYLVETTE. Monsieur[1] Percinet, how divinely beautiful!

PERCINET. Is it not? Listen to what Romeo answers: [*Reading*]

"It was the lark, the herald of the morn,
No nightingale: look, love, what envious streaks

Do lace the severing clouds in yonder east.
Night's candles are burnt out, and jocund day
Stands tiptoe on the misty mountain tops:
I must begone"—

SYLVETTE. [*Interrupts him, as she listens in the distance*] Sh!

PERCINET. [*Listens a moment, then*] No one! But, Mademoiselle, you must not take fright like some startled bird. Hear the immortal lovers:

"*Juliet.*—Yon light is not the daylight, I know it, I,
It is some meteor that the sun exhales,
To be to thee this night a torch-bearer,
And light thee on thy way to Mantua:[2]
Therefore stay yet, thou need'st not to be gone.

---

1. Monsieur (mə syʉr′): French title meaning Mister.

2. Mantua (man′ choo wə): A city in Italy.

Romeo.—Let me be ta'en, let me be put to
   death;
I am content, so thou will have it so.
I'll say, yon gray is not the morning's
   eye,
'Tis but the pale reflex of Cynthia's
   brow;
Nor that is not the lark, whose notes do
   beat
The vaulty[3] heaven so high above our
   heads:
I have more care to stay than will to go:
Come, death and welcome''—

SYLVETTE. No, he must not say such things,
or I shall cry—

PERCINET. Then let us stop and read no fur-
ther until tomorrow. We shall let Romeo live!
[*He closes the book and looks about him.*]
This charming spot seems expressly made,
it seems to me, to cradle the words of the
Divine Will![4]

SYLVETTE. The verses are divine, and the soft
air here is a divine accompaniment. And
see, these green shades! But, Monsieur Percinet, what makes them divine to me is the
way you read!

PERCINET. Flatterer!

SYLVETTE. [*Sighing*] Poor lovers! Their fate
was cruel! [*Another sigh*] I think—

PERCINET. What?

SYLVETTE. Nothing!

PERCINET. Something which made you blush
as red as a rose.

SYLVETTE. Nothing, I say.

PERCINET. Ah, that's too transparent. I see it
all: you are thinking of our fathers!

SYLVETTE. Perhaps—

PERCINET. Of the terrible hatred between
them.

SYLVETTE. The thought often pains me
and makes me cry when I am alone. Last
month, when I came home from the convent,[5] my father pointed out your father's
park, and said to me: "My dear child, you
behold there the domain of my mortal enemy, Bergamin. Never cross the path of
those two rascals, Bergamin and his son
Percinet. Mark well my words, and obey me
to the letter, or I cast you off as an enemy.
Their family has always been at swords'
points with our own." And I promised. But
you see how I keep my word!

PERCINET. Did I not promise my father to do
the same, Sylvette?—Yet I love you!

SYLVETTE. Holy saints!

PERCINET. I love you, my dearest!

SYLVETTE. It's sinful!

PERCINET. Very—but what can we do? The
greater the obstacles to be overcome, the
sweeter is the reward. Sylvette, kiss me!

SYLVETTE. Never! [*She jumps down from the
bench and runs off a few steps.*]

PERCINET. But you love me?

SYLVETTE. What?

PERCINET. My dear child: I, too, sometimes
think of ourselves and compare us with
those other lovers: of Verona.[6]

SYLVETTE. But *I* didn't compare—!

PERCINET. You and I are Juliet and Romeo—I
love you to despair, and I shall brave the

---

3. vaulty (vôlt′ ē) *adj.*: Arched.
4. Divine Will: William Shakespeare, the playwright
who wrote *Romeo and Juliet.*

5. convent (kän′ vənt) *n.*: A girls' boarding school
run by nuns.
6. Verona (və rō′ nə): The city in Italy where Romeo
and Juliet lived.

wrath of Pasquinot-Capulet and Bergamin-Montague![7]

SYLVETTE. [*Coming a little nearer to the wall*] Then we love? But how, Monsieur Percinet, has it happened so soon?

PERCINET. Love is born we know not how, because it must be born. I often saw you pass by my window—

SYLVETTE. I saw you, too!

PERCINET. And our eyes spoke in silence.

SYLVETTE. And one day I was gathering nuts in the garden by the wall—

PERCINET. One day I happened to be reading Shakespeare. See how everything conspired to unite two hearts!

SYLVETTE. And a little gust of wind blew my scarf in your direction.

PERCINET. I climbed to the wall in order to return it to you—

SYLVETTE. [*Climbing the wall again*] I climbed too—

PERCINET. And since that day, my dear, I have waited at the same hour, here by this wall, and each time my heart beat louder and faster, until I knew by your soft laugh that you were near!

SYLVETTE. Now since we love, we must be married.

PERCINET. I was just thinking about that.

SYLVETTE. [*Solemnly*] I, last of the Pasquinot, do solemnly pledge myself to you, last of the Bergamin.

PERCINET. What noble folly!

SYLVETTE. We shall be sung in distant ages!

PERCINET. Too tender children of too hard-hearted fathers!

SYLVETTE. But who knows whether the hour is not at hand when our fathers' hatred may come to an end?

PERCINET. I doubt it.

SYLVETTE. I have heard of more doubtful happenings. I can think of half a dozen—

PERCINET. What, for instance?

SYLVETTE. Imagine that the reigning prince comes riding past some day—I've read of stranger things in novels—I run to him and kneel, and tell him the story of our love and of our fathers' hatred. The prince asks to see my father and Bergamin, and they become reconciled—

PERCINET. And your father gives me your hand!

SYLVETTE. Yes.—Or else, you languish, the doctor declares you cannot live—

PERCINET. And my father asks: "What ails you?"

SYLVETTE. And you reply, "I must have Sylvette!"

PERCINET. And his pride is then forced to bend.

SYLVETTE. Yes.—Or else: an aged duke, having seen a portrait of me, falls in love with me, sends a 'squire to sue for my hand, and offers to make me a duchess—

PERCINET. And you say, "No!"

SYLVETTE. He is offended, and some dark night when I am in the garden, meditating,[8]

---

7. Pasquinot-Capulet and Bergamin-Montague: Percinet refers to their fathers as though they belonged to Juliet's and Romeo's feuding families, the Capulets and the Montagues.

---

8. meditating (med′ ə tāt′ iŋ) *v*.: Thinking deeply.

he springs forth out of the darkness! I scream!

PERCINET. And I lose not a second in springing over the wall, dagger in hand. I fight like a tiger, I—

SYLVETTE. You run through three or four men. Then my father rushes in and takes me in his arms. You tell him who you are. His heart softens, he gives me to my savior —your father consents, for he is proud of your bravery.

PERCINET. Then we live together for years, happy and content!

SYLVETTE. This is not at all impossible, is it?

PERCINET. Someone's coming!

SYLVETTE. [*Forgetting herself*] Kiss me!

PERCINET. [*Kissing her*] This evening, at eight, then? As usual? You will come?

SYLVETTE. No.

PERCINET. Yes!

SYLVETTE. [*Disappearing behind the wall*]

these festoons[10] make! The air is purer here than elsewhere.

BERGAMIN. By the side of this wall?

PERCINET. I love it!

BERGAMIN. I see nothing lovable about it!

SYLVETTE. [*Aside*] He can't see why!

PERCINET. But it is charming, all covered with ivy and creeper. See here, what honeysuckle! This hundred-year-old wall, with its clinging vines, its constellations[11] of flowers, looking through the crannies,[12] kissed by the summer sun, makes of the bench a throne fit for kings to sit on!

BERGAMIN. Nonsense, you hare-brained youth! Do you mean to tell me that this wall has eyes?

PERCINET. Ah, what eyes! [*Turns toward the wall*] Of soft azure, yet dazzlingly blue; let but a tear come to dim your brightness, a single kiss—

BERGAMIN. But the wall hasn't eyes, you idiot!

PERCINET. See this vine, though! [*He plucks part of the vine from the wall and graciously presents it to his father.*]

SYLVETTE. [*Aside*] How clever!

BERGAMIN. How stupid!—But I know now what has turned your silly head: you come here to read! [SYLVETTE *starts as she hears this.* PERCINET *also shows signs of fear as his father pulls forth the book from the youth's pocket.*] Plays! [*He drops the book in horror.*] And verse! Verse! That's what has turned your head. Now I see why you talk about eyes and honeysuckle. I tell you, to be

Your father! [PERCINET *jumps quickly from the wall.*]

[*Enter* BERGAMIN.]

BERGAMIN. Ah, ha, I find you here again, dreaming in this corner of the park!

PERCINET. Father, I love this old corner! I adore this bench over which the vines of the wall have so gracefully draped themselves. See—what graceful arabesques[9]

---

9. arabesques (ar′ ə besks′) *n.*: A complex and elaborate design of intertwined flowers or foliage.

10. festoons (fes toons′) *n.*: Wreaths or garlands of flowers or leaves.
11. constellations (kän′ stə lā′ shəns) *n.*: A brilliant cluster.
12. crannies (kran′ ēs) *n.*: Small, narrow openings.

useful, a wall doesn't have to be beautiful. I am going to have all this green stuff taken away, and the bricks re-laid and the holes stopped up. I want a white wall and a high one to keep our neighbors from looking into our park. I want no vines and honeysuckles. Along the top I'll sprinkle broken glass—

PERCINET. Pity!

BERGAMIN. No pity! I insist on it! Glass—all along the top of the wall! [SYLVETTE *and* PERCINET *are in despair.* BERGAMIN *sits down on the bench.*] And now, I have something to say to you. [*He rises and examines the wall.*] If the wall hasn't eyes, possibly it has ears? [*He is about to stand up on the bench, when* PERCINET *takes fright and* SYLVETTE *clings close to her side of the wall, making herself as small as she can.* BERGAMIN *decides not to scale the wall, but motions to his son to do so.*] See whether some curious listener—?

PERCINET. [*Climbing to the top and leaning over so that* SYLVETTE *can hear him*] Till tonight!

SYLVETTE. [*Giving him her hand, which he kisses*] I'll come as the clock is striking! I adore you!

BERGAMIN. [*To* PERCINET] Well?

PERCINET. [*Jumping down—to his father*] Well—no one!

BERGAMIN. [*Reseating himself*] Well, then, my boy, I should like to see you married.

SYLVETTE. [*Aside*] Oh!

BERGAMIN. What's that?

PERCINET. Nothing.

BERGAMIN. I thought I heard a little cry?

PERCINET. [*Looking into the air*] Some wounded bird, perhaps.

BERGAMIN. Well, I have given the matter my undivided attention, and I have chosen a wife for you. [PERCINET *whistles and walks away*] I tell you, I am in earnest and I intend to force you, if necessary—[PERCINET *continues whistling.*] Will you stop that confounded whistling! The young woman is rich—she's a jewel!

PERCINET. I want none of your jewels!

BERGAMIN. I'll show you, you young insolent[13]—

PERCINET. [*Grasping his father's cane, which is raised as if to strike him*] Spring has filled the bushes with the songs of birds; the brooklets accompany the love-notes of wild birds—

BERGAMIN. Rascal!

PERCINET. [*Still holding the cane*] The whole world laughs and sings farewell to April—The butterflies—

BERGAMIN. Ruffian!

PERCINET. [*As before*] Wing their way across the meadows, to make love to the adored flowers! Love—

BERGAMIN. Villain!

PERCINET. Love opens wide the heart of all nature. And you ask me to consent to a marriage of reason!

BERGAMIN. Of course I do!

PERCINET. [*Passionately*] No, no, no, Father. I swear by this wall—which hears me I hope—that my marriage will be more romantic than any dreamed of in the most poetic of the world's love stories! [*He runs out.*]

BERGAMIN. [*Pursuing him*] Ah, let me catch you—!

---

13. insolent (in′ sə lənt) *n.*: One who is boldly disrespectful or impertinent.

SYLVETTE. I can really understand now why Papa hates that old man—

[*Enter* PASQUINOT, *left*]

PASQUINOT. Well, Mademoiselle, what are you doing here?

SYLVETTE. Nothing. Taking the air.

PASQUINOT. Alone? But, you silly girl, are you not afraid?

SYLVETTE. Not in the least.

PASQUINOT. Near this wall? But I forbade you to come near it! You see that park over there? That belongs to my mortal enemy!

SYLVETTE. I know it, Father dear.

PASQUINOT. Why, here you are exposed to any insult, any—Why, if those rascals knew that my daughter were walking alone in this park—Brrr! It makes me shiver to think of! I'm going to have the wall repaired, and erect a huge iron grill on top of it.

SYLVETTE. [*Aside*] He'll never do it—it would cost too much!

PASQUINOT. Now go into the house—quick! [*She goes out,* PASQUINOT *glowering at her.*]

BERGAMIN. [*Heard from the other side of the wall, as he enters*] Take this note at once to Monsieur Straforel.

PASQUINOT. [*Running to the wall and climbing to the top of it*] Bergamin!

BERGAMIN. [*Doing likewise*] Pasquinot! [*They embrace.*]

PASQUINOT. How goes it?

BERGAMIN. Pretty well.

PASQUINOT. How's your gout?

BERGAMIN. Better. And how is your cold?

PASQUINOT. Still troubles me, devil take it!

BERGAMIN. Well, the marriage is sure!

PASQUINOT. What?

BERGAMIN. I heard everything—I was hidden in the bushes. They adore each other!

PASQUINOT. Bravo!

BERGAMIN. Now we must bring matters to a head! [*He rubs his hands.*] Ha, ha! Now we can do as we had planned—

PASQUINOT. Yes, and tear down the wall.

BERGAMIN. And live together.

PASQUINOT. Joining our properties.

BERGAMIN. By marrying our children. But I wonder, would they be so anxious if they knew we wished it? A marriage arranged beforehand is not so tempting to two young children so romantic as ours. That is why we kept our own wishes a secret. I felt sure that after they had been separated—Sylvette in the convent, Percinet at college—they would thrive on their guilty love. That is how I came to invent this hatred of ours. And you even doubted its success! Now all we have to do is to say Yes.

PASQUINOT. Yes, but how can it be done? Remember, I've called you a scoundrel, fool, idiot—

BERGAMIN. Idiot? Scoundrel was sufficient.

PASQUINOT. Now what pretext—?

BERGAMIN. Your daughter herself has given me an inspiration. This evening they are to meet here at eight. Percinet comes first. Now at the moment when Sylvette appears, mysterious men in black will emerge from the shadows and start to carry her off. A real abduction![14] She screams, then our young hero gives chase, draws his sword—the rav-

---

14. abduction (ab duk' shən) *n.*: Kidnapping.

ishers[15] pretend to flee—I arrive on the scene, then you—your daughter is safe and sound. You bless the couple and drop a few appropriate tears; my heart is softened. Tableau.[16]

PASQUINOT. A stroke of genius.

BERGAMIN. [*Modestly*] Yes—I think it really is. Look—see that man coming? It's Straforel, the bravado whom I wrote to a few minutes ago. He is to carry out the abduction.

[STRAFOREL, *in an elaborate swordsman's costume, appears at the back of* BERGAMIN'S park and swaggers downstage.]

BERGAMIN. [*Descending from the wall and bowing low to* STRAFOREL] Allow me to introduce you to my friend Pasquinot—

STRAFOREL. [*Bowing*] Monsieur—[*He raises his head and sees no* PASQUINOT.]

BERGAMIN. [*Pointing to* PASQUINOT *on the crest of the wall*] There, on the wall!—Now, my dear master, does my plan meet with your approval?

STRAFOREL. It does. It is most simple.

BERGAMIN. You must act quickly—you understand—

STRAFOREL. And say nothing!

BERGAMIN. A make-believe abduction and artificial fight with swords.

STRAFOREL. I understand perfectly.

BERGAMIN. You must have skillful swordsmen —I can't have my boy hurt. He is my only child!

STRAFOREL. I will see to that myself.

BERGAMIN. Good—in that case, I shall fear nothing.

PASQUINOT. [*Aside to* BERGAMIN] Ask him the price?

BERGAMIN. For an abduction, Maestro, how much do you charge?

STRAFOREL. That depends, Monsieur, on the kind you wish; we have them for all prices. In an affair of this kind, however, nothing should be spared. If I were in your place, I should have a first-class abduction.

BERGAMIN. [*Surprised*] Then you have many classes?

STRAFOREL. Indeed I have. I have the ordinary vulgar abduction in a cab, with two men dressed in black—that's rarely used—the daylight abduction, the midnight abduction; the pompous abduction in a court carriage, with powdered servants—wigs are extra —with brigands, musketeers, anything you like! The abduction in a post-chaise,[17] with two, three, four, five, horses, ad-lib.; the discreet and quiet abduction, in a small carriage—that one's rather lugubrious[18]—the rollicking[19] abduction, in which the victim is carried away in a sack; the romantic abduction in a boat—but a lake is necessary!—the Venetian[20] abduction, in a gondola[21]—ah, you have no lagoon! Moonlight abduction, or the abduction on a dark and starless night—those moonlight abductions are quite the style, though they are a little dear!—Besides these, there

---

15. ravishers (rav′ ish ərs) *n.*: Those who seize and carry someone away forcibly.
16. tableau (tab′ lō) *n.*: A striking, dramatic scene or picture.

17. post-chaise (pōst′ shāz′) *n.*: A closed, four-wheeled carriage drawn by fast horses.
18. lugubrious (loo gōō′ brē əs) *adj.*: Sad or mournful.
19. rollicking (räl′ ik iŋ) *adj.*: Lively.
20. Venetian (vi nē′ shən) *adj.*:Having to do with Venice, Italy.
21. gondola (gän′ də lə) *n.*: A long, narrow canalboat.

is the abduction lighted by torches, with cries and screams, the clash and shock of arms; the brutal abduction, the polite abduction; the classical one with masks; the gallant abduction to the accompaniment of music; but the latest, most stylish, gayest, of all, is the sedan-chair abduction![22]

BERGAMIN. [*Scratching his head—aside to* PASQUINOT] Well, what do you think?

PASQUINOT. Hm, well what do you?

BERGAMIN. I think that we should do everything in the best possible way, no expense spared. Let us give our young romancers something they'll not soon forget. Let's have it with masks, dark mantles, torches, music, and a sedan-chair!

STRAFOREL. [*Taking notes*] A first-class then, with all the extras.

BERGAMIN. That's it.

STRAFOREL. I shall return soon. [*To* PASQUINOT] Remember, Monsieur, to leave open the door of your park tonight.

BERGAMIN. Very well, it shall be done.

STRAFOREL. [*Bowing*] My compliments. [*Turning to go*] One first-class—with extras. [*He goes out.*]

PASQUINOT. The honest man, he went without telling us the price!

BERGAMIN. Everything is arranged. Now we'll live together, after demolishing the wall.

PASQUINOT. And in the winter we'll have but one hearth and home.

BERGAMIN. Our dearest wishes are about to be realized!

---

22. sedan-chair abduction: A kidnapping in which the victim is carried off in an enclosed chair, carried on poles by two men.

PASQUINOT. And we'll grow old together!

BERGAMIN. Dear old Pasquinot!

PASQUINOT. Dear old Bergamin! [*They embrace.* SYLVETTE *and* PERCINET *enter, from each side of the stage, and, seeing their fathers embrace*]

SYLVETTE. Oh!

BERGAMIN. [*Aside to* PASQUINOT] Your daughter!

PERCINET. Oh!

PASQUINOT. [*Aside to* BERGAMIN] Your son!

BERGAMIN. [*Aside to* PASQUINOT] We must pretend we are fighting! [*Their embrace is transformed into a struggle.*] Rascal!

PASQUINOT. Fool!

SYLVETTE. [*Pulling her father's coattails*] Papa!

PERCINET. [*Doing the same with his father*] Papa!

BERGAMIN. Let us be!

PASQUINOT. He insulted me!

BERGAMIN. He struck me!

PASQUINOT. Coward!

SYLVETTE. Papa!

BERGAMIN. Thief!

PERCINET. Papa!

PASQUINOT. Bandit!

SYLVETTE. Papa!! [SYLVETTE *and* PERCINET *finally succeed in separating the fathers.*]

PERCINET. [*Dragging his father away*] Go in now, it's late.

BERGAMIN. [*Trying to go to the wall again*] I can't control myself. Just let me—! [PERCINET *takes him out.*]

PASQUINOT. [*Also trying to return to the wall*] I'll kill him—!

SYLVETTE. [*Dragging* PASQUINOT *out*] The air is so damp! Think of your rheumatism! [*They go out.*]

[*Little by little it grows dark. For a moment the stage is empty. Then, in* PASQUINOT'S *park, enter* STRAFOREL *and swordsmen, musicians, and torch-bearers.*]

STRAFOREL. I see one star already. The day is dying—[*He places his men about.*] Stay there—you there—and you there. The hour is near. You will see, as the clock strikes eight, a figure in white enter on this side. Then I whistle—[*He looks at the sky again.*] The moon? Splendid! Every effect is perfect tonight! [*Examining the costumes of his band*] The capes and mantles are excellent. Look a little more dangerous, over there! Now, ready? [*A sedan-chair is*

mask, don't look so harmless—I want a villainous slouch! Good! Now, instruments, play softly—tune up!—Good—tra la la! [*He puts on his mask.*]

[PERCINET *enters slowly, from the other side of the stage. As he speaks the following lines, the stage becomes darker, until at the end, it is night.*]

PERCINET. My father is more calm now. The day is dying, and the odor of the elders is wafted to me, intoxicating me; the flowers close their petals in the gray of the evening—

STRAFOREL. [*Aside to the violins*] Music!

[*The musicians play softly until the end of the act.*]

PERCINET. I tremble like a reed. She is coming!

STRAFOREL. [*To the musicians*] Amoroso![23]

PERCINET. My first evening meeting—I can scarcely stand! The evening breeze sounds like the fluttering of her dress—Now I can't see a single flower—tears are in my eyes —but I can smell them. Ah, this great tree, with a star above it—Music? Who—? [*A pause*] Night has come. [*After another pause, a clock strikes eight in the distance.* SYLVETTE *appears at the back of her park.*]

SYLVETTE. The hour has struck. He must be waiting.

[*A whistle is heard.* STRAFOREL *rises in front of* SYLVETTE, *and torch-bearers appear in the background.* SYLVETTE *screams. The swordsmen seize* SYLVETTE *and place her in the sedan-chair.*]

brought in.] The chair over there in the shade. [*Speaking at a distance*] Torches, there, you understand you are not to come until you receive the signal? [*The faint reflection of the torches is seen at the back of the stage, through the underbrush. Enter the musicians.*] Musicians? There—at the back. Now, a little air of distinction and life! Vary your poses a little from time to time. Stand straight, mandolin! Sit down, alto! There. [*Severely to a swordsman*] You, first

---

23. amoroso (äm ə rō′ sō): An instruction to musicians to play with tenderness.

SYLVETTE. Help! Help!

PERCINET. Great Heavens!

SYLVETTE. Percinet, they are carrying me off!

PERCINET. [*Leaping toward the wall*] I come! [*When he reaches the top of the wall, he draws his sword, jumps down on the other side of the wall, and engages four or five swordsmen in combat. They flee before him.*] There, and there, and there!

STRAFOREL. [*To the musicians*] Tremolo![24]

[*The violins now play a dramatic tremolo.*]

STRAFOREL. Per Bacco, he's the devil, that child! [PERCINET *now engages* STRAFOREL *in a duel.* STRAFOREL, *after a few thrusts, puts his hand to his breast.*] I—I'm mortally wounded! [*He falls.*]

PERCINET. [*Running to* SYLVETTE, *who sits in the sedan-chair*] Sylvette! [*He kneels to her.*]

SYLVETTE. My savior!

PASQUINOT. [*Entering*] Bergamin's son?! Your savior? Your savior? You are his!

SYLVETTE and **PERCINET.** *Heavens!*

[BERGAMIN *now appears on his side of the wall.*]

PASQUINOT. [*To* BERGAMIN, *who is seen on top of the wall*] Bergamin, your son is a hero! Let us forget our quarrels, and make these children happy!

BERGAMIN. [*Solemnly*] I hate no more!

PERCINET. Sylvette, don't speak loud: I know I am dreaming. But don't wake me yet!

BERGAMIN. Our hatred is ended in the wedding of our dear ones. [*Indicating the wall*] Let there be no Pyrenees![25]

PERCINET. Who would have believed that my father could so change!

SYLVETTE. I told you that everything would come out all right! [*While the lovers go up-stage with* PASQUINOT, STRAFOREL *rises and extends a folded paper to* BERGAMIN.]

BERGAMIN. [*Aside*] Well, what is it? This paper —your signature? What is it, if you please?

STRAFOREL. [*Bowing*] Monsieur, it's my bill! [*He falls down again.*]

---

24. tremolo (trem′ ə lō′) *n*.: An instruction to a musician to produce a quivering effect or vibration in the music.

25. Pyrenees (pir′ ə nēz′): Mountain range between France and Spain.

Copies of this play, in individual paper-covered acting editions, are available from Samuel French, Inc., 45 W. 25th St., New York, N.Y. 10010 or 7623 Sunset Blvd., Hollywood, Calif. 90046, or in Canada, Samuel French (Canada) Ltd., 80 Richmond Street East, Toronto M5C 1P1, Canada.

THINKING ABOUT THE SELECTION

Recalling

1. How do Percinet and Sylvette think their fathers feel about each other? How do they really feel about each other?
2. What is the plan for the "abduction"?
3. What does the "abduction" accomplish?

Interpreting

4. The play *Romeo and Juliet* tells of a young man and woman who defy their parents and marry. Why did the playwright choose *Romeo and Juliet* for Percinet and Sylvette to read?
5. Why did the fathers build the wall?
6. How might the lovers feel if they knew their fathers had planned their marriage?
7. One definition of *romance* is "the tendency to derive great pleasure from adventures involving excitement and love." Who are the real romancers or romantics, the young couple or their fathers? Explain your answer.

Applying

8. The fathers use reverse psychology: They hope to unite the couple by forbidding them to see each other. How well does reverse psychology work in real life? Give examples.

ANALYZING LITERATURE

Appreciating Staging

Staging includes what costumes are used, where the props go, what lighting or sound effects are used, and where the actors should move.

The staging of *The Romancers* includes only one set, which is the arrangement of props and scenery for a scene in a play. The play takes place in a garden, in which the most important prop is a wall.

1. Describe the set as you imagine it. What would be the most important part of it? Why?

2. What mood, or feeling, should the lighting create? What lights would create this mood?
3. What sound effects would you use?
4. Describe the costumes you would use.
5. The abduction scene is a dramatic moment. Describe how you would stage this scene.

CRITICAL THINKING AND READING

Recognizing the Playwright's Purpose

A playwright's **purpose** or reason for writing, may be to entertain, to persuade, or to portray a particular aspect of life.

Rostand's purpose in *The Romancers* is to entertain. To entertain he uses humor, shown by exaggerated behavior, preposterous, or laughable situations, and information in stage directions. For example, the stage direction "Sighing" when Sylvette says, "Poor lovers! Their fate was cruel!" is exaggerated behavior.

1. Find two examples of exaggerated behavior.
2. Why is the fathers' plan preposterous?
3. What are the stage directions when Bergamin is trying to force Percinet to marry?
4. What do the stage directions tell Sylvette and Percinet to do when their fathers are fighting over the wall?
5. How do these stage directions create humor?

THINKING AND WRITING

Writing About Staging the Play

Imagine that you have an opportunity to stage a production of *The Romancers*. Write a memo to the producer telling him everything you would need for the staging. First make a list for yourself of the props, costumes, sound effects, and kind of lighting you would need. Include a detailed description of each item. Revise your memo to make sure the producer will have a clear idea of what you need. Then prepare a final draft.

GUIDE FOR READING

Let Me Hear You Whisper

Paul Zindel (1936–   ) was born in Staten Island, New York, where he later taught high-school chemistry for ten years. After the publication of his young-adult novels *The Pigman* (1968) and *My Darling, My Hamburger* (1969), Zindel turned to writing full time. He wrote several plays, including *The Effects of Gamma Rays on Man-in-the-Moon Marigolds.* In the television play *Let Me Hear You Whisper,* Zindel focuses on some controversies associated with science.

Conflict in Drama

Conflict is a struggle between opposing sides or forces. In a play, the characters *act out* the conflict, and ultimately their actions result in a resolution, or outcome. External conflict is a struggle between a character and an outside force, such as another person, nature, or fate. Internal conflict is a struggle within the character's own mind. A character can express internal conflict—as well as external conflict—through actions, facial expressions, and dialogue.

Look For

As you read *Let Me Hear You Whisper,* look for indications of what the main character, Helen, experiences. Try to understand the reasons for her conflict and the way she resolves it.

Writing

Science has found the answers to many problems. However, sometimes, it creates problems. Brainstorm with your classmates to form two lists. Label one list *Advances Brought About Through Science.* Label the second list *Problems Caused by Science.*

Vocabulary

Knowing the following words will help you as you read *Let Me Hear You Whisper.*

predecessor (pred′ ə ses′ ər) *n.*: Someone who comes before another in a position (p. 278)

incessantly (in ses′ 'nt lē) *adv.*: Without interruption (p. 279)

compulsory (kəm pul′ sər ē) *adj.*: Required (p. 280)

enunciated (i nun′ sē āt′ əd) *v.*: Spoken clearly (p. 282)

macabre (mə käb′ rə) *adj.*: Gruesome, suggesting the horror of death (p. 291)

benevolent (bə nev′ ə lənt) *adj.*: Kindly (p. 291)

gyrations (jī rā′ shənz) *n.*: Circling or spiral movements (p. 293)

Let Me Hear You Whisper

Paul Zindel

CHARACTERS

Helen . . . . A cleaning lady

Miss Moray . . . Her briskly efficient supervisor

Dr. Crocus . . . . A dedicated lady of science

Mrs. Fridge . . . . Her assistant

Danielle . . . . . . A talky lady porter

A Dolphin . . . . . . The subject of an experiment

[*The play is set in the laboratory of a building near the Hudson River in lower Manhattan—the home of American Biological Association Development For The Advancement of Brain Analysis.*]

Scene 1

[*Curtain rises on* DR. CROCUS *and* MRS. FRIDGE, *conducting an experiment on the* DOLPHIN *in the laboratory. The* DOLPHIN *is in a long narrow tank with little room to move. A head sling lifting its blowhole out of the water and several electrodes implanted in its brain further the impression of a trapped and sad animal.* DR. CROCUS *is observing closely as* MRS. FRIDGE *presses various buttons on cue. An oscilloscope is bleeping in the background.*]

DR. CROCUS. Pain.

[MRS. FRIDGE *presses a button. No response from* DOLPHIN.]

Pleasure.

[*Another button*]

Anger.

[*Another*]

Fear.

[*There has been no satisfactory response from the* DOLPHIN, *but an automatic recorder starts to play a charming melody. When the accompanying vocal commences, however, it is an eerily precise enunciation of the words.*]

RECORD.
> Let me call you sweetheart,
> I'm in love with you.
> Let me hear you whisper,
> That you love me, too.

[*Disappointed at the lack of response,* DR. CROCUS *crosses toward* MRS. FRIDGE.]

DR. CROCUS. Resistance to electrodic impulses. Possibly destroyed tissue. Continue impulse and auditory suggestion at intervals of seven minutes until end of week. If no response by Friday, termination.

[DOLPHIN'*s special discomfort at this word is unnoticed by others.* DR. CROCUS *and* MRS. FRIDGE *head toward elevator on other side of the stage. The elevator doors open and* MISS MORAY *emerges with* HELEN.]

MISS MORAY. Dr. Crocus. Mrs. Fridge. I'm so glad we've run into you. I want you to meet Helen.

HELEN. Hello.

[DR. CROCUS *and* MRS. FRIDGE *nod and get on elevator.*]

MISS MORAY. Helen is the newest member of our Custodial Engineering Team. So if you two "coaches" have any suggestions we'll be most grateful. We want everything to be perfect, don't we, Helen?

HELEN. I do the best I can.

MISS MORAY. Exactly. The doctor is one of the most remarkable . . . [*The elevator doors close and* MRS. FRIDGE *and* DR. CROCUS *are gone.*] Remarkable.

HELEN. She looked remarkable. [HELEN *looks like a peasant, kerchief and all. As they walk,* HELEN *begins to remove the kerchief and she would like to fold it properly, for that to be her only activity, but she is distracted by a shopping bag she carries, a bulky coat, and the voice of* MISS MORAY.]

MISS MORAY. Dr. Crocus is the guiding heart here at the American Biological Association Development For The Advancement of Brain Analysis. We call it ABADABA, for short.

HELEN. I guess you have to. [*They stop at a metal locker.*]

MISS MORAY. This will be your locker and your key. Mrs. Fridge has been with ABADABA only three months and already she's a much endeared part of our little family. Your equipment is in this closet.

[*She opens a closet next to the locker.*]

HELEN. I have to bring my own hangers, I suppose . . .

MISS MORAY. Although it was somewhat embarrassing to me, it was Mrs. Fridge's in-ventorial excellence that uncovered what Margaurita—your predecessor—did and why she had to leave us. She'd been drinking portions of the ethyl alcohol—there's a basin under the sink for rag rinsing—the undenatured ethyl alcohol, and she almost burned out her esophagus. [*Pause*] I wouldn't have minded so much if she had only asked. Didn't you find Personnel pleasant?

HELEN. They asked a lot of crazy questions.

MISS MORAY. For instance.

HELEN. They wanted to know how I felt watching TV.

MISS MORAY. What do you mean, *how you felt?*

HELEN. They wanted to know what went on in my head when I'm watching television in my living room and the audience laughs. They asked if I ever thought the audience was laughing at *me.*

MISS MORAY. [*Laughing*] My, oh, my! What did you tell them?

HELEN. I don't have a TV.

MISS MORAY. I'm sorry.

HELEN. I'm not.

MISS MORAY. Yes. Now, it's really quite simple. That's our special soap solution. One tablespoon to a gallon of hot water for ordinary cleaning, if I may suggest. I so much prefer to act as an assist to the Custodial Engineering Staff. New ideas. Techniques. I try to keep myself open.

[*Her mouth pauses wide open.* HELEN *has been busy familiarizing herself with the contents of the closet. She has culminated a series of small actions which have put things in order for her, by running water into a pail which fits into a metal stand on wheels.*]

HELEN. She left a dirty mop.

MISS MORAY. I beg your pardon?

HELEN. The one that drank. She left a dirty mop.

MISS MORAY. How ugly. I'll report it first thing in the morning. It may seem like a small point but if she ever tries to use us as a reference, she may be amazed at the specificity of our files.

HELEN. It's not that dirty.

MISS MORAY. I'll start you in the main laboratory area. We like it done first. The specimen section next. By that time we'll be well toward morning and if there are a few minutes left you can polish the brass strip. [*She points to brass strip which runs around halfway between ceiling and floor.*] Margaurita never once got to the brass strip.

[HELEN *has completed her very professional preparations and looks impatient to get moving.*]

Ready? Fine.

[*They start moving toward Dolphin area,* MISS MORAY *thumbing through papers on a clipboard.*]

You were with one concern for fourteen years, weren't you? Fourteen years with the Metal Climax Building. That's next to the Radio City Music Hall, isn't it, dear?

HELEN. Uh huh . . .

MISS MORAY. They sent a marvelous letter of recommendation—how you washed the corridor on the seventeenth floor . . . and the Metal Climax Building is a very long building. My! Fourteen years on the seventeenth floor. You must be very proud. Why did you leave?

HELEN. They put in a rug.

[MISS MORAY *leads* HELEN *into the laboratory area as* DANIELLE *enters.*]

MISS MORAY. Danielle, Helen will be taking Margaurita's place. Danielle is the night porter for the fifth through ninth floors. Duties you might find distasteful.

DANIELLE. Hiya!

HELEN. Hello. [HELEN *looks over the place.*]

MISS MORAY. By the way Danielle . . . there's a crock on nine you missed and the technicians on that floor have complained about the odor . . . [*Back to* HELEN] you can be certain we'll assist in every way possible.

HELEN. Maybe you could get me some hangers . . . ?

DANIELLE. I'll be glad to do anything. Just say the word and . . .

HELEN. What's behind there? [*Opening the Dolphin area*]

MISS MORAY. What? Oh, that's a dolphin, dear. But don't you worry about anything except the floor. Dr. Crocus prefers us not to touch either the equipment or the animals. That was another shortcoming of Margaurita's. Recently the doctor was . . . experimenting . . . with a colony of mice in that cage . . . [*She indicates cage.*] . . . and she was incessantly feeding them popcorn.

DANIELLE. Kinda a nice lady, though. Lived in the East Village.[1]

MISS MORAY. Yes, she did live in the East Village.

HELEN. [*Attention still on* DOLPHIN] Do you keep him cramped up in that all the time?

---

1. East Village: A neighborhood in Manhattan in New York City.

MISS MORAY. We have a natatorium[2] for it to exercise in at Dr. Crocus's discretion.

HELEN. He really looks cramped.

MISS MORAY. [*Closing the Dolphin area*] Well, you must be anxious to begin. I'll make myself available at the reception desk in the hall for a few nights in case any questions arise. Although my hunch is, that before you know it, I'll be coming to *you* with questions . . . coffee break at 2 and 6 A.M. Lunch at 4 A.M. All clear?

HELEN. I don't need a coffee break.

MISS MORAY. I beg your pardon?

HELEN. I said I don't need a coffee break.

MISS MORAY. Helen, we all need Perk-You-Ups. All of us. Perhaps you never liked them at the Metal Climax Building, but you'll learn to love them here. Perk-You-Ups make the employees much more efficient. Besides, Helen—

HELEN. I don't want one.

MISS MORAY. They're compulsory. Oh, Helen, I know, you're going to fit right in with our little family. You're such a *nice* person.

[*She exits.* HELEN *immediately gets to work moving her equipment into place and getting down on her hands and knees to scrub the floor.* DANIELLE *spots a ceiling bulb out and prepares to remove it by using a long stick with a grip on the end of it designed to unscrew bulbs one cannot reach.*]

DANIELLE. Margaurita wasn't half as bad as Miss Moray thought she was.

HELEN. I'm sure she wasn't.

DANIELLE. She was twice as bad. [*She laughs. Pause*] You live in the city? . . .

---

2. natatorium (nāt′ ə tôr′ ē əm) *n.:* An indoor swimming pool.

HELEN. Yes.

DANIELLE. That's nice. . . . my husband died two years ago.

HELEN. That's too bad.

DANIELLE. Yeah, two years in June. He blew up.

HELEN. Oh, I'm sorry.

DANIELLE. When you want that water changed, just lemme know. I'll take care of it.

HELEN. Thanks, but I just like to get the temperature right so my hands don't get boiled. You must miss your husband.

DANIELLE. Biggest mistake I ever made, getting married . . . you married?

HELEN. No.

DANIELLE. Good, if a woman ain't suited for it, she shouldn't do it.

HELEN. I didn't say I wasn't suited for it.

DANIELLE. My husband was set in his ways, too.

HELEN. If you'll excuse me, I have to get my work done.

DANIELLE. Guess I'd better see about that crock on nine. You don't like to talk, do you?

HELEN. I'm used to working alone and that's the way I get my work done.

[DANIELLE *exits. Not realizing she's already gone*]

What do you mean, your husband blew up?

[*But* DANIELLE *is gone. She glances at the curtain shielding the* DOLPHIN, *then continues scrubbing. After a beat, the record begins to play.*]

RECORD.

> Let me call you sweetheart,
> I'm in love with you.
> Let me hear you whisper,
> That you love me, too.

[HELEN *eyes the automatic machinery with suspicion, but goes on working. When the song is finished she looks at the curtain again and again until her curiosity makes her pull the curtain open and look at the* DOLPHIN. *He is looking right back at her. She becomes uncomfortable and starts to close the curtain again. She decides to leave it part-way open so she can still see the* DOLPHIN *while she scrubs. She glances out of the corner of her eye after a few moments of scrubbing and notices the* DOLPHIN *is looking at her. She pretends to look away and sings* Let Me Call You Sweetheart *to herself —missing a word or two here and there —but her eyes return to the* DOLPHIN. *She becomes uncomfortable again under his stare and crawls on her hands and knees to the other side of the room. She scrubs there for a moment or two and then shoots a look at the* DOLPHIN. *It is still looking at her. She tries to ease her discomfort by playing peek-a-boo with the* DOLPHIN *for a moment. There is no response and she resumes*

scrubbing and humming. The DOLPHIN *then lets out a bubble or two and moves in the tank to bring his blowhole to the surface. (Any sounds he does make, including words, are like a haunting whisper and never enunciated so they are absolute.)]*

DOLPHIN. Youuuuuuuuuuuuu. [HELEN *hears the sound, assumes she is mistaken, and goes on with her work.*] Youuuuuuuuuuuuu.

[HELEN *has heard the sound more clearly this time. She is puzzled, contemplates a moment, and then decides to get up off the floor. She closes the curtain on the* DOLPHIN'*s tank and is quite disturbed. The elevator door suddenly opens and* MISS MORAY *enters.*]

MISS MORAY. What is it, Helen?

HELEN. The fish is making some kinda funny noise.

MISS MORAY. Mammal, Helen. It's a mammal.

HELEN. The mammal's making some kinda funny noise.

MISS MORAY. Mammals are supposed to make funny noises.

HELEN Yes, Miss Moray.

[HELEN *hangs awkwardly a moment and then continues scrubbing.* MISS MORAY *exits officiously to another part of the floor. A moment later, from behind the curtains, the* DOLPHIN *is heard.*]

DOLPHIN. Youuuuuuuuuuuuuu.

[HELEN *is quite worried.*] Youuuuuuuuuuuuuu.

[*She apprehensively approaches the curtain, and opens it, when* DANIELLE *barges in. She goes to get her reaching pole and* HELEN *hurriedly returns to scrubbing the floor.*]

DANIELLE. Bulb out on ten.

HELEN. What do they have that thing for?

DANIELLE. What thing?

HELEN. That.

DANIELLE. Yeah, he's something, ain't he? They're tryin' to get it to talk.

HELEN. Talk?

DANIELLE. Uh-huh, but this one don't. They had one last year that used to laugh. It'd go heh heh heh heh heh heh heh heh. I'd be in here doing something and it'd start heh heh heh heh heh heh hehing. He died a year ago May. Then they got another one that used to say "Yeah, it's four o'clock." Everybody took pictures of that one. All the magazines.

HELEN. What'd it say "four o'clock" for?

DANIELLE. Nobody knows.

HELEN. It just kept saying "Yeah, it's four o'clock!"

DANIELLE. Until it died of pneumonia. [*Pause*] They talk outta their blowholes, when they can talk, that is. Did you see the blowhole?

HELEN. No.

DANIELLE. Come on and take a look. Look at it.

HELEN. I don't want to look at any blowhole.

DANIELLE. You can see it right there.

[HELEN *gets up and goes to the tank. As she and* DANIELLE *stand at the tank, their backs are to one of the entrances, and they don't see* MISS MORAY *open the door and watch them.*]

This one don't say anything at all. It bleeps, beeps, barks and blatts out of the mouth, but it don't talk out of the blowhole. They been playing that record every seven minutes for months and it can't learn beans.

MISS MORAY. Helen?

[HELEN *and* DANIELLE *turn around.*]

Helen, would you mind stepping over here a moment?

HELEN. Yes, Miss Moray.

DANIELLE. I was just showing her something.

MISS MORAY. Have you attended to the crock on nine?

DANIELLE. Yes, Ma'am.

MISS MORAY. Then hadn't we better get on with our duties? [MISS MORAY *guides* HELEN *aside putting her arm around her as though taking her into great confidence. She even whispers.*] Helen, I have to talk to you. Frankly, I need your help.

HELEN. She was just showing me . . .

MISS MORAY. It's something about Danielle I need your assistance with. I'm sure you've noticed that she . . .

HELEN. Yes?

MISS MORAY. Well, that she's the type of person who will do anything to breed idle chatter. Yes, an idle chatter breeder. How many times we've told her, "Danielle, this is a scientific atmosphere you're employed in and from Dr. Crocus all the way down to the most insignificant member of the Custodial Engineering Staff we would appreciate a minimum of subjective intercourse." So—if you can help, Helen—and I'm sure you can, enormously—we'd be so grateful. This is science—and science means progress. You do want progress, don't you, dear?

HELEN. Yes, Miss Moray.

MISS MORAY. I knew you did.

DANIELLE. I just wanted to show her the blowhole.

MISS MORAY. I'm sure that's all it was, Danielle. [DANIELLE *exits.*]

Helen, why don't you dust for a while? Vary your labors.

[*She swings open a shelf area to reveal rather hideously preserved specimens.* HELEN *looks ready to gag as she sees the jars of all sizes. Various animals and parts of animals are visible in their formaldehyde baths.*]

A feather duster—here—is marvelous for dusting though a damp rag may be necessary for the glass surfaces. But whatever —do be careful. Margaurita once dropped a jar of assorted North Atlantic eels.

[MISS MORAY *smiles and exits in the elevator, leaving Helen alone. She is most uncomfortable in the environment. The sound of music and voice from beyond the walls falls over.*]

RECORD.
> Let me call you sweetheart,
> I'm in love with you.
> Let me hear you whisper,
> That you love me, too.

Scene 2

[*It is the next evening.* HELEN *gets off the elevator carrying a few hangers and still wearing her kerchief and coat. She looks around for anyone, realizes she is alone, and then proceeds to her locker. She takes her coat off and hangs it up.* HELEN *pushes her equipment into the lab. The curtain on the* DOLPHIN's *tank has been closed. She sets her items up, then goes to the tank and pulls the curtain open a moment. The* DOLPHIN *is looking at her. She closes the curtain and starts scrubbing. The thought of the* DOLPHIN *amuses her a moment, relieving the tension she feels about the mammal, and she appears to be in good spirits as she* starts humming Let Me Call You Sweetheart and scrubs in rhythm to it. She sets a one-two-three beat for the scrub brush.

This mood passes quickly and she opens the curtain so she can watch the DOLPHIN as she works. She and the DOLPHIN stare at each other and HELEN appears to be more curious than worried.

Finally, she decides to try to imitate the sound she heard it make the night before.]

HELEN. Youuuuuuuuuuuuu. [*She pauses, watches for a response.*] Youuuuuuuuu-uuuuu. [*Still no response. She returns her attention to her scrubbing for a moment. Then:*]

Polly want a cracker?
Polly want a cracker?

[*She wrings out a rag and resumes work.*]

Yeah, it's four o'clock. Yeah, it's four o'clock. [*When her expectation is unfulfilled, she is slightly disappointed. Then:*] Polly want a cracker at four o'clock?

[*She laughs at her own joke, then is re-minded of the past success with laughter in working with dolphins. She can't resist trying it, so she goes to the DOLPHIN's tank and notices how sad it looks. She is divert-ed from her initial intention by a guilty feeling of leaving the scrubbing. She bends down and looks directly into the DOLPHIN's face. He lets out a bubble at her. She sticks her tongue out at him. She makes an exag-gerated smile, and is very curious about what his skin feels like. She reaches her hand in and just touches the top of his head. He squirms and likes it, but she's interested in drying off her finger. She even washes it in her soap solution. She returns to scrubbing for a minute, then can't resist more fully petting the DOLPHIN. This time he*

reacts even more enthusiastically. She is half afraid and half happy. She returns to scrubbing. Then, at the tank:]

Heh heh heh heh heh heh heh heh heh. [*Beat*] Heh heh heh heh. [*Beat*] Heh heh heh heh heh heh . . .

[MISS MORAY *enters. She sees what's going on. Then says, with exaggerated praise*]

MISS MORAY. Look how nicely the floor's com-ing along tonight! There's not a streak! Not a streak! You must have a special rinsing technique, Helen. You do, don't you? Why, you certainly do. I can smell something.

HELEN. Just a little . . . vinegar in the rinse water.

MISS MORAY. You brought that vinegar your-self just so the floors . . . they are sparkling, Helen. Sparkling! [*Jotting down in a pad*] This is going in your file, dear—and from now on, I'm going to requisition vinegar as a staple in the Custodial Engineering Depart-ment's supply list. [*She pauses—looks at the* DOLPHIN—*then at* HELEN.] It's marvelous, Helen, how well you've adjusted . . .

HELEN. Thank you, Miss Moray.

MISS MORAY. Not everyone does, you know. Just last week I had a problem with a porter on five, who became too fond of a St. Bernard they . . . worked on . . . and . . . [*Pause*] well, Helen a lot of people can't seem—

HELEN. [*Still scrubbing*] What do you mean, worked on?

MISS MORAY. Well . . . well, even Margaurita. She had fallen in love with the mice. All three hundred of them. She seemed shocked when she found out Dr. Crocus was . . .

using . . . them at the rate of twenty or so a day in connection with electrode implanting. She noticed them missing after a while and when I told her they'd been decapitated, she seemed terribly upset. It made one wonder if she'd thought we'd been sending them away on vacations or something. But, I'm sure you understand—you have such insight. [*She is at the tank.*] It's funny isn't it? To look at these mammals, you'd never suspect they were such rapacious carnivori . . .[3]

HELEN. What do they want with it?

[*The* Let Me Call You Sweetheart *record commences playing but* MISS MORAY *talks over it.*]

MISS MORAY. Well, they may have an intelligence equal to our own. And if we can teach them our language—or learn theirs—we'll be able to communicate. [*Raising her voice higher over record*] Wouldn't that be wonderful, Helen? To be able to communicate?

HELEN. I can't understand you.

MISS MORAY. [*Louder*] Communicate! Wouldn't it be wonderful?

HELEN. Oh, yeah.

MISS MORAY. [*With a cutting device*] When

---

3. rapacious (rə pā′ shəs) **carnivori** (kär nə vôr′ ī): Greedy flesh-eating mammals.

Margaurita found out they were using this . . . on the mice, she almost fainted. No end of trouble.

HELEN. They chopped the heads off three hundred mice?

MISS MORAY. Now, Helen, you wanted progress, remember?

HELEN. That's horrible.

MISS MORAY. Helen, over a thousand individual laboratories did the same study last year.

HELEN. A thousand labs chopping off three hundred mice heads. Three hundred thousand mice heads chopped off? That's a lot of mouse heads. Couldn't one lab cut off a couple and then spread the word?

MISS MORAY. Now, Helen, this is exactly what I mean. You will do best not to become fond of the subject animals. When you're here a little longer you'll learn—well, there are some things in this world you have to accept on faith.

[*She exits. After a moment, the* DOLPHIN *starts in again.*]

DOLPHIN. Whisper . . .

HELEN. What?

DOLPHIN. Whisper to me . . .

[DANIELLE *barges in, pushing a hamper.*]

DANIELLE. Hi, Helen.

HELEN. Hello.

DANIELLE. [*Emptying wastes into hamper*] Miss Moray said she's got almond horns for our Perk-You-Up tonight.

HELEN. That thing never said anything to anybody?

DANIELLE. What thing?

HELEN. That mammal fish.

DANIELLE. Nope.

HELEN. Not one word?

DANIELLE. Nope.

HELEN. Nothing that sounded like "Youuuuuu-uuuuuuuu."

DANIELLE. What?

HELEN. "Youuuuuuuuuuuuuu?" Or "Whisper?"

DANIELLE. I don't know what you're talking about. I got here an hour too early so I sat down by the docks. You can see the moon in the river.

[*The record goes on again, and* DANIELLE *exits without the hamper.*]

RECORD.

Let me call you sweetheart,
I'm in love with you.
Let me hear you whisper,
That you love me, too.

[HELEN *opens the curtain to see the* DOLPHIN. *It is staring at her. It is as though the* DOLPHIN *is trying to tell her something, and she can almost suspect this from the intensity of its stare. She goes to her locker, unwraps a sandwich she brought, and takes a slice of ham from it. She approaches the tank and offers the ham. The* DOLPHIN *moves and startles her, but the ham falls to the bottom of the tank.*]

DOLPHIN. Hear . . .

HELEN. Huh?

DOLPHIN. Hear me . . .

[DANIELLE *bursts back in carrying a crock, and Helen darts to her scrubbing.*]

DANIELLE. Ugh. This—gotta rinse this one out. Full of little gooey things.

HELEN. What do they eat?

DANIELLE. What?

HELEN. What do dolphins eat?

DANIELLE. Fish.

HELEN. What kind of fish?

DANIELLE. These. [*She opens a freezer chest packed with fish.*] Fly 'em up from Florida. [DANIELLE *is at* DOLPHIN*'s tank.*] Hiya, fella! How are ya? That reminds me. Gotta get some formaldehyde jars set up by Friday.

[*She exits with hamper.* HELEN *returns to the* DOLPHIN, *apprehensive about leaving the piece of ham at the bottom of the tank. She begins to reach her hand into the tank.*]

HELEN. You wouldn't bite Helen, would you? Helen's got to get that ham out of there. I wouldn't hurt you. You know that. Helen knows you talk. You do talk to Helen, don't you? Hear . . . hear me . . .

DOLPHIN. Hear . . .

HELEN. That's a good boy. That's a goodie goodie boy.

DOLPHIN. Hear me . . .

HELEN. Oh, what a pretty boy. Such a pretty boy.

[*At this point, the elevator doors zip open and* MISS MORAY *enters.*]

MISS MORAY. What are you doing, Helen?

[HELEN *looks ready to cry.*]

HELEN. I . . . uh . . .

MISS MORAY. Never mind. Go on with your work. [MISS MORAY *surveys everything, and then sits on a stool and calms herself. As* HELEN *scrubs:*] You know, Helen, you're such a sympathetic person. You have pets, I imagine? Cats? Lots of cats?

HELEN. They don't allow them in my building.

MISS MORAY. Then plants. I'm sure you have hundreds of lovely green things crawling up the windows?

HELEN. If there were green things crawling up my windows I'd move out.

MISS MORAY. No plants, either?

HELEN. Two gloxinias.[4]

MISS MORAY. Gloxinias! Oh, such trumpets! Such trumpets!

HELEN. They never bloom. My apartment's too cold.

MISS MORAY. Oh, that is a shame. [*Pause*] You live alone, don't you, Helen?

HELEN. [*Almost hurt*] Yes. I live alone.

MISS MORAY. But you have friends, of course. Other . . . custodial colleagues, perhaps . . . clubs, you belong to . . . social clubs . . . activities?

HELEN. [*Continuing to scrub*] I'm used to . . . being alone.

MISS MORAY. Nothing . . . ?

HELEN. I took a ceramic course . . . once.

MISS MORAY. Isn't that nice. A ceramic course . . . [*Pause*] Oh, Helen, you're such a nice person. So nice. [*Pause*] It does seem unjust that so much more than that is required. You must feel overwhelmed by this environment here . . . of oscilloscopes and sonar and salinity meters. To have so many personal delicacies and then be forced to behold the complexity of an electronic and chemical world must be devastating. Nevertheless, I can't—

[DANIELLE *rushes in with several large jars on a wheeled table.*]

---

4. gloxinias (gläk sin′ ē əz) *n.*: A tropical plant with colorful, trumpet-shaped flowers.

DANIELLE. 'Scuse me, but I figure I'll get the formaldehyde set up tonight so I'll only have to worry about the dissection stuff tomorrow.

MISS MORAY. Very good, Danielle.

DANIELLE. I'm gonna need a twenty-liter one for the lungs and there ain't any on this floor.

HELEN. [*Noticing the* DOLPHIN *is stirring*] What's the formaldehyde for?

MISS MORAY. That's what I'm trying to tell you, Helen . . . to make it easier on you. The experiment series on . . . the dolphin will . . . terminate . . . on Friday. Dr. Crocus left the orders with us tonight. That's why it has concerned me that you've apparently grown . . . fond . . . of the mammal.

HELEN. They're gonna kill it?

DANIELLE. Gonna sharpen the hand saws now. Won't have any trouble getting through the skull on this one, no sir. Everything's gonna be perfect. [*She exits.*]

HELEN. What for? Because it didn't say anything? Is that what they're killing it for?

MISS MORAY. [*So sweetly*] Of course, you wanted to be kind. You didn't know what harm you might have caused . . . what delicate rhythm you may have disturbed in the experiment. Helen, no matter how lovely our intentions, no matter how lonely we are and how much we want people or animals . . . to like us . . . we have no right to endanger the genius about us. Now, we've spoken about this before. And this time, we're going to remember, aren't you? Get your paraphernalia ready. In a minute you're going upstairs to the main specimen room.

[HELEN *is dumbfounded as* MISS MORAY *exits in the direction* DANIELLE *went.* HELEN *gathers her equipment and looks at the* DOLPHIN, *which is staring desperately at her.*]

DOLPHIN. Help. Please help me.

[MISS MORAY *returns, pauses a moment and then takes the mop to relieve* HELEN'*s burden.*]

MISS MORAY. Come, Helen. Let me help you up to the main specimen room.

[*As they get into the elevator, the record plays again.*]

RECORD.
> Let me call you sweetheart,
> I'm in love with you.
> Let me hear you whisper . . .

Scene 3

[*At rise,* MISS MORAY *is walking with* DR. CROCUS *and* MRS. FRIDGE *to the elevator. She is jotting items down on a clipboard.*]

MISS MORAY. You can be assured the Custodial Engineering Staff is anxious to contribute in every nontechnical way possible. Every nontechnical way. [*The elevator doors open and* HELEN *gets off.*] Just a moment, Helen. I'd like to talk with you. [*To the others as they get on*] If you think of anything else between now and morning please don't hesitate to call. Extra scalpels, dissection scissors, autoclaved glassware . . . pleasant dreams.

[*The doors close on* DR. CROCUS *and* MRS. FRIDGE, *and* MISS MORAY *turns to* HELEN.]

I hope you're well this evening.

HELEN. When they gonna kill it?

MISS MORAY. [*Going with her to her locker*] Don't say kill, Helen. You make it sound like murder. Besides, you won't have to go into the dolphin area at all this evening.

HELEN. When they gonna do it?

MISS MORAY. They'll be back, but don't worry. I've decided to let you go before they start so . . . you won't have to be in the building when . . .

HELEN. What do they do?

MISS MORAY. [*A hesitating laugh*] Why, what do you mean, what do they do?

HELEN. How do they kill it?

MISS MORAY. Nicotine mustard, Helen. Nicotine mustard. It's very humane. They inject it.

HELEN. Just 'cause it don't talk they've got to kill it?

MISS MORAY. There's that word again.

HELEN. Maybe he's a mute.

MISS MORAY. Do you have all your paraphernalia?

HELEN. Some human beings are mute, you know. Just because they can't talk we don't kill them.

MISS MORAY. It looks like you're ready to open a new box of steel wool.

HELEN. Maybe he can type with his nose. Did they try that?

MISS MORAY. Now, now, Helen . . .

HELEN. Miss Moray, I don't mind doing the dolphin area.

MISS MORAY. Absolutely not! I'm placing it off limits for your own good. You're too emotionally involved.

HELEN. I'm not emotionally involved.

MISS MORAY. Trust me, Helen. Trust me.

HELEN. Yes, Miss Moray.

[MISS MORAY *exits and* HELEN *makes a beeline for the Dolphin area which is closed off by portable walls. She opens the area enough to slide in. The lights are out and moonlight from the window casts many shadows.*]

DOLPHIN. Help. [HELEN *moves slowly toward the tank.*] Help me. [HELEN *opens the curtain. The* DOLPHIN *and she look at each other.*] Help me.

HELEN. You don't need me. Just say something to them. Whatever you want. Say "help." Anything. They just need to hear you say something . . . [*She waits for a response, which doesn't come.*] You want me to tell 'em? I'll tell them. I'll just say I heard you say "help." O.K.? I'll go tell them. [*She starts to leave the area, turning back to give opportunity for a response.*]

DOLPHIN. Noooooooooooo. [HELEN *stops. Moves back toward tank*] Noooooooooooo.

HELEN. They're gonna kill you! [*Puzzled,* HELEN *moves a bit closer to the tank. Pause*]

DOLPHIN. Booooooooooook.

HELEN. What? [*There is a long pause. No response. She moves closer.*]

DOLPHIN. Booooooooooook.

HELEN. Book?

DOLPHIN. Booooooooooook.

HELEN. Booooooooooook? What book?

[DANIELLE *charges through a door and snaps on the light.*]

DANIELLE. Uh oh. Miss Moray said she don't want you in here. Said you have to not be in the lab and I'm not to talk to you about what they're gonna do because I make you nauseous.

[HELEN *goes to* DR. CROCUS*'s desk in the lab and begins to look at various books on it.*]

HELEN. Do you know anything about a book, Danielle?

DANIELLE. She's gonna be mad. What book?

HELEN. Something to do with . . . [*She indicates the* DOLPHIN.]

DANIELLE. Hiya, fella! [*To* HELEN] Do I really make you nauseous?

HELEN. About the dolphin . . .

DANIELLE. You talking about the experiment folder? They got an experiment folder they write in.

HELEN. Where?

DANIELLE. I don't know.

HELEN. Find it, please.

DANIELLE. I don't know where she keeps that stuff. Sometimes she puts it in the top and other times she puts it in the bottom.

HELEN. Please find it. Please. [*She steps outside the area.*]

DANIELLE. I'll try. I'll try, but I got other things to do, you know. Can't spend time looking for what ain't any of my business anyway. I never knew I made anybody nauseous.

[DANIELLE *rummages through the desk mumbling to herself and finally finds the folder. She hands the folder out to* HELEN *as the elevator doors spring open and* MISS MORAY *enters.* DANIELLE *exits quickly through a door in the Dolphin area as* HELEN *conceals the folder.*]

MISS MORAY. Helen?

HELEN. Yes, Miss Moray?

MISS MORAY. Would you feel better if we talked about it?

HELEN. About what?

MISS MORAY. Helen, you're such a nice person. I understand just what you're going through. Really, I do. And . . . well, I'm going to tell you something I've never told anyone else . . . my first week at ABADABA, I fell in love with an animal myself. An alley cat. Pussy Cat. That's what I called it— Pussy Cat.

HELEN. Did they cut the head off it?

[MISS MORAY *removes a plastic covering from an object on a shelf to reveal an articulated[5] cat skeleton. As she talks she sets it in view and gently dusts it with the feather duster.*]

MISS MORAY. I sense a touch of bitterness in your voice, Helen, and don't think I wasn't bitter when I saw what had happened to Pussy Cat.

HELEN. I'll bet it didn't sit well with Pussy Cat either.

MISS MORAY. But when I thought about it for awhile, I had to realize that I was just being selfish. Before . . . what happened to Pussy Cat happened I was the only one benefiting from her—whereas now she's borrowed at least once a month. Last week she went to an anatomy seminar at St. Vincent's Medical School.

HELEN. It's nice you let her out once in a while.

MISS MORAY. In life, she was unnoticed and worthless except to me. Now she belongs to the ages. [*Then solemnly*] I hope that's some comfort to you.

HELEN. Oh, it's very comforting.

MISS MORAY. Well, Perk-You-Up time will be here soon.

---

5. articulated (är tik′ yə lāt′ əd) *adj.*: Connected by joints.

HELEN. Yes, Miss Moray.

MISS MORAY. We have lady fingers.

HELEN. Oh, good.

MISS MORAY. Such a strange thing to call a confectionary, isn't it? It's almost macabre.

HELEN. Miss Moray . . .

MISS MORAY. Yes, Helen?

HELEN. I was wondering . . .

MISS MORAY. Yes?

HELEN. I was wondering why they wanna talk with . . .

MISS MORAY. Now now now! I was the same way about Pussy Cat. Right up to the final moment I kept asking "What good is vivisection?"[6] "What good is vivisection?"

HELEN. What good is vivisection?

MISS MORAY. A *lot* of good, believe me.

HELEN. Like what?

MISS MORAY. Well, like fishing, Helen. If we could communicate with dolphins, they might be willing to herd fish for us. The fishing industry would be revolutionized. Millions of fish being rounded into nets by our little mammal friends.

HELEN. Is that all?

MISS MORAY. All? Heavens, no. They'd be a blessing to the human race. A blessing.

HELEN. What kind?

MISS MORAY. Oh. Why, oceanography. They would be worshipped in oceanography. Checking the Gulf Stream . . . taking water temperatures, depths, salinity readings. To say nothing of the contributions they could make in marine biology, navigation. Linguistics! Oh, Helen, it gives me the chills.

HELEN. It'd be good if they talked?

MISS MORAY. God's own blessing. God's own blessing.

[MISS MORAY *exits and* HELEN *returns to scrubbing for a moment. When she feels safe she sets the folder in front of her and begins reading. Commence fantasy techniques to establish the ensuing events are going on in* HELEN's *mind concerning the benevolent utilization of dolphins. Relate to what* MISS MORAY *had told her about uses. Sound: Sonar beeping underwater. It has the urgency of a beating heart. Sweet strains of* Let Me Call You Sweetheart *in. Projection: Underwater shot, dolphins and other fish gliding by. All voices echo. Doors open and* MISS MORAY, DR. CROCUS *and* MRS. FRIDGE *appear phantasmagorically.*][7]

And if we could make friends with them, talk to them, they might be willing to herd all those fish for us . . .

DR. CROCUS. [*Lovingly*] All right, little mammal friends—today we want swordfish. Fat meaty ones suitable for controlled portion sizing. Go and get 'em! [*Projection of dolphins swimming, a school of large fish panicking in the water*]

MRS. FRIDGE. My dear dolphin friends. My dear, dear dolphin friends. We're most curious about seismographic readings at the bottom of the Mariana Trench. But do be careful. We're unsure of the weather above that area.

[*Projection of dolphins racing, deep underwater shots, sounding bell noises*]

MISS MORAY. [*Sweetly*] Our linguistics lesson today will consider the most beautiful word

---

6. vivisection (viv′ ə sek′ shən) *n.*: Surgical operations performed on living animals to study the structure and function of living organs.

7. phantasmagorically (fan taz′ mə gôr′ ik lē) *adv.*: In a rapidly changing way, as in a dream.

in the English language: Love. Love is a strong, complex emotion or feeling causing one to appreciate and promote the welfare of another. Do you have a word like it in dolphinese? A word similar to love?

[*The fantasy disappears, leaving* MISS MORAY *and* HELEN *in the reality of the play.*]

It has a nice sheen.

HELEN. What?

MISS MORAY. It has a nice sheen. The floor. Up here where it's dried.

HELEN. Thank you. Miss Moray . . . ?

MISS MORAY. Yes, dear?

HELEN. You sure it would be good for us if . . . dolphins talked?

MISS MORAY. Helen, are you still thinking about that! Perhaps you'd better leave now. It's almost time.

HELEN. No! I'm almost finished.

[DANIELLE *opens the Dolphin area and yells over* HELEN*'s head to* MISS MORAY.]

DANIELLE. I got everything except the head vise.

MISS MORAY. I beg your pardon?

DANIELLE. The vise for the head. I can't find it. They can't saw through the skull bone without the head vise.

MISS MORAY. Did you look on five? They had it there for . . . what they did to the St. Bernard . . . they had.

[*The record plays again and the others try to talk over it.*]

RECORD.
>   Let me call you sweetheart,
>   I'm in love with you.
>   Let me hear you whisper,
>   That you love me, too.

DANIELLE. Can't hear you.

MISS MORAY. The St. Bernard. They used it for the St. Bernard.

DANIELLE. On five?

MISS MORAY. That's what I said.

DANIELLE. I looked on five. I didn't see any head vise.

MISS MORAY. You come with me. It must have been staring you in the face. Just staring you right in the face.

[DANIELLE *tiptoes over the wet portion of the floor and she and* MISS MORAY *get on the elevator.*]

We'll be right back, Helen.

[*The doors close and* HELEN *hurries into the Dolphin area. She stops just within the door and it is obvious that she is angry. There is a pause as she looks at the silhouette of the tank behind the closed curtain. Then:*]

DOLPHIN. Booooooooooooook.

[HELEN *charges to the curtain, pulls it open and prepares to reprimand the* DOLPHIN.]

HELEN. I looked at your book. I looked at your book all right!

DOLPHIN. Booooooooooooook.

HELEN. And you want to know what I think? I don't think much of you, that's what I think.

DOLPHIN. Booooooooooooook.

HELEN. Oh, shut up. Book book book book book. I'm not interested. You eat yourself silly—but to get a little fish for hungry humans is just too much for you. Well, I'm going to tell 'em you can talk.

[DOLPHIN *moves in the tank, lets out a few warning bubbles.*]

You don't like that, eh? Well, I don't like lazy selfish people, mammals or animals.

[*She starts away from the tank half intending to go and half watching for a reaction. The* DOLPHIN *looks increasingly desperate and begins to make loud blatt and beep sounds. He struggles a bit in the tank, starting to splash water.*]

Oh, you'd do anything to avoid a little work, wouldn't you?

[*In its most violent gyrations to date, the* DOLPHIN *blasts at her.*]

DOLPHIN. Booooooooooooook!

HELEN. Cut it out, you're getting water all over the floor.

DOLPHIN. Booooooooooooook!

[HELEN *is a little scared and stops moving toward the door. As she stops, the* DOLPHIN *calms down. She waits a moment and then moves closer to the tank again. They experience a sustained visual exchange.* HELEN's *anger and fear subside into frustration. When it appears the* DOLPHIN *is going to say nothing else,* HELEN *starts to leave the room. She turns around and looks back at the* DOLPHIN. *Then she looks at the folder on the desk. She is going to leave again when she decides to go to the folder once more. She picks it up, opens it, closes it, and sets it down again.*]

HELEN. I guess you don't like us. [*Pause*] I guess you don't like us enough to . . . die rather than help us . . .

DOLPHIN. Hate.

HELEN. [*Picking up the folder and skimming reflexively*] Yes.

DOLPHIN. Hate.

HELEN. I guess you do hate us . . . [HELEN

stops. She returns to the folder. Reading] Military implications . . . plants mines in enemy waters . . . useful as antipersonnel self-directing weapons . . . war . . . deliver atomic warheads . . . war . . . nuclear torpedoes . . . attach bombs to submarines or surface vessels . . . terrorize enemy waters, beaches . . . war . . . war . . . war . . .

[HELEN's *voice becomes echoed in the middle of the last speech, theatrical effects creeping in to establish fantasy sequence like the first, except now the characters enter and appear sinister. Their requests are all war oriented.*]

MISS MORAY. [*Demanding*] And if we could talk to them, we'd get them to herd fish all right. One way or another they'd do exactly as they were told!

[*Let Me Call You Sweetheart plays in background in a discordant version with projection of dolphins swimming.*]

DR. CROCUS. All right, you dolphins. Today we want you to herd fish. Herd all the fish you can away from the enemy's waters. Remove their food supply. Detonate underwater poison bombs and foul the enemy coastline. Make the water unfit for life of any kind.

[*A map is imposed over projection of dolphins.*]

MRS. FRIDGE. Enemy fleets are located here and here and here. You'll have twenty-seven hours to attach the nuclear warheads before automatic detonation. Our objective: total annihilation.

[*Projection of dolphins racing off, deep underwater shots, frogman examining ship's hulls, planting mines.*]

MISS MORAY. [*Fanatically*] Our linguistics lesson today will consider the most basic word in the English language: HATE. Hate is a strong emotion which means abhorrence, anger, animosity, detestation, hostility, malevolence, malice, malignity, odium, rancor, revenge, repugnance, and dislike. Do you have a word like it in dolphinese? If you don't, we'll teach you every nuance of ours. Every nuance of the word *hate*.

[*The fantasy sequence evaporates leaving* HELEN *alone on stage with the* DOLPHIN. *She sadly closes the folder and moves slowly to the tank a bit ashamed about the way she had reprimanded the* DOLPHIN. *They look sadly at each other. She reaches out her hand and just pets his head gently.*]

HELEN. They're already thinking about ways to use you for . . . war . . . is that why you can't talk to them? What did you talk to me for? You won't talk to them but you . . . you talk to me because . . . you want something . . . there's something . . . I can do? Something you want me to do?

DOLPHIN. Hamm . . .

HELEN. What?

DOLPHIN. Hamm . . .

HELEN. Ham? I thought you ate fish.

DOLPHIN. [*Moving with annoyance*] Ham . . . purrrrr.

HELEN. Ham . . . purrrrr? I don't know what you're talking about?

DOLPHIN. [*Even more annoyed*] Ham . . . purrrrr.

HELEN. Ham . . . purrrr. What's a purrrrr?

[HELEN *is most upset and recalls that* MISS MORAY *is due back. Confused and scared she returns to scrubbing the floor just as the doors of the elevator open revealing* MISS MORAY, DANIELLE *and* MRS. FRIDGE. DANIELLE *pushes a dissection table loaded with shiny instruments toward the lab.*]

MISS MORAY. Clean the vise up, Danielle. Immediately.

DANIELLE. I didn't leave the blood on it.

MISS MORAY. I'm not accusing you. I just said whoever was the porter the night they did you know what to the St. Bernard was . . . [*To* MRS. FRIDGE] it's the first dirty vise since I've led the Custodial Engineering Department! Is the good doctor in yet?

MRS. FRIDGE. She's getting the nicotine mustard on eighteen. I'll have to see if she needs assistance.

MISS MORAY. I'll come with you. Oh, Helen. You can go now. It's time. [*She smiles and the elevator doors close on* MRS. FRIDGE *and* MISS MORAY.]

DANIELLE. [*Pushing the dissection table into the Dolphin area*] I never left a dirty head vise. She's trying to say I left it like that. I know what she's getting at.

HELEN. Did you ever hear of Ham . . . purrrrr?

DANIELLE. Wait'll I get my hands on Kazinski. Kazinski does the fifth floor and he should be cleaning this, not me. It's all caked up.

HELEN. Would you listen a minute? Ham . . . purrrrr. Do you know what a ham . . . purrrrr is?

DANIELLE. The only hamper I ever heard of is out in the hall.

[HELEN *looks toward an exit indicated by* DANIELLE.]

Five scalpels, large clamps . . . small clamps . . . bone saws . . . scissors . . . dissection needles, two dozen . . . Kazinski left the high-altitude chamber dirty once and I got blamed for that, too. And that had mucus all over it. [DANIELLE *exits.*]

HELEN. [*Rushing to the* DOLPHIN] You want me to do something with the hamper. What? To get it? To put—You want me to put you in it? . . . But what'll I do with you? Where can I take you?

DOLPHIN. Sea . . .

HELEN. See? See what?

DOLPHIN. Sea . . . ham . . . purrrrr . . .

HELEN. See ham—I *saw* the hamper.

DOLPHIN. Sea . . .

HELEN. See what? What do you want me to see? [*She walks about the room, mumbling, looking for what the* DOLPHIN *could want her to see. Finally, she looks out the window.*]

DOLPHIN. Sea . . . sea . . .

HELEN. See? . . . The sea! That's what you're talking about! [*There is almost an atmosphere of celebration.*] The river . . . to the sea!

[*She darts into the hall and returns with hamper, pushes it next to the* DOLPHIN. *She pulls closed the curtain as . . .* MISS MORAY *gets off the elevator.* MISS MORAY *looks very calm. Everything is under control and on schedule from her point of view. She then notices that* HELEN *is not there, though her mop and pail are. She wonders if* HELEN *has gone and just carelessly left the items out.*]

MISS MORAY. [*Sweetly*] Helen? [*When there is no response she starts into the Dolphin area.*] Helen? [HELEN *is not there, though her coat is still hanging in her locker. She is a little concerned at this point. For a second she assumes it is unlikely* HELEN *would be in there, since it was strictly placed off limits, but then she decides to investigate. She notices the closed curtain in front of the tank.*] Helen? Are you there? [*Pause*] Helen?

Helen? [MISS MORAY *moves to the curtain and pulls it open. There is Helen with her arms around the front part of the* DOLPHIN, *lifting it a good part of the way out of the water.*]

Helen, what do you think you're hugging?

[HELEN *gets so scared she drops the* DOLPHIN *back into the tank, splattering* MISS MORAY *with water.* MISS MORAY *lets out a scream just as* DR. CROCUS *and* MRS. FRIDGE *enter.*]

MRS. FRIDGE. Is anything wrong, Miss Moray?

[MISS MORAY *is unable to answer at first.*]

Is anything wrong?

MISS MORAY. [*Not wishing to admit an irregularity.*] No . . . nothing wrong. Nothing at all.

[*She hurriedly composes herself, not wanting to hang any dirty wash of the Custodial Engineering Department.*]

Just a little spilled water. Right, Helen? Just a little spilled water. Get those sponges, Helen. Immediately!

[HELEN *and* MISS MORAY *grab sponges from the lab sink and begin to get up some of the water around the tank.* DR. CROCUS *begins to occupy herself with filling a hypodermic syringe while* MRS. FRIDGE *expertly gets all equipment into place.* DANIELLE *enters.*]

MRS. FRIDGE. Danielle, get the formaldehyde jars into position, please.

DANIELLE. I didn't spill anything. Don't try to blame *that* on me.

MISS MORAY. I didn't say you did.

DANIELLE. You spilled something?

MISS MORAY. Just do as Mrs. Fridge tells you. Hurry, Danielle, you're so slow.

DANIELLE. I'm tired of getting blamed for Kazinski.

MRS. FRIDGE. Would you like to get an encephalogram during the death process, Dr. Crocus?

DR. CROCUS. Why not?

[MRS. FRIDGE *begins to implant electrodes into the* DOLPHIN's *head. The* DOLPHIN *commences making high pitched distress signals which send shivers up and down* HELEN's *back.*]

MISS MORAY. That'll do it. No harm done. Step outside, Helen. [*To the* DOCTOR] I do hope everything is satisfactory, doctor. [DR. CROCUS *looks at her, gives no reaction.*] The Custodial Engineering Staff has done everything in its power . . . [*She is still ignored.*] Come, Helen. I'll see you to the elevator.

[HELEN *looks at the* DOLPHIN *as* MRS. FRIDGE *is sticking the electrodes into its head. Its distress signals are pathetic, and* HELEN *is terrified.*]

Let's go now.

[MISS MORAY *leads her out to the hall.* MISS MORAY *is trying to get control of herself, to resist yelling at* HELEN, *as she gets on her coat and kerchief.*]

You can leave that.

HELEN. I never left a dirty mop. Never. [HELEN *gives the mop a quick rinse and puts the things in their place. Cuts to the lab door and the sounds coming out of it show where her attention is.*]

MISS MORAY. Well, I hardly know what to say. Frankly, Helen, I'm deeply disappointed. I'd hoped that by being lenient with you—and heaven knows I have been—that you'd develop a heightened loyalty to our team. I mean, do you think for one minute that putting vinegar in rinse water really is more effective? If you ask me, it streaks. Streaks.

HELEN. [*Bursting into tears and going to the elevator*] Leave me alone.

MISS MORAY. [*Softening as she catches up to her*] You really are a nice person, Helen. A very nice person. But to be simple and nice in a world where great minds are giant-stepping the micro- and macrocosms, well —one would expect you'd have the humility to yield in unquestioning awe. I truly am very fond of you, Helen, but you're fired. Call Personnel after 9. And I was going to bring you in hangers. I want you to know that. [*As* MISS MORAY *heads back toward the Dolphin area, the record starts to play.*]

RECORD.

> Let me call you sweetheart,
> I'm in love with you.
> Let me hear you whisper . . .

[*The record is roughly interrupted. What* HELEN *is contemplating at that moment causes the expression on her face to turn from sadness to thought to strength to anger—and as the elevator doors open —to fury. Instead of getting on the elevator, she whirls around and marches back to the Dolphin area.* MISS MORAY, MRS. FRIDGE, DANIELLE, *and* DR. CROCUS (*with hypodermic needle poised to stick the* DOLPHIN) *turn and look at her with surprise.*]

HELEN. Who do you think you are? Who do you think you *are*? I think you're murderers, that's what I think.

MISS MORAY. Doctor, I assure you this is the first psychotic outburst the Custodial Engineering Department has ever had.

HELEN. I'm very tired of being a nice person, Miss Moray. You kept telling me how nice I was and now I know what you meant. [*Pause*] I'm going to report the bunch of you to the ASPCA—or somebody. Because . . . I've decided I don't like you cutting the heads off mice and sawing through skulls of St. Bernards . . . and if being a nice person is just not saying anything and letting you pack of butchers run around doing whatever you want, then I don't want to be nice any more. You gotta be very stupid people to need an animal to talk before you know just from looking at it that it's saying something . . . that it knows what pain feels like. I'd like to see you all with a few electrodes stuck in your heads. I really would. [HELEN *starts crying, though her features won't give way to weakness.*] Being nice isn't any good. [*Looking at* DOLPHIN] They just kill you off if you do that. And that's being a coward. You gotta talk back against what's wrong or you can't ever stop it. At least you've gotta try. [*She bursts into tears.*]

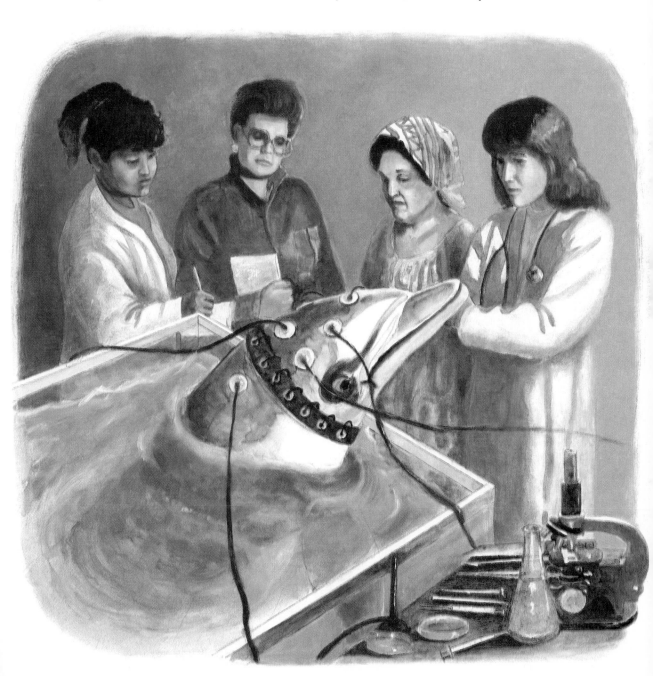

MISS MORAY. Nothing like this has ever happened with a member of the Custodial Engineering . . . Helen, dear . . .

HELEN. Get your hands off me. [*Yelling at the* DOLPHIN] You're a coward, that's what you are. [*She turns and starts to leave. A sound comes from the* DOLPHIN'*s tank.*]

DOLPHIN. [*Whispering*] Looooooooooooveeeeeee. [*Everyone turns to stare at the* DOLPHIN, *and freezes for a second.*] Love.

DR. CROCUS. Get the recorder going. [*The laboratory becomes a bustle of activity concerning the utterance of the* DOLPHIN. *Plans for dissection are obviously canceled and* HELEN *has a visual exchange with the* DOLPHIN. *Then she continues toward the elevator.*]

DOLPHIN. Love . . .

DR. CROCUS. Is the tape going?

MRS. FRIDGE. Yes, Doctor.

MISS MORAY. I'm enormously embarrassed about the incident, Doctor. Naturally, I've taken steps to see this won't . . .

MRS. FRIDGE. He's opening the blowhole sphincter.

DOLPHIN. Love . . .

DR. CROCUS. That scrub woman's got something to do with this. Get her back in here.

MISS MORAY. She won't be any more trouble. I fired her.

DOLPHIN. Love . . .

DR. CROCUS. Just get her. [*To* MRS. FRIDGE.] You're sure the machine's recording?

MISS MORAY. Doctor, I'm afraid you don't understand. That woman was hugging the mammal . . .

DR. CROCUS. Try to get another word out of it.

MISS MORAY. The water on the floor was her fault. [*The record starts.*]

DR. CROCUS. Try the fear button.

MISS MORAY. She could have damaged the rib cage if I hadn't stopped her.

DR. CROCUS. One more word . . . try anger.

MISS MORAY. The last thing in the world I want is for our problems in Custodial Engineering to . . .

DR. CROCUS. [*Furious*] Will you shut up and get her back here?

[MISS MORAY *appears stunned momentarily.*]

MISS MORAY. Immediately, Doctor. [*She hurries to* HELEN *waiting for the elevator.*] Helen? Oh, Helen? [*She goes to* HELEN, *who refuses to pay any attention to her.*] Don't you want to hear what the dolphin has to say? He's so cute! Dr. Crocus thinks that his talking might have something to do with you. Wouldn't that be exciting? [*Pause*] Please, Helen. The doctor . . .

HELEN. Don't talk to me, do you mind?

MISS MORAY. It was only in the heat of argument that I distorted the ineffectiveness of the vinegar and . . . of course, you won't be discharged. All right? Please, Helen, you'll embarrass me . . .

[*The elevator doors open and* HELEN *gets on to face* MISS MORAY. *She looks at her a moment and then lifts her hand to press the button for the ground floor.*]

Don't you dare . . . Helen, the team needs you, don't you see? Everyone says the corridors have never looked so good. Ever. Helen, please. What will I do if you leave?

HELEN. Why don't you put in a rug?

[*She presses the button. The elevator doors close.*]

THINKING ABOUT THE SELECTION

Recalling

1. According to Miss Moray, what is the purpose of the experiment on the dolphin?
2. How does Helen learn the dolphin can talk?
3. In what way does the dolphin want Helen to help him?
4. What are the results of Helen's trying to rescue the dolphin?
5. For what reason does the doctor want Helen to come back at the end of the play?

Interpreting

6. Compare and contrast Helen and Miss Moray.
7. Miss Moray uses many euphemisms, words that hide the true meaning of things. For example, she calls the cleanup crew the "custodial engineering team." Find three other euphemisms. What euphemism disguises the true nature of the experiment?
8. The researchers use a love song to teach the dolphin to talk. What contrast is shown by having the researchers use a love song?
9. Why does the dolphin talk to Helen instead of the researchers? What does this suggest about the theme of this play?
10. Explain the title of the play.

Applying

11. Imagine you are Helen. What would you have done in her place? Explain your answer.

ANALYZING LITERATURE

Understanding Conflict in Drama

In a play, the characters *act out* the **conflict,** or struggle between opposing sides or forces. A character must rely on actions, facial expressions, and dialogue to express conflict, especially internal conflict.

In *Let Me Hear You Whisper,* there is both external and internal conflict. You learn about Helen's conflict through her dialogue, actions, and facial expressions.

1. What conflict does Helen have with the scientific laboratory?
2. What evidence in the play helps you recognize this conflict?
3. What is Helen's conflict with the dolphin?
4. What helps you recognize this conflict?
5. How are Helen's conflicts resolved?

CRITICAL THINKING AND READING

Understanding Controversy

Controversy occurs when two sides hold opposing views. *Let Me Hear You Whisper* presents the controversial issue of using animals for scientific experimentation. One side of this controversy believes such experimentation yields beneficial results for human beings. The other side believes such experimentation is cruel to animals and violates animals' rights. Take a side on this issue and discuss it with your classmates.

UNDERSTANDING LANGUAGE

Appreciating Specialized Vocabulary

Professional people often use words that seem difficult to people outside the profession. In *Let Me Hear You Whisper,* for example, all of the technical terms would be understood by workers in a scientific laboratory. Use a dictionary to find the meaning of the following technical terms.

1. salinity
2. autoclave
3. seismograph
4. electroencephalogram

THINKING AND WRITING

Writing a Response to Critical Comment

Paul Zindel has said, "In each of my plays, there is an attempt to find some grain of truth, something to hang onto." Brainstorm about what "grain of truth" you found in *Let Me Hear You Whisper.* Then use these ideas to write a letter to Paul Zindel, explaining what "grain of truth" you found in the play. Revise your letter for clarity and proofread it.

ANNE FRANK: THE STORY BEHIND THE PLAY

The Diary of Anne Frank, the play by Frances Goodrich and Albert Hackett, is based on a real diary written by a young girl during World War II. Anne Frank was born in Frankfurt, Germany, on June 12, 1929, before World War II began. She had a normal, happy childhood until Adolf Hitler and his political party, the Nazis, gained control of the government of Germany in 1933.

Persecution of the Jews

The Nazis persecuted their political opponents and other groups. One group they particularly singled out was the Jews. Adolf Hitler blamed the Jews for the problems of the world. He had the Nazis round up German Jews and send them to prison camps, called concentration camps. Many Jews escaped from Germany to other countries to avoid this persecution. Even more, though, stayed behind.

Anne Frank's family was Jewish. They left their home in Germany in 1933 and moved to the Netherlands. In Amsterdam Mr. Frank reestablished his business, and Mrs. Frank set up their new household. Anne and her older sister, Margot, attended school and made new friends. Anne was known as a lively chatterbox who seemed to be a normal but not a particularly gifted child. World War II, however, affected the lives of millions of people on both sides of the fighting, and Anne Frank was no exception.

World War II

World War II officially began on September 1, 1939, when Germany, which had already occupied Czechoslovakia and taken over Austria, invaded Poland. Britain and France declared war on Germany two days later. Hitler's forces attacked Denmark, Norway, and Luxembourg; and by May 1940, they invaded and defeated the Netherlands, where the Franks were now living.

German forces continued to move through Europe and occupied Belgium and France. It was not until May 1945 that Germany was defeated and surrendered to the Allied powers, which included Great Britain, the Soviet Union, and the United States.

The Holocaust

Meanwhile during the war, everywhere the German army went, Jews were persecuted. Jews had to register with government authorities and wear yellow stars on their clothing to identify themselves as Jews. Nazis seized their property and businesses.

Amsterdam after a German bombing

People being rounded up to be sent to concentration camps by the Nazis

Millions of Jews throughout Europe were sent to concentration camps. There they were starved and put to death. About six million Jews died in what became known as the Holocaust, the systematic extermination of people by the Nazis. Gypsies, Slavs, political prisoners, and disabled people were also included in this systematic extermination.

In 1942, however, most Jews were unaware of the extent of the danger they faced. Most simply thought they would be temporarily imprisoned. To avoid this fate, the Frank family went into what they thought would be temporary hiding in the attic of a warehouse and office building that had been part of Mr. Frank's business in Amsterdam.

On her thirteenth birthday, Anne had received a diary as a gift. When her family went into hiding, she began to write regularly and often in her diary. The play *The Diary of Anne Frank,* which you are about to read, is based on this diary, which Mr. Frank recovered when he returned to the secret attic after the war.

The Diary of Anne Frank, Act I

Frances Goodrich (1890–1984) and **Albert Hackett** (1900–   )
spent two years writing *The Diary of Anne Frank,* which is based on
The Diary of a Young Girl by Anne Frank. As part of their background work, Goodrich and Hackett visited with Anne's father, Otto
Frank. Goodrich and Hackett's play won the Pulitzer Prize, the
Drama Critics Circle Award, and the Tony Award for best play of the
1955–1956 season. *The Diary of Anne Frank* shows the unconquer-
able spirit of a young girl.

Flashback

Most of this play is presented as a flashback. A **flashback** is a
technique that writers use to present events that happened at an
earlier time. The writer inserts a scene that presents the earlier
action as though it were taking place in the present. *The Diary of
Anne Frank* begins in 1945 as Mr. Frank returns to the warehouse
where he and his family hid from the Nazis. When Mr. Frank starts to
read Anne's diary, however, the time changes back to 1942. The
events of 1942 are presented as though they were taking place in
the present. Using a flashback lets the authors show you how Mr.
Frank is affected now by what has happened in the past.

Look For

As you read the first act of this play, look for the ways Anne's
reactions to being in hiding change as the act progresses.

Writing

Put yourself in Anne's place. Freewrite about what you would miss
most if you had to go into hiding.

Vocabulary

Knowing the following words will help you as you read *The Diary of
Anne Frank,* Act I.

conspicuous (kən spik' yoo
wəs) *adj.*: Noticeable (p. 307)
mercurial (mər kyoor' ē əl)
adj.: Quick or changeable in
behavior (p. 307)
unabashed (un ə bash' əd)
adj.: Unashamed (p. 311)
insufferable (in suf'ər ə b'l)
adj.: Unbearable (p. 317)

meticulous (mə tik'yoo ləs)
adj.: Extremely careful about
details (p. 326)
fatalist (fā'tə list) *n.*: One who
believes that all events are determined by fate and cannot be
changed (p. 334)
ostentatiously (äs' tən tā'
shəs lē) *adv.*: Showily (p. 339)

The Diary of Anne Frank

Frances Goodrich and Albert Hackett

CHARACTERS

Mr. Frank	**Mr. Van Daan**	**Margot Frank**	**Mr. Kraler**
Miep	**Peter Van Daan**	**Anne Frank**	**Mr. Dussel**
Mrs. Van Daan	**Mrs. Frank**		

ACT I

Scene 1

[*The scene remains the same throughout the play. It is the top floor of a warehouse and office building in Amsterdam, Holland. The sharply peaked roof of the building is outlined against a sea of other rooftops, stretching away into the distance. Nearby is the belfry[1] of a church tower, the Wester-toren, whose carillon[2] rings out the hours. Occasionally faint sounds float up from below: the voices of children playing in the street, the tramp of marching feet, a boat whistle from the canal.*

The three rooms of the top floor and a small attic space above are exposed to our view. The largest of the rooms is in the center, with two small rooms, slightly raised, on either side. On the right is a bathroom, out of sight. A narrow steep flight of stairs at the back leads up to the attic. The rooms are sparsely furnished with a few chairs, cots, a table or two. The windows are painted over, or covered with makeshift blackout curtains.[3] In the main room there is a sink, a gas ring for cooking and a woodburning stove for warmth.

The room on the left is hardly more than a closet. There is a skylight in the sloping ceiling. Directly under this room is a small steep stairwell, with steps leading down to a door. This is the only entrance from the building below. When the door is opened we see that it has been concealed on the outer side by a bookcase attached to it.

The curtain rises on an empty stage. It is late afternoon November, 1945.

The rooms are dusty, the curtains in rags. Chairs and tables are overturned.

The door at the foot of the small stairwell swings open. MR. FRANK *comes up the steps into view. He is a gentle, cultured European in his middle years. There is still a trace of a German accent in his speech.*

He stands looking slowly around, making a supreme effort at self-control. He is weak, ill. His clothes are threadbare.

---

1. belfry (bel′ frē) *n.*: The part of a tower that holds the bells.
2. carillon (kar′ ə län′) *n.*: A set of stationary bells, each producing one note of the scale.

3. blackout curtains: Draperies that conceal all lights that might otherwise be visible to enemy air raiders at night.

Dit is een foto, zoals
ik me zou wensen,
altijd zo te zijn.
Dan had ik nog wel
een kans om naar
Holywood te komen.

Anne Frank.
10 Oct. 1942

(translation)
"This is a photo as I would wish
myself to look all the time. Then
I would maybe have a chance to
come to Hollywood."
        Anne Frank, 10 Oct. 1942

Anne Frank and her opinion of this photo

After a second he drops his rucksack[4] on the couch and moves slowly about. He opens the door to one of the smaller rooms, and then abruptly closes it again, turning away. He goes to the window at the back, looking off at the Westertoren as its carillon strikes the hour of six, then he moves restlessly on.

From the street below we hear the sound of a barrel organ[5] and children's voices at play. There is a many-colored scarf hanging from a nail. MR. FRANK *takes it, putting it around his neck. As he starts back for his rucksack, his eye is caught by something lying on the floor. It is a woman's white glove. He holds it in his hand and suddenly all of his self-control is gone. He breaks down, crying.*

We hear footsteps on the stairs. MIEP GIES *comes up, looking for* MR. FRANK. MIEP *is a Dutch girl of about twenty-two. She wears a coat and hat, ready to go home. She is*

---

4. rucksack (ruk′ sak′) *n.*: A knapsack.
5. barrel organ *n.*: A mechanical musical instrument played by turning a crank.

pregnant. Her attitude toward MR. FRANK *is protective, compassionate.*]

MIEP. Are you all right, Mr. Frank?

MR. FRANK. [*Quickly controlling himself*] Yes, Miep, yes.

MIEP. Everyone in the office has gone home . . . It's after six. [*Then pleading*] Don't stay up here, Mr. Frank. What's the use of torturing yourself like this?

MR. FRANK. I've come to say good-bye . . . I'm leaving here, Miep.

MIEP. What do you mean? Where are you going? Where?

MR. FRANK. I don't know yet. I haven't decided.

MIEP. Mr. Frank, you can't leave here! This is your home! Amsterdam is your home. Your business is here, waiting for you . . . You're needed here . . . Now that the war is over, there are things that . . .

MR. FRANK. I can't stay in Amsterdam, Miep. It has too many memories for me. Everywhere there's something . . . the house we lived in . . . the school . . . that street organ playing out there . . . I'm not the person you used to know, Miep. I'm a bitter old man. [*Breaking off*] Forgive me. I shouldn't speak to you like this . . . after all that you did for us . . . the suffering . . .

MIEP. No. No. It wasn't suffering. You can't say we suffered. [*As she speaks, she straightens a chair which is overturned.*]

MR. FRANK. I know what you went through, you and Mr. Kraler. I'll remember it as long as I live. [*He gives one last look around.*] Come, Miep. [*He starts for the steps, then remembers his rucksack, going back to get it.*]

MIEP. [*Hurrying up to a cupboard*] Mr. Frank, did you see? There are some of your papers here. [*She brings a bundle of papers to him.*] We found them in a heap of rubbish on the floor after . . . after you left.

MR. FRANK. Burn them. [*He opens his rucksack to put the glove in it.*]

MIEP. But, Mr. Frank, there are letters, notes . . .

MR. FRANK. Burn them. All of them.

MIEP. Burn *this?* [*She hands him a paperbound notebook.*]

MR. FRANK. [*Quietly*] Anne's diary. [*He opens the diary and begins to read.*] "Monday, the sixth of July, nineteen forty-two." [*To* MIEP] Nineteen forty-two. Is it possible, Miep? . . . Only three years ago. [*As he continues his reading, he sits down on the couch.*] "Dear Diary, since you and I are going to be great friends, I will start by telling you about myself. My name is Anne Frank. I am thirteen years old. I was born in Germany the twelfth of June, nineteen twenty-nine. As my family is Jewish, we emigrated to Holland when Hitler came to power."

[*As* MR. FRANK *reads on, another voice joins his, as if coming from the air. It is* ANNE'S VOICE.]

MR. FRANK AND ANNE. "My father started a business, importing spice and herbs. Things went well for us until nineteen forty. Then the war came, and the Dutch capitulation,[6] followed by the arrival of the Germans. Then things got very bad for the Jews."

[MR. FRANK'S VOICE *dies out.* ANNE'S VOICE *continues alone. The lights dim slowly to darkness. The curtain falls on the scene.*]

---

6. capitulation (kə pich′ ə lā′ shən) *n.*: Surrender.

ANNE'S VOICE. You could not do this and you could not do that. They forced Father out of his business. We had to wear yellow stars.[7] I had to turn in my bike. I couldn't go to a Dutch school any more. I couldn't go to the movies, or ride in an automobile, or even on a streetcar, and a million other things. But somehow we children still managed to have fun. Yesterday Father told me we were going into hiding. Where, he wouldn't say.

---

7. yellow stars: Stars of David, which are six-pointed stars that are symbols of Judaism. The Nazis ordered all Jews to wear them sewn to their clothing so that Jews could be easily identified.

At five o'clock this morning Mother woke me and told me to hurry and get dressed. I was to put on as many clothes as I could. It would look too suspicious if we walked along carrying suitcases. It wasn't until we were on our way that I learned where we were going. Our hiding place was to be upstairs in the building where Father used to have his business. Three other people were coming in with us . . . the Van Daans and their son Peter . . . Father knew the Van Daans but we had never met them . . .

[*During the last lines the curtain rises on the scene. The lights dim on.* ANNE'S VOICE *fades out.*]

Front view and rear view of the building where the Franks and their friends hid

Scene 2

[*It is early morning, July, 1942. The rooms are bare, as before, but they are now clean and orderly.*

MR. VAN DAAN, *a tall, portly[8] man in his late forties, is in the main room, pacing up and down, nervously smoking a cigarette. His clothes and overcoat are expensive and well cut.*

MRS. VAN DAAN *sits on the couch, clutching her possessions, a hatbox, bags, etc. She is a pretty woman in her early forties. She wears a fur coat over her other clothes.*

PETER VAN DAAN *is standing at the window of the room on the right, looking down at the street below. He is a shy, awkward boy of sixteen. He wears a cap, a raincoat, and long Dutch trousers, like "plus fours."[9] At his feet is a black case, a carrier for his cat.*

The yellow Star of David is conspicuous on all of their clothes.]

MRS. VAN DAAN. [*Rising, nervous, excited*] Something's happened to them! I know it!

MR. VAN DAAN. Now, Kerli!

MRS. VAN DAAN. Mr. Frank said they'd be here at seven o'clock. He said . . .

MR. VAN DAAN. They have two miles to walk. You can't expect . . .

MRS. VAN DAAN. They've been picked up. That's what's happened. They've been taken . . .

[MR. VAN DAAN *indicates that he hears someone coming.*]

MR. VAN DAAN. You see?

[PETER *takes up his carrier and his schoolbag, etc., and goes into the main room as* MR. FRANK *comes up the stairwell from below.* MR. FRANK *looks much younger now. His movements are brisk, his manner confident. He wears an overcoat and carries his hat and a small cardboard box. He crosses to the* VAN DAANS. *shaking hands with each of them.*]

MR. FRANK. Mrs. Van Daan, Mr. Van Daan, Peter. [*Then, in explanation of their lateness*] There were too many of the Green Police[10] on the streets . . . we had to take the long way around.

[*Up the steps come* MARGOT FRANK, MRS. FRANK, MIEP (*not pregnant now*) *and* MR. KRALER. *All of them carry bags, packages, and so forth. The Star of David is conspicuous on all of the* FRANKS' *clothing.* MARGOT *is eighteen, beautiful, quiet, shy.* MRS. FRANK *is a young mother, gently bred, reserved. She, like* MR. FRANK, *has a slight German accent.* MR. KRALER *is a Dutchman, dependable, kindly.*

As MR. KRALER *and* MIEP *go upstage to put down their parcels,* MRS. FRANK *turns back to call* ANNE.]

MRS. FRANK. Anne?

[ANNE *comes running up the stairs. She is thirteen, quick in her movements, interested in everything, mercurial in her emotions. She wears a cape, long wool socks and carries a schoolbag.*]

MR. FRANK. [*Introducing them*] My wife, Edith. Mr. and Mrs. Van Daan . . . their son, Peter . . . my daughters, Margot and Anne.

[MRS. FRANK *hurries over, shaking hands with them.*]

[ANNE *gives a polite little curtsy as she shakes* MR. VAN DAAN'S *hand. Then she imme-*

---

8. portly (pôrt' lē) *adj.:* Large, heavy, and dignified.
9. plus fours *n.:* Loose knickers.

10. Green Police: The Nazi police who wore green uniforms.

Mr. and Mrs. Van Daan and Victor Kraler in happier times

diately starts off on a tour of investigation of her new home, going upstairs to the attic room.

MIEP *and* MR. KRALER *are putting the various things they have brought on the shelves.*]

MR. KRALER. I'm sorry there is still so much confusion.

MR. FRANK. Please. Don't think of it. After all, we'll have plenty of leisure to arrange everything ourselves.

MIEP. [*To* MRS. FRANK] We put the stores of food you sent in here. Your drugs are here . . . soap, linen here.

MRS. FRANK. Thank you, Miep.

MIEP. I made up the beds . . . the way Mr. Frank and Mr. Kraler said. [*She starts out.*] Forgive me. I have to hurry. I've got to go to the other side of town to get some ration books[11] for you.

MRS. VAN DAAN. Ration books? If they see our names on ration books, they'll know we're here.

MR. KRALER. There isn't anything . . .

MIEP. Don't worry. Your names won't be on them. [*As she hurries out*] I'll be up later.

---

11. ration books (rash' ən books') *n.*: Books of stamps given to ensure even distribution of scarce items, especially in wartime. Stamps as well as money must be given to obtain an item that is scarce.

MR. FRANK. Thank you, Miep.

MRS. FRANK. [*To* MR. KRALER] It's illegal, then, the ration books? We've never done anything illegal.

MR. FRANK. We won't be living here exactly according to regulations.

[*As* MR. KRALER *reassures* MRS. FRANK, *he takes various small things, such as matches, soap, etc., from his pockets, handing them to her.*]

MR. KRALER. This isn't the black market,[12] Mrs. Frank. This is what we call the white market . . . helping all of the hundreds and hundreds who are hiding out in Amsterdam.

[*The carillon is heard playing the quarter-hour before eight.* MR. KRALER *looks at his watch.* ANNE *stops at the window as she comes down the stairs.*]

ANNE. It's the Westertoren!

MR. KRALER. I must go. I must be out of here and downstairs in the office before the workmen get here. [*He starts for the stairs leading out.*] Miep or I, or both of us, will be up each day to bring you food and news and find out what your needs are. Tomorrow I'll get you a better bolt for the door at the foot of the stairs. It needs a bolt that you can throw yourself and open only at our signal. [*To* MR. FRANK] Oh . . . You'll tell them about the noise?

MR. FRANK. I'll tell them.

MR. KRALER. Good-bye then for the moment. I'll come up again, after the workmen leave.

MR. FRANK. Good-bye, Mr. Kraler.

MRS. FRANK. [*Shaking his hand*] How can we thank you?

---

12. black market: An illegal way of buying scarce items without ration stamps.

[*The others murmur their good-byes.*]

MR. KRALER. I never thought I'd live to see the day when a man like Mr. Frank would have to go into hiding. When you think—

[*He breaks off, going out.* MR. FRANK *follows him down the steps, bolting the door after him. In the interval before he returns.* PETER *goes over to* MARGOT, *shaking hands with her. As* MR. FRANK *comes back up the steps,* MRS. FRANK *questions him anxiously.*]

MRS. FRANK. What did he mean, about the noise?

MR. FRANK. First let us take off some of these clothes.

[*They all start to take off garment after garment. On each of their coats, sweaters, blouses, suits, dresses, is another yellow Star of David.* MR. *and* MRS. FRANK *are underdressed quite simply. The others wear several things, sweaters, extra dresses, bathrobes, aprons, nightgowns, etc.*]

MR. VAN DAAN. It's a wonder we weren't arrested, walking along the streets . . . Petronella with a fur coat in July . . . and that cat of Peter's crying all the way.

ANNE. A cat?

[*Finally, as they have all removed their surplus clothes, they look to* MR. FRANK, *waiting for him to speak.*]

MR. FRANK. Now. About the noise. While the men are in the building below, we must have complete quiet. Every sound can be heard down there, not only in the workrooms, but in the offices too. The men come at about eight-thirty, and leave at about five-thirty. So, to be perfectly safe, from eight in the morning until six in the evening we must move only when it is necessary, and then in stockinged feet. We must not speak above a whisper. We must not run any water. We cannot use the sink, or even, forgive me, the w.c.[13] The pipes go down through the workrooms. It would be heard. No trash . . .

[MR. FRANK *stops abruptly as he hears the sound of marching feet from the street below. Everyone is motionless, paralyzed with fear.* MR. FRANK *goes quietly into the room on the right to look down out of the window.* ANNE *runs after him, peering out with him. The tramping feet pass without stopping. The tension is relieved.* MR. FRANK, *followed by* ANNE, *returns to the main room and resumes his instructions to the group.*]

. . . No trash must ever be thrown out which might reveal that someone is living up here . . . not even a potato paring. We must burn everything in the stove at night. This is the way we must live until it is over, if we are to survive.

[*There is silence for a second.*]

MRS. FRANK. Until it is over.

MR. FRANK. [*Reassuringly*] After six we can move about . . . we can talk and laugh and have our supper and read and play games . . . just as we would at home. [*He looks at his watch.*] And now I think it would be wise if we all went to our rooms, and were settled before eight o'clock. Mrs. Van Daan, you and your husband will be upstairs. I regret that there's no place up there for Peter. But he will be here, near us. This will be our common room, where we'll meet to talk and eat and read, like one family.

MR. VAN DAAN. And where do you and Mrs. Frank sleep?

MR. FRANK. This room is also our bedroom.

MRS. VAN DAAN. That isn't right. We'll sleep here and you take the room upstairs.

MR. VAN DAAN. It's your place.

[*Together*]

MR. FRANK. Please. I've thought this out for weeks. It's the best arrangement. The only arrangement.

MRS. VAN DAAN. [*To* MR. FRANK] Never, never can we thank you. [*Then to* MRS. FRANK] I don't know what would have happened to us, if it hadn't been for Mr. Frank.

MR. FRANK. You don't know how your husband helped me when I came to this country . . . knowing no one . . . not able to speak the language. I can never repay him for that. [*Going to* VAN DAAN] May I help you with your things?

MR. VAN DAAN. No. No. [*To* MRS. VAN DAAN] Come along, *liefje.*[14]

MRS. VAN DAAN. You'll be all right, Peter? You're not afraid?

PETER. [*Embarrassed*] Please, Mother.

[*They start up the stairs to the attic room above.* MR. FRANK *turns to* MRS. FRANK.]

MR. FRANK. You too must have some rest, Edith. You didn't close your eyes last night. Nor you, Margot.

ANNE. I slept, Father. Wasn't that funny? I knew it was the last night in my own bed, and yet I slept soundly.

MR. FRANK. I'm glad, Anne. Now you'll be able to help me straighten things in here. [*To* MRS. FRANK *and* MARGOT] Come with me . . . You and Margot rest in this room for the time being.

---

13. w.c.: water closet; bathroom.

14. *liefje* (lēf´ hyə): Dutch for "little love."

[*He picks up their clothes, starting for the room on the right.*]

MRS. FRANK. You're sure . . . ? I could help . . . And Anne hasn't had her milk . . .

MR. FRANK. I'll give it to her. [*To* ANNE *and* PETER] Anne, Peter . . . it's best that you take off your shoes now, before you forget.

[*He leads the way to the room, followed by* MARGOT.]

MRS. FRANK. You're sure you're not tired, Anne?

ANNE. I feel fine. I'm going to help Father.

MRS. FRANK. Peter, I'm glad you are to be with us.

PETER. Yes, Mrs. Frank.

[MRS. FRANK *goes to join* MR. FRANK *and* MARGOT.]

[*During the following scene* MR. FRANK *helps* MARGOT *and* MRS. FRANK *to hang up their clothes. Then he persuades them both to lie down and rest. The* VAN DAANS *in their room above settle themselves. In the main room* ANNE *and* PETER *remove their shoes.* PETER *takes his cat out of the carrier.*]

ANNE. What's your cat's name?

PETER. Mouschi.

ANNE. Mouschi! Mouschi! Mouschi! [*She picks up the cat, walking away with it. To* PETER] I love cats. I have one . . . a darling little cat. But they made me leave her behind. I left some food and a note for the neighbors to take care of her . . . I'm going to miss her terribly. What is yours? A him or a her?

PETER. He's a tom. He doesn't like strangers. [*He takes the cat from her, putting it back in its carrier.*]

Star of David patch that the Nazis forced Jews to wear

ANNE. [*Unabashed*] Then I'll have to stop being a stranger, won't I? Where did you go to school?

PETER. Jewish Secondary.

ANNE. But that's where Margot and I go! I never saw you around.

PETER. I used to see you . . . sometimes . . .

ANNE. You did?

PETER. . . . in the school yard. You were always in the middle of a bunch of kids. [*He takes a penknife from his pocket.*]

ANNE. Why didn't you ever come over?

PETER. I'm sort of a lone wolf. [*He starts to rip off his Star of David.*]

ANNE. What are you doing?

PETER. Taking it off.

ANNE. But you can't do that. They'll arrest you if you go out without your star.

[*He tosses his knife on the table.*]

PETER. Who's going out?

ANNE. Why, of course! You're right! Of course we don't need them any more. [*She picks up his knife and starts to take her star off.*] I wonder what our friends will think when we don't show up today?

PETER. I didn't have any dates with anyone.

ANNE. Oh, I did. I had a date with Jopie to go and play ping-pong at her house. Do you know Jopie de Waal?

PETER. No.

ANNE. Jopie's my best friend. I wonder what she'll think when she telephones and there's no answer? . . . Probably she'll go over to the house . . . I wonder what she'll think . . . we left everything as if we'd suddenly been called away . . . breakfast dishes in the sink . . . beds not made . . . [*As she pulls off her star, the cloth underneath shows clearly the color and form of the star.*] Look! It's still there!

[PETER *goes over to the stove with his star.*]

What're you going to do with yours?

PETER. Burn it.

ANNE. [*She starts to throw hers in, and cannot.*] It's funny, I can't throw mine away. I don't know why.

PETER. You can't throw . . . ? Something they branded you with . . . ? That they made you wear so they could spit on you?

ANNE. I know. I know. But after all, it *is* the Star of David, isn't it?

[*In the bedroom, right,* MARGOT *and* MRS. FRANK *are lying down.* MR. FRANK *starts quietly out.*]

PETER. Maybe it's different for a girl.

[MR. FRANK *comes into the main room.*]

MR. FRANK. Forgive me, Peter. Now let me see. We must find a bed for your cat. [*He goes to a cupboard.*] I'm glad you brought your cat. Anne was feeling so badly about hers. [*Getting a used small washtub*] Here we are. Will it be comfortable in that?

PETER. [*Gathering up his things*] Thanks.

MR. FRANK. [*Opening the door of the room on the left*] And here is your room. But I warn you, Peter, you can't grow any more. Not an inch, or you'll have to sleep with your feet out of the skylight. Are you hungry?

PETER. No.

MR. FRANK. We have some bread and butter.

PETER. No, thank you.

MR. FRANK. You can have it for luncheon then. And tonight we will have a real supper . . . our first supper together.

PETER. Thanks. Thanks. [*He goes into his room. During the following scene he arranges his possessions in his new room.*]

MR. FRANK. That's a nice boy, Peter.

ANNE. He's awfully shy, isn't he?

MR. FRANK. You'll like him, I know.

ANNE. I certainly hope so, since he's the only boy I'm likely to see for months and months.

[MR. FRANK *sits down, taking off his shoes.*]

MR. FRANK. Annele,[15] there's a box there. Will you open it?

---

15. Annele (än′ ə lə): Nickname for *Anne.*

[*He indicates a carton on the couch.* ANNE *brings it to the center table. In the street below there is the sound of children playing.*]

ANNE. [*As she opens the carton*] You know the way I'm going to think of it here? I'm going to think of it as a boarding house. A very peculiar summer boarding house, like the one that we—[*She breaks off as she pulls out some photographs.*] Father! My movie stars! I was wondering where they were! I was looking for them this morning . . . and Queen Wilhelmina![16] How wonderful!

MR. FRANK. There's something more. Go on. Look further. [*He goes over to the sink, pouring a glass of milk from a thermos bottle.*]

ANNE. [*Pulling out a pasteboard-bound book*] A diary! [*She throws her arms around her father.*] I've never had a diary. And I've always longed for one. [*She looks around the room.*] Pencil, pencil, pencil, pencil. [*She starts down the stairs.*] I'm going down to the office to get a pencil.

MR. FRANK. Anne! No! [*He goes after her, catching her by the arm and pulling her back.*]

ANNE. [*Startled*] But there's no one in the building now.

MR. FRANK. It doesn't matter. I don't want you ever to go beyond that door.

ANNE. [*Sobered*] Never . . . ? Not even at nighttime, when everyone is gone? Or on Sundays? Can't I go down to listen to the radio?

MR. FRANK. Never. I am sorry, Anneke.[17] It isn't safe. No, you must never go beyond that door.

[*For the first time* ANNE *realizes what "going into hiding" means.*]

ANNE. I see.

MR. FRANK. It'll be hard, I know. But always remember this, Anneke. There are no walls, there are no bolts, no locks that anyone can put on your mind. Miep will bring us books. We will read history, poetry, mythology. [*He gives her the glass of milk.*] Here's your milk. [*With his arm about her, they go over to the couch, sitting down side by side.*] As a matter of fact, between us, Anne, being here has certain advantages for you. For instance, you remember the battle you had with your mother the other day on the subject of overshoes? You said you'd rather die than wear overshoes? But in the end you had to wear them? Well now, you see, for as long as we are here you will never have to wear overshoes! Isn't that good? And the coat that you inherited from Margot, you won't have to wear that any more. And the piano! You won't have to practice on the piano. I tell you, this is going to be a fine life for you!

[ANNE'S *panic is gone.* PETER *appears in the doorway of his room, with a saucer in his hand. He is carrying his cat.*]

PETER. I . . . I . . . I thought I'd better get some water for Mouschi before . . .

MR. FRANK. Of course.

[*As he starts toward the sink the carillon begins to chime the hour of eight. He tiptoes to the window at the back and looks*

---

16. Queen Wilhelmina (kwēn' wil' hel mē' nə): Queen of Holland from 1890 to 1948.

17. Anneke (än' ə kə): Nickname for *Anne.*

down at the street below. He turns to PETER, indicating in pantomime that it is too late. PETER *starts back for his room. He steps on a creaking board. The three of them are frozen for a minute in fear. As* PETER *starts away again,* ANNE *tiptoes over to him and pours some of the milk from her glass into the saucer for the cat.* PETER *squats on the floor, putting the milk before the cat.* MR. FRANK *gives* ANNE *his fountain pen, and then goes into the room at the right. For a second* ANNE *watches the cat, then she goes over to the center table, and opens her diary.*

In the room at the right, MRS. FRANK *has sat up quickly at the sound of the carillon.* MR. FRANK *comes in and sits down beside her on the settee, his arm comfortingly around her.*

Upstairs, in the attic room, MR. *and* MRS. VAN DAAN *have hung their clothes in the closet and are now seated on the iron bed.* MRS. VAN DAAN *leans back exhausted.* MR. VAN DAAN *fans her with a newspaper.*

ANNE *starts to write in her diary. The lights dim out, the curtain falls.*

In the darkness ANNE'S VOICE *comes to us again, faintly at first, and then with growing strength.*]

ANNE'S VOICE. I expect I should be describing what it feels like to go into hiding. But I really don't know yet myself. I only know it's funny never to be able to go outdoors . . . never to breathe fresh air . . . never to run and shout and jump. It's the silence in the nights that frightens me most. Every time I hear a creak in the house, or a step on the street outside, I'm sure they're coming for us. The days aren't so bad. At least we know that Miep and Mr. Kraler are down there below us in the office. Our protectors, we call them. I asked Father what would happen to them if the Nazis found out they were hiding us. Pim said that they would suffer the same

fate that we would . . . Imagine! They know this, and yet when they come up here, they're always cheerful and gay as if there were nothing in the world to bother them . . . Friday, the twenty-first of August, nineteen forty-two. Today I'm going to tell you our general news. Mother is unbearable. She insists on treating me like a baby, which I loathe. Otherwise things are going better. The weather is . . .

[*As* ANNE'S VOICE *is fading out, the curtain rises on the scene.*]

Scene 3

[*It is a little after six o'clock in the evening, two months later.*

MARGOT *is in the bedroom at the right, studying.* MR. VAN DAAN *is lying down in the attic room above.*

The rest of the "family" is in the main room. ANNE *and* PETER *sit opposite each other at the center table, where they have been doing their lessons.* MRS. FRANK *is on the couch.* MRS. VAN DAAN *is seated with her fur coat, on which she has been sewing, in her lap. None of them are wearing their shoes.*

Their eyes are on MR. FRANK, *waiting for him to give them the signal which will release them from their day-long quiet.* MR. FRANK, *his shoes in his hand, stands looking down out of the window at the back, watching to be sure that all of the workmen have left the building below.*

After a few seconds of motionless silence, MR. FRANK *turns from the window.*]

MR. FRANK. [*Quietly, to the group*] It's safe now. The last workman has left.

[*There is an immediate stir of relief.*]

ANNE. [*Her pent-up energy explodes.*] WHEE!

MRS. FRANK. [*Startled, amused*] Anne!

MRS. VAN DAAN. I'm first for the w.c.

[*She hurries off to the bathroom.* MRS. FRANK *puts on her shoes and starts up to the sink to prepare supper.* ANNE *sneaks* PETER'S *shoes from under the table and hides them behind her back.* MR. FRANK *goes in to* MARGOT'S *room.*]

MR. FRANK. [*To* MARGOT] Six o'clock. School's over.

[MARGOT *gets up, stretching.* MR. FRANK *sits down to put on his shoes. In the main room* PETER *tries to find his.*]

PETER. [*To* ANNE] Have you seen my shoes?

ANNE. [*Innocently*] Your shoes?

PETER. You've taken them, haven't you?

ANNE. I don't know what you're talking about.

PETER. You're going to be sorry!

ANNE. Am I?

[PETER *goes after her.* ANNE, *with his shoes in her hand, runs from him, dodging behind her mother.*]

MRS. FRANK. [*Protesting*] Anne, dear!

PETER. Wait till I get you!

ANNE. I'm waiting!

[PETER *makes a lunge for her. They both fall to the floor.* PETER *pins her down, wrestling with her to get the shoes.*]

Don't! Don't! Peter, stop it. Ouch!

MRS. FRANK. Anne! . . . Peter!

[*Suddenly* PETER *becomes self-conscious. He grabs his shoes roughly and starts for his room.*]

ANNE. [*Following him*] Peter, where are you going? Come dance with me.

PETER. I tell you I don't know how.

ANNE. I'll teach you.

PETER. I'm going to give Mouschi his dinner.

ANNE. Can I watch?

PETER. He doesn't like people around while he eats.

ANNE. Peter, please.

PETER. No! [*He goes into his room.* ANNE *slams his door after him.*]

MRS. FRANK. Anne, dear, I think you shouldn't play like that with Peter. It's not dignified.

ANNE. Who cares if it's dignified? I don't want to be dignified.

[MR. FRANK *and* MARGOT *come from the room on the right.* MARGOT *goes to help her mother.* MR. FRANK *starts for the center table to correct* MARGOT'S *school papers.*]

MRS. FRANK. [*To* ANNE] You complain that I don't treat you like a grownup. But when I do, you resent it.

ANNE. I only want some fun . . . someone to laugh and clown with . . . After you've sat still all day and hardly moved, you've got to have some fun. I don't know what's the matter with that boy.

MR. FRANK. He isn't used to girls. Give him a little time.

ANNE. Time? Isn't two months time? I could cry. [*Catching hold of* MARGOT] Come on, Margot . . . dance with me. Come on, please.

MARGOT. I have to help with supper.

Anne and her father, Otto Frank

ANNE. You know we're going to forget how to dance . . . When we get out we won't remember a thing.

[*She starts to sing and dance by herself.* MR. FRANK *takes her in his arms, waltzing with her.* MRS. VAN DAAN *comes in from the bathroom.*]

MRS. VAN DAAN. Next? [*She looks around as she starts putting on her shoes.*] Where's Peter?

ANNE. [*As they are dancing*] Where would he be!

MRS. VAN DAAN. He hasn't finished his lessons, has he? His father'll kill him if he catches him in there with that cat and his work not done.

[MR. FRANK *and* ANNE *finish their dance. They bow to each other with extravagant formality.*]

Anne, get him out of there, will you?

ANNE. [*At* PETER'S *door*] Peter? Peter?

PETER. [*Opening the door a crack*] What is it?

ANNE. Your mother says to come out.

PETER. I'm giving Mouschi his dinner.

MRS. VAN DAAN. You know what your father says. [*She sits on the couch, sewing on the lining of her fur coat.*]

PETER. For heaven's sake, I haven't even looked at him since lunch.

MRS. VAN DAAN. I'm just telling you, that's all.

ANNE. I'll feed him.

PETER. I don't want you in there.

MRS. VAN DAAN. Peter!

PETER. [*To* ANNE] Then give him his dinner and come right out, you hear?

[*He comes back to the table.* ANNE *shuts the door of* PETER'S *room after her and disappears behind the curtain covering his closet.*]

MRS. VAN DAAN. [*To* PETER] Now is that any way to talk to your little girl friend?

PETER. Mother . . . for heaven's sake . . . will you please stop saying that?

MRS. VAN DAAN. Look at him blush! Look at him!

PETER. Please! I'm not . . . anyway . . . let me alone, will you?

MRS. VAN DAAN. He acts like it was something to be ashamed of. It's nothing to be ashamed of, to have a little girl friend.

PETER. You're crazy. She's only thirteen.

MRS. VAN DAAN. So what? And you're sixteen. Just perfect. Your father's ten years older than I am. [*To* MR. FRANK] I warn you, Mr. Frank, if this war lasts much longer, we're going to be related and then . . .

MR. FRANK. *Mazeltov!*[18]

MRS. FRANK. [*Deliberately changing the conversation*] I wonder where Miep is. She's usually so prompt.

[*Suddenly everything else is forgotten as they hear the sound of an automobile coming to a screeching stop in the street below.*]

---

18. mazeltov (mä′ z'l tōv′): "Good luck" in Hebrew and Yiddish.

They are tense, motionless in their terror. The car starts away. A wave of relief sweeps over them. They pick up their occupations again. ANNE *flings open the door of* PETER'S *room, making a dramatic entrance. She is dressed in* PETER'S *clothes.* PETER *looks at her in fury. The others are amused.*]

ANNE. Good evening, everyone. Forgive me if I don't stay. [*She jumps up on a chair.*] I have a friend waiting for me in there. My friend Tom. Tom Cat. Some people say that we look alike. But Tom has the most beautiful whiskers, and I have only a little fuzz. I am hoping . . . in time . . .

PETER. All right, Mrs. Quack Quack!

ANNE. [*Outraged—jumping down*] Peter!

PETER. I heard about you . . . How you talked so much in class they called you Mrs. Quack Quack. How Mr. Smitter made you write a composition . . . "'Quack, quack,' said Mrs. Quack Quack."

ANNE. Well, go on. Tell them the rest. How it was so good he read it out loud to the class and then read it to all his other classes!

PETER. Quack! Quack! Quack . . . Quack . . . Quack . . .

[ANNE *pulls off the coat and trousers.*]

ANNE. You are the most intolerable, insufferable boy I've ever met!

[*She throws the clothes down the stairwell.* PETER *goes down after them.*]

PETER. Quack, quack, quack!

MRS. VAN DAAN. [*To* ANNE] That's right, Anneke! Give it to him!

ANNE. With all the boys in the world . . . Why I had to get locked up with one like you! . . .

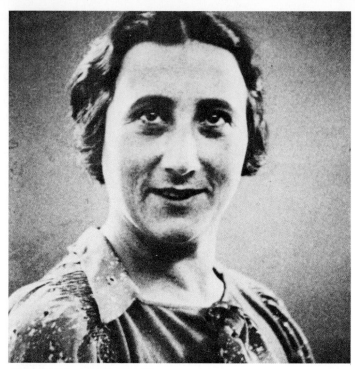

Edith Frank, Anne's mother

PETER. Quack, quack, quack, and from now on stay out of my room!

[*As* PETER *passes her,* ANNE *puts out her foot, tripping him. He picks himself up, and goes on into his room.*]

MRS. FRANK. [*Quietly*] Anne, dear . . . your hair. [*She feels* ANNE'S *forehead.*] You're warm. Are you feeling all right?

ANNE. Please, Mother. [*She goes over to the center table, slipping into her shoes.*]

MRS. FRANK. [*Following her*] You haven't a fever, have you?

ANNE. [*Pulling away*] No. No.

MRS. FRANK. You know we can't call a doctor here, ever. There's only one thing to do . . . watch carefully. Prevent an illness before it comes. Let me see your tongue.

ANNE. Mother, this is perfectly absurd.

MRS. FRANK. Anne, dear, don't be such a baby. Let me see your tongue. [*As* ANNE *refuses,* MRS. FRANK *appeals to* MR. FRANK.] Otto . . . ?

MR. FRANK. You hear your mother, Anne.

[ANNE *flicks out her tongue for a second, then turns away.*]

MRS. FRANK. Come on—open up! [*As* ANNE *opens her mouth very wide*] You seem all right . . . but perhaps an aspirin . . .

MRS. VAN DAAN. For heaven's sake, don't give that child any pills. I waited for fifteen minutes this morning for her to come out of the w.c.

ANNE. I was washing my hair!

MR. FRANK. I think there's nothing the matter with our Anne that a ride on her bike, or a visit with her friend Jopie de Waal wouldn't cure. Isn't that so, Anne?

[MR. VAN DAAN *comes down into the room. From outside we hear faint sounds of bombers going over and a burst of ack-ack.*][19]

MR. VAN DAAN. Miep not come yet?

MRS. VAN DAAN. The workmen just left, a little while ago.

MR. VAN DAAN. What's for dinner tonight?

MRS. VAN DAAN. Beans.

MR. VAN DAAN. Not again!

MRS. VAN DAAN. Poor Putti! I know. But what can we do? That's all that Miep brought us.

[MR. VAN DAAN *starts to pace, his hands behind his back.* ANNE *follows behind him, imitating him.*]

ANNE. We are now in what is known as the "bean cycle." Beans boiled, beans en casserole, beans with strings, beans without strings . . .

[PETER *has come out of his room. He slides into his place at the table, becoming immediately absorbed in his studies.*]

MR. VAN DAAN. [*To* PETER] I saw you . . . in there, playing with your cat.

MRS. VAN DAAN. He just went in for a second, putting his coat away. He's been out here all the time, doing his lessons.

MR. FRANK. [*Looking up from the papers*] Anne, you got an excellent in your history paper today . . . and very good in Latin.

ANNE. [*Sitting beside him*] How about algebra?

MR. FRANK. I'll have to make a confession. Up until now I've managed to stay ahead of you in algebra. Today you caught up with me. We'll leave it to Margot to correct.

ANNE. Isn't algebra *vile*, Pim!

MR. FRANK. Vile!

MARGOT. [*To* MR. FRANK] How did I do?

ANNE. [*Getting up*] Excellent, excellent, excellent, excellent!

MR. FRANK. [*To* MARGOT] You should have used the subjunctive[20] here . . .

MARGOT. Should I? . . . I thought . . . look here . . . I didn't use it here . . .

[*The two become absorbed in the papers.*]

ANNE. Mrs. Van Daan, may I try on your coat?

MRS. FRANK. No, Anne.

MRS. VAN DAAN. [*Giving it to* ANNE] It's all right . . . but careful with it.

[ANNE *puts it on and struts with it.*]

My father gave me that the year before he died. He always bought the best that money could buy.

ANNE. Mrs. Van Daan, did you have a lot of boy friends before you were married?

MRS. FRANK. Anne, that's a personal question. It's not courteous to ask personal questions.

MRS. VAN DAAN. Oh I don't mind. [*To* ANNE] Our house was always swarming with boys. When I was a girl we had . . .

---

19. ack-ack (ak′ ak′) *n.*: Slang for an antiaircraft gun's fire.

20. subjunctive (səb juŋk′ tiv) *n.*: A particular form of a verb.

MR. VAN DAAN. Oh, no. Not again!

MRS. VAN DAAN. [*Good-humored*] Shut up!

[*Without a pause, to* ANNE. MR. VAN DAAN *mimics* MRS. VAN DAAN, *speaking the first few words in unison with her.*]

One summer we had a big house in Hilversum. The boys came buzzing round like bees around a jam pot. And when I was sixteen! . . . We were wearing our skirts very short those days and I had good-looking legs. [*She pulls up her skirt, going to* MR. FRANK.] I still have 'em. I may not be as pretty as I used to be, but I still have my legs. How about it, Mr. Frank?

MR. VAN DAAN. All right. All right. We see them.

MRS. VAN DAAN. I'm not asking you. I'm asking Mr. Frank.

PETER. Mother, for heaven's sake.

MRS. VAN DAAN. Oh, I embarrass you, do I? Well, I just hope the girl you marry has as good. [*Then to* ANNE] My father used to worry about me, with so many boys hanging round. He told me, if any of them gets fresh, you say to him . . . "Remember, Mr. So-and-So, remember I'm a lady."

ANNE. "Remember, Mr. So-and-So, remember I'm a lady." [*She gives* MRS. VAN DAAN *her coat.*]

MR. VAN DAAN. Look at you, talking that way in front of her! Don't you know she puts it all down in that diary?

MRS. VAN DAAN. So, if she does? I'm only telling the truth!

[ANNE *stretches out, putting her ear to the floor, listening to what is going on below. The sound of the bombers fades away.*]

MRS. FRANK. [*Setting the table*] Would you mind, Peter, if I moved you over to the couch?

ANNE. [*Listening*] Miep must have the radio on.

[PETER *picks up his papers, going over to the couch beside* MRS. VAN DAAN.]

MR. VAN DAAN. [*Accusingly, to* PETER] Haven't you finished yet?

PETER. No.

MR. VAN DAAN. You ought to be ashamed of yourself.

PETER. All right. All right. I'm a dunce. I'm a hopeless case. Why do I go on?

MRS. VAN DAAN. You're not hopeless. Don't talk that way. It's just that you haven't anyone to help you, like the girls have. [*To* MR. FRANK] Maybe you could help him, Mr. Frank?

MR. FRANK. I'm sure that his father . . . ?

MR. VAN DAAN. Not me. I can't do anything with him. He won't listen to me. You go ahead . . . if you want.

MR. FRANK. [*Going to* PETER] What about it, Peter? Shall we make our school coeducational?

MRS. VAN DAAN. [*Kissing* MR. FRANK] You're an angel, Mr. Frank. An angel. I don't know why I didn't meet you before I met that one there. Here, sit down, Mr. Frank . . . [*She forces him down on the couch beside* PETER] Now, Peter, you listen to Mr. Frank.

MR. FRANK. It might be better for us to go into Peter's room.

[PETER *jumps up eagerly, leading the way.*]

MRS. VAN DAAN. That's right. You go in there, Peter. You listen to Mr. Frank. Mr. Frank is a highly educated man.

[*As* MR. FRANK *is about to follow* PETER *into his room*, MRS. FRANK *stops him and wipes the lipstick from his lips. Then she closes the door after them.*]

ANNE. [*On the floor, listening*] Shh! I can hear a man's voice talking.

MR. VAN DAAN. [*To* ANNE] Isn't it bad enough here without your sprawling all over the place?

[ANNE *sits up.*]

MRS. VAN DAAN. [*To* MR. VAN DAAN] If you didn't smoke so much, you wouldn't be so bad-tempered.

MR. VAN DAAN. Am I smoking? Do you see me smoking?

MRS. VAN DAAN. Don't tell me you've used up all those cigarettes.

MR. VAN DAAN. One package. Miep only brought me one package.

MRS. VAN DAAN. It's a filthy habit anyway. It's a good time to break yourself.

MR. VAN DAAN. Oh, stop it, please.

MRS. VAN DAAN. You're smoking up all our money. You know that, don't you?

MR. VAN DAAN. Will you shut up?

[*During this*, MRS. FRANK *and* MARGOT *have studiously kept their eyes down. But* ANNE, *seated on the floor, has been following the discussion interestedly.* MR. VAN DAAN *turns to see her staring up at him.*]

And what are you staring at?

ANNE. I never heard grownups quarrel before. I thought only children quarreled.

MR. VAN DAAN. This isn't a quarrel! It's a discussion. And I never heard children so rude before.

ANNE. [*Rising, indignantly*] I, rude!

MR. VAN DAAN. Yes!

MRS. FRANK. [*Quickly*] Anne, will you get me my knitting?

[ANNE *goes to get it.*]

I must remember, when Miep comes, to ask her to bring me some more wool.

MARGOT. [*Going to her room*] I need some hairpins and some soap. I made a list. [*She goes into her bedroom to get the list.*]

MRS. FRANK. [*To* ANNE] Have you some library books for Miep when she comes?

ANNE. It's a wonder that Miep has a life of her own, the way we make her run errands for us. Please, Miep, get me some starch. Please take my hair out and have it cut. Tell me all the latest news, Miep. [*She goes over, kneeling on the couch beside* MRS. VAN DAAN] Did you know she was engaged? His name is Dirk, and Miep's afraid the Nazis will ship him off to Germany to work in one of their war plants. That's what they're doing with some of the young Dutchmen . . . they pick them up off the streets—

MR. VAN DAAN. [*Interrupting*] Don't you ever get tired of talking? Suppose you try keeping still for five minutes. Just five minutes.

[*He starts to pace again. Again* ANNE *follows him, mimicking him.* MRS. FRANK *jumps up and takes her by the arm up to the sink, and gives her a glass of milk.*]

MRS. FRANK. Come here, Anne. It's time for your glass of milk.

MR. VAN DAAN. Talk, talk, talk. I never heard such a child. Where is my . . . ? Every evening it's the same talk, talk, talk. [*He looks around.*] Where is my . . . ?

MRS. VAN DAAN. What're you looking for?

MR. VAN DAAN. My pipe. Have you seen my pipe?

MRS. VAN DAAN. What good's a pipe? You haven't got any tobacco.

MR. VAN DAAN. At least I'll have something to hold in my mouth! [*Opening* MARGOT'S *bedroom door*] Margot, have you seen my pipe?

MARGOT. It was on the table last night.

[ANNE *puts her glass of milk on the table and picks up his pipe, hiding it behind her back.*]

MR. VAN DAAN. I know. I know. Anne, did you see my pipe? . . . Anne!

MRS. FRANK. Anne, Mr. Van Daan is speaking to you.

ANNE. Am I allowed to talk now?

MR. VAN DAAN. You're the most aggravating . . . The trouble with you is, you've been spoiled. What you need is a good old-fashioned spanking.

ANNE. [*Mimicking* MRS. VAN DAAN] "Remember, Mr. So-and-So, remember I'm a lady." [*She thrusts the pipe into his mouth, then picks up her glass of milk.*]

MR. VAN DAAN. [*Restraining himself with difficulty*] Why aren't you nice and quiet like your sister Margot? Why do you have to show off all the time? Let me give you a little advice, young lady. Men don't like that kind of thing in a girl. You know that? A man likes a girl who'll listen to him once in a while . . . a domestic girl, who'll keep her house shining for her husband . . . who loves to cook and sew and . . .

ANNE. I'd cut my throat first! I'd open my veins! I'm going to be remarkable! I'm going to Paris . . .

MR. VAN DAAN. [*Scoffingly*] Paris!

ANNE. . . . to study music and art.

MR. VAN DAAN. Yeah! Yeah!

ANNE. I'm going to be a famous dancer or singer . . . or something wonderful.

[*She makes a wide gesture, spilling the glass of milk on the fur coat in* MRS. VAN DAAN'S *lap.* MARGOT *rushes quickly over with a towel.* ANNE *tries to brush the milk off with her skirt.*]

MRS. VAN DAAN. Now look what you've done . . . you clumsy little fool! My beautiful fur coat my father gave me . . .

ANNE. I'm so sorry.

MRS. VAN DAAN. What do you care? It isn't yours . . . So go on, ruin it! Do you know what that coat cost? Do you? And now look at it! Look at it!

ANNE. I'm very, very sorry.

MRS. VAN DAAN. I could kill you for this. I could just kill you!

[MRS. VAN DAAN *goes up the stairs, clutching the coat.* MR. VAN DAAN *starts after her.*]

MR. VAN DAAN. Petronella . . . *liefje! Liefje!* . . . Come back . . . the supper . . . come back!

MRS. FRANK. Anne, you must not behave in that way.

ANNE. It was an accident. Anyone can have an accident.

MRS. FRANK. I don't mean that. I mean the answering back. You must not answer back. They are our guests. We must always show the greatest courtesy to them. We're all living under terrible tension.

[*She stops as* MARGOT *indicates that* VAN DAAN *can hear. When he is gone, she continues.*]

That's why we must control ourselves . . . You don't hear Margot getting into arguments with them, do you? Watch Margot. She's always courteous with them. Never familiar. She keeps her distance. And they respect her for it. Try to be like Margot.

ANNE. And have them walk all over me, the way they do her? No, thanks!

MRS. FRANK. I'm not afraid that anyone is going to walk all over you, Anne. I'm afraid for other people, that you'll walk on them. I don't know what happens to you, Anne. You are wild, self-willed. If I had ever talked to my mother as you talk to me . . .

ANNE. Things have changed. People aren't like that any more. "Yes, Mother." "No, Mother." "Anything you say, Mother." I've got to fight things out for myself! Make something of myself!

MRS. FRANK. It isn't necessary to fight to do it. Margot doesn't fight, and isn't she . . . ?

ANNE. [*Violently rebellious*] Margot! Margot! Margot! That's all I hear from everyone . . . how wonderful Margot is . . . "Why aren't you like Margot?"

MARGOT. [*Protesting*] Oh, come on, Anne, don't be so . . .

ANNE. [*Paying no attention*] Everything she does is right, and everything I do is wrong! I'm the goat around here! . . . You're all against me! . . . And you worst of all!

[*She rushes off into her room and throws herself down on the settee, stifling her sobs.* MRS. FRANK *sighs and starts toward the stove.*]

MRS. FRANK. [*To* MARGOT] Let's put the soup on the stove . . . if there's anyone who cares to eat. Margot, will you take the bread out?

[MARGOT *gets the bread from the cupboard.*]

I don't know how we can go on living this way . . . I can't say a word to Anne . . . she flies at me . . .

MARGOT. You know Anne. In half an hour she'll be out here, laughing and joking.

MRS. FRANK. And . . . [*She makes a motion upwards, indicating the* VAN DAANS.] . . . I told your father it wouldn't work . . . but no . . . no . . . he had to ask them, he said . . . he owed it to him, he said. Well, he knows now that I was right! These quarrels! . . . This bickering!

MARGOT. [*With a warning look*] Shush. Shush.

[*The buzzer for the door sounds.* MRS. FRANK *gasps, startled.*]

MRS. FRANK. Every time I hear that sound, my heart stops!

MARGOT. [*Starting for* PETER'S *door*] It's Miep. [*She knocks at the door.*] Father?

[MR. FRANK *comes quickly from* PETER'S *room.*]

MR. FRANK. Thank you, Margot. [*As he goes down the steps to open the outer door*] Has everyone his list?

MARGOT. I'll get my books. [*Giving her mother a list*] Here's your list.

[MARGOT *goes into her and* ANNE'S *bedroom on the right.* ANNE *sits up, hiding her tears, as* MARGOT *comes in.*]

Miep's here.

[MARGOT *picks up her books and goes back.* ANNE *hurries over to the mirror, smoothing her hair.*]

Aerial view of Amsterdam, Holland. The house where Anne Frank hid is tinted

MR. VAN DAAN. [*Coming down the stairs*] Is it Miep?

MARGOT. Yes. Father's gone down to let her in.

MR. VAN DAAN. At last I'll have some cigarettes!

MRS. FRANK. [*To* MR. VAN DAAN] I can't tell you how unhappy I am about Mrs. Van Daan's coat. Anne should never have touched it.

MR. VAN DAAN. She'll be all right.

MRS. FRANK. Is there anything I can do?

MR. VAN DAAN. Don't worry.

[*He turns to meet* MIEP. *But it is not* MIEP *who comes up the steps. It is* MR. KRALER, *followed by* MR. FRANK. *Their faces are grave.* ANNE *comes from the bedroom.* PETER *comes from his room.*]

MRS. FRANK. Mr. Kraler!

MR. VAN DAAN. How are you, Mr. Kraler?

MARGOT. This is a surprise.

MRS. FRANK. When Mr. Kraler comes, the sun begins to shine.

MR. VAN DAAN. Miep is coming?

MR. KRALER. Not tonight.

[KRALER *goes to* MARGOT *and* MRS. FRANK *and* ANNE, *shaking hands with them.*]

MRS. FRANK. Wouldn't you like a cup of coffee? . . . Or, better still, will you have supper with us?

MR. FRANK. Mr. Kraler has something to talk over with us. Something has happened, he says, which demands an immediate decision.

MRS. FRANK. [*Fearful*] What is it?

[MR. KRALER *sits down on the couch. As he talks he takes bread, cabbages, milk, etc., from his briefcase, giving them to* MARGOT *and* ANNE *to put away.*]

MR. KRALER. Usually, when I come up here, I try to bring you some bit of good news. What's the use of telling you the bad news when there's nothing that you can do about it? But today something has happened . . . Dirk . . . Miep's Dirk, you know, came to me just now. He tells me that he has a Jewish friend living near him. A dentist. He says he's in trouble. He begged me, could I do anything for this man? Could I find him a hiding place? . . . So I've come to you . . . I know it's a terrible thing to ask of you, living as you are, but would you take him in with you?

MR. FRANK. Of course we will.

MR. KRALER. [*Rising*] It'll be just for a night or two . . . until I find some other place. This happened so suddenly that I didn't know where to turn.

MR. FRANK. Where is he?

MR. KRALER. Downstairs in the office.

MR. FRANK. Good. Bring him up.

MR. KRALER. His name is Dussel . . . Jan Dussel.

MR. FRANK. Dussel . . . I think I know him.

MR. KRALER. I'll get him.

[*He goes quickly down the steps and out.* MR. FRANK *suddenly becomes conscious of the others.*]

MR. FRANK. Forgive me. I spoke without consulting you. But I knew you'd feel as I do.

MR. VAN DAAN. There's no reason for you to consult anyone. This is your place. You have a right to do exactly as you please. The only thing I feel . . . there's so little food as it is . . . and to take in another person . . .

[PETER *turns away, ashamed of his father.*]

MR. FRANK. We can stretch the food a little. It's only for a few days.

MR. VAN DAAN. You want to make a bet?

MRS. FRANK. I think it's fine to have him. But, Otto, where are you going to put him? Where?

PETER. He can have my bed. I can sleep on the floor. I wouldn't mind.

MR. FRANK. That's good of you, Peter. But your room's too small . . . even for *you.*

ANNE. I have a much better idea. I'll come in here with you and Mother, and Margot can take Peter's room and Peter can go in our room with Mr. Dussel.

MARGOT. That's right. We could do that.

MR. FRANK. No, Margot. You mustn't sleep in that room . . . neither you nor Anne. Mouschi has caught some rats in there. Peter's brave. He doesn't mind.

ANNE. Then how about *this?* I'll come in here with you and Mother, and Mr. Dussel can have my bed.

MRS. FRANK. No. No. *No!* Margot will come in here with us and he can have her bed. It's the only way. Margot, bring your things in here. Help her, Anne.

[MARGOT *hurries into her room to get her things.*]

ANNE. [*To her mother*] Why Margot? Why can't I come in here?

MRS. FRANK. Because it wouldn't be proper for Margot to sleep with a . . . Please, Anne. Don't argue. Please.

[ANNE *starts slowly away.*]

MR. FRANK. [*To* ANNE] You don't mind sharing your room with Mr. Dussel, do you, Anne?

ANNE. No. No, of course not.

MR. FRANK. Good.

[ANNE *goes off into her bedroom, helping* MARGOT. MR. FRANK *starts to search in the cupboards.*]

Where's the cognac?

MRS. FRANK. It's there. But, Otto, I was saving it in case of illness.

MR. FRANK. I think we couldn't find a better time to use it. Peter, will you get five glasses for me?

[PETER *goes for the glasses.* MARGOT *comes out of her bedroom, carrying her possessions, which she hangs behind a curtain in the main room.* MR. FRANK *finds the cognac and pours it into the five glasses that* PETER *brings him.* MR. VAN DAAN *stands looking on sourly.* MRS. VAN DAAN *comes downstairs and looks around at all the bustle.*]

MRS. VAN DAAN. What's happening? What's going on?

MR. VAN DAAN. Someone's moving in with us.

MRS. VAN DAAN. In here? You're joking.

MARGOT. It's only for a night or two . . . until Mr. Kraler finds him another place.

MR. VAN DAAN. Yeah! Yeah!

[MR. FRANK *hurries over as* MR. KRALER *and* DUSSEL *come up.* DUSSEL *is a man in his late fifties, meticulous, finicky . . . bewildered now. He wears a raincoat. He carries a*

briefcase, *stuffed full, and a small medicine case.*]

MR. FRANK. Come in, Mr. Dussel.

MR. KRALER. This is Mr. Frank.

DUSSEL. Mr. Otto Frank?

MR. FRANK. Yes. Let me take your things. [*He takes the hat and briefcase, but* DUSSEL *clings to his medicine case.*] This is my wife Edith . . . Mr. and Mrs. Van Daan . . . their son, Peter . . . and my daughters, Margot and Anne.

[DUSSEL *shakes hands with everyone.*]

MR. KRALER. Thank you, Mr. Frank. Thank you all. Mr. Dussel, I leave you in good hands. Oh . . . Dirk's coat.

[DUSSEL *hurriedly takes off the raincoat, giving it to* MR. KRALER. *Underneath is his white dentist's jacket, with a yellow Star of David on it.*]

DUSSEL. [*To* MR. KRALER] What can I say to thank you . . . ?

MRS. FRANK. [*To* DUSSEL] Mr. Kraler and Miep . . . They're our life line. Without them we couldn't live.

MR. KRALER. Please. Please. You make us seem very heroic. It isn't that at all. We simply don't like the Nazis. [*To* MR. FRANK, *who offers him a drink*] No, thanks. [*Then going on*] We don't like their methods. We don't like . . .

MR. FRANK. [*Smiling*] I know. I know. "No one's going to tell us Dutchmen what to do with our Jews!"

MR. KRALER. [*To* DUSSEL] Pay no attention to Mr. Frank. I'll be up tomorrow to see that they're treating you right. [*To* MR. FRANK] Don't trouble to come down again. Peter will bolt the door after me, won't you, Peter?

PETER. Yes, sir.

MR. FRANK. Thank you, Peter. I'll do it.

MR. KRALER. Good night. Good night.

GROUP. Good night, Mr. Kraler. We'll see you tomorrow, etc., etc.

[MR. KRALER *goes out with* MR. FRANK. MRS. FRANK *gives each one of the "grownups" a glass of cognac.*]

MRS. FRANK. Please, Mr. Dussel, sit down.

[MR. DUSSEL *sinks into a chair.* MRS. FRANK *gives him a glass of cognac.*]

DUSSEL. I'm dreaming. I know it. I can't believe my eyes. Mr. Otto Frank here! [*To* MRS. FRANK] You're not in Switzerland then? A woman told me . . . She said she'd gone to your house . . . the door was open, everything was in disorder, dishes in the sink. She said she found a piece of paper in the wastebasket with an address scribbled on it . . . an address in Zurich. She said you must have escaped to Zurich.

ANNE. Father put that there purposely . . . just so people would think that very thing!

DUSSEL. And you've been *here* all the time?

MRS. FRANK. All the time . . . ever since July.

[ANNE *speaks to her father as he comes back.*]

ANNE. It worked, Pim . . . the address you left! Mr. Dussel says that people believe we escaped to Switzerland.

MR. FRANK. I'm glad. . . . And now let's have a little drink to welcome Mr. Dussel.

[*Before they can drink,* MR. DUSSEL *bolts his drink.* MR. FRANK *smiles and raises his glass.*]

To Mr. Dussel. Welcome. We're very honored to have you with us.

MRS. FRANK. To Mr. Dussel, welcome.

[*The* VAN DAANS *murmur a welcome. The "grownups" drink.*]

MRS. VAN DAAN. Um. That was good.

MR. VAN DAAN. Did Mr. Kraler warn you that you won't get much to eat here? You can imagine . . . three ration books among the seven of us . . . and now you make eight.

[PETER *walks away, humiliated. Outside a street organ is heard dimly.*]

DUSSEL. [*Rising*] Mr. Van Daan, you don't realize what is happening outside that you should warn me of a thing like that. You don't realize what's going on . . .

[*As* MR. VAN DAAN *starts his characteristic pacing,* DUSSEL *turns to speak to the others.*]

Right here in Amsterdam every day hundreds of Jews disappear . . . They surround a block and search house by house. Children come home from school to find their parents gone. Hundreds are being deported . . . people that you and I know . . . the Hallensteins . . . the Wessels . . .

MRS. FRANK. [*In tears*] Oh, no. No!

DUSSEL. They get their call-up notice . . . come to the Jewish theater on such and such a day and hour . . . bring only what you can carry in a rucksack. And if you refuse the call-up notice, then they come and drag you from your home and ship you off to Mauthausen.[21] The death camp!

MRS. FRANK. We didn't know that things had got so much worse.

DUSSEL. Forgive me for speaking so.

---

21. Mauthausen (mou tou′ zən): A village in Austria that was the site of a Nazi concentration camp.

Dr. Albert Dussel

MR. FRANK. [*Interrupting, with a glance at* ANNE] I think we should put this off until later. We all have many questions we want to ask . . . But I'm sure that Mr. Dussel would like to get settled before supper.

DUSSEL. Thank you. I would. I brought very little with me.

MR. FRANK. [*Giving him his hat and briefcase*] I'm sorry we can't give you a room alone. But I hope you won't be too uncomfortable. We've had to make strict rules here . . . a schedule of hours . . . We'll tell you after supper. Anne, would you like to take Mr. Dussel to his room?

ANNE. [*Controlling her tears*] If you'll come with me, Mr. Dussel? [*She starts for her room.*]

DUSSEL. [*Shaking hands with each in turn*] Forgive me if I haven't really expressed my gratitude to all of you. This has been such a shock to me. I'd always thought of myself as Dutch. I was born in Holland. My father was born in Holland, and my grandfather. And now . . . after all these years . . . [*He breaks off.*] If you'll excuse me.

[DUSSEL *gives a little bow and hurries off after* ANNE. MR. FRANK *and the others are subdued.*]

ANNE. [*Turning on the light*] Well, here we are.

[DUSSEL *looks around the room. In the main room* MARGOT *speaks to her mother.*]

MARGOT. The news sounds pretty bad, doesn't it? It's so different from what Mr. Kraler tells us. Mr. Kraler says things are improving.

MR. VAN DAAN. I like it better the way Kraler tells it.

ANNE. [*Coming to* DUSSEL] Do you know the de Waals? . . . What's become of them? Their daughter Jopie and I are in the same class. Jopie's my best friend.

DUSSEL. They are gone.

ANNE. Gone?

DUSSEL. With all the others.

ANNE. Oh, no. Not Jopie!

[*She turns away, in tears.* MRS. FRANK *motions to* MARGOT *to comfort her.* MARGOT *goes to* ANNE, *putting her arms comfortingly around her.*]

MRS. VAN DAAN. There were some people called Wagner. They lived near us . . . ?

[*They resume their occupations, quietly.* PETER *goes off into his room. In* ANNE'S *room,* ANNE *turns to* DUSSEL.]

ANNE. You're going to share the room with me.

DUSSEL. I'm a man who's always lived alone. I haven't had to adjust myself to others. I hope you'll bear with me until I learn.

ANNE. Let me help you. [*She takes his brief-case.*] Do you always live all alone? Have you no family at all?

DUSSEL. No one. [*He opens his medicine case and spreads his bottles on the dressing table.*]

ANNE. How dreadful. You must be terribly lonely.

DUSSEL. I'm used to it.

ANNE. I don't think I could ever get used to it. Didn't you even have a pet? A cat, or a dog?

DUSSEL. I have an allergy for fur-bearing animals. They give me asthma.

ANNE. Oh, dear. Peter has a cat.

DUSSEL. Here? He has it here?

ANNE. Yes. But we hardly ever see it. He keeps it in his room all the time. I'm sure it will be all right.

DUSSEL. Let us hope so. [*He takes some pills to fortify himself.*]

ANNE. That's Margot's bed, where you're going to sleep. I sleep on the sofa there. [*Indicating the clothes hooks on the wall*] We cleared these off for your things. [*She goes over to the window.*] The best part about this room . . . you can look down and see a bit of the street and the canal. There's a houseboat . . . you can see the end of it . . . a bargeman lives there with his family . . . They have a baby and he's just beginning to walk and I'm so afraid he's going to fall into the canal some day. I watch him. . . .

DUSSEL. [*Interrupting*] Your father spoke of a schedule.

ANNE. [*Coming away from the window*] Oh, yes. It's mostly about the times we have to be quiet. And times for the w.c. You can use it now if you like.

DUSSEL. [*Stiffly*] No, thank you.

ANNE. I suppose you think it's awful, my talking about a thing like that. But you don't know how important it can get to be, especially when you're frightened . . . About this room, the way Margot and I did . . . she had it to herself in the afternoons for studying, reading . . . lessons, you know . . . and I took the mornings. Would that be all right with you?

DUSSEL. I'm not at my best in the morning.

ANNE. You stay here in the mornings then. I'll take the room in the afternoons.

DUSSEL. Tell me, when you're in here, what happens to me? Where am I spending my time? In there, with all the people?

ANNE. Yes.

DUSSEL. I see. I see.

ANNE. We have supper at half past six.

DUSSEL. [*Going over to the sofa*] Then, if you don't mind . . . I like to lie down quietly for ten minutes before eating. I find it helps the digestion.

ANNE. Of course. I hope I'm not going to be too much of a bother to you. I seem to be able to get everyone's back up.

[DUSSEL *lies down on the sofa, curled up, his back to her.*]

DUSSEL. I always get along very well with children. My patients all bring their children to me, because they know I get on well with them. So don't you worry about that.

[ANNE *leans over him, taking his hand and shaking it gratefully.*]

ANNE. Thank you. Thank you, Mr. Dussel.

[*The lights dim to darkness. The curtain falls on the scene.* ANNE'S VOICE *comes to us faintly at first, and then with increasing power.*]

ANNE'S VOICE. . . . And yesterday I finished Cissy Van Marxvelt's latest book. I think she is a first-class writer. I shall definitely let my children read her. Monday the twenty-first of September, nineteen forty-two. Mr. Dussel and I had another battle yesterday. Yes, Mr. Dussel! According to him, nothing, I repeat . . . nothing, is right about me . . . my appearance, my character, my manners. While he was going on at me I thought . . . sometime I'll give you such a smack that you'll fly right up to the ceiling! Why is it that every grownup thinks he knows the way to bring up children? Particularly the grownups that never had any. I keep wishing that Peter was a girl instead of a boy. Then I would have someone to talk to. Margot's a darling, but she takes everything too seriously. To pause for a moment on the subject of Mrs. Van Daan. I must tell you that her attempts to flirt with father are getting her nowhere. Pim, thank goodness, won't play.

[*As she is saying the last lines, the curtain rises on the darkened scene.* ANNE'S VOICE *fades out.*]

Scene 4

[*It is the middle of the night, several months later. The stage is dark except for a little light which comes through the skylight in* PETER'S *room.*

Everyone is in bed. MR. *and* MRS. FRANK *lie on the couch in the main room, which has been pulled out to serve as a makeshift double bed.*

MARGOT *is sleeping on a mattress on the floor in the main room, behind a curtain stretched across for privacy. The others are all in their accustomed rooms.*

From outside we hear two soldiers singing "Lili Marlene." A girl's high giggle is heard. The sound of running feet is heard coming closer and then fading in the distance. Throughout the scene there is the distant sound of airplanes passing overhead.

A match suddenly flares up in the attic. We dimly see MR. VAN DAAN. *He is getting his bearings. He comes quickly down the stairs, and goes to the cupboard where the food is stored. Again the match flares up, and is as quickly blown out. The dim figure is seen to steal back up the stairs.*

There is quiet for a second or two, broken only by the sound of airplanes, and running feet on the street below.

Suddenly, out of the silence and the dark, we hear ANNE *scream.*]

ANNE. [*Screaming*] No! No! Don't . . . don't take me!

[*She moans, tossing and crying in her sleep. The other people wake, terrified.* DUSSEL *sits up in bed, furious.*]

DUSSEL. Shush! Anne! Anne, for God's sake, shush!

ANNE. [*Still in her nightmare*] Save me! Save me!

[*She screams and screams.* DUSSEL *gets out of bed, going over to her, trying to wake her.*]

DUSSEL. Quiet! Quiet! You want someone to hear?

[*In the main room* MRS. FRANK *grabs a shawl and pulls it around her. She rushes in to* ANNE, *taking her in her arms.* MR. FRANK *hurriedly gets up, putting on his overcoat.* MARGOT *sits up, terrified.* PETER'S *light goes on in his room.*]

MRS. FRANK. [*To* ANNE, *in her room*] Hush, darling, hush. It's all right. It's all right. [*Over her shoulder to* DUSSEL] Will you be kind enough to turn on the light, Mr. Dussel? [*Back to* ANNE] It's nothing, my darling. It was just a dream.

[DUSSEL *turns on the light in the bedroom.* MRS. FRANK *holds* ANNE *in her arms. Gradually* ANNE *comes out of her nightmare still trembling with horror.* MR. FRANK *comes into the room, and goes quickly to the window, looking out to be sure that no one outside has heard* ANNE'S *screams.* MRS. FRANK *holds* ANNE, *talking softly to her. In the main room* MARGOT *stands on a chair, turning on the center hanging lamp. A light goes on in the* VAN DAANS' *room overhead.* PETER *puts his robe on, coming out of his room.*]

DUSSEL. [*To* MRS. FRANK, *blowing his nose*] Something must be done about that child, Mrs. Frank. Yelling like that! Who knows but there's somebody on the streets? She's endangering all our lives.

MRS. FRANK. Anne, darling.

DUSSEL. Every night she twists and turns. I don't sleep. I spend half my night shushing her. And now it's nightmares!

[MARGOT *comes to the door of* ANNE'S *room, followed by* PETER. MR. FRANK *goes to them, indicating that everything is all right.* PETER *takes* MARGOT *back.*]

MRS. FRANK. [*To* ANNE] You're here, safe, you see? Nothing has happened. [*To* DUSSEL] Please, Mr. Dussel, go back to bed. She'll be herself in a minute or two. Won't you, Anne?

DUSSEL. [*Picking up a book and a pillow*] Thank you, but I'm going to the w.c. The one place where there's peace!

[*He stalks out.* MR. VAN DAAN, *in underwear and trousers, comes down the stairs.*]

MR. VAN DAAN. [*To* DUSSEL] What is it? What happened?

DUSSEL. A nightmare. She was having a nightmare!

MR. VAN DAAN. I thought someone was murdering her.

DUSSEL. Unfortunately, no.

[*He goes into the bathroom.* MR. VAN DAAN *goes back up the stairs.* MR. FRANK, *in the main room, sends* PETER *back to his own bedroom.*]

MR. FRANK. Thank you, Peter. Go back to bed.

[PETER *goes back to his room.* MR. FRANK *follows him, turning out the light and looking out the window. Then he goes back to the main room, and gets up on a chair, turning out the center hanging lamp.*]

MRS. FRANK. [*To* ANNE] Would you like some water? [ANNE *shakes her head.*] Was it a very bad dream? Perhaps if you told me . . . ?

ANNE. I'd rather not talk about it.

MRS. FRANK. Poor darling. Try to sleep then. I'll sit right here beside you until you fall asleep. [*She brings a stool over, sitting there.*]

ANNE. You don't have to.

MRS. FRANK. But I'd like to stay with you . . . very much. Really.

ANNE. I'd rather you didn't.

MRS. FRANK. Good night, then.

[*She leans down to kiss* ANNE. ANNE *throws her arm up over her face, turning away.* MRS. FRANK, *hiding her hurt, kisses* ANNE'S *arm.*]

You'll be all right? There's nothing that you want?

ANNE. Will you please ask Father to come.

MRS. FRANK. [*After a second*] Of course, Anne dear.

[*She hurries out into the other room.* MR. FRANK *comes to her as she comes in.*]

Sie verlangt nach Dir![22]

MR. FRANK. [*Sensing her hurt*] Edith, *Liebe, schau . . .*[23]

MRS. FRANK. *Es macht nichts! Ich danke dem lieben Herrgott, dass sie sich wenigstens an Dich wendet, wenn sie Trost braucht! Geh hinein, Otto, sie ist ganz hysterisch vor Angst.*[24] [*As* MR. FRANK *hesitates*] *Geh zu ihr.*[25]

---

22. Sie verlangt nach Dir (sē fer′ länt′ näk dir′): German for "She is asking for you."
23. Liebe, schau (lē′ bə′ shou): German for "Dear, look."
24. Es macht . . . vor Angst (es mäkt nichts ich dän′ kə dəm lē′ bən här′ gôt däs sē sich ven ig stəns än dish ven′ dət ven sē träst broukt gē hē nīn ät tō sē ist gänz hi ste′ rik fär änst): German for "It's all right. I thank dear God that at least she turns to you when she needs comfort. Go in, Otto, she is hysterical because of fear."
25. Geh zu ihr (gē tsoo ēr): German for "Go to her."

[*He looks at her for a second and then goes to get a cup of water for* ANNE. MRS. FRANK *sinks down on the bed, her face in her hands, trying to keep from sobbing aloud.* MARGOT *comes over to her, putting her arms around her.*]

She wants nothing of me. She pulled away when I leaned down to kiss her.

MARGOT. It's a phase . . . You heard Father . . . Most girls go through it . . . they turn to their fathers at this age . . . they give all their love to their fathers.

MRS. FRANK. You weren't like this. You didn't shut me out.

MARGOT. She'll get over it . . .

[*She smooths the bed for* MRS. FRANK *and sits beside her a moment as* MRS. FRANK *lies down. In* ANNE'S *room* MR. FRANK *comes in, sitting down by* ANNE. ANNE *flings her arms around him, clinging to him. In the distance we hear the sound of ack-ack.*]

ANNE. Oh, Pim. I dreamed that they came to get us! The Green Police! They broke down the door and grabbed me and started to drag me out the way they did Jopie.

MR. FRANK. I want you to take this pill.

ANNE. What is it?

MR. FRANK. Something to quiet you.

[*She takes it and drinks the water. In the main room* MARGOT *turns out the light and goes back to her bed.*]

MR. FRANK. [*To* ANNE] Do you want me to read to you for a while?

ANNE. No. Just sit with me for a minute. Was I awful? Did I yell terribly loud? Do you think anyone outside could have heard?

MR. FRANK. No. No. Lie quietly now. Try to sleep.

ANNE. I'm a terrible coward. I'm so disappointed in myself. I think I've conquered my fear . . . I think I'm really grown-up . . . and then something happens . . . and I run to you like a baby . . . I love you, Father. I don't love anyone but you.

MR. FRANK. [*Reproachfully*] Annele!

ANNE. It's true. I've been thinking about it for a long time. You're the only one I love.

MR. FRANK. It's fine to hear you tell me that you love me. But I'd be happier if you said you loved your mother as well . . . She needs your help so much . . . your love . . .

ANNE. We have nothing in common. She doesn't understand me. Whenever I try to explain my views on life to her she asks me if I'm constipated.

MR. FRANK. You hurt her very much just now. She's crying. She's in there crying.

ANNE. I can't help it. I only told the truth. I didn't want her here . . . [*Then, with sud-*

Scene along a canal in Amsterdam after a bombing raid

den change] Oh, Pim, I was horrible, wasn't I? And the worst of it is, I can stand off and look at myself doing it and know it's cruel and yet I can't stop doing it. What's the matter with me? Tell me. Don't say it's just a phase! Help me.

MR. FRANK. There is so little that we parents can do to help our children. We can only try to set a good example . . . point the way. The rest you must do yourself. You must build your own character.

ANNE. I'm trying. Really I am. Every night I think back over all of the things I did that day that were wrong . . . like putting the wet mop in Mr. Dussel's bed . . . and this thing now with Mother. I say to myself, that was wrong. I make up my mind, I'm never going to do that again. Never! Of course I may do something worse . . . but at least I'll never do *that* again! . . . I have a nicer side, Father . . . a sweeter, nicer side. But I'm scared to show it. I'm afraid that people are going to laugh at me if I'm serious. So the mean Anne comes to the outside and the good Anne stays on the inside, and I keep on trying to switch them around and have the good Anne outside and the bad Anne inside and be what I'd like to be . . . and might be . . . if only . . . only . . .

[*She is asleep.* MR. FRANK *watches her for a moment and then turns off the light, and starts out. The lights dim out. The curtain falls on the scene.* ANNE'S VOICE *is heard dimly at first, and then with growing strength.*]

ANNE'S VOICE. . . . The air raids are getting worse. They come over day and night. The noise is terrifying. Pim says it should be music to our ears. The more planes, the sooner will come the end of the war. Mrs. Van Daan pretends to be a fatalist. What

will be, will be. But when the planes come over, who is the most frightened? No one else but Petronella! . . . Monday, the ninth of November, nineteen forty-two. Wonderful news! The Allies have landed in Africa. Pim says that we can look for an early finish to the war. Just for fun he asked each of us what was the first thing we wanted to do when we got out of here. Mrs. Van Daan longs to be home with her own things, her needle-point chairs, the Beckstein piano her father gave her . . . the best that money could buy. Peter would like to go to a movie. Mr. Dussel wants to get back to his dentist's drill. He's afraid he is losing his touch. For myself, there are so many things . . . to ride a bike again . . . to laugh till my belly aches . . . to have new clothes from the skin out . . . to have a hot tub filled to overflowing and wallow in it for hours . . . to be back in school with my friends . . .

[*As the last lines are being said, the curtain rises on the scene. The lights dim on as* ANNE'S VOICE *fades away.*]

Scene 5

[*It is the first night of the Hanukkah*[26] *celebration.* MR. FRANK *is standing at the head of the table on which is the Menorah.*[27] *He lights the Shamos,*[28] *or servant candle, and holds it as he says the blessing. Seated*

---

26. Hanukkah (khä′ noo kä′) *n.*: A Jewish celebration that lasts eight days.
27. menorah (mə nō′ rə) *n.*: A candle holder with nine candles, used during Hanukkah.
28. shamos (shä′ məs) *n.*: The candle used to light the others in a menorah.

listening is all of the "family," dressed in their best. The men wear hats, PETER *wears his cap.*]

MR. FRANK. [*Reading from a prayer book*] "Praised be Thou, oh Lord our God, Ruler of the universe, who has sanctified us with Thy commandments and bidden us kindle the Hanukkah lights. Praised be Thou, oh Lord our God, Ruler of the universe, who has wrought wondrous deliverances for our fathers in days of old. Praised be Thou, oh Lord our God, Ruler of the universe, that Thou has given us life and sustenance and brought us to this happy season." [MR. FRANK *lights the one candle of the Menorah as he continues.*] "We kindle this Hanukkah light to celebrate the great and wonderful deeds wrought through the zeal with which God filled the hearts of the heroic Maccabees, two thousand years ago. They fought against indifference, against tyranny and oppression, and they restored our Temple to us. May these lights remind us that we should ever look to God, whence cometh our help." Amen.

ALL. Amen.

[MR. FRANK *hands* MRS. FRANK *the prayer book.*]

MRS. FRANK. [*Reading*] "I lift up mine eyes unto the mountains, from whence cometh my help. My help cometh from the Lord who made heaven and earth. He will not suffer thy foot to be moved. He that keepeth thee will not slumber. He that keepeth Israel doth neither slumber nor sleep. The Lord is thy keeper. The Lord is thy shade upon thy right hand. The sun shall not smite thee by day, nor the moon by night. The Lord shall keep thee from all evil. He shall keep thy soul. The Lord shall guard thy going out and thy com-ing in, from this time forth and forever-more." Amen.

ALL. Amen.

[MRS. FRANK *puts down the prayer book and goes to get the food and wine.* MARGOT *helps her.* MR. FRANK *takes the men's hats and puts them aside.*]

DUSSEL. [*Rising*] That was very moving.

ANNE. [*Pulling him back*] It isn't over yet!

MRS. VAN DAAN. Sit down! Sit down!

ANNE. There's a lot more, songs and presents.

DUSSEL. Presents?

MRS. FRANK. Not this year, unfortunately.

MRS. VAN DAAN. But always on Hanukkah everyone gives presents . . . everyone!

DUSSEL. Like our St. Nicholas' Day.[29]

[*There is a chorus of "no's" from the group.*]

MRS. VAN DAAN. No! Not like St. Nicholas! What kind of a Jew are you that you don't know Hanukkah?

MRS. FRANK. [*As she brings the food*] I remember particularly the candles . . . First one, as we have tonight. Then the second night you light two candles, the next night three . . . and so on until you have eight candles burning. When there are eight candles it is truly beautiful.

MRS. VAN DAAN. And the potato pancakes.

MR. VAN DAAN. Don't talk about them!

MRS. VAN DAAN. I make the best *latkes* you ever tasted!

---

29. St. Nicholas' Day: December 6, the day Christian children in Holland receive gifts.

MRS. FRANK. Invite us all next year . . . in your own home.

MR. FRANK. God willing!

MRS. VAN DAAN. God willing.

MARGOT. What I remember best is the presents we used to get when we were little . . . eight days of presents . . . and each day they got better and better.

MRS. FRANK. [*Sitting down*] We are all here, alive. That is present enough.

ANNE. No, it isn't. I've got something . . .[*She rushes into her room, hurriedly puts on a little hat improvised from the lamp shade, grabs a satchel bulging with parcels and comes running back.*]

MRS. FRANK. What is it?

ANNE. Presents!

MRS. VAN DAAN. Presents!

DUSSEL. Look!

MR. VAN DAAN. What's she got on her head?

PETER. A lamp shade!

ANNE. [*She picks out one at random.*] This is for Margot. [*She hands it to* MARGOT, *pulling her to her feet.*] Read it out loud.

MARGOT. [*Reading*]
"You have never lost your temper.
You never will, I fear,
You are so good.
But if you should,
Put all your cross words here."

[*She tears open the package.*] A new crossword puzzle book! Where did you get it?

ANNE. It isn't new. It's one that you've done. But I rubbed it all out, and if you wait a little and forget, you can do it all over again.

MARGOT. [*Sitting*] It's wonderful, Anne. Thank you. You'd never know it wasn't new.

[*From outside we hear the sound of a streetcar passing.*]

ANNE. [*With another gift*] Mrs. Van Daan.

MRS. VAN DAAN. [*Taking it*] This is awful . . . I haven't anything for anyone . . . I never thought . . .

MR. FRANK. This is all Anne's idea.

MRS. VAN DAAN. [*Holding up a bottle*] What is it?

ANNE. It's hair shampoo. I took all the odds and ends of soap and mixed them with the last of my toilet water.

MRS. VAN DAAN. Oh, Anneke!

ANNE. I wanted to write a poem for all of them, but I didn't have time. [*Offering a large box to* MR. VAN DAAN] Yours, Mr. Van Daan, is *really* something . . . something you want more than anything. [*As she waits for him to open it*] Look! Cigarettes!

MR. VAN DAAN. Cigarettes!

ANNE. Two of them! Pim found some old pipe tobacco in the pocket lining of his coat . . . and we made them . . . or rather, Pim did.

MRS. VAN DAAN. Let me see . . . Well, look at that! Light it, Putti! Light it.

[MR. VAN DAAN *hesitates.*]

ANNE. It's tobacco, really it is! There's a little fluff in it, but not much.

[*Everyone watches intently as* MR. VAN DAAN *cautiously lights it. The cigarette flares up. Everyone laughs.*]

PETER. It works!

MRS. VAN DAAN. Look at him.

Margot and Anne Frank

MR. VAN DAAN. [*Spluttering*] Thank you, Anne. Thank you.

[ANNE *rushes back to her satchel for another present.*]

ANNE. [*Handing her mother a piece of paper*] For Mother, Hanukkah greeting.

[*She pulls her mother to her feet.*]

MRS. FRANK. [*She reads*]
"Here's an I.O.U. that I promise to pay.
Ten hours of doing whatever you say.
Signed, Anne Frank." [MRS. FRANK, *touched, takes* ANNE *in her arms, holding her close.*]

DUSSEL. [*To* ANNE] Ten hours of doing what you're told? *Anything* you're told?

ANNE. That's right.

DUSSEL. You wouldn't want to sell that, Mrs. Frank?

MRS. FRANK. Never! This is the most precious gift I've ever had!

[*She sits, showing her present to the others.* ANNE *hurries back to the satchel and pulls out a scarf, the scarf that* MR. FRANK *found in the first scene.*]

ANNE. [*Offering it to her father*] For Pim.

MR. FRANK. Anneke . . . I wasn't supposed to have a present! [*He takes it, unfolding it and showing it to the others.*]

ANNE. It's a muffler . . . to put round your neck . . . like an ascot, you know. I made it myself out of odds and ends . . . I knitted it in the dark each night, after I'd gone to bed. I'm afraid it looks better in the dark!

MR. FRANK. [*Putting it on*] It's fine. It fits me perfectly. Thank you, Annele.

[ANNE *hands* PETER *a ball of paper; with a string attached to it.*]

ANNE. That's for Mouschi.

PETER. [*Rising to bow*] On behalf of Mouschi, I thank you.

ANNE. [*Hesitant, handing him a gift*] And . . . this is yours . . . from Mrs. Quack Quack. [*As he holds it gingerly in his hands*] Well . . . open it . . . Aren't you going to open it?

PETER. I'm scared to. I know something's going to jump out and hit me.

ANNE. No. It's nothing like that, really.

MRS. VAN DAAN. [*As he is opening it*] What is it, Peter? Go on. Show it.

ANNE. [*Excitedly*] It's a safety razor!

DUSSEL. A what?

ANNE. A razor!

MRS. VAN DAAN. [*Looking at it*] You didn't make that out of odds and ends.

ANNE. [*To* PETER] Miep got it for me. It's not new. It's second-hand. But you really do need a razor now.

DUSSEL. For what?

ANNE. Look on his upper lip . . . you can see the beginning of a mustache.

DUSSEL. He wants to get rid of that? Put a little milk on it and let the cat lick it off.

PETER. [*Starting for his room*] Think you're funny, don't you.

DUSSEL. Look! He can't wait! He's going in to try it!

PETER. I'm going to give Mouschi his present!

[*He goes into his room, slamming the door behind him.*]

MR. VAN DAAN. [*Disgustedly*] Mouschi, Mouschi, Mouschi.

[*In the distance we hear a dog persistently barking.* ANNE *brings a gift to* DUSSEL.]

ANNE. And last but never least, my roommate, Mr. Dussel.

DUSSEL. For me? You have something for me?

[*He opens the small box she gives him.*]

ANNE. I made them myself.

DUSSEL. [*Puzzled*] Capsules! Two capsules!

ANNE. They're ear-plugs!

DUSSEL. Ear-plugs?

ANNE. To put in your ears so you won't hear me when I thrash around at night. I saw them advertised in a magazine. They're not real ones . . . I made them out of cotton and candle wax. Try them . . . See if they don't work . . . see if you can hear me talk . . .

DUSSEL. [*Putting them in his ears*] Wait now until I get them in . . . so.

ANNE. Are you ready?

DUSSEL. Huh?

ANNE. Are you ready?

DUSSEL. Oh! They've gone inside! I can't get them out! [*They laugh as* MR. DUSSEL *jumps about, trying to shake the plugs out of his ears. Finally he gets them out. Putting them away*] Thank you, Anne! Thank you!

MR. VAN DAAN. A real Hanukkah!

MRS. VAN DAAN. Wasn't it cute of her?

MRS. FRANK. I don't know when she did it.

MARGOT. I love my present.

[*Together*]

ANNE. [*Sitting at the table*] And now let's have the song, Father . . . please . . . [*To* DUSSEL] Have you heard the Hanukkah song, Mr. Dussel? The song is the whole thing! [*She sings.*] "Oh, Hanukkah! Oh Hanukkah! The sweet celebration . . ."

MR. FRANK. [*Quieting her*] I'm afraid, Anne, we shouldn't sing that song tonight. [*To* DUSSEL] It's a song of jubilation, of rejoicing. One is apt to become too enthusiastic.

ANNE. Oh, please, please. Let's sing the song. I promise not to shout!

MR. FRANK. Very well. But quietly now . . . I'll keep an eye on you and when . . .

[*As* ANNE *starts to sing, she is interrupted by* DUSSEL, *who is snorting and wheezing.*]

DUSSEL. [*Pointing to* PETER] You . . . You!

[PETER *is coming from his bedroom, ostentatiously holding a bulge in his coat as if he were holding his cat, and dangling* ANNE'S *present before it.*]

How many times . . . I told you . . . Out! Out!

MR. VAN DAAN. [*Going to* PETER] What's the matter with you? Haven't you any sense? Get that cat out of here.

PETER. [*Innocently*] Cat?

MR. VAN DAAN. You heard me. Get it out of here!

PETER. I have no cat. [*Delighted with his joke, he opens his coat and pulls out a bath towel. The group at the table laugh, enjoying the joke.*]

DUSSEL. [*Still wheezing*] It doesn't need to be the cat . . . his clothes are enough . . . when he comes out of that room . . .

MR. VAN DAAN. Don't worry. You won't be bothered any more. We're getting rid of it.

DUSSEL. At last you listen to me. [*He goes off into his bedroom.*]

MR. VAN DAAN. [*Calling after him*] I'm not doing it for you. That's all in your mind . . . all of it! [*He starts back to his place at the table.*] I'm doing it because I'm sick of seeing that cat eat all our food.

PETER. That's not true! I only give him bones . . . scraps . . .

MR. VAN DAAN. Don't tell me! He gets fatter every day! That cat looks better than any of us. Out he goes tonight!

PETER. No! No!

ANNE. Mr. Van Daan, you can't do that! That's Peter's cat. Peter loves that cat.

MRS. FRANK. [*Quietly*] Anne.

PETER. [*To* MR. VAN DAAN] If he goes, I go.

MR. VAN DAAN. Go! Go!

MRS. VAN DAAN. You're not going and the cat's not going! Now please . . . this is Hanukkah . . . Hanukkah . . . this is the time to celebrate . . . What's the matter with all of you? Come on, Anne. Let's have the song.

ANNE. [*Singing*]

"Oh, Hanukkah! Oh, Hanukkah!
The sweet celebration."

MR. FRANK. [*Rising*] I think we should first blow out the candle . . . then we'll have something for tomorrow night.

MARGOT. But, Father, you're supposed to let it burn itself out.

MR. FRANK. I'm sure that God understands shortages. [*Before blowing it out*] "Praised be Thou, oh Lord our God, who hast sustained us and permitted us to celebrate this joyous festival."

[*He is about to blow out the candle when suddenly there is a crash of something falling below. They all freeze in horror, motionless. For a few seconds there is complete silence.* MR. FRANK *slips off his shoes. The others noiselessly follow his example.* MR. FRANK *turns out a light near him. He motions to* PETER *to turn off the center lamp.* PETER *tries to reach it, realizes he cannot and gets up on a chair. Just as he is touching the lamp he loses his balance. The chair goes out from under him. He falls. The iron lamp shade crashes to the floor. There is a sound of feet below, running down the stairs.*]

MR. VAN DAAN. [*Under his breath*] Oh, oh!

[*The only light left comes from the Hanukkah candle.* DUSSEL *comes from his room.* MR. FRANK *creeps over to the stairwell and stands listening. The dog is heard barking excitedly.*]

Do you hear anything?

MR. FRANK. [*In a whisper*] No. I think they've gone.

MRS. VAN DAAN. It's the Green Police. They've found us.

MR. FRANK. If they had, they wouldn't have left. They'd be up here by now.

MRS. VAN DAAN. I know it's the Green Police. They've gone to get help. That's all. They'll be back!

MR. VAN DAAN. Or it may have been the Gestapo,[30] looking for papers . . .

MR. FRANK. [*Interrupting*] Or a thief, looking for money.

MRS. VAN DAAN. We've got to do something . . . Quick! Quick! Before they come back.

MR. VAN DAAN. There isn't anything to do. Just wait.

[MR. FRANK *holds up his hand for them to be quiet. He is listening intently. There is complete silence as they all strain to hear any sound from below. Suddenly* ANNE *begins to sway. With a low cry she falls to the floor in a faint.* MRS. FRANK *goes to her quickly, sitting beside her on the floor and taking her in her arms.*]

MRS. FRANK. Get some water, please! Get some water!

[MARGOT *starts for the sink.*]

MR. VAN DAAN. [*Grabbing* MARGOT] No! No! No one's going to run water!

MR. FRANK. If they've found us, they've found us. Get the water. [MARGOT *starts again for the sink.* MR. FRANK, *getting a flashlight*] I'm going down.

[MARGOT *rushes to him, clinging to him.* ANNE *struggles to consciousness.*]

MARGOT. No, Father, no! There may be someone there, waiting . . . It may be a trap!

---

30. Gestapo (gə stä′ pō) *n.*: The secret police force of the German Nazi state, known for its terrorism and atrocities.

MR. FRANK. This is Saturday. There is no way for us to know what has happened until Miep or Mr. Kraler comes on Monday morning. We cannot live with this uncertainty.

MARGOT. Don't go, Father!

MRS. FRANK. Hush, darling, hush.

[MR. FRANK *slips quietly out, down the steps and out through the door below.*]

Margot! Stay close to me.

[MARGOT *goes to her mother.*]

MR. VAN DAAN. Shush! Shush!

[MRS. FRANK *whispers to* MARGOT *to get the water.* MARGOT *goes for it.*]

MRS. VAN DAAN. Putti, where's our money? Get our money. I hear you can buy the Green Police off, so much a head. Go upstairs quick! Get the money!

MR. VAN DAAN. Keep still!

MRS. VAN DAAN. [*Kneeling before him, pleading*] Do you want to be dragged off to a concentration camp? Are you going to stand there and wait for them to come up and get you? Do something, I tell you!

MR. VAN DAAN. [*Pushing her aside*] Will you keep still!

[*He goes over to the stairwell to listen.* PETER *goes to his mother, helping her up onto the sofa. There is a second of silence, then* ANNE *can stand it no longer.*]

ANNE. Someone go after Father! Make Father come back!

PETER. [*Starting for the door*] I'll go.

MR. VAN DAAN. Haven't you done enough?

[*He pushes* PETER *roughly away. In his anger against his father* PETER *grabs a chair*

as if to hit him with it, then puts it down, burying his face in his hands. MRS. FRANK *begins to pray softly.*]

ANNE. Please, please, Mr. Van Daan. Get Father.

MR. VAN DAAN. Quiet! Quiet!

[ANNE *is shocked into silence.* MRS. FRANK *pulls her closer, holding her protectively in her arms.*]

MRS. FRANK. [*Softly, praying*] "I lift up mine eyes unto the mountains, from whence cometh my help. My help cometh from the Lord who made heaven and earth. He will not suffer thy foot to be moved . . . He that keepeth thee will not slumber . . ."

[*She stops as she hears someone coming. They all watch the door tensely.* MR. FRANK *comes quietly in.* ANNE *rushes to him, holding him tight.*]

MR. FRANK. It was a thief. That noise must have scared him away.

MRS. VAN DAAN. Thank goodness.

MR. FRANK. He took the cash box. And the radio. He ran away in such a hurry that he didn't stop to shut the street door. It was swinging wide open. [*A breath of relief sweeps over them.*] I think it would be good to have some light.

MARGOT. Are you sure it's all right?

MR. FRANK. The danger has passed.

[MARGOT *goes to light the small lamp.*]

Don't be so terrified, Anne. We're safe.

DUSSEL. Who says the danger has passed? Don't you realize we are in greater danger than ever?

MR. FRANK. Mr. Dussel, will you be still!

[MR. FRANK *takes* ANNE *back to the table, making her sit down with him, trying to calm her.*]

DUSSEL. [*Pointing to* PETER] Thanks to this clumsy fool, there's someone now who knows we're up here! Someone now knows we're up here, hiding!

MRS. VAN DAAN. [*Going to* DUSSEL] Someone knows we're here, yes. But who is the someone? A thief! A thief! You think a thief is going to go to the Green Police and say . . . I was robbing a place the other night and I heard a noise up over my head? You think a thief is going to do that?

DUSSEL. Yes. I think he will.

MRS. VAN DAAN. [*Hysterically*] You're crazy!

[*She stumbles back to her seat at the table.* PETER *follows protectively, pushing* DUSSEL *aside.*]

DUSSEL. I think some day he'll be caught and then he'll make a bargain with the Green Police . . . if they'll let him off, he'll tell them where some Jews are hiding!

[*He goes off into the bedroom. There is a second of appalled silence.*]

MR. VAN DAAN. He's right.

ANNE. Father, let's get out of here! We can't stay here now . . . Let's go . . .

MR. VAN DAAN. Go! Where?

MRS. FRANK. [*Sinking into her chair at the table*] Yes. Where?

MR. FRANK. [*Rising, to them all*] Have we lost all faith? All courage? A moment ago we thought that they'd come for us. We were sure it was the end. But it wasn't the end. We're alive, safe.

[MR. VAN DAAN *goes to the table and sits.* MR. FRANK *prays.*]

"We thank Thee, oh Lord our God, that in Thy infinite mercy Thou hast again seen fit to spare us." [*He blows out the candle, then turns to* ANNE.] Come on, Anne. The song! Let's have the song!

[*He starts to sing.* ANNE *finally starts falteringly to sing, as* MR. FRANK *urges her on. Her voice is hardly audible at first.*]

ANNE. [*Singing*]
"Oh, Hanukkah! Oh, Hanukkah!
The sweet . . . celebration . . ."

[*As she goes on singing, the others gradually join in, their voices still shaking with fear.* MRS. VAN DAAN *sobs as she sings.*]

GROUP.
"Around the feast . . . we . . . gather
In complete . . . jubilation . . .
Happiest of sea . . . sons
Now is here.
Many are the reasons for good cheer."

[DUSSEL *comes from the bedroom. He comes over to the table, standing beside* MARGOT, *listening to them as they sing.*]

"Together
We'll weather
Whatever tomorrow may bring."

[*As they sing on with growing courage, the lights start to dim.*]

"So hear us rejoicing
And merrily voicing
The Hanukkah song that we sing.
Hoy!"

[*The lights are out. The curtain starts slowly to fall.*]

"Hear us rejoicing
And merrily voicing
The Hanukkah song that we sing."
[*They are still singing, as the curtain falls.*]

THINKING ABOUT THE SELECTION

Recalling

1. How does going into hiding affect Anne at first?
2. Explain the special precautions the two families take in order to prevent discovery.
3. When does Anne realize what going into hiding really means?
4. In what ways do the families try to live their lives normally? Which events intrude, showing that their lives are not normal?
5. What are Anne's dreams for her future? What fears are revealed through her nightmares?
6. What special meaning does Hanukkah have for the families? How does Anne make the celebration particularly special?

Interpreting

7. Compare and contrast Peter and Anne. How do their differences account for the reaction of each to removing the yellow star?
8. Compare and contrast Margot and Anne. How does the difference between the two characters account for each's relationship with Mrs. Frank?
9. Mr. Frank tells Anne, "There are no walls, there are no bolts, no locks that anyone can put on your mind." Explain this statement. How does Anne prove its truth?
10. Describe the mood at the end of Act I. What event has caused this mood?

Applying

11. Like the Franks and Van Daans, many people turn to traditions and celebrations to give them courage in times of trouble. How do such traditions help us through difficult times?
12. Does the fact that Anne Frank was a real person make this play more meaningful for you? Explain your answer.

ANALYZING LITERATURE

Appreciating the Use of Flashback

The play opens with Mr. Frank returning to the warehouse apartment in 1945 after the war. Once he has begun reading the diary, the action flashes back to 1942.

1. From whose point of view are the events seen at the beginning of the play?
2. During the flashback, to what character does the point of view shift?
3. Why is using a flashback more effective than having Mr. Frank simply tell what had happened in 1942?

CRITICAL THINKING AND READING

Predicting Outcomes

As you read, you continually make predictions about what will happen next. You make predictions based on clues authors provide and on your own experiences and those about which you have read.

As you make the following predictions, give two clues from Act I on which you base your predictions.

1. Choose two characters from this play. How do you think being in hiding will affect the relationship of these characters?
2. What do you think will happen to Anne?

THINKING AND WRITING

Writing as a Character in the Play

Pretend you are either Anne or Peter. Write a letter to Jopie or to another friend about what life in hiding is like. Before you start writing, list several topics you want to include. The topics might be how you spend your day, how your relationships with people have changed, and so forth. When you have finished your letter, make sure your spelling and punctuation are correct.

GUIDE FOR READING

The Diary of Anne Frank, Act II

Characters and Theme

Act II begins a little more than a year after the end of Act I. The passage of time, along with the characters' living so closely together and always in fear, has changed the characters. Observing the changes in the characters can help you to understand the theme of the play.

When Anne Frank wrote the diary from which this play was created, she may not have set out to present a **theme,** or general observation about life. Nevertheless, the events in the play do point to a strong theme.

Look For

As you read Act II, notice the changes in the characters. Which have changed most? Which have changed least? Which have changed for the better? Which for the worse? How have these changes affected their relationships? What role does hope play in their lives?

Writing

O.S. Marden has written: "There is no medicine like hope, no incentive so great, and no tonic so powerful as expectation of something tomorrow." Freewrite for five minutes about hope. Think about a time when you or someone you know faced a difficult situation. What part did hope play in the situation? What enables people who face difficult circumstances to have hope in the future?

Vocabulary

Knowing the following words will help you as you read *The Diary of Anne Frank,* Act II.

inarticulate (in' är tik' yə lit) *adj.*: Speechless or unable to express oneself (p. 347)

apprehension (ap' rə hen' shən) *n.*: A fearful feeling about the future; dread (p. 349)

intuition (in'tŏŏ wish'ən) *n.*: Ability to know immediately, without reasoning (p. 354)

sarcastic (sär kas' tik) *adj.*: Speaking with sharp mocking intended to hurt another (p. 355)

indignant (in dig' nənt) *adj.*: Filled with anger over some meanness or injustice (p. 356)

inferiority complex (in fir'ē ôr'ə tē käm' pleks) *n.*: Tendency to belittle oneself (p. 356)

stealthily (stel' thi lē') *adv.*: In a secretive or sneaky manner (p. 359)

ineffectually (in'i fek'chŏŏ wə lē) *adv.*: Without producing the desired effect (p. 365)

ACT II

Scene 1

[*In the darkness we hear* ANNE'S VOICE, *again reading from the diary.*]

ANNE'S VOICE. Saturday, the first of January, nineteen forty-four. Another new year has begun and we find ourselves still in our hiding place. We have been here now for one year, five months and twenty-five days. It seems that our life is at a standstill.

[*The curtain rises on the scene. It is late afternoon. Everyone is bundled up against the cold. In the main room* MRS. FRANK *is taking down the laundry which is hung across the back.* MR. FRANK *sits in the chair down left, reading.* MARGOT *is lying on the couch with a blanket over her and the many-colored knitted scarf around her throat.* ANNE *is seated at the center table, writing in her diary.* PETER, MR. *and* MRS. VAN DAANS *and* DUSSEL *are all in their own rooms, reading or lying down.*

As the lights dim on, ANNE'S VOICE *continues, without a break.*]

ANNE'S VOICE. We are all a little thinner. The Van Daans' "discussions" are as violent as ever. Mother still does not understand me. But then I don't understand her either. There is one great change, however. A change in myself. I read somewhere that girls of my age don't feel quite certain of themselves. . . .

[*We hear the chimes and then a hymn being played on the carillon outside. The buzzer of the door below suddenly sounds. Everyone is startled,* MR. FRANK *tiptoes cautiously to the top of the steps and listens. Again the buzzer sounds, in* MIEP'S *V-for-Victory signal.[1]*]

---

1. V-for-Victory signal: Three short rings and one long one (the letter *V* in Morse code).

The Westertoren Church tower as seen through the window of the attic hiding place

MR. FRANK. It's Miep!

[*He goes quickly down the steps to unbolt the door.* MRS. FRANK *calls upstairs to the* VAN DAANS *and then to* PETER.]

MRS. FRANK. Wake up, everyone! Miep is here!

[ANNE *quickly puts her diary away.* MARGOT *sits up, pulling the blanket around her shoulders.* MR. DUSSEL *sits on the edge of his bed, listening, disgruntled.* MIEP *comes up the steps, followed by* MR. KRALER. *They bring flowers, books, newspapers, etc.* ANNE *rushes to* MIEP, *throwing her arms affectionately around her.*]

Miep . . . and Mr. Kraler . . . What a delightful surprise!

MR. KRALER. We came to bring you New Year's greetings.

MRS. FRANK. You shouldn't . . . you should have at least one day to yourselves. [*She goes quickly to the stove and brings down teacups and tea for all of them.*]

ANNE. Don't say that, it's so wonderful to see them! [*Sniffing at* MIEP'S *coat*] I can smell the wind and the cold on your clothes.

MIEP. [*Giving her the flowers*] There you are. [*Then to* MARGOT, *feeling her forehead*] How are you, Margot? . . . Feeling any better?

MARGOT. I'm all right.

ANNE. We filled her full of every kind of pill so she won't cough and make a noise.

[*She runs into her room to put the flowers in water.* MR. *and* MRS. VAN DAAN *come from upstairs. Outside there is the sound of a band playing.*]

MRS. VAN DAAN. Well, hello, Miep. Mr. Kraler.

MR. KRALER. [*Giving a bouquet of flowers to* MRS. VAN DAAN] With my hope for peace in the New Year.

PETER. [*Anxiously*] Miep, have you seen Mouschi? Have you seen him anywhere around?

MIEP. I'm sorry, Peter. I asked everyone in the neighborhood had they seen a gray cat. But they said no.

[MRS. FRANK *gives* MIEP *a cup of tea.* MR. FRANK *comes up the steps, carrying a small cake on a plate.*]

MR. FRANK. Look what Miep's brought for us!

MRS. FRANK. [*Taking it*] A cake!

MR. VAN DAAN. A cake! [*He pinches* MIEP'S

cheeks gaily and hurries up to the cupboard.] I'll get some plates.

[DUSSEL, *in his room, hastily puts a coat on and starts out to join the others.*]

MRS. FRANK. Thank you, Miepia. You shouldn't have done it. You must have used all of your sugar ration for weeks. [*Giving it to* MRS. VAN DAAN] It's beautiful, isn't it?

MRS. VAN DAAN. It's been ages since I even saw a cake. Not since you brought us one last year. [*Without looking at the cake, to* MIEP] Remember? Don't you remember, you gave us one on New Year's Day? Just this time last year? I'll never forget it because you had "Peace in nineteen forty-three" on it. [*She looks at the cake and reads*] "Peace in nineteen forty-four!"

MIEP. Well, it has to come sometime, you know. [*As* DUSSEL *comes from his room*] Hello, Mr. Dussel.

MR. KRALER. How are you?

MR. VAN DAAN. [*Bringing plates and a knife*] Here's the knife, *liefje*. Now, how many of us are there?

MIEP. None for me, thank you.

MR. FRANK. Oh, please. You must.

MIEP. I couldn't.

MR. VAN DAAN. Good! That leaves one . . . two . . . three . . . seven of us.

DUSSEL. Eight! Eight! It's the same number as it always is!

MR. VAN DAAN. I left Margot out. I take it for granted Margot won't eat any.

ANNE. Why wouldn't she!

MRS. FRANK. I think it won't harm her.

MR. VAN DAAN. All right! All right! I just didn't want her to start coughing again, that's all.

DUSSEL. And please, Mrs. Frank should cut the cake.

MR. VAN DAAN. What's the difference?

MRS. VAN DAAN. It's not Mrs. Frank's cake, is it, Miep? It's for all of us.

Together

DUSSEL. Mrs. Frank divides things better.

MRS. VAN DAAN. [*Going to* DUSSEL] What are you trying to say?

MR. VAN DAAN. Oh, come on! Stop wasting time!

Together

MRS. VAN DAAN. [*To* DUSSEL] Don't I always give everybody exactly the same? Don't I?

MR. VAN DAAN. Forget it, Kerli.

MRS. VAN DAAN. No. I want an answer! Don't I?

DUSSEL. Yes. Yes. Everybody gets exactly the same . . . except Mr. Van Daan always gets a little bit more.

[VAN DAAN *advances on* DUSSEL, *the knife still in his hand.*]

MR. VAN DAAN. That's a lie!

[DUSSEL *retreats before the onslaught of the* VAN DAANS.]

MR. FRANK. Please, please! [*Then to* MIEP] You see what a little sugar cake does to us? It goes right to our heads!

MR. VAN DAAN. [*Handing* MRS. FRANK *the knife*] Here you are, Mrs. Frank.

MRS. FRANK. Thank you. [*Then to* MIEP *as she goes to the table to cut the cake*] Are you sure you won't have some?

MIEP. [*Drinking her tea*] No, really, I have to go in a minute.

[*The sound of the band fades out in the distance.*]

PETER. [*To* MIEP] Maybe Mouschi went back to our house . . . they say that cats . . . Do you ever get over there . . . ? I mean . . . do you suppose you could . . . ?

MIEP. I'll try, Peter. The first minute I get I'll try. But I'm afraid, with him gone a week . . .

DUSSEL. Make up your mind, already someone has had a nice big dinner from that cat!

[PETER *is furious, inarticulate. He starts toward* DUSSEL *as if to hit him.* MR. FRANK *stops him.* MRS. FRANK *speaks quickly to ease the situation.*]

MRS. FRANK. [*To* MIEP] This is delicious, Miep!

MRS. VAN DAAN. [*Eating hers*] Delicious!

MR. VAN DAAN. [*Finishing it in one gulp*] Dirk's in luck to get a girl who can bake like this!

MIEP. [*Putting down her empty teacup*] I have to run. Dirk's taking me to a party tonight.

ANNE. How heavenly! Remember now what everyone is wearing, and what you have to eat and everything, so you can tell us tomorrow.

MIEP. I'll give you a full report! Good-bye, everyone!

MR. VAN DAAN. [*To* MIEP] Just a minute. There's something I'd like you to do for me.

[*He hurries off up the stairs to his room.*]

MRS. VAN DAAN. [*Sharply*] Putti, where are you going? [*She rushes up the stairs after him, calling hysterically.*] What do you want? Putti, what are you going to do?

MIEP. [*To* PETER] What's wrong?

PETER. [*His sympathy is with his mother.*] Father says he's going to sell her fur coat. She's crazy about that old fur coat.

DUSSEL. Is it possible? Is it possible that anyone is so silly as to worry about a fur coat in times like this?

PETER. It's none of your darn business . . . and if you say one more thing . . . I'll, I'll take you and I'll . . . I mean it . . . I'll . . .

[*There is a piercing scream from* MRS. VAN DAAN *above. She grabs at the fur coat as* MR. VAN DAAN *is starting downstairs with it.*]

MRS. VAN DAAN. No! No! No! Don't you dare take that! You hear? It's mine!

[*Downstairs* PETER *turns away, embarrassed, miserable.*]

My father gave me that! You didn't give it to me. You have no right. Let go of it . . . you hear?

[MR. VAN DAAN *pulls the coat from her hands and hurries downstairs.* MRS. VAN DAAN *sinks to the floor, sobbing. As* MR. VAN DAAN *comes into the main room the others look away, embarrassed for him.*]

MR. VAN DAAN. [*To* MR. KRALER] Just a little —discussion over the advisability of selling this coat. As I have often reminded Mrs. Van Daan, it's very selfish of her to keep it when people outside are in such desperate need of clothing . . . [*He gives the coat to* MIEP.] So if you will please to sell it for us? It should fetch a good price. And by the way, will you get me cigarettes. I don't care what kind they are . . . get all you can.

MIEP. It's terribly difficult to get them, Mr. Van Daan. But I'll try. Good-bye.

[*She goes.* MR. FRANK *follows her down the steps to bolt the door after her.* MRS. FRANK *gives* MR. KRALER *a cup of tea.*]

MRS. FRANK. Are you sure you won't have some cake, Mr. Kraler?

MR. KRALER. I'd better not.

MR. VAN DAAN. You're still feeling badly? What does your doctor say?

MR. KRALER. I haven't been to him.

MRS. FRANK. Now, Mr. Kraler! . . .

MR. KRALER. [*Sitting at the table*] Oh, I tried. But you can't get near a doctor these days . . . they're so busy. After weeks I finally managed to get one on the telephone. I told him I'd like an appointment . . . I wasn't feeling very well. You know what he answers . . . over the telephone . . . Stick out your tongue! [*They laugh. He turns to* MR. FRANK *as* MR. FRANK *comes back.*] I have some contracts here . . . I wonder if you'd look over them with me . . .

MR. FRANK. [*Putting out his hand*] Of course.

MR. KRALER. [*He rises*] If we could go downstairs . . . [MR. FRANK *starts ahead;* MR. KRALER *speaks to the others.*] Will you forgive us? I won't keep him but a minute. [*He starts to follow* MR. FRANK *down the steps.*]

MARGOT. [*With sudden foreboding*] What's happened? Something's happened! Hasn't it, Mr. Kraler?

[MR. KRALER *stops and comes back, trying to reassure* MARGOT *with a pretense of casualness.*]

MR. KRALER. No, really. I want your father's advice . . .

MARGOT. Something's gone wrong! I know it!

MR. FRANK. [*Coming back, to* MR. KRALER] If it's something that concerns us here, it's better that we all hear it.

MR. KRALER. [*Turning to him, quietly*] But . . . the children . . . ?

The bookcase moved aside to show the stairs leading to the attic hiding place; the bookcase hiding the stairs

MR. FRANK. What they'd imagine would be worse than any reality.

[*As* MR. KRALER *speaks, they all listen with intense apprehension.* MRS. VAN DAAN *comes down the stairs and sits on the bottom step.*]

MR. KRALER. It's a man in the storeroom . . . I don't know whether or not you remember him . . . Carl, about fifty, heavy-set, near-sighted . . . He came with us just before you left.

MR. FRANK. He was from Utrecht?

MR. KRALER. That's the man. A couple of weeks ago, when I was in the storeroom, he closed the door and asked me . . . how's Mr. Frank? What do you hear from Mr. Frank? I told him I only knew there was a rumor that you were in Switzerland. He said he'd heard that rumor too, but he thought I might know something more. I didn't pay any attention to it . . . but then a thing happened yesterday . . . He'd brought some invoices to the office for me to sign. As I was going through them, I looked up. He was standing staring at the bookcase . . . your bookcase. He said he thought he remembered a door there . . . Wasn't there a door there that used to go up to the loft? Then he told me he wanted more money. Twenty guilders[2] more a week.

---

2. guilders (gil′ dərz) *n.*: The monetary unit of Holland.

MR. VAN DAAN. Blackmail!

MR. FRANK. Twenty guilders? Very modest blackmail.

MR. VAN DAAN. That's just the beginning.

DUSSEL. [*Coming to* MR. FRANK] You know what I think? He was the thief who was down there that night. That's how he knows we're here.

MR. FRANK. [*To* MR. KRALER] How was it left? What did you tell him?

MR. KRALER. I said I had to think about it. What shall I do? Pay him the money? . . . Take a chance on firing him . . . or what? I don't know.

DUSSEL. [*Frantic*] Don't fire him! Pay him what he asks . . . keep him here where you can have your eye on him.

MR. FRANK. Is it so much that he's asking? What are they paying nowadays?

MR. KRALER. He could get it in a war plant. But this isn't a war plant. Mind you, I don't know if he really knows . . . or if he doesn't know.

MR. FRANK. Offer him half. Then we'll soon find out if it's blackmail or not.

DUSSEL. And if it is? We've got to pay it, haven't we? Anything he asks we've got to pay!

MR. FRANK. Let's decide that when the time comes.

MR. KRALER. This may be all my imagination. You get to a point, these days, where you suspect everyone and everything. Again and again . . . on some simple look or word, I've found myself . . .

[*The telephone rings in the office below.*]

MRS. VAN DAAN. [*Hurrying to* MR. KRALER] There's the telephone! What does that mean, the telephone ringing on a holiday?

MR. KRALER. That's my wife. I told her I had to go over some papers in my office . . . to call me there when she got out of church. [*He starts out*] I'll offer him half then. Good-bye . . . we'll hope for the best!

[*The group calls their good-byes half-heartedly.* MR. FRANK *follows* MR. KRALER, *to bolt the door below. During the following scene,* MR. FRANK *comes back up and stands listening, disturbed.*]

DUSSEL. [*To* MR. VAN DAAN] You can thank your son for this . . . smashing the light! I tell you, it's just a question of time now.

[*He goes to the window at the back and stands looking out.*]

MARGOT. Sometimes I wish the end would come . . . whatever it is.

MRS. FRANK. [*Shocked*] Margot!

[ANNE *goes to* MARGOT, *sitting beside her on the couch with her arms around her.*]

MARGOT. Then at least we'd know where we were.

MRS. FRANK. You should be ashamed of yourself! Talking that way! Think how lucky we are! Think of the thousands dying in the war, every day. Think of the people in concentration camps.

ANNE. [*Interrupting*] What's the good of that? What's the good of thinking of misery when you're already miserable? That's stupid!

MRS. FRANK. Anne!

[*As* ANNE *goes on raging at her mother,* MRS. FRANK *tries to break in, in an effort to quiet her.*]

ANNE. We're young, Margot and Peter and I! You grownups have had your chance! But look at us . . . If we begin thinking of all the horror in the world, we're lost! We're trying to hold onto some kind of ideals . . . when everything . . . ideals, hopes . . . everything, are being destroyed! It isn't our fault that the world is in such a mess! We weren't around when all this started! So don't try to take it out on us! [*She rushes off to her room, slamming the door after her. She picks up a brush from the chest and hurls it to the floor. Then she sits on the settee, trying to control her anger.*]

MR. VAN DAAN. She talks as if we started the war! Did we start the war?

[*He spots* ANNE'S *cake. As he starts to take it,* PETER *anticipates him.*]

PETER. She left her cake.

[*He starts for* ANNE'S *room with the cake. There is silence in the main room.* MRS. VAN DAAN *goes up to her room, followed by* VAN DAAN. DUSSEL *stays looking out the window.* MR. FRANK *brings* MRS. FRANK *her cake. She eats it slowly, without relish.* MR. FRANK *takes his cake to* MARGOT *and sits quietly on the sofa beside her.* PETER *stands in the doorway of* ANNE'S *darkened room, looking at her, then makes a little movement to let her know he is there.* ANNE *sits up, quickly, trying to hide the signs of her tears.* PETER *holds out the cake to her.*]

You left this.

ANNE. [*Dully*] Thanks.

[PETER *starts to go out, then comes back.*]

PETER. I thought you were fine just now. You know just how to talk to them. You know just how to say it. I'm no good . . . I never can think . . . especially when I'm mad . . . That Dussel . . . when he said that about Mouschi . . . someone eating him . . . all I could think is . . . I wanted to hit him. I wanted to give him such a . . . a . . . that he'd . . . That's what I used to do when there was an argument at school . . . That's the way I . . . but here . . . And an old man like that . . . it wouldn't be so good.

ANNE. You're making a big mistake about me. I do it all wrong. I say too much. I go too far. I hurt people's feelings . . .

[DUSSEL *leaves the window, going to his room.*]

PETER. I think you're just fine . . . What I want to say . . . if it wasn't for you around here, I don't know. What I mean . . .

[PETER *is interrupted by* DUSSEL'S *turning on the light.* DUSSEL *stands in the doorway, startled to see* PETER. PETER *advances toward him forbiddingly.* DUSSEL *backs out of the room.* PETER *closes the door on him.*]

ANNE. Do you mean it, Peter? Do you really mean it?

PETER. I said it, didn't I?

ANNE. Thank you, Peter!

[*In the main room* MR. *and* MRS. FRANK *collect the dishes and take them to the sink, washing them.* MARGOT *lies down again on the couch.* DUSSEL, *lost, wanders into* PETER'S *room and takes up a book, starting to read.*]

PETER. [*Looking at the photographs on the wall*] You've got quite a collection.

ANNE. Wouldn't you like some in your room? I could give you some. Heaven knows you

Anne's bedroom wall in the hiding place and the photographs she hung there

spend enough time in there . . . doing heaven knows what . . .

PETER. It's easier. A fight starts, or an argument . . . I duck in there.

ANNE. You're lucky, having a room to go to. His lordship is always here . . . I hardly ever get a minute alone. When they start in on me, I can't duck away. I have to stand there and take it.

PETER. You gave some of it back just now.

ANNE. I get so mad. They've formed their opinions . . . about everything . . . but we

. . . we're still trying to find out . . . We have problems here that no other people our age have ever had. And just as you think you've solved them, something comes along and bang! You have to start all over again.

PETER. At least you've got someone you can talk to.

ANNE. Not really. Mother . . . I never discuss anything serious with her. She doesn't understand. Father's all right. We can talk about everything . . . everything but one thing. Mother. He simply won't talk about her. I don't think you can be really intimate with anyone if he holds something back, do you?

PETER. I think your father's fine.

ANNE. Oh, he is, Peter! He is! He's the only one who's ever given me the feeling that I have any sense. But anyway, nothing can take the place of school and play and friends of your own age . . . or near your age . . . can it?

PETER. I suppose you miss your friends and all.

ANNE. It isn't just . . . [*She breaks off, staring up at him for a second.*] Isn't it funny, you and I? Here we've been seeing each other every minute for almost a year and a half, and this is the first time we've ever really talked. It helps a lot to have someone to talk to, don't you think? It helps you to let off steam.

PETER. [*Going to the door*] Well, any time you want to let off steam, you can come into my room.

ANNE. [*Following him*] I can get up an awful lot of steam. You'll have to be careful how you say that.

PETER. It's all right with me.

ANNE. Do you mean it?

PETER. I said it, didn't I?

[*He goes out.* ANNE *stands in her doorway looking after him. As* PETER *gets to his door he stands for a minute looking back at her. Then he goes into his room.* DUSSEL *rises as he comes in, and quickly passes him, going out. He starts across for his room.* ANNE *sees him coming, and pulls her door shut.* DUSSEL *turns back toward* PETER'S *room.* PETER *pulls his door shut.* DUSSEL *stands there, bewildered, forlorn.*

The scene slowly dims out. The curtain falls on the scene. ANNE'S VOICE *comes over in the darkness . . . faintly at first, and then with growing strength.*]

ANNE'S VOICE. We've had bad news. The people from whom Miep got our ration books have been arrested. So we have had to cut down on our food. Our stomachs are so empty that they rumble and make strange noises, all in different keys. Mr. Van Daan's is deep and low, like a bass fiddle. Mine is high, whistling like a flute. As we all sit around waiting for supper, it's like an orchestra tuning up. It only needs Toscanini[3] to raise his baton and we'd be off in the Ride of the Valkyries.[4] Monday, the sixth of March, nineteen forty-four. Mr. Kraler is in the hospital. It seems he has ulcers. Pim says we are his ulcers. Miep has to run the business and us too. The Americans have landed on the southern tip of Italy. Father looks for a quick finish to the war. Mr. Dussel is waiting every day for the warehouse man to demand more money. Have I been skipping too much from one subject to another? I can't help it. I feel that spring is coming. I feel it in my whole body and soul. I feel utterly confused. I am longing . . . so longing . . . for everything . . . for friends . . . for someone to talk to . . . someone who understands . . . someone young, who feels as I do . . .

[*As these last lines are being said, the curtain rises on the scene. The lights dim on.* ANNE'S VOICE *fades out.*]

Scene 2

[*It is evening, after supper. From outside we hear the sound of children playing. The "grownups," with the exception of* MR. VAN

---

3. Toscanini (täs′ kə nē′ nē): Arturo Toscanini, a famous Italian orchestral conductor.
4. Ride of the Valkyries (val′ ki rēs): a stirring selection from an opera by Richard Wagner, a German composer.

DAAN, *are all in the main room.* MRS. FRANK *is doing some mending,* MRS. VAN DAAN *is reading a fashion magazine.* MR. FRANK *is going over business accounts.* DUSSEL, *in his dentist's jacket, is pacing up and down, impatient to get into his bedroom.* MR. VAN DAAN *is upstairs working on a piece of embroidery in an embroidery frame.*

In his room PETER *is sitting before the mirror, smoothing his hair. As the scene goes on, he puts on his tie, brushes his coat and puts it on, preparing himself meticulously for a visit from* ANNE. *On his wall are now hung some of* ANNE'S *motion picture stars.*

In her room ANNE *too is getting dressed. She stands before the mirror in her slip, trying various ways of dressing her hair.* MARGOT *is seated on the sofa, hemming a skirt for* ANNE *to wear.*

In the main room DUSSEL *can stand it no longer. He comes over, rapping sharply on the door of his and* ANNE'S *bedroom.*]

ANNE. [*Calling to him*] No, no, Mr. Dussel! I am not dressed yet.

[DUSSEL *walks away, furious, sitting down and burying his head in his hands.* ANNE *turns to* MARGOT.]

How is that? How does that look?

MARGOT. [*Glancing at her briefly*] Fine.

ANNE. You didn't even look.

MARGOT. Of course I did. It's fine.

ANNE. Margot, tell me, am I terribly ugly?

MARGOT. Oh, stop fishing.

ANNE. No. No. Tell me.

MARGOT. Of course you're not. You've got nice eyes . . . and a lot of animation, and . . .

ANNE. A little vague, aren't you?

[*Outside,* MRS. FRANK, *feeling sorry for* DUSSEL, *comes over, knocking at the girls' door.*]

MRS. FRANK. [*Outside*] May I come in?

MARGOT. Come in, Mother.

MRS. FRANK. [*Shutting the door behind her*] Mr. Dussel's impatient to get in here.

ANNE. Heavens, he takes the room for himself the entire day.

MRS. FRANK. [*Gently*] Anne, dear, you're not going in again tonight to see Peter?

ANNE. [*Dignified*] That is my intention.

MRS. FRANK. But you've already spent a great deal of time in there today.

ANNE. I was in there exactly twice. Once to get the dictionary, and then three-quarters of an hour before supper.

MRS. FRANK. Aren't you afraid you're disturbing him?

ANNE. Mother, I have some intuition.

MRS. FRANK. Then may I ask you this much, Anne. Please don't shut the door when you go in.

ANNE. You sound like Mrs. Van Daan! [*She picks up her blouse, putting it on.*]

MRS. FRANK. No. No. I don't mean to suggest anything wrong. I only wish that you wouldn't expose yourself to criticism . . . that you wouldn't give Mrs. Van Daan the opportunity to be unpleasant.

ANNE. Mrs. Van Daan doesn't need an opportunity to be unpleasant!

MRS. FRANK. Everyone's on edge, worried about Mr. Kraler. This is one more thing . . .

ANNE. I'm sorry, Mother. I'm going to Peter's room. I'm not going to let Petronella Van Daan spoil our friendship.

[MRS. FRANK *hesitates for a second, then goes out, closing the door after her. She gets a pack of playing cards and sits at the center table, playing solitaire. In* ANNE'S *room* MARGOT *hands the finished skirt to* ANNE. *As* ANNE *is putting it on,* MARGOT *takes off her high-heeled shoes and stuffs paper in the toes so that* ANNE *can wear them.*]

MARGOT. [*To* ANNE] Why don't you two talk in the main room? It'd save a lot of trouble. It's hard on Mother, having to listen to those remarks from Mrs. Van Daan and not say a word.

ANNE. Why doesn't she say a word? I think it's ridiculous to take it and take it.

MARGOT. You don't understand Mother at all, do you? She can't talk back. She's not like you. It's just not in her nature to fight back.

ANNE. Anyway . . . the only one I worry about is you. I feel awfully guilty about you. [*She sits on the stool near* MARGOT, *putting on* MARGOT'S *high-heeled shoes.*]

MARGOT. What about?

ANNE. I mean, every time I go into Peter's room, I have a feeling I may be hurting you. [MARGOT *shakes her head.*] I know if it were me, I'd be wild. I'd be desperately jealous, if it were me.

MARGOT. Well, I'm not.

ANNE. You don't feel badly? Really? Truly? You're not jealous?

MARGOT. Of course I'm jealous . . . jealous that you've got something to get up in the morning for . . . But jealous of you and Peter? No.

[ANNE *goes back to the mirror.*]

ANNE. Maybe there's nothing to be jealous of. Maybe he doesn't really like me. Maybe I'm just taking the place of his cat . . . [*She picks up a pair of short white gloves, putting them on.*] Wouldn't you like to come in with us?

MARGOT. I have a book.

[*The sound of the children playing outside fades out. In the main room* DUSSEL *can stand it no longer. He jumps up, going to the bedroom door and knocking sharply.*]

DUSSEL. Will you please let me in my room!

ANNE. Just a minute, dear, dear Mr. Dussel. [*She picks up her mother's pink stole and adjusts it elegantly over her shoulders, then gives a last look in the mirror.*] Well, here I go . . . to run the gauntlet.[5]

[*She starts out, followed by* MARGOT.]

DUSSEL. [*As she appears—sarcastic*] Thank you so much.

[DUSSEL *goes into his room.* ANNE *goes toward* PETER'S *room, passing* MRS. VAN DAAN *and her parents at the center table.*]

MRS. VAN DAAN. My God, look at her!

[ANNE *pays no attention. She knocks at* PETER'S *door.*]

I don't know what good it is to have a son. I never see him. He wouldn't care if I killed myself.

[PETER *opens the door and stands aside for* ANNE *to come in.*]

Just a minute, Anne. [*She goes to them at the door.*] I'd like to say a few words to my son. Do you mind?

[PETER *and* ANNE *stand waiting.*]

---

5. to run the gauntlet (gônt' lit): Formerly, to pass between two rows of men who struck at the offender with clubs as he passed; here, a series of troubles or difficulties.

Peter, I don't want you staying up till all hours tonight. You've got to have your sleep. You're a growing boy. You hear?

MRS. FRANK. Anne won't stay late. She's going to bed promptly at nine. Aren't you, Anne?

ANNE. Yes, Mother . . . [*To* MRS. VAN DAAN] May we go now?

MRS. VAN DAAN. Are you asking me? I didn't know I had anything to say about it.

MRS. FRANK. Listen for the chimes, Anne dear.

[*The two young people go off into* PETER'S *room, shutting the door after them.*]

MRS. VAN DAAN. [*To* MRS. FRANK] In my day it was the boys who called on the girls. Not the girls on the boys.

MRS. FRANK. You know how young people like to feel that they have secrets. Peter's room is the only place where they can talk.

MRS. VAN DAAN. Talk! That's not what they called it when I was young.

[MRS. VAN DAAN *goes off to the bathroom.* MARGOT *settles down to read her book.* MR. FRANK *puts his papers away and brings a chess game to the center table. He and* MRS. FRANK *start to play. In* PETER'S *room,* ANNE *speaks to* PETER, *indignant, humiliated.*]

ANNE. Aren't they awful? Aren't they impossible? Treating us as if we were still in the nursery.

[*She sits on the cot.* PETER *gets a bottle of pop and two glasses.*]

PETER. Don't let it bother you. It doesn't bother me.

ANNE. I suppose you can't really blame them . . . they think back to what *they* were like at our age. They don't realize how much

more advanced we are . . . When you think what wonderful discussions we've had! . . . Oh, I forgot. I was going to bring you some more pictures.

PETER. Oh, these are fine, thanks.

ANNE. Don't you want some more? Miep just brought me some new ones.

PETER. Maybe later. [*He gives her a glass of pop and, taking some for himself, sits down facing her.*]

ANNE. [*Looking up at one of the photographs*] I remember when I got that . . . I won it. I bet Jopie that I could eat five ice-cream cones. We'd all been playing ping-pong . . . We used to have heavenly times . . . we'd finish up with ice cream at the Delphi, or the Oasis, where Jews were allowed . . . there'd always be a lot of boys . . . we'd laugh and joke . . . I'd like to go back to it for a few days or a week. But after that I know I'd be bored to death. I think more seriously about life now. I want to be a journalist . . . or something. I love to write. What do you want to do?

PETER. I thought I might go off some place . . . work on a farm or something . . . some job that doesn't take much brains.

ANNE. You shouldn't talk that way. You've got the most awful inferiority complex.

PETER. I know I'm not smart.

ANNE. That isn't true. You're much better than I am in dozens of things . . . arithmetic and algebra and . . . well, you're a million times better than I am in algebra. [*With sudden directness*] You like Margot, don't you? Right from the start you liked her, liked her much better than me.

PETER. [*Uncomfortably*] Oh, I don't know.

[*In the main room* MRS. VAN DAAN *comes from*

the bathroom and goes over to the sink, polishing a coffee pot.]

ANNE. It's all right. Everyone feels that way. Margot's so good. She's sweet and bright and beautiful and I'm not.

PETER. I wouldn't say that.

ANNE. Oh, no, I'm not. I know that. I know quite well that I'm not a beauty. I never have been and never shall be.

PETER. I don't agree at all. I think you're pretty.

ANNE. That's not true!

PETER. And another thing. You've changed . . . from at first, I mean.

ANNE. I have?

PETER. I used to think you were awful noisy.

ANNE. And what do you think now, Peter? How have I changed?

PETER. Well . . . er . . . you're . . . quieter.

[*In his room* DUSSEL *takes his pajamas and toilet articles and goes into the bathroom to change.*]

ANNE. I'm glad you don't just hate me.

PETER. I never said that.

ANNE. I bet when you get out of here you'll never think of me again.

PETER. That's crazy.

ANNE. When you get back with all of your friends, you're going to say . . . now what did I ever see in that Mrs. Quack Quack.

PETER. I haven't got any friends.

ANNE. Oh, Peter, of course you have. Everyone has friends.

PETER. Not me. I don't want any. I get along all right without them.

ANNE. Does that mean you can get along without me? I think of myself as your friend.

PETER. No. If they were all like you, it'd be different.

[*He takes the glasses and the bottle and puts them away. There is a second's silence and then* ANNE *speaks, hesitantly, shyly.*]

ANNE. Peter, did you ever kiss a girl?

PETER. Yes. Once.

ANNE. [*To cover her feelings*] That picture's crooked.

[PETER *goes over, straightening the photograph.*]

Was she pretty?

PETER. Huh?

ANNE. The girl that you kissed.

PETER. I don't know. I was blindfolded. [*He comes back and sits down again.*] It was at a party. One of those kissing games.

ANNE. [*Relieved*] Oh. I don't suppose that really counts, does it?

PETER. It didn't with me.

ANNE. I've been kissed twice. Once a man I'd never seen before kissed me on the cheek when he picked me up off the ice and I was crying. And the other was Mr. Koophuis, a friend of Father's who kissed my hand. You wouldn't say those counted, would you?

PETER. I wouldn't say so.

ANNE. I know almost for certain that Margot would never kiss anyone unless she was engaged to them. And I'm sure too that Mother never touched a man before Pim. But I don't know . . . things are so different now . . . What do you think? Do you think a girl shouldn't kiss anyone except if she's

Peter Van Daan

engaged or something? It's so hard to try to think what to do, when here we are with the whole world falling around our ears and you think . . . well . . . you don't know what's going to happen tomorrow and . . . What do you think?

PETER. I suppose it'd depend on the girl. Some girls, anything they do's wrong. But others . . . well . . . it wouldn't necessarily be wrong with them.

[*The carillon starts to strike nine o'clock.*]

I've always thought that when two people . . .

ANNE. Nine o'clock. I have to go.

PETER. That's right.

ANNE. [*Without moving*] Good night.

[*There is a second's pause, then* PETER *gets up and moves toward the door.*]

PETER. You won't let them stop you coming?

ANNE. No. [*She rises and starts for the door.*] Sometimes I might bring my diary. There are so many things in it that I want to talk over with you. There's a lot about you.

PETER. What kind of thing?

ANNE. I wouldn't want you to see some of it. I thought you were a nothing, just the way you thought about me.

PETER. Did you change your mind, the way I changed my mind about you?

ANNE. Well . . . You'll see . . .

[*For a second* ANNE *stands looking up at* PETER, *longing for him to kiss her. As he makes no move she turns away. Then suddenly* PETER *grabs her awkwardly in his arms, kissing her on the cheek.* ANNE *walks out dazed. She stands for a minute, her back to the people in the main room. As she regains her poise she goes to her mother and father and* MARGOT, *silently kissing them. They murmur their good nights to her. As she is about to open her bedroom door, she catches sight of* MRS. VAN DAAN. *She goes quickly to her, taking her face in her hands and kissing her first on one cheek and then on the other. Then she hurries off into her room.* MRS. VAN DAAN *looks after her, and then looks over at* PETER'S *room. Her suspicions are confirmed.*]

MRS. VAN DAAN. [*She knows.*] Ah hah!

[*The lights dim out. The curtain falls on the scene. In the darkness* ANNE'S VOICE *comes faintly at first and then with growing strength.*]

ANNE'S VOICE. By this time we all know each

other so well that if anyone starts to tell a story, the rest can finish it for him. We're having to cut down still further on our meals. What makes it worse, the rats have been at work again. They've carried off some of our precious food. Even Mr. Dussel wishes now that Mouschi was here. Thursday, the twentieth of April, nineteen forty-four. Invasion fever is mounting every day. Miep tells us that people outside talk of nothing else. For myself, life has become much more pleasant. I often go to Peter's room after supper. Oh, don't think I'm in love, because I'm not. But it does make life more bearable to have someone with whom you can exchange views. No more tonight. P.S. . . . I must be honest. I must confess that I actually live for the next meeting. Is there anything lovelier than to sit under the skylight and feel the sun on your cheeks and have a darling boy in your arms? I admit now that I'm glad the Van Daans had a son and not a daughter. I've outgrown another dress. That's the third. I'm having to wear Margot's clothes after all. I'm working hard on my French and am now reading *La Belle Nivernaise.*[6]

[*As she is saying the last lines—the curtain rises on the scene. The lights dim on, as* ANNE'S VOICE *fades out.*]

Scene 3

[*It is night, a few weeks later. Everyone is in bed. There is complete quiet. In the* VAN DAANS' *room a match flares up for a moment and then is quickly put out.* MR. VAN DAAN, *in bare feet, dressed in underwear and trousers, is dimly seen coming stealthily down the stairs and into the main room, where* MR. *and* MRS. FRANK *and* MARGOT *are sleep-*

ing. *He goes to the food safe and again lights a match. Then he cautiously opens the safe, taking out a half-loaf of bread. As he closes the safe, it creaks. He stands rigid.* MRS. FRANK *sits up in bed. She sees him.*]

MRS. FRANK. [*Screaming*] Otto! Otto! *Komme schnell!*[7]

[*The rest of the people wake, hurriedly getting up.*]

MR. FRANK. *Was ist los? Was ist passiert?*[8]

[DUSSEL, *followed by* ANNE, *comes from his room.*]

MRS. FRANK. [*As she rushes over to* MR. VAN DAAN] *Er stiehlt das Essen!*[9]

DUSSEL. [*Grabbing* MR. VAN DAAN] You! You! Give me that.

MRS. VAN DAAN. [*Coming down the stairs*] Putti . . . Putti . . . what is it?

DUSSEL. [*His hands on* VAN DAAN'S *neck*] You dirty thief . . . stealing food . . . you good-for-nothing . . .

MR. FRANK. Mr. Dussel! Oh! Help me, Peter!

[PETER *comes over, trying, with* MR. FRANK, *to separate the two struggling men.*]

PETER. Let him go! Let go!

[DUSSEL *drops* MR. VAN DAAN, *pushing him away. He shows them the end of a loaf of bread that he has taken from* VAN DAAN.]

DUSSEL. You greedy, selfish . . . !

[MARGOT *turns on the lights.*]

MRS. VAN DAAN. Putti . . . what is it?

---

6. *La Belle Nivernaise:* A story by Alphonse Daudet, a French author.

7. *Komme schnell* (käm′ ə shnel): German for "Come quick!"
8. *Was ist los? Was ist passiert?* (väs ist los väs ist päs′ ērt): German for "What's the matter? What happened?"
9. *Er stiehlt das Essen!* (er stēlt däs es′ ən): German for "He steals food!"

[*All of* MRS. FRANK'S *gentleness, her self-control, is gone. She is outraged, in a frenzy of indignation.*]

MRS. FRANK. The bread! He was stealing the bread!

DUSSEL. It was you, and all the time we thought it was the rats!

MR. FRANK. Mr. Van Daan, how could you!

MR. VAN DAAN. I'm hungry.

MRS. FRANK. We're all of us hungry! I see the children getting thinner and thinner. Your own son Peter . . . I've heard him moan in his sleep, he's so hungry. And you come in the night and steal food that should go to them . . . to the children!

MRS. VAN DAAN. [*Going to* MR. VAN DAAN *protectively*] He needs more food than the rest of us. He's used to more. He's a big man.

[MR. VAN DAAN *breaks away, going over and sitting on the couch.*]

MRS. FRANK. [*Turning on* MRS. VAN DAAN] And you . . . you're worse than he is! You're a mother, and yet you sacrifice your child to this man . . . this . . . this . . .

MR. FRANK. Edith! Edith!

[MARGOT *picks up the pink woolen stole, putting it over her mother's shoulders.*]

MRS. FRANK. [*Paying no attention, going on to* MRS. VAN DAAN] Don't think I haven't seen you! Always saving the choicest bits for him! I've watched you day after day and I've held my tongue. But not any longer! Not after this! Now I want him to go! I want him to get out of here!

MR. FRANK. Edith!

MR. VAN DAAN. Get out of here?

MRS. VAN DAAN. What do you mean?

} Together

MRS. FRANK. Just that! Take your things and get out!

MR. FRANK. [*To* MRS. FRANK] You're speaking in anger. You cannot mean what you are saying.

MRS. FRANK. I mean exactly that!

[MRS. VAN DAAN *takes a cover from the* FRANKS' *bed, pulling it about her.*]

MR. FRANK. For two long years we have lived here, side by side. We have respected each other's rights . . . we have managed to live in peace. Are we now going to throw it all away? I know this will never happen again, will it, Mr. Van Daan?

MR. VAN DAAN. No. No.

MRS. FRANK. He steals once! He'll steal again!

[MR. VAN DAAN, *holding his stomach, starts for the bathroom.* ANNE *puts her arms around him, helping him up the step.*]

MR. FRANK. Edith, please. Let us be calm. We'll all go to our rooms . . . and afterwards we'll sit down quietly and talk this out . . . we'll find some way . . .

MRS. FRANK. No! No! No more talk! I want them to leave!

MRS. VAN DAAN. You'd put us out, on the streets?

MRS. FRANK. There are other hiding places.

MRS. VAN DAAN. A cellar . . . a closet. I know. And we have no money left even to pay for that.

MRS. FRANK. I'll give you money. Out of my own pocket I'll give it gladly. [*She gets her purse from a shelf and comes back with it.*]

MRS. VAN DAAN. Mr. Frank, you told Putti you'd never forget what he'd done for you when you came to Amsterdam. You said you could never repay him, that you . . .

MRS. FRANK. [*Counting out money*] If my husband had any obligation to you, he's paid it, over and over.

MR. FRANK. Edith, I've never seen you like this before. I don't know you.

MRS. FRANK. I should have spoken out long ago.

DUSSEL. You can't be nice to some people.

MRS. VAN DAAN. [*Turning on* DUSSEL] There would have been plenty for all of us, if *you* hadn't come in here!

MR. FRANK. We don't need the Nazis to destroy us. We're destroying ourselves.

[*He sits down, with his head in his hands.* MRS. FRANK *goes to* MRS. VAN DAAN.]

MRS. FRANK. [*Giving* MRS. VAN DAAN *some money*] Give this to Miep. She'll find you a place.

ANNE. Mother, you're not putting *Peter* out. Peter hasn't done anything.

MRS. FRANK. He'll stay, of course. When I say I must protect the children, I mean Peter too.

[PETER *rises from the steps where he has been sitting.*]

PETER. I'd have to go if Father goes.

[MR. VAN DAAN *comes from the bathroom.* MRS. VAN DAAN *hurries to him and takes him to the couch. Then she gets water from the sink to bathe his face.*]

MRS. FRANK. [*While this is going on*] He's no father to you . . . that man! He doesn't know what it is to be a father!

PETER. [*Starting for his room*] I wouldn't feel right. I couldn't stay.

MRS. FRANK. Very well, then. I'm sorry.

ANNE. [*Rushing over to* PETER] No, Peter! No!

[PETER *goes into his room, closing the door after him.* ANNE *turns back to her mother, crying.*]

I don't care about the food. They can have mine! I don't want it! Only don't send them away. It'll be daylight soon. They'll be caught . . .

MARGOT. [*Putting her arms comfortingly around* ANNE] Please, Mother!

MRS. FRANK. They're not going now. They'll stay here until Miep finds them a place. [*To* MRS. VAN DAAN] But one thing I insist on! He must never come down here again! He must never come to this room where the food is stored! We'll divide what we have . . . an equal share for each!

[DUSSEL *hurries over to get a sack of potatoes from the food safe.* MRS. FRANK *goes on, to* MRS. VAN DAAN]

You can cook it here and take it up to him.

[DUSSEL *brings the sack of potatoes back to the center table.*]

MARGOT. Oh, no. No. We haven't sunk so far that we're going to fight over a handful of rotten potatoes.

DUSSEL. [*Dividing the potatoes into piles*] Mrs. Frank, Mr. Frank, Margot, Anne, Peter, Mrs. Van Daan, Mr. Van Daan, myself . . . Mrs. Frank . . .

[*The buzzer sounds in* MIEP'S *signal.*]

MR. FRANK. It's Miep! [*He hurries over, getting his overcoat and putting it on.*]

MARGOT. At this hour?

MRS. FRANK. It is trouble.

MR. FRANK. [*As he starts down to unbolt the door*] I beg you, don't let her see a thing like this!

MR. DUSSEL. [*Counting without stopping*] . . . Anne, Peter, Mrs. Van Daan, Mr. Van Daan, myself . . .

MARGOT. [*To* DUSSEL] Stop it! Stop it!

DUSSEL. . . . Mr. Frank, Margot, Anne, Peter, Mrs. Van Daan, Mr. Van Daan, myself, Mrs. Frank . . .

MRS. VAN DAAN. You're keeping the big ones for yourself! All the big ones . . . Look at the size of that! . . . And that! . . .

[DUSSEL *continues on with his dividing.* PETER, *with his shirt and trousers on, comes from his room.*]

MARGOT. Stop it! Stop it!

[*We hear* MIEP'S *excited voice speaking to* MR. FRANK *below.*]

MIEP. Mr. Frank . . . the most wonderful news! . . . The invasion has begun!

MR. FRANK. Go on, tell them! Tell them!

[MIEP *comes running up the steps ahead of* MR. FRANK. *She has a man's raincoat on over her nightclothes and a bunch of orange-colored flowers in her hand.*]

MIEP. Did you hear that, everybody? Did you hear what I said? The invasion has begun! The invasion!

[*They all stare at* MIEP, *unable to grasp what she is telling them.* PETER *is the first to recover his wits.*]

PETER. Where?

MRS. VAN DAAN. When? When, Miep?

MIEP. It began early this morning . . .

[*As she talks on, the realization of what she*

has said begins to dawn on them. Everyone goes crazy. A wild demonstration takes place. MRS. FRANK hugs MR. VAN DAAN.]

MRS. FRANK. Oh, Mr. Van Daan, did you hear that?

[DUSSEL *embraces* MRS. VAN DAAN. PETER *grabs a frying pan and parades around the room, beating on it, singing the Dutch National Anthem.* ANNE *and* MARGOT *follow him, singing, weaving in and out among the excited grown-ups.* MARGOT *breaks away to take the flowers from* MIEP *and distribute them to everyone. While this pandemonium is going on* MRS. FRANK *tries to make herself heard above the excitement.*]

MRS. FRANK. [*to* MIEP] How do you know?

MIEP. The radio . . . The B.B.C.![10] They said they landed on the coast of Normandy![11]

PETER. The British?

MIEP. British, Americans, French, Dutch, Poles, Norwegians . . . all of them! More than four thousand ships! Churchill spoke, and General Eisenhower! D-Day they call it!

MR. FRANK. Thank God, it's come!

MRS. VAN DAAN. At last!

MIEP. [*Starting out*] I'm going to tell Mr. Kraler. This'll be better than any blood transfusion.

MR. FRANK. [*Stopping her*] What part of Normandy did they land, did they say?

MIEP. Normandy . . . that's all I know now . . . I'll be up the minute I hear some more! [*She goes hurriedly out.*]

MR. FRANK. [*To* MRS. FRANK] What did I tell you? What did I tell you?

---

10. B.B.C.: British Broadcasting Corporation.
11. Normandy (nôr′ mən dē): A region in Northwest France, on the English channel.

Postage stamp of Anne Frank issued in 1979

[MRS. FRANK *indicates that he has forgotten to bolt the door after* MIEP. *He hurries down the steps.* MR. VAN DAAN, *sitting on the couch, suddenly breaks into a convulsive[12] sob. Everybody looks at him, bewildered.*]

MRS. VAN DAAN. [*Hurrying to him*] Putti! Putti! What is it? What happened?

MR. VAN DAAN. Please. I'm so ashamed.

[MR. FRANK *comes back up the steps.*]

DUSSEL. Oh!

MRS. VAN DAAN. Don't, Putti.

---

12. convulsive (kən vul′ siv) *adj.*: Having an involuntary contraction or spasm of the muscles; shuddering.

MARGOT. It doesn't matter now!

MR. FRANK. [*Going to* MR. VAN DAAN] Didn't you hear what Miep said? The invasion has come! We're going to be liberated! This is a time to celebrate! [*He embraces* MRS. FRANK *and then hurries to the cupboard and gets the cognac and a glass.*]

MR. VAN DAAN. To steal bread from children!

MRS. FRANK. We've all done things that we're ashamed of.

ANNE. Look at me, the way I've treated Mother . . . so mean and horrid to her.

MRS. FRANK. No, Anneke, no.

[ANNE *runs to her mother, putting her arms around her.*]

ANNE. Oh, Mother, I was. I was awful.

MR. VAN DAAN. Not like me. No one is as bad as me!

DUSSEL. [*To* MR. VAN DAAN] Stop it now! Let's be happy!

MR. FRANK. [*Giving* MR. VAN DAAN *a glass of cognac*] Here! Here! *Schnapps! L'chaim!*[13]

[VAN DAAN *takes the cognac. They all watch him. He gives them a feeble smile.* ANNE *puts up her fingers in a V-for-Victory sign. As* VAN DAAN *gives an answering V-sign, they are startled to hear a loud sob from behind them. It is* MRS. FRANK, *stricken with remorse. She is sitting on the other side of the room.*]

MRS. FRANK. [*Through her sobs*] When I think of the terrible things I said . . .

[MR. FRANK, ANNE *and* MARGOT *hurry to her, trying to comfort her.* MR. VAN DAAN *brings her his glass of cognac.*]

MR. VAN DAAN. No! No! You were right!

MRS. FRANK. That I should speak that way to you! . . . Our friends! . . . Our guests! [*She starts to cry again.*]

DUSSEL. Stop it, you're spoiling the whole invasion!

[*As they are comforting her, the lights dim out. The curtain falls.*]

ANNE'S VOICE. [*Faintly at first and then with growing strength*] We're all in much better spirits these days. There's still excellent news of the invasion. The best part about it is that I have a feeling that friends are coming. Who knows? Maybe I'll be back in school by fall. Ha, ha! The joke is on us! The warehouse man doesn't know a thing and we are paying him all that money! . . . Wednesday, the second of July, nineteen forty-four. The invasion seems temporarily to be bogged down. Mr. Kraler has to have an operation, which looks bad. The Gestapo have found the radio that was stolen. Mr. Dussel says they'll trace it back and back to the thief, and then, it's just a matter of time till they get to us. Everyone is low. Even poor Pim can't raise their spirits. I have often been downcast myself . . . but never in despair. I can shake off everything if I write. But . . . and that is the great question . . . will I ever be able to write well? I want to so much. I want to go on living even after my death. Another birthday has gone by, so now I am fifteen. Already I know what I want. I have a goal, an opinion.

[*As this is being said—the curtain rises on the scene, the lights dim on, and* ANNE'S VOICE *fades out.*]

Scene 4

[*It is an afternoon a few weeks later . . . Everyone but Margot is in the main room. There is a sense of great tension.*

Both MRS. FRANK *and* MR. VAN DAAN *are nervously pacing back and forth,* DUSSEL *is standing at the window, looking down fixedly at the street below.* PETER *is at the center table, trying to do his lessons.* ANNE *sits opposite him, writing in her diary.* MRS. VAN DAAN *is seated on the couch, her eyes on* MR. FRANK *as he sits reading.*

The sound of a telephone ringing comes from the office below. They all are rigid, listening tensely. MR. DUSSEL *rushes down to* MR. FRANK.]

---

13. Schnapps! L'chaim! (shnäps′ lə khä′ yim):
German for "a drink" and a Hebrew toast meaning
"To life."

DUSSEL. There it goes again, the telephone! Mr. Frank, do you hear?

MR. FRANK. [*Quietly*] Yes. I hear.

DUSSEL. [*Pleading, insistent*] But this is the third time, Mr. Frank! The third time in quick succession! It's a signal! I tell you it's Miep, trying to get us! For some reason she can't come to us and she's trying to warn us of something!

MR. FRANK. Please. Please.

MR. VAN DAAN. [*To* DUSSEL] You're wasting your breath.

DUSSEL. Something has happened, Mr. Frank. For three days now Miep hasn't been to see us! And today not a man has come to work. There hasn't been a sound in the building!

MRS. FRANK. Perhaps it's Sunday. We may have lost track of the days.

MR. VAN DAAN. [*To* ANNE] You with the diary there. What day is it?

DUSSEL. [*Going to* MRS. FRANK] I don't lose track of the days! I know exactly what day it is! It's Friday, the fourth of August. Friday, and not a man at work. [*He rushes back to* MR. FRANK, *pleading with him, almost in tears.*] I tell you Mr. Kraler's dead. That's the only explanation. He's dead and they've closed down the building, and Miep's trying to tell us!

MR. FRANK. She'd never telephone us.

DUSSEL. [*Frantic*] Mr. Frank, answer that! I beg you, answer it!

MR. FRANK. No.

MR. VAN DAAN. Just pick it up and listen. You don't have to speak. Just listen and see if it's Miep.

DUSSEL. [*Speaking at the same time*] Please . . . I ask you.

MR. FRANK. No. I've told you, no. I'll do nothing that might let anyone know we're in the building.

PETER. Mr. Frank's right.

MR. VAN DAAN. There's no need to tell us what side you're on.

MR. FRANK. If we wait patiently, quietly, I believe that help will come.

[*There is silence for a minute as they all listen to the telephone ringing.*]

DUSSEL. I'm going down.

[*He rushes down the steps.* MR. FRANK *tries ineffectually to hold him.* DUSSEL *runs to the lower door, unbolting it. The telephone stops ringing.* DUSSEL *bolts the door and comes slowly back up the steps.*]

Too late.

[MR. FRANK *goes to* MARGOT *in* ANNE's *bedroom.*]

MR. VAN DAAN. So we just wait here until we die.

MRS. VAN DAAN. [*Hysterically*] I can't stand it! I'll kill myself! I'll kill myself!

MR. VAN DAAN. Stop it!

[*In the distance, a German military band is heard playing a Viennese waltz.*]

MRS. VAN DAAN. I think you'd be glad if I did! I think you want me to die!

MR. VAN DAAN. Whose fault is it we're here?

[MRS. VAN DAAN *starts for her room. He follows, talking at her.*]

We could've been safe somewhere . . . in America or Switzerland. But no! No! You wouldn't leave when I wanted to. You couldn't leave your things. You couldn't leave your precious furniture.

MRS. VAN DAAN. Don't touch me!

[*She hurries up the stairs, followed by* MR. VAN DAAN. PETER, *unable to bear it, goes to his room.* ANNE *looks after him, deeply concerned.* DUSSEL *returns to his post at the window.* MR. FRANK *comes back into the main room and takes a book, trying to read.* MRS. FRANK *sits near the sink, starting to peel some potatoes.* ANNE *quietly goes to* PETER'S *room, closing the door after her.* PETER *is lying face down on the cot.* ANNE *leans over him, holding him in her arms, trying to bring him out of his despair.*]

ANNE. Look, Peter, the sky. [*She looks up through the skylight.*] What a lovely, lovely day! Aren't the clouds beautiful? You know what I do when it seems as if I couldn't stand being cooped up for one more minute? I *think* myself out. I think myself on a walk in the park where I used to go with Pim. Where the jonquils and the crocus and the violets grow down the slopes. You know the most wonderful part about *thinking* yourself out? You can have it any way you like. You can have roses and violets and chrysanthemums all blooming at the same time . . . It's funny . . . I used to take it all for granted . . . and now I've gone crazy about everything to do with nature. Haven't you?

PETER. I've just gone crazy. I think if something doesn't happen soon . . . if we don't get out of here . . . I can't stand much more of it!

ANNE. [*Softly*] I wish you had a religion, Peter.

PETER. No, thanks! Not me!

ANNE. Oh, I don't mean you have to be Orthodox[14] . . . or believe in heaven and hell and purgatory[15] and things . . . I just mean some religion . . . it doesn't matter what. Just to believe in something! When I think of all that's out there . . . the trees . . . and flowers . . . and seagulls . . . when I think of the dearness of you, Peter . . . and the goodness of the people we know . . . Mr. Kraler, Miep, Dirk, the vegetable man, all risking their lives for us every day . . . When I think of these good things, I'm not afraid any more . . . I find myself, and God, and I . . .

[PETER *interrupts, getting up and walking away.*]

PETER. That's fine! But when I begin to think, I get mad! Look at us, hiding out for two years. Not able to move! Caught here like . . . waiting for them to come and get us . . . and all for what?

ANNE. We're not the only people that've had to suffer. There've always been people that've had to . . . sometimes one race . . . sometimes another . . . and yet . . .

PETER. That doesn't make me feel any better!

ANNE. [*Going to him*] I know it's terrible, trying to have any faith . . . when people are doing such horrible . . . But you know what I sometimes think? I think the world may be going through a phase, the way I was with Mother. It'll pass, maybe not for hundreds of years, but some day . . . I still believe, in spite of everything, that people are really good at heart.

PETER. I want to see something now . . . Not a thousand years from now! [*He goes over, sitting down again on the cot.*]

ANNE. But, Peter, if you'd only look at it as

---

14. Orthodox (ôr′ thə däks′) *adj.*: Strictly observing the rites and traditions of Judaism.

15. purgatory (pŭr′ gə tôr′ ē) *n.*: A state or place of temporary punishment.

part of a great pattern . . . that we're just a little minute in the life . . . [*She breaks off.*] Listen to us, going at each other like a couple of stupid grownups! Look at the sky now. Isn't it lovely?

[*She holds out her hand to him.* PETER *takes it and rises, standing with her at the window looking out, his arms around her.*]

Some day, when we're outside again, I'm going to . . .

[*She breaks off as she hears the sound of a car, its brakes squealing as it comes to a sudden stop. The people in the other rooms also become aware of the sound. They listen tensely. Another car roars up to a screeching stop.* ANNE *and* PETER *come from* PETER'S *room.* MR. *and* MRS. VAN DAAN *creep down the stairs.* DUSSEL *comes out from his room. Everyone is listening, hardly breathing. A doorbell clangs again and again in the building below.* MR. FRANK *starts quietly down the steps to the door.* DUSSEL *and* PETER *follow him. The others stand rigid, waiting, terrified.*

In a few seconds DUSSEL *comes stumbling back up the steps. He shakes off* PETER'S *help and goes to his room.* MR. FRANK *bolts the door below, and comes slowly back up the steps. Their eyes are all on him as he stands there for a minute. They realize that what they feared has happened.* MRS. VAN DAAN *starts to whimper.* MR. VAN DAAN *puts her gently in a chair, and then hurries off up the stairs to their room to collect their things.* PETER *goes to comfort his mother. There is a sound of violent pounding on a door below.*]

MR. FRANK. [*Quietly*] For the past two years we have lived in fear. Now we can live in hope.

[*The pounding below becomes more insis-*

tent. *There are muffled sounds of voices, shouting commands.*]

MEN'S VOICES. *Auf machen! Da drinnen! Auf machen! Schnell! Schnell! Schnell!*[16] *etc., etc.*

[*The street door below is forced open. We hear the heavy tread of footsteps coming up.* MR. FRANK *gets two school bags from the shelves, and gives one to* ANNE *and the other to* MARGOT. *He goes to get a bag for* MRS. FRANK. *The sound of feet coming up grows louder.* PETER *comes to* ANNE, *kissing her good-bye, then he goes to his room to collect his things. The buzzer of their door starts to ring.* MR. FRANK *brings* MRS. FRANK *a bag. They stand together, waiting. We hear the thud of gun butts on the door, trying to break it down.*

ANNE *stands, holding her school satchel, looking over at her father and mother with a soft, reassuring smile. She is no longer a child, but a woman with courage to meet whatever lies ahead.*

The lights dim out. The curtain falls on the scene. We hear a mighty crash as the door is shattered. After a second ANNE'S *voice is heard.*]

ANNE'S VOICE. And so it seems our stay here is over. They are waiting for us now. They've allowed us five minutes to get our things. We can each take a bag and whatever it will hold of clothing. Nothing else. So, dear Diary, that means I must leave you behind. Good-bye for a while. P.S. Please, please, Miep, or Mr. Kraler, or anyone else. If you should find this diary, will you please keep it safe for me, because some day I hope . . .

---

16. Auf machen! . . . Schnell! (ɔuf măk ən dä dri nən ɔuf măk ən shnel shnel shnel): German for "Open up, you in there, open up, quick, quick, quick."

[Her voice stops abruptly. There is silence. After a second the curtain rises.]

Scene 5

[It is again the afternoon in November, 1945. The rooms are as we saw them in the first scene. MR. KRALER *has joined* MIEP *and* MR. FRANK. *There are coffee cups on the table. We see a great change in* MR. FRANK. *He is calm now. His bitterness is gone. He slowly turns a few pages of the diary. They are blank.]*

MR. FRANK. No more. [*He closes the diary and puts it down on the couch beside him.*]

MIEP. I'd gone to the country to find food. When I got back the block was surrounded by police . . .

MR. KRALER. We made it our business to learn how they knew. It was the thief . . . the thief who told them.

[MIEP *goes up to the gas burner, bringing back a pot of coffee.*]

MR. FRANK. [*After a pause*] It seems strange to say this, that anyone could be happy in a concentration camp. But Anne was happy in the camp in Holland where they first took us. After two years of being shut up in these rooms, she could be out . . . out in the sunshine and the fresh air that she loved.

MIEP. [*Offering the coffee to* MR. FRANK] A little more?

MR. FRANK. [*Holding out his cup to her*] The news of the war was good. The British and Americans were sweeping through France.

We felt sure that they would get to us in time. In September we were told that we were to be shipped to Poland . . . The men to one camp. The women to another. I was sent to Auschwitz.[17] They went to Belsen.[18] In January we were freed, the few of us who were left. The war wasn't yet over, so it took us a long time to get home. We'd be sent here and there behind the lines where we'd be safe. Each time our train would stop . . . at a siding, or a crossing . . . we'd all get out and go from group to group . . . Where were you? Were you at Belsen? At Buchenwald?[19] At Mauthausen? Is it possible that you knew my wife? Did you ever see my husband? My son? My daughter? That's how I found out about my wife's death . . . of Margot, the Van Daans . . . Dussel. But Anne . . . I still hoped . . . Yesterday I went to Rotterdam. I'd heard of a woman there . . . She'd been in Belsen with Anne . . . I know now.

[*He picks up the diary again, and turns the pages back to find a certain passage. As he finds it we hear* ANNE'S VOICE.]

ANNE'S VOICE. In spite of everything, I still believe that people are really good at heart. [MR. FRANK *slowly closes the diary.*]

MR. FRANK. She puts me to shame.

[*They are silent.*]

---

17. Auschwitz (ou′ shvitz): A Nazi concentration camp in Poland, notorious as an extermination center.
18. Belsen (bel′ z′n): A village in what is now West Germany that with the village of Bergen was the site of Bergen-Belsen, a Nazi concentration camp and extermination center.
19. Buchenwald (boo′ k′n wôld): A notorious Nazi concentration camp and extermination center in central Germany.

THINKING ABOUT THE SELECTION

Recalling

1. Why is Miep's cake such a treat? How does it also reveal rising tensions?
2. Give two other indications that tensions in the hideout are rising.
3. What gives the families hope? What troubling information does Mr. Kraler bring?
4. Why does Mrs. Frank want to turn out the Van Daans? How has the playwright prepared you for this aspect of her character?
5. What role does the thief play in the events?

Interpreting

6. How does Anne's friendship with Peter help her live through difficult times?
7. What does Mr. Frank mean when he says the people in hiding are Mr. Kraler's ulcers?
8. How does the families' behavior prove Mr. Frank's statement: "We don't need the Nazis to destroy us. We're destroying ourselves"?
9. How can Anne believe that "In spite of everything . . . people are really good at heart"?
10. Explain the meaning of Mr. Frank's last line: "She puts me to shame."

Applying

11. How might Anne's speech on page 351, beginning "We're young . . . ," express the attitudes of young people today?
12. How is Anne's diary a portrait of courage?

ANALYZING LITERATURE

Understanding Characters and Theme

The **theme** is the insight into life revealed by a work of literature. Sometimes a theme is stated directly. At other times you may have to figure out the theme by analyzing what the characters do and say. In this play the way characters cope with adversity reveals something about life.

1. How does Anne change during the the play?
2. What do the changes in the characters reveal about human beings in adversity?
3. What does the play reveal about hope?
4. What does it reveal about courage?

CRITICAL THINKING AND READING

Finding Support for Opinions

Opinions should be supported by reasons or evidence. For example, Anne tells Peter that he is wrong when he says she knows just how to talk to the adults. One piece of evidence that supports Anne's opinion is that she made her mother cry.

Anne wrote: "In spite of everything, I still believe that people are really good at heart."

1. Find three pieces of evidence in the play that support Anne's opinion about people.
2. Find three pieces of evidence in your own life that support Anne's opinion about people.

THINKING AND WRITING

Writing a Letter to the Editor

Imagine that it is the anniversary of Anne Frank's death. Write a letter to the editor of your local paper in which you explain why you feel it is good that the play based on her diary is read and performed regularly today

First, make an outline of points you want to include. Explain what the theme of the play is and why it is still an important one to consider.

Write a first draft of your letter. Then read it carefully. Make any needed revisions.

Finally, write a final draft of your letter, being careful to follow the correct form for a business letter. When you finish, reread your letter to make sure the spelling and punctuation are correct.

Mapping

Making a semantic map is a good way to remember and understand what you read. **Semantic mapping** is an easy, uncomplicated method of organizing information in graphic form. It is an excellent study technique that helps you to see how things are related to one another and provides a graphic pattern that is easy to remember. Creating and filling out a semantic map helps you understand, make your own assumptions, and evaluate information.

Steps

The first step in making a map is to decide what is the important information in the material you read. You must identify the major concepts or events that you want to organize. With a play you may want to make a map that organizes the plot, setting, and characters. You may choose to map the character traits of several characters or to show the development of one or more characters.

Once you have chosen your information, you should organize it into main ideas and relevant details. Now determine what type of diagram is best suited to organizing this information. The shape of the map should make it easy to see how everything is related. Different colors can be used to indicate these relationships. When your map is constructed, fill in all the information that you can recall. Then skim to find the information you couldn't remember and to check your facts. After skimming, fill in any blanks. Periodically review your map to recall the information.

The map on page 371 was constructed to give an overview of the play *The Diary of Anne Frank.* Look at it to understand what a semantic map is like and to see how the different parts of the plot structure relate to one another.

Note that this map is similar to an outline because everything is written concisely and is organized into main ideas or events and details. Events are listed in the order in which they occurred and under the appropriate part of the plot structure. You could have expanded this map by including sub-details under the details.

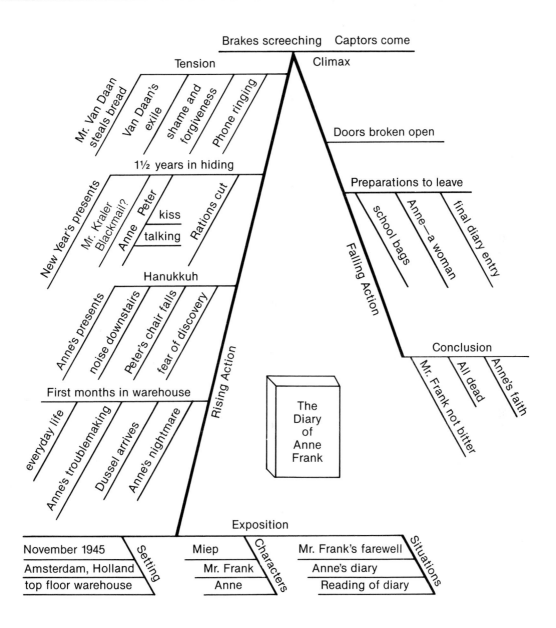

Brakes screeching   Captors come

Tension   Climax

Mr. Van Daan steals bread
Van Daan's exile
shame and forgiveness
Phone ringing

Doors broken open

1½ years in hiding

New Year's presents
Mr. Kraler
Blackmail?
Anne   Peter
kiss
talking
Rations cut

Preparations to leave

school bags
Anne—a woman
final diary entry

Falling Action

Hanukkuh

Anne's presents
noise downstairs
Peter's chair falls
fear of discovery

Conclusion

Mr. Frank not bitter
All dead
Anne's faith

First months in warehouse

everyday life
Anne's troublemaking
Dussel arrives
Anne's nightmare

Rising Action

The Diary of Anne Frank

Exposition

November 1945		Miep		Mr. Frank's farewell	
Amsterdam, Holland	Setting	Mr. Frank	Characters	Anne's diary	Situations
top floor warehouse		Anne		Reading of diary	

Activity

Now you are going to create your own map. Select a play. Brainstorm with your classmates to list the three most appropriate character traits for each of the major characters. Brainstorm some more to decide how you could organize this information so that your map would show which characters were most similar and which least alike. When you have created and filled in your map, compare it with those of your classmates.

YOU THE WRITER

Assignment

1. As an apprentice costume designer, you have been asked to create a costume for a minor character in one of the plays that you have read. Write a description of your design.

Prewriting. Review the plays, and select a minor character. Then brainstorm about the kind of costume this character might wear, noting each item.

Writing. Write the first draft of a description of a costume you would create. Provide detailed descriptions of each part of the costume. Include appropriate items from head to toe.

Revising. Make sure you have arranged your description so that it covers each item from head to toe.

Assignment

2. Your local community theater is producing "The Romancers." The director wants you to adapt the play to make it more contemporary. Write at least fifteen lines of dialogue between two characters.

Prewriting. Review the play. Jot down some lines of dialogue that you especially like between two characters. Think about how you could make the language seem more contemporary.

Writing. Write at least fifteen lines of dialogue. Use modern expressions, contemporary references, and slang. Use quotation marks and paragraph breaks to indicate a change of speakers.

Revising. Make certain you have used vivid language and modern expressions to make your dialogue seem realistic. Check your dialogue for spelling, grammar, and punctuation errors.

Assignment

3. Imagine one of the plays that you have read as a musical. Choose one scene from the play, and write a short description of the set, lighting, costumes, musical score, and songs that the characters might sing in this particular scene.

Prewriting. Freewrite until you have made some notes about adapting the scene. Then make notes about musicals that you have seen or read about.

Writing. Use your freewriting notes as the basis for your description. Describe how you would change this scene if the play were a musical. Include details about set, lighting, costumes, and musical numbers.

Revising. Make certain that your introductory sentence explains which play the scene you have adapted comes from. Have you provided adequate support for your ideas?

YOU THE CRITIC

Assignment

1. Write a summary of the plot of a play to appear on a theatrical poster. Your sentences will be printed on the poster as an enticement to come see this play.

    Prewriting. Choose one of the plays that you have read. Prepare a semantic map of the plot.

    Writing. Use your map as the basis for writing your summary. Make certain that each sentence in your summary reveals why the play is interesting or intriguing.

    Revising. Make certain that you have arranged events in chronological order.

Assignment

2. What makes a hero or a villain? Choose one character from the plays that you have read. Write an evaluation of this character, describing why he or she is mostly good or mostly evil.

    Prewriting. Review the plays that you have read, and select one character. List the characteristics and personality traits of that character.

    Writing. Write your character evaluation, using your prewriting list as a basis for your essay. Make certain to explain your reasons for identifying this character as a villain or a hero. Include a discussion of clues that the playwright gives you.

    Revising. Make certain that your opinions are supported by reasons and examples from the play. Check your evaluation for spelling, grammar, and punctuation errors.

Assignment

3. *Theater Scoop Magazine* has sent an interviewer to opening night. The interviewer asks you about the play that you just saw. Write a short essay to explain your reaction to one of the plays.

    Prewriting. Choose a play you found particularly interesting. Freewrite, exploring your reactions to it. Group your notes into negative and positive reactions.

    Writing. Write your reaction to the play, including reasons for your opinions. Write your negative reactions in one paragraph and your positive reactions in another. Prepare an introduction and a conclusion that summarize your overall impressions of the play.

    Revising. Make certain that you have written a strong introduction and conclusion and have provided reasons for your opinions. Are your opinions adequately supported by details from the play? Check your paragraphs for spelling, grammar, and punctuation errors.

MIRACLE OF NATURE
Thomas Moran
Three Lions

NONFICTION

Do you enjoy reading newspaper articles on sporting events? Do you take pleasure in reviews of performances you have seen? Do you particularly like stories of the lives of real people, both from the past and the present? Many people do. Newspaper articles, reviews, autobiographies, biographies—all are types of nonfiction.

Nonfiction deals with actual people, places, events, and topics based on real life. Autobiographies and biographies deal with the lives of real people, while essays provide a writer with room to express his or her thoughts and feelings on a particular subject. Nonfiction may inform, describe, persuade, or it may simply amuse.

In this unit you will encounter many types of nonfiction. The topics, too, will be varied; for example, a baseball player, a forest fire, shooting stars, and television.

Nonfiction

What are active readers? Active readers are people who bring their own experiences to what they read. They filter the information the author provides through what they already know. They become actively involved with the writing as they pause to ask questions about the information and to predict where the information is leading. By interacting with the writing in this way, active readers gain a greater understanding of it.

You, too, can become an active reader by using the following strategies.

Question
Ask questions about the information. What does the author reveal about the topic? Do conclusions seem based on the information given? In addition, question the author's purpose. Is the author trying to persuade you to act or to think a certain way?

Predict
Think about what you already know about the topic. Where is the information leading? Make predictions about the conclusions you think the author will reach based on this information. As you read, you will find out whether your predictions are accurate.

Clarify
As you read, try to find the answers to your questions and check the accuracy of your predictions. In this way, you will monitor, or guide, your own reading and so gain the fullest understanding of the information presented. If there is a word you do not know, look it up in a dictionary. If there is information that seems inaccurate, check it in a reference book.

Summarize
Every now and then, pause to summarize, or review, the information the author has presented so far. What important points has the author made? How has the author supported these points?

Pull It Together
Determine the main idea of the entire selection. What did you find out about the topic? What are your reactions to the information the author had presented?

On the following pages, you will find a model of how to read an essay actively.

from One Writer's Beginnings

Eudora Welty

Questions: What is the meaning of the title? Will the selection tell about this writer's youth? Will it tell how she became a writer?

Learning stamps you with its moments. Childhood's learning is made up of moments. It isn't steady. It's a pulse.

Questions: What does this mean? Isn't a pulse steady? Perhaps she means that there are intense moments of learning followed by slack periods followed again by intense moments.

In a children's art class, we sat in a ring on kindergarten chairs and drew three daffodils that had just been picked out of the yard; and while I was drawing, my sharpened yellow pencil and the cup of the yellow daffodil gave off whiffs just alike. That the pencil doing the drawing should give off the same smell as the flower it drew seemed part of the art lesson—as shouldn't it be? Children, like animals, use all their senses to discover the world. Then artists come along and discover it the same way, all over again. Here and there, it's the same world. Or now and then we'll hear from an artist who's never lost it.

Clarification: Here is one of the writer's intense moments of learning. She is learning through her sense of smell.

Prediction: Perhaps the author will discuss how she learns through each of her senses.

In my sensory[1] education I include my physical awareness of the *word*. Of a certain word, that is; the connection it has with what it stands for. At around age six, perhaps, I was standing by myself in our front yard waiting for supper, just at that hour in a late summer day when the sun is already below the horizon and the risen full moon in the visible sky stops being chalky and begins to take on light. There comes the moment, and I saw it then, when the moon goes from flat to round. For the first time it met my eyes as a globe. The word "moon" came into my mouth as though fed to me out of a silver spoon. Held in my mouth the moon became a word. It had the roundness of a Concord grape Grandpa took off his vine and gave me to suck out of its skin and swallow whole, in Ohio.

Clarification: She *does* discuss what she learned through the sense of taste. How unusual to taste a word! The image of the grape suggests the richness of the word *moon*.

---

1. sensory (sen′ sər ē) *adj.*: Of receiving sense impressions.

This love did not prevent me from living for years in foolish error about the moon. The new moon just appearing in the west was the rising moon to me. The new should be rising. And in early childhood the sun and moon, those opposite reigning powers, I just as easily assumed rose in east and west respectively in their opposite sides of the sky, and like partners in a reel[2] they advanced, sun from the east, moon from the west, crossed over (when I wasn't looking) and went down on the other side. My father couldn't have known I believed that when bending behind me and guiding my shoulder, he positioned me at our telescope in the front yard and, with careful adjustment of the focus, brought the moon close to me.

Clarification: Here she learns through her sense of sight, but the knowledge she gains is in error.

Question: What will she learn from her mistake?

The night sky over my childhood Jackson was velvety black. I could see the full constellations in it and call their names; when I could read, I knew their myths. Though I was always waked for eclipses and indeed carried to the window as an infant in arms and shown Halley's Comet[3] in my sleep, and though I'd been taught at our diningroom table about the solar system and knew the earth revolved around the sun, and our moon around us, I never found out the moon didn't come up in the west until I was a writer and Herschel Brickell, the literary critic, told me after I misplaced it in a story. He said valuable words to me about my new profession: "Always be sure you get your moon in the right part of the sky."

Summary: As a child, Welty learned of the world through her senses.

Question: What does Brickell's remark indicate?

2. **reel** (rēl) *n.*: A lively Scottish dance.
3. **Halley's Comet:** A famous comet that reappears every 75 years.

Pulling It Together: Young children, like artists, learn through their senses. Good writers use sensory details to enrich their work. However, they must be certain the details are accurate.

Eudora Welty (1909–   ) was born and raised in Jackson, Mississippi, and this environment has formed the backdrop for most of her writing. After college she returned to Mississippi where her first full-time job for the Works Progress Administration took her all over the state, writing articles and taking photographs. Welty's first published short story appeared in 1936, and since then her reputation has grown steadily. In 1973 she was awarded a Pulitzer Prize for her novel *The Optimist's Daughter*.

THINKING ABOUT THE SELECTION
Recalling

1. Explain the similarity Welty notices between the sharpened pencil and the daffodil.
2. According to Welty, how are children, animals, and artists alike?
3. What error does Welty make about the moon? Why does this error seem logical to her?
4. At what point does Welty learn that the moon is round? In what other way does the moon become round for her?

Interpreting

5. Why does Welty think it appropriate for the flower and the pencil to smell alike?
6. Explain the meaning of Herschel Brickell's advice.

Applying

7. Do you agree with Welty that the new should be rising? Explain your answer.
8. Do you think it necessary for an artist to see the world with a childlike sense of wonder? Explain your answer.

ANALYZING LITERATURE
Understanding the Informal Essay

An essay is a brief work of nonfiction in which a writer explores a topic and expresses an opinion or conclusion. It can be thought of as a kind of thinking aloud on paper. In an informal essay, writers use a conversational tone, injecting their personality into their observations.

1. What is the topic of this essay? What opinion does the writer express about this topic?
2. What impression do you form of Eudora Welty on the basis of this essay? Find evidence in the selection to support your answer.

CRITICAL THINKING AND READING
Comparing and Contrasting Opinions

An **opinion** is a personal view or a judgment or belief that rests on grounds insufficient to prove it true. People can consider the same topic and form different opinions. For example, Welty reached a special awareness of the meaning of words.

Compare and contrast Welty's understanding of words with those of the following writers.

1. Ellen Glasow: "I haven't much opinion of words . . . They're apt to set fire to a dry tongue, that's what I say."
2. Samuel Butler: "Words are like money; there is nothing so useless, unless in actual use."
3. Hermann Hesse: "Words are really a mask. They rarely express the true meaning; in fact they tend to hide it."
4. Aldous Huxley: "Words form the thread on which we string our experiences."

UNDERSTANDING LANGUAGE
Tracing Word Histories

Words have histories, just as people do. The word *lunatic,* for example, is based on *luna,* the Latin word for moon. A lunatic was thought to be moonstruck, or caused to go crazy by the influence of the moon.

Explain the meaning of each word. How does each relate to the Latin word for moon?

1. lunar
2. lunacy
3. lunation
4. lunarian

THINKING AND WRITING
Writing About Beginnings

Eudora Welty chose to write about a writer's beginnings. Think about another field—art, sports, teaching, medicine, or the like. Select a career. Then list the traits you think are necessary to be successful in that career. Using your list to guide you, write an essay entitled, "A _____'s Beginnings." In your essay explain how you think a young person comes to realize these traits. Revise your essay, making sure you have organized your information in a logical fashion. Proofread your essay and share it with your classmates.

Biographies and Personal Accounts

MANY BRAVE HEARTS
Charles Demuth
Hirshhorn Museum and Sculpture Garden, Smithsonian Institution

Harriet Tubman: Guide to Freedom

Ann Petry (1912–   ) worked as a newspaper reporter in New York City after college. Her first book, *The Street,* was set in Harlem, in northern New York City. Her short stories have appeared in magazines. Growing up in Old Saybrook, Connecticut, Petry decided that Harriet Tubman stood for everything indomitable, or not easily discouraged, in the human spirit. The following selection is from *Harriet Tubman: Conductor of the Underground Railroad.*

Biography

A **biography** is an account of a person's life as written by another person. A biography tells you about events in the person's life, focusing on his or her achievements and the difficulties that the person had to overcome. The biographer must create a living, believable character and stick to the known facts about the person. Usually an author chooses as a subject of a biography someone who has achieved something significant.

Look For

As you read "Harriet Tubman: Guide to Freedom," look for descriptions of Tubman that show that her spirit is not easily discouraged. Why would someone choose to write a biography about her?

Writing

In the selection you are about to read, Harriet Tubman shows great courage while facing many dangers. Imagine a situation in which a character faces danger with courage. Freewrite about this experience, describing what happens and how the character feels.

Vocabulary

Knowing the following words will help you as you read "Harriet Tubman: Guide to Freedom."

incentive (in sen′ tiv) *n.*: Something that stirs up people or urges them on (p. 385)
disheveled (di ѕhev′′ld) *adj.*: Untidy; messy (p. 385)
guttural (gut′ ər əl) *adj.*: Made in back of the throat (p. 386)
mutinous (myo͞ot′′n əs) *adj.*: Rebelling against authority (p. 387)

cajoling (kə jōl′ iŋ) *v.*: Coaxing gently (p. 389)
indomitable (in däm′ it ə b′l) *adj.*: Not easily discouraged (p. 389)
fastidious (fas tid′ ē əs) *adj.*: Not easy to please (p. 390)

Harriet Tubman: Guide to Freedom

Ann Petry

Along the Eastern Shore of Maryland, in Dorchester County, in Caroline County, the masters kept hearing whispers about the man named Moses, who was running off slaves. At first they did not believe in his existence. The stories about him were fantastic, unbelievable. Yet they watched for him. They offered rewards for his capture.

They never saw him. Now and then they heard whispered rumors to the effect that he was in the neighborhood. The woods were searched. The roads were watched. There was never anything to indicate his whereabouts. But a few days afterward, a goodly number of slaves would be gone from the plantation. Neither the master nor the overseer had heard or seen anything unusual in the quarter. Sometimes one or the other would vaguely remember having heard a whippoorwill call somewhere in the woods, close by, late at night. Though it was the wrong season for whippoorwills.

Sometimes the masters thought they had heard the cry of a hoot owl, repeated, and would remember having thought that the intervals between the low moaning cry were wrong, that it had been repeated four times in succession instead of three. There was never anything more than that to suggest that all was not well in the quarter. Yet when morning came, they invariably discov-ered that a group of the finest slaves had taken to their heels.

Unfortunately, the discovery was almost always made on a Sunday. Thus a whole day was lost before the machinery of pursuit could be set in motion. The posters offering rewards for the fugitives could not be print-ed until Monday. The men who made a living hunting for runaway slaves were out of reach, off in the woods with their dogs and their guns, in pursuit of four-footed game, or they were in camp meetings[1] saying their prayers with their wives and families beside them.

Harriet Tubman could have told them that there was far more involved in this matter of running off slaves than signaling the would-be runaways by imitating the call of a whippoorwill, or a hoot owl, far more involved than a matter of waiting for a clear night when the North Star was visible.

In December 1851, when she started out with the band of fugitives that she planned to take to Canada, she had been in the vicinity of the plantation for days, planning the trip, carefully selecting the slaves that she would take with her.

She had announced her arrival in the

---

1. camp meetings *n.:* Religious meetings held outdoors or in a tent.

HARRIET TUBMAN SERIES, #7
Jacob Lawrence
Hampton University Museum

quarter by singing the forbidden spiritual [2]—"Go down, Moses, 'way down to Egypt Land"—singing it softly outside the door of a slave cabin, late at night. The husky voice was beautiful even when it was barely more than a murmur borne on the wind.

Once she had made her presence known, word of her coming spread from cabin to cabin. The slaves whispered to each other, ear to mouth, mouth to ear, "Moses is here." "Moses has come." "Get ready. Moses is back again." The ones who had

agreed to go North with her put ashcake and salt herring in an old bandanna, hastily tied it into a bundle, and then waited patiently for the signal that meant it was time to start.

There were eleven in this party, including one of her brothers and his wife. It was the largest group that she had ever conducted, but she was determined that more and more slaves should know what freedom was like.

She had to take them all the way to Canada. The Fugitive Slave Law [3] was no longer a great many incomprehensible words written down on the country's lawbooks. The new law had become a reality. It was Thomas Sims, a boy, picked up on the streets of Boston at night and shipped back to Georgia. It was Jerry and Shadrach, arrested and jailed with no warning.

She had never been in Canada. The route beyond Philadelphia was strange to her. But she could not let the runaways who accompanied her know this. As they walked along she told them stories of her own first flight, she kept painting vivid word pictures of what it would be like to be free.

But there were so many of them this time. She knew moments of doubt when she was half-afraid, and kept looking back over her shoulder, imagining that she heard the sound of pursuit. They would certainly be pursued. Eleven of them. Eleven thousand dollars' worth of flesh and bone and muscle that belonged to Maryland planters. If they were caught, the eleven runaways would be whipped and sold South, but she—she would probably be hanged.

They tried to sleep during the day but they never could wholly relax into sleep. She

2. forbidden spiritual: In 1831 a slave named Nat Turner encouraged an unsuccessful slave uprising in Virginia, by talking about the Biblical story of the Israelites' escape from Egypt. Afterwards, the singing of certain spirituals was forbidden, for fear of encouraging more uprisings.

3. Fugitive Slave Law: This part of the Compromise of 1850 held that escaped slaves, even if found in free states, could be returned to their masters. As a result, fugitives were not safe until they were in Canada.

could tell by the positions they assumed, by their restless movements. And they walked at night. Their progress was slow. It took them three nights of walking to reach the first stop. She had told them about the place where they would stay, promising warmth and good food, holding these things out to them as an incentive to keep going.

When she knocked on the door of a farmhouse, a place where she and her parties of runaways had always been welcome, always been given shelter and plenty to eat, there was no answer. She knocked again, softly. A voice from within said, "Who is it?" There was fear in the voice.

She knew instantly from the sound of the voice that there was something wrong. She said, "A friend with friends," the password on the Underground Railroad.

The door opened, slowly. The man who stood in the doorway looked at her coldly, looked with unconcealed astonishment and fear at the eleven disheveled runaways who were standing near her. Then he shouted, "Too many, too many. It's not safe. My place was searched last week. It's not safe!" and slammed the door in her face.

She turned away from the house, frowning. She had promised her passengers food and rest and warmth, and instead of that, there would be hunger and cold and more walking over the frozen ground. Somehow she would have to instill courage into these eleven people, most of them strangers, would have to feed them on hope and bright dreams of freedom instead of the fried pork and corn bread and milk she had promised them.

They stumbled along behind her, half-dead for sleep, and she urged them on, though she was as tired and as discouraged as they were. She had never been in Canada but she kept painting wondrous word pictures of what it would be like. She man-aged to dispel their fear of pursuit, so that they would not become hysterical, panic-stricken. Then she had to bring some of the fear back, so that they would stay awake and keep walking though they drooped with sleep.

Yet during the day, when they lay down deep in a thicket, they never really slept, because if a twig snapped or the wind sighed in the branches of a pine tree, they jumped to their feet, afraid of their own shadows, shivering and shaking. It was very cold, but they dared not make fires because someone would see the smoke and wonder about it.

She kept thinking, eleven of them. Eleven thousand dollars' worth of slaves. And she had to take them all the way to Canada. Sometimes she told them about Thomas Garrett, in Wilmington. She said he was their friend even though he did not know them. He was the friend of all fugitives. He called them God's poor. He was a Quaker and his speech was a little different from that of other people. His clothing was different, too. He wore the wide-brimmed hat that the Quakers wear.

She said that he had thick white hair, soft, almost like a baby's, and the kindest eyes she had ever seen. He was a big man and strong, but he had never used his strength to harm anyone, always to help people. He would give all of them a new pair of shoes. Everybody. He always did. Once they reached his house in Wilmington, they would be safe. He would see to it that they were.

She described the house where he lived, told them about the store where he sold shoes. She said he kept a pail of milk and a loaf of bread in the drawer of his desk so that he would have food ready at hand for any of God's poor who should suddenly appear before him, fainting with hunger. There was a hidden room in the store. A whole wall

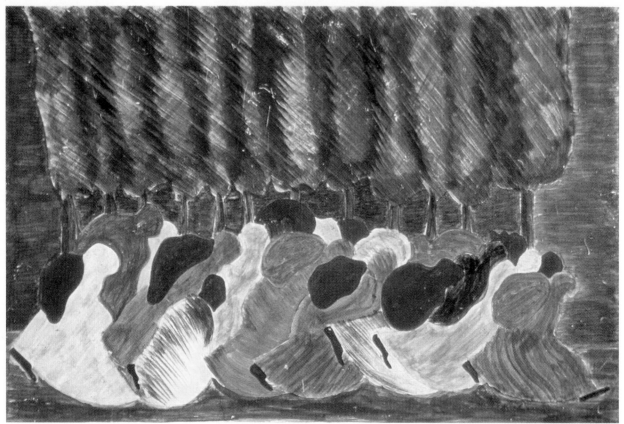

HARRIET TUBMAN SERIES, #16
Jacob Lawrence
Hampton University Museum

swung open, and behind it was a room where he could hide fugitives. On the wall there were shelves filled with small boxes —boxes of shoes—so that you would never guess that the wall actually opened.

While she talked, she kept watching them. They did not believe her. She could tell by their expressions. They were thinking. New shoes, Thomas Garrett, Quaker, Wilmington—what foolishness was this? Who knew if she told the truth? Where was she taking them anyway?

That night they reached the next stop—a farm that belonged to a German. She made the runaways take shelter behind trees at the edge of the fields before she knocked at the door. She hesitated before she approached the door, thinking, suppose that he, too, should refuse shelter, suppose—Then she thought, Lord, I'm going to hold steady on to You and You've got to see me through—and knocked softly.

She heard the familiar guttural voice say, "Who's there?"

She answered quickly, "A friend with friends."

He opened the door and greeted her warmly. "How many this time?" he asked.

"Eleven," she said and waited, doubting, wondering.

He said, "Good. Bring them in."

He and his wife fed them in the lamplit kitchen, their faces glowing, as they offered food and more food, urging them to eat, saying there was plenty for everybody, have more milk, have more bread, have more meat.

They spent the night in the warm kitchen. They really slept, all that night and until dusk the next day. When they left, it was with reluctance. They had all been warm and safe and well-fed. It was hard to exchange the security offered by that clean, warm kitchen for the darkness and the cold of a December night.

Harriet had found it hard to leave the warmth and friendliness, too. But she urged them on. For a while, as they walked, they seemed to carry in them a measure of contentment; some of the serenity and the cleanliness of that big warm kitchen lingered on inside them. But as they walked farther and farther away from the warmth and the light, the cold and the darkness entered into them. They fell silent, sullen, suspicious. She waited for the moment when some one of them would turn mutinous. It did not happen that night.

Two nights later she was aware that the feet behind her were moving slower and slower. She heard the irritability in their voices, knew that soon someone would refuse to go on.

She started talking about William Still and the Philadelphia Vigilance Committee.[4] No one commented. No one asked any questions. She told them the story of William and Ellen Craft and how they escaped from Georgia. Ellen was so fair that she looked as though she were white, and so she dressed up in a man's clothing and she looked like a wealthy young planter. Her husband, William, who was dark, played the role of her slave. Thus they traveled from Macon, Georgia, to Philadelphia, riding on the trains, staying at the finest hotels. Ellen pretended to be very ill—her right arm was in a sling, and her right hand was bandaged, because she was supposed to have rheumatism. Thus she avoided having to sign the register at the hotels for she could not read or write. They finally arrived safely in Philadelphia, and then went on to Boston.

No one said anything. Not one of them seemed to have heard her.

She told them about Frederick Douglass, the most famous of the escaped slaves, of his eloquence, of his magnificent appearance. Then she told them of her own first vain effort at running away, evoking the memory of that miserable life she had led as a child, reliving it for a moment in the telling.

But they had been tired too long, hungry too long, afraid too long, footsore too long. One of them suddenly cried out in despair, "Let me go back. It is better to be a slave than to suffer like this in order to be free."

She carried a gun with her on these trips. She had never used it—except as a threat. Now as she aimed it, she experienced a feeling of guilt, remembering that time, years ago, when she had prayed for the death of Edward Brodas, the Master, and then not too long afterward had heard that great wailing cry that came from the throats of the field hands, and knew from the sound that the Master was dead.

One of the runaways said, again, "Let me go back. Let me go back," and stood still, and then turned around and said, over his shoulder, "I am going back."

She lifted the gun, aimed it at the despairing slave. She said, "Go on with us or die." The husky low-pitched voice was grim.

He hesitated for a moment and then he joined the others. They started walking again. She tried to explain to them why none of them could go back to the plantation. If a

---

4. Philadelphia Vigilance Committee: A group of citizens who helped escaped slaves. Its secretary was a free black man named William Still.

runaway returned, he would turn traitor, the master and the overseer would force him to turn traitor. The returned slave would disclose the stopping places, the hiding places, the cornstacks they had used with the full knowledge of the owner of the farm, the name of the German farmer who had fed them and sheltered them. These people who had risked their own security to help runaways would be ruined, fined, imprisoned.

She said, "We got to go free or die. And freedom's not bought with dust."

This time she told them about the long agony of the Middle Passage on the old slave ships, about the black horror of the holds, about the chains and the whips. They too knew these stories. But she wanted to remind them of the long hard way they had come, about the long hard way they had yet to go. She told them about Thomas Sims, the boy picked up on the streets of Boston and sent back to Georgia. She said when they got him back to Savannah, got him in prison there, they whipped him until a doctor who was standing by watching said, "You will kill him if you strike him again!" His master said, "Let him die!"

Thus she forced them to go on. Sometimes she thought she had become nothing but a voice speaking in the darkness, cajoling, urging, threatening. Sometimes she told them things to make them laugh, sometimes she sang to them, and heard the eleven voices behind her blending softly with hers, and then she knew that for the moment all was well with them.

She gave the impression of being a short, muscular, indomitable woman who could never be defeated. Yet at any moment she was liable to be seized by one of those curious fits of sleep, which might last for a few minutes or for hours.[5]

Even on this trip, she suddenly fell asleep in the woods. The runaways, ragged, dirty, hungry, cold, did not steal the gun as they might have, and set off by themselves, or turn back. They sat on the ground near her and waited patiently until she awakened. They had come to trust her implicitly, totally. They, too, had come to believe her repeated statement, "We got to go free or die." She was leading them into freedom, and so they waited until she was ready to go on.

Finally, they reached Thomas Garrett's house in Wilmington, Delaware. Just as Harriet had promised, Garrett gave them all new shoes, and provided carriages to take them on to the next stop.

By slow stages they reached Philadelphia, where William Still hastily recorded their names, and the plantations whence they had come, and something of the life they had led in slavery. Then he carefully hid what he had written, for fear it might be discovered. In 1872 he published this record in book form and called it *The Underground Railroad.* In the foreword to his book he said: "While I knew the danger of keeping strict records, and while I did not then dream that in my day slavery would be blotted out, or that the time would come when I could publish these records, it used to afford me great satisfaction to take them down, fresh from the lips of fugitives on the way to freedom, and to preserve them as they had given them."

William Still, who was familiar with all the station stops on the Underground Railroad, supplied Harriet with money and sent her and her eleven fugitives on to Burlington, New Jersey.

Harriet felt safer now, though there were danger spots ahead. But the biggest part of her job was over. As they went farther and farther north, it grew colder; she was aware of the wind on the Jersey ferry and aware of the cold damp in New York. From New York they went on to Syracuse, where the temperature was even lower.

In Syracuse she met the Reverend J. W. Loguen, known as "Jarm" Loguen. This was the beginning of a lifelong friendship. Both Harriet and Jarm Loguen were to become friends and supporters of Old John Brown.[6]

From Syracuse they went north again, into a colder, snowier city—Rochester. Here they almost certainly stayed with Frederick Douglass, for he wrote in his autobiography:

"On one occasion I had eleven fugitives at the same time under my roof, and it was necessary for them to remain with me until

---

5. sleep . . . hours: When she was about 13, Harriet accidentally received a severe blow on the head. Afterwards, she often lost consciousness, and could not be woken until the episode was over.

6. John Brown: White abolitionist (1800–1859) who was hanged for leading a raid on the arsenal at Harpers Ferry, Virginia, as part of a slave uprising.

I could collect sufficient money to get them to Canada. It was the largest number I ever had at any one time, and I had some difficulty in providing so many with food and shelter, but, as may well be imagined, they were not very fastidious in either direction, and were well content with very plain food, and a strip of carpet on the floor for a bed, or a place on the straw in the barnloft.''

Late in December, 1851, Harriet arrived in St. Catharines, Canada West (now Ontario), with the eleven fugitives. It had taken almost a month to complete this journey; most of the time had been spent getting out of Maryland.

That first winter in St. Catharines was a terrible one. Canada was a strange frozen land, snow everywhere, ice everywhere, and a bone-biting cold the like of which none of them had ever experienced before. Harriet rented a small frame house in the town and set to work to make a home. The fugitives boarded with her. They worked in the forests, felling trees, and so did she. Sometimes she took other jobs, cooking or cleaning house for people in the town. She cheered on these newly arrived fugitives, working herself, finding work for them, finding food for them, praying for them, sometimes begging for them.

Often she found herself thinking of the beauty of Maryland, the mellowness of the soil, the richness of the plant life there. The climate itself made for an ease of living that could never be duplicated in this bleak, barren countryside.

In spite of the severe cold, the hard work, she came to love St. Catharines, and the other towns and cities in Canada where black men lived. She discovered that freedom meant more than the right to change jobs at will, more than the right to keep the money that one earned. It was the right to vote and to sit on juries. It was the right to be elected to office. In Canada there were black men who were county officials and members of school boards. St. Catharines had a large colony of ex-slaves, and they owned their own homes, kept them neat and clean and in good repair. They lived in whatever part of town they chose and sent their children to the schools.

When spring came she decided that she would make this small Canadian city her home—as much as any place could be said to be home to a woman who traveled from Canada to the Eastern Shore of Maryland as often as she did.

In the spring of 1852, she went back to Cape May, New Jersey. She spent the summer there, cooking in a hotel. That fall she returned, as usual, to Dorchester County, and brought out nine more slaves, conducting them all the way to St. Catharines, in Canada West, to the bone-biting cold, the snow-covered forests—and freedom.

She continued to live in this fashion, spending the winter in Canada, and the spring and summer working in Cape May, New Jersey, or in Philadelphia. She made two trips a year into slave territory, one in the fall and another in the spring. She now had a definite crystallized purpose, and in carrying it out, her life fell into a pattern which remained unchanged for the next six years.

THINKING ABOUT THE SELECTION
Recalling

1. How did Harriet Tubman announce her arrival in the slave quarter?
2. Why was it smart of Tubman to plan escapes on Saturday nights?
3. Why was no fugitive allowed to turn back?

Interpreting

4. Why was Moses an appropriate name for Harriet Tubman?
5. Why did Tubman never tell any of the fugitives that she was afraid?
6. In what sense was Tubman a "guide to freedom"? In what sense was she a "conductor on the railroad"?

Applying

7. Like the Israelites escaping Egypt, the slaves escaped to freedom. What other groups today have made similar escapes? What qualities do such people have?

ANALYZING LITERATURE
Understanding Biography

A biography, or account of a person's life written by another person, often focuses on the achievements of the person's life. The writer may tell you about the difficulties the person overcame.

1. How do you think the author wants you to feel about her subject—Harriet Tubman?
2. Find three details of Tubman's life that help create this impression.
3. For what reasons do you think Tubman is a good subject for a biography?

CRITICAL THINKING AND READING
Recognizing Subjective Details

Writers often include both objective and subjective details in a biography. **Objective details** are true-to-life descriptions that do not include personal feelings or judgments. For example, the writer says, "There were eleven in this party, including one of her brothers and his wife."

Subjective details are descriptions that tell you a person's feelings, attitudes, or judgments instead of external facts. An example is, ". . . she was determined that more and more slaves should know what freedom was like."

Identify which of the following contain subjective and which contain objective details.

1. "She knew moments of doubt when she was half-afraid, and kept looking back over her shoulder, imagining that she heard the sound of pursuit."
2. "In December 1851, when she started out with the band of fugitives that she planned to take to Canada, she had been in the vicinity of the plantation for days. . . ."

UNDERSTANDING LANGUAGE
Using Latin Roots

A **root** is a word or word part to which other parts may be added to make new words. The root *duct* comes from the Latin word *ducere*, meaning "to lead." For example, the word *conduct* means "to lead or direct an orchestra."

Explain how the root *duct* gives meaning to these English words.

1. educate 2. deduct 3. production

THINKING AND WRITING
Writing a Biography

Choose a person whom you admire. Select one incident in the person's life that portrays the qualities you most associate with that person. The incident may be one in which the person overcame an obstacle. Freewrite about this incident. Using the information from your freewriting, write a biographical sketch. Revise your sketch, making sure you have portrayed your subject vividly. Proofread your sketch.

Roberto Clemente: A Bittersweet Memoir

Jerry Izenberg (1930–   ), a graduate of Rutgers University, is a sportswriter and reporter. He is a syndicated sports columnist based at the *Newark Star Ledger,* whose daily column appears in newspapers around the country. He has written seven books and written or directed thirty-one television specials. In the following selection from *Great Latin Sports Figures,* published in 1976, he portrays the inspiration of Roberto Clemente, the former All-Star right fielder and record-making hitter for the Pittsburgh Pirates.

Memoir

A **memoir** is a biographical piece usually written by a relative or personal friend of the subject. The writer has based this memoir about Roberto Clemente on interviews and anecdotes.

An interview is a planned meeting at which writers obtain information about a topic from someone who is knowledgeable about it. Izenberg gathered first-hand information about Roberto Clemente through interviews with people who had known him well.

Answers to interview questions often provide anecdotes—brief stories about noteworthy incidents—that give information and show the person in a different light.

Look For

As you read "Roberto Clemente: A Bittersweet Memoir," look for the information gained from others through interviews and the anecdotes that help create this strong, personal memoir. Why does Clemente's life serve as an inspiration to others?

Writing

List five well-known people about whom you might like to write a memoir. Note the field or career of each person, for example, Alice Walker—American writer.

Vocabulary

Knowing the following words will help you as you read "Roberto Clemente: A Bittersweet Memoir."

delineate (di lin′ ē āt′) v.: Describe in detail (p. 393)

brace (brās) n.: A pair of like things (p. 393)

conjectured (kən jek′ chərd) v.: Guessed from very little evidence (p. 394)

banked (baŋkt) v.: Tilted an airplane to the side when turning, making one wing higher than the other (p. 395)

crypt (kript) n.: An underground vault or room, used as a burial place (p. 397)

prospect (präs′ pekt) n.: A likely candidate (p. 399)

Roberto Clemente:
A Bittersweet Memoir

Jerry Izenberg

I saw him play so often. I watched the grace of his movements and the artistry of his reflexes from who knows how many press boxes. None of us really appreciated how pure an athlete he was until he was gone. What follows is a personal retracing of the steps that took Roberto Clemente from the narrow, crowded streets of his native Carolina to the local ball parks in San Juan and on to the major leagues. But it is more. It is a remembrance formed as I stood at the water's edge in Puerto Rico and stared at daybreak into the waves that killed him. It is all the people I met in Puerto Rico who knew him and loved him. It is the way an entire island in the sun and a Pennsylvania city in the smog took his death. . . .

The record book will tell you that Roberto Clemente collected 3,000 hits during his major-league career. It will say that he came to bat 9,454 times, that he drove in 1,305 runs, and played 2,433 games over an eighteen-year span.

But it won't tell you about Carolina, Puerto Rico; and the old square; and the narrow, twisting streets; and the roots that produced him. It won't tell you about the Julio Coronado School and a remarkable woman named María Isabella Casares,

whom he called "Teacher" until the day he died and who helped to shape his life in times of despair and depression. It won't tell you about a man named Pedron Zarrilla, who found him on a country softball team and put him in the uniform of the Santurce club and who nursed him from promising young athlete to major-league superstar.

And most of all, those cold numbers won't begin to delineate the man Roberto Clemente was. To even begin to understand what this magnificent athlete was all about, you have to work backward. The search begins at the site of its ending.

The car moves easily through the pre-dawn streets of San Juan. A heavy all-night rain has now begun to drive, and there is that postrain sweetness in the air that holds the promise of a new, fresh, clear dawn. This is a journey to the site of one of Puerto Rico's deepest tragedies. This last says a lot. Tragedy is no stranger to the sensitive emotional people who make this island the human place it is.

Shortly before the first rays of sunlight, the car turns down a bumpy secondary road and moves past small shantytowns, where the sounds of the children stirring for the long walk toward school begin to drift out on the morning air. Then there is another turn, between a brace of trees and onto the hard-packed dirt and sand, and although the light has not yet quite begun to break, you can sense the nearness of the ocean. You can hear its waves, pounding harshly against the jagged rocks. You can smell its saltiness. The car noses to a stop, and the driver says, "From here you must walk. There is no other way." The place is called Puente Maldonado and the dawn does not slip into this angry place. It explodes in a million lights and colors as the large fireball of the sun begins to nose above the horizon.

"This is the nearest place," the driver tells me. "This is where they came by the thousands on that New Year's Eve and New Year's Day. Out there," he says, gesturing with his right hand, "out there, perhaps a mile and a half from where we stand. That's where we think the plane went down."

The final hours of Roberto Clemente were like this. Just a month or so before, he had agreed to take a junior-league baseball team to Nicaragua and manage it in an all-star game in Managua. He had met people and made friends there. He was not a man who made friends casually. He had always said that the people you wanted to give your friendship to were the people for whom you had to be willing to give something in return—no matter what the price.

Two weeks after he returned from that trip, Managua, Nicaragua exploded into flames. The earth trembled and people died. It was the worst earthquake anywhere in the Western Hemisphere in a long, long time.

Back in Puerto Rico, a television personality named Luis Vigereaux heard the news and was moved to try to help the victims. He needed someone to whom the people would listen, someone who could say what had to be said and get the work done that had to be done and help the people who had to be helped.

"I knew," Luis Vigereaux said, "that Roberto was such a person, perhaps the only such person who would be willing to help."

And so the mercy project, which would eventually claim Roberto's life, began. He appeared on television. But he needed a staging area. The city agreed to give him Sixto Escobar Stadium.

"Bring what you can," he told them. "Bring medicine . . . bring clothes . . . bring food . . . bring shoes . . . bring yourself to help us load. We need so much. Whatever you bring, we will use."

And the people of San Juan came. They walked through the heat and they drove old cars and battered little trucks, and the mound of supplies grew and grew. Within two days, the first mercy planes left for Nicaragua.

Meanwhile, a ship had been chartered and loaded. And as it prepared to steam away, unhappy stories began to drift back from Nicaragua. Not all the supplies that had been flown in, it was rumored, were getting through. Puerto Ricans who had flown the planes had no passports, and Nicaragua was in a state of panic.

"We have people there who must be protected. We have black-market types who must not be allowed to get their hands on these supplies," Clemente told Luis Vigereaux. "Someone must make sure—particularly before the ship gets there. I'm going on the next plane."

The plane they had rented was an old DC-7. It was scheduled to take off at 4 P.M. on December 31, 1972. Long before take-off time, it was apparent that the plane needed more work. It had even taxied onto the runway and then turned back. The trouble, a mechanic who was at the airstrip that day conjectured, "had to do with both port [left side] engines. We worked on them most of the afternoon.''

The departure time was delayed an hour, and then two, and then three. Across town, a man named Rudy Hernandez, who had been a teammate of Roberto's when they were rookies in the Puerto Rican League and who had later pitched for the Washington Senators, was trying to contact Roberto by telephone. He had just received a five-hundred-dollar donation, and he wanted to know where to send it. He called Roberto's wife, Vera, who told him that Roberto was going on a trip and that he might catch him at the airport. She had been there herself only moments before to pick up some friends who were coming in from the States, and she had left because she was fairly sure that the trouble had cleared and Roberto had probably left already.

"I caught him at the airport and I was surprised,'' Rudy Hernandez told me. "I said I had this money for Nicaraguan relief and I wanted to know what to do with it. Then I asked him where he was going.''

"Nicaragua,'' Clemente told him.

"It's New Year's Eve, Roberto. Let it wait.''

"Who else will go?'' Roberto told him. "Someone has to do it.''

At 9 P.M., even as the first stirrings of the annual New Year's Eve celebration were beginning in downtown San Juan, the DC-7 taxied onto the runway, received clearance, rumbled down the narrow concrete strip, and pulled away from the earth. It headed out over the Atlantic and banked toward Nicaragua, and its tiny lights disappeared on the horizon.

Just ninety seconds later, the tower at San Juan International Airport received this message from the pilot: "We are coming back around.''

Just that.

Nothing more.

And then there was a great silence.

"It was almost midnight,'' recalls Rudy Hernandez, a former teammate of Roberto's. "We were having this party in my restaurant, and somebody turned on the radio and the announcer was saying that Roberto's plane was feared missing. And then, because my place is on the beach, we saw these giant floodlights crisscrossing the waves, and we heard the sound of the helicopters and the little search planes.''

Drawn by a common sadness, the people of San Juan began to make their way toward the beach, toward Puente Maldonado. A cold rain had begun to fall. It washed their faces and blended with the tears.

They came by the thousands, and they watched for three days. Towering waves boiled up and made the search virtually impossible. The U.S. Navy sent a team of expert divers into the area, but the battering of the waves defeated them too. Midway through the week, the pilot's body was found in the swift-moving currents to the north. On Saturday bits of the cockpit were sighted.

And then—nothing else.

"I was born in the Dominican Republic," Rudy Hernandez said, "but I've lived on this island for more than twenty years. I have never seen a time or a sadness like that. The streets were empty, the radios silent, except for the constant bulletins about Roberto. Traffic? Forget it. All of us cried. All of us who knew him and even those who didn't, wept that week.

"Manny Sanguillen, the Pittsburgh catcher, was down here playing winter ball, and when Manny heard the news he ran to the beach and he tried to jump into the ocean with skin-diving gear. I told him, man, there's sharks there. You can't help. Leave it to the experts. But he kept going back. All of us were a little crazy that week.

"There will never be another like Roberto."

Who was he . . . I mean really?

Well, nobody can put together all the pieces of another man's life. But there are so many who want the world to know that it is not as impossible a search as you might think.

He was born in Carolina, Puerto Rico. Today the town has about 125,000 people, but when Roberto was born there in 1934, it was roughly one sixth its current size.

María Isabella Casares is a schoolteacher. She has taught the children of Carolina for thirty years. Most of her teaching has been done in tenth-grade history classes. Carolina is her home, and its children are her children. And among all of those whom she calls her own (who are all the children she taught), Roberto Clemente was something even more special to her.

"His father was an overseer on a sugar plantation. He did not make much money," she explained in an empty classroom at Julio Coronado School. "But then, there are no rich children here. There never have been. Roberto was typical of them. I had known him when he was a small boy because my father had run a grocery store in Carolina, and Roberto's parents used to shop there."

There is this thing that you have to know about María Isabella Casares before we hear more from her. What you have to know is that she is the model of what a teacher should be. Between her and her students even now, as back when Roberto attended her school, there is this common bond of mutual respect. Earlier in the day, I had watched her teach a class in the history of the Abolition Movement in Puerto Rico. I don't speak much Spanish, but even to me it was clear that this is how a class should be, this is the kind of person who should teach, and these are the kinds of students such a teacher will produce.

With this as a background, what she has to say about Roberto Clemente carries much more impact.

"Each year," she said, "I let my students choose the seats they want to sit in. I remember the first time I saw Roberto. He was a very shy boy and he went straight to the back of the room and chose the very last seat. Most of the time he would sit with his eyes down. He was an average student. But there was something very special about him. We would talk after class for hours. He wanted to be an engineer, you know, and perhaps he could have been. But then he began to play softball, and one day he came to me and said, 'Teacher, I have a problem.'

"He told me that Pedron Zarrilla, who was one of our most prominent baseball people, had seen him play, and that Pedron wanted him to sign a professional contract with the Santurce Crabbers. He asked me what he should do.

"I have thought about that conversation many times. I believe Roberto could have been almost anything, but God gave him a gift that few have, and he chose to use that gift. I remember that on that day I told him, 'This is your chance, Roberto. We are poor people in this town. This is your chance to do something. But if in your heart you prefer not to try, then, Roberto, that will be your problem—and your decision.' "

There was and there always remained a closeness between this boy-soon-to-be-a-man and his favorite teacher.

"Once, a few years ago, I was sick with a very bad back. Roberto, not knowing this, had driven over from Rio Piedras, where his house was, to see me."

"Where is the teacher?" Roberto asked Mrs. Casares' stepdaughter that afternoon.

"Teacher is sick, Roberto. She is in bed."

"Teacher," Roberto said, pounding on the bedroom door "get up and put on your clothes. We are going to the doctor whether you want to or not."

"I got dressed," Mrs. Casares told me, "and he picked me up like a baby and carried me in his arms to the car. He came every day for fifteen days, and most days he had to carry me, but I went to the doctor and he treated me. Afterward, I said to the doctor that I wanted to pay the bill.

"'Mrs. Casares', he told me, 'please don't start with that Clemente, or he will kill me. He has paid all your bills, and don't you dare tell him I have told you.'

"Well, Roberto was like that. We had been so close. You know, I think I was there the day he met Vera, the girl he later married. She was one of my students, too. I was working part-time in the pharmacy and he

was already a baseball player by then, and one day Vera came into the store.

"'Teacher,' Roberto asked me, 'who is that girl?'

"'That's one of my students,' I told him. 'Now don't you dare bother her. Go out and get someone to introduce you. Behave yourself.'

"He was so proper, you know. That's just what he did, and that's how he met her, and they were married here in Carolina in the big church on the square."

On the night Roberto Clemente's plane disappeared, Mrs. Casares was at home, and a delivery boy from the pharmacy stopped by and told her to turn on the radio and sit down. "I think something has happened to someone who is very close with you, Teacher, and I want to be here in case you need help."

María Isabella Casares heard the news. She is a brave woman, and months later, standing in front of the empty crypt in the cemetery at Carolina where Roberto Clemente was to have been buried, she said, "He was like a son to me. This is why I want to tell you about him. This is why you must make people—particularly our people, our Puerto Rican children—understand what he was. He was like my son, and he is all our sons in a way. We must make sure that the children never forget how beautiful a man he was."

The next person to touch Roberto Clemente was Pedron Zarrilla, who owned the Santurce club. He was the man who discovered Clemente on the country softball team, and he was the man who signed him for a four-hundred-dollar bonus.

"He was a skinny kid," Pedron Zarrilla recalls, "but even then he had those large, powerful hands, which we all noticed right away. He joined us, and he was nervous. But I watched him, and I said to myself, 'this kid can throw and this kid can run, and this kid

can hit. We will be patient with him.' The season had been through several games before I finally sent him in to play.''

Luis Olmo remembers that game. Luis Olmo had been a major-league outfielder with the Brooklyn Dodgers. He had been a splendid ballplayer. Today he is in the insurance business in San Juan. He sat in his office and recalled very well that first moment when Roberto Clemente stepped up to bat.

''I was managing the other team. They had a man on base and this skinny kid comes out. Well, we had never seen him, so we didn't really know how to pitch to him. I decided to throw him a few bad balls and see if he'd bite.

''He hit the first pitch. It was an outside fast ball, and he never should have been able to reach it. But he hit it down the line for a double. He was the best bad-ball hitter I have ever seen, and if you ask major-league pitchers who are pitching today, they will tell you the same thing. After a while it got so that I just told my pitchers

to throw the ball down the middle because he was going to hit it no matter where they put it, and at least if he decided not to swing, we'd have a strike on him.

''I played in the big leagues. I know what I am saying. He was the greatest we ever had . . . maybe one of the greatest anyone ever had. Why did he have to die?''

Once Pedron Zarrilla turned him loose, there was no stopping Roberto Clemente. As Clemente's confidence grew, he began to get better and better. He was the one the crowds came to see out at Sixto Escobar Stadium.

''You know, when Clemente was in the lineup,'' Pedron Zarrilla says, ''there was always this undercurrent of excitement in the ball park. You knew that if he was coming to bat, he would do something spectacular. You knew that if he was on first base, he was going to try to get to second base. You knew that if he was playing right field and there was a man on third base, then that man on third base already knew what a lot of men on third base in the majors were going to find out—you don't try to get home against Roberto Clemente's arm.''

''I remember the year that Willie Mays came down here to play in the same outfield with him for the winter season. I remember the wonderful things they did and I remember that Roberto still had the best of it.

''Sure I knew we were going to lose him. I knew it was just a matter of time. But I was only grateful that we could have him if only for that little time.''

The major-league scouts began to make their moves. Olmo was then scouting, and he tried to sign him for the Giants. But it was the Dodgers who won the bidding war. The Dodgers had Clemente, but in having him, they had a major problem. He had to be hidden.

This part takes a little explaining. Under the complicated draft rules that baseball used at that time, if the Dodgers were not prepared to bring Clemente up to their major-league team within a year (and because they were winning with proven players, they couldn't), then Clemente could be claimed by another team.

They sent him to Montreal with instructions to the manager to use him as little as possible, to hide him as much as possible, and to tell everyone he had a sore back, a sore arm, or any other excuse the manager could give. But how do you hide a diamond when he's in the middle of a field of broken soda bottles?

In the playoffs that year against Syracuse, they had to use Clemente. He hit two doubles and a home run and threw a man out at home the very first try.

The Pittsburgh Pirates had a man who saw it all. They drafted him at the season's end.

And so Roberto Clemente came to Pittsburgh. He was the finest prospect the club had had in a long, long time. But the Pirates of those days were spectacular losers, and even Roberto Clemente couldn't turn them around overnight.

"We were bad, all right," recalls Bob Friend, who later became a great Pirate pitcher. "We lost over a hundred games, and it certainly wasn't fun to go to the ball park under those conditions. You couldn't blame the fans for being noisy and impatient. Branch Rickey, our general manager, had promised a winner. He called it his five-year plan. Actually, it took ten."

When Clemente joined the club, it was Friend who made it his business to try to make him feel at home. Roberto was, in truth, a moody man, and the previous season hadn't helped him any.

"I will never forget how fast he became a superstar in this town," says Bob Friend. "Later he would have troubles because he was either hurt or thought he was hurt, and some people would say that he was loafing.

But I know he gave it his best shot and he helped make us winners."

The first winning year was 1960, when the Pirates won the pennant and went on to beat the Yankees in the seventh game of the World Series. Whitey Ford, who pitched against him twice in that Series, recalls that Roberto actually made himself look bad on an outside pitch to encourage Whitey to come back with it. "I did," Ford recalls, "and he unloaded. Another thing I remember is the way he ran out a routine ground ball in the last game, and when we were a little slow covering, he beat it out. It was something most people forget, but it made the Pirates' victory possible."

The season was over. Roberto Clemente had hit safely in every World Series game. He had batted over .300. He had been a superstar. But when they announced the Most Valuable Player Award voting, Roberto had finished a distant third.

"I really don't think he resented the fact that he didn't win it," Bob Friend says. "What hurt—and in this he was right —was how few votes he got. He felt that he simply wasn't being accepted. He brooded about that a lot. I think his attitude became one of 'Well, I'm going to show them from now on so that they will never forget.'

"And you know, he sure did."

Roberto Clemente went home and married Vera. He felt less alone. Now he could go on and prove what it was he had to prove. And he was determined to prove it.

"I know he was driven by thoughts like that," explains Buck Canel, a newspaper writer who covers all sports for most of the hemisphere's Spanish-language papers. "He would talk with me often about his feelings. You know, Clemente felt strongly about the fact that he was a Puerto Rican and that he was a black man. In each of these things he had pride.

"On the other hand, because of the early

language barriers, I am sure that there were times when he *thought* people were laughing at him when they were not. It is difficult for a Latin-American ballplayer to understand everything said around him when it is said at high speed, if he doesn't speak English that well. But, in any event, he wanted very much to prove to the world that he was a superstar and that he could do things that in his heart he felt he had already proven."

In later years, there would be people who would say that Roberto was a hypochondriac (someone who *imagined* he was sick or hurt when he was not). They could have been right, but if they were, it made the things he did even more remarkable. Because I can testify that I saw him throw his body into outfield fences, teeth first, to make remarkable plays. If he thought he was hurt at the time, then the act was even more courageous.

His moment finally came. It took eleven years for the Pirates to win a World Series berth again, and when they did in 1971, it was Roberto Clemente who led the way. I will never forget him as he was during that 1971 series with the Orioles, a Series that the Pirates figured to lose, and in which they, in fact, dropped the first two games down in Baltimore.

When they got back to Pittsburgh for the middle slice of the tournament, Roberto Clemente went to work and led this team. He was a superhero during the five games that followed. He was the big man in the Series. He was the MVP. He was everything he had ever dreamed of being on a ball field.

Most important of all, the entire country saw him do it on network television, and never again—even though nobody knew it would end so tragically soon—was anyone ever to doubt his ability.

The following year, Clemente ended the season by collecting his three thousandth hit. Only ten other men had ever done that in the entire history of baseball.

"It was a funny thing about that hit," Willie Stargell, his closest friend on the Pirates, explains. "He had thought of taking himself out of the lineup and resting for the playoffs, but a couple of us convinced him that there had to be a time when a man had to do something for himself, so he went on and played and got it. I'm thankful that we convinced him, because, you know, as things turned out, that number three thousand was his last hit.

"When I think of Roberto now, I think of the kind of man he was. There was nothing phony about him. He had his own ideas about how life should be lived, and if you didn't see it that way, then he let you know in so many ways, without words, that it was best you each go your separate ways.

"He was a man who chose his friends carefully. His was a friendship worth having. I don't think many people took the time and the trouble to try to understand him, and I'll admit it wasn't easy. But he was worth it.

"The way he died, you know, I mean on that plane carrying supplies to Nicaraguans who'd been dying in that earthquake, well, I wasn't surprised he'd go out and do something like that. I wasn't surprised he'd go. I just never thought what happened could happen to him.

"But I know this. He lived a full life. And if he knew at that moment what the Lord had decided, well, I really believe he would have said, 'I'm ready.'"

He was thirty-eight years old when he died. He touched the hearts of Puerto Rico in a way that few people ever could. He touched a lot of other hearts, too. He touched hearts that beat inside people of all colors of skin.

He was one of the proudest of The Proud People.

THINKING ABOUT THE SELECTION

Recalling

1. What roles do María Casares and Pedron Zarrilla play in Clemente's childhood?
2. Name two achievements of Roberto Clemente's baseball career.
3. Explain Clemente's view of friendship.
4. Why did Luis Vigereaux try to enlist Clemente's aid? How was Clemente trying to help when he died?
5. What do Roberto Clemente's friends remember most about him?

Interpreting

6. What inference do you make about Clemente based on his treatment of Mrs. Casares when she was ill?
7. Why is this called a "bittersweet memoir"?

Applying

8. How is Clemente a model for others?

ANALYZING LITERATURE

Understanding the Memoir

A **memoir,** or biographical piece often written by a relative or personal friend of the subject, can be about a well-known person or about someone important to the writer. A memoir can be one person's recollection, or based on interviews and anecdotes of several people.

An interview is a planned meeting at which writers obtain information about a topic from someone knowledgeable about it. Anecdotes are brief stories about noteworthy incidents.

1. List the people the writer interviewed.
2. What two anecdotes did María Casares tell about Roberto that no one else could tell?

CRITICAL THINKING AND READING

Identifying Primary Sources

A **primary source** is the original or direct source. For example, the wife of a famous ball-player would be a primary source of information about him. A **secondary source** is one that is based on primary sources. For example, a writer interviewing the friends of a famous ballplayer would be a secondary source.

Which of the following could give you primary-source information about Clemente?

1. María Casares
2. Jerry Izenberg
3. Manny Sanguillen
4. Rudy Hernandez

SPEAKING AND LISTENING

Doing an Interview

Before the **interview,** make an appointment for the meeting, research your topic, and prepare a list of simple and direct questions.

During the interview, listen attentively, take careful notes, and ask unprepared follow-up questions when a point needs to be made clearer. Immediately afterwards, look over your notes and pinpoint facts that need to be checked.

Think of a well-known person, and interview three classmates about their opinions about that person. Ask them to recall any anecdotes that show what that person means to them.

THINKING AND WRITING

Writing a Memoir

Write a memoir of someone you know well, based on your own knowledge of him or her. First freewrite about that person, including any details about his or her appearance or behavior. Include any anecdotes that help reveal this person's character. Then use this information in your memoir. Revise your memoir, making sure you have created a vivid portrait. Proofread your memoir and share it with your classmates.

GUIDE FOR READING

from I Know Why the Caged Bird Sings

Maya Angelou (1928–   ) was born Marguerite Johnson in St. Louis, Missouri. She and her older brother Bailey were raised by their grandmother, who owned a country store in Stamps, Arkansas. Angelou later became a journalist, a civil rights worker, and an author. In *I Know Why the Caged Bird Sings,* the first of four books of autobiography, she vividly recalls a woman from her childhood who influenced her life.

Autobiography

An **autobiography** is a person's own account of his or her life. Usually in an autobiography, a writer uses the first-person pronoun "I" to write about his or her experiences. You experience the writer's story through his or her eyes—knowing not only what he or she observes and recalls, but also what he or she thinks and feels about the experience. Unlike biography, autobiography provides you with information about the subject from the subject.

Look For

As you read this excerpt from *I Know Why the Caged Bird Sings,* look for the way in which Mrs. Flowers changes Maya's life. What does Maya learn from her?

Writing

Think of someone you consider special. Freewrite about that person, describing what they were like and what they did that made them special.

Vocabulary

Knowing the following words will help you as you read this excerpt from *I Know Why the Caged Bird Sings.*

fiscal (fis′ kəl) *adj.*: Having to do with finances (p. 403)

troubadours (trōō′ bə dôrz′) *n.*: Traveling singers, usually accompanying themselves on stringed instruments (p. 403)

taut (tôt) *adj.*: Tightly stretched (p. 405)

voile (voil) *n.*: A light cotton fabric (p. 405)

benign (bi nīn′) *adj.*: Kindly (p. 405)

infuse (in fyōōz′) *v.*: To put into (p. 406)

couched (koucht) *v.*: Put into words; expressed (p. 407)

wormwood (wʉrm′ wood′) *n.*: A plant that produces a bitter oil (p. 408)

from I Know Why the Caged Bird Sings

Maya Angelou

We lived with our grandmother and uncle in the rear of the Store (it was always spoken of with a capital s), which she had owned some twenty-five years.

Early in the century, Momma (we soon stopped calling her Grandmother) sold lunches to the sawmen in the lumberyard (east Stamps) and the seedmen at the cotton gin (west Stamps). Her crisp meat pies and cool lemonade, when joined to her miraculous ability to be in two places at the same time, assured her business success. From being a mobile lunch counter, she set up a stand between the two points of fiscal interest and supplied the workers' needs for a few years. Then she had the Store built in the heart of the Negro area. Over the years it became the lay center of activities in town. On Saturdays, barbers sat their customers in the shade on the porch of the Store, and troubadours on their ceaseless crawlings through the South leaned across its benches and sang their sad songs of The Brazos[1] while they played juice harps[2] and cigar-box guitars.

The formal name of the Store was the Wm. Johnson General Merchandise Store.

Customers could find food staples, a good variety of colored thread, mash[3] for hogs, corn for chickens, coal oil for lamps, light bulbs for the wealthy, shoestrings, hair dressing, balloons, and flower seeds. Anything not visible had only to be ordered.

Until we became familiar enough to belong to the Store and it to us, we were locked up in a Fun House of Things where the attendant had gone home for life. . . .

Weighing the half-pounds of flour, excluding the scoop, and depositing them dust-free into the thin paper sacks held a simple kind of adventure for me. I developed an eye for measuring how full a silver-looking ladle of flour, mash, meal, sugar or corn had to be to push the scale indicator over to eight ounces or one pound. When I was absolutely accurate our appreciative customers used to admire: "Sister Henderson sure got some smart grandchildrens." If I was off in the Store's favor, the eagle-eyed women would say, "Put some more in that sack, child. Don't you try to make your profit offa me."

Then I would quietly but persistently punish myself. For every bad judgment, the

---

1. The Brazos (bräz′ əs): An area in central Texas near the Brazos River.
2. juice (jew's) **harps:** Small musical instruments held between the teeth and played by plucking.

3. mash n.: A moist grain mixture fed to farm animals.

fine was no silver-wrapped kisses, the sweet chocolate drops that I loved more than anything in the world, except Bailey. And maybe canned pineapples. My obsession with pineapples nearly drove me mad. I dreamt of the days when I would be grown and able to buy a whole carton for myself alone.

Although the syrupy golden rings sat in their exotic cans on our shelves year round, we only tasted them during Christmas. Momma used the juice to make almost-black fruit cakes. Then she lined heavy soot-encrusted iron skillets with the pineapple rings for rich upside-down cakes. Bailey and I received one slice each, and I carried mine around for hours, shredding off the fruit until nothing was left except the perfume on my fingers. I'd like to think that my desire for pineapples was so sacred that I wouldn't allow myself to steal a can (which was possible) and eat it alone out in the garden, but I'm certain that I must have weighed the possibility of the scent exposing me and didn't have the nerve to attempt it.

Until I was thirteen and left Arkansas for good, the Store was my favorite place to be. Alone and empty in the mornings, it looked like an unopened present from a stranger. Opening the front doors was pulling the ribbon off the unexpected gift. The light would come in softly (we faced north), easing itself over the shelves of mackerel, salmon, tobacco, thread. It fell flat on the big vat of lard and by noontime during the summer the grease had softened to a thick soup. Whenever I walked into the Store in the afternoon, I sensed that it was tired. I alone could hear the slow pulse of its job half done. But just before bedtime, after numerous people had walked in and out, had argued over their bills, or joked about their neighbors, or just dropped in "to give Sister Henderson a 'Hi y'all,'" the promise of magic mornings returned to the Store and spread itself over the family in washed life waves. . . .

When Maya was about ten years old, she returned to Stamps from a visit to St. Louis with her mother. She had become depressed and withdrawn.

For nearly a year, I sopped around the house, the Store, the school and the church, like an old biscuit, dirty and inedible. Then I met, or rather got to know, the lady who threw me my first lifeline.

Mrs. Bertha Flowers was the aristocrat[4] of Black Stamps. She had the grace of control to appear warm in the coldest weather, and on the Arkansas summer days it seemed she had a private breeze which swirled around, cooling her. She was thin without the taut look of wiry people, and her printed voile dresses and flowered hats were as right for her as denim overalls for a farmer. She was our side's answer to the richest white woman in town.

---

4. aristocrat (ə ris′ tə krat) *n.:* A person belonging to the upper class.

Her skin was a rich black that would have peeled like a plum if snagged, but then no one would have thought of getting close enough to Mrs. Flowers to ruffle her dress, let alone snag her skin. She didn't encourage familiarity. She wore gloves too.

I don't think I ever saw Mrs. Flowers laugh, but she smiled often. A slow widening of her thin black lips to show even, small white teeth, then the slow effortless closing. When she chose to smile on me, I always wanted to thank her. The action was so graceful and inclusively benign.

She was one of the few gentlewomen I have ever known, and has remained throughout my life the measure of what a human being can be. . . .

One summer afternoon, sweet-milk fresh in my memory, she stopped at the Store to buy provisions. Another Negro woman of her health and age would have been expected to carry the paper sacks home in one hand, but Momma said, "Sister Flowers, I'll send Bailey up to your house with these things."

She smiled that slow dragging smile, "Thank you, Mrs. Henderson. I'd prefer Marguerite, though." My name was beautiful when she said it. "I've been meaning to talk to her, anyway." They gave each other age-group looks.

Momma said, "Well, that's all right then. Sister, go and change your dress. You going to Sister Flowers's. . . ."

There was a little path beside the rocky road, and Mrs. Flowers walked in front swinging her arms and picking her way over the stones.

She said, without turning her head, to me, "I hear you're doing very good school work, Marguerite, but that it's all written. The teachers report that they have trouble getting you to talk in class." We passed the triangular farm on our left and the path widened to allow us to walk together. I hung back in the separate unasked and unanswerable questions.

"Come and walk along with me, Marguerite." I couldn't have refused even if I wanted to. She pronounced my name so nicely. Or more correctly, she spoke each word with such clarity that I was certain a foreigner who didn't understand English could have understood her.

"Now no one is going to make you talk —possibly no one can. But bear in mind, language is man's way of communicating with his fellow man and it is language alone which separates him from the lower animals." That was a totally new idea to me, and I would need time to think about it.

"Your grandmother says you read a lot. Every chance you get. That's good, but not good enough. Words mean more than what is set down on paper. It takes the human voice to infuse them with the shades of deeper meaning."

I memorized the part about the human voice infusing words. It seemed so valid and poetic.

She said she was going to give me some books and that I not only must read them, I must read them aloud. She suggested that I try to make a sentence sound in as many different ways as possible.

"I'll accept no excuse if you return a book to me that has been badly handled." My imagination boggled at the punishment I would deserve if in fact I did abuse a book of Mrs. Flowers'. Death would be too kind and brief.

The odors in the house surprised me. Somehow I had never connected Mrs. Flowers with food or eating or any other common experience of common people. There must

have been an outhouse, too, but my mind never recorded it.

The sweet scent of vanilla had met us as she opened the door.

"I made tea cookies this morning. You see, I had planned to invite you for cookies and lemonade so we could have this little chat. The lemonade is in the icebox."

It followed that Mrs. Flowers would have ice on an ordinary day, when most families in our town bought ice late on Saturdays only a few times during the summer to be used in the wooden ice cream freezers.

She took the bags from me and disappeared through the kitchen door. I looked around the room that I had never in my wildest fantasies imagined I would see. Browned photographs leered or threatened from the walls and the white, freshly done curtains pushed against themselves and against the wind. I wanted to gobble up the room entire and take it to Bailey, who would help me analyze and enjoy it.

"Have a seat, Marguerite. Over there by the table." She carried a platter covered with a tea towel. Although she warned that she hadn't tried her hand at baking sweets for some time, I was certain that like everything else about her the cookies would be perfect.

They were flat round wafers, slightly browned on the edges and butter-yellow in the center. With the cold lemonade they were sufficient for childhood's lifelong diet. Remembering my manners, I took nice little ladylike bites off the edges. She said she had made them expressly for me and that she had a few in the kitchen that I could take home to my brother. So I jammed one whole cake in my mouth and the rough crumbs scratched the insides of my jaws, and if I hadn't had to swallow, it would have been a dream come true.

As I ate she began the first of what we later called "my lessons in living." She said that I must always be intolerant of ignorance but understanding of illiteracy. That some people, unable to go to school, were more educated and even more intelligent than college professors. She encouraged me to listen carefully to what country people called mother wit. That in those homely sayings was couched the collective wisdom of generations.

When I finished the cookies she brushed off the table and brought a thick, small book from the bookcase. I had read *A Tale of Two Cities* and found it up to my standards as a romantic novel. She opened the first page and I heard poetry for the first time in my life.

"It was the best of times and the worst of times . . ." Her voice slid in and curved down through and over the words. She was nearly singing. I wanted to look at the pages. Were they the same that I had read? Or were there notes, music, lined on the pages, as in a hymn book? Her sounds began cascading gently. I knew from listening to a thousand preachers that she was nearing the end of her reading, and I hadn't really heard, heard to understand, a single word.

"How do you like that?"

It occurred to me that she expected a response. The sweet vanilla flavor was still

on my tongue and her reading was a wonder in my ears. I had to speak.

I said, "Yes, ma'am." It was the least I could do, but it was the most also.

"There's one more thing. Take this book of poems and memorize one for me. Next time you pay me a visit, I want you to recite."

I have tried often to search behind the sophistication of years for the enchantment I so easily found in those gifts. The essence escapes but its aura[5] remains. To be allowed, no, invited, into the private lives of strangers, and to share their joys and fears, was a chance to exchange the Southern bitter wormwood for a cup of mead with Beowulf[6] or a hot cup of tea and milk with Oliver Twist. When I said aloud, "It is a far better thing that I do, than I have ever done . . ."[7] tears of love filled my eyes at my selflessness.

On that first day, I ran down the hill and into the road (few cars ever came along it) and had the good sense to stop running before I reached the Store.

I was liked, and what a difference it made. I was respected not as Mrs. Henderson's grandchild or Bailey's sister but for just being Marguerite Johnson.

Childhood's logic never asks to be proved (all conclusions are absolute). I didn't question why Mrs. Flowers had singled me out for attention, nor did it occur to me that Momma might have asked her to give me a little talking to. All I cared about was that she had made tea cookies for *me* and read to *me* from her favorite book. It was enough to prove that she liked me.

---

5. aura (ôr' ə) *n.*: An atmosphere or quality.
6. Beowulf (bā' ə woolf'): The hero of an old Anglo-Saxon epic. People in this poem drink mead, (mēd), a drink made with honey and water.

7. "It is . . . than I have ever done": A speech from *A Tale of Two Cities* by Charles Dickens.

THINKING ABOUT THE SELECTION
Recalling

1. According to Mrs. Flowers, for what two reasons is language so important?
2. Although Marguerite reads a great deal, what does she *not* do? According to Mrs. Flowers, why is reading a great deal not enough?
3. What does Mrs. Flowers tell Marguerite as the first of her "lessons in living"?
4. What does Mrs. Flowers want Marguerite to do with the book of poems she gives her?
5. What does Mrs. Flowers's making cookies and reading to Marguerite prove to Marguerite?

Interpreting

6. The word *sopped* means "to have been wet, like a piece of bread soaked in gravy." What does the use of the word "sopped" tell you about how Marguerite feels about herself before meeting with Mrs. Flowers?
7. Why does Mrs. Flowers tell Marguerite to read aloud and in as many different ways as possible?
8. After listening to *A Tale of Two Cities*, why does Marguerite write, "I said, 'Yes, ma'am.' It was the least I could do, but it was the most also"?
9. How do you think Marguerite changes as a result of her meetings with Mrs. Flowers?

10. Why has Mrs. Flowers remained "the measure of what a human being can be"?

Applying

11. Mrs. Flowers throws Marguerite a "lifeline" by inviting her to her house for lemonade and cookies and reading with her. In what other ways do people give others "lifelines"?

ANALYZING LITERATURE
Understanding Autobiography

An **autobiography** is the story of a person's life, written by that person. Through the writer's eyes, you see events unfold and come to understand his or her feelings and thoughts. The writer's view influences the telling of each incident. For example, Marguerite says, "I wanted to gobble up the room entire and take it to Bailey, who would help me analyze and enjoy it."

1. What does Marguerite tell you about the Store that only she could tell you?
2. What does Marguerite tell you about Mrs. Flowers that only she could tell you?

CRITICAL THINKING AND READING
Inferring the Author's Purpose

The autobiographer writes for a certain purpose, or reason. For example, authors may write autobiographies to entertain you, to preserve their memories, to inform you of their accomplishments, or for some other purpose. When you read, you usually infer, or draw conclusions about, the author's purpose. Of course, you can never get inside the author's mind, so your inference remains simply an intelligent guess.

Considering who the author is can help you infer his or her purpose. For example, a famous politician may want to emphasize in her autobiography that her policies improved people's lives. Therefore she will emphasize those incidents from her career that highlight this favorable effect, rather than those incidents that point out her drawbacks.

1. Why do you think Maya Angelou wrote about Mrs. Flowers? Explain the reason for your answer.
2. How is the author's purpose evident? Explain the reason for your answer.

THINKING AND WRITING
Writing an Autobiographical Sketch

Choose an incident in your life that is important to you. First, freewrite about this incident. Then, using this information, write an autobiographical account of it. Use the first-person point of view. Revise your writing, making sure you have presented the information clearly. Proofread your autobiography and share it with your classmates.

GUIDE FOR READING

Cub Pilot on the Mississippi

Mark Twain (1835–1910) was the pen name of Samuel Langhorne Clemens. A phrase used by boatmen in taking river soundings, *mark twain* means "two fathoms deep." Twain was known for his humorous writing and for novels of growing up like *The Adventures of Tom Sawyer.* Born in Florida, Missouri, he grew up in Hannibal on the Mississippi River. The influence the river had on Twain is evident in the following excerpt from *Life on the Mississippi,* published in 1883. In this excerpt, Twain tells of his experience steamboating.

Conflict in Autobiography

In autobiographical accounts, writers often describe how they have dealt with **conflicts,** or struggles. The conflicts they describe may be external or internal. An **external conflict** is one that takes place between the writer and a person or a natural force. An **internal conflict** is one that exists in the writer's mind, such as the struggle to make a difficult decision or to overcome an overwhelming fear. The outcome of a conflict is called its resolution. In "Cub Pilot on the Mississippi," Twain tells of the conflicts he faced as an apprentice —a person learning a trade while working for a master craftsman.

Look For

As you read "Cub Pilot on the Mississippi," look for the reasons behind the conflict Twain has with one of the pilots—a person who steers ships—and the way he resolves it. What do you learn about the life of a cub pilot from this excerpt?

Writing

Imagine some conflicts that a person could experience. Identify which are external conflicts with outside forces or other people, and which are internal conflicts within the person.

Vocabulary

Knowing the following words will help you as you read "Cub Pilot on the Mississippi."

furtive (fər′ tiv) *adj.*: Sly or done in secret (p. 412)
pretext (prē′ tekst) *n.*: A false reason or motive given to hide a real intention (p. 413)
intimation (in′ tə mā′ shən) *n.*: Hint or suggestion (p. 415)

indulgent (in dul′ jənt) *adj.*: Very mild and tolerant, not strict or critical (p. 416)
emancipated (i man′ sə pā′ təd) *v.*: Freed from the control or power of another (p. 418)

Cub Pilot
on the Mississippi

Mark Twain

THE GREAT MISSISSIPPI STEAMBOAT RACE, 1870
Currier and Ives
The Granger Collection

During the two or two and a half years of my apprenticeship[1] I served under many pilots, and had experience of many kinds of steamboatmen and many varieties of steamboats. I am to this day profiting somewhat by that experience; for in that brief, sharp schooling, I got personally and familiarly acquainted with about all the different types of human nature that are to be found in fiction, biography, or history.

The fact is daily borne in upon me that the average shore-employment requires as

---

1. apprenticeship (ə pren′ tis ship) *n.*: The time spent by a person working for a master craftsman in a craft or trade in return for instruction and, formerly, support.

much as forty years to equip a man with this sort of an education. When I say I am still profiting by this thing, I do not mean that it has constituted me a judge of men—no, it has not done that, for judges of men are born, not made. My profit is various in kind and degree, but the feature of it which I value most is the zest which that early experience has given to my later reading. When I find a well-drawn character in fiction or biography I generally take a warm personal interest in him, for the reason that I have known him before—met him on the river.

The figure that comes before me oftenest, out of the shadows of that vanished time, is that of Brown, of the steamer *Pennsylvania.* He was a middle-aged, long, slim, bony, smooth-shaven, horse-faced, ignorant, stingy, malicious, snarling, fault-hunting, mote[2]-magnifying tyrant. I early got the habit of coming on watch with dread at my heart. No matter how good a time I might have been having with the off-watch below, and no matter how high my spirits might be when I started aloft, my soul became lead in my body the moment I approached the pilothouse.

I still remember the first time I ever entered the presence of that man. The boat had backed out from St. Louis and was "straightening down." I ascended to the pilothouse in high feather, and very proud to be semiofficially a member of the executive family of so fast and famous a boat. Brown was at the wheel. I paused in the middle of the room, all fixed to make my bow, but Brown did not look around. I thought he took a furtive glance at me out of the corner of his eye, but as not even this notice was repeated, I judged I had been mistaken. By

this time he was picking his way among some dangerous "breaks" abreast the woodyards; therefore it would not be proper to interrupt him; so I stepped softly to the high bench and took a seat.

There was silence for ten minutes; then my new boss turned and inspected me deliberately and painstakingly from head to heel for about—as it seemed to me—a quarter of an hour. After which he removed his countenance[3] and I saw it no more for some seconds; then it came around once more, and this question greeted me: "Are you Horace Bigsby's cub?[4]"

"Yes, sir."

After this there was a pause and another inspection. Then: "What's your name?"

I told him. He repeated it after me. It was probably the only thing he ever forgot; for although I was with him many months he never addressed himself to me in any other way than "Here!" and then his command followed.

"Where was you born?"

"In Florida, Missouri."

A pause. Then: "Dern sight better stayed there!"

By means of a dozen or so of pretty direct questions, he pumped my family history out of me.

The leads[5] were going now in the first crossing. This interrupted the inquest.[6] When the leads had been laid in he resumed:

"How long you been on the river?"

I told him. After a pause:

"Where'd you get them shoes?"

---

2. mote (mōt) *n.*: A speck of dust or other tiny particle.

3. countenance (koun′ tə nəns) *n.*: Face.
4. cub (kub) *n.*: Beginner.
5. leads (lēdz) *n.*: Weights that were lowered to test the depth of the river.
6. inquest (in′ kwest) *n.*: Investigation.

I gave him the information.

"Hold up your foot!"

I did so. He stepped back, examined the shoe minutely and contemptuously, scratching his head thoughtfully, tilting his high sugar-loaf hat well forward to facilitate the operation, then ejaculated, "Well, I'll be dod derned!" and returned to his wheel.

What occasion there was to be dod derned about it is a thing which is still as much of a mystery to me now as it was then. It must have been all of fifteen minutes —fifteen minutes of dull, homesick silence —before that long horse-face swung round upon me again—and then what a change! It was as red as fire, and every muscle in it was working. Now came this shriek: "Here! You going to set there all day?"

I lit in the middle of the floor, shot there by the electric suddenness of the surprise. As soon as I could get my voice I said apologetically: "I have had no orders, sir."

"You've had no *orders!* My, what a fine bird we are! We must have *orders!* Our father was a *gentleman*—and *we've* been to *school.* Yes, *we* are a gentleman, *too,* and got to have *orders!* ORDERS, is it? ORDERS is what you want! Dod dern my skin, *I'll* learn you to swell yourself up and blow around *here* about your dod-derned *orders!* G'way from the wheel!" (I had approached it without knowing it.)

I moved back a step or two and stood as in a dream, all my senses stupefied by this frantic assault.

"What you standing there for? Take that ice-pitcher down to the texas-tender![7] Come, move along, and don't you be all day about it!"

The moment I got back to the pilothouse Brown said: "Here! What was you doing down there all this time?"

"I couldn't find the texas-tender; I had to go all the way to the pantry."

"Derned likely story! Fill up the stove."

I proceeded to do so. He watched me like a cat. Presently he shouted: "Put down that shovel! Derndest numskull I ever saw —ain't even got sense enough to load up a stove."

All through the watch this sort of thing went on. Yes, and the subsequent watches were much like it during a stretch of months. As I have said, I soon got the habit of coming on duty with dread. The moment I was in the presence, even in the darkest night, I could feel those yellow eyes upon me, and knew their owner was watching for a pretext to spit out some venom on me. Preliminarily he would say: "Here! Take the wheel."

Two minutes later: "*Where* in the nation you going to? Pull her down! pull her down!"

After another moment: "Say! You going to hold her all day? Let her go—meet her! meet her!"

Then he would jump from the bench, snatch the wheel from me, and meet her himself, pouring out wrath upon me all the time.

George Ritchie was the other pilot's cub. He was having good times now; for his boss, George Ealer, was as kind-hearted as Brown wasn't. Ritchie had steered for Brown the season before; consequently, he knew exactly how to entertain himself and plague me, all by the one operation. Whenever I took the wheel for a moment on Ealer's watch, Ritchie would sit back on the bench and play Brown, with continual ejaculations

---

7. texas tender: The waiter in the officers' quarters. On Mississippi steamboats, rooms were named after the states. The officers' area, which was the largest, was named after what was then the largest state, Texas.

ST. LOUIS FROM THE RIVER, 1832
George Catlin
The Granger Collection

of "Snatch her! Snatch her! Derndest mud-cat I ever saw!" "Here! Where are you going *now?* Going to run over that snag?" "Pull her *down!* Don't you hear me? Pull her *down!*" "There she goes! *Just* as I expected! I *told* you not to cramp that reef. G'way from the wheel!"

So I always had a rough time of it, no matter whose watch it was; and sometimes it seemed to me that Ritchie's good-natured badgering was pretty nearly as aggravating as Brown's dead-earnest nagging.

I often wanted to kill Brown, but this would not answer. A cub had to take everything his boss gave, in the way of vigorous comment and criticism; and we all believed that there was a United States law making it a penitentiary offense to strike or threaten a pilot who was on duty.

However, I could *imagine* myself killing Brown; there was no law against that; and that was the thing I used always to do the moment I was abed. Instead of going over my river in my mind, as was my duty, I threw business aside for pleasure, and killed Brown. I killed Brown every night for months; not in old, stale, commonplace ways, but in new and picturesque ones —ways that were sometimes surprising for freshness of design and ghastliness of situation and environment.

Brown was *always* watching for a pretext to find fault; and if he could find no plausible pretext, he would invent one. He would scold you for shaving a shore, and for not shaving it; for hugging a bar, and for not hugging it; for "pulling down" when not invited, and for *not* pulling down when not invited; for firing up without orders, and for waiting *for* orders. In a word, it was his invariable rule to find fault with *everything* you did and another invariable rule of his was to throw all his remarks (to you) into the form of an insult.

One day we were approaching New Madrid, bound down and heavily laden. Brown was at one side of the wheel, steering; I was at the other, standing by to "pull down" or "shove up." He cast a furtive glance at me every now and then. I had long ago learned what that meant; viz., he was trying to invent a trap for me. I wondered what shape it was going to take. By and by he stepped back from the wheel and said in his usual snarly way:

"Here! See if you've got gumption enough to round her to."

This was simply *bound* to be a success; nothing could prevent it; for he had never allowed me to round the boat to before; consequently, no matter how I might do the thing, he could find free fault with it. He stood back there with his greedy eye on me, and the result was what might have been foreseen: I lost my head in a quarter of a minute, and didn't know what I was about; I started too early to bring the boat around, but detected a green gleam of joy in Brown's eye, and corrected my mistake. I started around once more while too high up, but corrected myself again in time. I made other false moves, and still managed to save myself; but at last I grew so confused and anxious that I tumbled into the very worst blunder of all—I got too far *down* before beginning to fetch the boat around. Brown's chance was come.

His face turned red with passion; he made one bound, hurled me across the house with a sweep of his arm, spun the wheel down, and began to pour out a stream of vituperation[8] upon me which lasted till he was out of breath. In the course of this speech he called me all the different kinds of hard names he could think of, and once or twice I thought he was even going to swear —but he had never done that, and he didn't this time. "Dod dern" was the nearest he ventured to the luxury of swearing.

Two trips later I got into serious trouble. Brown was steering; I was "pulling down." My younger brother Henry appeared on the hurricane deck, and shouted to Brown to stop at some landing or other, a mile or so below. Brown gave no intimation that he had heard anything. But that was his way: he never condescended to take notice of an underclerk. The wind was blowing; Brown was deaf (although he always pretended he wasn't), and I very much doubted if he had heard the order. If I had had two heads, I would have spoken; but as I had only one, it seemed judicious to take care of it; so I kept still.

Presently, sure enough, we went sailing by that plantation. Captain Klinefelter appeared on the deck, and said: "Let her come around, sir, let her come around. Didn't Henry tell you to land here?"

"*No*, sir!"

"I sent him up to do it."

"He *did* come up; and that's all the good it done, the dod-derned fool. He never said anything."

"Didn't *you* hear him?" asked the captain of me.

---

8. vituperation (vī too′ pə rā′ shən) *n.*: Abusive language.

Of course I didn't want to be mixed up in this business, but there was no way to avoid it; so I said: "Yes, sir."

I knew what Brown's next remark would be, before he uttered it. It was: "Shut your mouth! You never heard anything of the kind."

I closed my mouth, according to instructions. An hour later Henry entered the pilothouse, unaware of what had been going on. He was a thoroughly inoffensive boy, and I was sorry to see him come, for I knew Brown would have no pity on him. Brown began, straightway: "Here! Why didn't you tell me we'd got to land at that plantation?"

"I did tell you, Mr. Brown."

"It's a lie!"

I said: "You lie, yourself. He did tell you."

Brown glared at me in unaffected surprise; and for as much as a moment he was entirely speechless; then he shouted to me: "I'll attend to your case in a half a minute!" then to Henry, "And you leave the pilothouse; out with you!"

It was pilot law, and must be obeyed. The boy started out, and even had his foot on the upper step outside the door, when Brown, with a sudden access of fury, picked up a ten-pound lump of coal and sprang after him; but I was between, with a heavy stool, and I hit Brown a good honest blow which stretched him out.

I had committed the crime of crimes—I had lifted my hand against a pilot on duty! I supposed I was booked for the penitentiary sure, and couldn't be booked any surer if I went on and squared my long account with this person while I had the chance; consequently I stuck to him and pounded him with my fists a considerable time. I do not know how long, the pleasure of it probably made it seem longer than it really was; but in the end he struggled free and jumped up and sprang to the wheel: a very natural solicitude, for, all this time, here was this steamboat tearing down the river at the rate of fifteen miles an hour and nobody at the helm! However, Eagle Bend was two miles wide at this bank-full stage, and correspondingly long and deep: and the boat was steering herself straight down the middle and taking no chances. Still, that was only luck—a body *might* have found her charging into the woods.

Perceiving at a glance that the *Pennsylvania* was in no danger, Brown gathered up the big spyglass, war-club fashion, and ordered me out of the pilothouse with more than ordinary bluster. But I was not afraid of him now; so, instead of going, I tarried, and criticized his grammar. I reformed his ferocious speeches for him, and put them into good English, calling his attention to the advantage of pure English over the dialect of the collieries[9] whence he was extracted. He could have done his part to admiration in a crossfire of mere vituperation, of course; but he was not equipped for this species of controversy; so he presently laid aside his glass and took the wheel, muttering and shaking his head; and I retired to the bench. The racket had brought everybody to the hurricane deck, and I trembled when I saw the old captain looking up from amid the crowd. I said to myself, "Now I *am* done for!" for although, as a rule, he was so fatherly and indulgent toward the boat's family, and so patient of minor shortcomings, he could be stern enough when the fault was worth it.

I tried to imagine what he *would* do to a cub pilot who had been guilty of such a crime as mine, committed on a boat guard-deep[10] with costly freight and alive with

---

9. collieries (käl′ yər ēz) *n*.: Coal mines.
10. guard-deep: Here, a wooden frame protecting the paddle wheel.

THE CHAMPIONS OF THE MISSISSIPPI
Currier & Ives
Scala/Art Resource

passengers. Our watch was nearly ended. I thought I would go and hide somewhere till I got a chance to slide ashore. So I slipped out of the pilothouse, and down the steps, and around to the texas-door, and was in the act of gliding within, when the captain confronted me! I dropped my head, and he stood over me in silence a moment or two, then said impressively: "Follow me."

I dropped into his wake; he led the way to his parlor in the forward end of the texas. We were alone now. He closed the afterdoor, then moved slowly to the forward one and closed that. He sat down; I stood before him. He looked at me some little time, then said: "So you have been fighting Mr. Brown?"

I answered meekly: "Yes, sir."

"Do you know that that is a very serious matter?"

"Yes, sir."

"Are you aware that this boat was plowing down the river fully five minutes with no one at the wheel?"

"Yes, sir."

"Did you strike him first?"

"Yes, sir."

"What with?"

"A stool, sir."

"Hard?"

"Middling, sir."

"Did it knock him down?"

"He—he fell, sir."

"Did you follow it up? Did you do anything further?"

"Yes, sir."

"What did you do?"

"Pounded him, sir."

"Pounded him?"

"Yes, sir."

"Did you pound him much? that is, severely?"

"One might call it that, sir, maybe."

"I'm deuced glad of it! Hark ye, never mention that I said that. You have been guilty of a great crime; and don't you ever be guilty of it again, on this boat. *But*—lay for him ashore! Give him a good sound thrashing, do you hear? I'll pay the expenses. Now go—and mind you, not a word of this to anybody. Clear out with you! You've been guilty of a great crime, you whelp!"[11]

I slid out, happy with the sense of a close shave and a mighty deliverance; and I heard him laughing to himself and slapping his fat thighs after I had closed his door.

---

11. whelp (hwelp) *n.*: A young dog or puppy; here, a disrespectful young man.

When Brown came off watch he went straight to the captain, who was talking with some passengers on the boiler deck, and demanded that I be put ashore in New Orleans—and added: "I'll never turn a wheel on this boat again while that cub stays."

The captain said: "But he needn't come round when you are on watch, Mr. Brown."

"I won't even stay on the same boat with him. *One* of us has got to go ashore."

"Very well," said the captain, "let it be yourself," and resumed his talk with the passengers.

During the brief remainder of the trip I knew how an emancipated slave feels, for I was an emancipated slave myself. While we lay at landings I listened to George Ealer's flute, or to his readings from his two Bibles, that is to say, Goldsmith and Shakespeare, or I played chess with him—and would have beaten him sometimes, only he always took back his last move and ran the game out differently.

THINKING ABOUT THE SELECTION

Recalling

1. Describe Mr. Brown when he meets the cub pilot, Twain.
2. What causes Twain's "serious trouble" with Mr. Brown? How is the trouble resolved?
3. Why does Twain feel like "an emancipated slave" at the end?
4. How does knowing the various kinds of steamboatmen profit Twain as a writer?

Interpreting

5. In what ways was Brown's treatment of the young Twain unfair?
6. Compare and contrast Brown's and Ritchie's treatment of Twain.
7. How does the Captain feel about Mr. Brown? What evidence supports your answer?

Applying

8. John Locke wrote: "It is easier for a tutor to command than to teach." Explain the mean-

ing of this quotation. How does it relate to this selection?

ANALYZING LITERATURE
Understanding Conflicts

Conflicts may provide the main element of a plot, or sequence of action, in an autobiography. For example, "Cub Pilot on the Mississippi" is based on the conflict between Mark Twain as a cub pilot and Mr. Brown. The outcome of the conflict is its resolution; however, a conflict may not always be resolved.

1. Why are the cub pilot and Mr. Brown in conflict?
2. What conflict does the cub pilot experience in his mind?
3. How are both conflicts resolved?

CRITICAL THINKING AND READING
Separating Fact from Opinion

Autobiographies may contain both facts and opinions. **Facts** are statements that can be proved true with reliable sources, such as an encyclopedia or an expert. For example, the statement that cub pilots were apprentices on Mississippi River steamboats can be verified with historical records.

Opinions are beliefs or judgments. The writer's opinions are not subject to verification, because they are based on the writer's attitudes or beliefs. For example, it is Twain's opinion that Mr. Brown is a "mote-magnifying tyrant."

Identify which of the following is fact and which is opinion. Indicate what source you might use to verify each fact.

1. The cub's brother Henry was a thoroughly inoffensive boy.

2. A cub pilot was required to obey a steamboat pilot on duty.
3. The cub pilot was born in Florida, Missouri.
4. George Ealer was as kind-hearted as Brown was not.

UNDERSTANDING LANGUAGE
Using Contrast Clues

You can often figure out the meaning of a word by using **contrast clues,** or other words in the sentence that are the opposite to or quite different from the unfamiliar word. The following sentence provides two contrast clues for the word *stern:*

". . . although, as a rule, he was . . . fatherly and indulgent toward the boat's family . . . he could be stern enough when the fault was worth it."

The clues *fatherly* and *indulgent* suggest a contrast to *stern.*

Find the meaning of each underlined word by using the contrast clues.

1. He was as *miserly* as she was generous.
2. It was *trivial* to me, but important to Joe.

THINKING AND WRITING
Writing About Conflict

Robert Keith Miller has said that in *Life on the Mississippi,* Mark Twain writes about the conflicting feelings of being attracted to and repulsed, or disgusted, by the world of the steamboat pilot. Write an essay explaining the conflicting feelings in the selection. First list some aspects of life on the Mississippi that attract Mark Twain and some that repulse him. Then develop your essay, showing the conflict between Mark Twain and Mr. Brown. Revise your essay, making sure that you use examples to support your views. Proofread your essay and share it with your classmates.

from Of Men and Mountains

William O. Douglas (1898–1980) was born in Maine, Minnesota, but grew up in Yakima, Washington. He is best known as a U.S. Supreme Court Justice who served for more than thirty-six years, and as a champion of conservation, the official care of natural resources. After recovering from polio as a child, he was drawn to nature. The following selection is from *Of Men and Mountains,* an autobiographical account of his mountain-climbing adventures.

The Narrator in Autobiography

A **narrator** is a person or character who tells a story. In an **autobiography** the author is the narrator, who tells his or her experiences from the first-person point of view, speaking as "I." When you read about William O. Douglas's climb, you experience it through his eyes and mind—knowing what he recalls, feels, and observes about his experience.

Look For

As you read "Of Men and Mountains," look for the way Douglas re-creates his experience by telling you what he recalls, feels, and observes. Why does the young Douglas want to face the challenge of climbing Kloochman, a rock on the southern side of the Tieton Basin?

Writing

Why do some people enjoy a challenge? Freewrite, exploring your answer.

Vocabulary

Knowing the following words will help you as you read "Of Men and Mountains."

shunned (shund) *v.*: Deliberately avoided (p. 421)

precarious (pri ker′ ē əs) *adj.*: Insecure and dangerous (p. 421)

tortuous (tôr′ cho͞o wəs) *adj.*: Winding with repeated twists and turns (p. 421)

bravado (brə va′ dō) *n.*: A show of bravery (p. 423)

laterally (lat′ ər əl ē) *adv.*: Toward the side (p. 425)

abyss (ə bis′) *n.*: A bottomless space (p. 426)

buoyant (boi′ ənt) *adj.*: Lighthearted (p. 427)

from Of Men and Mountains

William O. Douglas

It was in 1913 when Doug was 19 and I was not quite 15 that the two of us made this climb of Kloochman.[1] Walter Kohagen, Doug, and I were camped in the Tieton Basin at a soda spring. The basin was then in large part a vast rich bottomland. We were traveling light, one blanket each. The night, I recall, was so bitter cold that we took turns refueling the campfire so that we could keep our backs warm enough to sleep. We rose at the first show of dawn, and cooked frying-pan bread and trout for breakfast. We had not planned to climb Kloochman, but somehow the challenge came to us as the sun touched her crest.

After breakfast we started circling the rock. There are fairly easy routes up Kloochman, but we shunned them. When we came to the southeast face (the one that never has been conquered, I believe) we chose it. Walter decided not to make the climb, but to wait at the base of the cliff for Doug and me. The July day was warm and cloudless. Doug led. The beginning was easy. For 100 feet or so we found ledges six to twelve inches wide we could follow to the left or right. Some ledges ran up the rock ten feet or more at a gentle grade. Others were merely steps to another ledge higher up. Thus by hugging the wall we could either ease ourselves up-

ward or hoist ourselves from one ledge to another.

When we were about 100 feet up the wall, the ledges became narrower and footwork more precarious. Doug suggested we take off our shoes. This we did, tying them behind us on our belts. In stocking feet we wormed up the wall, clinging like flies to the dark rock. The pace was slow. We gingerly tested each toehold and fingerhold for loose rock before putting our weight on it. At times we had to inch along sidewise, our stomachs pressed tightly against the rock, in order to gain a point where we could reach the ledge above us. If we got on a ledge that turned out to be a cul-de-sac,[2] the much more dangerous task of going down the rock wall would confront us. Hence we picked our route with care and weighed the advantages of several choices which frequently were given us. At times we could not climb easily from one ledge to another. The one above might be a foot or so high. Then we would have to reach it with one knee, slowly bring the other knee up, and then, delicately balancing on both knees on the upper ledge, come slowly to our feet by pressing close to the wall and getting such purchase[3] with our fingers as the lava rock permitted.

In that tortuous way we made perhaps

---

1. Kloochman: An oval-shaped lava rock on the southern side of the Tieton Basin in the Cascades. The final third of it consists of a sheer cliff rising straight up 1,200 feet or more.

2. cul-de-sac (kul′ də sak′) *n.*: A passage with only one outlet.

3. purchase (pʉr′ chəs) *n.*: A tight hold to keep from slipping.

600 feet in two hours. It was late forenoon when we stopped to appraise our situation. We were in serious trouble. We had reached the feared cul-de-sac. The two- or three-inch ledge on which we stood ended. There seemed none above us within Doug's reach. I was longer-legged than Doug; so perhaps I could have reached some ledge with my fingers if I were ahead. But it was impossible to change positions on the wall. Doug was ahead and there he must stay. The problem was to find a way to get him up.

Feeling along the wall, Doug discovered a tiny groove into which he could press the tips of the fingers of his left hand. It might help him maintain balance as his weight began to shift from the lower ledge to the upper one. But there was within reach not even a lip of rock for his right hand. Just out

of reach, however, was a substantial crevice, one that would hold several men. How could Doug reach it? I could not boost him, for my own balance was insecure. Clearly, Doug would have to jump to reach it—and he would have but one jump. Since he was standing on a ledge only a few inches wide, he could not expect to jump for his hand-hold, miss it, and land safely. A slip meant he would go hurtling down some 600 feet onto the rocks. After much discussion and indecision, Doug decided to take the chance and go up.

He asked me to do him a favor: If he failed and fell, I might still make it, since I was longer-legged; would I give certain messages to his family in that event? I nodded.

"Then listen carefully. Try to remember my exact words," he told me. "Tell Mother that I love her dearly. Tell her I think she is the most wonderful person in the world. Tell her not to worry—that I did not suffer. Tell Sister that I have been a mean little devil but I had no malice towards her. Tell her I love her too—that some day I wanted to marry a girl as wholesome and cheery and good as she.

"Tell Dad I was brave and died unafraid. Tell him about our climb in full detail. Tell Dad I have always been very proud of him, that some day I had planned to be a doctor too. Tell him I lived a clean life, that I never did anything to make him ashamed. . . . Tell Mother, Sister, and Dad I prayed for them."

Every word burned into me. My heart was sick, my lips quivered. I pressed my face against the rock so Doug could not see. I wept.

All was silent. A pebble fell from the ledge on which I squeezed. I counted seconds before it hit 600 feet below with a faint, faraway tinkling sound. Would Doug drop through the same space? Would I follow? When you fall 600 feet do you die before you hit the bottom? Closing my eyes, I asked God to help Doug up the wall.

In a second Doug said in a cheery voice, "Well, here goes."

A false bravado took hold of us. I said he could do it. He said he would. He wiped first one hand then the other on his trousers. He placed both palms against the wall, bent his knees slowly, paused a split second, and jumped straight up. It was not much of a jump—only six inches or so. But that jump by one pressed against a cliff 600 feet in the air had daredevil proportions. I held my breath; my heart pounded. The suspense was over.

Doug made the jump, and in a second was hanging by two hands from a strong, wide ledge. There was no toehold; he would have to hoist himself by his arms alone. He did just that. His body went slowly up as if pulled by some unseen winch.[4] Soon he had the weight of his body above the ledge and was resting on the palms of his hands. He then put his left knee on the ledge, rolled over on his side, and chuckled as he said, "Nothing to it."

A greater disappointment followed. Doug's exploration of the ledge showed he was in a final cul-de-sac. There was no way up. There was not even a higher ledge he could reach by jumping. We were now faced with the nightmare of going down the sheer rock wall. We could not go down frontwards because the ledges were too narrow and the wall too steep. We needed our toes, not our heels, on the rock; and we needed to have our stomachs pressed tightly against it. Then we could perhaps feel our way. But as every rock expert knows, descent of a cliff without ropes is often much more difficult than ascent.

That difficulty was impressed on us by the first move. Doug had to leave the ledge he had reached by jumping. He dared not slide blindly to the skimpy ledge he had just left. I must help him. I must move up the wall and stand closer to him. Though I could not possibly hold his weight, I must exert sufficient pressure to slow up his descent and to direct his toe onto the narrow ledge from which he had just jumped.

I was hanging to the rock like a fly, twelve feet or more to Doug's left. I inched my way toward him, first dropping to a lower ledge and then climbing to a higher one, using such toeholds as the rock afforded and edging my way crabwise.

When I reached him I said, "Now I'll help."

Doug lowered himself and hung by his fingers full length. His feet were about six inches above the ledge from which he had

---

4. winch *n.*: A machine used for lifting.

jumped. He was now my responsibility. If he dropped without aid or direction he was gone. He could not catch and hold to the scanty ledge. I had little space for maneuvering. The surface on which I stood was not more than three inches wide. My left hand fortunately found an overhead crevice that gave a solid anchor in case my feet slipped.

I placed my right hand in the small of Doug's back and pressed upward with all my might. "Now you can come," I said.

He let go gently, and the full weight of his body came against my arm. My arm trembled under the tension. My left hand hung onto the crack in the rock like a grappling hook. My stomach pressed against the wall as if to find mucilage[5] in its pores. My toes dug in as I threw in every ounce of strength.

Down Doug came—a full inch. I couldn't help glancing down and seeing the rocks 600 feet below.

Down Doug moved another inch, then a third. My left hand seemed paralyzed. The muscles of my toes were aching. My right arm shook. I could not hold much longer.

Down came Doug a fourth inch. I thought he was headed for destruction. His feet would miss the only toehold within reach. I could not possibly hold him. He would plunge to his death because my arm was not strong enough to hold him. The messages he had given me for his family raced through my mind. And I saw myself, sick and ashamed, standing before them, testifying to my own inadequacy, repeating his last words.

"Steady, Doug. The ledge is a foot to your right." He pawed the wall with the toes of his foot, searching.

"I can't find it. Don't let go."

---

5. mucilage (myoo′ s'l ij) *n.*: Any watery solution of gum, glue, etc. used as an adhesive.

The crisis was on us. Even if I had been safely anchored, my cramped position would have kept me from helping him much more. I felt helpless. In a few seconds I would reach the physical breaking point and Doug would go hurtling off the cliff. I did not see how I could keep him from slipping and yet maintain my own balance.

I will never know how I did it. But I tapped some reserve and directed his right foot onto the ledge from which he had earlier jumped. I did it by standing for a moment on my left foot alone and then using my right leg as a rod to guide his right foot to the ledge his swinging feet had missed.

His toes grabbed the ledge as if they were the talons of a bird. My right leg swung back to my perch.

"Are you OK?" I asked.

"Yes," said Doug. "Good work."

My right arm fell from him, numb and useless. I shook from exhaustion and for the first time noticed that my face was wet with perspiration. We stood against the rock in silence for several minutes, relaxing and regaining our composure.

Doug said: "Let's throw our shoes down. It will be easier going." So we untied them from our belts and dropped them to Walter Kohagen, who was waiting at the rock field below us.

Our descent was painfully slow but uneventful. We went down backwards, weaving a strange pattern across the face of the cliff as we moved from one side to the other. It was perhaps midafternoon when we reached the bottom, retrieved our shoes, and started around the other side of the rock. We left the southeast wall unconquered.

But, being young, we were determined to climb the rock. So once more we started to circle. When we came to the northwest wall, we selected it as our route.

Here, too, is a cliff rising 1,000 feet like some unfinished pyramid. But close examination shows numerous toe- and finger-holds that made the start at least fairly easy. So we set out with our shoes on.

Again it was fairly easy going for a hundred feet or so, when Doug, who was ahead, came to a ledge to which he could not step. On later climbs we would send the longer-legged chap ahead. And on other occasions Doug himself has used a rope to traverse this spot. But this day success of the climb depended at this point on Doug's short legs alone. The ledge to which he must move was up to his hips. There were few fingerholds overhead, and none firm enough to carry his whole weight. Only a few tiny cracks were within reach to serve as purchase for him. But Doug would not give up.

He hitched up his trousers, and grasped a tiny groove of rock with the tips of the fingers of his left hand, pressing his right hand flat against the smooth rock wall as if it had magical sticking power. Slowly he lifted his left knee until it was slightly over the ledge above him. To do so he had to stand tiptoe on his right foot. Pulling with his left hand, he brought his right knee up. Doug was now on both knees on the upper ledge. If he could find good purchase overhead for his hands, he was safe. His hands explored the wall above him. He moved them slowly over most of it without finding a hold. Then he reached straight above his head and cried out, "This is our lucky day."

He had found strong rough edges of rock, and on this quickly pulled himself up. His hands were on a ledge a foot wide. He lay down on it on his stomach and grasped my outstretched hand. The pull of his strong arm against the drop of 100 feet or more was as comforting an experience as any I can recall. In a jiffy I was at his side. We pounded each other on the shoulders and laughed.

My own most serious trouble was yet to come. For a while Doug and I were separated. I worked laterally along a ledge to the south, found easier going, and in a short time was 200 feet or more up the rock wall. I was above Doug, 25 feet or so, and 50 feet to his right. We had been extremely careful to test each toe- and finger-hold before putting our trust in it. Kloochman is full of treacherous rock. We often discovered thin ledges that crumbled under pressure and showered handfuls of rock and dust down below. Perhaps I was careless; but whatever the cause, the thin ledge on which I was standing gave way.

As I felt it slip, I grabbed for a hold above me. The crevasse[6] I seized was solid. But there I was, hanging by my hands 200 feet in the air, my feet pawing the rock. To make

6. **crevasse** (kri vas′) *n.*: A deep crack.

matters worse, my camera had swung between me and the cliff when I slipped. It was a crude and clumsy instrument, a box type that I carried on a leather strap across my shoulders. Its hulk was actually pushing me from the cliff. I twisted in an endeavor to get rid of it, but it was firmly lodged between me and the wall.

I yelled to Doug for help. He at once started edging toward me. It seemed hours, though it was probably not over a few minutes. He shouted, "Hang on, I'll be there."

Hang on I did. My fingers ached beyond description. They were frozen to the rock. My exertion in pawing with my feet had added to the fatigue. The ache of my fingers extended to my wrists and then along my arms. I stopped thrashing around and hung like a sack, motionless. Every second seemed a minute, every minute an hour. I did not see how I could possibly hold.

I would slip, I thought, slip to sure death. I could not look down because of my position. But in my mind's eye I saw in sharp outline the jagged rocks that seemed to pull me toward them. The camera kept pushing my fingers from the ledge. I felt them move. They began to give way before the pull of a force too great for flesh to resist.

Fright grew in me. The idea of hanging helpless 200 feet above the abyss brought panic. I cried out to Doug but the words caught in my dry throat. I was like one in a nightmare who struggles to shout—who is then seized with a fear that promises to destroy him.

Then there flashed through my mind a family scene. Mother was sitting in the living room talking to me, telling me what a wonderful man Father was. She told me of his last illness and his death. She told me of his departure from Cleveland, Washington to Portland, Oregon for what proved to be a fatal operation. His last words to her were: "If I die it will be glory. If I live, it will be grace."

The panic passed. The memory of those words restored reason. Glory to die? I could not understand why it would be glory to die. It would be glory to live. But as Father said, it might take grace to live, grace from One more powerful than either Doug or I.

And so again that day I prayed. I asked God to save my life, to save me from destruction on this rock wall. I asked God to make my fingers strong, to give me strength to hang on. I asked God to give me courage, to make me unafraid. I asked God to give me guts, to give me power to do the impossible.

My fingers were as numb as flesh that is full of novocaine. They seemed detached from me, as if they belonged to someone else. My wrists, my shoulders, cried out for respite from the pain. It would be such welcome relief if they could be released from the weight that was on them.

Hang on? You can't hang on. You are a weakling. The weaklings die in the woods.

Weakling? I'll show you. How long must I hang on? All day? OK, all day then. I'll hang on, I'll hang on. O, help me hang on!

I felt someone pushing my left foot upwards. It was Doug. As if through a dream his voice was saying, "Your feet are 18 inches below your toehold." Doug found those toeholds for my feet.

I felt my shoes resting in solid cracks. I pulled myself up and leaned on my elbows on the ledge to which my hands had been glued. I flexed my fingers and bent my wrists to bring life back.

Doug came up abreast of me and said, "We're even Stephen now."

"Even Stephen?"

"Today each of us has saved the other's life."

It was shortly above the point where Doug saved my life that we discovered a classic path up Kloochman. It is a three-sided chimney chute,[7] a few feet wide, that leads almost to the top. There are several such chutes on Kloochman. In later years Cragg Gilbert and Louis Ulrich went up Devil's Chimney on the northeast face in a seven-hour nerve-wracking climb with ropes. Clarence Truitt and many others have gone up the chimney chute that Doug and I discovered. Then as now this chute was filled with loose rock that had to be cleared away. To negotiate the chute we took off our shoes and tied them to our belts. We climbed the chute in stocking feet, pressing our hands and feet against the opposing walls as we kept our backs to the abyss below us. This day we went up the chute with ease, stopping every eight feet or so to measure our progress.

The sun was setting when we reached the top. We were gay and buoyant. We talked about the glories of the scene in front of us. We bragged a bit about our skill in rock work—how we must be part mountain goat to have reached the top. We shouted and hallooed to the empty meadows far below us.

On Kloochman Rock that July afternoon both Doug and I valued life more because death had passed so close. It was wonderful to be alive, breathing, using our muscles, shouting, seeing.

We stayed briefly at the top. We went down as we came up, in stocking feet. We raced against darkness, propelled by the thought of spending the night on Kloochman's treacherous wall.

It was deep dusk when we rejoined Walter on the rock fields at the base. We put on

our shoes and hurried on. We entered the woods at double-quick time, seeking the trail that led toward the South Fork of the Tieton. We saw the trail from the edge of a clearing as a faint, light streak in a pitch-black night. We had two ways of keeping on it. We had no matches or torch or flashlight. But we could feel the edges with our feet. And we could search out the strip of night sky over the path.

We finally decided that it would take too long to follow the trail to camp in this groping way. We'd take a short cut to Westfall Rocks, whose formless shape we could see against the sky. We took to the brush on our right, and kept our hands out in front to ward off boughs and branches. We crossed a marshy bog where we went in up to our knees. We came to soft earth where we went in up to our hips.

There were animals in the brush. We could hear them in the thickets, disturbed by our approach, and going out ahead of us. Thinking they might be bear, we paused to listen. "Cattle," said Doug.

We reached the Tieton River, which we knew could not be forded in many places in that stretch. So we took off our pants, shoes, and shirts and rolled them in bundles which we held on our heads. We waded out into the dark, cold, swift river, Doug in the lead. We had by accident picked one of the few good fords in the Tieton. We were never in water over our waists.

Then we dressed and located the road leading back to camp. As we started along it Doug said: "You know, Bill, there is power in prayer."

That night I prayed again. I knelt on a bed of white fir boughs beside the embers of a campfire and thanked God for saving Doug's life and mine, for giving us the strength to save each other.

---

7. chimney (chim′ nē) **chute** (shoot): A vertical passage the size of a chimney.

THINKING ABOUT THE SELECTION

Recalling

1. What is the first serious problem that William and his friend Doug encounter? How do they solve this problem?
2. Describe the serious trouble that William gets into. How does he get out of this serious trouble?
3. How do the boys feel at the end of the climb?

Interpreting

4. What qualities enable the boys to get themselves out of difficulties when they are in trouble?
5. What role does luck play in saving the boys?
6. Explain the meaning of the title.

Applying

7. What is it about the impossible that makes people want to make it possible?

ANALYZING LITERATURE

Understanding Narrator in Autobiography

A **narrator** is the person telling his or her autobiography. A narrator tells a personal story from his or her own point of view. As a result, you find out what the narrator knows and feels and what the narrator guesses about the thoughts and feelings of others. For example, the narrator tells you his own thoughts and feelings as he is hanging by his fingers 200 feet in the air: "How long must I hang on? All day? OK, all day then. I'll hang on."

Find two passages in "Of Men and Mountains" that are good examples of ideas, feelings, and observations that only the narrator would know about the central character—himself.

CRITICAL THINKING AND READING

Recognizing the Effect of Point of View

When you read a selection written in the first person, you experience the events as the narrator experienced them. Although the experience is based on facts, what you read is subjective, that is, colored by the writer's views.

1. How might Doug have written the incident in which William almost falls?
2. How might the selection have been different if an objective observer had written it?

UNDERSTANDING LANGUAGE

Appreciating Words from Greek Myths

Many English words have their origins in Greek myths. The word *panic,* meaning "fear," comes from the name of the Greek god Pan, a noisy musician who was thought to play his pipes day and night in the woods. Long ago people thought Pan made the sounds that frightened travelers in the wilderness at night. The word *panic* soon came to describe their fear.

Use a dictionary to find the meaning and origin of the following words from Greek mythology.

1. arachnid
2. narcissus
3. titan
4. echo
5. ocean
6. herculean
7. protean

THINKING AND WRITING

Writing from Another Point of View

Select an event in this selection and retell it from Doug's point of view. What did Doug think about the event? What were his feelings? How will Doug's account be different from William's? Write your first draft of Doug's account. Revise it, making sure you have maintained a consistent point of view. Finally proofread your account and share it with your classmates.

Essays for Enjoyment

GIRL READING OUTDOORS
Fairfield Porter

GUIDE FOR READING

Sancho

J. Frank Dobie (1888–1964) grew up in the southwest Texas brush country. He pursued a writing and teaching career devoted to the folklore and history of his native state. Over the years he became, in his words, "a historian of the longhorns, the mustangs, the coyote, and the other characters of the West." In his book *The Longhorns,* he tells of some memorable Texas steers. He included the story of Sancho, which he heard from John Rigby, a trail boss on the Texas Range.

Narrative Essay

An essay is a short nonfiction composition exploring a topic. A **narrative essay** explores this topic by telling a true story. It discusses a topic of personal interest to the writer, giving the writer's view of the subject or personal experience with it. In "Sancho," the author J. Frank Dobie tells you about a Texas longhorn whose story he found unusual as well as interesting.

Look For

As you read "Sancho," look for details that make Sancho stand out from the herd. Why did the author choose to write about this Texas longhorn?

Writing

In this selection, Maria lives on a ranch in the latter part of the nineteenth century. Freewrite about what a day in her life might be like.

Vocabulary

Knowing the following words can help you as you read "Sancho." **dogie** (dō′ gē) **calves**: Motherless calves or strays in a range herd; used chiefly in the West (p. 431) **vigorous** (vig′ ər əs) *adj.*: Strong and energetic (p. 431) **yearling** (yir′ liŋ) *n.*: An animal that is between one and two years old (p. 433)

Sancho

J. Frank Dobie

A man by the name of Kerr had a little ranch on Esperanza Creek in Frio County, in the mesquite lands[1] south of San Antonio. He owned several good cow ponies, a few cattle, and a little bunch of goats that a dog guarded by day. At night they were shut up in a brush corral near the house. Three or four acres of land, fenced in with brush and poles, grew corn, watermelons and "kershaws"—except when the season was too drouthy.[2] A hand-dug well equipped with pulley wheel, rope and bucket furnished water for the establishment.

Kerr's wife was named María. They had no children. She was clean, thrifty, cheerful, always making pets of animals. She usually milked three or four cows and sometimes made cheese out of goat's milk.

Late in the winter of 1877, Kerr while riding over on the San Miguel found one of his cows dead in a bog-hole. Beside the cow was a mud-plastered little black-and-white paint bull calf less than a week old. It was too weak to run; perhaps other cattle had saved it from the coyotes. Kerr pitched his rope over its head, drew it up across the saddle in front of him, carried it home, and turned it over to María.

She had raised many dogie calves and numerous colts captured from mustang mares. The first thing she did now was to pour milk from a bottle down the orphan's throat. With warm water she washed the caked mud off its body. But hand-raising a calf is no end of trouble. The next day Kerr rode around until he found a thrifty brown cow with a young calf. He drove them to the pen. By tying this cow's head up close to a post and hobbling her hind legs, Kerr and María forced her to let the orphan suckle. She did not give a cup of milk at this first sucking. Her calf was kept in the pen next day, and the poor thing bawled herself hoarse. María began feeding her some prickly pear with the thorns singed off. After being tied up twice daily for a month, she adopted the orphan as a twin to her own offspring.

Now she was one of the household cows. Spring weeds came up plentifully and the guajilla brush put out in full leaf. When the brown cow came in about sundown and her two calves were released for their supper, it was a cheering sight to see them wiggle their tails while they guzzled milk.

The dogie was a vigorous little brute, and before long he was getting more milk than the brown cow's own calf. María called him Sancho, a Mexican name meaning "pet." She was especially fond of Sancho, and he grew to be especially fond of her.

---

1. mesquite (mes kēt') **lands** n.: Areas in which grow certain thorny trees and shrubs, common in the southwest U.S. and in Mexico.
2. drouthy (drouth' ē) adj.: Dried up due to drought—a lack of rain.

IN A STAMPEDE
Illustration by Frederic Remington
The Granger Collection

She would give him the shucks wrapped around tamales. Then she began treating him to whole tamales, which are made of ground corn rolled around a core of chopped-up meat, this banana-shaped roll, done up in a shuck, then being steam-boiled. Sancho seemed not to mind the meat. As everybody who has eaten them knows, Mexican tamales are highly seasoned with pepper. Sancho seemed to like the seasoning.

In southern Texas the little chiltipiquin peppers, red when ripe, grow wild in low, shaded places. Cattle never eat them, leaving them for the wild turkeys, mockingbirds and blue quail to pick off. Sometimes in the early fall wild turkeys used to gorge on them so avidly that their flesh became too peppery for human consumption. By eating tamales Sancho developed a taste for the little red peppers growing in the thickets along Esperanza Creek. In fact, he became a kind of chiltipiquin addict. He would hunt for the peppers.

Furthermore, the tamales gave him a tooth for corn in the ear. The summer after he became a yearling he began breaking through the brush fence that enclosed Kerr's corn patch. A forked stick had to be tied around his neck to prevent his getting through the fence. He had been branded and turned into a steer, but he was as strong as any young bull. Like many other pets, he was something of a nuisance. When he could not steal corn or was not humored with tamales, he was enormously contented with grass, mixed in summertime with the sweet mesquite beans. Now and then María gave him a lump of the brown *piloncillo* sugar, from Mexico, that all the border country used.

Every night Sancho came to the ranch pen to sleep. His bed ground was near a certain mesquite tree just outside the gate.

He spent hours every summer day in the shade of this mesquite. When it rained and other cattle drifted off, hunting fresh pasturage, Sancho stayed at home and drank at the well. He was strictly a home creature.

In the spring of 1880 Sancho was three years old and past, white of horn and as blocky of build as a long-legged Texas steer ever grew. Kerr's ranch lay in a big unfenced range grazed by the Shiner brothers. That spring they had a contract to deliver three herds of steers, each to number 2500 head, in Wyoming. Kerr was helping the Shiners gather cattle, and, along with various other ranchers, sold them what steers he had.

Sancho was included. One day late in March the Shiner men road-branded him 7 Z and put him in the first herd headed north. The other herds were to follow two or three days apart.

It was late in the afternoon when the "shaping up" of the herd was completed. It was watered and thrown out on open prairie ground to be bedded down. But Sancho had no disposition to lie down—there. He wanted to go back to that mesquite just outside the pen gate at the Kerr place on the Esperanza where he had without variation slept every night since he had been weaned. Perhaps he had in mind an evening tamale. He stood and roamed about on the south side of the herd. A dozen times during the night the men on guard had to drive him back. As reliefs were changed, word passed to keep an eye on that paint steer on the lower side.

When the herd started on next morning, Sancho was at the tail end of it, often stopping and looking back. It took constant attention from one of the drag drivers to keep him moving. By the time the second night arrived, every hand in the outfit knew Sancho, by name and sight, as being the stubbornest and gentlest steer of the lot. About dark one of them pitched a loop over his horns and staked him to a bush. This saved bothering with his persistent efforts to walk off.

Daily when the herd was halted to graze, spreading out like a fan, the steers all eating their way northward, Sancho invariably pointed himself south. In his lazy way he grabbed many a mouthful of grass while the herd was moving. Finally, in some brush up on the Llano, after ten days of trailing, he dodged into freedom. On the second day following, one of the point men of the second Shiner herd saw him walking south, saw his 7 Z road brand, rounded him in, and set him traveling north again. He became the chief drag animal of this herd. Somewhere north of the Colorado there was a run one night, and when morning came Sancho was missing. The other steers had held together; probably Sancho had not run at all. But he was picked up again, by the third Shiner herd coming on behind.

He took his accustomed place in the drag and continued to require special driving. He picked up in weight. He chewed his cud peacefully and slept soundly, but whenever he looked southward, which was often, he raised his head as if memory and expectation were stirring. The boys were all personally acquainted with him, and every night one of them would stake him.

One day the cattle balked and milled at a bank-full river. "Rope Old Sancho and lead him in," the boss ordered, "and we'll point the other cattle after him." Sancho led like a horse. The herd followed. As soon as he was released, he dropped back to the rear. After this, however, he was always led to the front when there was high water to cross.

By the time the herd got into No Man's Land, beyond Red River, the sand-hill plums and the low-running possum grapes were turning ripe. Pausing now and then to pick a little of the fruit, Sancho's driver saw the pet steer following his example.

Meantime the cattle were trailing, trailing, always north. For five hundred miles across Texas, counting the windings to find water and keep out of breaks, they had come. After getting into the Indian Territory, they snailed on across the Wichita, the South Canadian, the North Canadian, and the Cimarron. On into Kansas they trailed and across the Arkansas, around Dodge City, cowboy capital of the world, out of Kansas into Nebraska, over the wide, wide Platte, past the roaring cow town of Ogallala, up the North Platte, under the Black Hills, and then against the Big Horn Mountains. For two thousand miles, making ten or twelve miles a day, the Shiner herds trailed. They "walked with the grass." Slow, slow, they moved. "Oh, it was a long and lonesome go"—as slow as the long drawn-out notes of "The Texas Lullaby," as slow as the night herder's song on a slow-walking horse:

> It's a whoop and a yea, get along
> my little dogies,
>   For camp is far away.
> It's a whoop and a yea and a-
> driving the dogies,
>   For Wyoming may be your new
> home.

When, finally, after listening for months, day and night, to the slow song of their motion, the "dogies" reached their "new home," Sancho was still halting every now and then to sniff southward for a whiff of the Mexican Gulf. The farther he got away from home, the less he seemed to like the change. He had never felt frost in September before. The Mexican peppers on the Esperanza were red ripe now.

The Wyoming outfit received the cattle. Then for a week the Texas men helped brand C R on their long sides before turning them loose on the new range. When San-

THE AMERICAN COWBOY
Charlie Dye
Collection of Harold McCracken

Sancho   435

cho's time came to be branded in the chute,[3] one of the Texans yelled out, "There goes my pet. Stamp that *C R* brand on him good and deep." Another one said, "The line riders had better watch for his tracks."

And now the Shiner men turned south, taking back with them their saddle horses and chuck wagons—and leaving Sancho behind. They made good time, but a blue norther was whistling at their backs when they turned the remuda[4] loose on the Frio River. After the "Cowboys' Christmas Ball" most of them settled down for a few weeks of winter sleep. They could rub tobacco juice in their eyes during the summer when they needed something in addition to night rides and runs to keep them awake.

Spring comes early down on the Esperanza. The mesquites were all in new leaf with that green so fresh and tender that the color seems to emanate into the sky. The bluebonnets and the pink phlox were sprinkling every hill and draw. The prickly pear was studded with waxy blossoms, and the glades were heavy with the perfume of white brush. It was a good season, and tallow weed and grass were coming together. It was time for the spring cow hunts and the putting up of herds for the annual drive north. The Shiners were at work.

"We were close to Kerr's cabin on Esperanza Creek," John Rigby told me, "when I looked across a pear flat and saw something that made me rub my eyes. I was riding with Joe Shiner, and we both stopped our horses."

"Do you see what I see?" John Rigby asked.

"Yes, but before I say, I'm going to read the brand," Joe Shiner answered.

They rode over. "You can hang me for a horse thief," John Rigby will tell, "if it wasn't that Sancho paint steer, four years old now, the Shiner *7 Z* road brand and the Wyoming *C R* range brand both showing on him as plain as boxcar letters."

The men rode on down to Kerr's.

"Yes," Kerr said, "Old Sancho got in about six weeks ago. His hoofs were worn mighty nigh down to the hair, but he wasn't lame. I thought María was going out of her senses, she was so glad to see him. She actually hugged him and she cried and then she begun feeding him hot tamales. She's made a batch of them nearly every day since, just to pet that steer. When she's not feeding him tamales, she's giving him *piloncillo*."

Sancho was slicking off and certainly did seem contented. He was coming up every night and sleeping at the gate, María said. She was nervous over the prospect of losing her pet, but Joe Shiner said that if that steer loved his home enough to walk back to it all the way from Wyoming, he wasn't going to drive him off again, even if he was putting up another herd for the *C R* owners.

As far as I can find out, Old Sancho lived right there on the Esperanza, now and then getting a tamale, tickling his palate with chili peppers in season, and generally staying fat on mesquite grass, until he died a natural death. He was one of the "walking Texas Longhorns."

---

3. chute (shoot) *n.*: A narrow, high-walled device used to restrain cattle.
4. remuda (rə moo′ də) *n.*: Group of extra saddle horses kept as a supply of remounts.

THINKING ABOUT THE SELECTION

Recalling

1. Describe the Kerrs' ranch.
2. How does Sancho become Maria's pet?
3. What is unusual about Sancho's eating habits?
4. Why does Sancho leave the ranch?
5. Describe Sancho's behavior on the drive.
6. What finally happens to Sancho? Why does Joe Shiner agree to this decision?

Interpreting

7. What does Sancho learn from his early experiences on the ranch that makes him different from the other longhorn cattle?
8. Dobie said that Sancho's story was the best range story he had ever heard. Why do you think he liked the story so much?
9. Dobie felt that Sancho was an animal worth remembering. Find three examples of Sancho's almost human personality.

Applying

10. Think about where Maria lived and what her daily life must have been like. Why would a pet be so important to her?

ANALYZING LITERATURE

Understanding a Narrative Essay

A **narrative essay** is a nonfiction composition in which the writer explores the subject by telling a true story. People write essays to present their observations, views, or opinions about a topic. Dobie knew the section of Texas where Sancho lived, and he had written and studied about cattle drives like the one described in "Sancho." Dobie was able to include details that help make Sancho vivid to readers.

1. List three details about the section of Texas where Sancho lived that Dobie includes.
2. List three details about cattle drives that Dobie includes in the essay.

CRITICAL THINKING AND READING

Putting Events in Chronological Order

Chronological order is the order in which events happen in time. Authors use certain words and phrases to place events in time, such as "the first thing she did" and "the next day" to signal time order.

Write the numbers of the following events in the order in which they happened. Then list the phrases that signal the order in which they should appear.

1. When he was a yearling, Sancho broke into the corn patch.
2. Sancho lived on the ranch until he died.
3. Sancho at three years old was a handsome Texas steer.

UNDERSTANDING LANGUAGE

Understanding Words from Spanish

Many Spanish words such as *tortilla, taco,* and *rodeo* have become part of the English language. The following words from "Sancho" came from the Spanish language. Look up the meaning of each in a dictionary. Also copy the spellings of the original Spanish words.

1. chili
2. corral
3. ranch
4. tamale

THINKING AND WRITING

Writing a Letter

Look over the freewriting you did before you began this selection. Use ideas from it and from the selection as the basis for a letter to a friend telling about Sancho's return. Revise your letter, making sure you have presented the information from Maria's point of view. Proofread your letter and share it with your classmates.

Debbie

James Herriot (1916–   ), who was born in Glasgow, Scotland, studied veterinary medicine. Since 1940 he has been a veterinarian in England, the setting for his true stories about being a "country vet." British veterinarians are not allowed to use any form of advertising. Since writing under his own name would be considered advertising, he chose James Herriot as his pen name. The incidents Herriot describes, such as the one in "Debbie," have filled more than ten books and have inspired a popular television series.

Characters in a Narrative Essay

The characters in a narrative essay are real people. In fact, sometimes the author even appears as a character. You learn about these characters in the same way you learn about characters in a piece of fiction. You can read about their actions, listen to their words, share their thoughts, or read descriptive details about them. Finally, you can learn much about a character by reading what other characters say or think about him or her.

Look For

As you read, look for the details that make the characters come alive for you. What impression do you form of James Herriot, Mrs. Ainsworth, Debbie, and Buster?

Writing

Many people enjoy reading Herriot's true stories because he provides an insider's view of the daily life of a veterinarian. List the questions you would like to ask James Herriot about his work with animals.

Vocabulary

Knowing the following words can help you as you read "Debbie."

fretted (fret′ əd) *adj.*: Decoratively arranged (p. 440)

sage (sāj) *n.*: A plant used to flavor food (p. 440)

wafted (waf′ təd) *v.*: Moved lightly through the air (p. 440)

knell (nel) *n.*: The sound of a bell slowly ringing, as for a funeral (p. 441)

privations (prī vā′ shənz) *n.*: Lack of common comforts (p. 441)

ornate (ôr nāt′) *adj.*: Having fancy decorations (p. 442)

goading (gōd′ iŋ): *v.*: Urging to action (p. 442)

Debbie

James Herriot

I first saw her one autumn day when I was called to see one of Mrs. Ainsworth's dogs, and I looked in some surprise at the furry black creature sitting before the fire.

"I didn't know you had a cat," I said.

The lady smiled. "We haven't, this is Debbie."

"Debbie?"

"Yes, at least that's what we call her. She's a stray. Comes here two or three times a week and we give her some food. I don't know where she lives but I believe she spends a lot of her time around one of the farms along the road."

"Do you ever get the feeling that she wants to stay with you?"

"No." Mrs. Ainsworth shook her head. "She's a timid little thing. Just creeps in, has some food then flits away. There's something so appealing about her but she doesn't seem to want to let me or anybody into her life."

I looked again at the little cat. "But she isn't just having food today."

"That's right. It's a funny thing but every now and again she slips through here into the lounge and sits by the fire for a few minutes. It's as though she was giving herself a treat."

"Yes . . . I see what you mean." There was no doubt there was something unusual in the attitude of the little animal. She was sitting bolt upright on the thick rug which lay before the fireplace in which the coals glowed and flamed. She made no effort to curl up or wash herself or do anything other than gaze quietly ahead. And there was something in the dusty black of her coat, the half-wild scrawny look of her, that gave me a clue. This was a special event in her life, a rare and wonderful thing; she was lapping up a comfort undreamed of in her daily existence.

As I watched she turned, crept soundlessly from the room and was gone.

"That's always the way with Debbie," Mrs. Ainsworth laughed. "She never stays more than ten minutes or so, then she's off."

Mrs. Ainsworth was a plumpish, pleasant-faced woman in her forties and the kind of client veterinary surgeons dream of; well off, generous, and the owner of three cosseted[1] Basset hounds. And it only needed the habitually mournful expression of one of the dogs to deepen a little and I was round there posthaste.[2] Today one of the Bassets had raised its paw and scratched its ear a couple of times and that was enough to send its mistress scurrying to the phone in great alarm.

So my visits to the Ainsworth home were frequent but undemanding, and I had ample opportunity to look out for the little cat that had intrigued me. On one occasion I spotted her nibbling daintily from a saucer at the kitchen door. As I watched she turned and almost floated on light footsteps into the hall then through the lounge door.

---

1. **cosseted** (käs′ it əd) *adj.*: Pampered, indulged.
2. **posthaste** (pōst′ hāst′) *adv.*: With great quickness.

The three Bassets were already in residence, draped snoring on the fireside rug, but they seemed to be used to Debbie because two of them sniffed her in a bored manner and the third merely cocked a sleepy eye at her before flopping back on the rich pile.

Debbie sat among them in her usual posture; upright, intent, gazing absorbedly into the glowing coals. This time I tried to make friends with her. I approached her carefully but she leaned away as I stretched out my hand. However, by patient wheedling and soft talk I managed to touch her and gently stroked her cheek with one finger. There was a moment when she responded by putting her head on one side and rubbing back against my hand but soon she was ready to leave. Once outside the house she darted quickly along the road then through a gap in a hedge and the last I saw was the little black figure flitting over the rain-swept grass of a field.

"I wonder where she goes," I murmured half to myself.

Mrs. Ainsworth appeared at my elbow. "That's something we've never been able to find out."

It must have been nearly three months before I heard from Mrs. Ainsworth, and in fact I had begun to wonder at the Bassets' long symptomless run when she came on the phone.

It was Christmas morning and she was apologetic. "Mr. Herriot, I'm so sorry to bother you today of all days. I should think you want a rest at Christmas like anybody else." But her natural politeness could not hide the distress in her voice.

"Please don't worry about that," I said. "Which one is it this time?"

"It's not one of the dogs. It's . . . Debbie."

"Debbie? She's at your house now?"

"Yes . . . but there's something wrong. Please come quickly."

Driving through the marketplace I thought again that Darrowby on Christmas Day was like Dickens come to life; the empty square with the snow thick on the cobbles and hanging from the eaves of the fretted lines of roofs; the shops closed and the colored lights of the Christmas trees winking at the windows of the clustering houses, warmly inviting against the cold white bulk of the fells[3] behind.

Mrs. Ainsworth's home was lavishly decorated with tinsel and holly, rows of drinks stood on the sideboard and the rich aroma of turkey and sage and onion stuffing wafted from the kitchen. But her eyes were full of pain as she led me through to the lounge.

Debbie was there all right, but this time everything was different. She wasn't sitting upright in her usual position; she was stretched quite motionless on her side, and huddled close to her lay a tiny black kitten.

I looked down in bewilderment. "What's happened here?"

"It's the strangest thing," Mrs. Ainsworth replied. "I haven't seen her for several weeks then she came in about two hours ago—sort of staggered into the kitchen, and she was carrying the kitten in her mouth. She took it through to the lounge and laid it on the rug and at first I was amused. But I could see all was not well because she sat as she usually does, but for a long time—over an hour—then she lay down like this and she hasn't moved."

I knelt on the rug and passed my hand over Debbie's neck and ribs. She was thinner than ever, her fur dirty and mudcaked. She did not resist as I gently opened her mouth. The tongue and mucous membranes

---

3. fells *n.*: Rocky or barren hills.

were abnormally pale and the lips ice-cold against my fingers. When I pulled down her eyelid and saw the dead white conjunctiva[4] a knell sounded in my mind.

I palpated[5] the abdomen with a grim certainty as to what I would find and there was no surprise, only a dull sadness as my fingers closed around a hard lobulated[6] mass deep among the viscera.[7] Massive lymphosarcoma. Terminal and hopeless. I put my stethoscope on her heart and listened to the increasingly faint, rapid beat then I straightened up and sat on the rug looking sightlessly into the fireplace, feeling the warmth of the flames on my face.

Mrs. Ainsworth's voice seemed to come from afar. "Is she ill, Mr. Herriot?"

I hesitated. "Yes . . . yes, I'm afraid so. She has a malignant growth." I stood up. "There's absolutely nothing I can do. I'm sorry."

"Oh!" Her hand went to her mouth and she looked at me wide-eyed. When at last she spoke her voice trembled. "Well, you must put her to sleep immediately. It's the only thing to do. We can't let her suffer."

"Mrs. Ainsworth," I said. "There's no need. She's dying now—in a coma—far beyond suffering."

She turned quickly away from me and was very still as she fought with her emotions. Then she gave up the struggle and dropped on her knees beside Debbie.

"Oh, poor little thing!" she sobbed and stroked the cat's head again and again as the tears fell unchecked on the matted fur. "What she must have come through. I feel I ought to have done more for her."

For a few moments I was silent, feeling her sorrow, so discordant among the bright seasonal colors of this festive room. Then I spoke gently.

"Nobody could have done more than you," I said. "Nobody could have been kinder."

"But I'd have kept her here—in comfort. It must have been terrible out there in the cold when she was so desperately ill—I daren't think about it. And having kittens, too—I . . . I wonder how many she did have?"

I shrugged. "I don't suppose we'll ever know. Maybe just this one. It happens sometimes. And she brought it to you, didn't she?"

"Yes . . . that's right . . . she did . . . she did." Mrs. Ainsworth reached out and lifted the bedraggled black morsel. She smoothed her finger along the muddy fur and the tiny mouth opened in a soundless miaow. "Isn't it strange? She was dying and she brought her kitten here. And on Christmas Day."

I bent and put my hand on Debbie's heart. There was no beat.

I looked up. "I'm afraid she's gone." I lifted the small body, almost feather light, wrapped it in the sheet which had been spread on the rug and took it out to the car.

When I came back Mrs. Ainsworth was still stroking the kitten. The tears had dried on her cheeks and she was brighteyed as she looked at me.

"I've never had a cat before," she said.

I smiled. "Well, it looks as though you've got one now."

And she certainly had. That kitten grew rapidly into a sleek handsome cat with a boisterous nature which earned him the name of Buster. In every way he was the opposite to his timid little mother. Not for him the privations of the secret outdoor life; he stalked the rich carpets of the Ainsworth

---

4. conjunctiva (kän′ jəŋk tī′ və) n.: Lining of the inner surface of the eyelids.
5. palpated (pal′ pāt ed) v.: Examined by touching.
6. lobulated (läb′ yōo lāt′ əd) adj.: Subdivided.
7. viscera (vis′ ər ə) n.: Internal organs.

home like a king and the ornate collar he always wore added something more to his presence.

On my visits I watched his development with delight but the occasion which stays in my mind was the following Christmas Day, a year from his arrival.

I was out on my rounds as usual. I can't remember when I haven't had to work on Christmas Day because the animals have never got round to recognizing it as a holiday; but with the passage of the years the vague resentment I used to feel has been replaced by philosophical acceptance. After all, as I tramped around the hillside barns in the frosty air I was working up a better appetite for my turkey than all the millions lying in bed or slumped by the fire.

I was on my way home, bathed in a rosy glow. I heard the cry as I was passing Mrs. Ainsworth's house.

"Merry Christmas, Mr. Herriot!" She was letting a visitor out of the front door and she waved at me gaily. "Come in and have a drink to warm you up."

I didn't need warming up but I pulled in to the curb without hesitation. In the house there was all the festive cheer of last year and the same glorious whiff of sage and onion which set my gastric juices surging. But there was not the sorrow; there was Buster.

He was darting up to each of the dogs in turn, ears pricked, eyes blazing with devilment, dabbing a paw at them then streaking away.

Mrs. Ainsworth laughed. "You know, he plagues the life out of them. Gives them no peace."

She was right. To the Bassets, Buster's arrival was rather like the intrusion of an irreverent outsider into an exclusive London club. For a long time they had led a life of measured grace; regular sedate walks with their mistress, superb food in ample quanti-

ties and long snoring sessions on the rugs and armchairs. Their days followed one upon another in unruffled calm. And then came Buster.

He was dancing up to the youngest dog again, sideways this time, head on one side, goading him. When he started boxing with both paws it was too much even for the Basset. He dropped his dignity and rolled over with the cat in a brief wrestling match.

"I want to show you something." Mrs. Ainsworth lifted a hard rubber ball from the sideboard and went out to the garden, followed by Buster. She threw the ball across the lawn and the cat bounded after it over the frosted grass, the muscles rippling under the black sheen of his coat. He seized the ball in his teeth, brought it back to his mistress, dropped it at her feet and waited expectantly. She threw it and he brought it back again.

I gasped incredulously. A feline retriever!

The Bassets looked on disdainfully. Nothing would ever have induced them to chase a ball, but Buster did it again and again as though he would never tire of it.

Mrs. Ainsworth turned to me. "Have you ever seen anything like that?"

"No," I replied. "I never have. He is a most remarkable cat."

She snatched Buster from his play and we went back into the house where she held him close to her face, laughing as the big cat purred and arched himself ecstatically against her cheek.

Looking at him, a picture of health and contentment, my mind went back to his mother. Was it too much to think that that dying little creature with the last of her strength had carried her kitten to the only haven of comfort and warmth she had ever known in the hope that it would be cared for there? Maybe it was.

But it seemed I wasn't the only one with

such fancies. Mrs. Ainsworth turned to me and though she was smiling her eyes were wistful.

"Debbie would be pleased," she said.

I nodded. "Yes, she would . . . It was just a year ago today she brought him, wasn't it?"

"That's right." She hugged Buster to her again. "The best Christmas present I ever had."

THINKING ABOUT THE SELECTION
Recalling

1. Why does Herriot first visit Mrs. Ainsworth?
2. Describe Debbie and her life.
3. Explain the reason for Herriot's second visit.
4. How is the Ainsworth household different as a result of Buster?

Interpreting

5. What qualities does Mrs. Ainsworth show in her treatment of animals?

Applying

6. Mrs. Ainsworth receives an unexpected reward for her kindness to Debbie. She receives Buster. Why are unexpected rewards sometimes more valued than expected ones?

ANALYZING LITERATURE
Understanding Characters in an Essay

You can learn about characters by reading about their actions, by reading their words, by reading about their thoughts and feelings, by reading descriptive details about them, and by reading what other characters say or think about them.

Look back over "Debbie" and point out one example of information about Herriot that you found in each of the following ways.

1. By reading about his actions
2. By reading his words
3. By reading about his thoughts
4. By reading a descriptive detail
5. By reading what another character says or thinks about him

CRITICAL THINKING AND READING
Comparing and Contrasting Characters

When you **compare** characters, you discuss traits about each that are the same. When you **contrast** characters, you discuss traits that are different. Comparing and contrasting characters can help you to understand them better.

1. List traits that Debbie and Buster share.
2. List traits that differ between Debbie and Buster.
3. What was it about the presentation of Debbie that made her come alive for you?
4. What was it about the presentation of Buster that made him come alive for you?

THINKING AND WRITING
Comparing and Contrasting Cats

Using the lists of traits you wrote for Debbie and Buster, write an article for a pet journal comparing and contrasting the two cats. Describe one cat completely and follow that description with a complete description of the other cat. When you revise, check the organization of your article carefully. Finally, proofread your article and share it with your classmates.

GUIDE FOR READING

My Wild Irish Mother

Jean Kerr (1923–   ) was born in Scranton, Pennsylvania. She was eight years old when she decided that she wanted "to be able to sleep until noon," a goal she achieved partly by becoming a writer who begins each day "at the stroke of the noon whistle." Still, Jean Kerr has found time to write many humorous stories, essays, and plays—all works of "realistic comedy." The essay "My Wild Irish Mother," published in 1978, comes from a collection of her essays called *How I Got To Be Perfect.*

Humorous Essay

A **humorous essay** is a short nonfiction composition in which a writer presents a subject in a humorous way. In "My Wild Irish Mother," Kerr writes about her mother, a woman of Irish descent and spirit. Kerr reveals her mother's character in a series of anecdotes —brief, amusing incidents or stories that make a simple point. These anecdotes and the writer's skill make this essay like a funny Valentine: it talks of love while making you laugh.

Look For

As you read "My Wild Irish Mother," look for the humorous anecdotes and descriptive details that reveal Mother's character. What is Mother like? Why does Kerr consider her such a character?

Writing

Think of a person who would be an interesting subject for a humorous essay. It may be someone you know, someone you have read about, or someone you have seen on television or in the movies. Freewrite about that person, recalling amusing anecdotes that reveal his or her most outstanding character traits.

Vocabulary

Knowing the following words will help you as you read "My Wild Irish Mother."

conviction (kən vik′ shən) *n.:* Strong belief (p. 445)

indulgent (in dul′ jənt) *adj.:* Generous (p. 445)

protestations (prät′ is tā′ shənz) *n.:* Formal declarations or assertions (p. 447)

portentous (pôr′ ten′ təs) *adj.:* Pompous and self-consciously weighty (p. 447)

conspiratorial (kən spir′ ə tôr′ ē əl) *adj.:* Secretive (p. 448)

languorous (laŋ′ gər əs) *adj.:* Slow and lazy (p. 448)

beguiled (bi gīl′d′) *v.:* Charmed (p. 448)

credo (krē′ dō) *n.:* Set of personal beliefs (p. 449)

My Wild Irish Mother

Jean Kerr

I'm never going to write my autobiography and it's all my mother's fault. I didn't hate her, so I have practically no material. In fact, the situation is worse than I'm pretending. We were crazy about her—and you know I'll never get a book out of that, much less a musical.

Mother was born Kitty O'Neill, in Kinsale, Ireland, with bright red hair, bright blue eyes, and the firm conviction that it was wrong to wait for an elevator if you were only going up to the fifth floor. It's not just that she won't wait for elevators, which she really feels are provided only for the convenience of the aged and infirm. I have known her to reproach herself on missing one section of a revolving door. And I well remember a time when we missed a train from New York to Washington. I fully expected her to pick up our suitcases and announce, "Well, darling, the exercise will be good for us."

When I have occasion to mutter about the financial problems involved in maintaining six children in a large house, Mother is quick to get to the root of the problem. "Remember," she says, "you take cabs a lot."

The youngest daughter of wealthy and indulgent parents, Mother went to finishing schools in France and to the Royal Conservatory of Music in London. Thus, when she came to America to marry my father, her only qualifications for the role of housewife and mother were the ability to speak four languages, play three musical instruments, and make *blancmange*.[1] I, naturally, wasn't around during those first troubled months when Mother learned to cook. But my father can still recall the day she boiled corn on the cob, a delicacy unknown in Ireland at that time, for five hours until the cobs were tender. And, with a typical beginner's zeal, Mother "put up" twenty bushels of tomatoes for that first winter before it struck her that neither she nor Dad really liked canned tomatoes.

By the time I was old enough to notice things, Mother was an excellent cook. She would cook things she had no intention of eating. Where food is concerned, she is totally conservative. She will study the menu at an expensive restaurant with evident interest and then say, "Darling, where do you see lamb chops?" Or she will glance with real admiration at a man at a nearby table who seems actually to be consuming an order of cherrystone clams. "Aren't Americans marvelous?" she'll remark. "They will eat anything."

On the other hand she was always willing to prepare all manner of exotic dishes for Dad and the rest of us. In the old days the men who worked for my father frequently gave him gifts of game—venison, rabbit, and the like. Occasionally we children

---

1. blancmange (blə mänzh′) *n.*: A sweet, molded jellylike dessert.

AFTER THE MEETING, 1914
Cecelia Beaux
The Toledo Museum of Art

would protest. I recall becoming quite tearful over the prospect of eating deer, on the theory that it might be Bambi. But Mother was always firm. "Nonsense," she would say, "eat up, it's just like chicken."

But one night she went too far. I don't know where she got this enormous slab of meat; I don't think my father brought it home. It stood overnight in the icebox in some complicated solution of brine[2] and herbs. The next day the four of us were told that we could each invite a friend to dinner. Mother spent most of the day lovingly preparing her roast. That night there were ten of us around the dining-room table, and if Mother seemed too busy serving all the rest of us to eat anything herself, that was not at all unusual. At this late date I have no impression of what the meat tasted like. But I know that we were all munching away when Mother beamed happily at us and asked, "Well, children, how are you enjoying the bear?"

Forks dropped and certain of the invited guests made emergency trips to the bathroom. For once, all of Mother's protestations that it was just like chicken were unavailing. Nobody would touch another bite. She was really dismayed. I heard her tell Dad, "It's really strange, Tom—I thought all Americans liked bear."

Mother's education, as I have indicated, was rather one-sided. While she knew a great deal about such "useless" things as music and art and literature, she knew nothing whatever, we were quick to discover, about isosceles triangles[3] or watts and volts or the Smoot-Hawley Tariff.[4] As we were growing up, we made haste to repair these gaps.

One of the most charming things about Mother was the extraordinary patience with which she would allow us youngsters to "instruct" her. I remember my brother Hugh, when he was about eight, sitting on the foot of Mother's bed and giving her a half-hour lecture which began with the portentous question, "Mom, how much do you know about the habits of the common housefly?"

At that, it's remarkable how much of this unrelated information stayed with her. Just recently I was driving her to a train and she noticed, high up in the air, a squirrel that was poised on a wire that ran between two five-story buildings. "Look at that little squirrel 'way up on that wire," she said. "You know, if he gets one foot on the ground, he'll be electrocuted."

But if her knowledge of positive and negative electricity is a little sketchy, there is nothing sketchy about her knowledge of any subject in which she develops an interest. Mother always adored the theater and was a passionate playgoer from the time she was five years old. However, during the years when she was sobbing gently over *The Lily of Killarney* in Cork City, she was blissfully unaware of the menacing existence of American drama critics or the fact that their printed opinions had a certain measurable effect on the box office. Even when she came to America, she still had the feeling that five nights was probably an impressive run for a Broadway show.

Time passed, and my husband and I

---

2. brine (brīn) *n.*: Water full of salt and used for pickling.
3. isosceles triangles (ī säs′ ə lēz′ trī′ an′ g'ls) *n.*: Geometrical figures with three angles and three sides, two sides of which are equal in length.

4. Smoot-Hawley Tariff: A tax law that required people to pay high taxes or tariffs on goods imported into the country.

became involved in the theater. Mother began to get the facts. When, quite a few years ago, we were living in Washington and came up to New York for the opening of a revue[5] we had written, I promised Mother that I would send her all the reviews, special delivery, as soon as they appeared. In those days, before the demise[6] of *The Sun,* there were eight metropolitan dailies. Eventually we got hold of all the papers and I was able to assess the evidence. All but one of the morning papers were fine, and while there were certain quibbles in the afternoon papers, the only seriously negative notice appeared in *The Sun.* Ward Morehouse was then the critic on *The Sun* but happened to be out of town at the moment, and the review was written by his assistant, or, as I was willing to suppose, his office boy. So, with that special brand of feminine logic that has already made my husband prematurely gray, I decided to omit this particular notice in the batch I was sending to my mother, on the theory that (a) it wasn't written by the *real* critic, and (b) nobody in Scranton, Pennsylvania, knew there was a paper called *The Sun* anyway. This was a serious miscalculation on my part, as I realized later in the day when I got Mother's two-word telegram. It read, "Where's Morehouse?"

Let me say that her interest in the more technical aspects of the theater continues unabated. Not long ago we were in Philadelphia, deep in the unrefined bedlam that surrounds any musical in its tryout stage. The phone rang. It was Mother. Without any preliminary word of greeting, she asked in hushed, conspiratorial tones, "Darling, have you pointed and sharpened?"

"Good Lord, Mother," I said, "what are you talking about?"

"I'm talking about the show, dear," she said, sounding like a small investor, which she was. "*Variety*[7] says it needs pointing and sharpening, and I think we should listen to them."

To the four low-metabolism types[8] she inexplicably produced, Mother's energy has always seemed awesome. "What do you think," she's prone to say, "do I have time to cut the grass before I stuff the turkey?" But her whirlwind activity is potentially less dangerous than her occasional moments of repose. Then she sits, staring into space, clearly lost in languorous memories. The faint, fugitive smile that hovers about her lips suggests the gentle melancholy of one hearing Mozart played beautifully. Suddenly she leaps to her feet. "I know it will work," she says. "All we have to do is remove that wall, plug up the windows, and extend the porch."

It's undoubtedly fortunate that she has the thrust and the energy of a well-guided missile. Otherwise she wouldn't get a lick of work done, because everybody who comes to her house, whether to read the gas meter or to collect for UNICEF,[9] always stays at least an hour. I used to think that they were one and all beguiled by her Irish accent. But I have gradually gleaned[10] that they are telling her the story of their invariably unhappy lives. "Do you remember my lovely huckleberry man?" Mother will ask. "Oh, *yes* you do—he had red hair and ears. Well, his brother-in-law sprained his back and hasn't

---

5. revue (ri vyoo′) *n.*: A musical show with loosely connected skits, songs, and dances.
6. demise (di mīz′) *n.*: A ceasing to exist; death.

7. Variety: A newspaper that specializes in show-business news.
8. low-metabolism types: Less energetic people.
9. UNICEF: United Nations International Children's Emergency Fund.
10. gleaned (glēn′d) *v.*: Found out gradually bit by bit.

worked in six months, and we're going to have to take a bundle of clothes over to those children." Or, again: "Do you remember that nice girl in the Scranton Dry Goods? Oh, yes you do, she was in lamp shades and she had gray hair and wore gray dresses. Well, she's having an operation next month and you must remember to pray for her." Mother's credo, by the way, is that if you want something, anything, don't just sit there—pray for it. And she combines a Job-like[11] patience in the face of the mysterious ways of the Almighty with a flash of Irish rebellion which will bring her to say—and I'm sure she speaks for many of us—"Jean,

11. Job-like (jōb′ līk) *adj.*: Similar to the man named Job in the Old Testament who endured much suffering but did not lose his faith in God.

what I am really looking for is a blessing that's *not* in disguise."

She does have a knack for penetrating disguises, whether it be small boys who claim that they have taken baths or middle-aged daughters who swear that they have lost five pounds. She has a way of cutting things to size, particularly books, which she gobbles up in the indiscriminate[12] way that a slot machine gobbles up quarters. The first time I had a collection of short pieces brought out in book form, I sent an advance copy to Mother. She was naturally delighted. Her enthusiasm fairly bubbled off the pages of the letter. "Darling," she wrote, "isn't it marvelous the way those old pieces of yours finally came to the surface like a dead body!"

I knew when I started this that all I could do was list the things Mother says, because it's not possible, really, to describe her. All my life I have heard people break off their lyrical descriptions of Kitty and announce helplessly, "You'll just have to meet her."

However, I recognize, if I cannot describe, the lovely festive air she always brings with her, so that she can arrive any old day in July and suddenly it seems to be Christmas Eve and the children seem handsomer and better behaved and all the adults seem more charming and—

Well, you'll just have to meet her.

---

12. indiscriminate (in´ dis krim´ ə nit) *adj.*: Not based on careful choices; random.

THINKING ABOUT THE SELECTION
Recalling

1. What are Mother's three unlikely qualifications for the role of wife and mother?
2. Give two examples of Mother's unusual ideas about food.
3. Why does the writer finally stop listing her mother's qualities and comments and end the essay?

Interpreting

4. What do we mean when we call someone "a real character"? In what ways is Mother "a real character"?
5. Based on what you know about the mother and daughter from this essay, name one way in which they are alike and one way in which they differ.

6. The writer has borrowed the title of her essay from an old Irish love song, "My Wild Irish Rose." Knowing this, what meaning does the title of the essay convey?

Applying

7. Think of a song title that would be appropriate as the title of a humorous essay about the subject of your freewriting assignment. Explain why that song title would be appropriate for an essay about that person.

ANALYZING LITERATURE
Understanding the Humorous Essay

A **humorous essay** is a nonfiction composition that gives a writer's thoughtful but humorous view of a subject. Although the subject may be serious, its treatment is lighthearted and intended to make you laugh. Writers of humorous essays amuse their audiences in different ways. Some use amusing anecdotes as Jean Kerr does when she tells about her mother boiling the corn on the cob.

1. What is Kerr's attitude toward her mother? Find the statement that reveals this.
2. How do you think she wants you to feel about her mother? Explain your answer.
3. Name three examples of the ways she used to accomplish her purpose.

CRITICAL THINKING AND READING
Identifying Exaggeration

Writers often achieve comic effects through **exaggeration**—the act of making something appear greater, more important, or funnier than it really is. Kerr exaggerates, for example, when she tells you that her mother "has the thrust and the energy of a well-guided missile." Her exaggeration is a much funnier way of overstating a fact.

1. Find three examples of exaggeration in this essay.
2. Explain the effect of each of these examples.

UNDERSTANDING LANGUAGE
Finding Homophones

A **homophone** is a word that sounds like another word but is spelled differently and has a different meaning. For example, the words *cash* and *cache* are homophones. *Cash* refers to ready money, whereas *cache* refers to a place in which stores of supplies are hidden.

Complete each word analogy below by filling in the appropriate homophone.

1. write:right::red:_____
2. know:no::weight:_____
3. ewe:you::time:_____
4. roll:role::days:_____
5. four:for::deer:_____
6. meet:meat::bite:_____
7. eight:ate::hi:_____
8. son:sun::review:_____
9. one:won::morning:_____
10. reel:real::more:_____

THINKING AND WRITING
Writing a Humorous Essay

Choose one of the humorous events in the essay "My Wild Irish Mother." Rewrite this episode making the daughter the subject instead of the mother. Using the information about Jean Kerr in the essay, retell the event from the mother's point of view. When you have finished writing, make sure you have consistently had the mother tell the story about Jean Kerr. Revise your essay and read it aloud to your classmates. Try to tell it aloud in the mother's voice.

GUIDE FOR READING

Forest Fire

Anaïs Nin (1903–1977) was born in France but grew up in the United States. At age eleven, she began the writing that continued her whole life. Although she wrote novels and short stories, Nin was best known for her six published diaries spanning sixty years. "Forest Fire," from the fifth diary, illustrates how Nin looked at life "as an adventure and a tale." The incident she wrote about in "Forest Fire" happened when she was living in Sierra Madre, California.

Descriptive Essay

A **descriptive essay** is a short nonfiction composition in which an author describes or creates word pictures of a subject. Like most other kinds of essays, an author writes a descriptive essay to present his or her view of a subject. But in descriptive essays, authors achieve their purpose mainly by including images and details that show us how things look, sound, smell, taste, or feel. Such details work to allow you to share the writer's experience fully.

Look For

As you read "Forest Fire," look for specific details the writer uses to create vivid word pictures for you. What sensory impressions do these details create?

Writing

Imagine that you are a newspaper reporter. You are preparing to interview the people who have just survived a forest fire. They managed to put out the fire quickly and without much damage to their surroundings. Write a list of interview questions to ask these people about the fire and the precautions they took that helped lessen the effects of the fire. Write questions that begin with *who, what, when, where, why, how,* or *tell me about.*

Vocabulary

Knowing the following words will help you as you read "Forest Fire."

tinted (tint′ əd) *v.*: Colored (p. 453)

evacuees (i vak′ yoo wēz′) *n.*: People who leave a place, especially because of danger (p. 453)

pungent (pun′ jənt) *adj.*: Sharp and stinging to the smell (p. 454)

tenacious (tə nā′ shəs) *adj.*: Holding on firmly (p. 454)

dissolution (dis′ ə loo′ shən) *n.*: The act of breaking down and crumbling (p. 454)

ravaging (rav′ ij iŋ) *adj.*: Severely damaging or destroying (p. 454)

Forest Fire

Anaïs Nin

A man rushed in to announce he had seen smoke on Monrovia Peak.[1] As I looked out of the window I saw the two mountains facing the house on fire. The entire rim burning wildly in the night. The flames, driven by hot Santa Ana winds[2] from the desert, were as tall as the tallest trees, the sky already tinted coral, and the crackling noise of burning trees, the ashes and the smoke were already increasing. The fire raced along, sometimes descending behind the mountain where I could only see the glow, sometimes descending toward us. I thought of the foresters in danger. I made coffee for the weary men who came down occasionally with horses they had led out, or with old people from the isolated cabins. They were covered with soot from their battle with the flames.

At six o'clock the fire was on our left side and rushing toward Mount Wilson. Evacuees from the cabins began to arrive and had to be given blankets and hot coffee. The streets were blocked with fire engines readying to fight the fire if it touched the houses. Policemen and firemen and guards turned away the sightseers. Some were relatives concerned over the fate of the foresters, or the pack station family. The policemen lighted flares, which gave the scene a theatrical, tragic air. The red lights on the police cars twinkled alarmingly. More fire engines arrived. Ashes fell, and the roar of the fire was now like thunder.

We were told to ready ourselves for evacuation. I packed the diaries. The saddest spectacle, beside that of the men fighting the fire as they would a war, were the animals, rabbits, coyotes, mountain lions, deer, driven by the fire to the edge of the mountain, taking a look at the crowd of people and panicking, choosing rather to rush back into the fire.

The fire now was like a ring around Sierra Madre,[3] every mountain was burning. People living at the foot of the mountain were packing their cars. I rushed next door to the Campion children, who had been left with a baby-sitter, and got them into the car. It was impossible to save all the horses. We parked the car on the field below us. I called up the Campions, who were out for the evening, and reassured them. The baby-sitter dressed the children warmly. I made more coffee. I answered frantic telephone calls.

All night the fire engines sprayed water over the houses. But the fire grew immense, angry, and rushing at a speed I could not believe. It would rush along and suddenly leap over a road, a trail, like a monster, devouring all in its path. The firefighters cut breaks in the heavy brush, but when the wind was strong enough, the fire leaped

---

1. Monrovia (mən rō′ vē ə) **Peak:** Mountain in southwest California.
2. Santa (san′ tə) **Ana** (an′ ə) **winds:** Hot desert winds from the east or northeast in southern California.

---

3. Sierra (sē er′ ə) **Madre** (mä′ drā): Mountain range.

across them. At dawn one arm of the fire reached the back of our houses but was finally contained.

But high above and all around, the fire was burning, more vivid than the sun, throwing spirals of smoke in the air like the smoke from a volcano. Thirty-three cabins burned, and twelve thousand acres of forest still burning endangered countless homes below the fire. The fire was burning to the back of us now, and a rain of ashes began to fall and continued for days. The smell of the burn in the air, acid and pungent and tenacious. The dragon tongues of flames devouring, the flames leaping, the roar of destruction and dissolution, the eyes of the panicked animals, caught between fire and human beings, between two forms of death. They chose the fire. It was as if the fire had come from the bowels of the earth, like that of a fiery volcano, it was so powerful, so swift, and so ravaging. I saw trees become skeletons in one minute, I saw trees fall, I saw bushes turned to ashes in a second, I saw weary, ash-covered men, looking like men returned from war, some with burns, others overcome by smoke.

The men were rushing from one spot to another watching for recrudescence.[4] Some started backfiring up the mountain so that the ascending flames could counteract the descending ones.

As the flames reached the cities below, hundreds of roofs burst into flame at once. There was no water pressure because all the fire hydrants were turned on at the same time, and the fire departments were helpless to save more than a few of the burning homes.

The blaring loudspeakers of passing police cars warned us to prepare to evacuate in case the wind changed and drove the fire in our direction. What did I wish to save? I thought only of the diaries. I appeared on the porch carrying a huge stack of diary volumes, preparing to pack them in the car. A reporter for the Pasadena *Star News* was taking pictures of the evacuation. He came up, very annoyed with me. ''Hey, lady, next time could you bring out something more important than all those old papers? Carry some clothes on the next trip. We gotta have human interest in these pictures!''

A week later, the danger was over.

Gray ashy days.

In Sierra Madre, following the fire, the January rains brought floods. People are sandbagging their homes. At four A.M. the streets are covered with mud. The bare, burnt, naked mountains cannot hold the rains and slide down bringing rocks and mud. One of the rangers must now take photographs and movies of the disaster. He asks if I will help by holding an umbrella over the cameras. I put on my raincoat and he lends me hip boots which look to me like seven-league boots.

We drive a little way up the road. At the third curve it is impassable. A river is rushing across the road. The ranger takes pictures while I hold the umbrella over the camera. It is terrifying to see the muddied waters and rocks, the mountain disintegrating. When we are ready to return, the road before us is covered by large rocks but the ranger pushes on as if the truck were a jeep and forces it through. The edge of the road is being carried away.

I am laughing and scared too. The ranger is at ease in nature, and without fear. It is a wild moment of danger. It is easy to love nature in its peaceful and consoling moments, but one must love it in its furies too, in its despairs and wildness, especially when the damage is caused by us.

---

4. recrudescence (rē′ krōō des′ əns) *n.*: A fresh outbreak of something that has been inactive.

THINKING ABOUT THE SELECTION
Recalling

1. Describe the setting—the time and place—of the forest fire.
2. How does the writer respond to the fire?
3. What are the effects of the forest fire?

Interpreting

4. Why is a fire so particularly dangerous in this setting?
5. What does the writer's choice of saving only her diaries tell you about her?

Applying

6. Imagine a natural disaster in your community. Develop a list of rules or guidelines for helping people survive the disaster.

ANALYZING LITERATURE
Understanding Descriptive Essays

Authors write descriptive essays to present their personal view of or experience with a subject. **Descriptive essays** usually contain two important elements: many specific details and figurative language—language that makes comparison between unlike things and that is not intended to be interpreted strictly or literally. For example, when Anaïs Nin describes the *angry fire,* she does not mean that the fire is really angry. She is saying that the fire has a wild, out-of-control quality that makes it like an angry person. Sometimes Nin uses the words *like* or *as, is* or *was.* At other times she gives the fire the qualities and movements of a living creature.

1. Find two examples of figurative language that contain the words *like* or *as* in the essay.
2. Find two examples of figurative language that describe something nonliving with the qualities of a living creature.
3. Find one descriptive detail you found especially effective, or strong. Explain your reasons for choosing this detail.

CRITICAL THINKING AND READING
Separating Fact and Opinion

Facts are statements about things that have either happened or are happening. This information can always be proved true or false using reliable sources. For example, that the forest fire occurred near Sierra Madre is a fact; it can be proved by checking newspaper accounts or local records. **Opinions,** on the other hand, cannot be proved true or false because they are based on the writer's personal beliefs or attitudes. For example, the statement that the forest is a beautiful place is an opinion. This information cannot be proved true or false.

Identify which of the following are facts and which are the writer's opinions. Be prepared to support your answers.

1. "I rushed next door to the Campion children . . . and got them into the car."
2. "The . . . lighted flares . . . gave the scene a theatrical, tragic air."
3. "It is easy to love nature in its peaceful and consoling moments, but one must love it in its furies too."

THINKING AND WRITING
Writing a Descriptive Essay

Write a descriptive essay that you could read as a radio news report. Write about the forest fire at Sierra Madre from a human-interest angle —that is, based on the feelings and reactions of the people the fire affected. Refer to the list of interview questions that you wrote. Write answers that people might give to them. Develop these answers into your account. When you finish your first draft, check to see that you included descriptive details and figurative language. Finally, proofread your essay and deliver it to your classmates.

GUIDE FOR READING

The Indian All Around Us

Bernard DeVoto (1897–1955) was born in Ogden, Utah, and became a respected critic, novelist, editor, and magazine columnist during his varied literary career. Above all, however, Bernard DeVoto was a historian. His book *Across the Wide Missouri,* one of a series of books about America's westward movement, received the Pulitzer Prize for history in 1948. In his essay "The Indian All Around Us," Bernard DeVoto explains the history of many Native American words that are familiar to people of the United States.

Expository Essay

An **expository essay** is a short nonfiction piece that explains or gives information about a topic. The word *expository,* in fact, simply means to give information about something or to explain what is difficult to understand. In expository essays, writers not only explain information but may also express a particular point of view or opinion on their topic.

Look For

As you read "The Indian All Around Us," look for the information the writer gives to help you understand his topic. What words come from the Native Americans? What do you learn about these words?

Writing

Work with a group of students. Select a culture, such as Spanish or German, from which many words have come into English. You may want to choose your own cultural heritage. In the center of a piece of paper, write the culture you have chosen and circle it. Think of a number of words that this culture has added to English. Include place names, foods, objects, games, and so forth. Write these words around the circled word, circling each one and drawing a line from it to the center of the word cluster.

Vocabulary

Knowing the following words will help you as you read "The Indian All Around Us."

versatile (vur′ sə t'l) *adj.*: Having many uses (p. 457)

tangible (tan′ jəb'l) *adj.*: Capable of being perceived or of being precisely identified (p. 457)

alkaloid (al′ kə loid′) *adj.*: Re-

ferring to certain bitter substances found chiefly in plants (p. 458)

gutturals (gut′ ər əlz) *n.*: Sounds produced in the throat (p. 460)

The Indian All Around Us

Bernard DeVoto

The Europeans who developed into the Americans took over from the Indians many things besides their continent. Look at a few: tobacco, corn, potatoes, beans (kidney, string and lima and therefore succotash), tomatoes, sweet potatoes, squash, popcorn and peanuts, chocolate, pineapples, hominy, Jerusalem artichokes, maple sugar. Moccasins, snowshoes, toboggans, hammocks, ipecac,[1] quinine, the crew haircut, goggles to prevent snow blindness—these are all Indian in origin. So is the versatile boat that helped the white man occupy the continent, the birch-bark canoe, and the custom canoeists have of painting designs on its bow.

A list of familiar but less important plants, foods and implements would run to several hundred items. Another long list would be needed to enumerate less tangible Indian contributions to our culture, such as arts, crafts, designs, ideas, beliefs, superstitions and even profanity. But there is something far more familiar, something that is always at hand and is used daily by every American and Canadian without awareness that it is Indian: a large vocabulary.

Glance back over the first paragraph. "Potato" is an Indian word, so is "tobacco," and if "corn" is not, the word "maize" is

PAINTED BUFFALO HIDE SHIELD
Jémez, New Mexico
Museum of the American Indian

1. **ipecac** (ip′ ə kȧk′) *n.*: A medicine made from certain dried roots.

and we used it for a long time, as the English do still. Some Indians chewed tobacco, some used snuff, nearly all smoked pipes or cigars or cigarettes, and the white man gladly adopted all forms of the habit. But he spoke of "drinking" tobacco, instead of smoking it, for a long time. Squash, hominy, ipecac, quinine, hammock, chocolate, canoe are all common nouns that have come into the English—or rather the American—language from Indian languages. Sometimes the word has changed on the way, perhaps only a little as with "potato," which was something like "batata" in the original, or sometimes a great deal, as with "cocoa,"

PAINTED BOWL: DEER FIGURE
Mimbres, New Mexico
Museum of the American Indian

which began as, approximately, "caca-huatl."

Sometimes, too, we have changed the meaning. "Succotash" is a rendering of a Narraganset word that meant an ear of corn. The dish that the Indians ate was exactly what we call succotash today, though an Indian woman was likely to vary it as much as we do stew, by tossing in any leftovers she happened to have on hand. Similarly with "quinine." This is a modern word, made up by the scientists who first isolated the alkaloid substance from cinchona bark[2], but they derived it from the botanical name of the genus, which in turn was derived from the Indian name for it, "quinquina." The Indians, of course, used a decoction[3] made from the bark.

Put on your moccasins and take a walk in the country. If it is a cold day and you

wear a mackinaw, your jacket will be as Indian as your footwear, though "mackinaw" originally meant a heavy blanket of fine quality and, usually, bright colors. On your walk you may smell a skunk, see a raccoon or possum, hear the call of a moose. Depending on what part of the country you are in, you may see a chipmunk, muskrat, woodchuck or coyote. The names of all these animals are Indian words. (A moose is "he who eats off," that is, who browses on leaves. A raccoon is "he who scratches with his hands.") You may see hickory trees or catalpas,[4] pecans or mesquite,[5] and these too are Indian words. At the right season and place you may eat persimmons or paw-paws or scuppernongs.[6] All the breads and most of the puddings we make from corn-meal originated with the Indians but we haven't kept many of the original names, except "pone."

On a Cape Cod beach you may see clam-mers digging quahogs,[7] or as a Cape Codder would say, "coehoggin'." The Pilgrims learned the name and the method of getting at them from the Indians: they even learned the technique of steaming them with sea-weed that we practice at clambakes. The muskellunge[8] and the terrapin[9] were named for us by Indians. Your children may build a wigwam to play in—it was a brush hut or a lodge covered with bark—or they may ask you to buy them a tepee, which was original-

---

2. cinchona (sin kō′ nə) **bark** *n.*: bark from certain tropical South American trees.
3. decoction (di käk′ sћən) *n.*: An extract or flavor produced by boiling.

4. catalpas (kə tal′ pəs) *n.*: American and Asiatic trees with large, heart-shaped leaves, trumpet-shaped flowers, and beanlike pods.
5. mesquite (mes kēt′) *n.*: Thorny trees or shrubs common in the southwest U.S. and in Mexico.
6. pawpaws, scuppernongs *n.*: Kinds of fruit.
7. quahogs (kwô′ hôgz) *n.*: Edible clams of the east coast of North America.
8. muskellunge (mus′ kə lunj) *n.*: A very large pike fish of the Great Lakes and upper Mississippi drainages.
9. terrapin (ter′ ə pin) *n.*: Several kinds of North American turtles.

ly made of buffalo hide but can be canvas now. They may chase one another with tomahawks. And we all go to barbecues.

The people earliest in contact with the Indians found all these words useful, but some Indian sounds they found hard to pronounce, such as the *tl* at the end of many words in Mexico and the Southwest. That is why "coyotl" became "coyote" and "tomatl" our tomato. Or accidental resemblances to English words might deceive them, as with "muskrat." The animal does look like a rat and has musk glands, but the Indian word was "musquash," which means "it is red."

Some words were simply too long. "Succotash" began as "musickwautash," "hominy" as "rockahominy," and "mackinaw" as "michilimackinac." (The last, of course, was the name given to the strait, the fort, the island, and ended as the name of a blanket and a jacket because the fort was a trading post.) At that, these are comparatively short; remember the lake in Massachusetts whose name is Chargoggagoggmanchaugagoggchaubunagungamaugg.[10]

Twenty-six of our states have Indian names, as have scores of cities, towns, lakes, rivers and mountains. In Maine are Kennebec, Penobscot, Androscoggin, Piscataqua, Wiscasset and many others, from Arowsic to Sytopilock by way of Mattawamkeag. California, noted for its Spanish names, still is well supplied with such native ones as Yosemite, Mojave, Sequoia, Truckee, Tahoe, Siskiyou. Washington has Yakima, Walla Walla, Spokane, Snoqualmie, Wenatchee; and Florida has Okeechobee, Seminole, Manitee, Ocala and as many

more as would fill a page. So with all the other states.

Consider such rivers as the Arkansas, Ohio, Mohawk, Wisconsin, Rappahannock, Minnesota, Merrimack, Mississippi, Missouri and Suwannee. Or such lakes as Ontario, Cayuga, Winnipesaukee, Memphremagog, Winnebago. Or such mountain ranges and peaks as Allegheny, Wichita, Wasatch, Shasta, Katahdin. Or cities: Milwaukee, Chattanooga, Sandusky.

The meaning of such names is not always clear. Tourist bureaus like to make up translations like bower-of-the-laughing-princess or land-of-the-sky-blue-water, but Indians were as practical-minded as anyone

JAR WITH ANIMAL HEAD HANDLE
Socorro County, New Mexico
Museum of the American Indian

---

10. Char . . . maugg: The translation is "You fish your side of the lake, we'll fish our side, and nobody fishes in the middle."

else and usually used a word that would identify the place. Our unpoetic pioneers christened dozens of streams Mud Creek or Muddy River—and that is about what Missouri means. The Sauk or Kickapoo word that gave Chicago its name had something to do with a strong smell. There may be some truth in the contention of rival cities that it meant "place of the skunks," but more likely it meant "place where wild onions grow." Kentucky does not mean "dark and bloody ground" as our sentimental legend says, but merely "place of meadows," which shows that the blue grass impressed Indians, too. Niagara means "point of land that is cut in two." Potomac means "something brought." Since the thing brought was probably tribute, perhaps in wampum,[11] we would not be far off if we were to render it "place where we pay taxes."

Quite apart from their meaning, such words as Kentucky, Niagara and Potomac are beautiful just as sounds. Though we usually take it for granted, the beauty of our Indian place names impresses foreign visitors. But since some Indian languages abounded with harsh sounds or gutturals, this beauty is unevenly distributed. In New England such names as Ogunquit, Megantic and Naugatuck are commoner than such more pleasing ones as Housatonic, Narragansett and Merrimack. The Pacific Northwest is overbalanced with harsh sounds like Nootka, Klamath, Klickitat and Clackamas, though it has its share of more agreeable ones—Tillamook, for instance, and Umatilla, Willamette, Multnomah. (Be sure to pronounce Willamette right: accent the second syllable.)

Open vowels were abundant in the languages spoken in the southeastern states,

so that portion of the map is thickly sown with delightful names. Alabama, Pensacola, Tuscaloosa, Savannah, Okefenokee, Chattahoochee, Sarasota, Ocala, Roanoke—they are charming words, pleasant to speak, pleasanter to hear. One could sing a child to sleep with a poem composed of just such names. In New York, if Skaneateles twists the tongue, Seneca glides smoothly from it and so do Tonawanda, Tuscarora, Oneonta, Saratoga, Genessee, Lackawanna, even Chautauqua and Canajoharie.

What is the most beautiful Indian place name? A surprising number of English writers have argued that question in travel books. No one's choice can be binding on anyone else. But there is a way of making a kind of answer: you can count the recorded votes. In what is written about the subject certain names appear repeatedly. Niagara and Tuscarora and Otsego are on nearly all the lists. So are Savannah and Potomac, Catawba, Wichita and Shenandoah.

But the five that are most often mentioned are all in Pennsylvania. That state has its Allegheny and Lackawanna, and many other musical names like Aliquippa, Towanda, Punxsutawney. But five others run away from them all. Wyoming (which moved a long way west and named a state)[12] and Conestoga and Monongahela seem to be less universally delightful than the two finalists, Juniata and Susquehanna. For 150 years, most of those who have written on the subject have ended with these two, and in the outcome Juniata usually takes second place. According to the write-in vote, then, the most beautiful place name in the United States is Susquehanna. It may be ungracious to remember that it first came into the language as "Saquesahannock."

---

11. wampum (wäm′ pəm) *n.*: Small beads made of shells and used by North American Indians as money and as ornaments.

12. which . . . state: The name Wyoming was originally given to a valley in Pennsylvania.

THINKING ABOUT THE SELECTION

Recalling

1. What is an important native American contribution to life in the United States that we use every day? Explain the importance of this contribution.
2. Name two reasons why some Indian words were changed before becoming part of English.

Interpreting

3. How would you interpret the title, "The Indian All Around Us"?
4. Why does the writer tell you to "put on your moccasins and take a walk in the country"?

Applying

5. What foods mentioned in the essay are a regular part of your diet?
6. Based on what you learned in this essay, what criteria could you apply when you are naming something?

ANALYZING LITERATURE

Understanding an Expository Essay

Expository essays are usually written to inform or to explain. But many expository essays do both. For example, "The Indian All Around Us" not only informs us that the Indian word *coyotl* was changed to the American word *coyote,* but it also explains the reason why: because people found the *tl* sound hard to pronounce.

Give three examples of this essay informing the reader.

CRITICAL THINKING AND READING

Identifying Main Ideas

In an expository essay, each paragraph usually has a main idea. Looking again at the fourth paragraph of "The Indian All Around Us," for example, the main idea of it is expressed in the first sentence: "Sometimes, too, we have changed the meaning." **Main ideas** are general statements that need supporting details, such as specific examples or reasons, to explain them. For example, DeVoto supports the main idea in the fourth paragraph with two specific examples —succotash and quinine.

Read the eleventh paragraph that begins "The meaning of such names."

1. What is the main idea of the paragraph?
2. List the supporting details that appear in the paragraph.

UNDERSTANDING LANGUAGE

Investigating Word Origins

If you look at a map of the United States, you will find many place names that have their origins in other languages as well as in the names of famous people. For example, the *Rio Grande* (river) comes from the Spanish words meaning "great river." The city of Lincoln, Nebraska, was named for President Abraham Lincoln.

1. Using a map of your own state, find five place names and identify their origins—the language or the famous person from which the name was taken.
2. In a dictionary, look up the meanings of three of the names you found.

THINKING AND WRITING

Writing an Expository Essay

Write an expository essay about the contributions a particular culture has made to life in the United States. Before you write, be sure that you have narrowed your topic to fit what you can say in a short essay. For example, you may want to narrow your topic to foods, a sport, or place names. Revise your essay, making sure you have supported your main ideas. Then proofread your essay and share it with your classmates.

GUIDE FOR READING

The Trouble with Television

Robert MacNeil (1931–   ) was born in Montreal, Canada. He is a radio and television journalist. He has worked for NBC radio and for the British Broadcasting Corporation. In the mid-1970's, MacNeil came to public television station WNET to host his own news analysis program, which has grown into the highly regarded *MacNeil/Lehrer Newshour.* This differs from other news programs by offering more in-depth reports on important issues. In the following essay, MacNeil criticizes American television programming.

Persuasive Essay

A **persuasive essay** is a short nonfiction composition in which a writer presents his or her views in order to convince you to accept the author's opinion or to act a certain way. Since you may not share the writer's opinion, the writer usually offers arguments, or reasons, to support the position. Because you may not care enough to take any action, the writer tries to stir your concern and emotions so that you will act.

Look For

As you read "The Trouble with Television," look for ways MacNeil tries to persuade you about the value of television. Are the arguments convincing?

Writing

Write down the amount of time you spend watching different types of programs, such as news, science specials, situation comedies, quiz shows, and so on. Which programs do you get the most from? List possible alternatives to watching television.

Vocabulary

Knowing the following words will help you as you read "The Trouble with Television."

gratification (grat′ ə fi kā′ shən) *n.:* The act of pleasing or satisfying (p. 463)

diverts (də vʉrts′) *v.:* Distracts (p. 463)

kaleidoscopic (kə lī′ də skäp′ ik) *adj.:* Constantly changing (p. 463)

usurps (yo͞o sʉrps′) *v.:* Takes over (p. 463)

medium (mē′ dē əm) *n.:* Means of communication; television (p. 464)

august (ô gust′) *adj.:* Honored (p. 464)

pervading (pər vād′ iŋ) *v.:* Spreading throughout (p. 465)

trivial (triv′ ē əl) *adj.:* Of little importance (p. 465)

The Trouble with Television

Robert MacNeil

It is difficult to escape the influence of television. If you fit the statistical averages, by the age of 20 you will have been exposed to at least 20,000 hours of television. You can add 10,000 hours for each decade you have lived after the age of 20. The only things Americans do more than watch television are work and sleep.

Calculate for a moment what could be done with even a part of those hours. Five thousand hours, I am told, are what a typical college undergraduate spends working on a bachelor's degree. In 10,000 hours you could have learned enough to become an astronomer or engineer. You could have learned several languages fluently. If it appealed to you, you could be reading Homer[1] in the original Greek or Dostoevski[2] in Russian. If it didn't, you could have walked around the world and written a book about it.

The trouble with television is that it discourages concentration. Almost anything interesting and rewarding in life requires some constructive, consistently applied effort. The dullest, the least gifted of us can achieve things that seem miraculous to those who never concentrate on anything. But television encourages us to apply no effort. It sells us instant gratification. It diverts us only to divert, to make the time pass without pain.

Television's variety becomes a narcotic,[3] not a stimulus.[4] Its serial, kaleidoscopic exposures force us to follow its lead. The viewer is on a perpetual guided tour: thirty minutes at the museum, thirty at the cathedral, then back on the bus to the next attraction —except on television, typically, the spans allotted are on the order of minutes or seconds, and the chosen delights are more often car crashes and people killing one another. In short, a lot of television usurps one of the most precious of all human gifts, the ability to focus your attention yourself, rather than just passively surrender it.

Capturing your attention—and holding it—is the prime motive of most television programming and enhances its role as a profitable advertising vehicle. Programmers live in constant fear of losing anyone's attention—anyone's. The surest way to

---

1. Homer (hō′ mər): Greek epic poet of the eighth century B.C.
2. Dostoevski (dôs′ tô yef′ skē): Fyodor (fyô′ dôr) Mikhailovich (mi khī′ lô vich) Dostoevski (1821–1881), Russian novelist.

3. narcotic (när kät′ ik) n.: Something that has a soothing effect.
4. stimulus (stim′ yə ləs) n.: Something that rouses to action.

AFTERNOON TELEVISION
Maxwell Hendler
The Metropolitan Museum of Art

avoid doing so is to keep everything brief, not to strain the attention of anyone but instead to provide constant stimulation through variety, novelty, action and movement. Quite simply, television operates on the appeal to the short attention span.

It is simply the easiest way out. But it has come to be regarded as a given, as inherent[5] in the medium itself: as an imperative, as though General Sarnoff, or one of the other august pioneers of video, had be-

---

5. inherent (in hir′ ənt) *adj.*: Natural.

queathed to us tablets of stone commanding that nothing in television shall ever require more than a few moments' concentration.

In its place that is fine. Who can quarrel with a medium that so brilliantly packages escapist entertainment as a mass-marketing tool? But I see its values now pervading this nation and its life. It has become fashionable to think that, like fast food, fast ideas are the way to get to a fast-moving, impatient public.

In the case of news, this practice, in my view, results in inefficient communication. I question how much of television's nightly news effort is really absorbable and understandable. Much of it is what has been aptly described as "machine gunning with scraps." I think its technique fights coherence.[6] I think it tends to make things ultimately boring and dismissable (unless they are accompanied by horrifying pictures) because almost anything is boring and dismissable if you know almost nothing about it.

I believe that TV's appeal to the short attention span is not only inefficient communication but decivilizing as well. Consider the casual assumptions that television tends to cultivate: that complexity must be avoided, that visual stimulation is a substitute for thought, that verbal precision is an anachronism.[7] It may be old-fashioned, but I was taught that thought is words, arranged in grammatically precise ways.

There is a crisis of literacy in this country. One study estimates that some 30 million adult Americans are "functionally illiterate" and cannot read or write well enough to answer a want ad or understand the instructions on a medicine bottle.

6. **coherence** (kō hir′ əns) n.: The quality of being connected in an intelligible way.
7. **anachronism** (ə nak′ rə niz'm) n.: Anything that seems to be out of its proper place in history.

Literacy may not be an inalienable human right, but it is one that the highly literate Founding Fathers might not have found unreasonable or even unattainable. We are not only not attaining it as a nation, statistically speaking, but we are falling further and further short of attaining it. And, while I would not be so simplistic as to suggest that television is the cause, I believe it contributes and is an influence.

Everything about this nation—the structure of the society, its forms of family organization, its economy, its place in the world—has become more complex, not less. Yet its dominating communications instrument, its principal form of national linkage, is one that sells neat resolutions to human problems that usually have no neat resolutions. It is all symbolized in my mind by the hugely successful art form that television has made central to the culture, the thirty-second commercial: the tiny drama of the earnest housewife who finds happiness in choosing the right toothpaste.

When before in human history has so much humanity collectively surrendered so much of its leisure to one toy, one mass diversion? When before has virtually an entire nation surrendered itself wholesale to a medium for selling?

Some years ago Yale University law professor Charles L. Black, Jr. wrote: ". . . forced feeding on trivial fare is not itself a trivial matter." I think this society is being force fed with trivial fare, and I fear that the effects on our habits of mind, our language, our tolerance for effort, and our appetite for complexity are only dimly perceived. If I am wrong, we will have done no harm to look at the issue skeptically and critically, to consider how we should be resisting it. I hope you will join with me in doing so.

THINKING ABOUT THE SELECTION
Recalling

1. When the average viewer reaches the age of twenty, how many hours of television has he or she watched?
2. According to MacNeil, what is the major trouble with television?
3. MacNeil states that television's appeal is "decivilizing." What three assumptions does he give that contribute to this decivilization?

Interpreting

4. What action is MacNeil trying to persuade you to take?
5. What do you think MacNeil would want people to do instead of watching television?
6. If MacNeil were the president of a commercial television network, what changes in the programming do you think he would make?

Applying

7. How do you think television could be improved? In what ways is it a valuable tool for society?

ANALYZING LITERATURE
Understanding the Persuasive Essay

A **persuasive essay** is nonfiction in which writers strive to make readers accept a certain way of thinking about an issue. Whether or not they are successful depends on how strong their reasons are and what facts they use.

1. Write down three points MacNeil makes that caused you to think again about watching television. Explain why each was effective.
2. Write down any points in the essay that are not persuasive. Explain why you think each is not effective.
3. Explain why MacNeil is or is not successful in persuading you to think carefully about and possibly change your television viewing habits.

CRITICAL THINKING AND READING
Recognizing Connotative Language

Persuasive writers often use words that provoke an emotional response in their readers. These words have certain **connotations,** or associated ideas and images, beyond their literal meanings. If the writer is supporting something, the words chosen will have positive connotations. If the writer opposes something, the words will be negative. For example, MacNeil states that television is a "narcotic," and that viewers "passively surrender" to it. Both of these words create negative images.

Explain what connotations the italicized words in the following sentences have for you.
1. "In 10,000 hours you could have learned enough to become an *astronomer* or *engineer.*"
2. "Quite simply, television operates on the appeal to the short attention span. It is simply the *easiest way out.*"

UNDERSTANDING LANGUAGE
Using Combining Forms

The combining form *tele* comes from Greek and means "far off." This form is often combined with other word parts to form new words. The word *television* consists of *tele* combined with *vision.* A television is the receiving set that receives pictures or visions from far off. Explain the meaning of each of the following words:
(a) teletype   (c) telescope
(b) telephone   (d) telex

THINKING AND WRITING
Writing a Persuasive Essay

Make a list of suggestions about programming that would make television viewing a more worthwhile experience. Write the suggestions in a letter to a television network or producer. When you have finished, check to be sure you have used the correct form for a business letter. Proofread it and prepare a final draft. Mail your letter if you wish.

Essays in
the Content Areas

PAUL HELLEU SKETCHING WITH HIS WIFE, 1889
John Singer Sargent
The Brooklyn Museum, Museum Collection Fund

GUIDE FOR READING

Shooting Stars

Hal Borland (1900–1978), born in Sterling, Nebraska, was a naturalist, a person who studies animals and plants. He worked as a reporter for the *Denver Post* and the *Brooklyn Times*. He was also a writer of documentary film scripts, radio scripts, and other nonfiction. Borland loved the outdoors. The National Audubon Society honored him by creating the Hal Borland Trail in Connecticut. Borland's essay "Shooting Stars" blends his fascination with nature and his ability to report facts in a clear, captivating manner.

Observation

One of the skills required of a naturalist is observation. **Observation** is the act of looking at or noticing an object or event carefully and objectively. When you observe, you try to concentrate only on what you see, not on what you feel, think, or conclude about it. Observing allows you to report or describe clearly and factually what happens.

Look For

As you read "Shooting Stars," notice the factual way in which the writer tends to report what he and others have observed. What do you learn about meteors as a result of these observations?

Writing

Choose an incident from nature to describe. First describe it objectively, or factually, reporting only what you see. Then describe it personally, including your own thoughts.

Vocabulary

horizon (hə rī′ zən) *n*.: The line that forms the apparent boundary between the earth and the sky (p. 469)
friction (frik′ sнən) *n*.: The rub-

bing of the surface of one body against another (p. 469)
droves (drōvz) *n*.: Large numbers; crowds (p. 470)

Shooting Stars

Hal Borland

Most clear, dark nights you can see a shooting star, as we call it, if you keep looking. Those shooting stars are meteors. They are points of light that suddenly appear in the sky, like distant stars, race across the darkness, usually toward the horizon, and disappear.

For a long time nobody knew what a meteor was. But finally those who study stars and the sky decided that a meteor is a piece of a comet that exploded long ago. Those pieces are still wandering about the universe in huge, looping paths that follow the original comet's orbit. There are uncounted pieces of such comets out there in the depths of space. Periodically clusters of them come close to the earth's orbit, or path around the sun. Most meteors are small, probably only a few inches in diameter, but when they enter the earth's atmosphere the friction makes them white-hot. Then they look big as stars streaking across the darkness.

There are half a dozen meteor showers

each year. Each is named after the constellation from which it appears to come. The biggest of all, the Perseids, named for the constellation of Perseus, occurs on the 10th, 11th, and 12th of August. The next largest, the Leonids, named for the constellation of Leo, comes on the nights of November 14, 15, and 16. Another, the Andromedids, which is not quite so big, comes from November 17 through 23. There are other meteor showers in December, January, April, May, and July, but none of them is as big as those in August and November.

Most people watching meteors will be satisfied if they see ten or twenty in an hour of watching. On special occasions, however, the meteors seem to come in droves. The most remarkable meteor shower I ever heard of was seen by a distinguished astronomer, Professor Denison Olmstead, of New Haven, Connecticut, on the night of November 12, 1833. He was watching the Leonids, which seem to come from directly overhead and race downward toward the horizon in all directions. He reported that meteors fell "like flakes of snow." He estimated that he saw 240,000 meteors in nine hours that night. He said they ranged in size from mere streaks of light to "globes of the moon's diameter." If he had not been a notable astronomer whose accuracy was beyond question, such statements would seem ridiculous. But there is no reason to doubt what he reported. He had seen one of the most unusual meteor showers ever reported. What he watched should be called a meteor storm rather than a shower.

I once watched the August Perseids with an astronomer on a hilltop in open country, and in two hours we counted almost a thousand meteors. That was the most I ever saw at one time. And we were bitten by one mosquito for every meteor we saw. After that I tried watching for meteors in November,

when there were no mosquitoes. But the most I ever saw in November was about one hundred meteors in two hours of watching.

The amazing thing about these meteor showers is that they come year after year. Professor Olmstead saw all those Leonids in November of 1833, but if you watch for meteors this year you almost certainly will see them on the same nights he saw them. They will come next year, the year after that, and for countless years more. Your grandfather saw them, and your grandchildren will see them if they look for them.

Occasionally a meteor reaches the earth. Then it is called a meteorite and it is valued as a sample of the vast mystery of the deep space in the sky. Scientists examine it, try to guess what it was to begin with, where it came from, what it is like out there. Nobody ever learned very much from the meteorites except that they often contain a great deal of nickel and iron.

Only a few large meteorites have struck the earth. The largest we know about fell in Arizona many centuries ago and made what is now called Meteor Crater, a hole about a mile across and 600 feet deep. Some Indian legends of the Southwest tell of a big fire that fell from the sky and ate a huge hole in the earth, so this big meteorite may have fallen since man first arrived in America, perhaps twenty-five thousand years ago.

Other big meteorites have fallen, in ancient times, in Texas, in Argentina, in northern Siberia, in South-West Africa, and in Greenland. A meteorite weighing more than thirty-six tons was found in Greenland and now can be seen in the Hayden Planetarium in New York City. Millions of meteors have flashed across the night sky, but only a few large meteorites have ever reached the earth. Never in all the centuries of written history has there been a report of anyone being struck by a meteorite.

THINKING ABOUT THE SELECTION

Recalling

1. What are meteors?
2. When do the biggest meteor showers occur?
3. Describe the most unusual meteor shower ever reported.
4. Why are meteorites valued so much?
5. What was the effect of the largest meteorite that fell to earth?

Interpreting

6. Why do you think scientists collect meteorites? What is it about meteors that stirs the imagination?

Applying

7. What is the difference between a scientific explanation and an explanation offered by a legend or myth? What can scientists learn from legends or myths?

READING IN THE CONTENT AREAS

Understanding Observation

Observation, or the act of looking at or noticing an object or event objectively, or factually, is a skill that scientists use to gain information. When observing, they try to concentrate only on the facts, not on their opinions.

You too can use observation to learn. By screening out your personal reactions, you can think only about the facts.

Take notes on one of the following situations, reporting the facts. Summarize what you observe.

a. the view outside your classroom window
b. students changing class

CRITICAL THINKING AND READING

Recognizing Observation and Inference

An **observation** is an act of noticing and recording facts and events. An **inference** is a reasonable conclusion you can draw from given facts or clues. When you see storm clouds overhead and note that they are gray and gathering quickly, you are observing the facts. When you remark that it looks as though it will storm soon, you are inferring based on what you see and know about storm clouds.

State whether the following sentences from "Shooting Stars" are observations or inferences.

1. "I once watched the August Perseids with an astronomer on a hilltop in open country, and in two hours we counted almost a thousand meteors."
2. "Some Indian legends of the Southwest tell of a big fire that fell from the sky and ate a huge hole in the earth, so this big meteorite may have fallen since man first arrived in America, perhaps twenty-five thousand years ago."

UNDERSTANDING LANGUAGE

Appreciating Words from Myths

Some scientific phenomena are named after myths. The Perseids meteor shower and the constellation of Perseus are named for Perseus, the son of Zeus who slew Medusa.

Find the origins, based on myths, of the following words.

1. Orion   2. Mercury   3. Mars   4. Venus

THINKING AND WRITING

Observing

Choose a common object such as a safety pin or a pencil sharpener. Observe it carefully, making notes. Then write a description of it, but do not name it. Revise to make sure you have described the object so precisely that someone reading it could guess what it is. Finally, read your description to your classmates and see if they can identify the object.

GUIDE FOR READING

The Sounds of Richard Rodgers

Ellen Goodman (1941–) is a national columnist based at the *Boston Globe*. Her column is syndicated by the *Washington Post* Writers Groups and appears in more than 170 newspapers. Born in Newton, Massachusetts, Goodman graduated from Radcliffe College and is a former Nieman Fellow at Harvard University. In 1980 she received the Pulitzer Prize for distinguished commentary. "The Sounds of Richard Rodgers" shows her common-sense, realistic style of writing.

Setting a Purpose for Reading

A **purpose** is a reason for doing something. If you set a purpose before you read, you will read more efficiently. One way of setting a purpose is to get a general idea of what the selection is about, first by looking at the title. Then ask yourself basic questions about the topic of the essay. You might use the journalistic formula *who? what? when? where? why?* and *how?* For example: Who was Richard Rodgers? For what is he best known? When and where did he live? How did he achieve success? Why do we remember him?

Look For

As you read, look for answers to these questions: Who? What? When? Where? Why? and How?

Writing

Think of a famous composer of music, including rock and popular music. Freewrite about that composer and his or her music. Include your thoughts and any anecdotes you know about the composer.

Vocabulary

Knowing the following words will help you as you read "The Sounds of Richard Rodgers."

scores (skôrz) *n.*: The music for a stage production or film, apart from the lyrics and dialogue (p. 473)

esophagus (i saf′ ə gəs) *n.*: The tube through which food passes to the stomach (p. 473)

regimen (rej′ ə mən) *n.*: A regulated system of diet and exercise (p. 474)

legacy (leg′ ə sē) *n.*: Anything handed down, as from an ancestor (p. 474)

The Sounds of Richard Rodgers[1]

Ellen Goodman

He came into our house with the first Victrola[2] . . . and stayed. By the time I was ten I knew every song on our boxed and scratched "78" records: songs from *Oklahoma!* and *Carousel* and *South Pacific.* They were, very simply, the earliest tunes in a house that was more alive with the sound of politics than the sound of music.

As I grew older, I knew he was no Beethoven[3] or Verdi,[4] or John Lennon[5] for that matter. By then his songs had been orchestrally overkilled into the sort of Muzak that kept you company in elevators or "on hold" at the insurance company line.

But the fact is that from the time I was a child, to the time I sat with my own child watching the Trapp family escape again over the mountains,[6] there has always been a Richard Rodgers song in the background.

His work has been, very simply, our musical common exchange—as familiar and contagious as the composer ever hoped.

By the time he died, he was that rare man, someone who accomplished what he set out to do: "All I really want to do is to provide a hard-working man in the blouse business with a method of expressing himself. If he likes a tune, he can whistle it and it will make his life happier."

And, at seventy-seven, he was something even rarer, a man who remained centered in his work over six decades.

The numbers were overwhelming: 1,500 songs, 43 stage musical scores, 9 film scores, 4 television scores. He wrote music when he had a heart attack and music when he had cancer and music when he was learning to talk through his esophagus. He wrote music when his plays were huge successes and music when they were not; music when he needed the money and music when he didn't.

At fourteen, he composed his first song and at sixty-seven he still wrote to a friend: "I have a strong need to write some more music, and I just hope nothing stands in the way."

Yet when he was praised, he said, "I admit with no modesty whatever that not

---

1. Richard Rodgers (1902–1979): U.S. composer of musicals.
2. Victrola (vik trō′ lə) *n.*: A trademark for a phonograph.
3. Ludwig van Beethoven (lōōt′ viH vän bā′ tō vən) (1770–1827): German composer.
4. Giuseppe Verdi (jōō zep′ pe ver′ dē) (1813–1901): Italian operatic composer.
5. John Lennon (1940–1980): Leader of the British rock music group The Beatles, which achieved world renown in the 1960's and 1970's.
6. Trapp family . . . mountains: An Austrian family who fled over mountains to escape Hitler, dictator of Germany during World War II. The musical *The Sound of Music* is about their experiences.

many people can do it. But when they say, 'You're a genius,' I say, 'no, it's my job.' "

Music was his job. It is a curious phrase. Yet it seems to me, looking back over his career, how little attention we've paid recently to the relationship between a life and "a job." For the past several years we've been more intrigued by life styles than by work styles, more curious about how someone sustains a marriage or a health regimen than how someone sustains an interest in his work.

The magazines we read are more focused on how we play than how we produce. We assume now that work is what we do for a living and leisure is how we enjoy living. When we meet people who do not understand this split, we label them "workaholics."

But Richard Rodgers was never seen in *People* magazine wearing his jog-togs. His "job" was writing music and his hobby was listening to it.

Usually we think of creative work as either inspired or tortured. We remember both Handel[7] writing "The Messiah" in three weeks and Michelangelo mounting the scaffolding of the Sistine Chapel[8] year after year. Rodgers for his part once wrote a song in five minutes. But when asked about it, he said, "The song situation has probably been going around in my head for weeks. Sometimes it takes months. I don't believe that a writer does something wonderful spontaneously. I believe it's the result of years of living, or study, reading—his very personality and temperament."

The man knew something about the relationship between creativity and productivity. He knew something about the satisfactions of both, and managed to blend them. He could write music when handed the lyrics and write it before the lyrics. He could and would write a song to fit a scene. If Woody Allen is right in saying that "Eighty percent of life is showing up," well, Richard Rodgers showed up.

"Some Enchanted Evening" will never go into the annals of great classics. *The King and I* is not *Aida.*[9] Rodgers was a workaday artist and he knew it. But he also knew that for some people there is a fuzzy line between work and play, between what is hard and what is fun.

"I heard a very interesting definition of work from a lawyer. Work, he said, is any activity you'd rather not do. . . . I don't find it work to write music, because I enjoy it," said Rodgers. Yet he also said, "It isn't any easier than when I began, and by the same token it isn't any harder."

He was a man who was lucky in his work and lucky in his temperament. In an era when we tend to doubt the satisfactions that can come from work and tend to regard hard workers as a touch flawed in their capacity for pleasure, this composer showed what work can be: how it can sustain rather than drain, heighten rather than diminish, a full life. He leaves us a legacy in the sound of his life as well as his music.

---

7. George Frederick Handel (han' d'l) (1685–1759): English composer, born in Germany.

8. Michelangelo (mī' k'l an' jə lō') **. . . Sistine Chapel:** Italian sculptor, painter, architect and poet (1475–1564) who painted the ceiling of the Sistine Chapel, the principal chapel in the Vatican at Rome.

---

9. The King . . . Aida: *The King and I,* a musical by Rodgers and his partner Oscar Hammerstein (1895–1960), is not on the same level as *Aida,* an Italian opera by Verdi.

THINKING ABOUT THE SELECTION

Recalling

1. What was Rodgers' goal in life?
2. What is Rodgers' special talent? Give examples of how he used his abilities.
3. On what, according to Rodgers, is writing music or performing an artistic task based?

Interpreting

4. What is the difference between Muzak and music?
5. Why did Rodgers say that he wasn't a genius but simply someone doing his job?
6. The writer says that "We assume now that work is what we do for a living and leisure is how we enjoy living." What does this say about the way many people feel about their work? How was the way Rodgers felt about his work different?
7. How did Rodgers leave "a legacy in the sound of his life" as well as in his music?

Applying

8. What do you think is the relationship between creativity and productivity?

READING IN THE CONTENT AREAS

Setting a Purpose for Reading

Setting a purpose for reading can help you read more efficiently. One way of setting a purpose for reading is imagining you are a journalist acquiring information for an article. Reading this essay should give you the answers to the questions you asked before reading.

1. Who was Richard Rodgers?
2. For what is he best known?
3. When and where did he live?
4. How did he achieve success?
5. Why do we remember him?

CRITICAL THINKING AND READING

Recognizing Subjective Details

Writers often include both objective and subjective details in their descriptions. **Objective details** are factual statements that are free from personal feelings or opinions. For example, Ellen Goodman gives this objective detail about Richard Rodgers' work, "The numbers were overwhelming: 1,500 songs, 43 stage musical scores, 9 film scores, 4 television scores." **Subjective details** are based on a person's feelings, interests, or opinions rather than on outside facts. For example, Goodman includes this subjective detail: "As I grew older, I knew he was no Beethoven or Verdi, or John Lennon for that matter."

Find two objective details in the selection and two subjective details.

UNDERSTANDING LANGUAGE

Appreciating Music Terms

In writing about the composer Richard Rodgers, Goodman uses some music terms. Look up each of the following music terms in the dictionary, and then use each one in a sentence.

1. lyrics   2. opera   3. orchestrate

THINKING AND WRITING

Writing About an Artistic Person

Think of someone skilled at singing, dancing, painting, or playing a musical instrument. First answer *who, what, when, where, why,* and *how* about this person. Then use this information in an article about this person for the cultural section of a newspaper. Revise your article, keeping in mind the audience, and proofread it.

GUIDE FOR READING

Dial Versus Digital

Isaac Asimov (1920–   ) was born in the Soviet Union and came to the United States with his family in 1923. Asimov has written and edited more than four hundred books. His interests range from science to history, literature (especially science fiction), and humor —fields in which he has done research, teaching, writing, or editing. "Dial Versus Digital" shows a fascination with time and how time is measured.

Varying Rates of Reading

When you read, you can use **varying rates of reading:** scanning, skimming, or reading intensively. You can vary your rate of reading depending on your purpose. You **scan** to find specific facts or details. You **skim,** or look through without reading carefully, to get a general idea of what is written. You **read intensively,** that is, you read slowly and carefully, to get a clear understanding of what is written.

Look For

Skim "Dial Versus Digital" to get an overview of it. Then read it intensively—slowly and carefully—pausing frequently to question your understanding of what you have just read. Later, when you answer the questions that follow the essay, scanning it may prove helpful.

Writing

"Dial Versus Digital" discusses the replacement of dial clocks by digital clocks. What other object or activity can you think of that has been replaced by modern technology? List any such item that comes to mind.

Vocabulary

Knowing the following words will help you as you read "Dial Versus Digital."

digital (dij′ it′l) *adj.:* Giving a reading in digits, which are the numerals from 0 to 9 (p. 477)
hovering (huv′ər iŋ) *v.:* Staying suspended in the air (p. 478)
arbitrary (är′ bə trer′ ē) *adj.:* Based on one's preference or whim (p. 478)

Dial Versus Digital

Isaac Asimov

There seems no question but that the clock dial, which has existed in its present form since the seventeenth century and in earlier forms since ancient times, is on its way out. More and more common are the digital clocks that mark off the hours, minutes, and seconds in ever-changing numbers. This certainly appears to be an advance in technology. You will no longer have to interpret the meaning of "the big hand on the eleven and the little hand on the five." Your digital clock will tell you at once that it is 4:55. And yet there will be a loss in the conversion of dial to digital, and no one seems to be worrying about it.

When something turns, it can turn in just one of two ways, clockwise or counter-clockwise, and we all know which is which. Clockwise is the normal turning direction of the hands of a clock and counterclockwise is the opposite of that. Since we all stare at clocks (dial clocks, that is), we have no trouble following directions or descriptions that include those words. But if dial clocks disappear, so will the meaning of those words for anyone who has never stared at anything but digitals. There are no *good* substitutes for clockwise and counterclockwise. The nearest you can come is by a consideration of your hands. If you clench your fists with your thumbs pointing at your chest and

THE PERSISTENCE OF MEMORY 1931
Salvadore Dali
The Museum of Modern Art

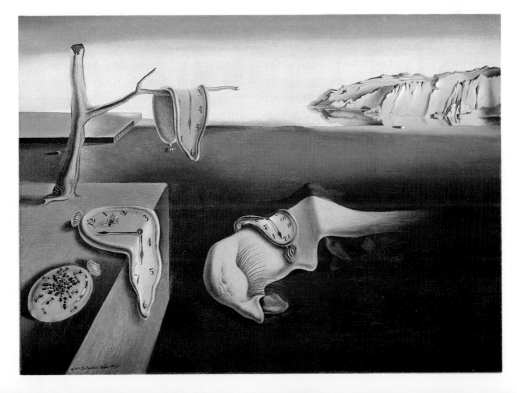

then look at your fingers, you will see that the fingers of your right hand curve counterclockwise from knuckles to tips while the fingers of your left hand curve clockwise. You could then talk about a "right-hand twist" and a "left-hand twist," but people don't stare at their hands the way they stare at a clock, and this will never be an adequate replacement.

Nor is this a minor matter. Astronomers define the north pole and south pole of any rotating body in such terms. If you are hovering above a pole of rotation and the body is rotating counterclockwise, it is the north pole; if the body is rotating clockwise, it is the south pole. Astronomers also speak of "direct motion" and "retrograde motion," by which they mean counterclockwise and clockwise, respectively.

Here is another example. Suppose you are looking through a microscope at some object on a slide or through a telescope at some view in the sky. In either case, you might wish to point out something to a colleague and ask him or her to look at it, too. "Notice that object at eleven o'clock," you might say—or five o'clock or two o'clock. Everyone knows exactly where two, five, or eleven—or any number from one to twelve—is located on the clock dial, and can immediately look exactly where he is told. (In combat, pilots may call attention to the approach of an enemy plane or the location of antiaircraft bursts or the target, for that matter, in the same way.)

Once the dial is gone, location by "o'clock" will also be gone, and we have nothing to take its place. Of course, you can use directions instead: "northeast," "southwest by south," and so on. However, you will have to know which direction is north to begin with. Or, if you are arbitrary and decide to let north be straight ahead or straight up, regardless of its real location, it still remains true that very few people are as familiar with a compass as with a clock face.

Here's still another thing. Children learn to count and once they learn the first few numbers, they quickly get the whole idea. You go from 0 to 9, and 0 to 9, over and over again. You go from 0 to 9, then from 10 to 19, then from 20 to 29, and so on till you reach 90 to 99, and then you pass on to 100. It is a very systematic thing and once you learn it, you never forget it. Time is different! The early Sumerians couldn't handle fractions very well, so they chose 60 as their base because it can be divided evenly in a number of ways. Ever since, we have continued to use the number 60 in certain applications, the chief one being the measurement of time. Thus, there are 60 minutes in an hour.

If you are using a dial, this doesn't matter. You simply note the position of the hands and they automatically become a measure of time: "half past five," "a quarter past three," "a quarter to ten," and so on. You see time as space and not as numbers. In a digital clock, however, time is measured *only* as numbers, so you go from 1:01 to 1:59 and then move directly to 2:00. It introduces an irregularity into the number system that is going to insert a stumbling block, and an unnecessary one, into education. Just think: 5.50 is halfway between 5 and 6 if we are measuring length or weight or money or anything but time. In time, 5:50 is nearly 6, and it is 5:30 that is halfway between 5 and 6.

What shall we do about all this? I can think of nothing. There is an odd conservatism among people that will make them fight to the death against making time decimal and having a hundred minutes to the hour. And even if we do convert to decimal time, what will we do about "clockwise," "counterclockwise," and locating things at "eleven o'clock"? It will be a pretty problem for our descendants.

THINKING ABOUT THE SELECTION

Recalling

1. For how long has the dial clock existed? By what is it being replaced?
2. In addition to showing time, what are two uses of the dial clock?
3. In what two ways do you see time if you are using a dial clock? In what way do you see time if you are using a digital clock?
4. Find three disadvantages of changing from dial to digital.

Interpreting

5. Why do you think many directions say to turn clockwise or counterclockwise?
6. The digital clock is a replacement for the dial clock. What did the dial clock replace?

Applying

7. Poll your classmates. How many have digital watches? How many have dial watches? How do you explain your findings?

READING IN THE CONTENT AREAS

Varying Your Rate of Reading

Varying rates of reading include reading intensively, or reading carefully to understand the meaning; scanning, or reading to locate specific information; and skimming, or looking over quickly without reading carefully.

Sometimes you **read intensively** for meaning, especially when reading a textbook. **Scanning** can be helpful when reading the newspaper or doing research to locate particular facts or details. **Skimming** is helpful for getting an idea of what a written work is about.

Indicate which rate of reading would be useful for the following tasks.

1. Looking through a magazine to find an article that interests you
2. Finding the author's date of birth in the encyclopedia entry

3. Reading a biography in preparation for an oral report on this person's life

CRITICAL THINKING AND READING

Finding Main Ideas

The **main idea** of each paragraph is the most important idea in it. Writers sometimes state the main idea directly in the topic sentence. However, when the main idea is not directly stated but is implied, you must discover it by making inferences from the **supporting details.**

1. Reread the second paragraph of the essay. What is the main idea?
2. What details support this main idea?

UNDERSTANDING LANGUAGE

Using the Prefix *Counter-*

The prefix *counter-* means "against." For example, a *counterattack* is an attack made against another attack.

Add the prefix *counter-* to the following words, and use each new word in a sentence.

1. clockwise
2. act
3. type
4. productive

THINKING AND WRITING

Writing About Technology

Write an article for a magazine called *Contemporary Life* about an object or activity in our culture that has been replaced by technology. You can choose your subject from the list you made earlier, or you can choose another. Explain how the object was used or the activity was done in the past, how it changed, and what is done now. Revise your article, supporting your main ideas. Proofread your article.

GUIDE FOR READING

Hokusai: The Old Man Mad About Drawing

Stephen Longstreet (1907-   ) is a writer of movie screenplays, art criticism, novels, television scripts, and detective stories. An accomplished artist, Longstreet studied painting in Paris, Rome, London, and Berlin. While living in Europe in the 1920's, he became acquainted with such famous artists as Marc Chagall, Henri Matisse, and Pablo Picasso. "Hokusai: The Old Man Mad About Drawing" combines Longstreet's interests in both writing and art.

Note Taking

Note taking is an important tool for learning. It is the jotting down of the important points of what you read. Taking notes can help you understand what you read and how it is organized, and can be an aid to writing an essay or a research paper.

Look For

As you read "Hokusai: The Old Man Mad About Drawing," look for the important points the author makes about the artist. What facts and details does he use to support his main ideas?

Writing

There are many different forms of art, dance, music, and literature. For example, two of the many forms of dance are ballet and folk dancing. Choose one of these arts: painting, dancing, singing, or writing. Then list all the forms of this art that come to mind.

Vocabulary

apprenticed (ə pren' tist) v.: Contracted to learn a trade under a skilled worker (p. 481)

commissioned (kə mish' ənd) v.: Ordered to make something (p. 481)

engulfing (in gulf' iŋ) v.: Flowing over and swallowing (p. 481)

mania (mā'nē ə) n.: Uncontrollable enthusiasm (p. 482)

Hokusai: The Old Man Mad About Drawing

Stephen Longstreet

Of all the great artists of Japan, the one Westerners probably like and understand best is Katsushika Hokusai. He was a restless, unpredictable man who lived in as many as a hundred different houses and changed his name at least thirty times. For a very great artist, he acted at times like P.T. Barnum[1] or a Hollywood producer with his curiosity and drive for novelty.

Hokusai was born in 1760 outside the city of Edo[2] in the province of Shimofusa. He was apprenticed early in life to a mirror maker and then worked in a lending library, where he was fascinated by the woodcut illustrations of the piled-up books. At eighteen he became a pupil of Shunsho, a great artist known mainly for his prints of actors. Hokusai was soon signing his name as Shunro, and for the next fifteen years he, too, made actor prints, as well as illustrations for popular novels. By 1795 he was calling himself Sori and had begun working with the European copper etchings which had become popular in Japan. Every time Hokusai changed his name, he changed his style. He drew, he designed fine surimino (greeting prints), he experimented with pure landscape.

Hokusai never stayed long with a period or style, but was always off and running to something new. A great show-off, he painted with his fingers, toothpicks, a bottle, an eggshell; he worked left-handed, from the bottom up, and from left to right. Once he painted two sparrows on a grain of rice. Commissioned by a shogun (a military ruler in 18th century Japan) to decorate a door of the Temple of Dempo-ji, he tore it off its hinges, laid it in the courtyard, and painted wavy blue lines on it to represent running water, then dipped the feet of a live rooster in red seal ink and chased the bird over the painted door. When the shogun came to see the finished job, he at once saw the river Tatsuta and the falling red maple leaves of autumn. Another time Hokusai used a large broom dipped into a vat of ink to draw the full-length figure of a god, over a hundred feet long, on the floor of a courtyard.

When he was fifty-four, Hokusai began to issue books of his sketches, which he called *The Manga*. He found everything worth sketching: radish grinders, pancake women, street processions, jugglers, and wrestlers. And he was already over sixty when he began his great series, *Thirty-six Views of Fuji*, a remarkable set of woodcut prints that tell the story of the countryside around Edo: people at play or work, great waves engulfing fishermen, silks drying in

---

1. P.T. Barnum: Phineas Taylor Barnum (1810–1891). U.S. showman and circus operator.
2. Edo (ē′ dō): Now Tokyo.

THE GREAT WAVE OFF KANAGAWA
Katsushika Hokusai
The Metropolitan Museum of Art

the sun, lightning playing on great mountains, and always, somewhere, the ash-tipped top of Fuji.

Hokusai did thirty thousand pictures during a full and long life. When he was seventy-five he wrote:

> From the age of six I had a mania for drawing the shapes of things. When I was fifty I had published a universe of designs. But all I have done before the age of seventy is not worth bothering with. At seventy-five I have learned something of the pattern of nature, of animals, of plants, of trees, birds, fish, and insects. When I am eighty you will see real progress. At ninety I shall have cut my way deeply into the mystery of life itself. At a hundred I shall be a marvelous artist. At a hundred and ten everything I create, a dot, a line, will jump to life as never before. To all of you who are going to live as long as I do, I promise to keep my word. I am writing this in my old age. I used to call myself Hokusai, but today I sign myself "The Old Man Mad About Drawing."

He didn't reach a hundred and ten, but he nearly reached ninety. On the day of his death, in 1849, he was cheerfully at work on a new drawing.

THINKING ABOUT THE SELECTION
Recalling

1. Where and when was Hokusai born?
2. What jobs did he have early in his life?
3. What types of art did Hokusai create?
4. How many pictures did Hokusai draw during his lifetime?
5. What was Hokusai doing the day he died?

Interpreting

6. What did Hokusai mean when he said, "At a hundred I shall be a marvelous artist"?
7. Hokusai called himself "The Old Man Mad About Drawing." Why is this name appropriate? Explain your answer.

Applying

8. According to the author, Westerners like and understand Hokusai best of all Japan's great artists. Why do you think this is?

READING IN THE CONTENT AREAS
Taking Notes

Note taking, or jotting down the important points of what you read, can help you understand what is written and how it is organized.

To take notes, you must be able to identify the main point, or important idea, of each paragraph. The writer may support the main point by giving details, examples, or quotes.

When you take notes, write in your own words, using words and phrases rather than complete sentences. Pay attention to words in italic, in boldface type, and in quotation marks. Notice words and phrases that may indicate main points; for example, *first, then, finally, most important, the reasons for, the result was.*

Reread the essay about Hokusai.
1. Take notes on the author's main points.
2. Compare your notes with your classmates'.

CRITICAL THINKING AND READING
Finding Implied Main Ideas

The **main idea** of each paragraph is the most important idea in it. Often the main idea is **implied** rather than stated. When this is the case, you must recognize it from the supporting details.

Look at the paragraph on page 481, beginning "When he was fifty-four." The implied main idea in this paragraph is that Hokusai continued to be a prolific painter throughout his life. The supporting details that tell you this are that Hokusai at age fifty-four issued books of numerous sketches.

Reread the paragraph on page 481, beginning "Hokusai never stayed long with a period."
1. What is the implied main idea?
2. What are the supporting details?

UNDERSTANDING LANGUAGE
Appreciating Art Terms

Every field has certain terms that are used to discuss it. Art terms describe the process of a particular art, the products of the type of art, or the materials used to create the art.

Use a dictionary to define the following art terms. Then use each one in a sentence.
a. woodcut prints   c. lithographs
b. still lifes   d. sketches

THINKING AND WRITING
Writing About Art

Look at Hokusai's print "Great Wave Off Kanagawa" on page 482. As you look at this work of art, freewrite about the thoughts and associations that come to mind. Then write several paragraphs describing the painting for someone who has never seen it. Include a description of its details, shapes, and colors.

Talking About Writing

Ursula K. Le Guin (1929-   ) was born in Berkeley, California, and grew up listening to Indian legends retold by her father, a scientist who worked with Native Americans. Le Guin's writing, which has been influenced also by Norwegian and Irish folk tales, includes imagined beings and invented places. Le Guin has won the Nebula Award of the Science Fiction Writers of America and the Hugo Award of the World Science Fiction Convention. In her speech "Talking About Writing," she expresses her love for writing.

Outlining

Outlining is the systematic listing of the most important points of a piece of writing. An outline lists the main points and supporting details in the order in which they occur.

I. First main topic
   A. First subtopic
      1. First supporting idea or detail
      2. Second supporting idea or detail
   B. Second Subtopic
II. Second main topic (The outline continues in the same way.)

Look For

As you read "Talking About Writing," pay attention to what the speaker believes are important points for writing.

Writing

In this selection, the speaker discusses her area of expertise —writing—and points to follow to succeed in it. Choose a skill or an area in which you have ability. Then list the points that you believe are important to follow to be successful in that skill or area.

Vocabulary

Knowing the following words will help you as you read "Talking About Writing."

snide (snīd) *adj.*: Intentionally mean (p. 485)

fluctuating (fluk' choo wāt' iŋ) *adj.*: Constantly changing; wavering (p. 485)

prerequisite (pri rek' wə zit) *n.*: An initial requirement (p. 486)

vicarage (vik' ər ij) *n.*: A place where the clergy live (p. 486)

premonition (prē mə nish' ən) *n.*: An omen; forewarning (p. 487)

communal (käm'yoon'l) *adj.*: Shared by members of a group or a community (p. 487)

axioms (ak' sē əmz) *n.*: Truths or principles that are widely accepted (p. 487)

Talking About Writing

Ursula K. Le Guin

Tonight we are supposed to be talking about writing. I think probably the last person who ought to be asked to talk about writing is a writer. Everybody else knows so much more about it than a writer does.

I'm not just being snide; it's only common sense. If you want to know all about the sea, you go and ask a sailor, or an oceanographer, or a marine biologist, and they can tell you a lot about the sea. But if you go and ask the sea itself, what does it say? Grumble grumble swish swish. It is too busy being itself to know anything about itself.

Anyway, meeting writers is always so disappointing. I got over wanting to meet live writers quite a long time ago. There is this terrific book that has changed your life, and then you meet the author, and he has shifty eyes and funny shoes and he won't talk about anything except the injustice of the United States income tax structure toward people with fluctuating income, or how to breed Black Angus cows, or something.

Well, anyhow, I am supposed to talk about writing, and the part I really like will come soon, when *you* get to talk to *me* about writing, but I will try to clear the floor for that by dealing with some of the most basic questions.

People come up to you if you're a writer, and they say, I want to be a writer. How do I become a writer?

I have a two-stage answer to that. Very often the first stage doesn't get off the ground, and we end up standing around the ruins on the launching pad, arguing.

The first-stage answer to the question, how do I become a writer, is this: You learn to type.

The only alternative to learning to type is to have an inherited income and hire a fulltime stenographer. If this seems unlikely, don't worry. Touch typing is easy to learn. My mother became a writer in her sixties, and realizing that editors will not read manuscripts written lefthanded in illegible squiggles, taught herself touch typing in a few weeks; and she is not only a very good writer but one of the most original, creative typists I have ever read.

Well, the person who asked, How do I become a writer, is a bit cross now, and he mumbles, but that isn't what I meant. (And I say, I know it wasn't.) I want to write short stories, what are the rules for writing short stories? I want to write a novel, what are the rules for writing novels?

Now I say Ah! and get really enthusiastic. You can find all the rules of writing in the book called Fowler's *Handbook of English Usage,* and a good dictionary. There are only a very few rules of writing not covered in those two volumes, and I can summarize them thus: Your story may begin in longhand on the backs of old shopping lists, but when it goes to an editor, it should be typed, double-spaced, on one side of the paper only, with generous margins—especially the left-hand one—and not too many really grotty corrections per page.

Your name and its name and the page number should be on the top of every single page; and when you mail it to the editor it should have enclosed with it a stamped, self-addressed envelope. And those are the Basic Rules of Writing.

I'm not being funny. Those are the basic requirements for a readable, therefore publishable, manuscript. And, beyond grammar and spelling, they are the only rules of writing I know.

All right, that is stage one of my answer. If the person listens to all that without hitting me, and still says All right all right, but how *do* you become a writer, then we've got off the ground, and I can deliver stage two. How do you become a writer? Answer: You write.

It's amazing how much resentment and disgust and evasion this answer can arouse. Even among writers, believe me. It is one of

those Horrible Truths one would rather not face.

The most frequent evasive tactic is for the would-be writer to say, But before I have anything to say, I must get *experience.*

Well, yes; if you want to be a journalist. But I don't know anything about journalism, I'm talking about fiction. And of course fiction is made out of the writer's experience, his whole life from infancy on, everything he's thought and done and seen and read and dreamed. But experience isn't something you go and *get*—it's a gift, and the only prerequisite for receiving it is that you be open to it. A closed soul can have the most immense adventures, go through a civil war or a trip to the moon, and have nothing to show for all that "experience"; whereas the open soul can do wonders with nothing. I invite you to meditate on a pair of sisters, Emily and Charlotte. Their life experience was an isolated vicarage in a small, dreary English village, a couple of bad years at a girls' school, another year or two in Brussels, which is surely the dullest city in all Europe, and a lot of housework. Out of that seething mass of raw, vital, brutal, gutsy Experience they made two of the greatest novels ever written: *Jane Eyre* and *Wuthering Heights.*

Now of course they were writing from experience; writing about what they knew, which is what people always tell you to do; but what was their experience? What was it they knew? Very little about "life." They knew their own souls, they knew their own minds and hearts; and it was not a knowledge lightly or easily gained. From the time they were seven or eight years old, they wrote, and thought, and learned the landscape of their own being, and how to describe it. They wrote with the imagination, which is the tool of the farmer, the plow you plow your own soul with. They wrote from inside, from as deep inside as they could get by using all their strength and courage and intelligence. And that is where books come from. The novelist writes from inside. What happens to him outside, during most of his life, doesn't really matter.

I'm rather sensitive on this point, because I write science fiction, or fantasy, or about imaginary countries, mostly—stuff that, by definition, involves times, places, events that I could not possibly experience in my own life. So when I was young and would submit one of these things about space voyages to Orion or dragons or something, I was told, at extremely regular intervals, "You should try to write about things you know about." And I would say, But I do; I know about Orion, and dragons, and imaginary countries. Who do you think knows about my own imaginary countries, if I don't?

But they didn't listen, because they don't understand, they have it all backward. They think an artist is like a roll of photographic film, you expose it and develop it and there is a reproduction of Reality in two dimensions. But that's all wrong, and if any artist tells you "I am a camera," or "I am a mirror," distrust him instantly, he's fooling you, pulling a fast one. Artists are people who are not at all interested in the facts —only in the truth. You get the facts from outside. The truth you get from inside.

OK, how do you go about getting at that truth? You want to tell the truth. You want to be a writer. So what do you do?

You write.

Honestly, why do people ask that question? Does anybody ever come up to a musician and say, Tell me, tell me—How should I become a tuba player? No! it's too obvious. If you want to be a tuba player you get a tuba, and some tuba music. And you ask the neighbors to move away or put cotton in their ears. And probably you get a tuba teacher, because there are quite a lot of objective rules and techniques both to written music and to tuba performance. And then you sit down and you play the tuba, every day, every week, every month, year after year, until you are good at playing the tuba; until you can—if you desire—play the truth on the tuba.

It is exactly the same with writing. You sit down and you do it, and you do it, and you do it, until you have learned how to do it.

Of course, there are differences. Writing makes no noise, except groans, and it can be done anywhere, and it is done alone.

It is the experience or premonition of that loneliness, perhaps, that drives a lot of young writers into this search for rules. I envy musicians very much, myself. They get to play together, their art is largely communal; and there are rules to it, an accepted body of axioms and techniques, which can be put into words or at least demonstrated, and so taught. Writing cannot be shared, nor can it be taught as a technique, except on the most superficial level. All a writer's real learning is done alone, thinking, reading other people's books, or writing— practicing. A really good writing class or workshop can give us some shadow of what musicians have all the time—the excitement of a group working together, so that each member outdoes himself—but what comes out of that is not a collaboration, a joint accomplishment, like a string quartet or a symphony performance, but a lot of totally separate, isolated works, expressions of individual souls. And therefore there are no rules, except those each individual makes up for himself.

I know. There are lots of rules. You find them in the books about The Craft of Fiction and The Art of the Short Story and so on. I know some of them. One of them says: Never begin a story with dialogue! People won't read it; here is somebody talking and they don't know who and so they don't care, so—Never begin a story with dialogue.

Well, there is a story I know, it begins like this:

"*Eh bien, mon prince!* so Genoa and Lucca are now no more than private estates of the Bonaparte family!*"*

It's not only a dialogue opening, the first four words are in *French,* and it's not even a French novel. What a horrible way to begin a book! The title of the book is *War and Peace.*

There's another Rule I know: Introduce all the main characters early in the book. That sounds perfectly sensible, mostly I suppose it is sensible, but it's not a rule, or if it is somebody forgot to tell it to Charles Dickens. He didn't get Sam Weller into the Pickwick Papers for ten chapters—that's five months, since the book was coming out as a serial in installments.

Now you can say, all right, so Tolstoy can break the rules, so Dickens can break the rules, but they're geniuses; rules are made for geniuses to break, but for ordinary, talented, not-yet-professional writers to follow, as guidelines.

And I would accept this, but very very grudgingly, and with so many reservations that it amounts in the end to nonacceptance. Put it this way: if you feel you need rules and want rules, and you find a rule that appeals to you, or that works for you, then follow it. Use it. But if it doesn't appeal to you or doesn't work for you, then ignore it; in fact, if you want to and are able to, kick it in the teeth, break it, fold staple mutilate and destroy it.

See, the thing is, as a writer you are free. You are about the freest person that ever was. Your freedom is what you have bought with your solitude, your loneliness. You are in the country where *you* make up the rules, the laws. You are both dictator and obedient populace. It is a country nobody has ever explored before. It is up to you to make the maps, to build the cities. Nobody else in the world can do it, or ever could do it, or ever will be able to do it again.

Absolute freedom is absolute responsibility. The writer's job, as I see it, is to tell the truth. The writer's truth—nobody else's. It is not an easy job. One of the biggest implied lies going around at present is the one that hides in phrases like "self-expression" or "telling it like it is"—as if that were easy, anybody could do it if they just let the words pour out and didn't get fancy. The "I am a camera" business again. Well, it just doesn't work that way. You know how hard it is to say to somebody, just somebody you know, how you *really* feel, what you *really* think—with complete honesty? You have to trust them; and you have to *know yourself:* before you can say anything anywhere near the truth. And it's hard. It takes a lot out of you.

You multiply that by thousands; you remove the listener, the live flesh-and-blood friend you trust, and replace him with a faceless unknown audience of people who may possibly not even exist; and you try to write the truth to them, you try to draw them a map of your inmost mind and feelings, hiding nothing and trying to keep all the distances straight and the altitudes right and the emotions honest. . . . And you never succeed. The map is never complete, or even accurate. You read it over and it may be beautiful but you realize that you have fudged here, and smeared there, and left this out, and put in some stuff that isn't really there at all, and so on—and there is nothing to do then but say OK; that's done; now I come back and start a new map, and try to do it better, more truthfully. And all of this, every time, you do alone—absolutely alone. The only questions that really matter are the ones you ask yourself.

You may have gathered from all this that I am not encouraging people to try to be writers. Well, I can't. You hate to see a nice young person run up to the edge of a cliff and jump off, you know. On the other hand, it is awfully nice to know that some other people are just as nutty and just as determined to jump off the cliff as you are. You just hope they realize what they're in for.

THINKING ABOUT THE SELECTION
Recalling

1. The speaker answers "How do I become a writer?" in two stages. What are they?
2. To what does the speaker compare writing?
3. How does the speaker feel about encouraging people to be writers?
4. What rules should writers follow?

Interpreting

5. What does the speaker mean by "I think probably the last person who ought to be asked to talk about writing is a writer"?
6. According to the author, why is experience not important to a writer of fiction?
7. How is telling the truth different from telling the facts?

Applying

8. Do you feel experienced people should not be asked about how to do their jobs? Explain.

READING IN THE CONTENT AREAS
Understanding Outlining

Outlining breaks down the most important points and their supporting details, following the order in which they are written. Begin an outline by listing the main point, or central idea, about each paragraph. The main points should be listed by roman numerals. Also note the support-ing details of each main point. Supporting details may include details, examples, or quotations. Indent and label them with a capital letter.

Make an outline of three consecutive para-graphs from "Talking About Writing."

CRITICAL THINKING AND READING
Sequencing Events

Sequencing events is putting a series of events in a particular order. The events might be in chronological order—the order in which they happened. The events might be in order of the least important to the most important, or vice versa. Similar events may be grouped together.
1. What steps does the writer describe in an-swering the question "How do I become a writer?" How does she arrange these steps?
2. What steps does the writer describe in the process of becoming a tuba player? How does she arrange these steps?

THINKING AND WRITING
Writing Advice About Performing a Skill

Refer to the skill you wrote about earlier, or choose another skill. Freewrite about how to accomplish that skill. Then prepare a how-to list of steps for a younger relative. Revise your steps, arranging your details chronologically. Proofread your steps.

Nonfiction

Nonfiction is based on real people and real events and presents factual information. A writer of nonfiction often sets out with a certain purpose in mind and directs the writing to a certain intended audience. For example, the writer may set out to explain, to persuade, or to entertain. The writer may direct the essay toward people already familiar with the subject or people who have little or no knowledge of it. You will gain more from reading nonfiction if you examine the techniques the writer uses to accomplish the purpose, the support the writer uses to back up the main idea, and the way the writer arranges the supporting information.

Purpose

By **purpose** we mean the writer's reason for writing. Usually a writer has both a general purpose and a specific purpose. For example, a writer may in general wish to give information about a topic, entertain readers, describe something, or even persuade readers to do something. In addition, the writer may want to make a specific point about the topic. This point, or main idea, may be stated in the topic sentence.

Techniques

Just as builders use tools to construct their buildings, writers use tools, or **techniques,** to accomplish their purpose. For example, writers may use vivid adjectives to describe a landscape or exaggeration to create humorous effects. They may use figurative language to create startling word pictures or words with strong connotations to stir up feelings and associations.

Support

Support is the information the writer uses to back up or clarify the main idea. This support may take several forms: facts, opinions, reasons, details, examples, or incidents. The better an idea is supported, the more likely the reader is to accept it.

Arrangement

The writer **arranges** the support to best accomplish the purpose. For example, the writer may arrange steps in chronological order, to show which should be done after the other. The writer may arrange reasons in order of importance, saving the most important reason for last and so building to a powerful conclusion.

On the following pages is a model of how an active reader might read an essay. As you read, pay close attention to the annotations.

A to Z in Foods as Metaphors:
Or, a Stew Is a Stew Is a Stew

Mimi Sheraton

Cooking styles may vary from one country to another, but certain foods inspire the same symbolism and human characteristics with remarkable consistency. The perception of food as metaphor is apparently more consistent than the perception of food as ingredient.

The inspiration for some of this imagery is easier to find than others. It is not too hard to understand, for example, why the big, compact, plebeian-tasting cabbage is widely regarded as being stupid, a role it shares with the starchy, inexpensive staple the potato. A cabbage head in this country is considered to be as dull-witted as a krautkopf in Germany, and a potato head indicates a similar, stodgy-brained individual, never mind that both are delicious and can be prepared in elegant ways.

Italians, on the other hand, consider the cucumber a symbol of ineptness, and to call a person a cetriolo is to cast him among the cabbages of the world.

Salt has been a highly regarded commodity throughout history, and so a valuable person is described as being the salt of the earth. Considering the bad press salt is getting these days, however, that remark may soon be taken as an insult.

It is difficult to understand why ham is the word for a bad actor who overacts. But no one has to explain why a pretty and delightful young woman is considered to be a peach, or why her adorable, accommodating brother is a lamb. With luck, he will not grow up to be a muttonhead, to be classified with the cabbage and potatoes. If he remains a lamb, he can

Purpose: The title provides a clue to the main idea of the essay. It will most likely express an idea about foods and how we use foods as metaphors. What could the subtitle mean?

Arrangement: The writer begins her essay by stating the main idea. What is the main idea?

Support: Here the writer offers three examples to support the main idea. What are they?

Techniques: Here the writer uses figurative language to make her points. What figurative expressions does she include? What is the meaning of these figurative expressions?

be counted on to bring home the bacon that is the bread and dough.

All things sweet, especially sugar and honey, inspire dozens of terms of endearment in every language; but the lemon, despite its sunny and piquant flavor, is best known for its sourness and so describes such things as an automobile always in need of repairs. In many countries the nut is, inexplicably, the metaphor for craziness, though it is easier to explain why someone who is sprightly and hot-tempered is said to be peppery.

Support: Notice the examples here that support the main idea. What are these examples?

Cooked foods or dishes also inspire such comparisons. To be in the soup (it's hot) is to be in trouble and to be in a stew indicates one is troubled. Stews and soups with many ingredients are the consistent metaphors in many languages for big, complicated events and procedures.

In New York the most commonly heard of such expressions is tsimmes,[1] referring to the Eastern European Jewish stew of carrots, sweet potatoes, prunes, onions and, often, beef. To make a whole tsimmes out of something is to create an event of endlessly involved complications. In English, a tsimmes is a hodgepodge, which in turn is named for the stew derived from the French hochepot, which became hotchpotch or hotpot.

Arrangement: Up until now, the writer has discussed individual foods. Here she shifts to cooked foods or dishes. What examples does she provide?

But a tsimmes is no more complicated than the New Orleans gumbo, also an event of dazzling complexities derived from the soup that may include okra, onions, peppers, shrimp, oysters, ham, sausage, chicken and at least a dozen other possibilities. Similarly used in their own countries are bouillabaisse,[2] the French soup of many fishes, and the Rumanian ghivetch, a baked or simmered stew that can be made with more than a dozen vegetables plus meat.

In Spain, to make an olla podrida[3] out of something is to make it as complex as that mixed boil of meats, poultry and onions. And though some Italians refer to a big mess as a big minestrone, the more popular metaphor is a pasticci,[4] a mess derived from the complicated preparations of the pastry chef,

---

1. tsimmes (tsim′ əs)
2. bouillabaisse (bōōl′ yə bäs′)
3. olla (äl′ ə) **podrida** (pə drē′ də)
4. pasticci (päs tē′ chē)

or pasticcere.[5] In Denmark it is the sailor's hash or stew known as labskaus that signifies complications, and no wonder when you consider that such a dish contains meat and herring in the same pot.

Some foods inspire conflicting metaphors. Fish is brain food, but a cold and unemotional person is a cold fish. You can beef up a program and make it better, but don't beef about the work that it involves or you will be marked a complainer. Instead of being given a promotion that is a plum you will be paid peanuts, even though you know your onions and are the apple of your boss's eye.

Arrangement: The writer concludes by expanding on her main idea. What new idea does she introduce? What details support this main idea?

Putting It Together: People use foods to describe a variety of things from character traits to situations.

---

5. pasticcere (päs′ tē cher′ ē)

Mimi Sheraton (1926–   ) was born in Brooklyn, New York. As a food critic for *The New York Times,* she traveled all over the world to do research on food and how it is prepared. One of her popular books is *Mimi Sheraton's Favorite New York Restaurants.* Sheraton traces her interest in food to her childhood in Brooklyn, where good food and family situations were important.

THINKING ABOUT THE SELECTION
Recalling

1. Explain what the cabbage and the potato have in common.
2. Why are valuable people considered "the salt of the earth"?
3. What idea is expressed by the word *stew*? Find three other words from other languages that express this same idea.
4. Explain the conflicting metaphors expressed by fish and beef.

Interpreting

5. Why would you call a promotion a "plum"?
6. Why would knowledgeable people be said to "know their onions"?
7. Why might you call a loved one "the apple of my eye"?

Applying

8. What foods would you use to describe someone with great physical strength? Explain.

ANALYZING LITERATURE
Understanding an Essay's Purpose

Sometimes writers will directly state their purpose for writing. At other times you must infer, or draw a conclusion from given facts or clues, what the writer's purpose is. The clues may be given in statements, quotes, examples, or tone.

For instance, a writer may use colorful, descriptive language and an emotional attitude to persuade; factual language and a serious attitude to inform; and humorous descriptions and a light attitude to entertain. In "A to Z in Foods as Metaphors," the writer sets the purpose directly.

1. What direct statement does the writer make that sets the purpose for writing?
2. List three quotes or examples the writer gives to support her purpose.
3. What tone does the writer use? Give examples.
4. Based on the writer's direct statement, examples and tone, what is her purpose?

CRITICAL THINKING AND READING
Interpreting Metaphorical Language

A **metaphor** is a way of comparing two seemingly unlike objects to highlight a characteristic of one of the objects. Metaphors can produce images in your mind. Read the following metaphor to see the image created.

The wind-tossed field was an ocean of grain.

Explain the following metaphors.
1. She is the Rock of Gibraltar.
2. He is the guiding light of the department.
3. She is a wizard of the stock market.

UNDERSTANDING LANGUAGE
Identifying Mixed Metaphors

A **mixed metaphor** consists of two or more metaphors that do not fit together. An example is this sentence: The *wave* of protest was *nipped in the bud*. Wave and *nipped in the bud* do not fit together. It would be more appropriate to say: A *wave* of protest *washed over* the crowd. In this case, *wave* and *washed over* fit together.

The following sentences contain mixed metaphors. Rewrite each sentence to make the metaphor consistent and effective.
1. A *roar* of approval *sifted* through the audience.
2. An *onslaught* of insults *besieged* him daily.

THINKING AND WRITING
Writing About Language Arts

List five metaphors that are used to compare people or situations to animals. Working with a group of students, research the origins of these metaphors. Then write a brief explanation of each one. Turn these explanations into an essay on "Animals as Metaphors," patterning the style in "A to Z in Foods as Metaphors." Revise your essay, making sure you have adequately supported your main idea. Then proofread your essay and share it with your classmates.

Understanding Persuasive Techniques

Writers of nonfiction often use **persuasive techniques** to convince readers to accept their opinions or to take some action. Understanding the persuasive techniques is helpful in determining whether or not to agree with the author or take the action.

Stated Position

To evaluate persuasive writing, you need to identify the stated position, or major opinion, that the author wants you to accept. This position should be stated in the topic sentence and should be written so that it is easily understood. Unfamiliar terms used in the position statement should be defined so that the reader can clearly understand what the author is proposing. The stated position is an opinion that is held by a writer and that is open to debate. It cannot be a fact because facts are verifiable and cannot be argued over.

Examine the following sentences:

Hokusai is a Japanese artist who painted over thirty thousand pictures.
Hokusai is my favorite artist.
Hokusai should be considered the Westerners' favorite Japanese artist.

Both the first and second sentences are unacceptable as stated positions. The first is a fact, which is not debatable, while the second is merely someone's personal opinion. It, too, cannot be disputed. The third sentence, however, is a good stated position because it is an opinion that can be sensibly argued. Facts can be used to support or dispute it.

Major Points

Repeating the major points is another effective persuasive technique. Writers often restate their position, especially at the conclusion of their essay. Consequently, looking for ideas that are repeated will help you identify the stated position and major points.

Once you understand the stated position, you must identify the facts the author uses to support it. Evaluate them in terms of their quality and quantity. Use the following criteria. The supporting facts should be accurate, logical, and relevant to the argument. If an expert is quoted, the person should be an outstanding authority in the field. The quotation by Hokusai is convincing because it emphasizes what the author is saying and is by the artist himself.

Organization

Organization is important in persuasive writing. Facts should be introduced in an appropriate order. For example, it would be best to discuss the work and contributions of Hokusai in the order in which he made them, as this would be the easiest order to follow.

Support

Another persuasive technique is to use examples, comparisons, and descriptions to support the facts. Using forceful, vivid language that appeals to the emotions makes these descriptions and comparisons more effective. For example, Hokusai is compared with P. T. Barnum, which reminds the reader of the excitement and novelty of the circus and thus creates a vivid image of the artist.

Piling up the evidence by using a series of examples or descriptions adds weight to the point being made. For instance, the author piles up evidence when he describes the woodcut prints Hokusai made. He says the prints "tell the story of the countryside around Edo: people at play or work, great waves engulfing fishermen, silks drying in the sun, lightning playing on great mountains, and always, somewhere, the ash-tipped top of Fuji." Piling up evidence is not only convincing; it also is a concise way of conveying a lot of ideas.

Finally a writer should include sufficient supporting facts or reasons to make a strong argument. The more supporting facts a writer includes, the more convincing is the argument.

Activity

Read "The Trouble with Television" by Robert MacNeil and answer the following questions about this essay.
1. What is the stated position of the author? Is this position clearly expressed? Give reasons to support your answer.
2. List the facts the author uses to back up his position.
3. Does the author use descriptions and examples to back up his facts? Has he used a series of examples or descriptions to make a more convincing argument? If so, give examples.
4. Does the author use comparisons to clarify and make his supporting facts more convincing? If so, give examples.
5. Based on your previous answers, how would you evaluate this persuasive essay?

YOU THE WRITER

Assignment

1. Choose an essay in which a person has a special gift or ability. Imagine what it would be like to be this person. Describe how it feels to paint, write music, and so on. Explain what motivates you and how creating something makes you feel.

Prewriting. Make word banks to collect the vocabulary you will need to write about your subject from the perspective of the creator.

Writing. Begin your own essay with a description of the person and the skill in which you are interested. Become that person and describe the creative process. Why do you write, paint, or write music, for example? Explain why you must do what you do.

Revising. Revise your essay. Add any information you think will strengthen it. Edit your sentences so that they are logically arranged.

Assignment

2. Choose one of the more scientific or technological essays in this unit and pretend you are a scientist researching a similar topic. As a scientist, do you agree or disagree with the basic premise of the essay? Explain why the essay is effective or why it is not.

Prewriting. List the scientific points in the essay. Use this list to build your argument for or against the premise of the essay.

Writing. Write the first draft of your own essay. Be sure to end your introductory paragraph with a thesis statement. Organize your ideas as you think a scientist would.

Revising. Revise your first draft. Check to see that your title suggests the main point and that this point is clearly made. Make sure your opinion is adequately supported.

Assignment

3. If you were a writer, about which of these subjects would you choose to write: science, music, math, art, or language arts? Why? What is it about the content area that appeals to you? Explain how you would go about writing an essay.

Prewriting. Freewrite about the content area that appeals to you. Explore why you would choose to write about a particular subject if you were a writer.

Writing. Write the first draft of your own essay. In your introductory paragraph, be sure to state the discipline in which you would write. Go on to discuss the reasons for your choice. Try to use the vocabulary appropriate to your subject.

Revising. Revise your first draft. Check to see that you have stated the reasons for your choice clearly and in logical order. Edit your sentences. Finally, proofread your final draft.

YOU THE CRITIC

Assignment

1. Choose two of the essays in this unit and compare or contrast their tones. Analyze the language in the essays and draw a conclusion about how the authors achieved their tones. Also discuss how the tone of each essay is appropriate for the subject.

Prewriting. Make word banks for each essay. List the key words that point to specific tones. Categorize them in logical order.

Writing. Begin your own essay with an explanation of tone. Examine one essay then the other. Compare or contrast their tones, using specific language from the essays. Summarize your main points in your last paragraph and reach a conclusion.

Revising. Read over your essay. Make sure your introduction provides an adequate explanation of tone. Check to see that you have compared or contrasted the tones of your chosen essays.

Assignment

2. Choose one of the essays and explore how the author makes his subject exciting and appealing. Analyze the language the author uses to make the subject of the essay come alive for the reader. Examine any other techniques, such as dialogue, that are used.

Prewriting. Brainstorm to form a list of the essay's appealing features. Organize the list to separate language and technique.

Writing. Begin your own essay with an introductory paragraph stating your premise. List and discuss the language that makes the essay exciting. Continue with a discussion of the author's technique. Summarize your main points and state a conclusion.

Revising. Read over your essay. Make sure your introduction arouses your reader's interest. Check to see that you have discussed both language and technique logically and cohesively.

Assignment

3. Choose one of the essays about a person and explain how the essay introduces the person to the reader. How does the author make the person interesting? What details are given to make the subject of the essay real to the reader?

Prewriting. Use a cueing technique to generate ideas about your topic. Jot down the questions *Who? What? Where? When?* and *Why?* Then answer each of the questions and explore how effectively the author presents information to answer each of the questions.

Writing. Present the subject, what he or she is famous for, where the person worked or works, when the person worked or works, and why the person does what he or she does. Continue with a discussion of how well you got to know the subject of the essay.

Revising. Revise your essay. Add any information you think will strengthen it. Edit your sentences so that they flow smoothly.

ABOVE VITEBSK, 1922
Marc Chagall
Three Lions

POETRY

Short stories, essays, autobiographies—all are examples of prose, the language that you hear in your daily life. Poetry, unlike prose, consists of language with a strong musical quality in which the words are highly charged with meaning. Usually poetry is written in lines, and these lines are grouped into stanzas.

Poetry is one of the oldest forms of literature. Before literature was written down, people told stories. They used rhythm and rhyme to help them remember the stories better. Ballads were actually stories in poetic form that were sung. Many narrative poems still use rhythm and rhyme to tell stories.

In addition to using rhythm and rhyme, poets use language in other special ways to appeal to a reader's senses and emotions. Because many poems are short, poets choose each word and phrase with care to create vivid images, or pictures, in the reader's mind.

The poems in this unit include narrative poems and poems in which language is used in unusual and creative ways.

Poetry

Reading poetry demands getting actively involved. The poet Wallace Stevens has written: "In poetry, you must love the words, the ideas, and the images and rhythms with all your capacity to love anything at all."

Use the following strategies to help you read a poem actively and discover the poem's full meaning.

Question

Poetry makes us look at the world with new eyes. As you read, ask questions about the meaning of the words and the effect of the language. Stop to think about the vivid images, or word pictures. What do they make you see and feel?

Clarify

The words in poetry are often easy to read, but getting the sense of the words is more difficult. Stop to clarify or clear up any questions you may have. If the words do not make sense to you, perhaps the poet is using them figuratively and intends to play with your imagination.

Listen

Listen to the musical quality created by the use of rhythm and rhyme. What effect is created by the use of repetition and alliteration?

Summarize

If a poem tells a story, stop at appropriate points to summarize what has happened so far.

Paraphrase

Put the poem in your own words. By doing so, you will make its meaning your own.

Pull It Together

Ralph Waldo Emerson has written: "A poem is made up of thoughts, each of which filled the whole sky of the poet in its turn." After you have read a poem, bring all these thoughts together. What did the poem say to you?

Mushrooms

Sylvia Plath

Question: Will this poem be about mushrooms?

Overnight, very
Whitely, discreetly,
Very quietly

Questions: Who is the speaker? Could it be the mushrooms?

Our toes, our noses
5 Take hold on the loam,[1]
Acquire the air.

Nobody sees us,
Stops us, betrays us;
The small grains make room.

Listening: Notice the way in which the short lines create a quiet but insistent rhythm.

10 Soft fists insist on
Heaving the needles,
The leafy bedding,

Clarification: The mushrooms *do* seem to be speaking. The poet presents them as an army.

Even the paving.
Our hammers, our rams,[2]
15 Earless and eyeless,

Clarification: These stanzas seem to describe how the caps of the mushrooms poke up through the ground.

Perfectly voiceless,
Widen the crannies,
Shoulder through holes. We

Diet on water,
20 On crumbs of shadow,
Bland-mannered,[3] asking

---

1. loam (lōm) *n.*: Rich, dark soil.
2. rams: Heavy beams used to break down gates, walls, doors, and so forth.
3. bland-mannered (bland′ man′ ərd) *adj.*: Having a smooth, mild way of acting.

Little or nothing.
So many of us!
So many of us!

25 We are shelves, we are
Tables, we are meek,
We are edible,

Nudgers and shovers
In spite of ourselves.
30 Our kind multiplies:

We shall by morning
Inherit the earth.
Our foot's in the door.

Questions: Why does the speaker repeat these two lines? Perhaps the repetition intensifies the effect!

Paraphrase: The mushrooms move quietly and meekly, but their presence is felt because they multiply.

Pulling It Together: The mushrooms are like a quiet army that takes over the world.

Sylvia Plath (1932–1963) was born in Boston. She developed an early interest in writing and published her first poems when she was only seventeen. A brilliant student, Plath attended Cambridge University on a Fulbright scholarship. While in England, she met and married Ted Hughes, who was to become one of the foremost British poets of his generation. Plath's own work is often noted for its gothic undertones. Did you notice the violent images as you read "Mushrooms"?

THINKING ABOUT THE SELECTION

Recalling

1. What is the mushrooms' purpose?
2. How long does it take them to accomplish their purpose?
3. Why does no one notice what the mushrooms are doing?

Interpreting

4. Explain the effect created by the words *discreetly, quietly,* and *voiceless.* Find one other word that also creates this impression.
5. Explain the effect created by the words *fists, hammers,* and *rams.* Find a verb that creates the same effect.
6. Explain the effect of the line: "Our kind multiplies."

Applying

7. The word *insidious* means "operating at a slow but relentless pace in a manner that is not readily apparent." Explain why an insidious attack can be even more dangerous than an open one.

ANALYZING LITERATURE

Understanding Personification

Personification is the process of giving human characteristics to nonhuman objects. For example, a gentle spring breeze can be personified as a child at play.

1. Explain how the poet personifies mushrooms.
2. Why is this use of personification effective?

CRITICAL THINKING AND READING

Reading Lines

The end of a line in poetry does not always signal the end of a sentence. Let the punctuation marks guide you. A period, question mark, or exclamation mark tells you to come to a full stop. A comma tells you to pause briefly, and a semicolon or colon tells you to take a slightly longer pause. If no punctuation mark appears at the end of a line, do not pause at all.

Answer each question below. Then read the poem aloud.

1. How many sentences are there in this poem? How many sentences end in the middle of a line?
2. Which lines should you read without stopping at the end?
3. Why do you think the poet used a colon at the end of line 30?
4. What effect is created by having you come to a full stop before reading the last line?

UNDERSTANDING LANGUAGE

Finding Synonyms

A **synonym** is a word that means the same or almost the same thing as another word. For example, the words *whole* and *complete* are synonyms, as are the words *injure* and *damage.* For each of the following words, find its synonym in the poem.

1. deceive
2. silently
3. carefully
4. mild

THINKING AND WRITING

Using Personification

A mushroom is a rapidly growing fungus that you may have eaten for dinner. By using personification, however, the poet makes you see this common food with new eyes. Select a fruit or vegetable that might appear as part of someone's dinner. For example, you might select the potato. Brainstorm to list as many qualities of this foodstuff as possible. Then, by using personification, write a poem making your classmates see this common food in a new light. When you revise, make sure you have given your foodstuff human traits that seem appropriate. Proofread your poem and share it with your classmates.

Narrative Poetry

HOLY MOUNTAIN III, 1945
Horace Pippin
Hirshhorn Museum and Sculpture Garden, Smithsonian Institution

GUIDE FOR READING

Paul Revere's Ride

Henry Wadsworth Longfellow (1807-1882) was born in Portland, in what is now the state of Maine. Longfellow published his first poem at the age of thirteen and two years later entered Bowdoin College, where he was a classmate of Nathaniel Hawthorne, who also became a famous writer. Longfellow's best-remembered works include the narrative poems "The Song of Hiawatha" and "Paul Revere's Ride." In "Paul Revere's Ride," he tells of a Revolutionary hero's historic ride.

The Narrative Poem

A **narrative poem** is a poem that tells a story. Like short stories, narrative poems have plot, setting, characters, dialogue, and theme. "Paul Revere's Ride" is set around Boston on the eve of the American Revolution. The main action is Revere's legendary midnight ride, during which he warned his fellow colonists of the approaching British army. His bravery gave the colonists time to get ready so they could turn back the British that night. The main characters are Paul Revere and his friend.

However, a poem is not a short story. A narrative poem is in poetic form, not in prose. It relies on rhythm and rhyme. It is usually organized in **stanzas,** groups of lines that form units in a poem, just as paragraphs are the units of a story.

Look For

As you read "Paul Revere's Ride," pay attention to the first time Paul Revere speaks because it will prepare you for what will happen in the rest of the poem. Why is his ride so important? How does it affect the fate of the colonists?

Writing

Most likely, you have heard of Paul Revere before this. Brainstorm with your classmates to list all the details you can recall about him.

Vocabulary

Knowing the following words will help you as you read "Paul Revere's Ride."

phantom (fan' təm) n.: Ghost-like (p. 509)

tread (tred) n.: Step (p. 510)

stealthy (stel' thē) adj.: Secret; quiet (p. 510)

somber (säm' bər) adj.: Dark; gloomy (p. 510)

impetuous (im pech' σο wəs) adj.: Impulsive (p. 511)

spectral (spek' trəl) adj.: Ghostly (p. 511)

aghast (ə gast') adj.: Horrified (p. 512)

Paul Revere's Ride

Henry Wadsworth Longfellow

Listen, my children, and you shall hear
Of the midnight ride of Paul Revere,
On the eighteenth of April, in Seventy-five;
Hardly a man is now alive
5   Who remembers that famous day and year.

He said to his friend, "If the British march
By land or sea from the town to-night,
Hang a lantern aloft in the belfry arch[1]
Of the North Church tower as a signal light,—
10 One, if by land, and two, if by sea;
And I on the opposite shore will be,
Ready to ride and spread the alarm
Through every Middlesex[2] village and farm,
For the country folk to be up and to arm."

15 Then he said, "Good night!" and with muffled oar
Silently rowed to the Charlestown[3] shore,
Just as the moon rose over the bay,
Where swinging wide at her moorings[4] lay
The Somerset, British man-of-war;[5]
20 A phantom ship, with each mast and spar[6]
Across the moon like a prison bar,
And a huge black hulk, that was magnified
By its own reflection in the tide.

---

1. belfry arch (bel' frē ärch): The curved top of a tower or steeple that holds the bells.
2. Middlesex (mid' 'l seks'): A county in Massachusetts.
3. Charlestown (chärl' stoun'): Part of Boston on the harbor.
4. moorings (moor' iŋs) n.: The lines, cables, or chains that hold a ship to the shore.
5. man-of-war: An armed naval vessel; warship.
6. mast and spar: Poles used to support sails.

Meanwhile, his friend, through alley and street,
25 Wanders and watches with eager ears,
Till in the silence around him he hears
The muster[7] of men at the barrack door,
The sound of arms, and the tramp of feet,
And the measured tread of the grenadiers,[8]
30 Marching down to their boats on the shore.

Then he climbed the tower of the Old North Church,
By the wooden stairs, with stealthy tread,
To the belfry-chamber overhead,
And startled the pigeons from their perch
35 On the somber rafters,[9] that round him made
Masses and moving shapes of shade,—
By the trembling ladder, steep and tall,
To the highest window in the wall,
Where he paused to listen and look down
40 A moment on the roofs of the town,
And the moonlight flowing over all.

Beneath, in the churchyard, lay the dead,
In their night-encampment on the hill,
Wrapped in silence so deep and still
45 That he could hear, like a sentinel's[10] tread,
The watchful night-wind, as it went
Creeping along from tent to tent,
And seeming to whisper, "All is well!"
A moment only he feels the spell
50 Of the place and the hour, and the secret dread
Of the lonely belfry and the dead;
For suddenly all his thoughts are bent
On a shadowy something far away,
Where the river widens to meet the bay,—
55 A line of black that bends and floats
On the rising tide, like a bridge of boats.

---

7. muster *v.*: An assembly of troops summoned for inspection, roll call, or service.
8. grenadiers (gren' ə dirz') *n.*: Members of a special regiment or corps.
9. rafters *n.*: The beams that slope from the ridge of a roof to the eaves and serve to support the roof.
10. sentinel (sen' ti n'l) *n.*: A person who keeps guard.

Meanwhile, impatient to mount and ride,
Booted and spurred, with a heavy stride
On the opposite shore walked Paul Revere.
60 Now he patted his horse's side,
Now gazed at the landscape far and near,
Then, impetuous, stamped the earth,
And turned and tightened his saddle-girth;[11]
But mostly he watched with eager search
65 The belfry-tower of the Old North Church,
As it rose above the graves on the hill,
Lonely and spectral and somber and still.
And lo! as he looks, on the belfry's height
A glimmer, and then a gleam of light!
70 He springs to the saddle, the bridle[12] he turns,
But lingers and gazes, till full on his sight
A second lamp in the belfry burns!

A hurry of hoofs in a village street,
A shape in the moonlight, a bulk in the dark,
75 And beneath, from the pebbles, in passing, a spark
Struck out by a steed flying fearless and fleet:
That was all! And yet, through the gloom and the light,
The fate of a nation was riding that night;
And the spark struck out by that steed[13] in his flight,
80 Kindled the land into flame with its heat.

He has left the village and mounted the steep,[14]
And beneath him, tranquil and broad and deep,
Is the Mystic,[15] meeting the ocean tides;
And under the alders[16] that skirt its edge,
85 Now soft on the sand, now loud on the ledge,
Is heard the tramp of his steed as he rides.

---

11. girth (gɑrth) *n.:* A band put around the belly of a horse for
holding a saddle.
12. bridle (brīd′ 'l) *n.:* A head harness for guiding a horse.
13. steed *n.:* A horse, especially a high-spirited riding horse.
14. steep *n.:* A slope or incline having a sharp rise.
15. Mystic (mis′ tik): A river in Massachusetts.
16. alders (ôl′ dərz) *n.:* Trees and shrubs of the birch family.

It was twelve by the village clock,
When he crossed the bridge into Medford[17] town.
He heard the crowing of the cock,
90   And the barking of the farmer's dog,
And felt the damp of the river fog,
That rises after the sun goes down.

It was one by the village clock,
When he galloped into Lexington.[18]
95   He saw the gilded weathercock[19]
Swim in the moonlight as he passed,
And the meeting-house windows, blank and bare,
Gaze at him with a spectral glare,
As if they already stood aghast
100   At the bloody work they would look upon.

---

17. Medford (med' fərd): A town outside of Boston.
18. Lexington (lek' siŋ tən): A town in eastern Massachusetts,
outside of Boston.
19. weathercock (weth' ər käk') *n.*: A weathervane in the form of a
rooster.

It was two by the village clock,
When he came to the bridge in Concord[20] town.
He heard the bleating[21] of the flock,
And the twitter of birds among the trees,
105 And felt the breath of the morning breeze
Blowing over the meadows brown.
And one was safe and asleep in his bed
Who at the bridge would be first to fall,
Who that day would be lying dead,
110 Pierced by a British musket-ball.

You know the rest. In the books you have read,
How the British Regulars[22] fired and fled,—

---

20. Concord (kän′ kôrd): A town in eastern Massachusetts. The
first battles of the Revolutionary War (April 19, 1775) were fought in
Lexington and Concord.
21. bleating (blēt′ iŋ) *n.*: The sound made by sheep.
22. British Regulars: Members of the army of Great Britain.

How the farmers gave them ball for ball,
From behind each fence and farm-yard wall,
115 Chasing the red-coats down the lane,
Then crossing the fields to emerge again
Under the trees at the turn of the road,
And only pausing to fire and load.

So through the night rode Paul Revere;
120 And so through the night went his cry of alarm
To every Middlesex village and farm,—
A cry of defiance and not of fear,
A voice in the darkness, a knock at the door,
And a word that shall echo forevermore!
125 For, borne on the night-wind of the Past,
Through all our history, to the last,
In the hour of darkness and peril and need,
The people will waken and listen to hear
The hurrying hoof-beats of that steed,
130 And the midnight message of Paul Revere.

THINKING ABOUT THE SELECTION
Recalling

1. When does Paul Revere make his ride? (lines 1–5)
2. What agreement does Revere make with his friend? (lines 6–14)
3. How many lamps does Paul Revere finally see in the belfry? (lines 70–72)
4. Through which towns does he ride? (lines 87–110) Name two things he passes in each.
5. Explain whether or not Paul Revere accomplished his purpose.

Interpreting

6. To what is the Somerset compared? (lines 15-23) What is the effect of this image?
7. From his position in the belfry-chamber, how does the friend feel at first? (lines 42–51)
8. What is the "shadowy something far away" that the friend suddenly sees? (lines 52–56)
9. How do lines 78 through 80 express the importance the poet places on the ride?

Applying

10. Do you think Revere's friend is also a hero? Explain your answer.

ANALYZING LITERATURE
Understanding a Narrative Poem

Although it is a poem, "Paul Revere's Ride" resembles a short story in several important ways. First, the poem has a **plot,** a sequence of events that take place and that present a conflict. Characters are introduced, and the setting is established. Next, the poem builds suspense as Revere and his friend wait. The poet writes first of one and then of the other, and the tension mounts. At last the signal appears, and the climax of the poem—the ride—begins.

1. What is the conflict in this narrative poem?
2. Describe Paul Revere's character.
3. How does the poet create suspense in his description of the friend's climb to the belfry-chamber?
4. Cite two specific details that describe the setting effectively. Explain why you chose each.

CRITICAL THINKING AND READING
Sequencing Events

Narrative poems present a **sequence of events,** or arrangement of actions. In the first stanza, the poet tells about Revere's agreement with his friend. That information prepares you for events that follow. Every other stanza builds on the information in the first two stanzas.

1. What does the friend do even before he climbs the belfry-tower?
2. How does stanza 7 relate to stanza 2?
3. How do stanzas 6 and 7 help build suspense?

SPEAKING AND LISTENING
Understanding Choral Reading

Poetry is especially effective when it is read aloud. A **choral reading** is a reading performed by a group, or chorus, of readers.

To perform a choral reading of "Paul Revere's Ride," divide the class into groups, each reading a stanza in turn. Or one group could read the stanzas that tell about Paul Revere; another could read those about his friend; a third could read the stanzas at the beginning and end, which contain the poet's own thoughts.

As you read, remember you are telling a story of adventure and heroism. Read each stanza with an appropriate tone of voice.

THINKING AND WRITING
Summarizing the Events in the Poem

Make a list of the main events in the poem. List them in the order in which they occur. Using this list as your guide, write a summary of the action. When you have finished, reread your summary, making sure you have covered all the important points. Proofread your summary.

GUIDE FOR READING

William Stafford

Ballad

A **ballad** is a narrative poem that tells a simple and dramatic story. It is usually intended to be sung or recited. Ballads generally have strong rhythms and rhymes. For example, read aloud these lines from "William Stafford":

> Through all its ups and downs
>   Some bitter days I saw,
> But never knew what misery was
>   Till I struck Arkansaw.

If you listen carefully as you read, you can hear the very regular rhythm. This regularity contributes to the musical, songlike quality of the ballad. The same is true of the ballad's strong rhymes: *saw/ Arkansaw.*

Many ballads were written by anonymous authors. They were passed along by word of mouth, often through singing, until someone finally wrote them down.

Look For

As you read "William Stafford," look for the ways it is similar to a song. What might the melody be like? Listen closely to the rhythms and rhymes. Finally, think about its story. Is it a sad story or a comical one? Or both?

Writing

Imagine an experience that was so unusual that it seemed "stranger than fiction." Or, imagine someone who seems larger than life. Freewrite about this experience or person, exploring what strikes you as strange or colorful.

Vocabulary

Knowing the following words will help you as you read "William Stafford."

sultry (sul′ trē) *adj.*: Hot and humid (p. 517)

crane (krān) *n.*: A large, slender bird with very long legs and neck (p. 518)

sassafras (sas′ ə fras′) *n.*: Dried root bark of the sassafras tree, usually used in cooking for flavoring (p. 518)

William Stafford

Anonymous

My name is William Stafford,
    Was raised in Boston Town;
For nine years as a rover
    I roved the wide world 'round;
5 Through all its ups and downs
    Some bitter days I saw,
But never knew what misery was
    Till I struck Arkansaw.

I started on my journey,
10   'Twas the merry month of June;
I landed in New Jersey
    One sultry afternoon.
Along came a walking skeleton
    With long and lantern jaw.[1]
15 He asked me to his hotel
    In the state of Arkansaw.

_____

1. lantern jaw: A long, thin, projecting lower jaw.

I followed up a great long rope
    Into his boarding place,
Where hunger and starvation
20   Were printed on his face;
His bread it was corn dodger;[2]
    His beef I could not chaw;[3]
He taxed me fifty cents for that
    In the state of Arkansaw.

25   I rose the next morning early
    To catch the early train.
He said, ''Young man, you'd better stay.
    I have some land to drain.
I'll give you fifty cents a day,
30   Your washing, board,[4] and all;
You'll find yourself a different lad
    When you leave Arkansaw.''

Six months I worked for this galoot;[5]
    Charles Tyler was his name;
35   He was six feet seven in his boots
    And thin as any crane.
His hair hung down like rat tails
    Around his lantern jaw;
He was the photograph of all the gents
40   That's raised in Arkansaw.

He fed me on corn dodgers
    As hard as any rock;
My teeth began to loosen;
    My knees began to knock.
45   I got so thin on sassafras,
    Could hide behind a straw,
So I sho' was a different lad
    When I left Arkansaw.

---

2. corn dodger: A small cake of cornmeal, baked or fried hard.
3. chaw: Chew.
4. board: Meals.
5. galoot (gə loot') n.: An awkward person.

THINKING ABOUT THE SELECTION

Recalling

1. What has William Stafford done for nine years? (lines 1–8)
2. How does he wind up in "Arkansaw"? (lines 9–16)
3. Describe the food there. (lines 21–24)
4. Describe Charles Tyler. (lines 33–40)

Interpreting

5. Why does Stafford stay in "Arkansaw"?
6. In what ways is Stafford "a different lad" when he leaves?
7. Do you thing the anonymous poet expected listeners to take the ballad seriously? Explain.

Applying

8. What people find humorous in one age may not be found amusing in another. Work with your classmates to list the things people find humorous today. Then list the things people might laugh at fifty years from now.

ANALYZING LITERATURE
Understanding Features of a Ballad

Generally, ballads tell about the adventures of colorful, larger-than-life characters. Often the main character is either a great hero or a terrible villain. Events and situations are exaggerated, or stretched to a nearly unrealistic degree. In "William Stafford," exaggeration creates humorous effects. Look, for example, at the description of William's main food—and its effects on him:

> He fed me on corn dodgers
>   As hard as any rock;
> My teeth began to loosen;
>   My knees began to knock.

1. Find two other exaggerations you found especially effective in the ballad. Explain your reason for each choice.
2. In what ways is Tyler a larger-than-life villain?
3. How is this ballad both funny and sad?

CRITICAL THINKING AND READING
Reading Inverted Sentences

In a sentence that is in normal word order, the subject precedes the predicate: *The hikers tramped up the mountain trail.* In an inverted sentence, the order is reversed. Sometimes the direct object comes before the subject and the predicate. In this case the verb follows the subject as it does in normal word order as in this example: *Some bitter days I saw.* To rewrite the example in normal word order, you must put the subject first: *I saw some bitter days.*

Find two sentences in "William Stafford" in which the direct object comes before the subject. Rewrite them in normal word order.

SPEAKING AND LISTENING
Selecting a Voice for a Dramatic Reading

Poetry was sung or recited aloud long before it was written down. Remember that a ballad is a special kind of narrative poem that was meant to be sung or read aloud. Perform a dramatic reading of "William Stafford." Choose an appropriate **tone of voice.** For example, your tone might be **dramatic** (serious or suspenseful). Or, it might be **parodic** (comical or as if you were telling a joke). Then take turns reading aloud.

THINKING AND WRITING
Evaluating the Ballad

You have probably reached an opinion as to whether "William Stafford" is an effective ballad or not. List reasons why you think this ballad is successful or unsuccessful. Then write an essay in which you explain your opinion. Be sure that you support your opinion with specific references from the poem. When you revise, make sure you have organized your supporting information logically. Then proofread your essay and share it with your classmates.

GUIDE FOR READING

Columbus

Joaquin Miller (1837–1913) was born near Liberty, Indiana, though he once claimed that his cradle was "a covered wagon pointed West." He lived in Oregon and California and worked as a teacher, lawyer, and journalist. Disappointed that poetry he had written was not well received, he left for England. In London, both he and his poetry won admiration. In 1886 he returned to America to live near Oakland, California, until his death. "Columbus," Miller's best-known poem, recounts the famous voyage of this daring explorer.

Elements of Poetry

Three basic elements of poetry are rhythm, rhyme, and refrain. **Rhythm** is the pattern of stressed and unstressed syllables in the lines of a poem. A poem's rhythm usually contributes to meaning. For example, the basic rhythm of "Columbus" is aggressive and forward-driving. It is a rhythm well suited to the poem's theme.

Rhyme is the repetition of sounds in words that appear close to one another in a poem. The commonest form of rhyme is **end rhyme,** which occurs at the end of two or more lines:

> This mad sea shows his teeth to-night.
> He curls his lip, he lies in wait,
> With lifted teeth as if to bite!

A **refrain** is a word, phrase, line, or group of lines that is repeated regularly in a poem. A refrain usually comes at the end of each stanza. Sometimes, as in "Columbus," the refrain recurs with small variations: "He said, 'Sail on! sail on! and on!'"

Look For

As you read "Columbus," listen to its rhythm. Look for the rhymes and see if they follow a regular pattern. Think, too, about the refrain. How does it convey the poem's theme?

Writing

Recall a person who kept trying until succeeding at some activity that seemed impossible at first. Freewrite for five minutes about this.

Vocabulary

Knowing the following words will help you as you read "Columbus."
mutinous (myo͞ot' 'n əs) *adj.*: Rebellious (p. 522)
wan (wan) *adj.*: Pale (p. 522)
swarthy (swôr' t͟hē) *adj.*: Having a dark complexion (p. 522)
unfurled (un fʉrld') *adj.*: Un-folded (p. 522)

THE LANDING OF COLUMBUS, 1876
Currier and Ives
Museum of the City of New York

Columbus

Joaquin Miller

> Behind him lay the gray Azores,[1]
> Behind the Gates of Hercules;[2]
> Before him not the ghost of shores;
> Before him only shoreless seas.
> 5   The good mate said: "Now must we pray,
> For lo! the very stars are gone.
> Brave Adm'r'l, speak; what shall I say?"
> "Why, say: 'Sail on! sail on! and on!'"

---

1. Azores (ā′ zôrz): A group of Portuguese islands in the North Atlantic west of Portugal.
2. Gates of Hercules (gāts uv hʊr′ kyə lēz′): Entrance to the Strait of Gibraltar, between Spain and Africa.

"My men grow mutinous day by day;
10 My men grow ghastly wan and weak."
The stout mate thought of home; a spray
Of salt wave washed his swarthy cheek.
"What shall I say, brave Adm'r'l, say,
If we sight naught[3] but seas at dawn?"
15 "Why, you shall say at break of day:
'Sail on! sail on! sail on! and on!'"

They sailed and sailed, as winds might blow,
Until at last the blanched mate said:
"Why, now not even God would know
20 Should I and all my men fall dead.
These very winds forget their way,
For God from these dread seas is gone.
Now speak, brave Adm'r'l; speak and say—"
He said: "Sail on! sail on! and on!"

25 They sailed. They sailed. Then spake[4] the mate:
"This mad sea shows his teeth to-night.
He curls his lip, he lies in wait,
With lifted teeth, as if to bite!
Brave Adm'r'l, say but one good word:
30 What shall we do when hope is gone?"
The words leapt like a leaping sword:
"Sail on! sail on! sail on! and on!"

Then, pale and worn, he kept his deck,
And peered through darkness. Ah, that night
35 Of all dark nights! And then a speck—
A light! A light! A light! A light!
It grew, a starlit flag unfurled!
It grew to be Time's burst of dawn.
He gained a world; he gave that world
40 Its grandest lesson: "On! sail on!"

---

3. naught (nôt) *n.*: Nothing.
4. spake (spāk) *v.*: Old-fashioned word for "spoke."

THINKING ABOUT THE SELECTION

Recalling

1. Who is the "Brave Adm'r'l"? What does he say each time in response to the mate?
2. What seems to frighten the mate in each of the first four stanzas?

Interpreting

3. To what does the poet compare the sea in lines 26–28? What is the effect of this comparison?
4. What is the light sighted in the last stanza?
5. Interpret line 38.
6. What is the "grandest lesson"?
7. In what ways is this poem about the great value of determination and perseverance?

Applying

8. What is the difference between perseverance and stubbornness? Explain why you do or do not think there is a point at which perseverance becomes foolish and dangerous.

ANALYZING LITERATURE

Understanding Rhythm and Refrain

A poem's **rhythm** is the pattern of stressed and unstressed syllables it contains. A **refrain** is a phrase or line or group of lines that is repeated several times in the poem. A refrain reinforces and helps express the meaning of the poem. The rhythm of "Columbus" creates a feeling of action; the refrain states the poet's main theme.

1. What general mood or feeling does the rhythm create?
2. What larger meaning does the refrain have?
3. How do the rhythm and refrain work together to convey the theme of the poem?

CRITICAL THINKING AND READING

Making Inferences About Theme

Theme is the main idea expressed in a literary work. Sometimes the theme is openly stated. More often it is implied, and you must **infer** it—you must draw a conclusion about it based on all the elements of the work. One way to infer the theme of a poem is to consider its refrain. In "Columbus," the simple refrain "sail on! and on!" expresses the theme of the poem.

1. How does the refrain apply to the actual events?
2. How does the refrain show what Columbus was like?
3. To what does the poet refer in his final use of the refrain?

UNDERSTANDING LANGUAGE

Appreciating Old-fashioned Words

This poem contains several old-fashioned words, words rarely used in writing or speech. It is useful to understand these words, however, as you are likely to encounter them again in your reading of American and English literature. Two such words, *naught* and *spake,* are defined in the footnotes. Others are *lo!* (line 6) and *blanched* (line 18). Find the definitions of these in a dictionary. Then use each of the four old-fashioned words mentioned here in an original sentence.

THINKING AND WRITING

Writing a Poem About a Historical Figure

List historical people who interest you. Next to each name, note one key idea that you associate with that figure.

From your list select one historical figure, and write a line or two that expresses the main idea you noted about him or her. Using these lines as a refrain, write a narrative poem that tells about the person you have chosen. After you have written one draft of your poem, read it over and make any corrections and improvements you feel are necessary. When you have finished your second draft, proofread it and read your poem aloud to the class.

GUIDE FOR READING

Barbara Frietchie

John Greenleaf Whittier (1807–1892) was born in Haverhill, Massachusetts. His poems are influenced by his Quaker upbringing and by his New England farm background. His most famous works express his political opinions, such as his opposition to slavery. Other works present the simple pleasures of country living. In the narrative poem "Barbara Frietchie," Whittier describes the courage and honor of people on both sides of the Civil War struggle.

Characters in Narrative Poems

In narrative poems, **characters** often stand for certain ideas or heroic qualities, which the poet wishes to celebrate. In order to understand a narrative poem, you must recognize the qualities that the characters in the poem represent. For example, in the poem about the Civil War that you are about to read, Barbara Frietchie, a Union supporter, is the subject, who represents human qualities that Whittier admires. He tells about her heroic action and Confederate General Stonewall Jackson's reaction to it to praise these qualities.

Look For

As you read, look for details about Barbara Frietchie and General Stonewall Jackson. How are they described? What are their actions? What human qualities did Whittier use them to represent?

Writing

Think of a person who has stood up for something he or she really believed in. It may be a figure from history or current events or someone you know, including yourself. What inspired that person? What actions did that person take? Did that person face disapproval or punishment from others? Freewrite for five minutes about this person's experience.

Vocabulary

Knowing the following words will help you as you read "Barbara Frietchie."

horde (hôrd) *n.*: Large moving group (p. 525)

banner (ban' ər) *n.*: Flag (p. 526)

Barbara Frietchie

John Greenleaf Whittier

Up from the meadows rich with corn,
Clear in the cool September morn,

The clustered spires of Frederick[1] stand
Green-walled by the hills of Maryland.

5   Round about them orchards sweep,
Apple and peach tree fruited deep,

Fair as the garden of the Lord
To the eyes of the famished rebel horde,

On that pleasant morn of the early fall
10   When Lee[2] marched over the mountain wall;

Over the mountains winding down,
Horse and foot, into Frederick town.

Forty flags with their silver stars,
Forty flags with their crimson bars,

15   Flapped in the morning wind: the sun
Of noon looked down, and saw not one.

Up rose old Barbara Frietchie then,
Bowed with her fourscore[3] years and ten;

Bravest of all in Frederick town,
20   She took up the flag the men hauled down

In her attic window the staff she set,
To show that one heart was loyal yet.

---

1. Frederick (fred' rik): A town in Maryland.
2. Lee (lē): Robert E. Lee, commander in chief of the Confederate
army in the Civil War.
3. fourscore (fôr' skôr') *adj.*: Four times twenty; eighty.

© Henri Cartier-Bresson/Magnum

Up the street came the rebel tread,
Stonewall Jackson[4] riding ahead.

25   Under his slouched hat left and right
He glanced; the old flag met his sight.

"Halt!"—the dust-brown ranks stood fast.
"Fire!"—out blazed the rifle-blast.

It shivered the window, pane and sash;[5]
30   It rent the banner with seam and gash.

Quick, as it fell, from the broken staff
Dame Barbara snatched the silken scarf.

---

4. Stonewall Jackson (stōn′ wôl′ jak′ s'n): Nickname of Thomas
Jonathan Jackson, Confederate general in the Civil War.
5. sash (sash) *n.*: The frame holding the glass panes of the window.

She leaned far out on the window-sill,
And shook it forth with a royal will.

35 "Shoot, if you must, this old gray head,
But spare your country's flag," she said.

A shade of sadness, a blush of shame,
Over the face of the leader came;

The nobler nature within him stirred
40 To life at that woman's deed and word;

"Who touches a hair of yon gray head
Dies like a dog! March on!" he said.

All day long through Frederick street
Sounded the tread of marching feet:

45 All day long that free flag tost[6]
Over the heads of the rebel host.[7]

Ever its torn folds rose and fell
On the loyal winds that loved it well;

And through the hill-gaps sunset light
50 Shone over it with a warm good-night.

Barbara Frietchie's work is o'er,
And the Rebel rides on his raids no more.

Honor to her! and let a tear
Fall, for her sake, on Stonewall's bier.[8]

55 Over Barbara Frietchie's grave,
Flag of Freedom and Union, wave!

Peace and order and beauty draw
Round thy symbol of light and law;

And ever the stars above look down
60 On thy stars below in Frederick town!

---

6. tost (tôst) *v.*: Old-fashioned form of *tossed.*
7. host (hōst) *n.*: An army; a multitude or great number.
8. bier (bir) *n.*: A coffin and its supporting platform.

THINKING ABOUT THE SELECTION

Recalling

1. Describe the time and place of the poem.
2. Who arrives in the town? What has happened before their arrival?
3. Why do the soldiers fire their guns? What does Barbara Frietchie do after they fire?
4. What is Stonewall Jackson's reaction to what Barbara Frietchie does?

Interpreting

5. What admirable human qualities does Barbara Frietchie represent?
6. What admirable human qualities does Stonewall Jackson represent?
7. Explain the last two lines of the poem.
8. What is the theme of this poem?

Applying

9. This poem has a patriotic theme. What other patriotic themes might be suitable for poetry? What might be the purpose of a poem with a patriotic theme?

ANALYZING LITERATURE

Creating Characters

A writer can create a character in several ways. Whittier directly describes Barbara Frietchie as ninety years old, "bowed" with age, and "Bravest of all in Frederick town."

Whittier also uses other methods to develop the character of Barbara Frietchie. He recounts her actions and he quotes her speech. Finally he shows the reactions of others to her and to her actions.

1. What method of developing a character does Whittier use in line 39?
2. What do Jackson's words in lines 41–42 tell you about his character?

CRITICAL THINKING AND READING

Making Inferences About Characters

To **infer** is to draw a conclusion based on available information. If a person always takes responsibility and completes given tasks, then it is reasonable to infer that this person is dependable.

1. List Barbara Frietchie's actions.
2. What does she say to Stonewall Jackson?
3. What does Stonewall Jackson's reaction to Barbara Frietchie tell you about *her*?
4. What inferences do you make about Stonewall Jackson?

UNDERSTANDING LANGUAGE

Choosing Meaning to Fit Context

If you come across a word you do not know, first check its meaning in a dictionary. If a dictionary is unavailable, try to figure out the word's meaning by looking at its **context**—the words and sentences around it.

In line 32 the poet writes that Barbara "snatched the silken scarf." Suppose you did not know the definition of *snatched*. Earlier lines explain that Barbara had held a flag from a window and that the flag had fallen. From the context you might then conclude that *snatched* means "caught" or "grabbed quickly."

Reread the context of each word below. Using the context, define each word. Then check your definitions in a dictionary.

1. famished (line 8)   3. tread (line 44)
2. rent (line 30)

THINKING AND WRITING

Writing a Definition of a Hero

Think about the admirable qualities that Barbara Frietchie has. Then make a list of other heroic qualities. Organize your list in order of increasing importance. Using your list as a guide, write an essay in which you define a true hero. Read your definition over after you have written it and make any changes you feel are needed. Proofread it and share it with your classmates.

Figurative Language and Imagery

THE BROOKLYN BRIDGE: VARIATION ON AN OLD THEME, 1939
Joseph Stella
Collection of Whitney Museum of American Art

Lyric 17

José Garcia Villa (1914–   ) was born in Manila, Philippines, and emigrated to the United States in 1930. He attended the University of New Mexico and Columbia University in New York City. Villa has published several volumes of poetry as well as short stories. "Lyric 17" reflects the judgment of one critic, who said that Villa's poems come "straight from the poet's being, from his blood, from his spirit, as a fire breaks from wood, or as a flower grows from its soil."

O Captain! My Captain!

Walt Whitman (1819–1892) was born in Long Island, New York, and grew up in Brooklyn. He worked as a printer and journalist in and around New York City. In 1848 he began working on *Leaves of Grass,* a long poem about America. Because of its unusual style, commercial publishers refused to publish it; therefore Whitman printed a first edition with his own money. Since then the style of Whitman's poetry has greatly influenced poets around the world. Whitman's most popular poem is "O Captain! My Captain!," which was inspired by the tragic death of President Lincoln.

Jetliner

Naoshi Koriyama (1926–   ) was born on Kikai Island in the southern part of Japan. He studied at Kagoshima Normal School in Japan, at a foreign language School in Okinawa, and at the University of New Mexico and graduated from the State University of New York at Albany. A member of the Poetry Society of Japan, Koriyama now teaches courses in English and American literature in a Tokyo university. Although his native language is Japanese, he writes some poems, such as "Jetliner," in English.

Figurative language is meant to be interpreted *imaginatively,* not literally. For example, if we write that the sun is like a golden eye, if we call a famous person an institution, or if we say that the summer night seems to whisper—then we are using figurative language.

In "Lyric 17," for example, the poet states that a poem must be "musical as a sea-gull." Poetry is compared with music; but it is beautiful music, music that darts, swoops, and soars. The comparison enables the poet to express this idea in an immediate, brief, and memorable way. This is an example of a particular form of figurative language called a simile. A **simile** is a comparison between two basically unlike things, using the words *like* or *as.*

Two other figures of speech are metaphor and personification. A **metaphor,** like a simile, is a comparison between two things. A metaphor, however, does not use the words *like* or *as* but simply identifies the two things. For example, according to "Lyric 17," a poem "must be a brightness moving." It must *shine,* and it must *move.* This radiance in motion is a metaphor for good poetry.

Personification is a figure of speech in which an animal, idea, or inanimate object is given human characteristics. In "Jetliner," a jet about to take off is personified as an athlete at the start of a race.

Imagery is the use of vivid language to describe people, places, things, and ideas. You must be able to picture in your mind what authors mean by their imagery in order for their writing to be effective.

Look For

As you read the following poems, look for ways that figurative language and imagery create fresh and memorable pictures.

Writing

The writer William Faulkner once wrote: "I would say that music is the easiest means in which to express . . . but since words are my talent, I must try to express clumsily in words what the pure music would have done better." Freewrite about the meaning of this quotation. How does it relate to poetry?

Vocabulary

Knowing the following words will help you as you read these poems.
luminance (lo͞o′ mə nəns) *n.:* Brightness; brilliance (p. 532)
exulting (ig zult′ iŋ) *v.:* Rejoicing (p. 534)
tread (tred) *n.:* Step (p. 534)

Lyric 17

José Garcia Villa

First, a poem must be magical,
Then musical as a sea-gull.
It must be a brightness moving
And hold secret a bird's flowering.
5   It must be slender as a bell,
And it must hold fire as well.
It must have the wisdom of bows
And it must kneel like a rose.
It must be able to hear
10   The luminance of dove and deer.
It must be able to hide
What it seeks, like a bride.
And over all I would like to hover
God, smiling from the poem's cover.

THINKING ABOUT THE SELECTION

Recalling

1. According to the poet, what must a poem be, first of all?
2. List ten other qualities that a poem must have.
3. Where does the poet imagine himself?

Interpreting

4. Look at the qualities the poet names. Which three do you consider the most important? Explain your answer.

Applying

5. The poet Emily Dickinson defined poetry as follows: "If . . . it makes my whole body so cold no fire can warm me, I know that is poetry." Explain the meaning of Dickinson's definition. How would you define poetry?

ANALYZING LITERATURE

Understanding Similes

A **simile** is a comparison between two basically unlike things that uses the word *like* or *as*. For example, José Garcia Villa uses a simile when he writes that a poem must be "Slender as a bell." The simile illustrates similarities between things we do not normally consider similar—a poem and a bell. But, through the simile, we see one way in which a poem and a bell *are* alike. The comparison connects the two things in a new way and extends our appreciation of *both*.

1. What simile occurs in line 2? What is the effect of this simile?
2. Explain the simile in line 8. What is the effect of this simile?
3. Explain the simile in lines 11–12. What is the effect of this simile?

UNDERSTANDING LANGUAGE
Appreciating Diction

José Garcia Villa has chosen his words with great care. For instance, in line 10 he says that a poem should *hear* the "luminance of dove and deer." This word choice is important. Normally, luminance is not something we hear, but *see*. The dove and the deer are quiet creatures that we usually see but do not hear. The poet suggests that true poetry shows us not only how to see, but also how to *hear* even quiet living things in nature.

1. Why do you think the author uses the word *flowering* in line 4?

2. Why do you think the author uses the word *kneel* in line 8?

THINKING AND WRITING
Writing Similes

Think again of your definition of poetry. Following the pattern of Villa's poem, write your own poem explaining the qualities you think poetry must have. Be sure to use similes to help clarify your points. When you revise, check that you have expressed the qualities of poetry in a vivid way. Then proofread your poem and read it aloud to your classmates.

O Captain! My Captain!

Walt Whitman

O Captain! my Captain! our fearful trip is done,
The ship has weather'd every rack,[1] the prize we sought is won,
The port is near, the bells I hear, the people all exulting,
While follow eyes the steady keel,[2] the vessel grim and daring;
5   But O heart! heart! heart!
      O the bleeding drops of red,
        Where on the deck my Captain lies,
        Fallen cold and dead.

O Captain! my Captain! rise up and hear the bells;
10 Rise up—for you the flag is flung—for you the bugle trills,
For you bouquets and ribbon'd wreaths—for you the shores a-crowding,
For you they call, the swaying mass, their eager faces turning;
    Here Captain! dear father!
      This arm beneath your head!
15   It is some dream that on the deck,
        You've fallen cold and dead.

My Captain does not answer, his lips are pale and still,
My father does not feel my arm, he has no pulse nor will,
The ship is anchor'd safe and sound, its voyage closed and done,
20 From fearful trip the victor ship comes in with object won;
    Exult O shores, and ring O bells!
      But I with mournful tread,
        Walk the deck my Captain lies,
        Fallen cold and dead.

---

1. rack *n.*: A great stress.
2. keel *n.*: The chief structural beam extending along the entire length of the bottom of a boat or ship and supporting the frame.

ABRAHAM LINCOLN
William Willard
National Portrait Gallery, Smithsonian Institution

THINKING ABOUT THE SELECTION

Recalling

1. What has happened to the Captain? Why is this event especially unfortunate?
2. What other name does the poet call the Captain?

Interpreting

3. What pronoun does the poet use to modify the world Captain? What is the significance of the pronoun?
4. What effect has the event described in this poem had on the poet? How would you describe the mood of the poem?

Applying

5. Do you think the fate of a nation ever rests entirely on one person? Explain your answer.

ANALYZING LITERATURE

Understanding Metaphors

A **metaphor** is a direct comparison between two unlike things. Throughout "O Captain! My Captain!," Whitman compares President Lincoln to the captain of a ship. The metaphor conveys and reinforces the poet's feelings about President Lincoln—that he was a great leader of the country and a hero.

1. Walt Whitman wrote this poem in response to the assassination of President Lincoln in 1865. If the Captain is a metaphor for Lincoln, explain the metaphor of the ship.
2. What is the "fearful trip" that the ship has "weathered"?
3. Explain why you do or do not think that a ship's captain is an appropriate metaphor for any kind of leader.

Jetliner

Naoshi Koriyama

now he takes his mark
at the very farthest end of the runway
looking straight ahead, eager, intense
with his sharp eyes shining

5   he takes a deep, deep breath
with his powerful lungs
expanding his massive chest
his burning heart beating like thunders

then . . . after a few . . . tense moments . . . of pondering[1]
10   he roars at his utmost
and slowly begins to jog
kicking the dark earth hard
and now he begins to run
kicking the dark earth harder
15   then he dashes, dashes like mad, like mad
howling, shouting, screaming, and roaring

then with a most violent kick
he shakes off the earth's pull
softly lifting himself into the air
20   soaring higher and higher and higher still
piercing the sea of clouds
up into the chandelier[2] of stars

---

1. pondering (pän′ dər iŋ) *n.*: Thinking deeply; considering carefully.
2. chandelier (shan′ də lir′) *n.*: A lighting fixture hanging from a
ceiling, with branches for several candles or electric bulbs.

THINKING ABOUT THE SELECTION

Recalling

1. Where does "he" take his mark? Where does "he" wind up?

Interpreting

2. Interpret lines 9–16. Describe what happened in this stanza. How is this poetic description different from a prose description?

Applying

3. What is it about flight that stirs the imagination? Explain your answer.

ANALYZING LITERATURE

Understanding Personification

Personification is a figure of speech in which an animal, object, or idea is given human qualities. Personification gives us new ways of thinking about things.

Through personification, the poet provides us with a kind of "double vision." We see both a jetliner *and* a runner at the same time. We imagine a great machine in human terms.

1. What are the "sharp eyes shining" in line 4?
2. What are the "powerful lungs" in line 6? What is the "massive chest" in line 7?
3. Find three other examples of figurative language in this poem.

THINKING AND WRITING

Writing About Figurative Language

Review the definitions of figurative language, simile, metaphor, and personification. Be sure you understand the differences between these terms. Choose a simile or a metaphor from "Jetliner," and write an analysis of it. What two things are compared? How does the simile or metaphor add to your appreciation of both elements? Revise, making sure your analysis is clear. Proofread your paper and share it with your classmates.

GUIDE FOR READING

By Morning

May Swenson (1919–   ) was born in Logan, Utah, and attended Utah State University. At the age of thirty, after working as a newspaper reporter, she moved to New York City. There she worked as an editor and lectured at colleges and universities. Swenson's poems have appeared in many magazines including *The New Yorker, Harper's,* and *The Nation.* She has written that enjoyment of poetry is based on our common desire to get through "the curtains of things as they *appear,* to things as they *are.*" "By Morning" is an example of her precise observations of the everyday world.

Reflections Dental

Phyllis McGinley (1905–1978), born in Ontario, Oregon, began writing poetry when she was a schoolteacher in Utah. After several of her poems were accepted by New York magazines, she moved to New Rochelle, New York, to teach and to write. Her early poems were serious and even sad in tone. She turned to lighter subjects only after an editor urged her to avoid "the same sad song all . . . poets sing." *Times Three: Selected Verse from Three Decades, with Seventy New Poems* (1960) is the only book of light verse ever to be awarded the Pulitzer Prize.

Ring Out, Wild Bells

Alfred, Lord Tennyson (1809–1892) was born in Somersby, Lincolnshire, England. Tennyson studied at Cambridge but never received a degree. He was an enthusiastic reader and worked hard to perfect his own craft as a poet. He composed short lyrics as well as longer works, such as *Idylls of the King* (a series of twelve narrative poems based on the King Arthur legends) and *In Memoriam* (a poem in memory of his closest friend Arthur Henry Hallam). In 1850 Lord Tennyson was named poet laureate of England, serving in this capacity for more than forty years.

Imagery is language that appeals to the senses. Imagery is the use of words and phrases to describe something so that a mental picture, or **image,** of it is created in your mind. Most images are visual, but often a writer may use language to suggest how something sounds, smells, tastes, or feels.

Images occur in all forms of writing, but they occur especially in poetry. For example, in "By Morning," May Swenson describes cars as "fumbling sheep." Phyllis McGinley portrays the teeth of television announcers as "rows of hybrid corn." Lord Tennyson evokes the *sound* of "wild bells" ringing "across the snow."

Look For

As you read these poems, keep your eyes open for visual images, but also be aware of imagery that appeals to your other senses. What is the effect of the use of imagery?

Writing

Look out your classroom window. What do you see? What images come to mind? Freewrite about this scene.

Vocabulary

Knowing the following words will help you as you read these poems.

airily (er′ ə lē) *adv.*: Lightly (p. 540)

gracious (grā′ shəs) *adj.*: Here, kind and generous (p. 540)

fleece (flēs) *n.*: Soft, warm covering made of sheep's wool (p. 540)

gleeful (glē′ fəl) *adj.*: Merry (p. 542)

hybrid (hī′ brid) *adj.*: Here, grown from different varieties (p. 542)

crooner (krōōn′ ər) *n.*: Singer (p. 542)

teem (tēm) *v.*: Swarm (p. 542)

strife (strīf) *n.*: Conflict (p. 544)

slander (slan′ dər) *n.*: Lies (p. 544)

By Morning

May Swenson

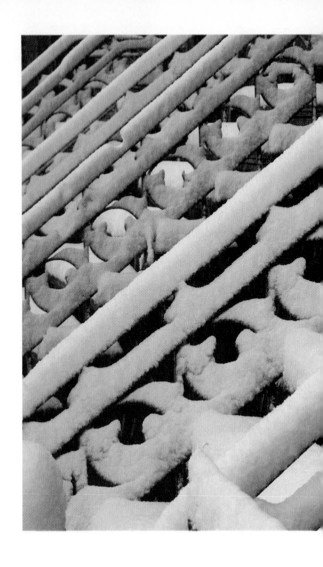

Some for everyone
   plenty

and more coming

Fresh   dainty   airily arriving
5   everywhere at once

Transparent at first
   each faint slice
   slow   soundlessly tumbling

   then quickly thickly a gracious fleece
10   will spread like youth   like wheat
   over the city

Each building will be   a hill
   all sharps made round

   dark worn noisy narrows made still
15   wide   flat   clean   spaces

Streets will be   fields
   cars be   fumbling sheep

A deep bright harvest will be seeded
   in a night

20 By morning we'll be   children
   feeding on manna[1]

   a new loaf on every doorsill

---

1. manna (man′ ə) *n.*: In the Bible, food that was miraculously provided for the Israelites in the wilderness.

THINKING ABOUT THE SELECTION
Recalling

1. Where is this poem set?
2. What will happen to the buildings?
3. What will the streets become?

Interpreting

4. What will arrive "everywhere at once"?
5. Why will sidewalks become "wide flat clean spaces"?
6. What is the poet actually describing?

Applying

7. How are we "children" *every* morning?

ANALYZING LITERATURE
Recognizing and Interpreting Imagery

Imagery can involve senses other than sight. A poet can describe a thing so that it evokes a sound, a smell, a taste, even a feeling (to the touch). Look, for instance, at Swenson's description:

> dark worn noisy narrows made still

The poet imagines city sidewalks at nightfall. Once noisy and crowded, they are now still, empty, quiet. With one image, the poet involves our senses of sight, hearing, and even touch.

1. Find two visual images in the poem.
2. What images of touch and of sound occur?
3. What image of taste and smell occurs?

THINKING AND WRITING
Using Images to Compose a Poem

Recall an experience you have had that stimulated your senses—for example, a movie, a swim, a visit to a zoo. Jot down a list of images related to that experience. Using your list as a reference, compose a poem telling about the experience. When you have finished, make sure you have given a clear picture of your experience. Proofread and share your poem.

Reflections Dental

Phyllis McGinley

How pure, how beautiful, how fine
Do teeth on television shine!
No flutist flutes, no dancer twirls,
But comes equipped with matching pearls.
5 Gleeful announcers all are born
With sets like rows of hybrid corn.
Clowns, critics, clergy, commentators,
Ventriloquists and roller skaters,
M.C.s who beat their palms together,
10 The girl who diagrams the weather,
The crooner crooning for his supper—
All flash white treasures, lower and upper.
With miles of smiles the airwaves teem,
And each an orthodontist's[1] dream.

15 'Twould please my eye as gold a miser's—
One charmer with uncapped incisors.[2]

---

1. orthodontist (ôr′ thə dän′ tist) *n.*: A dentist who
straightens teeth.
2. incisors (in sī′ zərz) *n.*: The front teeth.

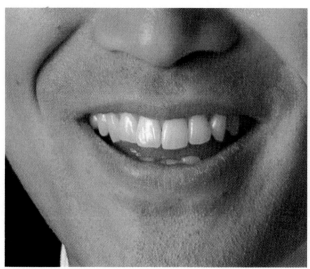
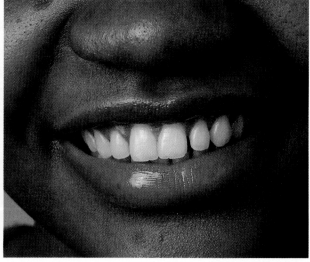

THINKING ABOUT THE SELECTION

Recalling

1. What has the poet observed about people on television?
2. Name three groups of people that the poet mentions.
3. What are two things to which she compares teeth?

Interpreting

4. The poet uses alliteration, the repetition of initial consonant sounds, to help her poke fun at her topic. For example, look at the repetition of the *c* sound in line 7. Find two other examples of alliteration in the poem. Explain how each of these helps create a humorous effect.
5. A *reflection* is usually a serious thinking about or consideration of a topic. Why is the title of this poem humorous?

Applying

6. Why do you think some viewers expect people on television to look perfect?

ANALYZING LITERATURE

Understanding Humorous Images

Images can be humorous in themselves if they are presented or put together in surprising ways. They can also be funny if they are exaggerated. Phyllis McGinley pictures an endless line of gleaming teeth: "miles of smiles." This is both a comical exaggeration and an unusual view of the behavior of television personalities.

1. List two other exaggerations the author uses.
2. What unusual image combinations occur in lines 3 through 6?

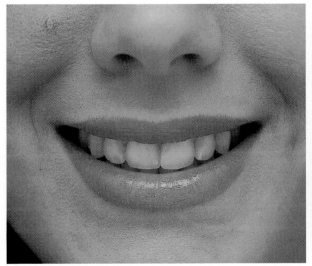
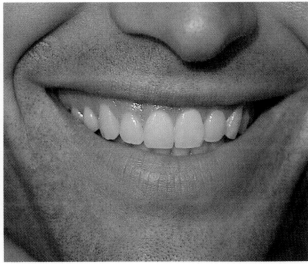

Ring Out, Wild Bells

Alfred, Lord Tennyson

Ring out, wild bells, to the wild sky,
   The flying cloud, the frosty light:
   The year is dying in the night;
Ring out, wild bells, and let him die.

5   Ring out the old, ring in the new,
   Ring, happy bells, across the snow:
   The year is going, let him go;
Ring out the false, ring in the true.

Ring out the grief that saps[1] the mind,
10   For those that here we see no more;
   Ring out the feud of rich and poor,
Ring in redress[2] to all mankind.

Ring out a slowly dying cause,
   And ancient forms of party strife;
15   Ring in the nobler modes[3] of life,
With sweeter manners, purer laws.

Ring out the want, the care, the sin,
   The faithless coldness of the times;
   Ring out, ring out thy mournful rhymes,
20   But ring the fuller minstrel[4] in.

Ring out false pride in place and blood,
   The civic[5] slander and the spite;
   Ring in the love of truth and right,
Ring in the common love of good.

25   Ring out old shapes of foul disease;
   Ring out the narrowing lust of gold;
   Ring out the thousand wars of old,
Ring in the thousand years of peace.

---

1. saps (saps) *v.*: Drains; exhausts.
2. redress (rē′ dres) *n.*: The righting of wrongs.
3. modes (mōdz) *n.*: Ways; forms.
4. fuller minstrel (min′ strəl) *n.*: A singer of the highest rank.
5. civic (siv′ ik) *adj.*: Of a city.

THINKING ABOUT THE SELECTION

Recalling

1. This poem celebrates the new year. What does the poet wish to "ring out"? What does he wish to "ring in"?

Interpreting

2. How does the poet seem to feel about the past? Support your answer.
3. What does he hope for the future? Support your answer.
4. What is this poem about in addition to the passing of the old year? What is its theme?
5. Would you describe this poem as sad and pessimistic, or hopeful and optimistic? Find details to support your answer.

Applying

6. Why does the start of a new year often make people feel hopeful?

THINKING AND WRITING

Writing a Patterned Poem

Write a poem that expresses your wishes for the new year. Begin by rereading all or part of "Ring Out, Wild Bells." Take note of the *pattern* of Tennyson's poem, especially the way every negative thing is balanced by something positive. Compose two or three stanzas following Tennyson's example. Tell what you would like to "ring out" and "ring in." After you have finished, read over your stanzas and make any corrections or improvements you feel are needed. Share your poem with your classmates.

The Secret Heart

Robert P. Tristram Coffin (1892–1955) was born in Brunswick, Maine, grew up on a farm, and got his early education in a rural schoolhouse. He attended Bowdoin College in Maine, Princeton University in New Jersey, and Oxford University in England. His poems often portray life on a farm or along the seacoast in Maine. Coffin illustrated many of his own books, including *Strange Holiness,* for which he won a Pulitzer Prize in 1936. Like many of Coffin's poems, "The Secret Heart" portrays the good in the world by describing the devoted love of a parent for his child.

Advice to a Girl

Sara Teasdale (1884–1933) was born in St. Louis, Missouri, and was educated at home and in private schools. Later she traveled extensively both in the United States and abroad. Teasdale's poetry was praised by critics and enjoyed by the public. In 1918 she won a Pulitzer Prize for a collection of poems entitled *Love Songs.* Generally, Teasdale's poems are short, graceful, and intense. She spent her last years in New York City, where her poems became simpler, more passionate, and deeply personal.

Taught Me Purple

Evelyn Tooley Hunt (1904–   ) was born in Hamburg, New York. In 1926 she graduated from William Smith College in Geneva, New York, where she had been an editor of the literary magazine. She received the Sidney Lanier Memorial Award for her first collection of poems, *Look Again, Adam,* published in 1961. Hunt's interest in different cultures is demonstrated in her writing. She is best known for her variations of haiku, a type of Asian poetry, which she writes under the pen name of Tao-Li. In "Taught Me Purple," Hunt writes of the lessons learned from a mother.

Symbols

A **symbol** is any person, place, or thing that has a meaning in itself and that also *stands for* something else. A symbol can be another living thing, an object, a situation, or an action. Usually symbols stand for ideas or qualities. You are probably familiar with certain common symbols: a flag symbolizing a nation; a dove symbolizing peace; the five interlocking rings (each ring symbolizing a continent) symbolizing the Olympic Games.

Symbols are a kind of figurative language. Like simile, metaphor, and personification, a symbol enables a writer to express a complicated idea or a deep feeling in few words, sometimes in a single image. For example, "The Secret Heart" begins with the image of a lighted match held between two hands in the dark. In the course of the poem, that image is gradually developed into a symbol of love.

Look For

As you read these poems, look for images, objects, situations, and places that might be symbolic. Think first about the literal meaning of what is being described. Then consider the overall mood and meaning of the poem. What might the object represent? In what way does it relate to the theme of the poem?

Writing

Choose a symbol with which you are familiar. The symbol may be one that represents a place, a holiday, a product, or an idea. Freewrite for five minutes about what the symbol you have chosen means.

Vocabulary

Knowing the following words will help you as you read these poems.

sire (sīr) *n.:* Father (p. 548)

kindled (kin′ d'ld) *v.:* Ignited (p. 548)

semblance (sem′ bləns) *n.:* Likeness; image (p. 548)

tenement (ten′ ə mənt) *n.:* Here, a rundown apartment building (p. 551)

molding (mōl′ diŋ) *n.:* Ornamental woodwork that projects from the walls of a room (p. 551)

The Secret Heart

Robert P. Tristram Coffin

Across the years he could recall
His father one way best of all.

In the stillest hour of night
The boy awakened to a light.

5   Half in dreams, he saw his sire
With his great hands full of fire.

The man had struck a match to see
If his son slept peacefully.

He held his palms each side the spark
10 His love had kindled in the dark.

His two hands were curved apart
In the semblance of a heart.

He wore, it seemed to his small son,
A bare heart on his hidden one,

15 A heart that gave out such a glow
No son awake could bear to know.

It showed a look upon a face
Too tender for the day to trace.

One instant, it lit all about,
20 And then the secret heart went out.

But it shone long enough for one
To know that hands held up the sun.

THINKING ABOUT THE SELECTION

Recalling

1. How does the boy best recall his father?
2. Why does the father strike a match? Where does he hold the match?

Interpreting

3. What do the two hands holding the flame seem to be? Is this image effective? Explain.
4. What do lines 16 and 18 mean?
5. Interpret the last two lines of the poem.

Applying

6. We say love fills us with warmth and unfriendliness leaves us feeling cold. Why are the sensations of warmth and cold appropriate for discussing love and unfriendliness?

ANALYZING LITERATURE

Interpreting Symbols Carefully

A symbol may mean something particular to the poet but not to everyone. Therefore it is important to think about a symbol in context (the words and ideas that surround it). For example, the image of "hands full of fire" could stand for many things. In "The Secret Heart," it becomes, for the boy, a symbol of his father's love.

1. How do the hands become a symbol of love?
2. In the last line, what does the sun symbolize?
3. Explain the meaning of the title of the poem.

Advice to a Girl

Sara Teasdale

No one worth possessing
Can be quite possessed;
Lay that on your heart,
My young angry dear;
5   This truth, this hard and precious stone,
Lay it on your hot cheek,
Let it hide your tear.
Hold it like a crystal
When you are alone
10   And gaze in the depths of the icy stone.
Long, look long and you will be blessed:
No one worth possessing
Can be quite possessed.

THINKING ABOUT THE SELECTION

Recalling

1. What is the advice the poet gives the girl?
2. To what does the poet compare the "truth"?
3. What does the poet tell the girl to do with the advice?

Interpreting

4. Why might the poet's "truth" be both precious and hard?
5. How do you think the girl is feeling? Support your answer with details from the poem.
6. Why do you think the poet begins and ends the poem with her words of advice?

Applying

7. Explain why you do or do not agree with the poet's advice.

THINKING AND WRITING

Paraphrasing a Poem

An effective way to clarify a poem for yourself is to **paraphrase** it—that is, restate it in your own words. You must be careful to paraphrase both accurately and *completely*. Reread "Advice to a Girl." Imagine that you are the speaker. Rewrite, or paraphrase, the poem as if you were writing a letter to a close friend. After you have finished, compare your letter with the poem to make sure you have paraphrased accurately and thoroughly. Proofread your letter and share it with your classmates.

Taught Me Purple

Evelyn Tooley Hunt

My mother taught me purple
    Although she never wore it.
Wash-gray was her circle,
    The tenement her orbit.

5   My mother taught me golden
    And held me up to see it,
Above the broken molding,
    Beyond the filthy street.

My mother reached for beauty
10   And for its lack she died,
Who knew so much of duty
    She could not teach me pride.

SUMMER MILLINERY, 1915
Charles W. Hawthorne
Chrysler Museum

THINKING ABOUT THE SELECTION

Recalling

1. What two things does the poet say her mother taught her?
2. What lack causes the mother to die?

Interpreting

3. The colors purple, gray, and golden are used in this poem. What does each color symbolize?
4. Compare and contrast the mother's surroundings with her goals.
5. Why could the mother not teach the daughter pride?
6. What is the theme of this poem?

Applying

7. We often use colors to symbolize qualities. What does the color red usually symbolize? Why is this symbol effective?

THINKING AND WRITING

Writing About Symbolism

Write an essay analyzing the use of symbols in "Taught Me Purple." First think of the meaning of the symbols. Then consider their effect on the theme. Write a first draft of your essay. When you revise, make sure your analysis is clear and well organized. Proofread your essay and share it with your classmates.

Lyric Poetry

INVITATION TO THE SIDESHOW, (LA PARADE)
Georges Pierre Seurat
The Metropolitan Museum of Art

Four Little Foxes

Lew Sarett (1888–1954) first began working at age twelve to support his family in Chicago. It was then that he developed a love for nature, which is shown in poems like "Four Little Foxes." Among those who encouraged him to write poetry was Carl Sandburg. Some of Sarett's poems echo the rhythms of Native American music and folklore. "Much of whatever is joyous and significant in life, timeless, true, and peculiarly American," he wrote, "tends to be rooted in the wild earth of America.".

Harlem Night Song

Langston Hughes (1902–1967) was the first black American to earn his living as a writer and public speaker. Hughes was part of the Harlem Renaissance of the 1920's—a period of intense creativity among black writers and artists living in the northern part of New York City. In his poems, short stories, and songs, Hughes wrote about the sorrows and joys of ordinary black people. "Harlem Night Song" shows how Hughes incorporated some aspects of black music, especially jazz themes, into his songs and poems.

Blue-Butterfly Day

Robert Frost (1874–1963) was an unofficial poet laureate of the United States. Born in San Francisco, he moved to New England at age ten. He did not attend college, but worked in a Massachusetts textile mill and began writing poetry. Frost's poetry was awarded the Pulitzer Prize four times. He read his poem "The Gift Outright" at the 1961 inauguration of President John F. Kennedy. In poems like "Blue-Butterfly Day," Frost deals with the relationship between human beings and nature.

For My Sister Molly Who in the Fifties

Alice Walker (1944–   ), the youngest of eight children, grew up in Georgia, where her parents were sharecroppers. Her novel *The Color Purple* is based on true stories about her great-grandmother and on research Walker did at Spelman College. Besides being active in the civil rights movement in the 1960's Walker has written works that deal with black heritage. This interest can be seen in "For My Sister Molly Who in the Fifties," which is from *Revolutionary Petunias and Other Poems.*

Lyric Poetry

Lyric poetry is poetry that expresses the poet's thoughts and feelings. It does not tell a story, as narrative poetry does, but creates a mood through vivid images—or pictures—descriptive words, and the musical quality of the lines. These means of creating mood help you remember the poet's thoughts and feelings, and "see" or "hear" the image the poet presents. Lyric poems may be made up of regular stanzas, like "Four Little Foxes," or they may have uneven stanzas, like "Harlem Night Song."

Originally, a lyric was a poem that was sung and accompanied by a lyre; today, lyric poetry reflects this musical heritage.

Look For

As you read these four poems, "see" the images and "hear" their musical quality. What is each poem about? What feelings does each poem arouse about its topic?

Writing

Many lyric poems use images, or pictures, from nature. These images may help create a mood, or show the poet's attitude toward nature or the relationship between people and nature. For example, the image of fresh snow on pine trees in winter may call up a peaceful feeling about nature. List five of your own vivid images of nature. They may appeal to the sense of sight, sound, smell, taste, or feeling.

Vocabulary

Knowing the following words will help you as you read these poems.
forbear (fôr ber') v.: To refrain from (p. 556)

suckled (suk' 'ld) v.: Sucked at the breast (p. 556)

rampant (ram' pənt) adj.: Violent and uncontrollable (p. 556)

Four Little Foxes

Lew Sarett

Speak gently, Spring, and make no sudden sound;
For in my windy valley, yesterday I found
New-born foxes squirming on the ground—
    Speak gently.

5 Walk softly, March, forbear the bitter blow;
Her feet within a trap, her blood upon the snow,
The four little foxes saw their mother go—
    Walk softly.

Go lightly, Spring, oh, give them no alarm;
10 When I covered them with boughs to shelter them from harm,
The thin blue foxes suckled at my arm—
    Go lightly.

Step softly, March, with your rampant hurricane;
Nuzzling one another, and whimpering with pain,
15 The new little foxes are shivering in the rain—
    Step softly.

THINKING ABOUT THE SELECTION

Recalling

1. What happened to the newborn foxes' mother?
2. What does the poet do to protect the foxes?

Interpreting

3. To what two things does the phrase "bitter blow" in line 5 refer?
4. Why does the poet plead with nature rather than with people to protect the animals?

5. What two kinds of relationships between people and nature are presented in the poem?

Applying

6. What is it about helpless creatures that makes us want to protect them? What other helpless creatures arouse strong protective feelings in people?

ANALYZING LITERATURE

Understanding Lyric Poetry

Lyric poetry expresses the poet's thoughts and feelings about a topic through vivid images and musical language.

In "Four Little Foxes," the phrase "The thin blue foxes suckled at my arm—" creates the vivid image of helpless creatures so hungry that they turn to a stranger's arm for milk.

1. What feeling does the image "Her feet within a trap, her blood upon the snow" suggest?
2. What is the effect of the repetition of such phrases as "Speak gently"?
3. What seems to be the poet's feelings or attitude about the foxes, who are "Nuzzling one another, and whimpering with pain"? What feelings do you think the poet wants to stir up in readers? Explain your answer.

Harlem Night Song

Langston Hughes

Come,
Let us roam the night together
Singing.

I love you.

5   Across
The Harlem[1] roof-tops
Moon is shining.
Night sky is blue.
Stars are great drops
10 Of golden dew.

Down the street
A band is playing.

I love you.

Come,
15 Let us roam the night together
Singing.

---

1. Harlem (här′ ləm) *n*.: Section of New York City, in the northern part of Manhattan.

THINKING ABOUT THE SELECTION

Recalling

1. What invitation does the poet give the friend?

Interpreting

2. What feeling do short lines give the poem?
3. Why does the speaker feel full of life?

Applying

4. Elizabeth Bowen wrote: "When you love someone all your saved up wishes start coming out." Do you agree that love makes people feel generous? Explain your answer.

CRITICAL THINKING AND READING

Making Inferences About Mood

An **inference about mood** is a reasonable conclusion you can draw about the overall feeling of a poem, based on clues.

Find three details that suggest a joyful mood.

Blue-Butterfly Day

Robert Frost

It is blue-butterfly day here in spring,
And with these sky-flakes down in flurry on flurry
There is more unmixed color on the wing
Than flowers will show for days unless they hurry.

5   But these are flowers that fly and all but sing:
And now from having ridden out desire
They lie closed over in the wind and cling
Where wheels have freshly sliced the April mire.[1]

---

1. mire (mīr) *n.*: Deep mud.

THINKING ABOUT THE SELECTION

Recalling

1. In what season does the poem take place?
2. What happens to the butterflies at the end of the poem?

Interpreting

3. To what does the poet compare the butterflies in line 2? Why is this comparison especially appropriate for New England in the early part of this season?
4. In what way are the butterflies also like birds? In what way are they like flowers?
5. What is suggested by the last two lines of the poem? What contrast do you find between the beginning of the poem and the end?

Applying

6. The poet describes the butterflies as "flowers that fly and all but sing." How else might you describe butterflies?

THINKING AND WRITING

Writing a Lyric Poem

"Blue-Butterfly Day" is a lyric poem about spring. The images of the color and movement of the butterflies, the descriptive language, and the musical quality suggest a mood of quiet, thoughtful delight.

Choose one of the other seasons and write a lyric poem about it. Describe what mood you would like to create in your poem. Then freewrite about the season, including descriptive words and phrases that create the mood you have chosen and that express your thoughts and feelings. Use this information to write a lyric poem. When you revise, make sure you have maintained a consistent mood. Proofread your poem and share it with your classmates.

For My Sister Molly Who in the Fifties

Alice Walker

Once made a fairy rooster from
Mashed potatoes
Whose eyes I forget
But green onions were his tail
5   And his two legs were carrot sticks
A tomato slice his crown.
Who came home on vacation
When the sun was hot
and cooked
10 and cleaned
And minded least of all
The children's questions
A million or more
Pouring in on her
15 Who had been to school
And knew (and told us too) that certain
Words were no longer good
And taught me not to say us for we
No matter what "Sonny said" up the
20 road.

FOR MY SISTER MOLLY WHO IN THE FIFTIES.
Knew Hamlet well and read into the night
And coached me in my songs of Africa
A continent I never knew
25 But learned to love
Because "they" she said could carry
A tune
And spoke in accents never heard
In Eatonton.[1]
30 Who read from *Prose and Poetry*
And loved to read "Sam McGee from Tennessee"
On nights the fire was burning low

---

1. Eatonton (ēt'n tən): A town in Georgia.

And Christmas wrapped in angel hair[2]
And I for one prayed for snow.

35 WHO IN THE FIFTIES
Knew all the written things that made
Us laugh and stories by
The hour   Waking up the story buds
Like fruit. Who walked among the flowers
40 And brought them inside the house
And smelled as good as they
And looked as bright.
Who made dresses, braided
Hair. Moved chairs about
45 Hung things from walls
Ordered baths
Frowned on wasp bites
And seemed to know the endings
Of all the tales
50 I had forgot.

---

2. angel hair: Fine, white, filmy Christmas tree decoration.

THINKING ABOUT THE SELECTION

Recalling

1. How does Molly act as a teacher to the children? Find three works she enjoys reading.
2. How does Molly take care of the house? How does she take care of the children?

Interpreting

3. Explain the title of this poem.
4. How does Molly reveal her creative spirit? How does she awaken the creative spirit in the children?
5. How do you know that being away at school has not separated Molly from the children?

6. What adjectives would you use to describe Molly?
7. What do the last three lines of the poem suggest about Molly?
8. How do you think the speaker feels about her sister Molly?

Applying

9. Think of a character in another work of literature who seems most like Molly. Explain how these characters are alike.
10. Think of an area in which you have expertise or experience. How might you interest a friend in this area?

Silver

Walter de la Mare (1873–1956), British poet and novelist, attended St. Paul's Cathedral Choir School in London. After graduation, for eighteen years he worked as a clerk; later a government grant allowed him to write full time. De la Mare believed that the world beyond human experience could best be understood through the imagination. His poems often stress the magical and the mysterious, as does "Silver," an enchanted look at a moonlit night.

Forgotten Language

Shel Silverstein (1932–   ) is a writer of children's books, a cartoonist, a folk singer, a composer, and an author of a one-act play, "The Lady or the Tiger" (1981). The critic William Cole has said that Silverstein's poems are "tender, funny, sentimental, philosophical, and ridiculous in turn, and they're for all ages." Youngsters delight in his poem's playful images, while older readers appreciate his observations about growing up. In "Forgotten Language" Silverstein vividly captures the magical moment called childhood.

Blow, Blow, Thou Winter Wind

William Shakespeare (1564–1616) was born in Stratford-upon-Avon, England. At eighteen he married Anne Hathaway; they had three children. In London he joined the Lord Chamberlain's Company, which performed plays at the Globe Theatre. Shakespeare wrote plays and poems that are among the best in the English language. They endure through the years because of his insight into human nature, his ability to lighten the tragic with the humorous, and his portrayal of kings and scoundrels with equal understanding. "Blow, Blow, Thou Winter Wind" is from his play *As You Like It*.

Sound Devices

Sound devices contribute to the musical quality of a poem. Including alliteration and repetition, sound devices are most noticeable when a poem is read aloud.

Alliteration is the repetition of a consonant at the beginning of words. For example, the phrase "casements catch" in "Silver" repeats the "k" sound at the beginning of each word.

There are various types of **repetition** in poetry. Parallel structure is the repetition of a grammatical structure. In "Forgotten Language" several of the beginning phrases, such as "Once I spoke," "Once I understood," are in parallel form. Like other sound devices, the repetition emphasizes the musical quality of the poem.

Look For

As you read the following three poems, look for alliteration and parallel structure. What effect does the use of these sound devices have on the poems?

Writing

Alliteration can add punch to ordinary speech as well as to poetry. "Pots and pans" and "sweet and sour" are examples of alliterative pairs of words used in everyday language. List other examples of alliteration that you hear or use in conversation.

Vocabulary

Knowing the following words will help you as you read these poems.

shoon (shoon) *n.*: Old-fashioned word for *shoes* (p. 564)

keen (kēn) *adj.*: Having a sharp cutting edge (p. 566)

feigning (fān'iŋ) *v.*: Making a false show of (p. 566)

Silver

Walter de la Mare

Slowly, silently, now the moon
Walks the night in her silver shoon;[1]
This way, and that, she peers, and sees
Silver fruit upon silver trees;
5 One by one the casements catch
Her beams beneath the silvery thatch;
Couched in his kennel, like a log,
With paws of silver sleeps the dog;
From their shadowy coat the white breasts peep
10 Of doves in a silver-feathered sleep;
A harvest mouse goes scampering by,
With silver claws, and silver eye;
And moveless fish in the water gleam,
By silver reeds in a silver stream.

---

1. shoon (sho͞on) *n.*: Old-fashioned word for "shoes."

THINKING ABOUT THE SELECTION

Recalling

1. At what time does this poem take place?
2. Name three human activities the moon does.
3. Describe the "silver" scene.
4. What is the only animal that moves in the poem? What do the other animals do?

Interpreting

5. Describe the effect of the moon's walk.
6. Find four details that create a picture of stillness. What mood is created by this?
7. In what way does the poem seem magical?

Applying

8. Find three other examples of "magic" in na-ture. Explain the reason for your choices.

ANALYZING LITERATURE

Understanding Alliteration

Alliteration, the repetition of consonants at the beginning of words, is one sound device poets use to heighten the musical quality of their work. The repetition of the sounds is especially striking when the poem is recited aloud. Read "Silver" aloud before answering the following questions.

1. Find two examples of alliteration in lines 1–2.
2. Find three other examples in the poem of the repetition of the sound of *s*.
3. What effect is created by the repetition of the sound of *s*?

Forgotten Language

Shel Silverstein

Once I spoke the language of the flowers,
Once I understood each word the caterpillar said,
Once I smiled in secret at the gossip of the starlings,[1]
And shared a conversation with the housefly
    in my bed.
5 Once I heard and answered all the questions
    of the crickets,
And joined the crying of each falling dying
    flake of snow,
Once I spoke the language of the flowers . . .
      How did it go?
      How did it go?

"FORGOTTEN LANGUAGE" *(Text only)*
from Where the Sidewalk Ends: The Poems & Drawings of Shel Silverstein.
Copyright © 1974 by Snake Eye Music, Inc. Reprinted by permission of Harper & Row, Publishers, Inc.

---

1. starlings (stär′ liŋs) *n.*: Dark-colored birds with short tails, long wings, and a sharp, pointed bill.

THINKING ABOUT THE SELECTION

Recalling

1. Name six languages from nature the poet once "understood."

Interpreting

2. When do you think the events in the poem took place?
3. Why are the snowflakes "crying"?
4. Explain the meaning of the lines "How did it go?" How would you answer this question?

Applying

5. In "Forgotten Language," the poet says that once he understood the language of flowers and animals. What other things might people forget as they grow older?

ANALYZING LITERATURE

Understanding Parallel Structure

Parallel structure is the repetition of a grammatical structure that allows the poet to emphasize important ideas and add to the musical quality of the poem. For example, the repetition of "Once I spoke," and "Once I understood," emphasizes the idea of time past.

1. Name the other beginning phrases that are in parallel form with "Once I spoke."
2. Which lines are not in parallel form with "Once I spoke"? Why do you think the poet chose to begin these lines in a different way?

Blow, Blow, Thou Winter Wind

William Shakespeare

Blow, blow, thou winter wind.
Thou art not so unkind
  As man's ingratitude.
Thy tooth is not so keen,
5   Because thou art not seen,
  Although thy breath be rude.[1]
Heigh-ho! Sing, heigh-ho! unto the green holly.
Most friendship is feigning, most loving mere folly.
  Then, heigh-ho, the holly!
10   This life is most jolly.

Freeze, freeze, thou bitter sky,
That dost not bite so nigh
  As benefits forgot.
Though thou the waters warp,[2]
15   Thy sting is not so sharp
  As friend remembered not.
Heigh-ho! Sing, heigh-ho! unto the green holly.
Most friendship is feigning, most loving mere folly.
  Then, heigh-ho, the holly!
20   This life is most jolly.

---

1. rude *adj.*: Rough, harsh.
2. warp *v.*: Freeze.

TRÈS RICHES HEURES DU DUC DE BERRY: FEBRUARY
Chantilly—Musée Conde
Giraudon/Art Resource

THINKING ABOUT THE SELECTION

Recalling

1. What is more unkind than the winter wind? Why is the wind's "tooth . . . not so keen"?
2. What does the poet think of friendship? What does the poet think of love?
3. What is sharper than the sting of the bitter sky?

Interpreting

4. Explain what the poem suggests about the harshness of nature compared to the pain of human relationships?
5. Keeping in mind the poet's views of human relationships, what do the phrases "Sing, heigh-ho!" and "This life is most jolly" tell you about the poet's attitude?

Applying

6. Do you agree with the poet that ingratitude is painful? Explain your answer.

GUIDE FOR READING

Hog Calling

Morris Bishop (1893–1973) was born in Willard, New York, and lived most of his life in Ithaca, New York. He attended Cornell University and went on to teach there from 1921 to 1973. Bishop translated plays by Molière and edited numerous collections of short stories. His diverse writings include histories, critical biographies, and light verse such as "Hog Calling."

I Raised a Great Hullabaloo

Anonymous. No one knows for sure how limericks came into being. It is believed that they were originally passed down by word of mouth.

Limerick

A **limerick** is a kind of light or humorous verse. Limericks follow a pattern. Generally, every limerick has five lines: three long lines (the first, second, and fifth) that rhyme with each other, and two short lines (the third and fourth) that rhyme. The lines also follow a particular rhythm. Each of the three long lines has three accented, or stressed, syllables; each of the two short lines has two stressed syllables. The purpose of most limericks is to make you laugh.

Look For

As you read these limericks, look for what they have in common. Why do they make you laugh?

Writing

Recall a comical incident that you recently observed or experienced. What made it funny? Freewrite about what happened.

Vocabulary

Knowing the following words will help you as you read these limericks.

meets (mētz) *n.*: A series of races or competitions held during a period of days at a certain place (p. 569)

applaud (ə plôd′) *v.*: To show approval or enjoyment by clapping the hands or by cheering (p. 569)

awed (ôd) *v.*: A mixed feeling of reverence, fear, and wonder (p. 569)

appalling (ə pôl′ iŋ) *adj.*: Causing horror or shock (p. 569)

Two Limericks

A bull-voiced young fellow of Pawling
Competes in the meets for hog-calling;
   The people applaud,
   And the judges are awed,
But the hogs find it simply appalling.

Morris Bishop

I raised a great hullabaloo[1]
When I found a large mouse in my stew,
   Said the waiter, "Don't shout
   And wave it about,
Or the rest will be wanting one, too!"

Anonymous

---

1. hullabaloo (hul′ ə bə lōō′) *n.:* Loud noise and confusion; hubbub.

THINKING ABOUT THE SELECTION
Recalling

1. In "I Raised a Great Hullabaloo," what does the speaker find in his stew?
2. What does the "young fellow" in "Hog Calling" do?

Interpreting

3. In "I Raised a Great Hullabaloo," how does the waiter's reply show cleverness and presence of mind?
4. Contrast the responses of the people and the judges with those of the hogs in "Hog Calling."

Applying

5. Humorists have a talent for looking at the everyday and seeing the ridiculous. Allow yourself to be silly for a few minutes. What would be ridiculous about an everyday bowl of soup? What could be ridiculous about a person with a beard? What could be ridiculous about a bath tub?

ANALYZING LITERATURE
Understanding Limericks

Limericks are meant to be funny, even foolish. Their writers observe, then poke good-natured fun at, human weaknesses and silly behavior. Generally, the humor of a limerick is delivered in a kind of "punch line"—a surprising and comical twist that comes at the end.

1. Explain the comical twist at the end of "Hog Calling."
2. What is surprising about the last line of "I Raised a Great Hullabaloo"?

THINKING AND WRITING
Writing a Limerick

Now that you are in a silly mood, choose a topic for a limerick. A good way to start a limerick is to introduce a character by name: for example, "There once was a fellow named Mo." When you revise your limerick, make sure you have followed the correct pattern. Share your completed limerick with your classmates.

Facets of Nature

SHADOWS OF EVENING, 1921-23
Rockwell Kent
Collection of Whitney Museum of American Art

GUIDE FOR READING

Haiku

Matsuo Bashō (1644–1694) of Japan is generally regarded as the greatest of all haiku poets. At the age of eight, he entered the service of a nobleman in Iga, in southern Japan. There he is believed to have composed his first poem when he was only nine. Later he lived for a time in a monastery. By the age of thirty, he had founded a school for the study of haiku, and he was revered as a master of the art. **Moritake** (1452–1540) was a priest as well as one of the leading Japanese poets of the sixteenth century.

Haiku

Haiku is a special type of poetry from Japan. A haiku consists of seventeen syllables arranged in three lines. The first line has five syllables, the second has seven, and the third has five. Haiku developed from an older thirty-one-syllable form, but it became an independent form in the latter part of the sixteenth century. It has remained the most popular of Japanese poetic forms.

Generally in a haiku, the poet describes a fleeting moment in nature—usually something he has observed and that has moved him. Through the haiku's simple image or series of images, the poet tries to arouse in the reader the same sensation that he experienced.

Look For

As you read each haiku, keep in mind that a haiku is a kind of "snapshot": an attempt to capture a fleeting moment of beauty in nature. Visualize, or picture, these two "snapshots." What is the poet describing? What emotion is he capturing?

Writing

List some scenes in nature that stay in your memory. Choose one and freewrite about how you felt and thought when you were in those surroundings.

Vocabulary

Haiku uses seemingly simple words that suggest vivid images, as do the following words from the haiku by Bashō.
slashing (slash'iŋ) *v.*: Cutting with a sweeping stroke (p. 573)
screech (skrēch) *n.*: A shrill, high-pitched shriek or sound (p. 573)

Two Haiku

The lightning flashes!
And slashing through the darkness,
A night-heron's[1] screech.
          Bashō

The falling flower
I saw drift back to the branch
Was a butterfly.
          Moritake

---

1. night-heron (nīt′ her′ ən) *n.*: A large wading bird with a long neck and long legs that is active at night.

Japanese Lacquered Box (19th century)
Inside Top Cover (detail)
The Metropolitan Museum of Art

THINKING ABOUT THE SELECTION

Recalling

1. What is the subject in the haiku by Bashō?
2. What is the subject in the haiku by Moritake?

Interpreting

3. How does the image in Bashō's haiku change by the third line?
4. How does the image in Moritake's haiku change by the third line?

Applying

5. Choose one of these two haiku and another poem about nature in this book. Compare and contrast the two views of nature. For example, you might compare and contrast Bashō's haiku with Frost's "Blue-Butterfly Day."

THINKING AND WRITING

Writing a Haiku

A haiku presents a moment in nature. It has three lines with five syllables in the first line, seven syllables in the second line, and five syllables in the third line.

Choose one of your freewritten impressions and observations about nature. Try to communicate your impression in a single image or two. Write a haiku to describe the image. As you write, keep in mind the emotion or sensation you felt. Try to involve at least two of your senses. Revise your haiku, making sure you have followed the correct form for a haiku. Proofread it and prepare a final draft that you illustrate. Place your illustrated haiku on the bulletin board.

GUIDE FOR READING

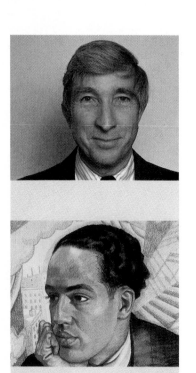

January

John Updike (1932–   ) was born in Shillington, Pennsylvania. In 1954 he graduated from Harvard, where he won numerous writing honors, and then studied art in England for a year. From 1955 to 1957 he was a cartoonist and staff writer for *The New Yorker,* where many of his short stories appeared. Also a distinguished essayist and respected poet, Updike is well known for such novels as *Rabbit Run* (1960) and *Rabbit Redux* (1971). In "January" he uses stark language to portray the coldness of a winter day.

Winter Moon

Langston Hughes (1902–1967) was born in Joplin, Missouri, and grew up in Lincoln, Illinois, and Cleveland, Ohio. He left Columbia University after a year to travel and write. In 1925 he met the poet Vachel Lindsay, who helped Hughes publish his first poetry collection, *The Weary Blues* (1926). Hughes also wrote two autobiographical works and humorous sketches about black city life called *The Best of Simple* (1961). "Winter Moon" depicts the moon as it might appear on a city night.

Song of the Sky Loom

The **Tewa Indians** were among the many Native Americans who flourished on the North American continent before the first European explorers arrived. The Tewa expressed their close relationship with nature through poetry. Native American poetry, like "Song of the Sky Loom," was not written; rather, it was chanted or sung along with music, dance, and colorful costumes. Native Americans believed this kind of poetry had magical power, and they performed it hoping to cause some good for the community.

New World

N. Scott Momaday (1934–   ), a Kiowa Indian, was born in Lawton, Oklahoma. His parents were teachers. Momaday was educated on Indian reservations and in 1952 entered the University of New Mexico. Today he is professor of English at Stanford University, California. He is best known for *The Way to Rainy Mountain* (1969). In 1968 his novel *House Made of Dawn* was awarded the Pulitzer Prize. In poems like "New World," Momaday reveals the Native American's rapport with nature.

Sensory language, or language that appeals to the senses—sight, hearing, smell, touch, and taste—is an important part of any kind of descriptive writing. A description of the visible features of a landscape, of a sound (or of a silence), of the taste or smell of an exotic food, of the way a fabric feels—all these involve the writer's use of sensory language.

For example, in "January" John Updike gives you images of "Fat snowy footsteps" and "trees of lace," word pictures that appeal to your sense of sight. N. Scott Momaday imagines winds that "lean upon mountains" and foxes that "stiffen in cold," images that appeal to your sense of touch. These examples of sensory language are used to create pictures in your imagination and help you experience what the poet describes.

Look For

As you read these poems, experience the poets' sensory language. Remember that an image, though usually visual, can also engage your senses of hearing, smell, taste, and touch. Look for words and phrases that appeal to the different senses. How do these poems make you feel—cold, wind-tossed, hungry, etc.?

Writing

Recall an experience in nature. Where were you? What do you remember seeing, hearing, smelling, tasting, and touching? Freewrite about the sensory impressions you remember from that experience.

Vocabulary

Knowing the following words will help you as you read these poems.

fittingly (fit' iŋ lē) adv.: Properly (p. 579)

glistens (glis' 'nz) v.: Shines (p. 580)

borne (bôrn) v.: Carried (p. 580)

low (lō) v.: Make the typical sound that a cow makes (p. 580)

hie (hī) v.: Hurry (p. 580)

recede (ri sēd') v.: Move farther away (p. 581)

January

John Updike

The days are short,
  The sun a spark
Hung thin between
  The dark and dark.

5 Fat snowy footsteps
   Track the floor.
Milk bottles burst
  Outside the door.

The river is
10 A frozen place
Held still beneath
  The trees of lace.

The sky is low.
  The wind is gray.
15 The radiator
  Purrs all day.

WINTER TWILIGHT NEAR ALBANY, NEW YORK, 1858
George Henry Boughton
Courtesy of The New York Historical Society

THINKING ABOUT THE SELECTION
Recalling

1. How does Updike describe the sun?
2. What happens to the milk bottles? Why?
3. What image of the river is delicate?
4. How does the poet describe the sky?
5. What sound fills the air at the poem's end?

Interpreting

6. Explain the image "dark and dark" in line 4.
7. Why do the trees appear to be made of "lace"?
8. Why did Updike write such short lines?

Applying

9. The poet uses the color gray to describe wind in winter. What colors do you associate with the other seasons? Explain your choices.

ANALYZING LITERATURE
Recognizing Sensory Language

"January" gives the poet's impressions of the month. For example, he refers to the sun as "a spark/ Hung thin . . ." This image of the sun as a mere spark barely hanging in the sky between morning and night expresses the poet's feeling.

1. To what sense does "purrs all day" appeal?
2. What does "fat snowy footsteps" mean?
3. To what senses does the last stanza appeal?
4. What impression do you form from this poem?

THINKING AND WRITING
Using Sensory Language

List impressions of your favorite month. Include impressions experienced through all your senses. Using this list, write a description of the month. Include sensory language, but do not state the name of the month. Check your description and make sure it portrays the month clearly. Then read your description to your classmates and let them guess which month you have described.

Winter Moon

Langston Hughes

How thin and sharp is the moon tonight!
How thin and sharp and ghostly white
Is the slim curved crook of the moon tonight!

the poet? Look at the exclamation mark at the end of the third line.

5. What is the poet's *tone,* or attitude toward what he sees?

Applying

6. What are some of your own impressions of the moon?

7. Notice the word *ghostly* in line 2. What is it about the moon that has suggested mystery to people throughout the ages?

THINKING ABOUT THE SELECTION
Recalling

1. What precisely does the poet describe?

Interpreting

2. What phrase is repeated? What effect does the poet achieve by repeating this phrase?

3. The moon goes through several phases during a month. What phase of the moon does the poet see?

4. What qualities of the moon seem to appeal to

THINKING AND WRITING
Writing a Poem

Reread "Winter Moon." Notice the pattern of the lines. Line 1 is a complete sentence. Lines 2 and 3, which make a second complete sentence, repeat the idea of line 1—but add to it.

Choose an aspect of nature that you free-wrote about earlier. Write three lines about it, following the pattern of "Winter Moon." Revise your poem, making sure you have created a vivid picture. Proofread your poem and share it with your classmates.

Song of the Sky Loom

Tewa Indian

Oh our Mother the Earth, oh our Father the Sky,
Your children are we, and with tired backs
We bring you the gifts that you love.
Then weave for us a garment of brightness;
5   May the warp¹ be the white light of morning,
May the weft² be the red light of evening,
May the fringes be the falling rain,
May the border be the standing rainbow.
Thus weave for us a garment of brightness
10 That we may walk fittingly where birds sing,
That we may walk fittingly where grass is green,
Oh our Mother the Earth, oh our Father the Sky!

---

1. warp (wôrp) *n.*: The threads running lengthwise in a loom.
2. weft (weft) *n.*: The threads carried horizontally by the shuttle back and forth across the warp in weaving.

THINKING ABOUT THE SELECTION
Recalling

1. Who are the Mother, Father and children?
2. What do the children bring? What do they want?

Interpreting

3. How is one's climate like a "garment"?
4. Explain the title of the poem.

Applying

5. Do you consider a close relationship to nature important? Explain your answer.

CRITICAL THINKING AND READING
Paraphrasing a Poem

Paraphrasing a poem, or restating it in your own words, can help you understand it. In "Song of the Sky Loom," the first three lines might be paraphrased: "Dear Mother Earth and Father Sky, we, your children, honor you with gifts."
1. How would you paraphrase lines 5 to 11?
2. What is the theme of this poem?

New World

N. Scott Momaday

1.

First Man,
behold:
the earth
glitters
5 with leaves;
the sky
glistens
with rain.
Pollen[1]
10 is borne
on winds
that low
and lean
upon
15 mountains.
Cedars
blacken
the slopes—
and pines.

2.

20 At dawn
eagles
hie and
hover
above
25 the plain
where light
gathers
in pools.
Grasses
30 shimmer
and shine.

---

1. pollen (päl′ ən) *n.*: The yellow, powderlike male cells formed in
the stamen of a flower.

Shadows
withdraw
and lie
35 away
like smoke.

3.

At noon
turtles
enter
40 slowly
into
the warm
dark loam.[2]
Bees hold
45 the swarm.
Meadows
recede
through planes
of heat
50 and pure
distance.

4.

At dusk
the gray
foxes
55 stiffen
in cold;
blackbirds
are fixed
in the
60 branches.
Rivers
follow
the moon,
the long
65 white track
of the
full moon.

---

2. loam (lōm) *n.*: Rich, dark soil.

THINKING ABOUT THE SELECTION

Recalling

1. To whom does the poet speak?
2. Where and when does the poem take place?
3. Explain the progression of time throughout the poem.

Interpreting

4. Find three details that suggest newness in the first stanza. Why are these details appropriate in this stanza?
5. What impression is created in the second stanza? In the third? In the last? Explain which details in each stanza help create this impression.
6. Explain the two meanings suggested by the title.

Applying

7. In what way is the world new every day? In what way are people new every day? What do we mean when we speak of renewing ourselves?

SPEAKING AND LISTENING

Giving a Choral Reading

The earliest poetry was chanted or sung aloud. Even today, poems gain in force and meaning when read aloud. A choral reading is one performed by a group, or *chorus,* of readers.

Give a choral reading of "New World." Your teacher may split the class into four groups, each reading one section of the poem in turn. Read with a tone of voice that communicates wonder at the beauty of the natural world seen for the first time.

Perceptions

HOUSES OF MURNAU AT OBERMARKT, 1908
Wassily Kandinsky
Lugano-Thyssen-Bornemisza Collection
Art Resource

GUIDE FOR READING

The City Is So Big

Richard García (1941–   ) writes poetry for adults and children. He has published *Selected Poetry* (1973) and a contemporary folk tale for children, *My Aunt Otilia's Spirits* (1978). García is the director of the Poets in the Schools program in Marin County, California. Born in San Francisco, California, he has also lived in Mexico and Israel. In "The City Is So Big" he describes the city as a child might see it.

Concrete Mixers

Patricia Hubbell (1928–   ) is a freelance journalist as well as a poet. She was born in Bridgeport, Connecticut, and attended the University of Connecticut. Her books include *The Apple Vendor's Fair* (1963), *8 A.M. Shadows* (1965), and *Catch Me a Wind* (1968). In "Concrete Mixers," she imagines these machines as elephants.

Southbound on the Freeway

May Swenson (1919–1989) was born in Logan, Utah, and attended Utah State University. After working for a while as a newspaper reporter, she moved to New York City, where she found employment as an editor and as a lecturer at colleges and universities. Her poems have been published in such magazines as *The New Yorker, Harper's,* and *The Nation.* Swenson believed that poetry is based on the desire to see things as they are, rather than as they appear. In "Southbound on the Freeway," however, she portrays an aspect of our culture as it might appear to an alien creature.

Free verse is poetry with irregular rhythms and varied line lengths. It is "free" of the traditional forms of poetry. Since it is written in a way that is similar to ordinary speech, if it uses rhyme, the rhymes are loose and also irregular.

A poem written in free verse may be long or short. It may or may not have stanzas. The stanzas may be long or short, or both. Sometimes, as in "Southbound on the Freeway," the stanzas may be regular. In general, the lines in free verse are organized according to the flow of the poet's thoughts, ideas, and images. For example, "Concrete Mixers" is arranged according to the natural pauses one makes when speaking normally.

> They rid the trunk-like trough of concrete,
> Direct the spray to the bulging sides,
> Turn and start the monsters moving.

As you read these poems, *listen* to them as if a friend were talking to you. Do most of the pauses sound natural and conversational?

You will read three poems about machinery in the modern world and will see technology in a new way. Freewrite about the new technology people encounter every day.

Knowing the following words will help you as you read these poems.
ponderous (pän' dər əs) *adj.*: Heavy, massive (p. 587)
perch (pʉrch) *v.*: Rest upon (p. 587)
trough (trôf) *n.*: Long, narrow container for holding water or food for animals (p. 587)
bellow (bel' ō) *v.*: Roar powerfully (p. 587)

The City Is So Big

Richard García

The city is so big
Its bridges quake with fear
I know, I have seen at night

The lights sliding from house to house
5 And trains pass with windows shining
Like a smile full of teeth

I have seen machines eating houses
And stairways walk all by themselves
And elevator doors opening and closing
10 And people disappear.

THINKING ABOUT THE SELECTION

Recalling

1. What has the speaker seen the bridges doing?
2. What do the passing trains resemble?

Interpreting

3. Describe the mood of this poem. Find five details that help create this mood.
4. Interpret lines 7–10. Explain how each of the three details is possible.

Applying

5. This poem presents one side of living in a big city. Discuss with your classmates the pros and cons of city living.

ANALYZING LITERATURE

Understanding Free Verse

Poetry that is written in free verse often follows its own form. In attempting to capture the sounds of natural speech, free verse often abandons any precise rhythmic pattern and regular rhyme scheme.

1. Read the poem aloud. How would you describe its rhythm?
2. What do you notice about the length of the lines?
3. How do these two features add to the mood of the poem?

Concrete Mixers

Patricia Hubbell

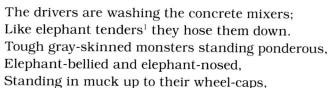

The drivers are washing the concrete mixers;
Like elephant tenders[1] they hose them down.
Tough gray-skinned monsters standing ponderous,
Elephant-bellied and elephant-nosed,
5   Standing in muck up to their wheel-caps,
Like rows of elephants, tail to trunk.
Their drivers perch on their backs like mahouts,[2]
Sending the sprays of water up.
They rid the trunk-like trough of concrete,
10 Direct the spray to the bulging sides,
Turn and start the monsters moving.
      Concrete mixers
      Move like elephants
      Bellow like elephants
15   Spray like elephants
   Concrete mixers are urban elephants,
   Their trunks are raising a city.

CITY AT THE SEA
Helmut Kies
Three Lions

1. **elephant tenders**: People in charge of elephants.
2. **mahouts** (mə hout´´s) *n*.: Elephant drivers or keepers.

THINKING ABOUT THE SELECTION
Recalling

1. What scene is being described in this poem?
2. What do the concrete mixers accomplish?

Interpreting

3. An extended metaphor is a figurative comparison carried throughout a poem. Describe how the two items here are alike.

Applying

4. Advertisers often use animal metaphors to describe cars. Tell what impression the advertiser is trying to create about two cars named for animals.

CRITICAL THINKING AND READING
Reading Free Verse

Let punctuation marks help you when you read free verse. Pause at commas and take a slightly longer pause at semicolons. Stop when you come to periods, question marks, and exclamation marks. If a line does not have a punctuation mark at the end of it, read on to the next line without pausing.

1. The punctuation marks in lines 1 through 11 tell you that these lines should be read one by one, pausing or stopping at the end of each. Given the subject, why do you suppose the poet chose this "step-by-step" arrangement?
2. How should lines 12 through 15 be read? Why?

Southbound on the Freeway

May Swenson

A tourist came in from Orbitville,
parked in the air, and said:

The creatures of this star
are made of metal and glass.

5   Through the transparent parts
you can see their guts.

Their feet are round and roll
on diagrams—or long

measuring tapes—dark
10 with white lines.

They have four eyes.
The two in the back are red.

Sometimes you can see a five-eyed
one, with a red eye turning

15 on the top of his head.
He must be special—

the others respect him,
and go slow,

when he passes, winding
20 among them from behind.

They all hiss as they glide,
like inches, down the marked

tapes. Those soft shapes,
shadowy inside.

25 the hard bodies—are they
their guts or their brains?

THINKING ABOUT THE SELECTION

Recalling

1. Who is the tourist in this poem?
2. According to the title, what does the tourist see?

Interpreting

3. Part of the humor in this poem comes from the tourist misinterpreting what he or she sees. How does the tourist misinterpret the creatures of this star?
4. What is the five-eyed creature? In what way is the tourist's analysis of the five-eyed creature actually correct?
5. Explain the question that the tourist asks. How would you answer this question?

Applying

6. Put yourself in the place of this tourist. For example, if this tourist were to see a parking lot, he or she might interpret it as a hotel. How might this tourist interpret a drive-through window at a fast-food restaurant? How might this tourist interpret a drive-in movie? List three other items and explain how this tourist might misinterpret them.

THINKING AND WRITING

Writing Free Verse

Imagine the tourist from Orbitville parked in the air above a football game. Freewrite about what the tourist would see and how the tourist might interpret what he or she sees. Then use your freewriting as the basis for writing a poem in free verse. When you revise your poem, make sure you have consistently described the game from the tourist's point of view. Then proofread your poem and share it with your classmates.

GUIDE FOR READING

400-Meter Free Style

Maxine Kumin (1925–   ) was born in Philadelphia, Pennsylvania. She attended Radcliffe College and taught there and at Tufts University, both in Massachusetts. Kumin has written novels, essays, and children's books, as well as several volumes of poetry. In 1973 she was awarded the Pulitzer Prize for *Up Country: Poems of New England*. In her poem "400-Meter Free Style," Kumin describes a swim race not only in words but also in shape.

Concrete Poetry

Concrete poetry is poetry in which the shape of the poem on the page resembles the subject of the poem. With concrete poetry, poets experiment with the way a poem *looks* on the page. They arrange the words so as to form a concrete, or actual, shape that is recognizable. Poems have been written in many shapes, including hearts, trees, wings, and even falling rain.

For example, the arrangement of the lines of "400-Meter Free Style" may confuse you at first. If so, just think about the poem's subject: a swimmer in a race.

Look For

As you read this concrete poem, look at its shape and consider its subject. Based on the title, what is the topic of this poem? What shape do you see as you look at the lines?

Writing

Imagine a simple physical action—a motion, a gesture, a series of movements; for example, the leap of a dancer, the downhill racing of a skier, or the uphill rocky scrambling of a mountain climber. On a blank sheet of paper, draw a simple shape of the action that you imagine.

Vocabulary

Knowing the following words will help you as you read "400-Meter Free Style."

catapults (kat′ ə pultz′) *v.*: Launches (p. 591)

cunningly (kun′ iŋ lē) *adv.*: Skillfully (p. 591)

extravagance (ik strav′ ə gəns) *n.*: Waste (p. 591)

compensation (käm′ pən sā′ shən) *n.*: Here, equal reaction (p. 591)

nurtures (nʉr′ chərz) *v.*: Nourishes (p. 591)

tick (tik) *v.*: Operate smoothly (p. 593)

expended (ik spend′ id) *v.*: Used up (p. 593)

plum (plum) *adj.*: Here, first-class (p. 593)

400-Meter Free Style

Maxine Kumin

The gun full swing the swimmer catapults and cracks
        s
        i
        x
feet away onto that perfect glass he catches at
a
n
d
throws behind him scoop[1] after scoop cunningly moving
        t
        h
        e
water back to move him forward. Thrift is his wonderful
s
e
c
5 ret; he has schooled out all extravagance. No muscle
        r
        i
        p
ples without compensation wrist cock[2] to heel snap to
h
i
s
mobile mouth that siphons[3] in the air that nurtures
        h
        i
        m
at half an inch above sea level so to speak.
T
h
e
astonishing whites of the soles of his feet rise
        a
        n
        d

---

1. scoop (sko͞op) *n.*: The amount taken up, in this case with a cupped hand.
2. wrist cock: The tilted position of the wrist.
3. siphons (sī′ fənz) *v.*: Draws; pulls.

10 salute us on the turns. He flips, converts, and is gone
a
l
l
in one. We watch him for signs. His arms are steady at
t
h
e
catch, his cadent[4] feet tick in the stretch, they know
t
h
e
lesson well. Lungs know, too; he does not list[5] for
a
i
r
he drives along on little sips carefully expended
b
u
t
15 that plum red heart pumps hard cries hurt how soon
i
t
s
near one more and makes its final surge   TIME 4:25:9

---

4. cadent (kā′ dənt) *adj.*: Rhythmic; beating.
5. list (list) *v.*: Wish; crave.

THINKING ABOUT THE SELECTION

Recalling

1. What three aspects of the swimmer's movements does the poet mention?
2. In lines 3 through 6, what does the poet admire about the swimmer's motion?
3. What hurts the swimmer?

Interpreting

4. Until the last four lines, the poet confines her observations to the swimmer's external movement. How does the poet move "inside" the swimmer at the end?
5. What does the shape of the poem show?
6. What is the effect of ending the poem with the swimmer's racing time?

Applying

7. How can the swimmer's training and discipline be helpful in daily living?

ANALYZING LITERATURE

Understanding Concrete Poetry

A **concrete poem** gives you another element—shape—to think about. The shape of a concrete poem not only reinforces the subject; it may also give you another way of understanding its meaning. Both the title and the shape tell you that "400-Meter Free Style" is about the idea of a swimming race.

In a concrete poem, punctuation may occur in places other than at the end of a line, and words may be placed other than horizontally. This may make the poem more difficult to read, but is meant to surprise you by the way the poem looks and sounds.

1. Read the poem aloud. What do you notice about your reading of a poem in this shape?
2. How might reading this poem aloud require the kind of concentration and effort that the swimmer has?

THINKING AND WRITING

Writing a Concrete Poem

Write a short concrete poem. Your subject can be the physical action and shape that you created earlier, or you may choose a person, a place, an event, or some form of movement. Think of a shape that in some way relates to your subject. For instance, if you wanted to write about the destruction of a fire, you could shape your poem like a flame. Draw the shape.

Freewrite about the subject you chose. Use this information to write your lines of poetry. Then fit the lines to the shape.

Choices

ON THE PROMENADE
August Macke
Three Lions

Identity

Julio Noboa Polanco (1949–   ) was born in The Bronx, New York, of Puerto Rican parents. The family moved to Chicago, and "Identity" was written while the poet was an eighth grader at a school on the west side of Chicago. As a bilingual poet who values his parents' Hispanic heritage, Julio Noboa Polanco has developed an interest in the variety of cultures in the world and has received a Bachelor's Degree in Anthropology as well as a Master's Degree in Education. Currently living in San Antonio, Texas, he administers a dropout prevention program in a barrio school in the city.

The Road Not Taken

Robert Frost (1874–1963) was born in San Francisco. In 1885, following the death of his father, his family moved to New England. There Frost attended school in Lawrence, Massachusetts, and then went on to Dartmouth and Harvard colleges. His experiences as a farmer and schoolteacher provided the material for many of his most famous poems. For twelve years, Frost met with little success in getting his poetry published. However, in 1913 and 1914 he put together two of his major collections, *A Boy's Will* and *North of Boston,* and these works brought him critical acclaim. Between 1913 and 1962, he won the Pulitzer Prize four times. In 1960 Congress gave him a special gold medal "in recognition of his poetry, which has enriched the culture of the United States and the philosophy of the world."

If you read a poem carefully, you will notice that someone–a speaker—is addressing you. Sometimes the speaker is the poet. Other times, however, the speaker is a character the poet has created. This character may be a man or a woman, a child, an animal, or even an inanimate object to whom the poet has chosen to give human qualities. For example, the poet may create a princess, a boxer, a baseball player, a cat, or even mushrooms that speak— all tell their own story from their unique point of view.

Look For

As you read, look for the speaker in each poem. What is the speaker like? How does the speaker reveal the world through his or her unique point of view?

Writing

In the poems you are about to read, each speaker makes a choice. George Moore has written, "The difficulty in life is the choice." Freewrite about choice. What is it? What types of choices do people have to make every day? Why do people find making a choice so difficult?

Vocabulary

Knowing the following words will help you as you read these poems.

harnessed (här′ nisd) v.: Tied (p. 598)

abyss (ə bis′) n.: Great depth (p. 598)

shunned (shund) v.: Avoided (p. 598)

fertile (fʉr′ t′l) adj.: Rich; productive (p. 598)

musty (mus′ tē) adj.: With a stale, damp smell (p. 598)

stench (stench) n.: Bad smell (p. 598)

diverged (də vʉrjd′) v.: Branched off (p. 600)

Identity

Julio Noboa Polanco

Let them be as flowers,
always watered, fed, guarded, admired,
but harnessed to a pot of dirt.

I'd rather be a tall, ugly weed,
5   clinging on cliffs, like an eagle
wind-wavering above high, jagged rocks.

To have broken through the surface of stone,
to live, to feel exposed to the madness
of the vast, eternal sky.
10   To be swayed by the breezes of an ancient sea,
carrying my soul, my seed, beyond the mountains of time
or into the abyss of the bizarre.

I'd rather be unseen, and if
then shunned by everyone,
15   than to be a pleasant-smelling flower,
growing in clusters in the fertile valley,
where they're praised, handled, and plucked
by greedy, human hands.

I'd rather smell of musty, green stench
20   than of sweet, fragrant lilac.
If I could stand alone, strong and free,
I'd rather be a tall, ugly weed.

SEASHORE AT PALAVAS, 1854
Gustave Courbet
Musée Fabre, Montpellier

THINKING ABOUT THE SELECTION

Recalling

1. According to the speaker, what benefits do flowers have? What two drawbacks make beings like flowers unattractive?
2. What would the speaker rather be? What benefit makes this choice extremely attractive to the speaker?

Interpreting

3. Explain what the speaker is really choosing between in this poem.
4. Which choice would be the easier to make? Support your answer.
5. What do you think is the theme of this poem? Explain how the title of the poem relates to the theme.

Applying

6. Provide three examples of how people make the choice the speaker makes in their daily lives.

ANALYZING LITERATURE

Hearing the Speaker's Voice

Hearing the speaker's voice when you read can help you understand the poem. In "Identity" the speaker is an individual who has made a choice about what kind of person to be.

1. Find three adjectives you think describe the speaker. Explain your reason for selecting each adjective.
2. Name three people from history or current affairs you think the speaker would admire. Explain the reason for each choice.
3. Look at the art that accompanies this poem. In what way does the figure in the painting capture the identity of the speaker?

The Road Not Taken

Robert Frost

Two roads diverged in a yellow wood,
And sorry I could not travel both
And be one traveler, long I stood
And looked down one as far as I could
5   To where it bent in the undergrowth;

Then took the other, as just as fair,
And having perhaps the better claim,
Because it was grassy and wanted wear;
Though as for that, the passing there
10   Had worn them really about the same,

And both that morning equally lay
In leaves no step had trodden black.
Oh, I kept the first for another day!
Yet knowing how way leads on to way,
15   I doubted if I should ever come back.

I shall be telling this with a sigh
Somewhere ages and ages hence:
Two roads diverged in a wood, and I—
I took the one less traveled by,
20   And that has made all the difference.

THINKING ABOUT THE SELECTION
Recalling

1. At the beginning of the poem the speaker is faced with a choice between two roads. Which choice does he make?
2. What reason does the speaker give for making this choice? Which lines tell you that he is not certain his reason is valid?
3. What does the speaker hope to be able to do later? Which lines tell you that he doubts he will be able to do this?

Interpreting

4. Find two details suggesting that the speaker feels this decision is significant.
5. What do the roads seem to symbolize? Find details from the poem to support your answer.
6. Explain the theme of the poem.

Applying

7. An old proverb states that opportunity is a short-lived visitor. Another old saying says that opportunity never knocks twice. How do these sayings relate to the poem? Do you agree with the sayings? Why or why not?

CRITICAL THINKING AND READING
Interpreting Differences in Metaphors

Many writers have used metaphors to describe life. Read each of the common metaphors below. Explain how each suggests a specific attitude toward life. For example, one common metaphor says that life is just a bowl of cherries. This metaphor suggests an optimistic view. However, the comedian Rodney Dangerfield has responded to this metaphor by saying that life is just a bowl of pits. His metaphor suggests a more pessimistic outlook.

1. Life is a long, hard road.
2. Life is a journey of discovery.
3. Life is a merry-go-round.
4. Life is an endless feast.

The Choice

Dorothy Parker (1893–1967) was born in West End (now part of Long Branch), New Jersey, and lived mostly in New York City. She began her literary career in 1916 as a magazine writer. For several years she was the regular book reviewer for *The New Yorker*. Today she is best remembered for her stories and poems, which are distinguished for their wit and sarcasm. Like "The Choice," Dorothy Parker's writing in general expresses a gentle cynicism toward life and its disappointments.

Journey to the Interior

Adrien Stoutenburg (1916–   ) was born in Darfur, Minnesota, and has lived in Mexico, New Mexico, and California. At various times she has worked as a librarian, journalist, editor, and freelance writer. Stoutenburg has written biographies and numerous other books for children, but she is best known for her poetry. She has won the Commonwealth Club of California Silver Medal and the Lamont Poetry Award from the Academy of American Poets.

Tone

The **tone** of any piece of writing is the attitude the writer takes toward the subject and audience. Just as you can hear someone's tone of voice in speech, you can infer it when reading. Tone is present in all writing, and many tones are possible. Usually, the speaker in a poem expresses the tone. The tone of a work may be formal or informal, serious or comic, angry or playful, sad or joyful.

Look For

As you read these two poems, listen for the speaker's tone of voice. How would you read these poems aloud to reflect the tone?

Writing

We all have to make many decisions living in our complex world. Some decisions are personal—affecting only the individual—while others are public—affecting other people. Freewrite about the tools we need to make wise decisions. In what way does education help us? In what way does sharing things with others help us?

Vocabulary

Knowing the following words will help you as you read these poems.

billowing (bil' ō iŋ) *adj.*: Large; spread-out (p. 604)

smoldering (smōl' dər iŋ) *adj.*: Here, fiery (p. 604)

lilting (lilt' iŋ) *adj.*: With a light, graceful rhythm (p. 604)

sheen (sͪhēn) *n.*: Shininess (p. 604)

garnets (gär' nits) *n.*: Deep red gems (p. 606)

tenure (ten' yər) *n.*: Time of residence (p. 606)

snickers (snik' ərz) *v.*: Laughs in a mean way (p. 606)

The Choice

Dorothy Parker

He'd have given me rolling lands,
    Houses of marble, and billowing farms,
Pearls, to trickle between my hands,
    Smoldering rubies, to circle my arms.
5 You—you'd only a lilting song.
    Only a melody, happy and high,
You were sudden and swift and strong,—
    Never a thought for another had I.

He'd have given me laces rare,
10   Dresses that glimmered with frosty sheen,
Shining ribbons to wrap my hair,
    Horses to draw me, as fine as a queen.
You—you'd only to whistle low,
    Gaily I followed wherever you led.
15 I took you, and I let him go,—
    Somebody ought to examine my head!

Recalling

1. What did the first man have to offer?
2. How did the second man differ from the first?
3. Whom did the speaker choose?

Interpreting

4. The speaker uses many image-producing words. Compare and contrast the imagery describing the two men.
5. Why is the last line surprising?
6. The last line tells you something about the character of the speaker. Until the last line, has her practical nature or romantic nature been speaking? Which side speaks in the last line?

Applying

7. Do you think decision making should be based on only practical considerations such as money and comfort? Explain your answer.

ANALYZING LITERATURE

Understanding Tone

Tone is the writer's attitude toward the subject. It may be angry, affectionate, comic, serious, sad, and so on.

1. What attitude toward romantic love does the speaker present?
2. How would you describe the tone of the poem?

Journey to the Interior

Adrien Stoutenburg

You will not live here,
nor your children,
nor the old, laughing coyotes
who once sang in these hills.
5   We are leaving here soon,
as the grizzly left, and the condor.
(Who has seen such claws or wings?)

There is a moment yet,
before the engineers arrive,
10   to watch hummingbirds
strung with garnets,
madronas brown as the wrists of Indians,
bay trees that smell like green candles,
and listen again for the silence
15   that made a darkness for owls
with horned mouths
speaking like the E string of a guitar.

The termite with his sad drill
opposed our tenure
20   but could not defeat us,
nor the bats strumming their teeth
within the wall where the telephone snickers—
(they have always been there,

in strange cradles,
25   a tiny echo of dark wires)—
nor the wood borer[1] on the sill
with his attic dream.

---

1. **wood borer**: An insect or worm that bores holes in wood.

Our trunks are ready,
a funeral of hinges and locks,
30   stuffed with snapshots, rose pips,[2] pencils,
and cool clothing for the desert—
the compass at hand,
the water bag hanging from the bumper
like a leaky, gray pillow.

---

2. rose pips: Pieces of roots with which to start new rose bushes.

THINKING ABOUT THE SELECTION
Recalling

1. What once sang in the hills? What animals have departed?
2. Who will soon arrive?
3. What obstacles had the people overcome?

Interpreting

4. Why are the people leaving? What will be lost once the engineers arrive?
5. What obstacle are the people unable to overcome?
6. What choice has been made?
7. Explain the title of the poem.

Applying

8. What other choices can people in a similar situation make?

ANALYZING LITERATURE
Understanding Speaker and Tone

The **speaker** is the voice the poet has chosen to present the poem. The **tone** of the poem expresses the poet's attitude or point of view toward the subject.

1. What can you tell about what the speaker likes from the first two stanzas?
2. What do stanzas 3 and 4 tell you about the speaker?
3. What can you tell about the speaker from the things that are packed in the trunks?
4. What descriptive words in the last stanza help set the tone of the poem?

UNDERSTANDING LANGUAGE
Appreciating Concrete Words

Concrete words are words that name or describe things that we can perceive through our senses. Many concrete words are nouns: *stone, whisper, mist, garlic, shadow*. Since concrete words are specific, immediate, and precise, writers tend to use them in description. For example, Adrien Stoutenburg writes of "bay trees that smell like green candles." The concrete words *bay trees* and *green candles* help make the description specific and sharp. They evoke a precise picture that we can envision clearly.

Find three more concrete words in the poem. First define each one. Then tell how each strengthens the overall imagery of the poem.

Staying Alive

David Wagoner (1926–   ) was born in Massillon, Ohio. He attended Pennsylvania State University and Indiana University and currently teaches English at the University of Washington in Seattle. He is respected not only as a poet, but also as a novelist. Collections of his verse include *Riverbed* (1972), *Sleeping in the Woods* (1974), and *Travelling Light* (1976). "Staying Alive," his most famous poem, has been called "one of the best American poems since World War II."

Figurative and Literal Language

Figurative language is language that appeals to the imagination. **Literal language,** on the other hand, is language that is to be interpreted in accordance with actual or strict meaning of the words.

We might, for example, describe an athlete in literal terms: "He ran with great speed and agility, eluding would-be tacklers on all sides." Or we might make the description figurative: "He ran like a jagged wind cutting through a field of limp, high grass." Both sentences describe the same thing. Yet the second description —the figurative one—is an image that appeals to our imagination.

Poems should be read both literally and figuratively. That is, first understand a poem's literal meaning. Then look for any additional meaning. Literally, "Staying Alive" is about how to survive in the woods. However, the poem contains helpful advice for all of us.

Look For

As you read "Staying Alive," first look for what the poem says literally about survival in the woods. What other meaning does the poem have? How might the instructions be applied to life in general?

Writing

Working with a group of your classmates, list rules for "staying alive" in a life-threatening situation.

Vocabulary

Knowing the following words will help you as you read "Staying Alive."

nuzzling (nuz′ liŋ) *v.*: Rubbing with the nose (p. 610)

uncanny (un kan′ ē) *adj.*: Strange (p. 610)

hoarse (hôrs) *adj.*: Sounding harsh (p. 610)

Staying Alive

David Wagoner

Staying alive in the woods is a matter of calming down
At first and deciding whether to wait for rescue,
Trusting to others,
Or simply to start walking and walking in one direction
5   Till you come out—or something happens to stop you.
By far the safer choice
Is to settle down where you are, and try to make a living
Off the land, camping near water, away from shadows.
Eat no white berries;
10   Spit out all bitterness. Shooting at anything
Means hiking further and further every day
To hunt survivors;
It may be best to learn what you have to learn without a gun,
Not killing but watching birds and animals go
15   In and out of shelter
At will. Following their example, build for a whole season:
Facing across the wind in your lean-to,[1]
You may feel wilder,
But nothing, not even you, will have to stay in hiding.
20   If you have no matches, a stick and a fire-bow[2]
Will keep you warmer,
Or the crystal[3] of your watch, filled with water, held up to the sun
Will do the same in time. In case of snow
Drifting toward winter,
25   Don't try to stay awake through the night, afraid of freezing—

---

1. lean-to (lēn' too') *n*.: A rough shelter with a sloping roof.
2. stick and a fire-bow: A way of starting a fire in which the string
of the bow is wrapped around a stick and the bow is pulled back and
forth rapidly, twirling the stick and thus creating sparks.
3. crystal (kris' t'l) *n*.: The transparent covering over the face of a
watch.

The bottom of your mind knows all about zero;
It will turn you over
And shake you till you waken. If you have trouble sleeping
Even in the best of weather, jumping to follow
30   With eyes strained to their corners
The unidentifiable noises of the night and feeling
Bears and packs of wolves nuzzling your elbow,
Remember the trappers
Who treated them indifferently and were left alone.
35   If you hurt yourself, no one will comfort you
Or take your temperature,
So stumbling, wading, and climbing are as dangerous as flying.
But if you decide, at last, you must break through
In spite of all danger,
40   Think of yourself by time and not by distance, counting
Wherever you're going by how long it takes you;
No other measure
Will bring you safe to nightfall. Follow no streams: they run
Under the ground or fall into wilder country.
45   Remember the stars
And moss when your mind runs into circles. If it should rain
Or the fog should roll the horizon⁴ in around you,
Hold still for hours
Or days if you must, or weeks, for seeing is believing
50   In the wilderness. And if you find a pathway,
Wheel-rut, or fence-wire,
Retrace it left or right: someone knew where he was going
Once upon a time, and you can follow
Hopefully, somewhere,
55   Just in case. There may even come, on some uncanny evening,
A time when you're warm and dry, well fed, not thirsty,
Uninjured, without fear,
When nothing, either good or bad, is happening.
This is called staying alive. It's temporary.
60   What occurs after
Is doubtful. You must always be ready for something to come bursting
Through the far edge of a clearing, running toward you,
Grinning from ear to ear
And hoarse with welcome. Or something crossing and hovering

---

4. horizon (hə rī′ z'n) *n*.: The line where the sky seems to meet the
earth.

65 Overhead, as light as air, like a break in the sky,
   Wondering what you are.
   Here you are face to face with the problem of recognition.
   Having no time to make smoke, too much to say,
   You should have a mirror
70 With a tiny hole in the back for better aiming, for reflecting
   Whatever disaster you can think of, to show
   The way you suffer.
   These body signals have universal meaning: If you are lying
   Flat on your back with arms outstretched behind you,
75 You say you require
   Emergency treatment; if you are standing erect and holding
   Arms horizontal, you mean you are not ready;
   If you hold them over
   Your head, you want to be picked up. Three of anything
80 Is a sign of distress. Afterward if you see
   No ropes, no ladders,
   No maps or messages falling, no searchlights or trails blazing,
   Then, chances are, you should be prepared to burrow
   Deep for a deep winter.

THINKING ABOUT THE SELECTION

Recalling

1. What situation does the poet imagine?
2. What decision must you make in this situation?
3. What, according to the poet, is the safest choice?
4. How can a watch crystal filled with water take the place of matches?
5. Why is it a good idea to keep track of time rather than distance when traveling?

Interpreting

6. How does the poet define "staying alive"?
7. What instructions for living are contained in lines 16, 26, and 34?
8. How might the poet's advice about "Shooting at anything" apply to life generally?
9. To stay alive means to *survive*. Given the poet's definition of "staying alive," what would you say is his view of life?

Applying

10. What is the difference between surviving and living? Is it enough to merely survive? Explain your answer.

ANALYZING LITERATURE

Understanding Figurative Language

To begin to understand any poem, you must try to comprehend its literal meaning first. For example, David Wagoner writes that in the woods, one should "Eat no white berries;/Spit out all bitterness." He means this literally: white berries are usually poisonous, as are many bitter-tasting things. Once you have understood this literal content, think further about the possible figurative meaning of these lines. What else might the poet mean by the suggestion that one ought to "spit out all bitterness"? Not only in the woods, but in life generally, one should avoid bitterness.

1. Give three examples of the poet's advice on survival in the woods.
2. How might any single piece of advice be extended to life in general?
3. How do you interpret lines 46 through 50?
4. How do you interpret the last six lines?
5. The first line begins "Staying alive in the woods . . .," yet the title is simply, "Staying Alive." What does this difference suggest about the true subject of this poem?

THINKING AND WRITING

Writing an Interpretation of a Poem

Write a simple outline of the literal content of this poem. Then jot down a few of the poem's suggestions for how to live life in general. Using your notes as a guide, write an essay in which you interpret the poem as completely as you can. Include specific references to the poem in your writing. Revise your essay to make sure you have organized your information logically. Proofread your essay and share it with your classmates.

Poetry

The poet A. E. Housman has written: "I could no more define poetry than a terrier can define a rat." Although like Housman you may not be able to define poetry, you probably can recognize a poem when you read one. You can fully appreciate it by putting all its elements together.

Types of Poetry

The most common **types of poetry** are the narrative poem and the lyric poem. A narrative poem tells a story, while a lyric poem expresses strong personal feelings about a subject.

Figurative Language

Figurative language consists of words used beyond their usual dictionary meaning. The words take on more imaginative implications. Three common types of figurative language are simile, metaphor, and personification. A **simile** is a figurative comparison between two basically unlike items. It uses the word *like* or *as* to make the comparison. A **metaphor** is a figurative comparison that does not use the word *like* or *as*. **Personification** means giving human qualities to nonhuman objects.

Imagery

Imagery refers to the use of language to create vivid word pictures. Usually these words have a sensory appeal.

Sound

Poetry has a musical quality created by the **sound** of the words, the use of rhythm and rhyme, and the use of repetition and alliteration. Onomatopoeia, or the use of words to imitate sounds, also helps create this musical effect.

Theme

Most poems provide an insight into life. As you read, ask yourself what **theme** the poem reveals.

On the following pages is a poem with annotations in the side column showing the elements of poetry that an active reader might note while reading.

GREEN VIOLINIST, 1923–24
Marc Chagall
Solomon R. Guggenheim Museum

The Story-Teller

Mark Van Doren

Title: The title indicates that the poem will be about a storyteller. What special insight about a storyteller will the poem provide?

He talked, and as he talked
Wallpaper came alive;
Suddenly ghosts walked,
And four doors were five;

Figurative Language: The poet is using language figuratively here. Certainly wallpaper doesn't come alive and ghosts don't walk. What does the use of figurative language indicate about the magic of the storyteller?

Sound: Notice the regular pattern of rhyme. How does this regular pattern fit the subject matter?

5   Calendars ran backward,
And maps had mouths;
Ships went tackward[1]
In a great drowse;[2]

Imagery: What effect is created by the odd images? To what senses do these images appeal?

Trains climbed trees,
10   And soon dripped down
Like honey of bees
On the cold brick town.

Theme: The poem provides an important insight into the magic of storytelling. What is this insight?

He had wakened a worm
In the world's brain,
15   And nothing stood firm
Until day again.

---

1. tackward (tak′ wərd) *adv.*: Against the wind.
2. drowse (drɑuz) *n.*: Sluggishness; doze.

Mark Van Doren (1894–1972) was a Pulitzer Prize-winning poet. Among his collections of poetry are *Collected Works* and *Good Morning: Last Poems by Mark Van Doren.* An English professor, Van Doren also wrote critical studies of major writers.

THINKING ABOUT THE SELECTION

Recalling

1. Find seven magical things that the storyteller is able to accomplish.
2. According to the last line, when do things return to normal?

Interpreting

3. What is the *worm* referred to in line 13? What is the *world's brain* in line 14?
4. Interpret lines 15–16.
5. Express the theme of this poem.

Applying

6. Why do you think that people like stories? Use details from life to support your answer.

ANALYZING LITERATURE

Understanding Rhyme

Rhyme is created by words sounding alike. In a poem, rhyme often occurs at the end of lines. The rhyme pattern of a poem helps give it a musical quality.

1. Look at the first stanza. Which words at the end of lines rhyme?
2. Look at the second stanza. Which words at the end of lines rhyme?
3. What conclusion do you draw about the rhyme pattern of this poem?

CRITICAL THINKING AND READING

Defining Poetry

Defining means giving the distinguishing characteristics of something. Read each definition of poetry below. Explain which one you think best captures the essential meaning of a poem.

1. Samuel Johnson: "Poetry is the art of uniting pleasure with truth."
2. Edgar Allan Poe: "Poetry is the rhythmical creation of beauty in words."
3. Gwyn Thomas: "Poetry is trouble dunked in tears."

UNDERSTANDING LANGUAGE

Finding Antonyms

An **antonym** is a word that means the opposite or nearly the opposite of another word. For example, the words *peaceful* and *warlike* are antonyms, as are the words *quiet* and *noise*. For each of the following words, find its antonym in the poem.

1. forward
2. listened
3. dead
4. slowly

THINKING AND WRITING

Retelling a Story

Think about the best story you have ever heard. What made this story come alive for you. Brainstorm, listing all the qualities that made this story special. Then retell the story in your own words. When you revise make sure you have included the features that made this story magical for you. Proofread your story and share it with your classmates.

Making Inferences

Reading actively is essential to enjoy and understand poetry because most poems are made up of only a few words. Poets often imply or suggest things rather than state them outright. You may have to make inferences, or intelligent guesses, to understand what a poet is saying in a poem. An **inference** is a conclusion based on evidence such as facts or clues provided by the author. It often requires using the reader's background knowledge and experience. To arrive at sound inferences, you must carefully weigh both types of evidence to determine if they support the inference that is being made. If the evidence does not support the inference, then you should discard it and make a different inference.

Character

Making inferences can help you understand the characters. Reread "O Captain! My Captain!" on page 534. Who is the Captain referred to in the poem? If you had read this poem when Walt Whitman wrote it, you would immediately know that the Captain was Abraham Lincoln. Since you cannot do that, you will have to find out when the poet wrote the poem and use your background knowledge to determine that Lincoln had just been assassinated. Now you have sufficient evidence to prove that Lincoln is the Captain.

What kind of man is this Captain, and what is the poet's attitude toward him? Like a detective, you need to search for clues. The poet calls him "my Captain" and "dear father," which indicates that the poet greatly respects and loves him. The reference to the poet's "mournful tread" and the terrible aching of his heart reinforces the idea that he loves the man. The greatness of the Captain is shown by the exulting eager crowds, the ringing bells and bugle trills, and the fact that the ship reached shore safely. Clearly, the evidence indicates that the Captain is a great, heroic man, loved and respected by the poet.

Plot

Now make inferences to understand the plot. Knowing that the Captain is Lincoln will help you. First you need to know what the ship represents. This is where your background knowledge will help you.

Remember that Lincoln was President during the Civil War, which was a time when the Union was threatened. The Southerners wanted to form their own Confederacy of states and break away from the Union. Therefore, you can figure out that the ship was the Union and the racks it weathered were the assaults from different groups of people and the forces of the war.

Now you need to find out why the voyage is over and why the people exult. Keeping in mind that the ship is the Union, you can see that "the prize we sought" is to keep the Union together. The voyage is over because "the prize . . . is won"—the Union has stayed together. And when you win a prize or succeed in doing something really important, you cheer and celebrate. Keeping the Union together makes the crowds exult and ring bells. Thus you can see that this poem is a tribute to Lincoln. It is telling how the poet and most Americans felt when the Civil War was over and President Lincoln had been shot for defending the Union. Using both evidence from the poem and your background knowledge has enabled you to make inferences that help explain the poem.

Mood

To understand the mood of a poem, you have to make inferences based on the words the poet uses and the way the events are described. The mood of "O Captain! My Captain!" is one of somber rejoicing. The poet rejoices because the Union is saved but mourns because the leader most responsible for saving it is dead.

Activity

Choose one of the narrative poems in this book. Reread it.
1. Make one inference about the main character. Find evidence to back up your inference.
2. Make one inference about the plot. Find evidence to back up your inference.
3. Make one inference about mood. Find evidence to back up your inference.

YOU THE WRITER

Assignment

1. Imagine that you are one of the characters in one of the poems. Write a poem describing yourself.

    Prewriting. Use a cueing technique to generate ideas about your character. Jot down the questions *Who? What? Where? When?* and *Why?* Then answer each of these questions.

    Writing. Write the first draft of your poem. Use a first-person speaker and have this character describe himself or herself. Begin each line of your poem with the words "I am."

    Revising. Read over your poem. Make sure your speaker has included vivid details.

Assignment

2. Choose one of the poems and write a different ending for it. You can describe a happier or sadder ending, but you must stay within the plot and time frame of the poem.

    Prewriting. Brainstorm for a list of possible alternative endings. They must all be in the realm of possibility for the poem. After you have your list, brainstorm for details for each item on your list.

    Writing. Write your new ending. If the poem you have chosen has a regular rhyme and rhythm pattern, be sure to stay within this pattern.

    Revising. Check to see that your details are consistent with the poem. Add anything else that would strengthen your ending.

Assignment

3. Choose a character from a poem set in an earlier time and place, and place him or her in a modern-day setting. Write a poem describing how the character would feel transported to our technological age. Explore how the character would react to such things as the automobile, space shuttle, and computer.

    Prewriting. Freewrite about your character transported to the present time. Explore any aspect of this idea that comes to mind.

    Writing. Begin your poem with a description of your character. Go on to develop situations in which to place your character. Then describe his or her feelings and reactions. Describe how the character's courage would enable him or her to meet the challenges of a new age.

    Revising. Revise your poem. Be sure your character acts consistently throughout. Check to see that you have included sufficient details. Edit your sentences. Proofread your final draft.

YOU THE CRITIC

Assignment

1. Choose a narrative poem from this unit and evaluate its plot, setting, characters, dialogue, and theme. Explain why the poem is or is not, in your opinion, effective. End your essay with an overall opinion of the poem's literary merit.

Prewriting. Prepare an outline of the poem. Be sure to include plot, setting, characters, dialogue, and theme.

Writing. Using your outline as a guide, write an evaluation of the poem. Discuss plot, setting, characters, dialogue, and theme. Finish with your general review of the poem's worth. Base your opinion on how effectively each of the elements was handled.

Revising. Check to see that you have evaluated the poem on the five basic elements. Be sure your opinion is supported by evidence from the poem itself. Add any information that you think will strengthen your opinion.

Assignment

2. The growth of character is a common literary theme. Choose one poem and show how the main character develops. Describe what the character goes through. Decide if the character has changed and, if so, in what way.

Prewriting. Choose a character from a poem. Freewrite, describing the character at the beginning of the poem and at the end.

Writing. Begin your essay by identifying and describing the character. Show how the character developed in the course of the poem. Organize your thoughts in an order-of-importance pattern. Discuss how the character has changed.

Revising. Be sure you have made your points clearly. If you feel the character has changed, verify your evidence to support your opinion.

Assignment

3. Choose two poems and compare and contrast the settings. In what ways are the settings alike and in what ways are they different?

Prewriting. Freewrite about the settings of the poems. Let your mind roam freely through the settings, exploring any detail that comes to mind.

Writing. Write the first draft of an essay. Begin by describing each setting in detail. Go on to describe how the two settings you have chosen are alike or how they are different from each other. Use evidence from the poems themselves to support your thesis.

Revising. Revise your first draft. Be sure you have consistently compared or contrasted the settings. Check the accuracy of your details.

WOODCUTTER ON A ROCK, 1891
Winslow Homer
Private Collection

AMERICAN MYTHS, LEGENDS, AND FOLKTALES

Myths, legends, and folktales are similar types of stories. They originated long ago when stories were all told orally, long before writing was invented. Their authors are unknown. Myths often explain early people's ideas about nature. Myths involve stories about gods, goddesses, and other supernatural beings, as well as the adventures of great heroes and heroines who serve as models for the way people in a particular culture are expected to behave. Legends differ from myths because they often involve heroes and heroines who may actually have existed. Folktales present the customs and beliefs of a culture but do not generally involve gods and goddesses. All cultures have their own myths, legends, and folktales. The ones in this unit are American. Some were told in early Native American cultures, while others are more recent.

American Myths, Legends, and Folktales

Background

Myths, legends, and folktales are three kinds of folklore. Folklore records the customs, traditions, and beliefs of a people and also consists of arts and crafts, dances, games, fairy tales, nursery rhymes; proverbs, riddles, songs, and superstitions. American folklore is as old as the country itself. Like its European counterpart, American folklore has been passed down orally from generation to generation. People have always told stories to entertain, to explain the mysterious, and to teach lessons or prove points. The stories recorded here are stories that were first heard around campfires or first told to pass the time on long winter nights or on wagons heading west.

Although the divisions are often blurred, there are distinct characteristics that make myths, legends, and folktales different from one another. Myths often explain how the world and its phenomena were created. Legends are rooted in historical events, even though they often have their heroes perform superhuman deeds. They are set in real and familiar environments and in relatively recent times. Folktales are fictional stories about animals or people that have been passed down from generation to generation orally. Often, they are not set in any particular time or place, and they often teach a lesson through the actions of the characters.

Reading Strategy

You may find colloquial language and clichés in American myths, legends, and folktales difficult to understand. Remember that in each tale, the flavor of the people who first told the story comes through. Identify the source of the story or the region of the country from which it comes. It will help you to understand the action and characters if you know whether it's an American Indian tale, a southern story, or a western story, for example. Think about why the story was probably first told.

Finally, interact with the literature by using the active reading strategies: question, predict, clarify, summarize, and pull together. The strategy that you may find particularly useful here is the questioning strategy. Ask yourself what the purpose of the story was when it was first told. Ask yourself why events are so exaggerated and why the characters have superhuman powers over nature and the elements. Using this strategy when you read will give you deeper insight into myths, legends, and folktales.

Themes

You will encounter the following themes.

- courage and bravery
- power over nature
- quick thinking to solve a problem
- superhuman strength and achievements
- exaggerated accomplishments

Characters

Become familiar with the following folk characters.

Indian boy—the boy who brought fire to his people

Indian girl—a maiden who hunts rabbits and encounters supernatural beings

Paul Bunyan—a lumberjack who could change the face of the earth and control the elements

Pecos Bill—a powerful cowboy who could control animals and nature and who created some of the most famous natural phenomena in the West

John Henry—a steel-driving man who could dig a tunnel faster than a steam drill

Stormalong—an ingenious sailor who blew his sailing ship out of the fog and doldrums into open water and safety

Johnny Appleseed—a frontiersman who traveled the Midwest planting apple trees

Davy Crockett—a real-life frontiersman and politician who became a folk hero

GUIDE FOR READING

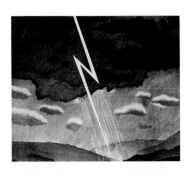

The Origin of Fire

The **Nez Percé** (nez′ pər sā′) were a powerful North American Indian tribe in Idaho, Oregon, and Washington. Their name, French for "pierced nose," was given them by a French interpreter who saw some of them wearing decorative shells in their noses.

"The Origin of Fire" is related by **Ella Elizabeth Clark** (1896–   ), born in Summertown, Tennessee, who has collected tales of the Pacific Northwest Indians.

Myth

A **myth** is an ancient story often involving supernatural beings that explains a natural phenomenon. For example, a myth may explain the origin of fire, the eruption of a volcano, or the shape of a lake. A myth explains these occurrences in familiar terms. It also reveals the culture itself: its beliefs, ideals, and gods.

Look For

As you read "The Origin of Fire," look for the explanation the Nez Percés provide for the origin of fire. Why is fire so important to people?

Writing

Do you ever wonder about how a river began, or why a nearby mountain has a certain shape, or why some dogs' tails curl? Think of something you see and wonder about, which a myth could explain. Brainstorm and write down your ideas for a possible imaginative explanation.

Vocabulary

Knowing the following words will help you as you read "The Origin of Fire."

fragrant (frā′ grənt) adj.: Covered with the odor of something (p. 627)
hurtling (hʉrt′ 'liŋ) v.: Moving quickly and forcefully (p. 627)
tipis (tē′ pēz′) n.: Cone-shaped tents made of animal skins (p. 627)
abalone (ab′ ə lō′ nē) **shell:** An oval shell with a pearly lining (p. 628)

The Origin of Fire

Ella E. Clark

Long ago the Nez Percé had no fire. They could see fire in the sky sometimes, but it belonged to the Great Power. He kept it in great black bags in the sky. When the bags bumped into each other, there was a crashing, tearing sound, and through the hole that was made fire sparkled.

People longed to get it. They ate fish and meat raw as the animals do. They ate roots and berries raw as the bears do. The women grieved when they saw their little ones shivering and blue with cold. The medicine men beat on their drums in their efforts to bring fire down from the sky, but no fire came.

At last a boy just beyond the age for the sacred vigil[1] said that he would get the fire. People laughed at him. The medicine men angrily complained, "Do you think that you can do what we are not able to do?"

But the boy went on and made his plans. The first time that he saw the black fire bags drifting in the sky, he got ready. First he bathed, brushing himself with fir branches until he was entirely clean and was fragrant with the smell of fir. He looked very handsome.

With the inside bark of cedar he wrapped an arrowhead and placed it beside his best and largest bow. On the ground he placed a beautiful white shell that he often wore around his neck. Then he asked his guardian spirit[2] to help him reach the cloud with his arrow.

All the people stood watching. The medicine men said among themselves, "Let us have him killed, lest he make the Great Power angry."

But the people said, "Let him alone. Perhaps he can bring the fire down. If he does not, then we can kill him."

The boy waited until he saw that the largest fire bag was over his head, growling and rumbling. Then he raised his bow and shot the arrow straight upward. Suddenly, all the people heard a tremendous crash, and they saw a flash of fire in the sky. Then the burning arrow, like a falling star, came hurtling down among them. It struck the boy's white shell and there made a small flame.

Shouting with joy, the people rushed forward. They lighted sticks and dry bark and hurried to their tipis to start fires with

---

1. vigil (vij′ əl), *n.*: Here, a religious period marking a young person's passage to adulthood.

2. guardian (gârd′ ē ən) **spirit:** A supernatural being that protects a person.

---

from *Indian Legends from the Northern Rockies* by Ella E. Clark. Copyright 1966 by the University of Oklahoma Press.

LIGHTNING, 1973
David Hockney
Gemini Gel

them. Children and old people ran around, laughing and singing.

When the excitement had died down, people asked about the boy. But he was nowhere to be seen. On the ground lay his shell, burned so that it showed the fire colors. Near it lay the boy's bow. People tried to shoot with it, but not even the strongest man and the best with bow and arrow could bend it.

The boy was never seen again. But his abalone shell is still beautiful, still touched with the colors of flame. And the fire he brought from the black bag is still in the center of each tipi, the blessing of every home.

THINKING ABOUT THE SELECTION

Recalling

1. What two difficulties or problems did the Nez Percé have before they had fire?
2. What was the medicine men's reaction to the boy's plan to bring down fire?
3. How did the boy bring down the fire?
4. After the excitement had died down, what did the people find?
5. Besides the origin of fire, what other natural phenomenon does the myth explain?

Interpreting

6. What were the great black bags in the sky?
7. What do you think happened to the boy after he captured the fire? Explain your answer.

Applying

8. The boy in this myth attempts to do what others consider impossible. What qualities might a person have who tries to do what others believe he or she cannot do?

ANALYZING LITERATURE

Understanding a Myth

A **myth** is an ancient story attempting to explain an aspect of the world, such as a custom or natural phenomenon. You can learn much about a culture from myths. In fact, researchers often gain valuable insights about cultures from studying myths. For example, "The Origin of Fire" tells you that when the Nez Percé bathed, they brushed themselves with fir branches to be clean and fragrant.

1. What job did the medicine men have?
2. What weapons did the Nez Percé use?
3. Who did the Nez Percé believe guided them?
4. In what did the Nez Percé live?
5. What does this myth—about how the Nez Percé get their fire—tell you about who or what they believed was responsible for the mysteries in their world?

CRITICAL THINKING AND READING

Understanding Cause and Effect

A **cause** makes something occur. An **effect** is the outcome of the cause.

Myths are a culture's attempts to explain the unknown; myths present imaginative causes for effects that seem unexplainable. "The Origin of Fire" is the Nez Percé's attempt to explain how they first came to use fire in their homes.

To identify an effect, ask yourself "What happened?" Ask "Why did this happen?" to identify its cause.

1. What causes the following events?
   a. The abalone shell was burned with color.
   b. The boy disappears.
2. What are the effects of the following events?
   a. The medicine men beat on their drums to bring fire down from the sky.
   b. The boy shot his arrow into the largest fire bag.
3. How do the causes science offers for natural phenomena differ from the causes offered by myths?

THINKING AND WRITING

Writing a Myth

Make up a myth that explains the topic you thought about before reading "The Origin of Fire." Your myth could explain your topic in terms of life as it was long ago or in terms of modern technology. List and describe the characters in your myth. Sketch out the plot—what will happen in the myth. Then write the story, using dialogue when needed. Reread your myth to see if it offers an imaginative explanation of the topic you chose.

GUIDE FOR READING

from The People, Yes

Carl Sandburg (1878–1967), born in Galesburg, Illinois, is best known for his poetry. Sandburg became a journalist, an author of children's books, and a historian, and also wrote and sang his own songs and ballads. He won the Pulitzer Prize in 1940 for his biography of Abraham Lincoln, and in 1950 for his *Complete Poems*. Sandburg's poetry celebrates the lives of ordinary people. In "The People, Yes," he uses the words, style, and rhythms of common speech to celebrate the tall tales of the American people.

Yarn

A **yarn** is a tale or story filled with exaggeration. The subject of a yarn is the tallest, fastest, strongest, longest, or most unusual of its kind. The yarnteller describes characteristics or actions that the listener knows are impossible but which, with only a small leap of the imagination, are fun to imagine as true.

Look For

As you read this selection from "The People, Yes," look for the feats or qualities that are exaggerated. Notice that this selection presents the *subjects* of various yarns, some of them well known. With which of these yarns are you familiar?

Writing

Have you ever used exaggeration to add effect to a story? Perhaps you were telling about how fast the roller coaster sped, or how far you swam. Brainstorm and write down your ideas for subjects or experiences that you could exaggerate in a yarn.

Vocabulary

Knowing the following words will help you as you read this selection from "The People, Yes."

shingled (shiŋ′ g'ld) *v*.: Covered the roof with shingles (p. 631)

mutineers (myoot′ 'n irz′) *n*.: People on a ship who revolt against their officers (p. 631)

runt (runt) *n*.: The smallest animal in a litter (p. 631)

flue (floo) *n*.: The pipe in a chimney that leads smoke outside (p. 631)

hook-and-eye: A fastening device in which a metal hook catches on to a loop (p. 632)

from The People, Yes

Carl Sandburg

They have yarns

Of a skyscraper so tall they had to put hinges

On the two top stories so to let the moon go by,

Of one corn crop in Missouri when the roots

Went so deep and drew off so much water

The Mississippi riverbed that year was dry,

Of pancakes so thin they had only one side,

Of "a fog so thick we shingled the barn and six feet out on the fog,"

Of Pecos Pete straddling a cyclone in Texas and riding it to the west coast where "it rained out under him,"

Of the man who drove a swarm of bees across the Rocky Mountains and the Desert "and didn't lose a bee,"

Of a mountain railroad curve where the engineer in his cab can touch the caboose and spit in the conductor's eye,

Of the boy who climbed a cornstalk growing so fast he would have starved to death if they hadn't shot biscuits up to him,

Of the old man's whiskers: "When the wind was with him his whiskers arrived a day before he did,"

Of the hen laying a square egg and cackling, "Ouch!" and of hens laying eggs with the dates printed on them,

Of the ship captain's shadow: it froze to the deck one cold winter night,

Of mutineers on that same ship put to chipping rust with rubber hammers,

Of the sheep counter who was fast and accurate: "I just count their feet and divide by four,"

Of the man so tall he must climb a ladder to shave himself,

Of the runt so teeny-weeny it takes two men and a boy to see him,

Of mosquitoes: one can kill a dog, two of them a man,

Of a cyclone that sucked cookstoves out of the kitchen, up the chimney flue, and on to the next town,

Of the same cyclone picking up wagon-tracks in Nebraska and dropping them over in the Dakotas,

Of the hook-and-eye snake unlocking itself into forty pieces, each piece two inches long, then in nine seconds flat snapping itself together again,

Of the watch swallowed by the cow—when they butchered her a year later the watch was running and had the correct time,

Of horned snakes, hoop snakes that roll themselves where they want to go, and rattlesnakes carrying bells instead of rattles on their tails,

Of the herd of cattle in California getting lost in a giant redwood tree that had hollowed out,

Of the man who killed a snake by putting its tail in its mouth so it swallowed itself,

Of railroad trains whizzing along so fast they reach the station before the whistle,

Of pigs so thin the farmer had to tie knots in their tails to keep them from crawling through the cracks in their pens,

Of Paul Bunyan's big blue ox, Babe, measuring between the eyes forty-two ax-handles and a plug of Star tobacco exactly,

Of John Henry's hammer and the curve of its swing and his singing of it as "a rainbow round my shoulder."

THINKING ABOUT THE SELECTION
Recalling

1. Find two yarns that involve exaggerated heights.
2. Find three yarns that involve cyclones.
3. Find two yarns that involve fantastic speed.
4. Find three yarns that involve snakes.

Interpreting

5. What does the statement "When the wind was with him his whiskers arrived a day before he did" tell you about the length of the man's whiskers?
6. Why is being made to chip rust with rubber hammers an effective punishment?
7. What did John Henry mean when he described the swing of his hammer as "a rainbow around my shoulder"?
8. Who are the people ("they") who told these yarns? What do these yarns suggest about these people?
9. Upon what characteristics of people, animals, or nature are these yarns built?

Applying

10. Why do you think people take pleasure in spinning yarns?

ANALYZING LITERATURE
Understanding a Yarn

A **yarn** is a tale or story that is exaggerated or incredible. Yarns usually start with everyday situations that then become so exaggerated as to be fantastic. For example, corn crops might have deep roots (true), but not actually so deep that the Mississippi riverbed would go dry (exaggerated).

1. What might a yarn exaggerate about the following topics?
   a. cats fighting
   b. a river overflowing
2. "The People, Yes" tells you about the way of life of Americans on the frontier. Find two yarns that reveal the dangers of nature. Find two yarns that reveal the need for hard work.

UNDERSTANDING LANGUAGE
Appreciating Compound Words

A **compound word** is formed by joining two words. Some words, such as *airplane,* are closed compounds because two words are joined together directly. Others, such as *baby-sit,* are hyphenated compounds. Still others, such as *major league,* are open compounds —although they are not actually joined, the two words are considered to mean one thing. You can usually learn the meaning of a compound word by breaking it into its parts.

1. Write the parts of the following compound words. Then write a sentence using each word correctly. Check the meaning in a dictionary.
   a. skyscraper
   b. riverbed
   c. pancakes
   d. ax handle
   e. West Coast
2. Add a second word to each of the following words to make a compound word. Check the dictionary if you need to.
   a. snow   b. night   c. bee

THINKING AND WRITING
Writing a Yarn

Refer to the list of subjects and experiences that you developed earlier. First freewrite about these subjects, including details that are as wild and exaggerated as you like. Then use these ideas to add eight lines to "The People, Yes" telling about some yarns that people could have in the 1980's and 1990's. Revise your writing, making sure you have used exaggeration effectively. Finally, proofread your work and share it with your classmates.

GUIDE FOR READING

The Girl Who Hunted Rabbits

The **Zuñi Indians** live in a harsh and unforgiving land, in northwestern New Mexico near Arizona. The early Zuñis were farmers. Their territory, governed by the United States after 1848, is parched by sun in summer and swept by wind and snow in winter. Yet there is beauty in the land: towering cliffs flaming red in the sunset; deep, cool canyons; and wide-open vistas. "The Girl Who Hunted Rabbits" tells of a courageous girl who faces the harsh elements to bring food home to her family.

Legend

A **legend** is an imaginative story believed to be based on an actual person or event, rather than on the supernatural. The story is passed from generation to generation, often by word of mouth. With retelling, the character's actions or the event may become more fantastic. The character becomes larger than life—a hero or heroine.

Legends also give you information about the people who tell them. "The Girl Who Hunted Rabbits" tells you how the Zuñis lived and some of the gods they believed in.

Look For

As you read "The Girl Who Hunted Rabbits," look for the dangers the girl faces. How is she finally saved from the demon?

Writing

Think of a time when a person did something brave. Freewrite, describing what happened. Describe how the brave person may have felt.

Vocabulary

Knowing the following words will help you as you read "The Girl Who Hunted Rabbits."

procured (prō kyoord') *adv.*: Obtained by some effort (p. 635)

sinew (sin' yoo) **n.**: A tendon, a band of fibrous tissue that connects muscles to bones or to other parts and can also be used as thread for sewing (p. 636)

mantle (man't'l) *n.*: Sleeveless cloak or cape (p. 636)

unwonted (un wun' tid) *adj.*: Not usual (p. 636)

bedraggled (bi drag' 'ld) *adj.*: Dirty and wet (p. 638)

voracious (vô rā' shəs) *adj.*: Eager to devour large quantities of food (p. 639)

devoured (di vourd') *v.*: Ate greedily (p. 639)

The Girl Who Hunted Rabbits

Zuñi Indian Legend

It was long ago, in the days of the ancients, that a poor maiden lived at "Little Gateway of Zuñi River." You know there are black stone walls of houses standing there on the tops of the cliffs of lava, above the narrow place through which the river runs, to this day.

In one of these houses there lived this poor maiden alone with her feeble old father and her aged mother. She was unmarried, and her brothers had all been killed in wars, or had died gently; so the family lived there helplessly, so far as many things were concerned, from the lack of men in their house.

It is true that in making the gardens— the little plantings of beans, pumpkins, squashes, melons, and corn—the maiden was able to do very well; and thus mainly on the products of these things the family were supported. But, as in those days of our ancients we had neither sheep nor cattle, the hunt was depended upon to supply the meat; or sometimes it was procured by barter[1] of the products of the fields to those who hunted mostly. Of these things this little family had barely enough for their own subsistence; hence, they could not procure their supplies of meat in this way.

Long before, it had been a great house, for many were the brave and strong young men who had lived in it; but the rooms were now empty, or at best contained only the leavings of those who had lived there, much used and worn out.

One autumn day, near wintertime, snow fell, and it became very cold. The maiden had gathered brush and firewood in abundance, and it was piled along the roof of the house and down underneath the ladder which descended from the top. She saw the young men issue forth the next morning in great numbers, their feet protected by long stockings of deerskin, the fur turned inward, and they carried on their shoulders and stuck in their belts stone axes and rabbit sticks. As she gazed at them from the roof, she said to herself, "O that I were a man and could go forth, as do these young men, hunting rabbits! Then my poor old mother and father would not lack for flesh with which to duly season their food and nourish their lean bodies." Thus ran her thoughts, and before night, as she saw these same young men coming in, one after another, some of them bringing long strings of rabbits, others short ones, but none of them empty-handed, she decided that she would set forth on the morrow to try what luck she might find in the killing of rabbits herself.

It may seem strange that, although this maiden was beautiful and young, the youths did not give her some of their rabbits. But

---

1. barter (bär′ tər), *v.*: To exchange goods.

their feelings were not friendly, for no one of them would she accept as a husband, although one after another of them had offered himself for marriage.

Fully resolved, the girl that evening sat down by the fireplace, and turning toward her aged parents, said, "O my mother and father, I see that the snow has fallen, whereby easily rabbits are tracked, and the young men who went out this morning returned long before evening heavily laden with strings of this game. Behold, in the other rooms of our house are many rabbit sticks, and there hang on the walls stone axes, and with these I might perchance strike down a rabbit on his trail, or, if he runs into a log, split the log and dig him out. So I have thought during the day, and have decided to go tomorrow and try my fortunes in the hunt."

"*Naiya*, my daughter," quavered the feeble, old mother, "you would surely be very cold, or you would lose your way, or grow so tired that you could not return before night, and you must not go out to hunt rabbits."

"Why, certainly not," insisted the old man, rubbing his lean knees and shaking his head over the days that were gone. "No, no; let us live in poverty rather than that you should run such risks as these, O my daughter."

But, say what they would, the girl was determined. And the old man said at last, "Very well! You will not be turned from your course. Therefore, O daughter, I will help you as best I may." He hobbled into another room, and found there some old deerskins covered thickly with fur; and drawing them out, he moistened and carefully softened them, and cut out for the maiden long stockings, which he sewed up with sinew and the fiber of the yucca[2] leaf. Then he selected

for her from among the old possessions of his brothers and sons, who had been killed or perished otherwise, a number of rabbit sticks and a fine, heavy stone ax. Meanwhile, the old woman busied herself in preparing a lunch for the girl, which was composed of little cakes of cornmeal, spiced with pepper and wild onions, pierced through the middle, and baked in the ashes. When she had made a long string of these by threading them like beads on a rope of yucca fiber, she laid them down not far from the ladder on a little bench, with the rabbit sticks, the stone ax, and the deerskin stockings.

That night the maiden planned and planned, and early on the following morning, even before the young men had gone out from the town, she had put on a warm, short-skirted dress, knotted a mantle over her shoulder and thrown another and larger one over her back, drawn on the deerskin stockings, had thrown the string of corncakes over her shoulder, stuck the rabbit sticks in her belt, and carrying the stone ax in her hand sallied[3] forth eastward through the Gateway of Zuñi and into the plain of the valley beyond, called the Plain of the Burnt River, on account of the black, roasted-looking rocks along some parts of its sides. Dazzlingly white the snow stretched out before her—not deep, but unbroken—and when she came near the cliffs with many little canyons in them, along the northern side of the valley, she saw many a trail of rabbits running out and in among the rocks and between the bushes.

Warm and excited by her unwonted exercise, she did not heed a coming snow-storm, but ran about from one place to another, following the trails of the rabbits, sometimes up into the canyons where the forests of pine and cedar stood, and where

---

2. yucca (yuk′ ə), *n.*: A desert plant with stiff leaves and white flowers.

3. sallied (sal′ ēd), *v.*: Set out energetically.

here and there she had the good fortune sometimes to run two, three, or four rabbits into a single hollow log. It was little work to split these logs, for they were small, as you know, and to dig out the rabbits and slay them by a blow of the hand on the nape of the neck, back of the ears; and as she killed each rabbit she raised it reverently to her lips, and breathed from its nostrils its expiring breath[4] and, tying its legs together, placed it on the string, which after a while began to grow heavy on her shoulders. Still

---

4. **expiring** (ik spīr′ ing) **breath:** Air breathed out as the rabbit dies.

she kept on, little heeding the snow which was falling fast; nor did she notice that it was growing darker and darker, so intent was she on the hunt, and so glad was she to capture so many rabbits. Indeed, she followed the trails until they were no longer visible, as the snow fell all around her, thinking all the while, "How happy will be my poor old father and mother that they shall now have flesh to eat! How strong will they grow! And when this meat is gone, that which is dried and preserved of it also, lo! another snowstorm will no doubt come, and I can go out hunting again."

At last the twilight came, and, looking

around, she found that the snow had fallen deeply, there was no trail, and that she had lost her way. True, she turned about and started in the direction of her home, as she supposed, walking as fast as she could through the soft, deep snow. Yet she reckoned not rightly, for instead of going eastward along the valley, she went southward across it, and entering the mouth of the Descending Plain of the Pines, she went on and on, thinking she was going homeward, until at last it grew dark and she knew not which way to turn.

"What harm," thought she, "if I find a sheltered place among the rocks? What harm if I remain all night, and go home in the morning when the snow has ceased falling, and by the light I shall know my way?"

So she turned about to some rocks which appeared, black and dim, a short distance away. Fortunately, among these rocks is the cave which is known as Taiuma's[5] Cave. This she came to, and peering into that black hole, she saw in it, back some distance, a little glowing light. "Ha, ha!" thought she, "perhaps some rabbit hunters like myself, belated yesterday, passed the night here and left the fire burning. If so, this is greater good fortune than I could have looked for." So, lowering the string of rabbits which she carried on her shoulder, and throwing off her mantle, she crawled in, peering well into the darkness, for fear of wild beasts; then, returning, she drew in the string of rabbits and the mantle.

Behold! there was a bed of hot coals buried in the ashes in the very middle of the cave, and piled up on one side were fragments of broken wood. The girl, happy in her good fortune, issued forth and gathered more sticks from the cliffside, where dead

pines are found in great numbers, and bringing them in little armfuls one after another, she finally succeeded in gathering a store sufficient to keep the fire burning brightly all the night through. Then she drew off her snow-covered stockings of deerskin and the bedraggled mantles, and, building a fire, hung them up to dry and sat down to rest herself. The fire burned up and glowed brightly, so that the whole cave was as light as a room at night when a dance is being celebrated. By and by, after her clothing had dried, she spread a mantle on the floor of the cave by the side of the fire, and, sitting down, dressed one of her rabbits and roasted it, and, untying the string of corncakes her mother had made for her, feasted on the roasted meat and cakes.

She had just finished her evening meal, and was about to recline and watch the fire for awhile, when she heard away off in the distance a long, low cry of distress — "Ho-o-o-o thlaia-a!"

"Ah!" thought the girl, "someone, more belated than myself, is lost; doubtless one of the rabbit-hunters." She got up, and went nearer to the entrance of the cavern.

"Ho-o-o-o thlaia-a!" sounded the cry, nearer this time. She ran out, and, as it was repeated again, she placed her hand to her mouth, and cried, as loudly as possible, "Li-i thlaia-a!" ("Here!")

The cry was repeated near at hand, and presently the maiden, listening first, and then shouting, and listening again, heard the clatter of an enormous rattle. In dismay and terror she threw her hands into the air, and, crouching down, rushed into the cave and retreated to its farthest limits, where she sat shuddering with fear, for she knew that one of the Cannibal Demons of those days, perhaps the renowned Atahsaia[6] of

---

5. Taiuma's (tī o͞o′ mɔz).

6. Atahsaia (ah′tə sī′ ə).

the east, had seen the light of her fire through the cave entrance, with his terrible staring eyes, and assuming it to be a lost wanderer, had cried out, and so led her to guide him to her place of concealment.

On came the Demon, snapping the twigs under his feet and shouting in a hoarse, loud voice, *"Ho lithlsh tā ime!"* ("Ho, there! So you are in here, are you?") *Kothl!* clanged his rattle, while, almost fainting with terror, closer to the rock crouched the maiden.

The old Demon came to the entrance of the cave and bawled out, "I am cold, I am hungry! Let me in!" Without further ado, he stooped and tried to get in; but, behold! the entrance was too small for his giant shoulders to pass. Then he pretended to be wonderfully civil, and said, "Come out, and bring me something to eat."

"I have nothing for you," cried the maiden. "I have eaten my food."

"Have you no rabbits?"

"Yes."

"Come out and bring me some of them."

But the maiden was so terrified that she dared not move toward the entrance.

"Throw me a rabbit!" shouted the old Demon.

The maiden threw him one of her precious rabbits at last, when she could rise and go to it. He clutched it with his long, horny hand, gave one gulp and swallowed it. Then he cried out, "Throw me another!" She threw him another, which he also immediately swallowed; and so on until the poor maiden had thrown all the rabbits to the voracious old monster. Every one she threw him he caught in his huge, yellow-tusked mouth, and swallowed, hair and all, at one gulp.

"Throw me another!" cried he, when the last had already been thrown to him.

So the poor maiden was forced to say, "I have no more."

"Throw me your overshoes!" cried he.

She threw the overshoes of deerskin, and these like the rabbits he speedily devoured. Then he called for her moccasins, and she threw them; for her belt, and she threw it; and finally, wonderful to tell, she threw even her mantle, and blanket, and her overdress, until, behold, she had nothing left!

Now, with all he had eaten, the old Demon was swollen hugely at the stomach, and, though he tried and tried to squeeze himself through the mouth of the cave, he could not by any means succeed. Finally, lifting his great flint ax, he began to shatter the rock about the entrance to the cave, and slowly but surely he enlarged the hole and the maiden now knew that as soon as he could get in he would devour her also, and she almost fainted at the sickening thought. Pound, pound, pound, pound, went the great ax of the Demon as he struck the rocks.

In the distance the two war-gods were sitting in their home at the Shrine amid the Bushes beyond Thunder Mountain, and though far off, they heard thus in the middle of the night the pounding of the Demon's hammer ax against the rocks. And of course they knew at once that a poor maiden, for the sake of her father and mother, had been out hunting—that she had lost her way and, finding a cave where there was a little fire, entered it, rebuilt the fire, and rested herself; that, attracted by the light of her fire, the Cannibal Demon had come and besieged her retreat,[7] and only a little time hence would he so enlarge the entrance to the cave that he could squeeze even his great overfilled paunch through it and come at the maiden to destroy her. So, catching up their wonderful weapons, these two

---

7. besieged (bi sējd') **her retreat:** Attacked her place of refuge.

war-gods flew away into the darkness and in no time they were approaching the Descending Plain of the Pines.

Just as the Demon was about to enter the cavern, and the maiden had fainted at seeing his huge face and gray shock of hair and staring eyes, his yellow, protruding tusks, and his horny, taloned hand, they came upon the old beast. Each one hitting him a blow with his war club, they "ended his daylight," and then hauled him forth into the open space. They opened his huge paunch and withdrew from it the maiden's garments, and even the rabbits which had been slain. The rabbits they cast away among the soap-weed plants that grew on the slope at the foot of the cliff. The garments they spread out on the snow, and cleansed and made them perfect, even more perfect than they had been before. Then, flinging the huge body of the giant Demon down into the depths of the canyon, they turned them about and, calling out gentle words to the maiden, entered and restored her. She, seeing in them not their usual ugly persons, but handsome youths, was greatly comforted; and bending low, and breathing upon their hands, thanked them over and over for the rescue they had brought her. But she crouched herself low with shame that her garments were but few, when, behold! the youths went out and brought in to her the garments they had cleaned, restoring them to her.

Then, spreading their mantles by the door of the cave, they slept there that night, in order to protect the maiden, and on the morrow wakened her. They told her many things, and showed her many things which she had not known before, and counseled her thus, "It is not fearful that a maiden should marry; therefore, O maiden, return unto thy people in the Village of the Gateway of the River of Zuñi. This morning we will slay rabbits unnumbered for you, and start you on your way, guarding you down the snow-covered valley. When you are in sight of your home we will leave you, telling you our names."

So, early in the morning the two gods went forth, flinging their sticks among the soap-weed plants. Behold! as though the soap-weed plants were rabbits, so many lay killed on the snow before these mighty hunters. And they gathered together great numbers of these rabbits, a string for each one of the party. When the Sun had risen clearer in the sky, and his light sparkled on the snow around them, they took the rabbits to the maiden and presented them, saying, "We will carry each one of us a string of these rabbits." Then taking her hand, they led her out of the cave and down the valley, until, beyond on the high black mesas[8] at the Gateway of the River of Zuñi, she saw the smoke rise from the houses of her village. Then turned the two war-gods to her, and they told her their names. And again she bent low, and breathed on their hands. Then, dropping the strings of rabbits which they had carried close beside the maiden, they swiftly disappeared.

Thinking much of all she had learned, she continued her way to the home of her father and mother. As she went into the town, staggering under her load of rabbits, the young men and the old men and women and children beheld her with wonder; and no hunter in that town thought of comparing himself with the Maiden Hunter of Zuñi River. The old man and the old woman, who had mourned the night through and sat up anxiously watching, were overcome with happiness when they saw their daughter had returned.

---

8. mesas (mā′ səz), *n.*: Small mountains with flat tops and steep sides.

THINKING ABOUT THE SELECTION

Recalling

1. For what reasons does the girl go hunting?
2. Why do the girl's parents at first resist her plans?
3. How does the girl become lost?
4. Explain the Cannibal Demon's plan to get the girl out of the cave.
5. How is the girl rescued?
6. How do the villagers regard the girl when she returns?

Interpreting

7. Why do the girl's parents help her when they really do not want her to go?
8. Why does the war god help the girl?
9. Why does the girl see the two "usually ugly" war gods as handsome youths?
10. What does the girl learn from the war gods? Do you think what she learns will affect the way she behaves in the future? Explain your answer.

Applying

11. In this legend the girl demonstrates bravery. Select one other character you have read about who is brave. Compare and contrast the girl and this character.

ANALYZING LITERATURE

Understanding a Legend

Legends are imaginative stories that are based on real people or real events. As the story is passed from generation to generation it often changes. Sometimes the retelling may result in downplaying the factual and highlighting the imaginative. "The Girl Who Hunted Rabbits" is probably based on a real incident.
1. What details of the legend could be based on fact?
2. What parts seem purely imaginative?

CRITICAL THINKING AND READING

Making Inferences from a Legend

An **inference** is a reasonable conclusion that can be drawn from evidence. In "The Girl Who Hunted Rabbits" you can infer that Zuñi girls were not expected to hunt based on the girl's statement, "O that I were a man and could go forth, as do these young men, hunting rabbits!"
1. Find evidence in this legend that suggests that young girls were expected to get married.
2. Find evidence that the Zuñi placed high value on children taking care of their parents.

UNDERSTANDING LANGUAGE

Choosing Meaning to Fit Context

Context is the surrounding words and ideas that can help you understand the meaning of an unfamiliar word.

From the context of the following sentences, figure out the meanings of the words in italics.
1. "But, as in those days of our ancients, we had neither sheep nor cattle, the hunt was depended upon to supply the meat; or sometimes it was *procured* by barter of the products of the fields to those who hunted mostly."
2. "Of these things this little family had barely enough for their own *subsistence;* hence, they could not procure their supplies of meat in this way."

THINKING AND WRITING

Retelling a Legend

Imagine you are the girl in this legend. Think about your feelings when the demon tried to devour you. Retell this episode from the girl's point of view. Use the pronoun *I* to identify yourself as the girl. Revise, making sure you have told events through the girl's eyes. Finally, proofread your story and share it with your classmates.

GUIDE FOR READING

Paul Bunyan of the North Woods

Paul Bunyan is a legendary frontiersman—a gigantic lumberjack known for his tremendous strength and fantastic logging feats. According to folklore, Paul Bunyan invented the idea of logging in the Pacific Northwest. He created the Great Lakes—to provide drinking water for his enormous blue ox, Babe.

Folktales about Paul Bunyan have been recorded by numerous writers, among them **Carl Sandburg** (1878–1967). (For more information on Carl Sandburg, see also page 630.)

Folktale

Folktales, like legends and myths, are stories that have been passed down orally, but today have been preserved in written form. They are not about gods and goddesses but often involve a hero who performs amazing feats of strength or daring or solves problems. Folktales often may last because they highlight qualities that a culture values.

Look For

As you read "Paul Bunyan of the North Woods," look for the traits about Paul Bunyan—strength, size, and cleverness—that make people enjoy hearing tales about him. Notice that this selection summarizes several folktales about Paul Bunyan. Which of the tales about him do you like the most?

Writing

Create an imaginary hero, such as the greatest football player or the most brilliant scientist. Brainstorm and write down your ideas about folktales that you could tell about that person.

Vocabulary

Knowing the following words will help you as you read "Paul Bunyan of the North Woods."

lumberjack (lum′ bər jak′) *n.*: A person employed to cut down timber (p. 643)

shanties (shan′ tēz) *n.*: Huts or shacks in which loggers lived (p. 643)

granite (gran′ it) *adj.*: Made of a type of very hard rock (p. 643)

hobnailed (häb′ nāld′) *adj.*: Having short nails put on the soles to provide greater traction (p. 643)

commotion (kə mō′ shən) *n.*: Noisy movement (p. 644)

bellowing (bel′ ō iŋ) *adv.*: Roaring (p. 644)

Paul Bunyan
of the North Woods

Carl Sandburg

Who made Paul Bunyan, who gave him birth as a myth, who joked him into life as the Master Lumberjack, who fashioned him forth as an apparition[1] easing the hours of men amid axes and trees, saws and lumber? The people, the bookless people, they made Paul and had him alive long before he got into the books for those who read. He grew up in shanties, around the hot stoves of winter, among socks and mittens drying, in the smell of tobacco smoke and the roar of laughter mocking the outside weather. And some of Paul came overseas in wooden bunks below decks in sailing vessels. And some of Paul is old as the hills, young as the alphabet.

The Pacific Ocean froze over in the winter of the Blue Snow and Paul Bunyan had long teams of oxen hauling regular white snow over from China. This was the winter Paul gave a party to the Seven Axmen. Paul fixed a granite floor sunk two hundred feet deep for them to dance on. Still, it tipped and tilted as the dance went on. And because the Seven Axmen

**PAUL BUNYAN CARRYING A TREE
ON HIS SHOULDER AND AN AX IN HIS HAND**
The Bettmann Archive

refused to take off their hobnailed boots, the sparks from the nails of their dancing feet lit up the place so that Paul didn't light the kerosene lamps. No women being on the Big Onion river at that time the Seven Axmen had to dance

---

1. apparition (ap′ə rish′ən), *n.*: A strange figure appearing suddenly or in an extraordinary way.

with each other, the one left over in each set taking Paul as a partner. The commotion of the dancing that night brought on an earthquake and the Big Onion river moved over three counties to the east.

One year when it rained from St. Patrick's Day till the Fourth of July, Paul Bunyan got disgusted because his celebration on the Fourth was spoiled. He dived into Lake Superior and swam to where a solid pillar of water was coming down. He dived under this pillar, swam up into it and climbed with powerful swimming strokes, was gone about an hour, came splashing down, and as the rain stopped, he explained, "I turned the dam thing off." This is told in the Big North Woods and on the Great Lakes, with many particulars.

Two mosquitoes lighted on one of Paul Bunyan's oxen, killed it, ate it, cleaned the bones, and sat on a grub shanty picking their teeth as Paul came along. Paul sent to Australia for two special bumblebees to kill these mosquitoes. But the bees and the mosquitoes intermarried; their children had stingers on both ends. And things kept getting worse till Paul brought a big boatload of sorghum[2] up from Louisiana and while all the bee-

mosquitoes were eating at the sweet sorghum he floated them down to the Gulf of Mexico. They got so fat that it was easy to drown them all between New Orleans and Galveston.

Paul logged on the Little Gimlet in Oregon one winter. The cookstove at that camp covered an acre of ground. They fastened the side of a hog on each snowshoe and four men used to skate on the griddle while the cook flipped the pancakes. The eating table was three miles long; elevators carried the cakes to the ends of the table where boys on bicycles rode back and forth on a path down the center of the table dropping the cakes where called for.

Benny, the Little Blue Ox of Paul Bunyan, grew two feet every time Paul looked at him, when a youngster. The barn was gone one morning and they found it on Benny's back; he grew out of it in a night. One night he kept pawing and bellowing for more pancakes, till there were two hundred men at the cookshanty stove trying to keep him fed. About breakfast time Benny broke loose, tore down the cook-shanty, ate all the pancakes piled up for the loggers' breakfast. And after that Benny made his mistake; he ate the red hot stove; and that finished him. This is only one of the hot-stove stories told in the North Woods.

_____

2. sorghum (sor'gəm), *n.*: Tropical grasses bearing flowers and seeds that are grown for use as grain or syrup.

THINKING ABOUT THE SELECTION

Recalling

1. How did Paul Bunyan show his cleverness?
2. How did Paul Bunyan use his strength?
3. How did Paul Bunyan solve the problem of serving pancakes at a table three miles long?
4. How often did Benny, the Little Blue Ox of Paul Bunyan, grow when a youngster?

Interpreting

5. Interpret the following statement: "And some of Paul is old as the hills, young as the alphabet"?
6. What qualities and abilities seem to be valued in this selection?

Applying

7. Explain how Paul's qualities of strength, cleverness, and size might be valuable for real lumberjacks.

ANALYZING LITERATURE

Understanding a Folktale

Before **folktales** were preserved in written form, they were simply stories retold whenever a group of people with the same interests gathered. Many times, the storyteller would claim to have witnessed the tale in order to make it seem more authentic. The tales that people chose to recount indicate something about what their lives were like. For example, this selection shows you the rugged lives that loggers lived.

1. Find three other details that indicate the ruggedness of the loggers' lives.
2. Find two details that indicate the need for courage.
3. Think about the landscape of the Pacific Northwest. Why would the people telling these folktales make Paul so big?

CRITICAL THINKING AND READING

Making Generalizations About a Folktale

A **generalization** is a general idea or statement derived from particular instances. For example, if every book you have read by a certain author is about science fiction, you can generalize that the author is a science-fiction writer.

1. What generalization do you make about the folktales based on "Paul Bunyan of the North Woods"?
2. Give the particular instances on which this generalization is based.

UNDERSTANDING LANGUAGE

Appreciating Homophones

Homophones are words that have the same sound, but differ in spelling and meaning. For example, *bough* sounds like *cow* and means "the branch of a tree." A homophone of *bough* is *bow,* which sounds the same, but is spelled differently and means "to bend the head or body in respect."

Write the homophone for each of the following words.

1. meet
2. site
3. pane
4. know

THINKING AND WRITING

Writing a Response to Critical Comment

A writer has said that the Paul Bunyan folktales were told matter-of-factly, as if by an eyewitness of commonly known events. This gives the tales a feeling of truthfulness. Choose which tales in this selection are told in a matter-of-fact manner. Then write an essay for your classmates explaining in what ways they seem matter-of-fact. Use examples to support your view. Revise your paragraphs to make sure your opinion is stated clearly. Finally, proofread your essay and share it with your classmates.

GUIDE FOR READING

Pecos Bill: The Cyclone

Pecos Bill is a legendary American cowboy. He is credited with the invention of branding, roping, and the six-shooter, and is said to have taught broncos how to buck. The tales tell that Pecos Bill was born in Texas in the 1830's. One of the most famous tales about Pecos Bill tells of the time he rode a cyclone in Oklahoma.

That exploit is recounted by **Harold W. Felton** (1902–   ), born in Neola, Iowa, who collected folklore of the West.

Conflict in a Folktale

A **conflict** is a struggle between opposing sides or forces. A conflict can be that of a person against another person, nature, fate, or society; or it can be between two opposing forces within a person.

The hero in a folktale may be in conflict with the fastest runner, the hardest worker, the best shot, the most courageous person, or the quickest thinker. Folktales are full of conflicts and competitions, such as shooting and boxing matches and encounters with nature, that the heroes win because of their extraordinary daring, skill, or strength.

Look For

As you read "Pecos Bill: The Cyclone," look for how Pecos Bill, the greatest of the cowboys, deals with conflicts in ways that are different from those of an average human being. Why is he able to win each of these conflicts?

Writing

Conflicts in folktales often involve a human being who is pitted against some overwhelming force or obstacle. Brainstorm and write down your ideas about the types of conflicts you could write a folktale about.

Vocabulary

Knowing the following words will help you as you read "Pecos Bill: The Cyclone."

usurped (yoo surpt´) v.: To take power or authority away from (p. 649)

invincible (in vin´ sə b'l) adj.: Unbeatable (p. 651)

futile (fyoot´ 'l) adj.: Useless, hopeless (p. 651)

inexplicable (in eks´ pli kə b'l) adj.: Without explanation (p. 652)

skeptics (skep´ tiks) n.: Persons who doubt (p. 652)

Pecos Bill: The Cyclone

Harold W. Felton

One of Bill's greatest feats, if not the greatest feat of all time, occurred unexpectedly one Fourth of July. He had invented the Fourth of July some years before. It was a great day for the cowpunchers.[1] They had taken to it right off like the real Americans they were. But the celebration had always ended on a dismal note. Somehow it seemed to be spoiled by a cyclone.

Bill had never minded the cyclone much. The truth is he rather liked it. But the other celebrants ran into caves for safety. He invented cyclone cellars for them. He even named the cellars. He called them "'fraid holes." Pecos wouldn't even say the word "afraid." The cyclone was something like he was. It was big and strong too. He always stood by musing[2] pleasantly as he watched it.

The cyclone caused Bill some trouble, though. Usually it would destroy a few hundred miles of fence by blowing the postholes away. But it wasn't much trouble for him to fix it. All he had to do was to go and get the postholes and then take them back and put the fence posts in them. The holes were rarely ever blown more than twenty or thirty miles.

In one respect Bill even welcomed the cyclone, for it blew so hard it blew the earth away from his wells. The first time this happened, he thought the wells would be a total loss. There they were, sticking up several hundred feet out of the ground. As wells they were useless. But he found he could cut them up into lengths and sell them for postholes to farmers in Iowa and Nebraska. It was very profitable, especially after he invented a special posthole saw to cut them with. He didn't use that type of posthole himself. He got the prairie dogs to dig his for him. He simply caught a few gross[3] of prairie dogs and set them down at proper intervals. The prairie dog would dig a hole. Then Bill would put a post in it. The prairie dog would get disgusted and go down the row ahead of the others and dig another hole. Bill fenced all of Texas and parts of New Mexico and Arizona in this manner. He took a few contracts and fenced most of the Southern Pacific right of way too. That's the reason it is so crooked. He had trouble getting the prairie dogs to run a straight fence.

As for his wells, the badgers dug them. The system was the same as with the prairie dogs. The labor was cheap so it didn't make much difference if the cyclone did spoil some of the wells. The badgers were digging all of the time anyway. They didn't seem to care whether they dug wells or just badger holes.

One year he tried shipping the prairie dog holes up north, too, for postholes. It was not successful. They didn't keep in storage

---

1. cowpunchers (kou′ pun chərz), *n.*: Cowboys.
2. musing (myoo̅z′ ing), *adv.*: Thinking deeply.

3. gross (grōs), *n.*: Twelve dozen.

and they couldn't stand the handling in shipping. After they were installed they seemed to wear out quickly. Bill always thought the difference in climate had something to do with it.

It should be said that in those days there was only one cyclone. It was the first and original cyclone, bigger and more terrible by far than the small cyclones of today. It usually stayed by itself up north around Kansas and Oklahoma and didn't bother anyone much. But it was attracted by the noise of the Fourth of July celebration and without fail managed to put in an appearance before the close of the day.

On this particular Fourth of July, the celebration had gone off fine. The speeches were loud and long. The contests and games were hard fought. The high point of the day was Bill's exhibition with Widow Maker, which came right after he showed off Scat and Rat. People seemed never to tire of seeing them in action. The mountain lion was almost useless as a work animal after his accident, and the snake had grown old and somewhat infirm, and was troubled with rheumatism in his rattles. But they too enjoyed the Fourth of July and liked to make a public appearance. They relived the old days.

Widow Maker had put on a good show, bucking as no ordinary horse could ever buck. Then Bill undertook to show the gaits[4] he had taught the palomino.[5] Other mustangs[6] at that time had only two gaits. Walking and running. Only Widow Maker could pace. But now Bill had developed and taught him other gaits. Twenty-seven in all. Twenty-three forward and three reverse. He

was very proud of the achievement. He showed off the slow gaits and the crowd was eager for more.

He showed the walk, trot, canter, lope, jog, slow rack, fast rack, single foot, pace, stepping pace, fox trot, running walk and the others now known. Both men and horses confuse the various gaits nowadays. Some of the gaits are now thought to be the same, such as the rack and the single foot. But with Widow Maker and Pecos Bill, each one was different. Each was precise and to be distinguished from the others. No one had ever imagined such a thing.

Then the cyclone came! All of the people except Bill ran into the 'fraid holes. Bill was annoyed. He stopped the performance. The remaining gaits were not shown. From that day to this horses have used no more than the gaits Widow Maker exhibited that day. It is unfortunate that the really fast gaits were not shown. If they were, horses might be much faster today than they are.

Bill glanced up at the cyclone and the quiet smile on his face faded into a frown. He saw the cyclone was angry. Very, very angry indeed.

The cyclone had always been the center of attention. Everywhere it went people would look up in wonder, fear and amazement. It had been the undisputed master of the country. It had observed Bill's rapid climb to fame and had seen the Fourth of July celebration grow. It had been keeping an eye on things all right.

In the beginning, the Fourth of July crowd had aroused its curiosity. It liked nothing more than to show its superiority and power by breaking the crowd up sometime during the day. But every year the crowd was larger. This preyed on the cyclone's mind. This year it did not come to watch. It deliberately came to spoil the celebration. Jealous of Bill and of his success,

---

4. gaits (gātz), *n*.: Any of the various foot movements of a horse.
5. palomino (pal'ə mē' nō), *n*.: A light tan or golden brown horse with a cream-colored mane and tail.
6. mustangs (mus' taŋz), *n*.: Wild horses of the American plains.

it resolved to do away with the whole institution of the Fourth of July once and for all. So much havoc and destruction would be wrought that there would never be another Independence Day Celebration. On that day, in future years, it would circle around the horizon leering[7] and gloating. At least, so it thought.

The cyclone was resolved, also, to do away with this bold fellow who did not hold it in awe and run for the 'fraid hole at its approach. For untold years it had been the most powerful thing in the land. And now, here was a mere man who threatened its position. More! Who had usurped its position!

When Bill looked at the horizon and saw the cyclone coming, he recognized the anger and rage. While a cyclone does not often smile, Bill had felt from the beginning that it was just a grouchy fellow who never had a pleasant word for anyone. But now, instead of merely an unpleasant character, Bill saw all the viciousness of which an angry cyclone is capable. He had no way of knowing that the cyclone saw its kingship tottering and was determined to stop this man who threatened its supremacy.

But Bill understood the violence of the onslaught even as the monster came into view. He knew he must meet it. The center of the cyclone was larger than ever before. The fact is, the cyclone had been training for this fight all winter and spring. It was in best form and at top weight. It headed straight for Bill intent on his destruction. In an instant it was upon him. Bill had sat quietly and silently on the great pacing mustang. But his mind was working rapidly. In the split second between his first sight of the monster and the time for action he had made his plans. Pecos Bill was ready! Ready and waiting!

Green clouds were dripping from the cyclone's jaws. Lightning flashed from its eyes as it swept down upon him. Its plan was to envelop Bill in one mighty grasp. Just as it was upon him, Bill turned Widow Maker to its left. This was a clever move for the cyclone was right-handed, and while it had been training hard to get its left in shape, that was not its best side. Bill gave rein to his mount. Widow Maker wheeled and turned on a dime which Pecos had, with great foresight[8] and accuracy, thrown to the ground to mark the exact spot for this maneuver. It was the first time that anyone had thought of turning on a dime. Then he urged the great horse forward. The cyclone, filled with surprise, lost its balance and rushed forward at an increased speed. It went so fast that it met itself coming back. This confused the cyclone, but it did not confuse Pecos Bill. He had expected that to happen. Widow Maker went into his twenty-first gait and edged up close to the whirlwind. Soon they were running neck and neck.

At the proper instant Bill grabbed the cyclone's ears, kicked himself free of the stirrups and pulled himself lightly on its back. Bill never used spurs on Widow Maker. Sometimes he wore them for show and because he liked the jingling sound they made. They made a nice accompaniment for his cowboy songs. But he had not been singing, so he had no spurs. He did not have his rattlesnake for a quirt.[9] Of course there was no bridle. It was man against monster! There he was! Pecos Bill astride a raging cyclone, slick heeled and without a saddle!

---

7. leering (lir'ing), *adv.*: Looking with malicious triumph.

8. foresight (fôr' sīt), *n.*: The act of seeing beforehand.

9. quirt (kwurt), *n.*: A short-handled riding whip with a braided rawhide lash.

The cyclone was taken by surprise at this sudden turn of events. But it was undaunted. It was sure of itself. Months of training had given it a conviction that it was invincible. With a mighty heave, it twisted to its full height. Then it fell back suddenly, twisting and turning violently, so that before it came back to earth, it had turned around a thousand times. Surely no rider could ever withstand such an attack. No rider ever had. Little wonder. No one had ever ridden a cyclone before. But Pecos Bill did! He fanned the tornado's ears with his hat and dug his heels into the demon's flanks and yelled, "Yipee-ee!"

The people who had run for shelter began to come out. The audience further enraged the cyclone. It was bad enough to be disgraced by having a man astride it. It was unbearable not to have thrown him. To have all the people see the failure was too much! It got down flat on the ground and rolled over and over. Bill retained his seat throughout this ruse.[10] Evidence of this desperate but futile stratagem[11] remains today. The great Staked Plains, or as the Mexicans call it, *Llano Estacado* is the result. Its small, rugged mountains were covered with trees at the time. The rolling of the cyclone destroyed the mountains, the trees, and almost everything else in the area. The destruction was so complete, that part of the country is flat and treeless to this day. When the settlers came, there were no landmarks to guide them across the vast unmarked space, so they drove stakes in the ground to mark the trails. That is the reason it is called "Staked Plains." Here is an example of the proof of the events of history by

---

10. ruse (rōoz), *n.*: Trick.
11. stratagem (stra′ tə jəm), *n.*: Plan for defeating an opponent.

careful and painstaking research. It is also an example of how seemingly inexplicable geographical facts can be explained.

It was far more dangerous for the rider when the cyclone shot straight up to the sky. Once there, the twister tried the same thing it had tried on the ground. It rolled on the sky. It was no use. Bill could not be unseated. He kept his place, and he didn't have a sky hook with him either.

As for Bill, he was having the time of his life, shouting at the top of his voice, kicking his opponent in the ribs and jabbing his thumb in its flanks. It responded and went on a wild bucking rampage over the entire West. It used all the bucking tricks known to the wildest broncos as well as those known only to cyclones. The wind howled furiously and beat against the fearless rider. The rain poured. The lightning flashed around his ears. The fight went on and on. Bill enjoyed himself immensely. In spite of the elements he easily kept his place. . . .

The raging cyclone saw this out of the corner of its eye. It knew then who the victor was. It was twisting far above the Rocky Mountains when the awful truth came to it. In a horrible heave it disintegrated! Small pieces of cyclone flew in all directions. Bill still kept his seat on the main central portion until that rained out from under him. Then he jumped to a nearby streak of lightning and slid down it toward earth. But it was raining so hard that the rain put out the lightning. When it fizzled out from under him, Bill dropped the rest of the way. He lit in what is now called Death Valley. He hit quite hard, as is apparent from the fact that he so compressed the place that it is still two hundred and seventy-six feet below sea level. The Grand Canyon was washed out by the rain, though it must be understood that this happened after Paul Bunyan had given it a good start

by carelessly dragging his ax behind him when he went west a short time before.

The cyclones and the hurricanes and the tornadoes nowadays are the small pieces that broke off of the big cyclone Pecos Bill rode. In fact, the rainstorms of the present day came into being in the same way. There are always skeptics, but even they will recognize the logic of the proof of this event. They will recall that even now it almost always rains on the Fourth of July. That is because the rainstorms of today still retain some of the characteristics of the giant cyclone that met its comeuppance at the hands of Pecos Bill.

Bill lay where he landed and looked up at the sky, but he could see no sign of the cyclone. Then he laughed softly as he felt the warm sand of Death Valley on his back. . . .

It was a rough ride though, and Bill had resisted unusual tensions and pressures. When he got on the cyclone he had a twenty-dollar gold piece and a bowie knife[12] in his pocket. The tremendous force of the cyclone was such that when he finished the ride he found that his pocket contained a plugged nickel[13] and a little pearl-handled penknife. His two giant six-shooters were compressed and transformed into a small water pistol and a popgun.

It is a strange circumstance that lesser men have monuments raised in their honor. Death Valley is Bill's monument. Sort of a monument in reverse. Sunk in his honor, you might say. Perhaps that is as it should be. After all, Bill was different. He made his own monument. He made it with his hips, as is evident from the great depth of the valley. That is the hard way.

---

12. bowie (bō′ ē) **knife:** A strong, single-edged hunting knife named after James Bowie (1799–1836), U.S. soldier.
13. plugged nickel: Fake nickel.

THINKING ABOUT THE SELECTION
Recalling

1. Before riding the cyclone, what feats had Pecos Bill performed?
2. Why does the cyclone want to spoil the Fourth of July celebration?
3. How does Pecos Bill get astride the cyclone?
4. What happens when the cyclone realizes that Pecos Bill is the victor?
5. What natural wonders or geographical sites are caused by Pecos Bill or the cyclone?

Interpreting

6. How is the cyclone similar to Pecos Bill?
7. How can Pecos Bill tell that the cyclone is very angry?
8. Bill laughs when he sees the cyclone is gone. What does this tell you about Bill?
9. Why does the writer call Death Valley a "monument in reverse" to Pecos Bill?

Applying

10. Bill makes his plans for this battle in "the split second between his first sight of the monster and the time for action." Do you believe anyone can think that quickly? Support your answer with examples of quick (or slow) thinking that you know about.

ANALYZING LITERATURE
Understanding Conflict in a Folktale

A **conflict,** or struggle between opposing sides or forces, is usually what a folktale is about. Often the hero of a folktale is thrown into conflict with another person or a natural force. After a significant struggle, the hero emerges as the winner.

1. What is the conflict in this folktale?
2. Write down your idea for a variation of this conflict.

CRITICAL THINKING AND READING
Identifying Reasons

A **reason** is the information that explains or justifies a decision, an action, or a conclusion. A reason may be a fact, an opinion, a situation, or an occurrence. For example, in "Pecos Bill: The Cyclone," the reason for Bill's welcoming the cyclone is that it blew the earth away from his wells, which Bill then sold for postholes.

Give the reasons for the following situations from "Pecos Bill: The Cyclone."
1. The cyclone wants to do away with Pecos Bill.
2. The cyclone is in top form.
3. The cyclone disintegrates.

UNDERSTANDING LANGUAGE
Appreciating Words from Spanish

Many words in English come from the Spanish language. For example, *chaps* comes from the Spanish *chaperejos,* meaning "leather trousers worn by cowboys to protect their legs."

Look up the original meanings of the following words from Spanish in an English dictionary. Then use each one in a sentence.
1. palomino 2. canyon 3. mustang 4. lasso

THINKING AND WRITING
Writing a Description of a Conflict

Choose one of the ideas about types of conflict that you wrote down earlier. Freewrite about how Pecos Bill might handle this conflict. Then use this information to write a description of the conflict and Pecos Bill's solving of it. Imagine that you are writing for a group of young children who are hearing about Pecos Bill for the first time. Revise your description, making sure you have used exaggeration effectively. Finally, proofread your description and share it with your classmates.

GUIDE FOR READING

Hammerman

Hammerman was the nickname for a black laborer named John Henry, who in the early 1870's helped construct the Big Bend Tunnel along the Chesapeake and Ohio Railroad in West Virginia. At the time, the workers used long-handled hammers to pound steel drills into rocks. One day a man arrived with a steam-powered drill, which he claimed could drill holes faster than twenty men using hammers.

This folktale is retold by **Adrien Stoutenburg** (1916–   ), a poet, biographer, and writer, who was born in Darfur, Minnesota.

Folk Hero

A **folk hero** is an extraordinary person who appears in folktales. Folktales glorify the hero for his or her wonderful qualities, which are far superior to those of most "folk," or ordinary, common people. There may be many tales about a hero, each focusing on a different aspect, such as strength, daring, or cunning. John Henry is an example of a folk hero.

Look For

As you read "Hammerman," look for John Henry's extraordinary qualities. What makes him stand out from ordinary people?

Writing

John Henry is one example of a folk hero. Brainstorm and write down your ideas about people, real or imaginary, who could be folk heroes in our society today.

Vocabulary

Knowing the following words will help you as you read "Hammerman."
whirl (hwʉrl) *adj.*: To drive with a rotating motion (p. 655)
hefted (hef′ tid) *v.*: Lifted; tested the weight of (p. 657)

Hammerman

Adrien Stoutenburg

People down South still tell stories about John Henry, how strong he was, and how he could whirl a big sledge[1] so lightning-fast you could hear thunder behind it. They even say he was born with a hammer in his hand. John Henry himself said it, but he probably didn't mean it exactly as it sounded.

The story seems to be that when John Henry was a baby, the first thing he reached out for was a hammer, which was hung nearby on the cabin wall.

John Henry's father put his arm around his wife's shoulder. "He's going to grow up to be a steel-driving man. I can see it plain as rows of cotton running uphill."

As John Henry grew a bit older, he practiced swinging the hammer, not hitting at things, but just enjoying the feel of it whooshing against the air. When he was old enough to talk, he told everyone, "I was born with a hammer in my hand."

John Henry was still a boy when the Civil War started, but he was a big, hard-muscled boy, and he could outwork and outplay all the other boys on the plantation.

"You're going to be a mighty man, John Henry," his father told him.

"A man ain't nothing but a man," young John Henry said. "And I'm a natural man, born to swing a hammer in my hand."

At night, lying on a straw bed on the floor, John Henry listened to a far-off train whistling through the darkness. Railroad tracks had been laid to carry trainloads of Southern soldiers to fight against the armies of the North. The trains had a lonesome, longing sound that made John Henry want to go wherever they were going.

When the war ended, a man from the North came to John Henry where he was working in the field. He said, "The slaves are free now. You can pack up and go wherever you want, young fellow."

"I'm craving to go where the trains go," said John Henry.

The man shook his head. "There are too many young fellows trailing the trains around now. You better settle down to doing what you know, like handling a cotton hook or driving a mule team."

John Henry thought to himself, there's a big hammer waiting for me somewhere, because I know I'm a steel-driving man. All I have to do is hunt 'til I find it.

That night, he told his folks about a dream he had had.

"I dreamed I was working on a railroad somewhere," he said, "a big, new railroad called the C. & O., and I had a mighty hammer in my hand. Every time I swung it, it made a whirling flash around my shoulder. And every time my hammer hit a spike,[2] the sky lit up from the sparks."

---

1. **sledge** (slej), *n.*: A heavy hammer, usually held with both hands.

2. **spike** (spīk), *n.*: A long, thick metal nail used for splitting rock.

HAMMER IN HIS HAND
Palmer C. Hayden
Museum of African American Art

"I believe it," his father said. "You were born to drive steel."

"That ain't all of the dream," John Henry said. "I dreamed that the railroad was going to be the end of me and I'd die with the hammer in my hand."

The next morning, John Henry bundled up some food in a red bandanna handkerchief, told his parents good-by, and set off into the world. He walked until he heard the clang-clang of hammers in the distance. He followed the sound to a place where gangs of men were building a railroad. John Henry watched the men driving steel spikes down into the crossties[3] to hold the rails in place. Three men would stand around a spike, then each, in turn, would swing a long hammer.

John Henry's heart beat in rhythm with the falling hammers. His fingers ached for the feel of a hammer in his own hands. He walked over to the foreman.

"I'm a natural steel-driving man," he said. "And I'm looking for a job."

---

3. crossties (krôs' tīz), *n*.: Beams laid crosswise under railroad tracks to support them.

"How much steel-driving have you done?" the foreman asked.

"I was born knowing how," John Henry said.

The foreman shook his head. "That ain't good enough, boy. I can't take any chances. Steel-driving's dangerous work, and you might hit somebody."

"I wouldn't hit anybody," John Henry said, "because I can drive one of those spikes all by myself."

The foreman said sharply, "The one kind of man I don't need in this outfit is a bragger. Stop wasting my time."

John Henry didn't move. He got a stubborn look around his jaw. "You loan me a hammer, mister, and if somebody will hold the spike for me, I'll prove what I can do."

The three men who had just finished driving in a spike looked toward him and laughed. One of them said, "Anybody who would hold a spike for a greenhorn[4] don't want to live long."

"I'll hold it," a fourth man said.

John Henry saw that the speaker was a small, dark-skinned fellow about his own age.

The foreman asked the small man, "D'you aim to get yourself killed, Li'l Willie?"

Li'l Willie didn't answer. He knelt and set a spike down through the rail on the crosstie. "Come on, big boy," he said.

John Henry picked up one of the sheep-nose hammers lying in the cinders. He hefted it and decided it was too light. He picked up a larger one which weighed twelve pounds. The handle was lean and limber and greased with tallow[5] to make it smooth.

Everyone was quiet, watching, as he stepped over to the spike.

John Henry swung the hammer over his shoulder so far that the hammer head hung down against the back of his knees. He felt a thrill run through his arms and chest.

"Tap it down gentle, first," said Li'l Willie.

But John Henry had already started to swing. He brought the hammer flashing down, banging the spike squarely on the head. Before the other men could draw a breath of surprise, the hammer flashed again, whirring through the air like a giant hummingbird. One more swing, and the spike was down, its steel head smoking from the force of the blow.

The foreman blinked, swallowed, and blinked again. "Man," he told John Henry, "you're hired!"

That's the way John Henry started steel-driving. From then on, Li'l Willie was always with him, setting the spikes, or placing the drills[6] that John Henry drove with his hammer. There wasn't another steel-driving man in the world who could touch John Henry for speed and power. He could hammer every which way, up or down or side-wise. He could drive for ten hours at a stretch and never miss a stroke.

After he'd been at the work for a few years, he started using a twenty-pound hammer in each hand. It took six men, working fast, to carry fresh drills to him. People would come for miles around to watch John Henry.

Whenever John Henry worked, he sang. Li'l Willie sang with him, chanting the rhythm of the clanging hammer strokes.

Those were happy days for John Henry. One of the happiest days came when he met a black-eyed, curly-haired girl called Polly Ann. And, on the day that Polly Ann said

---

4. greenhorn (grēn' hôrn), *n.*: An inexperienced person; a beginner.
5. tallow (tal' ō), *n.*: Solid fat obtained from sheep or cattle.

6. drills (drilz), *n.*: Pointed tools used for making holes in hard substances.

she would marry him, John Henry almost burst his throat with singing.

Every now and then, John Henry would remember the strange dream he had had years before, about the C. & O. Railroad and dying with a hammer in his hand. One night, he had the dream again. The next morning, when he went to work, the steel gang gathered round him, hopping with excitement.

"The Chesapeake and Ohio Railroad wants men to drive a tunnel through a mountain in West Virginia!" they said.

"The C. & O. wants the best hammer-men there are!" they said. "And they'll pay twice as much as anybody else."

Li'l Willie looked at John Henry. "If they want the best, John Henry, they're goin' to need you."

John Henry looked back at his friend. "They're going to need you, too, Li'l Willie. I ain't going without you." He stood a minute, looking at the sky. There was a black thundercloud way off, with sunlight flashing behind it. John Henry felt a small chill between his shoulder blades. He shook himself, put his hammer on his shoulder, and said, "Let's go, Willie!"

When they reached Summers County where the Big Bend Tunnel was to be built, John Henry sized up the mountain standing in the way. It was almost solid rock.

"Looks soft," said John Henry. "Hold a drill up there, Li'l Willie."

Li'l Willie did. John Henry took a seventy-pound hammer and drove the drill in with one mountain-cracking stroke. Then he settled down to working the regular way, pounding in the drills with four or five strokes of a twenty-pound sledge. He worked so fast that his helpers had to keep buckets of water ready to pour on his hammers so they wouldn't catch fire.

Polly Ann, who had come along to West Virginia, sat and watched and cheered him on. She sang along with him, clapping her hands to the rhythm of his hammer, and the sound echoed around the mountains. The songs blended with the rumble of dynamite where the blasting crews were at work. For every time John Henry drilled a hole in the mountain's face, other men poked dynamite and black powder into the hole and then lighted a fuse to blow the rock apart.

One day the tunnel boss Cap'n Tommy Walters was standing watching John Henry, when a stranger in city clothes walked up to him.

"Howdy, Cap'n Tommy," said the stranger. "I'd like to talk to you about a steam engine[7] I've got for sale. My engine can drive a drill through rock so fast that not even a crew of your best men can keep up with it."

"I don't need any machine," Cap'n Tommy said proudly. "My man John Henry can out-drill any machine ever built."

"I'll place a bet with you, Cap'n," said the salesman. "You race your man against my machine for a full day. If he wins, I'll give you the steam engine free."

Cap'n Tommy thought it over. "That sounds fair enough, but I'll have to talk to John Henry first." He told John Henry what the stranger had said. "Are you willing to race a steam drill?" Cap'n Tommy asked.

John Henry ran his big hands over the handle of his hammer, feeling the strength in the wood and in his own great muscles.

"A man's a man," he said, "but a machine ain't nothing but a machine. I'll beat that steam drill, or I'll die with my hammer in my hand!"

"All right, then," said Cap'n Tommy. "We'll set a day for the contest."

---

7. steam engine: Here, a machine that drives a drill by means of steam power.

Polly Ann looked worried when John Henry told her what he had promised to do.

"Don't you worry, honey," John Henry said. It was the end of the workday, with the sunset burning across the mountain, and the sky shining like copper. He tapped his chest. "I've got a man's heart in here. All a machine has is a metal engine." He smiled and picked Polly Ann up in his arms, as if she were no heavier than a blade of grass.

On the morning of the contest, the slopes around the tunnel were crowded with people. At one side stood the steam engine, its gears and valves and mechanical drill gleaming. Its operators rushed around, giving it final spurts of grease and oil and shoving fresh pine knots into the fire that fed the steam boiler.

John Henry stood leaning on his hammer, as still as the mountain rock, his shoulders shining like hard coal in the rising sun.

"How do you feel, John Henry?" asked Li'l Willie. Li'l Willie's hands trembled a bit as he held the drill ready.

"I feel like a bird ready to bust out of a nest egg," John Henry said. "I feel like a rooster ready to crow. I feel pride hammering at my heart, and I can hardly wait to get started against that machine." He sucked in the mountain air. "I feel powerful free, Li'l Willie."

Cap'n Tommy held up the starting gun. For a second everything was as silent as the dust in a drill hole. Then the gun barked, making a yelp that bounced against mountain and sky.

John Henry swung his hammer, and it rang against the drill.

At the same time, the steam engine gave a roar and a hiss. Steam whistled through its escape valve. Its drill crashed down, gnawing into the granite.

John Henry paid no attention to anything except his hammer, nor to any sound except the steady pumping of his heart. At the end of an hour, he paused long enough to ask, "How are we doing, Li'l Willie?"

Willie licked his lips. His face was pale with rock dust and with fear. "The machine's ahead, John Henry."

John Henry tossed his smoking hammer aside and called to another helper, "Bring me two hammers! I'm only getting warmed up."

He began swinging a hammer in each hand. Sparks flew so fast and hot they singed his face. The hammers heated up until they glowed like torches.

"How're we doing now, Li'l Willie?" John Henry asked at the end of another hour.

Li'l Willie grinned. "The machine's drill busted. They have to take time to fix up a new one. You're almost even now, John Henry! How're you feeling?"

"I'm feeling like sunrise," John Henry took time to say before he flashed one of his hammers down against the drill. "Clean out the hole, Willie, and we'll drive right down to China."

Above the clash of his hammers, he heard the chug and hiss of the steam engine starting up again and the whine of its rotary drill biting into rock. The sound hurt John Henry's ears.

"Sing me a song, Li'l Willie!" he gasped. "Sing me a natural song for my hammers to sing along with."

Li'l Willie sang, and John Henry kept his hammers going in time. Hour after hour, he kept driving, sweat sliding from his forehead and chest.

The sun rolled past noon and toward the west.

"How're you feeling, John Henry?" Li'l Willie asked.

"I ain't tired yet," said John Henry and

stood back, gasping, while Willie put a freshly sharpened drill into the rock wall. "Only, I have a kind of roaring in my ears."

"That's only the steam engine," Li'l Willie said, but he wet his lips again. "You're gaining on it, John Henry. I reckon you're at least two inches ahead."

John Henry coughed and slung his hammer back. "I'll beat it by a mile, before the sun sets."

At the end of another hour, Li'l Willie called out, his eyes sparkling, "You're going to win, John Henry, if you can keep on drivin'!"

John Henry ground his teeth together and tried not to hear the roar in his ears or the racing thunder of his heart. "I'll go until I drop," he gasped. "I'm a steel-driving man and I'm bound to win, because a machine ain't nothing but a machine."

The sun slid lower. The shadows of the crowd grew long and purple.

"John Henry can't keep it up," someone said.

"The machine can't keep it up," another said.

Polly Ann twisted her hands together and waited for Cap'n Tommy to fire the gun to mark the end of the contest.

"Who's winning?" a voice cried.

"Wait and see," another voice answered.

There were only ten minutes left.

"How're you feeling, John Henry?" Li'l Willie whispered, sweat dripping down his own face.

John Henry didn't answer. He just kept slamming his hammers against the drill, his mouth open.

Li'l Willie tried to go on singing. "Flash that hammer—uh! Wham that drill—uh!" he croaked.

Out beside the railroad tracks, Polly beat her hands together in time, until they were numb.

The sun flared an instant, then died behind the mountain. Cap'n Tommy's gun cracked. The judges ran forward to measure the depth of the holes drilled by the steam engine and by John Henry. At last, the judges came walking back and said something to Cap'n Tommy before they turned to announce their findings to the crowd.

Cap'n Tommy walked over to John Henry, who stood leaning against the face of the mountain.

"John Henry," he said, "you beat that steam engine by four feet!" He held out his hand and smiled.

John Henry heard a distant cheering. He held his own hand out, and then he staggered. He fell and lay on his back, staring up at the mountain and the sky, and then he saw Polly Ann and Li'l Willie leaning over him.

"Oh, how do you feel, John Henry?" Polly Ann asked.

"I feel a bit tuckered out," said John Henry.

"Do you want me to sing to you?" Li'l Willie asked.

"I got a song in my own heart, thank you, Li'l Willie," John Henry said. He raised up on his elbow and looked at all the people and the last sunset light gleaming like the edge of a golden trumpet. "I was a steel-driving man," he said, and lay back and closed his eyes forever.

Down South, and in the North, too, people still talk about John Henry and how he beat the steam engine at the Big Bend Tunnel. They say, if John Henry were alive today, he could beat almost every other kind of machine, too.

Maybe so. At least, John Henry would die trying.

THINKING ABOUT THE SELECTION

Recalling

1. Describe John Henry's dream.
2. Explain how John Henry wins his first job hammering steel.
3. How does Li'l Willie help John Henry with his work?
4. What events bring about John Henry's death?

Interpreting

5. Why is Li'l Willie willing to hold the spike for John Henry—a dangerous task—when no one else will?
6. Interpret the sentence: "A man's a man, but a machine ain't nothing but a machine."
7. What is the goal and the purpose of the quest?
8. What clues in the tale hint at the outcome?

Applying

9. Ever since the invention of machines, some people have felt threatened by them. Why? What machines today cause this reaction?

ANALYZING LITERATURE

Understanding the Folk Hero

A **folk hero** is an extraordinary person whose qualities are glorified in folktales. The fantastic qualities glorified in the folk hero give you an idea of the characteristics valued on the frontier.

1. What qualities of John Henry are glorified in the following sentences from "Hammerman"?
   a. "He brought the hammer flashing down, banging the spike squarely on the head . . . One more swing, and the spike was down, its steel head smoking from the force of the blow."
   b. "It took six men, working fast, to carry fresh drills to him."
2. What do these qualities say about the type of person who was admired on the frontier?

CRITICAL THINKING AND READING

Making Inferences About Characters

Inferences are conclusions drawn from evidence in a story. You make inferences about a character's traits and personality from clues given in the character's words and actions.

For example, L'il Willie goes with John Henry to work on the railroad, joins him in his competition against the machine, and sings to John Henry to urge him along. From these actions you can conclude that L'il Willie is a loyal friend.

What inferences about John Henry's character can you draw from the following?

1. ' "I feel like a rooster ready to crow. I feel pride hammering at my heart, and I can hardly wait to get started against that machine." '
2. "I'll go until I drop."

SPEAKING AND LISTENING

Dramatizing a Folktale

Prepare and dramatize a skit based on "Hammerman" for your class. List the cast of characters and devise simple dialogue and stage directions. Choose the cast and director from your classmates. After you rehearse, perform the skit for your class.

THINKING AND WRITING

Writing Another Adventure

Brainstorm and write down your ideas for other adventures that John Henry could have had. Select one to write about for your class. First freewrite about the adventure, including descriptions of John Henry, the challenge that confronts him, and what happens. Use this information to write about the adventure, including dialogue when necessary. Revise your story, making sure you have used the qualities that John Henry exhibits in "Hammerman." Read the adventure aloud to your class.

GUIDE FOR READING

John Henry

John Henry, also called Hammerman in folk tales, was a black laborer who helped build the Big Bend Tunnel on the Chesapeake & Ohio Railroad in West Virginia in the early 1870's. He was a huge man, capable of deeds that ordinary workers could only dream of doing, and he did race a steam drill.

John Henry appears in songs, poems, and folktales, sometimes as a dockworker. He is always the "superworker"—able to work all day and night, amazing others with his incredible feats.

Oral Tradition

Oral tradition is the developing and passing down by word of mouth stories, beliefs, and customs from generation to generation. Ballads, legends, myths, yarns, and folktales are all part of our oral tradition. They have been written down to be remembered.

This version about John Henry is a ballad—a song or poem in short stanzas that tells a story in simple words. A refrain, a phrase or verse repeated at intervals, emphasizes a point and adds to the poem's rhythmic quality.

Look For

As you read "John Henry," look for the ballad's refrain: "Lawd, Lawd," and the repetition of the last line of the stanza. Imagine that you are pounding spikes on a railroad or drilling a tunnel and that you are singing this ballad in time with the swinging of your hammer.

Writing

Today computers and humans play chess against each other. Think of other contests that could take place between a human and a modern machine. Describe what the competition would be about and how it might take place.

Vocabulary

Knowing the following words will help you as you read "John Henry."

drive (drīv) v.: To force by hitting (p. 663)

yonder (yän' dər) adj.: In the distance (p. 665)

flagged (flagd) v.: Signaled to a train to stop so a passenger can board (p. 666)

John Henry

Traditional

John Henry was a lil baby,
Sittin' on his mama's knee,
Said: 'The Big Bend Tunnel on the C. & O. road
Gonna cause the death of me,
5   Lawd, Lawd, gonna cause the death of me.'

Cap'n says to John Henry,
'Gonna bring me a steam drill 'round,
Gonna take that steam drill out on the job,
Gonna whop that steel on down,
10   Lawd, Lawd, gonna whop that steel on down.

John Henry tol' his cap'n,
Lightnin' was in his eye:
'Cap'n, bet yo' las' red cent on me,
Fo' I'll beat it to the bottom or I'll die,
15   Lawd, Lawd, I'll beat it to the bottom or I'll die.'

Sun shine hot an' burnin',
Wer'n't no breeze a-tall,
Sweat ran down like water down a hill,
That day John Henry let his hammer fall,
20   Lawd, Lawd, that day John Henry let his hammer fall.

John Henry went to the tunnel,
An' they put him in the lead to drive,
The rock so tall an' John Henry so small,
That he lied down his hammer an' he cried,
25   Lawd, Lawd, that he lied down his hammer an' he cried.

A MAN AIN'T NOTHIN' BUT A MAN
Palmer C. Hayden

John Henry started on the right hand,
The steam drill started on the lef'—
'Before I'd let this steam drill beat me down,
I'd hammer my fool self to death,
30 Lawd, Lawd, I'd hammer my fool self to death.'

John Henry had a lil woman,
Her name were Polly Ann,
John Henry took sick an' had to go to bed,
Polly Ann drove steel like a man,
35 Lawd, Lawd, Polly Ann drove steel like a man.

John Henry said to his shaker,[1]
'Shaker, why don' you sing?
I'm throwin' twelve poun's from my hips on down,
Jes' listen to the col' steel ring,
40 Lawd, Lawd, jes' listen to the col' steel ring.'

Oh, the captain said to John Henry,
'I b'lieve this mountain's sinkin' in.'
John Henry said to his captain, oh my!
'Ain' nothin' but my hammer suckin' win',
45 Lawd, Lawd, ain' nothin' but my hammer suckin' win'.'

John Henry tol' his shaker,
'Shaker, you better pray,
For, if I miss this six-foot steel,
Tomorrow'll be yo' buryin' day,
50 Lawd, Lawd, tomorrow'll be yo' buryin' day.'

John Henry tol' his captain,
'Look yonder what I see—
Yo' drill's done broke an' yo' hole's done choke,
An' you cain' drive steel like me,
55 Lawd, Lawd, an' you cain' drive steel like me.'

The man that invented the steam drill,
Thought he was mighty fine.
John Henry drove his fifteen feet,
An' the steam drill only made nine,
60 Lawd, Lawd, an' the steam drill only made nine.

---

1. shaker (shā′ kər), *n.*: Person who sets the spikes
and places the drills for a steel-driver to hammer.

The hammer that John Henry swung,
It weighed over nine pound;
He broke a rib in his lef'-han' side,
An' his intrels[2] fell on the groun',
65 Lawd, Lawd, an' his intrels fell on the groun'.

All the womens in the Wes',
When they heared of John Henry's death,
Stood in the rain, flagged the eas'-boun' train,
Goin' where John Henry fell dead,
70 Lawd, Lawd, goin' where John Henry fell dead.

John Henry's lil mother,
She was all dressed in red,
She jumped in bed, covered up her head,
Said she didn' know her son was dead,
75 Lawd, Lawd, didn' know her son was dead.

Dey took John Henry to the graveyard,
An' they buried him in the san',
An' every locomotive come roarin' by,
Says, 'There lays a steel-drivin' man,
80 Lawd, Lawd, there lays a steel-drivin' man.'

---

2. intrels: entrails (en' trālz), *n.*: Inner organs.

THINKING ABOUT THE SELECTION

Recalling

1. At what point in his life does John Henry make his prediction about his own death?
2. What happens in the contest between John Henry and the steam drill?
3. Which one wins the contest?
4. What injuries does John Henry suffer?
5. What tribute do trains give John Henry when they roll by his grave?

Interpreting

6. Why does John Henry say that if he misses the six-foot steel, tomorrow will be his shaker's burying day?
7. Why does John Henry's mother react as she does to the news of her son's death?
8. State what we learn from this tale about John Henry that explains why he is a folk hero.

Applying

9. What jobs today are as dangerous as driving steel was in John Henry's day? Give two examples, and explain why they are dangerous.

ANALYZING LITERATURE

Understanding the Oral Tradition

Oral tradition is the passing down by word of mouth stories, beliefs, and customs from generation to generation. Ballads, for example, are usually sung long before they are ever written down. A ballad's refrain—phrase or verse repeated at intervals—emphasizes a point and sounds like a chorus. In the first stanza of "John Henry," the refrain "Lawd, Lawd, gonna cause the death of me" adds the phrase "Lawd, Lawd," and repeats the line before it.

A ballad passed down in the oral tradition may have several different versions. It may often include the dialect, or particular manner of speaking, of its creators. For example, "Gonna whop that steel on down" is the way black laborers in the South in the late 1800's might have said, "I will hammer that spike into the ground." To get the full flavor of the dialect, you should read the ballad aloud.

Read "John Henry" aloud. Then answer the following questions.

1. What lines contain a refrain?
2. What are two other examples of dialect from "John Henry"?
3. What feelings for John Henry does this ballad arouse?

SPEAKING AND LISTENING

Sharing Other Ballads About Folk Heroes

John Henry is not the only folk hero about whom ballads have been written. Working with a group of students, think of a ballad you know about another American folk hero, or find one in the library. Read it aloud to the class.

THINKING AND WRITING

Comparing and Contrasting Selections

Compare and contrast "John Henry" with "Hammerman." First list the similarities and differences between the two selections. Consider the characters, situations, form of literature, and descriptions. Then use this information to write an essay for a school literary magazine. Revise your essay, making sure you use examples to support your views. Proofread your essay and share it with your classmates.

GUIDE FOR READING

The Foggy Stew

Alfred Bulltop Stormalong was a gigantic sea captain in New England folklore. In some stories he stood over four fathoms (twenty-four feet!) tall and picked his teeth with an eighteen-foot oar. His ship was so huge that its deck had to be traveled on horseback. The masts were hinged in order to let the sun and moon pass by. Young sailors who climbed its rigging returned with gray beards.

"The Foggy Stew," by **Harold Felton** (1902–   ), relates one of Stormalong's fantastic deeds before he became a captain.

Exaggeration in a Folk Tale

Exaggeration is overstatement. It is often used in tall tales, folktales, and legends for humorous effect. For instance, a story may be about a rainstorm so heavy that people have to wear scuba gear to walk outside. Rainstorms in actuality can be heavy, but a rainstorm so heavy as to require scuba gear is exaggerated. In "The Foggy Stew" the famous sailor Stormalong comes up against a fog so thick that fish are swimming in it.

Look For

As you read "The Foggy Stew," look for exaggeration. What effect is caused by the use of exaggeration?

Writing

Freewrite about another exaggerated situation. Let your mind wander freely, creating the most outrageous of details.

Vocabulary

Knowing the following words will help you as you read "The Foggy Stew."

notions (nō′ shənz) *n.:* Small, useful, household items (p. 669)

becalmed (bi kämd′) *v.:* Made motionless, as a sailing ship when there is no wind (p. 669)

galley (gal′ ē) *n.:* Cooking area on a ship (p. 669)

starboard (stär′ bərd) *adj.:* The right side of a ship, as one faces forward (p. 670)

poached (pōcht) *adj.:* Cooked gently in near-boiling water (p. 671)

prow (prou) *n.:* The frontmost part of a ship (p. 671)

promoted (prə mōt′ id) *v.:* Given a higher position (p. 672)

The Foggy Stew

Harold W. Felton

The *Lady of the Sea* was in the China trade. She was fully loaded with timber, metal goods, cotton cloth and notions. When she cast off the wind filled her sails, and soon the land was left far behind.

On the outward voyage the ship became becalmed in the doldrums.[1] For days she lay silent in a fog, with never a cat's paw of wind.[2]

The fog grew thicker. "It's the worst fog I ever saw," declared Captain Hardstone.

There seemed to be no sun or moon or stars. There seemed to be no day or night. Nothing but a gray curtain of fog. There seemed to be no fore or aft,[3] no up or down.

"The only way you can tell up from down," said the captain, "is to drop something. When it hits your foot, you can tell that way is down."

The fog got thicker still. "This ain't no pea soup fog," said the captain. "It's thicker than that."

"Speaking of pea soup, that's an uncommon good smell coming from the galley," said Stormalong.

"So it is. But it ain't pea soup. It's plum duff,[4]" said the captain. "A heaven-touched mixture of flour, water, and prunes."

"What's that?" asked Stormalong.

"Plum duff," said the captain.

"No. I know what plum duff is. I mean, what's that noise?"

Captain Hardstone cocked his head to listen better. "It's a kind of a flutterin' sound," he said.

"It's fish. That's what it is. It's fish! There are fish swimming in the fog!" said Stormalong.

"Fish?" the captain was puzzled.

Stormalong listened again. Then slowly the facts came to his mind, and as they did, he put them into words. "This fog is so thick a man can't tell where the water stops and the fog begins. So it stands to reason that a fish, which is no ways as smart as a man, can't tell either."

"Yes sir, it stands to reason. It certainly does," the captain muttered, still wondering how this strange fact could be true, as it undoubtedly was, and at the same time admiring Stormy for his quick logic and clear explanation.

Stormy continued. "They smell the plum duff cooking. It smells so good, they are swimming for it."

When he heard his own words, Stormy got an idea. Peering through the fog, he was dimly able to see a school of salmon[5] nosing around the cracks at the edge of the galley door.

---

1. doldrums (dol' drəmz), *n.*: Parts of the ocean near the equator where there is a lack of wind.
2. cat's paw of wind: A light wind that barely ruffles the water.
3. fore or aft: Front or back.
4. duff (duf), *n.*: A thick flour pudding boiled in a cloth bag.

5. school of salmon: A large number of salmon swimming together.

Softly he glided to the starboard porthole of the galley. "Cookie, are you there?" he whispered.

"Yes," the cook answered. "I shut the galley door so as to try to keep some of the fog out."

"You're keeping the salmon out too," Stormy told him.

"What?" The wonder in the cook's voice made it clear that he was not following Stormy.

"There are salmon sniffing at the galley door. They smell your plum duff cooking."

"Most everybody likes my plum duff," the cook said with pride in his voice. There was a pause. "But—fish! I never heard of fish caring one way or another about plum duff. As a matter of fact, I never heard of fish sniffing around a galley door!"

"Just take my word for it," said Stormy. "Listen. Put some plum duff in a big cooking pot, the biggest one you've got."

"Well, I don't know what you've got in mind. But I'll do what you say," the cook answered.

When the pot was ready, Stormalong opened the galley door. The salmon swam inside. They swam directly toward the plum duff in the pot.

Stormy followed closely behind them. Fortunately the salmon were so intent on the delicious-smelling plum duff, they ignored all signs of danger and forgot caution. They swam right into the waiting pot and greedily began to munch at the tasty plum duff.

Stormy stepped forward and slammed the lid on the pot. "Got 'em!" he declared.

The salmon were poached in the pot full of fog, and all the sailors agreed they had never had better poached salmon. And the plum duff was the perfect dessert for such a delicious meal.

Stormalong met the captain after dinner on the quarter deck. There was a happy, contented look in Captain Hardstone's eyes. "I do declare, that was the best poached salmon I ever put a tooth to. I tell you it makes a big difference when fish are fresh caught."

But the contentment did not last. A man can't remember a pleasant meal forever. Work must be done, and the captain was restless at the long delay in the fog. He tried to peer through the gray curtain that enveloped the ship, examining every quarter for a sign of a breeze.

But the sails hung limp, with no flap or flutter. She was a silent ship on a silent sea—as quiet as an eel swimming in oil.

"I certainly would admire to see a sign of a breeze," Captain Hardstone said. "I'd welcome any wind able to move, even enough to ripple up a fly's eyelashes would give me hope."

"Maybe I can help," said Stormalong.

"Poached salmon is fine, and I like it. I would enjoy eating a good many meals of it. But it's wind I want, boy." Captain Hardstone moved to the rail and stared over it into the gray fog. The captain was now a solemn man.

"That's what I mean," said Stormy. He turned and walked to the stern of the ship. Facing the bow, he planted his feet firmly on the planks that were wet from the dripping fog. He squared his shoulders, took a deep breath, and blew.

The slack sails fluttered a small flutter. "There's a show of a breeze," Captain Hardstone cried.

Stormy took another deep breath. His chest expanded and three buttons popped off and danced across the wet planks.

"What are you doing there, boy?" the captain shouted.

Stormy didn't answer. He blew again. The sails bent out.

"Never seen anything like it before," the captain exclaimed. "Man and boy, I never seen—"

His words were lost in the breeze as Stormy blew again. A small white crest began to trail along each side of the prow, as the *Lady of the Sea* moved slowly through the water.

The ship picked up speed. The prow pushed the seas aside.

Captain Hardstone and the crew

watched with amazement as Stormy blew the fog away. He blew the ship right out of the doldrums and into the trade winds.[6]

When the breeze of nature caught the sails, Stormy stopped his blowing. To tell the truth, his face was red, and he sat down because he needed a rest. But he soon caught his breath and grinned, well satisfied with what he had done.

"Hip, hip!" the captain cried.

"Hooray!" the crew replied.

"Stormalong!"

"Stormalong!"

Captain Hardstone promoted Stormy and made him boatswain.[7] When he blew his boatswain's whistle he blew it so loud the echo would dry the sailors' laundry on a rainy day.

---

6. trade winds: Either of two winds blowing in the same direction toward the equator.

7. boatswain (bō′ sən), *n.*: An officer of a ship in charge of the rigging and anchors. He calls the crew to duty with his whistle.

Recalling

1. Where does the ship become becalmed?
2. What problems does the heavy fog create for Captain Hardstone and his crew?
3. How does Stormalong take advantage of the heavy fog?
4. Why is the captain still discontented after the salmon dinner?
5. How does Stormalong solve the captain's problem?
6. What is Stormalong's reward?

Interpreting

7. Do you agree with Captain Hardstone that Stormalong has quick logic and a clear explanation about the fish swimming in the fog? Give reasons for your answer.
8. What does Stormalong's calm reaction to his getting the ship moving tell you about him?
9. What qualities of Stormalong does this folk tale glorify?

Applying

10. Captain Hardstone promotes Stormalong because his quick thinking and reactions were helpful. Think of examples of people from history or current affairs whose quick thinking and reactions were helpful.

ANALYZING LITERATURE

Understanding Exaggeration

Exaggeration, or overstatement, is often used for comic effect by treating the impossible as if it were real. Exaggeration can be expressed in a statement or through a description of an unbelievable situation.

1. Indicate which of the following statements contain exaggeration.
   a. "A man can't remember a pleasant meal forever."
   b. ' "This fog is so thick a man can't tell where the water stops and the fog begins." '
   c. "When he blew his boatswain's whistle he blew it so loud the echo would dry the sailors' laundry on a rainy day."
   d. "To tell the truth, his face was red, and he sat down because he needed a rest."
2. Find three examples of exaggeration you found especially effective. Explain your reason for selecting each.

CRITICAL THINKING AND READING

Interpreting the Storyteller's Purpose

A writer's purpose is his or her reason for writing. A writer may write to inform, entertain, or persuade. You must infer, or recognize, the writer's purpose from clues that are given. Sometimes the writer may use factual language and a serious tone, or attitude, to inform; exaggeration and a light tone to entertain; and strong, definite language and an emotional tone to persuade.

1. What tone, or attitude, does the writer use in "The Foggy Stew"?
2. What kind of language does the writer use?
3. What do you think is the writer's purpose in "The Foggy Stew"?
4. Do you think the author may have had more than one purpose? Explain your answer.

THINKING AND WRITING

Writing with Exaggeration in a Folktale

Choose one of the ideas for an exaggerated situation that you thought of earlier and write a folktale about it for your classmates. First free-write about the situation, including a description of your hero—like Stormalong or your own invention—what happens, and how your hero deals with the situation. Make sure you exaggerate your descriptions to create humor. Then write a folktale using the exaggerated situation. Revise each, making sure your writing is entertaining. Proofread your story and read it to your class.

GUIDE FOR READING

Johnny Appleseed

Johnny Appleseed (1774–1845) was a real-life frontiersman —John Chapman. Chapman was born in Leominster, Massachusetts. His life was so extraordinary that he became a folklore hero. In stories about him that blend truth and fantasy, he scattered apple seeds throughout Pennsylvania along the Allegheny River. His apple orchards spread through Ohio to northern Indiana!

This poem about him was written by the poet and editor **Rosemary Carr Benét** (1898–1962).

Characterization

Characterization is the way a writer shows you what a character is like. A writer can give you an idea of a character's personality through a description of his or her appearance and actions, through dialogue, or through direct statements. In "Johnny Appleseed," the writer portrays the character through his appearance and actions.

Look For

As you read "Johnny Appleseed," look for his character traits. Which traits might describe the real-life man? Which belong solely to the legendary hero?

Writing

Think of people you have heard about who have selflessly given of their time and abilities to others in some beneficial way. List these people and their accomplishments.

Vocabulary

Knowing the following words will help you as you read "Johnny Appleseed."

gnarled (närld) *adj.*: Knotty and twisted, as the trunk of an old tree (p. 675)

ruddy (rud′ ē) *adj.*: Healthy color (p. 675)

encumber (in kum′ bər) *v.*: Weigh down (p. 675)

stalking (stôk′ iŋ) *adj.*: Secretly approaching (p. 676)

tendril (ten′ drəl) *n.*: Thin shoot from a plant (p. 676)

lair (ler) *n.*: Den of a wild animal (p. 676)

Johnny Appleseed

Rosemary Carr Benét

Of Jonathan Chapman
Two things are known,
That he loved apples,
That he walked alone.

At seventy-odd
He was gnarled as could be,
But ruddy and sound
As a good apple tree.

For fifty years over
Of harvest and dew,
He planted his apples
Where no apples grew.

The winds of the prairie
Might blow through his rags,
But he carried his seeds
In the best deerskin bags.

From old Ashtabula
To frontier Fort Wayne,
He planted and pruned
And he planted again.

He had not a hat
To encumber his head.
He wore a tin pan
On his white hair instead.

He nested with owl,
And with bear-cub and possum,

JOHN CHAPMAN, 1871
The Granger Collection

Johnny Appleseed 675

And knew all his orchards
Root, tendril and blossom.

A fine old man,
As ripe as a pippin,[1]
His heart still light,
And his step still skipping.

The stalking Indian,
The beast in its lair
Did no hurt
While he was there.

For they could tell,
As wild things can,
That Jonathan Chapman
Was God's own man.

Why did he do it?
We do not know.
He wished that apples
Might root and grow.

He has no statue.
He has no tomb.
He has his apple trees
Still in bloom.

Consider, consider,
Think well upon
The marvelous story
Of Appleseed John.

---

1. pippin (pip' in), *n.*: An apple.

THINKING ABOUT THE SELECTION

Recalling

1. What are the two things that the speaker says are known about John Chapman?
2. Describe Chapman's life on the frontier.
3. What kind of relationship does Chapman have with animals?
4. What monument to Chapman stands today?

Interpreting

5. What is Chapman's most important possession?
6. How does Chapman feel about nature?

Applying

7. What areas in today's world would benefit from having someone provide help in growing food? Explain what those areas might need.

ANALYZING LITERATURE

Understanding Characterization

Characterization is the way a writer presents a character. A character's personality can be shown through his or her appearance, actions, and thoughts; through dialogue; or through the writer's direct statements about him or her.

1. Find a detail that shows that Chapman did not care about his appearance.
2. Find a detail that shows that Chapman did not care to live in town.
3. Find details that indicate Chapman's health.

CRITICAL THINKING AND READING

Making Inferences About Characters

An **inference** is a reasonable conclusion you draw from given evidence. You can make inferences about a character from his or her appearance and actions. For example, from "He nested with owl, and with bear-cub and possum" you can infer that Johnny Appleseed liked animals.

What can you infer from the following?

1. Although he wore rags, he carried his apple seeds in the best deerskin bags.
2. He has no tombstone or memorial, but the apple trees he planted still thrive.

UNDERSTANDING LANGUAGE

Completing Word Analogies

A **word analogy** shows a relationship that two pairs of words have in common. The relationship may be in terms of similar meaning, size, volume, use, appearance, or other aspect. On tests, word analogies are usually written with colons:

gnarled: straight :: roundabout: direct

This is stated: Gnarled is to straight as roundabout is to direct. The relationship is that of opposites.

To complete word analogy problems, determine the relationship in the given pair of words. Then look for a pair with the same relationship.

Select the pair of words that has the same relationship as the italicized pair.

1. *harvest: crop::*
   a. fertilize: field   c. preserve: fruit
   b. reap: grain
2. *prune: tree::*
   a. trim: hair   c. plant: seed
   b. hem: dress

THINKING AND WRITING

Comparing and Contrasting

Write down what you know about John Chapman. Also write down what you know about Johnny Appleseed. Then list the similarities and differences between the actual man and the legend he became. Use these lists to write an essay comparing and contrasting the two for your school literary magazine. Revise your essay, making sure you state your points clearly and support them with examples. Proofread your work and share it with your classmates.

GUIDE FOR READING

Davy Crockett

Davy Crockett (1786–1836) was a frontiersman from Jefferson County in Tennessee who served in the Army and was a colonel in the Tennessee militia. He also became a justice of the peace and was twice elected to Congress. Crockett is believed to have died in the battle against Mexican troops at the Alamo in March 1836, fighting for Texan independence. This account is by **Adrien Stoutenburg** (1916–   ), a poet and biographer born in Darfur, Minnesota, who has written about other larger-than-life figures.

Yarn

A **yarn** is an exaggerated, or overstated, story that captures the spirit and language of the times in which it was told. Yarns were commonly told on the American frontier for entertainment; a good yarn teller could hold an audience spellbound for hours. A yarn can be about any subject. It may include several anecdotes about the hero, mixing fact with imagination and exaggeration.

Look For

As you read this excerpt from "Davy Crockett," imagine that it is being told aloud by a yarn teller. Look for the language and the exaggeration the writer uses to hold your interest. What is the effect of this yarn?

Writing

Imagine that you are living on the frontier in the 1800's. What problems do you face? What is life like? Freewrite, expressing your thoughts and feelings.

Vocabulary

Knowing the following words will help you as you read this excerpt from "Davy Crockett."

bellowed (bel′ ōd) v.: Roared loudly (p. 679)

brimstone (brim′ stōn′) n.: Another name for *sulfur,* a foul-smelling mineral that burns with a blue flame (p. 680)

allies (al′ īz′) n.: Countries, persons, or groups joined for a common purpose (p. 681)

amble (am′ b'l) v.: To move at a smooth, easy pace (p. 683)

shinny (shin′ ē) v.: To climb by gripping with both hands and legs (p. 683)

from Davy Crockett

Adrien Stoutenburg

The state of Tennessee wasn't born too many years before Davy Crockett was. In a way, Tennessee and Davy grew up together, and they both grew fast. Davy never became quite as tall as the Great Smoky Mountains, but by the time he was eight years old, he had a good start. All the Crockett family were on the large side. They had to be. Clearing out the wilderness by the Nolachucky River,[1] where Davy first saw the sunrise, took grit and gumption.[2] Davy had plenty of that, and more.

When people wanted to push posts down into the Nolachucky's bed to make supports for a bridge, they called Davy to jump on the posts. Davy would leap from one post to another, pushing them down with his bare feet. He had to be careful not to jump on a single post more than once or it might disappear into the river bottom.

He was a handy boy with an ax, too. There was wonderful timber in Tennessee. Many of the trees were so thick that the settlers couldn't cut them down, but had to tie chains around them and let the trees choke themselves to death. Davy could chop down the biggest sycamores or gum trees with the dull side of his ax blade.

As for hunting, Davy was the terror of the forest. The wild animals who were smart would crawl off and hide in their holes, pulling in their shadows after them, when they saw Davy coming with his rifle. At other times, when Davy wasn't hunting, the animals liked to spend the time of day with him and even talk a little. Davy always did know how to talk to animals.

One of the most special things about Davy was his grin. He could grin from ear to ear, and since his ears were rather far apart, this made for a sizable grin. He inherited his grin from his father, who, it was said, could grin in the teeth of a blizzard and change it into a rainbow. Davy didn't know how powerful his own grin was, until one day he grinned at a raccoon sitting in a tree. The raccoon tumbled to the ground, dead right down to its striped tail.

From then on, Davy did most of his raccoon hunting that way. One night, he was out hunting with his hound dog Rattler. It was a clear, crisp night, with the moon spangling the trees and the wild pea vines, and the frogs croaking in a way that sounded like *Cr-r-r-ock-k-k-ket.* Davy stood admiring the scenery, slapping at a mosquito or two, when he saw a raccoon sitting high up in a big tulip tree. It seemed to be a sleek, shining raccoon, though the black mask across its eyes didn't look as dark as usual. Rattler, who generally bellowed when he saw game, didn't even bark.

Davy grinned up at the creature. He

---

1. **Nolachucky** (nō′ lə chuk′ ē) **River.**
2. **gumption** (gump′ shən), *n.*: Courage; boldness.

**DAVY CROCKETT, WITH THE HELP OF HIS DOG,
FIGHTING A BEAR**
Cover of the Crockett Almanac, 1841
The Granger Collection

grinned for several minutes, but the raccoon stayed where it was.

"Maybe he can't see me clearly enough," Davy said to Rattler, who had gone to sleep. Davy moved where the moonlight was brighter. He set himself to grinning again, looking straight up at the raccoon. The raccoon didn't even twitch a whisker.

Davy began to get a little mad. Also, his grin-muscles were growing tired.

"You fool raccoon!" Davy yelled and shook his fist. "Don't you know you're sup-

posed to fall dead when I grin at you? Ain't I the yallerest blossom in the forest, and all solid brimstone except for my head and ears? If I have to stand here much longer grinning at you, I'll spoil, unless somebody covers me up with salt."

Davy found a large fallen tree branch. He propped it up and leaned his chin against the top end so that he could rest and grin at the same time. He grinned his hardest, showing all his teeth. His grin was so wide it went past his ears and halfway around to the back of his head. It made no difference to the raccoon.

"Well, sir!" said Davy, mad enough to spit nails, but curious too, about the kind of raccoon that could be so stupid it didn't fall dead when it was supposed to. He went back for his ax. The raccoon was still in the tree when Davy returned. Since the tree was rather large, about ten feet thick, he had to hit it twice with the sharp side of the ax.

The tree crashed down. Davy ran to it. Rattler woke up and ran beside him. Davy searched, and Rattler sniffed. There was no sign of the raccoon. But there was something on a top branch that *looked* like a sleek, shining raccoon.

Davy stared at it, feeling foolish. He had been wasting his time grinning at a large knot on the tree branch. The knot was as bare of bark as a hound's tooth, for Davy had grinned the bark completely off the knot and off all one side of the tree.

Davy still used his rifle, named Betsy, now and then to keep in practice. Near a gap in the Cumberland Mountains one day, he saw a raccoon perched in a cottonwood. It was a real, live raccoon, but it was so sad-looking that Davy had tears in his eyes as he raised his gun.

The raccoon lifted one paw and said in a mournful voice, "Pardon me, mister, but do you happen to be Davy Crockett?"

"I'm one and the same," said Davy.

"In that case," said the raccoon, "I'm as good as dead already, so you can put your rifle away." The raccoon crawled down from the tree and stood with his head bowed as if he were already at his own funeral.

Davy had never met such a respectful raccoon before. He stooped and patted the animal. "You've got such fine manners, little fellow," said Davy, "I want you to go home and raise up more raccoons like yourself."

The raccoon raced off, then remembered his manners. "Thank you, Mister Crockett," he called.

The time came for Davy to get married; so he did. He found a girl called Polly Finley Thunder Whirlwind, who was just the right-size wife for him, being about half as tall as the Northern Lights and twice as good at dancing. Polly had a good-sized grin, too, and she could laugh the mud chinks out of a log cabin. She laughed so hard dancing with Davy one winter that the cabin was full of holes. The wind naturally poked all its fingers through the holes until everyone nearly froze. They were all too busy shivering to have time for anything else. Davy brought home a half-bald wolf to lie in front of the coldest blast and do the shivering for the whole family, which by then included several children.

Davy brought home another pet, a big, good-natured bear. Davy had gotten caught in an earthquake crack and couldn't get free. A bear passed by, and Davy hung on to him until the bear pulled him out of the crack. Davy was so thankful, he hugged the bear. The bear hugged Davy back and almost hugged him to death. Davy named the bear Death-Hug and told him that the next time either of them felt affectionate, it would be safer if they just shook hands.

Death-Hug grew tame enough to let Davy put a saddle on his back and ride him like a horse. They traveled and hunted all over Tennessee together, from Lick Creek to the Shakes Country to the Obion River. When they were through traveling around for the day, they would sit and smoke a pipe together. Death-Hug was as fond of smoking as a fireplace with the damper shut.

Around 1812 the War of 1812 began, and Davy went to fight the English and their allies, the Creek Indians. The leader of the American Army was General Andrew Jackson.[3] Jackson was as full of brimstone and dynamite as Davy, so they got along fine.

Davy and Andy Jackson beat the Indians so badly there wasn't much left except their war paint. Then Davy went down to New Orleans with Jackson and fought the British redcoats until the red coats turned pale gray.

When there wasn't any fighting left to do, Davy went home to his spring planting. With him, he took another pet he had picked up in the southern swamp country, a slithering, good-natured, grinning alligator called Old Mississippi.

Davy never lost his own grin in all that time. It was his grin that made him decide to go into politics. In those days, just like today, the politician with the biggest grin was apt to win. Davy went into the woods and practiced making speeches to his animal friends.

The animals figured life would be safer for them if Davy were elected to the state legislature and had to spend his time making laws instead of hunting. So they cheered and paraded, barking and howling. It sounded to Davy as if they were saying, "VOTE FOR CROCKETT." It sounded that way to his neighbors, too, so they went along with the animals and elected Davy to the Tennessee legislature.

Davy put on his foxskin cap, dusted off his fringed buckskin jacket, and set out for Nashville. He rode Death-Hug part of the way and Old Mississippi the rest. Some of the other politicians snickered when they saw him, but Davy paid no attention. All his life he had lived by his motto—*Be sure you're right, then go ahead.* That's what he did then. The Tennessee settlers liked what he did so well that they finally elected him to Congress and sent him to Washington.

---

3. **Andrew Jackson** (1767–1845), seventh president of the U.S. from 1829 to 1837.

Andrew Jackson was President by then. When he saw Davy, he wrapped his arms around him so hard, Davy felt as if Death-Hug had grabbed him. Davy hugged Andy right back. It seemed they might crush each other to death, but when they both got blue in the face, they let go.

Davy had heard about the wonderful dancing that went on in Washington, and had trained Death-Hug and Old Mississippi to dance. Old Mississippi danced on his tail, and Death-Hug danced on his hind legs. Davy, who was a first-class dancer himself, danced the legs off everyone.

When there wasn't any work to be done in Congress, and no dancing or parades, Davy kept busy at other things. One of his biggest jobs was a certain comet that pulled loose from its hinges and started speeding toward the earth. At first, it was only a yellowish speck far off in the sky, its tail sparkling like the tail of a horse on fire. Every day, however, it grew bigger and brighter, coming closer.

Andy Jackson called Davy aside. "Colonel Crockett," he said, "the government has to do something about that comet. If it hits us, we'll all be blown to smithereens, and then some."

"I'll look into the situation, Mr. President," said Davy.

He straddled Death-Hug and rode him to the top of the tallest mountain, figuring on meeting the comet half-way. He got so close to the comet, he began to sweat from its heat.

The comet came closer and closer, wiggling its flaming tail like a fish on a hook. Davy tried grinning it to death, but the comet grinned right back, its teeth like a thousand torches. Davy tried firing his rifle at it, but the bullets melted and dripped off like red butter.

"Well, sir!" said Davy. He bunched up

his muscles and prepared to jump. The comet whooshed past him, all set to smash into every one of the thirty states in the Union. Davy stretched his arm out to its full length and grabbed the comet's tail. The comet hissed and thrashed, shooting sparks up to the Milky Way.

Davy started whirling the comet around his head like a lasso.[4] He whirled until the comet grew dizzy and began to wobble. When the comet was too weak even to hiccough, Davy let go. The comet went flying back up into the sky, growing smaller until it was little bigger than a firefly running out of fuel. Then Davy and Death-Hug started back to Washington for a good night's rest.

Around that time, Davy moved his family to Tennessee's western border. The soil there was richer than a multimillionaire. Davy didn't bother to plant seeds in the regular way; he loaded his shotgun with the seeds and shot them into the ground. Pumpkin vines grew so fast that the pumpkins were worn out from being dragged across the soil. A man had to be a fast runner even to pick one.

Things went along fine, until the time of the Big Freeze. The winter started out cold and grew colder. By January, it was so cold that smoke froze in fireplace chimneys. Davy's hair froze so stiff he didn't dare comb it, for fear it would crack. One morning, daybreak froze solid. When that happened, it became so cold that people didn't even dare think about it, because their thoughts froze right inside their heads.

Davy told his wife Polly, "I reckon I better amble around the country and see what in tarnation the trouble is."

He put on a foxskin cap and several coonskin caps on over it. He piled on a half-dozen jackets and several pairs of bearskin mittens. He put on so many socks that he had to stand on his head between times to rest his feet. When he left, he took a homemade bear trap with him. Davy walked all day, going toward Cloud Mountain. To keep from freezing to death, he had to shinny up and down a tree all night.

In the morning, he saw what the trouble was. The machinery that kept the earth turning had frozen. The gears and wheels couldn't move, and the sun had been caught between two blocks of ice under the wheels. The sun had worked so hard to get loose that it had frozen in its own icy sweat.

Davy set the bear trap and caught an exceptionally fat bear. He took the bear and held him up over the earth's frozen machinery. Then Davy squeezed the bear until slippery, hot bear oil ran down over the wheels and gears. Next, he greased the sun's face until the oil melted the ice.

"Get moving!" Davy ordered and gave one of the wheels a kick with his heel.

There was a creak, which changed to a whir as the earth began to turn again. The sun rolled over and flipped free. As it circled past, Davy lit his pipe from its trailing sparks. Then he stuck an especially bright piece of sunrise in his pocket and started for home.

On the way, he decided to do a little hunting, since he had a double-barreled shotgun with him. He was just aiming the gun at a flock of wild geese flying near, when he saw a big buck deer. He waited for the geese to come near the buck, figuring he could get both the geese and the deer with one shot. Suddenly, a rattlesnake started rattling its loud tail right at Davy's feet, ready to strike. Davy gave the geese a blast from one barrel of his gun, and the buck a blast from the other. The gun kicked hard against Davy's shoulder and flew out of his

---

4. lasso (las′ ō), *n.*: A long rope or narrow strip of leather, used for catching horses and cattle.

hands. It flattened the snake and knocked Davy into a nearby river.

Davy climbed out of the water in such a hurry that his clothes were still dry. His pockets were loaded down with goggle-eyed perch. The weight of the fish pulled at his jacket and made the buttons pop off. One button hit a doe-deer, and the other hit a squirrel, and they both died immediately from surprise.

Davy reached home lugging a bundle of geese, a swarm of fish, two deer, a rattlesnake, and a squirrel in his free hand. When he told his neighbors he had killed them all with one shot, one of the settlers said, "You're a clapper-clawing liar, Davy Crockett."

"Oh, I only lie enough to keep myself happy," said Davy, and he pulled out the scrap of sunrise for the children to play with.

Most of the people were grateful to Davy for breaking the cold snap, but some began saying Davy wasted his time in Congress dancing, parading, and telling tall tales. When voting time came again, enough people voted against Davy for him to lose the election.

"Well, sir!" said Davy, feeling as hot around his collar as he had when he had fought the comet. "From now on, the people of Tennessee will get no help from me! Anyhow, the state's getting too crowded. I'm moving to Texas!"

When the Texas animals heard that Davy Crockett was coming, half of them fled across the border to Mexico. About a third of the buffalo—the meanest and toughest —remained. Buffalo didn't scare Davy, even the orneriest[5] of them. One day, he caught two of the biggest buffalo bulls in Texas and tied their tails together in a bow knot. Davy made a personal pet of one of the bulls and took the creature to church with him. This buffalo had such a fine bass voice, he was the best singer in the church choir.

Texas in those days was a part of Mexico. Davy and many of the other American settlers didn't like taking orders from the Mexican government. So Davy and his friends decided to make their own laws. When Santa Anna,[6] the President of Mexico, heard this, he ordered his army to go northward and beat the tar out of the rebel Americans.

According to some people, Davy killed enough buffalo to feed the whole Texas army. He roasted the meat by racing along behind the flames of a prairie fire. Also, they say, he talked so many of the animals over to the American side, including wildcats, snakes, wolves, and mountain lions, that he scared the Mexican soldiers out of their boots.

The people who write history books say that Davy died fighting the Mexicans in San Antonio, Texas, at a fort called the Alamo. No one has ever said whether Death-Hug and Old Mississippi were with him. The chances are that they were and fought beside him to the end, since they have never been seen since.

One thing is certain. The sun comes up in Texas and in Tennessee every day, summer or winter. And the earth keeps turning smoothly, the way it's supposed to. If it ever does get frozen fast again, Davy Crockett may come along to squeeze some bear oil over the works and give the wheels a kick to start everything humming once more.

---

5. orneriest (ôr′ nər ē əst), *n.*: Most contrary and stubborn; most hard to manage.

6. Santa Anna (1795–1876), Mexican general; president of Mexico from 1833 to 1835.

THINKING ABOUT THE SELECTION

Recalling

1. How does young Davy help build bridges?
2. How does Crockett hunt raccoons?
3. Describe two times that Crockett is unsuccessful when hunting.
4. Why is Polly Finley Thunder Whirlwind the "right-size wife" for Crockett?
5. What will help a politician win an election?
6. Name three of Crockett's pets.

Interpreting

7. Why do the forest animals like to talk with Crockett when he isn't trying to hunt them?
8. Later in his life, Crockett served three terms in the United States Congress. What qualities, besides those illustrated in "Davy Crockett," must he have had to win election?
9. The writer states, "When there wasn't any work to be done in Congress, and no dancing or parades, Davy kept busy at other things." What does this tell you about the frontiersman's view of Congress?

Applying

10. If Davy Crockett were alive today, what kind of activities might interest him?

ANALYZING LITERATURE

Understanding a Yarn

A **yarn** is an exaggerated story that captures the spirit and language of the times in which it was told. A yarn is told for entertainment; it does not have a "lesson." Through descriptions of fantastic events or heroic feats, a yarn can help you imagine what life was like at that time.

1. In what ways do you think the information you would learn about Davy Crockett from a biographical account would be different from the information you learn about him from a yarn?
2. Are there any ways in which the information would be similar? Explain your answer.

CRITICAL THINKING AND READING

Making Inferences About Audience

An **inference** is a conclusion you draw from evidence. Based on Crockett's qualities, you can make inferences about what Americans on the frontier were like and what was important to them. For example, "Davy could chop down the biggest sycamores or gum trees with the dull side of his ax blade" tells you that settlers chopped wood and that strength was admired.

1. Name three of Davy Crockett's traits that would have been important on the frontier.
2. Explain why each trait was important.
3. Are these traits as important today? Explain.

UNDERSTANDING LANGUAGE

Appreciating Dialect

Dialect is the pronunciation, grammar, and vocabulary used by a particular group of people in a region. An example of dialect is "Clearing out the wilderness . . . took grit and gumption." In standard English, we might say that it took courage and determination.

Rewrite in standard English the following.
1. "The knot was as bare of bark as a hound's tooth . . ."
2. '". . . I reckon I better amble around the country and see what in tarnation the trouble is."'

THINKING AND WRITING

Comparing and Contrasting Folk Heroes

Choose another hero in this unit you like. List the similarities in character traits, behavior, and circumstances between that hero and Davy Crockett. Also list differences between them. Then use these lists to write an essay for a literary magazine in which you compare and contrast the heroes. Revise, making sure you have organized information logically. Proofread and prepare a draft fit for publication.

Making Generalizations

A **generalization** is a general statement or rule drawn from specific facts or cases. For this conclusion to be considered sound, it must be true for a number of different cases or situations.

Evaluating Generalizations

It is important to evaluate a generalization by determining if the facts *do* support it and if it applies to a number of other situations or cases besides the one you are considering. Be aware that a generalization does not have to apply to all cases.

Activity

Reread the excerpt from *The People, Yes.* Then decide which of the following statements are sound generalizations and which are unsound ones.

1. All people have yarns.
2. Many people have yarns.
3. Yarns are written about many different topics.
4. Yarns are written about every imaginable topic.
5. People have created yarns about a variety of topics.

You should have selected sentences 2, 3, and 5 as sound generalizations because the facts support them and they apply to a number of other cases. Sentences 1 and 4 are too broad. While you can safely conclude that many people have yarns or have created yarns, you cannot conclude that all people have done so. Likewise, you cannot conclude that yarns have been written about every imaginable topic.

Overgeneralizations

An **overgeneralization** is a general statement that is too broad. Using words such as *never, always, everyone, all, must, no one,* and *never* in generalizations makes them too broad. These kinds of words do not allow for any exceptions.

Hasty Generalizations

When a generalization is based on insufficient evidence or too few cases, it is called a **hasty generalization.** It is difficult to make a sound general conclusion if it is based on too few cases or evidence. For instance, if you had said that most yarns were about cyclones, you would be making a hasty generalization. Carl Sandburg mentions only two yarns about cyclones. The rest of the yarns focus on other topics. You could correct this generalization by saying, "Some yarns are about cyclones."

Guidelines

- Make sure you understand the main idea and supporting details.
- Make sure the conclusions you draw are adequately supported by facts or evidence.
- Make sure the generalization you draw applies to many different cases or situations.
- Make sure you do not use words such as "always" or "must," which do not allow for any exceptions and which make the generalization too broad.

Activity

Read the following paragraph from "The Origin of Fire." Identify the numbered statements as either sound generalizations, hasty generalizations, or overgeneralizations. Give evidence to support each answer.

> Long ago the Nez Percé had no fire. They could see fire in the sky sometimes, but it belonged to the Great Power. He kept it in great black bags in the sky. When the bags bumped into each other, there was a crashing, tearing sound, and through the hole that was made fire sparkled.

1. The Nez Percé thought fire belonged to the Great Power.
2. The Nez Percé thought the Great Power owned everything.
3. The Nez Percé thought you could make fire if you bumped black bags together.
4. Fire originated in the sky.
5. Conclusions are always based on observations.
6. People often draw conclusions based on observations.

Activity

Read each set of statements below. Then make a generalization that is based on the set.

1. The tales about Paul Bunyan were created in the North because many people in Minnesota and Wisconsin were lumberjacks. The stories about Davy Crockett were invented on the frontier because many people had to struggle against harsh surroundings there. The tales about Pecos Bill began in the Southwest because there were many cowboys.
2. Paul Bunyan was a giant lumberjack whose dancing with some friends caused an earthquake and caused a river to move over three counties. Pecos Bill was a superhuman cowboy whose ride on a cyclone resulted in the creation of the Staked Plains.

YOU THE WRITER

Assignment

1. Many myths deal with the origin of some natural occurrence. Write a myth explaining an event in nature.

Prewriting. First brainstorm to list natural occurrences such as a sunset, a waterfall, or a volcanic eruption. Select one of these events and jot down as many details about it as you can.

Writing. Write the first draft of a myth, providing an imaginative explanation for the natural occurrence you have chosen. Be sure to include descriptive details in your myth. Proceed in chronological order.

Revising. Revise your myth, making sure you have provided an imaginative explanation. Proofread your myth and share it with your classmates.

Assignment

2. Many legends are based on real-life people. Create a character for a legend based on a contemporary figure.

Prewriting. Brainstorm to list contemporary figures who might be the subject of future legends. For example, you might list famous athletes, astronauts, or even computer experts. Select one of these figures, and freewrite about his or her deeds.

Writing. Write the first draft of a legend, using your figure as a folk hero and telling about one of his or her exploits. Use exaggeration to make the exploit seem larger than life.

Revising. Have you made the exploit seem larger than life? Revise your legend, making sure it presents your character in a vivid way. Proofread your legend and prepare a final draft.

Assignment

3. Imagine you are living in the early 1800's and you are traveling across the country by wagon train. Write a tall tale to entertain your fellow travelers sitting around the campfire at night.

Prewriting. Create a story map, showing the plot, characters, and setting of your tale.

Writing. Write the first draft of your tall tale. Since this tale is "tall," make sure you exaggerate events. Also include dialect to give your tale a regional flavor.

Revising. When you revise, make sure you have created vivid characters and have used exaggeration to describe them and their deeds. Have you included dialect? Check your spelling and punctuation, paying special attention to your use of quotation marks.

YOU THE CRITIC

Assignment

1. Write an essay explaining how one of the folkheroes you have read about presents traits considered especially "American."

Prewriting. Choose a folk hero from one of the selections in this unit. List words and phrases describing this hero. From the list select the trait that you think most characterizes this hero.

Writing. Write the first draft of your essay. Begin with a topic sentence explaining how this folk hero portrays a special aspect of the American character. Support your main idea with details from the selection.

Revising. When you revise, make sure you have provided adequate support for your main idea. Proofread your essay and prepare a final draft.

Assignment

2. Write an essay comparing and contrasting a mythical explanation with a scientific explanation.

Prewriting. Thumb through the selections you have read and list mythical explanations for events in nature. Do some research to find a scientific explanation of the same event.

Writing. Write the first draft of your essay, comparing and contrasting a mythical and a scientific explanation. Organize your essay so that one paragraph deals with the mythical explanation and the next deals with the scientific explanation.

Revising. When you revise, make sure you have organized your information logically. Proofread your essay and prepare a final draft.

Assignment

3. What is it about myths, legends, and folktales that stirs our imagination? Write an essay explaining the appeal of this type of literature.

Prewriting. Freewrite, exploring the appeal of myths, legends, and folktales. Review your freewriting, underlining important ideas and starring especially effective use of language.

Writing. Write the first draft of an essay explaining the appeal of myths, legends, and folktales. Support your main idea with examples or reasons drawn from real life.

Revising. When you revise your essay, make sure you have presented your main idea in a clear fashion. Have you supported it with examples or reasons? Proofread your essay and prepare a final draft.

CROSSING THE CHILKOOT PASS DURING THE GOLD RUSH IN ALASKA
O. E. Berninghaus
Three Lions

THE NOVEL

A novel is a work of fiction; that is, an author creates it from his or her imagination. A novel includes the same elements as a short story. These are plot, characters, setting, theme, and point of view. Because a novel is usually much longer than a short story, the author presents a plot, or sequence of events, that is more complicated than that of a short story. The author can also include more characters and develop them more thoroughly. A novel usually takes place in more than one setting, and more than one conflict, or struggle, may occur in addition to the main one.

Readers can gain greater insights about life and about a particular time and place from a novel than they can from most short stories. In *The Call of the Wild,* you will read about a time and place unfamiliar to most readers.

The Call of the Wild

Background

The Call of the Wild describes life in the Yukon Territory of northwestern Canada near the Klondike River during the great gold rush of 1896. The Klondike gold rush began when a man named Carmack found a large quantity of gold in the gravel of a creek. This discovery drew thousands of prospectors to the Yukon, and the town of Dawson sprang up overnight.

In his short novel The Call of the Wild, London describes gold rush fever through the eyes of the sled dog Buck. This device of having a dog tell the story allows the story to be told simply, without the complications introduced by human thought and emotion. Buck tells a simple tale of survival against the backdrop of men's greed and the perils of the frozen Yukon.

Reading Strategies

You may have difficulty reading the dialogue that's written in the regional dialects of some of the characters. A strategy for overcoming this difficulty is to read the dialogue aloud slowly and to think about what the character is trying to communicate. You can often determine what the words are by their context, or the situation in which the words are spoken.

Interact with the literature by using the active reading strategies: question, predict, clarify, summarize, and pull together. For this novel, the reading strategy that might prove particularly useful is summarizing. At intervals throughout the novel, stop and summarize for yourself the action that has taken place and the distinctive behavior of the characters that have been introduced.

Themes

You will encounter the following themes in The Call of the Wild.

- the law of club and fang
- survival of the fittest
- the relationship between humans and animals
- the destructive power of greed
- the powerful force of loyalty and love

The Call of the Wild

TRAPPER IN THE WILDS OF ALASKA
Sydney Laurence
The Shelburne Museum, Vermont

GUIDE FOR READING

The Call of the Wild, Chapters 1 and 2

Jack London (1876–1916) was born in San Francisco. As a teenager he went to sea to support himself. Later he worked in a canning factory, a mill, and a laundry. In 1897 he joined the Gold Rush to the Klondike. He was twenty-one years old, filled with the spirit of adventure, and determined to make his fortune. He was unsuccessful in his search for gold, but his trip brought him fame and fortune in a way he didn't expect: It provided the material for many of his stories and novels, the most famous of which is *The Call of the Wild*.

The Setting

In *The Call of the Wild,* the **setting,** the time and place of the action, is an essential element that affects characterization, plot, and theme. *The Call of the Wild* opens in the sunny Santa Clara Valley in California, but these surroundings only provide a strong contrast to the setting of most of the novel.

The Yukon Territory, where most of the novel takes place, was largely unsettled in 1897 when the rush for gold took place. Even today, the region is sparsely settled, but snowmobiles have replaced dog teams, and planes can now bring in supplies. During the years in which *The Call of the Wild* takes place, everything—food, clothing, tools—had to be carried in by dog sled.

Look For

As you read the first two chapters of *The Call of the Wild,* look for words and phrases the author uses to describe Buck's home. Then look for the ways he describes the environment at the Dyea beach. How are these two environments different? What effect do they have on Buck? Why do you think London started the novel as he did?

Writing

How do you think you would react if someone took you from your own familiar surroundings and placed you in a strange and threatening environment? Freewrite about facing such a situation.

Vocabulary

Knowing the following words will help you as you read Chapters 1 and 2 of *The Call of the Wild.*

unwonted (un wun′ tid) *adj.:* Not ordinary (p. 696)

primordial (prī môr′ dē əl) *adj.:* Primitive (p. 702)

prowess (prou′ is) *n.:* Superior ability (p. 704)

malingerer (mə lin′ gər ər) *n.:* One who pretends to be ill in order to escape work (p. 707)

The Call of the Wild

Jack London

1. Into the Primitive

Buck did not read the newspapers, or he would have known that trouble was brewing, not alone for himself, but for every tidewater[1] dog, strong of muscle and with warm, long hair, from Puget Sound[2] to San Diego.[3] Because men, groping in the Arctic[4] darkness, had found a yellow metal, and because steamship and transportation companies were booming the find,[5] thousands of men were rushing into the Northland. These men wanted dogs, and the dogs they wanted were heavy dogs, with strong muscles by which to toil, and furry coats to protect them from the frost.

Buck lived at a big house in the sun-kissed Santa Clara Valley.[6] Judge Miller's place, it was called. It stood back from the road, half hidden among the trees, through which glimpses could be caught of the wide, cool veranda that ran around its four sides. The house was approached by graveled driveways which wound about through wide-spreading lawns and under the interlacing boughs of tall poplars. At the rear things were on even a more spacious scale than at the front. There were great stables, where a dozen grooms and boys held forth, rows of vine-clad servants' cottages, an endless and orderly array of outhouses, long grape arbors, green pastures, orchards, and berry patches. Then there was the pumping plant for the artesian well, and the big cement tank where Judge Miller's boys took their morning plunge and kept cool in the hot afternoon.

And over this great demesne[7] Buck ruled. Here he was born, and here he had lived the four years of his life. It was true, there were other dogs. There could not but be other dogs on so vast a place, but they did not count. They came and went, resided in the populous kennels, or lived obscurely in the recesses of the house after the fashion of Toots, the Japanese pug, or Ysabel,[8] the Mexican hairless—strange creatures that rarely put nose out of doors or set foot to ground. On the other hand, there were the fox terriers, a score of them at least, who yelped fearful promises at Toots and Ysabel looking out of the windows at them and protected by a legion of housemaids armed with brooms and mops.

But Buck was neither house dog nor kennel dog. The whole realm was his. He plunged into the swimming tank or went

---

1. tidewater: Seacoast.
2. Puget (pyo͞o′ jit) **Sound:** Pacific Ocean inlet in northwestern Washington State.
3. San Diego (san′ dē ä′ go): Seaport in southern California.
4. Arctic (ärk′ tik): Near the North Pole.
5. booming the find: Rushing people to the site of the gold find.
6. Santa Clara Valley: Valley in western California.

---

7. demesne (di mān′), n.: Lands of an estate.
8. Ysabel (iz′ ə bel′).

hunting with the Judge's sons; he escorted Mollie and Alice, the Judge's daughters, on long twilight or early-morning rambles; on wintry nights he lay at the Judge's feet before the roaring library fire; he carried the Judge's grandsons on his back, or rolled them in the grass, and guarded their footsteps through wild adventures down to the fountain in the stable yard, and even beyond, where the paddocks[9] were, and the berry patches. Among the terriers he stalked imperiously, and Toots and Ysabel he utterly ignored, for he was king—king over all creeping, crawling, flying things of Judge Miller's place, humans included.

His father, Elmo, a huge St. Bernard, had been the Judge's inseparable companion, and Buck bid fair to follow in the way of his father. He was not so large—he weighed only one hundred and forty pounds—for his mother, Shep, had been a Scotch shepherd dog. Nevertheless, one hundred and forty pounds, to which was added the dignity that comes of good living and universal respect, enabled him to carry himself in right royal fashion. During the four years since his puppyhood he had lived the life of a sated[10] aristocrat; he had a fine pride in himself, was even a trifle egotistical, as country gentlemen sometimes become because of their insular[11] situation. But he had saved himself by not becoming a mere pampered house dog. Hunting and kindred outdoor delights had kept down the fat and hardened his muscles; and to him the love of water had been a tonic and a health preserver.

And this was the manner of dog Buck was in the fall of 1897, when the Klondike strike[12] dragged men from all the world into the frozen North. But Buck did not read the newspapers, and he did not know that Manuel, one of the gardener's helpers, was an undesirable acquaintance. Manuel had one besetting sin. He loved to play Chinese lottery. Also, in his gambling, he had one besetting weakness—faith in a system; and this made his doom certain. For to play a system requires money, while the wages of a gardener's helper do not lap over the needs of a wife and numerous progeny.[13]

The Judge was at a meeting of the Raisin Growers' Association, and the boys were busy organizing an athletic club, on the memorable night of Manuel's treachery. No one saw him and Buck go off through the orchard on what Buck imagined was merely a stroll. And with the exception of a solitary man, no one saw them arrive at the little flag station known as College Park. This man talked with Manuel, and money chinked between them.

"You might wrap up the goods before you deliver 'm," the stranger said gruffly, and Manuel doubled a piece of stout rope around Buck's neck under the collar.

"Twist it, an' you'll choke 'm plentee," said Manuel, and the stranger grunted a ready affirmative.

Buck had accepted the rope with quiet dignity. To be sure, it was an unwonted performance; but he had learned to trust in men he knew, and to give them credit for a wisdom that outreached his own. But when the ends of the rope were placed in the stranger's hands, he growled menacingly.

---

9. paddocks (pad' əkz), *n.*: Enclosed fields in which horses are exercised.
10. sated (sāt' əd), *adj.*: Fully satisfied.
11. insular (in' sə lər), *adj.*: Isolated; detached.

12. Klondike (Klän' dīk) **strike:** The discovery of gold near the Klondike River in the Yukon Territory of northwest Canada. This caused the Gold Rush in 1898.
13. progeny (präj' ə nē), *n.*: Children.

He had merely intimated[14] his displeasure, in his pride believing that to intimate was to command. But to his surprise the rope tightened around his neck, shutting off his breath. In quick rage he sprang at the man, who met him halfway, grappled him close by the throat, and with a deft twist threw him over on his back. Then the rope tightened mercilessly, while Buck struggled in a fury, his tongue lolling out of his mouth and his great chest panting futilely. Never in all his life had he been so vilely treated, and never in all his life had he been so angry. But his strength ebbed, his eyes glazed, and he knew nothing when the train was flagged and the two men threw him into the baggage car.

The next he knew, he was dimly aware that his tongue was hurting and that he was being jolted along in some kind of a conveyance. The hoarse shriek of a locomotive whistling a crossing told him where he was. He had traveled too often with the Judge not to know the sensation of riding in a baggage car. He opened his eyes, and into them came the unbridled anger of a kidnaped king. The man sprang for his throat, but Buck was too quick for him. His jaws closed on the hand, nor did they relax till his senses were choked out of him once more.

"Yep, has fits," the man said, hiding his mangled hand from the baggageman, who had been attracted by the sounds of struggle. "I'm takin' 'm up for the boss to 'Frisco. A crack dog doctor there thinks that he can cure 'm."

Concerning that night's ride, the man spoke most eloquently for himself, in a little shed back of a saloon on the San Francisco waterfront.

"All I get is fifty for it," he grumbled; "an' I wouldn't do it over for a thousand, cold cash."

His hand was wrapped in a bloody handkerchief, and the right trouser leg was ripped from knee to ankle.

"How much did the other mug get?" the saloonkeeper demanded.

"A hundred," was the reply. "Wouldn't take a sou[15] less, so help me."

"That makes a hundred and fifty," the saloonkeeper calculated; "and he's worth it, or I'm a squarehead."

Dazed, suffering intolerable pain from throat and tongue, with the life half throttled out of him, Buck attempted to face his tormentors. But he was thrown down and choked repeatedly, till they succeeded in filing the heavy brass collar from off his neck. Then the rope was removed, and he was flung into a cagelike crate.

There he lay for the remainder of the weary night, nursing his wrath and wounded pride. He could not understand what it all meant. What did they want with him, these strange men? Why were they keeping him pent up in this narrow crate? He did not know why, but he felt oppressed by the vague sense of impending calamity. Several times during the night he sprang to his feet when the shed door rattled open, expecting to see the Judge, or the boys at least. But each time it was the bulging face of the saloonkeeper that peered in at him by the sickly light of a tallow candle. And each time the joyful bark that trembled in Buck's throat was twisted into a savage growl.

But the saloonkeeper let him alone, and in the morning four men entered and picked up the crate. More tormentors, Buck decid-

---

14. intimated (in' tǝ māt ǝd), v.: Hinted or implied.

15. sou (so͞o), n.: French coin once worth about one cent.

ed, for they were evil-looking creatures, ragged and unkempt; and he stormed and raged at them through the bars. They only laughed and poked sticks at him, which he promptly assailed with his teeth till he realized that that was what they wanted. Whereupon he lay down sullenly and allowed the crate to be lifted into a wagon. Then he, and the crate in which he was imprisoned, began a passage through many hands. Clerks in the express office took charge of him; he was carted about in another wagon; a truck carried him, with an assortment of boxes and parcels, upon a ferry steamer; he was trucked off the steamer into a great railway depot, and finally he was deposited in an express car.

For two days and nights this express car was dragged along at the tail of shrieking locomotives; and for two days and nights Buck neither ate nor drank. In his anger he had met the first advances of the express messengers with growls, and they had retaliated by teasing him. When he flung himself against the bars, quivering and frothing, they laughed at him and taunted him. They growled and barked like detestable dogs, mewed, and flapped their arms and crowed. It was all very silly, he knew; but therefore the more outrage to his dignity, and his anger waxed and waxed. He did not mind the hunger so much, but the lack of water caused him severe suffering and fanned his wrath to fever pitch. For that matter, high-strung and finely sensitive, the ill treatment had flung him into a fever, which was fed by the inflammation[16] of his parched and swollen throat and tongue.

He was glad for one thing: the rope was off his neck. That had given them an unfair advantage; but now that it was off, he would show them. They would never get another rope around his neck. Upon that he was resolved. For two days and nights he neither ate nor drank, and during those two days and nights of torment, he accumulated a fund of wrath that boded[17] ill for whoever first fell foul of him. His eyes turned bloodshot, and he was metamorphosed[18] into a raging fiend. So changed was he that the Judge himself would not have recognized him; and the express messengers breathed with relief when they bundled him off the train at Seattle.

Four men gingerly carried the crate from the wagon into a small, high-walled back yard. A stout man, with a red sweater that sagged generously at the neck, came out and signed the book for the driver. That was the man, Buck divined, the next tormentor, and he hurled himself savagely against the bars. The man smiled grimly, and brought a hatchet and a club.

"You ain't going to take him out now?" the driver asked.

"Sure," the man replied, driving the hatchet into the crate for a pry.

There was an instantaneous scattering of the four men who had carried it in, and from safe perches on top of the wall they prepared to watch the performance.

Buck rushed at the splintering wood, sinking his teeth into it, surging and wrestling with it. Wherever the hatchet fell on the outside, he was there on the inside, snarling and growling, as furiously anxious to get out as the man in the red sweater was calmly intent on getting him out.

"Now, you red-eyed devil," he said, when he had made an opening sufficient for the passage of Buck's body. At the same

---

16. inflammation (in′ flə mā′ shən), *n.*: A state of redness, pain, and swelling.

17. boded (bōd′ əd), *v.*: Foretold a future event.
18. metamorphosed (met′ ə môr′ fōsd, *v.*: Changed or transformed.

time he dropped the hatchet and shifted the club to his right hand.

And Buck was truly a red-eyed devil, as he drew himself together for the spring, hair bristling, mouth foaming, a mad glitter in his bloodshot eyes. Straight at the man he launched his one hundred and forty pounds of fury, surcharged[19] with the pent passion of two days and nights. In midair, just as his jaws were about to close on the man, he received a shock that checked his body and brought his teeth together with an agonizing clip. He whirled over, fetching the ground on his back and side. He had never been struck by a club in his life, and did not understand. With a snarl that was part bark and more scream he was again on his feet and launched into the air. And again the shock came and he was brought crushingly to the ground. This time he was aware that it was the club, but his madness knew no caution. A dozen times he charged, and as often the club broke the charge and smashed him down.

After a particularly fierce blow, he crawled to his feet, too dazed to rush. He staggered limply about, the blood flowing from nose and mouth and ears, his beautiful coat sprayed and flecked with bloody slaver.[20] Then the man advanced and deliberately dealt him a frightful blow on the nose. All the pain he had endured was as nothing compared with the exquisite agony of this. With a roar that was almost lionlike in its ferocity, he again hurled himself at the man. But the man, shifting the club from right to left, coolly caught him by the under jaw, at the same time wrenching downward and backward. Buck described a complete circle in the air, and half of another, then crashed to the ground on his head and chest.

For the last time he rushed. The man struck the shrewd blow he had purposely withheld for so long, and Buck crumpled up and went down, knocked utterly senseless.

"He's no slouch at dog-breakin', that's wot I say," one of the men on the wall cried enthusiastically.

"Druther break cayuses[21] any day, and twice on Sundays," was the reply of the driver, as he climbed on the wagon and started the horses.

Buck's senses came back to him, but not his strength. He lay where he had fallen, and from there he watched the man in the red sweater.

"'Answers to the name of Buck,'" the man soliloquized,[22] quoting from the saloon-keeper's letter, which had announced the consignment of the crate and contents. "Well, Buck, my boy," he went on in a genial voice, "we've had our little ruction,[23] and the best thing we can do is to let it go at that. You've learned your place, and I know mine. Be a good dog and all'll go well and the goose hang high. Be a bad dog, and I'll whale the stuffin' outa you. Understand?"

As he spoke he fearlessly patted the head he had so mercilessly pounded, and though Buck's hair involuntarily bristled at touch of the hand, he endured it without protest. When the man brought him water he drank eagerly, and later bolted a generous meal of raw meat, chunk by chunk, from the man's hand.

He was beaten (he knew that); but he was not broken. He saw, once for all, that he stood no chance against a man with a club. He had learned the lesson, and in all his

---

19. surcharged (sur′ charjd), *adj.*: Overcharged.
20. slaver (slav′ ər), *n.*: Saliva.

21. cayuses (kī′ o͞os iz), *n.*: Small Western horses used by cowboys.
22. soliloquized (sə lil′ ə kwīzd), *v.*: Talked to himself.
23. ruction (ruk′ shən), *n.*: Quarrel or noisy disturbance.

after life he never forgot it. That club was a revelation. It was his introduction to the reign of primitive law, and he met the introduction halfway. The facts of life took on a fiercer aspect; and while he faced that aspect uncowed, he faced it with all the latent cunning of his nature aroused. As the days went by, other dogs came, in crates and at the ends of ropes, some docilely, and some raging and roaring as he had come; and, one and all, he watched them pass under the dominion of the man in the red sweater. Again and again, as he looked at each brutal performance, the lesson was driven home to Buck: a man with a club was a lawgiver, a master to be obeyed, though not necessarily conciliated.[24] Of this last Buck was never guilty, though he did see beaten dogs that fawned upon the man, and wagged their tails, and licked his hand. Also he saw one dog, that would neither conciliate nor obey, finally killed in the struggle for mastery.

---

24. conciliated (kən sil′ ē āt′ əd), *adv.*: Made friends with.

Now and again men came, strangers, who talked excitedly, wheedlingly and in all kinds of fashions to the man in the red sweater. And at such times that money passed between them the strangers took one or more of the dogs away with them. Buck wondered where they went, for they never came back; but the fear of the future was strong upon him, and he was glad each time when he was not selected.

Yet his time came, in the end, in the form of a little weazened[25] man who spat broken English and many strange and uncouth exclamations which Buck could not understand.

When his eyes lit upon Buck, he cried, "Dat one bully dog! Eh? How moch?"

"Three hundred, and a present at that,"

---

25. weazened: wizened (wēz′ 'nd), *adj.*: Shriveled; withered.

was the prompt reply of the man in the red sweater. "And seein' it's government money, you ain't got no kick coming, eh, Perrault?"[26]

Perrault grinned. Considering that the price of dogs had been boomed skyward by the unwonted demand, it was not an unfair sum for so fine an animal. The Canadian Government would be no loser, nor would its dispatches travel the slower. Perrault knew dogs, and when he looked at Buck he knew that he was one in a thousand. "One in ten t'ousand," he commented mentally.

Buck saw money pass between them, and was not surprised when Curly, a good-natured Newfoundland, and he were led away by the little weazened man. That was the last he saw of the man in the red sweater, and as Curly and he looked at receding Seattle from the deck of the *Narwhal*, it was the last he saw of the warm Southland. Curly and he were taken below by Perrault and turned over to a black-faced giant called François.[27] Perrault was a French-Canadian, and swarthy; but François was a French-Canadian half-breed, and twice as swarthy. They were a new kind of men to Buck (of which he was destined to see many more), and while he developed no affection for them, he nonetheless grew honestly to respect them. He speedily learned that Perrault and François were fair men, calm and impartial in administering justice, and too wise in the way of dogs to be fooled by dogs.

In the 'tween decks[28] of the *Narwhal*, Buck and Curly joined two other dogs. One of them was a big, snow-white fellow from Spitzbergen who had been brought away by a whaling captain, and who had later ac-

---

26. Perrault (pər ō′).
27. François (fran swä′).
28. 'tween decks: Any of the decks below the main deck.

companied a Geological Survey into the Barrens. He was friendly, in a treacherous sort of way, smiling into one's face the while he meditated some underhand trick, as, for instance, when he stole from Buck's food at the first meal. As Buck sprang to punish him, the lash of Francois's whip sang through the air, reaching the culprit first; and nothing remained to Buck but to recover the bone. That was fair of François, he decided, and the half-breed began his rise in Buck's estimation.

The other dog made no advances, nor received any; also, he did not attempt to steal from the newcomers. He was a gloomy, morose fellow, and he showed Curly plainly that all he desired was to be left alone, and further, that there would be trouble if he were not left alone. Dave he was called, and he ate and slept, or yawned between times, and took interest in nothing, not even when the *Narwhal* crossed Queen Charlotte Sound and rolled and pitched and bucked like a thing possessed. When Buck and Curly grew excited, half wild with fear, he raised his head as though annoyed, favored them with an incurious glance, yawned, and went to sleep again.

Day and night the ship throbbed to the tireless pulse of the propeller, and though one day was very like another, it was apparent to Buck that the weather was steadily growing colder. At last, one morning, the propeller was quiet, and the *Narwhal* was pervaded with an atmosphere of excitement. He felt it, as did the other dogs, and knew that a change was at hand. François leashed them and brought them on deck. At the first step upon the cold surface, Buck's feet sank into a white mushy something very like mud. He sprang back with a snort. More of this white stuff was falling through the air. He shook himself, but more of it fell upon him. He sniffed it curiously, then licked some up on his tongue. It bit like fire, and the next instant was gone. This puzzled him. He tried it again, with the same result. The onlookers laughed uproariously,[29] and he felt ashamed, he knew not why, for it was his first snow.

2. The Law of Club and Fang

Buck's first day on the Dyea beach was like a nightmare. Every hour was filled with shock and surprise. He had been suddenly jerked from the heart of civilization and flung into the heart of things primordial. No lazy, sun-kissed life was this, with nothing to do but loaf and be bored. Here was neither peace, nor rest, nor a moment's safety. All was confusion and action, and every moment life and limb were in peril. There was imperative need to be constantly alert; for these dogs and men were not town dogs and men. They were savages, all of them, who knew no law but the law of club and fang.

He had never seen dogs fight as these wolfish creatures fought, and his first experience taught him an unforgettable lesson. It is true, it was a vicarious[30] experience, else he would not have lived to profit by it. Curly was the victim. They were camped near the log store, where she, in her friendly way, made advances to a husky dog the size of a full-grown wolf, though not half so large as she. There was no warning, only a leap in like a flash, a metallic clip of teeth, a leap out equally swift, and Curly's face was ripped open from eye to jaw.

It was the wolf manner of fighting, to strike and leap away; but there was more to it than this. Thirty or forty huskies ran

---

29. uproariously (up rôr′ ē əs lē), *adv.*: Loudly and boisterously.
30. vicarious (vī kãr′ ē əs), *adj.*: Experienced by one person or animal in place of another.

to the spot and surrounded the combatants in an intent and silent circle. Buck did not comprehend that silent intentness, nor the eager way with which they were licking their chops. Curly rushed her antagonist, who struck again and leaped aside. He met her next rush with his chest, in a peculiar fashion that tumbled her off her feet. She never regained them. This was what the onlooking huskies had waited for. They closed in upon her, snarling and yelping, and she was buried, screaming with agony, beneath the bristling mass of bodies.

So sudden was it, and so unexpected, that Buck was taken aback. He saw Spitz run out his scarlet tongue in a way he had of laughing; and he saw François, swinging an ax, spring into the mess of dogs. Three men with clubs were helping him to scatter them. It did not take long. Two minutes from the time Curly went down, the last of her assailants were clubbed off. But she lay there limp and lifeless in the bloody, trampled snow, almost literally torn to pieces, the swart[31] half-breed standing over her and cursing horribly. The scene often came back to Buck to trouble him in his sleep. So that was the way. No fair play. Once down, that was the end of you. Well, he would see to it that he never went down. Spitz ran out his tongue and laughed again, and from that moment Buck hated him with a bitter and deathless hatred.

Before he had recovered from the shock caused by the tragic passing of Curly, he received another shock. François fastened upon him an arrangement of straps and buckles. It was a harness, such as he had seen the grooms put on the horses at home. And as he had seen horses work, so he was set to work, hauling François on a sled to the forest that fringed the valley, and returning with a load of firewood. Though his dignity was sorely hurt by thus being made a draft animal,[32] he was too wise to rebel. He buckled down with a will and did his best, though it was all new and strange. François was stern, demanding instant obedience, and by virtue of his whip receiving instant obedience; while Dave, who was an experienced wheeler, nipped Buck's hind quarters whenever he was in error. Spitz was the leader, likewise experienced, and while he could not always get at Buck, he growled sharp reproof now and again, or cunningly threw his weight in the traces[33] to jerk Buck into the way he should go. Buck learned easily, and under the combined tuition of his two mates and François made remarkable progress. Ere[34] they returned to camp he knew enough to stop at "ho," to go ahead at "mush," to swing wide on the bends, and to keep clear of the wheeler when the loaded sled shot downhill at their heels.

"T'ree vair' good dogs," François told Perrault. "Dat Buck, heem pool lak a devil. I tich heem queek as anyt'ing."

By afternoon, Perrault, who was in a hurry to be on the trail with his dispatches, returned with two more dogs. Billee and Joe he called them, two brothers, and true huskies both. Sons of the one mother though they were, they were as different as day and night. Billee's one fault was his excessive good nature, while Joe was the very opposite, sour and introspective,[35] with a perpetual snarl and a malignant eye. Buck received them in comradely fashion, Dave ignored them, while Spitz proceeded to

---

31. swart (swôrt), *adj.*: Having a dark complexion.

32. draft animal: An animal used for hauling heavy loads.
33. traces (trās′ əz) *n.*: Straps that connect the harness to the sled.
34. Ere (er), *prep.*: Before.
35. introspective (in′ trə spek′ tiv), *adj.*: Inclined to look into one's own mind and feelings.

thrash first one and then the other. Billee wagged his tail appeasingly, turned to run when he saw that appeasement was of no avail, and cried (still appeasingly) when Spitz's sharp teeth scored his flank. But no matter how Spitz circled, Joe whirled around on his heels to face him, mane bristling, ears laid back, lips writhing and snarling, jaws clipping together as fast as he could snap, and eyes diabolically gleaming—the incarnation of belligerent fear. So terrible was his appearance that Spitz was forced to forgo disciplining him; but to cover his own discomfiture he turned upon the inoffensive and wailing Billee and drove him to the confines of the camp.

By evening Perrault secured another dog, an old husky, long and lean and gaunt, with a battle-scarred face and a single eye which flashed a warning of prowess that commanded respect. He was called Sol-leks, which means The Angry One. Like Dave, he asked nothing, gave nothing, expected nothing; and when he marched slowly and deliberately into their midst, even Spitz left him alone. He had one peculiarity which Buck was unlucky enough to discover. He did not like to be approached on his blind side. Of this offense Buck was unwittingly guilty, and the first knowledge he had of his indiscretion was when Sol-leks whirled upon him and slashed his shoulder to the bone for three inches up and down. Forever after Buck avoided his blind side, and to the last of their comradeship had no more trouble. His only apparent ambition, like Dave's, was to be left alone; though, as Buck was afterward to learn, each of them possessed one other and even more vital ambition.

That night Buck faced the great problem of sleeping. The tent, illumined by a candle, glowed warmly in the midst of the white plain; and when he, as a matter of course, entered it, both Perrault and François bom-barded him with curses and cooking utensils, till he recovered from his consternation and fled ignominiously[36] into the outer cold. A chill wind was blowing that nipped him sharply and bit with especial venom into his wounded shoulder. He lay down on the snow and attempted to sleep, but the frost soon drove him shivering to his feet. Miserable and disconsolate, he wandered about among the many tents, only to find that one place was as cold as another. Here and there savage dogs rushed upon him, but he bristled his neck hair and snarled (for he was learning fast), and they let him go his way unmolested.

---

36. ignominiously (ig' nə min' ē əs lē), *adv.*: In a shameful way.

Finally an idea came to him. He would return and see how his own teammates were making out. To his astonishment, they had disappeared. Again he wandered about through the great camp, looking for them, and again he returned. Were they in the tent? No, that could not be, else he would not have been driven out. Then where could they possibly be? With drooping tail and shivering body, very forlorn indeed, he aim-lessly circled the tent. Suddenly the snow gave way beneath his forelegs and he sank down. Something wriggled under his feet. He sprang back, bristling and snarling, fearful of the unseen and unknown. But a friendly little yelp reassured him, and he went back to investigate. A whiff of warm air ascended to his nostrils, and there, curled up under the snow in a snug ball, lay Billee. He whined placatingly, squirmed and wriggled to show his good will and intentions, and even ventured, as a bribe for peace, to lick Buck's face with his warm, wet tongue.

Another lesson. So that was the way they did it, eh? Buck confidently selected a spot, and with much fuss and waste effort proceeded to dig a hole for himself. In a trice the heat from his body filled the confined space and he was asleep. The day had been long and arduous, and he slept soundly and comfortably, though he growled and barked and wrestled with bad dreams.

Nor did he open his eyes till roused by the noises of the waking camp. At first he did not know where he was. It had snowed during the night and he was completely buried. The snow walls pressed him on every side, and a great surge of fear swept through him—the fear of the wild thing for the trap. It was a token that he was harking back through his own life to the lives of his forebears; for he was a civilized dog, an unduly civilized dog, and of his own experience knew no trap and so could not of himself fear it. The muscles of his whole body contracted spasmodically and instinctively, the hair on his neck and shoulders stood on end, and with a ferocious snarl he bounded straight up into the blinding day, the snow flying about him in a flashing cloud. Ere he landed on his feet, he saw the white camp spread out before him and knew where he was and remembered all that had passed from the time he went for a stroll with Manuel to the hole he had dug for himself the night before.

A shout from François hailed his appearance. "Wot I say?" the dog driver cried to Perrault. "Dat Buck for sure learn queek as anyt'ing."

Perrault nodded gravely. As courier[37] for the Canadian Government, bearing important dispatches, he was anxious to secure the best dogs, and he was particularly gladdened by the possession of Buck.

Three more huskies were added to the team inside an hour, making a total of nine, and before another quarter of an hour had passed they were in harness and swinging up the trail toward the Dyea Canyon.[38] Buck was glad to be gone, and though the work was hard he found he did not particularly despise it. He was surprised at the eagerness which animated the whole team and which was communicated to him; but still more surprising was the change wrought in Dave and Sol-leks. They were new dogs, utterly transformed by the harness. All passiveness and unconcern had dropped from them. They were alert and active, anxious that the work should go well, and fiercely irritable with whatever, by delay or confusion, retarded that work. The toil of the traces seemed the supreme expression of their being, and all that they lived for and the only thing in which they took delight.

Dave was wheeler or sled dog, pulling in front of him was Buck, then came Sol-leks; the rest of the team was strung out ahead, single file, to the leader, which position was filled by Spitz.

Buck had been purposely placed between Dave and Sol-leks so that he might receive instruction. Apt scholar that he was, they were equally apt teachers, never allowing him to linger long in error, and enforcing their teaching with their sharp teeth. Dave was fair and very wise. He never nipped Buck without cause, and he never failed to nip him when he stood in need of it. As François's whip backed him up, Buck found it to be cheaper to mend his ways than to retaliate. Once, during a brief halt, when he got tangled in the traces and delayed the start, both Dave and Sol-leks flew at him and administered a sound trouncing. The resulting tangle was even worse, but Buck took good care to keep the traces clear

---

37. courier (kσor′ ē ər), *n*.: Messenger.

38. Dyea (dī′ ā) **Canyon:** Deep valley leading from the former village of Dyea (northwest of the present-day city of Skagway) toward Chilkoot Pass on the border of Alaska and Canada's Yukon Territory. It was the main trail to Dawson and the gold fields.

thereafter; and ere the day was done, so well had he mastered his work, his mates about ceased nagging him. François's whip snapped less frequently, and Perrault even honored Buck by lifting up his feet and carefully examining them.

It was a hard day's run, up the Canyon, through Sheep Camp, past the Scales and the timber line, across glaciers and snow-drifts hundreds of feet deep, and over the great Chilkoot Divide, which stands between the salt water and the fresh and guards forbiddingly the sad and lonely North. They made good time down the chain of lakes which fills the craters of extinct volcanoes, and late that night pulled into the huge camp at the head of Lake Bennett, where thousands of gold seekers were building boats against the break-up of the ice in the spring. Buck made his hole in the snow and slept the sleep of the exhausted just, but all too early was routed out in the cold darkness and harnessed with his mates to the sled.

That day they made forty miles, the trail being packed; but the next day, and for many days to follow, they broke their own trail, worked harder, and made poorer time. As a rule, Perrault traveled ahead of the team, packing the snow with webbed shoes to make it easier for them. François, guiding the sled at the gee pole,[39] sometimes exchanged places with him, but not often. Perrault was in a hurry, and he prided himself on his knowledge of ice, which knowledge was indispensable, for the fall ice was very thin, and where there was swift water, there was no ice at all.

Day after day, for days unending, Buck toiled in the traces. Always, they broke camp in the dark, and the first gray of dawn found them hitting the trail with fresh miles reeled off behind them. And always they pitched camp after dark, eating their bit of fish, and crawling to sleep into the snow. Buck was ravenous. The pound and a half of sun-dried salmon which was his ration for each day seemed to go nowhere. He never had enough, and suffered from perpetual hunger pangs. Yet the other dogs, because they weighed less and were born to the life, received a pound only of the fish and managed to keep in good condition.

He swiftly lost the fastidiousness[40] which had characterized his old life. A dainty eater, he found that his mates, finishing first, robbed him of his unfinished ration. There was no defending it. While he was fighting off two or three, it was disappearing down the throats of the others. To remedy this, he ate as fast as they; and, so greatly did hunger compel him, he was not above taking what did not belong to him. He watched and learned. When he saw Pike, one of the new dogs, a clever malingerer and thief, slyly steal a slice of bacon when Perrault's back was turned, he duplicated the performance the following day, getting away with the whole chunk. A great uproar was raised, but he was unsuspected; while Dub, an awkward blunderer who was always getting caught, was punished for Buck's misdeed.

This first theft marked Buck as fit to survive in the hostile Northland environment. It marked his adaptability, his capacity to adjust himself to changing conditions, the lack of which would have meant swift and terrible death. It marked, further, the decay or going to pieces of his moral nature, a vain thing and a handicap in the ruthless struggle for existence. It was all well enough in the Southland, under the law of love and fellowship, to respect private property and

---

39. gee (gē) pole: Pole at the front of the sled used for steering.

40. fastidiousness (fas tid′ ē əs′ nis) n.: Refinement; daintiness.

personal feelings; but in the Northland, under the law of club and fang, whoso took such things into account was a fool, and insofar as he observed them he would fail to prosper.

Not that Buck reasoned it out. He was fit, that was all, and unconsciously he accommodated himself to the new mode of life. All his days, no matter what the odds, he had never run from a fight. But the club of the man in the red sweater had beaten into him a more fundamental and primitive code. Civilized, he could have died for a moral consideration, say the defense of Judge Miller's riding whip; but the completeness of his decivilization was now evidenced by his ability to flee from the defense of a moral consideration and so save his hide. He did not steal for joy of it, but because of the clamor of his stomach. He did not rob openly, but stole secretly and cunningly, out of respect for club and fang. In short, the things he did were done because it was easier to do them than not to do them.

His development (or retrogression[41]) was rapid. His muscles became hard as iron, and he grew callous to all ordinary pain. He achieved an internal as well as external economy. He could eat anything, no matter how loathsome or indigestible; and, once eaten, the juices of his stomach extracted the last least particle of nutriment; and his blood carried it to the farthest reaches of his body, building it into the toughest and stoutest of tissues. Sight and scent became remarkably keen, while his hearing developed such acuteness that in his sleep he heard the faintest sound and knew whether it heralded peace or peril. He learned to bite the ice out with his teeth when it collected between his toes; and when he was thirsty and there was a thick scum of ice over the water hole, he would break it by rearing and striking it with stiff forelegs. His most conspicuous trait was an ability to scent the wind and forecast it a night in advance. No matter how breathless the air when he dug his nest by tree or bank, the wind that later blew inevitably found him to leeward, sheltered and snug.

And not only did he learn by experience, but instincts long dead became alive again. The domesticated generations fell from him. In vague ways he remembered back to the youth of the breed, to the time the wild dogs ranged in packs through the primeval forest and killed their meat as they ran it down. It was no task for him to learn to fight with cut and slash and the quick wolf snap. In this manner had fought forgotten ancestors. They quickened the old life within him, and the old tricks which they had stamped into the heredity of the breed were his tricks. They came to him without effort or discovery, as though they had been his always. And when, on the still, cold nights, he pointed his nose at a star and howled long and wolflike, it was his ancestors, dead and dust, pointing nose at star and howling down through the centuries and through him. And his cadences[42] were their cadences, the cadences which voiced their woe and what to them was the meaning of the stillness, and the cold, and dark.

Thus, as token of what a puppet thing life is, the ancient song surged through him and he came into his own again; and he came because men had found a yellow metal in the North, and because Manuel was a gardener's helper whose wages did not lap over the needs of his wife and divers small copies of himself.

---

41. retrogression (ret′ rə gresh′ ən), *n*.: A moving backward to a more primitive state.

42. cadences (kād′ʹns əz), *n*.: Rhythmic flow of sound.

THINKING ABOUT THE SELECTION

Recalling

1. Explain the events in the world outside of San Francisco that make dogs like Buck so valuable.
2. Describe Buck's life at Judge Miller's.
3. How does Buck get from his home at Judge Miller's to the Yukon?
4. Why does Buck hate Spitz?

Interpreting

5. What lesson does Buck learn from the man in the red sweater?
6. What does the following sentence tell you about Buck's character? "He buckled down with a will and did his best, though it was all new and strange."
7. Explain the passage beginning "This first theft marked Buck as fit to survive in the hostile Northland environment."
8. What is meant by "the law of club and fang"? In what way does the North represent this moral code?
9. What is the difference between development and retrogression? What is the implication of the statement: "His development (or retrogression) was rapid"?

Applying

10. Discuss a situation from history or current events where the tactics were adopted of fighting fiercely or of accepting situations in the way Buck does to survive.

ANALYZING LITERATURE

Visualizing Setting

The **setting** of a story is where and when it takes place. In *The Call of the Wild* the setting is an important element of the story, creating as it does a mood and an atmosphere.

Reread the description of Judge Miller's place. Now close your eyes and try to visualize the house and grounds.

1. What details of this setting do you see?
2. What mood is evoked?
3. Why do you think the author makes the reader so sharply aware of this setting?

CRITICAL THINKING AND READING

Using Inductive Reasoning

Inductive reasoning is looking at particular facts or instances and arriving at a general conclusion. For example, if a man at a resort sees people paying for dinner with beads, he might conclude that at this resort beads are used as money.

Explain what Buck learns from each of the following specific situations.

1. The man with the red sweater strikes Buck with a club.
2. Buck has a problem sleeping in the bitter cold.
3. Buck watches Pike steal a slice of bacon.

THINKING AND WRITING

Describing a Setting

The novel begins in the Santa Clara Valley in California, but the setting quickly changes to Dyea beach in the Yukon. Someone planning to make a movie of the novel would need to create the settings carefully. Make a list of the details describing one of those settings for a movie maker. Then write a short composition describing and creating the mood of the setting you have chosen. Try to make your words as vivid as a picture would be. Use your imagination to add sensory details: What can you hear, smell, see, feel? You may want to search for or draw a picture to illustrate your scene. When you have finished, check your paper to make sure you have included enough vivid details. Finally, proofread it and share it with your classmates.

The Call of the Wild, Chapters 3 and 4

Characterization

An essential element in a novel is characterization. An author has a number of ways to reveal the characters in a novel. They can be presented through dialogue, by means of their actions in various situations, by the way other characters react to them, or through information provided directly to the reader by the author.

In *The Call of the Wild* Jack London usually tells the reader directly what Buck is feeling and thinking. The actions of Buck and the other dogs also reveal information about them. Thus, London makes the animals important characters in *The Call of the Wild*. Although London sometimes describes the people in the novel directly, more often he reveals their character traits, emotions, and motivations through their words, actions, and relationships with others. The human characters are believable in part because London based them on people he had actually known.

Look For

As you read these chapters, look for the methods the author uses to acquaint the reader with the various characters. What is Buck's relationship to each of the other characters? Why did the author include each of these characters?

Writing

List all the characters, including both people and animals, presented in Chapters 1 and 2. Next to each one, write one word that could be used in a description of that character. Then describe how each character affected Buck. How was he or his life changed because of each character he met?

Vocabulary

Knowing the meaning of the following words will help you as you read Chapters 3 and 4 of *The Call of the Wild*.

adversary (ad′ vər ser′ ē) *n.:* Enemy (p. 712)

daunted (dônt′ əd) *adj.:* Made afraid or discouraged (p. 713)

pre-eminently (prē em′ ən ənt lē) *adv.:* Dominantly (p. 714)

covert (kuv′ ərt) *adj.:* Concealed; hidden; disguised (p. 716)

insubordination (in′ sə bor′ d'n ā′ shun) *n.:* Disobedience (p. 716)

paradox (par′ ə däks′) *n.:* A situation that seems to have contradictory or inconsistent qualities (p. 717)

obdurate (äb′ d <unk>oor ət) *adj.:* Unyielding; stubborn (p. 720)

3. The Dominant Primordial Beast

The dominant primordial beast was strong in Buck, and under the fierce conditions of trail life it grew and grew. Yet it was a secret growth. His newborn cunning gave him poise and control. He was too busy adjusting himself to the new life to feel at ease, and not only did he not pick fights, but he avoided them whenever possible. A certain deliberateness characterized his attitude. He was not prone to rashness and precipitate action; and in the bitter hatred between him and Spitz he betrayed no impatience, shunned all offensive acts.

On the other hand, possibly because he divined in Buck a dangerous rival, Spitz never lost an opportunity of showing his teeth. He even went out of his way to bully Buck, striving constantly to start the fight which could end only in the death of one or the other. Early in the trip this might have taken place had it not been for an unwonted accident. At the end of this day they made a bleak and miserable camp on the shore of Lake Laberge. Driving snow, a wind that cut like a white-hot knife, and darkness had forced them to grope for a camping place. They could hardly have fared worse. At their backs rose a perpendicular wall of rock, and Perrault and François were compelled to make their fire and spread their sleeping robes on the ice of the lake itself. The tent they had discarded at Dyea in order to travel light. A few sticks of driftwood furnished them with a fire that thawed down through the ice and left them to eat supper in the dark.

Close in under the sheltering rock Buck made his nest. So snug and warm was it, that he was loath to leave it when François distributed the fish which he had first thawed over the fire. But when Buck finished his ration and returned, he found his nest occupied. A warning snarl told him that the trespasser was Spitz. Till now Buck had avoided trouble with his enemy, but this was too much. The beast in him roared. He sprang upon Spitz with a fury which surprised them both, and Spitz particularly, for his whole experience with Buck had gone to teach him that his rival was an unusually timid dog, who managed to hold his own only because of his great weight and size.

François was surprised, too, when they shot out in a tangle from the disrupted nest and he divined the cause of the trouble. "A-a-ah!" he cried to Buck. "Gif it to heem, by Gar! Gif it to heem, the dirty t'eef!"

Spitz was equally willing. He was crying with sheer rage and eagerness as he circled back and forth for a chance to spring in. Buck was no less eager, and no less cautious, as he likewise circled back and forth for the advantage. But it was then that the unexpected happened, the thing which projected their struggle for supremacy far into the future, past many a weary mile of trail and toil.

An oath from Perrault, the resounding impact of a club upon a bony frame, and a shrill yelp of pain heralded the breaking forth of pandemonium. The camp was suddenly discovered to be alive with skulking furry forms—starving huskies, four or five score of them, who had scented the camp from some Indian village. They had crept in while Buck and Spitz were fighting, and when the two men sprang among them with stout clubs they showed their teeth and fought back. They were crazed by the smell of the food. Perrault found one with head buried in the grub box. His club landed heavily on the gaunt ribs, and the grub box was capsized on the ground. On the instant a score of the famished brutes were scrambling for the bread and bacon. The clubs fell upon them unheeded. They yelped and howled under the rain of blows, but struggled none the less madly till the last crumb had been devoured.

In the meantime the astonished team dogs had burst out of their nests only to be set upon by the fierce invaders. Never had Buck seen such dogs. It seemed as though their bones would burst through their skins. They were mere skeletons, draped loosely in draggled hides, with blazing eyes and slavered fangs. But the hunger madness made them terrifying, irresistible. There was no opposing them. The team dogs were swept back against the cliff at the first onset. Buck was beset by three huskies, and in a trice his head and shoulders were ripped and slashed. The din was frightful. Billee was crying as usual. Dave and Sol-leks, dripping blood from a score of wounds, were fighting bravely side by side. Joe was snapping like a demon. Once, his teeth closed on the foreleg of a husky, and he crunched down through the bone. Pike, the malingerer, leaped upon the crippled animal, breaking its neck with a quick flash of teeth and a jerk. Buck got a frothing adversary by the throat, and was sprayed with blood when his teeth sank through the jugular. The warm taste of it in his mouth goaded him to greater fierceness. He flung himself upon another, and at the same time felt teeth sink into his own throat. It was Spitz, treacherously attacking from the side.

Perrault and François, having cleaned out their part of the camp, hurried to save their sled dogs. The wild wave of famished beasts rolled back before them, and Buck shook himself free. But it was only for a moment. The two men were compelled to run back to save the grub, upon which the huskies returned to the attack on the team. Billee, terrified into bravery, sprang through the savage circle and fled away over the ice. Pike and Dub followed on his heels, with the rest of the team behind. As Buck drew himself together to spring after them, out of the tail of his eye he saw Spitz rush upon him with the evident intention of overthrowing him. Once off his feet and under that mass of huskies, there was no hope for him. But he braced himself to the shock of Spitz's charge, then joined the flight out on the lake.

Later, the nine team dogs gathered together and sought shelter in the forest. Though unpursued, they were in a sorry plight. There was not one who was not wounded in four or five places, while some were wounded grievously. Dub was badly injured in a hind leg; Dolly, the last husky added to the team at Dyea, had a badly torn throat; Joe had lost an eye; while Billee, the good-natured, with an ear chewed and rent to ribbons, cried and whimpered throughout the night. At daybreak they limped warily back to camp, to find the marauders gone and the two men in bad tempers. Fully half their grub supply was gone. The huskies had chewed through the sled lashings and canvas coverings. In fact, nothing, no matter how remotely eatable, had escaped them. They had eaten a pair of Perrault's moose-hide moccasins, chunks out of the leather traces, and even two feet of lash from the end of François's whip. He broke from a mournful contemplation of it to look over his wounded dogs.

"Ah, my frien's," he said softly, "mebbe it mek you mad dog, dose many bites. Mebbe all mad dog! Wot you t'ink, eh, Perrault?"

The courier shook his head dubiously. With four hundred miles of trail still between him and Dawson,[1] he could ill afford to have madness break out among his dogs. Two hours of cursing and exertion got the

---

1. Dawson: An important city in Yukon Territory during the Gold Rush.

harnesses into shape, and the wound-stiffened team was under way, struggling painfully over the hardest part of the trail they had yet encountered, and for that matter, the hardest between them and Dawson.

The Thirty Mile River was wide open. Its wild water defied the frost, and it was in the eddies only and in the quiet places that the ice held at all. Six days of exhausting toil were required to cover those thirty terrible miles. And terrible they were, for every foot of them was accomplished at the risk of life to dog and man. A dozen times Perrault, nosing the way, broke through the ice bridges, being saved by the long pole he carried, which he so held that it fell each time across the hole made by his body. But a cold snap was on, the thermometer registering fifty below zero, and each time he broke through he was compelled for very life to build a fire and dry his garments.

Nothing daunted him. It was because nothing daunted him that he had been chosen for government courier. He took all manner of risks, resolutely thrusting his little weazened face into the frost and struggling on from dim dawn to dark. He skirted the frowning shores on rim ice that bent and crackled under foot and upon which they dared not halt. Once, the sled broke through, with Dave and Buck, and they were half-frozen and all but drowned by the time they were dragged out. The usual fire was necessary to save them. They were coated solidly with ice, and the two men kept them on the run around the fire, sweating and thawing, so close that they were singed by the flames.

At another time Spitz went through, dragging the whole team after him up to Buck, who strained backward with all his strength, his forepaws on the slippery edge and the ice quivering and snapping all around. But behind him was Dave, likewise straining backward, and behind the sled was François, pulling till his tendons cracked.

Again, the rim ice broke away before and behind, and there was no escape except up the cliff. Perrault scaled it by a miracle, while François prayed for just that miracle; and with every thong and sled lashing and the last bit of harness rove into a long rope, the dogs were hoisted, one by one, to the cliff crest. François came up last, after the sled and load. Then came the search for a place to descend, which descent was ultimately made by the aid of the rope, and night found them back on the river with a quarter of a mile to the day's credit.

By the time they made the Hootalinqua and good ice, Buck was played out. The rest of the dogs were in like condition; but Perrault, to make up lost time, pushed them late and early. The first day they covered thirty-five miles to the Big Salmon; the next day thirty-five more to the Little Salmon; the third day forty miles, which brought them well up toward the Five Fingers.

Buck's feet were not so compact and hard as the feet of the huskies. His had softened during the many generations since the day his last wild ancestor was tamed by a cave dweller or river man. All day long he limped in agony, and camp once made, lay down like a dead dog. Hungry as he was, he would not move to receive his ration of fish, which François had to bring to him. Also, the dog driver rubbed Buck's feet for half an hour each night after supper, and sacrificed the tops of his own moccasins to make four moccasins for Buck. This was a great relief, and Buck caused even the weazened face of Perrault to twist itself into a grin one morning, when François forgot the moccasins and Buck lay on his back, his four feet waving appealingly in the air, and refused to budge without them. Later his feet grew hard to the trail, and the worn-out footgear was thrown away.

At the Pelly one morning, as they were harnessing up, Dolly, who had never been conspicuous for anything, went suddenly mad. She announced her condition by a long, heartbreaking wolf howl that sent every dog bristling with fear, then sprang straight for Buck. He had never seen a dog go mad, nor did he have any reason to fear madness; yet he knew that here was horror, and fled away from it in a panic. Straight away he raced, with Dolly, panting and frothing, one leap behind; nor could she gain on him, so great was his terror, nor could he leave her, so great was her madness. He plunged through the wooded breast of the island, flew down to the lower end, crossed a back channel filled with rough ice to another island, gained a third island, curved back to the main river, and in desperation started to cross it. And all the time, though he did not look, he could hear her snarling just one leap behind. François called to him a quarter of a mile away and he doubled back, still one leap ahead, gasping painfully for air and putting all his faith in that François would save him. The dog driver held the ax poised in his hand, and as Buck shot past him the ax crashed down upon mad Dolly's head.

Buck staggered over against the sled, exhausted, sobbing for breath, helpless. This was Spitz's opportunity. He sprang upon Buck, and twice his teeth sank into his unresisting foe and ripped and tore the flesh to the bone. Then François's lash descended, and Buck had the satisfaction of watching Spitz receive the worst whipping as yet administered to any of the teams.

"One devil, dat Spitz," remarked Perrault. "Some day heem keel dat Buck."

"Dat Buck two devils," was François's rejoinder. "All de tam I watch dat Buck I know for sure. Lissen: some fine day heem get mad an' den heem chew dat Spitz all up an' spit heem out on de snow. Sure. I know."

From then on it was war between them. Spitz, as lead dog and acknowledged master of the team, felt his supremacy threatened by this strange Southland dog. And strange Buck was to him, for of the many Southland dogs he had known, not one had shown up worthily in camp and on trail. They were all too soft, dying under the toil, the frost, and starvation. Buck was the exception. He alone endured and prospered, matching the husky in strength, savagery, and cunning. Then he was a masterful dog, and what made him dangerous was the fact that the club of the man in the red sweater had knocked all blind pluck and rashness out of his desire for mastery. He was pre-eminently cunning, and could bide his time with a patience that was nothing less than primitive.

It was inevitable that the clash for leadership should come. Buck wanted it. He wanted it because it was his nature, because he had been gripped tight by that nameless, incomprehensible pride of the trail and trace—that pride which holds dogs in the toil to the last gasp, which lures them to die joyfully in the harness, and breaks their hearts if they are cut out of the harness. This was the pride of Dave as wheel dog, of Sol-leks as he pulled with all his strength; the pride that laid hold of them at break of camp, transforming them from sour and sullen brutes into straining, eager, ambitious creatures; the pride that spurred them on all day and dropped them at pitch of camp at night, letting them fall back into gloomy unrest and uncontent. This was the pride that bore up Spitz and made him thrash the sled dogs who blundered and shirked in the traces or hid away at harness-up time in the morning. Likewise it was this pride that made him fear Buck as a possible lead dog. And this was Buck's pride, too.

He openly threatened the other's leadership. He came between him and the shirks he should have punished. And he did it deliberately. One night there was a heavy snowfall, and in the morning Pike, the malingerer, did not appear. He was securely hidden in his nest under a foot of snow. François called him and sought him in vain. Spitz was wild with wrath. He raged through the camp, smelling and digging in every likely place, snarling so frightfully that Pike heard and shivered in his hiding place.

But when he was at last unearthed, and Spitz flew at him to punish him, Buck flew, with equal rage, in between. So unexpected was it, and so shrewdly managed, that Spitz was hurled backward and off his feet. Pike, who had been trembling abjectly, took heart at this open mutiny, and sprang upon his overthrown leader. Buck, to whom fair play was a forgotten code, likewise sprang upon Spitz. But François, chuckling at the incident while unswerving in the administra-

tion of justice, brought his lash down upon Buck with all his might. This failed to drive Buck from his prostrate rival, and the butt of the whip was brought into play. Half-stunned by the blow, Buck was knocked backward and the lash laid upon him again and again, while Spitz soundly punished the many-times-offending Pike.

In the days that followed, as Dawson grew closer and closer, Buck still continued to interfere between Spitz and the culprits; but he did it craftily, when François was not around. With the covert mutiny of Buck, a general insubordination sprang up and increased. Dave and Sol-leks were unaffected, but the rest of the team went from bad to worse. Things no longer went right. There was continual bickering and jangling. Trouble was always afoot, and at the bottom of it was Buck. He kept François busy, for the dog driver was in constant apprehension of the life-and-death struggle between the two which he knew must take place sooner or later; and on more than one night the sounds of quarreling and strife among the other dogs turned him out of his sleeping robe, fearful that Buck and Spitz were at it.

But the opportunity did not present itself, and they pulled into Dawson one dreary afternoon with the great fight still to come. Here were many men, and countless dogs, and Buck found them all at work. It seemed the ordained order of things that dogs should work. All day they swung up and down the main street in long teams, and in the night their jingling bells still went by. They hauled cabin logs and firewood, freighted up to the mines, and did all manner of work that horses did in the Santa Clara Valley. Here and there Buck met Southland dogs, but in the main they were the wild wolf husky breed. Every night, regularly, at nine, at twelve, at three, they lifted a nocturnal song, a weird and eerie chant, in which it was Buck's delight to join.

With the aurora borealis[2] flaming coldly overhead, or the stars leaping in the frost dance, and the land numb and frozen under its pall of snow, this song of the huskies might have been the defiance of life, only it was pitched in minor key, with long-drawn wailings and half-sobs, and was more the pleading of life, the articulate travail[3] of existence. It was an old song, old as the breed itself—one of the first songs of the younger world in a day when songs were sad. It was invested with the woe of unnumbered generations, this plaint by which Buck was so strangely stirred. When he moaned and sobbed, it was with the pain of living that was of old the pain of his wild fathers, and the fear and mystery of the cold and dark that was to them fear and mystery. And that he should be stirred by it marked the completeness with which he harked back through the ages of fire and roof to the raw beginnings of life in the howling ages.

Seven days from the time they pulled into Dawson, they dropped down the steep bank by the Barracks to the Yukon Trail, and pulled for Dyea and Salt Water. Perrault was carrying dispatches if anything more urgent than those he had brought in; also, the travel pride had gripped him, and he purposed to make the record trip of the year. Several things favored him in this. The week's rest had recuperated the dogs and put them in thorough trim. The trail they had broken into the country was packed hard by later journeyers. And further, the police had arranged in two or three places deposits of grub for dog and man, and he was traveling light.

---

2. aurora borealis (ô rôr′ ə bôr′ ē al′ is), *n*.: Bands of colored light sometimes appearing in the night sky of the Northern Hemisphere.
3. articulate (är tik′ yə lit) **travail** (trə vāl′): Clearly expressed pain.

They made Sixty Mile, which is a fifty-mile run, on the first day; and the second day saw them booming up the Yukon well on their way to Pelly. But such splendid running was achieved not without great trouble and vexation on the part of François. The insidious[4] revolt led by Buck had destroyed the solidarity of the team. It no longer was as one dog leaping in the traces. The encouragement Buck gave the rebels led them into all kinds of petty misdemeanors. No more was Spitz a leader greatly to be feared. The old awe departed, and they grew equal to challenging his authority. Pike robbed him of half a fish one night, and gulped it down under the protection of Buck. Another night Dub and Joe fought Spitz and made him forgo the punishment they deserved. And even Billee, the good-natured, was less good-natured, and whined not half so placatingly as in former days. Buck never came near Spitz without snarling and bristling menacingly. In fact, his conduct approached that of a bully, and he was given to swaggering up and down before Spitz's very nose.

The breaking down of discipline likewise affected the dogs in their relations with one another. They quarreled and bickered more than ever among themselves, till at times the camp was a howling bedlam. Dave and Sol-leks alone were unaltered, though they were made irritable by the unending squabbling. François swore strange, barbarous oaths, and stamped the snow in futile rage, and tore his hair. His lash was always singing among the dogs, but it was of small avail. Directly his back was turned they were at it again. He backed up Spitz with his whip, while Buck backed up the remainder of the team. François knew he was behind all the trouble, and Buck knew he knew; but Buck was too clever ever again to be caught red-handed. He worked faithfully in the harness, for the toil had become a delight to him; yet it was a greater delight slyly to precipitate a fight amongst his mates and tangle the traces.

At the mouth of the Talkeetna, one night after supper, Dub turned up a snowshoe rabbit, blundered it, and missed. In a second the whole team was in full cry. A hundred yards away was a camp of the Northwest Police, with fifty dogs, huskies all, who joined the chase. The rabbit sped down the river, turned off into a small creek, up the frozen bed of which it held steadily. It ran lightly on the surface of the snow, while the dogs ploughed through by main strength. Buck led the pack, sixty strong, around bend after bend, but he could not gain. He lay down low to the race, whining eagerly, his splendid body flashing forward, leap by leap, in the wan, white moonlight. And leap by leap, like some pale frost wraith[5] the snowshoe rabbit flashed on ahead.

All that stirring of old instincts which at stated periods drives men out from the sounding cities to forest and plain to kill things by chemically propelled leaden pellets, the blood lust, the joy to kill—all this was Buck's, only it was infinitely more intimate. He was ranging at the head of the pack, running the wild thing down, the living meat, to kill with his own teeth and wash his muzzle to the eyes in warm blood.

There is an ecstasy that marks the summit of life, and beyond which life cannot rise. And such is the paradox of living, this ecstasy comes when one is most alive, and it comes as a complete forgetfulness that one is alive. This ecstasy, this forgetfulness of living, comes to the artist, caught up and out of himself in a sheet of flame; it comes to the soldier, war-mad on a stricken field and refusing quarter; and it came to Buck, leading the pack, sounding the old wolf cry,

---

4. insidious (in sid′ ē əs) *adj*.: Sly; crafty.

5. wraith (rāth), *n*.: Ghost.

straining after the food that was alive and that fled swiftly before him through the moonlight. He was sounding the deeps of his nature, and of the parts of his nature that were deeper than he, going back into the womb of Time. He was mastered by the sheer surging of life, the tidal wave of being, the perfect joy of each separate muscle, joint, and sinew in that it was everything that was not death, that it was aglow and rampant, expressing itself in movement, flying exultantly under the stars and over the face of dead matter that did not move.

But Spitz, cold and calculating even in his supreme moods, left the pack and cut across a narrow neck of land where the creek made a long bend around. Buck did not know of this, and as he rounded the bend, the frost wraith of a rabbit still flitting before him, he saw another and larger frost wraith leap from the overhanging bank into the immediate path of the rabbit. It was Spitz. The rabbit could not turn, and as the white teeth broke its back in midair it shrieked as loudly as a stricken man may shriek. At sound of this, the cry of Life plunging down from Life's apex[6] in the grip of Death, the full pack at Buck's heels raised a hell's chorus of delight.

Buck did not cry out. He did not check himself, but drove in upon Spitz, shoulder to shoulder, so hard that he missed the throat. They rolled over and over in the powdery snow. Spitz gained his feet almost as though he had not been overthrown, slashing Buck down the shoulder and leaping clear. Twice his teeth clipped together, like the steel jaws of a trap, as he backed away for better footing, with lean and lifting lips that writhed and snarled.

In a flash Buck knew it. The time had come. It was to the death. As they circled about, snarling, ears laid back, keenly

watchful for the advantage, the scene came to Buck with a sense of familiarity. He seemed to remember it all—the white woods, and earth, and moonlight, and the thrill of battle. Over the whiteness and silence brooded a ghostly calm. There was not the faintest whisper of air—nothing moved, not a leaf quivered, the visible breaths of the dogs rising slowly and lingering in the frosty air. They had made short work of the snowshoe rabbit, these dogs that were ill-tamed wolves; and they were now drawn up in an expectant circle. They, too, were silent, their eyes only gleaming and their breaths drifting slowly upward. To Buck it was nothing new or strange, this scene of old time. It was as though it had always been, the wonted way of things.

Spitz was a practiced fighter. From Spitzbergen through the Arctic, and across Canada and the Barrens, he had held his own with all manner of dogs and achieved to mastery over them. Bitter rage was his, but never blind rage. In passion to rend and destroy, he never forgot that his enemy was in like passion to rend and destroy. He never rushed till he was prepared to receive a rush; never attacked till he had first defended that attack.

In vain Buck strove to sink his teeth in the neck of the big white dog. Wherever his fangs struck for the softer flesh, they were countered by the fangs of Spitz. Fang clashed fang, and lips were cut and bleeding, but Buck could not penetrate his enemy's guard. Then he warmed up and enveloped Spitz in a whirlwind of rushes. Time and time again he tried for the snow-white throat, where life bubbled near to the surface, and each time and every time Spitz slashed him and got away. Then Buck took to rushing, as though for the throat, when, suddenly drawing back his head and curving in from the side, he would drive his shoulder at the shoulder of Spitz, as a ram

_____

6. apex (ā′ peks), *n.*: Highest point; peak.

by which to overthrow him. But instead, Buck's shoulder was slashed down each time as Spitz leaped lightly away.

Spitz was untouched, while Buck was streaming with blood and panting hard. The fight was growing desperate. And all the while the silent and wolfish circle waited to finish off whichever dog went down. As Buck grew winded, Spitz took to rushing, and he kept him staggering for footing. Once Buck went over, and the whole circle of sixty dogs started up; but he recovered himself, almost in midair, and the circle sank down again and waited.

But Buck possessed a quality that made for greatness—imagination. He fought by instinct, but he could fight by head as well. He rushed, as though attempting the old shoulder trick, but at the last instant swept low to the snow and in. His teeth closed on Spitz's left foreleg. There was a crunch of breaking bone, and the white dog faced him on three legs. Thrice he tried to knock him over, then repeated the trick and broke the right foreleg. Despite the pain and helplessness, Spitz struggled madly to keep up. He saw the silent circle, with gleaming eyes, lolling tongues, and silvery breaths drifting upward, closing in upon him as he had seen similar circles close in upon beaten antagonists in the past. Only this time he was the one who was beaten.

There was no hope for him. Buck was inexorable.[7] Mercy was a thing reserved for gentler climes. He maneuvered for the final rush. The circle had tightened till he could feel the breaths of the huskies on his flanks. He could see them, beyond Spitz and to either side, half-crouching for the spring, their eyes fixed upon him. A pause seemed to fall. Every animal was motionless as though turned to stone. Only Spitz quivered

and bristled as he staggered back and forth, snarling with horrible menace, as though to frighten off impending death. Then Buck sprang in and out; but while he was in, shoulder had at last squarely met shoulder. The dark circle became a dot on the moon-flooded snow as Spitz disappeared from view. Buck stood and looked on, the successful champion, the dominant primordial beast who had made his kill and found it good.

4. Who Has Won to Mastership

"Eh? Wot I say? I spik true w'en I say dat Buck two devils."

This was François's speech next morning when he discovered Spitz missing and Buck covered with wounds. He drew him to the fire and by its light pointed them out.

"Dat Spitz fight lak a devil," said Perrault, as he surveyed the gaping rips and cuts.

"An' dat Buck fight lak two devils," was Francois's answer. "An' now we make good time. No more Spitz, no more trouble, sure."

While Perrault packed the camp outfit and loaded the sled, the dog driver proceeded to harness the dogs. Buck trotted up to the place Spitz would have occupied as leader; but François, not noticing him, brought Sol-leks to the coveted position. In his judgment, Sol-leks was the best lead dog left. Buck sprang upon Sol-leks in a fury, driving him back and standing in his place.

"Eh? eh?" François cried, slapping his thighs gleefully. "Look at dat Buck. Heem keel dat Spitz, heem t'ink to take de job."

"Go 'way, Chook!" he cried, but Buck refused to budge.

He took Buck by the scruff of the neck, and though the dog growled threateningly, dragged him to one side and replaced Sol-leks. The old dog did not like it, and showed plainly that he was afraid of Buck. François

---

7. inexorable (in ek′ sər ə b'l), *adj.*: Unwilling to give in.

was obdurate, but when he turned his back Buck again displaced Sol-leks, who was not at all unwilling to go.

François was angry. "Now, by Gar, I feex you!" he cried, coming back with a heavy club in his hand.

Buck remembered the man in the red sweater, and retreated slowly; nor did he attempt to charge in when Sol-leks was once more brought forward. But he circled just beyond the range of the club, snarling with bitterness and rage; and while he circled he watched the club so as to dodge it if thrown by François, for he was become wise in the way of clubs.

The driver went about his work, and he called to Buck when he was ready to put him in his old place in front of Dave. Buck retreated two or three steps. François followed him up, whereupon he again retreated. After some time of this, François threw down the club, thinking that Buck feared a thrashing. But Buck was in open revolt. He wanted, not to escape a clubbing, but to have the leadership. It was his by right. He had earned it, and he would not be content with less.

Perrault took a hand. Between them they ran him about for the better part of an hour. They threw clubs at him. He dodged. He did not try to run away, but retreated around and around the camp, advertising plainly that when his desire was met, he would come in and be good.

François sat down and scratched his head. Perrault looked at his watch and swore. Time was flying, and they should have been on the trail an hour gone. François scratched his head again. He shook it and grinned sheepishly at the courier, who shrugged his shoulders in sign that they were beaten. Then François went up to where Sol-leks stood and called to Buck. Buck laughed, as dogs laugh, yet kept his distance. François unfastened Sol-lek's traces and put him back in his old place.

The team stood harnessed to the sled in an unbroken line, ready for the trail. There was no place for Buck save at the front. Once more François called, and once more Buck laughed and kept away.

"T'row down de club," Perrault commanded.

François complied, whereupon Buck trotted in, laughing triumphantly, and swung around into position at the head of the team. His traces were fastened, the sled broken out, and with both men running they dashed out on to the river trail.

Highly as the dog driver had forevalued Buck, with his two devils, he found, while the day was yet young, that he had undervalued. At a bound Buck took up the duties of leadership; and where judgment was required, and quick thinking and quick acting, he showed himself the superior even of Spitz, of whom François had never seen an equal.

But it was in giving the law and making his mates live up to it that Buck excelled. Dave and Sol-leks did not mind the change in leadership. It was none of their business. Their business was to toil, and toil mightily, in the traces. So long as that were not interfered with, they did not care what happened. Billee, the good-natured, could lead for all they cared, so long as he kept order. The rest of the team, however, had grown unruly during the last days of Spitz, and their surprise was great now that Buck proceeded to lick them into shape.

Pike, who pulled at Buck's heels, and who never put an ounce more of his weight against the breastband than he was compelled to do, was swiftly and repeatedly shaken for loafing; and ere the first day was done he was pulling more than ever before in his life. The first night in camp, Joe, the sour one, was punished roundly—a thing that Spitz had never succeeded in doing. Buck simply smothered him by virtue of superior weight, and cut him up till he ceased snapping and began to whine for mercy.

The general tone of the team picked up immediately. It recovered its old-time solidarity, and once more the dogs leaped as one dog in the traces. At the Rink Rapids two native huskies, Teek and Koona, were added; and the celerity with which Buck broke them in took away François's breath.

"Nevaire such a dog as dat Buck!" he cried. "No, nevaire! Heem worth one t'ousan' dollair, by Gar! Eh? Wot you say, Perrault?"

And Perrault nodded. He was ahead of the record then, and gaining day by day. The trail was in excellent condition, well packed and hard, and there was no new-fallen snow with which to contend. It was not too cold. The temperature dropped to fifty below zero and remained there the whole trip. The men rode and ran by turn, and the dogs were kept on the jump, with but infrequent stoppages.

The Thirty Mile River was comparatively coated with ice, and they covered in one day going out what had taken them ten days coming in. In one run they made a sixty-mile dash from the foot of Lake Laberge to the Whitehorse Rapids. Across Marsh, Tagish, and Bennett (seventy miles of lakes), they flew so fast that the man whose turn it was to run towed behind the sled at the end of a rope. And on the last night of the second week they topped White Pass and dropped down the sea slope with the lights of Skagway and of the shipping at their feet.

It was a record run. Each day for fourteen days they had averaged forty miles. For three days Perrault and François threw chests[8] up and down the main street of Skagway and were deluged with invitations to drink, while the team was the constant

---

8. threw chests: Boasted; bragged.

center of a worshipful crowd of dog busters and mushers.[9] Then three or four Western bad men aspired to clean out the town, were riddled like pepperboxes for their pains, and public interest turned to other idols. Next came official orders. François called Buck to him, threw his arms around him, wept over him. And that was the last of François and Perrault. Like other men, they passed out of Buck's life for good.

A Scotch half-breed took charge of him and his mates, and in company with a dozen other dog teams he started back over the weary trail to Dawson. It was no light running now, nor record time, but heavy toil each day, with a heavy load behind; for this was the mail train, carrying word from the world to the men who sought gold under the shadow of the Pole.

Buck did not like it, but he bore up well to the work, taking pride in it after the manner of Dave and Sol-leks, and seeing that his mates, whether they prided in it or not, did their fair share. It was a monotonous life, operating with machinelike regularity. One day was very like another. At a certain time each morning the cooks turned out, fires were built, and breakfast was eaten. Then, while some broke camp, others harnessed the dogs, and they were under way an hour or so before the darkness fell which gave warning of dawn. At night, camp was made. Some pitched the flies,[10] others cut firewood and pine boughs for the beds, and still others carried water or ice for the cooks. Also, the dogs were fed. To them, this was the one feature of the day, though it was good to loaf around, after the fish was eaten, for an hour or so with the other dogs, of which there were five score[11] and odd. There

were fierce fighters among them, but three battles with the fiercest brought Buck to mastery, so that when he bristled and showed his teeth they got out of his way.

Best of all, perhaps, he loved to lie near the fire, hind legs crouched under him, forelegs stretched out in front, head raised, and eyes blinking dreamily at the flames. Sometimes he thought of Judge Miller's big house in the sun-kissed Santa Clara Valley, and of the cement swimming tank, and Ysabel, the Mexican hairless, and Toots, the Japanese pug; but oftener he remembered the man in the red sweater, the death of Curly, the great fight with Spitz, and the good things he had eaten or would like to eat. He was not homesick. The Sunland was very dim and distant, and such memories had no power over him. Far more potent were the memories of his heredity that gave things he had never seen before a seeming familiarity; the instincts (which were but the memories of his ancestors become habits) which had lapsed in later days, and still later, in him, quickened and became alive again.

Sometimes as he crouched there, blinking dreamily at the flames, it seemed that the flames were of another fire, and that as he crouched by this other fire he saw another and different man from the half-breed cook before him. This other man was shorter of leg and longer of arm, with muscles that were stringy and knotty rather than rounded and swelling. The hair of this man was long and matted, and his head slanted back under it from the eyes. He uttered strange sounds, and seemed very much afraid of the darkness, into which he peered continually, clutching in his hand, which hung midway between knee and foot, a stick with a heavy stone made fast to the end. He was all but naked, a ragged and firescorched skin hanging partway down his back, but on his body there was much

---

9. busters and mushers: People who train and drive sled dogs.
10. pitched the flies: Set up the tents.
11. five score: One hundred.

hair. In some places, across the chest and shoulders and down the outside of the arms and thighs, it was matted into almost a thick fur. He did not stand erect, but with trunk inclined forward from the hips, on legs that bent at the knees. About his body there was a peculiar springiness, or resiliency, almost catlike, and a quick alertness as of one who lived in perpetual fear of things seen and unseen.

At other times this hairy man squatted by the fire with head between his legs and slept. On such occasions his elbows were on his knees, his hands clasped above his head as though to shed rain by the hairy arms. And beyond that fire, in the circling darkness, Buck could see many gleaming coals, two by two, always two by two, which he knew to be the eyes of great beasts of prey. And he could hear the crashing of their bodies through the undergrowth, and the noises they made in the night. And dreaming there by the Yukon bank, with lazy eyes blinking at the fire, these sounds and sights of another world would make the hair to rise along his back and stand on end across his shoulders and up his neck, till he whimpered low and suppressedly, or growled softly, and the half-breed cook shouted at him, "Hey, you Buck, wake up!" Whereupon the other world would vanish and the real world come into his eyes, and he would get up and yawn and stretch as though he had been asleep.

It was a hard trip, with the mail behind them, and the heavy work wore them down. They were short of weight and in poor condition when they made Dawson, and should have had a ten days' or a week's rest at least. But in two days' time they dropped down the Yukon bank from the Barracks, loaded with letters for the outside. The dogs were tired, the drivers grumbling, and to make matters worse, it snowed every day. This meant a soft trail, greater friction on the runners, and heavier pulling for the dogs; yet the drivers were fair through it all, and did their best for the animals.

Each night the dogs were attended to first. They ate before the drivers ate, and no man sought his sleeping robe till he had seen to the feet of the dogs he drove. Still, their strength went down. Since the beginning of the winter they had traveled eighteen hundred miles, dragging sleds the whole weary distance; and eighteen hundred miles will tell upon life of the toughest. Buck stood it, keeping his mates up to their work and maintaining discipline, though he, too, was very tired. Billee cried and whimpered regularly in his sleep each night. Joe was sourer than ever, and Sol-leks was unapproachable, blind side or other side.

But it was Dave who suffered most of all. Something had gone wrong with him. He became more morose and irritable, and when camp was pitched at once made his nest, where his driver fed him. Once out of the harness and down, he did not get on his feet again till harness-up time in the morning. Sometimes, in the traces, when jerked by a sudden stoppage of the sled, or by straining to start it, he would cry out with pain. The driver examined him, but could find nothing. All the drivers became interested in his case. They talked it over at mealtime, and over their last pipes before going to bed, and one night they held a consultation. He was brought from his nest to the fire and was pressed and prodded till he cried out many times. Something was wrong inside, but they could locate no broken bones, could not make it out.

By the time Cassiar Bar was reached, he was so weak that he was falling repeatedly in the traces. The Scotch half-breed called a halt and took him out of the team, making the next dog, Sol-leks, fast to the sled. His intention was to rest Dave, letting him run free behind the sled. Sick as he was, Dave resented being taken out, grunting and growling while the traces were unfastened, and whimpering brokenheartedly when he saw Sol-leks in the position he had held and served so long. For the pride of trace and trail was his, and, sick unto death, he could not bear that another dog should do his work.

When the sled started, he floundered in the soft snow alongside the beaten trail, attacking Sol-leks with his teeth, rushing against him and trying to thrust him off into the soft snow on the other side, striving to leap inside his traces and get between him and the sled, and all the while whining and yelping and crying with grief and pain. The half-breed tried to drive him away with the whip; but he paid no heed to the stinging lash, and the man had not the heart to strike harder. Dave refused to run quietly on the trail behind the sled, where the going was easy, but continued to flounder alongside in the soft snow, where the going was most difficult, till exhausted. Then he fell, and lay where he fell, howling lugubriously[12] as the long train of sleds churned by.

With the last remnant of his strength he managed to stagger along behind till the train made another stop, when he floundered past the sleds to his own, where he stood alongside Sol-leks. His driver lingered a moment to get a light for his pipe from the man behind. Then he returned and started his dogs. They swung out on the trail with remarkable lack of exertion, turned their heads uneasily, and stopped in surprise. The driver was surprised, too; the sled had not moved. He called his comrades to witness the sight. Dave had bitten through both of Sol-leks's traces, and was standing directly in front of the sled in his proper place.

He pleaded with his eyes to remain there. The driver was perplexed. His comrades talked of how a dog could break its heart through being denied the work that killed it, and recalled instances they had known, where dogs, too old for the toil, or injured, had died because they were cut out of the traces. Also, they held it a mercy, since Dave was to die anyway, that he should die in the traces, heart-easy and content. So he was harnessed in again, and proudly he pulled as of old, though more than once he cried out involuntarily from the bite of his inward hurt. Several times he fell down and was dragged in the traces, and once the sled ran upon him so that he limped thereafter in one of his hind legs.

But he held out till camp was reached, when his driver made a place for him by the fire. Morning found him too weak to travel. At harness-up time he tried to crawl to his driver. By convulsive efforts he got on his feet, staggered, and fell. Then he wormed his way forward slowly toward where the harnesses were being put on his mates. He would advance his forelegs and drag up his body with a sort of hitching movement, when he would advance his forelegs and hitch ahead again for a few more inches. His strength left him, and the last his mates saw of him he lay gasping in the snow and yearning toward them. But they could hear him mournfully howling till they passed out of sight behind a belt of river timber.

Here the train was halted. The Scotch half-breed slowly retraced his steps to the camp they had left. The men ceased talking. A revolver shot rang out. The man came back hurriedly. The whips snapped, the bells tinkled merrily, the sleds churned along the trail; but Buck knew, and every dog knew, what had taken place behind the belt of river trees.

---

12. lugubriously (loo goo' brē əs lē), *adv.*: Very sadly or mournfully.

THINKING ABOUT THE SELECTION

Recalling

1. What incident triggers the fight between Buck and Spitz? Describe this incident.
2. Describe Buck's conflict with François over the leadership of the team.

Interpreting

3. In what ways is Buck well equipped to survive in the North?
4. What is the "dominant primordial beast"? Find two examples of Buck's behavior that reveal this beast.
5. What is the significance of the man with long matted hair in Buck's daydream?

Applying

6. According to this story, is the law of club and fang ever justified? Support your answer with details from the story.

ANALYZING LITERATURE

Understanding Characterization

Jack London gives the reader information about how Buck thinks and feels. In addition, London shows how Buck acts in different situations. Seeing what Buck does in a variety of circumstances allows you to form an opinion about Buck's character.

1. List the traits that describe Buck's character as it develops under the hardships of the trail. Find an incident that reveals each trait.
2. What qualities made him a good leader?

CRITICAL THINKING AND READING

Identifying Cause and Effect

When you ask for an explanation of why something happened or why someone did something, you are looking for a cause. You are looking for an effect when you ask "What will happen because of this?" A **cause** produces an effect or result. An **effect** is the result produced

by a cause. For example, because the man in the red sweater beat Buck with a club, Buck was wary of men with clubs. The beating was the cause and Buck's wariness was the result.

Indicate which statement of each pair is the *cause* and which is the *effect*.

1. a. Buck attacked Spitz.
   b. Spitz trespassed on Buck's sleeping nest.
2. a. Dolly suddenly went mad.
   b. Buck fled from Dolly in a panic.
3. a. The dogs worked together again as a team.
   b. Buck excelled in making his mates obey.

UNDERSTANDING LANGUAGE

Finding Word Origins

Knowing a word's origins can help you understand and remember the meaning of that word. For example, the word *aver* means "to state positively." In a dictionary the origin of this word appears as follows: [ME. *averren* OFr. *averrer,* to confirm L. *ad,* to + *verus,* true]. This means that *aver* originally came from two Latin words meaning *to* and *true.* Later it appeared as an Old French word and then a Middle English word that meant "to confirm."

Find the following words in a dictionary. For each word write the origin and the meaning. Then use each word in a sentence.

1. primordial   3. canvas
2. paradox   4. moccasin

THINKING AND WRITING

Writing a Character Sketch

Choose one of the following: Perrault, François, Spitz, Dave. List details of appearance and any incidents that reveal the character you have chosen. Use your imagination to supply some details. Then write a character sketch without using the character's name. End your writing by drawing a conclusion evaluating the character's outstanding qualities. Exchange papers with a classmate and see if your partner can identify your character.

GUIDE FOR READING

The Call of the Wild, Chapters 5 and 6

Plot

All elements of a novel are present throughout it, and they constantly interact with each other. As you read this novel, first you focused on the setting. Then you paid special attention to characterization. Now you will investigate the element of plot.

The **plot** is the sequence of events in a novel. Each event is related to the others and all work together to create the effect the author has in mind. Often the author begins by supplying background information in the exposition and presenting the important characters. Soon a **conflict** or problem between opposing forces is introduced. The plot moves forward with events that make you wonder "Why did that happen?" or "What will happen next?" Unlike a short story, a novel is long enough to include many events in the plot before the story finally reaches a **climax,** the point of highest interest, and begins to be resolved. A novel may also include small climaxes as it progresses toward the main climax. Buck's fight with Spitz provides one of these minor climaxes in *The Call of the Wild.*

Look For

As you read these chapters, look for the development of conflict in the plot and the events that show it. Will Buck survive the conflict?

Writing

London uses a pattern to tell Buck's story that is often used in literature. This pattern includes a journey taken by the hero. The dangers and adventures the hero encounters result in both hero and reader gaining a deeper understanding of life. Freewrite about another story you have read or seen that uses the pattern of a journey in the plot.

Vocabulary

Knowing the following words will help you as you read Chapters 5 and 6 of *The Call of the Wild.*

salient (sāl′ yənt) *adj.:* Noticeable; prominent (p. 727)
callowness (kal′ ō nəs) *n.:* Youth and inexperience; immaturity (p. 727)
repugnance (ri pug′ nəns) *n.:* Extreme dislike (p. 729)
superfluous (soo pʉr′ floo wəs) *adj.:* More than is neces-

sary (p. 730)
jaded (jā′ did) *adj.:* Worn-out (p. 731)
amenities (ə men′ ə tēs) *n.:* Pleasant qualities (p. 732)
callous (kal′ əs) *adj.:* Unfeeling (p. 733)
transient (tran′ shənt) *adj.:* Not permanent (p. 738)

5. The Toil of Trace and Trail

Thirty days from the time it left Dawson, the Salt Water Mail, with Buck and his mates at the fore, arrived at Skagway. They were in a wretched state, worn out and worn down. Buck's one hundred and forty pounds had dwindled to one hundred and fifteen. The rest of his mates, though lighter dogs, had relatively lost more weight than he. Pike, the malingerer, who, in his lifetime of deceit, had often successfully feigned a hurt leg, was now limping in earnest. Sol-leks was limping, and Dub was suffering from a wrenched shoulder blade.

They were all terribly footsore. No spring or rebound was left in them. Their feet fell heavily on the trail, jarring their bodies and doubling the fatigue of a day's travel. There was nothing the matter with them except that they were dead tired. It was not the dead-tiredness that comes through brief and excessive effort, from which recovery is a matter of hours; but it was the dead-tiredness that comes through the slow and prolonged strength drainage of months of toil. There was no power of recuperation left, no reserve strength to call upon. It had been all used, the last least bit of it. Every muscle, every fiber, every cell, was tired, dead tired. And there was reason for it. In less than five months they had traveled twenty-five hundred miles, during the last eighteen hundred of which they had had but five days' rest. When they arrived at Skagway they were apparently on their last legs. They could barely keep the traces taut, and on the downgrades just managed to keep out of the way of the sled.

"Mush on, poor sore feets," the driver encouraged them as they tottered down the main street of Skagway. "Dis is de las'. Den we get one long res'. Eh? For sure. One bully long res'."

The drivers confidently expected a long stopover. Themselves, they had covered twelve hundred miles with two days' rest, and in the nature of reason and common justice they deserved an interval of loafing. But so many were the men who had rushed into the Klondike, and so many were the sweethearts, wives, and kin that had not rushed in, that the congested mail was taking on Alpine proportions; also, there were official orders. Fresh batches of Hudson Bay dogs were to take the places of those worthless for the trail. The worthless ones were to be got rid of, and, since dogs count for little against dollars, they were to be sold.

Three days passed, by which time Buck and his mates found how really tired and weak they were. Then, on the morning of the fourth day, two men from the States came along and bought them, harness and all, for a song. The men addressed each other as Hal and Charles. Charles was a middle-aged, lightish-colored man, with weak and watery eyes and a mustache that twisted fiercely and vigorously up, giving the lie to the limply drooping lip it concealed. Hal was a youngster of nineteen or twenty, with a big Colt's revolver and a hunting knife strapped about him on a belt that fairly bristled with cartridges. This belt was the most salient thing about him. It advertised his callowness—a callowness sheer and unutterable. Both men were manifestly out of place, and why such as they should adventure the North is part of the mystery of things that passes understanding.

Buck heard the chaffering,[1] saw the money pass between the man and the Government agent, and knew that the Scotch half-breed and the mail-train drivers were passing out of his life on the heels of Per-

---

1. chaffering (chaf' ər iŋ), n.: Haggling over terms or price.

rault and François and the others who had gone before. When driven with his mates to the new owners' camp, Buck saw a slipshod and slovenly affair, tent half-stretched, dishes unwashed, everything in disorder; also, he saw a woman. Mercedes[2] the men called her. She was Charles's wife and Hal's sister—a nice family party.

Buck watched them apprehensively as they proceeded to take down the tent and load the sled. There was a great deal of effort about their manner, but no businesslike method. The tent was rolled into an awkward bundle three times as large as it should have been. The tin dishes were packed away unwashed. Mercedes continually fluttered in the way of her men and kept up an unbroken chattering of remonstrance and advice. When they put a clothes sack on the front of the sled, she suggested it should go on the back; and when they had put it on the back, and covered it over with a couple of other bundles, she discovered overlooked articles which could abide nowhere else but in that very sack, and they unloaded again.

Three men from a neighboring tent came out and looked on, grinning and winking at one another.

"You've got a right smart load as it is," said one of them; "and it's not me should tell you your business, but I wouldn't tote that tent along if I was you."

"Undreamed of!" cried Mercedes, throwing up her hands in dainty dismay. "However in the world could I manage without a tent?"

"It's springtime, and you won't get any more cold weather," the man replied.

She shook her head decidedly, and Charles and Hal put the last odds and ends on top the mountainous load.

"Think it'll ride?" one of the men asked.

---

2. **Mercedes** (mer sā′ dēz).

"Why shouldn't it?" Charles demanded rather shortly.

"Oh, that's all right, that's all right," the man hastened meekly to say. "I was just a-wonderin', that is all. It seemed a mite top heavy."

Charles turned his back and drew the lashings down as well as he could, which was not in the least well.

"An' of course the dogs can hike along all day with that contraption behind them," affirmed a second of the men.

"Certainly," said Hal with freezing politeness, taking hold of the gee pole with one hand and swinging his whip from the other. "Mush!" he shouted. "Mush on there!"

The dogs sprang against the breast-bands, strained hard for a few moments, then relaxed. They were unable to move the sled.

"The lazy brutes, I'll show them," he cried, preparing to lash out at them with the whip.

But Mercedes interfered, crying, "Oh, Hal, you mustn't," as she caught hold of the whip and wrenched it from him. "The poor dears! Now you must promise you won't be harsh with them for the rest of the trip, or I won't go a step."

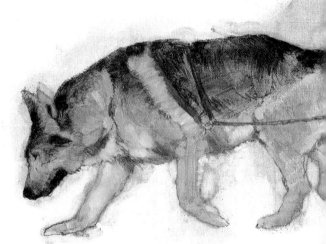

"Precious lot you know about dogs," her brother sneered; "and I wish you'd leave me alone. They're lazy, I tell you, and you've got to whip them to get anything out of them. That's their way. You ask anyone. Ask one of those men."

Mercedes looked at them imploringly, untold repugnance at sight of pain written in her pretty face.

"They're weak as water, if you want to know," came the reply from one of the men. "Plumb tuckered out, that's what's the matter. They need a rest."

"Rest be blanked," said Hal, with his beardless lips; and Mercedes said, "Oh!" in pain and sorrow at the oath.

But she was a clannish creature, and rushed at once to the defense of her brother. "Never mind that man," she said pointedly. "You're driving our dogs, and you do what you think best with them."

Again Hal's whip fell upon the dogs. They threw themselves against the breastbands, dug their feet into the packed snow, got down low to it, and put forth all their strength. The sled held as though it were an anchor. After two efforts, they stood still,

panting. The whip was whistling savagely, when once more Mercedes interfered. She dropped on her knees before Buck, with tears in her eyes, and put her arms around his neck.

"You poor, poor dears," she cried sympathetically, "why don't you pull hard?—then you wouldn't be whipped." Buck did not like her, but he was feeling too miserable to resist her, taking it as part of the day's miserable work.

One of the onlookers, who had been clenching his teeth to suppress hot speech, now spoke up:

"It's not that I care a whoop what becomes of you, but for the dogs' sakes I just want to tell you, you can help them a mighty lot by breaking out that sled. The runners are froze fast. Throw your weight against the gee pole, right and left, and break it out."

A third time the attempt was made, but this time, following the advice, Hal broke out the runners which had been frozen to the snow. The overloaded and unwieldy sled forged ahead, Buck and his mates struggling frantically under the rain of blows. A hundred yards ahead the path turned and sloped steeply into the main street. It would have required an experienced man to keep the top-heavy sled upright, and Hal was not such a man. As they swung on the turn the sled went over, spilling half its load through the loose lashings. The dogs never stopped. The lightened sled bounded on its side behind them. They were angry because of the ill treatment they had received and the unjust load. Buck was raging. He broke into a run, the team following his lead. Hal cried "Whoa! whoa!" but they gave no heed. He tripped and was pulled off his feet. The capsized sled ground over him, and the dogs dashed up the street, adding to the gaiety of Skagway as they scattered the remainder of the outfit along its chief thoroughfare.

Kindhearted citizens caught the dogs and gathered up the scattered belongings. Also, they gave advice. Half the load and twice the dogs, if they ever expected to reach Dawson, was what was said. Hal and his sister and brother-in-law listened unwillingly, pitched tent, and overhauled the outfit. Canned goods were turned out that made men laugh, for canned goods on the Long Trail are a thing to dream about. "Blankets for a hotel," quoth one of the men who laughed and helped. "Half as many is too much; get rid of them. Throw away that tent, and all those dishes—who's going to wash them, anyway? Good Lord, do you think you're traveling on a Pullman?"[3]

And so it went, the inexorable elimination of the superfluous. Mercedes cried when her clothes bags were dumped on the ground and article after article was thrown out. She cried in general, and she cried in particular over each discarded thing. She clasped hands about knees, rocking back and forth broken-heartedly. She averred[4] she would not go an inch, not for a dozen Charleses. She appealed to everybody and to everything, finally wiping her eyes and proceeding to cast out even articles of apparel that were imperative necessaries. And in her zeal, when she had finished with her own, she attacked the belongings of her men and went through them like a tornado.

This accomplished, the outfit, though cut in half, was still a formidable bulk. Charles and Hal went out in the evening and bought six Outside dogs. These, added to the six of the original team, and Teek and Koona, the huskies obtained at the Rink Rapids on the record trip, brought the team up to fourteen. But the Outside dogs, though

---

3. Pullman: A railroad car with private sleeping compartments.
4. averred (ə vʉrd'), *v.*: Declared.

practically broken in since their landing, did not amount to much. Three were short-haired pointers, one was a Newfoundland, and the other two were mongrels of indeterminate breed. They did not seem to know anything, these newcomers. Buck and his comrades looked upon them with disgust, and though he speedily taught them their places and what not to do, he could not teach them what to do. They did not take kindly to trace and trail. With the exception of the two mongrels, they were bewildered and spirit-broken by the strange, savage environment in which they found themselves and by the ill treatment they had received. The two mongrels were without spirit at all; bones were the only things breakable about them.

With the newcomers hopeless and forlorn, and the old team worn out by twenty-five hundred miles of continuous trail, the outlook was anything but bright. The two men, however, were quite cheerful. And they were proud, too. They were doing the thing in style, with fourteen dogs. They had seen other sleds depart over the Pass for Dawson, or come in from Dawson, but never had they seen a sled with so many as fourteen dogs. In the nature of Arctic travel there was a reason why fourteen dogs should not drag one sled, and that was that one sled could not carry the food for fourteen dogs. But Charles and Hal did not know this. They had worked the trip out with a pencil, so much to a dog, so many dogs, so many days, Q.E.D.[5] Mercedes looked over their shoulders and nodded comprehensively, it was all so very simple.

Late next morning Buck led the long team up the street. There was nothing lively about it, no snap or go in him and his fellows. They were starting dead weary.

Four times he had covered the distance between Salt Water and Dawson, and the knowledge that, jaded and tired, he was facing the same trail once more, made him bitter. His heart was not in the work, nor was the heart of any dog. The Outsides were timid and frightened, the Insides without confidence in their masters.

Buck felt vaguely that there was no depending upon these two men and the woman. They did not know how to do anything, and as the days went by it became apparent that they could not learn. They were slack in all things, without order or discipline. It took them half the night to pitch a slovenly camp, and half the morning to break that camp and get the sled loaded in fashion so slovenly that for the rest of the day they were occupied in stopping and rearranging the load. Some days they did not make ten miles. On other days they were unable to get started at all. And on no day did they succeed in making more than half the distance used by the men as a basis in their dog-food computation.

It was inevitable that they should go short on dog food. But they hastened it by overfeeding, bringing the day nearer when underfeeding would commence. The Outside dogs, whose digestions had not been trained by chronic famine to make the most of little, had voracious appetites. And when, in addition to this, the worn-out huskies pulled weakly, Hal decided that the orthodox ration[6] was too small. He doubled it. And to cap it all, when Mercedes, with tears in her pretty eyes and a quaver in her throat, could not cajole him into giving the dogs still more, she stole from the fish sacks and fed them slyly. But it was not food that Buck and the huskies needed, but rest. And though they were making poor time, the heavy

---

5. Q.E.D.: Abbreviation for the Latin *quod erat demonstrandum*—"that which was to be proved."

6. orthodox ration (ôr′ thə däks rash′ ən): The usual daily amount of food.

load they dragged sapped their strength severely.

Then came the underfeeding. Hal awoke one day to the fact that his dog food was half gone and the distance only quarter covered; further, that for love or money no additional dog food was to be obtained. So he cut down even the orthodox ration and tried to increase the day's travel. His sister and brother-in-law seconded him; but they were frustrated by their heavy outfit and their own incompetence. It was a simple matter to give the dogs less food; but it was impossible to make the dogs travel faster, while their own ability to get under way earlier in the morning prevented them from traveling longer hours. Not only did they not know how to work dogs, but they did not know how to work themselves.

The first to go was Dub. Poor blundering thief that he was, always getting caught and punished, he had none the less been a faithful worker. His wrenched shoulder blade, untreated and unrested, went from bad to worse, till finally Hal shot him with the big Colt's revolver. It is a saying of the country that an Outside dog starves to death on the ration of the husky, so the six Outside dogs under Buck could do no less than die on half the ration of the husky. The Newfoundland went first, followed by the three short-haired pointers, the two mongrels hanging more grittily on to life, but going in the end.

By this time all the amenities and gentlenesses of the Southland had fallen away from the three people. Shorn of its glamour and romance, Arctic travel became to them a reality too harsh for their manhood and womanhood. Mercedes ceased weeping over the dogs, being too occupied with weeping over herself and with quarreling with her husband and brother. To quarrel was the one thing they were never too weary to do. Their irritability arose out of their misery, increased with it, doubled upon it, outdistanced it. The wonderful patience of the trail which comes to men who toil hard and suffer sore, and remain sweet of speech and kindly, did not come to these two men and the woman. They had no inkling of such a patience. They were stiff and in pain; their muscles ached, their bones ached, their very hearts ached; and because of this they became sharp of speech, and hard words were first on their lips in the morning and last at night.

Charles and Hal wrangled whenever Mercedes gave them a chance. It was the cherished belief of each that he did more than his share of the work, and neither forbore to speak this belief at every opportunity. Sometimes Mercedes sided with her husband, sometimes with her brother. The result was a beautiful and unending family quarrel. Starting from a dispute as to which should chop a few sticks for the fire (a dispute which concerned only Charles and Hal), presently would be lugged in the rest of the family, fathers, mothers, uncles, cousins, people thousands of miles away, and some of them dead. That Hal's views on art, or the sort of society plays his mother's brother wrote, should have anything to do with the chopping of a few sticks of firewood, passes comprehension; nevertheless the quarrel was as likely to tend in that direction as in the direction of Charles's political prejudices. And that Charles's sister's tale-bearing tongue should be relevant to the building of a Yukon fire was apparent only to Mercedes, who disburdened herself of copious opinions upon that topic, and incidentally upon a few other traits unpleasantly peculiar to her husband's family. In the meantime the fire remained unbuilt, the camp half pitched, and the dogs unfed.

Mercedes nursed a special grievance—the grievance of sex. She was pretty and soft, and had been chivalrously treated all her days. But the present treatment by her husband and brother was everything save chivalrous. It was her custom to be helpless. They complained. Upon which impeachment of what to her was her most essential sex-prerogative, she made their lives unendurable. She no longer considered the dogs, and because she was sore and tired, she persisted in riding on the sled. She was pretty and soft, but she weighed one hundred and twenty pounds—a lusty last straw to the load dragged by the weak and starving animals. She rode for days, till they fell in the traces and the sled stood still. Charles and Hal begged her to get off and walk, pleaded with her, entreated, the while she wept and importuned Heaven with a recital of their brutality.

On one occasion they took her off the sled by main strength. They never did it again. She let her legs go limp like a spoiled child, and sat down on the trail. They went on their way, but she did not move. After they had traveled three miles they unloaded the sled, came back for her, and by main strength put her on the sled again.

In the excess of their own misery they were callous to the suffering of their animals. Hal's theory, which he practiced on others, was that one must get hardened. He had started out preaching it to his sister and brother-in-law. Failing there, he hammered it into the dogs with a club. At the Five Fingers the dog food gave out, and a toothless old squaw offered to trade them a few pounds of frozen horse hide for the Colt's revolver that kept the big hunting knife company at Hal's hip. A poor substitute for food was this hide, just as it had been stripped from the starved horses of the cattlemen six months back. In its frozen state it was more like strips of galvanized iron, and when a dog wrestled it into his stomach it thawed into thin and unnutritious leathery strings and into a mass of short hair, irritating and indigestible.

And through it all Buck staggered along at the head of the team as in a nightmare. He pulled when he could; when he could no longer pull, he fell down and remained down till blows from whip or club drove him to his feet again. All the stiffness and gloss had gone out of his beautiful furry coat. The hair hung down, limp and draggled, or matted with dried blood where Hal's club had bruised him. His muscles had wasted away to knotty strings, and the flesh pads had disappeared, so that each rib and every bone in his frame were outlined cleanly through the loose hide that was wrinkled in folds of emptiness. It was heartbreaking, only Buck's heart was unbreakable. The man in the red sweater had proved that.

As it was with Buck, so was it with his mates. They were perambulating[7] skeletons. There were seven altogether, including him. In their very great misery they had become insensible to the bite of the lash or the bruise of the club. The pain of the beating was dull and distant, just as the things their eyes saw and their ears heard seemed dull and distant. They were not half living, or quarter living. They were simply so many bags of bones in which sparks of life fluttered faintly. When a halt was made, they dropped down in the traces like dead dogs, and the spark dimmed and paled and seemed to go out. And when the club or whip fell upon them, the spark fluttered feebly up, and they tottered to their feet and staggered on.

There came a day when Billee, the good-natured, fell and could not rise. Hal had traded off his revolver, so he took the ax and

---

7. perambulating (per am′ byoo lāt′ iŋ), *adj.*: Walking.

knocked Billee on the head as he lay in the traces, then cut the carcass out of the harness and dragged it to one side. Buck saw, and his mates saw, and they knew that this thing was very close to them. On the next day Koona went, and but five of them remained: Joe, too far gone to be malignant; Pike, crippled and limping, only half conscious and not conscious enough longer to malinger; Sol-leks, the one-eyed, still faithful to the toil of trace and trail, and mournful in that he had so little strength with which to pull; Teek, who had not traveled so far that winter and who was now beaten more than the others because he was fresher; and Buck, still at the head of the team, but no longer enforcing discipline or striving to enforce it, blind with weakness half the time and keeping the trail by the loom of it and by the dim feel of his feet.

It was beautiful spring weather, but neither dogs nor humans were aware of it. Each day the sun rose earlier and set later. It was dawn by three in the morning, and twilight lingered till nine at night. The whole long day was a blaze of sunshine. The ghostly winter silence had given way to the great spring murmur of awakening life. This murmur arose from all the land, fraught with the joy of living. It came from the things that lived and moved again, things which had been as dead and which had not moved during the long months of frost. The sap was rising in the pines. The willows and aspens were bursting out in young buds. Shrubs and vines were putting on fresh garbs of green. Crickets sang in the nights, and in the days all manner of creeping, crawling things rustled forth into the sun. Partridges and woodpeckers were booming and knocking in the forest. Squirrels were chattering, birds singing, and overhead honked the wild fowl driving up from the south in cunning wedges that split the air.

From every hill slope came the trickle of running water, the music of unseen fountains. All things were thawing, bending, snapping. The Yukon was straining to break loose the ice that bound it down. It ate away from beneath; the sun ate from above. Air holes formed, fissures sprang and spread apart, while thin sections of ice fell through bodily into the river. And amid all this bursting, rending, throbbing of awakening life, under the blazing sun and through the soft-sighing breezes, like wayfarers to death, staggered the two men, the woman, and the huskies.

With the dogs falling, Mercedes weeping and riding, Hal swearing innocuously, and Charles's eyes wistfully watering, they staggered into John Thornton's camp at the mouth of White River. When they halted, the dogs dropped down as though they had all been struck dead. Mercedes dried her eyes and looked at John Thornton. Charles sat down on a log to rest. He sat down very slowly and painstakingly what of his great stiffness. Hal did the talking. John Thornton was whittling the last touches on an ax handle he had made from a stick of birch. He whittled and listened, gave monosyllabic replies, and, when it was asked, terse advice. He knew the breed, and he gave his advice in the certainty that it would not be followed.

"They told us up above that the bottom was dropping out of the trail and that the best thing for us to do was to lay over," Hal said in response to Thornton's warning to take no more chances on the rotten ice. "They told us we couldn't make White River, and here we are." This last with a sneering ring of triumph in it.

"And they told you true," John Thornton answered. "The bottom's likely to drop out at any moment. Only fools, with the blind luck of fools, could have made it. I tell you straight, I wouldn't risk my carcass on that ice for all the gold in Alaska.''

''That's because you're not a fool, I suppose,'' said Hal. ''All the same, we'll go on to Dawson.'' He uncoiled his whip. ''Get up there, Buck! Hi! Get up there! Mush on!''

Thornton went on whittling. It was idle, he knew, to get between a fool and his folly; while two or three fools more or less would not alter the scheme of things.

But the team did not get up at the command. It had long since passed into the stage where blows were required to rouse it. The whip flashed out, here and there, on its merciless errands. John Thornton compressed his lips. Sol-leks was the first to crawl to his feet. Teek followed. Joe came next, yelping with pain. Pike made painful efforts. Twice he fell over, when half up, and on the third attempt managed to rise. Buck made no effort. He lay quietly where he had fallen. The lash bit into him again and again, but he neither whined nor struggled. Several times Thornton started, as though to speak, but changed his mind. A moisture came into his eyes, and, as the whipping continued, he arose and walked irresolutely up and down.

This was the first time Buck had failed, in itself a sufficient reason to drive Hal into a rage. He exchanged the whip for the customary club. Buck refused to move under the rain of heavier blows which now fell upon him. Like his mates, he was barely able to get up, but, unlike them, he had made up his mind not to get up. He had a vague feeling of impending doom. This had been strong upon him when he pulled in to the bank, and it had not departed from him. What with the thin and rotten ice he had felt under his feet all day, it seemed that he sensed disaster close at hand, out there ahead on the ice where his master was trying to drive him. He refused to stir. So

greatly had he suffered, and so far gone was he, that the blows did not hurt much. And as they continued to fall upon him, the spark of life within flickered and went down. It was nearly out. He felt strangely numb. As though from a great distance, he was aware that he was being beaten. The last sensations of pain left him. He no longer felt anything, though very faintly he could hear the impact of the club upon his body. But it was no longer his body, it seemed so far away.

And then, suddenly, without warning, uttering a cry that was inarticulate and more like the cry of an animal, John Thornton sprang upon the man who wielded the club. Hal was hurled backward, as though struck by a falling tree. Mercedes screamed. Charles looked on wistfully, wiped his watery eyes, but did not get up because of his stiffness.

John Thornton stood over Buck, struggling to control himself, too convulsed with rage to speak.

''If you strike that dog again, I'll kill you,'' he at last managed to say in a choking voice.

''It's my dog,'' Hal replied, wiping the blood from his mouth as he came back. ''Get out of my way, or I'll fix you. I'm going to Dawson.''

Thornton stood between him and Buck, and evinced no intention of getting out of the way. Hal drew his long hunting knife. Mercedes screamed, cried, laughed, and manifested the chaotic abandonment of hysteria. Thornton rapped Hal's knuckles with the ax handle, knocking the knife to the ground. He rapped his knuckles again as he tried to pick it up. Then he stooped, picked it up himself, and with two strokes cut Buck's traces.

Hal had no fight left in him. Besides, his hands were full with his sister, or his arms, rather; while Buck was too near dead to be of further use in hauling the sled. A few minutes later they pulled out from the bank and down the river. Buck heard them go and raised his head to see. Pike was leading, Sol-leks was at the wheel, and between were Joe and Teek. They were limping and staggering. Mercedes was riding the loaded sled. Hal guided at the gee pole, and Charles stumbled along in the rear.

As Buck watched them, Thornton knelt beside him and with rough, kindly hands searched for broken bones. By the time his search had disclosed nothing more than many bruises and a state of terrible starvation, the sled was a quarter of a mile away. Dog and man watched it crawling along over the ice. Suddenly, they saw its back end drop down, as into a rut, and the gee pole, with Hal clinging to it, jerk into the air. Mercedes's scream came to their ears. They saw Charles turn and make one step to run back, and then a whole section of ice give way and dogs and humans disappear. A yawning hole was all that was to be seen. The bottom had dropped out of the trail.

John Thornton and Buck looked at each other.

"You poor devil," said John Thornton, and Buck licked his hand.

6.   For the Love of a Man

When John Thornton froze his feet in the previous December, his partners had made him comfortable and left him to get well, going on themselves up the river to get out a raft of saw logs for Dawson. He was still limping slightly at the time he rescued Buck, but with the continued warm weather even the slight limp left him. And here, lying by the river bank through the long spring days, watching the running water, listening lazily to the songs of birds and the hum of nature, Buck slowly won back his strength.

A rest comes very good after one has traveled three thousand miles, and it must be confessed that Buck waxed lazy as his wounds healed, his muscles swelled out, and the flesh came back to cover his bones. For that matter, they were all loafing —Buck, John Thornton, and Skeet and Nig —waiting for the raft to come that was to carry them down to Dawson. Skeet was a little Irish setter who early made friends with Buck, who, in a dying condition, was unable to resent her first advances. She had the doctor trait which some dogs possess; and as a mother cat washes her kittens, so she washed and cleansed Buck's wounds. Regularly, each morning after he had finished his breakfast, she performed her self-appointed task, till he came to look for her ministrations as much as he did for Thornton's. Nig, equally friendly, though less demonstrative, was a huge black dog, half bloodhound and half deerhound, with eyes that laughed and a boundless good nature.

To Buck's surprise these dogs manifested no jealousy toward him. They seemed to share the kindliness and largeness of John Thornton. As Buck grew stronger they enticed him into all sorts of ridiculous games, in which Thornton himself could not forbear to join; and in this fashion Buck romped through his convalescence and into a new existence. Love, genuine passionate love, was his for the first time. This he had never experienced at Judge Miller's down in the sun-kissed Santa Clara Valley. With the Judge's sons, hunting and tramping, it had been a working partnership; with the Judge's grandsons, a sort of pompous guardianship; and with the Judge himself, a stately and dignified friendship. But love that was feverish and burning, that was adoration, that was madness, it had taken John Thornton to arouse.

This man had saved his life, which was something; but, further, he was the ideal master. Other men saw to the welfare of their dogs from a sense of duty and business expediency; he saw to the welfare of his as if they were his own children, because he could not help it. And he saw further. He never forgot a kindly greeting or a cheering word, and to sit down for a long talk with them (gas, he called it) was as much his delight as theirs. He had a way of taking Buck's head roughly between his hands, and resting his own head upon Buck's, of shaking him back and forth, the while calling him ill names that to Buck were love names. Buck knew no greater joy than that rough embrace and the sound of murmured oaths, and at each jerk back and forth it seemed that his heart would be shaken out of his body so great was its ecstasy. And when, released, he sprang to his feet, his mouth laughing, his eyes eloquent, his throat vibrant with unuttered sound, and in that fashion remained without movement, John Thornton would reverently exclaim, "You can all but speak!"

Buck had a trick of love expression that was akin to hurt. He would often seize Thornton's hand in his mouth and close so fiercely that the flesh bore the impress of his teeth for some time afterward. And as Buck understood the oaths to be love words, so the man understood this feigned bite for a caress.

For the most part, however, Buck's love was expressed in adoration. While he went wild with happiness when Thornton touched him or spoke to him, he did not seek these tokens. Unlike Skeet, who was wont to shove her nose under Thornton's

hand and nudge and nudge till petted, or Nig, who would stalk up and rest his great head on Thornton's knee, Buck was content to adore at a distance. He would lie by the hour, eager, alert, at Thornton's feet, looking up into his face, dwelling upon it, studying it, following with keenest interest each fleeting expression, every movement or change of feature. Or, as chance might have it, he would lie farther away, to the side or rear, watching the outlines of the man and the occasional movements of his body. And often, such was the communion in which they lived, the strength of Buck's gaze would draw John Thornton's head around, and he would return the gaze, without speech, his heart shining out of his eyes as Buck's heart shone out.

For a long time after his rescue, Buck did not like Thornton to get out of his sight. From the moment he left the tent to when he entered it again, Buck would follow at his heels. His transient masters since he had come into the Northland had bred in him a fear that no master could be permanent. He was afraid that Thornton would pass out of his life as Perrault and François and the Scotch half-breed had passed out. Even in the night, in his dreams, he was haunted by this fear. At such times he would shake off sleep and creep through the chill to the flap of the tent, where he would stand and listen to the sound of his master's breathing.

But in spite of this great love he bore John Thornton, which seemed to bespeak the soft, civilizing influence, the strain of the primitive, which the Northland had aroused in him, remained alive and active. Faithfulness and devotion, things born of fire and roof, were his; yet he retained his wildness and wiliness. He was a thing of the wild, come in from the wild to sit by John Thornton's fire, rather than a dog of the soft Southland stamped with the marks of gene-rations of civilization. Because of his very great love, he could not steal from this man, but from any other man, in any other camp, he did not hesitate an instant; while the cunning with which he stole enabled him to escape detection.

His face and body were scored by the teeth of many dogs, and he fought as fiercely as ever and more shrewdly. Skeet and Nig were too good-natured for quarreling —besides, they belonged to John Thornton; but the strange dog, no matter what the breed or valor, swiftly acknowledged Buck's supremacy or found himself struggling for life with a terrible antagonist. And Buck was merciless. He had learned well the law of club and fang, and he never forwent an advantage or drew back from a foe he had started on the way to Death. He had lessoned from Spitz, and from the chief fighting dogs of the police and mail, and knew there was no middle course. He must master or be mastered; while to show mercy was a weakness. Mercy did not exist in the primordial life. It was misunderstood for fear, and such misunderstandings made for death. Kill or be killed, eat or be eaten, was the law; and this mandate, down out of the depths of Time, he obeyed.

He was older than the days he had seen and the breaths he had drawn. He linked the past with the present, and the eternity behind him throbbed through him in a mighty rhythm to which he swayed as the tides and seasons swayed. He sat by John Thornton's fire, a broad-breasted dog, white-fanged and long-furred; but behind him were the shades of all manner of dogs, half wolves and wild wolves, urgent and prompting, tasting the savor of the meat he ate, thirsting for the water he drank, scenting the wind with him, listening with him and telling him the sounds made by the wild life in the forest, dictating his moods, directing his actions, lying down to sleep with him when he lay down, and dreaming with him and beyond him and becoming themselves the stuff of his dreams.

So peremptorily[8] did these shades beckon him, that each day mankind and the claims of mankind slipped farther from him. Deep in the forest a call was sounding, and as often as he heard this call, mysteriously thrilling and luring, he felt compelled to turn his back upon the fire and the beaten earth around it, and to plunge into the forest, and on and on, he knew not where or why; nor did he wonder where or why, the call sounding imperiously, deep in the forest. But as often as he gained the soft unbroken earth and the green shade, the love for John Thornton drew him back to the fire again.

Thornton alone held him. The rest of mankind was as nothing. Chance travelers might praise or pet him; but he was cold under it all, and from a too demonstrative man he would get up and walk away. When Thornton's partners, Hans and Pete, arrived on the long-expected raft, Buck refused to notice them till he learned they were close to Thornton; after that he tolerated them in a passive sort of way, accepting favors from them as though he favored them by accepting. They were of the same large type as Thornton, living close to the earth, thinking simply and seeing clearly; and ere they swung the raft into the big eddy by the sawmill at Dawson, they understood Buck and his ways, and did not insist upon an intimacy such as obtained with Skeet and Nig.

For Thornton, however, his love seemed to grow and grow. He, alone among men, could put a pack upon Buck's back in the summer traveling. Nothing was too great for Buck to do, when Thornton commanded. One day (they had grubstaked[9] themselves from the proceeds of the raft and left Dawson for the headwaters of the Tanana) the men and dogs were sitting on the crest of a cliff which fell away, straight down, to naked bedrock three hundred feet below. John Thornton was sitting near the edge, Buck at his shoulder. A thoughtless whim seized Thornton, and he drew the attention of Hans and Pete to the experiment he had in mind. "Jump, Buck!" he commanded, sweeping his arm out and over the chasm. The next instant he was grappling with Buck on the extreme edge, while Hans and Pete were dragging them back into safety.

"It's uncanny," Pete said, after it was over and they had caught their speech.

Thornton shook his head. "No, it is splendid, and it is terrible, too. Do you know, it sometimes makes me afraid."

"I'm not hankering to be the man that lays hands on you while he's around," Pete announced conclusively, nodding his head toward Buck.

"Py Jingo!" was Hans's contribution. "Not mineself either."

It was at Circle City, ere the year was out, that Pete's apprehensions were realized. "Black" Burton, a man evil-tempered and malicious, had been picking a quarrel with a tenderfoot at the bar, when Thornton stepped good-naturedly between. Buck, as was his custom, was lying in a corner, head on paws, watching his master's every action. Burton struck out, without warning, straight from the shoulder. Thornton was sent spinning, and saved himself from falling only by clutching the rail of the bar.

Those who were looking on heard what was neither bark nor yelp, but a something which is best described as a roar, and they

---

8. peremptorily (pə remp′ tər i lē), *adv.*: Absolutely; without question.

9. grubstaked: Bought supplies for.

saw Buck's body rise up in the air as he left the floor for Burton's throat. The man saved his life by instinctively throwing out his arm, but was hurled backward to the floor with Buck on top of him. Buck loosed his teeth from the flesh of the arm and drove in again for the throat. This time the man succeeded only in partly blocking, and his throat was torn open. Then the crowd was upon Buck, and he was driven off; but while a surgeon checked the bleeding, he prowled up and down, growling furiously, attempting to rush in, and being forced back by an array of hostile clubs. A ''miners' meeting,'' called on the spot, decided that the dog had sufficient provocation, and Buck was discharged. But his reputation was made, and from that day his name spread through every camp in Alaska.

Later on, in the fall of the year, he saved John Thornton's life in quite another fashion. The three partners were lining a long and narrow poling boat down a bad stretch of rapids on the Forty Mile Creek. Hans and Pete moved along the bank, snubbing[10] with a thin Manila rope from tree to tree, while Thornton remained in the boat, helping its descent by means of a pole, and shouting directions to the shore. Buck, on the bank, worried and anxious, kept abreast of the boat, his eyes never off his master.

At a particularly bad spot, where a ledge of barely submerged rocks jutted out into the river, Hans cast off the rope, and, while Thornton poled the boat out into the stream, ran down the bank with the end in his hand to snub the boat when it had cleared the ledge. This it did, and was flying downstream in a current as swift as a millrace,[11]

---

10. snubbing: Checking the movement of the boat by turning the rope around a tree.
11. millrace (mil′ rās), *n.:* The current of water that drives a mill wheel.

when Hans checked it with the rope and checked too suddenly. The boat flirted over and snubbed in to the bank bottom up, while Thornton, flung sheer out of it, was carried downstream toward the worst part of the rapids, a stretch of wild water in which no swimmer could live.

Buck had sprung in on the instant; and at the end of three hundred yards, amid a mad swirl of water, he overhauled Thornton. When he felt him grasp his tail, Buck headed for the bank, swimming with all his splendid strength. But the progress shoreward was slow, the progress downstream amazingly rapid. From below came the fatal roaring where the wild current went wilder and was rent in shreds and spray by the rocks which thrust through like the teeth of an enormous comb. The suck of the water as it took the beginning of the last steep pitch was frightful, and Thornton knew that the shore was impossible. He scraped furiously over a rock, bruised across a second, and struck a third with crushing force. He clutched its slippery top with both hands, releasing Buck, and above the roar of the churning water shouted: ''Go, Buck! Go!''

Buck could not hold his own, and swept on downstream, struggling desperately, but unable to win back. When he heard Thornton's command repeated, he partly reared out of the water, throwing his head high, as though for a last look, then turned obediently toward the bank. He swam powerfully and was dragged ashore by Pete and Hans at the very point where swimming ceased to be possible and destruction began.

They knew that the time a man could cling to a slippery rock in the face of that driving current was a matter of minutes, and they ran as fast as they could up the bank to a point far above where Thornton was hanging on. They attached the line with which they had been snubbing the boat to Buck's neck and shoulders, being careful that it should neither strangle him nor impede his swimming, and launched him into the stream. He struck out boldly, but not straight enough into the stream. He discovered the mistake too late, when Thornton was abreast of him and a bare half-dozen strokes away while he was being carried helplessly past.

Hans promptly snubbed with the rope, as though Buck were a boat. The rope thus tightening on him in the sweep of the current, he was jerked under the surface, and under the surface he remained till his body struck against the bank and he was hauled out. He was half drowned, and Hans and Pete threw themselves upon him, pounding the breath into him and the water out of him. He staggered to his feet and fell down. The faint sound of Thornton's voice came to them, and though they could not make out the words of it, they knew that he was in his extremity.[12] His master's voice acted on Buck like an electric shock. He sprang to his feet and ran up the bank ahead of the men to the point of his previous departure.

Again the rope was attached and he was launched, and again he struck out, but this time straight into the stream. He had miscalculated once, but he would not be guilty of it a second time. Hans paid out the rope, permitting no slack, while Pete kept it clear of coils. Buck held on till he was on a line straight above Thornton; then he turned, and with the speed of an express train headed down upon him. Thornton saw him coming, and, as Buck struck him like a battering ram, with the whole force of the current behind him, he reached up and closed with both arms around the shaggy neck. Hans snubbed the rope around the tree, and Buck

and Thornton were jerked under the water. Strangling, suffocating, sometimes one uppermost and sometimes the other, dragging over the jagged bottom, smashing against rocks and snags, they veered in to the bank.

Thornton came to, belly downward and being violently propelled back and forth across a drift log by Hans and Pete. His first glance was for Buck, over whose limp and apparently lifeless body Nig was setting up a howl, while Skeet was licking the wet face and closed eyes. Thornton was himself bruised and battered, and he went carefully over Buck's body, when he had been brought around, finding three broken ribs.

"That settles it," he announced. "We camp right here." And camp they did, till Buck's ribs knitted and he was able to travel.

That winter, at Dawson, Buck performed another exploit, not so heroic, perhaps, but one that put his name many notches higher on the totem pole of Alaskan fame. This exploit was particularly gratifying to the three men; for they stood in need of the outfit which it furnished, and were enabled to make a long-desired trip into the virgin East, where miners had not yet appeared. It was brought about by a conversation in the Eldorado Saloon, in which men waxed boastful of their favorite dogs. Buck, because of his record, was the target for these men, and Thornton was driven stoutly to defend him. At the end of half an hour one man stated that his dog could start a sled with five hundred pounds and walk off with it; a second bragged six hundred for his dog; and a third, seven hundred.

"Pooh! pooh!" said John Thornton; "Buck can start a thousand pounds."

"And break it out! and walk off with it for a hundred yards?" demanded Matthewson, a Bonanza King, he of the seven hundred vaunt.

---

12. extremity (ik strem′ ə tē), *n.*: Dying stage.

"And break it out, and walk off with it for a hundred yards," John Thornton said coolly.

"Well," Matthewson said, slowly and deliberately, so that all could hear, "I've got a thousand dollars that says he can't. And there it is." So saying, he slammed a sack of gold dust of the size of a bologna sausage down upon the bar.

Nobody spoke. Thornton's bluff, if bluff it was, had been called. He could feel a flush of warm blood creeping up his face. His tongue had tricked him. He did not know whether Buck could start a thousand pounds. Half a ton! The enormousness of it appalled him. He had great faith in Buck's strength and had often thought him capable of starting such a load; but never, as now, had he faced the possibility of it, the eyes of a dozen men fixed upon him, silent and waiting. Further, he had no thousand dollars; nor had Hans or Pete.

"I've got a sled standing outside now, with twenty fifty-pound sacks of flour on it," Matthewson went on with brutal directness; "so don't let that hinder you."

Thornton did not reply. He did not know what to say. He glanced from face to face in the absent way of a man who has lost the power of thought and is seeking somewhere to find the thing that will start it going again. The face of Jim O'Brien, a Mastodon King and old-time comrade, caught his eyes. It was as a cue to him, seeming to rouse him to do what he would never have dreamed of doing.

"Can you lend me a thousand?" he asked, almost in a whisper.

"Sure," answered O'Brien, thumping down a plethoric[13] sack by the side of Matthewson's. "Though it's little faith I'm

having, John, that the beast can do the trick."

The Eldorado emptied its occupants into the street to see the test. The tables were deserted, and the dealers and gamekeepers came forth to see the outcome of the wager and to lay odds. Several hundred men, furred and mittened, banked around the sled within easy distance. Matthewson's sled, loaded with a thousand pounds of flour, had been standing for a couple of hours, and in the intense cold (it was sixty below zero) the runners had frozen fast to the hard-packed snow. Men offered odds of two to one that Buck could not budge the sled. A quibble arose concerning the phrase "break out." O'Brien contended it was Thornton's privilege to knock the runners loose, leaving Buck to "break it out" from a dead standstill. Matthewson insisted that the phrase included breaking the runners from the frozen grip of the snow. A majority of the men who had witnessed the making of the bet decided in his favor, whereat the odds went up to three to one against Buck.

There were no takers. Not a man believed him capable of the feat. Thornton had been hurried into the wager, heavy with doubt; and now that he looked at the sled itself, the concrete fact, with the regular team of ten dogs curled up in the snow before it, the more impossible the task appeared. Matthewson waxed jubilant.

"Three to one!" he proclaimed. "I'll lay you another thousand at that figure, Thornton. What d'ye say?"

Thornton's doubt was strong in his face, but his fighting spirit was aroused—the fighting spirit that soars above odds, fails to recognize the impossible, and is deaf to all save the clamor for battle. He called Hans and Pete to him. Their sacks were slim, and with his own, the three partners could rake together only two hundred dollars. In the

---

13. plethoric (plə thôr′ ik), *adj.*: Too full.

ebb of their fortunes, this sum was their total capital; yet they laid it unhesitatingly against Matthewson's six hundred.

The team of ten dogs was unhitched, and Buck, with his own harness, was put into the sled. He had caught the contagion of the excitement, and he felt that in some way he must do a great thing for John Thornton. Murmurs of admiration at his splendid appearance went up. He was in perfect condition, without an ounce of superfluous flesh, and the one hundred and fifty pounds that he weighed were so many pounds of grit and virility. His furry coat shone with the sheen of silk. Down the neck and across the shoulders, his mane, in repose as it was, half bristled and seemed to lift with every movement, as though excess of vigor made each particular hair alive and active. The great breast and heavy forelegs were no more than in proportion with the rest of the body, where the muscles showed in tight rolls underneath the skin. Men felt these muscles and proclaimed them hard as iron, and the odds went down to two to one.

"Gad, sir! Gad, sir!" stuttered a member of the latest dynasty, a king of the Skookum Benches. "I offer you eight hundred for him, sir, before the test, sir; eight hundred just as he stands."

Thornton shook his head and stepped to Buck's side.

"You must stand off from him," Matthewson protested. "Free play and plenty of room."

The crowd fell silent; only could be heard the voices of the gamblers vainly offering two to one. Everybody acknowledged Buck a magnificent animal, but twenty fifty-pound sacks of flour bulked too large in their eyes for them to loosen their pouch strings.

Thornton knelt down by Buck's side. He took his head in his two hands and rested cheek to cheek. He did not playfully shake him, as was his wont, or murmur soft love curses; but he whispered in his ear. "As you love me, Buck. As you love me," was what he whispered. Buck whined with suppressed eagerness.

The crowd was watching curiously. The affair was growing mysterious. It seemed like a conjuration.[14] As Thornton got to his feet, Buck seized his mittened hand between his jaws, pressing in with his teeth and releasing slowly, half-reluctantly. It was the answer, in terms, not of speech, but of love. Thornton stepped well back.

"Now, Buck," he said.

Buck tightened the traces, then slacked them for a matter of several inches. It was the way he had learned.

"Gee!" Thornton's voice rang out, sharp in the tense silence.

Buck swung to the right, ending the movement in a plunge that took up the slack and with a sudden jerk arrested his one hundred and fifty pounds. The load quivered, and from under the runners arose a crisp crackling.

"Haw!" Thornton commanded.

Buck duplicated the maneuver, this time to the left. The crackling turned into a snapping, the sled pivoting and the runners slipping and grating several inches to the side. The sled was broken out. Men were holding their breaths, intensely unconscious of the fact.

"Now, MUSH!"

Thornton's command cracked out like a pistol shot. Buck threw himself forward, tightening the traces with a jarring lunge. His whole body was gathered compactly together in the tremendous effort, the muscles writhing and knotting like live things under the silky fur. His great chest was low to the

---

14. conjuration (kän′ jə rā′ shən), *n.*: Making a magic spell.

ground, his head forward and down, while his feet were flying like mad, the claws scarring the hard-packed snow in parallel grooves. The sled swayed and trembled, half-started forward. One of his feet slipped, and one man groaned aloud. Then the sled lurched ahead in what appeared a rapid succession of jerks, though it never really came to a dead stop again . . . half an inch . . . an inch . . . two inches. . . . The jerks perceptibly diminished; as the sled gained momentum, he caught them up, till it was moving steadily along.

Men gasped and began to breathe again, unaware that for a moment they had ceased to breathe. Thornton was running behind, encouraging Buck with short, cheery words. The distance had been measured off, and as he neared the pile of firewood which marked the end of the hundred yards, a cheer began to grow and grow, which burst into a roar as he passed the firewood and halted at command. Every man was tearing himself loose, even Matthewson. Hats and mittens were flying in the air. Men were shaking hands, it did not matter with whom, and bubbling over in a general incoherent babel.[15]

But Thornton fell on his knees beside Buck. Head was against head, and he was shaking him back and forth. Those who hurried up heard him cursing Buck, and he cursed him long and fervently, and softly and lovingly.

"Gad, sir! Gad, sir!" spluttered the Skookum Bench king. "I'll give you a thousand for him, sir, a thousand, sir—twelve hundred, sir."

Thornton rose to his feet. His eyes were wet. The tears were streaming frankly down his cheeks. "Sir," he said to the Skookum Bench king, "no, sir. You can go to the devil, sir. It's the best I can do for you, sir."

Buck seized Thornton's hand in his teeth. Thornton shook him back and forth. As though animated by a common impulse, the onlookers drew back to a respectful distance; nor were they again indiscreet enough to interrupt.

---

15. babel (ba′ b'l), *n.*: A confusion of sounds.

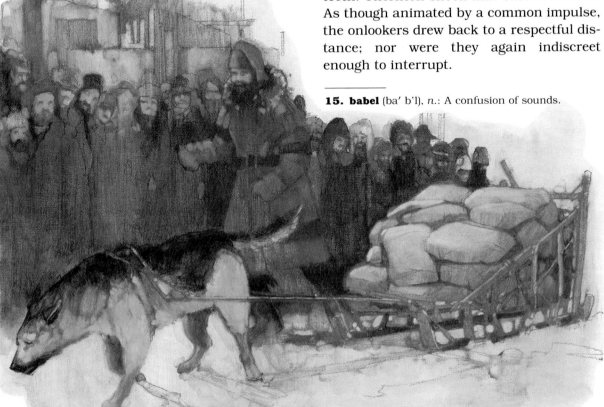

THINKING ABOUT THE SELECTION

Recalling

1. In what ways do Hal and Charles show their inexperience?
2. Describe what happens to Mercedes, Hal, and Charles.
3. How does Buck avoid the fate of the others?
4. Explain the bet Thornton makes with Matthewson.
5. How do Buck and John Thornton show their feeling for each other?

Interpreting

6. Why does Buck think it is a weakness to show mercy?
7. What is shown about Buck when he attacks "Black" Burton and when he saves Thornton from drowning?
8. What do you think is meant by "He was older than the days he had seen and the breaths he had drawn"?
9. Why is Chapter 6 called "For the Love of a Man"?

Applying

10. Explain how Thornton's having Buck pull a sled loaded with a thousand pounds to win a bet was or was not cruelty.

ANALYZING LITERATURE

Understanding Plot

Often the plot of a novel centers on a major conflict that is finally resolved.

1. What is the main conflict that Buck has faced?
2. How does the episode involving Hal, Mercedes, and Charles advance the plot?
3. How does Buck's great love for Thornton create another conflict for the dog?

CRITICAL THINKING AND READING

Identifying the Expert Opinion

One of the ways you can determine the truth of a statement is to seek the opinion of someone who is an expert in the matter. Expert opinion is based on knowledge, research, or experience.

1. Who in this episode is able to offer expert opinions?
2. What expert advice do Mercedes, Hal, and Charles ignore in loading the sled?
3. What expert advice does Hal accept when the dogs cannot move the sled?
4. How does Mercedes finally follow the advice of the "kind-hearted citizens"?
5. What qualifies those giving Mercedes, Hal, and Charles advice as experts?

UNDERSTANDING LANGUAGE

Understanding Word Parts

Words often include several parts. For example, the word *transfusion* contains a prefix (*trans-* meaning "across"), a root (*-fus-* meaning "to pour"), and a suffix (*-ion* meaning "the act of"). The meaning of *transfusion* is "the act of pouring something from one container into another."

1. Write another word using the prefix *trans-*.
2. Write another word using the root *-fus-*.
3. Write another word using the suffix *-ion*.

THINKING AND WRITING

Writing About Plot

Make a list of the major details of Buck's journey up to this point. Write a composition explaining how each of the events in the plot has helped Buck develop the characteristics he needs to survive. When you have finished writing, check your paper to make sure you have included information that would help someone who had never read *The Call of the Wild* understand what has happened to Buck as a result of his journey. Proofread your composition and share it with your classmates.

GUIDE FOR READING

The Call of the Wild, Chapter 7

Theme

The **theme** of a novel is the general idea about life presented through the characters and actions. To this point in *The Call of the Wild,* London has presented a variety of situations in which Buck must learn to survive. You have seen changes occurring in Buck as he learns to adapt to new conditions and to the environment. All of these events help to point out a theme.

Look For

As you read this final chapter, look for the ways that Buck completes his adaptation to a primitive environment. What in Buck enables him to survive? What statement about life is London making through Buck?

Writing

List six events that you have already read from *The Call of the Wild.* Next to each event, write the lesson Buck learned or the way in which the event changed Buck. For example, you might list the beating Buck received from the man in the red sweater. Then you might say Buck learned that not all people are kind or that he was no match for a man with a club or that he became more wary.

Vocabulary

Knowing the following words will help you as you read Chapter 7 of *The Call of the Wild.*

obliterated (ə blit′ ə rāt əd) *adj.:* Wiped out; leaving no traces (p. 747)

imperiously (im pir′ ē əs lē) *adv.:* Overbearing; arrogant; domineering (p. 750)

rampant (ram′ pənt) *adj.:* Unrestrained; spreading unchecked (p. 752)

wantonness (wän tən nəs) *n.:* Lack of discipline (p. 753)

cessation (se sā′ shən) *n.:* A ceasing or stopping (p. 756)

7. The Sounding of the Call

When Buck earned sixteen hundred dollars in five minutes for John Thornton, he made it possible for his master to pay off certain debts and to journey with his partners into the East after a fabled lost mine, the history of which was as old as the history of the country. Many men had sought it; few had found it; and more than a few there were who had never returned from the quest. This lost mine was steeped in tragedy and shrouded in mystery. No one knew of the first man. The oldest tradition stopped before it got back to him. From the beginning there had been an ancient and ramshackle cabin. Dying men had sworn to it, and to the mine the site of which it marked, clinching their testimony with nuggets that were unlike any known grade of gold in the Northland.

But no living man had looted this treasure house and the dead were dead; wherefore John Thornton and Pete and Hans, with Buck and half a dozen other dogs, faced into the East on an unknown trail to achieve where men and dogs as good as themselves had failed. They sledded seventy miles up the Yukon, swung to the left into the Stewart River, passed the Mayo and the McQuestion, and held on until the Stewart itself became a streamlet, threading the upstanding peaks which marked the backbone of the continent.

John Thornton asked little of man or nature. He was unafraid of the wild. With a handful of salt and a rifle he could plunge into the wilderness and fare wherever he pleased and as long as he pleased. Being in no haste, Indian fashion, he hunted his dinner in the course of the day's travel; and if he failed to find it, like the Indian, he kept on traveling, secure in the knowledge that sooner or later he would come to it. So, on this great journey into the East, straight meat was the bill of fare, ammunition and tools principally made up the load on the sled, and the time card was drawn upon the limitless future.

To Buck it was boundless delight, this hunting, fishing, and indefinite wandering through strange places. For weeks at a time they would hold on steadily, day after day; and for weeks upon end they would camp, here and there, the dogs loafing and the men burning holes through frozen muck and gravel and washing countless pans of dirt by the heat of the fire. Sometimes they went hungry, sometimes they feasted riotously, all according to the abundance of game and the fortune of hunting. Summer arrived, and dogs and men packed on their backs, rafted across blue mountain lakes, and descended or ascended unknown rivers in slender boats whipsawed from the standing forest.

The months came and went, and back and forth they twisted through the uncharted vastness, where no men were and yet where men had been if the Lost Cabin were true. They went across divides in summer blizzards, shivered under the midnight sun on naked mountains between the timber line and the eternal snows, dropped into summer valleys amid swarming gnats and flies, and in the shadows of glaciers picked strawberries and flowers as ripe and fair as any the Southland could boast. In the fall of the year they penetrated a weird lake country, sad and silent, where wild fowl had been, but where then there was no life nor sign of life—only the blowing of chill winds, the forming of ice in sheltered places, and the melancholy rippling of waves on lonely beaches.

And through another winter they wandered on the obliterated trails of men who had gone before. Once, they came upon a path blazed through the forest, an ancient path, and the Lost Cabin seemed very near. But the path began nowhere and ended nowhere, and it remained mystery, as the man who made it and the reason he made it remained mystery. Another time they chanced upon the time-graven wreckage of a hunting lodge, and amid the shreds of rotted blankets John Thornton found a long-barreled flintlock. He knew it for a Hudson Bay Company gun of the young days in the Northwest, when such a gun was worth its height in beaver skins packed flat. And that was all—no hint as to the man who in an early day had reared the lodge and left the gun among the blankets.

Spring came on once more, and at the end of all their wandering they found, not the Lost Cabin, but a shallow placer[1] in a broad valley where the gold showed like yellow butter across the bottom of the washing pan. They sought no farther. Each day they worked earned them thousands of dollars in clean dust and nuggets, and they worked every day. The gold was sacked in moose-hide bags, fifty pounds to the bag, and piled like so much firewood outside the spruce-bough lodge. Like giants they toiled, days flashing on the heels of days like dreams as they heaped the treasure up.

There was nothing for the dogs to do, save the hauling in of meat now and again that Thornton killed, and Buck spent long hours musing by the fire. The vision of the short-legged hairy man came to him more frequently, now that there was little work to be done; and often, blinking by the fire, Buck wandered with him in that other world which he remembered.

The salient thing of this other world seemed fear. When he watched the hairy man sleeping by the fire, head between his knees and hands clasped above, Buck saw that he slept restlessly, with many starts and awakenings, at which times he would peer fearfully into the darkness and fling more wood upon the fire. Did they walk by the beach of a sea, where the hairy man gathered shellfish and ate them as he gathered, it was with eyes that roved everywhere for hidden danger and with legs prepared to run like the wind at its first appearance. Through the forest they crept noiselessly, Buck at the hairy man's heels; and they were alert and vigilant, the pair of them, ears twitching and moving and nostrils quivering, for the man heard and smelled as keenly as Buck. The hairy man could spring up into the trees and travel ahead as fast as on the ground, swinging by the arms from limb to limb, sometimes a dozen feet apart, letting go and catching, never falling, never missing his grip. In fact, he seemed as much at home among the trees as on the ground; and Buck had memories of nights of vigil spent beneath trees wherein the hairy man roosted, holding on tightly as he slept.

And closely akin to the visions of the hairy man was the call still sounding in the depths of the forest. It filled him with a great unrest and strange desires. It caused him to feel a vague, sweet gladness, and he was aware of wild yearnings and stirrings for he knew not what. Sometimes he pursued the call into the forest, looking for it as though it were a tangible thing, barking softly or defiantly, as the mood might dictate. He would thrust his nose into the cool wood moss, or into the black soil where long grasses grew, and snort with joy at the fat earth smells; or he would crouch for hours, as if in concealment, behind fungus-covered trunks of fallen trees, wide-eyed and wide-eared to all that moved and sounded about him. It might be, lying thus, that he hoped to sur-

---

1. placer (plās' ər) n.: A deposit of sand mixed with gold.

prise this call he could not understand. But he did not know why he did these various things. He was impelled to do them, and did not reason about them at all.

Irresistible impulses seized him. He would be lying in camp, dozing lazily in the heat of the day, when suddenly his head would lift and his ears cock up, intent and listening, and he would spring to his feet and dash away, and on and on, for hours, through the forest aisles and across the open spaces. He loved to run down dry watercourses, and to creep and spy upon the bird life in the woods. For a day at a time he would lie in the underbrush where he could watch the partridges drumming and strutting up and down. But especially he loved to run in the dim twilight of the summer midnights, listening to the subdued and sleepy murmurs of the forest, reading signs and sounds as man may read a book, and seeking for the mysterious something that called —called, waking or sleeping, at all times, for him to come.

One night he sprang from sleep with a start, eager-eyed, nostrils quivering and scenting, his mane bristling in recurrent waves. From the forest came the call (or one note of it, for the call was many-noted), distinct and definite as never before—a long-drawn howl, like, yet unlike, any noise made by husky dog. And he knew it, in the old familiar way, as a sound heard before. He sprang through the sleeping camp and in swift silence dashed through the woods. As he drew closer to the cry he went more slowly, with caution in every movement, till he came to an open place among the trees, and looking out saw, erect on haunches, with nose pointed to the sky, a long, lean timber wolf.

He had made no noise, yet it ceased from its howling and tried to sense his presence. Buck stalked into the open, half-crouching, body gathered compactly together, tail straight and stiff, feet falling with unwonted care. Every movement advertised commingled threatening and overture of friendliness. It was the menacing truce that marks the meeting of wild beasts that prey. But the wolf fled at sight of him. He followed, with wild leapings, in a frenzy to overtake. He ran him into a blind channel, in the bed of the creek, where a timber jam barred the way. The wolf whirled about, pivoting on his hind legs after the fashion of Joe and of all cornered husky dogs, snarling and bristling, clipping his teeth together in a continuous and rapid succession of snaps.

Buck did not attack, but circled him about and hedged him in with friendly advances. The wolf was suspicious and afraid; for Buck made three of him in weight, while his head barely reached Buck's shoulder. Watching his chance, he darted away, and the chase was resumed. Time and again he was cornered, and the thing repeated, though he was in poor condition, or Buck could not so easily have overtaken him. He would run till Buck's head was even with his flank, when he would whirl around at bay, only to dash away again at the first opportunity.

But in the end Buck's pertinacity[2] was rewarded; for the wolf, finding that no harm was intended, finally sniffed noses with him. Then they became friendly, and played about in the nervous, half-coy way with which fierce beasts belie their fierceness. After some time of this the wolf started off at an easy lope in a manner that plainly showed he was going somewhere. He made it clear to Buck that he was to come, and they ran side by side through the somber twilight, straight up the creek bed, into

2. pertinacity (pŭr′ tə nas′ ə tē), *n.*: Stubbornness; perseverance.

the gorge from which it issued, and across the bleak divide where it took its rise.

On the opposite slope of the watershed they came down into a level country where were great stretches of forest and many streams, and through these great stretches they ran steadily, hour after hour, the sun rising higher and the day growing warmer. Buck was wildly glad. He knew he was at last answering the call, running by the side of his wood brother toward the place from where the call surely came. Old memories were coming upon him fast, and he was stirring to them as of old he stirred to the realities of which they were the shadows. He had done this thing before, somewhere in that other and dimly remembered world, and he was doing it again, now, running free in the open, the unpacked earth underfoot, the wide sky overhead.

They stopped by a running stream to drink, and, stopping, Buck remembered John Thornton. He sat down. The wolf started on toward the place from where the call surely came, then returned to him, sniffing noses and making actions as though to encourage him. But Buck turned about and started slowly on the back track. For the better part of an hour the wild brother ran by his side, whining softly. Then he sat down, pointed his nose upward, and howled. It was a mournful howl, and as Buck held steadily on his way he heard it grow faint and fainter until it was lost in the distance.

John Thornton was eating dinner when Buck dashed into camp and sprang upon him in a frenzy of affection, overturning him, scrambling upon him, licking his face, biting his hand—"playing the general tomfool," as John Thornton characterized it, the while he shook Buck back and forth and cursed him lovingly.

For two days and nights Buck never left camp, never let Thornton out of his sight. He followed him about at his work, watched him while he ate, saw him into his blankets at night and out of them in the morning. But after two days the call in the forest began to sound more imperiously than ever. Buck's restlessness came back on him

and he was haunted by recollections of the wild brother, and of the smiling land beyond the divide and the run side by side through the wide forest stretches. Once again he took to wandering in the woods, but the wild brother came no more; and though he listened through long vigils, the mournful howl was never raised.

He began to sleep out at night, staying away from camp for days at a time; and once he crossed the divide at the head of the creek and went down into the land of timber and streams. There he wandered for a week,

seeking vainly for fresh sign of the wild brother, killing his meat as he traveled and traveling with the long, easy lope that seems never to tire. He fished for salmon in a broad stream that emptied somewhere into the sea, and by this stream he killed a large black bear, blinded by the mosquitoes while likewise fishing, and raging through the forest helpless and terrible. Even so, it was a hard fight, and it aroused the last latent remnants of Buck's ferocity. And two days later, when he returned to his kill and found a dozen wolverines quarreling over the spoil, he scattered them like chaff;[3] and those that fled left two behind who would quarrel no more.

The blood longing became stronger than ever before. He was a killer, a thing that preyed, living on the things that lived, unaided, alone, by virtue of his own strength and prowess, surviving triumphantly in a hostile environment where only the strong survived. Because of all this he became possessed of a great pride in himself, which communicated itself like a contagion to his physical being. It advertised itself in all his movements, was apparent in the play of every muscle, spoke plainly as speech in the way he carried himself, and made his glorious furry coat if anything more glorious. But for the stray brown on his muzzle and above his eyes, and for the splash of white hair that ran midmost down his chest, he might well have been mistaken for a gigantic wolf, larger than the largest of the breed. From his St. Bernard father he had inherited size and weight, but it was his shepherd mother who had given shape to that size and weight. His muzzle was the long wolf muzzle, save

that it was larger than the muzzle of any wolf; and his head, somewhat broader, was the wolf head on a massive scale.

His cunning was wolf cunning, and wild cunning; his intelligence, shepherd intelligence and St. Bernard intelligence; and all this, plus an experience gained in the fiercest of schools, made him as formidable a creature as any that roamed the wild. A carnivorous animal, living on a straight meat diet, he was in full flower, at the high tide of his life, overspilling with vigor and virility. When Thornton passed a caressing hand along his back, a snapping and crackling followed the hand, each hair discharging its pent magnetism at the contact. Every part, brain and body, nerve tissue and fiber, was keyed to the most exquisite pitch; and between all the parts there was a perfect equilibrium or adjustment. To sights and sounds and events which required action, he responded with lightning-like rapidity. Quickly as a husky dog could leap to defend from attack or to attack, he could leap twice as quickly. He saw the movement, or heard sound, and responded in less time than another dog required to compass the mere seeing or hearing. He perceived and determined and responded in the same instant. In point of fact the three actions of perceiving, determining, and responding were sequential; but so infinitesimal were the intervals of time between them that they appeared simultaneous. His muscles were surcharged with vitality, and snapped into play sharply, like steel springs. Life streamed through him in splendid flood, glad and rampant, until it seemed that it would burst him asunder in sheer ecstasy and pour forth generously over the world.

"Never was there such a dog," said John Thornton one day, as the partners watched Buck marching out of camp.

---

3. chaff (chaf), *n.*: Husks of grain that are separated when the grain is beaten during threshing.

"When he was made, the mold was broke," said Pete.

"Py jingo! I t'ink so mineself," Hans affirmed.

They saw him marching out of camp, but they did not see the instant and terrible transformation which took place as soon as he was within the secrecy of the forest. He no longer marched. At once he became a thing of the wild, stealing along softly, cat-footed, a passing shadow that appeared and disappeared among the shadows. He knew how to take advantage of every cover, to crawl on his belly like a snake, and like a snake to leap and strike. He could take a ptarmigan[4] from its nest, kill a rabbit as it slept, and snap in midair the little chipmunks fleeing a second too late for the trees. Fish, in open pools, were not too quick for him; nor were beaver, mending their dams, too wary. He killed to eat, not from wantonness; but he preferred to eat what he killed himself. So a lurking humor ran through his deeds, and it was his delight to steal upon the squirrels, and, when he all but had them, to let them go, chattering in mortal fear to the treetops.

As the fall of the year came on, the moose appeared in greater abundance, moving slowly down to meet the winter in the lower and less rigorous valleys. Buck had already dragged down a stray part-grown calf; but he wished strongly for larger and more formidable quarry, and he came upon it one day on the divide at the head of the creek. A band of twenty moose had crossed over from the land of streams and timber, and chief among them was a great bull. He was in a savage temper, and, standing over six feet from the ground, was as formidable an antagonist as even Buck could desire. Back and forth the bull tossed his great palmated[5] antlers, branching to fourteen points and embracing seven feet within the tips. His small eyes burned with a vicious and bitter light, while he roared with fury at sight of Buck.

From the bull's side, just forward of the flank, protruded a feathered arrow end, which accounted for his savageness. Guided by that instinct which came from the old hunting days of the primordial world, Buck proceeded to cut the bull out from the herd. It was no slight task. He would bark and dance about in front of the bull, just out of reach of the great antlers and of the terrible splay hoofs which could have stamped his life out with a single blow. Unable to turn his back on the fanged danger and go on, the bull would be driven into paroxysms[6] of rage. At such moments he charged Buck, who retreated craftily, luring him on by a simulated inability to escape. But when he was thus separated from his fellows, two or three of the younger bulls would charge back upon Buck and enable the wounded bull to rejoin the herd.

There is a patience of the wild—dogged, tireless, persistent as life itself—that holds motionless for endless hours the spider in its web, the snake in its coils, the panther in its ambuscade;[7] this patience belongs peculiarly to life when it hunts its living food; and it belonged to Buck as he clung to the flank of the herd, retarding its march, irritating the young bulls, worrying the cows with their half-grown calves, and driving the

---

4. ptarmigan (tär′ mə gən), *n.*: A northern or alpine game bird.

5. palmated (pal′ māt əd), *adj.*: Shaped like a hand with the fingers spread.
6. paroxysms (par′ ək siz′mz), *n.*: Outbursts or convulsions.
7. ambuscade (am′ bəs kād′), *n.*: Place of surprise attack.

wounded bull mad with helpless rage. For half a day this continued. Buck multiplied himself, attacking from all sides, enveloping the herd in a whirlwind of menace, cutting out his victim as fast as it could rejoin its mates, wearing out the patience of creatures preyed upon, which is a lesser patience than that of creatures preying.

As the day wore along and the sun dropped to its bed in the northwest (the darkness had come back and the fall nights were six hours long), the young bulls retraced their steps more and more reluctantly to the aid of their beset leader. The downcoming winter was harrying them on to the lower levels, and it seemed they could never shake off this tireless creature that held them back. Besides, it was not the life of the herd, or of the young bulls, that was threatened. The life of only one member was demanded, which was a remoter interest than their lives, and in the end they were content to pay the toll.

As twilight fell the old bull stood with lowered head, watching his mates—the cows he had known, the calves he had fathered, the bulls he had mastered—as they shambled on at a rapid pace through the fading light. He could not follow, for before his nose leaped the merciless fanged terror that would not let him go. Three hundredweight more than half a ton he weighed; he had lived a long, strong life, full of fight and struggle, and at the end he faced death at the teeth of a creature whose head did not reach beyond his great knuckled knees.

From then on, night and day, Buck never left his prey, never gave it a moment's rest, never permitted it to browse the leaves of trees or the shoots of young birch and willow. Nor did he give the wounded bull opportunity to slake his burning thirst in the slender trickling streams they crossed. Often, in desperation, he burst into long stretches of flight. At such times Buck did not attempt to stay him, but loped easily at his heels, satisfied with the way the game was played, lying down when the moose stood still, attacking him fiercely when he strove to eat or drink.

The great head drooped more and more under its tree of horns, and the shambling trot grew weak and weaker. He took to standing for long periods, with nose to the ground and dejected ears dropped limply; and Buck found more time in which to get water for himself and in which to rest. At such moments, panting with red lolling tongue and with eyes fixed upon the big bull, it appeared to Buck that a change was coming over the face of things. He could feel a new stir in the land. As the moose were coming into the land, other kinds of life were coming in. Forest and stream and air seemed palpitant[8] with their presence. The news of it was borne in upon him, not by sight, or sound, or smell, but by some other and subtler sense. He heard nothing, saw nothing, yet knew that the land was somehow different; that through it strange things were afoot and ranging; and he resolved to investigate after he had finished the business in hand.

At last, at the end of the fourth day, he pulled the great moose down. For a day and a night he remained by the kill, eating and sleeping, turn and turn about. Then, rested, refreshed and strong, he turned his face toward camp and John Thornton. He broke into the long easy lope, and went on, hour after hour, never at loss for the tangled way,

---

8. palpitant (pal′ pə tənt), *adj.*: Quivering; trembling.

heading straight home through strange country with a certitude of direction that put man and his magnetic needle to shame.

As he held on he became more and more conscious of the new stir in the land. There was life abroad in it different from the life which had been there throughout the summer. No longer was this fact borne in upon him in some subtle, mysterious way. The birds talked of it, the squirrels chattered about it, the very breeze whispered of it. Several times he stopped and drew in the fresh morning air in great sniffs, reading a message which made him leap on with greater speed. He was oppressed with a sense of calamity happening, if it were not calamity already happened; and as he crossed the last watershed and dropped down into the valley toward camp, he proceeded with greater caution.

Three miles away he came upon a fresh trail that sent his neck hair rippling and bristling. It led straight toward camp and John Thornton. Buck hurried on, swiftly and stealthily, every nerve straining and tense, alert to the multitudinous details which told a story—all but the end. His nose gave him a varying description of the passage of the life on the heels of which he was traveling. He remarked the pregnant silence of the forest. The bird life had flitted. The squirrels were in hiding. One only he saw—a sleek gray fellow, flattened against a gray dead limb so that he seemed a part of it, a woody excrescence[9] upon the wood itself.

As Buck slid along with the obscureness of a gliding shadow, his nose was jerked suddenly to the side as though a positive force had gripped and pulled it. He followed the new scent into a thicket and found Nig. He was lying on his side, dead where he had dragged himself, an arrow protruding, head and feathers, from either side of his body.

A hundred yards farther on, Buck came upon one of the sled dogs Thornton had bought in Dawson. This dog was thrashing about in a death struggle, directly on the trail, and Buck passed around him without stopping. From the camp came the faint sound of many voices, rising and falling in a singsong chant. Bellying forward to the edge of the clearing, he found Hans, lying on his face, feathered with arrows like a porcupine. At the same instant Buck peered out where the spruce-bough lodge had been and saw what made his hair leap straight up on his neck and shoulders. A gust of overpowering rage swept over him. He did not know that he growled, but he growled aloud with a terrible ferocity. For the last time in his life he allowed passion to usurp[10] cunning and reason, and it was because of his great love for John Thornton that he lost his head.

The Yeehats were dancing about the wreckage of the spruce-bough lodge when they heard a fearful roaring and saw rushing upon them an animal the like of which they had never seen before. It was Buck, a live hurricane of fury, hurling himself upon them in a frenzy to destroy. He sprang at the foremost man (it was the chief of the Yeehats), ripping the throat wide open till the rent jugular spouted a fountain of blood. He did not pause to worry the victim, but ripped in passing, with the next bound tearing wide the throat of a second man. There was no withstanding him. He plunged about in their very midst, tearing, rending, destroying, in constant and terrific motion which

---

9. excrescence (iks kres′ ′ns), *n.*: A natural outgrowth.

10. usurp (yo͞o sʉrp′), *v.*: Take control over.

defied the arrows they discharged at him. In fact, so inconceivably rapid were his movements, and so closely were the Indians tangled together, that they shot one another with the arrows; and one young hunter, hurling a spear at Buck in midair, drove it through the chest of another hunter with such force that the point broke through the skin of the back and stood out beyond. Then a panic seized the Yeehats, and they fled in terror to the woods, proclaiming as they fled the advent of the Evil Spirit.

And truly Buck was a fiend, raging at their heels and dragging them down like deer as they raced through the trees. It was a fateful day for the Yeehats. They scattered far and wide over the country, and it was not till a week later that the last of the survivors gathered together in a lower valley and counted their losses. As for Buck, wearying of the pursuit, he returned to the desolated camp. He found Pete where he had been killed in his blankets in the first moment of surprise. Thornton's desperate struggle was fresh-written on the earth, and Buck scented every detail of it down to the edge of a deep pool. By the edge, head and forefeet in the water, lay Skeet, faithful to the last. The pool itself, muddy and discolored from the sluice boxes,[11] effectually hid what it contained, and it contained John Thornton; for Buck followed his trace into the water, from which no trace led away.

All day Buck brooded by the pool or roamed restlessly about the camp. Death, as a cessation of movement, as a passing out and away from the lives of the living, he knew, and he knew John Thornton was dead. It left a great void in him, somewhat akin to hunger, but a void which ached and

ached, and which food could not fill. At times, when he paused to contemplate the carcasses of the Yeehats, he forgot the pain of it; and at such times he was aware of a great pride in himself—a pride greater than any he had yet experienced. He had killed man, the noblest game of all, and he had killed in the face of the law of club and fang. He sniffed the bodies curiously. They had died so easily. It was harder to kill a husky dog than them. They were no match at all, were it not for their arrows and spears and clubs. Thenceforward he would be unafraid of them except when they bore in their hands their arrows, spears, and clubs.

Night came on, and a full moon rose high over the trees into the sky, lighting the land till it lay bathed in ghostly day. And with the coming of the night, brooding and mourning by the pool, Buck became alive to a stirring of the new life in the forest other than that which the Yeehats had made. He stood up, listening and scenting. From far away drifted a faint, sharp yelp, followed by a chorus of similar sharp yelps. As the moments passed the yelps grew closer and louder. Again Buck knew them as things heard in that other world which persisted in his memory. He walked to the center of the open space and listened. It was the call, the many-noted call, sounding more luringly and compellingly than ever before. And as never before, he was ready to obey. John Thornton was dead. The last tie was broken. Man and the claims of man no longer bound him.

Hunting their living meat, as the Yeehats were hunting it, on the flanks of the migrating moose, the wolf pack had at last crossed over from the land of streams and timber and invaded Buck's valley. Into the clearing where the moonlight streamed, they poured in a silvery flood; and in the center of the

---

11. sluice (slo͞os) **boxes:** Long channels through which water is run, leaving the gold.

clearing stood Buck, motionless as a statue, waiting their coming. They were awed, so still and large he stood, and a moment's pause fell, till the boldest one leaped straight for him. Like a flash Buck struck, breaking the neck. Then he stood, without movement, as before, the stricken wolf rolling in agony behind him. Three others tried it in sharp succession; and one after the other they drew back, streaming blood from slashed throats or shoulders.

This was sufficient to fling the whole pack forward, pell-mell, crowded together, blocked and confused by its eagerness to pull down the prey. Buck's marvelous quickness and agility stood him in good stead. Pivoting on his hind legs, and snapping and gashing, he was everywhere at once, presenting a front which was apparently unbroken so swiftly did he whirl and guard from side to side. But to prevent them from getting behind him, he was forced back, down past the pool and into the creek bed, till he brought up against a high gravel bank. He worked along to a right angle in the bank which the men had made in the course of mining, and in this angle he came to bay, protected on three sides and with nothing to do but face the front.

And so well did he face it, that at the end of half an hour the wolves drew back discomfited. The tongues of all were out and lolling, the white fangs showing cruelly white in the moonlight. Some were lying down with heads raised and ears pricked forward; others stood on their feet, watching him; and still others were lapping water from the pool. One wolf, long and lean and gray, advanced cautiously, in a friendly manner, and Buck recognized the wild brother with whom he had run for a night and a day. He was whining softly, and, as Buck whined, they touched noses.

Then an old wolf, gaunt and battle-scarred, came forward. Buck writhed his lips into the preliminary of a snarl, but sniffed noses with him. Whereupon the old wolf sat down, pointed nose at the moon, and broke out the long wolf howl. The others sat down and howled. And now the call came to Buck in unmistakable accents. He, too, sat down and howled. This over, he came out of his angle and the pack crowded around him, sniffing in half-friendly, half-savage manner. The leaders lifted the yelp of the pack and sprang away into the woods. The wolves swung in behind, yelping in chorus. And Buck ran with them, side by side with the wild brother, yelping as he ran.

And here may well end the story of Buck. The years were not many when the Yeehats noted a change in the breed of timber wolves; for some were seen with splashes of brown on head and muzzle, and with a rift of white centering down the chest. But more remarkable than this, the Yeehats tell of a Ghost Dog that runs at the head of the pack. They are afraid of this Ghost Dog, for it has cunning greater than they, stealing from their camps in fierce winters, robbing their traps, slaying their dogs, and defying their bravest hunters.

Nay, the tale grows worse. Hunters there are who fail to return to the camp, and hunters there have been whom their tribesmen found with throats slashed cruelly open and with wolf prints about them in the snow greater than the prints of any wolf. Each fall, when the Yeehats follow the movement of the moose, there is a certain valley which they never enter. And women there are who become sad when the word goes over the fire of how the Evil Spirit came to select that valley for an abiding place.

In the summers there is one visitor, however, to that valley, of which the Yeehats do not know. It is a great gloriously coated wolf, like, and yet unlike, all other wolves. He crosses alone from the smiling timber land and comes down into an open space among the trees. Here a yellow stream flows from rotted moose-hide sacks and sinks into the ground, with long grasses growing through it and vegetable mold overrunning it and hiding its yellow from the sun; and here he muses for a time, howling once, long and mournfully, ere he departs.

But he is not always alone. When the long winter nights come on and the wolves follow their meat into the lower valleys, he may be seen running at the head of the pack through the pale moonlight or glimmering borealis, leaping gigantic above his fellows, his great throat a-bellow as he sings a song of the younger world which is the song of the pack.

THINKING ABOUT THE SELECTION

Recalling

1. What makes it possible for John Thornton to search for the lost mine?
2. How does Buck overcome the wolf's suspicions and win his confidence?
3. What happens to John Thornton?
4. What does Buck do after Thornton is gone?
5. Describe the legends that grow up among the Yeehats concerning Buck?

Interpreting

6. What mood does the author invoke as he describes the setting in this chapter?
7. What does London mean by "the instant and terrible transformation" that takes place in Buck when he leaves Thornton's camp?
8. Why does Buck survive?
9. To what does the title of the novel refer?

Applying

10. Think about what qualities Buck had at the beginning of the novel that helped him to survive. What qualities do you think help people adapt to new and difficult situations?

ANALYZING LITERATURE

Recognizing a Theme

The Call of the Wild reveals a general idea about life—a **theme**. Buck's character changes in a way that reveals the theme.
1. List two incidents in this chapter that caused Buck to change.
2. After each incident you have listed, write how Buck was changed by it.
3. Look at the titles for each of the seven chapters. Explain how each title relates to the theme.
4. In your own words state the theme of *The Call of the Wild*.
5. How are your atittudes toward the theme of the novel the same as or different from Jack London's attitudes?

CRITICAL THINKING AND READING

Determining Causes

In any situation that demands critical thinking, it is important to determine the causes of events and situations.

Choose two of the following situations and list the causes that led to it.
1. John Thornton decides to search for the lost mine.
2. Buck's "wild brother," the wolf, becomes friendly with Buck.
3. Buck decides to return to the camp from the wild.
4. Buck finally responds to the call of the wild.

UNDERSTANDING LANGUAGE

Using a Dictionary

A dictionary can provide much more than definitions of words. A dictionary can help you with the spelling of a word, with its pronunciation, with its syllabification, and with tracing its origin.

Look up each of the following words and give the information requested.
1. conveyence/conveyance (correct spelling)
2. metamorphosed (meaning and pronunciation)
3. inarticulate (syllabification)
4. arctic (origin)

THINKING AND WRITING

Writing About Theme

Think about your reaction to the novel and its theme. Would you have preferred a different outcome? If so, persuade your classmates to agree with you by writing a new ending to the story. Make sure that any change in the novel's theme will be clear to your classmates from what you write. If you would not prefer a different ending, persuade your classmates to agree by explaining why you think the novel and its theme are effective just as they are. Revise your writing, making sure you have organized information logically. Proofread your work and share it with your classmates.

Reading a Map

Sometimes writers present information through various types of maps. They may want to show the distances their characters have traveled or the geographical features of the area such as mountain ranges and waterways. To be able to understand and appreciate this information, it is necessary to know how to read a map.

Information

The first step in reading a map is to understand what kind of information the map presents. A **road map** shows the highways, cities, county and state boundaries, and recreational areas. A **population or historical map** is used to show information about population, political boundaries, industry, and farm production. **Physical maps** indicate the geographical features. The map on page 761 shows cities and geographical features such as mountains, rivers, and bodies of water.

Layout

Next you need to understand how maps are laid out. The top part of the map is the north and the bottom the south. The area to the right is the east, while that to the left is the west.

Keys

Most maps contain keys, or legends, which are located at the bottom right or left of the map. These keys provide important information to help you interpret a map. The map on page 761 provides a scale of distance at the bottom left. This scale helps you measure distance by telling what distances represent.

Let's use the map to locate Dyea. Remember that this is the place where Curly was savagely attacked and killed. To help someone find it, you could explain that it was north of Skagway, south of Fort Selkirk, and east of the St. Elias Mountains. You could further explain that it is about 100 miles northeast of the coast of the Gulf of Alaska. You could describe the region surrounding it as rather mountainous. You could identify it as a city or town because a dot accompanies it. By knowing how to read the map, you could understand the information it provides.

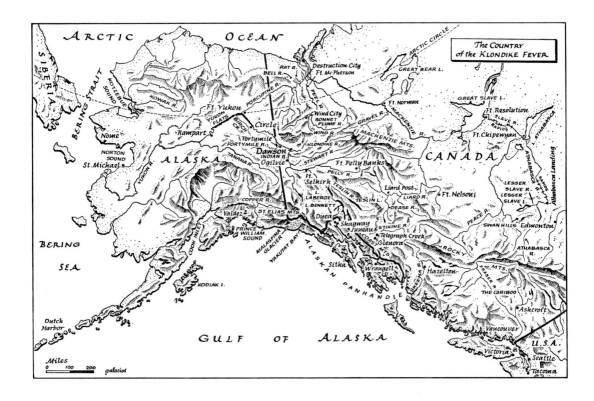

Activity

Use The Country of the Klondike Fever map to answer the following questions.

1. Buck defended Thornton in the city of Circle, which is located
   a. northwest of Dawson   b. north of Dawson
   c. northeast of Dawson

2. St. Michael is on a. Katzebue Sound   b. Norton Sound
   c. Prince William Sound

3. What country borders on Alaska?

4. The Gravel River is near what range of mountains?

5. What city is located on the Arctic Circle?

YOU THE WRITER

Assignment

1. Imagine that you are Buck. Compare and contrast your life as it was with Judge Miller, François and Perrault, and John Thornton.

Prewriting. Use a cueing technique to generate the details. Answer the questions *Who? What? Where? When?* and *Why?*

Writing. Begin by describing life with each of your masters. Remember to write from Buck's perspective. Perhaps devote a paragraph to each lifestyle. Summarize your main points in your last paragraph and reach a conclusion.

Revising. Read over your narrative. Check your details against the story for accuracy. Edit your sentences.

Assignment

2. Imagine that you are John Thornton. Describe your feelings for Buck. Explore why you have these feelings. Discuss the incidents that won Buck your love and respect. Include the details surrounding Buck's life-saving feats and the time he won the bet for you.

Prewriting. Brainstorm to form a list of Buck's extraordinary traits. List the incidents of Buck's stamina, loyalty, and courage. Add details as they occur to you for each incident.

Writing. From Thornton's point of view, describe your feelings for Buck. Show why you have these feelings. Relate the incidents in which Buck's performance impressed you the most. Conclude with a summary of why you think Buck is an extraordinary animal.

Revising. Revise your narrative. Make sure you have written from Thornton's point of view. Add any information you think will strengthen your narrative.

Assignment

3. Rewrite the ending of *The Call of the Wild*. Some possible alternatives would be to develop details surrounding John Thornton's survival, Judge Miller's finding Buck after a long search, or Buck and Thornton's leaving the Klondike.

Prewriting. Freewrite about the alternative plot of your choice. Write down whatever occurs to you that you might use to flesh out a new and different ending to Buck's story.

Writing. Begin your story at the point at which Buck has finished with the moose and has "turned his face toward camp and John Thornton." Try to write in London's style so that your ending will blend easily into the rest of the story. Write as much as is necessary to develop the plot of your ending and bring the story to a satisfactory close.

Revising. Read over your story. Be sure the writing style parallels London's so that your ending fits seamlessly into the novel. Add any details that will make your conclusion more dramatic.

Assignment

1. Write an essay discussing how London develops Buck's relationship with Judge Miller, François and Perrault, and John Thornton.

Prewriting. Outline the three major dog-human relationships in the novel. Your outline can include as many details as is necessary to make the writing of your essay easier.

Writing. Using your detailed outline, begin your essay with a general statement about the relationship between people and animals in literature. Go on to discuss Buck's three main relationships in any order you choose. Be sure to progress logically from one relationship to the next.

Revising. Read over your essay. Make sure your introduction will arouse your reader's interest and prepare them for the subject of your essay. See that you have presented your points clearly.

Assignment

2. Discuss how London uses suspense in the novel to reveal more about Buck in a most effective way.

Prewriting. Prepare a word bank for each suspenseful incident you choose. List the words that create suspense as well as those that describe the incident. Categorize your words logically.

Writing. Begin your essay with an extended definition of the word *suspense*. Go on to describe how London creates suspense in each of the incidents you choose to write about. Describe the incident as well as how suspense works to make it most effective.

Revising. Check to see that your title suggests the main point you are presenting and that this point is clearly made at the end of the first paragraph. Make sure that all the points you make about London's use of suspense are adequately supported.

Assignment

3. Write an essay discussing how Buck's character is developed, even though he is not human. Analyze what caused Buck to change during the course of the novel.

Prewriting. Brainstorm for a list of all the ways in which Buck's character developed. Next to each item in the list, jot down key words from the incident that caused his character to develop.

Writing. Write the first draft of an essay. Be sure to end your introductory paragraph with a thesis statement. Organize your ideas in a chronological pattern. Show how Buck's character changes over time. Finally, discuss how Buck's development of character parallels human character development.

Revising. Be sure your ideas are arranged in chronological order, as events unfold in the novel.

HANDBOOK OF WRITING ABOUT LITERATURE

SECTION 1: UNDERSTANDING THE WRITING PROCESS

Lesson 1: Prewriting

The writing process can be divided into five stages, as follows.

1. *Prewriting:* planning the writing project
2. *Drafting:* writing your ideas in sentences and paragraphs
3. *Revising:* making improvements in your draft
4. *Proofreading:* checking for errors in spelling and mechanics
5. *Publishing,* or *sharing:* allowing others to read your writing

In this lesson you will learn about the steps involved in prewriting.

STEP 1: ANALYZE THE SITUATION

A writing situation can be analyzed in six parts: topic, purpose, audience, voice, content, and form. As you begin thinking about a writing project, ask yourself the following questions about these six parts.

1. *Topic* (the subject you will be writing about): What, exactly, is this subject? Can you state it in a sentence? Is your subject too broad or too narrow?
2. *Purpose* (what you want the writing to accomplish): Is your purpose to explain? to describe? to persuade? to tell a story? What do you want the reader to take away from the writing?
3. *Audience* (the people who will be reading or listening to your work): What are the backgrounds of these people? Do they already know a great deal about your subject, or will you have to provide basic information?
4. *Voice* (the way the writing will sound to the reader): What impression do you want to make on your readers? What tone should the writing have? Should it be formal or informal?

Should it be cool and reasoned or charged with emotion?

5. *Content* (the subject and all the information provided about the subject): How much do you already know about the subject? What will you have to find out? Will you have to do some research? What people, books, magazines, newspapers, or other sources should you consult?
6. *Form* (the shape that the writing will take, including its organization and length): What will the final piece of writing look like? How long will it be? Will it be a single paragraph or several paragraphs? Will it take some special form such as verse or drama? In what order will the content be presented?

The answers to some of these questions will usually be obvious from the start. For example, your teacher may assign you a particular topic and may require that your writing be of a specified length or form. However, the answers to many of these questions will be up to you to decipher. Writing always involves making decisions, setting goals, and then making a plan for achieving these goals.

STEP 2: MAKE A PLAN

Your answers to the questions listed under Step 1 will help you determine what your plan of action will be. For example, if you discover that you are undecided about your topic, your plan of action will have to include clarifying what your topic will be. Your plan of action might also include doing research to find out more about your topic. Depending on what you need to know before you begin writing, choose one or more of the prewriting techniques described in the next section to help you.

STEP 3: GATHER INFORMATION

The following are some techniques for gathering ideas and information for use in your writing.

1. *Freewriting:* Think about your topic, and as you do so, write down everything that comes to your mind. Do not pause to think about proper spelling, grammar, or punctuation. Just write, nonstop, for one to five minutes. Then read your freewriting to find ideas that you can use in your paper.

2. *Clustering:* Write your topic in the middle of a piece of paper and circle it. Then, in the space around your topic, write down ideas that are related to it and circle these ideas. Draw lines to show how the ideas are connected to each other and to the main topic. This technique is especially useful for broadening or narrowing a topic. If your topic is too broad, you might use one of the related ideas as a new main topic. If your topic is too narrow, you might include some of the related ideas in your main topic.

3. *Analyzing:* Divide your topic into parts. Then think about each part separately and write down your thoughts about it in your notes. Also think about how the parts relate to each other and how they relate to the topic as a whole.

4. *Questioning:* Make a list of questions about your topic in your notes. Begin your questions with the words *who, what, when, where, why,* and *how.* Then do some research to find the answers to your questions.

5. *Using outside sources:* Consult books, magazines, newspapers, pamphlets, and reference works such as encyclopedias and atlases. Talk to people who are knowledgeable about your topic. Record in your notes any information that you gather from these sources.

6. *Making charts or lists:* Create charts or lists of information related to your topic. For example, you might list all the parts or characteristics of your topic, or you might make a time line or a pros-and-cons chart.

STEP 4: ORGANIZE YOUR NOTES

To make sense of the information you have gathered, you will need to put it into some kind of logical order. The following are ways to organize your notes.

1. *Chronological order,* or *time order:* the order in which events occur

2. *Spatial order:* the order in which objects appear in space, as from left to right, top to bottom, or near to far

3. *Degree order:* in increasing or decreasing order, as of size, importance, or familiarity

After you have organized your notes, make a rough outline for your paper.

CASE STUDY: PREWRITING

Mia's English teacher asked the class to write a paragraph on the topic of animals. Mia knew that the topic was too broad for a one-paragraph composition, so she tried clustering to narrow the topic. See her chart on the next page.

Since Mia had two cats of her own, she decided that the topic of her paper would be *Why Cats Make Good Pets.* Her purpose would be to explain why it is worthwhile to own a cat, and her audience would be her classmates and her teacher. She decided that her tone would be informal, since a very formal, serious tone would not suit her topic.

Mia's next plan of action was to gather ideas about why she thought cats made good house pets. She made a list in her notes of the reasons why she believed this:

- They don't take up the whole chair like big dogs.

- They don't make a lot of noise.

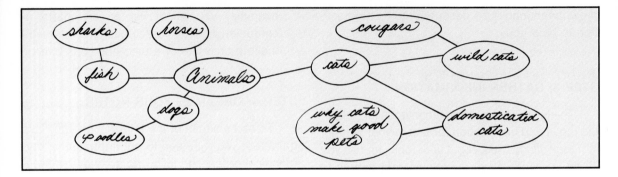

- You don't have to walk them.
- They clean themselves and don't have to be bathed.
- They're easy to clean up after.
- They're cuddly.
- They can play with each other and not be too mad at you when you're out all day.

Mia made a rough outline for her paper. She showed in the outline that she would first introduce her topic, then would give three reasons why cats make good house pets, and finally would conclude with a summarizing sentence. She also decided that she would organize her three reasons by degree, from least to most important.

ACTIVITIES AND ASSIGNMENTS

A. Answer the following questions about the case study:

1. How did Mia analyze the writing situation? What was her plan of action after she had analyzed it?
2. Why did Mia use the clustering technique? How did it help her?
3. Why did Mia make a list in her notes?

B. Choose one of the following topics or think of one of your own:

        School   Weekends
        Hobbies   Writing

Prepare to write a paragraph on the topic by following these steps.

1. Analyze the writing situation by answering the questions listed in this lesson.
2. Make a plan of action for gathering information and ideas to use in your paper. Use one of the prewriting techniques described in this lesson to gather information. Record this information in your notes.
3. Organize your notes and make a rough outline for your paragraph. Save your notes and outline in a folder.

Lesson 2: Drafting and Revising

CHOOSING A METHOD FOR DRAFTING

Drafting is the second stage in the writing process. After you have gathered information and made a rough outline, the next step is to put your ideas down on paper. As you draft, keep the following points in mind:

1. Choose a drafting method that feels right to you. There are many different ways of writing a draft. Some writers like to work from a detailed outline and to write very slowly and carefully. Other writers prefer to make only a very brief outline and to write quickly. Then they go back over their work and take care of the details. Whichever method works best for you is the method you should use.

2. Do not expect your first draft to be a finished product. Drafting gives you the chance to work out your ideas on paper. At this stage you should not worry about proper spelling, grammar, punctuation, and so on. You can take care of these details later.

3. Refer to your prewriting notes and to your outline as you write. Work from your notes and outline, keeping your audience and your purpose in mind.

4. Be flexible. Do not be afraid to discard old ideas as better ones come to mind. You may need to stop in the middle of your draft and do some more prewriting to develop your new ideas.

5. Write as many rough drafts as you need. You may have to make several attempts at drafting before you come up with a draft that is satisfactory. If you write a draft that does not seem to have a well-defined purpose or doesn't contain enough information to support your main idea, go back to the prewriting stage. Define your purpose more clearly, review your notes to discard irrelevant ideas, and gather any additional ideas and facts that you need.

REVISING YOUR DRAFT

Once you have a draft that pleases you, you can begin refining and polishing it. This process of reworking a draft is known as *revising*. As you revise, ask yourself the questions in the following Checklist for Revision. If your answer to any

CHECKLIST FOR REVISION

Topic and Purpose
- ☐ Is my topic clear?
- ☐ Does my writing have a specific purpose?
- ☐ Does my writing achieve its purpose?

Audience
- ☐ Will everything that I have written be clear to my audience?
- ☐ Will my audience find the writing interesting?
- ☐ Will my audience respond in the way that I would like?

Voice and Word Choice
- ☐ Is the impression that my writing conveys the one I intended it to convey?
- ☐ Is my language appropriately formal or informal?
- ☐ Have I avoided vague, undefined terms?
- ☐ Have I avoided jargon that my audience will not understand?
- ☐ Have I avoided clichés?
- ☐ Have I avoided slang, odd connotations, euphemisms, and gobbledygook except for novelty or humor?

Content/Development
- ☐ Have I avoided including unnecessary or unrelated ideas?
- ☐ Have I developed my topic completely?
- ☐ Have I supplied examples or details that support the statements I have made?
- ☐ Are my sources of information unbiased, up-to-date, and authoritative?

Form
- ☐ Have I followed a logical method of organization?
- ☐ Have I used transitions, or connecting words, to make the organization clear?
- ☐ Does the writing have a clear introduction, body, and conclusion?

of the questions is "no," revise your draft until you can answer "yes."

Editorial Symbols

Use the following symbols to edit, or revise, your draft:

SYMBOL	MEANING	EXAMPLE
℺↑	move text	She (however) was not at home.
℮	delete	I ~~also~~ went, too.
∧	insert	OUR of ∧car
⌒	close up; no space	every ⌣ where
⊙	insert period	ran ⊙ I
⅄	insert comma	mice, bats ⅄ and rats
⅌	add apostrophe	they⅌re here
℣ ℣	add quotation marks	℣The Tell-Tale Heart℣
⌐⌐⌙	transpose	to (clearly) (see)
¶	begin paragraph	crash. ¶The man
/	make lower case	the /Basketball player
≡	capitalize	president Truman ≡

CASE STUDY: DRAFTING AND REVISING

Mia used her prewriting notes from the pre-ceding lesson to begin drafting her paragraph. Here is her first draft:

> Cats are grate housepets. They don't bark, you can take care of them easy and they're cud-dly. I love my two cats.

Mia stopped writing and looked at her draft. She had given the three reasons why she thought cats were good pets, and now she had nothing more to say. She set a goal for her next draft: to give examples that would support each of her reasons.

Mia wrote several more drafts. Here is the last draft that she wrote, which she revised, using standard editorial symbols:

ACTIVITIES AND ASSIGNMENTS

A. Answer the following questions about the revised draft in the case study:

1. Why hasn't Mia corrected all of her grammar and spelling errors? When will these errors be corrected?

2. Why did Mia delete material in the first two sentences?

3. Why did Mia add the sentence "They're pleasant to have around"?

4. Why did Mia change the words "fool around with"?
5. What transitional words did Mia add to indicate that she was about to tell the last reason why cats are good house pets?
6. Why did Mia move the original last sentence in her paragraph?
7. Why did Mia add a new last sentence?
8. What other revisions did Mia make? Why did she make them?

B. Using your prewriting notes from the last lesson, write a draft of a paragraph on your topic. Then revise your draft. Follow these steps:
1. Read over your outline to see how your paragraph will be organized. Then write a thesis statement of one or two sentences to introduce your topic.
2. Write the rest of your draft, based on your outline and your prewriting notes. Make sure that you support your statements with evidence from your notes. Do not worry about spelling and mechanics at this point.
3. Write a conclusion that sums up the main point of your paragraph.
4. Revise your draft, using the Checklist for Revision in this lesson. If you answer "no" to any of the questions on the checklist, use standard editorial symbols to make the necessary corrections.

Lesson 3: Proofreading and Publishing

PROOFREADING YOUR FINAL DRAFT

Before a draft is ready to be shared with a reader, it must be checked for errors in grammar and usage, spelling, punctuation, capitalization, and manuscript form. This process of final checking is called *proofreading*. When you proofread, ask yourself the questions in the checklist at the left. If your answer to any of the questions is "no," make the necessary corrections on your revised draft.

If you need to check your spelling or to review rules for mechanics, refer to a dictionary, writing textbook, or handbook of style.

CHECKLIST FOR PROOFREADING

Grammar and Usage
- ☐ Are all of my sentences complete? That is, have I avoided sentence fragments?
- ☐ Does each of my sentences express only one complete thought? That is, have I avoided run-on sentences?
- ☐ Do the verbs I have used agree with their subjects?
- ☐ Have all the words in my paper been used correctly? Am I sure about the meanings of all of these words?
- ☐ Is the person or thing being referred to by each pronoun clear?
- ☐ Have I used adjectives and adverbs correctly?

Spelling
- ☐ Am I absolutely sure that each word has been spelled correctly?

Punctuation
- ☐ Does every sentence end with a punctuation mark?
- ☐ Have I correctly used commas, semicolons, colons, hyphens, dashes, parentheses, quotation marks, and apostrophes?

Capitalization
- ☐ Have I capitalized any words that should not be capitalized?
- ☐ Should I capitalize any words that I have not capitalized?

Manuscript Form
- ☐ Have I indented the first line(s) of my paragraph(s)?
- ☐ Have I written my name and the page number in the top right-hand corner of each page?
- ☐ Have I double-spaced the manuscript?
- ☐ Is my draft neat and legible?

PUBLISHING OR SHARING YOUR WORK

After you have proofread your revised draft, you are ready to share your writing with other people. When you write for school, you generally submit your work to your teachers. However, there are many other ways to share, or publish, your writing. The following is a list of possibilities:

1. Share your work in a small discussion group.
2. Read your work aloud to the class.
3. Share copies of your writing with members of your family, or with friends.
4. Display your work on the class bulletin board.
5. Save your work in a folder for later publication. At the end of the year, work from the entire class can be bound together into a booklet.
6. Submit your writing to the school literary magazine, or start a literary magazine for your school or for your class.
7. Submit your writing to your school or community newspaper.
8. Enter your writing in literary contests for student writers.
9. Submit your writing to a magazine that publishes work by young people.

CASE STUDY: PROOFREADING AND PUBLISHING

After revising her final draft, Mia made a fresh, clean copy for proofreading. She read the Checklist for Proofreading in this lesson and applied each question to her revised draft. Here is Mia's paragraph, with the proofreading corrections that she made, marked with editorial symbols:

¶ Cats make wonderful housepets. They're pleasant to have around. They make soft, purring sounds when ~~their~~ *they're* happy; they sound like little engines when you're close up. They curl up peaceful*ly* in a warm ball in your lap or against your foot. They're also independent. *— all they need is* A little ball to chase or a piece of bright*ly* colored yarn. Best of all, they're easy to care for. *If you have two they play together and keep each other happy.* You don't have to rush home, get up early or stay up late to walk a cat. Cats are delightful, easy pets.

Mia made a clean final copy of her paragraph. Then she read it aloud to a few of her classmates in a small discussion group.

ACTIVITIES AND ASSIGNMENTS

A. Answer the following questions about the case study:
1. What errors in spelling did Mia correct during proofreading?
2. Why did Mia change "peaceful" to "peacefully"?
3. What sentence fragment did Mia correct? How did she do this?
4. What punctuation error did Mia correct?
5. What error in manuscript form did Mia make? How did she correct it?
6. Are there any changes you think should still be made in Mia's paragraph? Explain.

B. Make a clean copy of your revised paragraph from the preceding lesson. Then use the Checklist for Proofreading to correct any errors in grammar and usage, spelling, punctuation, capitalization, and manuscript form that remain in your draft.

Make a final copy of your paragraph, and share this copy with your classmates and with your teacher.

SECTION 2: UNDERSTANDING THE PARTS OF A LITERARY WORK: ANALYSIS AND INTERPRETATION

Lesson 4: Writing About Images

WHAT IS AN IMAGE?

An *image* is a word or phrase that appeals to one of the five senses. These senses include sight, hearing, touch, taste, and smell. Consider this line from William Melvin Kelley's short story "A Good Long Sidewalk":

The barbershop was warm enough to make Carlyle Bedlow sleepy, and smelled of fragrant shaving soap.

In this line Kelley uses images that appeal to the senses of touch ("the barbershop was warm") and smell ("fragrant shaving soap").

WHY DO WRITERS USE IMAGES?

Writers use images for two purposes:
1. To portray scenes that include people, places, and things, and
2. To create feelings, or moods.

Look again at the line from William Kelley's short story. Notice that the images in the line help to create a picture of the barbershop. They create a mood of relaxation and coziness.

Now consider the use of images in the following passage from Maya Angelou's autobiography *I Know Why the Caged Bird Sings*:

Throughout the year, until the next frost, we took our meals from the smokehouse . . . and from the shelves of canned foods. There were choices on the shelves that could set a hungry child's mouth to watering. Green beans, snapped always the right length, collards, cabbage, juicy red tomato preserves that came into their own on steaming buttered biscuits, and sausage, beets, berries, and every fruit grown in Arkansas.

The images in this passage

1. Create a picture of jars of colorful, delicious-tasting, fragrant foods sitting on pantry shelves, waiting to be enjoyed, and
2. Create feelings of pleasure and happiness.

CASE STUDY: WRITING ABOUT IMAGES

Prewriting

Tenetia's English teacher asked the class to write an analysis of a favorite poem. Tenetia chose to write about the use of images in the following poem:

DRIVING TO TOWN LATE TO MAIL A LETTER

Robert Bly

It is a cold and snowy night. The main
   street is deserted.
The only things moving are swirls of snow.
As I lift the mailbox door, I feel its
   cold iron.
There is a privacy I love in this snowy
   night.
Driving around, I will waste more time.

Tenetia checked to see if there were any words she needed to look up in the dictionary. There weren't. She then read the poem again, paying close attention to its images. Next she made a list of the images in the poem:

- Images of sight:
  Dark, "snowy night"
  "street is deserted"
  "swirls of snow" moving around
  Speaker mailing letter in mailbox
  Speaker's car waiting

- Images of sound:
  Silence—no people, only silent snow

- Images of touch:
  "cold iron" of mailbox door
  Softness of "swirls of snow"
  Coldness of night

- Images of taste:
  None

- Images of smell:
  None

Then Tenetia asked herself, "What picture do these images create and what mood do they suggest?" She wrote her responses in her prewriting notes:

- Picture created by images in the poem:
  Cold, snowy, deserted corner of town at night by a mailbox
  Speaker has parked a car by the mailbox to mail a letter
  Snow swirling around

- Mood created by the images:
  Alone but not lonely
  What the speaker calls "a privacy I love"

Tenetia decided to write about how Bly used images to create a mood of wonderful privacy. She made the following rough outline of her paper:

- Introduction:
  Tell what poem I'm writing about.
  State my purpose (to show that Bly uses images to create a mood of wonderful privacy).

- Body:
  Describe the images of sight, sound, and touch in the poem.

- Conclusion:
  Point out how the last two lines sum up the mood created by the poem's images.

Drafting and Revising

Using her outline and her prewriting notes, Tenetia wrote a draft of her analysis. Then she carefully revised and proofread her work. At right is her rough draft with the handwritten corrections that she made.

In the poem "Driving to Town Late to Mail a Letter," Robert Bly uses images to create a mood of wonderful privacy; the images of sight show the speaker, who has driven downtown late at night to mail a letter. The "main street is deserted," for workers and shoppers have gone home. However, the lively "swirls of snow" keep the scene from being lonely.

Also, images of touch also reinforce the pleasure of this mood, that the speaker calls "the privacy I love." The swirling snow suggests a soft, pleasant touch. The cold night air seems refreshing and energizing, but not chilling. Not even the "cold iron" of the mailbox door is unpleasant in this setting. Instead the cold iron suggests strength. The speaker's privacy is enhanced by the snow's softness and charged by the bracing cold.

The night's silence, too, emphasises the privacy. No sounds break intrude. Moreover, this is the magical silence of the noiseless snow. Little wonder the speaker loves this privacy. When he says, "Driving around, I will waste more time," the reader realizes it cannot be the speaker who judges this mood a waste of time. It must be those who are not poets.

Proofreading and Publishing

After making a clean final copy of her paper, Tenetia proofread it carefully. As she did so, she caught several punctuation errors and one spelling error. She corrected these. Then she shared her paper with a small group of classmates. First she read the poem to them, and then she read her analysis.

ACTIVITIES AND ASSIGNMENTS

A. Study the corrections Tenetia made in her paragraph. Identify each of the following:
1. Places where Tenetia corrected errors in spelling
2. A place where Tenetia corrected an error in subject and verb agreement
3. A place where Tenetia eliminated unnecessary repetition
4. A place where Tenetia fixed a sentence fragment
5. Places where Tenetia corrected errors in punctuation
6. Errors in punctuation and spelling that were not corrected on Tenetia's revised draft (Hint: Check her use of quotation marks.)

B. Choose one of the poems from the poetry unit of your anthology. Then write a short paper about its images and the mood that the images create. Follow these steps:
1. Read the poem carefully. Look up any words that you don't know and write out their definitions.
2. Make a chart showing the images of sight, sound, touch, taste, and smell used in the poem.
3. Make notes telling what picture is created by the images and what mood, or feeling, the images convey.
4. Write an introduction that gives the name of the poem and tells what mood is created by the images.
5. In the body of your paper, explain what images are used in the poem.
6. Write a conclusion that sums up the poem's mood.
7. Revise and proofread your paragraph carefully. Add any important details that you left out. Delete any unnecessary words. Proofread for errors in organization, grammar, spelling, usage, punctuation, and capitalization.
8. Make a clean final copy for handing in and for sharing.

Lesson 5: Writing About Sound

SOUND AND MEANING

Sometimes when you hear a writer's words read aloud, you discover a new dimension of meaning. The sounds made by the words are part of what the writer wants to communicate. For example, note how the following poem sounds when read aloud:

WINTER OCEAN

John Updike

Many-maned scud-thumper, tub
of male whales, maker of worn wood,
shrub-ruster, sky-mocker, rave!
portly pusher of waves, wind-slave.

The sound of the poem gives the reader a strong sense of the choppy violence and power of an ocean in winter. In both prose and poetry, sound and meaning are often closely related.

TECHNIQUES INVOLVING SOUND

Writers use many techniques to enrich the way their writing sounds. The chart below lists some common literary devices of sound.

Read the entries for the terms in the Sound Devices chart below in the Handbook of Literary Terms. Then read the following case study.

CASE STUDY: WRITING ABOUT SOUND

Arthur's English class was studying the use of sound in poetry. For an assignment to write about sound in a poem, Arthur chose the following poem, which he had enjoyed reading:

A LAZY THOUGHT

Eve Merriam

There go the grownups
To the office,
To the store,
Subway rush,
Traffic crush;
Hurry, scurry,
Worry, flurry.

No wonder
Grownups
Don't grow up
Any more.

It takes a lot
Of slow
To grow.

Prewriting

Arthur read the poem aloud several times,

SOUND DEVICES	
Onomatopoeia: words that sound like what they mean, such as "whoosh" or "buzz"	*Assonance:* repetition of vowel sounds, as in "the flat sad face of a rather fat man"
Euphony: flowing, pleasant sounds, as in "graceful lilies floating by"	*Meter:* a regular rhythmical pattern, as in "The soup is on the stove"
Cacophony: harsh, jarring sounds, as in this line from the Updike poem: "shrub-ruster, sky-mocker, rave!"	*Parallelism:* repetition of groups of words with similar grammatical structures, as in "over the river and through the woods" (Both are prepositional phrases.)
Alliteration: repetition of initial consonant sounds, as in "*bright beauty*"	
Consonance: repetition of internal consonant sounds, as in "Donkeys, turkeys, and monkeys all gathered around."	*Repetition:* a repeated sound, word, phrase, or sentence. Examples of repetition include rhyme, consonance, assonance, and parallelism.

listening carefully to its sounds. Then, to gather information, he made a copy of the poem and marked the copy as follows:

1. He underlined examples of onomatopoeia.
2. He circled the rhyming words.
3. He underlined, twice, all the repeated sounds he could find.
4. In the margins he noted examples of alliteration, consonance, assonance, parallelism, and repeated words.
5. He marked the stresses and feet in the first and last stanzas to show the meter of the poem.

Here is Arthur's marked copy of "A Lazy Thought":

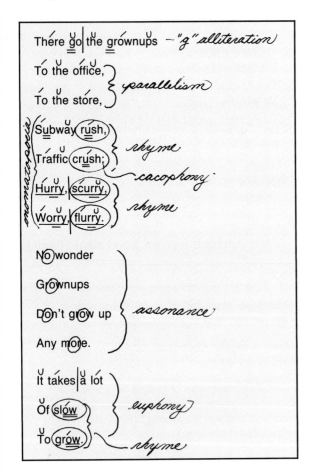

Arthur made some further notes about the meter and the rhyme in the poem:

- Meter: The first stanza has a heavy, drumming meter that echoes the footsteps of the grownups going to work.
- Rhyme: The first stanza has lots of rhyme, which accentuates the abrupt rhythm of the grownups rushing. The second stanza doesn't rhyme—makes the reader stop and listen to the poet. The third stanza rhymes and gives the poem a smooth ending.

Arthur reviewed the poem and his notes. Then he made the following generalizations about the poem:

- First stanza: sounds rushed, like the grownups' world
- Last stanza: sounds lazy and a slow, like kids' time

Next Arthur made a rough outline for his composition. He decided to organize his information by topic—he would discuss one sound device at a time and give examples of each.

Drafting and Revising

Arthur used his prewriting notes and his outline to write a draft of his composition. Here is the beginning of his unrevised first draft:

In her poem "A Lazy Thought," Eve Merriam uses many sound devices, especially meter and repetition, to show what time is like for rushing grownups contrasted with the lazy pleasent, slow time of others. First of all, the fast-paced meter in the first stanza emphasizes the frantic pace of grownups. Lines 2–7 start with heavy beats and each have two stressed beats. The rhythm of the first stanza is like the grownups pounding footsteps. In contrast, the last stanza has a lovely rhythm. Each line begins with a soft beat. And it is followed by a gentley accented beat. The repetition of sounds emphasize the same contrast, between grownup time and kid time. Onomatopoia, for example, lets the reader hear the "rush,/ . . . crush;/Hurry, scurry,/Worry, flurry" of the grownups. In addition, the assonance and rhyme in the last two stanzas, with the repeated long o sounds, contrast with the rushing feeling and emphasize slowness.

Arthur finished his draft and then revised it.

Proofreading and Publishing

Arthur carefully proofread his revised draft. Then he made a clean final copy of his composition and shared it with a small group of his classmates before handing it in to his teacher.

ACTIVITIES AND ASSIGNMENTS

A. Finish writing Arthur's rough draft. Then revise the entire draft, making sure that all of the ideas are expressed clearly and are supported with examples. Finally, proofread the draft and make a final copy of it. Share the composition with a small group of your classmates.

B. Write a two-paragraph composition on the use of sound in one of the following poems: "By Morning," on page 540; "Ring Out, Wild Bells," on page 544; "Four Little Foxes," on page 556; or "Silver," on page 564. Follow these steps:

1. Select a poem and read it aloud several times. Listen to the way the poem sounds, and think about how the sounds affect the poem's meaning.

2. Make a copy of the poem. If the poem is particularly long, copy only one or two stanzas.

3. Mark the copy as Arthur did in the case study, showing examples of onomatopoeia, rhyme, repeated sounds, alliteration, consonance, assonance, parallelism, and repeated words.

4. Read the entry for Meter in the Handbook of Literary Terms and Techniques. Then choose one stanza of the poem and mark its stresses and feet.

5. Organize your notes and make a rough outline for your composition. In the introduction, tell what poem you are writing about and explain that you are going to discuss the poet's use of sound. In the body of your composition, discuss each device of sound in turn, giving at least one example of each. Conclude your composition with a summary of your main point.

6. Revise and proofread your composition. Then make a final copy of it, and share this copy with your classmates and with your teacher.

Lesson 6: Writing About Figures of Speech

WHAT IS A FIGURE OF SPEECH?

Sometimes a writer uses words to convey more than just a literal meaning. When a word or group of words is used in a special, nonliteral way, it is called a *figure of speech*. In the opening lines of the excerpt from *One Writer's Beginnings,* on page 377, Eudora Welty uses several figures of speech:

> Learning stamps you with its moments. Childhood's learning is made up of moments. It isn't steady. It's a pulse.

Learning doesn't literally "stamp" anyone, nor is it really a "pulse." These are figures of speech used to describe, vividly and imaginatively, the process of learning.

The following are some of the most frequently used figures of speech.

```
┌──────────────────────────────────────┐
│          FIGURES OF SPEECH           │
├──────────────────────────────────────┤
│ Hyperbole: exaggeration for emphasis: │
│                                      │
│ "My brother makes the best chocolate │
│ chip cookies in the world."          │
│                                      │
│ Personification: speaking or writing │
│ about a nonhuman subject as though   │
│ it were human:                       │
│                                      │
│ "That wallpaper pattern reaches right│
│ out and grabs you!"                  │
│                                      │
│ Simile: a comparison of two very     │
│ different things, using like or as:  │
│                                      │
│ "Your thoughtful gift was like       │
│ sunshine on a cold winter's day."    │
│                                      │
│ Metaphor: writing or speaking of one │
│ thing as though it were something    │
│ very different:                      │
│                                      │
│ "The engine of my mother's new car   │
│ purrs."                              │
└──────────────────────────────────────┘
```

WHY WRITERS USE FIGURES OF SPEECH

Figures of speech can be much more vivid and interesting than literal language. For example, here is one way to describe how someone feels after a long day at work:

> Feeling very tired, Maria took a nap.

The statement is accurate, but not very striking. Here is an example of a figure of speech—a simile—used to describe the same subject:

> Feeling like someone who had just run the Boston Marathon, Maria collapsed on the couch.

The comparison in the second sentence helps the reader to feel Maria's exhaustion.

HOW WRITERS CREATE FIGURES OF SPEECH

To create a hyperbole, a writer first thinks of a subject and then of a particular quality of that subject.

Subject: myself
Quality: energetic

Then the writer writes a sentence that exaggerates the quality:

> Today I could run around the world.

Personifications, similes, and metaphors are slightly more challenging to write. Again the writer begins with a subject and with a particular quality of that subject.

Subject: publishing the school newspaper
Quality: satisfying

Then the writer chooses a second subject that shares the same quality:

Second subject: making a slam dunk

Finally, the writer uses the second subject to describe the first:

> Publishing the school newspaper is as satisfying as making a slam dunk.

CASE STUDY: WRITING ABOUT FIGURES OF SPEECH

Mario's English teacher asked the class to write a paragraph about the figures of speech in a favorite poem. Mario decided to write about Sylvia Plath's "Mushrooms," on page 503.

Prewriting

Mario read the poem several times. Then he listed the following figures of speech in his prewriting notes:

- Personification: Mushrooms are personified throughout the poem. Specific examples include:
  "discreetly" (line 2)
  "Our toes, our noses" (line 4)
  "fists" (line 10)
  "Our hammers, our rams" (line 14)
  "We/Diet on water" (line 19)
  "Bland-mannered" (line 21)
  "we are meek" (line 26)
  "Nudgers and shovers" (line 28)
  "We shall.../Inherit the earth" (lines 31–32)
  "Our foot's in the door" (line 33)

- Metaphor: Personification is a type of metaphor. Other examples of metaphors include:
  "crumbs of shadow" (line 20)
  "We are shelves, we are/Tables" (lines 25–26)

Now that Mario had gathered enough information for his paragraph, he needed to organize it. He made the following rough outline:

- Introduction: Tell what poem I'm writing about. Introduce topic: figures of speech in the poem.

- Body: Give examples of personification and then examples of metaphor. Tell how each gives poem deeper meaning.

- Conclusion: Sum up main idea of paragraph—say that figures of speech make this poem especially vivid and imaginative.

Drafting and Revising

Mario wrote a draft of his paragraph, based on his outline and his prewriting notes. Then he revised his draft, making sure that his points were clear. He made a fresh copy of his revised draft for proofreading.

Proofreading and Publishing

Mario proofread his paragraph, correcting his errors in grammar, usage, spelling, and punctuation. Then he made a final copy and shared this copy with his parents before turning it in to his English teacher.

ACTIVITIES AND ASSIGNMENTS

A. Use Mario's notes and outline to write a paragraph about the figures of speech in Sylvia Plath's "Mushrooms," on page 503. Follow these steps:

1. Read the poem several times. Then reread Mario's prewriting notes. Write a topic sentence that introduces the main point of the paragraph.

2. Draft the rest of the paragraph. First discuss the use of personification in the poem and give examples. Then discuss how metaphor is used and cite specific examples.

3. Write a conclusion of one or two sentences, summarizing the main idea of your paragraph.

4. Revise your paragraph, using the Checklist for Revision on page 769. Then proofread your work carefully and make a clean final copy. Share your final copy with a small group of your classmates and with your teacher.

B. Write a paragraph about the figures of speech in one of the following poems: "Harlem Night Song," on page 558; "Blue-Butterfly Day," on page 559; "Silver," on page 564; "January," on page 576; "Winter Moon," on page 578; "The City Is So Big," on page 586; "Concrete Mixers," on page 587; or "The Story-Teller," on page 615. Follow these steps:

1. Select a poem and read it several times. Then copy the poem by hand onto a separate sheet of paper. This will help you to become familiar with the exact words and punctuation used by the poet.

2. On the copy, underline all the examples of figures of speech that you can find. List them in your notes under the following headings: Hyperbole, Personification, Simile, and Metaphor.

3. Decide which figure of speech you think is most important to the meaning of the poem. Begin your rough draft with a topic sentence that gives the title and author of the poem and introduces the central figure of speech.

4. Make an outline for the rest of your paragraph that shows the order in which you will present your information. Then finish your draft. Conclude with a summary of the main point of your paragraph.

5. Revise your draft. Make sure that all of your ideas are clear. Also check to see that your statements are supported by examples from the poem.

6. Proofread your paragraph for errors in spelling and mechanics. Then make a clean final copy for sharing with your classmates and with your teacher.

Lesson 7: Writing About Setting

WHAT IS SETTING?

The *setting* of a literary work is the time and place in which the action occurs. Setting is revealed by details that describe furniture, scenery, customs, transportation, clothing, dialects, weather, time of day, and time of year. Writers use images of sight, sound, touch, taste, and smell to create vivid settings.

The following passage is from the opening of Dorothy M. Johnson's short story, "The Day the Sun Came Out," on page 101. To create the setting for the story, the author uses details about transportation, scenery, historical time, economic conditions, and weather as well as images of sight and sound.

> We left the home place behind, mile by slow mile, heading for the mountains, across the prairie where the wind blew forever.
>
> At first there were four of us with the one-horse wagon and its skimpy load. Pa and I walked, because I was a big boy of eleven. My two little sisters romped and trotted until they got tired and had to be boosted up into the wagon bed.
>
> That was no covered Conestoga, like Pa's folks came West in, but just an old farm wagon, drawn by one weary horse, creaking and rumbling westward to the mountains, toward the little woods town where Pa thought he had an old uncle who owned a little two-bit sawmill.

THE FUNCTIONS OF A SETTING

A writer may use setting to serve one or more functions in a literary work. The chart on uses of setting in the right column lists some of the possible functions of setting.

CASE STUDY: WRITING ABOUT SETTING

Nora's English teacher asked the class to write about the setting in a literary work. Nora decided to write about the setting of "Paul Revere's Ride," on page 509.

USES OF SETTING

To create a mood: A description of an open wagon traveling across a huge expanse of windy prairie creates a lonely mood. Details about a sunny, fragrant field of flowers might create a happy, carefree mood.

To show the reader a different way of life: For example, through details about customs, furniture, and transportation, a reader can get a sense of what life was like in a different time in history or of how people live in a foreign country.

To make the action seem more real: Through vivid details and images, the reader is transported to the scene of the action. The reader can imagine the setting almost as if he or she were participating in the story.

To be the source of the conflict, or struggle, in a work: A character fighting a snowstorm, the heat of a desert, or a high mountain is in conflict with an element of the setting.

To symbolize an idea: For example, the ocean might symbolize the immense power of nature as compared to the puny strength of one person, or a springtime setting might symbolize new life and growth.

Prewriting

First Nora read the poem several times. Then she listed some of the details that helped to create the poem's setting:

- Time: midnight; April 18, 1775

- Historical Setting: just before the outbreak of the American Revolution

- Images of sight:
  "Just as the moon rose over the bay" (line 17)
  "A phantom ship, with each mast and spar/Across the moon like a prison bar" (lines 20–21)

"moonlight flowing over all" (line 41)

- Images of sound:
  "muffled oar" (line 15)
  "Silently rowed" (line 16)
  "his friend.../Wanders and watches with eager ears,/Til in the silence around him he hears" (lines 24–26)
  "startled the pigeons from their perch" (line 34)
  "Beneath...lay the dead/.../Wrapped in silence so deep and still/That he could hear.../The watchful night-wind" (lines 42–46)

Nora looked over the information she had gathered from the poem and thought about what function the setting served. She decided that it did two things: (1) It showed the reader what Boston was like in 1775, and (2) it created a mood.

Nora thought the second function was more important, so she decided that the topic of her composition would be how setting created a mood in "Paul Revere's Ride." To gather more ideas about this mood, Nora did some freewriting:

> The mood of the poem is one of waiting—there is a great deal of suspense, as if the setting—including the moon, the bay, the houses, etc.—is holding its breath in anticipation. The reader feels this tension, and when Paul Revere starts his ride, there is a sharp contrast—the silence is broken. The fact that the action takes place at midnight is important to the setting because midnight is a time of stillness.

Next Nora wrote a topic sentence for her composition:

> The setting of Henry Wadsworth Longfellow's "Paul Revere's Ride" creates a mood of stillness and anticipation.

Nora made an outline for her composition that showed the order in which she would present her information.

Drafting and Revising

Nora wrote a draft of her composition. When she reread her draft, she decided that she needed more specific examples to support her ideas. As she revised her paper, she added these examples.

Proofreading and Publishing

Nora proofread her composition, correcting errors in grammar, spelling, and punctuation. Then she made a clean copy of her paper and shared this copy with her classmates and with her teacher.

ACTIVITIES AND ASSIGNMENTS

A. Using Nora's prewriting notes from the case study, write a one- or two-paragraph composition about the setting of "Paul Revere's Ride." Follow these steps:

1. Read the poem carefully at least twice. Then read Nora's notes and add to your own notes any important details that she left out.
2. Make an outline for your composition. You may use Nora's topic sentence in your paper, or you may write your own.
3. Write a draft of your composition, based on your notes and your outline. Then revise your draft, making sure that it is clear and well organized.
4. Proofread your revised draft for errors in grammar, usage, spelling, punctuation, capitalization, and manuscript form. Then make a clean final copy of your composition, and share this copy with a small group of your classmates.

B. Select one of the following short stories for a one- or two-paragraph composition on setting: "The Land and the Water," on page 119; "Grass Fire," on page 129; "Crime on Mars," on page 137; "The Tell-Tale Heart," on page 145; or "The Drummer Boy of Shiloh," on page 151. Follow these steps when writing your paper:

1. Read the story once, and then freewrite about the impression the setting has made on you. Then read the story again, and list in your notes specific details from the story that help to create the setting.

2. Decide what you think is the most important function of the setting. Write a topic sentence that tells the title and author of the story and that introduces this function of the setting. Then make a rough outline for the rest of your composition.
3. Write a draft of your paper. Then revise the draft, using the Checklist for Revision on page 769.
4. Proofread your revised draft carefully. When you are certain that you have corrected all your errors, make a clean final copy. Share your composition with a small group of your classmates before handing it in to your teacher.

Lesson 8: Writing About Plot

WHAT IS PLOT?

Plot is what happens and how it happens in a narrative. A *narrative* is any work that tells a story, such as a short story, a novel, a drama, or a narrative poem. To understand a narrative work, a reader must first understand its plot.

THE PARTS OF A PLOT

The following is a list of events that might take place in a simple plot:

> A boy passes a pet store and sees a dog that he would like to own. The boy has no money, and his parents will not buy him the dog because they do not think that he is responsible enough to take care of it. The boy gets a job after school and earns enough money to buy the dog. The boy asks his parents if he can buy the dog with the money he has earned. The boy's parents see that he is responsible enough to earn the money for the dog, so they give him permission to buy it. The boy buys the dog.

These events may be grouped into parts of the plot, as follows:

1. *Inciting incident:* The inciting incident is an event that gives rise to the conflict. In the example, this event takes place when the boy sees the dog in the window of the pet store.
2. *Development:* In this part of the plot, events occur as a result of the central conflict. The development in the example includes all the events that occur while the boy is struggling to earn money to buy the dog.
3. *Climax:* The climax is the high point of interest or suspense in a story. In the example, the climax occurs when the boy asks his parents for permission to buy the dog. The reader wonders whether the boy's hard work will pay off.
4. *Resolution:* When the conflict ends, the plot has reached its resolution. In the example, the resolution occurs when the boy finally gets his dog.

Most narratives also have an *introduction*, or *exposition*, which is the section at the beginning of the work that introduces the setting and the major characters. Some narratives also have a *denouement*, which is made up of the events that take place after the resolution. In this section, the writer answers any questions about the plot that remain in the reader's mind.

A writer may use other variations on the standard plot form as well. For example, in some narratives the inciting incident occurs before the opening of the story. If the example had opened with the boy already working, the inciting incident would have occurred before the start of the narrative.

Sometimes the climax and the resolution are the same event. This would have been the case in the example if the boy had gone to ask his parents whether he could buy the dog and had found that they had already bought it for him.

A standard plot may be represented in diagram form as follows:

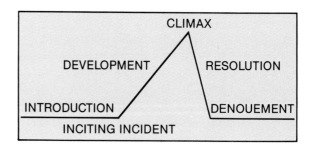

SPECIAL TECHNIQUES OF PLOT

Writers often use the following techniques to make their plots more interesting:

1. *Suspense:* This is the excitement or tension that keeps the reader interested in the plot of a narrative. A writer creates suspense by raising questions in the reader's mind about what will happen next.

2. *Foreshadowing:* This is a hint, or clue, about something that will happen later in the story.
3. *Flashback:* This is a section of a story that interrupts the normal sequence of events to tell about something that happened in the past.
4. *Surprise ending:* This is a conclusion to a story that the reader does not expect.

CONFLICT

Conflict is a struggle between opposing forces. Every plot must contain some kind of conflict—otherwise there would be no action. Although a story might have several different conflicts, short narratives usually have one central conflict involving the main character.

Conflicts can be external or internal. An *external conflict* takes place between a person or a group and some outside force. The outside force might be another person, a group, or a nonhuman obstacle such as a hurricane or a difficult homework assignment. An *internal conflict* takes place within a character's mind. For example, a character may struggle against the temptation to tell a lie.

Read the entries for Conflict and Plot in the Handbook of Literary Terms. Then read the following case study.

CASE STUDY: WRITING ABOUT PLOT

Gabe's English teacher asked the class to write a paragraph about plot. Gabe had enjoyed reading Shirley Jackson's "Charles," on page 73, so he decided to write about the plot of this short story.

Prewriting

First Gabe reread the story, paying special attention to details of the plot. Then he made the following chart of the parts of the plot:

- Introduction: The narrator introduces the main character, her son Laurie, who has just started kindergarten.
- Inciting incident: Laurie announces that

there is a boy at school named Charles who is very fresh and who was spanked by the teacher.

- Development: Laurie comes home from school every day with a new story about Charles. Laurie's parents become increasingly curious about this little boy.
- Climax and resolution: The narrator goes to a PTA meeting, hoping to meet Charles's mother. She asks Laurie's teacher about Charles, and the teacher says that there is no Charles in the class. (The reader and the narrator realize at once that Laurie is the one who has been misbehaving.)

Next Gabe looked for special plot techniques in the story. He made another list in his notes, as follows:

- Suspense: During the development, the reader wonders along with the narrator what Charles is really like and what his mother would be like.
- Foreshadowing: Laurie's story of how the entire class stayed after school with Charles sounds fishy. Also, at the beginning of the narrator's conversation with the teacher, the teacher says, "We had a little trouble adjusting, the first week or so, but now he's a fine little helper."
- Surprise ending: Charles turns out to be Laurie.

Gabe used his notes to make a rough outline for his paragraph.

Drafting and Revising

Gabe wrote a draft of his paragraph, based on his prewriting notes. Then he revised the draft to improve its wording and organization.

Proofreading and Publishing

Gabe proofread his paragraph carefully and

made a clean final copy of it. Then he shared his paragraph with his parents and with his teacher.

ACTIVITIES AND ASSIGNMENTS

A. Using Gabe's notes from the case study, write a paragraph about the plot of "Charles." Read the story carefully, review Gabe's notes, and write a topic sentence that tells how the plot makes the story interesting to read. Make an outline for the rest of your paragraph. Then finish your draft, revise it, and proofread it. Share your work with your classmates and with your teacher.

B. Choose one of the following short stories for a paragraph on plot: "Rain, Rain, Go Away," on page 13; "Christmas Day in the Morning," on page 21; "The Adventure of the Speckled Band," on page 27; "Accounts Settled," on page 47; "A Retrieved Reformation," on page 55; or "The Rule of Names," on page 63. Follow these steps:

1. Read the story twice. In your notes, list the events of the plot under the following headings: Introduction, Inciting Incident, Development, Climax, Resolution, and Denouement. Also make a list of the special plot techniques used in the story.

2. Write a topic sentence that tells the title and author of the story and that introduces the reason why you think the plot makes the story worth reading. Make a rough outline for the rest of your paragraph.

3. Finish the draft of your paragraph. Then revise and proofread your draft. Share your final copy with your classmates and with your teacher.

Lesson 9: Writing About Character

TYPES OF CHARACTER

The people and animals who take part in the action of a literary work are called *characters*. Some characters play very important roles in the plot. These are the *major characters*. Other characters play lesser roles and are known as *minor characters*. Normally a narrative focuses on the actions of a single major character, the *protagonist*. Sometimes there is another major character, called the *antagonist*, who is in conflict with the protagonist.

CHARACTERIZATION

A writer reveals what a character is like and how the character changes through the process of *characterization*. There are two primary methods of characterization: direct and indirect. In *direct characterization*, the writer simply tells the reader what the character is like. A statement such as "Sheila was a cheerful conspirator in many harmless pranks" is an example of direct characterization.

In *indirect characterization*, the writer shows what a character is like by describing what the character looks like, by telling what the character says and does, and by telling what other characters say about and do in response to the character. Some of these methods of characterization are very subtle. Tiny details that the writer provides about a character may contain important clues to the character's personality.

ELEMENTS OF CHARACTER

To analyze a character, a reader must think about many factors. These factors appear in the following list:

1. *Appearance:* What does the character look like? What kinds of clothing does the character wear? What do these aspects of appearance reveal about the character?

2. *Personality:* Does the character tend to be emotional or rational? shy or outgoing? skillful or clumsy? happy or depressed? caring or cold? honest or dishonest? a leader or a follower?

3. *Background:* Where did the character grow up? What experiences has he or she had? Is the character experienced or naive? What is the character's social status? How has the character been educated? What does the character do for a living? What are the character's hobbies or skills?

4. *Motivation:* What makes the character act as he or she does? What does the character like and dislike? What are the character's wishes, goals, desires, dreams, and needs?

5. *Relationships:* How is the character related to other characters in the narrative? How does he or she interact with these characters? What happens as a result of these interactions.

6. *Conflict:* Is the character involved in some conflict? If so, is this an internal conflict—one that takes place within the character's mind—or an external conflict—a struggle between the character and some outside force? Is the conflict ever resolved? If so, how?

7. *Change:* Does the character change in the course of the narrative? Does he or she learn or grow? In other words, is the character static (unchanging) or dynamic (changing)?

CASE STUDY: WRITING ABOUT CHARACTER

Ben's English class learned about the methods used by writers to characterize the people and animals in their works. Then his teacher asked the class to write a paragraph about the characterization of the protagonist in a short story. Ben decided to write about the main character in Juan A. A. Sedillo's "Gentleman of Río en Medio," on page 87.

Prewriting

Ben read the short story once. He did some freewriting to gather ideas about the main character, Anselmo:

> This character is very proud. He has lots of dignity. I would really trust him. He is a man of principle, although sometimes his principles seem a little strange... he refused to take more money for the land—he would only stick to the original bargain.

Ben read the story a second time and listed in his notes some specific examples from the story to support the ideas he had gathered in his freewriting. Then he made a rough outline for his paragraph.

Drafting and Revising

Ben wrote a draft of his paragraph, based on his prewriting notes and his outline. Then he revised his draft, using standard editorial symbols. Here is Ben's draft and the revisions that he made in it:

~~What a great guy!~~ The protagonist in Juan A. A. Sedillo's short story, "Gentleman of Río en Medio," is a very honest and principaled character. <ins>Anselmo</ins> Never tries to cheat anybody—he just wants to do the right thing. ~~You can tell~~ <ins>The reader knows</ins> this ~~cause of~~ <ins>by</ins> the way he ~~won't take~~ <ins>refuses to</ins> take more than the original ~~agreed on~~ <ins>(by set)</ins> price <ins>for his land.</ins> Anselmo is also a very proud man<ins>;</ins> his clothes are old and ragged<ins>,</ins> but he wears them like a gentleman. For example, he takes off his gloves, which have no fingers left in them, ~~very slow~~ <ins>in a</ins> and <ins>manner</ins> dignified<ins>.</ins> He is very civilized<ins>,</ins> too. He doesn't ~~jump right into~~ <ins>talk about</ins> business <ins>right away, but</ins> ~~He~~ discusses the weather first. This strange old man truly is a gentleman.

Proofreading and Publishing

Ben made a fresh copy of his draft and proofread it for errors in grammar, usage, spelling, and punctuation. Then he made a final copy of his paragraph and shared this copy with his class discussion group.

ACTIVITIES AND ASSIGNMENTS

A. Answer the following questions about the case study:
1. Why did Ben delete the first sentence in his rough draft?
2. What spelling errors did Ben correct?
3. Why did Ben add "Anselmo" to the beginning of the second sentence? Why did he not simply add "He"?
4. Why did Ben change "You can tell" to "The reader knows"?
5. What run-on sentence did Ben correct? How did he do this?
6. Why did Ben change "jump right into" to "talk about... right away"?
7. What other changes did Ben make? Why did he make them?

B. Choose one of the following short stories for a paragraph on character: "The House Guest," on page 79; "Raymond's Run," on page 91; "The Day the Sun Came Out," on page 101; "What Stumped the Blue-Jays," on page 107; or "The Day I Got Lost," on page 113. Follow these steps when planning and writing your paragraph:
1. Read the story and select a major character to write about. Freewrite about your impression of the character. Focus your freewriting on the character's outstanding qualities.
2. Reread the story and make a list of specific details from the story that reveal the character. After each detail, write down what it tells you about that character.
3. Look over your prewriting notes and decide what you think is the most interesting aspect of the character. Write a topic sentence that introduces this aspect as the main idea of your paragraph.

4. Organize your notes. For each idea you want to convey about the character, make sure that you have specific details from the story to support it. Then make a rough outline for your paragraph.

5. Write a draft of your paragraph, referring to your prewriting notes and to your outline as you write. Make sure to conclude with a sentence that summarizes the main point of your paper.

6. Use the Checklist for Revision, on page 769, to revise your rough draft. Then proofread your revised draft for errors in grammar, usage, spelling, punctuation, capitalization, and manuscript form.

7. Share the final copy of your paragraph with a small group of classmates before turning it in to your teacher.

Lesson 10: Writing About Point of View

WHAT IS NARRATION?

The act of telling a story is called *narration*. Literary works that tell stories are called *narratives*. Short stories, novels, plays, and narrative poems are types of narratives.

The writer of a narrative creates a voice to tell the story. This voice is the *narrator*. The type of narrator a story has determines the story's point of view.

WHAT IS POINT OF VIEW?

Point of view is the perspective from which a narrative is told. Imagine that a friend is telling you about a basketball game in which she played. Because your friend is a character in her own story, she will refer to herself as "I" and will describe what happened as she herself experienced it. Such a narrative, in which the narrator participates in the action, is told from the *first-person point of view*.

Now imagine that your friend is telling you a made-up story about a boy who wants a pet skunk. In this case the narrator will not refer to herself as "I" but will use third-person pronouns such as *he*, *her*, *them*, and *their* to refer to the characters in the story. This type of narrative, in which the narrator tells the story from outside the action, is told from the *third-person point of view*.

Once a writer has decided whether to use the first-person or the third-person point of view, he or she must then decide how much the narrator will know about the thoughts and feelings of each character in the story. A story told from the first-person point of view is almost always *limited*. The narrator knows only what is going on inside his or her own mind. A *first-person limited narrator* can report the words and actions of the other characters but not their thoughts or feelings.

A story told from the third-person point of view can also be limited. A *third-person limited narrator* can tell the reader what *one* of the characters is thinking and feeling but only what the other characters say and do.

A third-person narrator who knows what every character is thinking is called *omniscient*, or "all-knowing." A story told from the third-person omniscient point of view will include details not only about the words and actions of all its characters but also about their thoughts and feelings.

WHY WRITERS USE POINT OF VIEW

The point of view from which a story is told affects the way the reader experiences the narrative. For example, a story told from the point of view of a small child will be quite different from one told from the point of view of a college student. Even if the events of the stories are the same, the two points of view will give them completely different flavors.

CASE STUDY: WRITING ABOUT NARRATION AND POINT OF VIEW

Joyce's English teacher asked the class to write a paragraph about the point of view in a short story. Joyce selected Pearl S. Buck's "Christmas Day in the Morning," on page 21.

Prewriting

Joyce read the story and then thought about the point of view from which it was told. She knew that the voice telling the story had not referred to itself as "I," so the point of view was definitely not first-person. Next she asked herself whether the point of view was limited or omniscient. She recalled that the narrator had been able to tell about the thoughts and feelings of one of the characters, Rob. However, the voice related only the actions and words of the other characters in the story. Joyce decided that "Christmas Day in the Morning" was told from the third-person limited point of view.

Joyce did some freewriting to gather ideas about the story's point of view. Then she made a rough outline to organize her notes.

Drafting and Revising

Joyce used her notes and her outline to write the following draft of her paragraph:

> The point of view of Pearl S. Buck's short story, "Christmas Day in the Morning," is third-person limited. Because the narrator can look inside the head of the protagonist, Rob—none of the other characters. I guess she used this point of view to show how Rob saw things, both as an old man and as a fifteen-year-old kid. Even though so many years have past, Rob has similar feelings about Christmas, he has learned the true meaning of Christmas: love. He wants to show his love to his wife as he did to his pa. Also the point of view makes the flashback which takes place in Rob's mind possible.

Joyce revised her paragraph and made a fresh copy of it for proofreading.

Proofreading and Publishing

Joyce proofread her revised draft for errors in grammar, spelling, and punctuation. Then she made a final copy of her paragraph and shared it with her family before turning it in to her teacher.

ACTIVITIES AND ASSIGNMENTS

A. Revise and proofread Joyce's rough draft. Follow these steps:

1. Find Joyce's topic sentence. Does it express clearly the main point of her paragraph? If not, change it as necessary.
2. Read the rest of Joyce's paragraph. Is it well organized? Are there any sentences that should be moved? Are the main ideas supported by evidence from the story? Make the necessary revisions.

3. Has Joyce used appropriate language, avoiding slang and informal expressions? Correct any errors in word choice that you find in her paragraph.
4. When you have finished revising the paragraph, make a clean copy of it for proofreading. Then use the Checklist for Proofreading on page 772.
5. Make a final copy of the paragraph, and share this copy with your classmates and with your teacher.

B. Select one of the following short stories for a paragraph on point of view: "The Adventure of the Speckled Band," on page 27; "Accounts Settled," on page 47; "The House Guest," on page 79; "Raymond's Run," on page 91; "The Drummer Boy of Shiloh," on page 151; or "Grass Fire," on page 129. Follow these steps:

1. Read the story once and determine the point of view from which the story is told. Then read the story a second time, keeping in mind the question, "Why did the writer use this point of view?"
2. Freewrite about the point of view, or list ways in which the point of view contributes to the effect of the story. Then write a topic sentence that tells the most important way in which the point of view makes the story effective.
3. Make an outline for your paragraph that shows how you will organize your information.
4. Following your outline, write a draft of the paragraph. First write your topic sentence. Then write the body of your paragraph, supporting the main idea of your paper with evidence from the story. Finally, write a conclusion that summarizes the main point of your paragraph.
5. Revise your draft, making sure that all your ideas are clear.
6. Proofread your paragraph for errors in grammar, usage, spelling, punctuation, capitalization, and manuscript form. Make a clean final copy of your paragraph for sharing with your classmates and with your teacher.

Lesson 11: Writing About Theme

WHAT IS THEME?

The central idea or insight into life provided by a literary work is called its *theme*. The theme usually reveals an important point about human beings or about life. A statement of theme is a sentence that tells what message a writer wants to convey through a work.

Consider the theme of this poem by an unknown author:

The lightning bug has wings of gold,
The goldbug wings of flame;
The bedbug has no wings at all,
But it gets there just the same.

The poem is about bugs, but it also has a meaning beyond what it says about bugs. One way of stating the poem's theme is, "A person doesn't have to be wealthy or beautiful to make it through life."

Not every literary work has a theme. A complex mystery novel, for example, might be intended merely to entertain. It might contain no deeper meaning beyond the level of the plot.

HOW WRITERS PRESENT THEMES

In some cases a writer simply states the theme of a work. For example, in a short story, a character may make a statement that expresses the theme. A theme that is stated directly is said to be *explicit*.

In other cases, there is no statement of theme included in the work itself. The reader must infer the theme from clues in the work, such as what happens to the characters and how the conflicts are resolved. A theme that is not stated directly is *implicit*, or *implied*.

IDENTIFYING THE THEME OF A LITERARY WORK

It is not always easy to discover an implicit theme in a literary work. You might have to read a work several times to figure out what message the writer wants to communicate. The following list contains questions about several elements of a work that will help you to identify the theme:

1. *Title:* What does the title mean? Does it contain a clue to the theme of the work?
2. *Characters:* What is each of the characters like? Which characters are arrogant? Which are honest? Which are foolish? What happens to each of the characters as a result of his or her personality or actions? What does each character learn from his or her experiences? What can the reader learn from the experiences of the characters?
3. *Conflict:* How is the central conflict in the work resolved, or ended? Does the resolution contain a message about a particular moral or ethical issue?

Some literary works contain more than one theme. One reader might read a work and come to a certain understanding of its meaning, while another reader might read the same work and derive a completely different meaning. Both interpretations would be valid if they could be supported by evidence in the work.

CASE STUDY: WRITING ABOUT THEME

Marita's English teacher asked the class to select a short story and to write a paragraph about its theme. Marita decided to write about "The Ninny," by Anton Chekhov, on page 159.

Prewriting

Marita read the short story twice. Then she thought about the theme of the work. She tried to state the theme in a single sentence, as follows:

The governess in "The Ninny" is spineless and won't stand up for her rights.

Marita read her sentence and realized that it was too narrow. It did not tell what important message the story conveyed to its readers. She rewrote her sentence as follows:

> People who are spineless can be taken advantage of by stronger, dishonest people.

Marita rewrote her sentence several more times before she had a statement she was satisfied with. Then she read the story again and made notes of specific details that supported the theme. Next she organized her notes and made a rough outline for her paragraph.

Drafting and Revising

Marita used her notes and her outline to write a draft of her paragraph. Then she revised her draft, using standard editorial symbols. Here is Marita's first draft, with her revisions:

¶The theme of Anton Chekhov's "The Ninny" can be ~~put~~ *stated as follows:* "By refusing to stand up for your rights, you make your life very difficult and risk being taken advantage of." In the story, the narrator plays a trick on his spineless governess. He ~~says~~ *asks her to* come into ~~my~~ *his* study. He ~~is very forceful and~~ tells her *very forcefully* that ~~he~~ is *they* deducting ~~from her~~ *pay* money for every Sunday and holiday and ~~because Kolya tore~~ *for "allowing" his son to tear* his coat. *He even lies about agreements that they made.* The young woman doesn't protest, ~~she just~~ *her eyes merely fill up with tears and* ~~looks sad. You can tell that she's upset.~~ Finally the ~~boss~~ *narrator* tells her that he's only *playing a trick* kidding and ~~she gets~~ *gives her* the full amount. ~~How can anyone be so meek?~~ *As she leaves, he wonders why anyone would make life so hard by being meek.*

Proofreading and Publishing

Marita proofread her paragraph carefully. Then she made a clean final copy and shared it with her class discussion group.

ACTIVITIES AND ASSIGNMENTS

A. Answer the following questions about the case study:

1. Why did Marita change "put" to "stated as follows"?
2. What spelling error did Marita correct?
3. How did Marita revise the original sentence "He says come into my study"? Why did she change it?
4. Why did Marita change "because Kolya tore" to "for 'allowing' his son to tear"?
5. Why did Marita change "she just looks sad" to "her eyes merely fill up with tears" and delete the sentence "You can tell that she's upset"?
6. Why did she change "boss" to "narrator"?
7. How did Marita revise the last sentence of her paragraph? Why is her new sentence a better conclusion to her paper?
8. What other changes did Marita make? Why did she make them?
9. Are there any changes that you think should still be made in Marita's paragraph? What are these changes?

B. Choose one of the following short stories for a one- or two-paragraph composition on theme: "The Six Rows of Pompons," on page 163; "Thank You, M'am," on page 169; "The Gift-Giving," on page 175; "The Man Without a Country," on page 185; or "Flowers for Algernon," on page 201. Follow these steps when planning and writing your composition:

1. Read the short story once and write down a sentence that explains what you think the story means. Then reread the story and look for evidence to support your statement of theme. List this evidence in your prewriting notes.
2. Organize your notes in a logical order. Then make an outline for your composition.
3. Write a draft of your composition from your notes and your outline. First write a topic sentence that tells the title and author of the story and briefly describes the theme. Then write the body of your paper, giving specific

details from the story that support your topic statement. Conclude with a sentence or two that summarize the main point of your paper.

4. Revise your draft. Make sure that all of your points are clear and that they are supported by examples from the story.

5. Proofread your composition for errors in grammar and usage, spelling, punctuation, capitalization, and manuscript form.

6. Make a clean final copy of your composition. Share it with a small group of your classmates before handing it in to your teacher.

SECTION 3: UNDERSTANDING THE WORK AS A WHOLE: INTERPRETATION AND SYNTHESIS

Lesson 12: Writing About a Short Story

There are many elements that must be covered when writing about a short story as a whole. The following list of elements and questions about them will help you to gather information for a composition about a short story.

1. *Author:* Who is the author of the story?
2. *Title:* What is the story's title? Does this title suggest the story's subject or theme?
3. *Setting:* What are the time and place of the story? What mood is created by the setting? Does the setting determine the action or conflict of the story?
4. *Point of view:* Is the story written from the first-person or third-person point of view? Is the narrator limited or omniscient?
5. *Central conflict:* What is the central conflict of the story? Is this conflict internal or external? If the conflict is external, is it a conflict between two people, between a person and nature, between a person and society, or between a person and a supernatural force?
6. *Plot:* What are the major events of the story? What happens in the introduction? What is the inciting incident? What happens during the development? What is the climax of the story? How is the central conflict resolved? What, if anything, happens after the resolution? That is, does the story have a denouement?

   What special plot devices are used in the story? Does the story make use of foreshadowing or flashbacks? Is the story suspenseful? If so, what expectations on the part of the reader create this suspense? Does the story have a surprise ending?
7. *Characterization:* Who is the main character, or protagonist? Who are the other major and minor characters? What is revealed in the story about each character's appearance, personality, background, motivations, and relationships? What conflicts do these characters face? Which of these characters changes in the course of the story and in what ways? What roles do the minor characters play in advancing the action of the story?
8. *Devices of sound and figures of speech:* Does the story make use of special devices of sound such as onomatopoeia or parallelism? of figures of speech such as metaphor or hyperbole?
9. *Theme:* What is the theme, or message, of the story? How is this theme revealed?

When you write about a short story, you will probably want to select one of the elements from the above list as the focus of your composition. Then you can discuss how the other elements relate to it. For example, you might decide to focus on the theme of a particular short story. In your introductory paragraph, you would tell the title and author of the story and introduce its theme. In the first body paragraph, you might give a brief summary of the story's plot. In the second body paragraph, you might describe the main character and the conflict that he or she faces in the story. You would devote other body paragraphs to other important elements in the story that related to the theme. Finally, you would write a concluding paragraph that explained how the theme was significant for real people.

CASE STUDY: WRITING ABOUT A SHORT STORY

Chuck's English class had studied all the

different elements of short stories. His teacher asked the class to write a composition of three to five paragraphs that analyzed an entire short story. Chuck decided to write about Edward Everett Hale's "The Man Without a Country," on page 185.

Prewriting

Chuck read the story once. He felt that the theme was an especially important one, so he decided that this theme would be the focus of his composition. Chuck did some freewriting to gather ideas about the theme:

> This story is so emotional! I never thought that a story about patriotism could be so moving. I really felt compassion for Nolan, even if he did swear that he didn't ever want to hear about the U.S. again—the story really made me think about what it means to be an American.

Next, to make sure that he had a clear idea of exactly what the theme was, he tried to state it in a sentence in his own words:

> Americans should realize how lucky they are to be citizens of the United States.

Chuck reread the story. He then made a chart in his notes listing other elements of the story and telling how they related to the theme. Here is a section from Chuck's prewriting notes:

- Author: Edward Everett Hale

- Title: "The Man Without a Country." The title suggests both the subject and the theme of the story.

- Point of view: First-person limited. This point of view allows the author to tell the story from the perspective of someone who had met Nolan and could appreciate his suffering.

- Central conflict: Nolan vs. his punishment. Nolan struggles to keep his feelings of longing for home under control. The conflict is internal, but the reader can see how painful it is for Nolan. This adds to the power of the theme.

Plot:

- Introduction: The young Nolan blindly joins Aaron Burr in his rebel activities.

- Inciting incident: When standing trial for his crime, Nolan says that he would like never to hear of the United States again.

- Development: The court grants Nolan his wish. He is transferred from ship to ship for the rest of his life, never being allowed to discuss his country with anyone. On one of these ships, he meets the narrrator and tells him that he should realize how much the United States means to him.

- Resolution: On his deathbed, Nolan begs the captain of the ship to tell him what has happened in the United States in the last fifty years. The captain does, and Nolan dies in peace.

- Denouement: The captain discovers a note left by Nolan asking that a gravestone be erected in the U.S. with his name and some patriotic words on it.

- Characterization: Nolan, the protagonist, is characterized as lonely and withdrawn after losing his country. This shows how important the United States really is—it's tragic that Nolan has to lose it before he appreciates it.

Chuck made an outline for his composition. The outline showed that his composition would have four paragraphs, as follows:

- Introductory paragraph:
  Author
  Title
  Theme

- First body paragraph:
  Summarize plot.
  Tell how plot reveals theme.

- Second body paragraph:
  Describe characterization of Nolan.
  Tell how this relates to theme.

- Concluding paragraph:
  Restate theme.
  Tell how theme is significant for all Americans.

Drafting and Revising

Chuck used his outline and his prewriting notes to write a draft of his composition. Then he revised his draft.

Proofreading and Publishing

Chuck proofread his composition and then made a clean copy of it. He shared his final copy with his classmates and his teacher.

ACTIVITIES AND ASSIGNMENTS

A. Read "The Man Without a Country," on page 185. Then use Chuck's notes and outline from the case study to write a four-paragraph composition on the short story. Revise and proofread the composition. Share your final copy with your classmates and your teacher.

B. Select one of the following short stories for a three- to five-paragraph composition: "Christmas Day in the Morning," on page 21; "The Day the Sun Came Out," on page 101; "The Tell-Tale Heart," on page 145; "The Six Rows of Pompons," on page 163; "The Gift-Giving," on page 175; or "Flowers for Algernon," on page 201. Follow the same steps that Chuck followed in the case study. Share the final copy of your composition with a small group of your classmates and with your English teacher.

Lesson 13: Writing About a Poem

In this handbook you have learned about some elements found in poetry—images, special devices of sound, figures of speech, theme, and so on. When you write about a poem, you must consider all of these elements and how they contribute to the poem as a whole.

It is important to understand a poem fully before you begin writing about it. Therefore, you should read the poem several times, both silently and aloud, to familiarize yourself with the way the poem achieves its effect. Make sure that you understand the meanings of all the words in the poem—if any are unfamiliar, look them up in a dictionary. Listen to the way the poem sounds, noticing the effect of the particular words the author has chosen. If the poem is a concrete poem, look carefully at the arrangement of the words on the page and think about how the shape relates to the poem's meaning. To make sure that you understand each line of the poem, try to paraphrase it, or put it into your own words.

The following list of questions will be helpful when you gather information for writing about a poem:

1. *Author:* Who is the poem's author?
2. *Title:* What is the title of the poem? Does the title suggest the poem's subject or theme?
3. *Genre:* What is the poem's genre, or type? Is it a lyric poem—a highly musical work that expresses emotion? Is it a narrative poem— one that tells a story? Is it a concrete poem— one with a shape that suggests its meaning?
4. *Stanza form:* Is the poem divided into stanzas? If so, how many lines does each stanza have? Is the poem written in some standard stanza form such as couplet, quatrain, sonnet, haiku, or limerick? Does each stanza function as a separate unit of meaning, like a paragraph in a composition?
5. *Devices of sound:* Is the poem in free verse or in some regular meter? If the poem has some regular meter, how many feet are there in an average line? What kind of foot is most common in the poem?

   Does the poem have a regular rhyme scheme? If so, what is this rhyme scheme?

   Does the poem make use of onomatopoeia? alliteration? consonance? assonance? internal rhyme? euphony? cacophony? parallelism? repetition? Does it have a refrain? What examples can you find of these devices?
6. *Imagery:* What images of sight are used in the poem? of sound? of taste? of touch? of smell? What effects do these images have?
7. *Figures of speech:* Does the poem contain examples of metaphor? of simile? of personification? of hyperbole? of understatement? Does the poet make use of symbols? puns? allusions? paradoxes? irony?
8. *Other literary devices:* What is the poem's general mood? Does this mood change in the course of the poem?

   What is the poem's setting? How is the setting related to the poem's mood? to the action of the poem?

   What seems to be the poem's central message, or theme? What do you think the writer's purpose was?

   Is the poem written in complete sentences?

   Does the poem use punctuation, capitalization, or spacing in special ways?

   Does the poem invite the reader to contrast two or more things?

CASE STUDY: WRITING ABOUT A POEM

Cory's English teacher asked the class to write a composition analyzing a favorite poem. Cory decided to write about Naoshi Koriyama's "Jetliner," on page 536.

Prewriting

First Cory read the poem silently. He took note of the words *pondering* and *chandelier*, which were defined in the footnotes. Then he read the poem aloud, listening to the sounds of the words as he read them. He read the poem a third time and looked for examples of images and figures of speech. Cory then read the chart in this lesson and answered the questions in his notes. Here is a section from Cory's prewriting notes:

- Author: Naoshi Koriyama

- Title: "Jetliner"

- Stanza form: The poem has four stanzas of unequal length. Each stanza describes a distinct part of the process of an airplane's taking off.

- Devices of sound: The poem is written in free verse. There is no rhyme scheme.
  Onomatopoeia:
  "burning heart beating like thunders" (line 8);
  "howling, shouting, screaming, and roaring" (line 16)
  Alliteration:
  "*sh*arp eyes *sh*ining" (line 4);
  "*b*urning heart *b*eating" (line 8);
  "*s*oftly lifting . . . *s*oaring higher" (lines 19-20)
  Euphony:
  "soaring higher and higher and higher still/piercing the sea of clouds/up into the chandelier of stars" (lines 20-22)
  Cacophony:
  "kicking the dark earth hard" (line 12);
  "violent kick" (line 17)
  Repetition:
  "deep, deep breath" (line 5);
  "kicking the dark earth hard/. . ./kicking the dark earth harder" (lines 12-14);
  "then he dashes, dashes like mad,

like mad" (line 15);
"soaring higher and higher and higher still" (line 20)

Cory finished answering the questions and then made a rough outline for his composition. He decided that the main point of his paper would be how the poem uses devices of sound and figures of speech to create a vivid picture of an airplane taking off.

Drafting and Revising

Cory wrote a draft of his composition from his outline and his prewriting notes. Then he revised his composition to make it clearer and more focused.

Proofreading and Publishing

Cory proofread his paper carefully. He made a clean final copy of his composition and shared it with his class discussion group.

ACTIVITIES AND ASSIGNMENTS

A. Finish Cory's prewriting and then write a composition about the poem "Jetliner." Follow these steps:
1. Read the poem several times, both silently and aloud. Then answer the questions in the list above under the headings Imagery, Figures of speech, and Other literary devices. Organize your information into an outline for your composition.
2. Write a draft of the composition according to your outline. Then revise your draft, making sure that your main points are clear.
3. Proofread the composition for errors in spelling and mechanics. Then make a clean copy of your paper and share it with a small group of your classmates.

B. Select one of the following poems for a two- or three-paragraph analysis: "Barbara Frietchie," on page 525; "Lyric 17," on page 532; "Reflections Dental," on page 542; "Ring Out, Wild Bells," on page 544; "Taught Me Purple," on page 551; "Four Little Foxes," on page 556;

"Blow, Blow, Thou Winter Wind," on page 566; "January," on page 576; "Southbound on the Freeway," on page 588; "Identity," on page 598; or "The Choice," on page 604. Follow these steps when planning and writing your paper:

1. Read the poem silently. Look up any unfamiliar words in a dictionary. Read the poem aloud, paying attention to the way the poem sounds. Then read the poem silently again and look for examples of imagery and figurative language. In your prewriting notes, answer the questions from the chart in this lesson.

2. Decide what you think is the purpose of the poem. Write a topic sentence for your composition that tells this purpose. Then organize your notes to show how the writer accomplishes the purpose through specific techniques used in the poem. Make a rough outline that shows what information you will present in each paragraph of your paper.

3. Write a draft of your composition. Revise your draft, making sure that it has an introduction with a clear topic sentence, a body with supporting evidence for the topic sentence, and a solid conclusion.

4. Proofread your composition using the Checklist for Proofreading on page 772.

5. Make a clean final copy of your paper and share it with your classmates and with your teacher.

Lesson 14: Writing About Drama

DRAMA AS LITERATURE

One way to experience a drama is to read it as you would any other form of literature. Drama shares many common elements with short stories, novels, and narrative poetry. Dramas have plots, conflicts, settings, and characters. Like other types of writing, dramas have themes and use imagery, devices of sound, and figurative language.

DRAMA AS PERFORMANCE

There is one aspect of drama that sets it apart from all other types of literature. Drama is written specifically to be performed by actors in front of an audience. To experience the full effect of a drama, you must see it as a stage production. When you read a drama, you should constantly be thinking about what the work would be like in a performance.

The printed form of a drama is called its *script*, and it is composed of dialogue and stage directions. *Dialogue* simply means the words spoken by the characters. There are no quotation marks around the dialogue in a drama; each line follows the name of the character who speaks it. *Stage directions* are instructions for how the performance should appear and sound to the audience. When reading a drama, you will see the stage directions in brackets or parentheses; they will be italicized or underlined. They give such information as how the stage should look; how the characters should move and speak; what special effects of sound and lighting should be used; and what properties, or movable objects, should appear on stage.

Since a drama may be experienced in two very different ways—as literature or as performance—there are many possible approaches to writing about a drama. You could simply analyze one aspect of the drama, such as characteriza-tion, plot, conflict, or setting. A paper focusing on one of these topics would be very similar to the compositions you have written in the other parts of this handbook. Another approach to writing about a drama is to write about some aspect of its performance. You might describe how you would go about constructing the set for a particu-lar scene in the drama or what costumes a cer-tain character would wear. If you were able to attend an actual performance of the drama, you could write a critique of that performance, telling what you thought was good about it and what you thought should have been done differently.

CASE STUDY: WRITING ABOUT DRAMA

Pauline's English class studied how drama was similar to and different from other types of literature. Then her teacher asked the class to write an analysis of a drama. Pauline decided to write about *The Ugly Duckling,* the play by A. A. Milne, on page 245.

Prewriting

Pauline read the drama very carefully. Since she had not seen a performance of the play, she decided to write about it as a work of literature. She made the following list of plot elements:

- Introduction: In the conversation between the King and the Chancellor, we learn that Prince Simon is on his way to meet Princess Camilla. The Princess is not beautiful, and the King and Queen are worried that the Prince will refuse to marry her.

- Inciting incident: This takes place before the opening of the play. The King and Queen have decided to let Dulcibella stand in for the Princess at her first meeting with the Prince.

- Development: Their Majesties' plan goes into action. Prince Simon and Princess Camilla meet accidentally and fall in love.

- Climax and resolution: Prince Simon's attendant must solve a riddle, but he is too stupid to figure it out. The Prince steps in and makes an excuse for him, and the wedding can go on as planned.

- Denouement: Princess Camilla tells her parents that she adores the Prince and leaves to prepare for the wedding. The King remarks that she doesn't look quite so plain any longer.

- Special techniques: The focus of the plot is the irony of situation that arises from the chance meeting of the Prince and Princess.

Pauline made one further note about *The Ugly Duckling*:

> This play is especially enjoyable in its written form because many of the stage directions contain many witty remarks that an audience would not experience.

Pauline decided that the main point of her paper would be to explain why *The Ugly Duckling* is a pleasure to read as well as to see performed. She made an outline for her composition showing how she would organize the information in her prewriting notes into three paragraphs.

Drafting and Revising

Pauline wrote a draft of her composition. She read her draft and realized that it did not really accomplish her purpose, which was to show why the drama was enjoyable to read. When she revised her composition, she added more specific details about the plot of the drama to make her writing more convincing.

Proofreading and Publishing

Pauline made a fresh copy of her revised draft and proofread it for errors in spelling and mechan-ics. Then she shared the final copy of her composition with her parents and her English teacher.

ACTIVITIES AND ASSIGNMENTS

A. Use Pauline's notes to write a three-paragraph composition about *The Ugly Duckling*. Follow these steps:

1. Read the drama carefully. Add to Pauline's notes any important details that you find are missing. Then make an outline for your composition. Your outline should have one section for each paragraph of your composition. In the introductory paragraph, tell what drama you're writing about and introduce the main point of your paper. In the body paragraph, give evidence to support your main point. In the concluding paragraph, summarize the main idea of your composition and perhaps comment on the theme of the play.

2. Use your outline to write a draft of your composition.

3. Revise your paper using the Checklist for Revision on page 769.

4. Proofread your composition and make a clean copy of it. Then share your final copy with your classmates and your teacher.

B. Select one of the following dramas for an original composition: *The Romancers,* on page 263; *Let Me Hear You Whisper,* on page 277; or *The Diary of Anne Frank,* on page 303. Follow these steps:

1. Read the drama carefully. Decide what approach you will take in writing about it—you can analyze it strictly as literature, or you can write about some aspect of its performance.

2. Decide on a single element of the drama—a particular character, the plot, the setting, and so on—that will serve as the focus of your composition. Write a topic sentence that explains the main idea of your paper.

3. Make an outline for your composition. Be sure that you plan for a clear introduction, body, and conclusion.

4. Write a draft of your paragraph. Then revise it, making sure that all of your ideas are expressed clearly and are supported with evidence from the drama.
5. Proofread your composition using the Checklist for Proofreading on page 772. Then make a clean final copy of your paper for sharing with a small group of your classmates and with your teacher.

SECTION 4: JUDGING A LITERARY WORK: EVALUATION

Lesson 15: Evaluating a Literary Work

WHAT IS AN EVALUATION?

An *evaluation* of a literary work is a judgment about its quality or value. Consider the following poem on page 578:

WINTER MOON

Langston Hughes

How thin and sharp is the moon tonight!
How thin and sharp and ghostly white
Is the slim curved crook of the moon tonight!

Here is a statement that evaluates the poem:

Langston Hughes's poem, ''Winter Moon,'' is effective because it uses sense images so well. The poem gives readers a vivid, intense experience of the painful emotions surrounding a winter moon.

The evaluation expresses an opinion about the poem, not a fact. However, the opinion must be supported by facts. Consider the following evaluation of the same poem:

Langston Hughes's poem, ''Winter Moon,'' is effective because it uses sense images so well. The poem gives readers a vivid, intense experience of how comforting and cheerful a winter moon can be.

This statement also expresses an opinion, but it is not a valid opinion. That is, the opinion cannot be backed up by facts about the poem. The moon's ''thin and sharp'' edges suggest a painful image of touch, and the ''ghostly white'' color of the moon evokes a frightening, eerie feeling. Therefore, the evidence from the poem does not support the claim that it gives the reader a ''comforting and cheerful'' experience.

CRITERIA FOR EVALUATION

When you evaluate something, you need a set of *criteria*, or standards, for your judgment. The following list includes some of the most common criteria used for evaluating literature:

1. *Originality:* A work that deals with a subject never dealt with before or that approaches a topic in a new and different way is said to show originality. Writers who avoid trite or cliched material and who show their readers fresh ways of looking at the world generally receive favorable evaluations of their work.

2. *Consistency or completeness of effect:* A writer usually tries to create a certain effect in a literary work. If the effect is spoiled through the author's carelessness, the overall quality of the work is lowered. For example, consider the following haiku:

Loose creaking floorboards—
I tiptoe through dark shadows.
    Boy, am I hungry!

The first two lines create a serious, suspenseful mood, but the third line does not complete this effect. Therefore, the poem probably would not be evaluated favorably.

3. *Importance:* Some works are considered to be of higher value than others because they deal with topics of greater importance. A nonsense poem about how many jellybeans a boy can eat would not be valuable in terms of its message. A poem whose theme was world hunger, on the other hand, might be evaluated favorably because of the importance of its message.

4. *Moral or ethical message:* In many works, the theme contains a message about how people should live their lives. A reader who agrees with the message will consider the work to be of greater value than a reader who does not agree with the message. For example, a per-

son who believed the statement "It is important to stand up for one's own rights" would probably place a high value on the short story, "The Ninny," on page 159.

5. *Clarity:* Good literature should present the writer's ideas clearly. This does not mean that works that are difficult to understand at first are inferior to simple ones. Some of the best literary works require careful study before the reader can understand and appreciate what the writer has intended. However, if a work is difficult to make sense of because it is simply written in a careless or confusing manner, then the work will probably be judged to be of poor quality.

CASE STUDY: EVALUATING A LITERARY WORK

Cara's English teacher asked the class to write an evaluation of a poem. Cara decided to write about Walter de la Mare's "Silver," on page 564.

Prewriting

Cara read the poem several times, silently and aloud. Then she did some freewriting about the effect that the poem created:

> The title says it all—everything in this poem turns silver when the moon's beams hit it. Even things you wouldn't think of like a dog's paws and a mouse's claws. The poem makes me think of moonlight as especially beautiful—I hadn't ever really thought about how things looked in it before. Every line in the poem shows how the moonlight turns something silver.

Next Cara applied the criteria for evaluation in this lesson to the poem. Here is a section from Cara's prewriting notes:

- Originality: The topic—moonlight—isn't particularly original. However, the way the poet describes it is—for example, he says that even a mouse's claws look silver in the moonlight.

- Completeness of effect: The poem never strays from its purpose of describing the moonlight. The theme of silver is carried throughout the poem.
  The mood—one of quiet, peaceful beauty—is consistent throughout the poem.

- Clarity: The poem is not confusing or unclear. It is fairly simple, but very effective.

Cara decided that what made the poem especially valuable was the completeness of the effect that it created through images of sight. She made this the main point of her evaluation, and she wrote a topic sentence that introduced this idea. Then she made an outline for her paper that showed how she would organize the information she had gathered in her prewriting.

Drafting and Revising

Cara wrote a draft of her evaluation. When she read what she had written, she realized that some of her ideas would be unclear to her readers. She revised her draft, adding more specific details to make her main points clearer.

Proofreading and Publishing

Cara proofread her draft, correcting errors in grammar and usage, spelling, punctuation, and capitalization. Then she made a final copy of her evaluation for sharing with her classmates and with her teacher.

ACTIVITIES AND ASSIGNMENTS

A. Use Cara's prewriting notes to write an evaluation of "Silver." Follow these steps:

1. Read the poem several times. Review Cara's notes and add any important details that you find are missing from them.

2. Decide what criterion will be the focus of your evaluation. Write a topic sentence that tells the author and title of the poem and the main criteria that you will be using to evaluate it. Make a rough outline for your paper.

3. Write a draft of your paper. Make sure that it has a clear introduction, body, and conclusion. In the conclusion, make a general statement about the quality of the work as a whole.

4. Revise and proofread your composition. Make a final copy to share with your classmates in a small discussion group. Then turn your evaluation in to your teacher.

B. Select one of the following works for a one- to three-paragraph evaluation: "Charles," on page 73; "Gentleman of Río en Medio," on page 87; "The Day I Got Lost," on page 113; "The Tell-Tale Heart," on page 145; "Thank You, M'am," on page 169; *Let Me Hear You Whisper*, on page 277; "Harriet Tubman: Guide to Freedom," on page 383; "The Trouble with Television," on page 463; "Dial Versus Digital," on page 477; "Paul Revere's Ride," on page 509; "The Secret Heart," on page 548; "Blue-Butterfly Day," on page 559; "Forgotten Language," on page 565; "The City Is So Big," on page 586; or "Identity," on page 598. Follow these steps:

1. Read the work carefully—if it is a poem, read it several times. Then freewrite about why you liked or did not like the work.

2. Apply the criteria listed in this lesson to the work. In your notes, write down how the work meets or does not meet each criterion.

3. Decide which criterion is the most appropriate for evaluating the work. Write a topic sentence that introduces the work and the central criterion that you will use to judge it. Then make an outline for the rest of your composition.

4. Draft, revise, and proofread your evaluation. Share your final copy with your classmates and with your teacher.

Lesson 16: Writing a Comparative Evaluation

WHAT IS A COMPARATIVE EVALUATION?

You learned in the last lesson that an evaluation is a judgment about the quality of a literary work. A *comparative evaluation* is one in which two or more works are evaluated side by side, exploring what makes one better or worse than the other(s).

One way to write a comparative evaluation is simply to apply the criteria listed in the preceding lesson to each of the works. For example, you might explain why one short story was more original than another short story.

Another approach to writing a comparative evaluation is to select a literary element that the works have in common—such as a subject, a theme, or a special technique—and to write about why one work is a better example of that element. For example, if you were comparing two poems that were both about a baseball game, you might tell why one was more vivid and interesting than the other.

STEPS IN WRITING A COMPARATIVE EVALUATION

Begin by selecting the works that you will compare. The works must have something in common. You might choose to compare two short stories, three poems, or a drama and a short story with similar themes. When you have decided what specific works you will compare, list in your notes their authors and titles and the feature they have in common as follows:

- Works to be compared: John Greenleaf Whittier's poem, "Barbara Frietchie," and Henry Wadsworth Longfellow's poem, "Paul Revere's Ride"
- Feature to be compared: originality in presenting a historical event

The next step is to study each of the works carefully and to decide which author has done the best job of handling the feature. Gather evidence from the works to support your opinion.

When you write your comparative evaluation, begin with an introductory paragraph that tells what works you will be comparing and what feature you will be discussing. Then write body paragraphs about each work. In each body paragraph, give details from the work to show how the author has dealt with the feature you are comparing. Make sure that the details you give support your opinion about which work is superior. Finally, write a concluding paragraph that sums up your opinion about the comparative values of the works.

CASE STUDY: WRITING A COMPARATIVE EVALUATION

Joanna's English teacher asked the class to write a comparative evaluation of two poems.

Prewriting

Joanna decided to compare two poems with similar subjects. She selected Robert Frost's "Blue-Butterfly Day," on page 559, and John Updike's "January," on page 576, because each described a particular season. She wrote the following information in her prewriting notes:

- Works to be compared: "Blue-Butterfly Day," by Robert Frost, and "January," by John Updike
- Feature to be compared: imagery used to portray a season

Joanna studied the poems very carefully and decided that she liked the Updike poem better because it had more images of scenery. She then gathered evidence from the poems to support her evaluation. Joanna made a rough outline for her paper showing how she would organize her information into four paragraphs.

Drafting and Revising

Joanna wrote a draft of her evaluation from her notes and her outline. Here are the first two paragraphs of her paper:

> Robert Frost's poem, "Blue-Butterfly Day," and John Updike's poem January both describe a certain season. Both are excellent, but maybe Updike's might be called "better" due to there are more images of scenery. The Frost one describes mainly only the butterflies.
>
> The images in "Blue-Butterfly Day" include "sky-flakes" in line 2, "unmixed color on the wing" in line 3, and "flowers that fly" in line 5. Their nice images. There are also images of touch as well. Like in the Last two lines: "They lie closed over in the wind and cling/Where wheels have freshly sliced the April mire." These images are farely specific—they describe the butterflies but not much info about the scenery around.

Joanna finished her draft. She then revised it, adding more details from the poems and making her sentences clearer. Then she made a fresh copy of her revised draft for proofreading.

Proofreading and Publishing

Joanna proofread her composition carefully. Then she shared the final copy of her comparative evaluation with her parents, her classmates, and her teacher.

ACTIVITIES AND ASSIGNMENTS

A. Finish writing Joanna's draft from the case study. Follow these steps:
1. Read the poems very carefully. Decide whether or not you agree with Joanna's evaluation. If you do agree, gather information to support it; if you do not, gather information to support your own evaluation.

2. Rewrite the first two paragraphs of Joanna's evaluation if you disagree with her comparison of the poems. Finish the composition, writing another body paragraph discussing the Updike poem and a concluding paragraph.

3. Revise the draft. Make sure that your ideas will be understood by your readers. Then proofread the paper for errors in spelling and mechanics. Share the final copy of your evaluation with a small group of your classmates and with your teacher.

B. Write a comparative evaluation of one of the following pairs of literary works (suggestions for features to compare are in parentheses): "Barbara Frietchie," on page 525, and "Paul Revere's Ride," on page 509 (effective presentation of historical events); "Jetliner," on page 536, and "Song of the Sky Loom," on page 579 (effective use of figures of speech); "Four Little Foxes," on page 556, and "Ring Out, Wild Bells," on page 544 (effective use of devices of sound); or "Identity," on page 598, and "The Choice," on page 604 (effective examination of the subject of choices). Follow these steps:

1. Read both works carefully. Freewrite about why you liked one better than the other. Then select one literary element or criterion of evaluation that shows how the two works differ in quality. Write a topic sentence that explains why you think this criterion shows one work to be better than the other.

2. Gather information from both works that supports your topic sentence. Then organize your notes and make an outline for a four-paragraph composition. The first paragraph should introduce the two works and include your topic sentence. The second and third paragraphs—the body paragraphs—should each discuss one of the works and give examples that support your topic sentence. The concluding paragraph should summarize the main point of your evaluation.

3. Revise and proofread your draft. Then make

a final copy of your comparative evaluation and share it with a small group of your classmates who also wrote about the two works that you selected. Finally, share your paper with your teacher.

SECTION 5: WRITING CREATIVELY
Lesson 17: Writing a Short Story

In the preceding lessons of this handbook, you have learned how to analyze literature written by other writers. Now you will have the chance to write your own literary works. In this lesson you will learn about the process of writing a short story.

FINDING A STORY IDEA

The first step in planning a short story is to think of a subject to write about. It is sometimes helpful to brainstorm about the elements of short stories that you have studied in this handbook—setting, conflict, character, and theme, for example. The following are some suggestions for finding an idea for your short story:

1. Think of a particular time and place that interest you. The setting of a short story often gives rise to the action. For example, if you decided to set your story in the distant future, you might write about a conflict between characters over whether or not to place an earth colony on the planet Venus.
2. Imagine an interesting conflict that might involve the main character of your short story. The conflict might be internal—within the mind of the character—or external—between the character and another character, a group, or a nonhuman force such as a tornado.
3. Think of an interesting person whom you know in real life and create a character that has some of the qualities of this person.
4. Take an idea that you believe in strongly and think of a situation that would illustrate this idea. For example, if you think that honesty is an important value, create a story that will show why it is important.

DEVELOPING YOUR IDEA

When you have found an idea for one part of your story, start planning the other parts and thinking about how they will all fit together. The following list of questions will help you to develop the various parts of your story:

1. *Setting:* When and where does the story take place? What images of sight, sound, touch, taste, and smell can I use to describe the setting?
2. *Character:* Who is the main character? What is he or she like? How will I show what the character is like in the story? What other major characters will appear in the story? What will they be like? How will these characters relate to the main character? What minor characters will appear in the story? What roles will they play?
3. *Conflict:* What conflict will the main character be involved in? Will the conflict be internal—within the character's mind—or external—between the character and some outside force?
4. *Plot:* What events will take place in the story, and in what order?
   Introduction: What background information will I need to supply about the setting? about the characters?
   Inciting incident: What event will cause the central conflict of the story?
   Development: What events will occur as a result of the inciting incident?
   Climax: What will be the high point of interest or suspense in the story?
   Resolution: How will the conflict in the story end?
   Denouement: What events, if any, will occur after the resolution?
5. *Theme:* What will be the main idea of my story? How will I reveal this idea?
6. *Point of view:* Will the story be told from the

first-person point of view—by a narrator who is a character in the story? Or will the story be told from the third-person point of view—by a narrator who is outside the action of the story? Will the narrator be limited or omniscient?

CASE STUDY: WRITING A SHORT STORY

Peter's English teacher asked the class to write an original short story for a literary contest in the school. Peter was excited about entering the contest, so he began thinking about the assignment right away.

Prewriting

First Peter needed an interesting idea for his story. He read the suggestions for finding a story idea in this lesson and brainstormed about setting, conflict, character, and theme. Here is a section from Peter's prewriting notes:

- Setting: the school cafeteria; a hut in the jungle; a deserted island; my dad's office building; on board a submarine

- Conflict: a fight with my best friend; a tiger is about to attack; there's no food or water; stuck in an elevator; deciding whether to attack an aircraft carrier

- Character: myself; my sister; my English teacher; an exchange student from India; the man who owns the candy store near the school

- Theme: friendship is really important; going to school isn't as bad as it seems sometimes; being in a position of authority means you have to make difficult decisions

Peter looked over his prewriting and decided that he would write a story about how he and his best friend got stuck in an elevator one day. He then made a list of the events that would take place in his story:

- Introduction: David and I skip school and go to my dad's office building. Dad was a kid once, so we hope he'll think it's funny. He works on the fourteenth floor, so we get into the elevator.

- Inciting incident: The elevator gets stuck somewhere near the ninth floor.

- Development: At first we think it's neat to be stuck, but then we start to get scared. We talk about what would happen if we never got out of the elevator. We wonder what our English teacher, Mrs. Mehl, would say tomorrow in class if we had died while skipping school.

- Climax: The elevator starts to shake. We're certain that we're going to fall to the bottom of the elevator shaft and die.

- Resolution: The elevator door opens. We take the stairs down to the ground floor.

- Denouement: We decide to go back to school, and we return just in time for English class. After class, we talk about how we've never enjoyed a class so much!

Peter planned to tell the story from the perspective of a character who takes part in the section, so the point of view would be first-person limited. Now that he had gathered all of his information, he was ready to begin writing his short story.

Drafting and Revising

Peter wrote a draft of his story, telling each of the events in order. Then he revised his draft, adding details that would create suspense for the reader.

Proofreading and Publishing

Peter proofread the revised draft of his story for errors in spelling and mechanics. Then he made three final copies of his short story—one for his friend David, one for his English teacher, and one for the literary contest.

ACTIVITIES AND ASSIGNMENTS

A. Use Peter's notes from the case study to write a short story. Revise and proofread the story. Then share it with your classmates and with your teacher.

B. Write an original short story about any subject that interests you. Follow these steps when planning and writing your story.

1. To think of an idea for your story, brainstorm about setting, conflict, character, and theme as Peter did in the case study. Pick one or two of the best ideas. Then develop the other parts of your story.

2. Make a list in your notes of the events that will take place in your story under the following heading: Introduction, Inciting incident, Development, Climax, Resolution, and Denouement. If you wish to do so, you may also include any of the following elements: Suspense, Foreshadowing, Flashbacks, and Surprise ending.

3. Write a draft of your short story. Revise the draft, making sure that your writing is vivid and keeps the reader interested in the story.

4. Proofread your story for errors in grammar and usage, spelling, punctuation, capitalization, and manuscript form. Then make a final copy of your short story and share it with your classmates and with your teacher.

Lesson 18: Writing a Poem

The type of poem a writer chooses to write depends upon his or her subject and purpose. For example, if a poet wanted to describe a brief scene in a striking, vivid manner, a haiku would be an appropriate choice. A haiku consists of three short lines. The first and third lines have five syllables, and the second line has seven syllables. Haiku often use images of sight, sound, touch, taste, and smell. The following is an example of a haiku:

> The spring lingers on
> In the scent of a damp log
> Rotting in the sun
>
> —Richard Wright

Sometimes the subject of a poem is one that can be represented by a simple shape. In this case, a writer may decide to write a concrete poem. The letters, words, and punctuation in a concrete poem are arranged in a shape on the page that suggests its subject or meaning. For example, the following traditional Native American poem, is a concrete poem:

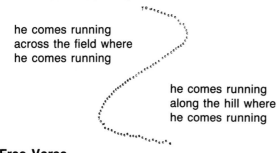

A POEM ABOUT A WOLF MAYBE TWO WOLVES

he comes running
across the field where
he comes running

he comes running
along the hill where
he comes running

Free Verse

Many modern poets write a type of poetry known as *free verse*. Free verse has no formal restrictions—that is, it does not have a specific meter, rhyme scheme, or stanza form. It is usually written in unrhymed lines of varying lengths, and it may or may not be broken up into stanzas. Punctuation is sometimes used in unusual ways to create certain effects. Naoshi Koriyama's

poem, "Jetliner," on page 536, is written in free verse. Here is the third stanza from that poem:

> then...after a few...tense moments.../
> of pondering
> he roars at his utmost
> and slowly begins to jog
> kicking the dark earth hard
> and now he begins to run
> kicking the dark earth harder
> then he dashes, dashes like mad, like/
>   mad
> howling, shouting, screaming, and/
>   roaring

Notice that Koriyama has used ellipses in the first line of the stanza to emphasize the "tense moments...of pondering." The poem is not divided into sentences, nor is the first word in each line capitalized.

The lack of formal structure does not mean that writing a poem in free verse does not require much thought, however; it simply means that the effect of the poem is created from something other than regular meter and rhyme scheme. After reading the following case study, you will have the chance to write your own poem in free verse.

CASE STUDY: WRITING A POEM

Aimee's English class learned about several different types of poems. Then her teacher asked the class to write an original poem in free verse.

Prewriting

Aimee needed to think of a subject for her poem. She brainstormed to gather a number of possible ideas. Then she selected the idea she liked best—she decided to write about her favorite hobby, horseback riding.

To gather ideas about her topic that she could use in her poem, Aimee freewrote for three minutes. She wrote down everything that came into her mind when she thought about horseback riding without worrying about punctuation or spelling.

Here is Aimee's freewriting:

> I love the exhilarating feeling of the wind in my face as I ride along—it's so refreshing and exciting and the horse—my favorite horse is named Comet—is so powerful but he's under my control—I can move along so effortlessly but I feel like I'm part of the horse at the same time and it's *my* legs that are galloping not just his. We're like one unit moving as a single person-horse.

Next Aimee wrote down the ideas she wanted to include in her poem in complete sentences, as if she were writing a paragraph about the topic. Here is what she wrote:

> I stand looking at my favorite horse, Comet. He is a graceful yet powerful animal. Then I get into the saddle, and when I give the signal, we start to move. We are no longer a person and a horse—we are a single person-horse. Comet moves into a gallop at my command—I'm in complete control—and we glide along effortlessly. I feel the wind in my face and I feel exhilaration and excitement at the same time. Somehow I'm more "me" when I'm riding Comet.

Aimee then made a list of the images of sight, sound, and touch that she would use in her poem.

Drafting and Revising

Aimee wrote a draft of her poem in free verse form. Here is her unrevised draft:

> I face him—
> A massive, powerful Other
> With muscles rippling under
> A shimering coat of hair.
> He looks at me calmly,
> As if giving consent,
> And I climb aboard his great back.
> A tiny signal that only he and I
> Know about
> And we are moving—
> No longer a person
>   and
>   a horse
> But now a single person-horse.
> We glide along the ground—
> His legs that are my legs
> Beat out a regular rhythm

> On the hard ground.
> The wind slaps onto my face
> To remind me that now I'm really
> Alive—
> Perhaps more alive then when
> I was just me
> Stumbling around
> On two legs.

Aimee gave her poem a title: "Comet." Then she revised her draft, changing some words to make the poem flow more smoothly. When she was sure that her poem achieved the effect she intended it to, she made a clean copy of her revised draft for proofreading.

Proofreading and Publishing

Aimee proofread her poem for errors in spelling and punctuation. Then she made two final copies of her poem, one for her teacher and one for the school literary magazine.

ACTIVITIES AND ASSIGNMENTS

A. Revise the first draft of Aimee's poem in the case study. Change any words that you feel spoil the effect of the poem, and add a few more images of sight, sound, or touch where appropriate. Then proofread the poem and make a clean final copy of it. Share this copy with a small group of your classmates and with your teacher.

B. Write an original poem in free verse. Follow these steps:

1. To gather possible ideas for your poem, brainstorm for three to five minutes. Then select the best idea to be the subject of your poem.

2. Freewrite about your subject. Write down everything that comes to mind, especially any personal experiences you've had with the subject.

3. Using your freewriting as a guide, write down in paragraph form what you want to say in your poem. Organize your paragraph in the order in which you plan to present your ideas in your poem.

4. Make a list of images of sight, sound, touch, taste, and smell that could be used to describe the subject. Also write down any figures of speech—hyperbole, personification, metaphor, or simile—that you might use in your poem.

5. Write a draft of your poem in free verse. Feel free to use punctuation and capitalization in innovative ways to express your ideas. Remember—you do not have to write in complete sentences if you do not wish to do so.

6. Revise your poem. Make sure that there are no lines or words that spoil the effect you are trying to create. If your poem is not very vivid, add more images or figures of speech.

7. Proofread your poem carefully. Then make a final copy of it for sharing. Read your poem aloud to a small group of your classmates before turning it in to your English teacher.

Lesson 19: Writing a Short Dramatic Sketch

A *dramatic sketch* is a short scene, serious or comic, that makes a single point. Like a full-length drama, a dramatic sketch can be read in its written form or performed by actors before an audience.

ELEMENTS OF A DRAMATIC SKETCH

The title of a dramatic sketch is followed by a list of characters. The sketch itself is made up of dialogue and stage directions. The *dialogue*, or the words spoken by each character, follows the name of the character that speaks it. The characters' names are capitalized, as in these lines of dialogue from *The Romancers*, on page 264:

PERCINET. What?
SYLVETTE. Nothing!
PERCINET. Something which made you blush as
          red as a rose.
SYLVETTE. Nothing, I say.

The *stage directions* in a dramatic sketch tell how the sketch is to be performed on stage. They give information about how the setting should appear to the audience; how the characters should move and speak; what *properties*, or movable objects, should be used in the performance; and what special effects of lighting and sound should be used. Stage directions are italicized or underlined, and they appear in brackets or parentheses. Here are stage directions from Act I, Scene 2 of *The Diary of Anne Frank*, on page 303:

[MR. FRANK *stops abruptly as he hears the sound of marching feet from the street below. Everyone is motionless, paralyzed with fear.* MR. FRANK *goes quietly into the room on the right to look down out of the window.* ANNE *runs after him, peering out with him. The tramping feet pass without stopping. The tension is relieved.* MR. FRANK, *followed by* ANNE, *returns to the main room and resumes his instructions to the group.*]

PLANNING A DRAMATIC SKETCH

When you plan to write a dramatic sketch, you must give careful consideration to all the elements that will make up the sketch. You must decide what the setting of the sketch will be and how that setting will be reproduced on stage. You must think about what you want each of the characters to look like and what costumes they will wear. You must decide how each character will move and speak. As in planning any narrative work, you must decide what events will take place in the sketch and in what order.

WRITING A DRAMATIC SKETCH

As you draft the sketch, you should bear in mind that it is meant to be performed for an audience. Stop from time to time and read the dialogue aloud to make sure that it sounds natural. Be sure that the setting is one that can be represented fairly easily on a stage. Where necessary, include stage directions to instruct the actors how to move and speak and the stage crew how to use special effects of lighting and sound.

CASE STUDY: WRITING A SHORT DRAMATIC SKETCH

Shirley's English teacher asked the class to write a short dramatic sketch based on a folk tale or a narrative poem. Shirley decided to use John Greenleaf Whittier's poem, "Barbara Frietchie," on page 525.

Prewriting
Shirley read the narrative poem several times. She thought about the setting and made the following notes about it:

- Time: cool September morning; 1860's
- Place: Frederick, Maryland

- Description of setting: cobblestone street with homes on both sides; lots of church spires in the distance

- Lighting: morning sun

- Properties: United States flag of the 1860's

Next Shirley thought about the characters and how she would portray each of them in a stage production. She made the following chart describing the characters in her prewriting notes:

Barbara Frietchie

- Appearance: old; bent over; gray hair; wearing a long skirt with an apron and a blouse

- Personality: proud; stubborn; brave

- Speech: loud, spirited, high-pitched voice

- Movement: slow, but deliberate and unafraid

Stonewall Jackson

- Appearance: tall and strong; wearing a slouched hat and a Confederate uniform; riding on horseback

- Personality: noble; a tough leader, but sensitive

- Speech: loud, strong voice, but a man of few words

- Movement: self-confident; gestures are bold and definite

Confederate soldiers

- Appearance: wearing Confederate uniforms

- Movement: obedient

Shirley listed, in order, the events that would take place in her dramatic sketch. Here are her notes:

- Barbara Frietchie appears on the empty street and picks up an American flag that is lying on the ground.

- She disappears into her house with the flag.

- The flag appears on a staff emerging from Barbara Frietchie's attic window.

- Stonewall Jackson leads rebel troops into the town; he looks around.

- Jackson sees the flag and orders his men to shoot it down.

- The Confederate soldiers aim their rifles at the house and shoot down the flag.

- When the firing has stopped, Barbara Frietchie appears at her window and says to Jackson and his men that they should shoot her instead of the flag.

- Jackson is moved by the old woman's courage and orders his men not to fire. The troop moves on through the town.

- The flag, now in shreds, flies from Barbara Frietchie's attic window all day while rebel troops march through the streets.

Drafting and Revising

Shirley wrote a draft of her dramatic sketch. First she wrote its title and the list of characters. Then she wrote the dialogue and stage directions that described the action of the sketch. When she had finished writing, she revised her draft, making sure that the dialogue sounded natural. She also added more stage directions to make the action clear.

Proofreading and Publishing

Shirley proofread her sketch for errors in spelling and mechanics. She and some of her friends performed the sketch for the rest of the class.

ACTIVITIES AND ASSIGNMENTS

A. Use Shirley's prewriting notes from the case study to write a short dramatic sketch based on "Barbara Frietchie." Start by creating a title and list of characters. Then write the dialogue and the stage directions. Revise and proofread the sketch, and share it with your classmates and your teacher.

B. Write an original dramatic sketch based on one of the following works: "The Adventure of the Speckled Band," on page 27; "Harriet Tubman: Guide to Freedom," on page 383; "Paul Revere's Ride," on page 509; "William Stafford," on page 517; "Hammerman," on page 655; "The Foggy Stew," on page 669; "Davy Crockett," on page 679; or The Call of the Wild, on page 695. Follow these steps:

1. Select a single scene from the narrative to portray in your sketch. Make a list of the characters in the scene and describe how each will look, act, and speak.

2. Think about how the setting of the scene could be reproduced on a stage. Write down your ideas for making the set in your notes.

3. List, in order, the events that will take place in your sketch.

4. Think of a title for your sketch and write it at the top of your paper. Then list the characters and give a brief description of each.

5. Write the dialogue and the stage directions for your sketch. Stop writing from time to time to read the dialogue aloud. Make sure that you include enough stage directions to make the action clear.

6. Revise and proofread your sketch. Suggest to your teacher that the sketch be performed or read aloud in front of the class.

Lesson 20: Writing a Personal Essay

A *personal essay* is a form of nonfiction writing that allows a writer to share his or her thoughts, feelings, and experiences with others. When you write a personal essay, you speak in your own voice about something important to you.

A personal essay is similar in some ways to the compositions about literature that you have learned about in preceding lessons. When you write, you must be sure that your essay has a clear introduction, body, and conclusion. You need a topic sentence that is supported by evidence. However, the evidence that you will use in a personal essay will not be from a literary work—it will be from your own thoughts and experiences.

The topic of a personal essay should be something especially important to you. Once you have decided on a topic, try freewriting to gather information for your essay. Write everything that you know and feel about the topic. Next you must decide what the purpose of your writing will be. Ask yourself whether you want to tell a story, to explain or describe something, or to persuade your readers to do or to believe something. Once you have a definite purpose in mind, you should write a sentence that tells what this purpose is. This sentence will be your thesis statement.

Include your thesis statement in the introduction of your essay. Then, in the body of your essay, give evidence to support the thesis statement. For example, if your thesis statement were something like ''Yellowstone National Park is a great place to go for a family vacation,'' you might list in the body all the interesting things you and your family did when you went there. In the last section of your essay, the conclusion, summarize your main point.

When you revise your essay, make sure that you have made all of your ideas very clear. Also check to see that each statement in your writing is supported by evidence. Finally, proofread your essay and make a final copy for sharing.

CASE STUDY: WRITING A PERSONAL ESSAY

Howard's English class learned how personal essays are a way to share one's thoughts and feelings with others. Then his teacher asked the class to write an essay on any topic that was important to them.

Prewriting

Howard needed to come up with a topic for his essay. He tried brainstorming for five minutes, writing down all the possible topics he could think of. Here are some of the ideas that Howard considered:

- The time my paintings were displayed in the lobby of the school and everyone liked them

- Why math is my favorite subject in school

- How to draw birds

- Why it's important to treat people fairly

- The time I tried out for the basketball team and didn't make it

Howard decided to write about his experience of trying out for the basketball team. He wasn't sure that he could state in a sentence exactly why the event was significant to him, so he tried freewriting to gather ideas. Here is Howard's freewriting:

When I didn't make the basketball team I was a mess. I vowed I'd never play basketball ever again. I was sure I was going to make the team. It was all I could do not to cry. I thought I'd never play hoop again but my friends were really nice about it though. When my mom and dad came home from work it was awfull—they marched in with big grins—thinking I had made the team. After about a week though I realized being so down in the dumps wasn't worth it. And I missed playing basketball just for fun—so I just lived with my disappointment and life went on as usual. Now I think back and realize that what I thought was so terrible really wasn't. Its OK to be disappointed sometimes. I got over it. I still play basketball and it's still fun and I still do my best. I'm even going to try out again for the team next year.

Howard read his freewriting and thought about the significance of his experience. He drafted the following thesis statement for his essay:

> I was really counting on making the basketball team, but when I didn't, it wasn't the end of the world.

He realized that the sentence was a bit too narrow, so he rewrote his thesis statement as follows:

> When you count on something and it doesn't come through, it's not the end of the world.

This sentence would inform his readers that his story had significance for everyone, not just for himself.

Howard made a rough outline for his essay. The outline showed how he would organize the introduction, body, and conclusion of his writing.

Drafting and Revising

Howard wrote a draft of his essay and then revised it, as shown in the box, with Howard's changes marked with standard editorial symbols.

Proofreading and Publishing

Howard proofread his draft. Then he made a final copy of it and shared it with his classmates and with his teacher.

ACTIVITIES AND ASSIGNMENTS

A. Answer the following questions about the case study.
1. What run-on sentence did Howard correct when he revised his draft? What sentence fragments?
2. Where did Howard change language that was too informal?

Last year I tried out for the basketball team, Sure I'd make it. I didn't. Although it took me a while to get over it, I realized that when you count on something and it doesn't come through, it's not the end of the world.

I got to school early the day the team list was posted outside the gym, eager to see my name. My name wasn't there, and I was really upset. I felt like walking out of school and going home and hiding in my room.

My friends saw that I was upset about something. When I told them I hadn't made the team, they said all kinds of things. They said, "Well, at least you tried your best." Or they said, "Gee, I'm sorry to hear it." They seemed to understand how much it meant to me, which helped. Soon I even wanted to played basket ball again.

I could have stopped doing things where I might not succeed, but then I wouldn't do very much. I'm still disappointed when things don't turn out the way I want, but I know I can handle it. In fact I still practice my jump shot and plan to try out for next years team.

3. Where did Howard combine sentences to make his writing smoother?

4. What corrections would Howard still have to make during proofreading?

B. Write your own personal essay. Follow these steps:

1. Think of a topic that is very important to you. If you need to do so, try brainstorming to gather ideas for possible topics.

2. When you have decided on a topic, try prewriting techniques such as freewriting, clustering, analyzing, questioning, or making charts and lists to gather information for your essay.

3. Decide what the purpose of your writing will be—to tell a story, to explain or describe something, or to persuade. Write a thesis statement that tells this purpose.

4. Make an outline that shows what information you will include in the introduction, body, and conclusion of your essay.

5. Use your outline to write a draft of your essay. Write as many drafts as you need to write. Then revise the draft that you are most pleased with. Make sure that your writing accomplishes its purpose.

6. Proofread your essay using the Checklist for Proofreading on page 772. Then make a clean final copy of your essay and share it with your classmates and with your teacher.

HANDBOOK OF LITERARY TERMS AND TECHNIQUES

ACT   See *Drama.*

ALLITERATION   *Alliteration* is the repetition of initial consonant sounds. Advertisers use alliteration to catch the ear of the reader or viewer, as in "*Books for a Buck.*" In poetry alliteration is used to create a musical or rhythmic effect, to emphasize key words, or to imitate sounds. Consider the alliteration in Kenyan poet John Roberts's "The Searchers":

> I remember a dog ran out from an alley,
> *S*niffed my trousers, *s*cented rags
> And as I stooped to pat him ran back,
> *Cl*aws *cl*icking on the asphalt.

In these lines alliteration of the *s* sounds links two images of smell, while the consecutive *cl* sounds in the last line mimic the "clicking" of the dog's claws.
See *Onomatopoeia* and *Repetition.*

ALLUSION   An *allusion* is a reference to a well-known person, place, event, literary work, or work of art. The title of A. A. Milne's play *The Ugly Duckling*, on page 245, alludes to a fairy tale by Hans Christian Andersen. The allusion invites the reader to compare the character Princess Camilla to the swan in Andersen's fairy tale. The Bible and classical mythology provide two of the most common sources of literary allusions. May Swenson's poem "By Morning" alludes to a famous Biblical story of the miraculous feeding of the Israelites:

> By morning we'll be children
>   feeding on manna
>
> a new loaf on every doorsill

Writers usually do not explain their allusions. They expect that their readers will be familiar with the things to which they refer. An active reader will think about the meaning of every allusion that he or she encounters.

ANAPEST   See *Meter.*

ANECDOTE   An *anecdote* is a brief story about an interesting, amusing, or strange event. Writers and speakers use anecdotes to entertain and to make specific points. In the excerpt from *Davy Crockett*, on page 679, Adrien Stoutenburg tells a series of anecdotes about a legendary American folk hero, including a story about how Davy Crockett met and named his pet bear, Death Hug. The bear rescued Davy from a crack left by an earthquake. Davy hugged the bear in gratitude, and the bear nearly hugged Davy to death.

ANTAGONIST   An *antagonist* is a character or force in conflict with the main character, or protagonist. A character who acts as an antagonist usually desires some goal that is at odds with the goals of the protagonist. The struggle between the two, or central conflict, is the foundation of the story's plot. In Ursula K. Le Guin's "The Rule of Names," on page 63, the protagonist, Mr. Underhill, wants to guard and keep his treasure. Blackbeard, the antagonist, wants to take the treasure away from the wizard.

ATMOSPHERE   See *Mood.*

AUTOBIOGRAPHY   *Autobiography* is a form of nonfiction in which a person tells his or her own life story. An autobiographer may tell his or her entire life story or may concentrate on only part of it. Maya Angelou writes about her childhood in *I Know Why the Caged Bird Sings*. Eudora Welty's *One Writer's Beginnings* describes how she became a writer. Autobiographies often include most of the elements of good fiction: interesting stories and events, well-developed characters, and vivid description of settings.

BALLAD   A *ballad* is a songlike poem that tells

a story, often one dealing with adventure and romance. Ballads have four- to six-line stanzas, with regular rhythms and rhyme schemes. Many ballads have a *refrain*, a line or group of lines repeated at the end of each stanza.

The earliest ballads, such as "Lord Randall" and "Barbara Allan," were not written down but rather were composed orally and then sung. Then they were passed by word of mouth from singer to singer and from generation to generation. Thus the ballads often changed dramatically over the course of time. By the time modern scholars began to collect folk ballads, most ballads existed in many different versions. Many writers of the modern era have created *literary ballads*, imitating the simplicity, structure, and diction of the ancient ballads. For example, Henry Wadsworth Longfellow's "Paul Revere's Ride," on page 509, borrows many elements from the folk ballad tradition.

BIOGRAPHY *Biography* is a form of nonfiction in which a writer tells the life story of another person. People often write biographies of people who are famous for their achievements. Ann Petry's *Harriet Tubman: Guide to Freedom* is an example of biography. Biographies are considered nonfiction because they deal with real people and events. Still, a good biography shares many of the qualities of all good narrative writing.
See *Autobiography*.

BLANK VERSE *Blank verse* is poetry written in unrhymed iambic pentameter lines. This form should not be confused with *free verse*, which is poetry that has no regular meter. A great deal of English poetry is written in blank verse because its meter is natural to the English language and because serious subjects are often best dealt with in unrhymed lines. William Wordsworth's "There Was a Boy" is in blank verse:

There was a boy; ye knew him well, ye cliffs
And islands of Winander! Many a time,
At evening, when the earliest stars began

To move along the edges of the hills,
Rising or setting, would he stand alone.

CENTRAL CONFLICT See *Conflict.*

CHARACTER A *character* is a person or animal who takes part in the action of a literary work. The *main character*, or protagonist, is the most important character in the story, the focus of the reader's attention. Often the protagonist changes in some important way during the course of the story. A *minor character* takes part in the story's events but is not the main focus of attention. Minor characters sometimes help the reader learn about the main character.

Fictional characters are sometimes described as either round or flat. A *round character* is fully developed. The writer reveals the character's background and his or her personality traits, both good and bad. A *flat character*, on the other hand, seems to possess only one or two personality traits and little, if any, personal history. Characters can also be described as dynamic or static. A *dynamic character* changes in the course of a story. A *static character* does not change. Philip Nolan, in Edward Everett Hale's "The Man Without a Country," on page 185, is a round, dynamic character. In contrast, Paul Revere, in Longfellow's poem, on page 509, is flat and static. See *Characterization, Hero/Heroine,* and *Motivation.*

CHARACTERIZATION *Characterization* is the act of creating and developing a character. Writers use two methods to create and develop characters—direct and indirect. When using *direct characterization*, the writer actually states a character's traits, or characteristics. Paul Annixter used direct characterization in the following passage from "Accounts Settled," on page 47:

Timber-bred, he knew the woods and creatures as well as his father, and never before had he feared any of them. But something about this valley had filled him with dread from the first.

When using *indirect characterization*, the writer allows the reader to draw his or her own conclusions based on information presented by the author. In ''The Adventures of the Speckled Band,'' on page 35, Arthur Conan Doyle provides indirect characterization of Dr. Roylott by means of his appearance, words, and actions:

> He stepped swiftly forward, seized the poker, and bent it into a curve with his huge brown hands.

> ''See that you keep yourself out of my grip,'' he snarled, and hurling the twisted poker into the fireplace he strode out of the room.

CINQUAIN   See *Stanza.*

CLIMAX   See *Plot.*

CONCRETE POEM   A *concrete poem* is one with a shape that suggests its subject. The poet arranges the letters, punctuation, and lines to create a visual image on the page. Guillaume Apollinaire's ''Crown'' is a concrete poem. Its letters and words are arranged in the shape of a jeweled crown.

CONFLICT   A *conflict* is a struggle between opposing forces. Conflict is one of the most important elements of stories, novels, and dramas because it causes the actions that form the plot. In an *external conflict* a character struggles against some outside person or force, such as a storm, a jealous enemy, or a social convention. The conflict between Mr. Underhill and Blackbeard, in ''The Rule of Names,'' on page 63, is an external conflict.

In an *internal conflict* the struggle takes place within the protagonist's mind. The character struggles to reach some new understanding or to make an important decision. Philip Nolan, in ''The Man Without a Country,'' on page 185, experiences an inner conflict as he comes to realize the importance of home and country. Literary works can have at the same time, several conflicts, both internal and external. The most important conflict in a work is called the *central conflict.* See *Plot.*

COUPLET   See *Stanza.*

DACTYL   See *Meter.*

DENOUEMENT   See *Plot.*

DESCRIPTION   A *description* is a portrait, in words, of a person, place, or object. Descriptive writing uses images that appeal to the five senses—sight, hearing, taste, smell, and touch.

In her poem ''Desert Noon,'' Elizabeth Coatsworth uses images of sight to create a description of a desert scene in southwestern California:

> When the desert lies
> Pulsating with heat
> And even the rattlesnakes
> Coil among the roots of the mesquite
> And the coyotes pant at the waterholes—
> Far above,
> Against the sky,
> Shines the summit of San Jacinto,
> Blue-white and cool as a hyacinth
> With snow.

See *Image.*

DEVELOPMENT   See *Plot.*

DIALECT   A *dialect* is a form of a language spoken by people in a particular region or group. English, for example, has numerous dialects. The English spoken in London differs from the English spoken in Liverpool. Likewise, the English spoken in Boston differs from the English spoken in Texas. Dialects differ in pronunciation, grammar, and word choice. Often they reflect the economic, geographc, and cultural differences among speakers of the same language.

Writers use dialects to make their characters seem true to life. For example, in ''The House Guest,'' on page 82, the character named Bridgie speaks in the dialect of Northern Ireland:

> ''Ya won't peach on me? Ya won't tell? Sometimes I just like swingin' around the neighborhood. I won't get lost and shame ya.''

Mark Twain, Rudyard Kipling, and Zora Neale

Hurston are three well-known writers who make effective use of dialect in their works.

DIALOGUE   A *dialogue* is a conversation between characters. Dialogue helps to make stories more interesting and more realistic. In poems, novels, and short stories, dialogue is usually set off by quotation marks, as in this example from "The Day the Sun Came Out," by Dorothy M. Johnson:

> "Mushrooms ain't good eating," I said. "They can kill you."
> "Maybe," Mary answered. "Maybe they can. I don't set up to know all about everything, like some people do."

In a play, dialogue simply follows the name of the character who is speaking, as in these lines from *Let Me Hear You Whisper*, by Paul Zindel:

HELEN: I don't have a TV.
MISS MORAY: I'm sorry.
HELEN: I'm not.

See *Dialect* and *Drama*.

DIMETER   See *Meter*.

DRAMA   A *drama* is a story written to be performed by actors. Although a drama is meant to be performed, one can also read the written version, or script, which contains the dialogue and stage directions. *Dialogue* is the words spoken by the actors. *Stage directions*, usually printed in brackets or parentheses and in italics, tell how the actors should look, move, and speak. They also describe the setting and desired effects of sound and lighting. Dramas are often divided into major sections called *acts*. These acts are then further divided into smaller sections called *scenes*.

In contemporary usage the term *drama* is often used to refer to serious or tragic plays, as opposed to lighter, comic plays.

See *Character*, *Dialogue*, and *Plot*.

DRAMATIC IRONY   See *Irony*.

DYNAMIC CHARACTER   See *Character*.

ESSAY   An *essay* is a short, nonfiction work about a particular subject. An *expository essay* presents information, discusses ideas, or explains a process. "The Indian All Around Us," on page 457, is an example of an expository essay. A *narrative essay* tells a true story. "Forest Fire," on page 453, tells the story of Anaïs Nin's actual experiences during a forest fire near her Sierra Madre home. A *persuasive essay* tries to convince the reader to do something or to accept a particular conclusion. Robert MacNeil's "The Trouble With Television," on page 463, tries to convince the reader that television is a harmful influence. Finally, a *descriptive essay* presents a portrait, in words, of a person, place, or object. Travel writing provides many examples of descriptive essays. Few essays, however, are purely descriptive. It is important to remember, too, that an essay may combine elements of all four types of writing.

See *Description*, *Exposition*, *Narration*, and *Persuasion*.

EXPOSITION   *Exposition* is writing or speech that explains or informs. Exposition may occur in both fiction and nonfiction writing. This Handbook of Literary Terms is an example of expository nonfiction because it explains the meanings of important literary terms and ideas.

The term *exposition* is also used to refer to the part of a story that introduces the basic elements of the plot: the characters, the setting, and the initial situation leading to the conflict. The exposition of *The Ugly Duckling*, on page 245, occurs in the opening conversation between the King and the Chancellor. Here the reader learns the identity of both characters and learns, too, that Prince Simon is arriving that day to ask Princess Camilla to marry him.

See *Plot*.

EXTENDED METAPHOR   In an *extended metaphor*, as in a regular metaphor, a subject is spoken

or written of as though it were something else. However, an extended metaphor differs from a regular metaphor in that several points of comparison are suggested by the writer or speaker. Naoshi Koriyama uses extended metaphor in his poem "Jetliner," on page 536, to compare a jet plane to a runner.
See *Metaphor*.

FABLE   A *fable* is a brief story, usually with animal characters, that teaches a lesson, or moral. The moral is usually stated at the end of the fable. The Greek slave Aesop wrote many fables in the sixth century B.C. that are still widely read today. Many familiar expressions, such as "cry wolf" and "sour grapes," come from Aesop's fables. Modern writers such as James Thurber and Mark Twain have also written fables.
See *Irony* and *Moral*.

FANTASY   *Fantasy* is highly imaginative writing that contains elements not found in real life. Fantasy involves not only invented characters and situations but sometimes also invented worlds and creatures. Many science-fiction stories, such as Isaac Asimov's "Rain, Rain, Go Away," on page 13, contain elements of fantasy.
See *Science Fiction*.

FICTION   *Fiction* is prose writing that tells about imaginary characters and events. Short stories and novels are works of fiction. Some writers base their fictional tales on actual experiences and real people, to which they add invented characters, dialogue, and settings. Other writers of fiction work entirely from their own imaginations.
See *Narration*, *Nonfiction*, and *Prose*.

FIGURATIVE LANGUAGE   *Figurative language* is writing or speech that is not meant to be taken literally. The many types of figurative language are called *figures of speech*. These include hyperbole, simile, metaphor, and personification. Writers use figurative language to express their meanings in fresh, vivid, surprising ways.

See *Hyperbole*, *Metaphor*, *Personification*, *Simile*, and *Symbol*.

FIGURE OF SPEECH   See *Figurative Language*.

FLASHBACK   A *flashback* is a section of a literary work that interrupts the sequence of events to relate an event from an earlier time. All the action in *The Diary of Anne Frank*, on page 303, except for the first and last scenes, is a flashback to events that occurred more than three years before the opening scene. Pearl Buck's "Christmas Day in the Morning," on page 21, is largely flashback. The story begins and ends with Rob as an elderly man, but the story's main action is a flashback to the Christmas of Rob's fifteenth year.

FLAT CHARACTER   See *Character*.

FOLK BALLAD   See *Ballad*.

FOLKTALE   A *folktale* is a story that was composed orally and then was passed from person to person by word of mouth. Types of folktales include fables, legends, myths, and tall tales. Most folktales are *anonymous:* no one knows who first composed them. In fact, folktales originated among people who could neither read nor write. These people entertained themselves by telling stories aloud, often ones dealing with heroes, adventure, romance, and magic.

In the modern era, scholars like the brothers Wilhelm and Jakob Grimm began collecting folktales and writing them down. Their collection, published as *Grimm's Fairy Tales*, includes such famous tales as "Cinderella," "Rapunzel," and "The Bremen Town Musicians."

American scholars have also collected folktales, often ones dealing with fanciful heroes such as Pecos Bill, Paul Bunyan, and Davy Crockett. See Carl Sandburg's retelling, "Paul Bunyan of the North Woods," on page 643.
See *Fable*, *Legend*, *Myth*, and *Oral Tradition*.

FOOT See *Meter*.

FORESHADOWING *Foreshadowing* is the use, in a literary work, of clues that suggest events that have yet to occur. Foreshadowing creates *suspense* by making the reader wonder what will happen next. In the short story, "A Retrieved Reformation," on page 55, O. Henry foreshadows later events in the story by means of certain details earlier in the tale. That Jimmy is no ordinary criminal but is rather an expert safecracker will become an important detail. The fact that he falls in love with a banker's daughter is a clue that his former trade might play a role in his new life. The fact that the prison warden told Jimmy, "You're not a bad fellow at heart," is another clue. Thus foreshadowing is a means of linking seemingly minor or unconnected details with important developments later in a work.

FREE VERSE *Free verse* is poetry not written in a regular rhythmical pattern, or meter. The following lines, from the South African poet Mongameli Mabona's "The Sea," are in free verse:

Ocean,
Green or blue or iron-gray,
As the light
Strikes you.
Primordial flood,
Relentless and remorseless
Like a woman in a rage.

In a free verse poem the poet is free to write lines of any length or with any number of rhythmic stresses, or beats. Thus free verse is less constraining than *metrical verse*, which requires set patterns of stresses.
See *Meter*.

GENRE A *genre* is a division or type of literature. Literature is generally divided into three major genres: poetry, prose, and drama. Each, in turn, is further divided into such standard literary categories as the following:
1. *Poetry:* lyric, epic, narrative, and dramatic poetry.

2. *Prose:* fiction (novels, short stories) and nonfiction (essays, letters, biographies, autobiographies, and reports).
3. *Drama:* serious drama and tragedy, comic drama, farce, and melodrama.
See *Drama, Poetry,* and *Prose*.

HAIKU *Haiku* is a three-line Japanese verse form. The first and third lines have five syllables; the second line has seven syllables. A haiku usually presents a single, vivid image drawn from nature. See the two examples by Bashō and Moritake, on page 573.

HEPTAMETER See *Meter*.

HEPTASTITCH See *Stanza*.

HERO/HEROINE A *hero* or *heroine* is a character whose actions are inspiring or noble. In very old myths and stories, heroes and heroines often have superhuman powers. Hercules and Achilles are two examples of this type of hero. In modern literature, heroes and heroines tend to be ordinary people. All heroes and heroines struggle to overcome some great obstacle or problem. For example, in "The Day the Sun Came Out," on page 101, Mary is a heroine because she risks her life by eating wild mushrooms to determine if they are safe for the children to eat. In Jack London's *The Call of the Wild*, the hero is Buck, the sled dog. In order to become a leader, Buck must overcome cruel treatment, a harsh climate, and rival dogs. By the end of the novel, Buck has turned from a pampered pet into the leader of a wolf pack.

The word *hero* was originally used for male characters and *heroine* for females. However, it is now acceptable to use the term *hero* to refer both to male and to female characters.

HEXAMETER See *Meter*.

HUBRIS *Hubris* is the fault of excessive pride. In tragic works the hubris of the main character is usually the cause of the protagonist's downfall. In the famous Greek play *Oedipus Rex*, the hero's downfall is partly caused by his hubris. Likewise, in the contemporary novel *Things Fall Apart*, by the Nigerian writer Chinua Achebe, the hubris of the main character, Okonkwo, leads to his exile and eventual death.

HYPERBOLE *Hyperbole* is exaggeration for effect. Because it makes a statement that is not meant to be taken literally, hyperbole is considered a figure of speech. Everyday speech is full of examples of hyperbole, such as "I'm so hungry I could eat a horse." Writers use hyperboles to create humor, to emphasize particular points, and to create dramatic effects. For example, a famous novel by Ralph Ellison begins with this powerful example of hyperbole, which gives his book its name:

I am an invisible man.

See *Figurative Language*.

IAMB See *Meter*.

IMAGE An *image* is a word or a phrase that appeals to one or more of the five senses. Writers use images to create specific descriptions—to show how their subjects look, sound, smell, taste, and feel. The following lines from "Nightsong City," by the South African poet Dennis Brutus, contain several images of sound:

The sound begins again:
The siren in the night
The thunder at the door
The shriek of nerves in pain.
Then the keen crescendo
Of faces split by pain
The wordless, endless wail
Only the unfree know.

IMAGERY See *Image*.

INCITING INCIDENT See *Plot*.

IRONY *Irony* is the general name given to literary techniques that involve surprising, interesting, or amusing contradictions. In *verbal irony*, words are used to suggest the opposite of their usual meaning, as when a weak person is called "a born leader." In *dramatic irony*, there is a contradiction between what a character thinks and what the audience or reader knows to be true. An example can be found in "The Tell-Tale Heart," on page 145, in which the reader knows that the beating heart exists only in the main character's imagination. In *irony of situation*, an event occurs that directly contradicts the expectations of the characters or the reader. *The Ugly Duckling,* on page 245, provides an example of irony of situation. Princess Camilla and Prince Simon send good-looking substitutes to stand in for them at their arranged first meeting. When the Prince and Princess accidentally meet, they fall in love despite their appearances and despite the fact that they do not know each other's true identity. Note that this is also an example of dramatic irony, for the reader or audience does know these characters' true identities.

IRONY OF SITUATION See *Irony*.

LEGEND A *legend* is a widely told story about the past, one that may or may not have a foundation in fact. The stories of King Arthur of Britain and his knights of the Round Table are legends. Likewise, the stories that have survived about American folk heroes such as Pecos Bill and Paul Bunyan are legends. Legends usually contain fantastic details, such as incredible feats of strength or supernatural beings. "The Girl Who Hunted Rabbits," on page 635, is a Zuñi Indian legend about a brave young maiden who risks her life to find food for her family. In this legend the maiden is menaced by a cannibal demon, but she is saved by two war gods.
See *Folktale*, *Myth*, and *Oral Tradition*.

LIMERICK A *limerick* is a humorous, rhyming

five-line poem with a specific meter and rhyme scheme. Most limericks have three strong stresses in lines one, two, and five, and two strong stresses in lines three and four. Most follow the rhyme scheme *aabba*. See the two limericks on page 569.

LYRIC POEM   A *lyric poem* is highly musical verse that expresses the observations and feelings of a single speaker. They are called lyrics because they were, in ancient times, sung to the accompaniment of a lyre, a stringed instrument. Langston Hughes's ''Harlem Night Song,'' on page 558, and Shakespeare's ''Blow, Blow, Thou Winter Wind,'' on page 566 are examples of lyric poetry.

MAIN CHARACTER   See *Character.*

METAMORPHOSIS.   A *metamorphosis* is a change in shape or form. In many ancient Greek and Roman myths, human beings are transformed by the gods into animals, trees, or flowers, as in the story of Daphne and Apollo. Daphne, a beautiful huntress who was being chased one day by the god Apollo, was transformed into a laurel tree by her father, the river god Peneus. The Roman poet Ovid incorporated many of these myths into his great Latin poem, *The Metamorphoses.* This poem is an important source of literary allusions to classical mythology.

Metamorphosis remains an important theme in contemporary literature as well. For example, the Australian writer B. Wongar begins his short story ''Babaru, the Family'' with this metamorphosis:

> Our mother has left us. She has not died or run away but has changed into a crocodile. Maybe it is better that way—not that we will see much of her, but it helps to know that she is not far off; should anything like that happen to any of us, we will be around in the bush together again.

See *Allusion* and *Myth.*

METAPHOR   A *metaphor* is a figure of speech in which something is described as though it were something else. A metaphor, like a simile, works by pointing out a similarity between two things. For example, in Robert Frost's ''The Road Not Taken,'' on page 600, the diverging roads are a metaphor for the major choices that people must make in their lives.

An *extended metaphor* is one that makes more than one point of comparison. Walt Whitman uses extended metaphor in his poem ''O Captain! My Captain!'' on page 534. He compares the United States to a ship, President Lincoln (who is not actually named in the poem) to the ship's captain, and national events to a ship's voyage.
See *Extended Metaphor* and *Figurative Language.*

METER   The *meter* of a poem is its rhythmical pattern. The pattern is determined by the number and types of stresses, or beats, in each line. To describe the meter of a poem, you must *scan* its lines. Scanning involves marking the stressed and unstressed syllables of a poem. A slash mark (´) is used to signify a strong stress, while a weak stress is marked with a horseshoe symbol (˘). Here is an example of *scansion* using Elizabeth Barrett Browning's ''The Cry of the Children'':

> Dŏ yĕ hĕar thĕ chíldrĕn weépĭng, Ó mў
>   bróthĕrs,
> Érĕ thĕ sórrŏw cŏmĕs wĭth yĕars?
> Theў ărĕ leánĭng thĕir yŏung héadś ăgainst
>   thĕir mothĕrs,
> Ănd thăt cánnŏt stŏp thĕir tears.

Each group of stresses within a line is called a *foot.* The following types of feet are common in English poetry:
1. *Iamb:* a foot with one weak stress followed by one strong stress, as in the word ''rĕfórm''
2. *Trochee:* a foot with one strong stress followed by one weak stress, as in the word ''flówĕr''
3. *Anapest:* a foot with two weak stresses followed by one strong stress, as in the phrase ''tŏ thĕ stóre''

4. *Dactyl:* a foot with one strong stress followed by two weak stresses, as in the word "fórmŭlă"

5. *Spondee:* a foot with two strong stresses, as in the word "eíghteén"

6. *Pyrrhic:* a foot with two weak stresses, as in the last foot of the word "fórtŭ|nătěly"

7. *Amphibrach:* a foot with a weak syllable, one strong syllable, and another weak syllable, as in "thĕ wándĕr|ĭng mínstrěl"

8. *Amphimacer:* a foot with one strong syllable, one weak syllable, and another strong syllable, as in "bláck ănd whíte"

Depending on the type of foot that is most common in them, lines of poetry are described as being *iambic*, *trochaic*, *anapestic*, or *dactylic*.

Lines of poetry are also described in terms of the number of feet they contain:

1. *Monometer:* verse written in one-foot lines

   Óne crów
   mélting snów
   —Elizabeth Coatsworth, "March"

2. *Dimeter:* verse written in two-foot lines

   Thĕ pítch | pĭnes fáde
   ĭntŏ ă | whítenĕss
   thăt hăs blót|tĕd thĕ mársh.
   —Marge Piercy, "The Quiet Fog"

3. *Trimeter:* verse written in three-foot lines

   Ă sát|ŭrát|ĕd meádŏw,
     Sún-shápĕd | ănd jéw|ĕl smáll
   Ă cír|clĕ scárce|lў wídĕr
     Thăn thĕ treés | ăroúnd | wĕre táll
   —Robert Frost, "Rose Pogonias"

4. *Tetrameter:* verse written in four-foot lines

   Ĭ hăve wrápped | mў dreáms ĭn | sílkĕn |
     clóth,
   Ănd laíd | thĕm ăwáy | ĭn ă bóx | ŏf góld;
   Whĕre lóng | wĭll clíng | thĕ líps | ŏf thĕ
     móth,
   Ĭ hăve wrápped | mў dreáms | ĭn sílkĕn |
     clóth.
   —Countee Cullen, "For a Poet"

5. *Pentameter:* verse written in five-foot lines

   Ăll thíngs | wĭthín | thĭs fád|ĭng wórld | hăth
     énd,
   Ădvér|sĭtў | dŏth stíll | ŏur jóys | ătténd;

No tíes | sŏ stróng, | nŏ friénds | sŏ deár|
  ănd sweét,
Bŭt wĭth | deáth's párt|ĭng blów | ĭs súre | tŏ
  meet.
    —Anne Bradstreet, "Before the Birth of One of
    Her Children"

A six-foot line is called a *hexameter*. A line with seven feet is called a *heptameter*. A complete description of the meter of a poem tells both how many feet each line contains and what kind of foot occurs most often in the lines. Thus the lines from Anne Bradstreet's poem would be described as *iambic pentameter*. Poetry that does not have a regular meter is called *free verse*.

See *Blank Verse* and *Free Verse*.

MINOR CHARACTER See *Character*.

MOOD *Mood,* or atmosphere, is the feeling created in the reader by a literary work or passage. Writers use many methods to create mood, including images, dialogue, descriptions, characterization, and plot events. Often a writer creates a particular mood at the beginning of a work and then sustains this mood throughout. For example, the mood of Edgar Allan Poe's "The Tell-Tale Heart," on page 145, is one of nervous dread and terror. Sometimes, however, the mood of a work will change with each new twist of the plot.

For example, the mood of "Flowers for Algernon," on page 201, changes according to the fortunes of the main character. Notice how the mood of the following poem by Mari Evans changes in the last three lines:

   if you have had your midnights
   and they have drenched your barren guts with
     tears
   I sing you sunrise and love and someone to
   touch

MONOMETER See *Meter*.

MORAL A *moral* is a lesson taught by a literary work. A fable usually ends with a moral that is directly stated. For example, the moral of Aesop's famous fable of the hare and the tortoise is this: "Sure and steady wins the race."

Novels, short stories, and poems often suggest certain lessons or morals, but these are rarely stated directly. Such morals must be inferred by readers from details contained in the works. See *Fable*.

MOTIVATION   A *motivation* is a reason that explains or partially explains a character's thoughts, feelings, actions, or speech. Writers try to make their characters' motivations, or motives, as clear as possible so that the characters will seem believable and lifelike. If a character's motives are not clear, then the character will seem flat and unconvincing.

Characters are often motivated by such common human feelings as love, greed, hunger, revenge, and friendship. For example, in "The Adventure of the Speckled Band," on page 27, fear motivates Miss Stoner to ask for Holmes's help. Holmes, in turn, is motivated by his intellectual interest in the case and by his sympathy for Miss Stoner.
See *Character*.

MYTH   A *myth* is a fictional tale that explains the actions of gods or heroes or the origins of elements of nature. Myths were generally handed down by word of mouth for generations. "The Origins of Fire," on page 627 is a native American myth that explains how human beings came to use fire. The ancient Greek myth of Prometheus also seeks to explain the origins of fire.

Every ancient culture has its own *mythology*, or collection of myths. Those of the Greeks and the Romans are called *classical mythology*. Myths often reflect the values of the cultures that give birth to them.
See *Oral Tradition*.

NARRATION *Narration* is writing that tells a story. Novels, short stories, biographies, histories,

and autobiographies are common types of *prose narration*, or narrative. Epics and ballads are standard types of *verse narrative*. Whether in verse or prose, a good narrative usually contains interesting events, settings, and characters.
See *Narrative Poem* and *Narrator*.

NARRATIVE   See *Narration*.

NARRATIVE POEM   A *narrative poem* is a story told in verse. It often possesses the elements of fiction, such as characters, conflict, and plot. The events are usually told in *chronological order*, the order in which they happen. Narrative poems may be serious, like Longfellow's "Paul Revere's Ride," on page 509, or humorous, like "William Stafford," on page 517.

NARRATOR   A *narrator* is a speaker or character who tells a story. There are several types of narrator, and the type that a writer chooses determines the story's *point of view*. If the narrator is a character who takes part in the story and who refers to herself or himself as *I*, this is *first-person narration*. For example, the narrator of Paul Darcy Boles's "The House Guest," on page 79, is the older brother in the household. He is a first-person narrator. If the narrator stands outside the action of the story, then this speaker is a *third-person narrator*. Loula Grace Erdman's "Grass Fire," on page 129, uses a third-person narrator.
See *Point of View*.

NONFICTION   *Nonfiction* is prose writing that presents and explains ideas or that tells about real people, places, objects, or events. Histories, biographies, autobiographies, essays, and newspaper articles are all types of nonfiction.
See *Fiction*

NOVEL   A *novel* is a long work of fiction. Novels, like short stories, contain plot, character, conflict, and setting, but they are much longer than short stories. Thus they usually contain more

characters, a greater variety of settings, and more complicated plots than do most short stories. A novel often contains, in addition to its major plot, one or more lesser stories, or subplots. Some famous novels include *Moby-Dick*, *David Copperfield*, and *The Red Badge of Courage*. Jack London's novel *The Call of the Wild* is included in this book.
See *Fiction*.

OCTAVE   See *Stanza*.

ONOMATOPOEIA   *Onomatopoeia* is the use of words that imitate sounds. *Hiss*, *crash*, *buzz*, *neigh*, *ring*, and *jingle* are examples of onomatopoeia. In William Shakespeare's ''Full Fathom Five,'' onomatopoeia is used to imitate the sound of a bell:

> Sea nymphs hourly ring the knell:
>   Ding-Dong.
> Hark! Now I hear them.
>   Ding-dong, bell.

ORAL TRADITION   The *oral tradition* is the passing of songs, stories, and poems from generation to generation by word of mouth. Folk songs, ballads, fables, and myths are often the products of oral tradition. No one knows who created them. That is, they are *anonymous*. The ballad ''John Henry,'' on page 663, is a product of the oral tradition. No one knows who first wrote this ballad. It has been passed from singer to singer for many years and, like most products of the oral tradition, exists in many different versions.
See *Folktale*, *Legend*, and *Myth*.

PARALLELISM   See *Repetition*.

PENTAMETER   See *Meter*

PERSONIFICATION   *Personification* is a type of figurative language in which a nonhuman subject is given human characteristics. The expressions ''Father Time'' and ''Mother Earth'' are examples of personification. The poem by Sylvia Plath on page 503 personifies mushrooms as meek, yet slightly sinister, creatures:

> Nudgers and shovers
> In spite of ourselves.
> Our kind multiplies:
> We shall by morning
> Inherit the earth.
> Our foot's in the door.

See *Figurative Language*.

PERSUASION   *Persuasion* is writing or speech that attempts to convince the reader to adopt an opinion or a course of action. Advertisements are the most common forms of persuasion: they try to persuade people to buy certain products or services. Newspaper editorials, political speeches, and essays are other common forms of persuasive writing. In his essay ''Dial Versus Digital,'' on page 477, Isaac Asimov tries to persuade his readers that something important has been lost in the change from dial to digital clocks and watches.

PLOT   *Plot* is the sequence of events in a literary work. In most novels, short stories, dramas, and narrative poems, the plot involves two basic elements—characters and conflict. The plot usually begins with the *exposition*, which establishes the setting, identifies the major characters, and introduces the basic situation. This is usually followed by the *inciting incident*, which introduces the *central conflict*. The *development* of the central conflict shows how the characters are affected by it. Eventually, the development reaches a high point of interest or suspense, the *climax*. The *resolution*, or end, of the conflict then follows. Any events that occur after the resolution make up the *denouement*.

Some plots do not contain all of these parts. Short stories, for example, often do not include an exposition and a denouement. Sometimes, too, the inciting incident in a short story or novel has occurred before the opening of the story.

All the events that occur before the climax of

a story make up its *rising action*. All the events that occur after the climax make up the *falling action*.
See *Conflict*.

POETRY   *Poetry* is one of the three major types of literature, the others being prose and drama. Poetry is not easy to define, but we might say that poetry is language used in special ways. Most poems make use of concise, rhythmic, and emotionally charged language. The language of poetry usually emphasizes the re-creation of experiences over analysis of these experiences. Traditionally, poetry has differed from prose in making use of formal structural devices such as rhyme, meter, and stanzas. Some poems, however, are written out just like prose.

Major types of poetry include lyrics, narrative poems, dramatic poems, and epics. Walter de la Mare's "Silver," on page 564, and Lew Sarett's "Four Little Foxes," on page 556, are lyrics. Joaquin Miller's "Columbus," on page 521, and John Greenleaf Whittier's "Barabara Frietchie," on page 525, are narrative poems. In dramatic poetry, characters speak the poem in their own voices. An epic poem, such as Homer's *Iliad*, is a long, involved narrative poem about the exploits of gods and heroes.

POINT OF VIEW   *Point of view* is the perspective, or vantage point, from which a story is told. The three most common points of view in narrative literature are first person, omniscient third-person, and limited third-person.

In a story from the *first-person point of view*, the narrator is a character in the story. We see the story through his or her eyes. Most of the Sherlock Holmes stories, such as "The Adventure of the Speckled Band," on page 27, are told from a first-person point of view—that of Dr. Watson.

In a story written from the *omniscient*, or "all knowing," *third-person point of view*, the narrator is not a character in the story but views the events of the story through the eyes of more than one of the characters. Saki's "The Story-Teller," on page 3, uses the third-person omniscient point of view.

In a *third-person limited point of view*, the narrator is not a character, but he or she presents the story from the perspective of one of the characters. That character's thoughts, feelings, and experiences are the focus of attention. Pearl S. Buck's "Christmas Day in the Morning," on page 21, is an example of limited third-person narration.
See *Narrator*.

PROSE   *Prose* is the ordinary form of written language. Most writing that is not poetry, drama, or song is considered prose. Prose fiction includes novels and short stories. Nonfiction prose includes essays, biography, autobiography, journalism, scientific reports, and historical writing.
See *Fiction, Genre*, and *Nonfiction*.

PROTAGONIST   The *protagonist* is the main character in a literary work. Normally, the reader sympathizes with or at least learns to understand the protagonist. For example, in "The Man Without a Country," on page 185, the reader sympathizes with the protagonist, Philip Nolan, who has been exiled for life to a ship. In *The Call of the Wild*, on page 695, the reader sympathizes with the protagonist, Buck, who must overcome many obstacles in order to survive in the harsh North Country.

PYRRHIC   See *Meter*.

QUATRAIN   See *Stanza*.

REFRAIN   A *refrain* is a regularly repeated line or group of lines in a poem or song. In Joaquin Miller's "Columbus," on page 521, the refrain is "Sail on! sail on! sail on!"

REPETITION   *Repetition* is the use, more than once, of any element of language—a sound, a word, a phrase, a sentence, a grammatical pattern, or a rhythmical pattern. Repetition is used both in prose and in poetry. In prose fiction, a plot may be repeated, with variations, in a subplot, or a minor character may be similar to a major character in important ways. In poetry, repetition often involves the recurring use of certain words, images, structures, and devices. Rhyme and alliteration, for example, repeat sounds. A repeating rhyme pattern is called a *rhyme scheme*. A *refrain* is a repeated line or group of lines.

Another form of repetition, used in both prose and poetry, is *parallelism*, in which a grammatical pattern is repeated, though with some changes over time. José Garcia Villa's poem "Lyric 17" which appears on page 532, contains parallel repetition of the phrase "It must":

> It must be slender as a bell,
> And it must hold fire as a well.
> It must have the wisdom of bows
> And it must kneel like a rose.

RESOLUTION   See *Plot*.

RHYME   *Rhyme* is the repetition of sounds at the end of words. Poets use rhyme to create musical effects, and to emphasize and to link certain words and ideas. The most traditional type of rhyme is *end rhyme*, or rhyming words at the end of the lines. Alfred, Lord Tennyson, uses end rhyme in "Ring Out, Wild Bells" on page 544:

> Ring out, wild bells, to the wild *sky*,
>   The flying cloud, the frosty *light*:
>   The year is dying in the *night*;
> Ring out, wild bells, and let him *die*.

Internal rhyme occurs when rhymes occur within lines. Notice, for example, the internal rhymes in this poem by Oliver Wendell Holmes:

> In the street I heard a *thumping*; and I knew it
>   was the *stumping*
> Of the Corporal, our old *neighbor*, on that leg
>   he *wore*,
> With a knot of women *round him*,—it was lucky
>   I had *found him*,
> So I followed with the others, and the Corporal
>   marched before.

RHYME SCHEME   A *rhyme scheme* is a regular pattern of rhyming words in a poem. To indicate the rhyme scheme of a poem, one uses lower case letters. For example, the following stanza, from Robert Frost's "Blue-Butterfly Day," on page 559, has an *abab* rhyme scheme:

> It is blue-butterfly day here in *spring*,   a
> And with these sky-flakes down in flurry
>   on *flurry*   b
> There is more unmixed color on the *wing*   a
> Than flowers will show for days unless
>   they *hurry*.   b

RHYTHM   *Rhythm* is the pattern of stresses, or beats, in spoken or written language.
See *Meter*.

ROUND CHARACTER   See *Character*.

SCAN/SCANNING   See *Meter*.

SCENE   See *Drama*.

SCIENCE FICTION   *Science fiction* is writing that tells about imaginary events that involve science or technology. Much science fiction is set in the future, often on planets other than Earth. Arthur C. Clarke's "Crime on Mars," on page 137, is a science-fiction story about a crime that takes place in a large Earth colony on Mars.
See *Fiction*.

SENSORY LANGUAGE   *Sensory language* is writing or speech that appeals to one or more of the five senses. Writers use sensory language to make the ideas and events they describe more vivid and clear.
See *Image*.

SESTET   See *Stanza*.

SETTING   The *setting* of a literary work is the time and place of the action. The time includes not only the historical period—past, present, or future—but also the year, the season, the time of day, and even the weather. The place may be a specific country, state, region, community, neighborhood, building, institution, or home. Details such as dialects, clothing, customs, and modes of transportation are often used to establish setting. In most stories, the setting serves as a backdrop against which the characters act out the actions of the narrative. The setting of Ray Bradbury's "The Drummer Boy of Shiloh," on page 151, is an April night in 1862, during the Civil War, at a place named "Shiloh" near the Tennessee River, close to a church.

The setting of a story often helps to create a particular mood, or feeling. The mood of Ray Bradbury's story is one of nervous expectation—of fear mingled with resolve.
See *Conflict*, *Plot*, and *Theme*.

SHORT STORY A *short story* is a brief work of fiction. Like novels, most short stories contain a central conflict and one or more characters, the most important of which is the protagonist. Like lyric poems, short stories usually create a single effect, or dominant impression. The main idea, message, or subject of a short story is its *theme*.
See *Fiction*.

SIMILE A *simile* is a figure of speech that makes a direct comparison between two unlike subjects, using *like* or *as*. Everyday speech contains many similes, as in "quiet as a mouse," "like a duck out of water," "good as gold," and "old as the hills."

Writers use similes to create vivid, telling descriptions. Poetry, especially, relies on similes to point out new and interesting ways of looking at the world. For example, Richard García's poem "The City is So Big," on page 586, contains this striking simile:

And trains pass with windows shining
Like a smile full of teeth.

SPEAKER The *speaker* is the imaginary voice assumed by the writer of a poem. In other words,

the speaker is the character who tells the poem. Sometimes this speaker will identify himself or herself by name. At other times the speaker is more vague. Interpreting a poem often depends on inferring what the speaker is like based on the details that he or she provides.

SPONDEE See *Meter*.

STAGE DIRECTIONS *Stage directions* are notes included in a drama to describe how the work is to be performed and staged. Stage directions are usually printed in italics and enclosed within parentheses or brackets. They may indicate how the actors should speak their lines, how they should move, how the characters should be dressed, what the stage should look like, or what special effects of lighting or sound should be used. Here is an excerpt from Edmond Rostand's play *The Romancers*, on page 263, which includes stage directions:

> SYLVETTE. [*Aside*] He'll never do it—it would cost too much!
> PASQUINOT. Now go into the house—quick!
> [*She goes out,* PASQUINOT *glowering at her*]
> BERGAMIN. [*Heard from the other side of the wall, as he enters*] Take this note at once to Monsieur Straforel.

See *Drama*.

STANZA A *stanza* is a group of lines in a poem, considered as a unit. Many poems are divided into stanzas of equal length, with the stanzas separated by spaces. Stanzas are often like paragraphs in prose: Each presents a single thought or idea.

Stanzas are usually named according to the number of lines they contain, as follows:
1. *Couplet:* a two-line stanza
2. *Tercet:* a three-line stanza
3. *Quatrain:* a four-line stanza
4. *Cinquain:* a five-line stanza
5. *Sestet:* a six-line stanza
6. *Heptastitch:* a seven-line stanza

7. *Octave:* an eight-line stanza

In traditional poetry stanzas are often rhymed. However, not all rhyming poems use stanzas, nor do all poems that are divided into stanzas rhyme. Less traditional poetry contains stanzas of varying length, sometimes with, sometimes without, rhyme.

STATIC CHARACTER   See *Character*.

SUBPLOT   See *Novel*.

SURPRISE ENDING   A *surprise ending* is a conclusion that violates the expectations of the reader. For example, the ending of Shirley Jackson's short story "Charles," on page 73, is a complete surprise to the reader. Laurie's parents are so convinced that Charles exists that the reader is as astonished as the narrator to discover that there is no Charles. The stories that Laurie has been telling to his parents are probably stories about himself. Often a writer *foreshadows* the surprise ending by including seemingly minor details earlier in the story that will make the later surprise appear a fair, if unexpected, ending.
See *Foreshadowing* and *Plot*.

SUSPENSE   *Suspense* is a feeling of anxious uncertainty about the outcome of events in a literary work. Writers create suspense by raising questions in the minds of their readers. For example, in Paul Annixter's "Accounts Settled," on page 47, the most suspenseful moment occurs when Gordon confronts the cougar. The reader wonders—and perhaps even worries—whether Gordon will escape and, if so, how. The suspense in a story can be especially intense if the writer has created convincing, interesting characters about whom the reader cares strongly.
See *Plot*.

SYMBOL   A *symbol* is anything that stands for or represents something else. Symbols are usually concrete objects or images that represent abstract ideas. For example, the eagle is often used as a symbol of freedom. Likewise, chains can symbolize slavery and oppression. In literature, concrete images are often used to represent, or symbolize, the themes of a literary work. For example, in Edgar Allan Poe's "The Tell-Tale Heart," on page 145, the beating heart of the old man could be a symbol of the old man's vengeance or of the main character's guilt. Symbols generally differ from metaphors or similes in that the reader or listener must infer what the symbol stands for. The writer or speaker does not explicitly make the comparison.
See *Figurative Language*.

TERCET   See *Stanza*.

TETRAMETER   See *Meter*.

THEME   A *theme* is a central message, concern, or insight into life expressed in a literary work. A theme can usually be expressed by a one- or two-sentence statement about human beings or about life. For example, the theme of Edward Everett Hale's short story, "The Man Without A Country," on page 185, might be this: "Every man needs to feel allegiance to his native country, whether he always appreciates that country or not."

A theme may be stated directly or may be implied. In poems and in works of prose fiction the theme is rarely stated directly. More often, the other elements of the work—its language, imagery, plot, tone, and structure—suggest the theme. *Interpretation* involves uncovering the theme of a literary work by carefully considering the parts, or elements, of the work.

In the nonfiction works, and especially in essays, theme is often stated directly. The title of Robert MacNeil's "The Trouble With Television," on page 463, suggests in a general way what the theme of the essay is, and the essay itself states the theme explicitly: Television oversimplifies, distorts, and ultimately "decivilizes" human existence.

TONE *Tone* is the attitude toward the subject and audience conveyed by the language and rhythm of the speaker in a literary work. For example, the tone of Edgar Allan Poe's "The Tell-Tale Heart," on page 145, is frantic and sinister. The narrator of the story reveals, by his tone and by his actions, that he is dangerously insane. In contrast, the tone of John Updike's poem "January," on page 576, is light and humorous. See *Mood*.

TRIMETER See *Meter*.

TROCHEE See *Meter*.

VERBAL IRONY See *Irony*.

HANDBOOK OF CRITICAL THINKING AND READING TERMS

ABSTRACT *adj.* Anything that is not concrete or definite is *abstract*. Writers make their abstract ideas clear by using specific examples and illustrations. Suppose, for instance, that a writer wants to convey the abstract idea that a character is happy. The writer might do this by showing the character smiling, whistling, walking briskly, and greeting others enthusiastically. Another way to express abstract ideas clearly is to use figures of speech, such as similes, metaphors, and personifications. For example, the simile "quiet as a mouse" uses a concrete image—a mouse—to convey the abstract idea of quietness.

ANALOGY *n.* An *analogy* is a comparison that explains one subject by pointing out its similarities to another subject. In "Concrete Mixers," on page 587, Patricia Hubbell compares concrete mixers to elephants:

> The drivers are washing the concrete mixers;
> Like elephant tenders they hose them down.
> Tough gray-skinned monsters standing ponderous,
> Elephant-bellied and elephant-nosed

To understand an analogy a reader must consider what qualities or characteristics the two subjects have in common.

An analogy may be expressed using a variety of literary techniques, including simile, metaphor, and extended metaphor. See the explanations of these techniques in the Handbook of Literary Terms and Techniques.

ANALYSIS *n.* *Analysis* is the process of studying the parts of a whole. By studying the parts, you can often come to understand what the whole is all about. The process of analysis consists of the following steps:

1. Separate the whole into its parts.

2. Describe each part.

3. Look for connections between the parts and between each part and the whole.

For example, you might analyze Robert MacNeil's essay "The Trouble with Television," on page 463, by dividing it into these parts: the introduction, the body, the conclusion, and the main idea. Then you would think about these parts and how they are interrelated. See Sections 2 and 3 of Handbook of Writing About Literature, on page 764, for more information about analyzing literary works.

ARGUMENT *n.* An *argument* is a set of statements consisting of a conclusion and one or more premises, or reasons for accepting the conclusion. In "Hokusai: The Old Man Mad About Drawing," on page 481, Stephen Longstreet presents the argument that Katsushika Hokusai is the Japanese artist whom westerners most like and understand. In the essay Longstreet supports his claim with specific reasons.

When you write about a literary work, you present arguments supporting conclusions that you have come to based on your reading. For example, you might argue that Robert Frost's "The Road Not Taken," on page 600, is about the choices that people make and the consequences of these choices. Of course, you would have to present evidence, or reasons, to support your conclusion. Never simply make claims about a work without supporting these claims with evidence.

Note that the term *argument* is also sometimes used to describe a brief summary, or synopsis, of a literary work. Thus a paragraph summarizing the plot of Paul Zindel's *Let Me Hear You Whisper*, on page 277, might be described as presenting the argument of the play.
See *Conclusion, Deduction, Evidence, Induction,* and *Inference.*

BANDWAGON   See *Propaganda Technique.*

BEGGING THE QUESTION   See *Logical Fallacy.*

CATEGORIZATION *n.*   *Categorization* is the process of placing objects or ideas into groups, or categories. To categorize something, follow these steps:

1. Note the characteristics of the thing that you are studying.
2. Think of other things that share these characteristics.
3. Think of a name to refer to the whole group of things.

   For example, to categorize Henry Wadsworth Longfellow's "Paul Revere's Ride," on page 509, you might begin by noting that the poem tells a story. Then you would think of other poems that share this characteristic. Finally, you would come up with a general term to describe all such poems, such as the term *narrative poem.*

CAUSE AND EFFECT *n. phrase*   When an event precedes and brings about a second event, the first is said to be a *cause* and the second an *effect.* The plot of a literary work often depends on cause-and-effect relationships. In a plot, one event causes another event, which causes another, and so on to the end of the work. For example, in O. Henry's "A Retrieved Reformation," on page 55, the main character, Jimmy, ceases to commit burglaries when he falls in love with Annabel. Falling in love is the cause, and Jimmy's reformation is the effect.

   Cause-and-effect relationships also exist between the parts of a work and the reponses of a reader. Writers choose their materials and techniques carefully to cause readers to feel certain effects. For example, in "The City Is So Big," on page 586, Richard García chooses his images carefully to cause the reader to feel how frightening a city can be.

CIRCULAR REASONING   See *Logical Fallacy.*

COMPARISON *n.*   *Comparison* is the process of observing and pointing out similarities. For example, a comparison of the American folk heroes Paul Bunyan and Davy Crockett might point out the following similarities: Each possessed great strength and courage. Each lived on the frontier. Each preferred a rugged life in the wilderness to life in a city or town. A comparison is often signaled by one of the following words or phrases: *similarly, likewise, also, in the same manner,* or *in the same way.*
See *Contrast.*

CONCLUSION *n.*   A *conclusion* is any idea that follows reasonably from another idea or group of ideas. The conclusion of an argument should follow reasonably from the supporting statements, facts, and reasons. For example, in the essay "Dial Versus Digital," on page 477, Isaac Asimov presents several reasons to support his conclusion that something important has been lost in the change from dial clocks to digital clocks.

   The word *conclusion* is also used, of course, to describe the ending of any written or spoken work. Whenever you write, you should make sure that your written product has a clear conclusion. That is, when a reader finishes your work, he or she should have a feeling of completeness. There are many ways to create this sense of an ending. The following are some common ways in which writers conclude their works:

1. By telling about the last of a series of events
2. By summarizing what has been said
3. By making a general statement about what has been said
4. By calling on readers to form some opinion or to take some action
5. By explaining the importance or value of what has been said
6. By connecting what has been said to something else of importance or value

CONTRAST *n.*   *Contrast* is the process of observing and pointing out differences. When you contrast two things, you first note their individual characteristics. Then you note any differences in these characteristics. For example, you might note the following differences between people and computers:

1. People are conscious, but computers are not.
2. People have feelings, but computers do not.
3. People can act on their own, but computers cannot.

In writing, a contrast is often signaled by one of the following words or phrases: *in contrast*, *on the contrary*, *however*, *but*, or *on the other hand*.

DEDUCTION *n.* *Deduction* is a form of argument in which the conclusion has to be true if the premises are true. The following is an example of a deductive argument:

> Premise 1: All lyric poems express the feelings of a speaker.
> Premise 2: "The Secret Heart," by Robert P. Tristram Coffin, is a lyric poem.
> Conclusion: "The Secret Heart," by Robert P. Tristram Coffin, expresses the feelings of a speaker.

As this example shows, if you accept the premises of a deductive argument, then you must accept the conclusion.

DEFINITION *n.* *Definition* is the process of explaining the meaning of a word or a phrase. Definition makes communication possible by establishing agreed-upon meanings for words.

The simplest type of definition, called *ostensive definition*, involves pointing to something and saying its name. If, for example, you point to an object and say, "bicycle" you are giving an ostensive definition of the word *bicycle*. Ostensive definition is often used to teach new words to small children.

Another common type of definition is *lexical definition*—the kind of definition found in dictionaries. A lexical definition uses words to explain the meanings of other words. Some types of lexical definition include definition by synonym, definition by antonym, definition by example, and genus and differentia definition.

In a *definition by synonym*, you use a word or a phrase that has the same meaning as the word or phrase that you are defining: A *film* is a "motion picture."

In a *definition by antonym*, you use a word or phrase that has an opposite meaning, along with a negative word such as *not*: *Tepid* water is water that is "neither very hot nor very cold."

In a *definition by example*, you list things to which the term being defined applies: *Scandinavia* includes Denmark, Sweden, Norway, and Finland.

In a *genus and differentia definition*, you first place the thing to be defined into a general category, or *genus*. Then you tell how the thing differs from other things in the same category:

> To be defined: daisy
> Genus, or group: flowers
> Differentia: many white petals
>   round yellow center
>   petals extend out from middle
> Definition: A daisy is "a flower with many white petals extending from a round, yellow middle."

The purpose of a definition is to make a reader or listener understand what is being said. Whenever you write, make sure that you define any terms that your audience might not otherwise understand. Use the methods of lexical definition explained here.

EITHER/OR FALLACY   See *Logical Fallacy*.

EVALUATION *n.* *Evaluation* is the process of making judgments about the quality or value of something. The statement " 'Flowers for Algernon' is an excellent short story" is an evaluation. To evaluate a literary work, you must first analyze it. Once you identify the parts of a work and understand how these components contribute to the whole, you can then evaluate the work.

Tastes vary from person to person, and intelligent readers can disagree on the merits of a particular work. Still, some judgments about literary works are more reasonable than others because

they are based on sensible standards, or criteria. Most readers agree that literary works should contain believable plots, imaginative language, and interesting, convincing characters. Criteria such as these make evaluations of literary works possible. An effective, persuasive evaluation uses elements in the work—such as plot details, characters, and descriptions—as evidence to support the evaluation. Judgments such as "I hated it" or "It's the best" are unacceptable because they are too vague.
See *Opinion* and *Judgment*.

EVIDENCE *n.* *Evidence* is factual information presented to support an argument. In criminal trials, lawyers present known or new facts as evidence to prove or disprove the innocence of the defendant. In literary analysis or evaluation, the parts of a work—such as language, plot, characters, and tone—are the evidence that must be used to support an interpretation or judgment. For example, consider the statement, "The main character in Poe's 'The Tell-Tale Heart' is mad." You might support this interpretation by pointing out that he thinks the old man in the tale possesses an "evil eye" and that he thinks he hears his dead victim's heart beating.
See *Fact*, *Reason*, and *Support*.

FALSE ANALOGY See *Logical Fallacy*.

FACT *n.* A *fact* is a statement that can be proved true or false by evidence. For example, the following facts are true by definition:

$9/_3 = 3$
A novel is a long, fictional prose narrative.

The following facts are true by observation:

William O. Douglas was a justice on the United States Supreme Court.
Tunisia is in Africa.

Facts are extremely important in literary works. An author uses them to develop charac-

ters, settings, and plots. A reader uses them as the evidence with which to make predictions, inferences, and evaluations.
See *Opinion*.

GENERALIZATION *n.* A *generalization* is a statement that applies to more than one thing. The following are generalizations:

John Greenleaf Whittier's poems usually rhyme.
Newspapers are reliable sources of information.

The first statement applies to more than one of Whittier's poems, and the second to more than one newspaper. *Deductive arguments* often begin with generalizations. Consider the following deductive argument:

Premise: (generalization) Mark Twain did not write any stories set in Sri Lanka.
Premise: Mark Twain wrote the story "What Stumped the Blue-Jays."
Conclusion: The story "What Stumped the Blue-Jays" is not set in Sri Lanka.

Inductive arguments, on the other hand, often end with generalizations. Consider the following argument:

Premise: Last month Mary read a book about Roberto Clemente.
Premise: Last week Mary read a book about Babe Ruth.
Premise: Now Mary is reading a history of the World Series.
Conclusion: (generalization) Mary likes to read about baseball.

Generalizations are useful for summarizing observations. True generalizations usually assert only that something is frequently or usually the case, not that it is always so. Be careful not to overgeneralize. For example, the statement "All of Ray Bradbury's stories are set on Mars" is an overgeneralization because many exceptions can be found. One way to avoid overgeneralizing is to limit your general statements by using qualifiers, such as *usually*, *often*, *generally*, *a few*, and *many*.
See *Conclusion* and *Stereotype*.

INDUCTION *n.* *Induction* is a form of argument in which the conclusion is probably but not necessarily true. For example, if you read several poems by Shel Silverstein and find that each is humorous, then you might conclude, "All of Shel Silverstein's poems are humorous." This conclusion may be true, but it is not necessarily true because you have not read all of Silverstein's poems. You would have to limit your conclusion by using a qualifier: "Many of Shel Silverstein's poems are humorous."
See *Generalization* and *Inference*.

INFERENCE *n.* An *inference* is any logical or reasonable conclusion based on known facts or accepted premises. Detectives such as Sherlock Holmes continually make inferences on the basis of the facts known to them. The conclusions of inductive and deductive arguments—Sherlock Holmes uses both kinds of reasoning—are inferences. In thinking about a literary work, the reader must constantly draw inferences from the details presented by the author. The author wants and expects the reader to do so. For example, Walt Whitman expected the readers of his "O Captain! My Captain!" on page 534 to infer that the real subject and inspiration of his poem was Abraham Lincoln. The emotional, heartrending nature of the poem and its repeated references to a beloved, nameless leader, coupled with the reader's knowledge of its background, or *context*, make this inference reasonable.

INTERPRETATION *n.* *Interpretation* is the process of determining the meaning or significance of speech, writing, art, music, or actions. The interpretation of a literary work involves many different processes. These include the following:

1. Reading carefully and actively and responding to each new detail, character, and plot incident

2. Breaking down the work into its parts, describing each and looking for patterns, connections, and similarities among the parts

3. Examining your own responses to the work

and identifying the details that help to create these responses

4. Unifying your observations by making generalizations, based on them, about the meaning or purpose of the work as a whole

Interpretation is usually aimed at identifying the theme of a literary work. For example, your reading of Pearl S. Buck's "Christmas Day in the Morning," on page 21, might lead you to this statement of theme: "Buck affirms the mysterious yet very practical ability of love to bring people together." Reasonable interpretations will take into account, directly or indirectly, all important parts of a work.
See *Analysis*.

JUDGMENT *n.* A *judgment* is a statement about the quality or value of something. Like arguments, judgments must be supported by facts and reasons. A sound judgment of a literary work, therefore, must be based on evidence from the text.
See *Evaluation* and *Opinion*.

LOGICAL FALLACY *n. phrase* A *logical fallacy* is an error in reasoning. People often commit such errors when they are attempting to persuade others to adopt some opinion or to take some action. The following logical fallacies are quite common:

1. *Begging the question*: This fallacy occurs when someone assumes the truth of the statement to be proved without providing any supporting evidence. For example: "All students who receive A's in algebra will go on to become great mathematicians." (No evidence is given to support the claim.)

2. *Circular reasoning*: This fallacy occurs when the evidence given to support a claim is simply a restatement of the claim in other words. For example: "I think the cafeteria food is delicious because it tastes good." (The second part of the sentence simply restates the original claim in different words.)

3. *Either/or fallacy*: This fallacy occurs when

someone claims that there are only two alternatives when there are actually more. For example: "A high-school graduate can either get a job or join the armed forces." (This statement ignores other possibilities such as going to college.)

4. *False analogy*: This fallacy occurs when someone falsely assumes that two subjects are similar in some respect just because they are similar in some other respect. For example: "Paul lives in Iowa, and he is a farmer. Janet also lives in Iowa. Therefore, Janet must be a farmer." (The false assumption is made that because Paul and Janet live in the same state, they must also have the same occupation.)

5. *Post hoc, ergo propter hoc*: (a Latin phrase meaning "After this, therefore because of this") This fallacy occurs when someone falsely assumes that an event is caused by another event simply because of the order of the events in time. For example: "After Rose entered the room, Claire left. Claire must have left because she doesn't like Rose." (The two events might be completely unrelated. One cannot assume a cause-and-effect relationship on such flimsy evidence.)

6. *Overgeneralization*: This fallacy occurs when someone makes a statement that is too broad or too inclusive. For example: "All baseball players chew bubble gum." (While this statement might be true of some baseball players, it is certainly not true of all of them.)

When you do persuasive writing or speaking, try to avoid these logical fallacies. Also be on guard against these fallacies in the speech and writing of others.

MAIN IDEA *n. phrase*   The *main idea* is the central point that a speaker or writer wants to communicate. For example, the main idea of Robert Frost's "The Road Not Taken," on page 600, is that making a difficult or unpopular choice can make a great difference in one's life. As in most works of poetry and fiction, however, this main idea is implied rather than stated directly. In es-

says that seek to persuade the reader, the thesis is usually directly stated early in the essay. This is especially true of essays that analyze or interpret a work of literature.
See *Purpose*.

OBJECTIVE *adj.*   Something is *objective* if it has to do with a reality that exists independently of any particular person's mind or personal, internal experiences. Statements of fact are objective because anyone can, at least in theory, determine whether they are true. For example, the statement "Jack London wrote *The Call of the Wild*" is objective because it deals with an impersonal , external reality. On the other hand, the statement "*The Call of the Wild* is an exciting, powerful book" is subjective because it reports one individual's personal, internal experience of the novel.

To be objective is to be fair. Judges and jurors in legal trials are expected to evaluate cases fairly and objectively by taking all the facts into account. Similarly, in writing about literature a critic will seem fair if he or she takes into account the important facts and details contained in the work.
See *Subjective*.

OPINION *n.*   An *opinion* is a statement that can be supported by facts but that is not itself a fact. Opinions usually fall into one of three categories: judgments, predictions, or statements of obligation.

A *judgment* offers an evaluation of something:

Mr. García is an excellent teacher.

A *prediction* is a statement about the future:

New baseball teams will be added to the major leagues.

A *statement of obligation* tells how one should act:

Do unto others as you would have them do unto you.
A good citizen should keep up with current events.

Whenever you express an opinion, you should be prepared to support it with facts and with reasoned arguments. An opinion that you cannot back up is merely a prejudice.
See *Fact*, *Judgment*, and *Prediction*.

OVERGENERALIZATION   See *Logical Fallacy*.

PARAPHRASE *n.*   A *paraphrase* is a restatement in other words. Paraphrasing is an excellent way to test your understanding of a literary work. A paraphrase can also be used to support an interpretive argument when the exact words of the original are not essential to the argument. When you paraphrase a passage, be careful not to alter the meaning of the original. Simply put into your own words what the writer has said.

POST HOC, ERGO PROPTER HOC   See *Logical Fallacy*.

PREDICTION *n.*   *Prediction* is the act of making statements about the future. An active reader of a literary work continually makes predictions about what is going to happen next. These predictions are based on details provided in the work and on the reader's general knowledge about how people act and how the world operates.

Prediction is possible because of the use in literary works of foreshadowing. *Foreshadowing* is the technique of providing clues about what is going to happen later in a work. See the definition of foreshadowing in the Handbook of Literary Terms and Techniques.
See *Opinion*.

PROBLEM SOLVING *n. phrase*   *Problem solving* is the process by which a person comes up with a solution to some difficulty. Interpreting a literary work is a type of problem solving. So is planning a piece of writing. The following are some general guidelines for solving problems:
1. State the problem as clearly as you can.
2. Identify the goal that you want to reach. That is, determine what situation will exist when the problem is solved.

3. Examine the differences between the goal state (the situation that will exist when the problem is solved) and the initial state (the situation at the time when you begin working on the problem).
4. Take steps to reduce the differences between the initial state and the goal state.

The following are some rules of thumb, or *heuristics*, that are useful in solving problems:
1. Break the problem down into parts and solve the parts separately.
2. Think of a time when you solved a simpler problem of the same type. See if you can use the same solution.
3. Restate the problem in various ways. Doing so may give you some additional insight into the problem.
4. Ask someone to help you with parts of the problems that are especially difficult.
5. Ask "What if" questions to come up with possible solutions. Test each of your solutions.
6. Define the key terms or concepts involved in the problem.
7. Use general thinking strategies such as diagramming, freewriting, clustering, and brainstorming to come up with possible solutions.
8. Use means/ends analysis. That is, at each step in the solution, compare where you are with where you want to be. Take steps to reduce the differences between where you are and the desired goal.

PROPAGANDA TECHNIQUE *n. phrase*   A *propaganda technique* is an improper appeal to emotion used for the purpose of swaying the opinions of an audience. The following propaganda techniques are quite common:
1. *Bandwagon*: This technique involves encouraging people to think or act in some way simply because other people are doing so. For example: "All your neighbors are rushing down to Mistri Motors to take advantage of this year-end sale. You come, too!"
2. *Loaded words*: This technique involves using words with strong positive or negative conno-

tations, or associations. Name-calling is an example of the use of loaded words. So is any use of words that are charged with emotion. For example: "No really *intelligent* voter would support his candidacy."

3. *Snob appeal*: This technique involves making a claim that one should act or think in a certain way because of the high social status associated with the action or thought. For example: "Felson's Furs—the feeling of luxury, for those who can afford the very best."

4. *Transfer*: This technique involves making an illogical association between one thing and something else that is generally viewed as positive or negative. For example: "The American pioneers worked hard because they cared about the future. If you care about the future of your family, then see your agent at Pioneer Insurance."

5. *Unreliable testimonial*: This technique involves having an unqualified person endorse a product, action, or opinion. For example: "Hi! I'm Bart Bearson. As a pro-football quarterback, I have to be concerned about my health. That's why I take Pro-Ball Vitamin Supplements."

6. *Vague, undefined terms*: This technique involves promoting or challenging an opinion by using words that are so vague or so poorly defined as to be almost meaningless. For example: "Try our *new* and *improved*, *all-natural* product!"

Avoid using propaganda techniques in your own speech and writing, and be on the alert for these techniques in the speech and writing of others.

PURPOSE *n.* The *purpose* is the goal or aim of a literary work. A writer's purpose may be to tell a story, to describe something, to explain or inform, to persuade, or simply to entertain. Often a work will combine several of these purposes. In her essay "The Sounds of Richard Rodgers," on page 473, Ellen Goodman has two major purposes: First, Goodman wants to explain Richard Rodgers's work. Second, she wants to persuade

readers that it is possible for people to blend their work lives with their personal lives, as Richard Rodgers did.

In an essay the writer's purpose is often stated directly. The sentence or sentences that tell the purpose, or main idea, of the essay are called the thesis statement.
See *Main Idea*.

REALISTIC DETAILS/FANTASTIC DETAILS *n. phrases* A *realistic detail* is one that is drawn from actual or possible experience. A *fantastic detail* is one that is not based on actual experience and that is highly improbable or imaginary. Realistic details make plots, characters, descriptions, and statements seem true to life, or believable. Writers often use fantastic details to capture the reader's interest or imagination. Folk tales, such as those about Paul Bunyan and Pecos Bill, often contain fantastic details about the hero's strength or courage. Fantastic details are also found in science fiction stories, such as Arthur C. Clarke's "Crime on Mars," on page 137.

Few works consist entirely of fantastic details. More often fantastic and realistic details are combined. In "Crime on Mars," for example, Clarke sets the realistic details of a human crime against the fantastic background of a colony on another planet.

REASON *n.* A *reason* is a statement made in support of some conclusion. The term *reason* is also used to signify the human ability to think logically and rationally.
See *Argument* and *Conclusion*.

SOURCE *n.* A *source* is anything from which ideas and information are taken. Books, magazines, speeches, television programs, conversations, and personal experience may all serve as sources. Some books, such as dictionaries, encyclopedias, almanacs, and atlases, are specifically designed to be used as sources. A good source is one that is thorough, objective, and up-to-date.

There are two types of sources, primary and secondary. *Primary sources* are first-hand accounts. Conversations, speeches, documents, and letters are examples of primary sources. *Secondary sources* are accounts written by others, after the fact. For example, *One Writer's Beginnings* is a primary source of information about Eudora Welty's life because Welty wrote this book herself. On the other hand, a biography of Eudora Welty, written by another writer, is a secondary source of information about Welty. It merely summarizes or repeats information gained from other sources, such as *One Writer's Beginnings*.

Whenever you borrow facts and ideas from other sources, be sure to credit your sources by means of footnotes or end notes. If you do not credit them, you are committing the dishonest act called plagiarism.

STEREOTYPE *n.* A *stereotype* is a fixed or conventional notion or characterization. It is a type of overgeneralization or oversimplification. Some examples include the mad scientist, the absent-minded professor, and the beautiful princess. Although writers occasionally use stereotypes when they do not have sufficient space to develop a character fully, good writers generally avoid stereotyping. They know that carefully drawn characters and situations are more interesting to read about than tired, simplistic stereotypes.
See *Generalization*.

SUBJECTIVE *adj.* Something is *subjective* if it is based on personal reactions or emotions rather than on some objective reality. A reader's reaction to a work of literature is subjective because another reader may have a different reaction. Opinions are subjective statements, but not all opinions are equally valid. Sensible subjective statements about a literary work are based on evidence from the text. For example, if you find Goodrich and Hackett's play *The Diary of Anne Frank* powerful and moving, you should be able to identify some of the details in the play that make you feel this way.

When authors invent thoughts, dialogue, and actions for their characters, they are depicting the subjective experiences of their characters. *The Diary of Anne Frank*, for example, recreates the subjective feelings and experiences of a young girl who, along with her family, is hiding from the Nazis during World War II.
See *Objective*.

SUMMARIZE *v.* To *summarize* something is to restate it briefly in different words. A brief summary of Pearl S. Buck's story, "Christmas Day in the Morning," might be as follows:

> The main character, an older man named Rob, recalls the Christmas when he was fifteen and gave his father a special gift: He got up early and milked the family's cows all by himself, a chore he had always helped his father with and had always hated. His father was delighted by this "present." Thinking back on this incident gives Rob the idea of doing something similar for his wife. So, Rob gets up early on Christmas morning to trim the Christmas tree and to write a love letter to his wife. Rob learned when he was fifteen how to give the gift of love, and he has remembered that lesson all of his life.

SUPPORT *v.* To *support* something is to provide evidence for it.
See *Argument* and *Evidence*.

TIME ORDER *n.* *Time order* is organization by order of occurrence, that is, by chronological order. Many fiction and nonfiction works use time order to organize and present the events they describe.

TRANSFER See *Propaganda Technique*.

UNRELIABLE TESTIMONIAL See *Propaganda Technique*.

READING THE GLOSSARY ENTRIES

The words in this glossary are from selections appearing in your textbook. Each entry in the glossary contains the following parts:

1. The Entry Word. This word appears at the beginning of the entry, in boldface type.

2. The Pronunciation. The symbols in parentheses tell how the entry word is pronounced. If a word has more than one possible pronunciation, the most common of these pronunciations is given first.

3. The Part of Speech. Appearing after the pronunciation, in italics, is an abbreviation that tells the part of speech of the entry word. The following abbreviations have been used:

n. noun	**p.** pronoun	**v.** verb
adj. adjective	**adv.** adverb	**conj.** conjunction

4. The Definition. This part of the entry follows the part-of-speech abbreviation and gives the meaning of the entry word as used in the selection in which it appears.

KEY TO PRONUNCIATION SYMBOLS USED IN THE GLOSSARY

The following symbols are used in the pronunciations that follow the entry words:

Symbol	Key Words	Symbol	Key Words
a	asp, fat, parrot	b	bed, fable, dub
ā	ape, date, play	d	dip, beadle, had
ä	ah, car, father	f	fall, after, off
		g	get, haggle, dog
		h	he, ahead, hotel
e	elf, ten, berry	j	joy, agile, badge
ē	even, meet, money	k	kill, tackle, bake
		l	let, yellow, ball
i	is, hit, mirror	m	met, camel, trim
ī	ice, bite, high	n	not, flannel, ton
		p	put, apple, tap
ō	open, tone, go	r	red, port, dear
ô	all, horn, law	s	sell, castle, pass
o͞o	ooze, tool, crew	t	top, cattle, hat
oo	look, pull, moor	v	vat, hovel, have
yo͞o	use, cute, few	w	will, always, swear
yoo	united, cure, globule	y	yet, onion, yard
oi	oil, point, toy	z	zebra, dazzle, haze
ou	out, crowd, plow		
		ch	chin, catcher, arch
u	up, cut, color	sh	she, cushion, dash
ur	urn, fur, deter	th	thin, nothing, truth
		th	then, father, lathe
ə	a in ago	zh	azure, leisure
	e in agent	ŋ	ring, anger, drink
	i in sanity	'	[see explanatory note
	o in comply		below and also *For-*
	u in focus		*eign sounds* below]
ər	perhaps, murder		

This pronunciation key is from *Webster's New World Dictionary*, Second College Edition. Copyright © 1986 by Simon & Schuster. Used by permission.

A

abalone (ab′əlō′nē) shell *n.* An oval shell with a pearly lining

abandonment (ə ban′ dən mənt) *n.* Unrestrained freedom of actions or emotions

abduction (ab duk′ shən) *n.* Kidnapping

aboriginal (ab′ ə rij′ ə n′l) *adj.* First; native

abyss (ə bis′) *n.* Great depth

acquiescent (ak′ wē es′ ənt) *adj.* Agreeing without protest

acrid (ak′ rid) *adj.* Sharp; bitter

acute (ə kyo͞ot′) *adj.* Sensitive

ad-lib (ad′ lib′) *v.* To say or do things not in a script

adversary (ad′ vər ser′ē) *n.* Enemy

affectation (af′ ek tā′ shən) *n.* Behavior not natural to a person intended to impress others

aghast (ə gast′) *adj.* Horrified

airy (er′ ə) *adj.* Lightness

alkaloid (al′ kə loid′) *adj.* Referring to certain bitter substances found chiefly in plants

ally (al′ ī) *v.* To join or to unite, connection between country, person, or group for a common purpose

allure (ə loor′) *v.* To tempt; attract

alterative (ôl′ tə rāt′ iv) *adj.* Causing a change

amble (am′ b'l) *v.* To move at a smooth, easy pace

ambuscade (am′ bəs kād′) *n.* Place of surprise attack

amenity (ə men′ ə tē) *n.* Pleasant quality

anachronism (ə nak′ rə niz′m) *n.* Anything that seems to be out of its proper place in history

anemometer (an′ ə mäm′ ə tər) *n.* An instrument that determines wind speed

antagonist (an tag′ ə nist) *n.* Opponent

anxious (aŋk′ shəs) *adj.* Eagerly wishing

apathetic (ap′ ə thet′ ik) *adv.* Indifferent

apex (ā′ peks) *n.* Highest point; peak

appall (ə pôl′) *v.* To overwhelm with horror or shock

apparition (ap′ ə rish′ ən) *n.* A strange figure appearing suddenly or in an extraordinary way

applaud (ə plôd′) *v.* To show approval or enjoyment by clapping the hands

appraisal (ə prā′ z'l) *n.* Evaluation; judgment

apprehension (ap′ rə hen′ shən) *n.* A fearful feeling about the future; dread

apprentice (ə pren′ tist) *v.* To contract to learn a trade under a skilled worker

arbitrary (är′ bə trer′ ē) *adj.* Based on one's preference or whim

archaeologist (är′ kē äl′ ə jist) *n.* Scientist who studies the life and culture of ancient people

archer (är′ chər) *n.* A person who shoots with bow and arrow

archipelago (ar′ kə pel′ ə gō′) *n.* A chain of many islands

ardent (är′ d'nt) *adj.* Passionate

aristocrat (ə ris′ tə krat′) *n.* A person belonging to the upper class

armory (är′ mər ē) *n.* A storehouse for weapons

articulated (är tik′ yə lāt′ əd) *adj.* Connected by joints

artifact (är′ tə fakt′) *n.* Any object made by human work, left behind by a civilization

askew (ə skyo͞o′) *adv.* Crookedly

assiduous (ə sij′ yoo wəs) *adj.* Careful and busy

august (ô gust′) *adj.* Honored

aura (ô′ ə) *n.* An atmosphere or quality

avail (ə vāl′) *v.* To be of use

aver   (ə vur')   *v.* To declare

awed   (ôd)   *adj.* Having a mixed feeling of reverence, fear, and wonder

axioms   (ak' sē əmz)   *n.* Truths or principles that are widely accepted

B

babel   (ba'b'l)   *n.* A confusion of sounds

backfire   (bak' fīr')   *n.* A fire started to stop an advancing fire

bane   (bān)   *n.* Ruin

bank   (baŋk)   *v.* To tilt an airplane to the side when turning

banner   (ban' ər)   *n.* Flag

barter   (bär' tər)   *v.* To exchange goods

becalm   (bi käm')   *v.* Not to move

bedraggle   (bi drag''l)   *v.* To wet and soil

beguile   (bi gīl')   *v.* To charm

belfry   (bel' frē)   *n.* The part of a tower that holds the bells

bellow   (bel' ō)   *v.* Roar powerfully

benediction   (ben' ə dik' shən)   *n.* A blessing

benevolent   (bə nev' ə lənt)   *adj.* Kindly

benign   (bi nīn')   *adj.* Kindly

billow   (bil' ō)   *n.* Large; spread out

bleating   (blēt' iŋ)   *n.* The sound made by sheep

blunder   (blun' dər)   *n.* A foolish or stupid mistake

bode   (bōd')   *v.* To foretell a future event

borne   (bôrn)   *v.* Carried

brace   (brās)   *n.* A pair of like things

bravado   (brə vä' dō)   *n.* Bold, bragging behavior

bridle   (brīd''l)   *n.* A head harness for guiding a horse

brimstone   (brim' stōn')   *n.* Another name for sulfur, a foul-smelling mineral

brine   (brīn)   *n.* Water full of salt and used for pickling

broach   (brōch)   *n.* Start a discussion about a topic

bullpen   (bool' pen)   *n.* A barred room in a jail, where prisoners are kept temporarily

buoyant   (boi' ənt)   *adj.* Lighthearted

C

cadence   (kād''ns)   *n.* Rhythmic flow of sound

cajole   (kə jōl')   *v.* To coax gently

callous   (kal' əs)   *adj.* Unfeeling

callowness   (kal' ō nəs)   *n.* Youth and inexperience; immaturity

capitulation   (kə pich' ə lā' shən)   *n.* Surrender

carcass   (kär' kəs)   *n.* The dead body of an animal

carillon   (kar' ə län')   *n.* A set of stationary bells, each producing one note of the scale

catapult   (kat' ə pult')   *v.* To launch

cataract   (kat' ə rakt')   *n.* Large waterfall

celestial   (səl es' chəl)   *adj.* Of the sky

centrifugal   (sen trif' yə gəl)   *adj.* Describing something that tends to move away from the center

cessation   (se sā' shən)   *n.* A stopping

chancellor   (chan' sə lər)   *n.* An official secretary

civic   (siv' ik)   *adj.* Of a city

coherence   (kō hir' əns)   *n.* The quality of being connected in an intelligible way

commission   (kə mish')   *n.* Authority given to make something

commotion   (kə mō' shən)   *n.* Noisy movement

communal   (käm yoon' 'l)   *adj.* Shared by members of a group

compassionate   (kəm pash' ə nit)   *adj.* Sympathizing deeply

compensation   (käm' pən sā' shən)   *n.* Equal reaction

compliance   (kəm plī' əns)   *n.* Agreeing to a request

compound   (käm pound')   *adj.* Mix

compulsory   (kəm pul' sər ē)   *adj.* Required

conciliate   (kən sil' ē āt)   *v.* To make friends with

condemn   (kən dem')   *v.* To disapprove of

confederate   (kən fed' ər it)   *adj.* Accomplice; partner in crime

conjecture   (kən jek' chər)   *v.* To guess from very little evidence

conjuration   (kän' jə rā' shən)   *n.* The making of a magic spell

conspicuous   (kən spik' yoo əs)   *adj.* Noticeable

conspiratorial   (kən spir' ə tôr' ē əl)   *adj.* Secretive

constellation   (kän' stə lā' shən)   *n.* Brilliant cluster

convent   (kän' vənt)   *n.* A girls' boarding school run by nuns

conviction   (kən vik' shən)   *n.* Strong belief

convolutions   (kän' və lū' shənz)   *n.* Uneven ridges on the brain's surface

convulse   (kən vuls')   *v.* To suffer a violent, involuntary spasm

cosseted   (käs' it əd)   *adj.* Pampered; indulged

couch   (kouch)   *v.* To put into words

countenance   (koun' tə nəns)   *n.* The face

covert   (kuv' ərt)   *adj.* Concealed; hidden

cower   (kou' ər)   *v.* To crouch or huddle from fear

cowling   (kou'liŋ)   *n.* A removable metal covering for an engine

cowpuncher   (kou' pun cher)   *n.* Cowboy

crane   (krān)   *n.* A large, slender bird with very long legs and neck

cranny   (kran' ē)   *n.* Small, narrow opening

credo   (krē' dō)   *n.* Set of personal beliefs

crevasse   (kri vas')   *n.* A deep, narrow opening, as in a cliff

crevice   (krev' is)   *n.* A narrow opening

crockery   (kräk' ər ē)   *n.* Earthenware dishes, pots, and so on

crooner   (kroon' ər)   *n.* Singer

crooning   (kroon' iŋ)   *v.* Singing or humming in a low, gentle way

crosstie   (krôs' tī)   *n.* Beam laid crosswise under railroad tracks to support them

crustaceans   (krus tā' shənz)   *n.* Shellfish, such as lobsters, crabs, or shrimp

crypt   (kript)   *n.* An underground vault, used as a burial place

cryptic   (krip' tik)   *adj.* Having hidden meaning

crystal   (kris' t'l)   *n.* The transparent covering over the face of a watch

cunning   (kun' iŋ)   *adj.* Skillful

cynical   (sin' ik l)   *adj.* Disbelief as to the sincerity of people's intentions or actions

D

damask   (dam' əsk)   *n.* A fine fabric of silk or linen with a woven design

daunt   (dônt')   *v.* To intimidate or discourage

defray   (di frā')   *v.* To pay the money for the cost of

delineate   (di lin' ē āt)   *v.* To describe in detail

demise (di mīz′) *n.* Death
derision (di rizh′ ən) *n.* Contempt; ridicule
destine (des′ tin) *v.* To determine by fate
devour (di vour′) *v.* To eat up greedily
digital (dij′ it əl) *adj.* Giving a reading in digits, which are the numerals from 0 to 9
dinghy (din′ gē) *n.* Small rowboat
dirge (dʉrj) *n.* Slow, sad song of mourning
discreet (dis krēt′) *adj.* Careful about what one says or does
discreet surveillance (dis krēt′ sər vā′ ləns) *n.* Careful, unobserved watch kept over a person
disheveled (di shev′ ld) *adj.* Untidy; messy
dissemble (di sem′ b'l) *v.* To conceal under a false appearance
dissentient (di sen′ shənt) *adj.* Differing from the majority
dissimulation (di sim′ yə lā′ shən) *n.* The hiding of one's feelings or purposes
dissolute (dis′ ə lo͞ot′) *adj.* Unrestrained
dissolution (dis′ ə lo͞o′ shən) *n.* The act of breaking down and crumbling
distend (dis tend′) *v.* To stretch out; to become swollen
diverge (də vʉrj′) *v.* To branch off
divert (də vʉrt′) *v.* To distract
divest (də vest′) *v.* To strip; to get rid of
doggedness (dôg′ id nis) *n.* Stubborness
dogie (dō′ gē)   **calves** *n.* Motherless calves
drill (dril) *n.* Pointed tool used for making holes in hard substances
drive (drīv) *v.* To force by hitting
drowse (drouz) *n.* Sluggishness; doze
drove (drōv) *n.* Large number; crowd
dugout (dug′ out′) *n.* A shelter built into a hillside

E

elaborate (i lab′ ər it) *adj.* Careful; painstaking
elder (el′ dər) *n.* Shrub or small tree
elixir (i lik′ sər) *n.* Magic potion
elusive (i lo͞o′ siv) *adj.* Hard to grasp mentally
emancipate (i man′ sə pāt) *v.* To free from the control or power of another
eminent (em′ ə nənt) *adj.* Well-known
encumber (in kum′ bər) *v.* To weigh down
engulf (in gulf′) *v.* To flow over; to swallow up
enigma (ə nig′ mə) *n.* An unexplainable event
enthusiasm (in tho͞o′ zē az'm) *n.* Intense or eager interest
enunciate (i nun′ sē āt′) *v.* To speak clearly and carefully
esophagus (i säf′ ə gəs) *n.* The tube through which food passes to the stomach
eternal (i tʉr′ n'l) *adj.* Everlasting
evacuee (i vak′ yo͞o wē′) *n.* One who leaves a place because of danger
evasion (i vā′ zhən) *n.* Avoidance
exception (ik sep′ shən) *n.* Exclusion
excrescence (iks kres′ ns) *n.* A natural outgrowth
exodus (ek′ sə dəs) *n.* Departure
expend (ik spend′) *v.* To use up
expound (ik spound′) *v.* To explain in careful detail
extravagance (ik strav′ ə gəns) *n.* Waste
extremity (ik strem′ ə tē) *n.* Dying stage
exult (ig zult′) *v.* To rejoice

F

fastidious (fas tid′ ē əs) *adj.* Not easy to please
fatalist (fā′ tə list) *n.* One who believes that all events are determined by fate
fatuous (fach′ o͞o wəs) *adj.* Foolish; blandly inane
feign (fān′) *v.* To make a false show of
fell (fel) *n.* Rocky or barren hill
fertile (fʉr′ t'l) *adj.* Rich; productive
fiscal (fis′ kəl) *adj.* Having to do with finances
fissure (fish′ ər) *n.* Narrow opening
fitting (fit′ iŋ) *adj.* Proper
flag (flag) *v.* To signal to a train to stop
fleece (flēs) *n.* Soft, warm covering made of sheep's wool
fluctuate (fluk′ cho͞o wāt′) *v.* To be constantly changing
flue (flo͞o) *n.* The pipe in a chimney
flush (flush) *n.* A blush or glow
forbear (fôr ber′) *v.* To refrain from
foresight (fôr′ sīt) *n.* The act of seeing beforehand
forestall (fôr stôl′) *v.* To prevent
forsaken (fər sā′ kən) *adj.* Abandoned
fragrant (frā′ grənt) *adj.* Covered with the odor of something
fretted (fret′ əd) *adj.* Decoratively arranged
friction (frik′ shən) *n.* The rubbing of the surface of one body against another
furtive (fʉr′ tiv) *adj.* Sly or done in secret
futile (fyo͞ot′ 'l) *adj.* Useless; hopeless

G

galley (gal′ ē) *n.* Cooking area on a ship
garnet (gär′ nit) *n.* Deep red gem
garrison (gar′ ə s'n) *n.* Military post or station
gentian (jen′ chən) *n.* Herb with blue flowers
gesticulation (jes tik′ yə lā′ shən) *n.* Energetic hand or arm gesture
glean (glēn) *v.* To find out gradually bit by bit
gleeful (glē′ fəl) *adj.* Merry
glisten (glis′ 'n) *v.* To shine
glockenspiel (gläk′ ən spēl′) *n.* Musical instrument, like xylophone
gnarled (närld) *adj.* Knotty and twisted
goad (gōd) *v.* To urge to action
gout (gout) *n.* Inflammation of the joints
gracious (grā′ shəs) *adj.* Kind and generous
granite (gran′ it) *adj.* Made of a type of very hard rock
gratification (grat′ ə fi kā′ shən) *n.* The act of pleasing
gross (grōs) *n.* Twelve dozen
guffaw (gə fô′) *v.* To laugh in a loud, coarse way
guile (gīl) *n.* Craftiness
gumption (gump′ shən) *n.* Courage, boldness
guttural (gut′ ər əl) *adj.* Made in back of the throat; *n.* Sound produced in the throat
gyration (jī rā′ shən) *n.* Circling or spiral movement

H

haggard (hag′ ərd) *adj.* Having a tired look
harness (här′ nis'd) *v.* To tie
hasp (hasp) *n.* Hinged metal fastening of a window

heft (heft) *v.* To lift; test the weight of
hie (hī) *v.* To hurry
hoarse (hôrs) *adj.* Sounding harsh
hobnailed (häb′ nāld) *adj.* Having short nails put on the soles to provide greater traction
homage (häm′ ij) *n.* Public expression of honor
homesteader (hōm′ sted′ ər) *n.* Settler in America in the 1800's
hook-and-eye (hook′ and ī′) *n.* A fastening device
horde (hôrd) *n.* Large moving group
horizon (hə rī′ zən) *n.* The line that forms the apparent boundary between the earth and the sky
host (hōst) *n.* An army; a multitude
hover (huv′ ər) *v.* To stay suspended in the air
hummock (hum′ ək) *n.* Mound or small hill
hurtle (hurt′ 'l) *v.* To move quickly
hybrid (hī′ brid) *adj.* Grown from different varieties

I

ignominious (ig′ nə min′ ē əs) *adj.* Humiliating; degrading
impenetrable (im pen′ i trə b'l) *adj.* Not able to be passed through
imperious (im pir′ ē əs) *adj.* Overbearing, arrogant
imperturbable (im′ pər tur′ bə bl) *adj.* Unexcited; calm
impetuous (im pech′ oo wəs) *adj.* Impulsive
inarticulate (in′ är tik′ yə lit) *adj.* Speechless or unable to express oneself
incantation (in′ kantā′ shən) *n.* Magic words used to cast a spell
incentive (in sen′ tiv) *n.* Something that stirs up people or urges them on
incessant (in ses′ 'nt) *adj.* Without interruption
incisors (in sī′ zərz) *n.* The front teeth
incredulous (in krej′ oo ləs) *adj.* Doubt or disbelief
indignant (in dig′ nənt) *adj.* Filled with anger over some injustice
indiscriminate (in′ dis krim′ ə nit) *adj.* Random
indomitable (in däm′ it ə b'l) *adj.* Not easily discouraged
indulgent (in dul′ jənt) *adj.* Very tolerant
ineffectual (in′ i fek′ choo əl) *adj.* Without any effect
inevitable (in ev′ ə tə b'l) *adj.* Unavoidable
inexorable (in ek′ sər ə b'l) *adj.* Unwilling to give in
inexplicable (in eks′ pli kə b'l) *adj.* Without explanation
inferiority complex (in fir′ ē or′ ə tē käm′ pleks) *n.* Constant sense of worthlessness
inflammation (in′ flə mā′ shən) *n.* A state of redness, pain and swelling
infuse (in fyooz′) *v.* To put into
ingot (iŋ′ gət) *n.* A mold in which metal is cast
inherent (in hir′ ənt) *adj.* Natural
initiation (i nish′ ē ā′ shən) *n.* The events during which a person becomes admitted as a member of a club
innumerable (i noo′ mər ə b'l) *adj.* Too many to be counted
inquest (in′ kwest) *n.* Investigation
inquisitive (in kwiz′ ə tiv) *adj.* Curious
insidious (in sid′ ē əs) *adj.* Sly; crafty
insolent (in′ sə lənt) *n.* One who is boldly disrespectful

insolent (in′ sə lənt) *adj.* In a bold disrespectful way
insubordination (in′ sə bor′ d'n ā′ shən) *n.* Disobedience
insufferable (in suf′ ər ə b'l) *adj.* Unbearable
insular (in′ sə lər) *adj.* Isolated; detached
intercourse (int′ ər kôrs) *n.* Communication between people
intern (in′ tərn) *n.* A doctor serving a training period
intimation (in′ tə mā′ shən) *n.* Hint or suggestion
introspective (in′ trə spek′ tiv) *adj.* Looking into one's own thoughts and feelings
intuition (in′ too wish′ ən) *n.* Ability to know immediately without reasoning
invariable (in ver′ ē ə b'l) *adj.* Not changing
invincible (in vin′ sə b'l) *adj.* Unbeatable

J

jaded (jā′ did) *adj.* Worn-out
jocund (jäk′ ənd) *adj.* Cheerful; merry

K

kaleidoscopic (kə lī′ də skäp′ ik) *adj.* Constantly changing
keel (kēl) *n.* The chief structural beam extending along the entire length of the bottom of a boat or ship supporting the frame
keen (kēn) *adj.* Having a sharp cutting edge
keystone (kē′ stōn) *n.* A wedge-shaped piece at the top of an arch that locks other pieces into place
kindle (kin′ d'l) *v.* To ignite
kitchenette-furnished (kich ə net′ fur′ nisht) *adj.* Having a small, compact kitchen
knell (nel) *n.* The sound of a bell slowly ringing
knothole (nät′ hōl) *n.* A hole in a board where a knot has fallen out

L

lag (lag) *v.* To fall behind
lair (ler) *n.* Den of a wild animal
languorous (laŋ′ gər əs) *adj.* Slow and lazy
lateral (lat′ ər əl) *adj.* Toward the side
lee (lē) *n.* Sheltered place; the side away from the wind
leer (lir′) *v.* To look with malicious triumph
legacy (leg′ ə sē) *n.* Anything handed down, as from an ancestor
lichen (lī′ kən) *n.* Small plants of fungus and algae growing on rocks, wood, or soil
lilting (lilt′ iŋ) *adj.* With a light, graceful rhythm
limned (lim'd) *adj.* Outlined
loam (lōm) *n.* Rich, dark soil
lobulated (läb′ yoo lāt′ əd) *adj.* Subdivided
lockjaw (läk′ jô′) *n.* A disease that causes jaw and neck muscles to become rigid
low (lō) *v.* To make the typical sound that a cow makes
lugubrious (loo goo′ brē əs) *adj.* Sad
lumberjack (lum′ bər jak′) *n.* A person employed to cut down timber
luminance (loo′ mə nəns) *n.* Brightness
luminous (loo′ mə nəs) *adj.* Glowing in the dark

M

macabre (mə käb′ rə) *adj.* Gruesome

malingerer (mə lin′ gər ər) *n.* One who pretends to be ill in order to escape work

mammoth (mam′ əth) *adj.* Huge

maneuver (mə noo′ vər) *v.* To move in a planned way

mania (mā′ nē ə) *n.* Uncontrollable enthusiasm

manifold (man′ ə fōld′) *adj.* Many and varied

mantle (man′ t′l) *n.* Sleeveless cloak or cape

meditate (med′ ə tāt′) *v.* To think deeply

medium (mē′ dē əm) *n.* Means of communication

meets (mētz) *n.* A series of races or competitions

mercurial (mər kyoor′ ē əl) *adj.* Quick or changeable in behavior

Mercury (mur′ kyoo rē) *n.* In Roman mythology, the messenger of the gods.

metamorphose (met′ ə môr′ fōs) *v.* To change or transform

meticulous (mə tik′ yoo ləs) *adj.* Extremely careful about details

mire (mīr) *n.* Deep mud

moccasin (mäk′ ə s′n) *n.* Heelless slipper of soft flexible leather

mode (mōd) *n.* Way; form

molding (mōl′ diŋ) *n.* Ornamental woodwork

morose (mə rōs′) *adj.* Gloomy

mote (mōt) *n.* A speck of dust or other tiny particle

mucilage (myoo′ s′l ij) *n.* Any watery solution of gum, glue, etc. used as an adhesive

muse (myooz′) *v.* To think deeply

muslin (muz′ lin) *n.* Plain-woven, cotton fabric

musty (mus′ tē) *adj.* Having a stale, damp smell

muted (myoot′ əd) *adj.* Muffled; subdued

mutineers (myoot′ ′n irz′) *n.* People on a ship who revolt against their officers

mutinous (myoot′ ′n əs) *adj.* Rebellious

mutual (myoo′ choo wəl) *adj.* Having the same relationship toward each other

N

narcotic (när kät′ ik) *n.* Something that has a soothing effect

negotiation (ni gō′ shē ā′ shən) *n.* Bargaining, or discussing to reach an agreement

nester (nest′ ər) *n.* A homesteader on the prairies in the mid-1800's

neurosurgeon (noor′ō sur′ jən) *n.* A doctor who operates on the nervous system

ninny (nin′ ē) *n.* Fool

nitwit (nit′ wit′) *n.* Stupid or silly person

nonchalant (nän′ shə länt′) *adj.* Casual

notions (nō′ shənz) *n.* Small, useful household items

nurture (nur′ chər) *v.* To nourish

nuzzle (nuz′ l) *v.* To rub with the nose

O

obdurate (äb′ door ət) *adj.* Stubborn; unyeilding

obliterate (ə blit′ ə rāf) *v.* To wipe out; leaving no traces

obscure (äb skyoor′) *adj.* Hidden; *v.* Hide

omen (ō′ mən) *n.* A thing or happening supposed to foretell a future event

ominous (äm′ ə nəs) *adj.* Threatening

oratorical (ôr′ ə tôr′ i k′l) *adj.* Of or characteristic of an orator, lofty, high-sounding

ornate (ôr nāt′) *adj.* Having fancy decorations

orthodontist (ôr′ thə dän′ tist) *n.* A dentist who straightens teeth

ostentatious (äs′ ten tā′ shəs) *adj.* Showy

P

paleontologist (pā′ lē än täl′ ə jist) *n.* Scientist who investigates prehistoric forms of life

palmated (pal′ māt əd) *adj.* Shaped like a hand with the fingers spread

palpate (pal′ pāt) *v.* To examine by touch

palpitant (pal′ pə tənt) *adj.* Quivering

pandemonium (pan′ də mō′ nē əm) *n.* A scene of wild disorder

panoply (pan′ə plē) *n.* Magnificent covering or array

paradox (par′ ə däks′) *n.* A situation that seems to have contradictory qualities

paraphernalia (par′ ə fər näl′ yə) *n.* Equipment

paroxysm (par′ ək siz′m) *n.* Outburst or convulsion

pelt (pelt) *n.* The skin and fur of an animal

perambulating (peram′ byoo lāt′ iŋ) *adj.* Walking

perch (purch) *v.* To rest upon

peremptory (pə remp′ tər ï) *adj.* Absolute, without question

periscope (per′ ə skōp′) *n.* An instrument containing mirrors and lenses to see objects not in a direct line from the viewer; often used in submarines

perspiration (pur′ spə rā′ shən) *n.* Sweat

pertinacity (pur′ tə nas′ ə tē) *n.* Stubbornness

pervade (pər vād′) *v.* To spread throughout

petulant (pech′ oo lənt) *adj.* Impatient

phantasmagorical (fan taz′ mə gôr′ ik l) *adj.* A rapid change, as in a dream

phantom (fan′ təm) *n.* Ghost-like figure

phoenix (fē′ niks) *n.* In Egyptian mythology, a beautiful bird

pinafore (pin′ ə fôr′) *n.* A sleeveless garment worn by little girls over a dress

pittance (pit′ ′ns) *n.* A small or barely sufficient allowance of money

placid (plas′ id) *adj.* Calm; quiet

platform (plat′ fôrm) *n.* Statement of intention

plethoric (plə thôr′ ik) *adj.* Too full

plum (plum) *adj.* Here, first-class

poach (pōch) *v.* To cook gently in near-boiling water

pollen (päl′ ən) *n.* The yellow, powderlike cells formed in the stamen of a flower

ponder (pän′ dər) *v.* To think deeply

ponderous (pän′ dər əs) *adj.* Heavy; massive

portentous (pôr ten′ təs) *adj.* Pompous

portly (pôrt′ lē) *adj.* Large, heavy, and dignified

posterity (päs ter′ ə tē) *n.* Future generations

posthaste (pōst′ hāst′) *adv.* With great quickness

precarious (pri ker′ ē əs) *adj.* Insecure and dangerous

precipitate (pri sip′ ə tāt) *v.* To cause to happen

predecessor (pred′ ə ses′ ər) *n.* Someone who comes before another in a position

pre·eminent (prē em′ ən ənt) *adj.* Dominant
premonition (prē mə nish′ ən) *n.* An omen
prerequisite (pri rek′ wə zit) *n.* An initial requirement
presentable (pri zen′ tə b′l) *adj.* Suitable to be seen by others
pretext (prē′ tekst) *n.* A false reason or motive given to hide a real intention
primordial (prī môr′ dē əl) *adj.* Primitive
privation (prī vā′ shən) *n.* Lack of common comfort
procure (prō kyoor′) *v.* To obtain by some effort
prodigy (präd′ ə jē) *n.* A child of extraordinary genius
profound (prə found′) *adj.* Deep
progeny (präj′ ə nē) *n.* Children
promote (prə mōt′) *v.* To give a higher position
propound (prə pound′) *v.* To propose; put forward for consideration
prospect (präs′ pekt) *n.* A likely candidate
protestation (prät′ is tā′ shən) *n.* Formal declaration or assertion
prow (prou) *n.* The frontmost part of a ship
prowess (prou′ is) *n.* Superior ability
pungent (pun′ jənt) *adj.* Sharp and stinging to the smell
purchase (pʉr′ chəs) *n.* A tight hold to keep from slipping
purgatory (pʉr′ gə tôr′ ē) *n.* A state or place of temporary punishment

R

rafter (raf′ tər) *n.* One of the beams that slopes from the ridge of a roof to the eaves and supports the roof
ram (ram) *v.* Heavy beams used to break down gates
rampage (ram′ pāj) *n.* An outbreak of violent behavior
rampant (ram′ pənt) *adj.* Unrestrained
raucous (rô′ kəs) *adj.* Boisterous; disorderly
ravaging (rav′ ij iŋ) *adj.* Severely damaging or destroying
recede (ri sēd′) *v.* To move farther away
reconnoiter (rē′ kə noit′ ər) *v.* To make an exploratory examination to get information about a place
recrudescence (rē′ kroo des′ əns) *n.* A fresh outbreak of something that has been inactive
redress (rē′ dres) *n.* The righting of wrongs
refute (ri fyoot′) *v.* To disprove
regimen (rej′ ə mən) *n.* A regulated system of diet and exercise
remote (ri mōt′) *adj.* Distant
renounce (ri nouns′) *v.* To give up
replica (rep′li kə) *n.* A copy of a work of art
repugnance (ri pug′ nəns) *n.* Extreme dislike
resolute (rez′ ə loot′) *adj.* Showing a firm purpose; determined
retribution (ret′ rə byoo′ shən) *n.* A punishment deserved for a wrong done
retrogression (ret′ rə gresh′ ən) *n.* A moving backward to a more primitive state
reverie (rev′ ər ē) *n.* Daydream
revue (ri vyoo′) *n.* A musical show with loosely connected skits, songs and dances
riveted (riv′ it əd) *adj.* Fastened or made firm
rollicking (räl′ ik iŋ) *adj.* Lively

ruction (ruk′ shən) *n.* Quarrel or noisy disturbance
ruddy (rud′ ē) *adj.* Having a healthy color
runt (runt) *n.* The smallest animal in a litter
ruse (rooz) *n.* A trick or plan for fooling someone

S

sagacity (sə gas′ ə tē) *n.* High intelligence and sound judgment
sage (sāj) *n.* A plant used to flavor food
salient (sāl′ yənt) *adj.* Noticeable; prominent
sap (sap) *v.* To drain; to exhaust
sarcastic (sär kas′ tik) *adj.* Having a sharp, mocking tone intended to hurt another
sash (sash) *n.* The frame holding the glass panes of the window
sassafras (sas′ ə fras′) *n.* Dried root bark of the sassafras tree
sated (sāt′ əd) *adj.* Fully satisfied
savor (sā′ vər) *v.* To enjoy; appreciate
scores (skôrz) *n.* The music for a stage production or film, apart from the lyrics and dialogue
screech (skrēch) *n.* A shrill, high-pitched shriek or sound
scuttle (skut′ ′l) *v.* To run or move quickly
sect (sekt) *n.* Small group of people with the same leader and belief
semblance (sem′ bləns) *n.* Likeness; image
sensory (sen′ sər ē) *adj.* Of receiving sense impressions
shanty (shan′ tē) *n.* Hut or shack
sheen (shēn) *n.* Shininess
shingle (shiŋ′ g′l) *v.* To cover the roof with shingles
shinny (shin′ ē) *v.* To climb by gripping with both hands and legs
shoal (shōl) *n.* Sand bar
shoon (shoon) *n.* Old-fashioned words for shoes
shun (shun) *v.* To avoid
simultaneous (sī′ məl tā′ nē əs) *adj.* Taking place at the same time
sinew (sin′ yoo) *n.* A band of fibrous tissue that connects muscles to bones or to other parts and can also be used as thread for sewing
singular (sin′ gyə lər) *adj.* Exceptional; peculiar
sinister (sin′ is tər) *adj.* Threatening harm, evil, or misfortune
sire (sīr) *n.* Father
skeptic (skep′ tik) *n.* Person who doubts
slander (slan′ dər) *n.* Lies
slash (slash) *v.* To cut with a sweeping stroke
smoldering (smōl′ dər iŋ) *adj.* Fiery
snicker (snik′ ər) *v.* To laugh in a mean way
snide (snīd) *adj.* Intentionally mean
soliloquize (sə lil′ ə kwīz) *v.* To talk to oneself
somber (säm′ bər) *adj.* Dark; gloomy
specious (spē′ shəs) *adj.* Seeming to be true without really being so
specter (spek′ tər) *n.* A disturbing thought
spectral (spek′ trəl) *adj.* Ghostly
spike (spīk) *n.* A long thick metal nail used for splitting rock
spume (spyoom) *n.* Foam; froth
squall (skwôl′) *v.* To cry out or scream

stalk (stôk′) *v.* To secretly approach

starboard (stär′ bərd) *adj.* The right side of a ship, as one faces forward

starling (stär′ liŋ) *n.* Dark-colored bird

stealthy (stel′ thē) *adj.* Secret; quiet

steep (stēp) *adj.* A slope or incline having a sharp rise

stench (stench) *n.* An offensive smell

stifled (stī′ f'ld) *adj.* Muffled; suppressed

stilted (stil′ təd) *adj.* Unnatural; very formal

stimulus (stim′ yə ləs) *n.* Something that rouses to action

stolid (stäl′ id) *adj.* Showing little or no emotion

stratagem (stra′ tə jəm) *n.* Plan for defeating an opponent

strife (strīf) *n.* Conflict

suavity (swä′ və tē) *n.* Graceful politeness

subjunctive (səb juŋk′ tiv) *n.* A particular form of a verb

successor (sək ses′ ər) *n.* A person that follows or comes after another

suckle (suk′'l) *v.* To nurse at the breast

suitor (soot′ ər) *n.* A man courting a woman

sultry (sul′ trē) *adj.* Hot and humid

superfluous (soo pur′ floo wəs) *adj.* More than is necessary

surcharged (sur′ charjd) *adj.* Overcharged

surveillance (sər vā′ ləns) *n.* Watch, inspection

swagger (swag′ ər) *n.* Arrogance or boastfulness; *v.* To strut; walk with a bold step

swamp (swämp) *v.* To sink by filling with water

swarthy (swôr′ thē) *adj.* Having a dark complexion

swoon (swoon) *v.* Faint

T

taciturn (tas′ ə turn′) *adj.* Not likely to talk

tangible (tan′ jə bəl) *adj.* Observable; understandable

taunt (tônt′) *v.* To jeer at; to mock

taut (tôt) *adj.* Tightly stretched

teamster (tēm′ stər) *n.* One who drives a team of horses to haul a load

teem (tēm) *v.* To swarm

tenacious (tə nā′ shəs) *adj.* Holding on firmly

tendril (ten′ drəl) *n.* Thin shoot from a plant

tenement (ten′ ə mənt) *n.* A run-down apartment building

tenure (ten′ yər) *n.* Time of residence

tepee (tē′pē) *n.* A cone-shaped tent of animal skins

tick (tik) *v.* To operate smoothly

tint (tint′) *v.* To color

tipis (tē′ pēz) *n.* Cone-shaped tents made of animal skins

tolerate (täl′ ə rāt′) *v.* To allow; permit

tortuous (tôr′ choo wəs) *adj.* Winding with repeated twists and turns

tousled-looking (tou′ z'ld loo′ kiŋ) *adj.* Rumpled or mussed

transient (tran′ shənt) *adj.* Not permanent

tread (tred) *n.* Step

tremor (trem′ ər) *n.* Shaking or vibration

trivial (triv′ ē əl) *adj.* Of little importance

troubadour (troo′ bə dôr′) *n.* Traveling singer, usually accompanying himself on a stringed instrument

trough (trôf) *n.* Long, narrow container for holding water or food for animals

U

unabashed (un ə bash′ əd) *adj.* Unashamed

uncanny (un kan′ ē) *adj.* Strange

unfurled (un furld′) *adj.* Unfolded

unobtrusive (un əb troo′ siv) *adj.* Not calling attention to oneself

unwonted (un wun′ tid) *adj.* Not usual

uproariously (up rôr′ ē əs lē) *adv.* Loudly and boisterously

usurp (yoo surp′) *v.* To take over

V

vacuous (vak′ yoo wəs) *adj.* Empty; shallow

venture (ven′ chər) *v.* To express oneself at the risk of criticism, objection, or denial

versatile (vur′ sə t'l) *adj.* Having many uses

vicarage (vik′ ər ij) *n.* A place where a member of the clergy lives

vicarious (vī kâr′ ē əs) *adj.* Experienced by one person or animal in place of another

vigorous (vig′ ər əs) *adj.* Strong and energetic

viscera (vis′ ər ə) *n.* Internal organs

vituperation (vī too′ pə rā′ shən) *n.* Abusive language

voile (voil) *n.* A light cotton fabric

voracious (vô rā′ shəs) *adj.* Eager to devour large quantities of food

W

waft (waf′ t) *v.* To move lightly through the air

walleyed (wôl′ īd′) *adj.* Having eyes that turn outward

wan (wän) *adj.* Pale

wantonness (wän′ tən nəs) *n.* Lack of discipline

whirl (hwurl) *v.* To drive with a rotating motion

willow-wild (wil′ ō wild′) *adj.* Slender and pliant, like a reed blowing in the wind

winch (winch) *n.* A machine used for lifting

wizened (wiz′ ənd) *adj.* Shrunken, and wrinkled with age

wormwood (wurm′ wood) *n.* A plant that produces a bitter oil

wraith (rāth) *n.* Ghost

Y

yearling (yir′ liŋ) *n.* An animal that is between one and two years old

yonder (yon′ dər) *adj.* In the distance

yucca (yuk′ ə) *n.* A desert plant with stiff leaves and white flowers

INDEX OF FINE ART

INDEX OF SKILLS

INDEX OF TITLES BY THEMES

INDEX OF AUTHORS AND TITLES

Page numbers in italics refer to biographical information.

ACKNOWLEDGMENTS (continued)

Doubleday & Co., Inc. (continued)
Reprinted by permission of Doubleday.

Mari Evans
"if you have had your midnights" from *Nightstar* by Mari Evans, published by CAAS, the University of California at Los Angeles, 1981. Reprinted by permission of the author.

Farrar, Straus and Giroux, Inc.
Adapted from "Charles" from *The Lottery* by Shirley Jackson. Copyright 1948, 1949 by Shirley Jackson; copyright © renewed 1976, 1977 by Laurence Hyman, Barry Hyman, Mrs. Sarah Webster, and Mrs. Joanne Schnurer. Reprinted by special permission of Farrar, Straus and Giroux, Inc. "The Day I Got Lost" from *Stories for Children* by Isaac Bashevis Singer. Copyright © 1962, 1967, 1968, 1970, 1972, 1973, 1974, 1975, 1976, 1979, 1980, 1984 by Isaac Bashevis Singer. Reprinted by permission of Farrar, Straus and Giroux, Inc.

Samuel French, Inc.
Act I of *The Romancers* by Edmond Rostand, translated by Barrett H. Clark. Copyright 1915 by Barrett H. Clark; copyright 1943 (in renewal) by Barrett H. Clark. Reprinted by permission of Samuel French, Inc.

Richard García
"The City Is So Big" by Richard Garcia, © 1973 by Richard Garcia. Reprinted by permission of the author.

Harcourt Brace Jovanovich, Inc.
"Crime on Mars" copyright © 1960 by Davis Publications. Reprinted from *The Nine Billion Names of God* by Arthur C. Clarke. "Forest Fire" from *The Diary of Anais Nin 1947-1955* edited by Gunther Stuhlmann, copyright © 1974 by Anais Nin. "Paul Bunyan of the North Woods" and "They Have Yarns" from *The People, Yes* by Carl Sandburg, copyright 1936 by Harcourt Brace Jovanovich, Inc.; renewed 1964 by Carl Sandburg. From "For My Sister Molly Who In The Fifties" copyright © 1972 by Alice Walker, in her volume *Revolutionary Petunias & Other Poems*. Reprinted by permission of Harcourt Brace Jovanovich, Inc.

Harper & Row, Publishers, Inc.
Text of "Shooting Stars" from *This World Of Wonder* by Hal Borland (J. B. Lippincott), copyright © 1972, 1973 by Hal Borland. Lines from "For a Poet" from *On These I Stand: The Best-Loved Poems of Countee Cullen* by Countee Cullen. Copyright 1925 by Harper & Row, Publishers, Inc.; renewed 1953 by Ida M. Cullen. Slightly adapted from pp. 314–325 of *Of Men and Mountains* by William O. Douglas, copyright 1950 by William O. Douglas. "New World" from *The Gourd Dancer* by N. Scott Momaday, copyright © 1976 by N. Scott Momaday. Haiku, "The Falling Flower," by Moritake from *Poetry Handbook: A Dictionary of Terms*, 4th edition, by Babette Deutsch (Thomas Y. Crowell), copyright © 1957, 1962, 1969, 1974 by Babette Deutsch. Reprinted by permission of Harper & Row, Publishers, Inc.

Harper & Row, Publisher, Inc., Joan Aiken, Jonathan Cape Ltd., and A. M. Heath & Company Ltd.
"The Gift Giving" from *Up the Chimney Down and Other Stories* by Joan Aiken, copyright © 1984 by Joan Aiken Enterprises Limited. Reprinted by permission.

Harvard University Press
"The Tell-Tale Heart" by Edgar Allan Poe from *Collected Works of Edgar Allan Poe* edited by Thomas Ollive Mabbott, copyright © 1978 by the President and Fellows of Harvard College. From *One Writer's Beginnings* by Eudora Welty, copyright © 1983, 1984 by Eudora Welty. Reprinted by permission of Harvard University Press.

John Hawkins & Associates, Inc.
Hokku poem ("The spring lingers on") by Richard Wright. Copyright by Richard Wright. Reprinted by permission of John Hawkins & Associates, Inc., New York.

Hill and Wang, a division of Farrar, Straus and Giroux, Inc.
"The Story-Teller" from *Collected and New Poems 1924-1963* by Mark Van Doren, copyright © 1963 by Mark Van Doren. Reprinted by permission of Hill and Wang, a division of Farrar, Straus and Giroux, Inc.

Henry Holt and Company, Inc.
"Blue-Butterfly Day" and "The Road Not Taken" copyright 1916, 1923, © 1969 by Holt, Rinehart and Winston, Inc. Copyright 1944, 1951 by Robert Frost. Reprinted from *The Poetry of Robert Frost* edited by Edward Connery Lathem. Lines from "Rose Pogonias" copyright © 1969 by Holt, Rinehart and Winston, Inc. Reprinted from *The Poetry of Robert Frost* edited by Edward Connery Lathem, by permission of Henry Holt and Company, Inc.

Evelyn Tooley Hunt and Negro Digest
"Taught Me Purple" by Evelyn Tooley Hunt from *Negro Digest*, February 1964, © 1964 by Johnson Publishing Company, Inc. Reprinted by permission.

Indiana University Press
"Staying Alive" from *Collected Poems 1956-1976* by David Wagoner. Copyright © 1976 by Indiana University Press.

Daniel Keyes
"Flowers For Algernon" (short story version) by Daniel Keyes. Copyright © 1959 and 1987 by Daniel Keyes. Reprinted by permission of the author. Edited for this edition.

Alfred A. Knopf, Inc.
"The Ninny" from *The Image of Chekhov* by Anton Chekhov, translated by Robert Payne. Copyright © 1963 by Alfred A. Knopf, Inc. "The Cyclone" from *Pecos Bill: Texas Cowpuncher* by Harold W. Felton. Copyright 1949 by Alfred A. Knopf, Inc. "Harlem Night Song" and "Winter Moon" from *Selected Poems of Langston Hughes* by Langston Hughes. Copyright 1926 by Alfred A. Knopf, Inc. and renewed 1954 by Langston Hughes. Lines from "The Quiet Fog" copyright © 1975 by Marge Piercy, reprinted from *The Twelve Spoked Wheel Flashing* by Marge Piercy. "January" from *A Child's Calendar* by John Updike. Copyright © 1965 by John Updike and Nancy Burkert. "Winter Ocean" copyright © 1960 by John Updike from *Telephone Poles* by John Updike. Reprinted by permission of Alfred A. Knopf, Inc.

Alfred A. Knopf, Inc. and Pierre Berton
Two maps ("The Country of the Klondike Fever" and "The Trail of '98") from *The Klondike Fever* by Pierre Berton. Copyright © 1958 by Pierre Berton. Reprinted by permission.

right © 1971 by Toni Cade Bambara. Reprinted from *Gorilla, My Love* by Toni Cade Bambara. From *The Diary of Anne Frank* by Frances Goodrich and Albert Hackett. Copyright 1954, 1956 as an unpublished work. Reprinted by permission of Random House, Inc. CAUTION: *The Diary of Anne Frank* is the sole property of the dramatists and is fully protected by copyright. It may not be acted by professionals or amateurs without written permission and the payment of a royalty. All rights, including professional, amateur, stock, radio broadcasting, television, motion picture, recitation, lecturing, public reading, and the rights of translation into foreign languages are reserved.

Reader's Digest
"The Indian All Around Us" by Bernard DeVoto. Reprinted with permission from the April 1953 *Reader's Digest.* Copyright 1953 by The Reader's Digest Association, Inc.

Reader's Digest and Robert MacNeil
"The Trouble with Television" by Robert MacNeil. Reprinted with permission from the March 1985 *Reader's Digest.*

Marian Reiner for Eve Merriam
"A Lazy Thought" from *Jamboree: Rhymes for All Times* by Eve Merriam. Copyright © 1962, 1964, 1966, 1973, 1984 by Eve Merriam. All rights reserved. Reprinted by permission of Marian Reiner for the author.

Andrea Reynolds, attorney-in-fact for André Milos
"The Adventure of the Speckled Band" by Sir Arthur Conan Doyle.

Russell and Volkening, Inc. as agents for the author
From *Harriet Tubman: Conductor on the Underground Railroad* by Ann Petry. Copyright © 1955, renewed 1983 by Ann Petry. Reprinted by permission of Russell and Volkening, Inc. as agents for the author.

St. Martin's Press, Inc., New York, and Harold Ober Associates Inc.
"Debbie" from *All Things Wise and Wonderful* by James Herriot. Copyright © 1976, 1977 by James Herriot.

Scholastic Inc.
"Accounts Settled" by Paul Annixter. Copyright © 1966 by Scholastic Magazines, Inc. Reprinted by permission of Scholastic Inc.

Argelia Sedillo
"Gentleman of Rio en Medio" by Juan A. A. Sedillo, published in *New Mexico Quarterly*, 1939.

Simon & Schuster, Inc.
"The Drummer Boy of Shiloh" from *The Machineries of Joy* by Ray Bradbury. Copyright © 1949, 1952, 1953, 1957, 1960, 1962, 1963, 1964 by Ray Bradbury. Reprinted by permission of Simon & Schuster, Inc. Pronunciation key from *Webster's New World Dictionary*—Second College Edition. Copyright © 1984 by Simon & Schuster, Inc. Reprinted by permission.

Virginia Driving Hawk Sneve
"The Medicine Bag" by Virginia Driving Hawk Sneve, published in *Boy's Life*, March 1975. Reprinted by permission of the author.

Lloyd Sarett Stockdale
"Four Little Foxes" from *Slow Smoke* by Lew Sarett, copyright 1953 by Lew Sarett; Henry Holt and Company. Reprinted by permission of Lloyd Sarett Stockdale.

Sterling Lord Literistic, Inc.
"A Poem About a Wolf Maybe Two Wolves" from *Shaking the Pumpkin* edited by Jerome Rothenberg. Copyright © 1972 by Jerome Rothenberg. Reprinted by permission of Sterling Lord Literistic, Inc.

Summit Books, a division of Simon & Schuster, Inc.
"The Sounds of Richard Rodgers" from *At Large* by Ellen Goodman. Copyright © 1981 by The Washington Post Company. Reprinted by permission of Summit Books, a division of Simon & Schuster, Inc.

Sunstone Press
"Song of the Sky Loom" from Herbert Spinden's *Songs of the Tewa*, published by Sunstone Press, Santa Fe, New Mexico.

May Swenson
"By Morning" by May Swenson is reprinted by permission of the author, copyright © 1954, renewed © 1982 by May Swenson, and originally appeared in *The New Yorker* under the title, "Snow By Morning." "Southbound on the Freeway" by May Swenson is reprinted by permission of the author, copyright 1968 by May Swenson, and was originally printed in *The New Yorker.*

Viking Penguin Inc.
"400-Meter Free Style" from *Our Ground Time Here Will Be Brief* by Maxine Kumin. Copyright 1959 by Maxine Kumin. "Reflections Dental" from *Times Three* by Phyllis McGinley. Copyright 1953 by Phyllis McGinley; copyright renewed © 1978 by Julie Elizabeth Hayden and Phyllis Hayden Blake. Originally published in *The New Yorker.* "The Choice" from *Enough Rope* by Dorothy Parker. Copyright 1926 by Dorothy Parker; copyright renewed 1953 by Dorothy Parker. "Frontier Fighter" (retitled, "Davy Crockett") and "Hammerman" from *American Tall Tales* by Adrien Stoutenburg. Copyright © 1966 by Adrien Stoutenburg. "Lyric 17" from *Have Come, Am Here* by José Garcia Villa. Copyright 1942 by José Garcia Villa; copyright renewed © 1969 by José Garcia Villa. Reprinted by permission of Viking Penguin Inc.

Viking Penguin Inc. and The Bodley Head Ltd.
"The Story-Teller" from *The Complete Short Stories of Saki (H. H. Munro).* Copyright 1930, renewed © 1958 by The Viking Press, Inc. Reprinted by permission.

Note: Every effort has been made to locate the copyright owner of material reprinted in this book. Omissions brought to our attention will be corrected in subsequent editions.

ART CREDITS

Sea, Helmut Kies, Three Lions; **p. 595:** *On the Promenade,* August Macke, Three Lions; **pp. 598–99:** *Seashore at Palavas,* 1854, Gustave Courbet, Musée Fabre, Montpellier; **p. 615:** Marc Chagall, *Green Violinist,* Solomon R. Guggenheim Museum, New York, Photo, David Heald; **pp. 622–23:** *Woodcutter on a Rock,* 1891, Winslow Homer, Private Collection; **pp. 626** (detail), **628:** Lightning, 1973, from the Weather Series, color lithograph, 39 × 32″, © Gemini Gel/David Hockney, 1973; **p. 630:** *Carl Sandburg* (detail), Miriam Svet, National Portrait Gallery, Smithsonian Institution; **p. 642:** New York Public Library; **p. 643:** *Paul Bunyan Carrying a Tree on His Shoulder and an Ax in His Hand,* The Bettmann Archive; **pp. 654** (detail), **656:** Museum of African American Art, Palmer C. Hayden, Collection, Gift of Miriam A. Hayden, Photograph by Armando Solis; **p. 664:** *A Man Ain't Nothin' but a Man,* Palmer C. Hayden, Palmer C. Hayden Collection, Gift of Miriam A. Hayden, Photograph by Armando Solis; **p. 674:** New York Public Library Picture Collection; **p. 680:** *Davy Crockett, with the Help of His Dog, Fighting a Bear,* cover of the Crockett Almanac, 1841, The Granger Collection; **pp. 690–91:** *Crossing the Chilkoot Pass During the Gold Rush in Alaska,* O. E. Berninghaus, Three Lions; **p. 693:** *Trapper in the Wilds of Alaska,* Sydney Laurence, The Shelburne Museum, Vermont.

PHOTOGRAPH CREDITS

p. 9: The Granger Collection; **p. 12:** Thomas Victor; **pp. 16–17:** Ann and Myron Sutton/Shostal; **p. 46:** New York Public Library Picture Collection; **p. 47:** Ken Karp; **p. 49:** Roy Morsch/Bruce Coleman; **p. 50:** E. R. Degginger/Bruce Coleman; **p. 54:** UPI/Bettmann Newsphotos; **p. 62:** Thomas Victor; **p. 72:** AP/Wide World Photos; **p. 90:** Nikky Finney; **p. 91:** Cliff Feulner/The Image Bank; **p. 92:** Co Tentmeester/The Image Bank; **p. 95:** Audrey Gottlieb/Monkmeyer; **p. 97:** Steven E. Sutton/Duomo CWG VIII; **p. 100:** Montana Historical Society, Helena; **p. 112:** Thomas Victor; **p. 113:** Ken Karp; **p. 118:** AP/Wide World; **p. 128:** Bradford Bachrach; **p. 136:** UPI/Bettmann Newsphotos; **p. 144:** UPI/Bettmann Newsphotos; **p. 150:** Thomas Victor; **p. 158:** The Bettmann Archive; **p. 162:** Steven Y. Mori; **p 164:** Steve Solum/Bruce Coleman; **p. 200:** Harry Snaveley; **p. 203:** The Memory Shop; **pp. 208, 217:** Phototeque; **p. 221:** The Memory Shop; **p. 229:** Ken Karp; **p. 233:** Tom Bean/The Stock Market; **p. 262:** The Bettmann Archive; **p. 276:** AP/Wide World; **pp. 300, 301, 302:** UPI/Bettmann Newsphotos; **p. 304:** The Bettmann Archive; **pp. 306, 308, 311, 316, 328:** © by Anne Frank-Fonds/COSMOPRESS, Genève; **p. 333:** UPI/Bettmann Newsphotos; **pp. 337, 345, 349, 352, 358:** © by Anne Frank-Fonds/COSMOPRESS, Genève; **p. 363:** The Granger Collection; **p. 378:** J. P. Nacivet/Leo de Wys, Inc.; **p. 379:** Thomas Victor; **p. 395:** Ken McVey/After Image; **p. 398:** Jerry Wachter/Focus on Sports; **p. 402:** Wake Forest University; **p. 420:** UPI/Bettmann Newsphotos; **p. 422:** Jonathan T. Wright/Bruce Coleman; **p. 425:** Gordon Wiltsie/Bruce Coleman; **p. 430:** The Bettmann Archive; **p. 438:** John Wyand; **p. 444:** The Granger Collection; **p. 452:** AP/Wide World Photos; **p. 456:** The Bettmann Archive; **p. 462:** The Bettmann Archive; **p. 468:** Les Line; **p. 469:** Dennis diCicco/Peter Arnold, Inc.; **p. 472:** UPI/Bettmann Newsphotos; **p. 476:** Thomas Victor; **p. 480:** AP/Wide World; **p. 484:** Thomas Victor; **p. 486:** Simon Warner/The Brontë Society; **p. 494:** AP/Wide World; **p. 504:** E. R. Degginger; **p. 505:** AP/Wide World; **p. 520:** The Granger Collection; **p. 526:** © Henri Cartier-Bresson/Magnum; **p. 530:** (top) NYT Pictures, (middle) UPI/Bettmann Newsphotos; **p. 537:** George Hall/Woodfin Camp; **p. 538:** (top) Thomas Victor; (middle) AP/Wide World; **pp. 540–41:** Charles West/The Stock Market; **p. 542:** (left and right) Joel Gordon; **p. 543:** (left) Roy Morsch/The Stock Market, (right) Richard Dunoff/The Stock Market; **p. 545:** G. Cigolini/The Image Bank; **p. 546:** (top) AP/Wide World, (middle) The Bettmann Archive; **p. 549:** Ken Karp; **p. 554:** (top) Courtesy of Helen Sarett Stockdale and Lloyd Sarett Stockdale, (third from top) Dmitri Kessel/*Life* magazine, © Time Inc.; (bottom) Thomas Victor; **p. 557:** Kenneth W. Fink/Bruce Coleman; **p. 559:** Jane Burton/Bruce Coleman; **p. 562:** (top) © Faber & Faber Ltd., (middle) AP/Wide World; **p. 564:** Aram Gesar/The Image Bank; **p. 574:** (top) Thomas Victor, (bottom) Thomas Victor; **p. 578:** A. & J. Verkaik/The Stock Market; **pp. 580–81:** David Fitzgerald/After Image; **p. 584:** (middle) Harold Hornstein, (bottom) Thomas Victor; **pp. 588–89:** Tardos Camesi/The Stock Market; **p. 590:** AP/Wide World; **p. 592:** Focus on Sports; **p. 596:** (bottom) Dmitri Kessel/*Life* Magazine © Time, Inc.; **pp. 600–601:** Julius Fekete/The Stock Market; **p. 602:** (top) The Granger Collection; **p. 608:** Robin Seyfried; **p. 611:** Michael Melford/Wheeler Pictures; **p. 616:** Thomas Victor; **p. 662:** The Granger Collection; **p. 675:** The Granger Collection; **p. 678:** The Granger Collection; **p. 694:** The Bettmann Archive.

ILLUSTRATION CREDITS

pp. 4, 7, 28–29, 34, 38–39, 59, 63, 68–69, 80, 83, 109, 128, 140–41, 146, 160, 170, 176–77, 180–81, 245, 249, 250–51, 256, 260, 266–67, 272–73, 281, 285, 297, 404, 407, 492, 509, 512–13, 517, 569, 631, 632, 633, 637, 646, 647, 654, 656, 668, 670, 672, 700–01, 705, 715, 721, 728–29, 737, 744, 750–51, 758: The Art Source